FILM HISTORY

An Introduction
Second Edition

Kristin Thompson
David Bordwell

University of Wisconsin-Madison

Boston   Burr Ridge, IL   Dubuque, IA   Madison, WI   New York
San Francisco   St. Louis   Bangkok   Bogotá   Caracas   Kuala Lumpur
Lisbon   London   Madrid   Mexico City   Milan   Montreal   New Delhi
Santiago   Seoul   Singapore   Sydney   Taipei   Toronto

McGraw-Hill Higher Education

A Division of The McGraw-Hill Companies

Film History: An Introduction

Published by McGraw-Hill, an imprint of The McGraw-Hill Companies, Inc., 1221 Avenue of the Americas, New York, NY 10020. Copyright © 2003, 1994, by The McGraw-Hill Companies, Inc. All rights reserved. No part of this publication may be reproduced or distributed in any form or by any means, or stored in a database or retrieval system, without the prior written consent of The McGraw-Hill Companies, Inc., including, but not limited to, in any network or other electronic storage or transmission, or broadcast for distance learning.
Some ancillaries, including electronic and print components, may not be available to customers outside the United States.

This book is printed on acid-free paper.

Domestic 1 2 3 4 5 6 7 8 9 0 QPD/QPD 0 9 8 7 6 5 4 3 2
International 1 2 3 4 5 6 7 8 9 0 QPD/QPD 0 9 8 7 6 5 4 3 2

ISBN 0-07-038429-0

Publisher: *Chris Freitag*
Sponsoring editor: *Allison McNamara*
Marketing manager: *Lisa Berry*
Project manager: *David Sutton*
Senior production supervisor: *Richard DeVitto*
Director of design: *Jeanne Schreiber*
Senior designer: *Jean Mailander*
Art editor: *Emma Ghiselli*
Cover design: *Joan Greenfield*
Interior design: *Glenda King*
Photo research coordinator: *Nora Agbayani*
Compositor: *Thompson Type*
Typeface: *10/13 Sabon*
Printer: *Quebecor World Dubuque Inc.*

Because this page cannot legibly accommodate all the copyright notices, page 738 constitutes an extension of this copyright page.

Library of Congress Cataloging-in-Publication Data

Thompson, Kristin, 1950–
   Film history: An Introduction / Kristin Thompson, David Bordwell.–2nd ed.
      p. cm.
   Includes bibliographical references and index.
   ISBN: 0-07-038429-0 (alk. paper)
   1. Motion pictures—History. I. Bordwell, David. II. Title.

PN1993.5.A1 T45 2002
791.43'09–dc21

2002070976

International Edition ISBN 0-07-115141-9
Copyright © 2003. Exclusive rights by the McGraw-Hill Companies, Inc. for manufacture and export. This book cannot be re-exported from the country to which it is sold by McGraw-Hill. The International Edition is not available in North America.

http://www.mhhe.com

FILM HISTORY

An Introduction

To Gabrielle

Chez Léon tout est bon

CONTENTS

Part One EARLY CINEMA 11

Part Two   THE LATE SILENT ERA, 1919–1929   81

Part Three   THE DEVELOPMENT OF SOUND CINEMA, 1926–1945   191

Part Four   THE POSTWAR ERA: 1945–1960s   323

Part Five THE CONTEMPORARY CINEMA SINCE THE 1960s   509

Part Six   CINEMA IN THE AGE OF ELECTRONIC MEDIA   677

ABOUT THE AUTHORS

Kristin Thompson and David Bordwell are married and live in Madison, Wisconsin.

Kristin Thompson is an Honorary Fellow in the Department of Communication Arts at the University of Wisconsin—Madison. She holds a master's degree in film from the University of Iowa and a doctorate in film from the University of Wisconsin—Madison. She has published *Eisenstein's Ivan the Terrible* (Princeton University Press, 1981), *Exporting Entertainment: America's Place in World Film Markets, 1901–1934* (British Film Institute, 1985), *Breaking the Glass Armor: Neoformalist Film Analysis* (Princeton University Press, 1988), *Wooster Proposes, Jeeves Disposes; or, Le Mot Juste* (James H. Heinemann, 1992), a study of P. G. Wodehouse, and *Storytelling in the New Hollywood: Understanding Classical Narrative Technique* (Harvard University Press, 1999). She is currently at work on a study of Ernst Lubitsch's silent features. She is also an amateur Egyptologist and a member of an expedition to Egypt.

David Bordwell is Jacques Ledoux Professor of Film Studies in the Department of Communication Arts at the University of Wisconsin—Madison. He also holds a Hilldale Professorship in the Humanities. He completed a master's degree and a doctorate in film at the University of Iowa. His books include *The Films of Carl-Theodor Dreyer* (University of California Press, 1981), *Narration in the Fiction Film* (University of Wisconsin Press, 1985), *Ozu and the Poetics of Cinema* (Princeton University Press, 1988), *Making Meaning: Inference and Rhetoric in the Interpretation of Cinema* (Harvard University Press, 1989), *The Cinema of Eisenstein* (Harvard University Press, 1993), *On the History of Film Style* (Harvard University Press, 1997), *Planet Hong Kong: Popular Cinema and the Art of Entertainment* (Harvard University Press, 2000), and *Visual Style in Cinema: Vier Kapitel Filmgeschichte* (Verlag der Autoren, 2001).

The authors have previously collaborated on *Film Art: An Introduction* (McGraw-Hill, 6th ed., 2001) and, with Janet Staiger, on *The Classical Hollywood Cinema: Film Style and Mode of Production to 1960* (Columbia University Press, 1985).

PREFACE

Summing up a hundred years in the development of a major mass medium is a daunting task. We have tried, within the compass of a single volume, to construct a readable history of the principal trends within mainstream fictional filmmaking, documentary filmmaking, and experimental cinema. Our Introduction, "Film History and How It Is Done," lays out in more detail the assumptions and frame of reference that have guided our work. We hope this book will prove a useful initiation to an endlessly fascinating subject.

We have been studying film history for over thirty years, and we are well aware of how much a historian owes to archives, libraries, and individuals. Many archivists helped us gain access to films and photographs. We thank Elaine Burrows, Jackie Morris, Julie Rigg, and the staff of the National Film and Television Archive of the British Film Institute; Paul Spehr, Kathy Loughney, Patrick Loughney, Cooper Graham, and the staff of the Motion Picture, Television, and Recorded Sound Division of the Library of Congress; Enno Patalas, Jan Christopher-Horak, Klaus Volkmer, Gerhardt Ullmann, Stefan Droessler, and the staff of the München Filmmuseum; Mark-Paul Meyer, Eric de Kuyper, and the staff of the Nederlands Filmmuseum; Eileen Bowser, Charles Silver, Mary Corliss, and the staff of the Film Study Center of the Museum of Modern Art; Ib Monty, Marguerite Engberg, and the staff of the Danish Film Museum; Vincent Pinel and the staff of the Cinémathèque Française of Paris; Robert Rosen, Eddie Richmond, and the staff of the UCLA Film Archive; Bruce Jenkins, Mike Maggiore, and the staff of the Walker Art Center Film Department; Robert A. Haller, Carol Pipolo, and the staff of Anthology Film Archives; and Edith Kramer and the staff of the Pacific Film Archive. We owe special thanks to Jan-Christopher Horak and Paolo Cherchai Usai of the Motion Picture Division of George Eastman House, who assisted our work "beyond the call of duty." Finally, this book could not have been as comprehensive and detailed as it has become without the generosity of the late Jacques Ledoux and his successor Gabrielle Claes. Along with their staff at the Cinémathèque Royale de Belgique, they kindly supported our work in innumerable ways.

In addition, we wish to thank others who shared information and films with us: Jacques Aumont, John Belton, Edward Branigan, Carlos Bustamente, Chen Mei, David Desser, Michael Drozewski, Michael Friend, André Gaudreault, Kevin Heffernan, Richard Hincha, Kyoko Hirano, Donald Kirihara, Hiroshi Komatsu, Richard Maltby, Albert Moran, Charles Musser, Peter Parshall, William Paul, Richard Peña, Tony Rayns, Donald Richie, David Rodowick, Phil Rosen, Barbara Scharres, Alex Sesonske, Alissa Simon, Cecille Starr, Yuri Tsivian, Alan Upchurch, Ruth Vasey, Marc Vernet, and Chuck Wolfe. Jerry Carlson went out of his way to assist our work on eastern European and Latin American topics, while Diane and Kewal Verma helped us get access to obscure Hindi films. Tom Gunning waded through the entire manuscript and offered many valuable suggestions.

Our coverage of silent cinema was enhanced by the annual "Giornate del cinema muto" events at Pordenone, Italy. These gatherings have revolutionized the study of silent cinema, and we are grateful to Davide Turconi, Lorenzo Codelli, Paolo Cherchi Usai, David Robinson, and their associates for inviting us to participate in them.

We are also grateful to our readers in the discipline, who provided helpful criticism and suggestions: Jonathan Buchsbaum, Queens College; Jeremy Butler, University of Alabama; Diane Carson, St. Louis Community College; Thomas D. Cooke, University of Missouri; David A. Daly,

Southwest Missouri State University; Peter Haggart, University of Idaho; Brian Henderson, State University of New York at Buffalo; Scott L. Jensen, Weber State College; Kathryn Kalinak, Rhode Island College; Jay B. Korinek, Henry Ford Community College; Sue Lawrence, Marist College; Karen B. Mann, Western Illinois University; Charles R. Myers, Humboldt State University; John W. Ravage, University of Wyoming; Jere Real, Lynchburg College; Lucille Rhodes, Long Island University; H. Wayne Schuth, University of North Orleans; J. P. Telotte, Georgia Tech University; Charles C. Werberig, Rochester Institute of Technology; and Ken White, Diablo Valley College. Additional suggestions and corrections for this new edition came from several of the above, as well as Geneviève van Cauwenberg, Université de Liège; Neil Rattigan, The University of New England; Scott Simmon, University of California–Davis; Cecile Starr; and Tom Stempel, Los Angeles City College. Our new research was aided by Robert Chen, the National Taiwan College of Arts; Li Cheuk-to; Stephen Teo; Athena Tsui; James Schamus, of Good Machine; Shu Kei; and Yeh Yueh-yu of Hong Kong Baptist University.

This project could not have come into being without the resources and people of the University of Wisconsin–Madison. Much of this volume derives from our teaching and scholarly work, activities that have been generously supported by the Department of Communication Arts, the Graduate School, and the Institute for Research in the Humanities. Moreover, we have come to rely on the Wisconsin Center for Film and Theater Research, its collections and its staff supervised by our archivist, the ever-cooperative Maxine Fleckner Ducey. Joe Beres and Brad Schauer helped us immeasurably with the new illustrations.

In addition, our Madison colleagues lent their expertise to this book. Tino Balio's suggestions improved our coverage of the film industry; Ben Brewster scrutinized our chapters on early cinema; Noël Carroll offered detailed comments on experimental cinema and Hollywood film; Don Crafton supplied suggestions and photographic materials on animation and early French cinema; Lea Jacobs improved our understanding of Hollywood film and women's cinema; Vance Kepley advised us on Russian and Soviet film; J. J. Murphy informed our discussion of the avant-garde; Marc Silberman helped us nuance our treatment of German film history. Our newest colleagues, Kelley Conway, Michael Curtin, and Ben Singer, have helped us refine this edition. Our intellectual debts to these colleagues are deepened by our admiration and affection.

Kristin Thompson
David Bordwell

INTRODUCTION
Film History and How It Is Done

WHY DO WE CARE ABOUT OLD MOVIES?

Around the world, at any instant, millions of people are watching movies. They watch mainstream entertainment, serious "art films," documentaries, cartoons, experimental films, educational shorts. They sit in air-conditioned theaters, in village squares, in art museums, in college classrooms, or in their homes before a television screen. The world's film theaters attract around 15 billion customers each year. With the availability of films on video—whether broadcast, fed from cable or satellites or the Internet, or played back from cassette or DVD—the audience has multiplied far beyond that.

Nobody needs to be convinced that film has been one of the most influential media for over one hundred years. Not only can you recall your most exciting or tearful moments at the movies, you can also probably remember moments in ordinary life when you tried to be as graceful, as selfless, as tough, or as compassionate as those larger-than-life figures on the screen. The way we dress and cut our hair, the way we talk and act, the things we believe or doubt—all these aspects of our lives are shaped by films. Films also provide us with powerful aesthetic experiences, insights into diverse cultures, and glimpses of new ways of thinking.

So we aren't surprised that people rush to see the latest hit or rent a cult favorite from the video store. Why, though, should anybody care about *old* movies?

For one thing, they provide the same sorts of insights that we get from watching contemporary movies. Some offer intense artistic experiences or penetrating visions of human life in other times and places. Some

are documents of everyday existence or of extraordinary historical events that continue to reverberate in our times. Still other old movies are resolutely strange. They resist assimilation to our current habits of thought. They force us to acknowledge that films can be radically different from what we are used to and that we must adjust our own field of view to accommodate what was, astonishingly, taken for granted by others.

Film history encompasses more than just films. By studying how films were made and received, we discover the range of options available to filmmakers and film viewers. By studying the social and cultural influences on films, we understand better the ways in which films may bear the traces of the societies that made and consumed them. Film history opens up a range of issues in politics, culture, and the arts—both "high" and "popular."

Yet another answer to our question is this: studying old movies and the times in which they were made is intrinsically fun. As a relatively new field of academic research (no more than forty years old), film history has the excitement of a young discipline. Over the past few decades, many lost films have been recovered, little-known genres explored, and neglected filmmakers reevaluated. Ambitious retrospectives have revealed entire national cinemas that had been largely ignored. Even television, with cable stations devoted wholly to cinema, brings previously rare and obscure silent and foreign films into viewers' living rooms. And much more remains to be discovered. Simply put, there are more old movies than new ones and, hence, many more chances for fascinating viewing experiences.

In the space of this one volume, we aim to introduce the history of film as it is presently conceived, written, and taught by its most accomplished scholars. This book assumes no specialized knowledge of film aesthetics or theory, although some acquaintance with these areas would certainly benefit the reader.[1] We limit our scope to those realms of filmmaking that are most frequently studied. We consider theatrical fiction films, documentary films, experimental or avant-garde filmmaking, and animation. There are other types of cinema—most notably educational, industrial, and scientific films—but, whatever their intrinsic interest, for the moment they play secondary roles in most historians' concerns.

Film History: An Introduction is not, however, exactly a distillation of an "essential" film history. Researchers are fond of saying that there is no film *history,* only film *histories.* For some, this means that there can be no intelligible, coherent "grand narrative" that puts all the facts into place. The history of avant-garde film does not fit neatly into the history of color technology or the development of the Western or the life of John Ford. For others, *film history* means that historians work from various perspectives and with different interests and purposes.

We agree with both points. There is no Big Story of Film History that accounts for all events, causes, and consequences. And the variety of historical approaches guarantees that historians will draw diverse and dissenting conclusions. We also think that film history is more aptly thought of as a set of film histories, because research into film history involves asking a series of *questions* and searching for *evidence* in order to answer them in the course of an *argument.* When historians focus on different questions, turn up different evidence, and formulate different explanations, we derive not a single history but a diverse set of historical arguments. In this introduction we will explain what film historians do and the particular approach *Film History: An Introduction* takes.

WHAT DO FILM HISTORIANS DO?

While millions are watching movies at this moment, a few thousand are studying the films of the past. One person is trying to ascertain whether a certain film was made in 1904 or 1905. Another is tracing the fortunes of a short-lived Scandinavian production company. Another is poring over a 1927 Japanese film, shot by shot, to find out how it tells its story. Some researchers are comparing prints of an obscure film to determine which one can be considered the original. Other scholars are studying a group of films signed by the same director or

set designer or producer. Some are scrutinizing patent records and technical diagrams, legal testimony, and production files. And still others are interviewing retired employees to discover how the Bijou Theater in their hometown was run during the 1950s.

Why?

Questions and Answers

One reason is evident. Most film historians—teachers, archivists, journalists, and freelancers—are *cinephiles,* lovers of cinema. Like bird-watchers, fans of 1960s television, art historians, and other devotees, they enjoy acquiring knowledge about the object of their affection.

Movie fans may stop there, regarding the accumulating of facts about their passion as an end in itself. But whatever the pleasure of knowing the names of all the Three Stooges' wives, most film historians are not trivia buffs.

Film historians mount *research programs,* systematic inquiries into the past. A historian's research program is organized around questions that require answers. A research program also consists of assumptions and background knowledge. For a film historian, a fact takes on significance only in the context of a research program.

Consider the image at the top of the page, from a film of the silent era. A film archivist—that is, someone who works in a library devoted to collecting and preserving motion pictures—often finds a film she cannot identify. Perhaps the title credit is missing or the print carries a title that differs from that of the original film. The archivist's research program is, broadly, identification. The film presents a series of questions: What is the date of production or of release? In what country was it made? Who made the film? Who are the actors?

Our mysterious film carries only the title *Wanda l'espione* ("Wanda the Spy")—most likely a title given to it by a distributor. It was probably imported rather than made in the small country in which the print was discovered. Fortunately there are some clues in the print itself that a knowledgeable historian can spot. Its lead actress, seated in the foreground, is a famous star, Francesca Bertini. Identifying her makes it almost certain that the film is Italian, made during the height of her career in the 1910s. The film's style allows the researcher to narrow the range of dates even more. The camera frames straight toward the back wall of the set, and the actors seldom move closer to the camera than they are seen here. The editing pace is slow, and the action is staged so that performers enter and exit through a rear doorway. All these stylistic features are typical of European filmmaking of the mid-1910s. Such clues can be followed up by referring to a *filmography* (a list of films) of Bertini's career. A plot description of a 1915 film in which she starred, *Diana l'affascinatrice* ("Diana the Seductress"), matches the action of the unidentified print.

Note that the identification depended on certain assumptions. For example, the researcher would have assumed that it is extremely unlikely, if not impossible, for, say, a 1977 filmmaker to scheme to bedevil archivists and make a fake 1915 Italian film. (Film historians seldom need worry about forgeries, as art historians must.) Note, too, that background knowledge was indispensable. The researcher had reason to believe that films staged and cut a certain way are characteristic of the mid-1910s, and the researcher recognized a star from other films of the period.

Consider another possibility. An archive holds many films made by the same production company, and it also has numerous filing cabinets bulging with documents concerning that company's production process. Its collection also includes scripts in various drafts; memos passed among writers, directors, producers, and other staff; and sketches for sets and costumes. This is a rich lode of data—too rich, in fact, for one researcher to tackle. The historian's problem is now selecting relevant data and salient facts.

What makes a datum relevant or a fact salient is the historian's research program and its questions. One scholar might be interested in tracing common features of the company's production process; he might ask something like, "In general, how did this firm typically go about making movies?" Another historian's research program might concentrate on the films of a certain director who worked for the company. She might ask, "What aspects of visual style distinguish the director's films?"

Some facts would be central to one program but peripheral to another. The historian interested in the company's production routines might not particularly care about a daring stylistic innovation introduced by the director who is the focus of the other historian's inquiry. Conversely, the latter historian might be uninterested in how the company's producers promoted certain stars.

Again, assumptions exert pressure on the researcher's framing of questions and pursuit of information. The company historian assumes that he can trace general tendencies of production organization, largely because film companies tend to make films by following fairly set routines. The director-centered researcher assumes—perhaps initially only as a hunch—that her director's films do have a distinct style. And both historians would mobilize background knowledge, about how companies work and how directors direct, to guide their research.

Historians in any discipline do more than accumulate facts. No facts speak for themselves. Facts are interesting and important only as part of research programs. But facts help us ask and answer questions.

Film History as Description and Explanation

Inevitably, a historian needs at least a little information to prod him to ask questions. But the historian does not necessarily sift through mountains of facts and then judiciously ask a question. A historian may begin with a question, and sometimes that question might be better described as a hunch or an intuition or even just an itch.

For example, one young historian saw a few of the "anarchic" American comedies of the 1930s and noticed that their vulgar gags and absurd situations were very different from the more sophisticated comedy of the period. Suspecting that stage comedy might have been a source, he framed a question: "Might vaudeville and its performance style have shaped these particular comedies of the early 1930s?" He began to gather information, examining films, reading coverage of the comedians in the Hollywood trade press, and studying shifts in American taste in humor. The process of research led him to refine his question and to mount a detailed account of how comedians introduced a vaudeville aesthetic into sound films but then muted it in accord with Hollywood's standards of taste.[2]

Nonhistorians often visualize the historical researcher as a cousin to Indiana Jones, braving library stacks and crawling through attics in quest of the treasure-lode of documents that overturn popular opinion. Certainly new documentation has a key role to play in historical research. One scholar gained entry to the long-inaccessible files of Hollywood's self-censorship agency, the Hays Office, and she was able to put forth a new account of the office's procedures and functions.[3]

Similarly, the increasing availability of films from cinema's earliest era has created an entire subfield of cinema history.[4]

Still, many research programs rely more on asking new questions than on unearthing new data. In some cases, the research question seems to have been answered by previous historians, but another researcher comes along and suggests a more complete or complex answer. For example, no historian disputes the fact that Warner Bros. was quick to invest in talking pictures in the mid-1920s. For a long time most historians believed that the firm took this risky step because it was on the verge of bankruptcy and was desperate to save itself. But another historian with more knowledge of economics and how to read companies' balance sheets concluded that evidence—which had long been publicly available to researchers—strongly indicated a quite different situation. He argued that, far from facing bankruptcy, Warners was quickly expanding and that investing in sound films was part of a carefully planned strategy for breaking into the ranks of the major studios.[5]

Our examples all indicate that the historian's research program aims to do at least two things. First, the historian tries to *describe* a process or state of affairs. She asks *What* and *who* and *where* and *when*. What is this film, and who made it, and where and when? In what ways does this director's work differ from that of others? What was the vaudeville comedic style? What evidence is there that a studio was nearly bankrupt? Who is the actor in this shot? Who was responsible for scripts at this company? Where was this film shown, and who might have seen it? Here the historian's problem is largely one of finding information that will answer such questions.

Accurate description is indispensable for all historical research. Every scholar is indebted to descriptive work for identifying films, collating versions, compiling filmographies, establishing timelines, and creating reference works that supply names, dates, and the like. The more sophisticated and long-lived a historical discipline is, the richer and more complete its battery of descriptive reference material is.

Second, the historian tries to *explain* a process or state of affairs. He asks, How does this work? and Why did this happen? How did this company assign tasks, lay out responsibilities, carry a project to completion? How did this director's work influence other films from the company? Why did Warners pursue talkies when larger companies were reluctant to do so? Why did some sound comedians adopt the vaudeville comedic style while others did not?

The film historian, like a historian of art or politics, proposes an *explanatory argument*. Having asked *how* or *why*, she puts forward an answer, based on an examination of evidence in light of assumptions and background knowledge. In reading historical writings, we need to recognize that the essay or book is not just a mass of facts but an argument. The historian's argument consists of evidence marshaled to create a plausible explanation for an event or state of affairs. That is, the argument aims to answer some historical question.

Evidence

Most arguments about empirical matters—and the history of film is principally an empirical matter—rely on evidence. Evidence consists of information that gives grounds for believing that the argument is sound. Evidence supports the expectation that the historian has presented a plausible answer to the original question.

Film historians work with evidence of many sorts. For many, copies of the films they study are central pieces of evidence. Historians also rely on print sources, both published (books, magazines, trade journals, newspapers) and unpublished (memoirs, letters, notes, production files, scripts, court testimony). Historians of film technology study cameras, sound recorders, and other equipment. A film studio or an important location might also serve as a source of evidence.

Usually historians must verify their sources of evidence. Often this depends on the sort of descriptive research we have already mentioned. The problem is particularly acute with film prints. Films have always circulated in differing versions. In the 1920s, Hollywood films were shot in two versions, one for the United States and one for export. These could differ considerably in length, content, and even visual style. To this day, many Hollywood films are released in Europe in more erotic or violent versions than are screened in the United States. In addition, many old films have deteriorated and been subject to cutting and revision. Even modern "restorations" do not necessarily result in a film identical to the original release version. (See "Notes and Queries," Chapter 4.) Many current video versions of old films have been trimmed, expanded, or otherwise altered from their theatrical release format.

Often, then, the historian does not know whether the print she is seeing represents anything like an original, if indeed there can be said to be a single "original" version. Historians try to be aware of the differences among the versions of the films they are studying and try to account for them; indeed, the fact that there are different versions can itself be a source of questions.

Historians generally distinguish between *primary* and *secondary* sources. As applied to film, *primary* usually refers to the people directly involved in whatever objects or events are being studied. For example, if you were studying Japanese cinema of the 1920s, films, interviews with filmmakers or audience members, and contemporary trade journals would count as primary material. Later discussions concerning the period, usually by an earlier historian, would be considered secondary.

Often, though, one scholar's secondary source is another's primary source, because the researchers are asking different questions. A critic's 1960s' essay about a 1925 film would be a secondary source if your question centered on the 1925 film. If, however, you were writing a history of film criticism during the 1960s, the critic's essay would be a primary source.

Explaining the Past: Basic Approaches

There are distinct types of explanation in film history. A standard list would include

Biographical history: focusing on an individual's life history

Industrial or economic history: focusing on business practices

Aesthetic history: focusing on film art (form, style, genre)

Technological history: focusing on the materials and machines of film

Social/cultural/political history: focusing on the role of cinema in the larger society

This sort of inventory helps us understand that there is not *one* history of film but many possible histories, each adopting a different perspective. Typically, the researcher begins with an interest in one of these areas, which helps him to formulate his initial question.

Nevertheless, such typologies can be restricting if they are taken too rigidly. Not all questions the historian may ask will fall neatly into only one of these pigeonholes. If you want to know *why* a film looks the way it does, the question may not be purely aesthetic; it might be linked to the biography of the filmmaker or to the technological resources available when the film was made. A study of film genres might involve both aesthetic and cultural factors, and a person's life cannot easily be separated from his or her working condi-

tions within a film industry or from the contemporary political context.

We propose that the student of film history think chiefly in terms of questions, keeping in mind that these might well cut across typological boundaries. Indeed, one could argue that the most interesting questions will.

Explaining the Past: Organizing the Evidence

Finding an answer to a historical question may involve both description and explanation, in different mixtures. The techniques of descriptive research are specialized and require a wide range of background knowledge. For example, some experts on early silent cinema can determine when a film copy was made by examining the stock on which it is printed. The number and shape of the sprocket holes, along with the manner in which a manufacturer's name is printed along the edge of the film strip, can help date the print. Knowing the age of the stock can in turn help narrow down the film's date of production and country of origin.

Historical explanation also involves concepts to organize the evidence produced by specialized knowledge. Here are some of them.

Chronology Chronology is essential to historical explanation, and descriptive research is an indispensable aid to establishing the sequence of events. The historian needs to know that this film was made before that one or that event B took place after event A. But history is not mere chronology. A chronology stops short of explanation, just as a record of high and low tides gives no hint as to why tides change. History, as we have already seen, centrally involves explanation.

Causality Much historical explanation involves cause and effect. Historians work with conceptions of various kinds of causes.

Individual Causes People have beliefs and desires that affect how they act. In acting, they make things happen. It is often reasonable to explain a historical change or a past state of affairs in light of the attitudes or behavior of individuals. This is not to say that individuals make everything happen or that things always happen as people originally intended or that people always understand just why they did what they did. It is simply to say that historians may justifiably appeal to what people think and feel and do as part of an explanation.

Some historians believe that *all* historical explanation must appeal to person-based causes sooner or later.

This position is usually called *methodological individualism*. A different, and even more sweeping, assumption is that only individuals, and exceptional individuals at that, have the power to create historical change. This view is sometimes called the Great Man theory of history, even though it is applied to women as well.

Group Causes   People often act in groups, and at times we speak of the group as having a kind of existence over and above the individuals who compose it. Groups have rules and roles, structures and routines, and often these factors make things happen. We speak of a government's declaring war, yet this act may not be reducible to more detailed statements about what all the individuals involved believed and did.

When we say that Warner Bros. decided to adopt sound, we are making a meaningful claim, even if we have no information about the beliefs and desires of the individual decision makers at the company; we may not even fully know who they were. Some historians assert that any historical explanation must, sooner or later, ground itself in group-based causes. This position is usually called *holism*, or *methodological collectivism*, as opposed to methodological individualism.

Several sorts of groups are important to the history of cinema. Throughout this book we will be talking about *institutions*—government agencies, film studios, distribution firms, and other fairly formal, organized groups. We will also be talking about more informal affiliations of filmmakers. These are usually called *movements* or *schools,* small assemblies of filmmakers and critics who share the same interests, beliefs about cinema, conceptions of film form and style, and the like. (Movements are discussed in more detail in the introduction to Part 2.)

Influence   Most historians use some notion of influence to explain change. Influence describes the inspiration that an individual, a group, or a film can provide for others. Members of a movement can deliberately influence a director to make a film a certain way, but a chance viewing of a movie can also influence a director.

Influence does not mean simple copying. You may have been influenced by a parent or a teacher, but you have not necessarily mimicked his or her behavior. In the arts, influence is often a matter of one artist's getting ideas from other artists' work but then pursuing those ideas in a personal way. The result may be quite different from the initial work that stimulated it. The contemporary director Jean-Luc Godard was influenced by Jean Renoir, although their films are markedly dif-

ferent. Sometimes we can detect the influence by examining the films; sometimes we rely on the testimony of the filmmaker.

A body of work by a group of directors may also influence later films. Soviet cinema of the 1920s influenced the documentary director John Grierson. The Hollywood cinema, as a set of films, has been enormously influential throughout film history, although all the directors influenced by it certainly did not see exactly the same films. Influences are particular kinds of causes, so it is not surprising that influences may involve both individual activity and group activity.

Trends and Generalizations   Any historical question opens up a body of data for investigation. Once the historian starts to look closely at the data—to go through a studio's records, examine the films, page through the trade press—she discovers that there is much more to explore than the initial question touches on. It is like looking into a microscope and discovering that a drop of water teems with organisms of confounding variety, all going about very different business.

Every historian omits certain material. For one thing, the historical record is already incomplete. Many events go unrecorded, and many documents are lost forever. Further, historians inevitably select. They reduce the messy complications of history to a more coherent, cogent story. A historian simplifies and streamlines according to the question he is pursuing.

One principal way historians go about such simplification is by postulating *trends*. Lots of things are going on, they admit, but "by and large" or "on the whole" or "for the most part," we can identify a general tendency. Most Hollywood films of the 1940s were made in black and white, but most Hollywood films today are in color. On the whole, there has been a change, and we can see a trend toward the increasing use of color film stock between the 1940s and the 1960s. Our task is to explain how and why this trend occurred.

By positing trends, historians generalize. They necessarily set aside interesting exceptions and aberrations. But this is no sin, because the answer to a question is necessarily pitched at a certain level of generality. All historical explanations pull back from the throbbing messiness of reality. By recognizing that tendencies are "for-the-most-part" generalizations, the scholar can acknowledge that there is more going on than she is going to explain.

Periods   Historical chronology and causation are without beginning or end. The child who incessantly asks what came before that or what made that happen soon discovers that we can trace out a sequence of events indefinitely. Historians necessarily limit the stretch of time they will explore, and they go on to divide that stretch into meaningful phases or segments.

For example, the historian studying American silent cinema already assumes that this period within film history ran from about 1894 to around 1929. The historian will probably further segment this stretch of time. She might break it down by decade (the 1900s, the 1910s, the 1920s), by changes external to film (say, pre–World War I, World War I, post–World War I), or by phases in the development of storytelling style (say, 1894–1907, 1908–1917, 1918–1929).

Every historian periodizes according to the research program he adopts and the question he asks. Historians recognize that periodization can't be rigid: trends do not follow in neat order. It is illuminating to think of the American "structural" film of the early 1970s as a kind of response to the "underground" film of the 1960s, but underground films were still being made well into the 1970s. Histories of genres often mark periods by innovative films, but this is not to deny that there may be a great deal of continuity in less innovative works across periods.

Similarly, we ought not to expect that the history of technology or styles or genres will necessarily march in step with political or social history. The period after World War II was indeed distinctive, because this global conflict had major effects on film industries and filmmakers in most countries; but not all political events demarcate distinct periods in relation to changes in film form or the film market. The assassination of President Kennedy was a wrenching event, but it had little if any effect on the film world. Here, as ever, the historian's research program and central question will shape her sense of the relevant periods and parallel events. (This is one reason that scholars often speak of film *histories* rather than a single film history.)

Significance   In mounting explanations, historians of all arts make assumptions about the significance of the artworks they discuss. We might treat a work as a "monument," studying it because it is a highly valued accomplishment. Alternatively, we might study a work as a "document" because it records some noteworthy historical activity, such as the state of a society at a given moment or a trend within the art form itself.

In this book, we assume that the films we discuss have significance on any or all of the following three criteria:

Intrinsic excellence: Some films are, simply, outstanding by artistic criteria. They are rich, moving, complex, thought-provoking, intricate, meaningful, or the like. At least partly because of their quality, such films have played a key role in the history of cinema.

Influence: A film may be historically significant by virtue of its influence on other films. It may create or change a genre, inspire filmmakers to try something new, or gain such a wide popularity that it spawns imitations and tributes. Since influence is an important part of historical explanations, this sort of film plays a prominent role in this book.

Typicality: Some films are significant because they vividly represent instances or trends. They stand in for many other films of the same type.

A particular film might be significant on two or even all three of these counts. A highly accomplished genre film, such as *Singin' in the Rain* or *Rio Bravo*, is often considered both excellent and highly typical. Many acclaimed masterworks, such as *The Birth of a Nation* or *Citizen Kane*, were also highly influential, and some also typify broader tendencies.

OUR APPROACH TO FILM HISTORY

Although this book surveys the history of world cinema, we could hardly start with the question What is the history of world cinema? That would give us no help in setting about our research and organizing the material we find.

Following the aspects of film history outlined here, we have pursued three principal questions.

1. *How have uses of the film medium changed or become normalized over time?* Within "uses of the medium" we include matters of film form: the part/whole organization of the film. Often this involves telling a story, but a film's overall form might also be based on an argument or an abstract pattern. The term "uses of the medium" also includes matters of film style, the patterned uses of film techniques (*mise-en-scène*, or staging, lighting, setting, and costume; camerawork; editing; and sound). In addition, any balanced conception of how the medium has been used must also consider film modes (documentary, avant-garde, fiction, animation) and genres (the Western, the thriller, the musical). So we also examine these phenomena. All such matters are central to most college and university survey courses in film history.

A central purpose of *Film History: An Introduction* is to survey the uses of the medium in different times and places. Sometimes we dwell on the creation of stable norms of form and style, as when we examine how Hollywood standardized certain editing options in the first two decades of filmmaking. At other times, we examine how filmmakers have proposed innovative ways of structuring form or using film technique.

2. *How have the conditions of the film industry—production, distribution, and exhibition—affected the uses of the medium?* Films are made within *modes of production,* habitual ways of organizing the labor and materials involved in creating a movie. Some modes of production are industrial. In these circumstances, companies make films as a business. The classic instance of industrial production is the *studio system,* in which firms are organized in order to make films for large audiences through a fairly detailed division of labor. Another sort of industrial production might be called the *artisanal,* or *one-off,* approach, in which a production company makes one film at a time (perhaps only one film, period). Other modes of production are less highly organized, involving small groups or individuals who make films for specific purposes. In any event, the ways in which films are made have had particular effects on the look and sound of the finished products.

So have the ways in which films are shown and consumed. For example, the major technological innovations associated with the early 1950s—wide-screen picture, stereophonic sound, increased use of color—were actually available decades earlier. Each could have been developed before the 1950s, but the U.S. film industry had no pressing need to do so since film attendance was so high that spending money on new attractions would not have significantly increased profits. Only when attendance dropped precipitously in the late 1940s were producers and exhibitors impelled to introduce new technologies to lure audiences back into theaters.

3. *How have international trends emerged in the uses of the film medium and in the film market?* In this book we try to balance the consideration of important national contributions with a sense of how international and cross-cultural influences were operating. Many nations' audiences and film industries have been influenced by directors and films that have migrated across their borders. Genres are vagabond as well. The Hollywood Western influenced the Japanese samurai film and the Italian Western, genres that in turn influenced the Hong Kong kung-fu films of the 1970s; interestingly,

Hollywood films then began incorporating elements of the martial arts movie.

Just as important, the film industry itself is significantly transnational. At certain periods, circumstances closed off countries from the flow of films, but most often there has been a global film market, and we understand it best by tracing trends across cultures and regions. We have paid particular attention to conditions that allowed people to see films made outside their own country.

Each of these *how* questions accompanies a great many *why* questions. For any part of the processes we focus on, we can ask what conditions caused them to operate as they did. Why, for instance, did Soviet filmmakers undertake their experiments in disturbing, aggressive narrative? Why did Hollywood's studio system begin to fragment in the late 1940s? Why did "new waves" and "young cinemas" arise in Europe, the Soviet Union, and Japan around 1960? Why are more films produced now with international investment than in the 1930s or 1940s? Historians are keen to know what factors made a change occur, and our general questions include a host of subquestions about causes and effects.

Recall our five general explanatory approaches: biographical, industrial, aesthetic, technological, and social. If we had to squeeze our book into one or more of these pigeonholes, we could say that its approach is predominantly aesthetic and industrial. It examines how types of films, film styles, and film forms have changed in relation to the conditions of film production, distribution, and exhibition within certain countries and within the international flow of films. But this summary of our approach is too confining, as even a cursory look at what follows will indicate. Sometimes we invoke the individual—a powerful producer, an innovative filmmaker, an imaginative critic. Sometimes we consider technology. And we often frame our account with discussions of the political, social, and cultural context of a period.

Take, for example, our central question: How have uses of the film medium changed or become normalized over time? This is a question about aesthetic matters, but it also impinges on factors of technology. For instance, conceptions of "realistic" filmmaking changed with the introduction of portable cameras and sound equipment in the late 1950s. Similarly, our second question—How have the conditions of the film industry affected the uses of the medium?—is at once economic, technological, and aesthetic. Finally, asking how international trends have emerged in the uses of the film medium and in the film market concerns both economic and social/cultural/political factors. In the early era of cinema, films circulated freely among countries, and viewers often did not know the nationality of a film they were seeing. In the 1910s, however, war and nationalism blocked certain films from circulating. At the same time, the growth of particular film industries, notably Hollywood, depended on access to other markets, so the degree to which films could circulate boosted some nations' output and hindered that of others. In addition, the circulation of U.S. films abroad served to spread American cultural values, which in turn created both admiration and hostility.

In sum, we have been guided, as we think most historians are, by research questions rather than rigid conceptions of the "kind" of history we are writing. And what we take to be the most plausible answer to a given question will depend on the strength of the evidence and the argument we can make for it—not on a prior commitment to writing only a certain kind of history.

History as Story

Our answers to historical questions are, however, not simply given in a list or summary. Like most historical arguments, ours takes a narrative form.

Historians use language to communicate their arguments and evidence to others. Descriptive research programs can do this through a summary of findings: this film is *Diana l'affascinatrice,* made in Italy by Caesar-Film in 1915, directed by Gustavo Serena, and so on. But historical explanations require a more complicated crafting.

Sometimes historians frame their explanations as persuasive arguments. To take an example already cited, a historian investigating the development of sound by Warner Bros. might start by considering the various explanations already offered and taken for granted. Then he might set forth the reasons for believing his alternative interpretation. This is a familiar form of rhetorical argument, eliminating unsatisfactory beliefs before settling on a more plausible one.

More often, historians' explanations take the form of stories. *Narrative history,* as it is called, seeks to answer *how* and *why* questions by tracing the relevant circumstances and conditions over time. It produces a chain of causes and effects, or it shows how a process works, by telling a story. For instance, if we are trying to answer the question How did the Hays Office negotiate with firms to arrive at an agreement about an ac-

ceptable film? we can frame a step-by-step narrative of the censorship process. Or, if we are seeking to explain what led the Hays Office to be created, we might lay out the causal factors as a story. As these examples indicate, the story's "players" might be individuals or groups, institutions or even films; the "plot" consists of the situations in which the players operate and the changes they initiate and undergo.

Narrative is one of the basic ways in which humans make sense of the world, and so it is not surprising that historians use stories to make past events intelligible. We have accordingly framed this book as a large-scale narrative, one that includes several stories within it. This is partly because of custom: virtually all introductory historical works take this perspective, and readers are comfortable with it. But we also believe that there are advantages to working on a wide canvas. New patterns of information may leap to the eye, and fresh connections may become more visible when we consider history as a dynamic, ongoing process.

We divide film history into five large periods—early cinema (to about 1919), the late silent era (1919–1929), the development of sound cinema (1926–1945), the period after World War II (1946–1960s), and the contemporary cinema (1960s to the present). These divisions reflect developments in (1) film form and style; (2) major changes in film production, distribution, and exhibition; and (3) significant international trends. The periodization cannot be exactly synchronized for all three areas, but it does indicate approximate boundaries for the changes we try to trace.

In our attempt to systematically answer the three principal questions outlined earlier, we have relied on secondary sources, principally other historians' writings on the matters we consider. We have also used primary sources: trade papers, the writings of filmmakers, and films. Because films constitute our major primary source, we need to say a few more words about how they serve as evidence in writing film history.

Although the cinema is a relatively young medium, invented only a little over a century ago, many films have already been lost or destroyed. For decades, movies were seen as products with temporary commercial value, and companies did little to ensure their preservation. Even when film archives were founded, beginning in the 1930s, they faced a daunting task of collecting and sheltering the thousands of films that had already been made. Moreover, the nitrate film stock, upon which most films up to the early 1950s were shot and printed, was highly flammable and deteriorated over time. Deliberate destruction of films, archive and warehouse fires,

A frame from
Knocknagow
(Film Company
of Ireland, 1918)

and the gradual decomposition of nitrate stored in bad conditions have led to the loss of many titles. (In the frame above, severe nitrate deterioration has all but obliterated the figures.) According to rough estimates, only about 20 percent of silent films are known to survive. Many of these are still sitting in vaults, unidentified or unpreserved due to lack of funds.

Even more recent films may be inaccessible to the researcher. Films made in some small countries, particularly in Third World nations, do not circulate widely. Small archives may not have the facilities to preserve films or show them to researchers. In some cases, political regimes may choose to suppress certain films and promote others. We have attempted to examine a great range of types of international films. Inevitably we could not track down every film we hoped to see, and sometimes we were unable to include photographs from those we did see.

Nevertheless, we have surveyed a large number of films, and we offer this book as both an overview of the history of cinema and an attempt to see it in a somewhat new light. Film history, for us, is less an inert body of knowledge than an *activity* of inquiry. After a researcher has made a serious argument in an attempt to answer a question, "film history" is no longer quite what it was before. The reader gains not only new information and a new point of view. New patterns emerge that can make even familiar facts stand out with fresh force.

If film history is a generative, self-renewing activity, then we cannot simply offer a condensation of "all previous knowledge." We are, in a sense, casting what we find into a new form. Throughout the years spent researching and writing this book, we have come to believe that it of-fers a fairly novel version of the shape of film history, both its overall contour and its specific detail. We have relied on the research of a great many scholars in gathering the information and arguments presented here, but we are chiefly responsible for the particular story we tell.

Recognizing that there are many stories to be told about cinema, we have appended to each chapter a section titled "Notes and Queries." In these we raise side issues, explore recent discoveries, and trace some more specialized historiographic matters.

We have taken the opportunity of this second edition of *Film History: An Introduction* to update its coverage and to take into account historical work that has appeared since its initial publication in 1994. We thank the scholars whose research initially made it possible for us to rethink the history of the medium we love, as well as those who contributed to this revision and those who will continue to challenge us to hone the ideas we offer here.

REFERENCES

1. The survey of film aesthetics most appropriate to our undertaking here is David Bordwell and Kristin Thompson, *Film Art: An Introduction*, 6th ed. (New York: McGraw-Hill, 2001).
2. This research program is described in Henry Jenkins, *What Made Pistachio Nuts? Early Sound Comedy and the Vaudeville Aesthetic* (New York: Columbia University Press, 1992).
3. See Lea Jacobs, *The Wages of Sin: Censorship and the Fallen Woman Film* (1991; reprint Berkeley: University of California Press, 1997).
4. See, for example, Yuri Tsivian, et al., *Silent Witnesses: Russian Films 1908–1919* (Pordenone: Giornate del Cinema Muto, 1989); Charles Musser, *Before the Nickelodeon: Edwin S. Porter and the Edison Manufacturing Company* (Berkeley: University of California Press, 1991); Tom Gunning, *D. W. Griffith and the Origins of American Narrative Film: The Early Years at Biograph* (Urbana: University of Illinois Press, 1991); and Ben Brewster and Lea Jacobs, *Theatre to Cinema: Stage Pictorialism and the Early Feature Film* (Oxford: Oxford University Press, 1997).
5. Douglas Gomery, "The Coming of Sound: Technological Change in the American Film Industry," in Tino Balio, ed., *The American Film Industry*, rev. ed. (Madison: University of Wisconsin Press, 1985), pp. 229–51. (See "Notes and Queries," Chapter 9.)

ONE

EARLY CINEMA

The medium of cinema appeared in the mid-1890s, an era when the United States was still expanding into one of the world's major colonialist powers. The Spanish-American War of 1898 resulted in the United States' gaining control of Puerto Rico, the Philippines, Guam, Hawaii, and part of Samoa. The United States itself was still in the process of formation. Idaho, Montana, and North and South Dakota had become states in 1889, and Arizona and New Mexico would not enter the Union until 1912. During the late nineteenth century, railroad, oil, tobacco, and other industries were expanding rapidly, and, in 1890, the Sherman Antitrust Act was passed in an attempt to limit the growth of monopolies.

Due to hard times in southern and eastern Europe, a new wave of immigrants arrived on American shores after 1890. Living mostly in ethnic communities within large cities, these non-English speakers would form a sizable audience for the silent cinema.

The first decade of the new century saw a progressivist impulse in America, under the presidency of Theodore Roosevelt. There were movements to give women the vote, to prohibit child labor, to enforce antitrust laws, and to institute regulations to protect consumers. This era was also one of virulent racism, scarred by many lynchings. African American progressives formed the National Association for the Advancement of Colored People in 1909.

American expansion came at a time when the major European powers had already established far-flung empires and were engaged in an intricate game of jockeying for further power in such unstable areas as the Balkan States and the decaying Ottoman Empire. Tensions over such maneuvering, as well as mutual distrust, especially between France and Germany, led to the outbreak of World War I in 1914. This conflict gradually drew countries from all over the globe into the fighting. Although many citizens wanted no involvement, the United States entered the fray in 1917 and broke the stalemate that had developed, ultimately forcing Germany to surrender in 1918.

The global balance of power had shifted. Germany lost many of its colonies, and the United States emerged as the world's leading financial force. President Woodrow Wilson tried to expand progressivist principles on an international scale, proposing a League of Nations to foster world unity. The League, formed in 1919, helped build a spirit of international cooperation during the 1920s, but it proved too weak to prevent lingering tensions from eventually causing a second international conflict.

During the three decades before World War I, the cinema was invented and grew from a small amusement-arcade business to an international industry. Films began as brief moving views presented as novelties, and, by the mid-1910s, the lengthy narrative feature film became the basis for cinema programs.

The invention of the cinema was a lengthy process, involving engineers and entrepreneurs in several countries. Struggles among patent holders in the United States slowed the development of the industry here, while French companies quickly seized the lead in markets throughout the world (Chapter 1).

From 1905 on, a rapid expansion in demand for motion-picture entertainment in the United States led to the spread of small movie theaters called nickelodeons. This demand was fueled in part by the rising immigrant population and in part by the shorter work hours gained by the increasingly militant labor-union movement. Soon America was far and away the world's largest market for films—a situation that would allow it to increase its selling power abroad as well.

During the period of the "nickelodeon boom," the story film became the main type of fare offered on programs. Films made in France, Italy, Denmark, the United Kingdom, the United States, and elsewhere circulated widely around the world. Narrative traits and stylistic techniques changed rapidly as influences passed back and forth among countries. Movies grew longer, employed more editing, added explanatory intertitles, and featured a greater variety of camera distances. Adaptations from literature and lavish historical spectacles added prestige to the new art form (Chapter 2).

World War I had enormous effects on the cinema. The outbreak of hostilities triggered a severe cutback in French production, and the country lost its leading position in world markets. Italy soon encountered similar problems. The growing Hollywood film industry stepped in to fill the gap in supply, expanding its distribution system abroad. By the war's end, American films had an international grip that other countries would struggle, usually with limited success, to loosen.

During this era, filmmakers in many countries explored film form. Film editing grew subtle and complex, acting styles became varied, and directors exploited long takes, realistic decor, and camera movement. By the end of World War I, many of today's film conventions had been established (Chapter 3).

CHAPTER 1

THE INVENTION AND EARLY YEARS OF THE CINEMA, 1880s–1904

The nineteenth century saw a vast proliferation of visual forms of popular culture. The industrial era offered ways of mass-producing lantern slides, books of photographs, and illustrated fiction. The middle and working classes of many countries could visit elaborate *dioramas*—painted backdrops with three-dimensional figures depicting famous historical events. Circuses, "freak shows," amusement parks, and music halls provided other forms of inexpensive entertainment. In the United States, numerous dramatic troupes toured, performing in the theaters and opera houses that existed even in small towns.

Hauling entire theater productions from town to town, however, was expensive. Similarly, most people had to travel long distances to visit major dioramas or amusement parks. In the days before airplane travel, few could hope to see firsthand the exotic lands they glimpsed in static view in books of travel photographs or in their *stereoscopes*, hand-held viewers that created three-dimensional effects by using oblong cards with two photographs printed side by side.

The cinema was to offer a cheaper, simpler way of providing entertainment to the masses. Filmmakers could record actors' performances, which then could be shown to audiences around the world. Travelogues would bring the sights of far-flung places, with movement, directly to spectators' hometowns. Movies would become the most popular visual art form of the late Victorian age.

The cinema was invented during the 1890s. It appeared in the wake of the industrial revolution, as did the telephone (invented in 1876), the phonograph (1877), and the automobile (developed during the 1880s and 1890s). Like them, it was a technological device that became the basis of a large industry. It was also a new form of entertainment and a new artistic medium. During the first decade of the cinema's existence, inventors worked to improve the machines for making and showing films.

Filmmakers also had to explore what sorts of images they could record, and exhibitors had to figure out how to present those images to audiences.

THE INVENTION OF THE CINEMA

The cinema is a complicated medium, and before it could be invented, several technological requirements had to be met.

Preconditions for Motion Pictures

First, scientists had to realize that the human eye will perceive motion if a series of slightly different images is placed before it in rapid succession—minimally, around sixteen per second. During the nineteenth century, scientists explored this property of vision. Several optical toys were marketed that gave an illusion of movement by using a small number of drawings, each altered somewhat. In 1832, Belgian physicist Joseph Plateau and Austrian geometry professor Simon Stampfer independently created the optical device that came to be called the Phenakistoscope (**1.1**). The Zoetrope, invented in 1833, contained a series of drawings on a narrow strip of paper inside a revolving drum (**1.2**). The Zoetrope was widely sold after 1867, along with other optical toys. Similar principles were later used in films, but in these toys, the same action was repeated over and over.

A second technological requirement for the cinema was the capacity to project a rapid series of images on a surface. Since the seventeenth century, entertainers and educators had been using "magic lanterns" to project glass lantern slides, but there had been no way to flash large numbers of images fast enough to create the illusion of motion.

A third prerequisite for the invention of the cinema was the ability to use photography to make successive pictures on a clear surface. The exposure time would have to be short enough to take sixteen or more frames in a single second. Such techniques came about slowly. The first still photograph was made on a glass plate in 1826 by Claude Niépce, but it required an exposure time of eight hours. For years, photographs were made on glass or metal, without the use of negatives, so only one copy of each image was possible; exposures took several minutes each. In 1839, Henry Fox Talbot introduced negatives made on paper. At about this same time, it became possible to print photographic images on glass lantern slides and project them. Not until 1878, however, did split-second exposure times become feasible.

Fourth, the cinema would require that photographs be printed on a base flexible enough to be passed through a camera rapidly. Strips or discs of glass could be used, but only a short series of images could be registered on them. In 1888, George Eastman devised a still camera that made photographs on rolls of sensitized paper. This camera, which he named the Kodak, simpli-

1.1 A phenakistoscope's spinning disc of figures gives the illusion of movement when the viewer looks through a slot in the stationary disc.

1.2 Looking through the slots in a revolving Zoetrope, the viewer receives an impression of movement.

1.3   One of Muybridge's earliest motion studies, photographed on June 19, 1878.

fied photography so that unskilled amateurs could take pictures. The next year Eastman introduced transparent celluloid roll film, creating a breakthrough in the move toward cinema. The film was intended for still cameras, but inventors could use the same flexible material in designing machines to take and project motion pictures (though it was apparently about a year before the stock was improved enough to be practical).

Fifth, and finally, experimenters needed to find a suitable intermittent mechanism for their cameras and projectors. In the camera, the strip of film had to stop briefly while light entered through the lens and exposed each frame; a shutter then covered the film as another frame moved into place. Similarly, in the projector, each frame stopped for an instant in the aperture while a beam of light projected it onto a screen; again a shutter passed behind the lens while the filmstrip moved. At least sixteen frames had to slide into place, stop, and move away each second. (A strip of film sliding continuously past the gate would create a blur unless the light source was quite dim.) Fortunately, other inventions of the century also needed intermittent mechanisms to stop and start quickly. For example, the sewing machine (invented in 1846) advanced strips of fabric several times per second while a needle pierced them. Intermittent mechanisms usually consisted of a gear with slots or notches spaced around its edge.

By the 1890s, all the technical conditions necessary for the cinema existed. The question was Who would bring the necessary elements together in a way that could be successfully exploited on a wide basis?

Major Precursors of Motion Pictures

Some inventors made important contributions without creating moving photographic images. Several men were simply interested in analyzing motion. In 1878, ex-governor of California Leland Stanford asked photographer Eadweard Muybridge to find a way of photographing running horses to help study their gaits. Muybridge set up a row of twelve cameras, each making an exposure in one-thousandth of a second. The photos recorded one-half-second intervals of movement (**1,3**). Muybridge later made a lantern to project moving images of horses, but these were drawings copied from his photographs onto a revolving disc. Muybridge did not go on to invent motion pictures, but he made a major contribution to anatomical science through thousands of motion studies using his multiple-camera setup.

In 1882, inspired by Muybridge's work, French physiologist Étienne Jules Marey studied the flight of birds and other rapid animal movements by means of a photographic gun. Shaped like a rifle, it exposed twelve images around the edge of a circular glass plate that

1.4 Using long flexible bands of drawings, Reynaud's Praxinoscope rear-projected cartoon figures onto a screen on which the scenery was painted.

made a single revolution in one second. In 1888, Marey built a box-type camera that used an intermittent mechanism to expose a series of photographs on a strip of paper film at speeds of up to 120 frames per second. Marey was the first to combine flexible film stock and an intermittent mechanism in photographing motion. He was interested in analyzing movements rather than in reproducing them on a screen, but his work inspired other inventors. During this same period, many other scientists used various devices to record and analyze movement.

A fascinating and isolated figure in the history of the invention of the cinema was Frenchman Émile Reynaud. In 1877, he had built an optical toy, the Projecting Praxinoscope. This was a spinning drum, rather like the Zoetrope, but one in which viewers saw the moving images in a series of mirrors rather than through slots. Around 1882, he devised a way of using mirrors and a lantern to project a brief series of drawings on a screen. In 1889, Reynaud exhibited a much larger version of the Praxinoscope. From 1892 on, he regularly gave public performances using long, broad strips of hand-painted frames (**1.4**). These were the first public exhibitions of moving images, though the effect on the screen was jerky and slow. The labor involved in making the bands meant that Reynaud's films could not easily be reproduced. Strips of photographs were more practical, and in 1895 Reynaud started using a camera to make his Praxinoscope films. By 1900, he was out of business, however, due to competition from other, simpler motion-picture projection systems. In despair,

he destroyed his machines, though replicas have been constructed.

Another Frenchman came close to inventing the cinema as early as 1888—six years before the first commercial showings of moving photographs. That year, Augustin Le Prince, working in England, was able to make some brief films, shot at about sixteen frames per second, using Kodak's recently introduced paper roll film. To be projected, however, the frames needed to be printed on a transparent strip; lacking flexible celluloid, Le Prince apparently was unable to devise a satisfactory projector. In 1890, while traveling in France, he disappeared, along with his valise of patent applications, creating a mystery that has never been solved. Thus his camera was never exploited commercially and had virtually no influence on the subsequent invention of the cinema.

An International Process of Invention

It is difficult to attribute the invention of the cinema to a single source. There was no one moment when the cinema emerged. Rather, the technology of the motion picture came about through an accumulation of contributions, primarily from the United States, Germany, England, and France.

Edison, Dickson, and the Kinetoscope In 1888, Thomas Edison, already the successful inventor of the phonograph and the electric lightbulb, decided to design machines for making and showing moving photographs. Much of the work was done by his assistant, W. K. L.

Dickson. Since Edison's phonograph worked by recording sound on cylinders, the pair tried fruitlessly to make rows of tiny photographs around similar cylinders. In 1889, Edison went to Paris and saw Marey's camera,

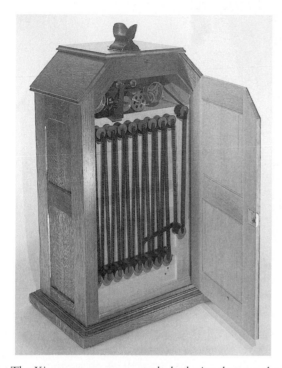

1.5   The Kinetoscope was a peephole device that ran the film around a series of rollers. Viewers activated it by putting a coin in a slot.

which used strips of flexible film. Dickson then obtained some Eastman Kodak film stock and began working on a new type of machine. By 1891, the Kinetograph camera and Kinetoscope viewing box (**1.5**) were ready to be patented and demonstrated. Dickson sliced sheets of Eastman film into strips 1 inch wide (roughly 35 millimeters), spliced them end to end, and punched four holes on either side of each frame so that toothed gears could pull the film through the camera and Kinetoscope. Dickson's early decisions influenced the entire history of the cinema; 35mm film stock with four perforations per frame has remained the norm. (Amazingly, an original Kinetoscope film can be shown on a modern projector.) Initially, however, the film was exposed at about forty-six frames per second—much faster than the average speed later adopted for silent filmmaking.

Edison and Dickson needed films for their machines before they could exploit them commercially. They built a small studio, called the Black Maria, on the grounds of Edison's New Jersey laboratory and were ready for production by January 1893 (**1.6**). The films lasted only twenty seconds or so—the longest run of film that the Kinetoscope could hold. Most films featured well-known sports figures, excerpts from noted vaudeville acts, or performances by dancers or acrobats (**1.7**). Annie Oakley displayed her riflery and a bodybuilder flexed his muscles. A few Kinetoscope shorts were knockabout comic skits, forerunners of the story film.

1.6   Edison's studio was named after the police paddy wagons, or Black Marias, that it resembled. The slanted portion of the roof opened to admit sunlight for filming, and the whole building revolved on a track to catch optimal sunlight.

1.7   Amy Muller danced in the Black Maria on March 24, 1896. The black background and patch of sunlight from the opening in the roof were standard traits of Kinetoscope films.

1.8 A typical entertainment parlor, with phonographs (note the dangling earphones) at left and center and a row of Kinetoscopes at the right.

Edison had exploited his phonograph by leasing it to special phonograph parlors, where the public paid a nickel to hear records through earphones. (Only in 1895 did phonographs become available for home use.) He did the same with the Kinetoscope. On April 14, 1894, the first Kinetoscope parlor opened in New York. Soon other parlors, both in the United States and abroad, exhibited the machines (**1.8**). For about two years the Kinetoscope was highly profitable, but it was eclipsed when other inventors, inspired by Edison's new device, found ways to project films on a screen.

European Contributions Another early system for taking and projecting films was invented by the Germans Max and Emil Skladanowsky. Their Bioscop held two strips of film, each 3½ inches wide, running side by side; frames of each were projected alternately. The Skladanowsky brothers showed a fifteen-minute program at a large vaudeville theater in Berlin on November 1, 1895—nearly two months before the famous Lumière screening at the Grand Café (see below). The Bioscop system was too cumbersome, however, and the Skladanowskys eventually adopted the standard 35mm, single-strip film used by more influential inventors. The brothers toured Europe through 1897, but they did not establish a stable production company.

The Lumière brothers, Louis and Auguste, invented a projection system that helped make the cinema a commercially viable enterprise internationally. Their family company, Lumière Frères, based in Lyon, France, was the biggest European manufacturer of pho-

tographic plates. In 1894, a local Kinetoscope exhibitor asked them to produce short films that would be cheaper than the ones sold by Edison. Soon they had designed an elegant little camera, the Cinématographe, which used 35mm film and an intermittent mechanism modeled on that of the sewing machine (**1.9**). The camera could serve as a printer when the positive copies were made. Then, mounted in front of a magic lantern, it formed part of the projector as well. One important decision the Lumières made was to shoot their films at sixteen frames

1.9 Unlike many other early cameras, the Lumière Cinématographe was small and portable. This 1930 photo shows Francis Doublier, one of the firm's representatives who toured the world showing and making films during the 1890s, posing with his Cinématographe.

1.10, *left*   The Lumière brothers' first film, *Workers Leaving the Factory*, was a single shot made outside their photographic factory. It embodied the essential appeal of the first films: realistic movement of actual people.

1.11, *right*   Birt Acres's *Rough Sea at Dover*, one of the earliest English films, showed large waves crashing against a seawall.

per second (rather than the forty-six frames per second used by Edison); this rate became the standard international film speed for about twenty-five years. The first film made with this system was *Workers Leaving the Factory*, apparently shot in March 1895 (**1.10**). It was shown in public at a meeting of the Société d'Encouragement à l'Industrie Nationale in Paris on March 22. Six further showings to scientific and commercial groups followed, including additional films shot by Louis.

On December 28, 1895, one of the most famous film screenings in history took place. The location was a room in the Grand Café in Paris. In those days, cafés were gathering spots where people sipped coffee, read newspapers, and were entertained by singers and other performers. That evening, fashionable patrons paid a franc to see a twenty-five minute program of ten films, about a minute each. Among the films shown were a close view of Auguste Lumière and his wife feeding their baby, a staged comic scene of a boy stepping on a hose to cause a puzzled gardener to squirt himself (later named *Arroseur arrosé*, or "The Waterer Watered"), and a shot of the sea.

Although the first shows did moderate business, within weeks the Lumières were offering twenty shows a day, with long lines of spectators waiting to get in. They moved quickly to exploit this success, sending representatives all over the world to show and make more short films.

At the same time that the Lumière brothers were developing their system, a parallel process of invention was going on in England. The Edison Kinetoscope had premiered in London in October 1894, and the parlor that displayed the machines did so well that it asked R. W. Paul, a producer of photographic equipment, to make some extra machines for it. For reasons that are still not clear, Edison had not patented the Kinetoscope outside the United States, so Paul was free to sell copies to anyone who wanted them. Since Edison would supply films only to exhibitors who had leased his own machines, Paul also had to invent a camera and make films to go with his duplicate Kinetoscopes.

By March 1895, Paul and his partner, Birt Acres, had a functional camera, which they based partly on the one Marey had made seven years earlier for analyzing motion. Acres shot thirteen films during the first half of the year, but the partnership broke up. Paul went on improving the camera, aiming to serve the Kinetoscope market, while Acres concentrated on creating a projector. On January 14, 1896, Acres showed some of his films to the Royal Photographic Society. Among these was *Rough Sea at Dover* (**1.11**), which would become one of the most popular first films. Seeing such one-shot films of simple actions or landscapes today, we can hardly grasp how impressive they were to audiences who had never seen moving photographic images. A contemporary review of Acres's Royal Photographic Society program hints, however, at their appeal:

> The most successful effect, and one which called forth rounds of applause from the usually placid members of the "Royal," was a reproduction of a number of breaking waves, which may be seen to roll in from the sea, curl over against a jetty, and break into clouds of snowy spray that seemed to start from the screen.[1]

Acres gave other demonstrations, but he did not systematically exploit his projector and films.

Projected films were soon shown regularly in England, however. The Lumière brothers sent a representative who opened a successful run of the Cinématographe in London on February 20, 1896, about a month after Acres's first screening. Paul went on improving his camera and invented a projector, which he used in several theaters to show copies of the films Acres had shot the year before. Unlike other inventors, Paul sold his machines rather than leasing them. By doing so, he not only speeded up the spread of the film industry in Great Britain but also supplied filmmakers and exhibitors abroad who were unable to get other machines. Among them was one of the most important early directors, Georges Méliès.

American Developments   During this period, projection systems and cameras were also being devised in the United States. Three important rival groups competed to introduce a commercially successful system.

Woodville Latham and his sons Otway and Gray began work on a camera and projector in 1894 and were able to show one film to reporters on April 21, 1895. They even opened a small storefront theater in May, where their program ran for years. The projector did not attract much attention, because it cast only a dim image. The Latham group did make one considerable contribution to film technology, however. Most cameras and projectors could use only a short stretch of film, lasting less than three minutes, since the tension created by a longer, heavier roll would break the film. The Lathams added a simple loop to create slack and thus relieve the tension, allowing much longer films to be made. The Latham loop has been used in most cameras and projectors ever since. Indeed, so important was the technique that a patent involving it was to shake up the entire American film industry in 1912. An improved Latham projector was used by some exhibitors, but other systems able to cast brighter images gained greater success.

A second group of entrepreneurs, the partnership of C. Francis Jenkins and Thomas Armat, first exhibited their Phantoscope projector at a commercial exposition in Atlanta in October 1895, showing Kinetoscope films. Partly due to competition from the Latham group and a Kinetoscope exhibitor, who also showed films at the exposition, and partly due to dim, unsteady projection, the Phantoscope attracted skimpy audiences. Later that year, Jenkins and Armat split up. Armat improved the projector, renamed it the Vitascope, and obtained backing from the entrepreneurial team of Norman Raff and Frank Gammon. Raff and Gammon were nervous about offending Edison, so in February they demonstrated the machine for him. Since the Kinetoscope's initial popularity was fading, Edison agreed to manufacture Armat's projector and supply films for it. For publicity purposes, it was marketed as "Edison's Vitascope," even though he had had no hand in devising it.

The Vitascope's public premiere was at Koster and Bial's Music Hall in New York on April 23, 1896. Six films were shown, five of them originally shot for the Kinetoscope; the sixth was Acres's *Rough Sea at Dover*, which again was singled out for praise. The showing was a triumph, and although it was not the first time films had been projected commercially in the United States, it marked the beginning of projected movies as a viable industry there.

1.12   At the right, a Mutoscope, a penny-in-the-slot machine with a crank that turned a drum containing a series of photographs. The stand at the left shows the circular arrangement of the cards, each of which flipped down and was briefly held still to create the illusion of movement.

The third major early invention in the United States began as another peepshow device. In late 1894, Herman Casler patented the Mutoscope, a flip-card device (**1.12**). He needed a camera, however, and sought advice from his friend W. K. L. Dickson, who had terminated his working relationship with Edison. With other partners, they formed the American Mutoscope Company. By early 1896, Casler and Dickson had their camera, but the market for peepshow movies had declined, and they decided to concentrate on projection. Using several films made during that year, the American Mutoscope Company soon had programs playing theaters around the country and touring with vaudeville shows.

The camera and projector were unusual, employing 70mm film that yielded larger, sharper images. By 1897, American Mutoscope was the most popular film company in the country. That year the firm also began showing its films in penny arcades and other entertainment spots, using the Mutoscope. The simple card holder of the Mutoscope was less likely to break down than was the Kinetoscope, and American Mutoscope soon dominated the peepshow side of film exhibition as well. (Some Mutoscopes remained in use for decades.)

By 1897, the invention of the cinema was largely completed. There were two principal means of exhibition: peepshow devices for individual viewers and projection systems for audiences. Typically, projectors used 35mm film with sprocket holes of similar shape and placement, so most films could be shown on different brands of projectors. But what kinds of films were being made? Who was making them? How and where were people seeing them?

EARLY FILMMAKING AND EXHIBITION

The cinema may have been an amazing novelty in the 1890s, but it came into being within a larger and varied context of Victorian leisure-time activities. During the late nineteenth century, many households had optical toys like the Zoetrope and stereoscope. Sets of cards depicted exotic locales or staged narratives. Many middle-class families also owned pianos, around which they gathered to sing. Increased literacy led to the spread of cheap popular fiction. The newfound ability to print photographs led to the publication of travel books that took the reader on vicarious tours of distant lands.

A great assortment of public entertainments was also available. All but the tiniest towns had theaters, and traveling shows crisscrossed the country. These included dramatic troupes putting on plays, lecturers using magic-lantern slides to illustrate their talks, and even concerts featuring the newly invented phonograph to bring the sounds of big-city orchestras to a wide public. Vaudeville offered middle-class audiences a variety of acts on a single program, ranging from performing animals to plate-spinning jugglers to slapstick comedians. Burlesque offered a similar potpourri of acts, though less family-oriented with their vulgar comedy and occasional nudity. People living in large cities also could go to amusement parks, like Coney Island in New York, which offered such attractions as roller coasters and elephant rides.

Scenics, Topicals, and Fiction Films

The new medium of film moved smoothly into this spectrum of popular entertainment. Like the early films that we have already mentioned, most subjects were nonfiction, or *actualities*. These included *scenics,* or short travelogues offering views of distant lands. News events might be depicted in brief *topicals.*

In many cases, cinematographers covered news events in the locations where they occurred. Often, however, filmmakers recreated current events in the studio—both to save money and to make up for the fact that cameramen had not been on the scene. In 1898, for example, both American and European producers used model ships in miniature landscapes to re-create the sinking of the battleship *Maine* and other key occurrences relating to the Spanish-American War. Audiences probably did not believe that these faked scenes were actual records of real incidents. Instead, they accepted them as representations of those incidents, comparable to engravings in newsmagazines.

From the beginning, *fiction films* were also important. Typically these were brief staged scenes. The Lumières' *Arroseur arrosé,* presented in their first program in 1895, showed a boy tricking a gardener by stepping on his hose. Such simple jokes formed a major genre of early filmmaking. Some of these fiction films were shot outdoors, but simple painted backdrops were quickly adopted and remained common for decades.

Creating an Appealing Program

Looking at the earliest films, we may find them so alien that we wonder what sort of appeal they held for audiences. With a little imagination, though, we can see that people then were probably interested in films for much the same reasons that we are. Every type of early film has some equivalent in contemporary media. The glimpses of news events, for example, may seem crude, yet they are comparable to the short clips shown on television news programs. Early scenics gave viewers glimpses of faraway lands, just as today college and church lectures and televised documentaries utilize films to show similarly exotic views. An evening of television offers a mix of shows that is somewhat comparable to early film programs. Despite the variety of early genres, fiction films gradually became the most popular attraction—a position they have held ever since.

Most films in this early period consisted of a single shot. The camera was set up in one position, and the action unfolded during a continuous take. In some cases, filmmakers did make a series of shots of the same subject. The resulting shots were then treated as a series of separate films. Exhibitors had the option of buying the whole series of shots and running them together, thus approximating a multishot film, or they might choose to buy only a few of the shots, combining them with other films or lantern slides to create a unique program. During this early period, exhibitors had considerable control over the

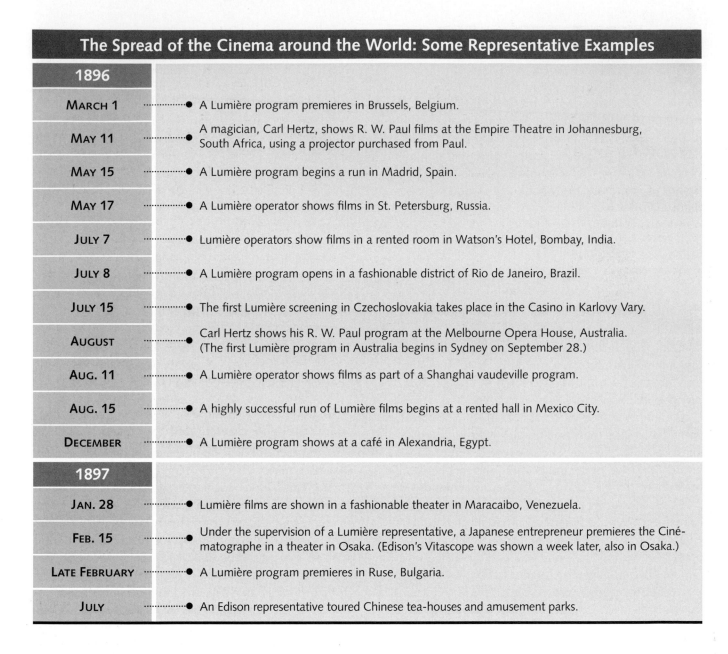

The Spread of the Cinema around the World: Some Representative Examples

1896

MARCH 1	A Lumière program premieres in Brussels, Belgium.
MAY 11	A magician, Carl Hertz, shows R. W. Paul films at the Empire Theatre in Johannesburg, South Africa, using a projector purchased from Paul.
MAY 15	A Lumière program begins a run in Madrid, Spain.
MAY 17	A Lumière operator shows films in St. Petersburg, Russia.
JULY 7	Lumière operators show films in a rented room in Watson's Hotel, Bombay, India.
JULY 8	A Lumière program opens in a fashionable district of Rio de Janeiro, Brazil.
JULY 15	The first Lumière screening in Czechoslovakia takes place in the Casino in Karlovy Vary.
AUGUST	Carl Hertz shows his R. W. Paul program at the Melbourne Opera House, Australia. (The first Lumière program in Australia begins in Sydney on September 28.)
AUG. 11	A Lumière operator shows films as part of a Shanghai vaudeville program.
AUG. 15	A highly successful run of Lumière films begins at a rented hall in Mexico City.
DECEMBER	A Lumière program shows at a café in Alexandria, Egypt.

1897

JAN. 28	Lumière films are shown in a fashionable theater in Maracaibo, Venezuela.
FEB. 15	Under the supervision of a Lumière representative, a Japanese entrepreneur premieres the Cinématographe in a theater in Osaka. (Edison's Vitascope was shown a week later, also in Osaka.)
LATE FEBRUARY	A Lumière program premieres in Ruse, Bulgaria.
JULY	An Edison representative toured Chinese tea-houses and amusement parks.

shape of their programs—a control that would gradually disappear from 1899 onward, as producers began making longer films consisting of multiple shots.

Quite a few of these early exhibitors had experience running lantern-slide programs or other forms of public entertainment. Many mixed scenics, topicals, and fiction films in a single, varied program. The typical program had musical accompaniment. In the more modest presentations, a pianist might play; in vaudeville theaters, the house orchestra provided music. In some cases, exhibitors had noises synchronized with the actions on the screen. The exhibitor might lecture during part of the program, describing the exotic landscapes, the current events, and the brief stories passing across the screen. At the least, the exhibitor would announce the titles, since early films had no credits at the beginning or intertitles

to explain the action. Some showmen mixed films with lantern slides or provided musical interludes using a phonograph. During these early years, the audience's response depended significantly on the exhibitor's skill in organizing and presenting the program.

During the first decade of cinema, films were shown in many countries around the world. But the making of films was concentrated largely in the three principal countries where the motion-picture camera had originated: France, England, and the United States.

The Growth of the French Film Industry

The Lumières' early screenings were successful, but the brothers believed that film would be a short-lived fad. As a result, they moved quickly to exploit the Ciné-

1.13   Lumière operator Eugène Promio influenced many filmmakers by placing his camera in moving boats to make several of his films, including *Egypte: Panorama des rives du Nil* ("Egypt: Panorama of the Banks of the Nile," 1896).

matographe. They initially avoided selling their machines, instead sending operators to tour abroad, showing films in rented theaters and cafés. These operators also made one-shot scenics of local points of interest. From 1896 on, the Lumière catalogue rapidly expanded to include hundreds of views of Spain, Egypt, Italy, Japan, and many other countries. Although the Lumière brothers are usually remembered for their scenics and topicals, they also produced many staged films, usually brief comic scenes.

Some of the Lumière operators' films were technically innovative. Eugène Promio, for example, is usually credited with originating the moving camera. The earliest cameras were supported by rigid tripods that did not allow the camera to swivel and make panorama, or panning, shots. In 1896, Promio introduced movement into a view of Venice by placing the tripod and camera in a gondola. Promio and other filmmakers continued this practice, placing their cameras in boats and on trains (**1.13**). Traveling shots of this type (and soon panning movements as well) were associated mainly with scenics and topicals during this era.

Because the Lumières quickly began exhibiting their films abroad, the first showings of projected motion pictures in many countries were put on by their representatives. Thus the history of the cinema in many nations begins with the arrival of the Cinématographe. This is apparent from the previous box, which samples the earliest known public screenings in several countries.

Of course, the Lumières and their rivals concentrated on the more lucrative markets and avoided some smaller countries. No screenings are known to have taken place in Bolivia, for example, until 1909, when two Italian entrepreneurs took films there. Ideological pressures kept the cinema out of some markets. In 1900, Iran's royal family obtained a camera and projector in Europe and began making home movies. A the-

ater that opened in Tehran in 1905, however, was soon forced by religious leaders to close.

On the whole, though, the Lumières and a few other firms made the cinema an international phenomenon. The Lumières further aided the spread of cinema when, in 1897, they began selling their Cinématographes.

The same year saw a setback for their firm, however. On May 4, 1897, during a film screening at the Charity Bazaar in Paris, a curtain was ignited by the ether being used to fuel the lamp of the projector (which was not a Cinématographe). The resulting blaze was one of the worst tragedies in the history of the cinema, killing about 125 people, most of them from the upper class. As a result, the cinema lost some of its attraction for fashionable city dwellers. In France, for several years, films were mainly exhibited in less lucrative traveling fairground shows (*fêtes foraines*). The Lumières continued producing films, but gradually more innovative rivals made their films seem old-fashioned. Their firm ceased production in 1905, though Louis and Auguste remained innovators in the area of still photography.

Following the initial success of the Lumière Cinématographe in 1895, other film production firms appeared in France. Among these was a small company started by a man who was perhaps the single most important filmmaker of the cinema's early years, Georges Méliès (see box).

Two other firms that were to dominate the French film industry were formed shortly after the invention of the cinema. Charles Pathé was a phonograph seller and exhibitor in the early 1890s. In 1895, he purchased some of R. W. Paul's imitation Kinetoscopes, and the following year formed Pathé Frères, which initially made most of its money on phonographs. From 1901, however, Pathé concentrated more on film production, and profits soared. The firm expanded rapidly. In 1902, it built a glass-sided studio and began selling the Pathé camera, which became the world's most widely used camera until the end of the 1910s.

At first Pathé's production was somewhat derivative, borrowing ideas from Méliès and from American and English films. For example, in 1901, Ferdinand Zecca, the company's most important director, made *Scenes from My Balcony*. It picked up on the vogue, recently started in England, for shots presenting things as if seen through telescopes or microscopes (**1.17, 1.18**). Pathé's films were extremely popular. While it only took a sale of 15 prints of a film to break even, actual sales averaged 350 prints. Pathé expanded abroad, opening sales offices in London, New York, Moscow, Berlin, and St. Petersburg in 1904 and 1905 and others in later years. Selling both projectors and films, Pathé encouraged people to

GEORGES MÉLIÈS, MAGICIAN OF THE CINEMA

Méliès was a performing magician who owned his own theater. After seeing the Lumière Cinématographe in 1895, he decided to add films to his program, but the Lumière brothers were not yet selling machines. In early 1896, he obtained a projector from English inventor R. W. Paul and by studying it was able to build his own camera. He was soon showing films at his theater.

Although Méliès is remembered mainly for his delightful fantasy movies, replete with camera tricks and painted scenery, he made films in all the genres of the day. His earliest work, most of which is lost, included many Lumière-style scenics and brief comedies, filmed outdoors. During his first year of production, he made seventy-eight films, including his first trick film, *The Vanishing Lady* (1896). In it, Méliès appears as a magician who transforms a woman into a skeleton. The trick was accomplished by stopping the camera and substituting the skeleton for the woman. Later, Méliès used stop-motion and other special effects to create more complex magic and fantasy scenes. These tricks had to be accomplished in the camera, while filming;

prior to the mid-1920s, few laboratory manipulations were possible. Méliès also acted in many of his films, recognizable as a dapper and spry figure with a bald head, moustache, and pointed beard.

In order to be able to control the mise-en-scène and cinematography of his films, Méliès built a small glass-enclosed studio. Finished by early 1897, the studio permitted Méliès to design and construct sets painted on canvas flats (**1.14**). Even working in this studio, however, Méliès continued to create various kinds of films. In 1898, for example, he filmed some reconstructed topicals, such as *Divers at Work on the Wreck of the "Maine"* (**1.15**). His 1899 film, *The Dreyfus Affair,* told the story of the Jewish officer convicted of treason in 1894 on the basis of false evidence put forth through anti-Semitic motives. The controversy was still raging when Méliès made his pro-Dreyfus picture. As was customary at the time, he released each of the ten shots as a separate film. When shown together, the shots combined into one of the most complex works of the cinema's early years. (Modern prints of *The Dreyfus Affair*

1.14   The interior of the Star studio, with Méliès on the balcony lifting a rolled backdrop while assistants arrange a large painted shell and trapdoors. Painted theater-style flats and smaller set elements are stored at the right rear or hang on the back wall.

enter the exhibition business, thus creating more demand for Pathé films. As we shall see in the next chapter, within a few years, Pathé Frères would be the single largest film company in the world.

Its main rival in France was a smaller firm formed by inventor Léon Gaumont. Like Lumière Frères, Gaumont initially dealt in still photographic equipment. The firm began producing films in 1897. These were mostly actualities made by Alice Guy, the first female film-maker. Gaumont's involvement in film production re-

mained limited in this era, since Léon was more concerned with technical innovations in film equipment. Building a production studio in 1905 made Gaumont more prominent, largely through the work of director Louis Feuillade.

England and the Brighton School

After the first public film screenings in early 1896, film exhibition spread quickly in England, largely because

1.15 One of many reconstructed documentaries relating to the sinking of the American battleship *Maine,* which began the Spanish-American War. Georges Méliès's *Divers at Work on the Wreck of the "Maine"* used a painted set with actors playing the divers. A fish tank in front of the camera suggested an undersea scene.

1.16 The space capsule lands in the Man in the Moon's eye in Méliès's fantasy *A Trip to the Moon.*

typically combine all the shots in a single reel.) With his next work, *Cinderella* (1899), Méliès began joining multiple shots and selling them as one film.

Méliès's films, and especially his fantasies, were extremely popular in France and abroad, and they were widely imitated. They were also commonly pirated, and Méliès had to open a sales office in the United States in 1903 to protect his interests. Among the most celebrated of his films was *A Trip to the Moon* (1902), a comic science-fiction story of a group of scientists traveling to the moon in a space capsule and escaping after being taken prisoner by a race of subterranean creatures (**1.16**). Méliès often enhanced the beauty of his elaborately designed mise-en-scène by using hand-applied tinting (**Color Plate 1.1**).

Except in Méliès's first years of production, many of his films involved sophisticated stop-motion effects. Devils burst out of a cloud of smoke, pretty women vanish, and leaping men change into demons in midair. Some historians have criticized Méliès for depending on static theatrical sets instead of editing. Yet recent research has shown that in fact his stop-motion effects also utilized editing. He would cut the film in order to match the movement of one object perfectly with that of the thing into which it was transformed. Such cuts were designed to be unnoticeable, but clearly Méliès was a master of one type of editing.

For a time, Méliès's films continued to be widely successful. After 1905, however, his fortunes slowly declined. His tiny firm was hard put to supply the burgeoning demand for films, especially in the face of competition from bigger companies. He continued to produce quality films, including his late masterpiece *Conquest of the Pole* (1912), but eventually these came to seem old-fashioned as filmmaking conventions changed. In 1912, deep in debt, Méliès stopped producing, having made 510 films (about 40 percent of which survive). He died in 1938, after decades of working in his wife's candy and toy shop.

1.17, 1.18 One of many mildly risqué films made in this early period, Zecca's *Scenes from My Balcony* shows a man looking through a telescope, followed by shots of what he sees, including a woman undressing.

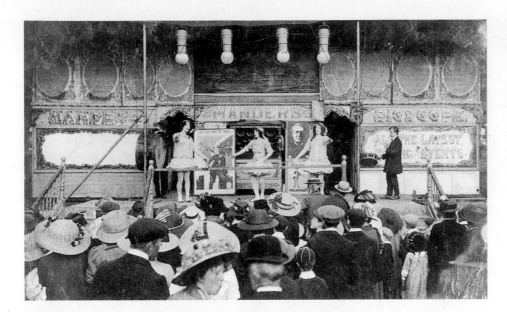

1.19 A typical fairground film show in England, about 1900. Behind the elaborate painted façades, the auditoriums were simple tents. Note here the picture of Thomas Edison in the center and the use of a drum to attract spectators.

R. W. Paul was willing to sell projectors. At first, most films were grouped together to be shown as a single act on the program of a music hall (the British equivalent of American vaudeville theaters). Beginning in 1897, short, cheap film shows were also widely presented in fairgrounds, appealing to working-class audiences (**1.19**).

At first, most English filmmakers offered the usual novelty subjects. For example, in 1896, Paul made *Twins' Tea Party* (**1.20**). Topicals showing the annual Derby were popular, and both the parade celebrating Queen Victoria's Jubilee in 1897 and events relating to the Boer War in South Africa were widely circulated. Some of these early newsreels consisted of more than one shot. The operator might simply stop and restart the camera to capture only highlights of the action, or he might actually splice bits of film together to hurry the action along. Similarly, some scenics were influenced by the Lumière films' placement of the camera on moving vehicles. *Phantom rides*, designed to give the spectator the illusion of traveling, became popular in England and other countries (**1.21**). As elsewhere, in England exhibitors gathered many types of films into a varied program.

Early English films became famous for their imaginative special-effects cinematography. For example, Cecil Hepworth began producing on a small scale in 1899. At first he concentrated on actualities, but he soon directed trick films as well (**1.22**). Hepworth went on to become the most important British producer from 1905 to 1914.

1.20 Paul's *Twins' Tea Party* appealed to audiences by showing two cute toddlers squabbling and then kissing and making up. It was typical of many films of this era: a single shot taken on an open-air stage in direct sunlight, against a neutral backdrop.

1.21 *View from an Engine Front—Barnstaple,* made by the Warwick Trading Company in 1898, was typical of a popular genre, the phantom ride.

1.22 In Hepworth's *Explosion of a Motor Car* (1900), stop-motion changes a real car into a fake one, which promptly blows up. A passing bobbie dutifully inventories the body parts that rain in from above, creating a grim but amusing film.

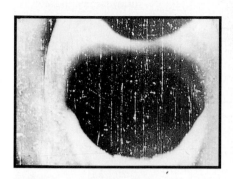

1.23, 1.24 Two stages of Williamson's *The Big Swallow,* as the irritated subject "eats" the cinematographer and camera.

1.25, 1.26 In *Mary Jane's Mishap,* close views alternate with long shots to show such detail as the maid's accidentally smearing a "moustache" on her face while shining some shoes.

There were other producers scattered around England, but the most notable were those in the small, but influential, group later dubbed the Brighton School because they worked in or near that resort town. Chief among them were G. A. Smith and James Williamson, both of whom were still photographers who branched into filmmaking in 1897. They also built small studios that opened at one side to admit sunlight. Both explored special effects and editing in ways that influenced filmmakers in other countries.

Williamson's 1900 film *The Big Swallow* is a good example of the ingenuity of the Brighton filmmakers. It begins with a view of a man, seen against a blank background, gesturing angrily because he does not want his picture taken. He walks forward until his wide-open mouth blots out the view (**1.23**). An imperceptible cut then substitutes a black backdrop for his mouth, and we see the cinematographer and his camera pitch forward into this void. Another concealed cut returns us to the open mouth, and the man backs away from the camera, laughing and chewing triumphantly (**1.24**).

Smith's 1903 grotesque comedy *Mary Jane's Mishap* uses editing in a remarkably sophisticated way. One basic distant framing of a slovenly maid in a kitchen is interrupted by several cut-ins to medium shots that show her amusing facial expressions (**1.25, 1.26**). Although the actor's position is usually not matched well at the cuts, there is a general attempt to create a continuous action while using closer shots to guide our attention.

This principle would become one basis for the dominant continuity style of filmmaking that developed over approximately the next fifteen years (see Chapter 2)

The English cinema was innovative and internationally popular for several years early in the history of motion pictures, though it would soon weaken in the face of French, Italian, American, and Danish competition.

The United States: Competition and the Resurgence of Edison

The United States was by far the largest market for motion pictures since it had more theaters per capita than any other country. For over fifteen years American and foreign firms competed vigorously here. Although American films were sold abroad, U.S. firms concentrated on the domestic market. As a result, France and Italy were soon to move ahead of the United States and control the international film trade until the mid-1910s.

Exhibition Expands   After the first New York presentation of Edison's Vitascope in April 1896, film venues spread rapidly across the country. The Vitascope was not for sale, but individual entrepreneurs bought the rights to exploit it in different states. During 1896 and 1897, however, many small companies marketed their own projectors, all designed to show 35mm prints. Since movies were not yet copyrighted and prints were sold rather than rented, it was difficult to control the

1.27 "The Messiah's Entry into Jerusalem," one of the single-shot tableaux that made up *The Passion Play of Oberammergau*, produced by the Eden Musée, an important New York entertainment establishment.

circulation of films. Edison's pictures were often duplicated and sold, while Edison profited by duping films imported from France and England. Firms also frequently made direct imitations of each other's movies.

Soon hundreds of projectors were in use, and films were shown at vaudeville houses, amusement parks, small storefront theaters, summer resorts, fairs, even churches and opera houses. The years from 1895 to 1897 were the novelty period of the cinema, because the primary appeal was simply the astonishment of seeing movement and unusual sights reproduced on the screen. By early 1898, however, films' novelty had worn off. As attendance declined, many exhibitors went out of business. One event that helped revive the industry was the Spanish-American War of 1898. Patriotic fervor made audiences eager to see anything relating to the conflict, and companies in the United States and abroad profited by making both authentic and staged films.

Another type of film that helped revive the industry was the Passion Play. Beginning in 1897, filmmakers made series of single-shot scenes from Jesus' life—views that resembled illustrations in Bibles or magic-lantern slides. One such series of shots was released in February 1898 as *The Passion Play of Oberammergau* (**1.27**). (The title lent the film respectability, though it in fact had no connection with the traditional German spectacle.) As with many of the more elaborate films of the day, the exhibitor had the option of buying some or all of the shots and combining them, along with lantern slides and other religious material, to make a lengthy program. Prizefight films were also popular, especially since they often could be shown in places where live bouts were prohibited.

From 1898, then, the American film industry enjoyed a certain stability, with most films being shown in vaudeville theaters. Production increased during this period to meet the high demand.

1.28 Eugène Lauste, an American Mutoscope Company employee who had helped invent the Biograph camera, by the camera booth in the Casino de Paris, where he showed films in 1897 and 1898. The hall, with its potted palms and chandeliers, indicates the sort of elegant venue in which some early film screenings were held.

Growing Rivalry The American Mutoscope Company did particularly well during the late 1890s, partly because of its clear 70mm images, displayed by the company's own touring operators in vaudeville houses. By 1897, American Mutoscope was the most popular film company in America, and it attracted audiences abroad as well (**1.28**). American Mutoscope began filming in a new rooftop studio (**1.29**). The firm changed its name in 1899 to American Mutoscope and Biograph (AM&B), reflecting its double specialization in peepshow Mutoscope reels and projected films. Over the next several years, AM&B was hampered by a lawsuit brought against it by Edison, who consistently took competitors to court for infringing patents and copyrights. In 1902, however, AM&B won the suit, because its camera used rollers rather than sprocketed gears to move the film. The company's prosperity grew. In 1903 it began to make and sell films in 35mm rather than 70mm, a change that boosted sales. Beginning in 1908, it employed one of the most important silent-era directors, D. W. Griffith.

1.29 Officials of the American Mutoscope Company (including W. K. L. Dickson, second from right) in the firm's new rooftop studio. Like the Black Maria, the studio rotated on rails to catch the sun. The camera was sheltered in the metal booth, and simple painted sets were built against the framework.

1.30 At the City Hall in New York, Vitagraph personnel (J. Stuart Blackton, to the right of the central camera, and Albert E. Smith, second from left) ready to film an important topical event: the triumphal return of Admiral George Dewey after the Battle of Manila, 1898.

Another important company that got its start during the early years of the cinema was American Vitagraph, founded in 1897 by J. Stuart Blackton and Albert E. Smith as an advertising firm. Vitagraph began producing popular films relating to the Spanish-American War (**1.30**). Like other production companies of this period, Vitagraph was threatened with patent- and copyright-infringement lawsuits by Edison, who hoped to control the American market. Vitagraph survived by agreeing to cooperate with Edison, making films for the Edison firm and in turn dealing in Edison films itself. AM&B's 1902 legal triumph over Edison briefly reduced the risk of lawsuits throughout the industry by establishing that Edison's patents did not cover all types of motion-picture equipment (see Chapter 2). As a result, Vitagraph expanded production. Within a few years, it would emerge as an important firm making artistically innovative films. Blackton would also make some of the earliest animated films.

Edwin S. Porter, Edison's Mainstay   The rise in production at AM&B and Vitagraph in the wake of Edison's failed lawsuit obliged Edison's company to make more films to counter their competition. One successful

1.31, 1.32 Porter's *Uncle Tom's Cabin* used an intertitle to introduce each shot. Here "The Escape of Eliza" leads to a single shot of the famous episode in the novel in which Eliza flees across the ice floes on a river.

tactic was to make longer films shot in the studio. In this endeavor, it had the assistance of the most important American filmmaker of this early period, Edwin S. Porter.

Porter was a film projectionist and an expert at building photographic equipment. In late 1900, he went to work for Edison, whom he greatly admired. He was assigned to improve the firm's cameras and projectors. That year the Edison Company built a new glass-enclosed rooftop studio in New York, where films could be shot using the typical painted stage-style scenery of the era. In early 1901, Porter began operating a camera there. At this point in cinema history, the cameraman was also the film's director, and soon Porter was responsible for many of the company's most popular films.

Porter has often been credited with virtually all the innovations of the pre-1908 period, including making the first story film (*Life of an American Fireman*) and inventing editing as we know it. In fact, he often drew upon techniques already used by Méliès, Smith, and Williamson. He imaginatively developed his models, however, and he undoubtedly introduced some original techniques. His position as the foremost filmmaker of the preeminent American production company gave his works wide exposure and made them popular and influential.

There had been many, indeed hundreds, of staged fictional films made before *Life of an American Fireman* (1903). Porter himself had done several, including a version of *Jack and the Beanstalk* in 1902. He had access to all the foreign films that the Edison Company was duping, so he could study the latest innovations. He examined Méliès's *A Trip to the Moon* closely and decided to copy its manner of telling a story in a series of shots. From 1902 on, many of his films contained several shots, with significant efforts to match time and space across cuts.

Porter's *Life of an American Fireman* is a notable attempt at such storytelling. It begins with a long shot of a dozing fireman dreaming of a woman and child threatened by fire; the dream is rendered as a sort of *thought balloon*, a circular vignette superimposed in the upper part of the screen. A cut to a close-up shows a hand pulling a public fire alarm. Several shots, mixing studio and location filming, show the firemen racing to the scene. The film ends with two lengthy shots that show the same action from two vantage points: in the first, a fireman comes in a bedroom window to rescue a mother and then returns to save her baby; in the second, we see both rescues again, from a camera position outside the house. To a modern audience, this repetition of events may seem strange, but such displays of the same event from different viewpoints were not uncommon in the early cinema. (In Méliès's *A Trip to the Moon*, we see the explorers' capsule land in the Man in the Moon's eye [see 1.16] and then see the landing again from a camera position on the moon's surface.) *Life of an American Fireman* was based on earlier films and lantern slides depicting fire-fighting techniques. Brighton School director James Williamson had made a similar film, *Fire!*, in 1901.

Porter made several significant films in 1903, among them an adaptation of the popular stage version of the novel *Uncle Tom's Cabin*. Porter's film was a series of one-shot scenes of famous episodes in the novel, linked by printed intertitles—the first known to have been used in an American film (**1.31, 1.32**). (Porter derived this technique from a G. A. Smith film.) His most important film, *The Great Train Robbery*, also made in 1903, used eleven shots to tell the story of a gang of bandits who hold up a train. A telegraph operator, whom they tie up at the beginning, alerts authorities, and a posse ambushes the thieves as they divide the loot. After the lengthy robbery scene, the action returns to the telegraph office seen earlier, then moves to a dance hall as the telegraph operator runs in to alert the local townspeople, and finally switches back to the robbers in a forest. Although Porter never cuts back and forth among these locales, a few years later filmmakers would begin to do so, thus creating a technique called *intercutting* (see pp. 46–48). Porter's film was, nonetheless, gripping in its depiction of violent action (**1.33**). Indeed, a novel extra shot, showing one of the robbers in a close

1.33 To make this shot for *The Great Train Robbery,* Porter exposed the film twice, showing most of the action of the holdup staged in the studio, with the view of the train as seen through the window filmed separately.

view firing a gun toward the camera, was included; exhibitors had the option of placing it at the beginning or end of the film. Perhaps no film of the pre-1905 period was as popular as *The Great Train Robbery.*

Porter worked for Edison for several more years. In 1905 he directed *The Kleptomaniac,* a social critique that contrasted the situations of two women who commit theft. The first part shows a rich kleptomaniac stealing goods at a department store; we then see shots of a poor woman impulsively taking a loaf of bread. The final courtroom scene shows the poor woman being sentenced, while the rich one is let off. In Porter's 1906 film *The Dream of a Rarebit Fiend,* superimposition and a rocking camera depict a drunkard's dizziness while Méliès-style special effects show his dream of flying above a city. In 1909, Porter left Edison to become an independent producer, but he was soon outshone by others just entering the field.

From 1902 to 1905, Porter was one of many filmmakers who contributed to an industrywide concentration on fiction filmmaking. Unlike topicals, which were dependent on unpredictable news events, fiction films could be carefully planned in advance. While scenics involved expensive travel to distant locales, fiction films allowed their makers to stay at or near the studio. Both of these factors enabled companies to create films steadily and on schedule. Moreover, audiences seemed to prefer films with stories. Some of these were still one-shot views, but filmmakers increasingly used a series of shots to depict comic chases, extravagant fantasies, and melodramatic situations.

By 1904, major changes were taking place in the new medium and art form of the cinema. Fiction films were becoming the industry's main product. Increasingly, movies were rented to exhibitors, a practice that established the division among production, distribution, and exhibition that was to shape the expansion of the film industry. Exhibition was spreading internationally, so films would soon be seen in most countries.

Although we have stressed production in France, England, and the United States, small-scale production also occurred in other parts of the world from an early date. Enterprising exhibitors made scenics and topicals of local interest to mix into their programs of imported films. In Spain, for instance, the first films were taken by Eugène Promio when he brought the Lumière Cinématographe to Madrid in June of 1896. By October of the same year, however, Eduardo Jimeno shot the first Spanish-made film, *Worshippers Leaving the Noon Mass at Pilar de Zaragoza;* similar imitations of Lumière actualities and even fiction films were produced in 1897. In India, exhibitor Harishchandra Sakharam Bhatwadekar ordered a European camera and filmed wrestling matches, circus monkeys, and local events, showing these actualities alongside imported films beginning in 1899. Entrepreneurs in other countries made similar films, but since only one or a few prints were made, hardly any survive.

During the first ten years of the commercial exploitation of the cinema, conditions were established for international growth of the industry. Moreover, filmmakers had begun to explore the creative possibilities of the new medium. These explorations were to intensify over the next decade.

- -

Notes and Queries

IDENTIFICATION AND PRESERVATION OF EARLY FILMS

In the silent era, there were no archives devoted to preserving films. The great majority of films from the first decade of the cinema are lost or incomplete, and even those that survive are often difficult to identify. Many had no title at the beginning, and there were seldom stars or other distinctive traits that would provide clues to the source.

Fortunately, however, some segments of this era of film history have been preserved. In the United States, there was a method of copyrighting films by printing every frame on a long roll of paper. This practice lasted from 1894 to 1912, although only a small proportion of films produced were copyrighted in this fashion. These "paper prints" were discovered in the 1940s at the Library of Congress and rephotographed onto film. In France, many negatives of the Lumière company were preserved, and even now hundreds have yet to be printed as positive viewing prints. In some cases, release copies of early films were stored away and found later, so archivists can now duplicate them.

Historians have also combed catalogues of early sales and distribution companies, trying to create filmographies of the movies made in a country or by a single studio. For a description of the paper prints, see Kemp Niver, *Early Motion Pictures: The Paper Print Collection in the Library of Congress* (Washington, D.C.: The Library of Congress, 1985), and Charles "Buckey" Grimm's "A Paper Print Prehistory," *Film History* 11, no. 2 (1999): 204–16. Niver's *Biograph Bulletins 1896–1908* (Los Angeles: Locare Research Group, 1971) reproduces the American Mutoscope and Biograph catalogues for this era; it provides a good example of the type of material historians work with. Denis Gifford's *The British Film Catalogue 1895–1985: A Reference Guide* (London: David & Charles, 1986) represents one of the most ambitious attempts to document a country's entire fiction-film production.

REVIVING INTEREST IN EARLY CINEMA: THE BRIGHTON CONFERENCE

For many years, the earliest period of the cinema was treated as relatively unimportant. Historians dealt with the invention of cameras and projectors but dismissed early films as crude. Overgeneralizations abounded. Edwin S. Porter, for example, was credited with being virtually the only stylistic forerunner of the American cinema's system of editing.

A major event in 1978 helped change many notions about the early cinema. The Fédération International des Archives du Film (FIAF, the International Federation of Film Archives) held its annual conference in Brighton, as a salute to the Brighton School. Many film historians were invited, and nearly six hundred pre-1907 films were screened. The result was a new appreciation of the variety and fascination of early films. To this day, the silent cinema remains one of the liveliest research areas of film history.

The proceedings of the Brighton Conference, along with a tentative filmography of surviving prints, were published as *Cinema 1900/1906: An Analytical Study,* 2 vols., ed. Roger Holman (Brussels: FIAS, 1982). For a description of the Brighton Conference and its effects on historians' work, see Jon Gartenberg, "The Brighton Project: Archives and Historians," *Iris* 2, no. 1 (1984): 5–16. *Early Cinema: Space, Frame, Narrative*, ed. Thomas Elsaesser, with Adam Barker (London: British Film Institute, 1990) contains several essays influenced by the Brighton event and written by historians who participated, including Charles Musser, Tom Gunning, André Gaudreault, Noël Burch, and Barry Salt.

Since 1982, the Cineteca de Fruili has carried on the Brighton tradition by holding an annual festival of silent cinema, Le Giornate del Cinema Muto ("The Days of Silent Cinema") in Pordenone and later Sacile, Italy.

- -

REFERENCE

1. From *The Photogram*, quoted in John Barnes, *The Beginnings of the Cinema in England* (New York: Barnes & Noble, 1976), p. 64.

FURTHER READING

Barnes, John. *The Beginnings of the Cinema in England 1894–1901*. Vol. 1: *The Beginnings of the Cinema in England*. New York: Barnes & Noble, 1976. Vol. 2: *Pioneers of the British Film*. London: Bishopgate Press, 1983. Vol. 3: *The Rise of the Cinema in Great Britain*. London: Bishopgate Press, 1983. Vol. 4: *Filming the Boer War*. London: Bishopgate Press, 1992. Vol. 5: *1900*. Exeter: University of Exeter Press, 1997.

Bottomore, Stephen, ed. "Cinema Pioneers" issue of *Film History* 10, no. 1 (1998).

Fell, John L. *Film before Griffith*. Berkeley: University of California Press, 1983.

Guibbert, Pierre, ed. *Les premiers ans de cinema français*. Perpignon: Institut Jean Vigo, 1985.

Hammond, Paul. *Marvelous Méliès*. New York: St. Martin's, 1975.

Hendricks, Gordon. *Beginnings of the Biograph: The Story of the Invention of the Mutoscope and Biograph and Their Supplying Camera*. New York: The Beginnings of the American Film, 1964.

_____. *The Edison Motion Picture Myth*. Berkeley: University of California Press, 1961.

Komatsu, Hiroshi. "The Lumière Cinématographe and the Production of the Cinema in Japan in the Earliest Period," *Film History* 8, no. 4 (1996): 431–38.

Leyda, Jay, and Charles Musser. *Before Hollywood: Turn-of-the-Century Films from American Archives*. New York: American Federation of the Arts, 1986.

McKernan, Luke, and Mark van den Tempel, eds. "The Wonders of the Biograph" issue of *Griffithiana* 66/70 (1999/2000).

Musser, Charles. *Before the Nickelodeon: Edwin S. Porter and the Edison Manufacturing Company*. Berkeley: University of California Press, 1991.

_____. *The Emergence of Cinema: The American Screen to 1907*. New York: Scribners, 1990.

Rossell, Deac. "A Chronology of Cinema, 1889–1896" issue of *Film History* 7, no. 2 (summer 1995).

_____. *Living Pictures: The Origins of the Movies*. Albany: State University of New York Press, 1998.

Turconi, Davide. "'Hic Sunt Leones': The First Decade of American Film Comedy, 1894–1903," *Griffithiana* 55/56 (September 1996): 151–215.

THE INTERNATIONAL EXPANSION OF THE CINEMA, 1905–1912

Before 1904, the cinema led a somewhat vagrant existence. Producers sold film prints, and exhibitors showed them in vaudeville houses, music halls, rented theaters, and fairground tents. The same prints were often resold and continued to circulate for years, becoming ever more battered. Around 1905, however, the film industry expanded and stabilized. Permanent theaters were devoted especially to film, and production expanded to meet increased demand. Italy and Denmark joined the ranks of important producing countries, and filmmaking on a smaller scale emerged in many other lands.

After 1905, films grew longer, using more shots and telling more complex stories. Filmmakers explored new techniques for conveying narrative information. Perhaps no other era has seen such extensive changes in films' formal and stylistic traits.

FILM PRODUCTION IN EUROPE

France: Pathé versus Gaumont

During this period, the French film industry was still the largest, and its movies were the ones most frequently seen around the world. The two main firms, Pathé Frères and Gaumont, continued to expand, and other companies were formed in response to an increased demand from exhibitors. As in many western countries, workers were winning a shorter workweek and thus had more leisure time for inexpensive entertainments. The French firms also courted a wider middle-class audience.

From 1905 to 1906, the French film industry grew rapidly. Pathé was already a large company, with three separate studios. It was also one of the earliest film companies to become *vertically integrated*. A vertically integrated firm is one controlling the production, distribution, and exhibition of a film. As we shall see time and again in this book, vertical integration has been a major strategy pursued by film companies and often a measure of their strength. Pathé made its own cameras and projectors, produced films, and manufactured the film stock for release prints. In 1906, Pathé also began buying theaters. The following year, the firm began to distribute its own films by renting rather than selling them to exhibitors. By then, it was the largest film company in the world. Over the next few years, it started distributing films made by other companies as well.

By 1905, Pathé employed six filmmakers, still overseen by Ferdinand Zecca, each making a film a week. The films encompassed a variety of genres: actualities, historical films, trick films, dramas, vaudeville acts, and chases. During 1903 and 1904, Pathé created an elaborate system for hand-stenciling color onto release prints. Stencils were painstakingly cut from a copy of the film itself, with a different stencil for each color. Assembly lines of women workers then painted the colors frame by frame on each release print. Pathé reserved color for trick films and films displaying flowers or elegantly dressed women (**Color Plate 2.1**). Such hand-coloring continued until the early sound era.

Among Pathé's most profitable films were series starring popular comics: the "Boireau" series (with André Deed), the "Rigadin" films (with the music-hall star Prince), and, above all, the Max Linder series. Linder's films reflected the industry's growing bid for respectability by being set in a middle-class milieu (**2.1**). Max typically suffered embarrassment in social situations, such as wearing painfully tight shoes to an elegant dinner. He was often thwarted in love; in *Une ruse de mari* ("The Husband's Ruse"), he unsuccessfully tries to commit suicide in various ways, calling upon his valet to fetch a knife, a gun, and so on. Linder's films were enormously influential. Charles Chaplin once referred to Linder as his "professor" and himself as Linder's "disciple."[1] Linder worked in both the United States and France from 1909 until his death in 1925.

Aside from being a vertically integrated firm, Pathé also used the strategy of *horizontal integration*. This term means that a firm expands within one sector of the film industry, as when one production firm acquires and absorbs another one. Pathé enlarged its film production by opening studios in such places as Italy, Russia, and the United States. From 1909 to 1911, its Moscow branch made about half the films produced in Russia.

Pathé's main French rival, Gaumont, also expanded rapidly. After finishing its new studio in 1905, the firm took on additional filmmakers. Alice Guy trained this

2.1 Max Linder in *Une ruse de mari* ("The Husband's Ruse," directed by Linder in 1913). Linder's distinctive appearance—elegant clothes, top hat, and dapper moustache—influenced other comics to adopt trademark outfits.

2.2 Alice Guy collaborated with designer Victorin Jasset on *La Naissance, la vie et la mort de Notre-Seigneur Jésus-Christ* ("The Birth, Life, and Death of Our Lord Jesus Christ," 1906). This scene of the scourging of Christ indicates the elaborate staging and sets used for some prestige films of this period.

staff and turned to making longer films herself (**2.2**). Among the new filmmakers was scriptwriter and director Louis Feuillade, who took over the supervision of Gaumont's films when Guy left in 1908. He became one of the silent cinema's most important artists, and his career paralleled Gaumont's fortunes until the 1920s. Feuillade was extraordinarily versatile, making comedies, historical films (see Color Plate 2.3), thrillers, and melodramas.

Following Pathé's lead, other companies and entrepreneurs opened film theaters, aiming at affluent consumers. Such theaters often showed longer and more prestigious films. Prosperity in the French industry and in film exports led to the formation of several smaller firms during this period.

One of these had a significant impact. As its name suggests, the Film d'Art company, founded in 1908, identified itself with elite tastes. One of its first efforts was *The Assassination of the Duc de Guise* (1908, Charles Le Bargy and André Calmettes). Using stage stars, a script by a famous dramatist, and an original score by classical composer Camille Saint-Saëns, the film told the

2.3, 2.4 The sets and acting in *The Assassination of the Duc de Guise* derived from the theater. Its shots, however, showed characters moving smoothly from one space to another, as when the Duc de Guise walks through a curtained doorway to confront his enemies.

2.5, *left* The large sets, crowd scenes, and lavish historical costumes of *The Fall of Troy* were typical of Italian epics.

2.6, *right* French-born clown Ferdinand Guillaume as the popular Polidor in *Polidor coi baffi* ("Polidor's Moustache," 1914).

story of a famous incident in French history (2.3, 2.4). It was widely shown and had a successful release in the United States. *The Assassination of the Duc de Guise* and similar works created a model of what art films should be like. The Film d'Art company, however, lost money on most of its productions and was sold in 1911.

On the whole, the French industry prospered. By 1910, the traveling *fêtes foraines* had dwindled, and large film theaters were the rule. During the same era, however, French firms were facing challenges in the lucrative American market and would soon lose their dominance over world markets.

Italy: Growth through Spectacle

Italy came somewhat late to the film production scene, but beginning in 1905 its film industry grew rapidly and within a few years, somewhat resembled that of France. Although films were produced in several cities, Rome's Cines firm (founded in 1905) and Turin's Ambrosio (1905) and Itala (1906) soon emerged as the principal companies. The new firms were handicapped by a lack of experienced personnel, and some lured artists away from French firms. For example, Cines hired one of Pathé's main filmmakers, Gaston Velle, as its artistic director. As a result, some Italian films were imitations, even remakes, of French movies.

Exhibition also expanded rapidly. Italy depended less than other European countries on films being shown in traveling fairs and other temporary venues.

Instead, many permanent theaters opened. Thus, in Italy, cinema won respect as a new art form earlier than in other countries. Italian producers moved toward art films at about the same time that Film d'Art was making *The Assassination of the Duc de Guise*. In 1908, the Ambrosio company made *The Last Days of Pompeii*, the first of many adaptations of Edward Bulwer-Lytton's historical novel. As a result of this film's popularity, the Italian cinema became identified with historical spectacle.

By 1910, Italy was probably second only to France in the number of films it sent around the world. Partly because Italian producers catered to permanent film theaters, they were among the first who consistently made films of more than one reel (that is, longer than fifteen minutes). For example, in 1910, a major director of the period, Giovanni Pastrone, made *Il Caduta de Troia* ("The Fall of Troy"; 2.5) in three reels. The triumph of this and similar films encouraged Italian producers to make longer, more expensive epics, a trend that culminated in the mid-1910s.

Not all Italian films were epics, however. For example, beginning in 1909, producers again imitated the French by creating several comic series. Itala hired Pathé's actor André Deed, who briefly abandoned his Boireau character to become Cretinetti ("Little Cretin"). Other companies found French or Italian comics to build series around, such as Ambrosio's Robinet and Cines's Polidor (2.6). These films were much cheaper than epics. They were also livelier and more sponta-

2.7 Nordisk's second studio was typical of such buildings in many countries during the silent era. Glass walls and roofs permitted sunlight to illuminate scenes.

neous, and they became internationally popular. Hundreds of such films were made, but the fad gradually declined during the 1910s.

Denmark: Nordisk and Ole Olsen

That a small country like Denmark became a significant player in world cinema was largely due to entrepreneur Ole Olsen. He had been an exhibitor, initially using a peepshow machine and later running one of the first movie theaters in Copenhagen. In 1906, he formed a production company, Nordisk, and immediately began opening distribution offices abroad. Nordisk's breakthrough came in 1907 with *Lion Hunt,* a fiction film about a safari. Because two lions were actually shot during the production, the film was banned in Denmark, but the publicity generated huge sales abroad. The company's New York branch, established in 1908, sold Nordisk films under the brand name Great Northern. In the same year, Olsen completed the first of four glass studios for indoor production (**2.7**).

Nordisk films quickly established an international reputation for excellent acting and production values. Nordisk specialized in crime thrillers, dramas, and somewhat sensationalistic melodramas, including "white-slave" (prostitution) stories. Olsen had a circus set permanently installed, and some of the firm's major films were melodramas of circus life, such as *The Four Devils* (1911, Robert Dinesen and Alfred Lind) and *Dødsspring til Hest fra Cirkus-Kuplen* ("Death Jump

on Horseback from the Circus Dome," 1912, Eduard Schnedler-Sørensen). The latter film concerns a count who loses his fortune through covering the gambling debts of a friend. His skill at riding horses allows him to work in a circus, where he becomes romantically involved with two women (**2.8**). One of them jealously tries to kill him by causing his horse to plunge from a high platform; the second nurses him back to health. Rival producers admired such films for compressing abrupt plot twists and highly emotional situations into two or three reels.

Although a few smaller companies started up during this period, Olsen eventually managed either to buy them or to drive them out of business. Nevertheless, it was one of these short-lived small firms that made the two-reeler *The Abyss* (1910, Urban Gad), which brought instant fame to actress Asta Nielsen. Indeed, like Max Linder, she was one of the first international film stars. Dark and thin, with large, intense eyes, she possessed an unconventional beauty. She often played women destroyed by love: seduced and abandoned, or sacrificing themselves for the happiness of the men they love (see 2.15–2.17). Nielsen was equally adept at comedy, however, and, although she had trained in the theater, she was one of the earliest screen performers whose style seemed to owe nothing to the stage. Nielsen went on to work in Germany, where she became one of the mainstays of the industry.

The Danish industry remained healthy until World War I cut off many of its export markets.

2.8 A dramatic staging in depth in *Dødsspring til Hest fra Cirkus-Kuplen*: the heroine watches from the foreground as the hero demonstrates his equestrian skills in the circus ring.

Other Countries

Led by Cecil Hepworth's production company, England remained a significant force in world film markets. Its 1905 film *Rescued by Rover* was one of the biggest international hits of its day. Filmmaking spread to other countries as well. The earliest systematic production in Japan, for example, was launched in 1908. Most films made there were apparently records of kabuki plays, filmed in static long shots. A few German production companies started up, though the industry did not begin to flourish until 1913. Pathé dominated Russian filmmaking, but several domestic firms also established themselves. In other countries, small production companies appeared, produced a few films, and vanished. None challenged France, Italy, Denmark, and the United States as the ruling industries on the international scene.

THE STRUGGLE FOR THE EXPANDING AMERICAN FILM INDUSTRY

Today, Hollywood dominates the international market in entertainment media, as it does in many other industries. Before World War I, however, the United States was not yet the world's most economically important country. Great Britain still ruled the waves; its ships carried more goods than did those of any other country, and London was the globe's financial center. It was the war that allowed the United States to surpass England and other European countries.

Prior to the war, American film firms concentrated on the swiftly expanding domestic demand and paid less attention to foreign markets. U.S. companies were also still struggling among themselves for power in the new industry. Between 1905 and 1912, American producers, distributors, and exhibitors tried to bring some stability to the shifting and confused film business. Only then would they be able to turn greater attention to export.

The Nickelodeon Boom

By 1905, films were showing in most of the available vaudeville houses, local theaters, and other venues. The main trend in the American film industry from 1905 to 1907 was the rapid multiplication of film theaters. These were typically small stores, installed with fewer than two hundred seats. Admission was usually a nickel (hence the term *nickelodeon*) or a dime for a program running fifteen to sixty minutes. Most nickelodeons had only one projector. During reel changes a singer might perform a current song, accompanied by lantern slides.

Nickelodeons spread for several reasons. When production companies turned away from actualities toward story films, moviegoing became less a novelty and more a regular entertainment. Shorter workweeks left more time for entertainment. In addition, film producers took to renting rather than selling films. Since exhibitors no longer had to keep running the same films until they made back their purchase price, they could change their programs two, three, even seven times a week. As a result, some of their patrons returned regularly. Nickelodeons could run the same brief programs over and over continuously, from late morning to midnight. Many exhibitors made huge profits.

Nickelodeons had advantages over earlier forms of exhibition. Unlike amusement parks, they were not seasonal. They were cheaper than vaudeville houses and more regularly available than traveling exhibitions. Expenses were low. Spectators typically sat on benches or in simple wooden seats. There were seldom newspaper advertisements to alert patrons in advance concerning programs. Patrons usually either attended on a regular basis or simply dropped in. The front of the theater displayed hand-painted signs with the names of the films, and there might be a phonograph or barker attracting the attention of passersby.

There was almost always some sound accompaniment. The exhibitor might lecture along with the film, but piano or phonograph accompaniment was probably more common. In some cases, actors stood behind the screen and spoke dialogue in synchronization with the action on the screen. More frequently, people used noisemakers to create appropriate sound effects (**2.9**).

In the days before 1905, when films had mainly been shown in vaudeville theaters or by touring lecturer-exhibitors, admission prices were often twenty-five cents or more—too much for most blue-collar workers. Nickel theaters, however, opened films to a mass audience, many of them immigrants. Nickelodeons clustered in business

2.9   A drawing from a 1909
Gaumont catalogue, showing how
sound effects could be produced
behind the screen. The hanging
sheet of metal at the left, when
shaken, created the sound of
thunder.

districts and working-class neighborhoods in cities. Blue-
collar workers could attend theaters near their homes,
while secretaries and office boys caught a show during
the lunch hour or before taking public transport home
after work. Women and children made up a significant
proportion of city audiences, stopping in for a break
while shopping. In small towns, a nickelodeon might be
the only place showing films, and people from all strata
of society would watch movies together.

Although films continued to be shown in vaudeville
houses and by a few touring exhibitors, by 1908, nickelodeons had become the main form of exhibition. As a
result, many more movies were needed by the new distributors, or *film exchanges,* that bought prints from
the producers. A single nickelodeon, using three films in
a program that changed three times a week, would rent
about 450 titles a year!

During the nickelodeon boom, most films came
from abroad. Pathé, Gaumont, Hepworth, Cines, Nordisk, and other European firms flooded the weekly release schedules. Since there were far more theaters in the
United States than in any other country, a huge number
of copies could be sold to exchanges there. Such sales
helped keep the English industry healthy and allowed
the Italian and Danish industries to expand quickly.

The nickelodeons also launched the careers of several important businessmen. The Warner brothers
got their start as nickelodeon exhibitors (**2.10**). Carl

2.10   The Cascade Theater in Newcastle, Pennsylvania was
the first nickelodeon acquired by Jack, Albert, Sam, and
Harry Warner. A sign promises "Refined Entertainment for
Ladies, Gentlemen, and Children." The Warners went on to
careers in exhibition and production, eventually establishing
Warner Bros.

Laemmle, later the founder of Universal, opened his first nickelodeon in Chicago in 1906. Louis B. Mayer, who became the second "M" of MGM (Metro-Goldwyn-Mayer), ran a small theater in Haverhill, Massachusetts. Other studio executives who started out running nickelodeons included Adolph Zukor (later head of Paramount), William Fox (who formed the company that became 20th Century-Fox), and Marcus Loew (whose Loew's was the parent company of MGM). These men would help create the basic structure of the Hollywood studio system during the 1910s.

The Motion Picture Patents Company versus the Independents

In the meantime, however, the nickelodeon boom spurred intense competition. The more established leaders of the industry consolidated power among themselves and tried to exclude newcomers. They realized that control of the burgeoning film industry would be highly profitable.

1907–1908: Control through Litigation

Since 1897, the Edison company had tried to force its competitors out of business by suing them for patent infringement. Edison claimed to own the basic patents on motion-picture cameras, projectors, and film stock. Some companies, like Vitagraph, paid Edison a license fee to be able to go on producing. After a court decision went in Edison's favor in 1904, other companies joined in paying such fees. American Mutoscope & Biograph (AM&B), however, refused to cooperate with Edison, since its Biograph camera had a different mechanism and separate patents.

In early 1907, an appeals court handed down an important decision. Edison had again sued AM&B for infringement of its camera patent. The decision reaffirmed that AM&B's roller-driven camera was sufficiently different and did not infringe Edison's patent, based on sprocket gears. The decision also stated, however, that other camera designs currently in use *did* infringe that patent. As a result, all production companies and importers assumed that they had to pay either AM&B or Edison to stay in business.

The rivalry between Edison and AM&B became more intense in 1908. Edison decided to sue AM&B yet again, this time claiming that the latter had infringed its patents on film stock. AM&B countered by buying the patent for the Latham loop and suing Edison for using this device in its cameras and projectors. The two firms set up rival licensing arrangements in early 1908: members of the Association of Edison Licensees paid Edison in order to go on making films, and the Biograph Association of Licensees collected money mostly from foreign companies and importers who wanted to bring films into the American market.

The film market approached chaos. Exhibitors needed a great many films, but producers were so busy fighting each other that they could not release enough titles. During this same period, however, Edison and AM&B decided to cooperate. They created a separate company that would control all competitors by owning and charging licensing fees on the existing key patents. In December of 1908, the Motion Picture Patents Company (MPPC), headed by Edison and AM&B, was created. Several other production companies belonged to the MPPC: Vitagraph, Selig, Essanay, Lubin, and Kalem. To keep operating, each of these had to pay fees to the two main companies (though Vitagraph, which had contributed a patent to the arrangement, got back a portion of the license fees).

In an attempt to gain a larger share of the U.S. market, the MPPC strictly limited the number of foreign firms that could join and import films. Pathé, the largest importer, and Méliès were allowed into the MPPC, as was George Kleine, a major Chicago firm that imported European films by Gaumont and Urban-Eclipse (an English-French company). Several European companies, such as Great Northern (Nordisk) and all Italian firms, were shut out. Although foreign companies continued to operate in the United States, both in the MPPC and as independents, they never regained the large share of the market that they had enjoyed before 1908. France and Italy continued to be the leaders in markets outside the United States until World War I.

The MPPC hoped to control all three phases of the industry: production, distribution, and exhibition. Only licensed companies could make films. Only licensed distribution firms could release them. And all theaters wanting films made by members of the MPPC had to pay a weekly fee for the privilege. Eastman Kodak agreed to sell film stock only to members of the MPPC, and in return they would buy no stock except from Kodak.

This arrangement set the stage for control over the entire U.S. film market by an *oligopoly*. When one company dominates its market, that firm has a monopoly. In an oligopoly, a small number of firms cooperate to control the market and block the entry of new companies. Members of the MPPC's oligopoly tried to eliminate all other firms by threatening to sue for patent infringement. A producer who used a film camera without paying the MPPC risked being taken to court. The same was true for exhibitors, since the MPPC claimed to control the patents covering their projectors.

During 1909, the American film industry stabilized somewhat. MPPC members set up a regular schedule of weekly releases. Newer films cost more and declined in value after they had been shown for a while (a situation that has survived to the present in a system of *runs* and *windows*). One reel became the standard film length. Each reel rented for the same price, whatever the film was, since producers viewed films as standard products, like sausages.

1909–1915: The Independents Fight Back

Still, the MPPC encountered challenges. Not all producers, distributors, and exhibitors were willing to pay fees to Edison and AM&B. Exhibitors who had purchased their projectors outright were particularly annoyed. It is estimated that about 6,000 theaters agreed to pay the weekly fee, but another 2,000 refused. The unlicensed theaters provided a market that unlicensed producers and distributors could serve. This portion of the industry was soon identified as the *independents*.

In April 1909, the first effective blow against the MPPC was dealt when Carl Laemmle, who ran the largest American distribution firm, turned in his license. He started the Independent Motion Picture Company (IMP), a small firm that would later form the basis for the Universal studio. Within the next few years, more than a dozen other independent companies started up across the country, including Thanhouser, Solax (run by Alice Guy Blaché, formerly of Gaumont in France), and the New York Motion Picture Company, headed by Thomas H. Ince, who would become one of the most important producers of the 1910s. Independent theaters could rent films from the European companies shut out of the MPPC arrangement. Trying to avoid patent-infringement suits by the MPPC, independent companies claimed to be using cameras that employed different mechanisms.

Responding to the independent movement, the MPPC created the General Film Company in 1910 as an attempt to monopolize distribution. The General Film Company was to release all the films made by MPPC producers. The MPPC also hired detectives to gain evidence that producers were using cameras with the Latham loop and other devices patented by the MPPC. Between 1909 and 1911, the MPPC brought lawsuits against nearly all of the independent producers for using patent-infringing cameras. One such suit, against Laemmle's IMP, was based on the Latham-loop patent.

In 1912, the courts ruled against the MPPC, on the grounds that the technique of the Latham loop had been anticipated in earlier patents. Consequently, independent companies could use any camera without fearing litigation. This court decision was a severe blow to the MPPC.

Also in 1912, the American government began proceedings against the MPPC as a trust (a group of companies acting in unfair constraint of trade). The case was decided against the MPPC in 1915. By that point, however, a number of the independent firms had wisely allied themselves with national distributors and opted for the new feature-film format. In contrast, some former members of the MPPC had become victims of mismanagement. As a result, during the early 1910s, several members of the independent sector of the industry began to create the new, stabler oligopoly that would form the Hollywood film industry.

Social Pressures and Self-Censorship

The quick spread of nickelodeons led to social pressures aimed at reforming the cinema. Many religious groups and social workers considered the nickel theaters sinister places where young people could be led astray. The movies were seen as a training ground for prostitution and robbery. French films were criticized for treating adultery in a comic fashion. Violent subject matter such as reenacted executions and murders were common fare early in the nickelodeon boom.

In late 1908, the mayor of New York briefly succeeded in closing down all the city's nickelodeons, and local censorship boards were formed in several towns. A concerned group of New York citizens formed the Board of Censorship in March 1909. This was a private body, aimed at improving the movies and thus forestalling the federal government from passing a national censorship law. Producers were to submit films voluntarily, and films that passed could include a notice of approval. As a way of gaining respectability, MPPC members allowed their films to be examined, and they even supported the board financially. This cooperation led the group to change its name to the National Board of Censorship (and, in 1915, to the National Board of Review). Although censorship boards continued to be formed on the municipal and state levels, no national censorship law was—or ever has been—passed. Variants of this policy of voluntary self-censorship have existed in the American film industry ever since.

Both the MPPC and the independents also tried to improve the public image of the movies by releasing more prestigious films that would appeal to middle- and upper-class spectators. Films became longer and more complex in their narratives. Stories derived from celebrated literature or portraying important historical events counterbalanced the popular slapstick chases and crime films. Some of these prestigious films, such as *The Assassination of the Duc de Guise* and *The Fall of Troy*, came from abroad. American producers increasingly turned to similar source material. In 1909, D. W. Griffith, on his way to becoming the most important American silent director, filmed Robert Browning's verse play *Pippa Passes*, quoting lines from the original as intertitles. Adaptations of Shakespeare's plays condensed to one or two reels became common.

Along with this move to appeal to refined audiences came a change in the theaters where films were shown. Some nickelodeons continued to operate well into the 1910s, but from 1908 on, exhibitors also began to build or convert larger theaters for showing films. These establishments might charge ten or twenty-five cents, or even more, for longer programs. Some theaters combined films and live vaudeville acts. Popular song slides, which were perceived as lower class, gradually disappeared as the better-class theaters began to use two projectors—and hence had no need for a song to cover the change of reels. Musical accompaniment by orchestras or pipe organs, ornate decorations, and occasional educational lectures accompanying the films were all designed to create an atmosphere very different from that of the nickel movie houses.

The Rise of the Feature Film

Part of the move toward longer programs and more prestigious films involved increasing the length of the films. In the early years of the twentieth century, *feature* simply meant an unusual film that could be featured in the advertising. During the nickelodeon boom, when the one-reel length became standard, *feature* still had the same meaning. But the term also came to be associated with longer films. Before 1909, these were typically prizefight films or religious epics and were often shown in legitimate theaters rather than nickelodeons.

By 1909, some American producers started making multireel films. Because the MPPC's rigid release system allowed for only single reels, such films had to be released in one part per week. In late 1909 and early 1910, for example, Vitagraph sold *The Life of Moses* as five separate reels. Once all five were out, however, some exhibitors showed them as a single program.

In Europe, the exhibition system was more flexible, and multireel films were common there. When these were imported into the United States, they were typically shown in their entirety in legitimate theaters, at higher admission prices. As we have seen, Itala's three-reel *The Fall of Troy* (see 2.5) had a great success in 1911. In 1912, Adolph Zukor triumphantly imported *Queen Elizabeth* and *Camille*, French productions starring the famous stage actress Sarah Bernhardt. Such pressure from imports led American firms to release longer films as a unit. In 1911, Vitagraph brought out its three-reel *Vanity Fair* as one film. By the mid-1910s, the feature film would become the standard basis for programming in more prestigious theaters, and the mixture of short films preferred by nickelodeon managers would decline.

The Star System

In the earliest years of the cinema, films were advertised as novelties. Once the nickelodeon boom and the formation of the Motion Picture Patents Company had regularized the American industry, companies sold films by brand name. Spectators knew that they were seeing an Edison or a Vitagraph or a Pathé picture, but filmmakers and actors received no screen credit. In vaudeville, the legitimate theater, and the opera, the star system was well established. Film actors' names, however, were not publicized—in part because fame would allow them to demand higher wages.

Indeed, before 1908, few actors worked regularly enough in films to be recognized. At about that time, however, producers started signing actors to longer contracts, and audiences began to see the same faces in film after film. By 1909, viewers were spontaneously demonstrating interest in their favorites, asking theater managers the actors' names or writing to the studios for photographs. Fans made up names for the most popular stars: Florence Lawrence, who regularly appeared in Griffith's films, became "the Biograph Girl"; Florence Turner was "the Vitagraph Girl"; and Vitagraph's heartthrob, Maurice Costello, was dubbed "Dimples." Reviewers picked up this way of referring to anonymous stars. Of Griffith's 1909 film *Lady Helen's Escapade*, a commentator remarked, "Of course, the chief honors of the picture are borne by the now famous Biograph girl, who must be gratified by the silent celebrity she has achieved. This lady combines with very great personal attractions very fine dramatic abilities indeed."[2]

By 1910, some companies responded to audience demand and began exploiting their popular actors for

2.11 An advertisement from October 1911 names Owen Moore and Mary Pickford as the stars of an upcoming release by an independent producer, Majestic.

publicity purposes. Kalem supplied theaters with photographs to display in their lobbies. Personal appearances by stars in theaters became an institution. In 1911, the first fan magazine, *The Motion Picture Story Magazine,* appeared. That same year, an enterprising firm began selling photo postcards of popular players. Stars were named in advertisements aimed at exhibitors (**2.11**). Still, films seldom included credits until 1914.

The Movies Move to Hollywood

The first American film companies were located in New Jersey and New York. Other producers emerged in Chicago (Selig, Essanay), Philadelphia (Lubin), and elsewhere in the East and the Midwest. Because filmmakers worked outdoors or in sunlit glass studios, poor weather could hamper production. After the formation of the MPPC in 1908, some film companies sent pro-

duction units to sunnier climes for the winter: New York–based firms might head to Florida, while Chicago companies tended to go west.

As early as 1908, a producing unit from the Selig company filmed on location in the Los Angeles area. It returned there to set up a makeshift studio in 1909 and a more substantial one in 1910. In 1909, New York Motion Picture Company also established operations there. Several other firms began working around Los Angeles in 1910. American Biograph began sending Griffith there during the winter season.

During the early 1910s, the Los Angeles area emerged as the country's major production center. It had several advantages. Its clear, dry weather permitted filming outdoors most days of the year. Southern California offered a variety of landscapes, including ocean, desert, mountain, forest, and hillside. The Western had emerged as one of the most popular American genres and such films looked more authentic when filmed in the real West rather than in New Jersey.

The small suburb of Hollywood was one of several where studios were established, and its name eventually came to stand for the entire American filmmaking industry—despite the fact that many decisions were still made in New York, in the head offices of the companies. Studios in the Hollywood area would soon grow from small open-air stages to sizable complexes with large enclosed studios and numerous departments.

In 1904, the American film industry had consisted of several small companies trying to put each other out of business. By 1912, it had gone through an unsuccessful attempt by one group, the MPPC, to monopolize the market. Now more film firms existed, and they were on the brink of building the business into something much larger and stabler.

THE PROBLEM OF NARRATIVE CLARITY

Beginning in 1904, American commercial filmmaking became increasingly oriented toward storytelling. Moreover, with the new emphasis on one-reel films, narratives became longer and necessitated a series of shots. Filmmakers faced the challenge of making story films that would be comprehensible to audiences. How could techniques of editing, camerawork, acting, and lighting be combined so as to clarify what was happening in a film? How could the spectator grasp where and when the action was occurring?

Early Moves toward Classical Storytelling

Over the span of several years, filmmakers solved such problems. Sometimes they influenced each other, while at other times two filmmakers might happen on the same technique. Some devices were tried and abandoned. By 1917, filmmakers had worked out a system of formal principles that were standard in American filmmaking. That system has come to be called the *classical Hollywood cinema*. Despite this name, many of the basic principles of the system were being worked out before filmmaking was centered in Hollywood, and, indeed, many of those principles were first tried in other countries. In the years before World War I, film style was still largely international, since films circulated widely outside their countries of origin.

The basic problem that confronted filmmakers early in the nickelodeon era was that audiences could not understand the causal, spatial, and temporal relations in many films. If the editing abruptly changed locales, the spectator might not grasp where the new action was occurring. An actor's elaborate pantomime might fail to convey the meaning of a crucial action. A review of a 1906 Edison film lays out the problem:

> Regardless of the fact that there a number of good motion pictures brought out, it is true that there are some which, although photographically good, are poor because the manufacturer, being familiar with the picture and the plot, does not take into consideration that the film was not made for him but for the audience. A subject recently seen was very good photographically, and the plot also seemed to be good, but could not be understood by the audience.[3]

In a few theaters, a lecturer might explain the plot as the film unrolled, but producers could not rely on such aids.

Filmmakers came to assume that a film should guide the spectator's attention, making every aspect of the story on the screen as clear as possible. In particular, films increasingly set up a chain of narrative causes and effects. One event would plainly lead to an effect, which would in turn cause another effect, and so on. Moreover, an event was typically caused by a character's beliefs or desires. Character psychology had not been particularly important in early films. Slapstick chases or brief melodramas depended more on physical action or familiar situations than on character traits. Increasingly after 1907, however, character psychology motivated actions. By following a series of characters' goals and resulting conflicts, the spectator could comprehend the action.

2.12 *The Arrival of a Train at la Ciotat Station* (France, 1897): the Lumière cameraman has chosen a vantage point that emphasizes many planes of activity.

2.13 *The Skyscrapers* (United States, 1906): as the foreman steps forward, he discovers that his purse had been stolen.

Every aspect of silent film style came to be used to enhance narrative clarity. Staging in depth could show the spatial relationships among elements. Intertitles could add narrative information beyond what the images conveyed. Closer views of the actors could suggest their emotions more precisely. Color, set design, and lighting could imply time of day, the milieu of the action, and so on.

Some of the most important innovations of this period involved the ways in which shots were put together to create a story. In one sense, editing was a boon to the filmmaker, permitting instant movement from one space to another or cuts to closer views to reveal details. But if the spectator could not keep track of the temporal and spatial relations between one shot and the next, editing might lead to confusion. In some cases, intertitles could help. Editing also came to emphasize *continuity* among shots. Certain cues indicated that time was flowing uninterruptedly across cuts. Between scenes, other cues might suggest how much time had been skipped over. When a cut moved from one space to another, the director found ways to orient the viewer.

Staging in Depth Filmmakers had been framing action in depth since the earliest years (**2.12**). Particularly in scenes staged outdoors, an important plot development might be emphasized by having the actor step toward the viewer (**2.13**). In chase films, the pursuers often ran diagonally from the distance into the

2.14 Village dancers in *Le Moulin maudit.*

foreground. Similarly, Alfred Machin's *Le Moulin maudit* ("The Accursed Mill," Belgium, 1909) shows villagers dancing up to and past the camera along a curved path (**2.14**).

From 1906 or so onward, filmmakers began giving more depth to indoor scenes as well. The results could be quite complex, with figures moving or halting to create vivid compositions and to highlight an actor's gesture or facial expression. In Urban Gad's *Afgrunden* ("Downfall," Denmark, 1910), the heroine's effort to reunite with her fiancé is blocked by her past involvement with a thug. Gad presents the thug's arrival so as to emphasize the fiancé's helpless response (**2.15–2.17**). In such ways, as the drama unfolded moment by moment, depth staging could guide the viewer's eye to the most important parts of the action.

Intertitles   Before 1905, most films had no intertitles. Their main titles often gave information concerning the basic situations in the simple narratives to come. In 1904, for example, the Lubin company released *A Policeman's Love Affair,* a six-shot comedy about a rich woman who catches a policeman wooing her maid and throws a bucket of water on him. In Chapter 1, we saw that Edwin S. Porter's 1903 *Uncle Tom's Cabin* used a

separate intertitle to introduce the situation of each shot (see 1.31, 1.32). The longer film length standardized during the nickelodeon era led to an increasing number of intertitles.

There were two types of intertitles. *Expository titles* were initially more common. Their texts were written in the third person, summarizing the upcoming action or simply setting up the situation. A typical one-reeler of 1911, *Her Mother's Fiancé* (made by Yankee, a small independent), introduced one scene with this title: "Home from School. The Widow's daughter comes home unexpectedly and surprises her mother." Other expository intertitles were more laconic, like the chapter titles in a book. In a 1911 Vitagraph film, *The Inherited Taint,* a scene begins with the title "An engagement broken." Intertitles could also signal time gaps between scenes; titles such as "The following day" and "One month later" became common.

Filmmakers also sought a type of intertitle that could convey narrative information less baldly. Information presented in *dialogue titles* seemed to come from within the story action. Moreover, because films increasingly focused on character psychology, dialogue titles could suggest characters' thoughts more precisely than gestures could. At first filmmakers were not quite sure where to insert dialogue titles. Some put the title before the shot in which the character delivered the line. Other filmmakers placed the dialogue title in the middle of the shot, just after the character had begun to speak. The latter placement became the norm by 1914, as filmmakers realized that the spectator could better understand the scene if the title closely coincided with the speech in the image.

Camera Position and Acting   Decisions about where to place the camera were important for ensuring that

2.15   In *Afgrunden,* the lovers are interrupted by the thug.

2.16   The fiancé moves away, leaving the heroine unprotected. By making him turn from us, Gad forces us to pay more attention to her and her former lover.

2.17   The thug moves to frame center, balancing the composition and asserting his control of the situation.

2.18, *left*   Griffith's *The Painted Lady* was an early instance of a film that concentrated on the virtuosic acting of its star, Blanche Sweet. Here she portrays the heroine's madness.

2.19, *right*   A camera framing from a slightly high angle enhances the drama of the final guillotine scene in Vitagraph's 1911 three-reel feature *A Tale of Two Cities*.

the action would be comprehensible to the viewer. The edges of the image created a frame around the events depicted. Objects or figures at the center tended to be more noticeable. Methods of framing the action changed after 1908.

In order to convey the psychology of the characters, for example, filmmakers began to put the camera slightly closer to the actors so that their facial expressions would be more visible. This trend seems to have started about 1909, when the *9-foot line* was introduced. This meant that the camera, instead of being 12 or 16 feet back and showing the actors from head to toe, was placed only 9 feet away, cutting off the actors just below the hips. Some reviewers complained that this looked unnatural and inartistic, but others praised the acting in films by Vitagraph, which pioneered this technique.

Griffith, in particular, explored the possibilities of enlarging facial expressions. In early 1912, he began training his talented group of young actresses, including Lillian Gish, Blanche Sweet, Mae Marsh, and Mary Pickford, to register a lengthy series of emotions using only slight gestures and facial changes. An early result of these experiments was *The Painted Lady,* in 1912, a tragic story of a demure young woman who is courted by a man who turns out to be a thief. After she shoots him during a robbery attempt, she goes mad and relives their romance in fantasy. Throughout much of *The Painted Lady,* Griffith places the camera relatively close to the heroine, framing her from the waist up so her slightest expressions and movements are visible (**2.18**). During the early teens, conventional pantomime gestures continued to be used but were more restrained and were increasingly used in combination with facial expressions.

Another technique of framing that changed during this period was the use of high and low camera angles. In early fiction films, the camera usually viewed the action at a level angle, about chest- or waist-high. By about 1911, however, filmmakers began occasionally to frame the action from slightly above or below when

doing so provided a more effective vantage point on the scene (**2.19**).

During these same years, camera tripods with swiveling heads were introduced. With such tripods, the camera could be turned from side to side to make *pan* shots or swiveled up and down to create *tilts.* Tilts and pans were often used to make slight adjustments, or *reframings,* when the figures moved about. This ability to keep the action centered also enhanced the comprehensibility of scenes.

Color   Although most of the prints of silent films that we see today are black and white, many were colored in some fashion when they first appeared. Two techniques for color release prints became common. *Tinting* involved dipping an already-developed positive print into a dye bath that colored the lighter portions of the images while the dark ones remained black. In *toning,* the already-developed positive print was placed in a different chemical solution that saturated the dark areas of the frame while the lighter areas remained nearly white.

Why add an overall color to the images? Color could provide information about the narrative situation and hence make the story clearer to the spectator. Vitagraph's *Jepthah's Daughter* uses tinting for a miracle scene by firelight; the pink color suggests the light of the flames (**Color Plate 2.2**). Blue tinting was frequently used to indicate night scenes (**Color Plate 2.3**). Amber tints were common for night interiors, green for scenes in nature, and so on. Similar color codes held for toning. For ordinary daylight scenes, toning in sepia or purple was typical (**Color Plate 2.4**). Color was also used to enhance realism. After Pathé introduced its stencil system, other companies applied similar techniques (**Color Plate 2.5**).

Set Design and Lighting   Between 1905 and 1912, as production companies were making more money from their films, some built larger studio buildings to replace the earlier open-air stages and cramped interior studios.

2.20   In this scene from *The 100-to-One Shot* (1906, Vitagraph), the table and chairs are real, but the fireplace, wall, door frame, window, flowerpots—even the sunlight coming in through the window—are painted on a backdrop. Note also the stark shadows cast on the floor by the sunlight used to illuminate the scene.

2.21   In *Shamus O'Brien* (1912, IMP), much of the scene is dark, while an arc lamp low and offscreen right simulates the light from a fire. (Contrast the set design and lighting of this scene with those of 2.20).

Most of these had glass walls to admit sunlight but also included some type of electric lighting. As a result, many films used deeper, more three-dimensional settings, and some used artificial light.

At the beginning of the nickelodeon era, many fiction films were still using painted theatrical-style backdrops, or flats, with some real furniture or props mixed in (**2.20;** see also 1.15, 1.25, 1.32, 2.23). Over the next several years, however, more three-dimensional sets, without painted furniture, windows, and so on, came into use (see 2.5, 2.27, 2.40). The set in *The Lonely Villa* (see 2.27), with its two sidewalls, gives a greater sense of depth than does the set in *The 100-to-One Shot* (see 2.20).

Most lighting in early films was even and flat, provided by sunshine or banks of electric lights (see 2.23, 2.26, and 2.40). During this era, however, filmmakers sometimes used a single arc lamp to cast a strong light from one direction. Such lamps could be placed in a fireplace to suggest a fire (**2.21**). The control of artificial studio lighting would be an important development in American film style of the late 1910s.

By 1912, American filmmakers had established many basic techniques for telling a clear story. Spectators could usually see the characters clearly and understand where they were in relation to each other, what they could see, and what they were saying. These techniques would be elaborated and polished over the next decade, until the Hollywood narrative system was sophisticated indeed.

The Beginnings of the Continuity System   When editing links a series of shots, narrative clarity will be enhanced if the spectator understands how the shots relate to each other in space and time. Is time continuing uninterruptedly, or has some time been skipped (creating an ellipsis)? Are we still seeing the same space, or

has the scene shifted to a new locale? As Alfred Capus, a scriptwriter for the French firm Film d'Art, put it in 1908, "If we wish to retain the attention of the public, we have to maintain unbroken connection with each preceding [shot]."[4] From about 1906 onward, filmmakers developed techniques for maintaining this "unbroken connection." By 1917, these techniques would come together in the *continuity system* of editing. This system involved three basic ways of joining shots: *intercutting, analytical editing,* and *contiguity editing.*

Intercutting   Before 1906, narrative films did not move back and forth between actions in separate spaces. In most cases, one continuous action formed the whole story. The popular chase genre provides the best example. Here an event triggers the chase, and the characters keep running through one shot after another until the culprit is caught. If a narrative involved several actions, the film would concentrate on one in its entirety and then move on to the next.

One of the earliest known cases where the action cuts back and forth between locales, with at least two shots in each place, occurs in *The 100-to-One Shot* (1906, Vitagraph). The situation is a last-minute race to pay the mortgage before the landlord evicts a family. The last four shots show the hero speeding toward and arriving at the house:

Shot 29 A street, with a car driving forward.

Shot 30 Inside the house, the landlord starts to force the old father to leave.

Shot 31 The street in front of the house, with the hero pulling up in the car.

Shot 32 Inside the house, the hero pays the landlord and tears up the eviction notice. General rejoicing.

2.22–2.24 Intercutting in *The Runaway Horse* allowed the filmmakers to give the impression that the horse grows healthy and fat by eating a whole bag of oats.

2.25–2.27 Successive shots from near the end of the intercut rescue scene in *The Lonely Villa* show simultaneous action in three locales.

Presumably the filmmakers hoped that when cutting moved back and forth between two different spaces, the spectator would understand that the actions were taking place simultaneously.

Early intercutting (also known as *parallel editing* and *crosscutting*) could be used for actions other than rescues. French films, especially Pathé's, were influential in developing this technique. A clever chase film of 1907, *The Runaway Horse*, for example, shows a cart horse eating a bag of oats outside a shop while his driver delivers laundry inside an apartment building. In the first shot, the horse is scrawny and the bag full (**2.22**). In the next shot, we see the driver inside the building (**2.23**). Four more shots of the horse are interspersed with six of the driver inside. The filmmakers substituted successively more robust animals, so the cart horse seems to get fatter as the sack empties (**2.24**). By the end of the scene, the horse is very lively, and a chase ensues.

D. W. Griffith is the early director most often associated with the development of intercutting (see "Notes and Queries" at the end of this chapter). After working as a minor stage and film actor, Griffith started making films at AM&B in 1908. He soon began using various techniques in extraordinarily original ways. Despite the fact that filmmakers were not credited, viewers soon recognized that films from American Biograph (the name

the company assumed in 1909) were consistently among the best coming from American studios.

Griffith was undoubtedly influenced by earlier films, including *The Runaway Horse*, but of all directors of the period, he explored the possibilities of intercutting most daringly. One of his most extended and suspenseful early uses of the technique came in *The Lonely Villa* (1909). The plot involves thieves who lure a man away from his isolated country home by sending a false message. Griffith cuts among three elements: the man, the thieves, and the family inside the house. Having car trouble, the man calls home and learns that the thieves are breaking into a room where his wife and daughters are barricaded. He hires a wagon, and a series of shots continues to connect the husband's rescue group, the thieves, and the terrified family (**2.25–2.27**). In less than 15 minutes, *The Lonely Villa* presents over fifty shots, most of which are linked by intercutting. A contemporary reviewer described the electrifying effect of the film's suspense sequence:

"Thank God, they're saved!" said a woman behind us at the conclusion of the Biograph film bearing the above name. Just like this woman, the entire audience were in a state of intense excitement as this picture was being shown. And no wonder, for it is one of the

2.28, 2.29 In *After One Hundred Years* (1911, Selig), a cut-in to a closer view shows a man discovering a bullet hole in a mantelpiece, a detail that would not be visible in the distant framing.

2.30, 2.31 *Rescued by Rover:* running consistently toward the left foreground, Rover leads his master through a clearly defined series of contiguous spaces to reach the kidnapper's hideout.

most adroitly managed bits of bloodless film drama that we have seen.[5]

Griffith experimented with intercutting, especially in rescue scenes, for several years. By 1912, intercutting was a common technique in American films.

Analytical Editing   This terms refers to editing that breaks down a single space into separate framings. One simple way of doing this is to cut in closer to the action. Thus a long shot shows the entire space, and a closer one enlarges small objects or facial expressions. Cut-ins in the period before 1905 were rare (see 1.25, 1.26).

During the nickelodeon era, filmmakers began inserting closer views into the middles of scenes. Often these were notes or photographs that the characters examined. These were called *inserts* and were usually seen from a character's point of view. They helped make the action comprehensible to the viewer.

Between 1907 and 1911, simple cut-ins to small gestures or objects were occasionally used (**2.28, 2.29**). Cut-ins did not become common until the mid-1910s, however. As we shall see in Chapter 3, longer features led to longer individual scenes, with filmmakers cutting more freely within a single space.

Contiguity Editing   In some scenes, characters move out of the space of one shot and reappear in a nearby locale. Such movements were crucial to the chase genre. Typically, a group of characters would run through the

shot and then out of sight; the film would then cut to an adjacent locale, where the process would be repeated as they ran through again. A series of such shots made up most of the film. A similar pattern occurs in an early model of clear storytelling, *Rescued by Rover* (produced in 1905 by Cecil Hepworth in England, and probably directed by Lewin Fitzhamon). After a baby is kidnapped, the family dog races from the house and through the town, finds the baby, runs back to fetch the father, and leads him to the kidnapper's lair. In all the shots of Rover running toward the lair, the dog moves forward through the space of one shot, exits to the left of the camera, and comes into the space of the next shot, still running forward and exiting left (**2.30, 2.31**).

Not all films of this early period show the characters moving in consistent directions in the contiguous spaces. By the teens, however, many filmmakers seem to have realized that keeping the direction of movement constant helped the audience keep track of spatial relations. In 1911, a reviewer complained about inconsistencies:

Attention has been called frequently in *Mirror* film reviews to apparent errors of direction or management as to exits and entrances in motion picture production. . . . A player will be seen leaving a room or locality in a certain direction, and in the very next connecting [shot], a sixteenth of a second later, he will enter in exactly the opposite direction. . . . Any one who has watched pictures knows how often his sense of reality has been shocked by this very thing. To him it is as

2.32, 2.33 In *Alma's Champion* (1912, Vitagraph), the first shot shows the hero exiting leftward. In the next shot, he moves into a nearby space along the tracks. His continued leftward movement, plus the presence of the train in the background, helps the spectator understand where the actions are taking place.

2.34, 2.35 In the 1905 Pathé comedy *The Scholar's Breakfast,* a shot of the scientist looking through his microscope leads to a point-of-view shot.

2.36, 2.37 Two shots from *A Friendly Marriage* (1911, Vitagraph). After the wife looks offscreen in the first shot, we understand that the framing through the window in the second represents her point of view.

if the player had turned abruptly around in a fraction of a second and was moving the other way.[6]

Within the next few years, filmmakers more consistently kept characters moving in the same direction (2.32, 2.33)

As we shall see, during the mid-1910s the idea of keeping screen direction consistent became an implicit rule in Hollywood-style editing. So important is this rule that the Hollywood approach to editing is also termed the *180-degree system,* meaning that the camera should stay within a semicircle on one side of the action in order to maintain consistent screen direction.

Another way of indicating that two contiguous spaces are near each other is to show a character looking offscreen in one direction and then cut to what that character sees. In the earliest cases where characters'

viewpoints were used to motivate a cut, we would see exactly what the character saw, from his or her optical *point of view.* The earliest point-of-view shots simulated views through microscopes, telescopes, and binoculars to show that we are seeing what characters see (2.34, 2.35). By the early teens, a new type of point-of-view shot was becoming common. A character simply looks offscreen, and we know from the camera's position in the second shot that we are seeing what the character sees (2.36, 2.37).

The second shot might, however, reveal what the character is looking at but not show it from his or her exact point of view. Such a cut is called an *eyeline match* (2.38, 2.39). Such editing was an excellent way of showing that one space was near another, thus clarifying the dramatic action. During the early 1910s, the eyeline match became a standard way of showing the

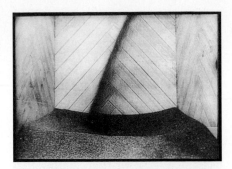

2.38, 2.39 In Griffith's *A Corner in Wheat* (1909, American Biograph), visitors touring the wheat warehouse glance down into a bin. The next shot shows what they see—the bin—but not from their point of view.

2.40, 2.41 In *The Gambler's Charm* (1910, Lubin), the gambler shoots through the door of a bar. He and the other characters look off toward the right, and in the second shot it is clear that they are looking offscreen left at the wounded man.

2.42, 2.43 In *The Loafer* (1911, Essanay), two characters argue in a field. The cutting employs a shot/reverse-shot technique: one character looks off left, shouting at the other, and then we see his opponent reacting, looking off right.

relationship between successive shots. The eyeline match also depended on the 180-degree rule. For example, if a character glances off to the right, he or she is assumed to be offscreen left in the next shot (**2.40, 2.41**).

At about the same time that the eyeline match came into occasional use, filmmakers also used a double eyeline match: one character looking offscreen and then a cut to another character looking in the opposite direction at the first. This type of cutting, with some further elaboration, has come to be known as the *shot/reverse shot*. It is used in conversations, fights, and other situations in which characters interact with each other. One of the earliest known shot/reverse shots occurs in an Essanay Western (**2.42, 2.43**). The shot/reverse-shot technique became more common over the next decade. Today it remains the principal way of constructing conversation scenes in narrative films.

AN INTERNATIONAL STYLE

Many aspects of film style were used in similar ways internationally. French, Italian, Danish, English, and American films and, to a lesser extent, films of other countries circulated widely outside the countries in which they were made. Two examples from very different places should suffice to suggest how widely some techniques were disseminated.

The chase film, so typical of the years from 1904 to 1908, was an international genre. In the Netherlands, where production was miniscule, a chase film called *De Mesavonture van een fransch Heertje zonder Pantalon aan het Strand te Zandvoort* ("The Misadventures of a Frenchman without Pants on the Beach of Zandvoort," c. 1905, Alberts Frères) followed a comic formula: a man falls asleep on the beach, the tide rises to wet his trousers, he removes them, and indignant bystanders

2.44, 2.45 In *De Mesavonture van een fransch Heertje zonder Pantalon aan heet Strand te Zandvoort,* a pair of shots show the unfortunate hero being chased along the beach.

2.46 In the Indian fantasy film, *Raja Harischandra,* the king explains to his queen that he has given his kingdom to an old sage whom he had offended. The shot uses a close framing typical of western filmmaking.

2.47, 2.48 In *Raja Harischandra,* Phalke uses consistent screen direction as the king walks rightward through the forest and, in a cut to a contiguous space, arrives at the hut of the villainous sage.

and police chase him through a series of adjacent locales (**2.44, 2.45**).

The early techniques of continuity developed later in this period also proved widely influential. The earliest Indian fiction feature film, *Raja Harischandra,* was made in 1912 and released in 1913; its director was the first major Indian filmmaker, D. G. Phalke. Like many later Indian films, its subject matter was derived from traditional mythology. Only the first and last of the film's four reels survive, but they indicate that Phalke had grasped the 9-foot line, contiguity cutting, and other current principles of western filmmaking (**2.46–2.48**).

After 1912, filmmakers continued to explore techniques for telling stories clearly. As we shall see in the next chapter, however, World War I interrupted the international circulation of films, and some nations developed distinctive film styles.

Notes and Queries

GRIFFITH'S IMPORTANCE IN THE DEVELOPMENT OF FILM STYLE

If this book had been written several years earlier, this chapter's discussion of changing film style would probably have centered on D. W. Griffith. Griffith himself helped to create the myth that he had invented virtually every important technique for film storytelling. In late 1913, just after he had left American Biograph, he ran a newspaper advertisement claiming to have created the close-up, intercutting, fade-outs, and restrained acting. Early historians, unable to see many films from the pre-1913 period, took him at his word, and Griffith became the father of the cinema.

More recent research, especially since the 1978 Brighton Conference (see "Notes and Queries," Chapter 1), has brought hundreds of overlooked films to light. Historians

THE BEGINNINGS OF FILM ANIMATION

Films using some aspects of animation existed from the beginnings of the cinema. Émile Reynaud's drawn images for his projecting Praxinoscope were important forerunners for cinematic animation (p. 16). Quick-draw artists from vaudeville—among them J. Stuart Blackton, one of the founders of Vitagraph—performed in several early films. There is some evidence that in 1890s' advertising films and films made for toy projectors, filmmakers created movement of objects or drawings by photographing them one frame at a time.

Animation within the film industry seems to have begun in 1906, when Blackton made *Humorous Phases of Funny Faces* for Vitagraph. It consisted mostly of drawings of faces that developed frame by frame, as Blackton added bits of lines. Thus the drawings gradually appeared but did not move—until the end, when the faces roll their eyes. That same year, Pathé produced *Le Théâtre de Petit Bob* (*Little Bob's Theater*), for which Spanish filmmaker Segundo de Chomón patiently moved objects between single-frame exposures to make the contents of a boy's toybox appear to come to life. Such animation of objects is called *pixillation*.

Creating animated films took a great deal of time and effort. In this early period, they usually were the painstaking creations of individual artists, working alone or with an assistant. Animation involved either making objects seem to move or bringing many separate drawings to life.

The earliest major film animating objects was Vitagraph's *The Haunted Hotel* (1907), directed by Blackton. Here the "magical" movement occurred within a live-action film. A hotel patron is plagued by supernatural forces, rendered onscreen through double exposures, wires, stop-motion, and other tricks. In one scene, we see a close view of objects on a table. A knife moves on its own to cut and butter bread (**2.49**). *The Haunted Hotel* was one of the first releases by Vitagraph's new Paris office, and it was widely imitated abroad.

Émile Cohl, who worked primarily for Gaumont from 1908 to 1910, was the first person to devote his energies to drawn animation. His earliest cartoon was *Fantasmagorie* (1908; **2.50**). In order to create steady movement, Cohl placed each drawing on a plate of glass illuminated from beneath and then traced the image onto the next sheet of paper, making slight changes in the figures. His many films were often based on bizarre, stream-of-consciousness transformations of a series of shapes, one

2.49 In Blackton's *The Haunted Hotel,* a meal prepares itself through frame-by-frame animation.

2.50 Cohl's *Fantasmagorie* was drawn in black ink on white paper and then printed in negative to give the impression of moving chalk figures on a blackboard.

into another. Cohl also made live-action films, often incorporating some animated sequences. Like Méliès, Cohl retired from filmmaking in the teens and lived a life of poverty; he died in 1938.

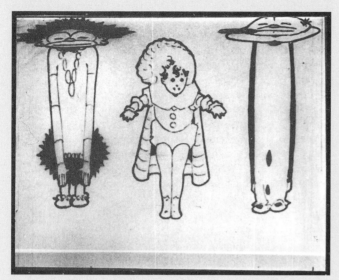

2.51 In *Little Nemo,* the characters move about, but there is no story line. The lack of scenery saved McCay considerable time in redrawing the backgrounds on each sheet.

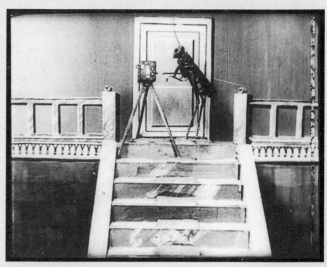

2.52 The grasshopper hero of *The Revenge of a Kinematograph Cameraman* films the adulterous activities of a beetle who has insulted him. Later the beetle and his wife see the film in a movie program, whereupon she thrashes him with her umbrella.

In the United States, eminent comic-strip artist and vaudevillian Winsor McCay also began making drawn animated films, initially to project in his stage act. His first film was *Little Nemo,* completed in 1911; it featured characters from his famous newspaper strip "Little Nemo in Slumberland" (**2.51**). The film contains a live-action prologue that shows how the enormous number of drawings necessary for the animation were made. McCay made a second cartoon, *The Story of a Mosquito,* in 1912, and a third, *Gertie,* in 1914. (Modern prints of these films contain live-action shots that McCay added after their use in his stage act.) *Mosquito* and *Gertie* contain sketchy background settings, which an assistant traced on every page. McCay made a few more films, utilizing new labor-saving techniques created after 1912.

In 1910, perhaps the greatest puppet animator of all time began his work. In Russia, Polish-born Ladislav Starevicz made some fiction shorts "acted" by insects. The realistic movements in these films baffled audiences and reviewers:

> What is so amazing about this film is that the beetles portray the situation with such plausibility. When angry they shake their feelers and raise their horns, they march just like people. . . .

How is it all done? Not one of the viewers could explain it. If the beetles were performing then their trainer must be a man of magical endurance and patience. That the actors were indeed beetles is clear from careful examination of their appearance.[7]

Like other animators, Starevicz was indeed a man of "magical patience," but he was manipulating plastic puppets with wire joints, changing their positions from frame to frame. His most famous early film is *The Revenge of a Kinematograph Cameraman* (1912; **2.52**). Its witty story and detailed movements of the insect puppets remain engrossing today. Starevicz made many more animated and live-action films in Russia; then he fled to Paris in the wake of the 1917 Bolshevik Revolution. There he remained active for many decades.

After 1912, animation was to become a more regular part of filmmaking as labor-saving techniques were invented and patented. The early individual animators largely gave way to staffs of specialists in various phases of the process. Even so, to this day there are still animators who work alone, following the tradition of Cohl, McCay, Starevicz, and others.

have also realized that many of Griffith's contemporaries were exploring similar techniques. His importance now seems to rest in his ability to combine these techniques in daring ways (as when he extended the number of shots in the intercutting of *The Lonely Villa*). Most historians now agree that Griffith's artistic ambitions, not his sheer originality, made him the foremost American filmmaker of this era.

Traditional accounts of Griffith as the inventor of the modern cinema appear in some of the earliest film histories, including Terry Ramsaye's *A Million and One Nights* (1926; reprint, New York: Simon & Schuster, 1964), chap. 50, "Griffith Evolves Screen Syntax"; and Lewis Jacobs's *The Rise of the American Film* (1939; reprint, New York: Teachers College Press, 1968), chap. 7, "D. W. Griffith: New Discoveries."

More recent accounts of the early development of film style stress typical films rather than highlighting those by masters like Griffith: Barry Salt, *Film Style & Technology: History and Analysis*, 2d ed. (London: Starword, 1992), chaps. 7–8; David Bordwell, Janet Staiger, and Kristin Thompson, *The Classical Hollywood Cinema: Film Style and Mode of Production to 1960* (New York: Columbia University Press, 1985), chaps. 14, 16–17; and Charlie Keil, *Early American Cinema in Transition: Story, Style, and Filmmaking, 1907–1913* (Madison: University of Wisconsin Press, 2002). Salt's *"The Physician of the Castle," Sight & Sound* 54, no. 4 (autumn 1985): 284–85, revealed that the intercutting in this Pathé film probably influenced Griffith. The article also provides insight into how historians make such discoveries. Tom Gunning's *D. W. Griffith and the Origins of American Narrative Film* (Urbana: University of Illinois Press, 1991) balances a detailed examination of Griffith's first two years of filmmaking with a look at the larger context within which he worked. See also Joyce E. Jesionowski, *Thinking in Pictures: Dramatic Structure in D. W. Griffith's Biograph Films* (Berkeley: University of California Press, 1987), which suggests (especially in the introduction) that the discovery of other filmmakers' contributions may have led historians to deemphasize Griffith too much.

- -

REFERENCES

1. Inscription on a photograph reproduced in Charles Ford, *Max Linder* (Paris: Éditions Seghers, 1966), opposite p. 65.
2. Quoted in Tom Gunning, *D. W. Griffith and the Origins of American Narrative Film: The Early Years at Biograph* (Urbana: University of Illinois Press, 1991), pp. 219–20.
3. Quoted in Charles Musser, *Before the Nickelodeon: Edwin S. Porter and the Edison Manufacturing Company* (Berkeley: University of California Press, 1991), p. 360.
4. Quoted in Eileen Bowser, *The Transformation of Cinema, 1907–1915* (New York: Scribners, 1990), p. 57. The original word used by Capus was *scene*, which was the term used during the period to mean *shot*.
5. Quoted in Gunning, *D. W. Griffith*, p. 204. The word *bloodless* refers to the fact that no actual violence is committed in the film.
6. "Spectator" [Frank Woods], "Spectator's Comments," *New York Dramatic Mirror* 65, no. 1681 (8 March 1911): 29.
7. Quoted in Yuri Tsivian et al., *Silent Witnesses: Russian Films 1908–1919* (London: British Film Institute, 1989), p. 586.

FURTHER READING

Abel, Richard. "In the Belly of the Beast: The Early Years of Pathé Frères." *Film History* 5, no. 4 (December 1993): 363–85.

_____. *The Red Rooster Scare: Making Cinema American, 1900–1910.* Berkeley: University of California Press, 1999.

Azlant, Edward. "Screenwriting for the Early Silent Films: Forgotten Pioneers, 1897–1911." *Film History* 9, no. 3 (1997): 228–56.

Bernardini, Aldo. "An Industry in Recession: The Italian Film Industry 1909–1909." *Film History* 3, no. 4 (1989): 341–68.

Bowser, Eileen. *The Transformation of Cinema: 1907–1915.* New York: Scribners, 1990.

Crafton, Donald. *Emile Cohl, Caricature and Film.* Princeton, NJ: Princeton University Press, 1990.

Färber, Helmut. *"A Corner in Wheat* by D. W. Griffith, 1909: A Critique." Issue of *Griffithiana* 59 (May 1997).

High, Peter B. "The Dawn of Cinema in Japan." *Journal of Contemporary History* 19, no. 1 (1984): 23–57.

Mottram, Ron. *The Danish Cinema before Dreyer.* Metuchen, NJ: Scarecrow, 1988.

Musser, Charles. "Pre-classical American Cinema: Its Changing Modes of Film Production." *Persistence of Vision*, no. 9 (1991): 46–65.

Slide, Anthony. *The Big V: A History of the Vitagraph Company.* Rev. ed. Metuchen, NJ: Scarecrow, 1987.

CHAPTER 3

NATIONAL CINEMAS, HOLLYWOOD CLASSICISM, AND WORLD WAR I, 1913–1919

The years just before World War I marked a turning point in the history of the cinema. In 1913 alone, an extraordinary array of important feature films were made in Europe: in France, Léonce Perret's *L'Enfant de Paris;* in Germany, Paul von Woringen's *Die Landstrasse* and Stellan Rye's *The Student of Prague;* in Denmark, August Blom's *Atlantis* and Benjamin Christensen's *The Mysterious X;* in Sweden, Victor Sjöström's *Ingeborg Holm;* in Italy, Giovanni Pastrone's *Cabiria* (released in early 1914). Also in 1913, the serial emerged as a major film form, and labor-saving techniques were introduced into animation. During the mid-teens, the feature film was becoming standardized internationally. A few directors brought Swedish cinema into a "golden age" that would last into the 1920s. Some countries saw the creation and consolidation of major firms and studios that would dominate film history for decades; most crucially, the Hollywood industry was taking shape. In other countries, problems caused the decline of major industries. The war forced both France and Italy to reduce their high levels of film production.

During this period, filmmakers around the world were exploring the expressive possibilities of film style. In its first decade or so, cinema relied on the display of action for its novelty value. Then, during the nickelodeon era, filmmakers tested ways of telling stories clearly. From about 1912 on, some directors increasingly realized that distinctive lighting, editing, acting, staging, set design, and other film techniques could not only clarify the unfolding of the action but also heighten the film's impact. Time and again in this chapter, we will see filmmakers creating striking compositions by backlighting subjects, using lengthy takes to create a realistic sense of ordinary time passing, or cutting among widely disparate elements to make a conceptual point. Such techniques could enhance the narrative by lending atmosphere, meaning, and suspense.

In August 1914, during these important changes, World War I began. The war had profound effects on the international cinema, some of which are still felt today. The war effort severely curtailed filmmaking in the two leading producing countries, France and Italy. American companies stepped in to fill the vacuum. As of 1916, the United States became the major supplier of films to the world market, and it has held that position ever since. Much of the history of world cinema has been bound up with the struggles of various national industries to compete with Hollywood's domination. The war also limited the free flow of films and influences across borders. The result was the isolation of several film-producing countries, where, for the first time, distinctive national cinemas evolved.

THE AMERICAN TAKEOVER OF WORLD MARKETS

As we saw in the previous chapter, up until 1912, American film companies were largely absorbed in the competition for the domestic market. They were hard put to satisfy the huge demand for films created by the nickelodeon boom. Edison, American Biograph, and other Motion Picture Patents Company members also hoped to limit competition from French, Italian, and other imported films.

Still, it was obvious that a great deal of money was to be made in exporting films. The first American company to open its own distribution offices in Europe was Vitagraph, which had a branch in London in 1906 and soon a second in Paris. By 1909, other American firms were moving into foreign markets as well. This expansion of American distribution abroad continued until the mid-1920s. Initially, most companies sold their films indirectly. Inexperienced with overseas trading, they simply sold the foreign rights to their films to export agents or foreign distribution firms. London became a center for the international circulation of U.S. films. Many British firms profited by acting as the agents for this business, though in doing so they weakened British production by turning over a large share of the U.K. market to American films.

France, Italy, and other producing countries still provided stiff competition around the world. Nonetheless, even before the war began, U.S. films were becoming very popular in some nations. By 1911, for example, an estimated 60 to 70 percent of films imported into Great Britain were American. The United States was also doing well in Germany, Australia, and New Zealand. In most other markets, however, the American share was much smaller. Without the war, Hollywood might not have gained a preeminent global position.

The beginning of the war caused a near cessation of French filmmaking. Many industry personnel were immediately sent to the front. Pathé's raw-stock factory switched to manufacturing munitions, and studios were converted into barracks. As it became apparent that the fighting would drag on for years, the French industry gradually resumed production, but never on the scale of the prewar era. A less extreme cutback in production affected Italy once it entered the war in 1916.

Hollywood firms seized the opportunity to expand in foreign markets. Cut off from European films, many countries found a new source in the United States. By 1916, American exports had risen dramatically. Over the next few years, American firms sold fewer films through London agents. They began to market their own products directly, opening distribution branches in South America, Australia, the Far East, and European countries not isolated by the hostilities. In this way, American companies collected all the profits themselves and were soon in a strong position in many countries. About 60 percent of Argentina's imports during 1916, for example, were American films, and in subsequent years South American nations bought more and more Hollywood films. About 95 percent of screenings in Australia and New Zealand consisted of American films. The U.S. shares of even the French and Italian markets were rising.

After the war, the U.S. industry maintained its lead abroad partly because of certain economic factors. A film's production budget was based on how much it could be expected to earn. Up to the mid-1910s, when most of an American film's income came from the domestic market, budgets were modest. Once a film could predictably earn more money abroad, its budget could be higher. It could then recover its costs in the United States and be sold cheaply abroad, undercutting local national production. By 1917, Hollywood firms were estimating costs based on both domestic and foreign sales. Accordingly, producers invested in big sets, lavish costumes, and more lighting equipment. Highly paid stars like Mary Pickford and William S. Hart were soon idolized around the world (3.1). By late 1918, Hollywood also had a backlog of films to flood the markets of countries formerly cut off by the war.

Other countries found it hard to compete against Hollywood production values. Low budgets led to low sales, which in turn perpetuated the low budgets. Moreover, it was usually cheaper to buy an American film than to finance a local production. Over time, some countries managed to counter these disadvantages, at least temporarily. Throughout this book, we shall see

3.1 The Elphinstone Picture Palace in Colombo, Ceylon, shows Paramount's big-budget adaptation of *Beau Geste* (1926), starring Ronald Colman. Native drivers wait outside for their colonialist employers.

how alternatives to Hollywood cinema have arisen. Basically, however, Hollywood has had two advantages since the mid-1910s: the average production budget has remained higher in Hollywood than anywhere else in the world, and importing an American film is still often cheaper than producing one locally.

THE RISE OF NATIONAL CINEMAS

Before World War I, the cinema was largely an international affair. Technical and artistic discoveries made in one country were quickly seen and assimilated elsewhere. The war, however, disrupted the free flow of films across borders. Some national industries benefited from this disruption. A few countries were partially or wholly cut off from imports, yet the demand for films remained. Hence domestic production rose in such countries, especially Sweden, Russia, and Germany. Other countries, such as France, Denmark, and Italy, suffered a decline from prewar levels but managed to continue and improve on prewar traditions. In many cases, stylistic influences could not circulate so freely across borders. For example, the singular filmmaking practice that developed in Russia during the war had virtually no impact

abroad and remained almost entirely unknown in the West for over seventy years. (See "Notes and Queries".)

Germany

Before 1912, the German film industry was relatively insignificant. Its films were not widely exported, and imports dominated its domestic market. The cinema also had a low reputation in Germany. During the early 1910s, reformers and censors attacked film as immoral. Theatrical and arts journals portrayed it as a lowbrow form of entertainment, primarily because competition from films had caused theater attendance to decline. In May 1912, organizations of playwrights, directors, and actors went so far as to boycott the cinema.

By late 1912, however, the boycott was broken, as film producers competed to sign those same playwrights, directors, and actors to exclusive contracts. Similarly, film firms sought to adapt prestigious literary works and to have established authors write original screenplays. During 1913 there arose the *Autorenfilm,* or "authors' film." The term *author* did not mean then what *auteur* means today—the director of the film. Rather, the Autorenfilm was publicized largely on the basis of a famous writer who had written the script or the original literary work from which the film was adapted. The director of the film was seldom mentioned. The Autorenfilm was, in effect, Germany's equivalent of the Film d'Art in France (p. 34) and other attempts at creating an artistic cinema. Similarly, stage stars were hired and featured prominently in the publicity for such films. A few leading theatrical directors, most notably Max Reinhardt, worked briefly in the cinema.

The Autorenfilm was established with *Der Andere* ("The Other," 1913, Max Mack), adapted from a drama by playwright Paul Lindau and starring a major theatrical performer, Albert Bassermann. *Der Andere* was reviewed favorably by theater journals. Another important Autorenfilm was *Die Landstrasse* ("The Country Road," 1913, Paul von Woringen). This time Lindau wrote an original script, dealing with an escaped convict who commits a murder in a small village. The murder is blamed on a passing beggar, who is finally cleared by the convict's deathbed confession. From a modern perspective, *Die Landstrasse* seems an unusually sophisticated film. It proceeds at a slow pace, carefully setting up parallelisms between the convict and the beggar. There are a number of very long takes that deemphasize action in favor of concentration on minute details—an early exploration of expressive cinematic techniques. One framing simply shows a forest setting, with the beggar wandering in from the background and sitting by a bush in the foreground to eat the scraps of food he has obtained in the village. More dramatically, the revelation of the dying convict's guilt comes in a minutes-long shot that encompasses the beggar's anguished reaction and the reactions of the onlookers (**3.2**).

The most successful and famous Autorenfilm is *The Student of Prague* (1913, Stellan Rye). It was based on an original screenplay by the popular writer Hanns Heinz Ewers and marked the entry of theater star Paul Wegener into the cinema. For decades, Wegener was to remain a major force in German filmmaking. *The Student of Prague* is a Faust-like story of a student who gives his mirror image to a demonic character in exchange for wealth. The image dogs the hero and finally provokes a fatal duel. Aided by the great cameraman Guido Seeber, Rye and Wegener used special effects to create scenes of the student and his double confronting each other (**3.3**). The fantasy elements of this film would become a prominent trait of German cinema, culminating in the German Expressionist movement of the 1920s (see Chapter 5).

The Autorenfilm lent respectability to the cinema, but most of the films were not successful with the public, and the notion of basing films on works by famous authors declined during 1914. During the same period,

however, the German industry was expanding. Domestic films were gaining popular success, largely due to the rise of the star system. Two very different female stars became widely known. The blonde Henny Porten was the ideal of German womanhood. Her films were soon export successes, and she was on the verge of becoming internationally famous as the war began. Her worldwide fame would finally come during the 1920s. The Danish actress Asta Nielsen had quickly caught on in Germany after moving there in 1911. Her Danish husband, Urban Gad, directed her in many short films until their separation in 1915. These were notable for Nielsen's varied portrayals, ranging from comic adolescents to betrayed lovers (**3.4**), and she had a great influence on acting styles in other countries.

During the early years of the war, Germany continued to import films, especially from Denmark. Officials soon concluded, however, that the anti-German content of some of these films was hurting the war effort. In 1916, Germany banned film imports. This ban would later stimulate the domestic film industry, helping it to become powerful internationally during the war.

Italy

Italian cinema flourished in the first half of the teens. The success of exported films and the establishment of the feature film attracted talented people to the industry and led producing companies to compete energetically.

Historical epics continued to have the most significant triumphs abroad. In 1913, Enrico Guazzoni's *Quo Vadis?* was an enormous hit and confirmed the epic as the main Italian genre. *Quo Vadis?* was followed in 1914 by one of the most internationally popular films of the era, Giovanni Pastrone's *Cabiria*. Set in the Roman Empire of the third century B.C., *Cabiria* involved kidnapping and human sacrifice, as the hero Fulvio and his strongman slave Maciste try to rescue the heroine. Mammoth scenes showed a palace destroyed by an erupting volcano and a huge temple within which children are thrown into a fiery figure of the pagan god Moloch (**3.5**). *Cabiria* also consistently used innovative slow tracking shots toward or away from static action. Camera movement had appeared in the early years of the cinema, particularly in scenics (pp. 23, 26). Filmmakers had also occasionally used mobile framing for expressive purposes in narrative films, as when D. W. Griffith began and ended *The Country Doctor* (1909) with pans across a rural landscape. *Cabiria*'s tracking shots were more influential, however, and the "Cabiria movement" became a common technique in films of the mid-1910s.

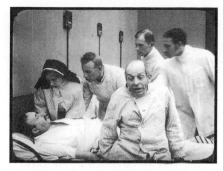

3.2 The climactic scene of *Die Landstrasse* consists primarily of a lengthy take concentrating on gradual changes in the characters' expressions.

3.3 In *The Student of Prague*, exposure of separate portions of the same shot during filming allowed two characters, both played by Paul Wegener, to confront each other.

3.4 Part of a complex scene in Urban Gad's last film with Asta Nielsen, *Weisse Rosen* ("White Roses," 1916), filmed into a mirror. Characters enter and exit from offscreen, seen directly or as reflections, as the plot develops.

3.5 The large interior of the temple in *Cabiria*.

3.6 Lyda Borelli, as an actress alone in her dressing room, strikes a dramatic pose reflected by her mirror in *Ma l'amor mio non muore!*

3.7 The faithful Maciste, seen here in a shot from *Cabiria*, inspired the strongman genre in Italian cinema.

A second distinctively Italian genre resulted from the rise of the star system. Several beautiful female stars became wildly popular. These were the *divas* ("goddesses"). They typically starred in what are sometimes known as *frock-coat films*—stories of passion and intrigue in upper-middle-class and aristocratic settings. The situations were unrealistic and often tragic, usually featuring eroticism and death, and were initially influenced by the importation of Asta Nielsen's German films.

The diva films played up luxurious settings, fashionable costumes, and the heightened acting of the performers. *Ma l'amor mio non muore!* ("But My Love Does Not Die!" 1913, Mario Caserini) established the genre (3.6). It made Lyda Borelli an instant star, and she remained one of the most celebrated divas. Borelli's main rival was Francesca Bertini, whose 1915 *Assunta Spina* (Gustavo Serena) was a rare diva film set in a working-class milieu. Bertini went on to make a series of more luxurious films based on her star persona. These included a spy melodrama, *Diana l'affascinatrice* ("Diana the Seductress," 1915, Gustavo Serena), that displayed Bertini's histrionic talents and elegant costumes (see p. 10). Diva films remained popular during the second half of the 1910s and then quickly declined in the 1920s.

The male equivalent of the diva was the strongman. The characters of Ursus in *Quo Vadis?* and of the slave Maciste in *Cabiria* started this trend. Maciste was played by a muscular dockworker, Bartolomeo Pagano (3.7). His character so fascinated audiences that Pagano went on to star in a series of Maciste films that lasted into the 1920s. Unlike *Cabiria*, these and other strongman films were set in the present rather than the historical past. This genre declined temporarily after 1923, as Italian filmmaking sank into crisis. The *peplum film,* or the heroic historical epic, often involving brawny heroes, resurfaced decades later with such films as *Hercules* (1957).

After the war, Italy tried to regain its place on world markets but could not make inroads against American films. In 1919, a large new firm called the Unione Cinematografica Italiana (UCI) attempted to revive Italian production. Its dependence on formulaic filmmaking, however, exacerbated the industry's decline during the 1920s.

3.8, *left*   In *Child of the Big City* (1914), Evgenii Bauer places a gauzy curtain in the foreground as the *femme fatale* dines with her friends. This curtain is subsequently drawn aside, and the camera tracks back as the characters move forward.

3.9, *right*   In *Father Sergius*, Protazanov uses sidelighting and staging in depth to enhance the tragic atmosphere as the protagonist resists seduction by a jaded society woman.

Russia

Like Germany, Russia developed a distinctive national cinema in near isolation as a result of World War I. Before the war, Russian production had been largely dominated by Pathé, which opened a studio in Russia in 1908, and Gaumont, which followed suit in 1909. The first Russian-owned filmmaking company, started in 1907 by photographer A. O. Drankov, was able to compete reasonably well. A second Russian firm, Khanzhonkov, appeared in 1908. During the early 1910s, exhibition expanded, and other, smaller Russian producers opened companies.

As in other European countries, between 1912 and 1913, the cinema was gaining respectability, with famous authors writing scenarios. Since Tsar Nikolai II and his family were ardent film fans, fashionable audiences as well as the masses went to the cinema. Although most audiences favored imported films, by 1914 Russia had a small, but healthy, film industry.

When Russia prepared for World War I in late July of 1914, the borders were closed, and many foreign distribution firms—primarily the German ones—closed their Moscow offices. With competition reduced, new Russian companies were formed, most significantly the Yermoliev firm. In 1916, when Italy entered the war, its films also dwindled in the Russian market, and the domestic industry continued to grow.

During this era, Russian filmmakers innovated a unique approach to the new art. First, they explored subject matter with a melancholy tone. Even before the war, Russian audiences favored tragic endings. As one film trade journal put it, " 'All's well that ends well!' This is the guiding principle of foreign cinema. But Russian cinema stubbornly refuses to accept this and goes its own way. Here it's 'All's well that ends badly'— we need tragic endings."[1] The pace of many Russian films was slow, with frequent pauses and deliberate gestures enabling the players to linger over each action.

This slow pace derived from a fascination with psychology. One appeal of these films was the display of intense, virtuosic acting. In this, Russian filmmaking was heavily influenced by Italian, German, and Danish films. Russian producers consciously sought actors and actresses who could duplicate Asta Nielsen's popularity. Many Russian films of this period were also somewhat comparable to the Italian diva films, which made intensity of acting the main appeal. Russian acting, however, was less flamboyant and more internalized.

The two most important Russian directors of the war period, Evgenii Bauer and Yakov Protazanov, were masters of the brooding melodrama. From a training in art, Bauer entered the cinema in 1912 as a set designer and soon became a director. His mise-en-scène was characterized by deep, detailed sets (**3.8**) and an unusually strong sidelighting; he also occasionally used complex tracking shots. Several of Bauer's films carried the Russian love for melancholy to extremes, centering on morbid subject matter. In *The Dying Swan* (1917), an obsessed artist tries to capture death in his painting of a melancholy ballerina; when she is suddenly transformed by love, he strangles her in order to finish his masterpiece. Bauer was the main director at the Khanzhonkov company, where he was given free artistic rein.

Protazanov began directing in 1912, and he worked mostly for Yermoliev. Several of his main films of this period were prestigious adaptations from Pushkin and Tolstoy. They starred Ivan Mozhukhin, a stage actor who had become immensely popular in films. Mozhukhin was the epitome of the Russian ideal in acting; tall and handsome, with hypnotic eyes, he cultivated a slow, fervent style. He starred in the title role of Protazanov's adaptation of Tolstoy's novel *Father Sergius*, made in 1917 between the February and October Revolutions and released in early 1918 (**3.9**). After a brief self-exile in Paris, Protazanov returned to become one of the most successful directors in the USSR when filmmaking revived there during the 1920s.

THE BRIEF HEYDAY OF THE SERIAL

Today the serial is usually remembered as a trivial form of cinema, consisting largely of low-budget thrillers aimed at youthful matinee audiences from the 1930s to the 1950s. Yet the serial originated as the main attraction in many theaters during the 1910s. Serial episodes can be seen as a kind of transitional form between the one-reeler and the feature film. Though some early serial episodes were quite short, others lasted forty-five minutes or more. They were shown with other short films—newsreels, cartoons, comic or dramatic narratives—but they formed the core of the program. Serials were usually action oriented, offering thrilling elements like master criminals, lost treasures, exotic locales, and daring rescues.

The true serial carried a story line over all its episodes. Typically, each episode ended at a high point, with the main characters in danger. These *cliffhangers* (so called because characters often ended up suspended from cliffs or buildings) lured the spectator back for the next installment.

Serials originated at almost the same time in the United States and France. The earliest American serial was *The Adventures of Kathlyn* (1914), made by the Selig company and starring Kathlyn Williams. Its episodes, set in India, were self-contained, but there was also an overall plot line. The same was true of *The Perils of Pauline*, made by Pathé in 1914. This hugely successful serial made a star of Pearl White and inspired other firms to make similar films. Williams and White established the pattern of the *serial queen*, a heroine (often described as plucky) who survives numerous outlandish plots against her life (**3.10**). By late 1915, American serials were highly profitable and were technically on a par with feature films of the era.

The greatest filmmaker associated with this form was Louis Feuillade. This prolific Gaumont director made around eighty short films a year between 1907 and 1913, working in various genres. A turning point in his career, however, was the "Fantômas" crime serial, beginning in 1913 with *Fantômas* and continuing through 1914 with four additional feature-length episodes. (Even then, however, he continued to direct comedies as well.) The "Fantômas" serial adapted the successful writings of Pierre Souvestre and Marcel Allain, whose books have become classics.

Fantômas was the ultimate criminal, master of many disguises, who constantly eluded his determined rival, the detective Juve (**3.11**). Feuillade filmed this crime story in the streets of Paris and in conventional studio sets, creating a bizarre juxtaposition of an everyday milieu and fantastic, nightmarish events. His subsequent thriller serials, including *Juve contra Fantômas* ("Juve versus Fantômas," 1913), *Les Vampires* (1915), and *Judex* (1916), continued this style. Feuillade was extremely popular with the general public, but he was also embraced by the Surrealists for the

3.10   Near the end of the first episode of *The Perils of Pauline*, the heroine shinnies down a rope from a balloon that has been set adrift by the villain.

3.11   The first episode of *Fantômas* ends as Juve sees a vision of the escaped Fantômas, in his famous evening clothes and mask, tauntingly holding out his hands to be handcuffed.

(perhaps unconscious) poetic quality of his work. This side of Feuillade's films makes them seem highly modern today; in fact, the 1990s saw a growing Feuillade revival.

Serials also became significant in Germany during the 1910s. *Homunculus* (1916, Otto Rippert) told the story of a laboratory-created humanoid who manipulated stock markets and ultimately tried to control the world. After the war, producer-director Joe May specialized in lavish serials starring his wife, Mia May, Germany's serial queen. His eight-part epic, *The Mistress of the World* (1919–1920), was perhaps the most expensive German project in the immediate postwar years. During seven episodes, the heroine undergoes ordeals in Chinese, Mayan, and African locales

(continued)

THE BRIEF HEYDAY OF THE SERIAL, continued

3.12 One of the many large, exotic sets constructed for *The Mistress of the World.*

(3.12). In the seventh installment she is rescued; the eighth wittily depicts the making of a sensationalistic film about her adventures.

Serial production continued to be important in France and some other countries into the 1920s, but in the United States it became a way of creating inexpensive programs in smaller theaters and of attracting children. During the sound era, the action serial played the same roles.

Serial films had a great influence on twentieth-century narrative form in general. Serials, especially soap operas, were a staple of radio for decades. Television picked up soap operas, and the continuing story with cliffhangers made its way into prime-time dramas in the 1980s. Modern films have also been influenced, as when Steven Spielberg deliberately based the episodic story of *Raiders of the Lost Ark* (1981) on adventure serials. The *Back to the Future, Star Wars, Matrix,* and *Lord of the Rings* films all revive the serial format.

By 1916, the Russian film industry had grown to thirty production firms. The 1917 Bolshevik Revolution brought filmmaking to a near standstill, however, and the slow, intense style that had developed in Russia during the war soon looked old-fashioned. Since the revolution's principal impact on the cinema was felt during the 1920s, we shall examine the events of the late 1910s in Chapter 6.

France

During the early 1910s, the French film industry was still thriving. Many new theaters were being built, and demand was high. Although imported American films were beginning to encroach on the market, French production remained robust.

In 1913, however, the largest company, Pathé Frères, took the first of several steps that ultimately would harm the French industry. It cut back on the increasingly costly production side of the business to concentrate on the profitable areas of distribution and exhibition. In the United States, French films were being squeezed out by the growth of independent firms. Pathé dropped its membership in the Motion Picture Patents Company, forming an independent distribution firm in 1913. This firm released several widely successful serials during the 1910s, including *The Perils of Pauline*

(see box). By 1919, however, Pathé's concentration on serials and shorts put it on the margins of the American industry, which was dominated by big firms making features.

Unlike Pathé, Gaumont expanded production in the years just before the war. Two important Gaumont directors, Léonce Perret and Louis Feuillade, did some of their best work during this period. Perret had come to fame in 1909 as a comic actor, directing his own series of "Léonce" films. During the mid-1910s, he also made some major features. *L'Enfant de Paris* ("Child of Paris," 1913) and *Roman d'un mousse* ("Tale of a Cabin Boy," 1914) were intensely melodramatic narratives of abducted children. They were notable for their beautiful cinematography, including skillful location filming and an unusual use of backlighting (3.13). Perret also varied his camera angles considerably and broke scenes down into more shots than was then typical. He thus helped expand the cinema's expressive possibilities. Perret's style became more formulaic later on, when he worked in Hollywood in the second half of the decade and returned to France to make historical epics in the 1920s.

Feuillade continued to work in a variety of genres, including comedies and a naturalistic series, "La vie telle qu'elle est" ("Life as It Is"). His main achievements, however, were in the new serial format.

Despite Pathé's and Gaumont's dominance of French production, they made no attempt to monopolize the industry, and smaller companies coexisted peacefully with them, staying in business by specializing in certain types of films. All this activity came to an abrupt halt when World War I began. By the end of 1914, it had become apparent that the fighting would continue for quite a while, and some theaters reopened. In early 1915, production resumed on a limited basis. Newsreels became more important, and all the firms made highly patriotic fiction films, such as *Mères français* ("French Mothers," 1917, René Hervil and Louis Mercanton).

Pathé's response to the war was to focus its efforts on its American distribution wing, releasing films made by independent producers in the United States. With the huge success of *The Perils of Pauline* and subsequent serials, Pathé remained profitable. It was, however, no longer providing a stable leadership for French film production. Through its distribution, Pathé was also helping American films gain a greater share of the French market.

French intellectuals and the general public alike adored the new American stars they discovered during the war: Charlie Chaplin, Douglas Fairbanks, William S. Hart, and Lillian Gish. Writer Philippe Soupault suggests how suddenly and intensely American films affected Parisian viewers:

> Then one day we saw hanging on the walls great posters as long as serpents. At every street-corner a man, his face covered with a red handkerchief, leveled a revolver at the peaceful passersby. We imagined that we heard galloping hoofs, the roar of motors, explosions, and cries of death. We rushed into the cinema, and realized immediately that everything had changed. On the screen appeared the smile of Pearl White—that almost ferocious smile which announced the revolution, the beginning of a new world.[2]

Serial queen Pearl White was idolized in France after the release of *Les Mystères de New York*, the French title of her second Pathé serial, *The Exploits of Elaine* (1915). During 1917, American films passed the 50-percent mark in French exhibition.

The real effect of American films in France was not apparent until after the war. From 1918 to 1919, French firms attempting to bring production back up to its old levels found it virtually impossible to reduce the American share of their market. The next chapter will examine how the French industry reacted, trying to create competitive alternatives to Hollywood cinema.

3.13 Filming inside a real building without using artificial light, Perret created dramatic silhouette effects in *L'Enfant de Paris*.

3.14 A set depicting a hallway in a sculptor's house attracts the eye in August Blom's *Atlantis*.

Denmark

In Denmark, Ole Olsen's Nordisk films continued to dominate production, though a small number of other firms operated during the 1910s. From 1913 to 1914, Nordisk and other companies were moving toward longer films of two, three, even four reels. One historian has summarized the typical style of Nordisk's films: "The lighting effects, the stories, the realism of interior settings, the extraordinary use of natural and urban locations, the intensity of the naturalistic acting style, the emphasis on fate and the passions."[3]

The work of August Blom, Nordisk's top director of the early teens, typifies this style. His most important film was *Atlantis* (1913), at eight reels the longest Danish film to date. Its plot offered a fairly conventional psychological melodrama, but the film dwelt on beautifully designed sets (**3.14**) and spectacular scenes, such as the sinking of an ocean liner (inspired by the *Titanic* disaster of the previous year). *Atlantis* was triumphantly successful abroad.

Another Nordisk director, Forest Holger-Madsen, made an outstanding film, *The Evangelist* (1914). The narrative involves a frame story and lengthy flashback, as a preacher tells a young man about his time in prison as a result of being wrongfully convicted of murder. His tale saves the young man from a life of crime. The

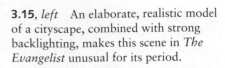

3.15, *left* An elaborate, realistic model of a cityscape, combined with strong backlighting, makes this scene in *The Evangelist* unusual for its period.

3.16, *right* Shooting into the sun creates a dramatic silhouette of an old mill, whose blades form part of the "X" motif in Christensen's *The Mysterious X*.

3.17, 3.18 A suspenseful tracking shot in *Night of Revenge*, beginning on the frightened heroine as she sees something outside her window and moving back rapidly to reveal an intruder forcing his way in and rushing to her.

preacher's dark, grim room, in which he relates his story, exemplifies the use of setting to create mood (**3.15**).

One of the most original and eccentric directors of the silent cinema also began working in the Danish industry. Benjamin Christensen started as an actor at the small Dansk Biografkompagni in 1911 and soon became president of the firm. His impressive debut as a director was *The Mysterious X* (1913), in which he also starred. It was a melodramatic story of spies and false accusations of treason, shot in a particularly bold visual style. Stark sidelighting and backlighting created silhouette effects (**3.16**); few films of this period contain such striking compositions. Christensen went on to make an equally virtuosic drama, *Night of Revenge* (1916). Here he added tracking shots that intensify the suspense and shock as a convict terrorizes a family (**3.17, 3.18**).

Christensen did not complete another film until the 1920s, when his *Witchcraft through the Ages* (1922) was financed by Svensk Filmindustri. It was a bizarre, episodic quasi-documentary tracing the history of witchcraft. After censorship difficulties with this film, Christensen moved into more conventional filmmaking, directing dramas and thrillers in Germany and Hollywood during the 1920s.

World War I had a mixed effect on the Danish cinema. Initially Denmark benefited, since, as a neutral northern country, it was in a unique position to furnish films to markets like Germany and Russia, which were cut off from their normal suppliers. But in 1916 Germany banned film imports. In 1917, the Russian Revolution eliminated that market, and the United States cut back on its imports from Denmark. During the 1910s, many top Danish directors and actors were also lured away, mainly to Germany and Sweden. By the war's end, Denmark was no longer a significant force in international distribution.

Sweden

In 1912, Sweden suddenly began producing a string of innovative, distinctive films. Remarkably, most of these were made by only three directors: Georg af Klercker, Mauritz Stiller, and Victor Sjöström. Moreover, the Swedish cinema initially had little impact abroad, and so its filmmakers were working without the larger budgets made possible by export. Sweden was among the first countries to create a major cinema by drawing deliberately on the particular traits of its national culture. Swedish films were characterized by their dependence on northern landscapes and by their use of local literature, costumes, customs, and the like. After the war's end, their specifically Swedish qualities made these films novel and popular in other countries.

The success of Nordisk in Denmark had been one inspiration for the formation of a small Swedish firm, the Svenska Biografteatern, in 1907. It eventually would form the basis of the leading Swedish film firm, still in existence. Located in the small provincial city of Kris-

3.19 Offscreen space in *Mysteriet natten till den 25:e* ("Mysterious Night of the 25th," 1917): the robber realizes by glancing into a mirror that the detective has hidden to wait for him.

3.20 The heroine of *Thomas Graal's Best Film* finds out she is to star in a film and practices acting—in a flamboyant style that parodies contemporary Italian diva films.

tianstad, the firm was initially a theater chain. In 1909, Charles Magnusson took over its management and built it into the country's main production company. In 1910, Julius Jaenzon, a cinematographer who had mainly made topicals, joined the firm. He was to photograph most of Stiller's and Sjöström's films of the 1910s. Under Magnusson and Jaenzon's guidance, the firm produced films on a small scale in a tiny studio above its main cinema in Kristianstad. (This building is one of the few early glass-sided studios that can still be visited; it houses a small cinema museum.)

In 1912, Svenska moved to a larger studio near Stockholm. The first director hired was Georg af Klercker, who became head of production. That same year, actors Mauritz Stiller and Victor Sjöström were hired to boost Svenska's production. All three directed, wrote scripts, and acted. They made many short films with modest budgets during the next few years.

After the beginning of the war, Germany blocked film imports to several northern European countries. Since few films got past this blockade, Swedish production was boosted and filmmakers were relatively free of foreign influences for a few years.

Until recently, the work of af Klercker was largely overshadowed by the contributions of Stiller and Sjöström. In the mid-1980s, however, several of his films were restored and shown in retrospectives. They revealed a skillful and versatile director with a strong sense of pictorial beauty. Af Klercker had begun as an actor, and he also did set designs when he first joined Svenska. He was soon directing but did not get on well with Magnusson and quit in 1913. He then worked at smaller production firms, primarily Hasselbladfilm (founded in 1915). There he was the undisputed leader, directing most of the firm's output.

Af Klercker made comedies, crime thrillers, war films, and melodramas, usually with fairly conventional stories. In all of them, however, he displays a distinctive eye for landscape, light, and a variety of framing within scenes. His films contain some of the most beautiful sets

of this period, defined by simple lines but richly furnished with details. Af Klercker skillfully suggests offscreen space: background rooms are often just visible through beaded curtains, and mirrors reveal action occurring outside the frame (**3.19**). He also elicited subtle, restrained performances from his actors. From 1918 to 1919, Hasselblad went through mergers that made it a part of Svenska Bio, which then became Svensk Filmindustri (the name it has kept ever since). At that point af Klercker gave up filmmaking to go into business.

Af Klercker's more famous colleagues, Stiller and Sjöström, both stayed at Svenska, directing, acting, and writing scripts. They were extremely prolific until both went to Hollywood, Sjöström in 1923, Stiller in 1925. Unfortunately, however, most of the negatives of the films made by Svenska were destroyed in a fire in 1941. This disaster, one of the most tragic losses among many nitrate fires, means that few of Svenska's early films have survived. Most existing prints of Stiller and Sjöström films have been copied from early positive release prints; hence their visual quality is often mediocre. Still, even such prints indicate the films' high artistic merits.

So many of Mauritz Stiller's early films are lost that it is difficult to judge his career before the mid-1910s. He is mainly remembered for the urbane wit of several films he made between 1916 and 1920, as well as for his adaptations of the works of Nobel prize–winning Swedish novelist Selma Lagerlöf.

The wit was well displayed in the comedy *Thomas Graal's Best Film* (1917). In it, an eccentric scriptwriter-actor (played delightfully by Victor Sjöström) glimpses and falls in love with a young woman, Bessie, and refuses to finish his overdue scenario unless she can be found and persuaded to star in it. Meanwhile, the free-spirited Bessie rejects her wealthy parents' choice of a fiancé and decides to accept the movie role (**3.20**). The film alternates between the two main characters, including scenes representing the scenario the hero writes, which fantasizes a love story between himself and Bessie. Eventually the two actually meet and become

3.21 At the end of *Sir Arne's Treasure*, the heroine's body is borne past the icebound ship on which the mercenaries had hoped to escape.

engaged. The result was one of the cleverest films about filmmaking made in the silent era. It was so successful that a sequel was made: *Thomas Graal's Best Child* (1918), in which the pair marry and have a baby.

Stiller's most famous film was the antithesis of these comedies. A tragedy set in Renaissance-period Sweden, *Sir Arne's Treasure* (1919) was adapted from a Lagerlöf story. Three fugitive mercenaries pillage the castle of Sir Arne, trying to escape with his treasure. The town's harbor is icebound, however, trapping them until spring. The young woman Elsalill, the sole survivor of the massacre, falls in love with Sir Archie, not realizing that he is one of the killers. Despite his love for Elsalill, Sir Archie uses her as a shield in a vain escape attempt. The final scene shows the townspeople bearing her coffin across the ice as spring approaches (**3.21**).

Stiller continued making both comedies and dramas. In 1920, he directed *Erotikon,* often credited as the first sophisticated sex comedy. It treated romantic relations casually, as a neglected young wife flirts with and finally starts an affair with a handsome suitor while her middle-aged husband, an absentminded professor, pairs off with his pretty niece. *Erotikon* may well have influenced German director Ernst Lubitsch, who later became famous for clever sexual innuendo in his films in Hollywood in the 1920s. Stiller also adapted another Lagerlöf novel in his two-part epic, *The Story of Gösta Berling* (1924; available in the United States only in an abridged version). This story of a defrocked minister torn between a dissolute life and the love of an unhappily married countess contains several remarkable scenes and performances; among these is the first major role of the young Greta Garbo, as the countess. She was discovered by Stiller, and they both soon went to Hollywood, where her career was more successful than his.

Victor Sjöström was one of the most important directors of the entire silent era. His style was austere and naturalistic. He used restrained acting and staged scenes in considerable depth, both in location shots and in sets.

His narratives frequently traced in great detail the grim consequences of a single action. Sjöström's early masterpiece, *Ingeborg Holm* (1913), for example, begins with a happy middle-class family; the father suddenly falls ill and dies, and the plot follows the wife's descent into poverty and madness as she struggles vainly to keep her children. The film consists primarily of lengthy shots that hold on a series of actions that unfold within deep spaces (**3.22–3.26**). The slow, steady pace conveys a remarkable impression of the heroine's decades of misfortune, despite the fact that *Ingeborg Holm* lasts only about seventy minutes.

Terje Vigen (1916) demonstrates Sjöström's mastery of landscape as an expressive element in the action. During wartime, Terje Vigen, a sailor, attempts to fetch food in his rowboat but is captured by the enemy. During his lengthy imprisonment, his wife and child die of starvation. Years later, the embittered protagonist gains power over the family of the man who captured him and must decide whether to wreak his revenge by killing them. Again the narrative traces out the long-term results of an event, suggesting an implacable fate guiding the characters. Sjöström heightens the effect of his narrative by using the sea as a prominent backdrop for much of the action, seeming to reflect the hero's anger (**3.27**).

Landscapes were also prominent in *The Outlaw and His Wife* (1917). Again a single desperate action, the hero's theft of a sheep to feed his family, affects his entire life. Fleeing arrest (**3.28**), Berg-Ejvind finds temporary safety working on the farm of a rich widow, Halla. They fall in love, but he is again pursued by the authorities. Abandoning her estate, Halla follows Berg-Ejvind into the mountains, where they live together for many years before dying in each other's arms in a blizzard. Sjöström daringly undercut the intense romanticism of this story by making the final scene in a snowbound cabin involve an ugly, petty quarrel between the couple; they reconcile at the end, just before they die.

The war had restricted exports of Swedish films, and *The Outlaw and His Wife* was the first to burst onto the international scene. The French, reeling from the recent flood of American films, reacted with delight. Critic and future filmmaker Louis Delluc praised *The Outlaw and His Wife:*

> And the public is swept away with emotion. For the public is awestruck by the barren landscapes, the mountains, the rustic costumes, both the austere ugliness and the acute lyricism of such closely observed feelings, the truthfulness of the long scenes which focus exclusively on the couple, the violent struggles, the

3.22   **3.23**   **3.24**

3.25   **3.26**

3.22–3.26 In *Ingeborg Holm*, a long-shot framing shows the heroine parting from her son. Reluctant to leave her, he returns to hug her again as the gatekeeper opens the gate (**3.22**). As the boy moves away again with his foster mother, Ingeborg quickly ducks into the doorway (**3.23**). The boy turns back once more (**3.24**) and, not seeing his mother, sadly follows his foster mother (**3.25**). Once the pair has gone, the gatekeeper locks the gate and returns just in time to catch Ingeborg as she emerges again and begins to faint (**3.26**). The staging with the heroine's back to the camera displays Sjöström's refusal to overemphasize emotions.

3.27, *left*   Years after the deaths of his family, the vengeful protagonist rages against the tempestuous sea in *Terje Vigen*.

3.28, *right*   The fugitive hero (played by Sjöström) wanders in the vast countryside in *The Outlaw and His Wife*.

high tragic end of the two aged lovers who escape life through a final embrace in a desertlike snowscape.[4]

In general, the Swedish cinema was recognized as the first major alternative to Hollywood to emerge after the war.

Even more successful was Sjöström's 1920 film *The Phantom Chariot*, again adapted from Lagerlöf. It uses remarkably complex means to tell the story of a drunken lout who nearly dies in a cemetery at midnight on New Year's Eve. He is given a chance to ride a ghostly carriage driven by death and witness how his behavior has ruined the lives of two women who love him. The ghostly superimpositions (accomplished entirely in the camera during filming) were some of the most elaborate yet attempted. Similarly, the story was

told in an intricately interwoven set of flashbacks that became highly influential in European cinema of the 1920s. *The Phantom Chariot* quickly came to be considered a classic and was often revived.

Ironically, the very success of the Swedish cinema abroad contributed to its decline. After about 1920, Svenska concentrated on expensive prestige pictures designed for export. Only a few of these, like *The Story of Gösta Berling*, were artistic successes. Sjöström's and Stiller's growing reputations led Hollywood firms to lure them away from Svensk Filmindustri. Moreover, other countries were entering the international marketplace, and the small Swedish cinema could not compete. After 1921, film production in Sweden fell precipitously.

THE CLASSICAL HOLLYWOOD CINEMA

The Motion Picture Patents Company had dominated the American film industry between 1908 and 1911, but it lost much of its power after a 1912 court decision rendered the Latham-loop patent void (see p. 40). Independent firms soon regrouped and expanded into a studio system that would form the basis for American filmmaking for decades. Certain filmmaking roles—chiefly the role of the producer—became central. In addition, the star system gained full strength, as celebrities came to command enormous salaries and even began producing in their own right.

The Major Studios Begin to Form

The process of building the Hollywood studio system often involved the combination of two or more small production or distribution firms. In 1912, independent producer Carl Laemmle, who had doggedly fought the MPPC, was pivotal in forming the Universal Film Manufacturing Company, a distribution firm to release the output of his own Independent Motion Picture Company and several other independent and foreign firms. By 1913, Laemmle had gained control of the new company, and in 1915 he opened Universal City, a studio north of Hollywood (3.29), forming the basis of a complex that still exists. By that point, Universal was partially vertically integrated, combining production and distribution in the same firm.

Also in 1912, Adolph Zukor scored a tremendous success by importing and distributing *Queen Elizabeth*, a French feature starring Sarah Bernhardt. Zukor then formed Famous Players in Famous Plays to exploit the star system and prestigious literary adaptations. Famous Players would soon become part of the most powerful studio in Hollywood. Another step toward the studio system came in 1914, when W. W. Hodkinson banded eleven local distributors together into Paramount, the first national distributor devoted solely to features. Zukor was soon distributing his Famous Players films through Paramount.

Another feature-film company originated in 1914. The Jesse L. Lasky Feature Play Company was centered primarily around the films of former playwright Cecil B. De Mille. Lasky also distributed through Paramount. In 1916, Zukor took over Paramount, merged Famous Players in Famous Plays and the Jesse L. Lasky Feature Play Company into Famous Players–Lasky and made Paramount this new firm's distribution subsidiary. This was another key move in fusing smaller American producers and distributors into larger, vertically integrated

firms. Paramount soon controlled many of the most popular silent stars, including Gloria Swanson, Mary Pickford, and Douglas Fairbanks, as well as top directors like D. W. Griffith, Mack Sennett, and De Mille.

Other firms formed during the 1910s would be crucial in the industry. Sam, Jack, and Harry Warner moved from exhibiting to distributing, founding Warner Bros. in 1913. By 1918, they began producing but remained a relatively small firm until the 1920s. William Fox, who had small exhibition, distribution, and production operations, merged all three in 1914 to form the Fox Film Corporation. The new firm would be a major player in 1920s Hollywood (eventually being renamed 20th-Century Fox). Three smaller firms that would merge into MGM in 1924 all began during this era: Metro in 1914 and Goldwyn and Mayer in 1917.

A major challenge to Paramount's growing power soon arose. Paramount was releasing about 100 features a year and requiring theaters to show all of them (with two programs per week) in order to get any. This was an early instance of *block booking*, a practice that was later repeatedly challenged as monopolistic. In 1917, a group of exhibitors resisted this tactic by banding together to finance and distribute independent features. They formed the First National Exhibitors Circuit, which soon was supplying films to hundreds of theaters nationwide. Zukor responded by beginning to buy up theaters for his own company in 1919, preparing the way for one of the main trends in the industry during the 1920s: increasing vertical integration through the growth of national theater chains.

Vertical integration was an important factor that contributed to Hollywood's international power. During this same period, Germany was just beginning to develop a vertically integrated film industry (see Chapter 5). France's leading firm, Pathé, was backing away from vertical integration by moving out of production. No other country developed a studio system as strong as that of the United States.

Controlling Filmmaking

The Hollywood studios have often been referred to as factories, turning out strings of similar films as if on assembly lines. This characterization is only partly true. Each film was different and so required specific planning and execution. The studios did, however, develop methods of making films as efficiently as possible. By 1914, most big firms had differentiated between the director, who was responsible for shooting the film, and the producer, who oversaw the entire production.

3.29 A row of open-air filmmaking stages at Universal City, c. 1915. A series of films could be made simultaneously on sets built side by side. The overhead framework held sheets of translucent material to diffuse the strong California sunlight.

3.30 Producer Thomas H. Ince stands in his studio at Inceville. The glass roof and walls are covered with cloth to permit the use of artificial light. Later studios had no windows.

The labor of filmmaking was increasingly divided among expert practitioners. There were separate scenario departments, for example, and a writer might specialize in plotting, dialogue, or intertitles. The version used during filming was the *continuity script*, and it broke the action down into individual, numbered shots. The script allowed the producer to estimate how much a given film would cost. The continuity script also allowed people working on the film to coordinate their efforts, even though they might never communicate directly with each other. In the planning stage, the set designer would use the script to determine what types of sets were necessary. After the shooting was done, the editor put the film together, guided by the numbers shown on a slate at the beginning of each shot, which corresponded to the numbers in the script. These shots were designed to match at each cut, creating a continuity of narrative action.

The big film companies also built studio facilities during the 1910s, mostly in the Los Angeles area. Initially, these primarily involved outdoor filming on covered stages (see 3.29). By the late 1910s, however, large *dark studios* were also constructed, either by covering the glass walls or building windowless enclosures (3.30). Here filmmakers controlled lighting with electric lamps. These studios also had extensive *backlots*, where large outdoor sets could be constructed; to save money, the production firms often kept some of these standing, using them over and over.

Again, no other country could match Hollywood's approach. Few firms employed so many different film specialists, and only a small number of studios outside the United States could boast of facilities as extensive as those of big companies like Paramount.

Filmmaking in Hollywood during the 1910s

During the late 1910s, foreign audiences, many of whom had been cut off from the Hollywood product during the war, marveled at how American films had changed. Aside from having appealing stars and splendid sets, they were fast-paced and stylistically polished. One reason for this appeal was that American filmmakers had gone on exploring the classical Hollywood style, linking technique to clear storytelling (see pp. 43–50).

Filmmakers continued to use intercutting in increasingly complex ways. In addition, by the mid-1910s, individual scenes within a single space were likely to be broken into several shots, beginning with an establishing shot, followed by one or more cut-ins to show portions of the action. Directors and cine-

3.31, 3.32 A conversation between the hero, played by Douglas Fairbanks, and the villain of *Manhattan Madness* (1916, Allan Dwan), edited in shot/reverse shot.

3.33, 3.34 A cut from a man looking downward to a high angle shows us his point of view on the characters at the bottom of the staircase in *The On-the-Square Girl* (1917, Frederick J. Ireland).

3.35–3.37 A typical continuity editing pattern in *Her Code of Honor* (1919, John Stahl). An establishing shot of a tea party (not shown) leads to a closer view of a young man and woman conversing and then an eyeline match to a medium shot of her stepfather, delighted at their courtship. Finally, a more distant framing reestablishes the space by showing all three characters.

matographers were expected to match the positions and movements of actors and objects at each cut so that the shift in framing would be less noticeable. Point-of-view shots were used more commonly and with greater flexibility. The use of shot/reverse-shot editing for conversation situations had been rare in the early 1910s (see p. 50), but by 1917 it occurred at least once in virtually every film (**3.31, 3.32**). Similarly common were cuts that alternated from shots of people looking at something to point-of-view shots revealing what they saw (**3.33, 3.34**). Indeed, by 1917, the fundamental techniques of continuity editing, including adherence to the 180-degree rule, or axis of action, had been worked out. Filmmakers would typically break even a simple scene into several shots, cutting to closer

views and placing the camera at various vantage points within the action itself (**3.35–3.37**). This editing-based manner of constructing a space contrasted considerably with the approach being used in Europe at the same time (see box).

The look of individual shots also changed. As we have seen in previous chapters, most early films were shot using flat, overall light, from either the sun or artificial lights or from a combination of both. During the mid-1910s, filmmakers experimented with *effects lighting*, that is, selective lighting over only part of the scene, motivated as coming from a specific source. The most influential film to include this technique was Cecil B. De Mille's *The Cheat* (1915; **3.44–3.46**), which utilized arc lamps derived from the theater. By the end of the 1910s

PRECISION STAGING IN EUROPEAN CINEMA • • • • • • • • • • • • • • •

How might you direct the audience's attention in the course of a scene? The Hollywood system favored editing together closer views of the characters, usually seen against an inconspicuous background. During the 1910s, some European filmmakers explored a rich alternative style: the dramatic and pictorial possibilities of depth-staging techniques (p. 43).

European filmmakers used editing more sparingly, tending to favor complex staging within quite lengthy shots. By creating deep sets, framing action in windows or other aper-

tures, and moving actors slightly to block and reveal key details, directors choreographed the flow of the action with great precision.

In *Assunta Spina* (p. 59), the accused criminal Michele is on trial, and the director, Gustavo Serena, carefully shifts our attention from his plaintive expression in the distance to his distraught mother's reaction in the foreground (**3.38–3.40**). By the mid-1910s directors were employing much deeper interior sets than we saw in *Afgrunden* from 1910 (see 2.15–2.17).

3.38 *Assunta Spina:* after the lawyer sits, a woman rushes into the court, and Michele looks up toward the camera.

3.39 More women crowd into the foreground, blocking out the other figures in court but leaving Michele fully visible.

3.40 Finally, as Michele's mother turns in frame center to reveal her anguish, the other women comfort her, blocking out Michele so that we can concentrate on her reaction.

(continued)

PRECISION STAGING IN EUROPEAN CINEMA, continued

Louis Feuillade often used depth to give Parisian locales mysteriously haunting qualities. The crime thriller *Fantômas* allowed him to display surprising and ingenious uses of depth on location (**3.41**, **3.42**) and in the vast sets he built at Gaumont Studios (**3.43**).

For further examples, compare the European-style depth staging in 3.4, 3.7–3.9, and 3.22–3.26 with the American propensity to edit together shots of figures in a shallow playing space in 3.31–3.37 and 3.44–3.46.

During the early 1920s, the continuity system was increasingly adopted in Europe as well, and depth staging in long-held shots was becoming a rare option. Such shots would become more common in the 1930s, when sound filming encouraged them.

3.41 *Fantômas:* as Inspector Juve and his sidekick Fandor investigate a dockside, Fantômas's gang pop up behind them and fire.

3.42 Inspector Juve awaits his prey, who approaches, visible through the bars of the gate.

3.43 At the theater, Lady Beltham turns to leave, but we still glimpse the actor taking his bow far behind her.

3.44–3.46 Light from a single, powerful spotlight offscreen left creates a dramatic silhouette on a translucent wall after the villain is shot in *The Cheat.*

and the early 1920s, large film studios boasted a great array of different types of lamps for every purpose.

As feature films became standardized, Hollywood filmmakers established firmer guidelines for creating intelligible plots. These guidelines have changed little since then. Hollywood plots consist of clear chains of causes and effects, and most of these involve character psychology (as opposed to social or natural forces). Each major character is given a set of comprehensible, consistent traits. The Hollywood protagonist is typically goal-oriented, trying to achieve success in work, sports, or some other activity. The hero's goal conflicts with the desires of other characters, creating a struggle that is resolved only at the end—which is typically a happy one. Hollywood films usually intensify interest by presenting two interdependent plot lines. Almost inevitably one of these involves romance, which gets woven in with the protagonist's quest to achieve a goal.

3.47 The figure of Christ superimposed on a battlefield in the pacifist drama *Civilization*.

3.48 The southern son's return home is filmed at an oblique angle so that the doorway conceals his mother and sister as they embrace him in *The Birth of a Nation*. Such understatement enhances the emotional power of the moment.

The plot also arouses suspense through deadlines, escalating conflicts, and last-minute rescues. These principles of storytelling have contributed to the enduring international success of American films.

Films and Filmmakers

During this period, the big Hollywood firms grew enormously. Feature-length films (running on average about 75 minutes) dominated exhibition by 1915. The studios competed to sign up the most popular actors to long-term contracts. Some stars, like Mary Pickford and Charles Chaplin, were making thousands, even tens of thousands, of dollars a week by the end of the decade. Studios also bought the rights to many famous literary works and adapted them as vehicles for their stars.

The huge expansion of American production required many directors. Some of these had begun working earlier, but a younger generation entered the cinema at this time.

Thomas H. Ince and D. W. Griffith   Thomas H. Ince had started by directing many short films in the early 1910s, but he also became a producer in the ranks of the independents. As the decade progressed, he focused more on producing. Today he is remembered primarily for having contributed to the move toward efficiency in studio filmmaking, particularly the use of the continuity script to control production. He still directed occasionally, however. His 1916 *Civilization* (codirected with Raymond B. West and Reginald Barker) is notable as one of a number of pacifist films made in the years before America entered World War I. The story takes place in a mythical kingdom ruled by a warmongering king. Christ enters the resurrected body of a young pacifist who died in battle and converts the king with a message of peace (**3.47**). This was Ince's last directorial effort, however, and he concentrated on producing—including most of the Westerns of William S. Hart—until his death in 1924.

In 1913, D. W. Griffith left the Biograph Company, where he had made over four hundred short films since 1908. Biograph was reluctant to allow Griffith to make films longer than two reels. Despite the firm's resistance, he completed a four-reel historical epic, *Judith of Bethulia* (1913), in the wake of the success of the Italian import *Quo Vadis?*, but it was his last film for Biograph. During 1914, he made four feature films for Mutual, the independent distribution firm he managed; among these, *The Avenging Conscience* was an imaginative film that employed fantasy scenes inspired by Edgar Allan Poe's short story "The Tell-Tale Heart" and poem "Annabel Lee."

That same year, however, he was at work on a far more ambitious project. Independently financed from various sources, the twelve-reel *The Birth of a Nation* told an epic tale of the American Civil War by centering on two families who befriend each other but are on opposite sides in the conflict. During Reconstruction, Stoneman, Leader of the House and the head of the northern family, pushes through legislation that gives rights to freed slaves, while the elder son of the southern family helps start the Ku Klux Klan in response to outrages committed in his town. Using many actors from his Biograph days, Griffith created subtle portrayals of the two families. His regular cinematographer, Billy Bitzer, designed shots ranging from epic views of battles to intimate details of the characters' lives (**3.48**). Later scenes expanded Griffith's technique of intercutting for last-minute rescue situations. The Klan races to save the southern family, trapped in a cabin by attacking blacks, and to free the heroine from the grip of the villainous mulatto leader, who threatens her virtue (**3.49**). Accompanied by a special orchestral score Griffith had commissioned, the film previewed in Los Angeles and San Francisco and then opened in New York and Boston early in 1915. It played in large legitimate theaters at high prices, was enormously successful, and brought a new respectability to the movies.

3.49 Griffith mounted his camera on a car to create fast tracking shots before the galloping Klan members in the climactic rescue sequence.

Not surprisingly, given its bigoted account of African Americans' role in southern history, *The Birth of a Nation* also aroused heated controversy. Many editorials in white- and black-owned newspapers alike denounced its racism. The film was based on a novel, *The Clansman,* by a well-known racist author, Thomas Dixon. Although Griffith had toned down the worst excesses of the novel in favor of a concentration on the white families, many commentators treated the film as primarily a creation of Dixon. The National Association for the Advancement of Colored People (NAACP) had been founded in 1909, and the struggle for civil rights was under way by the time the film appeared. Realizing that the artistic qualities of *Birth* made it all the more effective as racist propaganda, NAACP officials pressured the censorship boards in New York and Boston to cut the most offensive scenes or to ban the film outright. (Ironically, segregation meant that these NAACP members could not even attend the film in theaters but had to see it at a screening arranged for them.) Supporters of the film won out, however, and *The Birth of a Nation* was exhibited all over the country. Black leaders realized the desirability of African American–produced films to counter such racism, but lack of funding delayed the implementation of this idea. Only somewhat later would a few black filmmakers emerge (see Chapter 7).

In his next film, Griffith tried to outdo himself. *Intolerance,* released in 1916, was even longer (fourteen reels, or roughly three and a half hours). Griffith used an abstract theme, the idea of intolerance through the ages, to link four separate stories set in different historical epochs: the fall of Babylon, the last part of Christ's life, the St. Bartholomew's Day Massacre in France, and a tale of a labor strike and gangster activity in modern-day America. To stress the unchanging nature of intolerance, Griffith intercut these stories rather than telling them one after the other. Through most of the film, intertitles and an allegorical figure of a woman

rocking a cradle announce the shifts from one story to the next. In the final section, however, as four separate rescues are attempted, Griffith suddenly cut among them without such signals. The result is a daring experiment in the use of editing to join disparate spaces and times (**3.50, 3.51**). *Intolerance* was also innovative in its cinematography, as when Bitzer mounted the camera on a movable elevator to create swooping movements over the huge set of the Babylonian court.

Intolerance was not as successful as *The Birth of a Nation,* and Griffith's subsequent features of the 1910s were less experimental. Griffith went on location to film war footage for *Hearts of the World* (1918), a story set in a French village during World War I. He made delightful country romances with *A Romance of Happy Valley* and *True Heart Susie* (both 1919) and a drama that used unusual hazy soft-focus cinematography, *Broken Blossoms* (1919).

Griffith was the most famous director of this era. He quickly came to be credited with innovating most of the major film techniques—something he encouraged in publicizing himself. Some modern historians have treated *The Birth of a Nation* and *Intolerance* as almost the only important American films of this period. Without detracting from Griffith's prestige, however, we should realize that many excellent filmmakers worked during this era, some of whose work is only beginning to be explored (see "Notes and Queries" at the end of this chapter).

A New Generation of Directors Griffith managed to keep considerable control over his productions, despite the growing supervision of the studio producers. Other directors who began working in this era also became powerful creative figures. In 1914, Maurice Tourneur emigrated from France and became known as a distinctive filmmaker with a strong sense of pictorial beauty. One of his first American films, *The Wishing Ring* (1914), was subtitled "An Idyll of Old England." It is a fanciful story of a poor girl who naively believes that a ring a gypsy has given her is magical. She tries to use it to reconcile a local earl and his estranged son and does so simply by befriending both. Tourneur managed to create a remarkable atmosphere of a rustic English village, even though the entire film was made in New Jersey. Tourneur was one of the many filmmakers testing the expressive possibilities of the film medium during this era. In 1918, he experimented with using modernist theatrical set design in *The Blue Bird* and *Prunella,* though these were less popular than most of his films of the 1910s. He also made some highly intelligent

3.50, 3.51 In *Intolerance*, Griffith boldly cut directly from galloping chariots in the Babylonian story to a speeding train in the modern story.

3.52, *left* Tourneur used a tent opening to create a dynamic composition for a dramatic moment in *The Last of the Mohicans*.

3.53, *right* Keystone comedies often parodied conventional melodramas, as when villain Ford Sterling threatens to saw Mabel Normand in half in *Mabel's Awful Mistake* (1913, Mack Sennett). The white streaks at the sides are nitrate deterioration.

literary adaptations, including *Victory* (1919, from Joseph Conrad's novel) and *The Last of the Mohicans* (1920, by James Fenimore Cooper). The latter, often considered his finest film, fully displays Tourneur's visual style, including his characteristic use of foreground shapes silhouetted against a landscape, often framed in a cave or doorway (3.52). During the 1920s, Tourneur increasingly had trouble retaining control over his productions as the studio system grew, and he returned to Europe in 1926.

Unlike Tourneur, Cecil B. De Mille survived within the studio system and managed to control many of his own productions throughout a long and prolific career. De Mille is often thought of today primarily for his historical epics of the sound era, but during his early career, he made many innovative films in various genres. *The Cheat* and several other pictures he made in 1915 were influential in popularizing directional, selective lighting (see 3.44–3.46). De Mille made a number of unpretentious, well-acted period films during the mid-1910s, including *The Warrens of Virginia* (1915) and *The Girl of the Golden West* (1916). In 1918, he made *Male and Female*, adapted from J. M. Barrie's play *The Admirable Crichton* and starring Gloria Swanson. The enormous success of this film led De Mille to concentrate on romantic comedies, often set in sophisticated society. His films of the 1920s became more extravagant, exploiting elaborate sets and fashionable costumes.

Other major Hollywood directors also began their careers in the 1910s. Actor Raoul Walsh, who had directed several two-reel films, made an impressive feature debut in 1915 with *Regeneration*, a realistic story set in a slum milieu. John Ford began making low-budget Westerns in 1917 and directed dozens of them over the next few years. Unfortunately, nearly all are lost, but two surviving films, *Straight Shooting* (1917) and *Hell Bent* (1918), indicate that Ford had a rare feeling for landscape and a flexible understanding of the continuity system from the beginning.

Slapstick Comedies and Westerns Some of the most popular directors and stars of this era were associated with the genre of slapstick comedy. Once feature films were standardized, they were typically shown on a program that included shorts, such as comedies, newsreels, and brief dramas. Among the most successful shorts were the films of producer-director Mack Sennett. Sennett headed the Keystone company, which specialized in slapstick comedy. Sennett used a great deal of fast action, including chases with the bumbling "Keystone Kops." His small stable of comic stars, who often directed their own pictures, included Charlie Chaplin, Ben Turpin, and Mabel Normand (3.53).

Chaplin, an English music-hall performer, became an international star with Keystone, going on to direct his own films at Essanay, Mutual, and First National

3.54 In *His New Job* (1915, Essanay, Charles Chaplin), Chaplin provided a look behind the scenes of comic filmmaking at the "Lockstone" film company, a reference to his beginnings at Keystone.

3.55 *The City Slicker* (1918) displays Harold Lloyd's typical persona, a brash young fellow in spectacles and a straw hat.

3.56 The protagonist of *Hell's Hinges* (1916, William S. Hart and Charles Swickard) epitomizes Hart's "good-badman" character, as he reads the Bible given to him by the heroine—with a bottle of whiskey at his elbow.

over the course of the 1910s (**3.54**). Chaplin's style was notable for his comically inappropriate use of objects, as in *The Pawnshop* (1916), where he gauges the value of a clock by listening to its ticking with a stethoscope. His dexterity led to many elaborately choreographed fights, chases, and mix-ups, such as the breakneck shenanigans on roller skates in *The Rink* (1916). In a few of his films, such as *The Vagabond* (1916) and *The Immigrant*, Chaplin also introduced an element of pathos unknown in slapstick films. Chaplin's "Little Tramp," with his bowler, cane, and oversized shoes, was soon one of the most widely recognized figures in the world.

One of Sennett's rivals was Hal Roach, who produced films with the young Harold Lloyd. Although Lloyd's initial series character, "Lonesome Luke," was basically an imitation of Chaplin, he soon donned a pair of dark-rimmed glasses and developed his own persona (**3.55**). Other comics of the period included Roscoe "Fatty" Arbuckle and his sidekick Buster Keaton, who would come into his own as a star in the 1920s.

The Western also continued to be popular during the 1910s. William S. Hart, one of its most prominent stars, had been a stage actor and did not enter films until he was nearly fifty. His age, plus his long, lean face, allowed him to play weather-beaten, world-weary roles. His characters were often criminals or men with shady pasts; the plots frequently involved his redemption by love. As a result, Hart's persona became known as the "good-badman," an approach taken up by many subsequent Western stars (**3.56**). His worn clothing and other realistic touches gave Hart's Westerns a sense of historical authenticity, despite their often conventional plots.

Another cowboy star of this period was in many ways Hart's opposite. Tom Mix came out of a background of rodeos and Wild West shows. His films were less realistic than Hart's and emphasized fast action, fancy riding, and stunts. After years of making low-budget shorts for Selig, Mix moved to Fox in 1917 and soon became the most popular cowboy star of the late silent era.

One event at the end of this decade indicates the importance that major stars and directors had assumed by this time. In 1919, three of the most popular actors—Mary Pickford, Douglas Fairbanks, and Charles Chaplin—joined the leading director D. W. Griffith in establishing a new firm, United Artists. This was a prestigious distribution company, dealing only in films that these four produced independently. (Later, other independent producers and stars, such as Samuel Goldwyn and Buster Keaton, also distributed through United Artists.) Although Griffith had to drop out a few years later, the new firm did give some stars and producers a high degree of control that was quite unlike the experiences of filmmakers working for the big studios. We shall see some of its results in Chapter 7.

The development of the Hollywood studio system during the 1910s and the accompanying American takeover of world film markets were among the most influential changes in cinema history. The events of these years defined standard commercial filmmaking. Some of the U.S. companies that began in this era are still making films. The division of labor into specialized tasks has continued to the present day. The star system is still one of the primary means of appealing to audiences, and directors continue to coordinate the process

3.57 In *The Artist's Dream* (1913), the animated dog is painted onto a background setting printed on a series of sheets of paper.

3.58 A frame from *Bobby Bumps and His Goatmobile* (1917), in which the moving figures are drawn on transparent celluloid sheets placed over a single painting of the setting.

3.59 An Edison cartoon of 1915, *Cartoons in the Hotel,* animated by Barré. The head of the cow has been "slashed" off its body, which remains static, while separate drawings allow the head to move.

of filmmaking. The basic principles of the classical Hollywood style of filmmaking have changed remarkably little. For better or worse, during this era, *Hollywood* and *the movies* became almost synonymous for many audiences around the world.

Streamlining American Animation

In the same manner that the labor involved in live-action filmmaking was being divided, animated filmmaking was also becoming standardized within the American industry. Several filmmakers realized that cartoons could be made more economically and quickly if the work could be broken down on an assembly-line system. The main animator could design and supervise the work while subsidiary workers drew most of the pictures needed for the film's movement. In addition, during the 1910s, technical innovations speeded up the process of animation: the mechanical printing of background settings, the use of transparent cels, and the slash technique of drawing action.

Early animators like Émile Cohl and Winsor McCay worked by making huge numbers of drawings (see Chapter 2). McCay had an assistant to trace the unmoving background settings onto sheets of paper. In 1913, John Randolph Bray devised a method of mechanizing the process of animation: he printed the same background on many sheets of paper, then animated painted shapes on top of that background to create *The Artist's Dream* (**3.57**).

In December 1914, Bray started his own animation studio, hiring a young man named Earl Hurd. That same month, Hurd applied for a patent on the idea of drawing the moving figures in animated cartoons on sheets of transparent celluloid. (The individual sheets are called

cels, giving rise to the term *cel animation.*) This technique meant that each moving portion could be redrawn bit by bit on separate cels while the background remained constant. Hurd's "Bobby Bumps" series were among the most popular cartoons of the decade (**3.58**).

During this same period, Raoul Barré developed the *slash system* of animation. A figure would be drawn on paper, and then the portion of the body that moved would be cut away and redrawn on the sheet of paper below the remaining portion of the figure. In order to keep the shapes steady on the screen when moving portions were redrawn, Barré proposed steadying the sheets of paper on a pair of pegs at the top of the drawing. This peg system of registration has remained central to drawn animation ever since, because it allows cels drawn by different animators to fit together smoothly. During 1915, Barré used the slash system to create a brief series of "Animated Grouch Chasers" for the Edison Company. These were live-action shorts with embedded animated sequences (**3.59**).

During the 1910s, animation was done by independent firms that sold the rights to their films to distributors. Cartoons were sometimes among the shorts shown on programs before features. During the 1920s, thanks in part to the labor-saving devices developed during the 1910s, animated shorts would become a much more regular element of movie programs.

SMALLER PRODUCING COUNTRIES

During the 1910s, many countries began producing fiction films. These films and the circumstances of their making were extremely varied. Unfortunately, it is

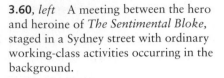

3.60, *left*   A meeting between the hero and heroine of *The Sentimental Bloke*, staged in a Sydney street with ordinary working-class activities occurring in the background.

3.61, *right*   The staging of a historical battle on location gives a nearly documentary quality to some scenes of *Ul Ultimo Malon.*

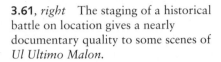

3.62, *left*   A set representing the interior of a tenant cottage, shot on an open-air stage in full daylight, in *Willy Reilly and His Colleen Bawn.*

3.63, *right*   Nell Shipman and a bear on location in the Canadian wilderness in *Back to God's Country.*

presently impossible to write adequate histories of such filmmaking practices, since few films from minor producing countries survive. The production companies, usually small and often short-lived, seldom could preserve the negatives of their films. In many cases only a few prints were distributed, so the chances of one surviving were slim. Many countries, such as Mexico, India, Colombia, and New Zealand, only relatively recently have established archives to save their cinematic heritage. Even the rare films that do survive are usually hard to see today except in large cities where archives schedule historical retrospectives.

Despite such problems, most countries have managed to salvage at least a few silent films. On the basis of these, we can make some generalizations about filmmaking in the less prominent producing countries during the silent era.

Firms in such countries had little hope of exporting their films. This meant that they could afford only small budgets, so production values were usually relatively low. Filmmakers concentrated on movies that would appeal primarily to domestic audiences.

Films made in the smaller producing nations share two general traits. First, many were shot on location. Since production was sporadic, large studio facilities simply did not exist, and filmmakers made a virtue of necessity, exploiting distinctive natural landscapes and local historical buildings for interesting mise-en-scène.

Those studio facilities that did exist were small and technologically limited. Little artificial lighting was available, and many interior scenes of this period were shot on simple open-air stages, in sunlight.

Second, filmmakers frequently sought to differentiate their low-budget films from the more polished imported works by using national literature and history as sources for their stories. In many cases, such local appeal worked, since audiences wanted at least occasionally to see films that reflected their own culture. In some cases these films were novel enough to be exported.

A good example of a film that used these tactics is *The Sentimental Bloke*, perhaps the most important Australian silent film (1919, Raymond Longford). Based on a popular book of dialect verses by Australian author C. J. Dennis, the film presented a working-class romance. The intertitles quoted passages from the poem, and the scenes were shot in the inner-city Woolloomooloo district of Sydney (**3.60**). The film was very popular in Australia. "It is a blessed relief and refreshment," wrote one reviewer, "after much of the twaddlesome picturing and camouflaged lechery of the films that come to us from America."[5] *The Sentimental Bloke* received some distribution in Great Britain, the United States, and other markets—though the local dialect in the intertitles had to be revised so that foreign viewers could understand the story.

Other films of the era drew upon similar appeals. In Argentina, Alcides Greca directed *Ul Ultimo Malon* ("The Last Indian Attack," 1917), based on a historical incident of 1904 (**3.61**). Similarly, a 1919 production by the small, newly formed Film Company of Ireland, *Willy Reilly and His Colleen Bawn* (released 1920, John Mac-Donagh), was based on an Irish novel by William Carleton, which in turn was based on traditional ballads and events of the Catholic-Protestant conflicts of 1745. Many of the film's scenes were filmed outdoors in the countryside of Ireland. Some interior scenes were also shot outdoors (**3.62**). In 1919, the Canadian producer Ernest Shipman made a film called *Back to God's Country* (director, David M. Hartford). The screenplay was written by Nell Shipman, the film's star, who in the 1920s became a notable independent producer and director. Much of the film was made in the Canadian wilderness, and the story stressed the heroine's love of animals and natural landscapes (**3.63**). Again, the distinctive Canadian subject matter and scenery made the film successful abroad.

The strategies of using national subject matter and exploiting picturesque local landscapes have remained common in countries with limited production to the present day.

The 1910s, then, were a crucial transitional period for the cinema. International explorations of storytelling techniques and stylistic expressivity led to a cinema that was surprisingly close to what we know today. Indeed, in many ways, early as they are, the films of the mid- to late 1910s are much more like modern movies than they are like the novelty-oriented short subjects made only a decade or so earlier.

Similarly, the postwar international situation in the film industry would have long-range consequences. In 1919, Hollywood dominated world markets, and most countries had to struggle to compete with it, either by imitating its films or by finding alternatives to them. The Swedish filmmakers had created a powerful national cinema, but it was too small to make real headway against the Americans after the war. Russia's distinctive film style was cut off by the 1917 Russian Revolution. The struggle against Hollywood domination would shape much of what happened within national film industries for decades to come. The next three chapters will examine some important styles of filmmaking that arose shortly after World War I. Chapter 7 will then describe Hollywood in the late silent period.

* * *

Notes and Queries

THE ONGOING REDISCOVERY OF THE 1910s

The work of understanding film history continues. For many years, historians considered the 1910s important for only a few events. It was widely known that World War I strangled European production, permitting Hollywood's worldwide dominance. Griffith and Ince were studied as major American producer-directors; silent comedies, particularly those of Chaplin and Sennett, were also praised. Among foreign films, a few by Stiller and Sjöström were considered classics.

The widespread revision of film history that has occurred in recent decades initially concentrated on pre–World War I cinema. Since the 1980s, however, scholars have paid increasing attention to the 1910s. A crucial contribution to this rediscovery has been the annual festival of silent film, Le Giornate del Cinema Muto, held in Pordenone and Sacile, Italy, since 1982. Although the festival screens films from the entire silent period, some of its most dramatic revelations have come during its retrospectives concentrating on the 1910s. In 1986, an extensive program of pre-1919 Scandinavian films was shown. Among other revelations, this was the occasion for the international

discovery of Georg af Klercker. Ironically, af Klercker's departure from Svenska meant that the negatives of his films were not among those in the tragic Svenska fire of 1941; Hasselblad kept the negatives in its own vault, and twenty of his twenty-eight films for Hasselblad survive, many in nearly pristine condition. Similar programs have dealt with Hollywood cinema of the 1910s (1988), prerevolutionary Russian films (1989), and German cinema of the pre-1920 era (1990). Each festival was accompanied by a collection of important essays in Italian and English. See Paolo Cherchi Usai and Lorenzo Codelli, eds., *Sulla via di Hollywood 1911–1920* (Pordenone: Edizioni Biblioteca dell'Immagine, 1988); Yuri Tsivian, ed., *Silent Witnesses: Russian Films 1908–1919* (London: British Film Institute, 1989); and Paolo Cherchi Usai and Lorenzo Codelli, eds., *Before Caligari: German Cinema, 1895–1920* (Madison: University of Wisconsin Press, 1990).

Events like Le Giornate del Cinema Muto emphasize how crucial the preservation and availability of early films are to our knowledge of cinema history. Early synoptic histories were based on the few masterpieces available in film archives. While important in themselves, these films seldom gave an accurate indication of national cinemas as wholes. Moreover, some important filmmakers have been virtually forgotten. Le Giornate has been crucial in bringing such directors as Georg af Klercker and Evgenii Bauer to historians' attention. Similarly, masterpieces like *Die Landstrasse* have been all but forgotten until a discovery (in this case by the Filmmuseum of the Netherlands) of a single copy. Today, many national archives take the opportunity of Le Giornate to display prints of newly discovered or restored films, which are then shown in other archives and museums around the world. Undoubtedly some unknown directors and lost films will occasionally resurface and modify our view of film history.

· ·

REFERENCES

1. Quoted in Yuri Tsivian, "Some Preparatory Remarks on Russian Cinema," in Tsivian, ed., *Silent Witnesses: Russian Films 1908–1919* (London: British Film Institute, 1989), p. 24.
2. Quoted in Richard Abel, *French Cinema: The First Wave, 1915–1929* (Princeton, NJ: Princeton University Press, 1984), p. 10.
3. Ron Mottram, *The Danish Cinema before Dreyer* (Metuchen, NJ: Scarecrow, 1988), p. 117.
4. Louis Delluc, "Cinema: *The Outlaw and His Wife*," (1919) in Richard Abel, ed., *French Film Theory and Criticism 1907–1939*, vol. 1 (Princeton, NJ: Princeton University Press, 1988), p. 188.
5. Quoted in Graham Shirley and Brian Adams, *Australian Cinema: The First Eighty Years* (Australia: Angus & Robertson Publishers and Currency Press, 1983), p. 56.

FURTHER READING

Brewster, Ben. "*Traffic in Souls:* An Experiment in Feature-Length Narrative Construction." *Cinema Journal* 31, no. 1 (fall 1991): 37–56.
DeBauche, Leslie Midkiff. *Reel Patriotism: The Movies and World War I.* Madison: University of Wisconsin Press, 1997.
"Feuillade and the French Serial." Issue of *The Velvet Light Trap*, 37 (spring 1996).

Forslund, Bengt. *Victor Sjöström: His Life and His Work.* Trans. Peter Cowie. New York: New York Zoetrope, 1988.
Jacobs, Lea. "Belasco, De Mille and the Development of Lasky Lighting." *Film History* 5, no. 4 (December 1993): 405–18.
Koszarski, Richard, ed. *Rivals of D. W. Griffith: Alternate Auteurs, 1913–1918.* Minneapolis: Walker Art Center, 1976.
Lacassin, François. *Louis Feuillade: Maitre des lions et des Vampires.* Paris: Pierre Bordas et Fils, 1995.
Langer, Mark. "The Reflections of John Randolph Bray: An Interview with Annotations." *Griffithiana* 53 (May 1995): 95–131.
Olsson, Jan. "'Classical' vs. 'Pre-Classical': *Ingeborg Holm* and Swedish Cinema in 1913." *Griffithiana* 50 (May 1994): 113–23.
Quaresima, Leonardo. "*Dichter, heraus!* The Autorenfilm and German Cinema of the 1910s." *Griffithiana* 38/39 (October 1999): 101–20.
Robinson, David. "The Italian Comedy." *Sight and Sound* 55, no. 2 (spring 1990): 105–12.
Silva, Fred, ed. *Focus on* The Birth of a Nation. Englewood Cliffs, NJ: Prentice-Hall, 1971.
Singer, Ben. "Female Power in the Serial-Queen Melodrama: The Etiology of an Anomaly." *Camera Obscura* 22 (January 1990): 90–129.
Youngblood, Denise J. *The Magic Mirror: Moviemaking in Russia, 1908–1918.* Madison: University of Wisconsin Press, 1999.

TWO

THE LATE SILENT ERA, 1919–1929

Although classical Hollywood form and style have been pervasive since the 1910s, we shall find many alternative approaches to filmmaking in different periods and places. So far we have looked at styles associated with a single filmmaker (such as Georges Méliès or D. W. Griffith), with a company (Pathé), or with a national industry (the huge classical Hollywood cinema or the small Swedish production). Some groups of films belong to a unified *movement*. A movement involves several filmmakers, working for a limited period and usually in a single country, whose films share significant formal traits.

Because film movements arise as alternatives to the ordinary filmmaking of their day, they often employ unusual techniques. Since few commercial film industries encourage the use of techniques that might alienate the broad audience, how can such movements arise? For each movement, the reasons are different, and, for each one that we study, we shall look briefly at the conditions in the film industry and the country as a whole that permitted the movement to exist.

One broad trend in the arts began in the late nineteenth century and was causing a great ferment as the cinema was spreading. This trend has been labeled *modernism*. It signaled a major shift in cultural attitudes that arose largely as a response to modern life—the late phases of the industrial revolution, especially the new modes of transportation and communication that were swiftly transforming people's lives. Telephones, automobiles, and airplanes were considered great advances, yet they also seemed threatening, especially in their capacity to be used in warfare.

Photography, in particular, revolutionized the visual arts. Photographs could provide realistic portraits and show landscapes and cityscapes in enormous detail. Many painters moved away from the traditions of realism, portraiture, and subjects drawn from history and classical myth.

A new value was placed on experimentation and even shock value. The many movements that arose during the early twentieth century can all loosely be summed up as *avant-garde* (literally, the "advance watch," or those at the forefront of a military unit). These new styles, which originated primarily in Europe, rejected the realistic depiction of a concrete world. The first such movement took place in the late nineteenth century and was termed French Impressionism; its practitioners abandoned painting the solid, permanent appearance of things and instead attempted to capture the fleeting patterns of light and shadow as they struck the eye.

During the early twentieth century, more modernist trends in painting quickly arose. Fauvism in France encouraged the use of bold colors and exaggerated shapes to elicit strong emotions rather than serene contemplation. At the same time, other French painters more coolly depicted several sides of objects, as if they were being seen in an impossible space from several viewpoints at once. This movement became known as Cubism. Beginning in 1908, proponents of German Expressionism attempted to express raw, extreme emotions, in painting through garish colors and distortion and in theater through emphasized gestures, loud declamation of lines, staring eyes, and choreographed movements.

The 1910s saw the beginnings of abstract painting, pioneered by Wassily Kandinsky and quickly spreading internationally. In Italy, the Futurists tried to capture the hectic pace of modern life by rendering the swirl and blur of movement. In Russia and, after the 1917 Russian Revolution, the Soviet Union, some artists championed purely abstract compositions of simple shapes, a style known as Suprematism. In the 1920s, as Lenin called for swift industrial progress, Soviet artists based their works around the machine in a movement termed Constructivism.

In France during the 1920s, practitioners of Surrealism favored bizarre, irrational, artfully contrived juxtapositions of objects and actions. Going even further, the Dadaists advocated purely random mixtures of elements in artworks, reflecting what they saw as the madness of the postwar world. All of these styles, along with modernist movements and trends in literature, drama, and music, created a radical break with traditional artistic realism in a remarkably short time. The modernist tradition would dominate the arts throughout much of the twentieth century.

Given the liveliness and prominence of these modernist movements, it is not surprising that they sometimes influenced the cinema. The years from 1918 to 1933 saw an astonishing variety of explorations in alternative film styles. No fewer than three avant-garde movements arose within commercial industries and flourished briefly: French Impressionism (1918–1929), German Expressionism (1920–1927), and Soviet Montage (1925–1933). Moreover, the 1920s saw the beginnings of an independent experimental cinema—including Surrealism, Dadaism, and abstract films.

There are many reasons for such intense, varied activity in this period. One of the most important involves the new prominence of the Hollywood cinema as a stylistic and commercial force. Chapters 2 and 3 described the establishment of the narrative and stylistic premises of the classical Hollywood cinema during the 1910s. We also saw how the wartime decline in European production allowed American firms to expand into world markets.

After the war, widely differing situations existed in other producing nations, but all faced one common factor: a need to compete with Hollywood in the local market. In some countries, like Great Britain, such competition usually involved imitating Hollywood films. Other national cinemas followed this strategy but also encouraged filmmakers to experiment, in the hope that innovative films could compete with the Hollywood product. Some postwar avant-garde films became successful, partly on the basis of their novelty.

Since the invention of the cinema, virtually everyone thought of the new medium primarily as a form of entertainment and as a commercial product. Although some filmmakers, like Maurice Tourneur and Victor Sjöström, took the cinema seriously as an art form, few observers conceived that filmmakers could experiment with modernist styles derived from the other arts. In the late 1910s and 1920s, however, this idea caught on in a number of European countries.

Many of the institutions we now consider integral parts of the film world first came into being then. For example, the specialized film journal, publishing theoretical and analytical articles, arose in France in the 1910s and proliferated internationally over the next decade. Similarly, the earliest groups of enthusiasts devoted to alternative cinema were formed—taking their name, the "ciné-club," from French groups that started the trend. Until the mid-1920s, there were no theaters devoted to the showing of art films. Whether a theater was large or small, first-run or second-run, it showed ordinary commercial films. Gradually, however, the "little cinema" movement spread, again beginning in France. Such theaters catered to a small but loyal portion of the public interested in foreign and avant-garde films. Finally, the first conferences and exhibitions devoted to the cinema as an art were held during the 1920s.

Many of the circumstances that allow any film movement to come into being, however, are unique to its time and place. No single set of circumstances will predictably give rise to a movement. Indeed, as we shall see in the next three chapters, the conditions in France, Germany, and the Soviet Union differed vastly in the postwar era.

We shall go on to examine Hollywood in the 1920s, a period during which it continued to expand and to polish the classical narrative style developed during the previous decade (Chapter 7). Finally, we will look at international trends of this period, including efforts to resist Hollywood competition and attempts to create an international experimental cinema (Chapter 8).

FRANCE IN THE 1920s

THE FRENCH FILM INDUSTRY AFTER WORLD WAR 1

French film production declined during World War I, as many resources were drained away to support the fighting. Moreover, American films increasingly entered France. In the years immediately following the war's end, only 20 to 30 percent of films screened there were French, with Hollywood supplying most of the rest.

French producers faced an uphill struggle in trying to regain their prewar strength. Throughout the late silent era, industry experts believed that French production was in a crisis. In 1929, for instance, France made 68 features, while Germany produced 220 and the United States 562. Even in 1926, the worst pre-Depression year for European production, Germany had managed 202 films to France's 55, while Hollywood outstripped both with about 725. In 1928, one of the best years for the Europeans, France made 94 films, compared to 221 for Germany and 641 for the United States. As such figures suggest, France's "crisis" fluctuated in its severity, but the struggle to boost production gained little ground in the postwar decade.

Competition from Imports

What created the problems confronting French film production between 1918 and 1928? For one thing, imported films continued to pour into France in the 1920s. American films were the most numerous, especially early in the decade. Even though America's share declined steadily throughout the mid- to late 1920s, other countries, primarily Germany and Great Britain, gained ground faster than did France.

YEAR	TOTAL NUMBER OF FEATURES	PERCENT RELEASED IN FRANCE			
		FRENCH	AMERICAN	GERMAN	OTHER
1924	693	9.8	85	2.9	2.3
1925	704	10.4	82	4.1	3.5
1926	565	9.7	78.6	5.8	5.9
1927	581	12.7	63.3	15.7	8.3
1928	583	16.1	53.7	20.9	9.3
1929	438	11.9	48.2	29.7	10.2

The situation for exports was little better. The domestic French market itself was relatively small, and films seldom could recover their costs without going abroad. Foreign films, however, were difficult to place in the lucrative American market, and only a tiny number of French films had any success there during this period. With American films dominating most other markets, the French could count on only limited export—primarily to areas that already had cultural exchange with France, such as Belgium, Switzerland, and French colonies in Africa and Southeast Asia. Thus there was a continuous call for a distinctively French cinema that might help counter foreign competition, both at home and abroad. Companies were apparently willing to experiment, and several directors central to the fledgling French Impressionist movement—Abel Gance, Marcel L'Herbier, Germaine Dulac, and Jean Epstein—made their early films for large firms.

Disunity within the Film Industry

French production was also hampered by disunity. Before World War I two big companies, Pathé and Gaumont, controlled the French film industry. After the war, both cut back severely on production, the riskiest sector of the industry, and concentrated instead on surer profits from distribution and exhibition. Thus the largest French firms backed off from vertical integration just as vertically integrated firms were strengthening the Hollywood industry. France's production sector consisted of a few large and medium-size firms and of many small companies. The latter often made only one or a few films each and then disappeared. This artisanal production strategy offered little hope for successful competition with America.

Why were there so many small companies in France? The answer lies partly in domestic business traditions. In the 1920s, French business was still dominated by small companies; the move toward mergers and big corporations in other industrialized countries had not yet caught hold. During this decade, between 80 and 90 percent of French cinemas were owned by individuals. Because it was easier to make money in distribution and exhibition, people investing in the film industry usually put their money into one of these areas, avoiding the risks of production.

As a result, the French tendency toward small production companies persisted. Someone, often a director or star, would raise money for a film. If it failed, the company went out of business or struggled along for another film or two. Many films of this era also had low budgets. Even by the late twenties, when the film industry was slightly better off, one expert estimated the average cost of a French feature at $30,000 (in 1927) to $40,000 (in 1928). (During the late 1920s, budgets for Hollywood features averaged more than $400,000.)

Thus, the interests of the three sectors of the industry—production, distribution, and exhibition—often conflicted. Most important, small exhibitors had no stake in French production. They wanted to show whatever would bring them the most money—usually American imports. Responding to the demands of theater owners, distributors provided Hollywood films. Moreover, it was often cheaper to purchase a foreign film than to produce a French film.

Producers repeatedly called for the government to limit imported films. Inevitably, however, the more powerful distributors and exhibitors, who made most of their money on imports, opposed any quota, and they typically won out. Despite some minor measures to limit importation in the late 1920s, a strong quota was not passed until the 1930s.

Not only did the government fail to protect producers from foreign competition, it also assailed the industry with high taxes on movie tickets. During the 1920s, these taxes ran anywhere from 6 to 40 percent, depending on a theater's size and income. Such taxes hurt every level of the industry, since exhibitors could not risk losing patrons by raising admission prices and hence they could not pay as much to the distributors and producers of the films.

Outdated Production Facilities

To make matters worse, technical facilities were outdated. As in other European countries, French producers depended on the glass studios built before the war. The lack of capital investment hampered companies in reequipping these studios to catch up with the technological innovations American firms had made during the 1910s, particularly in lighting (see pp. 70–72).

As a result, French filmmakers were unaccustomed to using artificial lighting extensively. In the late teens, French visitors to Hollywood were awed by the vast lighting systems. As director Henri Diamant-Berger observed in early 1918, "Lighting effects are sought and achieved in America by the addition of strong light sources, and not, as in France, by the suppression of other sources. In America, lighting effects are created; in France, shadow effects are created."[1] That is, French filmmakers would typically start with sunlight and block off parts of the light to create dark patches within the set. American filmmakers had more flexibility, eliminating sunlight altogether and creating exactly the effects they wanted with artificial light.

There were some attempts to bring this kind of control to French filmmaking. In 1919 director Louis Mercanton rigged up portable lighting equipment to take on location for his realist filmmaking. For the epic *The Three Musketeers* (1921–1922), Diamant-Berger installed American-style overhead lighting in a studio at Vincennes, which thus became one of the earliest studios in France to be so equipped. Modern lighting technology became increasingly available during the 1920s, but it remained too expensive for widespread use.

Although some new studios were built, few had extensive backlots of the sort owned by the larger American and German producers. Most studios were in the Parisian suburbs, surrounded by houses rather than by open space. Large sets often had to be constructed in rented studios. Partly as a result of this and partly through a desire for realism, French filmmakers went on location more often than did their counterparts in Germany or the United States. Chateaux, palaces, and other historic landmarks appear as the backdrops of many French silent films; filmmakers also made a virtue of necessity by using natural landscapes and scenes shot in French villages.

MAJOR POSTWAR GENRES

Despite foreign competition, industry disunity, lack of capital, government indifference, and limited technical resources, the French industry produced a variety of films. In most countries, serials declined in prestige during the late teens, but in France, they remained among the most lucrative films well into the 1920s. Big firms like Pathé and Gaumont found that a high-budget costume drama or literary adaptation could make a profit only when shown in several parts. Because moviegoers regularly attended their local theater, they were willing to return for all the episodes.

4.1 Some scenes in *L'Agonie des aigles* ("The Agony of the Eagles," 1921), a Pathé film about Napoléon, were shot on location outside Fontainebleau.

Some French serials of the postwar era followed the established pattern, with cliffhanger endings, master criminals, and exotic locales, as in Louis Feuillade's *Tih-Minh* (1919). But social pressures against the glorification of crime and perhaps also a sense that the formula was becoming stale led to changes. Feuillade, whose films were now virtually Gaumont's sole output, turned to serials based on popular sentimental novels with *Les Deux gamines* ("The Two Kids," 1921) and continued in this vein until his death in 1925. Diamant-Berger's epic adaptation of *The Three Musketeers* was among the decade's most successful films. Henri Fescourt directed *Mandrin* (1924), whose twelve episodes continued the traditions of kidnaps, disguises, and rescues—but presented them as swashbuckling feats in an eighteenth-century setting.

Whether made in serial format or not, many prestigious and expensive productions were historical epics. In many cases film companies economized by using French monuments as settings (**4.1**). Such films were often intended for export. *The Miracle of the Wolves* (1924, Raymond Bernard) was the most lavish French historical film yet made; while its interiors used sets, many scenes were shot in the medieval town of Carcassone. The film's producer, the Société des Films Historiques, gave it a gala New York run, but, as often happened with such attempts, no American distributor purchased *The Miracle of the Wolves*.

A modest genre was the fantasy film, and its most prominent practitioner was René Clair. His first film, *Paris qui dort* ("Sleeping Paris," aka *The Crazy Ray*, 1924), was a comic story of a mysterious ray that paralyzes Paris. Clair used freeze-frame techniques and unmoving actors to create the sense of an immobile city. Several characters flying above the city escape the ray and proceed to live luxuriously by looting whatever they want; soon they track down the source of the problem and set things moving again. In Clair's *Le Voyage imaginaire* ("The Imaginary Journey," 1926), the hero dreams that he is transported by a witch to a fairyland, created with fancifully painted sets (**4.2**). Such fantasies revived

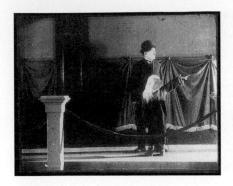

4.2, *left* Among the supernatural events in *Le Voyage imaginaire* is a scene in which a waxworks museum comes to life—including figures of Charlie Chaplin and Jackie Coogan as they appeared in Chaplin's 1921 film *The Kid.*

4.3, *right* Max Linder's comic feature *Le Petit café* combines intertitles with live action.

a popular tradition of the early cinema in France, drawing upon camera tricks and stylized sets somewhat as Georges Méliès and Gaston Velle had done.

Comedies continued to be popular after the war. Max Linder, who had been lured briefly to Hollywood, returned to make comedies in France, including one of the earliest comic features, *Le Petit café* (1919, Raymond Bernard). Linder played a waiter who inherits a large sum of money but must go on working to fulfill his contract; comic scenes follow as he tries to get himself fired. The film's witty touches (**4.3**) made it a surprise hit and helped give the comic genre more respectability in France. Other important comedies were made by Clair, whose *The Italian Straw Hat* (1928) brought him an international fame that would grow in the sound era.

THE FRENCH IMPRESSIONIST MOVEMENT

Between 1918 and 1929, a new generation of filmmakers sought to explore the cinema as an art. These directors considered French filmmaking stodgy and preferred the lively Hollywood films that had flooded into France during the war. Their films displayed a fascination with pictorial beauty and an interest in intense psychological exploration.

The Impressionists' Relation to the Industry

These filmmakers were aided by the crises that plagued the French industry. Because companies would often shift their policies or reorganize, filmmakers had various ways of obtaining financing. Some Impressionist directors also divided their time between avant-garde projects and more profit-oriented films. Germaine Dulac made some important Impressionist films, including *The Smiling Madame Beudet* and *Gossette* (both 1923), but she spent much of her career making more conventional dramas. Similarly, Jean Epstein directed costume pictures in

between some of his most experimental works. Jacques Feyder was among the more commercially successful of French directors in the 1920s, making a huge hit, *L'Atlantide,* in 1921; yet he made Impressionist films from 1923 to 1926. Few Impressionists had the luxury of working full-time in their preferred style, yet they kept the movement going for over a decade.

Despite their avant-garde proclivities, these directors had to make their way within the regular commercial firms. The first to depart from established stylistic traditions was Abel Gance, who had entered filmmaking in 1911 as a scenarist and then began directing. Aside from making an unreleased Méliès-like fantasy, *La Folie du Dr. Tube* ("Dr. Tube's Madness," 1915), he had worked on commercial projects. With a passion for Romantic literature and art, however, Gance aspired to make more personal works. His *La Dixième symphonie* (1918) is the first major film of the Impressionist movement. It concerns a composer who writes a symphony so powerful that his friends consider it a successor to Beethoven's nine symphonies. Gance suggests the listeners' emotional reactions to the score by a series of visual devices (**4.4**). Such attempts to convey sensations and emotional "impressions" would become central to the Impressionist movement.

La Dixième symphonie was produced by Charles Pathé, who continued to finance and distribute Gance's films after the director formed his own production

4.4 In *La Dixième symphonie*, Gance superimposes a dancer over piano keys to suggest the subjective effect of a musical passage.

A Chronology of French Impressionist Cinema

1918 ....● November: Germany and Austria surrender, ending World War I.
La Dixième symphonie ("The Tenth Symphony"), Abel Gance

1919 ....● Summer: Independent company, Films Abel Gance, is formed.
J'Accuse ("I Accuse"), Abel Gance
Rose-France, Marcel L'Herbier

1920 ....● January: Louis Delluc publishes *Le Journal du Ciné-Club*, then starts *Cinéa* in April.
Le Carnival des vérités ("Carnival of Truths"), Marcel L'Herbier
L'Homme du large ("The Man of the Open Sea"), Marcel L'Herbier

1921 ....● *Fièvre* ("Fever"), Louis Delluc
El Dorado, Marcel L'Herbier

1922 ....● Yermoliev's émigré company becomes Films Albatros.
La Femme de nulle part ("The Woman from Nowhere"), Louis Delluc
La Roue ("The Wheel"), Abel Gance

1923 ....● *L'Auberge rouge* ("The Red Inn"), Jean Epstein
Don Juan et Faust ("Don Juan and Faust"), Marcel L'Herbier
La Souriante Madame Beudet (The Smiling Madame Beudet), Germaine Dulac
Coeur fidèle ("Faithful Heart"), Jean Epstein
Crainquebille, Jacques Feyder
Le Marchand de plaisir ("The Seller of Pleasure"), Jaque Catelain
Gossette ("The Little Kid"), Germaine Dulac
Le Brasier ardent ("The Burning Brazier"), Ivan Mosjoukine and Alexandre Volkoff

1924 ....● March: Louis Delluc dies.
La Galérie des monsters ("The Freak Show"), Jaque Catelain
L'Inondation ("The Flood"), Louis Delluc
l'Inhumaine ("The Inhuman One"), Marcel L'Herbier
Kean, Alexandre Volkoff
Catherine, Albert Dieudonné (script by Jean Renoir)
La Belle Nivernaise ("The Beautiful Nivernaise"), Jean Epstein
L'Ironie du destin ("The Irony of Destiny"), Dimitri Kirsanoff

1925 ....● *L'Affiche* ("The Poster"), Jean Epstein
Visages d'enfants ("Children's Faces"), Jacques Feyder
Feu Mathias Pascal ("The Late Mathias Pascal"), Marcel L'Herbier
La Fille de l'eau ("The Daughter of the Water"), Jean Renoir

1926 ....● Les Films Jean Epstein is formed.
Gribiche, Jacques Feyder
Menilmontant, Dimitri Kirsanoff

1927 ....● *6½ × 11*, Jean Epstein
La Glace à trois faces ("The Three-Sided Mirror"), Jean Epstein
Napoléon vu par Abel Gance ("Napoléon as Seen by Abel Gance"), Abel Gance

1928 ....● Les Films Jean Epstein goes out of business.
L'Herbier's company, Cinégraphic, is absorbed by Cinéromans.
Brumes d'automne ("Autumn Mists"), Dimitri Kirsanoff
La Chute de la maison Usher (The Fall of the House of Usher), Jean Epstein
La Petite marchande d'allumettes (The Little Match Girl), Jean Renoir

1929 ....● *L'Argent* ("Money"), Marcel L'Herbier
Finis Terrae ("The End of the Earth"), Jean Epstein

4.5 Gance's *La Roue* contains many oval and round masks to change the rectangular shape of the image.

4.6 In L'Herbier's *Rose-France*, an elaborate mask divides the frame into three images, centering the heroine as if in a traditional triptych painting.

4.7 As the hero of L'Herbier's *Feu Mathias Pascal* sits in a moving train, we see what he is thinking through a series of images of his village and family, superimposed over the moving train tracks.

4.8 When the heroine of *Menilmontant* stands on a bridge and contemplates suicide, the superimposition of the river over her face suggests her mental turmoil.

4.9, 4.10 A filter creates a subjective effect in *El Dorado*.

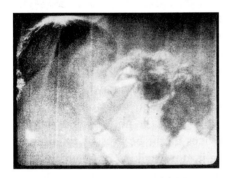

4.11 Filters achieve a subjective effect in the wedding-night scene in *Napoléon*.

4.12 In a POV shot of M. Beudet, his wife's dislike leads her to see him as grotesque.

4.13 A shot made using a curved mirror, from L'Herbier's *El Dorado*

from anyone's point of view. In Gance's *Napoléon*, the passion of Napoléon and Josephine as they kiss on their wedding night is conveyed by a series of gauze filters that drop one by one between the couple and the lens, gradually blurring the screen to gray (**4.11**).

Occasionally the Impressionists would shoot into a curved mirror to distort the image. Such distortions

could create a POV shot, as in Dulac's *The Smiling Madame Beudet;* this film contains many optical devices that convey the heroine's unhappiness with her boorish husband (**4.12**). L'Herbier uses a similar mirror shot in *El Dorado* (**4.13**), but here the framing is not from anyone's point of view; it simply conveys the man's drunkenness subjectively.

4.14, 4.15 In *Le Brasier ardent*, the image goes out of focus to suggest the heroine's mental abstraction.

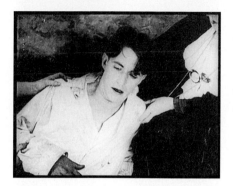 

4.16, 4.17 A POV shot in *La Fille de l'eau* shows the hero's vision blurred as a result of a beating.

4.18 In Jacques Feyder's *Visages d'enfants*, a low camera height and slightly low angle show the optical point of view of a child being scolded.

4.19 A drunken woman's dizziness is conveyed in *Feu Mathias Pascal* through a canted framing as she staggers along a hallway.

4.20 In *Feu Mathias Pascal*, Mathias dreams of leaping on his enemy.

Throwing the lens out of focus could also convey subjectivity, whether we see the characters or see through their eyes. In *Le Brasier ardent*, the heroine and her husband have just agreed to divorce, and she sadly stands thinking (**4.14, 4.15**). After the hero of Renoir's *La Fille de l'eau* has been in a fight, he sits groggily as a POV shot conveys his mental state (**4.16, 4.17**). Similarly, the framing of a shot may suggest characters' points of view or inner states (**4.18, 4.19**).

Virtually any manipulation of the camera could be used subjectively. Slow motion was common in rendering mental images (**4.20**). In *Napoléon*, Gance divided the frame into a grid of smaller, distinct images (**4.21**). He also used three cameras side by side to create an

4.21 In a split-screen process he called Polyvision, Gance conveyed the chaos of a pillow fight in *Napoléon*.

4.22   In *Napoléon*, three images joined horizontally create an epic vista of the hero surveying his troops.

4.23, *left*   In *Napoléon*, Gance mounted the camera on a horse's back, putting us in the hero's position as he flees from pursuing soldiers.

4.24, *right*   In *Coeur fidèle*, the camera is mounted on the swing along with the couple so that the background whirls past as the woman and her fiancé sit unmoving in the foreground.

extremely wide format called a *triptych* (**4.22**). This functioned to create wide vistas, symbolic juxtapositions of images, and occasional subjective effects.

Impressionist films also feature camera movements that convey subjectivity and enhance photogénie. Moving shots could suggest the character's optical point of view (**4.23**). The moving camera could also convey subjectivity without optical point of view, as in the carnival scene in Epstein's *Coeur fidèle*. Here the heroine sits miserably on a carnival ride with the fiancé her parents have forced on her (**4.24**).

Devices of Editing   Until 1923, camera devices for achieving photogénie and expressing subjectivity were the main distinguishing traits of Impressionism. In that year, however, two films appeared that experimented with quick editing to explore characters' mental states. Gance's *La Roue* (which premiered in December of 1922 but was released in February of 1923) contains several scenes with very fast cutting. In one sequence, many short shots convey the overwrought emotions of the hero, Sisif. A railway engineer, he has fallen in love with Norma, a woman whom he has raised from a child and who thinks she is his daughter. He is driving the train upon which she is riding into the city to be mar-

ried. In despair, he opens the throttle of the train, planning to crash it and kill himself and everyone aboard (**4.25–4.31**). Figures 4.25 through 4.31 are respectively eleven, fourteen, fourteen, seven, six, five, and six frames long. Given that projection speeds were about twenty frames per second at this time, each shot would last less than a second, and the shortest would remain on the screen for only about a quarter of a second. Here excitement is conveyed less through acting than through a rhythmic rush of swift details.

Later in *La Roue*, Sisif's son Elie, who also loves Norma, has fallen over a cliff during a fight with her husband. As he dangles, he hears Norma calling and running to his rescue. Suddenly a close-up of his face introduces a radically abbreviated series of shots. Each is only one frame in length, showing Elie and Norma in situations from earlier scenes in the film. This barrage of instantaneous flashbacks is too brief to register on the eye (since twenty of them would pass in a single second). The effect is a flicker, suggesting the confusion of Elie's emotions as he recognizes Norma's voice and then falls to his death. This scene is the first known use of single-frame shots in film history. Such segments of rhythmic montage made *La Roue* an enormously influential film during the 1920s.

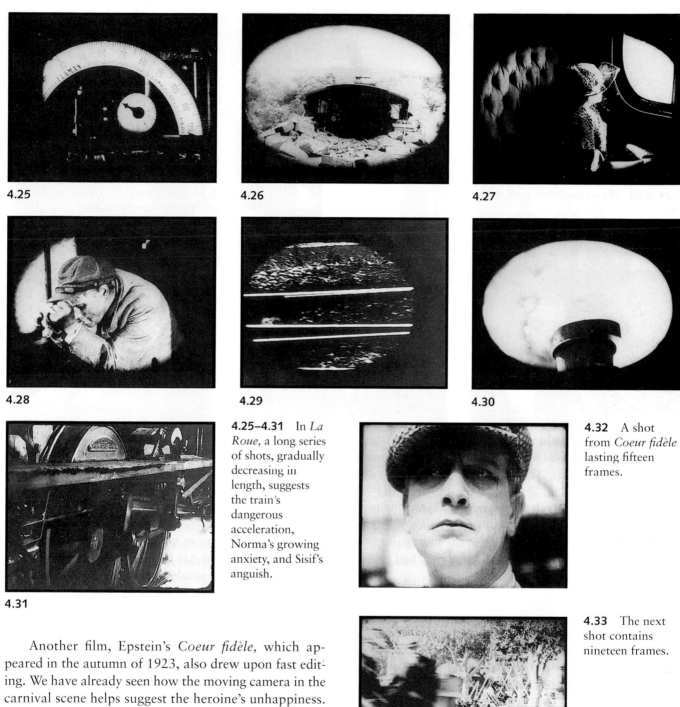

4.25

4.26

4.27

4.28

4.29

4.30

4.25–4.31 In *La Roue*, a long series of shots, gradually decreasing in length, suggests the train's dangerous acceleration, Norma's growing anxiety, and Sisif's anguish.

4.31

4.32 A shot from *Coeur fidèle* lasting fifteen frames.

4.33 The next shot contains nineteen frames.

Another film, Epstein's *Coeur fidèle*, which appeared in the autumn of 1923, also drew upon fast editing. We have already seen how the moving camera in the carnival scene helps suggest the heroine's unhappiness. The editing enhances this effect. As in *La Roue*'s train scene, details appear in a series of about sixty brief shots of the objects around the whirling-swings ride. Most of these shots are well under one second, and many are only two frames long. One brief segment, for example, shows the man the woman actually loves looking on from the ground (**4.32**), a quick long shot of the ride and crowd (**4.33**), then quick flashes of two frames each of the heroine and her thuggish fiancé (**4.34, 4.35**).

After the release of *La Roue* and *Coeur fidèle*, fast rhythmic editing became a staple of Impressionist film-

making. It appears in the disorienting opening sequence of *Menilmontant*, where the violence of a double murder is conveyed through details caught in close, short shots. Gance pushed the technique he had innovated even further in the final scene of *Napoléon* by using

5.5   In the Burgundian court in *Siegfried*, ranks of soldiers and decor alike form geometric shapes that combine into an overall composition.

5.6   In *The Golem*, an animated clay statue emerges onto a rooftop, looking as if he is made of the same material as his surroundings.

5.7   A symmetrical shot in *Algol* shows a corridor made up of repeated abstract black and white shapes and lines.

fashion possible. Similar goals led to extreme stylization in literature, and narrative techniques such as frame stories and open endings were adopted by scriptwriters for Expressionist films.

By the end of the 1910s, Expressionism had gone from being a radical experiment to being a widely accepted, even fashionable, style. Thus when *The Cabinet of Dr. Caligari* premiered, it hardly came as a shock to critics and audiences. Other Expressionist films quickly followed. The resulting stylistic trend lasted until the beginning of 1927.

What traits characterize Expressionism in the cinema? Historians have defined this movement in widely differing ways. Some claim that the true Expressionist films resemble *The Cabinet of Dr. Caligari* in using a distorted, graphic style of mise-en-scène derived from theatrical Expressionism. Of such films only perhaps half a dozen were made. Other historians classify a larger number of films as Expressionist because the films all contain some types of stylistic distortion that *function* in the same ways that the graphic stylization in *Caligari* does. By this broader definition (which we use here), there are close to two dozen Expressionist films, released between 1920 and 1927. Like French Impressionism, German Expressionism uses the various techniques of the medium—mise-en-scène, editing, and camerawork—in distinctive ways. We shall look first at these techniques, then go on to examine the narrative patterns that typically helped motivate the extreme stylization of Expressionism.

While the main defining traits of French Impressionism lay in the area of camerawork, German Expressionism is distinctive primarily for its use of mise-en-scène. In 1926, set designer Hermann Warm (who worked on *Caligari* and other Expressionist films) was

quoted as believing that "the film image must become graphic art."[1] Indeed, German Expressionist films emphasize the composition of individual shots to an exceptional degree. Any shot in a film creates a visual composition, of course, but most films draw our attention to specific elements rather than to the overall design of the shot. In classical films, the human figure is the most expressive element, and the sets, costume, and lighting are usually secondary to the actors. The three-dimensional space in which the action occurs is more important than are the two-dimensional graphic qualities on the screen.

In Expressionist films, however, the expressivity associated with the human figure extends into every aspect of the mise-en-scène. During the 1920s, descriptions of Expressionist films often referred to the sets as "acting" or as blending in with the actors' movements. In 1924, Conrad Veidt, who played Cesare in *Caligari* and acted in several other Expressionist films, explained, "If the decor has been conceived as having the same spiritual state as that which governs the character's mentality, the actor will find in that decor a valuable aid in composing and living his part. He will blend himself into the represented milieu, and both of them will *move* in the same rhythm."[2] Thus, not only did the setting function as almost a living component of the action, but the actor's body became a visual element.

In practice, this blend of set, figure behavior, costumes, and lighting fuses into a perfect composition only at intervals. A narrative film is not like the traditional graphic arts of painting or engraving. The plot must advance, and the composition breaks up as the actors move. In Expressionist films the action often proceeds in fits and starts, and the narrative pauses or slows

5.8 The old, sagging house in G. W. Pabst's *Der Schatz*.

5.9 The leaning buildings and lamppost in Wiene's *Raskolnikow,* an adaptation of *Crime and Punishment*.

5.10 A stairway in *Torgus* seems to lean dizzily, with a slender black triangle painted on each tread.

5.11, *left* In this famous shot from *The Cabinet of Dr. Caligari*, the diagonal composition of the wall dictates the movement of the actor, with his tight black clothes contributing to the compositional effect.

5.12, *right* In *Kriemhild's Revenge*, Marguerithe Schön's wide-eyed stare, her heavy makeup, the abstract shapes in her costume, and the blank background create a stylized composition completely in keeping with the rest of the film.

briefly for moments when the mise-en-scène elements align into eye-catching compositions. (Such compositions need not be wholly static. An actor's dancelike movement may combine with a stylized shape in the set to create a visual pattern.)

Expressionist films had many tactics for blending the settings, costumes, figures, and lighting. These included the use of stylized surfaces, symmetry, distortion, and exaggeration and the juxtaposition of similar shapes.

Stylized surfaces might make disparate elements within the mise-en-scène seem similar. For example, Jane's costumes in *Caligari* are painted with the same jagged lines as are the sets (see 5.2). In *Siegfried,* many shots are filled with a riot of decorative patterns (5.5). In *The Golem,* texture links the Golem to the distorted ghetto sets: both look as if they are made of clay (5.6).

Symmetry offers a way to combine actors, costumes, and sets so as to emphasize overall compositions. The Burgundian court in *Siegfried* (see 5.5) uses symmetry, as do scenes in most of Fritz Lang's films of this period. Another striking instance occurs in Hans Werckmeister's *Algol* (5.7).

Perhaps the most obvious and pervasive trait of Expressionism is the use of distortion and exaggeration. In Expressionist films, houses are often pointed and

twisted, chairs are tall, staircases are crooked and uneven (compare 5.8–5.10).

To modern viewers, performances in Expressionist films may look simply like extreme versions of silent-film acting. Yet Expressionist acting was deliberately exaggerated to match the style of the settings. In long shots, gestures could be dancelike as the actors moved in patterns dictated by the sets. Conrad Veidt "blend[s] himself into the represented milieu" in *Caligari* when he glides on tiptoe along a wall, his extended hand skimming its surface (**5.11**). Here, a tableau involves movement rather than a static composition.

This principle of exaggeration governed close-ups of the actors as well (**5.12**). In general, Expressionist actors worked against an effect of natural behavior, often moving jerkily, pausing, and then making sudden gestures. Such performances should be judged not by standards of realism but by how the actors' behavior contributed to the overall mise-en-scène.

A crucial trait of Expressionist mise-en-scène is the juxtaposition of similar shapes within a composition. Along with Robert Wiene and Fritz Lang, F. W. Murnau was one of the major figures of German Expressionism,

5.13, *left* Count Orlak and his guest are placed within a nested set of four archways, with the hunched back of the vampire and the rounded arms of Hutter echoing the innermost arch. (Arches become an important motif in *Nosferatu*, associated closely with the vampire and his coffin.)

5.14, *right* In Murnau's *Tartuffe*, the title character's pompous walk is set off against the legs of a huge cast-iron lamp.

5.15, *left* A woman's stance in *Der steinere Reiter* echoes the shape of the stylized tree behind her.

5.16, *right* In *Nosferatu*, the vampire creeps up the stairway toward the heroine, but we see only his shadow, huge and grotesque.

5.17 In *Tartuffe*, a high angle places an actor against a swirl of abstract lines created by a stairway.

yet his films contain relatively few of the obviously artificial, exaggerated sets that we find in other films of this movement. He did create, however, numerous stylized compositions in which the figures blended in with their surroundings (**5.13, 5.14**). A common ploy in Expressionist films is to pose human figures beside distorted trees to create similar shapes (**5.15**).

For the most part, Expressionist films used simple lighting from the front and sides, illuminating the scene flatly and evenly to stress the links between the figures and the decor. In some notable cases, shadows were used to create additional distortion (**5.16**).

Although the main traits of Expressionist style come in the area of mise-en-scène, we can make a few generalizations about its typical use of other film techniques. Such techniques usually function unobtrusively to display the mise-en-scène to best advantage. Most editing is simple, drawing upon continuity devices like

shot/reverse shot and crosscutting. In addition, German films are noted for having a somewhat slower pace than other films of this period. Certainly in the early twenties they have nothing comparable to the quick rhythmic editing of French Impressionism. This slower pace gives us time to scan the distinctive compositions created by the Expressionist visual style.

Similarly, the camerawork is typically functional rather than spectacular. Many Expressionist sets used false perspective to form an ideal composition when seen from a specific vantage point. Thus camera movement and high or low angles were relatively rare, and the camera tended to remain at a straight-on angle and an approximately eye-level or chest-level height. In a few cases, however, a camera angle could create a striking composition by juxtaposing actor and decor in an unusual way (**5.17**).

Like the French Impressionists, Expressionist filmmakers gravitated to certain types of narratives that suited the traits of the style. The movement's first film, *The Cabinet of Dr. Caligari*, used the story of a madman to motivate the unfamiliar Expressionist distortions for movie audiences. Because *Caligari* has remained the most famous Expressionist film, there is a lingering impression that the style was used mainly for conveying character subjectivity.

This was not the case in most films of the movement, however. Instead, Expressionism was often used for narratives that were set in the past or in exotic locales or that involved elements of fantasy or horror—genres that remained popular in Germany in the 1920s. *Der Schatz* takes place at an unspecified point in the past and concerns a search for a legendary treasure. The two feature-length parts of *Die Nibelungen, Siegfried* and *Kriemhild's Revenge,* are based on the national German epic and include a dragon and other magical elements in a medieval setting. *Nosferatu* is a vampire story set in the mid-nineteenth century, and in *The Golem,* the rabbi of the medieval ghetto in Prague animates a superhuman clay statue to defend the Jewish population against persecution. In a variant of this emphasis upon the past, the last major Expressionist film, *Metropolis,* is set in a futuristic city where the workers labor in huge underground factories and live in apartment blocks, all done in Expressionist style.

In keeping with this emphasis on remote ages and fantastic events, many Expressionist films have frame stories or self-contained stories embedded within the larger narrative structure. *Nosferatu* is supposedly told by the town historian of Bremen, where much of the action takes place. Within the narrative, the characters read books: the *Book of the Vampires* explains the basic premises of vampire behavior (exposition that would have been necessary, since this was the first of many vampire films), and entries in the log of the ship that carries Count Orlak to Bremen recount additional action. The central story of *Warning Shadows* (1923) consists of a shadow play that a showman puts on during a dinner party, with the shadow figures coming to life and acting out the guests' secret passions. *Tartuffe* begins and ends with a frame story in which a young man tries to warn his aging father that the housekeeper is out to marry him for his money; his warning takes the form of a film of Molière's play *Tartuffe,* which constitutes the inner story.

Some Expressionist films do take place in the present. Lang's *Dr. Mabuse, the Gambler* uses Expressionist style to satirize the decadence of modern German society: the characters patronize drug and gambling dens in nightclubs with Expressionist decor, and one couple lives in a lavish house decorated in the same style. In *Algol,* a greedy industrialist receives supernatural aid from the mysterious star Algol and builds up an empire; the sets representing his factories and the star are Expressionist in style. Thus, in the cinema, Expressionism had the same potential for social comment that it did on the stage. In most cases, however, filmmakers used the style to create exotic and fantastic settings that were remote from contemporary reality.

Kammerspiel

Another German trend of the early 1920s had less international influence but led to the creation of a number of major films. This was the *Kammerspiel,* or "chamber-drama" film. The name derives from a theater, the Kammerspiele, opened in 1906 by the major stage director Max Reinhardt to stage intimate dramas for small audiences. Few Kammerspiel films were made, but nearly all are classics: Lupu Pick's *Shattered* (1921) and *Sylvester* (aka *New Year's Eve* or *St. Sylvester's Eve,* 1923), Leopold Jessner's *Backstairs* (1921), Murnau's *The Last Laugh* (1924), and Carl Dreyer's *Michael* (1924). Remarkably, all these films except *Michael* were scripted by the important scenarist Carl Mayer, who also coscripted *The Cabinet of Dr. Caligari* and wrote other films, both Expressionist and non-Expressionist. Mayer is considered the main force behind the Kammerspiel genre.

In many ways these films contrasted sharply with Expressionist drama. A Kammerspiel film concentrated on a few characters and explored a crisis in their lives in detail. The emphasis was on slow, evocative acting and telling details, rather than extreme expressions of emotion. The chamber-drama atmosphere came from the use of a small number of settings and a concentration on character psychology rather than spectacle. Some Expressionist-style distortion might appear in the sets, but it typically suggested dreary surroundings rather than the fantasy or subjectivity of Expressionist films. (One Kammerspiel, *Erdgeist,* also scripted by Mayer and directed by Jessner, applied Expressionist sets and acting to an intimate, modern drama of lust and betrayal.) Indeed, the Kammerspiel avoided the fantasy and legendary elements so common in Expressionism; these were films set in everyday, contemporary surroundings, and they often covered a short span of time.

Sylvester takes place during a single evening in the life of a café owner. His mother visits his family for a New Year's Eve celebration. Jealousies and conflicts between the mother and the wife intensify until, as midnight strikes, the man commits suicide. Brief scenes of people celebrating in hotels and in the streets create an ironic contrast with the tensions of these three characters, but most of the action occurs in the small apartment (**5.18**). As with most major Kammerspiel films, *Sylvester* uses no intertitles, depending on simple situations, details of acting and setting, and symbolism to convey the narrative events.

Similarly, *Backstairs* balances two settings. The boardinghouse kitchen in which the housekeeper works

5.18 In *Sylvester,* a motif of shots using a mirror on the wall emphasizes the relationships among the characters within the family's drab home.

5.19 Much of the action in *Backstairs* consists of the mailman's trips back and forth across the courtyard as he visits the heroine.

and the apartment of her secret admirer, the mailman, stand opposite each other in a grubby courtyard (**5.19**). The film's action never moves outside this area. When the heroine's departed fiancé mysteriously fails to write to her, the mailman tries to console her by forging letters from him. Finally she visits the mailman in his little apartment—at which point the fiancé returns and is killed in a struggle with the mailman. The heroine then commits suicide by throwing herself into the courtyard from the top of the building.

As these examples suggest, the narratives of the Kammerspiel films concentrated on intensely psychological situations and concluded unhappily. Indeed, *Shattered, Backstairs,* and *Sylvester* all end with at least one violent death, and *Michael* closes with the death of its protagonist from illness. Because of the unhappy endings and claustrophobic atmospheres, these films intrigued mostly critics and highbrow audiences. Erich Pommer recognized this fact when he produced *The Last Laugh,* insisting that Mayer add a happy ending. This story of a hotel doorman who is demoted from his lofty post to that of lavatory attendant was to have concluded with the hero sitting in the rest room in despair, possibly dying. Mayer, upset at having to change what he saw as the logical outcome of his script's situation, added a blatantly implausible final scene in which a sudden inheritance turns the doorman into a millionaire to

whom all the hotel staff cater. Whether this ludicrously upbeat ending was the cause, *The Last Laugh* became the most successful and famous of the Kammerspiel films. By late 1924, however, the trend ceased to be a prominent genre in German filmmaking.

German Films Abroad

The historical spectacle, the Expressionist film, and the Kammerspiel drama helped the German industry break down prejudices abroad and gain a place on world film markets. Lubitsch's *Madame Dubarry* was one of the first postwar German films to succeed abroad. It showed in major cities in Italy, Scandinavia, and other European countries in 1920, becoming famous even in countries like England and France, where exhibitors had pledged not to show German films for a lengthy period after the war. In December 1920, *Madame Dubarry,* retitled *Passion,* broke box-office records in a major New York theater and was released throughout the United States by one of the largest distributors, First National. Suddenly American film companies were clamoring to buy German films, though few found the success of *Passion.*

More surprisingly, German Expressionism also proved an export commodity. There was particularly strong anti-German sentiment in France. Yet *The Cabinet of Dr. Caligari* had an international reputation by late 1921 (having already had a mildly successful release in America after its triumph in Germany). In September, French critic and filmmaker Louis Delluc arranged for *Caligari* to be shown as part of a program to benefit the Red Cross. So great was the film's impact that it opened in a regular Parisian cinema in April 1922. A fashion for German film followed. Works by Lubitsch, as well as virtually all the Expressionist and Kammerspiel films, played in France over the next five years. A similar fad for Expressionism hit Japan in the early twenties, and in many countries, these distinctive films had at least limited release in art houses.

MAJOR CHANGES IN THE MID- TO LATE 1920s

Despite these early successes, the German industry could not continue making films in the same way. Many factors led to major changes. Foreign technology and style conventions had considerable influence. Moreover, the protection afforded the industry by the high postwar inflation ended as the German currency was stabilized in

5.20   An elaborate use of false perspective in *The Last Laugh*.

5.21   Hollywood-style backlighting in *The Loves of Pharaoh*.

5.22   One portion of an elaborate tracking shot through a street in *Sylvester*.

1924. Success also created new problems, as prominent filmmakers were lured away to work in Hollywood. Continued emphasis on export led some studios to imitate Hollywood's product rather than seek alternatives to it. In the middle of the decade, a major trend called *Neue Sachlichkeit*, or "New Objectivity," displaced Expressionism in the arts. By 1929, the German cinema had changed greatly from its postwar situation.

The Technological Updating of the German Studios

Unlike in France, German technological resources for filmmaking developed rapidly over the course of the 1920s. Because inflation encouraged film companies to invest their capital in facilities and land, many studios were built or expanded. Ufa, for example, enlarged its two main complexes at Tempelhof and Neubabelsberg and soon owned the best-equipped studios in Europe, with an extensive backlot at Neubabelsberg that could accommodate several enormous sets. Here were made such epic productions as Lang's *The Nibelungen* and Murnau's *Faust*. Foreign producers, primarily from England and France, rented Ufa's facilities for shooting large-scale scenes. In 1922, an investment group converted a zeppelin hangar into the world's largest indoor production facility, the Staaken studio. The studio was rented to producing firms for sequences requiring large indoor sets. Scenes from such films as Lang's monumental *Metropolis* were shot at Staaken.

Other innovations during the 1920s responded to German producers' desire to give their films impressive production values. Designers pioneered the use of false perspectives and models to make sets look bigger. A marginal Expressionist film, *The Street* (1923) used an elaborate model to represent a cityscape in the background of one scene, with a real car and actors in the foreground. Tiny cars and dolls moving on tracks in the

distance in *The Last Laugh* made the street in front of the hotel set seem bigger than it really was (**5.20**). In this area, the Germans were ahead of the Americans, and Hollywood cinematographers and designers picked up tips on models and false perspective by watching German films and visiting the German studios.

Aside from making more spectacular scenes, German producers wanted to light and photograph their films using techniques innovated by Hollywood during the 1910s. Since the Germans were eager to export films to the United States, a widespread assumption arose that filmmakers should adopt the new elements of American style, such as backlighting and the use of artificial illumination for exterior shots. Articles in the trade press urged companies to build better facilities: dark studios in place of the old glass-walled ones, endowed with the latest in lighting equipment.

The installation of American-style lighting equipment began in 1921, when Paramount made a short-lived attempt at producing in Berlin. It outfitted a Berlin studio with the latest technology, painting over the glass roof to permit artificial lighting. There Lubitsch made one of his last German films, *Das Weib des Pharao* ("The Pharaoh's Wife," released in the United States as *The Loves of Pharaoh*, 1921), which was shot with extensive backlighting and effects lighting (**5.21**). By mid-decade, most major German films had the option of filming entirely with artificial light.

One German technological innovation of the 1920s became internationally influential: the *entfesselte camera* (literally, the "unfastened camera," or the camera moving freely through space). During the early 1920s, some German filmmakers began experimenting with elaborate camera movements. In the script for the Kammerspiel film *Sylvester*, Carl Mayer specified that the camera should be mounted on a dolly to take it smoothly through the revelry of a city street (**5.22**). The

Bolshevik party, which favored a Marxist revolution to bring the worker and peasant classes to power. When the provisional government failed to halt Russia's hopeless and unpopular struggle against Germany in World War I, the Bolshevik cause gained support, especially from the military. In October, Vladimir Lenin led a second revolution that created the Union of Soviet Socialist Republics.

The February Revolution had relatively little effect on the Russian film industry, which had expanded during the war. Films made just prior to the revolution appeared, and a few films with political subject matter were rushed through production. Evgenii Bauer, a leading prerevolutionary director, made *The Revolutionary,* released in April; it supported Russia's continued participation in World War I. Yakov Protazanov's *Father Sergius,* produced between the two revolutions, was released in 1918. This film carried on the tradition of the mid-1910s Russian cinema, with its emphasis on psychological melodrama (see pp. 60–62).

The Bolshevik Revolution in October created a far greater disruption in Russian life in general. Given that the Communists favored state ownership of all companies, existing film firms waited nervously to see what would happen. Coincidentally, Bauer died in the spring of 1917, and the illness of his producer, Alexander Khanzhonkov, ended that company's existence. Another major prerevolutionary producer, Alexander Drankov, left the USSR in the summer of 1918 and tried vainly to reestablish his business abroad. After a brief trial period of producing propaganda films commissioned by the new government, the Yermoliev troupe fled to Paris via the Crimea in 1919; there they established a successful company, Films Albatros (p. 90).

The logical first step for the new Marxist regime would have been for the government to acquire, or nationalize, the film industry. The Bolsheviks, however, were not yet powerful enough for this step. Instead, a new regulatory body, the People's Commissariat of Education (generally known as Narkompros), was assigned to oversee the cinema. The commissar, or head, of Narkompros was Anatoli Lunacharsky. He was interested in film and occasionally wrote scripts. Lunacharsky's sympathetic attitude later helped create favorable conditions for the Montage directors.

During the first half of 1918, Narkompros struggled to gain control over film production, distribution, and exhibition. A few Soviets, or local workers' governing bodies, set up their own production units, making propaganda films promoting the new society. For example, the Petrograd Cinema Committee produced *Cohab-*

6.1 *Cohabitation* ends with documentary shots of cheerful revolutionary soldiers, giving this rather crudely made early Soviet film an air of historical immediacy.

itation (1918), made by a collective of directors and scripted by Lunacharsky. Under Soviet rule, large houses that had previously belonged to rich families were divided to provide dwellings for poorer families. In *Cohabitation,* a well-to-do professor and a poor janitor work at the same school; when the janitor and his daughter are assigned to live in the professor's large home, the latter's wife objects. Eventually all learn to live together in harmony (**6.1**).

The year 1918 also saw the first directorial efforts of two young men who were to become major directors in the 1920s. In June, Dziga Vertov took charge of Narkompros's first newsreel; later he would be an important documentarist working in the Montage movement. Before the October Revolution, Lev Kuleshov made *Engineer Prite's Project* (released 1918) for the Khanzhonkov firm, where he had previously worked as a set designer. Only a few scenes from the film survive, but they indicate that, unlike his contemporaries in Russia, Kuleshov employed Hollywood-style continuity guidelines (**6.2–6.6**). Kuleshov's later teachings and writings explored the implications of Hollywood continuity style in detail.

Despite these tentative signs of progress, however, Soviet production received two serious blows during 1918. Because the companies that had fled after the revolution had taken whatever they could with them, the USSR badly needed production equipment and raw stock. (Neither was manufactured there.) In May, the government entrusted $1 million in credit to a film distributor who had operated in Russia during World War I, Jacques Cibrario. On a buying mission to the United States, Cibrario purchased worthless used material and absconded with most of the money. Russia had little foreign currency, and the loss was serious. It is little wonder that the government was reluctant to give the film industry further large sums. Another problem arose in June 1918, when a decree required that all raw stock held by private firms be registered with the government. The

6.2 A scene in *Engineer Prite's Project* uses continuity editing, as a woman seated at a window drops something to attract the attention of two men passing below.

6.3 A long shot shows them noticing the object.

6.4 In a cut-in, the hero picks it up.

6.5 In another shot, he looks up and right.

6.6 In the reverse shot, the woman looks back at him. The rest of the scene proceeds in standard continuity fashion.

remaining producers and dealers promptly hid what little raw film remained, and a severe shortage developed.

From 1918 to 1920, Soviet production, distribution, and exhibition were disorganized. Production remained low at first. Only six films were produced under state auspices in 1918. Sixty-three were made in 1919, but most of these were short newsreels and *agitki,* brief propaganda films with simple pro-Soviet messages. *Workers of All Lands, Unite!* (1919), for example, showed scenes from the history of the struggle of workers across the ages, linked by quotes from Karl Marx's *Communist Manifesto* (**6.7**). Conditions remained bleak, however, especially for the few private firms still producing films. When the Russ company set out in 1919 to adapt Tolstoy's *Polikushka,* lack of food, heat, and positive film stock created incredible difficulties. The film did not reach theaters until late 1922.

These were the years of the civil war in the USSR, as the Reds, or Bolshevik forces, fought the Whites, Russians opposed to the revolutionary government and supported by Britain, the United States, and other countries. In 1920, the Bolsheviks won, but at a terrible cost.

During the civil war, a major concern was to get films out to troops and villagers in the countryside. Many of

6.7 An actor playing Karl Marx sits before a map of Europe, writing the *Communist Manifesto.* The superimposed clasping workers' hands symbolize his inspiration for the famous command (and the film's title) *Workers of All Lands, Unite!*

6.16 Biomechanical acting, work clothes, and a machine-like set in *The Magnanimous Cuckold*.

of some enduring higher truth, as many nineteenth-century views of art had held. The artist was not an inspired visionary; he or she was a skilled artisan using the materials of the medium to create an artwork. Artists were often compared to engineers, using tools and a rational, even scientific approach.

The Constructivists also often compared the artwork to a machine. While earlier views of art frequently saw the artwork as analogous to a plant, with an organic unity and growth, the Constructivists stressed that it was put together from parts. This process of assemblage was sometimes referred to as *montage*, from the French word for the assembly of parts into a machine. (As we have seen, filmmakers applied the term *montage* to the editing of shots into a film.) This analogy between artwork and machine was seen positively. Because Soviet society focused on enhancing the USSR's industrial output, and also because communism stressed the dignity of human labor, the factory and the machine became symbols of the new society. Artists' studios were often seen as factories where laborers built useful products.

Because all human response was seen as based on scientifically determinable processes, the Constructivists considered that an artwork could be calculated to elicit a particular reaction. Thus artworks could be used for propagandistic and educational purposes promoting the new communist society—if only the right ways of making them could be discovered. Many artists therefore jettisoned the notion that elite art forms (like opera and

painting) were superior to popular art forms (like circus and poster). Art should be understandable to all, particularly to the workers and peasants so central to the Bolshevik cause.

Constructivism resulted in an extraordinary fusion of abstract graphic design and practical function. For example, El Lissitsky used a geometric composition straight out of Suprematism for a 1920 propaganda poster supporting the Bolshevik side in the civil war (**Color Plate 6.1**). Constructivist artists designed textiles, book covers, workers' uniforms, street kiosks, even ceramic cups and saucers—many using modernist abstract shapes.

In the early 1920s, Constructivism also affected the theater. The most important Constructivist theatrical director was Vsevolod Meyerhold, an established figure who offered his services to the Bolshevik government immediately after the revolution. Meyerhold's bold methods of staging were to influence Soviet film directors. Set and costume designs in several major Meyerhold productions incorporated Constructivist design principles. In his 1922 production of *The Magnanimous Cuckold*, for example, the set somewhat resembled a large factory machine; it consisted of a series of bare platforms, with their supporting legs visible and a large propeller turning during the play. The actors performed in ordinary work clothes (**6.16**). Meyerhold also pioneered the principle of *biomechanical acting*. The actor's body was assumed to be like a machine, and thus a performance consisted of carefully controlled physical movements rather than of the expression of inner emotions. Meyerhold's actors trained by doing exercises to gain mastery over their bodies, and their performances had an acrobatic quality.

A New Generation: The Montage Filmmakers

During the first half of the 1920s, when all these sweeping changes were revolutionizing the arts, a new generation of filmmakers was moving into the cinema. For them, the revolution was a crucial formative event—partly because they were extraordinarily young. Indeed, Sergei Eisenstein was nicknamed "the old man" by his younger friends because he was all of twenty-six when he began his first feature film. Born in 1898, Eisenstein came from a middle-class family in Riga, Latvia. His education gave him fluency in Russian, English, German, and French. He recalled that, while on a visit to Paris at age 8, he saw a Méliès film and became interested in the cinema. Two years later he visited the circus and became similarly obsessed with this popular spectacle. Following his father's wishes, he began studying engineering in 1915. Eisenstein participated in the revolution and during the civil war put his engineering skills to work building bridges. He was drawn to the arts, however, and during this same period he also decorated agit-trains and helped design many theatrical skits for the Red Army. The combination of engineering and artistic work seemed anything but contradictory in the era of Constructivism, and throughout his life Eisenstein likened the production of his films to the building of those bridges.

In 1920, at the end of the civil war, Eisenstein went to Moscow and joined the Proletkult Theater (short for Proletarian, or Workers', Cultural Theater). There he designed and codirected many plays. In 1921, Eisenstein (along with his friend, Sergei Yutkevich, another future Montage film director) enrolled in a theater workshop under the supervision of Meyerhold, whom he would always consider his mentor. In 1923, Eisenstein directed his first theatrical production, *Enough Simplicity in Every Wise Man*. Although the play was a nineteenth-century farce, Eisenstein staged it as a circus. The actors dressed in clown costumes and performed in the acrobatic biomechanical style, walking on a tightrope above the audience or doing handstands as they spoke their lines. Eisenstein also produced *Glumov's Diary*, a short film to be shown on a screen on the stage (**6.17**). At the same time that this play was performed, Eisenstein gained some early experience as a film editor: along with Esfir Shub (soon to become an important maker of compilation documentaries), he reedited a

6.17   At the end of *Glumov's Diary*, Eisenstein takes a bow in front of a poster for the play *Enough Simplicity in Every Wise Man*. At his chin level are written "Montage of Attractions" and "Eisenstein."

German Expressionist film, Fritz Lang's *Dr. Mabuse, the Gambler*, for Soviet release.

Eisenstein always maintained that his move from the theater to film came in 1924, when he directed a production of playwright S. M. Tretyakov's *Gas Masks*, not in a theater but in a real gas factory. According to Eisenstein, the contrast between the reality of the setting and the artifice of the drama was too great. A few months later, he began work on *Strike* (released in early 1925)—a film set and shot in a factory. It was the first major film of the Montage movement, and Eisenstein went on to make three more important works in that style: *Potemkin, October* (aka *Ten Days That Shook the World* in an abridged version), and *Old and New*. *Potemkin* was extremely successful abroad, which gave Eisenstein and his colleagues considerable leeway for experimentation over the next few years. Many Montage films proved more popular abroad than in the USSR, where they were often accused of being too difficult for workers and peasants to understand.

The oldest Montage director in years and experience was Lev Kuleshov, who had designed and directed films before the revolution and then taught at the State Film School. Kuleshov's own Soviet films were only mildly experimental in style, but his workshop produced two important Montage directors.

Vsevolod Pudovkin had intended to train as a chemist until he saw D. W. Griffith's *Intolerance* in 1919. Convinced of the cinema's importance, he soon joined Kuleshov's workshop and trained as both an actor and a director. His first feature film typified the Constructivist interest in the physical bases of psychological response; he made *Mechanics of the Brain*, a documentary about Ivan Pavlov's famous experiments on stimulus-response physiology. In 1926, Pudovkin (born in 1893) helped

A Chronology of the Soviet Montage Movement

1917 — February: Tsar Nicholas II is overthrown; the provisional government is established.
October: The Bolshevik Revolution

1918 — Narkompros (the People's Commissariat of Education) takes charge of regulating the film industry.

1919 — August: Nationalization of the film industry
Foundation of the State Film School

1920 — Lev Kuleshov joins the State Film School and forms his workshop.

1921 — The New Economic Policy is instituted.

1922 — Formation of Goskino, the state film distribution monopoly

1923 — Publication of Sergei Eisenstein's essay, "Montage of Attractions"

1924 — *Kino-Eye*, Dziga Vertov
The Extraordinary Adventures of Mr. West in the Land of the Bolsheviks, Lev Kuleshov

1925 — January: Formation of Sovkino, the new government distribution monopoly and production company
Strike, Sergei Eisenstein
Potemkin, Sergei Eisenstein

1926 — *Mother*, Vsevolod Pudovkin
The Devil's Wheel, Grigori Kozintsev and Leonid Trauberg
The Cloak, Grigori Kozintsev and Leonid Trauberg

1927 — *Zvenigora*, Alexander Dovzhenko
The House on Trubnoya, Boris Barnet
The End of St. Petersburg, Vsevolod Pudovkin
Moscow in October, Boris Barnet
SVD, Grigori Kozintsev and Leonid Trauberg

1928 — March: The First Communist Party Conference on Film Questions is held.
October (aka *Ten Days That Shook the World*), Sergei Eisenstein
The Heir of Ghenghis-Khan (aka *Storm over Asia*), Vsevolod Pudovkin
Lace, Sergei Yutkevich

1929 — Sergei Eisenstein begins travels that will keep him abroad until 1932.
The New Babylon, Grigori Kozintsev and Leonid Trauberg
My Grandmother, Kote Mikaberidze
China Express (aka *Blue Express*), Ilya Trauberg
Man with a Movie Camera, Dziga Vertov
Arsenal, Alexander Dovzhenko
Old and New (aka *The General Line*), Sergei Eisenstein

1930 — Formation of Soyuzkino, a centralized company to control all production, distribution, and exhibition
Earth, Alexander Dovzhenko

1931 — *Alone*, Grigori Kozintsev and Leonid Trauberg
Golden Mountains, Sergei Yutkevich

1932 — *A Simple Case*, Vsevolod Pudovkin

1933 — *Deserter*, Vsevolod Pudovkin

found the Montage movement with his first fiction feature, *Mother*. Within the USSR, *Mother* was the most popular of all Montage films. As a result, Pudovkin enjoyed the highest approval from the government of any of the movement's directors, and he was able to keep up his experiments with Montage longer than any of the others—up until 1933. Another Kuleshov workshop member, Boris Barnet (born 1902) had studied painting and sculpture, and he trained as a boxer after the revolution. He acted in *The Extraordinary Adventures of Mr. West in the Land of the Bolsheviks* and other mid-1920s films, and he also directed *The House on Trubnoya* (1927) and other Montage-style films.

The other important filmmaker who, along with Kuleshov, had started directing about the time of the revolution was Dziga Vertov (born 1896). During the mid-1910s, he wrote poetry and science fiction, composed what we now call *musique concrète*, and became influenced by the Cubo-Futurists. From 1916 to 1917, however, he studied medicine until becoming the supervisor of Narkompros's newsreel series in 1917. He went on, in 1924, to make feature-length documentaries, some employing the Montage style.

The youngest Montage directors came out of the Leningrad theater milieu of the early 1920s. In 1921, while still in their teens, Grigori Kozintsev (born 1905), Leonid Trauberg (born 1902), and Sergei Yutkevich (born 1904) formed the Factory of the Eccentric Actor (FEKS). This theatrical troupe enthusiastically embraced the circus, the popular American cinema, the cabaret, and other entertainments. They issued provocative manifestos in the manner of the Cubo-Futurists' "Slap in the Face of Public Taste" (1912). In 1922, the FEKS group defined how their approach to acting departed from that of the traditional theater: "from emotion to the machine, from anguish to the trick. The technique—circus. The psychology—head over heels."[1] They staged theatrical events that adopted the techniques of popular entertainments, and by 1924, they moved into the cinema with a short parody of American serials, *The Adventures of Oktya brina* (now lost). Yutkevich went on to make Montage films on his own; Kozintsev and Trauberg codirected several important films of the movement. Because of their taste for bizarre experimentation, the FEKS group were criticized by government officials from the start of their careers.

Eisenstein, Kuleshov, Pudovkin, Vertov, and the FEKS group were the principal early exponents of Soviet Montage. Other directors picked up their influences and developed the style. In particular, filmmakers working in the non-Russian republics enriched the Montage movement. Foremost among these was Alexander Dovzhenko, the principal Ukrainian director. Dovzhenko had been in the Red Army during the civil war and served as a diplomatic administrator in Berlin in the early 1920s. There he studied art, returning to the Ukraine as a painter and cartoonist. In 1926, he suddenly switched to filmmaking and made a comedy and a spy thriller before directing his first Montage film, *Zvenigora*, in 1927. Based on obscure Ukrainian folk legends, *Zvenigora* baffled audiences but demonstrated an original style that emphasizes lyrical imagery above narrative. Dovzhenko went on to make two more important Montage films, *Arsenal* and *Earth*, also set in the Ukraine.

The Theoretical Writings of Montage Filmmakers

The mid-1920s saw a burgeoning in Soviet film theory, as critics and filmmakers sought to understand cinema scientifically. Like the French Impressionists, several Montage directors considered theory and filmmaking to be closely linked, and they wrote about their conceptions of cinema. They were united in an opposition to traditional films. All saw in Montage the basis of revolutionary films that would inspire audiences. But the writings of the Montage directors differed in important ways.

In many respects, Kuleshov was the most conservative theorist of the group. He admired the succinct storytelling of American films, and he discussed Montage chiefly as techniques of editing for clarity and emotional effects. This conception of Montage influenced Pudovkin, whose two 1926 pamphlets on filmmaking were soon translated into western languages (in English as *Film Language*, 1929). Through Pudovkin, *Montage* came to refer generally to dynamic, often discontinuous, narrative editing.

Vertov was far more radical. A committed Constructivist, he emphasized the social utility of documentary film. Vertov saw the fiction films of his contemporaries as "cine-nicotine," a drug that dulled the viewer's awareness of social and political reality. For him, "life caught unawares" would be the basis of a cinema of fact. Montage was less a single technique than the entire production process: choosing a subject, shooting footage, and assembling the film all involved selection and combination of "cine-facts." As for editing, Vertov emphasized that the filmmaker should calculate the differences between shots—light versus dark, slow motion versus fast motion, and so on. These differences, or "intervals," would be the basis of the film's effect on the audience.

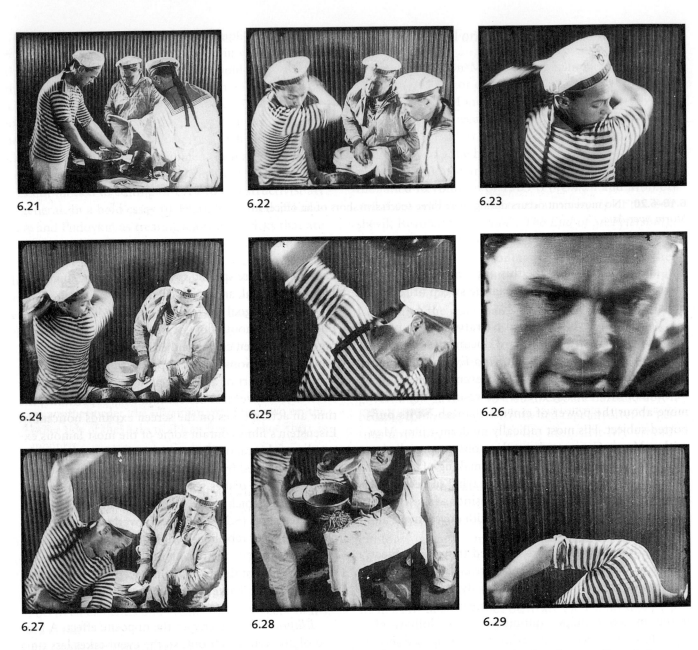

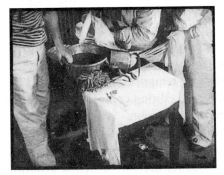

6.21–6.30 Ten shots in the plate-smashing scene from *Potemkin*, showing the repeated action of the sailor raising his arm in contradictory directions.

Then, after *La Roue* and other fast-cut French Impressionist films were shown in the USSR in 1926, Montage filmmakers began to use strings of two- and one-frame shots. In most cases, however, rapid editing does not convey characters' subjective perceptions, as it would in French films. Instead, fast cutting may suggest rhythmic sound (**6.32**) or enhance the effect of explosive, often violent, action (**6.33**).

As these examples of temporal relationships among shots suggest, Montage editing can also create conflict through spatial relationships. Again, the filmmakers do not guide the spectator through a clear, straightforward locale, as in a Hollywood film. Rather, the viewer must actively piece together what is going on. In the plate-

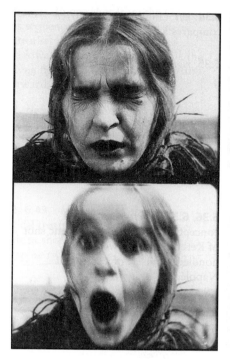

6.31, *left*   A jump cut in *The House on Trubnoya*: two successive close-ups show a woman's terrified face as she sees a streetcar bearing down on her; in the first her eyes are tightly closed, but a cut reveals them suddenly open.

6.32, *center*   In *October*, a rapid burst of two-frame shots suggests the rat-tat of a machine gun.

6.33, *right*   Near the end of *Storm over Asia*, the Mongolian hero rebels against the British colonialists who have exploited him; single-frame shots alternate between him swinging his sword and the sword itself flashing against a dark background.

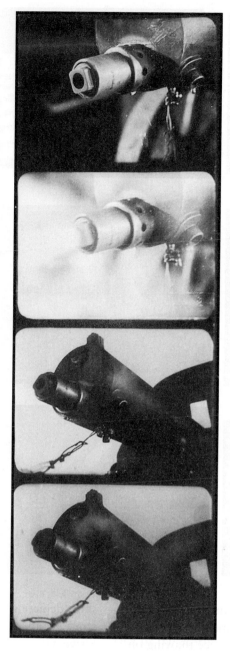

smashing scene from *Potemkin*, for example, Eisenstein creates a contradictory space by mismatching the sailor's position from shot to shot. The sailor swings the plate down from behind his left shoulder (see 6.24) and then is seen in the next shot with the plate already lifted above his right shoulder (see 6.25).

The Soviet filmmakers also used intercutting to create unusual spatial relationships. As we have seen, intercutting was common in the cinema from the early teens, and it most often presented simultaneous actions in different spaces (as in Griffith's *The Birth of a Nation*, p. 73). In the USSR, it also served more abstract purposes, linking two actions for the sake of a thematic point. Near the end of *Strike*, for example, Eisenstein cuts from a police officer bringing his fists down violently as he orders a massacre of the strikers (**6.34**) to a butcher's hands bringing a knife down to kill a bull (**6.35**). The scene continues to cut between the death of the animal and the attack on the workers—not to suggest that these two events are happening simultaneously,

6.46, 6.47 Two quick shots from the demonstration scene in *Mother*.

6.48 A dynamic angle in *China Express*.

6.49 The heroine of *Mother* in the demonstration scene.

6.50 In *Arsenal*, a train carrying Ukrainian soldiers seems to rush upward at a steep angle, emphasizing its dynamic thrust.

6.51 In *The End of St. Petersburg*, Pudovkin satirized profiteers who wanted to carry on with Russia's participation in World War I by showing them only from the neck down.

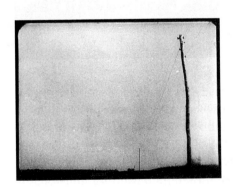 

6.52, *left* In *Earth*, Dovzhenko repeatedly emphasized the vast farmlands of the Ukraine through framings that show almost nothing but sky.

6.53, *right* Pudovkin used a similar device in *Deserter* to suggest the vulnerability of a workers' demonstration about to be attacked by police.

threatening (**6.48**) or heroic (**6.49**). Canted or decentered framings dynamize the image (**6.50, 6.51**). The Montage directors were also fond of placing the horizon line extremely low in the frame (**6.52, 6.53**).

Special Effects Montage directors also exploited special effects cinematography. Vertov's playful documentary *Man with a Movie Camera* shows off the power of the cinema through split-screen framing and superimpositions (**6.54**). Eisenstein's film about collective farming, *Old and New*, uses a superimposition of a bull towering above a field full of cows to suggest how important this one animal has been to the building of a successful farm (**6.55**). While such camera tricks were likely used for subjective effects in French Impressionism, Soviet directors often employed them to make symbolic

6.54 In *Man with a Movie Camera*, Vertov makes a huge building split like a broken egg by exposing each side of the frame separately and rolling the camera in opposite directions for each.

6.55 A conceptual use of special effects in *Old and New*.

6.56 In *Potemkin*, an officer glances suspiciously at some sailors. The composition splits into two distinct halves, dark and bright, with the lighting on the figures' faces matching the color of their costumes.

6.57 In *The New Babylon*, the heroine stands atop a barricade built by the Paris communards; her plain dress contrasts with the lacy frills on a department-store mannequin.

6.58 In *Potemkin*, a high-angle shot down the side of the battleship shows men on the upper level, moving left to right, while the group on the deck below move right to left.

6.59 A contrast in volumes in *Old and New*, as a bull looms hugely in the foreground while farmers and a cow appear as tiny figures below it.

points. (The building that "splits" in *Man with a Movie Camera* is the Bolshoi Theater in Moscow, home of traditional prerevolutionary opera and ballet.)

Mise-en-Scène   Because many Soviet films dealt with historical and social situations, some elements of their mise-en-scène tended to be realistic. Scenes might be shot on location in a factory, as *Strike* and *Mother* were. Costumes often served primarily to indicate class position. Yet the Montage filmmakers also realized that dynamic tension between elements was not solely a matter of joining shots. Juxtapositions could be made within the shot as well, using mise-en-scène elements to heighten the impact on the viewer. Contrasting textures, shapes, volumes, colors, and the like could be placed within a single frame (**6.56, 6.57**).

We have seen how shots containing opposed directions of movement might be edited together. A single

shot can use this principle by setting up more than one direction of figure movement (**6.58**). Patterns might also create oppositions within the shot; in the plate-smashing scene from *Potemkin* (see 6.21–6.30), the horizontal stripes of the sailor's shirt clash with the vertical stripes of the wall behind him. Although the precise effect of the juxtaposition is difficult to define, we can imagine that our impression of the scene would be very different if the wall were simply blank. Also, mise-en-scène elements arranged in different planes in the depth of the shot could create juxtapositions of volume (**6.59, 6.60**). When shots with visual juxtapositions are edited together with other shots, the multiple conflicting relationships can be complex indeed.

Lighting also gives Montage films a distinctive look. Soviet films frequently used no fill light on the sets, so characters appeared against black backgrounds. Note in **6.61** how the front of the officer's face is relatively

6.60 Similarly, *A Simple Case* arranges rows of mounted soliders in depth, so that some appear large and some small.

6.61 A typical use of an unlit background in *Mother*.

6.62 For the unglamorous role of the peasant heroine of *Old and New*, Eisenstein cast a real peasant.

6.63, *left* In *The Extraordinary Adventures of Mr. West in the Land of the Bolsheviks*, Khokhlova uses eccentric acting in playing a crook who vamps Mr. West.

6.64, *right* A Montage-style framing in a non-Montage film, *The White Eagle*.

dark, while the sides are strongly lit; this approach to lighting actors is common in Montage films.

Montage films used a variety of types of acting, ranging from realistic to highly stylized—often within the same film. Because so many characters in Soviet films represented certain social classes or professions, directors used *typage*, casting nonactors whose physical appearances would instantly suggest what sort of people they were playing (**6.62**). There was no need for the nonactor to have the same job in real life; for *Potemkin*, Eisenstein chose the small, fastidious man who plays the doctor because he "looked" like a doctor—though he actually made his living shoveling coal.

Typage was a gesture toward realism, but many performers in Montage films borrowed stylized techniques from Constructivist theater and from the circus: *biomechanics* and *eccentricity*. As in the theater, biomechanical film acting stressed physical control rather than subtle emotion. The Montage filmmakers delighted in having their actors punch one another or scramble about over factory equipment. Eccentricity emphasized the grotesque; performers behaved almost like clowns or slapstick comics. Alexandra Khokhlova, Kuleshov's

wife and a member of his workshop, offered vivid instances of eccentric acting. Tall and gangly, she avoided the glamorous image of the female star; instead, she grimaced and used angular gestures (**6.63**). Eisenstein's *Strike* and Kozintsev and Trauberg's silent films all contain eccentric performances.

Of the three avant-garde movements we have examined in Chapters 4 through 6, only the Soviet Montage style lasted into the early sound era. In Chapter 9 we shall discuss how the Montage filmmakers applied their approach to sound.

OTHER SOVIET FILMS

During the Montage movement's existence, perhaps fewer than thirty films were made in the style. Nevertheless, as in France and Germany, these avant-garde films were prestigious and influential. Many more conventional films contain a few Montage techniques, usually employed in a milder fashion. For example, Protazanov's *The White Eagle* (1928) begins with several dynamic

6.65, 6.66 In *The Tailor from Torzhok*, the star mugs broadly, at one point glancing at the camera and crossing his eyes.

6.67, *left* In 1926, the acclaimed theater actor, Leonid Leonidov appeared as Ivan the Terrible in Yuri Tarich's *Wings of a Serf;* his performance aided the film's widespread success abroad.

6.68, *right* Lavish production values in a conventional Soviet film, *Decembrists.*

views of statues against the sky (**6.64**), a device that had become a cliché. Although *The White Eagle* story is similar to those of some Montage films—the brutal repression of a strike by a provincial Tsarist governor—the rest of the film is done in the modified continuity style typical of European filmmaking in the 1920s.

Non-Montage films covered a wide range of genres. Although Soviet silent comedies are seldom seen today, there were plenty of them. Slapstick comedian Igor Ilinsky, a sort of Russian Jim Carrey, was the decade's most popular star. In *The Tailor from Torzhok* (made by Protazanov in 1925 to publicize the government lottery), Ilinsky plays a tailor frantically seeking a winning lottery ticket he has lost (**6.65, 6.66**). A light tone also prevails in the crime serial *Miss Mend* (codirected by veteran filmmakers Fyodor Ozep and Barnet, a Kuleshov alumnus, in 1925). In this fantasy, three American workers from the "Rockefeller" company hear of a plot to poison the Soviet Union's water supply and, in a spirit of class solidarity, foil the villain.

Despite the Montage directors' downplaying of major stars, other films exploited the fame of established stage actors by casting them in dramas. In a few cases, top stars of the famous Moscow Art Theater, established by Konstantin Stanislavsky in 1898 (and considered by many young filmmakers to be a bastion of conservative style), agreed to act in films (**6.67**). Other

Moscow Art Theater actors such as Ivan Moskvin and Mikhail Chekhov starred in films, and the only surviving film performance by the great Constructivist stage director Meyerhold is in *The White Eagle.*

A similar attempt at prestige came with historical epics and literary adaptations. Two popular films of this type were Viktor Gardin's *Poet and Tsar* (1927), a biography of the poet Aleksandr Pushkin, and *Decembrists* (1927, Alexander Ivanovsky). In a 1927 meeting to discuss the problems of Sovkino, Cubo-Futurist poet Vladimir Mayakovsky dismissed the former film contemptuously: "Take 'Poet and Tsar' for example. The picture is liked—but when you stop to think about it, what bosh, what a monstrosity."[3] Similarly, *Decembrists*, with its large ballroom set (**6.68**), looked like a tired version of Russian historical dramas of the prerevolutionary era. The Montage directors found such films conservative and thus diametrically opposed to their own approaches to filmmaking.

THE FIRST FIVE-YEAR PLAN AND THE END OF THE MONTAGE MOVEMENT

As we have seen, several of the early Montage films were successfully exported and were praised at home for their political content. As a result, between 1927 and 1930, the movement's activities intensified. At the same time, however, criticisms were increasingly being leveled at the Montage filmmakers by government and film-industry officials. The main charge was *formalism*, a vague term implying that a film was too complex for mass audiences and that its makers were more interested in film style than in correct ideology.

Ironically, the very recovery of the film industry, which the export of Montage films helped create, led to criticisms of the movement. In 1927, for the first time, the industry made more money from its own films than from imported ones. Official policy encouraged the industry to cut back its foreign trade. Sovkino and Lunacharsky came under attack for making films—including those of the Montage movement—that were more appropriate for sophisticated foreigners than for the uneducated peasant population at home. And as Montage filmmakers experimented with increasingly complex techniques, accusations of formalism intensified.

Criticized by the press, the major filmmakers had difficulties getting scripts approved and projects funded. Kuleshov came under fire first. Then Vertov had to move from his base in Moscow to make *Man with a Movie Camera* for the Ukrainian national company Vufku. Critics also charged that Kozintsev and Trauberg's eccentric stylization was frivolous and obscure. Eisenstein's early prestige, gained through *Potemkin*, protected him at first, but as he explored the possibility of creating abstract ideas through intellectual montage in the late 1920s, he too faced growing criticisms. For a time, Pudovkin was spared such attacks, and he managed to keep making Montage-style films until 1933, when his *Deserter* brought the movement to a close.

A turning point for the Soviet film industry came in March 1928, when the First Communist Party Conference on Film Questions was held. Until now, the government had left film matters largely to the control of Narkompros and other, smaller film organizations scattered through the republics. Now the Soviet Union was instituting the First Five-Year Plan, a major push toward expanding industrial output. As part of the plan, the cinema was to be centralized. The goal was to increase the number of films made and to build equipment factories to supply all the industry's needs. Eventually, it was hoped, imports of raw film stock, cameras, lighting fixtures, and other equipment would be eliminated. Similarly, exportation would not be necessary, and all films could be tailored strictly to the needs of the workers and peasants.

The implementation of the First Five-Year Plan in the cinema came slowly. Over the next two years, the government still put little money into the industry. This delay probably helped prolong the Montage movement. Soon, however, circumstances changed. In 1929, Eisenstein left the country to study sound filmmaking abroad. Spending most of his time working on abortive projects, first in Hollywood and then in Mexico, he did not return until 1932. Also in 1929, control over the cinema was taken away from Narkompros and turned over to the Movie Committee of the Soviet Union. Now Lunacharsky had little input, being only one of many members of the new body. In 1930, the film industry was further centralized by the formation of Soyuzkino, a company that was to supervise all production by the studios in the different republics and to handle all distribution and exhibition of films. The head of Soyuzkino was Boris Shumyatsky, a Communist party bureaucrat without film experience. Unlike Lunacharsky, Shumyatsky had no sympathy for the Montage filmmakers.

Soon the attacks on those filmmakers intensified. In 1931, for example, while Eisenstein was still in North America, an article criticized his films for their supposed "petty bourgeois" tendencies. If Eisenstein could strengthen his ties to the proletariat, the author concluded, he might "create real revolutionary cinema productions. But we must on no account minimize the difficulties confronting him. The way out of this crisis is possible only through a stubborn campaign for reeducation, through merciless exposure and criticism of his first films."[4] All the major Montage filmmakers, and, indeed, modernist artists in every medium, eventually adopted more accessible styles.

The Soviet Montage movement's influence lingered, however. Leftist filmmakers in other countries, especially documentarists like Scottish-born John Grierson and Dutch Joris Ivens, adopted heroic, low-angle framings and dynamic cutting for similar propaganda purposes. Pudovkin's and Eisenstein's theoretical writings have been read by critics and filmmakers ever since they were translated, and more recently Kuleshov's essays have become available in English (see "Notes and Queries" following). Few filmmakers have used the full range of radical Montage devices, but in a modified fashion, the movement has had a broad influence.

During the early 1930s, the Soviet film industry moved toward an official policy that required all films to follow an approach called *Socialist Realism*. We shall examine the early era of intensified government control and Socialist Realism, from 1933 to 1945, in Chapter 12.

Notes and Queries

FILM INDUSTRY AND GOVERNMENTAL POLICY: A TANGLED HISTORY

The film industry of any major producing country has a complex history, of course, but the Soviet situation in the fifteen years after the Russian Revolution was particularly volatile. Many organizations disappeared soon after being formed. Government regulations attempted to make the industry both profitable and ideologically acceptable.

Several books offer detailed overviews. Jay Leyda's *Kino: A History of the Russian and Soviet Film,* 3rd ed. (Princeton, NJ: Princeton University Press, 1983) provides an anecdotal account that gives a vivid sense of the events of the period. In his *The Politics of the Soviet Cinema 1917–1929* (Cambridge: Cambridge University Press, 1979), Richard Taylor explores the workings of the industry and government policy. Denise Youngblood's *Soviet Cinema in the Silent Era, 1918–1935* (Ann Arbor: UMI Research Press, 1985) examines the kinds of criticism leveled at the Montage filmmakers, and she takes the history up to the institution of Socialist Realism as the film industry's official style. An older, but still interesting, source is Paul Babitsky and John Rimberg's *The Soviet Film Industry* (New York: Praeger, 1955). Many contemporary decrees and essays are translated in an anthology covering all aspects of Soviet cinema, *The Film Factory: Russian and Soviet Cinema in Documents 1896–1939,* ed. Richard Taylor and Ian Christie (Cambridge, MA: Harvard University Press, 1988).

THE KULESHOV EFFECT

Lev Kuleshov was an important theorist and teacher as well as a filmmaker. Modern historians have investigated the Kuleshov experiments and the "films without film," which the Kuleshov workshop staged in the early 1920s. Kuleshov's own accounts are available in English, in *Kuleshov on Film: Writings of Lev Kuleshov,* tr. and ed. Ronald Levaco (Berkeley: University of California Press, 1974); and *Lev Kuleshov: Fifty Years in Films,* tr. Dmitri Agrachev and Nina Belenkaya (Moscow: Raduga, 1987). Vance Kepley, Jr., discusses "The Kuleshov Workshop" in *Iris* 4, no. 1 (1986), an issue devoted to Kuleshov (with most of the articles in French). A lengthy essay by Stephen P. Hill, "Kuleshov—Prophet without Honor?" appears in *Film Culture* 44 (spring 1967). On Kuleshov's experiment *The Created Surface of the Earth,* see Yuri Tsivian, Ekaterina Khokhlova, and Kristin Thompson, "The Rediscovery of a Kuleshov Experiment: A Dossier," *Film History* 8, no. 3 (1996): 357–64.

THE RUSSIAN FORMALISTS AND THE CINEMA

During the period from 1914 to around 1930, a group of literary critics with close ties to the Cubo-Futurist and Constructivist movements created an important theoretical school called Russian Formalism. The Russian Formalists believed that artworks obeyed different principles than did other kinds of objects and that the theorist's task was to study how artworks were constructed to create certain effects. Working in Leningrad and Moscow, which were also the two centers of Russian film production, these critics wrote film reviews, essays on film theory, and even some scenarios for both Montage and non-Montage films. (For instance, Osip Brik scripted *Storm over Asia* and Viktor Shklovsky cowrote Kuleshov's 1926 *By the Law.*) Several Soviet filmmakers, including Eisenstein, the FEKS group, and Kuleshov, had close links to Russian Formalism, which influenced their theoretical writings. Like the Montage directors, the Russian Formalists were attacked and forced after 1930 into more conventional approaches.

One volume of the Russian Formalists' film theory, *The Poetics of Cinema,* was published in 1927; it has been translated by Herbert Eagle as *Russian Formalist Film Theory* (Ann Arbor: Michigan Slavic Publications, 1981) and by Richard Taylor as *The Poetics of Cinema* in *Russian Poetics in Translation,* no. 9 (1982). Essays by both Montage directors and Russian Formalist critics have been published in *Screen* 12, no. 4 (winter 1971/1972) and *Screen* 15, no. 3 (autumn 1974). Material on the FEKS group, Russian Formalism, and eccentrism is available in *Futurism, Formalism, FEKS: 'Eccentrism' and Soviet Cinema 1918–36,* ed. Ian Christie and John Gillett (London: British Film Institute, n.d.). Several essays by Viktor Shklovsky appear in Taylor and Christie's *The Film Factory* (cited above),

REFERENCES

1. Grigori Kozintsev, Leonid Trauberg, Sergei Yutkevich, and Georgi Kryzhitsky, "Eccentrism," tr. Richard Taylor, in *The Film Factory: Russian and Soviet Cinema in Documents 1896–1939,* ed. Taylor and Ian Christie (Cambridge, MA: Harvard University Press, 1988), p. 58.

2. Sergei Eisenstein, "The Cinematographic Principle and the Ideogram," in his *Film Form,* tr. and ed. Jay Leyda (New York: Harcourt, Brace & World, 1949), p. 37.

3. Quoted in Jay Leyda, *Kino: A History of the Russian and Soviet Film,* 3rd ed. (Princeton, NJ: Princeton University Press, 1983), p. 229.

4. Ivan Anisimov, "The Films of Eisenstein," *International Literature* 3 (1931): 114.

FURTHER READING

Kepley, Vance. "'Cinefication': Soviet Film Exhibition in the 1920s." *Film History* 6, no. 2 (summer 1994): 262–77.

———. "Federal Cinema: The Soviet Film Industry, 1924–32." *Film History* 8, no. 3 (1996): 344–56.

———. *In the Service of the State: The Cinema of Alexander Dovzhenko*. Madison: University of Wisconsin Press, 1986.

Michelson, Annette, ed. *Kino-Eye: The Writings of Dziga Vertov*. Berkeley: University of California Press, 1984.

Nebesio, Bhodan Y., ed., "The Cinema of Alexander Dovzhenko," special issue of *Journal of Ukrainian Studies* 19, no. 1 (summer 1994).

Taylor, Richard, and Ian Christie, eds. *Inside the Film Factory: New Approaches to Russian and Soviet Cinema*. London: Routledge, 1991.

Tsivian, Yuri. "Between the Old and the New: Soviet Film Culture in 1918–1924." *Griffithiana* 55/56 (September 1996): 15–63.

Youngblood, Denise J. *Movies for the Masses: Popular Cinema and Soviet Society in the 1920s*. Cambridge, England: Cambridge University Press, 1992.

THE LATE SILENT ERA IN HOLLYWOOD, 1920–1928

During World War I, the United States became a global economic leader. The center of world finance shifted from London to New York, and American ships carried goods all over the world. Despite a brief, intense recession in 1921, resulting primarily from the shift back to a peacetime economy, the 1920s were a period of prosperity for many sectors of society. Republican administrations were in power, and a conservative, probusiness approach dominated the country. American consumer goods, including movies, continued to make inroads in many foreign countries.

In contrast to this fiscal conservatism, society seemed to lose much of its restraint during the Roaring Twenties. The passage of the Volstead Act (1919), outlawing all forms of alcoholic beverages, led to the excesses of the age of Prohibition. Bootleg liquor was readily available, and flouting the law by visiting speakeasies or attending wild drinking parties became common even among the upper classes. Before the war, women had grown their hair long, worn floor-length dresses, and danced sedately. Now they created scandals by bobbing their hair, wearing short skirts, doing the Charleston, and smoking in public.

Many sectors of society, though, were shut off from the general prosperity and sophistication of the 1920s. Racism was rampant, with the Ku Klux Klan growing after its revival in 1915 and the stiffening of immigration quotas to keep certain groups out of the United States. Workers in agriculture and mining fared poorly. The film industry, however, benefited from the high level of capital available during this period, and its films reflected the fast pace of life in the Jazz Age.

THEATER CHAINS AND THE STRUCTURE OF THE INDUSTRY

The American film industry, expanding hugely during World War I, continued to grow during the postwar decade. Despite the short recession of 1921, the era was one of general prosperity and intensive business investment. For the first time, major Wall Street investment firms became interested in the young film industry, fueling its expansion. Between 1922 and 1930, total investment in the industry leaped from $78 to $850 million. The average weekly attendance at American movie theaters doubled from 1922 (40 million) to 1928 (80 million). Hollywood's exports continued to grow nearly unchecked until the mid-1920s and leveled off only because virtually all foreign markets were sated.

Central to the industry's expansion was a strategy of buying and building movie theaters. By owning theater chains, the big producers ensured an outlet for their films. Producers could then confidently raise budgets for individual films. Studios competed in offering eye-catching production values. A new generation of directors came to prominence, and Hollywood also attracted more foreign filmmakers, who brought stylistic innovations. If the 1910s had seen the basic formation of the film industry, the next decade witnessed its expansion into a sophisticated set of institutions.

Vertical Integration

The most obvious indication of the growth of the film industry was its increasing vertical integration. The biggest firms jockeyed for power by combining production and distribution with expanding chains of theaters.

At first, the main theater chains were regional. In 1917, in an attempt to challenge the power of the big Hollywood firms, a group of local theater chains formed its own production company, First National Exhibitors' Circuit. Its main member was the Stanley Company of America, a Philadelphia-based regional chain. Thus Hollywood firms like Famous Players–Lasky, Universal, and Fox were suddenly faced with a competitor that combined production, distribution, and exhibition.

This three-tiered vertical integration guaranteed that a company's films would find distribution and exhibition. The bigger the theater chain owned by the firm, the wider its films' exposure would be.

Although First National's production wing never became really profitable, it goaded other firms to integrate vertically. Adolf Zukor, head of Famous Players–Lasky and its distribution wing, Paramount, began buying theaters in 1920. In 1925, during a second wave of theater-buying by the major firms, Famous Players–Lasky merged with Balaban & Katz, a Chicago-based theater chain controlling many of the biggest auditoriums in the Midwest. The result was the first production-distribution-exhibition firm with a truly national theater chain. Zukor marked the change by naming the theater circuit Publix Theaters. The firm as a whole became Paramount-Publix. By the early 1930s, it owned 1,210 North American theaters, as well as some theaters abroad. Paramount-Publix's extensive holdings made it the subject of repeated government antitrust investigation and litigation that would lead to major changes in the film industry after World War II.

Another important firm that achieved vertical integration during this era was Loew's, Inc. Marcus Loew had begun as a nickelodeon owner, expanded into vaudeville, and built up a large chain of movie theaters by the late 1910s. In 1919, he moved into production by acquiring a medium-size firm, Metro, run by Louis B. Mayer. With the purchase of Goldwyn Pictures in 1924, Loew combined his production wing into Metro-Goldwyn-Mayer (MGM). After Paramount, MGM became the second largest of the Hollywood companies.

The chains owned by the vertically integrated firms encompassed a small portion of the nation's 15,000 theaters. In the mid-1920s, the Publix chain had roughly 500 houses, while MGM had a mere 200. Yet the three main chains included many of the big first-run theaters, with seating capacities in the thousands and higher admission prices. By late in the decade, about three-quarters of box-office receipts came from these large theaters. Smaller urban theaters and those in rural areas had to wait to get a film on a subsequent run and often received worn prints.

As the big Hollywood companies expanded, they developed a system of distribution that would maximize their profits and keep other firms at the margins of the market. In dealing with the theaters they did not own, they employed *block booking*, which meant that any exhibitor who wanted certain films with high box-office potential had to rent other, less desirable films from the same company. Some exhibitors might be forced to book an entire year's program in advance. Since most theaters changed programs at least twice a week and each big firm usually made only around fifty films a year, a theater could deal with more than one firm. Similarly, the big companies needed films from other firms to keep their theater programs full. Thus the biggest firms cooperated among themselves. The movie business developed into a mature oligopoly during the 1920s.

Picture Palaces

Because the big theaters were so important, the major companies made them opulent to attract patrons, not simply through the films being shown but through the promise of an exciting moviegoing experience. The 1920s were the age of the picture palace, seating thousands of patrons and offering fancy lobbies, uniformed ushers, and orchestral accompaniment to the films. The Balaban & Katz chain pioneered the use of air-conditioning in 1917; this was a major draw in a period when home air-conditioning was unknown and theater business ordinarily dropped off sharply in the summer months. Balaban & Katz houses and other big theaters also offered a lengthy film program in addition to the feature, including newsreels and comic shorts. Silent films always had musical accompaniment. In the big palaces, this would usually entail a live orchestra; a smaller palace might have a chamber group or pipe organ; and small-town and second-run houses could offer only a piano player. Any of these might perform an overture and musical interludes. Some theaters even had live-action playlets and musical numbers interspersed with the film program.

The architecture of the picture palaces gave working- and middle-class patrons an unaccustomed taste of luxury. There were two types of design: conventional and atmospheric. Conventional palaces were imitations of legitimate theaters, often incorporating elaborate ornamentation based on Italian baroque and rococo styles. Huge chandeliers, domes, and balconies were covered with stucco and gilt. The atmospheric palace gave the spectator the impression of sitting in an auditorium that opened onto a night sky. The dark-blue dome would have lightbulb stars, and moving clouds were cast onto the ceiling by projectors. The decor might imitate exotic places, such as a Spanish villa or an Egyptian temple. As the 1920s progressed, theaters got more and more flamboyant (**7.1**). The Depression would soon put an end to such extravagant theater building.

The Big Three and the Little Five

The vertically integrated firms that controlled big theater chains—Paramount-Publix, Loew's (MGM), and First National—constituted the Big Three at the top of the American film industry. Trailing behind them, but still important, were the Little Five, firms that owned few or no theaters: Universal, Fox, the Producers Dis-

7.1 Part of the interior of the Brooklyn Paramount (built in 1928). This theater combined conventional and atmospheric approaches to picture-palace design, incorporating trees and false sky glimpsed through the alcoves, topping it all with an elaborately decorated ceiling.

tributing Corporation, the Film Booking Office, and Warner Bros.

Under founder Carl Laemmle, Universal continued into the 1920s to concentrate on relatively low-budget films aimed at smaller theaters. Despite a strong distribution wing, the firm had few theaters. Universal attempted to build a chain in the mid-1920s but found the venture unprofitable and soon sold the theaters off. Several major directors (John Ford, Erich von Stroheim) and stars (Lon Chaney) worked there early in the decade, but they were soon drawn away by higher salaries. For a time Universal employed the successful young producer Irving Thalberg, who helped the firm move into higher-quality, big-budget films; soon Thalberg also left, becoming a major force in shaping MGM's policies. Later in the decade, German-born Laemmle was in the forefront in hiring émigré directors, who brought a brooding, distinctive style to the studio's output.

Fox also continued to concentrate on lower-budget popular fare, including its Westerns with William Farnum and Tom Mix. Fox began to create a modest theater chain in 1925, making it one of the strongest of the Little Five. The company had a small stable of prestige directors: John Ford, Raoul Walsh, F. W. Murnau, and Frank Borzage.

Warner Bros. was smaller, possessing neither theaters nor a distribution wing. It scored a considerable success, however, with a series of films starring a German shepherd, Rin-Tin-Tin. More surprisingly, Warners hired German director Ernst Lubitsch, and he made several important films there. In 1924, Warners drew upon the new willingness of Wall Street investors to put money into the film industry. It began a major expansion, acquiring theaters and other assets. The firm's investment in new sound technology would thrust it to the forefront of the industry within a few years.

The two other members of the Little Five were relatively small firms. The short-lived Producers Distributing Corporation (1924–1928) was notable mainly for producing a series of Cecil B. De Mille's films after he left Famous Players–Lasky in 1925. The Film Booking Office was formed in 1922 and turned out popular action films for several years. In 1929, it became the basis for the production portion of a much more important new firm, RKO.

Standing apart from both the Big Three and the Little Five was United Artists (UA), formed by Mary Pickford, Charles Chaplin, Douglas Fairbanks, and D. W. Griffith in 1919. UA, which was an umbrella distribution firm, owned neither production facilities nor theaters. It existed to distribute films produced independently by its four owners, who each had a small production company. Prior contractual commitments by the four founders delayed the firm's initial releases for a year, and Chaplin's first UA film, *A Woman of Paris*, was not a hit. In 1924, producer Joseph Schenck took over management of the firm. By adding stars Rudolph Valentino, Norma Talmadge, Buster Keaton, and Gloria Swanson, as well as prestigious producer Samuel Goldwyn, Schenck stepped up the rate of release of UA films. However, UA still failed to make a profit in most years.

THE MOTION PICTURE PRODUCERS AND DISTRIBUTORS OF AMERICA

As the American film industry expanded, so too did efforts on the part of various social groups to increase censorship. By the late 1910s and early 1920s, there was increasing pressure for a national censorship law, and more local boards were being formed. Many postwar films used the sort of subject matter associated with the Roaring Twenties: bootleg liquor, jazz music, flappers, and wild parties. Cecil B. De Mille's sex comedies presented adultery as a frivolous, even glamorous, pastime. Erich von Stroheim's *Blind Husbands* (1919) similarly treated a married woman's flirtation as a fascinating violation of social norms.

Soon a series of scandals focused attention on the less palatable aspects of the lifestyles of famous filmmakers, including sex scandals and flagrant violations of the new Prohibition law. Mary Pickford's image as America's sweetheart received a blow in 1920 when she divorced her first husband to marry Douglas Fairbanks. In 1921, comedian Roscoe "Fatty" Arbuckle was charged with rape and murder when a young actress died during a drunken party; although he was ultimately acquitted, the charges wrecked his career. The following year, director William Desmond Taylor was mysteriously murdered in circumstances that revealed his affairs with several well-known actresses. In 1923, the handsome, athletic star Wallace Reid died of morphine addiction. The public increasingly viewed Hollywood as promoting excess and decadence.

Partly in an effort to forestall censorship and clean up Hollywood's image, the main studios banded together to form a trade organization, the Motion Picture Producers and Distributors of America (MPPDA). To head it, in early 1922 they hired Will Hays, then postmaster general under Warren Harding. Hays had already proved his flair for publicity by chairing the Republican National Committee when Harding was elected president. That flair, combined with Hays's access to powerful figures in Washington and his Presbyterian background, made him useful to the film industry.

Hays's strategy was to pressure the producers to eliminate the offensive content of their films and to include morals clauses in studio contracts. Despite Arbuckle's acquittal on the rape and murder charges, Hays banned his films. In 1924, the MPPDA issued the "Formula," a vague document urging studios not to make the "kind of picture which should not be produced." Predictably, this had little effect, and in 1927 the Hays office (as the MPPDA came to be known) adopted the more explicit "Don'ts and Be Carefuls" list. "Don'ts" included "the illegal traffic in drugs," "licentious or suggestive nudity," and "ridicule of the clergy." "Be Carefuls" involved "the use of the flag," "brutality and possible gruesomeness," "methods of smuggling," and "deliberate seduction of girls." The list was as concerned with the depiction of how various crimes were committed as it was with sexual content. Producers continued to circumvent the guidelines, however, and in the early 1930s the list would be replaced by the much more elaborate Production Code (see Chapter 10).

Although the Hays Office is usually thought of as a strategy to block domestic censorship, the organization also performed other services for the industry. The MPPDA gathered information on film markets at home and abroad, keeping up, for example, with censorship regulations in various countries. Hays established a foreign department that battled several European quotas that stifled American exports. In 1926, Hays's group successfully lobbied Congress to form the Motion Picture Division of the Department of Commerce. That division then helped promote the sale of American films abroad by gathering information and bringing more pressure against harmful regulations. Indeed, the formation of the MPPDA provided a clear signal that motion pictures had become a major American industry.

STUDIO FILMMAKING

Style and Technological Changes

The expansion and consolidation of the Hollywood film industry was paralleled by a polishing of the classical continuity style that had developed in the 1910s.

By the 1920s, the big production firms had *dark studios* that kept out all sunlight and allowed entire scenes to be illuminated by artificial lights. Scenes' backgrounds were kept inconspicuous with a low *fill light,* while the main figures were outlined with a glow of *backlight,* usually cast from the rear top of the set (**7.2**). The *key,* or brightest light, came from one side of the camera, while a dimmer secondary light from the other side created fill that softened shadows and kept backgrounds visible but inconspicuous. This *three-point lighting system* (fill, backlighting, and key) became standard in Hollywood cinematography. It created glamorous, consistent compositions from shot to shot.

By the 1920s, the continuity editing system had become sophisticated indeed. Eyeline matches, cut-ins, and small variations of framing could successively reveal the most important portions of a scene's space. In John Ford's 1920 Western *Just Pals,* for example, a mother waits in anguish as her son supposedly drowns a litter of unwanted kittens. In fact, he only pretends that he has killed them. This complex action is gradually revealed without intertitles through a series of carefully framed details observed by the heroine (**7.3–7.11**).

7.2 Light coming from the upper rear of the set outlines the characters in *The Marriage Circle.*

By the late 1910s, most of the major technological innovations in American filmmaking had been made. One distinct change in the next decade was a new approach to cinematography. Before about 1919, most films were shot with a hard-edge, sharp-focus look. Some filmmakers began to place gauzy fabrics or filters in front of their lenses to create soft, blurry images. Special lenses could keep the foreground action in focus while making the background less distinct. This technique enhanced the classical narrative style by concentrating the spectator's attention on the main action while deemphasizing less important elements. The result of such techniques was the *soft style* of cinematography, used most extensively during the 1920s and 1930s. This style derived from still photography and especially the Pictorialist school, pioneered by such photographers as Alfred Stieglitz and Edward Steichen early in the century.

D. W. Griffith was one of the early proponents of this style. He worked with cinematographer Hendrick Sartov, who had begun as a still photographer, to film soft-focus shots of Lillian Gish and some landscapes in *Broken Blossoms* (1919). They further explored the approach in *Way Down East* (1920; **7.12, 7.13**). Other filmmakers pushed such techniques further. Erich von Stroheim sometimes placed coarse filters in front of the lens so that the scene was viewed through a textured screen (**7.14**). During the 1920s, the soft style became more common in cinematography. It was dominant by the early sound era and remained prominent until a new hard-edged style became fashionable in the 1940s.

Another major innovation of this era came with the gradual adoption of a new *panchromatic* type of film stock. The film stock used previously had been *orthochromatic*; that is, it was sensitive only to the purple, blue, and green portions of the visible spectrum. Yellow and red light barely registered on it, so objects of these colors appeared nearly black in the finished film. For example, the lips of actors wearing ordinary red lipstick appear very dark in many silent films. Purple and blue registered on the film stock as nearly white, so it was

7.3   Walking near town, the heroine of *Just Pals* pauses and looks off left.

7.4   An eyeline match reveals what she sees, a little boy with a bag by a fence, looking off right.

7.5   Another cut takes us to a medium shot of the boy's mother, also by the fence, weeping.

7.6   A second shot of the boy shows him looking through the fence apprehensively and beginning to empty the bag onto the ground.

7.7   A cut to the ground shows a litter of kittens falling out of the bag.

7.8   A long shot shows the whole space: the mother and son are by a river, and he throws the empty bag into the water.

7.9   We see the bag hit the water in a closer view.

7.10   The long-shot framing shows the pair moving away, the boy comforting his mother, who has not turned around to watch any of his actions.

7.11   After seven shots of their actions, we return to a closer view of the heroine, reacting in horror.

difficult to photograph cloudy skies: a blue sky with clouds simply washed out to a uniform white.

Panchromatic film stock, available by the early 1910s, registered the whole range of the visible spectrum, from purple to red, with nearly equal sensitivity. Thus it could record a sky with the clouds visible against the blue background, or red lips as shades of gray. But panchromatic stock had problems as well: it was expensive, it deteriorated quickly if not used right away, and it demanded much greater illumination to expose a satisfactory image. During the 1910s and early 1920s, it was primarily used outdoors in bright sunlight

7.12 A shimmering soft-focus landscape shot in *Way Down East* resembles high-art still photographs of the period.

7.13 Soft-focus cinematography also considerably enhanced glamorous shots, as in this medium close-up of Lillian Gish.

7.14 The entire wedding scene in *Greed* was filmed through a textured scrim placed in front of the lens.

for landscape shots (to capture cloud scenes) or indoors for studio close-ups that could be brightly lit. By 1925, Eastman Kodak had made its panchromatic motion-picture stock cheaper and stabler; soon the stock was also made more sensitive, requiring less light for proper exposure. By 1927, the Hollywood studios were quickly switching over to panchromatic stock. The result was not a radical change in the look of films, but panchromatic did permit filmmakers to make shots of actors who were not wearing makeup and to shoot a greater variety of subjects without having to worry about using filters, special paint, makeup, and the like. Panchromatic soon became the standard in other countries as well.

In the years after World War I, the technical sophistication of the Hollywood studios was the envy of the world. In addition, income from the huge American exhibition market and from expanded exports allowed higher budgets for the most prestigious films. These could cost in the neighborhood of ten times more than comparable films made in Europe.

Such resources, in combination with the fully formulated classical Hollywood style, gave filmmakers considerable flexibility. They could apply the same stylistic methods to many types of movies.

During the 1920s, a new generation of filmmakers came to the fore, and they would dominate American filmmaking for the next three decades and more. Some of them, like John Ford and King Vidor, had started directing on a modest scale in the 1910s, but they now rose to fame. Similarly, although a few stars of earlier years retained their popularity, new ones now came forward. Older genres developed, as when slapstick comedies and Westerns, typically relegated to short subjects, became more respected. New genres also appeared, such as the antiwar film.

7.15 The final scene of *The Four Horsemen of the Apocalypse* shows a military cemetery with innumerable crosses, suggesting the horrors of war.

Big-Budget Films of the 1920s

A film that typified several trends of the decade was *The Four Horsemen of the Apocalypse*, directed by Rex Ingram and released in 1921. It was made by Metro, the production firm recently purchased by Loew's in its expansion. Ingram, who had directed several minor films, gained considerable control over this project, based on a best-selling novel. The film dealt with a South American family's changing fortunes during World War I, and it shed new light on the war. Although it still showed the Germans as evil "Huns," it presented the conflict as destructive rather than glorious (**7.15**). The film's triumph was probably mainly due, however, to the fact that its doomed lovers were played by Rudolph Valentino and Alice Terry, who rose to immediate stardom (**7.16**).

7.16   Glamorous photography in *The Four Horsemen of the Apocalypse* helped make Rudolph Valentino and Alice Terry stars.

7.17, 7.18   In *Why Change Your Wife?* Gloria Swanson plays a mousy wife who saves her marriage to Thomas Meighan by adopting a daring wardrobe.

Valentino was soon hired by Paramount and became one of the matinee idols of the era, further popularizing the "Latin lover" image in such films as *Blood and Sand* (1922, Fred Niblo). He was willing to play in extremely melodramatic roles but also to mock his own image. His early death in 1926 provoked frenzied grief among his many fans. Alice Terry, who was married to Ingram, went on to act primarily in his later films. Ingram was ill suited to the restrictions of Hollywood, especially when Metro became part of the MGM merger in 1924. Unable to work under the strict regime of Louis B. Mayer and Irving Thalberg, Ingram made several films in France for the firm, including *Mare Nostrum* (1926). As with several nonconformist directors who worked for MGM, however, his career declined by the end of the 1920s.

Cecil B. De Mille had been extraordinarily prolific from 1914 on. During the 1920s, he moved on to more sumptuous films at Paramount. One of his primary genres was the sex comedy, often starring Gloria Swanson, one of the top stars. De Mille's sophisticated comedies helped earn Hollywood a reputation for being inordinately risqué. He exploited expensive women's fashions, rich decors, and sexually provocative situations, as in *Why Change Your Wife?* (1920; **7.17, 7.18**). (Swanson's silent-film stardom later added resonance to her role as an aging diva in Billy Wilder's *Sunset Blvd.* [1950], in which De Mille briefly appeared as the heroine's former director.)

When his films came under fire from censorship groups, De Mille responded with films that mixed equally steamy melodrama with religious subject matter. *The Ten Commandments* (1923) had an introductory story depicting a young man who scoffs at morality and vows to break all the commandments; the main part of the film was a historical epic showing Moses leading the Jews out of Egypt (**7.19**). De Mille's biggest

religious production of this era was *The King of Kings* (1927), controversial for its onscreen depiction of Christ. In the sound era, De Mille would become identified with historical epics.

Similarly, after D. W. Griffith cofounded United Artists, he made several large-scale historical films. Just as he had been inspired by Italian epics like *Cabiria* to make *The Birth of a Nation* and *Intolerance,* now he was influenced by Ernst Lubitsch's postwar German films. Griffith's greatest success of the era was *Orphans of the Storm* (1922), set during the French Revolution. It starred the Gish sisters, Lillian and Dorothy, both affiliated with Griffith since the early 1910s (**7.20**). Lillian's career in particular flourished during this decade, as she worked with such major directors as King Vidor (*La Bohème,* 1926) and Victor Sjöström. Griffith made another historical epic, *America* (1924), concerning the American Revolutionary War. His next film, however, was quite different: a naturalistic tale of difficulties in postwar Germany called *Isn't Life Wonderful* (1924). Griffith's mid-1920s films were increasingly unprofitable, and he soon abandoned independent production to make a few films for Paramount. He made two films in the early sound era, including the ambitious *Abraham Lincoln* (1930), but then was forced into retirement until his death in 1948.

As Griffith's case suggests, not all filmmakers who commanded large budgets in Hollywood during the 1920s fit comfortably into its efficient system. Erich von Stroheim had begun in the mid-1910s as an assistant to Griffith. He also acted, typically playing the "evil Hun" figure in World War I films. Universal elevated him to director in 1919 with *Blind Husbands,* the story of a couple on a mountaineering holiday; the wife is nearly seduced away from her complacent husband by a scoundrel, played by von Stroheim (**7.21**). The success of this film led Universal to give von Stroheim a larger budget

7.19   The Egyptian forces set out in pursuit of the fleeing Jews in front of a massive set in *The Ten Commandments*.

7.20   A poignant moment in *Orphans of the Storm*, as the two separated sisters briefly encounter and then lose each other again in the streets of Paris.

7.21, *left*   Erich von Stroheim as the villainous seducer (termed by publicists "the man you love to hate") in *Blind Husbands*.

7.22, *right*   The ending of *Greed*, with the protagonist trapped in Death Valley and killing his old enemy, manifests the bleak tone that made *Greed* unpopular with its initial audiences.

for his second film, *Foolish Wives* (1922), in which he played another predatory role. Von Stroheim exceeded the budget considerably, partly by building a large set reproducing Monte Carlo on the studio backlot. Universal turned this to its advantage by advertising *Foolish Wives* as the first million-dollar movie. More problematically, von Stroheim's first version ran over six hours. The studio pared it down to roughly two and a half hours.

Von Stroheim's Hollywood career involved several such problems with excessive length and budgets. Producer Irving Thalberg replaced him when cost overruns threatened his next project, *The Merry-Go-Round* (1923). Von Stroheim then moved to the independent production firm Goldwyn (which Samuel Goldwyn had sold) to make *Greed*, an adaptation of Frank Norris's naturalistic novel *McTeague*. The result was a nine-hour film, which von Stroheim cut by about half. By this point Goldwyn had become part of MGM, and von Stroheim again encountered constraints imposed by Thalberg. The final release print, taken out of von Stroheim's control, ran about two hours, shorn of one major

plot line and many scenes. This story of an uneducated dentist and his miserly wife was filled with naturalistic touches and was perceived as grim, even sordid, by most critics and audiences (**7.22**). The excised footage was apparently destroyed, and *Greed* remains one of the great mutilated films.

Von Stroheim achieved brief success at MGM with *The Merry Widow* (1925), a film that gained popularity mainly as a result of its sexual subject matter. He then moved to Paramount to make *The Wedding March* (1928), yet another film in which he starred as a seducer, this time nearly redeemed by love. Again von Stroheim contemplated a lengthy film that he hoped to release as two features; the studio reduced it to one, which did poor business. Von Stroheim's last major Hollywood project, an independent production for Gloria Swanson, was *Queen Kelly* (1928–1929), which was unfinished and only much later restored and shown. Von Stroheim ceased to direct in the sound era, but he acted in many important films, including Jean Renoir's *Grand Illusion* (1937).

7.23   Large sets and trick photography re-created Rome's Circus Maximus for the chariot race in *Ben-Hur*.

7.24   The hero and heroine's romantic interlude ends as they are wrenched apart when he must leave for the front in *The Big Parade*.

7.25   The "big parade" of men and equipment moving up to the front.

New Investment and Blockbusters

During the mid-1920s, Wall Street investment allowed the Hollywood studios to produce even more big-budget films. Epic films followed the trend typified by *The Ten Commandments,* with colossal sets and lavish costume design. The newly formed MGM was particularly committed to prestige pictures. It undertook one of the decade's most ambitious projects, an adaptation of General Lew Wallace's novel *Ben-Hur* (a best-selling book and an enormous stage hit as well). The production had originated in 1922 at the Goldwyn company, and the planners tried to give the film greater authenticity by filming on location in Italy—where, incidentally, labor costs were lower. Shooting in Italy, however, lacked the efficiency of studio work, and one accident during the filming of a naval battle may have resulted in the deaths of some extras. In 1924, MGM inherited the project when it absorbed Goldwyn, and the process of completing the film was long and troubled. *Ben-Hur* finally appeared in 1926. Its chariot race was filmed in huge sets; a battery of cameras covered the action from many angles, permitting a breakneck pace in the editing (**7.23**).

MGM also made an important pacifist war film, *The Big Parade* (1925). Its director, King Vidor, had learned his craft by studying the emerging classical Hollywood style in his hometown theater in Texas. He began his career by acting in and directing minor films in the 1910s. Moving to MGM when it formed in 1924, he worked in several genres. His *Wine of Youth* (1924) was a subtle story of three generations of women: a wise grandmother looks on helplessly as her daughter nearly divorces, and her granddaughter takes this as a cue that she can settle for love outside marriage. *The Big Parade* was a much more ambitious project. It starred John Gilbert, the main romantic idol of the period after Valentino's death, as a rich young man who volunteers during World War I. The early portion of the story depicts his time behind the lines, as he falls in love with a French farm woman (**7.24**). An abrupt switch moves the film into epic scenes of the war (**7.25**). But, even more than *The Four Horsemen of the Apocalypse, The Big Parade* depicts the horrors of war. Now German soldiers are seen simply as other human victims of the combat. Alone in a foxhole with a dying German boy, the hero finds himself unable to kill the lad and instead lights him a cigarette. Other war films of the late 1920s and the 1930s followed this pattern, portraying war as grim and unglorious. *The Big Parade* became the first film to run more than a year on Broadway, and its success abroad was enor-

7.26 In *Wings*, the death of a German pilot and the attacking American plane in the background were filmed in the air without trick photography.

7.27 Douglas Fairbanks, as Zorro, soars over a host of pursuers in *The Mark of Zorro*.

mous. Vidor made a very different sort of film with *The Crowd* (1928). A working-class woman marries a clerk, but they nearly break up when one of their children dies in a traffic accident. *The Crowd* stood apart from most Hollywood films in its nonglamorous depiction of everyday life.

Other studios than MGM carried on the trend toward big-budget films. In 1927, Paramount released *Wings* (William Wellman), another bittersweet tale of World War I, this time centering on two friends, Jack and David, who love the same girl and become pilots together. Jack fails to realize that his neighbor, Mary, is in love with him, and she follows him to France as a Red Cross driver. Mary was played by Clara Bow, who enjoyed a brief but intense period of stardom from the mid-1920s to early 1930s. She epitomized the Jazz Age flapper, with an uninhibited natural sexuality; her most famous film, *It* (1927, Clarence Badger), earned her the name the "It girl" ("It" being a current euphemism for sex appeal).

Wings, like *The Big Parade,* combined its romantic elements with spectacular battle footage. Portable cameras were mounted on airplanes to capture aerial combats with an immediacy that trick photography could not equal (**7.26**). Its careful use of motifs and sophisticated use of continuity editing, selective lighting, and camera movement made *Wings* the epitome of late silent filmmaking in Hollywood. When the Academy of Motion Picture Arts and Sciences was formed in 1927 and began giving out annual awards (later dubbed "Oscars"), *Wings* was the first winner as best picture.

Genres and Directors

After United Artists was started in 1919, Douglas Fairbanks was the first of its founders to release a film through the new company. *His Majesty, the American* (1919, Joseph Henabery) was one of the unpretentious, clever comedies that made Fairbanks a star. Soon, however, he moved from comedy to a more ambitious costume picture, *The Mark of Zorro* (1920, Fred Niblo). This film retained the star's comic flair but was longer and placed more emphasis on historical atmosphere, a conventional romance, dueling, and other dangerous stunts (**7.27**). *The Mark of Zorro* was so successful that Fairbanks soon gave up comedy and concentrated on swashbucklers such as *The Three Musketeers* (1921, Fred Niblo), *The Thief of Bagdad* (1924, Raoul Walsh), and *The Black Pirate* (1926, Albert Parker). Fairbanks remained one of the most consistently popular stars of the 1920s, though his success dissipated in the early sound era.

Fairbanks had been unusual as a silent comedian who worked exclusively in features from the beginning of his film career in 1915. In the 1920s, however, several of the great slapstick stars of the earlier period also aspired to work in longer films (see box).

Another genre that gained in prestige during the 1920s was the Western. Previously, Westerns had been cheap, short features shown primarily in small-town theaters. Then, in 1923, Paramount released *The Covered Wagon* (James Cruze), an epic of the westward trip of a wagon train. With a large cast, including major stars, and a thrilling scene of the wagons crossing a river, the film was a hit. The low-budget Western continued to be a staple of Hollywood production, but for decades the large-scale Western would command respect.

John Ford had made his start directing stylish, modest Westerns (p. 75). *Just Pals* (1920) was an unconventional film, the story of a loafer in a small western town who befriends a hobo boy and eventually becomes a

SILENT COMEDY IN THE 1920s

During the 1910s, most comedies that were based on physical action, or slapstick, were shorts that accompanied more prestigious features (though the popular comic stars often proved bigger draws than those of the "main attraction"). During the 1920s, feature-length slapstick comedies became more common. Stars like Charles Chaplin, Harold Lloyd, and Buster Keaton concentrated on creating stronger stories that would support their elaborate physical gags. With their mastery of purely visual action, these comedians developed one of the most prominent and enduring genres of the decade.

Charles Chaplin continued to make hugely successful films in the early 1920s, when his contract with First National kept him from releasing through United Artists. In 1914, Chaplin had appeared in the first slapstick feature, *Tillie's Punctured Romance,* but subsequently he concentrated on shorts. In 1921, he returned to features with extraordinary success in *The Kid.* Here Chaplin played the familiar Little Tramp but shared the spotlight with the expressive child actor Jackie Coogan, who appeared as a foundling whom the Tramp raises (**7.28**).

Chaplin soon became even more ambitious, making a drama, *A Woman of Paris,* in which he played only a walk-on role. This bitterly ironic romance satirized high society. Its droll, even risqué, humor (**7.29**) influenced other directors of sophisticated comedies. The public, however, stayed away from a Chaplin film without the Little Tramp. Chaplin brought back that beloved character in two very popular features, *The Gold Rush* (1925) and *The Circus* (1927).

7.28   In *The Kid,* the Little Tramp coaches the foundling on tactics of street fighting, unaware that the rival's muscular father is looking on.

Harold Lloyd quickly joined the vogue for slapstick features. Using the "glasses" character he had developed in the late teens, he made *A Sailor-Made Man* (1921, Fred Newmeyer), the story of a brash young man who wins his love through a series of adventures. Although Lloyd starred in various types of comedies, he is best remembered for his "thrill" comedies. In *Safety Last* (1923, Newmeyer and Sam Taylor), he played an ambitious young man who has

7.29   The heroine's rich lover fetches one of his own handkerchiefs from a drawer in her apartment, a touch that establishes their intimate relationship visually, in *A Woman of Paris.*

7.30   In *Safety Last,* Harold Lloyd created one of the most memorable comic images of the cinema when he dangled from a clock high up the side of a building.

7.31 Trapped on a horse-drawn moving van in a passing police parade, the hero calmly lights his cigarette with a bomb tossed by an anarchist in *Cops* (1922, codirected by Keaton and Eddie Cline).

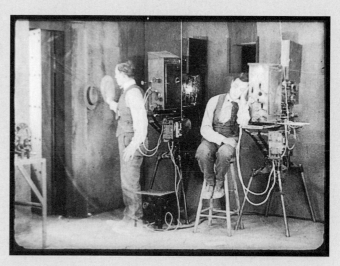

7.32 The hero of *Sherlock Junior,* a projectionist, dreams while his superimposed dream image goes out to enter the film being shown in the theater.

to climb the side of a skyscraper as a publicity stunt for the store where he works (**7.30**). Some of Lloyd's films of this era featured him as the bumbling small-town boy who becomes a hero when confronted with a great challenge, as in *Girl Shy* (1924, Newmeyer and Taylor), *The Freshman* (1925, Newmeyer and Taylor), and *The Kid Brother* (1927, Ted Wilde). Lloyd's career lasted into the early sound era, but eventually the aging actor did not fit his youthful image, and he retired.

Buster Keaton's show-business career began when as a child he joined his parents' vaudeville act. In the late 1910s, he moved into films as an actor in Fatty Arbuckle's short films of the late 1910s. When Arbuckle shifted to features in the early 1920s, Keaton took over his film production unit and directed and starred in a series of popular two-reelers. His trademark was his refusal to smile, and he became known as "the Great Stone Face." Keaton's early films revealed a taste for bizarre humor that bordered at times on Surrealism (**7.31**).

Keaton soon moved into features, though his offbeat humor and complex plots made him less popular than his main rivals, Chaplin and Lloyd. His first feature-length hit was *The Navigator* (1924, codirected with Donald Crisp), a story of a couple cast adrift alone on a huge ocean liner. Keaton was fond of stories that exploited the cinematic medium, as in *Sherlock Junior* (1924), which contained an elaborate film-within-a-film dream sequence (**7.32**). Keaton's finest film may be *The General* (1927, codirected with Clyde Bruckman), a story of a daring rescue during the Civil War. Keaton and Bruckman created an almost perfectly

balanced plot structure, evoked period detail, and staged elaborate gags within single shots. Nonetheless, *The General* failed to win popularity.

In 1928, Keaton moved to MGM, where he made one film that was up to his old standard—*The Cameraman* (1928, Edward Sedgwick, Jr.). After the coming of sound, however, he was not allowed his customary freedom in improvising gags on the set. Keaton's career gradually declined in the early 1930s, when MGM began costarring him with more aggressive comics like Jimmy Durante. From the

7.33 In a long take in *The Luck of the Foolish* (1924, Harry Edwards), Harry Langdon slowly eats a sandwich, registering his dawning realization that a shingle has accidentally fallen into it.

(continued)

mid-1930s, Keaton played in many minor films and took small roles during the sound era, but his career never revived before his death in 1966.

Harry Langdon came to the cinema somewhat later than the other major comics of this era. From 1924 to 1927, he made short comedies for Mack Sennett. In these he developed his typical persona, one quite different from those of his rivals. Langdon cultivated a baby-faced image, playing naive characters who react slowly to whatever happens to them (**7.33**). By the mid-1920s, he also began making features: *Tramp, Tramp, Tramp* (1926, Harry Edwards), *The Strong Man* (1926, Frank Capra), and *Long Pants* (1927, Capra). Langdon continued to appear in small roles into the 1940s, but, as with many other comics of this era, his appeal came primarily through visual humor.

Although these major actors entered features, the comic short remained a popular part of theater programs. The most important producers of shorts remained Hal Roach, who had discovered Harold Lloyd, and Mack

Sennett, formerly of Keystone. Under their guidance, a new generation of stars emerged. The most famous of these were Stan Laurel and Oliver Hardy, who had worked separately in minor comedies for years before being teamed by Roach in *Putting Pants on Philip* (1927). This short film about an American (Hardy) trying to deal with the turmoil caused by his aggressively flirtatious, kilt-wearing Scottish cousin (Laurel) remains one of their most hilarious. Unlike some other silent comedians, Laurel and Hardy made an effortless transition to sound, and Roach graduated them to feature films in 1931. Another star of this period was Charlie Chase, who worked for Sennett. Chase was a thin, ordinary-looking man with a small moustache who depended not so much on his comic appearance as on his talent for staging elaborate indoor chases. Comics from the teens who had played supporting roles in Chaplin's and other stars' films, such as Chester Conklin and Mack Swain, now acquired series of their own under Sennett.

7.34 The odd heroes of *Just Pals* awake after a night spent in a hayloft.

hero by exposing a local embezzler (**7.34**). In 1921, he moved from Universal to the Fox Film Corporation. His first major success there was *The Iron Horse* (1924), a high-budget Western made in the wake of *The Covered Wagon*. This story of the building of the first transcontinental railroad exploited Ford's feeling for landscape. He soon became Fox's top director, working in a variety of genres. Ford's other Western at Fox was *3 Bad Men* (1926), with an impressive land-rush sequence. Surprisingly, he did not return to the genre until *Stagecoach* (1939), but he was identified with Westerns throughout his long career.

Frank Borzage had also directed a number of low-budget Westerns during the 1910s. These include *The Gun Woman* (1918), an intense story of a rugged dance-hall owner, the Tigress, who shoots the man she loves

when he turns out to be a stagecoach bandit. Like Ford, Borzage moved into more prestigious filmmaking at the larger studios during the 1920s, though he quickly abandoned Westerns. Today he is often thought of in connection with melodramas, such as *Humoresque* (1920), a sentimental account of a Jewish violinist wounded in World War I. Some of Borzage's best films of the decade, however, were in other genres. *The Circle* (1925, MGM) was a sophisticated romantic comedy. In 1924, Borzage moved to Fox, where he joined Ford as a leading director. His first film there, *Lazybones* (1925), was a rambling, low-key comedy about a lazy young man who—unlike most Hollywood protagonists—has no goals but sacrifices his already shaky reputation to raise a child for the sister of the woman he loves.

After *The Cabinet of Dr. Caligari* was shown in the United States in 1921, horror films gradually became a minor American genre. Universal pioneered this type of film, primarily because one of its main stars was Lon Chaney. Chaney was a master of makeup—"the Man of a Thousand Faces"—and had a flair for macabre roles. He played Quasimodo in the original adaptation of *The Hunchback of Notre Dame* (1923, Wallace Worsley), for which Universal built extravagant sets recreating medieval Paris, and the Phantom in the 1925 version of *The Phantom of the Opera* (Rupert Julian). Chaney's most consistently disturbing films, however, were made at MGM with director Tod Browning,

7.35   Lon Chaney as the protagonist of *The Unknown*.

7.36   Josef von Sternberg used backlight and smoke to create this atmospheric moment as the protagonist of *Underworld* guns down a rival. The film's style anticipated the later brooding *films noirs* ("dark films") of the 1940s.

7.37   Lulu's brother-in-law complains about her buying a small plant out of her meager earnings.

whose taste for stories with perverse twists matched his own. In *The Unknown* (1927), for example, Chaney played a circus knife thrower, Alonzo, who pretends to be armless as part of his act. His beautiful partner (played by the young Joan Crawford) has a pathological fear of being touched by men and trusts only Alonzo. To gain her lasting love, he actually has his arms amputated, only to discover that she has now fallen in love with another man (**7.35**). Chaney died prematurely in 1930, but Browning went on in the 1930s to make some notable horror films, such as *Dracula* (1931) and *Freaks* (1932). The horror film also received a boost in the late 1920s, when German directors began moving to Hollywood.

The gangster genre had not been particularly important in American filmmaking before the mid-1920s. There had been some films about petty gang crime, such as Griffith's *The Musketeers of Pig Alley* (1912) and Walsh's *Regeneration* (1915). It was the rise of organized criminal activity associated with Prohibition, however, that helped make the flashily dressed, heavily armed gangster a prominent image in Hollywood films. One film did a great deal to establish the genre: Josef von Sternberg's *Underworld* (1927), made for Paramount.

Von Sternberg had started by independently producing and directing a gloomy naturalistic drama, *The Salvation Hunters* (1925), on a shoestring budget. It was championed by Charles Chaplin, and although the film failed at the box office, von Sternberg was hired by MGM for a brief and unfruitful period. *Underworld* was a big hit, however, in part due to its offbeat stars. Its odd hero is a homely, lumbering jewel thief, played by George Bancroft. He picks up a drunken Britisher (Clive Brook) and makes him into a refined assistant. The hero's world-weary mistress (Evelyn Brent) falls in love with the Britisher, and the hero, after plotting to kill the pair, magnanimously holds off a police raid to allow them to escape together. Von Sternberg filmed this story with the dense, dazzling cinematography that was to become his hallmark (**7.36**). Von Sternberg went on to make another quirky gangster film starring Bancroft, an early talkie called *Thunderbolt* (1929). He also worked in other genres during the 1920s. *The Docks of New York* (1928) was a sordid story of a ship's stoker (Bancroft again) and a prostitute redeemed by each other's love; again the crowded scenery and textured, atmospheric lighting set von Sternberg's work apart. *The Docks of New York* prefigured the romantic melodramas that were to be the director's specialty in the 1930s.

Another unconventional director of this period was William C. de Mille, who has been overshadowed by his brother Cecil B. (the two spelled their surnames differently). A former playwright, William made several distinctive films during the decade after World War I, mostly centering on gentle idiosyncratic characters. In *Conrad in Quest of His Youth* (1920), for example, a British soldier returns from India to find himself without any aim in life. In an amusing scene, he reunites his cousins in an attempt to re-create exactly their childhood existence; the adults, however, find the pleasures of their youth (oatmeal, games) unsatisfactory and uncomfortable. *Miss Lulu Bett* deals with a plain spinster forced into a subservient position to earn her keep with her sister's family. Jolted out of her unquestioning acceptance by a false marriage to a bigamist, she rebels and achieves a happy marriage to the local teacher (**7.37**).

Another isolated, but noteworthy, talent of the period was Karl Brown, a cinematographer who had worked with Griffith in the 1920s. For Paramount he

7.38, *left*   Location photography in a scene where the hero of *Stark Love* teaches the heroine to read.

7.39, *right*   The large sets and deep stagings of *Rosita* made it more a Lubitsch film than a Mary Pickford star vehicle.

directed *Stark Love* (1927), a film outstanding for its realism. *Stark Love* was a rural drama, filmed entirely on location in North Carolina with nonactors. It went against gender stereotypes of the period, telling the story of a backwoods culture in which women are utterly oppressed. A young man who manages to get an education decides to give up his tuition money to send a neighbor girl to college in his place (**7.38**). When his brutal father decides to marry the girl, she fends him off with an ax, and the young couple escape their primitive surroundings. After *Stark Love,* Brown returned to cinematography.

Unconventional films were not ruled out in Hollywood, but they had to make money. The American production companies also proved their willingness to experiment by importing many successful foreign filmmakers.

Foreign Filmmakers in Hollywood

Before 1920, filmmakers from abroad had occasionally made their way into the American industry. Most notably, Charles Chaplin had gone from touring as a British music-hall star to making his own comedies, and Maurice Tourneur had come from France. The 1920s, however, were the first decade during which American firms systematically sought foreign talent and in which émigrés had a major influence on Hollywood filmmaking.

As important filmmaking trends emerged in Sweden, France, Germany, and elsewhere in Europe, American studio executives realized that these countries could be a source of fresh talent. Moreover, hiring the best European personnel was a way of ensuring that no country would grow powerful enough to challenge Hollywood in world film markets.

American firms also bought up the rights to European plays and literary works and in some cases brought their authors to work as scriptwriters in the United States. In 1921, for example, a Paramount advertisement boasted

Every form of printed or spoken drama that might be suitable for Paramount Pictures is examined. Everything useful published in Italian, Spanish, German or French is steadily translated. Synopses are made of every stage play produced in America, Paris, Berlin, Vienna, London and Rome.[1]

Studio representatives regularly visited Europe and viewed the latest films, looking for promising stars and filmmakers. In 1925, MGM executives who had seen *The Story of Gösta Berling* in Berlin signed its two stars, Greta Garbo and Lars Hansen, to contracts and also brought its director, Mauritz Stiller, to Hollywood. Similarly, Harry Warner saw two of Hungarian director Mihály Kertész's early films in London and wired him an offer that led to his lengthy career at Warner Bros. under the name Michael Curtiz. Since Germany had the most prominent foreign film industry, the largest number of émigré filmmakers came from that country.

Lubitsch Comes to Hollywood   The regular flow of European (and, later, Latin American) talent to Hollywood began after Ernst Lubitsch's *Madame Dubarry* was released in the United States (as *Passion,* see p. 103) to great success. Star Pola Negri was soon acquired by Paramount. Lubitsch himself followed her to Hollywood in 1923. Already the most successful director in Germany, Lubitsch quickly adapted his style to incorporate the classical narrative approach. He became one of the most highly respected filmmakers in Hollywood. Mary Pickford asked him to direct her in her 1923 production, *Rosita*. Although it allowed Pickford many amusing scenes, the film had the grandiose manner of Lubitsch's German pictures (**7.39**).

Despite the success of *Rosita*, United Artists was in financial difficulties and could not fund further Lubitsch productions. Surprisingly, he moved to Warner Bros. and became the minor studio's most prestigious director. Inspired by Chaplin's *A Woman of Paris,* he made a series

7.40   **7.41**   **7.42**

7.43

7.40–7.43 Four shots from the racetrack scene of *Lady Windermere's Fan* (1925), during which the views of various characters through binoculars reveal their attitudes toward a woman of shady reputation.

7.44 This trapeze scene in *The Devil's Circus* exemplifies the kinds of "European" special effects and daring camera angles the Hollywood cinema was beginning to adopt in the mid-1920s.

of sophisticated society comedies. These hinted at sexual appetites and rivalries bubbling beneath the surface of polite veneers. This suggestiveness and Lubitsch's clever visual jokes came to be known as "the Lubitsch touch." He mastered continuity editing and was able to indicate characters' attitudes simply by the ways in which they shifted position in the frame or through the directions of their glances from shot to shot (**7.40–7.43**). Lubitsch's principal films for Warner Bros. were *The Marriage Circle* (1924; see 7.2), *Lady Windermere's Fan* (1925), and *So This Is Paris* (1926). He also returned to his old genre, the historical film, with *The Student Prince in Old Heidelberg* (1927) at MGM and *The Patriot* at Paramount (1928). He later proved to be one of the most imaginative directors during the early sound era.

The Scandinavians Come to America Hollywood, and specifically MGM, also picked up on the important Scandinavian directors of the 1910s and early 1920s (pp. 63–67). The studio imported Benjamin Christensen, whose first American film, appropriately enough, was *The Devil's Circus* (1926); it harked back to the circus genre that had been so common in Scandinavian films of the 1910s (**7.44**). Christensen went on to make several gothic thrillers, most notably *Seven Footprints to Satan* (1929). During the 1930s he returned to Denmark.

Mauritz Stiller was hired by MGM after the success of *The Story of Gösta Berling* in Berlin. With him went Greta Garbo, whom Stiller had discovered. MGM set the pair to work on *The Torrent*, but Stiller's eccentricities and inability to conform to strict accounting methods soon led to his replacement. German producer Erich Pommer, then working in a brief stint at Paramount, hired him to make *Hotel Imperial*, starring Pola Negri. This was Stiller's most notable Hollywood production, including some "Germanic" camera movements that involved placing the camera on an elaborate elevator system. It did not recapture the wit or intensity of his Swedish films, however, and after a few more aborted projects, Stiller returned to Sweden, where he died in 1928.

7.45 The Reverend Arthur Dimmesdale walks through a forest of stumps in *The Scarlet Letter.*

7.46 In *Broadway,* the camera pulls far back from the hero during a musical number in the Expressionistic nightclub.

In 1923, Victor Sjöström also accepted an offer from MGM, which renamed him Victor Seastrom. His first American film, *Name the Man,* was a bit stiff but contained several landscape shots that recalled his earlier feeling for natural environments. His next project, *He Who Gets Slapped* (1924), was a vehicle for Lon Chaney; another Scandinavian-influenced circus film, it proved highly popular. Seastrom then made two films starring Lillian Gish, who had recently come to MGM after her long association with Griffith. She wanted to do an adaptation of *The Scarlet Letter* (1926), directed by Seastrom, who seemed perfectly suited to Nathaniel Hawthorne's tale of love and retribution. His sense of landscape emerged even more strongly here (7.45). Similarly, the performances of Gish and Swedish actor Lars Hansen were strong, but MGM insisted on a comic subplot that vitiated the austere drama.

Gish and Hansen starred again in Seastrom's final American film, *The Wind* (1928). The story involves a woman who moves to the desolate, windswept western frontier to marry a naive rancher. She kills and buries a would-be rapist but then is driven to the brink of madness by visions of the wind uncovering his body. Despite a hopeful ending imposed by the studio, *The Wind* was a powerful, bleak film. Its grimness and its release as a silent film as sound was coming in doomed it to failure, however, and Seastrom returned to Sweden, to his original name, and to a long career acting in sound films.

European Directors at Universal Universal, one of the larger studios among the Little Five, lent prestige to its production output by hiring several European directors. Among these was Paul Fejos, a Hungarian who had made his mark in Hollywood by directing an experimental independent feature, *The Last Moment* (1927), which consisted primarily of a drowning man's final vision, portrayed in a lengthy, rapidly edited passage almost certainly influenced by French Impressionist style. *Lonesome* (1928) was a simple story of a working-class couple's romance, portrayed with a naturalism that was

unusual for Hollywood. His next film, the elaborate early musical *Broadway* (1929, which survives only in its silent version) used a huge Expressionist-style nightclub set through which the camera swooped on a giant crane built for this production (7.46). After a few more minor Hollywood projects, including the foreign-language versions of some early talkies, Fejos returned to work in various European countries in the 1930s.

Universal also hired Paul Leni, director of one of the main German Expressionist films, *Waxworks*. Leni's dark, vaguely expressionist adaptation of the hit Broadway gothic thriller *The Cat and the Canary* (1927) became an enormous success. He then directed a big-budget historical epic with overtones of the horror genre, *The Man Who Laughs* (1928), starring German actor Conrad Veidt in an Expressionist performance as a man whose mouth has been cut into a permanent grotesque grin. These two films reinforced Universal's orientation toward horror films—a tendency that had begun with *The Hunchback of Notre Dame* and *The Phantom of the Opera* and which was to intensify in the sound era with such films as *Dracula* and *Frankenstein.* Leni's premature death in 1929, however, meant that others would take over the exploration of the genre.

Murnau and His Influence at Fox Aside from Lubitsch, F. W. Murnau was the most prestigious European director to come to Hollywood in the 1920s. Fox hired him in 1925, in the wake of the critical acclaim for *The Last Laugh.* Murnau lingered at Ufa only long enough to make *Faust* (which proved popular in the United States). Fox allowed him an enormous budget to make its biggest picture of 1927, *Sunrise.* Scripted by Carl Mayer,

7.47, *left* Deep space and skewed false perspectives create an Expressionist composition in *Sunrise*.

7.48, *right* The huge city square constructed for *Sunrise* (with help from German false-perspective techniques that made it seem even larger).

7.49 Diane and her sister in their garret apartment in *7th Heaven*. The upwardly slanting floor shows the influence of German set design.

7.50 This elevator allowed the camera to move with Diane and Chico seven flights up as they approached his apartment, which their love transforms into "heaven."

who had written so many German Expressionist and Kammerspiel films, and designed by Rochus Gliese, who had worked with Murnau in Germany, the film was virtually a German film made in America. It was a simple but intense psychological drama of a farmer who attempts to murder his wife in order to run away with his lover from the city. When he cannot bring himself to commit the deed, he must regain his horrified wife's trust. The film was full of Germanic mise-en-scène with Expressionist touches (**7.47**). Even the American stars, Janet Gaynor and George O'Brien, were induced to give Expressionist-style performances.

Sunrise was perhaps too sophisticated to be really popular, and its huge city sets (**7.48**) made it so expensive that it did only moderately well for Fox. As a result, Murnau's fortunes declined. He went on to increasingly more modest projects: *Four Devils* (1929), yet another circus film, now lost; and *City Girl* (1930), a part-talkie that was taken out of Murnau's control and altered considerably. His last film began as a collaboration with documentarist Robert Flaherty (pp. 184–185). The two worked on a fiction film about Tahiti, *Tabu* (1931). After Flaherty abandoned the project, Murnau completed a flawed but beautiful love story made on location in the South Seas. He died in a car accident shortly before the film's release.

Despite Murnau's lack of popular success during his Hollywood career, *Sunrise* had an enormous effect on American filmmakers, especially at Fox. Both John

Ford and Frank Borzage were encouraged to imitate it. Ford's sentimental World War I drama *Four Sons* (1928) looks very much like a German film, and signs of Ufa's studio-bound style were to crop up in his sound films, such as *The Informer* (1935) and *The Fugitive* (1947).

Borzage's late-1920s films show even more directly the influence of Murnau's work. Borzage's *7th Heaven* is an affecting melodrama about a forlorn Parisian prostitute, Diane, and a woman-hating sewer cleaner, Chico, who gradually gain each other's love and trust only to be separated by World War I. None of the film crew was European, but the set designs by Harry Oliver incorporated the sorts of false-perspective backgrounds that Murnau had used in *Sunrise* and some of his German films (**7.49**). German-style virtuosic camera movements were imitated, most spectacularly in an elaborate verti-

7.51, *left*   The duel scene in *Flesh and the Devil*, handled with a rapid tracking movement back from a silhouetted scene. The opponents end offscreen at either side, with puffs of smoke coming into the frame, briefly leaving the result uncertain.

7.52, *right*   A tiny spotlight created a romantic moment as John Gilbert lights a cigarette for Greta Garbo; the pair were cast as lovers in several more films.

cal shot made from an elevator (7.50). Borzage followed up the tremendous success of *7th Heaven* with a similar film, *Street Angel* (1928), starring the same actors, Janet Gaynor and Charles Farrell. They became the ideal romantic couple of the late 1920s. She won the first Best Actress award from the Academy of Motion Picture Arts and Sciences for these two films and *Sunrise* (at a time when the rules allowed an actor's entire year's output to be nominated). They starred together again in Borzage's late silent film *Lucky Star* (1929), a dark, romantic love story that again displayed German influence and remained one of the rare Hollywood films with a wheelchair-bound hero.

European films, and especially those from Germany, also affected Hollywood filmmaking more generally. *Flesh and the Devil* (1926), directed by the well-established filmmaker Clarence Brown, was full of fancy camera movement, subjective camera effects, and other techniques derived from European avant-garde cinema (7.51). It also starred the single most successful of the imported European stars, Greta Garbo. Here she was teamed with matinee idol John Gilbert, with whom she was linked romantically in real life (7.52). *Flesh and the Devil* was only one production of the 1920s to borrow from European cinema. Many other Hollywood films of the late 1920s and the 1930s also reflected influences from European films, particularly those of the French Impressionist, German Expressionist, and Soviet Montage movements.

FILMS FOR AFRICAN AMERICAN AUDIENCES

In Chapters 4 through 6, we saw how alternatives to classical Hollywood cinema arose in the form of stylistic movements. Other alternatives to mainstream Hollywood fare also appeared. In the United States, such alternatives have usually been specialty films aimed at specific audiences. During the silent era, a small circuit of theaters for African American audiences developed, along with a number of regional producers making films with all-black casts.

In 1915, the release of Griffith's *The Birth of a Nation* led to many protests and boycotts on the part of African Americans. Some envisioned the creation of black-controlled production firms that could provide an alternative perspective on race relations. A few sporadic attempts at production were initiated during the latter half of the 1910s, but the results were usually short films that were relegated to a minor role on programs. They either showed positive images of black heroism during World War I or perpetuated traditional black comic stereotypes.

During the 1920s, black roles in mainstream Hollywood films were minor and still based on stereotypes. African Americans appeared as servants, wastrels, comic children, and the like. Black actors seldom found regular work and had to fill in with other jobs, usually menial, to survive.

As moviegoers, African Americans had little choice but to attend theaters that showed films designed for white audiences. Most theaters in the United States were segregated. In the South, laws required that exhibitors separate their white and black patrons. In the North, despite civil rights statutes in many localities, the practice was for the races to sit in separate parts of auditoriums. Some theaters, usually owned by whites, were in black neighborhoods and catered to local viewers. In such theaters, any films with black-oriented subject matter proved popular.

There were even a small number of films produced specifically for African American audiences. These used all-black casts, even though the directors and other filmmakers were usually white. The most prominent company of this kind in the 1920s was the Colored Players, which made several films, including two particularly significant ones. *The Scar of Shame* (1929?, Frank Perugini) dealt with the effects of environment and upbringing on black people's aspirations. The hero, a struggling composer, strives to live a respectable middle-class existence; he is "a credit to his race,"

7.53 The conservatively dressed hero of *Scar of Shame* confronts the villainous gambler, marked by his sporty checked suit.

7.54 The hero of *Ten Nights in a Barroom* holds his fatally wounded daughter.

7.55 Paul Robeson as the villain in *Body and Soul*.

despite the attempts of sordid characters to corrupt him (**7.53**).

The Colored Players also made a less preachy film that has survived, *Ten Nights in a Barroom* (1926, Charles S. Gilpin), an adaptation of a classic stage melodrama that had traditionally been played by white casts. Its complex flashback structure tells the story of a drunkard who reforms when he accidentally contributes to the death of his daughter in a barroom brawl (**7.54**). Despite its low budget, *Ten Nights in a Barroom* was skillfully lit and edited in the classical style.

In rare cases, black filmmakers were able to work behind the camera. Oscar Micheaux was for several decades the most successful African American producer-director. He began as a homesteader in South Dakota, where he wrote novels and sold them door to door to his white neighbors. He used the same method to sell stock to adapt his writings into films, creating the Micheaux Book and Film Company in 1918. Over the next decade, he made thirty films, concentrating on such black-related topics as lynching, the Ku Klux Klan, and interracial marriage.

The energetic and determined Micheaux worked quickly with low budgets, and his films have a rough, disjunctive style that boldly depicts black concerns on the screen. *Body and Soul* (1924) explores the issue of the religious exploitation of poor blacks. Paul Robeson, one of the most successful black actors and singers of the century, plays a false preacher who extorts money and seduces women (**7.55**). Micheaux went bankrupt in the late 1920s and had to resort to white financing in the sound era. Nevertheless, he continued to average a film a year up to 1940 and made one more in 1948. Although much of his work is lost, Micheaux demonstrated that a black director could make films for black audiences.

The opportunities for African Americans would improve somewhat during the sound era. Talented black entertainers were in greater demand in musicals, and major studios experimented with all-black casts. As we shall see in Chapter 9, one of the most important early sound films, King Vidor's *Hallelujah!*, attempted to explore African American culture (p. 200).

THE ANIMATED PART OF THE PROGRAM

The basic techniques of animated films had been invented during the 1910s (p. 77), and the post–World War I period saw a boom in animation. New independent animation studios appeared, creating greater output and applying a division of labor that made the process of animation more efficient. Typically, head animators laid out the basic poses for the scene, the "inbetweeners" filled in the movements with additional drawings, other workers traced the drawings onto cels, still others filled in with paint, and a cinematographer photographed the images frame by frame. The result could be a series of cartoons released monthly or even biweekly. A whole new generation of animators set up shop as technical information about cels and the slash system was disseminated.

Most animation companies produced series with continuing characters or themes. These films would be released through an independent distributor, but that distributor might sign a contract with one of the big Hollywood firms to put the cartoons on its own program. The most successful independent distributor of this era was Margaret J. Winkler Mintz. By the early 1920s, she was financing and releasing the decade's three most popular series: the Fleischer brothers' "Out of the Inkwell" films, the cartoons based on Bud Fisher's beloved "Mutt and Jeff" comics, and some of Walt Disney's earliest efforts.

The Fleischer brothers, Max and Dave, had experimented with a new film technique called *rotoscoping* in the mid-1910s. The rotoscope allowed a filmmaker to take live-action films, project each frame onto a piece of paper, and trace the outlines of its figures. Originally, the brothers seem to have intended the device to be used for military purposes. Although the rotoscope was patented in 1915, World War I delayed further work on it. After the war, Max and Dave returned to work, this time tracing the live-action images as cartoon figures. They used a live-action prologue for each film in their series, featuring Max Fleischer as a cartoonist who creates Koko, a clown who pops "out of the inkwell." The first cartoon was released in late 1919, and several others followed sporadically through 1920.

Rotoscoping was not intended to increase efficiency, as earlier inventions in cartooning were. Instead, by tracing the action one image at a time on cels, the cartoonist could easily produce characters that moved naturally *as whole figures*, rather than stiffly, moving only one or a few parts of their bodies, as in the slash and other simple cel systems. The Fleischer's new character, Koko the Clown, swung his limbs through space freely, and his loose outfit swirled about him as he went (7.56). A reviewer of the period commented on this ease of movement:

> [Koko's] motions, for one thing, are smooth and graceful. He walks, dances and leaps as a human being, as a particularly easy-limbed human being might. He does not jerk himself from one position to another, nor does he move an arm or a leg while the remainder of his body remains as unnaturally stiff as—as if it were fixed in ink lines on paper.[2]

The Fleischers also employed the standard techniques of cels, slashing, and retracing, but rotoscoping gave these devices new freedom. The "Out of the Inkwell" series prospered during the 1920s. In the early sound era, however, the Fleischers replaced Koko with the equally popular Betty Boop and Popeye.

The "Mutt and Jeff" series had begun as a comic strip in 1911. Its hapless stars were two moustached fellows, one tall, one short. The strip's artist, Bud Fisher, agreed in 1916 to allow the celebrated strip to be animated. His name was invariably given as the creator of the cartoon series, even though over the years Raoul Barré, Charles Bowers, and various other animation veterans actually drew the cartoons. Distributor Mintz contracted the series for release through Fox, and it remained popular through the 1920s (7.57).

The young Walt Disney and his friend Ub Iwerks started their own commercial-arts firm in Kansas City in 1919. Failing to make money, they then worked for an ad agency, making simple animated films. There they started "Newman's Laugh-o-grams," a series of short animated films for local distribution. After this venture also failed, Disney moved to Hollywood. In 1923, he received backing from Mintz to create a series of "Alice Comedies," which proved to be his first success. With his brother Roy, he formed the Disney Brothers Studios, which would eventually grow into one of the world's biggest entertainment conglomerates.

During the 1920s, the staff of the firm included several of the major animators who would create series for Warner Bros. and MGM in the 1930s: Hugh Harman, Rudolf Ising, and Isadore "Friz" Freleng. They all worked on the Alice series, which combined live action and cartoon images—a technique that was not new to cartooning (7.58). In 1927, the Disney studio switched to full animation with the "Oswald the Rabbit" series. In a legal battle, however, Charles Mintz, husband of Disney's distributor, seized control of the character. Walt's solution was to invent a new character called Mickey Mouse. The first two Mickey cartoons failed to find a distributor. A third, *Steamboat Willie*, incorporated the new sound technology and proved a huge hit. It helped catapult Disney to the head of the animation business in the 1930s.

Other series of this period proved highly popular. Paul Terry, who had worked at various animation studios during the 1910s, started his own firm, Fables Pictures Inc., in 1921. He launched a series called "Aesop's Fables." For these modern retellings of the classic fables Terry used a virtual assembly-line division of labor to turn out one film per week; the results were amusing but usually conventional (7.59). Terry left the company in 1928 to create Terrytoons, a firm he ran until 1955, when he sold it to television producers.

The most popular series of the 1920s starred Felix the Cat. Its nominal creator, Pat Sullivan, had opened his own studio in 1915, making ads and animated films. He began making Felix cartoons for Paramount around 1918. Although Sullivan signed all the films, the head of animation was actually Otto Messmer, who originated the character of Felix and handled the animation process. Mintz signed to distribute the series in 1922. The films were hugely successful, partly through the appeal of the feline hero and partly through the flexible animation style. In these films, Felix's tail could fly off his body and become a question mark or a cane for him to lean on (7.60). By the mid-1920s, the films had achieved a

7.56 In *The Clown's Little Brother* (1919 or 1920), Koko struts across the frame in a rotoscoped motion that seemed effortless and lively in the context of 1910s animation.

7.57 Mutt's attempts to help Jeff get out of the pot attached to his head soon leads to dizzy escapades on a half-built skyscraper in *Where Am I?* (1925).

7.58 In *Alice in the Wooly West* (1926), animated exclamation points express the live-action heroine's astonishment as she confronts the world of cartoon characters.

7.59, *left*   The nightclub in which the protagonist fritters away his paycheck in *The Spendthrift* (1922), with the moral "A spendthrift blames everybody but himself for his misfortune."

7.60, *right*   Felix politely tips his ears in *Felix the Cat in Futuritzy* (1928).

huge audience. Sullivan was also a pioneer in the use of tie-in products like dolls to further exploit the success of his cartoon character. Like most of the major animated series of the 1920s, Felix did not carry over well into the sound era, though there have been many later imitations of this character.

The U.S. film industry's push into foreign markets during World War I gave it an enormous economic base for its expansion and consolidation during the 1920s. Most national film industries were too small to offer any significant resistance to American domination. Yet the cinema continued to be an international phenomenon, and many countries managed to make at least a few films of their own. Some countries in Europe were strong enough to support national industries and even to consider banding together to challenge American power. Moreover, for the first time, filmmakers in several countries were creating short experimental films that challenged the classical narrative approach of Hollywood cinema. We shall examine these trends in the next chapter.

Notes and Queries

THE REDISCOVERY OF BUSTER KEATON

After the great age of silent comedy ended, Charles Chaplin remained the most revered of the era's clowns. Although he controlled the rights to most of his features and refused to circulate them, most of his dozens of short comedies were commonly available. By contrast, few of the films of Buster Keaton circulated. As a result, a great deal was written about Chaplin, and he was generally ranked as much better than Keaton or Harold Lloyd.

The balance shifted dramatically in the mid-1960s, when Keaton films began to surface. Distributor Raymond Rohauer made new prints of most of Keaton's silent work. These were shown at the Venice Film Festival in 1965, where Keaton appeared to tremendous applause. That same year the British Film Institute presented him with a special award. Interviews and retrospectives followed. Keaton lived just long enough to enjoy this acclaim. He died in 1966, shortly before the publication of Rudi Blesh's biography, *Keaton* (New York: Macmillan, 1966). Blesh documented the decline in Keaton's career during the 1930s and helped revive interest in his early work.

Critics and historians recognized that Keaton had been a major director as well as a brilliant performer. His ability to arrange complex gags all within a single long-shot framing, his compositions in depth, his careful use of motifs, and the balanced structure of his scenarios all received attention.

For a description of Keaton's appearance at Venice and an interview with him, see John Gillett and James Blue, "Keaton at Venice," *Sight & Sound* 35, no. 1 (winter 1965/1966): 26–30. Studies of Keaton done in the wake of this revival include J.-P. Lebel's *Buster Keaton* (New York: Barnes, 1967) and David Robinson's *Buster Keaton* (Bloomington: Indiana University Press, 1969). Further information and sources can be found in Joanna E. Rapf and Gary L. Green, *Buster Keaton: A Bio-Bibliography* (Westport, CT: Greenwood Press, 1995).

- -

REFERENCES

1. Advertisement, Paramount Pictures, *Photoplay* 19, no. 4 (March 1921): 4.
2. From the *New York Times*, quoted in Donald Crafton, *Before Mickey: The Animated Film 1898–1928* (Cambridge, MA: MIT Press, 1982), p. 174.

FURTHER READING

Bernstein, Matthew, with Dana F. White. " 'Scratching Around' in a 'Fit of Insanity': The Norman Film Manufacturing Company and the Race Film Business in the 1920s." *Griffithiana* 62/63 (May 1998): 81–127.

Bowser, Pearl, Jane Gaines, and Charles Musser, *Oscar Micheaux & His Circle: African-American Filmmaking and Race Cinema of the Silent Era.* Bloomington: Indiana University Press, 2001.

Bowser, Pearl, and Louise Spence. *Writing Himself into History: Oscar Micheaux, His Silent Films, and His Audiences.* New Brunswick: Rutgers University Press, 2000.

Canemaker, John. *Felix: The Twisted Tale of the World's Most Famous Cat.* New York: Pantheon, 1991.

"Frank Borzage: Hollywood's Lucky Star." Entire issue of *Griffithiana* 46 (December 1992).

Koszarski, Richard. *An Evening's Entertainment: The Age of the Silent Feature Picture, 1915–1928.* New York: Scribners, 1990.

_____. *Von: The Life and Times of Erich von Stroheim.* New York: Limelight, 2001.

O'Leary, Liam. *Rex Ingram: Master of the Silent Cinema.* New York: Barnes & Noble, 1980. Reprint, London: British Film Institute, 1994.

Reilly, Adam. *Harold Lloyd: The King of Daredevil Comedy.* New York: Collier, 1977.

CHAPTER 8

INTERNATIONAL TRENDS OF THE 1920s

As we saw in Chapters 4 to 6, major alternatives to the classical film-making style of Hollywood arose in the years after World War I: French Impressionism, German Expressionism, and Soviet Montage. These three movements occurred within the context of a general reaction against the domination of international markets by Hollywood films. Some European companies united to resist American encroachment. At the same time, artists in other media and dedicated filmmakers worked outside the commercial establishment to create alternative types of cinema, both experimental and documentary. Less dramatically, several countries tried to compete with the United States by producing films more regularly.

"FILM EUROPE"

After World War I, many countries struggled against American films' continued domination of their markets. At first, nations competed against each other as well as against Hollywood, hoping to prosper in the international film market. The German government fostered the growth of its film industry by continuing the wartime ban on imported films. In France, despite many efforts, adverse conditions kept production low. For a few years, Italy continued to produce many films but could not regain its strong pre-1914 position. Other countries sought to establish even a small amount of steady production.

Postwar Animosities Fade

This competition was exacerbated by lingering animosities. Great Britain and France were determined not to let German production expand abroad. Theater owners in both countries agreed not to show German

8.1 A 1922 French advertisement for F. W. Murnau's *Nosferatu* called it "more powerful than *Caligari*."

films after the war, for a period of five years in Britain and for fifteen in France. Unofficial boycotts existed in Belgium and other countries that had suffered during the war.

Yet by 1921, glowing reviews of German films like Lubitsch's *Madame Dubarry* and Wiene's *The Cabinet of Dr. Caligari* made French and British audiences feel that they were missing important developments. In November, Louis Delluc held a Paris screening of *The Cabinet of Dr. Caligari* (at a charity benefit to forestall objections). The film created a sensation, and a distributor quickly bought the French rights. *Caligari* opened in March 1922 and became an enormous hit. The exhibitors' ban was forgotten, and a vogue for German Expressionist films developed (**8.1**). In late 1922, *Madame Dubarry* premiered in London, breaking that country's boycott. Postwar hostility was waning.

Moreover, by the early 1920s, European producers realized that American competition was too great for any one country to counter. The United States, with around 15,000 theaters, was the world's largest film market. Thus American producers garnered a huge, predictable income from domestic rentals alone. They could afford to sell films cheaply abroad because most foreign income was pure profit. Commentators noted, however, that if the movie theaters of all European countries were

gathered into a single continental market, it would be comparable in size to that of the United States. What if European film industries could cooperate by guaranteeing to import each other's films? European films might make as much money as Hollywood films did. Then their budgets could be raised, their production values would improve, and they might even be able to compete with American films in other world markets. This idea was gradually formulated as the "pan-European" cinema, or "Film Europe."

Concrete Steps toward Cooperation

By 1922 to 1923, European film trade journals were calling for such cooperation, and, in 1924, the first steps were taken to create a practical cooperation among European producing nations. Erich Pommer, head of the powerful German company Ufa, concluded a pact with Louis Aubert, a major Parisian distributor. Ufa agreed to release in Germany French films provided by the Aubert company, in exchange for Aubert's distribution of Ufa films in France. Previously, French-German deals had meant the sale of a film or two, but now mutual distribution became regular.

The Ufa-Aubert deal attracted wide notice. Pommer declared, "I think that European producers must at last think of establishing a certain cooperation among themselves. It is imperative to create a system of regular trade which will enable the producers to amortise their films rapidly. It is necessary to create 'European films,' which will no longer be French, English, Italian, or German films, but entirely 'continental' films."[1] The Ufa-Aubert agreement provided the model for later transactions. Exchange of films among France, Germany, Britain, and other countries increased during the second half of the 1920s.

Pommer's statement that producers should make "European films" reflects other tactics used to increase the international circulation of films. Firms imported stars, directors, and other personnel to give an international flavor to their output. Similarly, a coproduction, in which a film would be financed and made by companies in two countries, guaranteed release in at least those two markets. A combination of these tactics might increase a film's breadth of circulation even further.

For example, British producer-director Graham Wilcox made *Decameron Nights* (1924), with Ufa providing its studio facilities and half the financing (**8.2**). Actors from several countries participated, including American star Lionel Barrymore, English actress Ivy Close, and Werner Krauss (famous as Dr. Caligari). The

8.2 Ufa's large, technically sophisticated studios permitted the construction of epic-style sets of Renaissance Venice for the British-German coproduction, *Decameron Nights*.

result was highly popular in several countries, including the United States. Producers and filmmakers from abroad often worked in Germany, since the production facilities there were the best in Europe. In 1924, the young Alfred Hitchcock began working as a designer on British films made at Ufa, where he watched Murnau working on *The Last Laugh* (p. 110). His first two films as a director, *The Pleasure Garden* (1925) and *The Mountain Eagle* (1926), were British-German coproductions shot in Germany.

Success Cut Short

By mid-decade, Germany's film industry was the leader in an increasingly cooperative pan-European effort. To be sure, many big coproductions failed to gain the anticipated international success, since cautious producers tended to use standard formulas. "International appeal" also too often meant imitations of Hollywood-style films, with a loss of the distinctive national qualities that attracted viewers to movies like *Caligari* and *Potemkin*. Tactics like coproductions and international casts, however, gradually made European films more competitive internationally. Cross-border arrangements created Spanish-French, German-Swedish, and other multinational films. The wider circulation of films allowed production budgets to rise.

The Film Europe effort also led to import quotas in some countries. After Germany lifted its import ban in 1921, it had strictly limited the number of films admitted to the country. In 1925, it changed to a system whereby a distributor could import one film for every German film

it had circulated the previous year. France imitated this plan in 1928 by introducing a modest limit of seven imported films for each French one distributed.

In 1927, Great Britain instituted a cautious quota calling for a small percentage of British footage to be distributed and exhibited in the United Kingdom. Over the years, this percentage was to increase gradually, allowing the production sector to grow to meet the demand. Even countries with more limited production created quotas. In Portugal, for example, one-tenth of screen time had to be reserved for domestic films—usually newsreels or travelogues preceding an imported feature. Although these quotas were purportedly directed against all imported films, it was common knowledge that their main target was Hollywood films. Such quotas contributed to the Film Europe drive.

Between 1924 and 1927, the Europeans, led by Germany, Britain, and France, built the base for a continental market. Slowly their efforts reduced the number of American film imports and replaced them with European ones. This table shows the percentage of feature films released in Germany, France, and Britain in 1926 and 1929, by the main countries of origin.

COUNTRY OF ORIGIN	PERCENT OF FILMS RELEASED IN					
	GERMANY		FRANCE		BRITAIN	
	1926	1929	1926	1929	1926	1929
United States	45	33	79	48	84	75
Germany	39	45	6	30	6	9
France	4	4	10	12	3	2
Britain	0.4	4	0.4	6	5	13

Germany, already the strongest film industry, benefited most from cooperative efforts. France, struggling in a production crisis, gained least; the decline in American films there was largely offset by other imports. Still, Film Europe might gradually have improved Europe's situation had the effort continued.

Abrupt changes cut it short, such as the introduction of sound in 1929. Dialogue created language barriers, and each country's producers began to hope that they could succeed locally because English-language imports would decline. Several countries did benefit from audiences' desire for sound films in their own languages, and some national industries became major forces as a result of sound. Competitiveness among European nations reappeared.

In addition, the Depression began to hit Europe in 1929. Faced by hard times, many businesses and

8.3 Expressionist mise-en-scène in L'Herbier's *Don Juan et Faust*.

8.4 A corner in a room of Usher's mansion in Epstein's *The Fall of the House of Usher* displays the influence of German Expressionism.

8.5 In *The Street*, Impressionist-style superimpositions depict the hero's visions of delights that await him in the city.

governments became more nationalistic and less interested in international cooperation. The rise of extreme left-wing and right-wing dictatorships in Europe and Asia increased divisiveness and territorial rivalries, a trend that would eventually lead to another global war. Film Europe was moribund by the early 1930s, but some of its effects lingered. Some films still circulated, and firms collaborated on productions.

THE "INTERNATIONAL STYLE"

The Blending of Stylistic Traits

Stylistic influences also circulated among countries. French Impressionism, German Expressionism, and Soviet Montage began as largely national trends, but soon the filmmakers exploring these styles became aware of each other's work. By the mid-1920s, an international avant-garde style blended traits of all three movements.

Caligari's success in France in 1922 led French directors to add Expressionist touches to their work. Impressionist director Marcel L'Herbier told two parallel stories of famous characters in *Don Juan et Faust* (1923), using Expressionist-style sets and costumes in the Faust scenes (**8.3**). In 1928, Jean Epstein combined Impressionist camera techniques with Expressionist set design to create an eerie, portentous tone in *The Fall of the House of Usher*, based on Edgar Allen Poe's story (**8.4**).

At the same time, French Impressionist traits of subjective camera devices were cropping up in German films. Karl Grune's *The Street*, an early example of the street film (p. 115), used multiple superimpositions to show the protagonist's visions (**8.5**). *The Last Laugh* and *Variety* popularized subjective cinematographic effects that had originated in France (see 5.23–5.25). By

the mid-1920s, the boundaries between the French Impressionist and German Expressionist movements were blurred.

The Montage movement started somewhat later, but imported films soon allowed Soviet directors to pick up on European stylistic trends. The rapid rhythmic editing pioneered by Epstein and Abel Gance in 1923 was pushed further by Soviet filmmakers after 1926 (p. 133). Grigori Kozintsev and Leonid Trauberg's 1926 adaptation of Nikolay Gogol's *The Cloak* contained exaggerations in the acting and mise-en-scène that were reminiscent of major German Expressionist films (**8.6**). In turn, from 1926 onward, Soviet Montage films wielded an influence abroad. Leftist filmmakers in Germany embraced the Soviet style as a means of making politically charged cinema. A shot from the final march scene in *Mutter Krausens Fahrt ins Gluck* ("Mother Krausen's Journey to Happiness," 1929, Piel Jutzi; **8.7**) echoes the climactic demonstration scene in Pudovkin's *Mother* (see 6.49). Soviet influence would intensify in the 1930s, when leftist filmmaking responded to the rise of fascism.

French, German, and Soviet techniques had an impact in many countries. Two of the most notable English directors of the 1920s reflected the influence of French Impressionism. Anthony Asquith's second feature, *Underground* (1928), used a freely moving camera and several subjective superimpositions to tell a story of love and jealousy in an ordinary working-class milieu (**8.8**). Alfred Hitchcock's boxing picture, *The Ring* (1927), demonstrated his absorption of Impressionist techniques in its many subjective passages (**8.9**). Hitchcock also acknowledged his debts to German Expressionism, an influence evident in *The Lodger* (1926). For decades, he would draw upon avant-garde techniques he learned in the 1920s.

8.6 *The Cloak* contains grotesque elements that recall German Expressionism, such as this giant steaming teapot that heralds the beginning of a strange dream sequence.

8.7 In *Mutter Krausens Fahrt ins Gluck,* a low angle isolates the major characters against the sky in Soviet Montage fashion as they march in protest.

8.8 As the heroine (not shown) of *Underground* looks up at a building, a superimposition reminiscent of French Impressionism conveys her vision of the villain.

8.9 In *The Ring,* Hitchcock used distorting mirrors in this shot of dancers to suggest the hero's mental turmoil during a party.

8.10 An enigmatic scene in *A Page of Madness,* in which an inmate obsessed with dancing appears in an elaborate costume, performing in an Expressionist set containing a whirling, striped ball.

8.11 In *The President* and other early films, Dreyer often calls as much attention to the set and incidental props as to the main action (compare with 3.14).

The international influence of the commercial avant-garde reached as far as Japan. By the 1920s, Japan was absorbing western modernism in various arts, primarily literature and painting. Futurism, Expressionism, Dada, and Surrealism were all welcomed. One young filmmaker, Teinosuke Kinugasa, was already well established in commercial production, having made over thirty low-budget pictures. He was also associated with modernist writers in Tokyo, however, and, with their help, in 1926 he independently produced a bizarre film, *A Page of Madness,* that carried Expressionist and Impressionist techniques to new extremes. Taking a cue from *Caligari,* Kinugasa set the action in a madhouse, with distorting camera devices and Expressionist mise-en-scène frequently reflecting the deranged visions of the inmates (**8.10**; compare this with shots from *Caligari* and other German Expressionist films in Chapter 5). The plot that motivates these strange scenes is full of flashbacks and fantasy passages. Kinugasa's next film, *Crossroads*

(1928), was less difficult but still reflected influences from European avant-garde films. It was the first Japanese feature to receive a significant release in Europe

Carl Dreyer: European Director

The epitome of the international director of the late silent era was Carl Dreyer. He began in Denmark as a journalist and then worked as a scriptwriter at Nordisk from 1913 on, when the company was still a powerful force. Dreyer's first film as a director, *The President* (1919), used traditional Scandinavian elements, including eye-catching sets (**8.11**), a relatively austere style, and dramatic lighting. His second film, *Leaves from Satan's Book* (1920), was also made for Nordisk; influenced by D. W. Griffith's *Intolerance,* it told a series of stories of suffering and faith.

At this point, one of the pioneers of Nordisk, Lau Lauritzen, departed, and the company declined. Both

8.12, *left*   A decentered close-up against a blank background in *The Passion of Joan of Arc* both disconcerts and allows us to watch Falconetti's moving performance in the title role.

8.13, *right*   Mismatched windows in the courtroom set of *The Passion of Joan of Arc* recall Hermann Warm's earlier career in German Expressionist filmmaking.

8.14, *left*   In *Vampyr*, the hero trails the disembodied shadow of a wooden-legged man and sees it rejoin its owner.

8.15, *right*   This shot shows the "dead" protagonist's point of view through a window in his coffin as the vampiric old woman he has been investigating peers down at him.

Dreyer and Benjamin Christensen left to work in Sweden for Svenska, Christensen making *Witchcraft through the Ages* while Dreyer did a bittersweet comedy, *The Parson's Widow* (1920). Over the next few years, Dreyer moved between Denmark and Germany, making *Michael* (1924) at the Ufa studio. Back in Denmark, he moved to the rising Palladium firm and made *Thou Shalt Honor Thy Wife* (aka *The Master of the House*, 1925). This chamber comedy shows a family deceiving an autocratic husband in order to make him realize how he has bullied his wife. It established Dreyer's reputation internationally and particularly in France. After a brief sojourn in Norway making a Norse-Swedish coproduction, Dreyer was hired by the prestigious Société Générale de Films (which was also producing Gance's *Napoléon*) to make a film in France.

The result was perhaps the greatest of all international-style silent films, *The Passion of Joan of Arc* (1928). The cast and crew represented a mixture of nationalities. The Danish director supervised designer Hermann Warm, who had worked on *Caligari* and other German Expressionist films, and Hungarian cinematographer Rudolph Maté. Most of the cast was French.

Joan of Arc blended influences from the French, German, and Soviet avant-garde movements into a fresh, daring style. Concentrating his story on Joan's trial and execution, Dreyer used many close-ups, often decentered and filmed against blank white backgrounds. The dizzying spatial relations served to concentrate attention intensely on the actors' faces. Dreyer used the newly available panchromatic film stock (p. 149), which made it possible for the actors to do without makeup. In the close framings, the images revealed every facial detail. Renée Falconetti gave an astonishingly sincere, intense performance as Joan (**8.12**). The sparse settings contained touches of muted Expressionist design (**8.13**), and the dynamic low framings and the accelerated subjective editing in the torture-chamber scene suggested the influence of Soviet Montage and French Impressionism.

Despite criticisms that *Joan of Arc* depended too much on lengthy conversations for a silent film, it was widely hailed as a masterpiece. The producer, however, was in financial difficulties after *Napoléon*'s extravagances and was unable to support another Dreyer project. Since Danish production was deteriorating, Dreyer turned to a strategy common among experimental filmmakers: he found a patron. A rich nobleman underwrote *Vampyr* (1932) in exchange for being allowed to play its protagonist.

As the name suggests, *Vampyr* is a horror film, but it bears little resemblance to such Hollywood examples of that genre as *Dracula* (which Universal had produced the previous year). Instead of presenting bats, wolves, and clear-cut rules about vampires' behavior, this film evokes unexplained, barely-glimpsed terrors. A tourist who stays at a country inn in a foggy landscape encounters a series of supernatural events as he wanders around the neighborhood. (**8.14**). He finds that the illness of a local landowner's daughter seems to be connected with her mysterious doctor and a sinister old lady who appears at intervals. The protagonist's investigation brings on a dream in which he imagines himself dead (**8.15**). Many scenes in *Vampyr* give a sense of dreadful events occurring just offscreen, with the camera tracking and panning just too late to catch them. Many visually degraded cut prints of *Vampyr* circulate, but good 35mm copies reveal Dreyer's use of lighting, misty landscapes, and camera movement to enhance the macabre atmosphere.

Vampyr was so different from other films of the period that it was greeted with incomprehension. It marked the end of Dreyer's international wanderings. He returned to Denmark and, unable to find backing for another project, to his original career as a journalist. During World War II, he recommenced feature filmmaking.

FILM EXPERIMENTS OUTSIDE THE MAINSTREAM INDUSTRY

As specialized art films became distinct from the popular entertainment cinema during the 1920s, an even more radical type of filmmaking appeared. This was *experimental*, or independent avant-garde, cinema. Experimental films were usually short, and they were produced outside the film industry. Indeed, they were often deliberate attempts to undercut the conventions of commercial narrative filmmaking.

To support their work, filmmakers might use their own money, find a rich patron, or work part-time within the mainstream industry. Moreover, the ciné-clubs and specialized theaters that had arisen to promote and exhibit art cinema also provided venues for more experimental cinema (see box). As with other types of alternative filmmaking, experimental trends emerged soon after World War I as isolated phenomena in different countries before becoming more international.

During the early decades of the century, painters and writers innovated a wide variety of modernist styles, including Cubism, abstract art, Futurism, Dadaism, and Surrealism. In many cases, artists already established in these movements made one or two films. In other cases, young filmmakers became enchanted with the idea of creating an alternative, noncommercial cinema.

During the 1910s, a few experimental films resulted from these stylistic movements, but unfortunately none of these is known to survive. Even before 1910, Italian artists Bruno Corra and Arnaldo Ginna reportedly made short films using hand-colored abstract shapes. In 1914, a group of Russian Futurist painters made a parodic film called *Drama in the Futurists' Cabaret No. 13,* but little is known about this intriguing work.

A few Futurist films were made in Italy. One was *Vita futurista* ("Futurist Life"), made by a group of Futurist artists during 1916 and 1917. The movement was concerned with celebrating the new "machine age." Artists avoided conventional logic and were fascinated with capturing rapid actions, even portraying successive events as happening simultaneously. *Vita futurista* consisted of several unconnected, absurd segments, including the painter Giacomo Balla's courting and marrying a chair. Surviving illustrations show that the film used distorting mirrors and superimpositions in ways that may have anticipated the French Impressionists and later avant-garde filmmakers. A commercial producer made two films directed by Anton Bragaglia, a Futurist photographer: *Il perfido canto* and *Thais* (both 1916). The first, which Bragaglia claimed contained innovative techniques, is lost. *Thais* survives, but it is less radical than the others, using a continuing narrative and sets, blurred focus, and costume designs that lend it a mildly Futuristic look.

Lacking sufficient evidence about these early experimental films, we must start our account of the independent avant-garde cinema with the 1920s. There were six major trends in experimental filmmaking: abstract animation, Dada-related production, Surrealism, cinéma pur, lyrical documentaries, and experimental narrative.

Abstract Animation

During the late nineteenth and early twentieth centuries, artists had moved toward works with increasingly nonobjective styles. Sometimes only the title enabled the viewer to tell what the shapes in a painting represented. In 1910, Wassily Kandinsky's *Abstract Watercolor* made the final break: the painting contained shapes and colors, but it depicted nothing. Other artists quickly followed suit, and pictorial abstraction became one of the major trends of modern art.

The nonrepresentational style took some time to make its way into film. In the late 1910s in Germany, a few artists believed that since film was a visual art like painting, its purest form would be abstract. One of

THE SPREAD OF "ART CINEMA" INSTITUTIONS

During the years after World War I, French Impressionist and German Expressionist films led many observers to distinguish between mainstream commercial cinema and a separate *art cinema*. Valid or not, the distinction has been widely used ever since.

Art films, with their more limited appeal, gave rise to a new set of institutions during the 1920s—what one historian has termed "the alternative cinema network."[2] Intellectually oriented journals, ciné-clubs, small art cinemas, exhibitions, and lectures all aimed at promoting film as an art form. Filmmakers often supported these endeavors, writing essays, appearing at clubs and art houses, and even making films aimed solely at these small, elite venues.

The origins of this network can be traced to Louis Delluc, who wrote theoretical essays and criticism for a serious fan magazine called *Le Film*, which he edited from 1917 to 1918. In it he championed early Impressionist films by Abel Gance and Marcel L'Herbier and published the latter's first theoretical writings on the cinema. In 1919, Delluc called for the formation of a ciné-club devoted to artistic films, and in 1920 he started *Le Journal de Ciné-Club*. After three sporadic meetings of the first ciné-club, Delluc started another journal, *Cinéa*, which he later sold to finance his shoestring filmmaking. It became *Cinéa-Ciné pour tous* and published many essays by the Impressionists and by critics sympathetic to the movement.

In 1921, the author Ricciotto Canudo organized the Club des Amis du Septième Art ("Club of Friends of the Seventh Art"), known as CASA. The membership included artists and critics from Paris's artistic elite, and the meetings mixed discussions of films with programs of music, poetry readings, and dance: film had gained a high-art cachet.

Canudo tirelessly promoted the cinema, and, through his connections in the Paris art world, he persuaded the prestigious annual arts exhibition, the Salon d'Automne, to devote two evenings to the cinema annually from 1921 to 1923. These evenings included lectures and clips from important films—often from the French Impressionist and German Expressionist movements. Despite Canudo's premature death in late 1923, and the subsequent decline of CASA, his colleagues continued his work. In 1924, the cinema moved up another step in respectability when a Paris art gallery, the Musée Galliera, held an exhibition on the art of the French cinema. Besides offering lectures and screenings, the exhibit displayed designs, posters, photographs, costumes, and other artifacts from recent French films—again, many of them Impressionist in style.

The climax of cinema's participation in exhibitions came in 1925, when one of this century's major art events, the Exposition International des Arts Décoratifs et Industriels Modernes, was held in Paris. This exposition was like a world's fair of decorative arts, and it popularized the modernist Art Deco style throughout the world. The cinema had its own gallery space, and a new film society was formed to show major recent films. Again, the Impressionists' work featured prominently.

Alternative cinema networks appeared in other countries as well. In 1924, a prestigious German art show, the Grossen Berliner Kunstausstellung, included a cinema section consisting of original set designs and models. Many Expressionist films, like *Caligari* and *Destiny*, were represented. The following year, a large exposition devoted entirely to photography and the cinema was held in Berlin. The Kino und Photo Ausstellung (or Kipho), mixed commerce and art. The big companies publicized forthcoming films, and visitors saw displays of German Expressionist film design, including the full-sized dragon from *The Nibelungen*.

In keeping with the Film Europe effort, exhibitions in the later 1920s were more international. A major event in the Hague in 1928, the Internationale Tentoonstelling op Filmgebied, helped introduce the young Soviet Montage movement more fully to Europeans. In 1929, the Deutsche Werkbund organized a big exposition in Stuttgart, Film und Foto. Here several programs of features and shorts surveyed the history of the avant-garde cinema, from *Caligari*

them, Hans Richter, had studied art and worked with an Expressionist group. During World War I, Richter encountered a group of Dadaists in Switzerland, including a Swedish artist, Viking Eggeling, who had also lived in Germany. Eggeling was fascinated with the idea of using art as a universal means of spiritual communication. Richter and Eggeling returned to Germany, and each worked on "scrolls," long strips of paper containing series of slightly different drawings. Both sought ways of transforming these into moving images that would be a sort of "visual music." The pair was allowed to use Ufa's facilities, and from 1910 to 1921, they experimented with animating short strips of frames photographed from the scrolls. Richter claims to have made the first abstract animated film, *Rhythmus 21*, in 1921, but it was not shown publicly until years later.

The earliest abstract animated film was apparently made in Germany by Walter Ruttmann. Ruttmann had

on. By the end of the silent era, the important art films were already gaining the status of classics.

Another major component of the alternative cinema network appeared in 1924, when Jean Tedesco opened the first of Paris's *salles specialisées* ("specialized theaters," known today as *art theaters*). Tedesco, a critic, had bought Delluc's magazine *Cinéa* and transformed it into *Cinéa-Ciné pour tous.* He had long campaigned for a theater that would revive classics and show new offbeat films. His Théâtre du Vieux-Colombier created a repertory of classics that were shown in rotation; a few films that could find no commercial distributor premiered there. In 1928, that theater even produced Renoir's Impressionist film *The Little Match Girl.* By the second half of the 1920s, there were several specialized cinemas like the Théâtre du Vieux-Colombier, as well as a growing number of ciné-clubs in Paris and provincial towns. Soon ciné-clubs and small specialized cinemas could be found abroad.

In 1925, a group of London intellectuals, including Iris Barry, who later headed the Museum of Modern Art's film archive, and filmmaker Ivor Montagu, started the Film Society. It showed old films, imports without distributors, and, especially, given England's strict censorship laws, films that were not approved for public screening. The Film Society and other clubs became vital in showing banned Soviet films in Britain. The group lasted until 1938, even though by the early 1930s, some art cinemas, including the long-lived Academy, had made it easier to see special-interest films and film clubs existed in many parts of Britain.

The art-cinema trend reached the United States in 1925, when Symon Gould began the Film Arts Guild, renting a small New York theater for Sunday matinees of imported films. Within the next three years, the guild was able to move to full-time screenings, and additional art cinemas opened in New York and other cities. In 1928, the Filmarte opened in Hollywood, giving filmmakers there increased access to European avant-garde cinema. These theaters initially relied heavily on Expressionist and other German films, both new and old. Late in the decade, Soviet films became a staple of art-house programs. Émigré moviegoers helped support these theaters, and by the early 1930s, there was a healthy alternative cinema market in the United States.

Ciné-clubs and art theaters spread to Belgium, Japan, Spain, and many other countries. A filmmaker who failed to find a distributor could deal directly with these groups, shipping prints around the globe. As long as films remained fairly cheap to make, this limited circulation could generate a modest profit.

A growing number of journals promoted art films. Tedesco's *Cinéa-Ciné pour tous* continued to offer a forum for discussion of Impressionism and other artistic tendencies. It was supplemented by other French journals, including *L'Art Cinématographique*, which published only eight issues but served as an important outlet for Impressionist theory. The main international periodical of the era, *Close Up,* ran from 1927 to 1933. Its driving forces were editor Kenneth Macpherson and his wife Bryher, wealthy Britishers living in Switzerland. Frequent contributors included their friends, notably the American poet H. D. (Hilda Doolittle), who wrote passionate, personal accounts of European art films. *Close Up* championed unconventional cinema of all types, including the films of G. W. Pabst and the Soviet cinema, on which Bryher wrote the first book in English. Many small journals came and went during this period.

Art theaters, clubs, expositions, and publications helped support alternative types of films. Moreover, they affected decisions about which films would be saved as classics. During the 1930s, several major archives were formed, including the National Film Archive in London, the Museum of Modern Art in New York, and the Cinémathèque Française in Paris. Most people working in these archives were sympathetic to alternative movements of the 1920s. Thus many films of this era were preserved, revived, and circulated in later decades.

---

also studied as a painter, working in abstract and Expressionist styles. From an early date, however, he was also interested in film. In 1913, he condemned the Autorenfilm (p. 57) as a pointless attempt to inject quality into the cinema by drawing on literature:

> You can't turn film into a work of art by augmenting and exalting it with "quality." You can gather together the best mimes in the world, you can let them perform in the most exquisite paradise, you can adorn the programs of your film dramas with the names of the most eminent poets—art will never result *that way.* A work of art will result only if it is born of the possibilities and demands of its material.[3]

Ruttmann's attitude would be shared by many experimental filmmakers in the 1920s. In 1918, he too became intrigued with the idea of "moving paintings" and

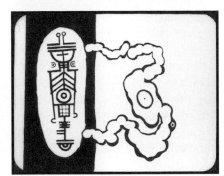

8.16, *left* In *Opus 2*, Ruttmann creates subtle gradations of texture as abstract shapes slide across each other, blending and separating rhythmically.

8.17, *right* In *Diagonal Symphony*, complicated curved shapes swirl around the basic diagonal motif that organizes the abstract patterns throughout the film.

8.18, *left* In *The Adventures of Prince Achmed*, shades of gray suggest the depth in a setting; the moving figures consist of jointed silhouette puppets.

8.19, *right* Len Lye based the abstract figures in *Tusalava* on Australian Aboriginal art.

began to cast about for a means of creating them through film.

Apparently knowing little of commercial animation techniques, Ruttmann painted with oil on glass, wiping off portions of the wet paint and replacing them. He photographed each change from above with illumination from beneath the glass. His *Lichtspiel Opus 1* was previewed in Frankfurt in early April 1921 and given a gala premiere in Berlin later that month. Ruttmann went on the make three similar short films, *Lichtspiel Opus 2* (1921), *Ruttmann Opus 3* (1924), and *Ruttmann Opus 4* (1925). (These are now known as *Opus 1, Opus 2,* and so on.) In each, abstract forms grow, shrink, and transmute in a lively fashion (**8.16**). Ruttmann intended that his films be shown with original musical scores and with hand-coloring. These delightful short films earned him commissions to make theatrical commercials and special sequences in feature films, such as Kriemhild's "Dream of the Falcon" in Fritz Lang's *Siegfried*.

In the meantime, Richter had managed to make three similar short animated films, the *Rhythmus* series (tentatively dated 1921, 1923, and 1925). His partner, Eggeling, met an experienced animator, Erna Niemeyer; she traced his scroll drawings and photographed them to make *Diagonalsymphonie* (*Diagonal Symphony*). Eggeling saw his moving abstract images as the equivalent of music, dictating that the short film be shown without any sound accompaniment. It presents a series of variations on parallel white diagonal lines moving in complex patterns against a black background (**8.17**). *Diagonal Symphony* was first shown in late 1924, a year before Eggeling died.

The technique of abstract animation influenced commercial cinema, most notably in the work of a distinctive filmmaker, Lotte Reiniger. Trained as an actress during the 1910s, she was also skilled at cutting out elaborate and delicate silhouettes. During the early 1920s, she created special-effects sequences and advertisements. From 1923 to 1926, she worked on her most important film, *The Adventures of Prince Achmed,* assisted by Ruttmann and others. *Prince Achmed* was the first major animated feature (preceding Disney's *Snow White and the Seven Dwarfs*). *Prince Achmed* told an Arabian Nights fairy tale by means of silhouette figures photographed against subtly shaded backgrounds (**8.18**). Reiniger created such silhouette fantasy films for decades in several countries.

On May 3, 1925, an important matinee of abstract films was held at an Ufa theater in Berlin. It included *Diagonal Symphony*, three of Ruttmann's *Opus* shorts, and Richter's *Rhythmus* series. Also on the program were two French films, René Clair's *Entr'acte* and Dudley Murphy and Fernand Léger's *Ballet mécanique* (see 8.28). German filmmakers recognized a fresh experimental impulse. Richter and Ruttmann abandoned abstract animation to make films using real objects, and the tradition nearly disappeared at this point.

It resurfaced unexpectedly in 1929. The London Film Society provided a young New Zealander, the ab-

8.20, *left* Man Ray created "Rayogram" images without a camera by scattering objects like pins and tacks directly on the film strip, exposing it briefly to light, and developing the result.

8.21, *right* Clair's Dadaist fantasy *Entr'acte* concludes with an irreverent funeral scene in which the hearse is pulled, often at dizzying speed and over roller-coaster tracks, by a camel.

stract painter and scriptwriter Len Lye, with the funds for a short film. The drawings occupied Lye from 1927 to 1929, while he supported himself as a curtain drawer in a theater. *Tusalava*, which premiered at the Film Society in 1929, baffled most spectators with its esoteric imagery (**8.19**). Despite the film's initial reception, Lye went on to become one of the most important abstract animators of the sound era. During the 1920s, Oskar Fischinger was also trying out different animation techniques, including drawn abstract images, but his work, too, flourished primarily after the introduction of sound.

Dada Filmmaking

Dada was a movement that attracted artists in all media. It began around 1915, as a result of artists' sense of the vast, meaningless loss of life in World War I. Artists in New York, Zurich, France, and Germany proposed to sweep aside traditional values and to elevate an absurdist view of the world. They would base artistic creativity on randomness and imagination. Max Ernst displayed an artwork and provided a hatchet so that spectators could demolish it. Marcel Duchamp invented "ready-made" artwork, in which a found object is placed in a museum and labeled; in 1917, he created a scandal by signing a urinal "R. Mutt" and trying to enter it in a prestigious show. Dadaists were fascinated by collage, the technique of assembling disparate elements in bizarre juxtapositions. Ernst, for example, made collages by pasting together scraps of illustrations from advertisements and technical manuals.

Under the leadership of poet Tristan Tzara, Dadaist publications, exhibitions, and performances flourished during the late 1910s and early 1920s. The performance "soirées" included such events as poetry readings in which several passages were performed simultaneously. On July 7, 1923, the last major Dada event, the "Soirée du 'Coeur à Barbe'" ("Soirée of the 'Bearded Heart'"), included three short films: a study of New York by

American artists Charles Sheeler and Paul Strand, one of Richter's *Rhythmus* abstract animated works, and the American artist Man Ray's first film, the ironically titled *Retour à la raison* ("Return to Reason"). The element of chance certainly entered into the creation of *Retour à la raison*, since Tzara gave Ray only twenty-four hours' notice that he was to make a film for the program. Ray combined some hastily shot live footage with stretches of "Rayograms" (**8.20**). The soirée proved a mixed success, since Tzara's rivals, led by poet André Breton, provoked a riot in the audience.

This riot was symptomatic of the disagreements that were already bringing Dada to an end. By 1922, it was in serious decline, but key Dada films were still to come. In late 1924, Dada artist Francis Picabia staged his ballet *Relâche* (meaning "performance called off"). Signs in the auditorium bore such statements as "If you are not satisfied, go to hell." During the intermission (or *entr'acte*), René Clair's *Entr'acte* was shown, with music by composer Erik Satie, who had done the music for the entire show. The evening began with a brief film prologue (seen as the opening segment of modern prints of *Entr'acte*) in which Satie and Picabia leap in slow motion into a scene and fire a cannon directly at the audience. The rest of the film, appearing during the intermission, consisted of unconnected, wildly irrational scenes (**8.21**). Picabia summed up the Dada view when he characterized Clair's film: "*Entr'acte* does not believe in very much, in the pleasure of life, perhaps; it believes in the pleasure of inventing, it respects nothing except the desire to *burst out laughing*."[4]

Dada artist Marcel Duchamp made one foray into cinema during this era. By 1913, Duchamp had moved away from abstract painting to experiment with such forms as ready-mades and kinetic sculptures. The latter included a series of motor-driven spinning discs. With the help of Man Ray, Duchamp filmed some of these discs to create *Anémic cinéma* in 1926. This brief film undercuts traditional notions of cinema as a visual, narrative art. All its shots show either turning abstract

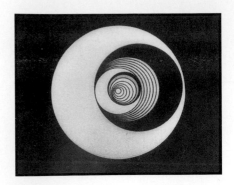 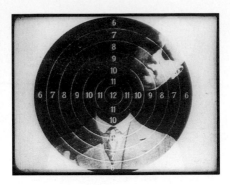

8.22, *left*   One of the spinning discs that create the "anemic" form of *Anémic cinéma.*

8.23, *right*   In *Ghosts before Breakfast*, a man's head flies off his body as a target is superimposed over him.

disks (**8.22**) or disks with sentences containing elaborate French puns. By emphasizing simple shapes and writing, Duchamp created an "anemic" style. (*Anémic* is also an anagram for *cinéma*.) In keeping with his playful attitude, he signed the film "Rrose Sélavy," a pun on *Eros c'est la vie* ("Eros is life").

Entr'acte and other dada films were on the 1925 Berlin program, and they convinced German filmmakers like Ruttman and Richter that modernist style could be created in films without completely abstract, painted images. Richter, who had been linked with virtually every major modern art movement, dabbled in Dada. In his *Ghosts before Breakfast* (1928), special effects show objects rebelling against their normal uses. In reverse motion, cups shatter and reassemble. Bowler hats take on a life of their own and fly through the air, and the ordinary laws of nature seem to be suspended (**8.23**).

Riven by internal dissension, the European Dada movement was largely over by 1922. Many of its members formed another group, the Surrealists.

Surrealism

Surrealism resembled Dada in many ways, particularly in its disdain for orthodox aesthetic traditions. Like Dada, Surrealism sought out startling juxtapositions. André Breton, who led the break with the Dadaists and the creation of Surrealism, cited an image from a work by the Comte de Lautréamont: "Beautiful as the unexpected meeting, on a dissection table, of a sewing machine and an umbrella."[5] The movement was heavily influenced by the emerging theories of psychoanalysis. Rather than depending on pure chance for the creation of artworks, Surrealists sought to tap the unconscious mind. In particular, they wanted to render the incoherent narratives of dreams directly in language or images, without the interference of conscious thought processes. Max Ernst, Salvador Dalí, Joan Miró, and Paul Klee were important Surrealist artists.

The ideal Surrealist film differed from Dada works in that it would not be a humorous, chaotic assemblage of events. Instead, it would trace a disturbing, often sexually charged story that followed the inexplicable logic of a dream. With a patron's backing, Dadaist Man Ray moved into Surrealism with *Emak Bakia* (1927), which used many film tricks to suggest a woman's mental state. At the end she is seen in a famous image, her eyes closed, with eyeballs painted on them; she opens her eyes and smiles at the camera. Many Surrealists denounced the film as containing too little narrative. Ray's next film, *L'Étoile de mer* ("The Starfish," 1927), hinted at a story based on a script by Surrealist poet Robert Desnos. It shows a couple in love, interspersed with random shots of starfish, trains, and other objects (**8.24**). At the end the woman leaves with another man, and her cast-off lover consoles himself with a beautiful starfish.

Germaine Dulac, who had already worked extensively in regular feature filmmaking and French Impressionism, turned briefly to Surrealism, directing a screenplay by poet Antonin Artaud. The result was *The Seashell and the Clergyman* (1928), which combines Impressionist techniques of cinematography with the disjointed narrative logic of Surrealism. A clergyman carrying a large seashell smashes laboratory beakers; an officer intrudes and breaks the shell, to the clergyman's horror. The rest of the film consists of the priest's pursuing a beautiful woman through an incongruous series of settings. His love seems to be perpetually thwarted by the intervention of the officer (**8.25**). Even after the priest marries the woman, he is left alone drinking from the shell. The initial screening of the film provoked a riot at the small Studio des Ursulines theater, though it is still not clear whether the instigators were Artaud's enemies or his friends, protesting Dulac's softening of the Surrealist tone of the scenario.

Perhaps the quintessential Surrealist film was created in 1928 by novice director Luis Buñuel. A Spanish film enthusiast and modernist poet, Buñuel had come

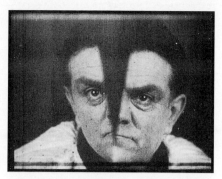

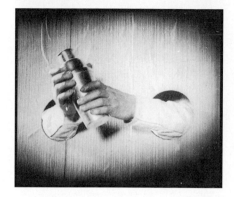

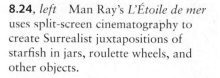

8.24, *left*   Man Ray's *L'Étoile de mer* uses split-screen cinematography to create Surrealist juxtapositions of starfish in jars, roulette wheels, and other objects.

8.25, *right*   A split-screen technique creates a bizarre effect in *The Seashell and the Clergyman*: the officer, dressed in baby clothes, seems to split in two.

8.26, *left*   In *Un Chien andalou*, a doorbell is inexplicably represented by hands shaking a cocktail.

8.27, *right*   During an elegant party, the heroine of *L'Age d'or* finds an ox in her bed.

to France and been hired as an assistant by Jean Epstein. Working in collaboration with Salvador Dalí, he made *Un Chien andalou* (*An Andalusian Dog*). Its basic story concerned a quarrel between two lovers, but the time scheme and logic are impossible. The film begins with a sequence in which a man inexplicably slices the heroine's eye with a razor—yet she appears, unharmed, in the next scene. As the quarrel goes on, ants crawl from a hole in a man's hand, the hero hauls a piano stuffed with rotting mules' carcasses across a room, and a pair of hands protrudes through the wall to shake a cocktail (**8.26**). Throughout, intertitles announce meaningless intervals of time passing, as when "sixteen years earlier" appears within an action that continues without pause.

Dalí and Buñuel followed this film with a longer, even more provocative one, *L'Age d'or* ("The Age of Gold," 1930). The tenuous plot concerns two lovers kept apart by the woman's wealthy parents and a disapproving society. An early scene shows a pompous ceremony at the seaside in which presiding bishops wither to skeletons. Later, a man who is shot falls up to the ceiling, and the heroine sucks on the toes of a statue to express her sexual frustration. The film teems with erotic imagery (**8.27**), and the ending portrays a figure clearly intended to represent Christ emerging from a sadistic orgy. *L'Age d'or,* which provoked riots during its initial screenings, was banned. It remained almost impossible to see for over four decades.

During the early 1930s, Surrealism as a unified movement was breaking up. Some artists became involved in leftist or anarchist politics, and Dalí earned their wrath through his fascination with Hitler. By 1933, the European phase of the movement was over, but, as with Dada, Surrealism's influence was felt strongly in the era after World War II.

Cinéma Pur

In 1924, a casual collaboration of artists resulted in an abstract film that did not use animated drawings but rather everyday objects and rhythmic editing. American set designer Dudley Murphy had decided to mount a series of "visual symphonies," the first of which was a rather literal-minded ballet film, *Danse macabre* (1922). In Paris, he encountered Man Ray and modernist poet Ezra Pound, who inspired him to do a more abstract work. Ray actually shot some footage, but the French painter Fernand Léger completed the filming of *Ballet mécanique*. Murphy did the cinematography, and Léger directed a complex film juxtaposing shots of objects like pot lids and machine parts with images of his own paintings. There were prismatic shots of women's faces, as well as an innovative shot of a washerwoman climbing

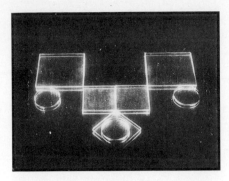

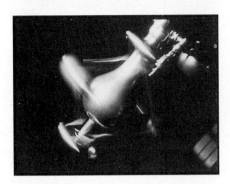

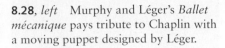

8.28, *left* Murphy and Léger's *Ballet mécanique* pays tribute to Chaplin with a moving puppet designed by Léger.

8.29, *right* *Cinq minutes de cinema pur* begins by dissolving among shots of shiny crystals in changing patterns against a black background.

8.30, 8.31 *Thème et variations* alternates machine parts and plants (not shown) with a ballerina's dance, suggesting an abstract graphic similarity between different kinds of movements and shapes.

a flight of steps, repeated identically many times. Léger had hoped to make a film about Charlie Chaplin, and he opened and closed *Ballet mécanique* with an animated figure of the comedian rendered in his own painting style (**8.28**).

In the wake of works like *Ballet mécanique,* some filmmakers realized that they could organize nonnarrative films around abstract visual qualities of the physical world. Since commercial cinema, especially that of Hollywood, was strongly associated with narrative, such abstract films seemed untainted, owing nothing to literary or theatrical influences. These filmmakers were not unified by membership in any modernist movement, like Dada or Surrealism. Indeed, they largely avoided the irreverence of Dada and the psychic explorations of Surrealism. These diverse, widely scattered filmmakers wanted to reduce film to its most basic elements in order to create lyricism and pure form.

Indeed, French proponents of this approach soon termed it *cinéma pur,* or "pure cinema." One of these was Henri Chomette, who had worked as an assistant director for commercial filmmakers like Jacques de Baroncelli and Jacques Feyder. In 1925, a commission from a rich count for an experimental short led to *Jeux des reflets et de la vitesse* ("The Play of Reflections and Speed," 1925). For the "speed" portion Chomette mounted his camera at various angles on a moving subway car, often filming in fast motion. He juxtaposed

these shots with views of a series of shiny objects. His next film, *Cinq minutes de cinéma pur* ("Five Minutes of Pure Cinema," 1926), was made for the growing circuit of specialized cinemas (**8.29**; compare with **8.17**). After these two films, Chomette became a commercial director.

Following her venture into Surrealism, Germaine Dulac embraced cinéma pur in *Disque 927* (1928), *Thème et variations* (1928), and *Arabesque* (1929). As the titles suggest, Dulac tried to make her short, lyrical studies equivalent to musical pieces (**8.30, 8.31**). With the coming of sound, Dulac could not finance her films independently, and, unwilling to return to mainstream filmmaking, she worked primarily in newsreels after 1929.

The concept of pure cinema surfaced in other countries, though seldom under that name. Some photographers experimented briefly with cinema. Laszló Moholy-Nagy, a Hungarian photographer and sculptor, created several films in the late 1920s and early 1930s. Among these was *Lichtspiel, schwarz-weiss-grau* ("Play of Light, Black-White-Gray," 1930), made while he was teaching at the Bauhaus. The title is a pun: *Lichtspiel* means both "movie" and "play of light" (**8.32**). American photographer Ralph Steiner's H_2O (1929) consisted of increasingly abstract images of water (**8.33**). Steiner made two similar films and then went on to photograph some of the most important documentaries of the next decade.

8.32 Filming one of his own kinetic sculptures, the *Light-Space Modulator,* Moholy-Nagy created shifting patterns of shadows and reflected light, produced by its moving metallic parts, for *Lichtspiel, schwarz-weiss-grau.*

8.33 In this shot from Steiner's H_2O, the reflections on the surface of the water create an image so abstract that we can barely recognize its subject.

8.34 A dramatic view of the street far below through a balustrade in *Manhatta.*

8.35 A drunken, perhaps dying, old woman wandering the streets forms one motif in *Rien que les heures.*

8.36, 8.37 In *Berlin,* Ruttmann cuts from an abstract moving image of bars forming an "X" to a similar composition created by a railroad crossing gate.

The pure-cinema impulse has had a strong influence on experimental filmmakers since the 1920s.

Lyrical Documentaries: The City Symphony

Some filmmakers experimented by taking their cameras outdoors and capturing poetic aspects of urban landscapes. Their films formed another new genre, the *city symphony*. These works were part documentary, part experimental film.

The earliest known city symphony, and, indeed, perhaps the first experimental film made in the United States, was created by modern artist Charles Sheeler and photographer Paul Strand in 1920. It was shown as a scenic short in a commercial theater in New York the following year under the title *New York the Magnificent,* but the filmmakers later dubbed it *Manhatta,* and that is the title by which it has come to be known. The pair filmed scenes near the Battery Park area of southern Manhattan, creating evocative, often nearly abstract views of the city (**8.34**). Although the film had little distribution initially, it was revived in art theaters during the second half of the decade and probably inspired later filmmaking.

By that era, the city symphony had become more common. In 1925, Brazilian director Alberto Cavalcanti, working in France, made *Rien que les heures* ("Nothing but the Hours," 1926). It juxtaposes two different types of material: candid documentary shots and staged scenes. Shopkeepers open their shutters, patrons eat at cafés, a pimp kills a woman, an old lady staggers through the streets (**8.35**). Cavalcanti refuses to develop any of these situations into a coherent plot, instead weaving together motifs to suggest the passage of time all over Paris.

Cavalcanti's film was followed by Walter Ruttmann's feature, *Berlin: die Symphonie der Grosstadt* (*Berlin, Symphony of a Great City,* 1927). It also provided a cross section of life in a city during one day. Coming from the tradition of abstract animation, Ruttmann begins the film with some geometric shapes, matching them graphically with documentary images (**8.36, 8.37**). Subsequent shots explore the abstract

8.38, *left*   Ivens captures the effects of the last few drops of a shower in a puddle on a brick pavement in *Rain*.

8.39, *right*   A split-screen effect in *The Life and Death of 9413—a Hollywood Extra* juxtaposes the hero's naive face with his abstract vision of Hollywood.

qualities of machines, building façades, store-window displays, and the like. Ruttmann also includes social commentary, as when during the noontime segment he cuts from a homeless woman with her children to plates of food in a fancy restaurant. *Berlin* circulated widely in commercial theaters and was one of the silent era's most influential documentaries.

The poetic city symphony proved fertile ground for young filmmakers working for the art-cinema and ciné-club circuit. For example, the Dutch documentarist Joris Ivens began as cofounder of a major club, the Filmliga, in Amsterdam in 1927. His first completed film was a lyrical, abstract study of a drawbridge, *The Bridge* (1928). Its success in art-film circles led to other films, including *Rain* (1929). *Rain* explores the changing look of Amsterdam before, during, and after a shower: the sheen of water on tile roofs and windows and the spatter of raindrops in the canals and in puddles (**8.38**). Again, *Rain* was well received among art-cinema audiences across Europe and inspired many imitations.

The city-symphony genre was diverse. The film might be lyrical, displaying the effects of wind and water. Henri Storck, who had formed the ciné-club for the Belgian seaside town of Ostende, recorded the town's summertime sights in his *Images d'Ostende* (1929). In contrast, Dziga Vertov's *Man with a Movie Camera* commented on Soviet society by weaving together several cities in a "day-in-the-life-of" documentary. Vertov demonstrated the power of the cinema by showing the filmmaking process within his film and by using extensive special effects (see 6.54). The city symphony has proved an enduring genre among documentarists and experimental filmmakers.

Experimental Narrative

By the late 1920s, filmmakers in several countries were using the techniques and styles of the independent experimental cinema to question narrative conventions.

In the United States, some experimental directors adapted techniques from German Expressionism and French Impressionism into cinematic forms suited to low-budget, independent production. During the late 1920s, noncommercial European filmmakers pushed both narrative and abstract techniques still further.

In the United States, some filmmakers outside the commercial industry wanted to treat film as a modern art. Few of the more radical experimental films made in Europe during this era were shown in America, however. Experimental filmmakers were inspired mainly by German Expressionist and French Impressionist films.

Like Dreyer, Robert Florey was an international director, though on a more modest scale. Born in France, he was thoroughly familiar with both the Impressionist and the Expressionist movements. He came to Hollywood in 1921, serving as United Artists' technical adviser on French subjects and eventually directing minor features. In 1927, he turned to experimental filmmaking, directing the short *The Life and Death of 9413—a Hollywood Extra* (aka *Life and Death of a Hollywood Extra*). This ingenious film, made for a reported $100, combined close shots of actors against black backgrounds with stylized miniature scenes, made of simple paper cut-outs and erector-set objects, shot with an ordinary light on a kitchen table (**8.39**). The film was a witty satire on Hollywood's uncaring treatment of aspiring talent. Florey's cinematographer, Gregg Toland, went on to photograph many major films, including *Citizen Kane*. The special effects were devised by Slavko Vorkapich, another émigré fascinated with avant-garde technique; during the 1930s, he created elaborate montage sequences for several Hollywood movies. *Hollywood Extra* was given a commercial release, through the intervention of Charles Chaplin, and Florey went on to make three more experimental shorts. The only one that survives, *The Love of Zero* (1928), contains many innovative camera techniques, but it is not as appealing as the earlier film. Florey soon moved back into commer-

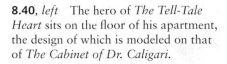

8.40, *left*   The hero of *The Tell-Tale Heart* sits on the floor of his apartment, the design of which is modeled on that of *The Cabinet of Dr. Caligari*.

8.41, *right*   An Expressionist set, apparently depicting a crypt, in *The Fall of the House of Usher*.

8.42, *left*   Paul Robeson in *Borderline*.

8.43, *right*   *Impatience* seems to suggest a narrative situation, yet its insistent repetition of shots like this one of the woman against a blank background also forces us to see it as abstract.

cial production, directing many stylish middle- and low-budget features, ranging from the Marx Brothers' first film, *The Coconuts* (1929), to the horror film *Murders in the Rue Morgue* (1932). Some of these show the influence of German Expressionism.

Almost simultaneously, some filmmakers drew upon the idea of using German Expressionism to bring stories by Edgar Allan Poe to the screen. Amateur director Charles Klein's *The Tell-Tale Heart* (1928) imitated *Caligari* by explicitly presenting its story as the vision of an insane man (**8.40**). Klein's film circulated among the newly formed art cinemas. In Rochester, New York, two film and photography enthusiasts, James Sibley Watson and Melville Webber, codirected *The Fall of the House of Usher* (1928). This film's oblique narrative technique depends on the spectator's foreknowledge of Poe's story. Impressionist-style subjective camera techniques and Expressionist decor are combined in an attempt to capture the eerie atmosphere of the original (**8.41**). Watson and Webber went on to make an even more obscure story, *Lot in Sodom* (1933), replete with superimpositions, painted faces, and black backgrounds.

A few European works pushed even further in exploring narrative conventions during the late 1920s. One such film was the short feature *Borderline*, created by the group around the international intellectual journal *Close Up* (p. 175). Its editor, Kenneth Macpherson, directed, and the poet H. D. was one of the actors. *Borderline* centers on two couples, one black, one white,

living in a small Swiss town. When the white man begins an affair with the black woman, sexual and racial tensions escalate. The film mixes objective and subjective scenes without clear-cut transitions. The African American stage actor and singer Paul Robeson played the black husband, and H. D. gave an intense performance as the jealous white woman. Dynamic compositions reflected the influence of the Soviet cinema (**8.42**), but the film was unique in its elliptical style. It remained the *Close Up* group's only completed experiment.

The Belgian Charles Dekeukeleire discovered the cinema through the work of the French Impressionists. After working as a critic, he turned to filmmaking in 1927, just as the ciné-club movement was spreading. Planning, shooting, and even processing his own footage, he made four silent experimental films over the next few years. Outstanding among these were *Impatience* (1929) and *Histoire de détective* ("Detective Story," 1930), bold films that had little precedent in any artistic tradition. *Impatience* lasts nearly forty-five minutes but consists of relentless repetitions of only four elements: a woman (alternately naked and dressed in a motorcyclist's outfit), a motorcycle, mountain scenery, and a set of three swinging abstract blocks. No two of these elements is ever seen in the same shot. Although the film seems to hint at a minimal narrative situation (perhaps the woman is riding the motorcycle through the mountains?), it simply shows us the same sorts of shots over and over (**8.43**).

8.44 Carefully staged action in *Nanook of the North* as the hero prepares to launch his kayak and join his friends in the hunt.

8.45 A documentary spectacle as thousands of nomads brave frigid mountains in a search for pastureland in *Grass*.

Histoire de détéctive is even more complex. Purportedly a film made by a detective investigating why a man has lost all interest in life, it consists mainly of lengthy written passages, punctuated by banal images of the lives of the man and his wife, which add little to the intertitles. In a period when cinematic stories were supposed to be told visually, Dekeukeleire's film was widely condemned. He made one more silent film, *Flamme blanche* ("White Flame," 1931), a semidocumentary story of police brutality during a Communist party rally. Faced with an uncomprehending reaction to his work, Dekeukeleire turned to documentary filmmaking during the sound era. His two silent masterpieces, however, were indications of how far experimental films could go in defying the norms of narrative cinema.

Independent avant-garde cinema depended on the fact that silent filmmaking was relatively inexpensive. The advent of sound increased costs considerably, and even ciné-clubs and art cinemas usually preferred to show sound films. The rise of fascism led several experimental directors to move toward political documentaries. Still, the tradition of experimentation outside commercial institutions continued, albeit in changed form, in the 1930s and beyond.

DOCUMENTARY FEATURES GAIN PROMINENCE

Before the 1920s, documentary filmmaking had largely been confined to newsreels and scenic shorts. Occasional feature-length documentaries had been made, but these had not established the genre as significant. During the 1920s, however, the documentary achieved new stature as it increasingly became identified with artistic cinema. We can distinguish three main tendencies in the documentaries of this era: the exotic film, the attempt at direct recording of reality, and the compilation documentary.

The exotic documentary was particularly important in the United States. It came dramatically to public attention in 1922 with the release of Robert Flaherty's *Nanook of the North*. An explorer and prospector in Alaska and Canada, Flaherty had shot some amateur footage of Eskimo culture. He determined to make a feature film following the life of an Eskimo family. Eventually, in 1920, a fur company agreed to finance the venture. Flaherty spent sixteen months in the region of Hudson Bay, filming Nanook and his wife and son. Every scene was planned in advance, with Nanook making many suggestions about what sorts of action to include (**8.44**). Flaherty balanced authenticity with arranged scenes, as when the Eskimos built an oversize igloo with one side open so that the family could be filmed going to bed.

The major Hollywood film firms refused to distribute *Nanook,* but the independent Pathé Exchange released it. It met with great success, undoubtedly in part because of the engaging personality of its hero. As a result, Paramount supported Flaherty in an expedition to Samoa to direct a similar film, *Moana*. He set out in 1923, only to find that the natives had adopted western-style customs. Flaherty persuaded his "actors" to return to traditional clothing and, in order to inject drama into the film, to reenact a painful, obsolete tattoo ritual. Flaherty had by now fallen into his lifelong habit of running far beyond schedule and shooting immense amounts of footage. *Moana* was not ready for release until 1926 and did not duplicate the success of *Nanook*. Flaherty would not complete another film for eight years.

8.46 In *Kino-Pravda* (number 21, 1925), Lenin's face is superimposed in the sky above his tomb.

8.47 In *The Fall of the Romanov Dynasty,* Esfir Shub includes newsreel footage of the destruction of the statue of Tsar Alexander III in Moscow in 1921.

8.48 The new railroad is used to tether a camel in *Turksib.*

Nanook's triumph also enabled the producer-director-photographer team of Ernest B. Schoedsack and Merian Cooper to create their first feature, *Grass: A Nation's Battle for Life* (1925). Also financed and distributed by Paramount, it recorded a dangerous migration of Iranian nomads seeking pastures for their flocks (**8.45**). *Grass* was popular enough to permit Schoedsack and Cooper to make *Chang* (1928), a staged account, shot on location, of a peasant family battling dangers in their native Siamese jungle. *Chang* reflected a move toward fiction-based filmmaking, and Schoedsack and Cooper were to push their interest in exoticism completely into fiction in producing the immensely successful *King Kong* in 1933.

The documentary form was particularly important in the Soviet Union. There all three types of documentary—exoticism, recording of reality, and compilation—found expression.

Dziga Vertov had taken charge of Soviet newsreel filmmaking during the Russian Revolution. By the early 1920s he had formulated his theory of the "kino eye," claiming that the camera lens, due to its recording abilities, was superior to the human eye. He put this claim to the test in 1922, establishing a new newsreel series, *Kino-Pravda.* (The name was derived from the national Bolshevik newspaper, *Pravda* ["Truth"], started by Lenin in 1912.) Each installment of the newsreel focused on two or three episodes of current events or ordinary life. Vertov also, however, believed that special effects were part of the camera's superior ability to report the truth. Thus he often used split-screen effects or superimpositions to comment on his subjects (**8.46**). Vertov also made feature-length documentaries, mixing footage photographed directly from life with special effects that conveyed ideological points (see 6.54). When

sound was introduced in the Soviet Union, Vertov insisted on having a mobile recording machine that could be taken on location in factories and mines for use in making *Enthusiasm* (1931), a documentary on the First Five-Year Plan in steel production.

During this era, Soviet filmmaker Esfir Shub virtually single-handedly invented the compilation film. She had reedited foreign films for Soviet release during the early 1920s. Her real interest, however, was in documentary. She aspired to assemble scenes from old newsreels into new films. The Soviet authorities refused to give her access to such footage until 1926. Among the old reels, she found the home movies of Tsar Nicholas II, around which she based *The Fall of the Romanov Dynasty* (1927; **8.47**). The favorable reception of this film allowed her to make two additional features: *The Great Road* (1927), on the Russian Revolution, and *The Russia of Nicholas II and Leo Tolstoy* (1928), on the prerevolutionary era. Having used much of the footage she had discovered, Shub continued her career as an editor in the sound era.

Aware of the many ethnic groups living in the new Soviet Union, directors fostered an exoticism not unlike that of Flaherty's *Nanook.* In 1929, Viktor Turin made *Turksib,* chronicling the epic construction of the Turkestan-Siberian railway. Although the film emphasized the achievements of the Soviet state, it also recorded the reactions of the indigenous peoples living along the railway's route (**8.48**). This exotic appeal made *Turksib* popular on the art-cinema circuit in the West. Similarly, in *Salt for Svanetia* (1930) Mikhail Kalatozov recorded in sparse but beautiful detail the efforts to bring salt to a remote mountain village near the Black and Caspian Seas.

The work of Flaherty, Schoedsack and Cooper, Vertov, Shub, and others would have a considerable impact during the 1930s, when the documentary became more prominent.

COMMERCIAL FILMMAKING INTERNATIONALLY

As we emphasized in Part 1, the cinema has always been an international phenomenon. Even while Hollywood dominated world markets and some countries developed distinctive styles, hundreds of other films aimed at a popular market continued to be made annually worldwide. Some countries' industries imitated Hollywood cinema fairly directly, while a few devised recognizable (though not avant-garde) styles. Several countries that previously had only sporadic production began making films more regularly, while production in some declined.

Japan

One of the most powerful studio systems grew up in Japan, where filmmakers forged a distinctive style. The first studios were built during the Russo-Japanese War (1904–1905). Japan's victory in the conflict established it as a world power. Soon industrial growth intensified. Japan supplied the warring nations of Europe with matériel and began dominating Asia with consumer goods. U.S. films entered the market, but Japanese audiences, though fond of American films, preferred the domestic product and sustained local production.

The two most powerful companies were Nikkatsu and Shochiku. Nikkatsu (short for Nippon Katsudo Shashin) was organized in 1912 out of several smaller firms. Shochiku was founded in 1920 by two brothers who ran a conglomerate of kabuki theaters and vaudeville houses. Both Nikkatsu and Shochiku were vertically integrated, owning distribution companies and theaters. The industry gained a professional identity by forming a trade association and by publishing a film magazine, *Kinema Jumpo* ("Movie Times").

In September 1923, an earthquake devastated Tokyo, but the movie business emerged stronger than before. In rebuilding theaters, exhibitors expanded and modernized them. Vertical integration allowed Japanese firms to control and profit from American imports.

Shooting a feature in two weeks or less, Shochiku, Nikkatsu, and dozens of smaller studios pumped out 600 to 800 films per year. By 1928, Japan was producing more films than any other country, a position it would hold for a decade and reassume after World War

II. Production was sustained through tight vertical integration, the big firms' investments in other entertainment businesses, and an eager urban audience.

As in other countries, the earliest Japanese features drew upon indigenous theater. The two major genres were the *jidai-geki,* or historical film, and the *gendai-geki,* or the film of contemporary life. Jidai-geki borrowed heavily from the kabuki theater, particularly in the swordfight films (*chambara*) featuring bold samurai and acrobatic action. Gendai-geki films were typically melodramas of romance or family life, influenced by the *shimpa* theater, which was modeled on nineteenth-century western drama. All genres adhered to the kabuki convention of having women's roles played by men.

Film exhibition also bore the marks of traditional theater. Exibitors had to compete with kabuki performances, which consumed half a day or more. Movie programs in the largest cities tended to be long, sometimes running over five hours. In addition, all films were accompanied by a commentator, the *katsuben* or *benshi*. Standing near the screen, the benshi (usually a man) would explain the action, imitate the dialogue of all the characters, and comment on their behavior. Carrying on the tradition of onstage narrators in kabuki and puppet theater, the benshi added the excitement of live performance to the film show. Some benshi became stars, attracting audiences regardless of what film was playing.

After World War I, companies cast off theatrical traditions and started to modernize their films. In the early 1920s, women began playing female parts. The fast-paced U.S. imports encouraged directors to break with the predominant long-shot style. Directors adopted Hollywood continuity principles, and close-ups and shot/reverse-shot editing became widespread. The jidai-geki directors, notably Masahiro Makino, intensified action sequences by using American-style rapid editing. Some directors, such as Kaoru Osanai and Minoru Murata in their *Souls on the Road* (1921), blended theatrical performance with more American-style cutting and flashback construction.

New genres sprang up as well. The modern comedy centering on young people was initiated by *Amateur Club* (1920). Its director, Thomas Kurihara, had worked in Hollywood as an assistant to Thomas Ince. With the modern reconstruction of Tokyo after the 1923 earthquake, the urban comedy of manners became an important genre. American imports also accelerated modernization, as when Yutaka Abe modeled *Woman Who Touched the Legs* (1926) on Lubitsch's *The Marriage Circle* (1924). A genre of *sarariman* ("salaryman") comedies portrayed the tribulations of the downtrodden

8.49 Dyamic swordfighting in *Komatsu Riyuzo* (1930).

8.50 The blind factory owner in *Town of Love* (1928, Tomotaka Tosaka) is given hard crosslighting.

8.51 The rye field Hepworth planted for *Comin' Thro' the Rye*. Its cycle, from plowing to harvesting, creates a bucolic background for key scenes of the central love story.

company employee trying to succeed. One master of the salaryman film was Yasujiro Shimazu (*Sunday,* 1924).

The few films that survive from this period indicate that, despite low budgets, Japan's studios created one of the world's most innovative cinemas. Kinugasa's *A Page of Madness* (p. 171) represents an experimental extreme, but mainstream films also displayed great pictorial dynamism. Swordfight scenes relied on fast-motion, abrupt cutting, hand-held camera movements, and carefully choreographed swordplay (**8.49**); and many films flaunted deep-space compositions and striking angles and lighting (**8.50**). The imaginative storytelling and style pioneered in the 1920s would be elaborated in the outstanding accomplishments of Japanese cinema in the following decade.

Great Britain

In the postwar years, the British film industry also optimistically set out to compete directly with Hollywood, largely by imitating its methods. Pioneer producer-director Cecil Hepworth expanded his company in 1919, and a few other important firms, such as Stoll and Ideal, both formed during the war, made ambitious films that they hoped would be released in the United States. Among these, Hepworth was the main figure to make distinctively British films. As he put it, "It was always in the back of my mind from the very beginning that *I was to make English pictures, with all the English countryside for background and with English atmosphere and English idiom throughout.*"[6] His own favorite was *Comin' Thro' the Rye* (1924), which exploited the beauties of the English countryside to tell an old-fashioned love story (**8.51**). Despite its location photography, however, the film proved unable to compete with the livelier

Hollywood films that still commanded around 90 percent of British screen time. Shortly after its completion, Hepworth's firm was bankrupt, and he turned to running a film laboratory. As we have seen, the young man who would become England's most famous director, Alfred Hitchcock, was making films that were more European than British in style (p. 170).

Other British filmmakers, imitating Hollywood films but unable to command the high budgets of American productions, also found it difficult to compete. By the mid-1920s, production slumped. Finally, in 1927, the government passed a quota to support British production. Investment picked up slowly in the last years of the decade, though the expenses connected with the introduction of sound in 1929 set the recovery back somewhat. The growth of the British industry into a mature studio system would occur during the 1930s.

Italy

A somewhat similar situation existed in Italy after the war. Initially producers tried to revive the palmy days of Italian prewar production, mostly by relying on the formulas of that period. Expensive costume pictures remained a staple. In 1923, the Unione Cinematografica Italiana (UCI), a large firm started four years earlier, produced a lavish remake of the 1913 hit *Quo Vadis?* Drawing upon tactics associated with the budding Film Europe movement, UCI brought in a German, Georg Jacoby, to codirect with Gabriellino D'Annunzio. A German cinematographer was also imported, and the cast was multinational (**8.52**). The film's lukewarm reception suggested that epics would not regain Italy its former glory. Further attempts were made, however. In 1924, one of the most important Italian directors,

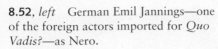

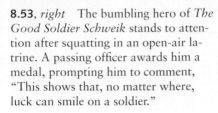

8.52, *left*   German Emil Jannings—one of the foreign actors imported for *Quo Vadis?*—as Nero.

8.53, *right*   The bumbling hero of *The Good Soldier Schweik* stands to attention after squatting in an open-air latrine. A passing officer awards him a medal, prompting him to comment, "This shows that, no matter where, luck can smile on a soldier."

8.54, 8.55   In *Curro Vargas*, the hero's entry into a building shows him moving from the street to a sunlit interior setting built on an open-air stage.

Augusto Genina, made *Cirano di Bergerac*, from Edmond Rostand's play *Cyrano de Bergerac*. The producers took the unusual step of adding hand-stenciled color to the entire lengthy feature (**Color Plate 8.1**). Another genre prominent in this period was the strongman film, including *Maciste all'inferno* ("Maciste in Hell," 1926).

The competition from American and other imported films was too great, however. During the early 1920s, Italian films made up only 6 percent of those screened. In 1926, output sank to a mere twenty features.

In 1922, the government was taken over by the Fascist party, whose leader, Benito Mussolini, considered the cinema "the strongest weapon" of the state. In 1923, the government formed L'Unione Cinematografica Educativa (LUCE) to make documentaries. Fiction films responded little to the Fascist regime, however, until the 1930s.

One notable event occurred at the end of the silent era. Alessandro Blasetti, the leader of a group of young critics and theorists who opposed the continued reliance on old formulas, made his first film, *Sole* ("Sun") in 1929. For this tale of the reclamation of marshes for farmland, Blasetti drew heavily upon influences from Soviet Montage films and other European avant-garde cinema. The brief surviving portion displays rapid editing for maximum conflict, subjective techniques, and unusual camera angles, all combined with dazzling photography of the marshland settings. Blasetti's film received considerable praise as the first major Fascist

fiction film. During the next few years, when the introduction of sound and increasing government support revived Italian filmmaking, he was to become one of Italy's most important directors.

Some Smaller Producing Countries

A number of countries began producing on a more stable basis. Often their films were inexpensively made and designed primarily for the domestic market. Such industries continued to draw heavily upon national literature and to use local scenery and customs to set their films apart from the dominant Hollywood product.

For example, although films had regularly been made in Czechoslovakia since 1908, the first well-equipped filmmaking studio was not built until 1921. In 1924, actor-director Karel Lamač constructed a second, the Kavalírka studios. Here Lamač made *The Good Soldier Schweik* (1926), which helped create a national film tradition. It was based on Jaroslav Hašek's popular satire on militarism: Lamač chose a few episodes from the sprawling tale and found an actor who resembled the Schweik of the original illustrations (8.53).

Spanish cinema also expanded slightly during this period. During the 1910s, Spanish films were usually adaptations of plays. Small firms came and went, as investors dabbled in producing a film or two. During the 1920s, longer lasting filmmaking companies formed, notably Film Española. Among its most prolific and

8.56 Location shooting in Brussels in *Le Portrait de l'amiral.*

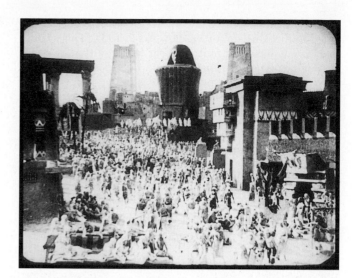

8.57   An Egyptian crowd scene in *Die Sklavenkönigen.*

popular directors was José Buchs. His *Curro Vargas* (1923), a costume picture set in the nineteenth century, typifies small national film production. It mixes picturesque exterior locales with interiors filmed in sets built on open-air stages (**8.54, 8.55**). Spanish audiences enjoyed seeing locally made films, and production rose to fifty-nine features in 1928. The coming of sound, however, temporarily brought the industry to a virtual standstill.

Production was even more sporadic in Belgium, but a few small companies made occasional features. In 1919, André Jacquemin formed a firm, Le Film Cinématographique Belge, which produced the feature *Le Portrait de l'amiral* (1922, directed by François Le Forestier). Adapted from a Belgian novel, the film used local settings to enhance its appeal (**8.56**). Although this film was aimed mainly at the domestic audience, it also did well in other French-speaking markets.

Occasionally, a firm in a smaller producing country would make a big-budget costume picture in order to break into the world market. The Austrian producer Alexander Joseph "Sascha" Kolowrat-Krakowsky took this tack. He had begun as a producer in the early 1910s, forming the Sascha firm in 1914. In 1918, Kolowrat visited the United States to study production methods. He decided that making spectacles was the way to succeed in the Austrian and even the U.S. markets. He produced two big-budget pictures, *Sodom and Gomorrah* (1922)

and *Die Sklavenkönigen* ("The Slave Queen," 1924), both directed by Hungarian Mihály Kertész. (By the end of the decade, he would go to work in Hollywood under the name Michael Curtiz, directing many films, including *Casablanca*.) *Die Sklavenkönigen* was a typical epic designed for international appeal. Based on an adventure novel by H. Rider Haggard, it highlighted crowds of extras and large sets (**8.57**), as well as impressive special effects depicting Moses parting the Red Sea. Such films occasionally succeeded on world markets, but they were not enough to form the basis for regular production in a minor industry.

During the 1920s, the strength of America's hold on world markets became apparent. Many countries, however, resisted that hold. Moreover, a new set of institutions assumed that artistic cinema was distinct from the commercial product. Challenging alternatives to Hollywood filmmaking arose. The introduction of sound at the end of the decade massively altered many countries filmmaking, sometimes adversely, sometimes positively.

· ·

Notes and Queries

DIFFERENT VERSIONS OF SILENT CLASSICS

Dudley Murphy and Fernand Léger's *Ballet mécanique* is commonly seen in museum and classroom screenings in the United States today—yet almost invariably we see it in a shortened version. The film premiered at the Internationale Ausstellung für Theatertechnik ("International Exhibition of Theater Technology") in Vienna in 1924. A copy of this full version—which contained additional footage not seen in most prints, including several shots of Léger's paintings—was preserved by Frederick Kiesler, a modernist architect (who designed a small art theater for the Film Guild in New York in 1929). His widow donated it to the Anthology Film Archives (New York) in 1976.

Léger had reedited a shorter version, which he donated to the Museum of Modern Art in 1935. This abridgment is the basis for most current prints, although other versions of *Ballet mécanique* exist. For an account of the film's production and subsequent career, see Judi Freeman, "Léger's *Ballet mécanique*," in Rudolf E. Kuenzli, ed., *Dada and Surrealist Film* (New York: Willis Locker & Owens, 1987), pp. 28–45.

The distribution history of *The Passion of Joan of Arc* has been even more confusing. Dreyer himself claimed that he was unable to prepare the final version of the film released in France, Denmark, and elsewhere, yet there is evidence that he did edit it. The film's negative was apparently burned in a laboratory fire. A shortened sound version of the film was released in the United States in 1933, and another sonorized version was released in France in 1952. The Cinémathèque Française in Paris preserved a lengthy print, which was copied and widely circulated. On the assumption that this print was still missing significant portions, the Dansk Filmmuseum in Copenhagen undertook a painstaking reconstruction. Then, in the early 1980s, a print made in 1928 from the original negative was discovered in Norway. Surprisingly, this print turned out to be only slightly different from the standard Cinémathèque version that had been circulating for decades. A few shots were longer, and the visual quality was clearer, but in this case the familiar version of a silent classic was apparently quite close to the original. See Tony Pipolo, "The Spectre of *Joan of Arc*: Textual Variations in the Key Prints of Carl Dreyer's Film," *Film History* 2, no. 4 (November/December 1988): 301–24. For more on reconstructions of early films, see "Notes and Queries," Chapter 4.

. . . .

REFERENCES

1. C. de Danilowicz, "Chez Erich Pommer," *Cinémagazine* 4, no. 27 (4 July 1924): 11.
2. Richard Abel, *French Film: The First Wave, 1915–1929* (Princeton, NJ: Princeton University Press, 1985), p. 239ff.
3. Quoted in Walter Schobert, *The German Avant-Garde Film of the 1920's* (Munich: Goethe-Institut, 1989), p. 10.
4. Quoted in Rudolf E. Kuenzli, *Dada and Surrealist Film* (New York: Willis Locker & Owens, 1987), p. 5.
5. Quoted in Patrick Waldberg, *Surrealism* (New York: McGraw-Hill, n.d.), pp. 24–25.
6. Cecil Hepworth, *Came the Dawn: Memories of a Film Pioneer* (London: Phoenix House, 1951), p. 144. Emphasis in original.

FURTHER READING

Higson, Andrew, and Richard Maltby, eds. *"Film Europe" and "Film America": Cinema, Commerce and Cultural Exchange 1920–1939*. Exeter: University of Exeter Press, 1999.

Horak, Jan-Christopher. *Lovers of Cinema: The First American Avant-Garde, 1919–1945*. Madison: University of Wisconsin Press, 1995.

Komatsu, Hiroshi. "The Fundamental Change: Japanese Cinema before and after the Earthquake of 1923." *Griffithiana* 38/39 (October 1999): 186–196.

Lawder, Standish D. *The Cubist Cinema*. New York: New York University Press, 1975.

Peterson, James. "A War of Utter Rebellion: Kinugasa's *Page of Madness* and the Japanese Avant-Garde of the 1920s." *Cinema Journal* 29, no. 1 (fall 1989): 35–63.

Thompson, Kristin. "National or International Films? The Debate during the 1920s." *Film History* 8, no. 3 (1996): 281–96.

———. "(Re)Discovering Charles Dekeukeleire." *Millennium Film Journal* 7/8/9 (fall/winter 1980/1981): 115–29.

PART THREE

THE DEVELOPMENT OF SOUND CINEMA, 1926–1945

Two major social upheavals dominated the period from 1930 to 1945: the Great Depression and World War II.

On October 29, 1929—Black Tuesday—a Wall Street crash signaled the beginning of the Depression in America. The slump quickly spread to other countries and lasted through most of the 1930s. Countless workers lost their jobs, banks failed in record numbers, farms were foreclosed, manufacturing declined, and currencies plunged in value. Fierce competition on international markets shattered the cooperative spirit that had been developing among European countries during the 1920s.

These economic disturbances took place in a threatening political climate. Italy had had a fascist government since 1922. In 1933, Adolf Hitler became chancellor of Germany, instituting the Nazi regime. The Japanese government was also moving to the extreme right and asserted its imperialist goals by invading Manchuria in 1931. In many countries, socialist parties' resistance to the spread of fascism led to political polarization.

The United States and its western European allies tried to appease Hitler, but Germany's invasion of Poland on September 3, 1939, precipitated World War II. The German-Italian-Japanese Axis powers would battle the United States, western European countries, and other Allies until 1945. Although the war caused massive destruction in some parts of the world, it boosted the U.S. economy, as the country recovered from the Depression partly by expanding its armaments industry.

The spread of sound in the cinema coincided with the early years of the Great Depression. Warner Bros. had successfully added music and sound effects to some of its films in 1926 and 1927. By 1929, sound had been adopted throughout the American studios, and theaters were quickly being converted. During that same year, early American sound films were enjoying long runs in European capitals.

9.28, 9.29 A cut-in in *The Blue Angel* maintains lip synchronization, though the scene was shot with one camera. Note that Lola's head is in a slightly different position after the cut and that Rath is holding her powder case higher. Their poses would have remained identical across the cut with multiple-camera shooting.

shot in the outdoor set, while those that needed synchronized sound were shot in the studio.

A very different sort of musical became one of the most widely seen of German sound films. Hollywood director Josef von Sternberg directed Emil Jannings (who had worked with Sternberg in Hollywood before the arrival of talkies forced him to return to Germany) in *The Blue Angel* (1930). The film also brought world fame to Marlene Dietrich, until then a minor actress.

Jannings plays Professor Rath, a repressed, unpopular high-school teacher. In the first scene, street sounds establish Rath's dreary neighborhood and his morning routine. The first break in his routine is in fact a moment of silence, when he whistles to his beloved canary and receives no response. The bird has died. Rath is plunged into a completely different world when he tries to catch some of his students at the Blue Angel, a sordid bar where they have gone to hear the sexy singer Lola-Lola. He falls in love with Lola himself, gives up his job to marry her, and becomes a clown in order to help earn money. Eventually he dies in despair after Lola is unfaithful to him.

Von Sternberg avoided multiple-camera shooting almost entirely, yet he still managed to create dialogue scenes with excellent lip synchronization (**9.28, 9.29**). *The Blue Angel* is also famous for its realistically motivated offscreen sound. A ringing bell becomes a motif associated with Rath's routinized life. When he assigns his students a punitive essay, there is silence as they write; he opens a window, and we hear a boys' choir singing nearby. Aside from its ingenious use of sound, *The Blue Angel*'s international success was based in part on Dietrich's sultry performance as Lola. It led her to a Hollywood career, and there she made several more important films with Josef von Sternberg in the 1930s.

By 1933, all of these German directors—Lang, Pabst, Ophüls, Sagan, Charell, Thiele, and von Sternberg—were working outside Germany, largely because the Nazi regime had gained power (see Chapter 12).

THE USSR PURSUES ITS OWN PATH TO SOUND

While western countries struggled with incompatible systems and patent disputes, the Soviet filmmaking establishment remained relatively isolated. In 1926, two inventors, P. T. Tager and A. Shorin, independently began working on sound-on-film systems. In the same year, the German Tri-Ergon demonstrated its equipment in Moscow, but it was unsuccessful in contractualizing with Soviet companies. In 1929, just as the Soviet industry was arranging to obtain sound equipment from western companies, Tager and Shorin declared their systems ready. Vsevolod Pudovkin tried to use Tagefon for *A Simple Case*, but technical problems forced him to release the film silent. Dziga Vertov managed to use Shorinfon on location in his documentary feature *Enthusiasm*, but there were many difficulties, and the film, begun in 1929, was not released until April 1931.

The first Soviet sound films were released in March 1930: Abram Room's *Plan for Great Works* (a compilation documentary with postdubbed sound only) and some vaudeville and musical shorts. At that point only two theaters were wired for sound. By 1931, however, enough theaters were equipped that sound films came out more frequently. Following *Enthusiasm*, Yuri Raizman's silent Montage-style film *The Earth Thirsts* (originally 1930) was re-released in May with a track of music, songs, and sound effects. Other silent films soon received the same treatment. New sound films also appeared: in the fall of 1931, Grigori Kozintsev and Leonid Trauberg's *Alone* was released, soon followed by Sergei Yutkevich's *Golden Mountains*.

The transition to sound began during the First Five-Year Plan, when the Soviet film industry was trying to expand and become self-sufficient in all areas. Moreover, the Depression hit the Soviet Union hard; prices and demand for its principal exports, grain and other raw ma-

1.1 *Faust aux Enfers* (*The Damnation of Faust*, 1903)

2.1 An unidentified Pathé film, e. 1905

2.2 An unidentified Urban-Eclipse film, e. 1907

2.3 *The Will* (1912, Éclair)

2.4 *La Fille du Margrave* ("Margrave's Daughter," 1912)

2.5 Jephtah's Daughter (1909)

5.1 "Dodo with a Feather Hat" (1911, Ernst Ludwig Kirchner)

5.2 "In a Village near Paris" (or "Street in Paris, Pink Sky," 1909, Lyonel Feininger)

6.1 El Lissitsky's Constructivist composition, "Beat the Whites with the Red Wedge."

8.1 *Cirano di Bergerac*

10.1 *Under a Texas Moon* (1930)

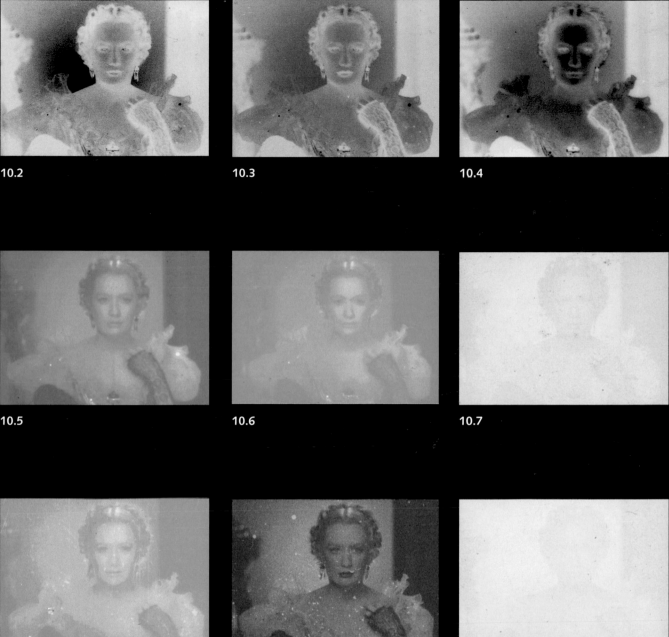

10.2

10.3

10.4

10.5

10.6

10.7

10.8

10.9

10.10

10.11

10.12

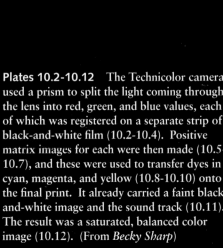

Plates 10.2-10.12   The Technicolor camera used a prism to split the light coming through the lens into red, green, and blue values, each of which was registered on a separate strip of black-and-white film (10.2-10.4). Positive matrix images for each were then made (10.5-10.7), and these were used to transfer dyes in cyan, magenta, and yellow (10.8-10.10) onto the final print. It already carried a faint black-and-white image and the sound track (10.11). The result was a saturated, balanced color image (10.12). (From *Becky Sharp*)

10.13 *La Cucaracha*

10.14 *The Three Little Pigs*

10.15 *Bambi*

10.16 *Thugs with Dirty Mugs*

9.30, 9.31 A scene in *Alone* that creates counterpoint by using contradictory sound sources.

terials, fell sharply. Consequently, as late as 1935, some theaters could show only silent versions of sound films; a few films were shot only in silent versions that year. By 1936, however, the USSR had completed the transition to sound with virtually no help from abroad.

While many western observers resisted sound film, fearing that static, dialogue-ridden scripts would ruin the artistic qualities achieved by the silent cinema, a more flexible view emerged from the famous 1928 "Statement on Sound," signed by Sergei Eisenstein, his associate Grigori Alexandrov, and V. I. Pudovkin. Indeed, they warned against sound's "unimaginative use for 'dramas of high culture' and other photographed presentations of a theatrical order." Simply filming characters talking, they asserted, would destroy the concept of Montage, which depended on abrupt juxtapositions. But they recognized that "*Only the contrapuntal use* of sound vis-à-vis the visual fragment of montage will open up new possibilities for the development and perfection of montage."[2] That is, sound should not simply duplicate the image but should add to the image in some way: offscreen sound could add narrative information, incongruous sound effects or music could change the tone of a scene, and nondiegetic sounds could comment ironically on the action.

The filmmakers of the Montage movement welcomed sound as a way of creating juxtapositions to affect audiences more powerfully. For example, Kozintsev and Trauberg's *Alone* had been almost completed as a silent film before they added a sound track. Rather than using simple postsynchronized dialogue and effects, they took advantage of the new technology by employing startling and contradictory sound. In one scene, the heroine makes a phone call (**9.30, 9.31**). As cuts move us inside and outside the phone booth, we hear an inconsistent succession of sounds: outside we hear a babble of voices and typewriters clacking in a nearby office; inside, the voices continue at the same volume level, but the typewriters are not heard. After the heroine hangs up—

9.32 Sound counterpoint in Pudovkin's *Deserter*.

viewed from outside the booth—there is a sudden and unmotivated silence. At no point do we hear her voice.

Pudovkin's first sound film, *Deserter* (1933), proved to be the last film of the Montage movement. It uses sound in vivid ways. In one scene the sound track is edited very rapidly. The heroine is selling a workers' newspaper on the street; during this, a cheery nondiegetic waltz alternates with diegetic women's voices. These sounds are heard in quicker succession, until only a single note of the music and a single word are heard, passing back and forth. Another scene uses sound ironically. At an outdoor café, a desperate man on strike tries to steal food from a rich man's table. The shot of the rich man lasts for about half a minute with virtually no movement, yet loud, cheerful music plays (**9.32**). As the food arrives, the music switches to a conga rhythm for the attempted theft and the worker's expulsion. This inappropriate music creates a bitter conceptual irony comparable to Eisenstein's visual treatment of Kerensky in *October* (p. 134).

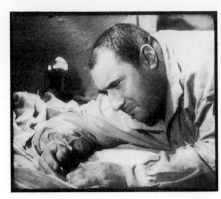

9.33, *left* In *La Petite Lise*, distant framings eliminate the problem of lip synchronization; voices could be post-dubbed in an exterior scene shot silent.

9.34, *right* Berthier's intense longing to return to Lise is conveyed simply in a lengthy shot of him staring at her picture, accompanied by the offscreen sounds of other prisoners.

Such experimentation with sound, however, ran counter to the official policy of Socialist Realism instituted in 1934 (see Chapter 12), and in later years sound was put to far more straightforward uses.

THE INTERNATIONAL ADOPTION OF SOUND

Synchronized sound movies were invented in just a few countries, but they soon became an international phenomenon. Three other countries produced important sound films in the early years. At the same time, language barriers were surmounted—through dubbing, subtitles, and so on—so that dialogue films could circulate around the world.

France

During the silent era, Léon Gaumont had persistently tried to devise a French sound system. In October 1928, Gaumont presented a program of sound shorts and a feature with postdubbed songs. Like the Warner brothers, he wanted to replace the live music and other entertainment that typically accompanied silent films. The early sound market in France, however, was dominated by American and German systems. Also in October, Paramount wired its first-run Paris theater and showed a short film starring the French music-hall star Maurice Chevalier. Other successful screenings, such as *The Jazz Singer* in January 1929, led to a race by French producers to make sound features. Since French studios were still being wired, the earliest, largely undistinguished, films were produced in London (including the first French sound feature, *Les Trois masques* ("The Three Masks," 1929) and in Berlin (e.g., *L'Amour chante*, "Singing Love," 1930).

Since France was an important market, German interests sought to capture part of the production sector.

In early 1929, Tobis-Klangfilm set up a subsidiary, the Société Française des Films Sonores Tobis, in Paris. Tobis produced many major French films, including the highly influential first three sound features of René Clair, which we shall discuss shortly.

Uncertainty concerning sound led to a dip in French production. By 1930, however, most of the main studio buildings were wired, using either American or German systems or one of several minor French brands. Wiring went on until 1934, since many theaters were small and independently owned.

Despite the weakness of the French film industry during this period, several filmmakers experimented with the new technique. *La Petite Lise* ("Little Lise," 1930, Jean Grémillon) tells a simple, melodramatic story of Berthier, a convicted murderer released after a long term in a South American prison; he returns to Paris to find his fragile daughter, Lise, who has secretly become a prostitute. Grémillon shot some scenes in the studio with synchronized dialogue, but he achieved variety by filming others silent, adding sound later. For example, in the opening scene at the prison in Cayenne, he cut freely among several striking exterior compositions of officers calling the roll (9.33). The film also makes powerful use of offscreen sound (9.34). Much of the dreary atmosphere of Lise's hotel room is conveyed by a sonic motif of trains passing.

Other scenes avoid simple synchronization of sound and image. In a transition from Lise's room to a factory where Berthier seeks work, the sound of a buzz saw in the factory begins before the cut to the new location, creating an early example of a sound bridge. Later in the film, sound creates a flashback. As Berthier contemplates confessing to the killing, there is a cut from him to the prison in Cayenne and then back to him. Only then, as we see his thoughtful face again, do we hear his memory: the warden's telling him he is to be freed, a line spoken in the film's first scene.

9.35, 9.36 René Clair uses tracking shots to compare work in a prison and in a factory in *À nous, la liberté!*

9.37 In *À nous, la liberté!* a "singing" flower's shape recalls the horns of the gramophones manufactured in Emile's factory.

René Clair became the most widely known of early French sound directors, as *Sous les toits de Paris* (*Under the Roofs of Paris*, 1930), *Le Million* (1930), and *À nous, la liberté!* ("For Us, Liberty," 1931) found an international audience. His imaginative use of camera movements, stretches of silence, and sonic puns helped quiet the fears of critics who believed that sound would result in static dialogue pictures. We shall see his influence cropping up in national cinemas from Hollywood to China.

À nous, la liberté! involves two escapees from prison. Emile becomes a rich but miserable gramophone manufacturer, while Louis remains a happy, Chaplinesque hobo. The opening uses several lengthy tracking shots to show the prisoners working on an assembly line making toy horses (**9.35**). These shots establish

camera movements and industrial tedium as important motifs. Later, the workers in Emile's factory are shown in similar shots of boring assembly lines (**9.36**).

Although *À nous, la liberté!* uses dialogue, it also employs music extensively—something many filmmakers favored in the early sound period. Clair also liked to surprise his audience by using the "wrong" sound for an object. In one scene, Louis lounges in a field overlooking the factory. We hear music and singing—the sounds of nature itself, which Louis "conducts." A close shot of a flower trembling in the wind is accompanied by a soprano voice so that it seems to be singing (**9.37**).

Clair, Grémillon, and other early sound directors like Jean Renoir laid the foundations for important French trends during the 1930s (Chapter 13).

Great Britain

In the mid-1920s, British film theaters began imitating American practice by adding vaudeville acts and prologues to their programs. The 1928 premiere of Vitaphone shorts aroused some interest, but there was no rush to convert to sound. Even *The Jazz Singer*, in September, failed to create a stir. Jolson's next film, *The Singing Fool*, however, opened to enormous acclaim in early 1929, and the push to wire theaters and studios began.

Western Electric's and RCA's were the principal systems on the market. Under the terms of the 1930 Paris agreement, 25 percent of the British market was reserved for Tobis-Klangfilm equipment, while 75 percent belonged to the American firms. But Tobis encountered technical difficulties as a result of having allied itself with the small British Phototone, and it could not exploit its share of the market. Several British companies offered cheaper sound outfits, but these provided poor reproduction. British Thomson-Houston (a subsidiary of General Electric) introduced reliable equipment in 1930, but it ran third behind the two American firms in the number of theaters wired. By 1933, all but the smallest British cinemas could reproduce sound.

The production companies, the weakest segment of the industry, had more trouble coping with the expense of converting to sound. The flow of investments into the British film industry after the 1927 Quota Act (p. 240) had slowed. By 1929, most of the new "quota" companies were in trouble, and their problems were compounded by the fact that their recent silent films were of little value in the big first-run cinemas. The main exception to this pattern was British International Pictures (BIP), which had been founded in 1927 by John Maxwell. Maxwell quickly wired his Elstree studio facility with RCA equipment. Rather than aiming for the largely closed American market, as other companies did, he concentrated on Europe and the British Commonwealth countries. His first production, Alfred Hitchcock's *Blackmail,* was released in both sound and silent versions and was a big hit in 1929. BIP went on to make inexpensive sound films aimed at the British market, and the company remained profitable.

Blackmail was one of the most imaginative early sound films. Refusing to surrender the camera movement and rapid editing of the silent era, Hitchcock avoided multiple-camera shooting, finding a variety of other ways to work sound into his scenes. The opening sequence is a fast-cut episode in which the heroine's policeman boyfriend helps apprehend a criminal; the many shots of the police van speeding through the streets and the criminal trying to trick his pursuers were all shot silent, with only music added. Later, in the jail, the camera tracks forward behind the two police officers in another scene shot silent and postdubbed (**9.38**).

Such devices functioned mainly to circumvent the problems of early sound, but Hitchcock also uses sound to enhance the style of *Blackmail.* For example, in one scene the heroine sees a homeless man lying with outstretched hand, in a posture that reminds her of the body of the would-be rapist she has recently stabbed to death. A scream begins on the sound track, and a cut takes us immediately to the dead man's apartment, where his landlady is screaming upon discovering the body (**9.39, 9.40**). In another scene, Hitchcock holds the shot on the heroine's distraught face as a gossipy neighbor babbles on about the killing. We hear the neighbor's speech subjectively, as the heroine does, with all the words becoming inaudible except the repeated "knife . . . knife . . . knife." Hitchcock would continue such deft manipulations of sound throughout his career.

Synchronized sound also provided the basis for a series of prestigious literary and historical films that

9.38 By filming the policemen from the back in *Blackmail,* Hitchcock could add their dialogue to silent footage without having to synchronize the sound with their lip movements.

British producers hoped would gain entry into the lucrative American market.

Japan

Musical accompaniment gave most national cinemas "sound" films in the silent era, but Japan's industry was one of the few to have "talkies." The *katsuben,* or *benshi,* performer was a mainstay of exhibition, sitting in the theater near the screen, explaining the action and vocally portraying the characters. Not surprisingly, the Japanese cinema was one of the last major film industries to convert to synchronized sound movies, and the process involved a protracted struggle.

Although Japanese inventors had tinkered with sound systems in the mid-1920s, the big firms displayed no interest until Fox exhibited Movietone films in the spring of 1929. Major urban theaters, particularly those co-owned by Hollywood companies, were quickly wired. By the end of 1930, most imported films were talkies.

Japanese production proceeded more cautiously. Financial problems of the Depression made the two major companies, Nikkatsu and Shochiku, reluctant to pay the high royalty fees demanded by U.S. equipment suppliers. Japanese studios also feared that giving the Americans control of sound would lead to foreign domination of the market, so the studios devised their own sound

9.39, 9.40 A cut from one woman's back to another makes it unclear whether one or both are the source of a scream that acts as an imaginative sonic transition in *Blackmail*.

technology. Nikkatsu's sound-on-disc system was tried on a few films, but it proved a failure. Shochiku's *Tsuchihashi* system, modeled on RCA's Photophone, was launched with Heinosuke Gosho's *Madam and Wife* (aka *The Neighbor's Wife and Mine*), which premiered in August 1931.

Madam and Wife is a domestic comedy that carefully integrates dialogue, music, and sound effects. A writer forever looking for excuses not to work is distracted by his neighbor's jazz band and the man's smoking, drinking modern wife. Gosho makes clever use of offscreen sounds (even mice), of subjective sound (the jazz dims when the writer puts cotton in his ears), and of thematic contrasts (the neighbor's wife is associated with jazz, while the writer's wife hums a traditional Japanese tune). The film also exploits the audience's fascination with American talkies. Invited next door, the writer staggers back home drunk and singing, "That's the Broadway melody!" His family is last seen walking home to the strains of "My Blue Heaven." Gosho shot the lip-synchronized scenes in multiple-camera fashion, but other passages were filmed and cut quite fluidly.

The popularity of *Madam and Wife* helped convince the film industry to convert to talkies. In 1933, Nikkatsu allied itself with Western Electric, while Shochiku stuck with its Tsuchihashi system. Smaller firms used sound technology to break into the market; most notable were PCL (Photo-Chemical Laboratories) and JO, both of which began talkie production in 1932. On the whole, however, sound production proceeded more slowly in Japan than in any other major filmmaking nation. Sound films did not account for over half the feature output until 1935, and many of these had only music tracks. As late as 1936, one-quarter of Japanese films were still silent.

The delay was due to several factors. Many small firms could not sustain the costs of sound production, many rural theaters remained unwired for years, and, as in other countries, labor resisted the introduction of sound. In 1929, the powerfully unionized benshi went on strike at the theater premiering the Fox Movietone process. Producers and exhibitors sought to get rid of the benshi. When, in 1932, Shochiku fired ten benshi from major Tokyo theaters, they struck and won reinstatement. Three years of battles followed, during which sound pictures became dominant.

In 1935, when a violent benshi strike against Shochiku was settled by police intervention, the struggle ended. Many benshi took up storytelling in variety halls or in street performances. Still, even at the end of the 1930s, one might be found accompanying a silent movie in a remote rural theater or in a neighborhood screening in Hawaii. For such remote locations, the Japanese industry was still making a few silent films.

Wiring the World's Theaters for Sound

Sound spread through the world's film theaters at an uneven pace. Some small countries, especially in eastern Europe and the Third World, produced no films, but their few theaters were wired relatively quickly. This was the case in Albania, for example, where there were a mere fourteen theaters—all showing sound films—in 1937. Venezuela had around a hundred theaters, as well as occasional open-air shows in bullrings and similar venues; even for these casual screenings, portable sound equipment was brought in.

Interestingly, silent screenings lingered on longer in some middle-size markets with small production sectors. In 1937, about 800 of Belgium's nearly 1,000 theaters had been equipped for sound. Only 100 more were still considered real possibilities for wiring. Belgium produced a small number of sound films, six in 1937. In Portugal, 185 of the country's 210 theaters were wired; it had one sound studio that made four features and about a hundred shorts in the first nine months of 1937. Brazil had 1,246 theaters, 1,084 of which had sound capability; in 1937 it produced just four sound features.

Ultimately many of those theaters that had not bought sound systems by the mid-1930s went out of business. They had survived primarily by showing old silent films or silent versions of sound films, but these became increasingly hard to get. By the mid-1930s sound films dominated international exhibition, as well as production in those countries that could afford it.

Crossing the Language Barrier

Sound filming created a problem for all producing countries: the language barrier threatened to limit export possibilities. Silent films could be translated through the simple substitution of intertitles, but talkies were another matter.

The earliest screenings of sound films explored several solutions to the problem. Sometimes films were shown abroad with no translation at all. Since sound was still a novelty, this occasionally worked, as when the German version of *The Blue Angel* met success in Paris. During the early sound era, Hollywood made several big *revue musicals,* such as *King of Jazz* (1929), that consisted of strings of musical numbers that could be enjoyed without a knowledge of English.

Because postproduction mixing of sound was impossible in the early years, dubbing a new sound track in a foreign language was clumsy and expensive. It involved, for example, rerecording all the music at the same time that the dialogue was put in, making lip synchronization difficult. Some dubbed films were successful in 1929, but others failed because the voices matched badly with the lip movements. Firms also added subtitles to some films, but these were often rejected as distracting. Other solutions, like eliminating the dialogue and substituting intertitles or even editing in narrators explaining the action in a different language, proved wholly unacceptable.

By 1929, many producers decided that the only way to preserve foreign markets was to reshoot additional versions of each film, with the actors speaking different languages in each. Advertised as the world's first "multilingual" film, the British production *Atlantic* was released in German and English (1929, E. A. Dupont). Similarly, the first German talkie, *Das Land ohne Frauen,* also appeared in an English version, *The Land without*

Women. In 1929, MGM set up an elaborate program of multilingual production, importing actors and directors to make French, German, and Spanish versions of its pictures. Paramount attempted to economize by producing its multilinguals in France, purchasing its Joinville studio, near Paris, in 1929. The Joinville facilities were equipped like a big Hollywood studio, and there Paramount turned out dozens of films in as many as fourteen languages. Germany's Tobis-Klangfilm also made many multilinguals.

The assumption was that multilinguals would be relatively cheap to make, since the same scripts, sets, and lighting plans could be used. As each scene was finished, a new team of actors would move in, and the same scene would be done again. The cast and crew were usually changed for each version, though in some cases directors and stars who could speak two or more languages would work on more than one version. Occasionally stars learned their lines phonetically, as when Laurel and Hardy were called upon to make Spanish versions of their films.

After about two years, it became apparent that multilinguals would not solve the language problem. Multilingual production's main drawback was that it required so many people to be at the studio at the same time, most just waiting their turn to work. The market for each version was too small to warrant the additional expense, and audiences did not welcome minor actors in roles made famous by stars like Gary Cooper and Norma Shearer.

By 1931, the technique of mixing separate sound tracks after shooting had been refined. The original music and sound effects could be combined with new voices, and methods of synchronizing voice and lip movements had improved. Moreover, subtitles were accepted more widely. By 1932, dubbing and subtitles enabled talkies to cross the language barrier, and they have remained in use ever since.

Despite its technical problems, sound boosted film production in several countries, since audiences wanted to hear native performers speaking their own languages. France, for example, gained a bigger share of its own exhibition market than it had enjoyed during the 1920s. Many small countries in eastern Europe and Latin America began producing more films. Most spectacularly, Indian production, which had been limited in the silent era, developed during the 1930s into one of the world's major studio systems. We shall examine some of these results of the coming of sound in Chapter 11.

Notes and Queries

FILMMAKERS ON THE COMING OF SOUND

From 1928 to 1933, sound seemed to many filmmakers both promising and threatening. Most realized that it offered new aesthetic possibilities, but many feared that static versions of plays might dominate production. Some directors offered views of how sound could be used creatively.

Predictably, the Soviet Montage filmmakers, who had written extensively on film theory in the silent era, discussed sound. *The Film Factory: Russian and Soviet Cinema in Documents 1896–1939*, ed. Richard Taylor and Ian Christie (Cambridge, MA: Harvard University Press, 1988), contains essays by several filmmakers, including Vsevolod Pudovkin ("On the Principle of Sound in Film," pp. 264–67), Esfir Shub ("The Advent of Sound in Cinema," p. 271), and Dziga Vertov ("Speech to the First All-Union Conference on Sound Cinema," pp. 301–05).

Writings on sound by several major French filmmakers of the 1920s and 1930s, such as Jacques Feyder (pp. 38–39), René Clair (pp. 39–40), Abel Gance (pp. 41–42), and Marcel Pagnol (pp. 55–57) are available in English in Richard Abel's *French Film Theory and Criticism 1907–1939: A History/Anthology,* vol. 2 (Princeton, NJ: Princeton University Press, 1988). The most successful and influential of French directors in the early sound era, Clair blended his writings from the period with commentary added years later, reflecting on his own initial reactions to sound; see his *Cinema Yesterday and Today,* ed. R. C. Dale and trans. Stanley Appelbaum (New York: Dover, 1972), pp. 126–58.

Hollywood directors wrote relatively little on the subject, but two significant articles appear in Richard Koszarski, ed., *Hollywood Directors 1914–1940* (London: Oxford University Press, 1976): Edmund Goulding's "The Talkers in Close-Up" (pp. 206–13) and Frank Borzage's "Directing a Talking Picture" (pp. 235–37). Writing from a very different perspective, Carl Dreyer offered thoughts on how filmmakers could adapt plays as sound films and still avoid static dialogue scenes in his "The Real Talking Film," in Donald Skoller, ed., *Dreyer in Double Reflection* (New York: Dutton, 1973), pp. 51–56.

SOUND AND THE REVISION OF FILM HISTORY

The topic of the introduction of sound illustrates how historians can overturn widely accepted accounts by discovering new data or devising new arguments to accommodate existing evidence. For instance, one historical puzzle was how a small firm like Warner Bros., whose financial records show heavy losses in the mid-1920s, managed to introduce sound and grow quickly into a major company. In 1939, Lewis Jacobs suggested that Vitaphone was "a desperate effort to ward off bankruptcy." (See his *The Rise of the American Film* [reprint, New York: Teachers College Press, 1968], p. 297.) Other historians repeated and embroidered this account; in *The Movies* (New York: Bonanza Books, 1957), Richard Griffith and Arthur Mayer even attributed Sam Warner's 1927 death to the strain of the "grim race with time" to save his debt-ridden company (pp. 240–41). In the mid-1970s, however, economic historian Douglas Gomery argued that Warners' debts were a sign of the firm's healthy expansion and that the introduction of sound was far from a frantic bid to avoid ruin. (Gomery's numerous articles on this topic include "The Coming of Sound: Technological Change in the American Film Industry," in Tino Balio, ed., *The American Film Industry,* 2nd ed. [Madison: University of Wisconsin Press, 1985], pp. 229–51.)

Similarly, the widespread resistance to the coming of sound on the part of filmmakers and critics has led some historians to treat its introduction as a major break in the cinema's stylistic history. By this account, early talkies virtually eliminated editing and camera movement. In the 1950s, however, André Bazin took a novel approach by asking "if the technical revolution created by the sound track was in any sense an aesthetic revolution" ("The Evolution of the Language of Cinema," in Hugh Gray, trans. and ed., *What Is Cinema?* [Berkeley: University of California Press, 1967], p. 23). David Bordwell, Janet Staiger, and Kristin Thompson offered evidence to support Bazin's view, showing that many aspects of visual style in the classical Hollywood cinema changed surprisingly little with the introduction of sound. (See their *The Classical Hollywood Cinema: Film Style and Mode of Production to 1960* [New York: Columbia University Press, 1985].)

REFERENCES

1. Stephen Watts, "Alfred Hitchcock on Music in Films," *Cinema Quarterly* 2, no. 2 (winter 1933/1934): 81.
2. Sergei Eisenstein, Vsevolod Pudovkin, and Grigori Alexandrov, "Statement on Sound," in Richard Taylor and Ian Christie, eds., *The Film Factory: Russian and Soviet Cinema in Documents 1896–1939* (Cambridge, MA: Harvard University Press, 1988), p. 234.

FURTHER READING

Abel, Richard, and Charles Altman, eds. "Global Experiments in Early Synchronous Sound." Special issue of *Film History* 11, no. 4 (1999).

Andrew, Dudley. "Sound in Focus: The Origins of a Native School." In Mary Lea Bandy, ed., *Rediscovering French Film.* New York: Museum of Modern Art, 1983, pp. 57–65.

Belaygue, Christien, ed. *Le passage du muet au parlant.* Toulouse: Cinémathèque de Toulouse, 1988.

Crafton, Donald. *The Talkies: American Cinema's Transition to Sound 1926–1931.* New York: Scribner's, 1997.

Gitt, Robert. "Bringing Vitaphone Back to Life." *Film History* 5, no. 3 (September 1993): 262–74.

Jossé, Harald. *Die Entstehung des Tonfilms.* Munich: Freiburg, 1984.

Murphy, Robert. "Coming of Sound to the Cinema in Britain." *Historical Journal of Film, Radio and Television* 4, no. 2 (1984): 143–60.

Thompson, Kristin. "Early Sound Counterpoint." *Yale French Studies* 60 (1980): 115–40.

CHAPTER 10

THE HOLLYWOOD STUDIO SYSTEM, 1930–1945

Between 1930 and 1945, the United States experienced a severe economic depression and then a spectacular recovery during World War II. In 1932, as the Great Depression was entering its depths, unemployment reached 23.6 percent. In 1933, nearly 14 million people were out of work. The dollar's buying power was high—admission at some local movie theaters might be only a dime—but many people had little to spend on anything but necessities.

The stock market hit its lowest level in mid-1932, just before the presidential election, and Franklin Roosevelt swept to the first of four victories by blaming the disaster on Herbert Hoover. Roosevelt's administration moved to bolster the economy. The National Recovery Administration, established in 1933, cast a lenient eye on big-business practices, such as trusts and oligopolies, while also displaying a new tolerance of labor unions. Both policies had a major impact on Hollywood. The government also fostered economic growth by financing roads, buildings, the arts, and other areas under the Works Progress Administration (WPA; established in 1935). The WPA put 8.5 million people back to work, thus building up buying power and aiding industries to recuperate.

Recovery was uneven, and a recession during 1937 and 1938, though not as severe as the original crisis, caused similar problems. By 1938, however, increased government intervention was pulling the country out of the Depression. The outbreak of war in parts of Europe accelerated that process. Although the United States remained neutral until the Japanese attack on Pearl Harbor on December 7, 1941, armaments companies were allowed to sell abroad beginning in November 1939. America declared itself "the arsenal of democracy," selling arms to its allies around the world and then building up its own combat capability. This increased manufacturing gradually absorbed the available labor force. Although there were still 3 million unemployed when the United States entered the war in 1941, by late in the war some jobs remained unfilled.

The war expanded the American economy. Between 1940 and 1944, for example, the output of manufactured goods quadrupled. Fully 40 percent of the nation's gross national product supported the war effort, but the newly employed workers at home (including many who had previously been housewives or servants) gained purchasing power and a higher standard of living. Despite shortages of some products, most American industries increased their sales, often by 50 percent or more. The film industry shared in this wartime boom, as movie theater attendance rose dramatically.

THE NEW STRUCTURE OF THE FILM INDUSTRY

During the silent era, the Hollywood film industry had developed into an oligopoly in which a small number of companies cooperated to close the market to competition. While the structure of this oligopoly remained relatively stable into the 1930s, the coming of sound and the onset of the Depression caused some changes.

Only one large new company was formed as a result of the coming of sound: RKO, created to exploit RCA's sound system, Photophone. Fox's successful innovation of sound-on-film led it to expand considerably during the late 1920s, but the beginning of the Depression forced Fox to cut back on its investments. Most notably, it sold its newly acquired controlling interest in First National to Warner Bros. Thus Warners, which had been a small company, grew into one of the largest firms of the 1930s.

By 1930, the Hollywood oligopoly had settled into a structure that would change little for nearly twenty years. Eight large companies dominated the industry. First were the Big Five, also called the *Majors*. In order of size, they were Paramount (formerly Famous Players–Lasky), Loew's (generally known by the name of its production subsidiary, MGM), Fox (which became 20th Century-Fox in 1935), Warner Bros., and RKO. To be a Major, a company had to be vertically integrated, owning a theater chain and having an international distribution operation. Smaller companies with few or no theaters formed Little Three, or the *Minors:* Universal, Columbia, and United Artists. There were also several independent firms. Some of these (such as Samuel Goldwyn and David O. Selznick) made expensive, or "A," pictures comparable to those of the Majors. Those firms (such as Republic and Monogram) making only inexpensive B pictures were collectively known as *Poverty*

Row. We shall survey each of the Majors and Minors briefly and then look at the phenomenon of independent production.

The Big Five

Paramount   Paramount began as a distribution firm and expanded by buying up large numbers of theaters (pp. 68 and 144–145). This strategy succeeded in the 1920s, but once the Depression hit, the company earned far less money and owed sizable amounts on the mortgages of its theaters. As a result, Paramount declared bankruptcy in 1933 and underwent court-ordered reorganization until 1935. During that time it produced films but at a loss. In 1936, Paramount theater executive Barney Balaban became president of the entire company and made it profitable again (so successfully that he retained his post until 1964).

In the early 1930s, Paramount was known partly for its European-style productions. Josef von Sternberg made his exotic Marlene Dietrich films there, Ernst Lubitsch continued to add a sophisticated touch with his comedies, and French import Maurice Chevalier was one of its major stars. The studio also depended heavily on radio and vaudeville comedians. The Marx Brothers made their earliest, most bizarre films there (notably *Duck Soup,* directed by Leo McCarey in 1933), and Mae West's suggestive dialogue attracted both audiences and controversy.

In the second half of the decade, Balaban turned paramount in a more mainstream direction. Bob Hope and Bing Crosby, consistently among the top box-office attractions of the World War II period, helped sustain the studio, as did tough guy Alan Ladd and comedian Betty Hutton. One of the studio's popular wartime directors, Preston Sturges, made several satirical comedies. Throughout the 1930s and 1940s, Cecil B. De Mille continued as a mainstay of the studio he had helped start, with a series of big-budget historical films.

Loew's/MGM   Unlike Paramount, MGM did well all the way through the period from 1930 to 1945. With a smaller theater chain, it had fewer debts and was the most profitable American film firm. This was partly due to the quiet guidance of Nicholas Schenck, who managed Loew's from New York. Louis B. Mayer ran the West Coast studio on a policy of high-profile, big-budget films (supervised by Irving Thalberg until his early death in 1936), backed up by mid-range films (mostly supervised by Harry Rapf) and B pictures.

MGM's films (even the Bs) often looked more luxurious than those of other studios. Budgets for features averaged $500,000 (higher, for example, than the $400,000 Paramount and 20th Century-Fox were spending). Cedric Gibbons, head of the art department, helped create an MGM look with large, white, brightly lit sets. MGM boasted that it had under contract "more stars than there are in heaven." Important directors who worked consistently for MGM included George Cukor and Vincente Minnelli.

In the early 1930s, MGM's biggest star was the unglamorous, middle-aged Marie Dressler, remembered today mainly for her Oscar-winning performance in *Min and Bill* (1930) and her sardonic role in *Dinner at Eight* (1933). Later in the decade, Clark Gable, Spencer Tracy, Mickey Rooney, and Judy Garland all became major drawing cards. It is some measure of MGM's emphasis on quality that Rooney, who was acting in A musicals like Busby Berkeley's *Strike Up the Band* (1940), could simultaneously be delegated to the relatively low-budget, but popular, "Andy Hardy" series. Greta Garbo was more a prestige star than a box-office draw in the United States, but her films did well in Europe; once the war broke out and European markets were closed to American films, MGM let her go. During the war, new stars emerged for the studio, including Greer Garson, Gene Kelly, and Katharine Hepburn—the latter teaming up with Spencer Tracy.

20th Century-Fox   Party as a result of its expansion after the innovation of sound, Fox entered the Depression in worse shape than the other Majors. The company remained in trouble until 1933, when Sidney Kent, former head of distribution for Paramount, took over and helped turn the firm around. One crucial step was a merger with a smaller company, Twentieth Century, in 1935. This deal brought in Darryl F. Zanuck as head of the West Coast studio, which he ran with an iron hand.

20th Century-Fox had relatively few long-term stars. Folk humorist Will Rogers was immensely popular up to his death in 1935; skating star Sonja Henie and singer Alice Faye were both famous for a few years. But the studio's biggest draw was child-star Shirley Temple, who topped national box-office polls from 1935 to 1938. Her popularity waned as she grew up, and 20th Century-Fox's biggest wartime profits came instead from Betty Grable musicals. (A photograph of Grable in a bathing suit was the favorite pin-up among the troops.) Major directors who worked steadily at Fox during this period included Henry King, Allan Dwan, and John Ford.

Warner Bros.   Like Fox, Warner Bros. had been borrowing and expanding just before the Depression began. It coped with its debts not by declaring bankruptcy but by selling off some holdings and cutting costs. Harry Warner ran the company from New York, insisting on making a relatively large number of low-budget projects resulting in modest but predictable profits.

The effects on the films were apparent. Although in total assets Warners was as big as MGM, its sets were much smaller, and its stable of popular actors—James Cagney, Bette Davis, Humphrey Bogart, Errol Flynn, and others—worked in more films. Plots were recycled frequently (the screenwriting department was known as the "echo chamber"), and the studio concentrated on creating popular genres and then mining them: the Busby Berkeley musical, the gangster film, the problem film based on current headlines, the "bio-pic"—and, once the war began, a series of successful combat films. Warners depended on prolific, solid directors like William Wellman, Michael Curtiz, and Mervyn LeRoy to keep the releases flowing. The many Warners films of the era that have become classics attest to the ability of the studio's filmmakers to succeed with limited resources.

RKO   This was the shortest-lived of the Majors. In 1928, the Radio Corporation of America (RCA), unable to convince any studio to adopt its sound system, went into the movie-making business itself as RKO (p. 195). Unfortunately, RKO always lagged behind the other Majors. By 1933 the firm was in bankruptcy, and it was not reorganized until 1940. At that point, the general wartime prosperity helped RKO achieve profitability—though its problems would return shortly after the war's end.

RKO had no stable policy during this period, and it lacked big stars. Katharine Hepburn, for example, was popular during the early 1930s, but a series of indifferent and eccentric films labeled her "box-office poison." RKO had isolated hits, such as the 1933 fantasy *King Kong*, but the studio's only consistent moneymakers during the 1930s were Fred Astaire and Ginger Rogers, whose series of musicals ran from 1934 to 1938. To a considerable extent, RKO's slim profits depended on its distribution of animated films made by an independent firm, Walt Disney.

During the early 1940s, RKO turned to producing prestigious Broadway plays, including *Abe Lincoln in Illinois* (1940). One controversial young theatrical producer hired at this time was Orson Welles. His *Citizen Kane* (1941) would later be remembered as the most important RKO film, though it was considered financially disappointing at the time. During the early 1940s, RKO's B unit, supervised by Val Lewton, produced some of the most creative low-budget films of Hollywood's studio era.

THE HAYS CODE: SELF-CENSORSHIP IN HOLLYWOOD

The popular image of Will Hays and other officials of the Motion Picture Producers and Distributors of America (MPPDA) casts them as sour puritans imposing censorship on the film industry. The reality is more complex. The MPPDA was a corporation owned jointly by the film companies themselves. One of the MPPDA's tasks was to help *avoid* censorship from the outside.

The MPPDA was formed in 1922 to improve public relations after a series of Hollywood scandals, to provide a lobbying link to the era's sympathetic Republican administrations, and to handle foreign problems like quotas. Similar functions continued into the 1930s, but the MPPDA became more famous for its policy of industry self-censorship: the Production Code (often called the Hays Code).

The early 1930s were an age of conservatism. Many believed that lax morality during the 1920s Jazz Age had been one cause of the Depression. State and municipal film censorship boards, formed in the silent era, tightened standards. Pressure groups promoting religious beliefs, children's welfare, and the like protested against sex, violence, and other types of subject matter. In 1932 and 1933, a series of studies by the Payne Fund investigated the effects of filmgoing on audiences—particularly children. More voices demanded regulation of filmmaking.

By early 1930, outside pressure for censorship forced the MPPDA to adopt the Production Code as industry policy. The Code was an outline of moral standards governing the depiction of crime, sex, violence, and other controversial subjects. Provisions of the Code demanded, for example, that "methods of crime should not be explicitly presented" and that "sexual perversion or any inference to it is forbidden." (In this period, "sexual perversion" referred primarily to homosexuality.) All Hollywood films were expected to obey the Code or risk local censorship. In enforcing the

Code, MPPDA censors often went to absurd lengths. Even respectably married couples had to be shown sleeping in twin beds (to suit British censors), and the mildest profanity was forbidden. When *Gone with the Wind* was filmed in 1939, there was lengthy controversy before the MPPDA finally permitted Clark Gable to speak the famous line "Frankly, my dear, I don't give a damn."

The MPPDA's efforts were initially resisted by the film companies. Most of the firms were in financial trouble, some moving into or near bankruptcy as theater attendance fell; they knew sex and violence could boost theater patronage. Gangster films and sex pictures, however, drew the wrath of censors and pressure groups. Films like *The Public Enemy* (1931), *Little Caesar* (1930), and *Scarface* (1932) were seen as glorifying criminals. Although the protagonists were killed in the end, it was feared that youngsters would copy the tough-guy images of James Cagney and Edward G. Robinson. More notoriously, several films centered on women who traded sexual favors for material gain. *Baby Face* (1933) and *Red-Headed Woman* (1932) showed women attaining elegant apartments, clothes, and cars through a series of affairs. Even *Back Street* (1932, John M. Stahl), in which the heroine lives modestly and truly loves the man who keeps her, was found offensive. According to the Code's author, the film approved "of extramarital relationship, thereby reflecting adversely on the institution of marriage and belittling its obligations."[1]

Mae West presented a formidable challenge to the MPPDA. She was a successful Broadway performer and playwright whose fame rested on sensational plays like *Sex* (1926). Although the MPPDA fought to keep her out of films, Paramount, facing bankruptcy, hired her; for a few years she was the company's top moneymaker. Her first star vehicle, *She Done Him Wrong* (1933, Lowell Sherman),

The Little Three

Universal   Although it had an extensive distribution system and was the largest of the Little Three, Universal had constant money problems from 1930 to 1945 (and beyond). It had few major stars, and its successful filmmakers tended to move to bigger studios. Universal's early strategy was to promote new stars in visually striking horror films. The firm made stars of Bela Lugosi (*Dracula*, 1931), Boris Karloff (*Frankenstein*, 1931), and Claude Rains (*The Invisible Man*, 1933). After

1935, Universal increasingly targeted small-town audiences, building up another new star, the cheerful teenage singer Deanna Durbin. B series were important to the studio, such as the Sherlock Holmes films of the 1940s, starring Basil Rathbone, and the slapstick Abbott and Costello series.

Columbia   Under the consistent leadership of studio head Harry Cohn, Columbia weathered the Depression and remained profitable. Despite low budgets, it turned out popular films, often by borrowing stars or directors

10.1   The seal of approval as it appeared in the 1930s at the beginning of films passed by the MPPDA.

took in many times its cost. A typical bit of dialogue occurs as the virtuous young hero chides the heroine, Lou, by asking her, "Haven't you ever met a man that could make you happy?" Lou replies, "Sure . . . lots of times." West's drawling delivery could make any line seem salacious.

The timing of the premiere of *She Done Him Wrong* could not have been worse. The first Payne Fund studies had just appeared. Moreover, in early 1933, the Roosevelt administration took over, severing Hays's ties to Republican officials in Washington. With growing ferment against the film industry, a national censorship law seemed to be in the offing. As a result, in March 1933, Hays pushed the film industry to enforce the Code.

Still, studios hungry for patrons tested the Code's limits. Mae West's films continued to cause problems. *Belle of the Nineties* (1934) was recut at the insistence of the New York State Censorship Board. The negotiations concerning this film coincided with mounting pressure from religious groups, especially the Catholic Legion of Decency. (The legion had a rating system that could condemn films either for young people or for all Catholics. This stigma could cause the industry considerable lost revenues.)

The danger of increased official censorship was too great to be ignored, and, in June 1934, the MPPDA established a new set of rules. Member studios releasing films without MPPDA seals of approval (**10.1**) now had to pay a $25,000 fine. More important, a film without a seal was barred from any MPPDA member's theaters—which included most first-run houses. This rule forced most producers to comply with the Code. Of course, "objectionable" material was still used, but it became more indirect. A strategic fade-out might hint that a couple was about to make love; extreme violence could occur just offscreen; sophisticated dialogue could suggest much without violating the Code.

The MPPDA may have been repressive, but it blocked potentially more extreme national censorship. In practical terms, the Code was not a tool of the prudish minds of MPPDA officials but a summary of the types of subject matter that could get movies cut by local censors or banned for Catholic viewers. The Code saved Hollywood money by pressuring filmmakers to avoid shooting scenes that would be snipped out. The MPPDA did not seek to eliminate every risqué line or violent moment. Instead, it allowed the studios to go just far enough to titillate the public without crossing the lines defined by local censorship authorities.

from bigger studios (thus avoiding the costs of keeping them under contract). The studio's most important director, Frank Capra, remained there throughout the 1930s. His 1934 film *It Happened One Night* starred Claudette Colbert (loaned out from Paramount) and Clark Gable (from MGM); film, director, and stars all won Oscars, and the picture was one of Columbia's biggest hits.

Although several major directors worked briefly at Columbia—most notably John Ford for *The Whole Town's Talking* (1935), George Cukor for *Holiday* (1938), and Howard Hawks for *Only Angels Have Wings* (1939) and *His Girl Friday* (1940)—they did not stay. The studio was largely dependent on its B Westerns and other cheaper fare (including Three Stooges films) during this era.

United Artists   The sound era saw the beginning of a slow decline for UA. D. W. Griffith, Mary Pickford, and Douglas Fairbanks all retired in the early to mid-1930s, and Charles Chaplin released a feature only about once every five years. UA distributed films for other prominent independent producers such as Alexander Korda, David O. Selznick, Walter Wanger, and Samuel Goldwyn—who all switched to other firms by the end of World War II. As a result, UA was the only company whose profits fell during most of the wartime boom years.

UA's releases from 1930 to 1945 reflect their origins from a batch of diverse independent producers. Prestigious British imports like *The Private Life of Henry VIII*, slapstick musicals with popular Broadway star Eddie Cantor, a few of Alfred Hitchcock's American films (including *Rebecca* and *Spellbound*), and some of William Wyler's finest works (*Dodsworth, Wuthering Heights*) provided a varied output. Unlike in the silent period, however, UA now had to fill out its feature schedule with mid-budget, or even B, pictures.

The Independents

There was little real competition among the Majors, the Minors, and the independents. Each group had a different function within the industry. The Majors provided the bulk of the A pictures for big theaters. The Minors supplied the extra films needed and catered to smaller theaters that did not belong to the Majors. A few independent firms made prestige films, while others, like Monogram and Republic, filled in the second halves of double features with B pictures, most of them falling into the action genres, like Westerns, crime thrillers, and serials.

Some small independent producers were even further removed from the Hollywood mainstream, producing low-budget films for specific ethnic groups. Oscar Micheaux (p. 163) continued making films with black casts. The introduction of sound led to production in a variety of languages. In cities where there were large enclaves of Jewish immigrants, for example, there was a demand for films in Yiddish. While there had been silent films distributed with Yiddish intertitles, the talkies fostered a brief flowering of Jewish-oriented production in the 1930s. Films such as *Uncle Moses* (produced by Yiddish Talking Pictures in 1932) were shown in theaters that also exhibited movies imported from the two other centers of Yiddish filmmaking, the USSR and Poland. Edgar G. Ulmer, who had worked briefly in Hollywood, made one of the most internationally successful Yiddish films, *Green Fields* (1937). Other directors adapted works from the popular theater. Many Yiddish films centered on family crises and the clash between traditional values and modern urban life. The films featured frequent musical interludes. The outbreak of World War II crushed Yiddish filmmaking in Poland

in 1939, and, by 1942, Yiddish-language production had ceased in the United States as well.

Despite the limited successes of various types of independent production, it would have been virtually impossible for a new company—large or small—to gain a significant share of the film market. The existing Hollywood firms had created a secure, stable situation in which they loaned each other stars, played each other's films in their theaters, and cooperated in other ways. In one of their most prominent joint actions, they worked through the Motion Picture Producers and Distributors of America to fight outside pressure for censorship of movies (see box p. 216).

EXHIBITION PRACTICE IN THE 1930s

Sound and the Depression significantly changed the way theaters presented movies. Warner Bros. initially viewed sound as a way of eliminating live orchestral accompaniment of features and stage acts in the theater. Its effort was successful, and by 1930 most theaters showed only filmed entertainment. In effect, creative control of programming had at last been taken entirely out of the hands of local theater managers, who received their entire shows in the form of films.

The Depression cut short the age of the movie palace. Many theaters no longer could afford ushers to show patrons to their seats. Managers also needed to bring in extra income, and so they offered candy, popcorn, and beverages in the lobbies. Since many moviegoers had little to spend on entertainment, exhibitors resorted to playing double and even triple features, in addition to the usual short films. The second film was often a cheap B picture, but it gave the moviegoer the impression of getting twice as much. Just as important, the double feature had an intermission during which the spectator could buy refreshments.

Managers also lured patrons with giveaways. There might be a drawing for a door prize, or a souvenir pillow might come with every ticket. Most effective were "dish nights," when each ticket came with a piece of chinaware (purchased in bulk by the theater). Families were thus encouraged to attend weekly to collect the whole set of crockery.

As attendance expanded during World War II, some of these incentives declined. B-film production was less important, but the double feature remained, as did the concession stand. Many big movie houses had deteriorated during the Depression, but they were still ready to accommodate the renewed crowds of moviegoers.

10.2 A lightweight boom aims a small microphone directly at the actors during production of Lloyd Bacon's *San Quentin* (1937).

CONTINUED INNOVATION IN HOLLYWOOD

During the 1920s, the expansion of the industry had included the formation of many technical companies and studio departments. The innovation of sound, which created such an upheaval in the business, had been one result of this growth in the technological-support side of the industry. During the 1930s and 1940s, advances in filmmaking continued. Through the efforts of the studios, key manufacturers, and coordinating institutions like the Academy of Motion Picture Arts and Sciences, film technology became more versatile and sophisticated.

Sound Recording

Methods of sound recording improved steadily. Early microphones were omnidirectional, picking up unwanted noise from crew and equipment. Gradually, unidirectional microphones, which could be aimed specifically at the desired sound source, were developed. While early booms to hang and move the microphone above the set had been large and clumsy, lighter booms soon made recording more flexible (**10.2**). By late 1932, innovations in multiple-track recording permitted music, voices, and sound effects to be registered separately and later mixed onto one track. (Songs were generally recorded first, with the singers moving their lips to a playback.) Also in 1932, identical edge numbers began to be printed on both the image and sound negatives, permitting close synchronization even of short shots.

By 1932, the results of such improvements were apparent in many films. Actors no longer had to move gingerly or to slowly enunciate their dialogue, and the lugubrious pace of many early talkies gave way to a livelier rhythm. The new flexibility in sound recording is apparent in such disparate films of 1932 as *Trouble in Paradise* (Ernst Lubitsch), *I Am a Fugitive from a Chain Gang* (Mervyn LeRoy), and *Dr. Jekyll and Mr. Hyde* (Rouben Mamoulian).

While early sound films had often avoided using much nondiegetic atmospheric music, multiple-track recording fostered the introduction of what came to be called the *symphonic score*, in which lengthy musical passages played under the action and dialogue. Several composers who were trained in the tradition of post-Romantic European classical music, including Max Steiner, Erich Wolfgang Korngold, Miklós Rózsa, David Raksin, and Bernard Herrmann, wrote scores to heighten moods of romance or suspense.

Steiner in particular helped establish the norms for studio music. His emphatic score for *King Kong* (1933) was an influential early use of the symphonic approach. Steiner also commonly quoted easily recognizable tunes to emphasize a scene's meaning, as in *Sergeant York* (1940), where "Give Me That Old Time Religion" forms

10.3   The crane Busby Berkeley used at Warner Bros. to film elaborate musical numbers, seen here between takes of *Wonder Bar* (1934).

a motif associated with the hero's religious faith. Like many musical techniques in the sound cinema, this quotation practice derived from live accompaniment of silent films. Composers usually tried to make the music unobtrusive; like continuity editing, set design, and other techniques, most music was supposed to serve the narrative without drawing attention to itself.

Camera Movement

Many early sound films contained camera movements, but to execute them, filmmakers often had to shoot silent and add sound later or create elaborate means to move the bulky camera booth. Moving shots tended to stand out from the rest of the film, which might well be made with multiple cameras. Such disparities were not good for continuity. Once blimps came into use, a new problem surfaced: the cameras were too heavy for traditional tripods, and they were difficult to move between shots. The solution was a camera support that was both strong and mobile, and individual cinematographers and service firms created new versions of the sorts of dollies and cranes used at the end of the silent era.

Again, 1932 was a breakthrough year, with the introduction of the Bell & Howell Rotambulator. This was a 700-pound dolly that could raise the camera vertically from 18 inches to 7 feet, and the operator could pan, tilt, or track with ease. The Fearless Company's compact

Panoram Dolly (1936) could pass through a 36-inch doorway. The spectacular tracking shots of some late 1930s and 1940s films, where the camera traverses two or more rooms of a set, depended on such equipment.

Craning movements also became more common. Universal's *All Quiet on the Western Front* (1931) used the giant 50-foot crane that had been built in 1929 for *Broadway.* The famous movement of pulling back above a huge railway platform full of wounded Confederate soldiers in *Gone with the Wind* employed a building crane. Large cranes could also be used in the studio, usually to create spectacular shots in historical epics, musicals, or fantasies (**10.3**). In MGM's 1939 musical fantasy *The Wizard of Oz,* the camera swooped over the Munchkin City and the Yellow Brick Road. Most cranes, however, were small models suitable for unobtrusive vertical and diagonal movements.

Technicolor

Undoubtedly the most striking innovation of this era was color filmmaking. We have seen how silent films employed various nonphotographic processes that colored the film after it had been shot. There were also several attempts to introduce photographic color processes in the silent period. The Technicolor firm's two-strip system had been used occasionally in Hollywood films during the 1920s, and it survived into the early sound era. It was

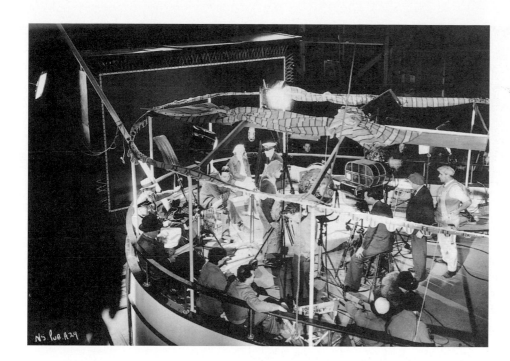

10.4 The actors in *The Woman in Red* (1935) sit in front of a back-projection screen, upper left, on which an ocean background will be projected during filming.

costly to use, however, and it rendered colors mainly as pinkish orange and greenish blue (**Color Plate 10.1**).

In the early 1930s, Technicolor introduced a new system involving prisms to split the light coming through the camera lens onto three strips of black-and-white film, one for each primary color (**Color Plates 10.2–10.12**). This technique was introduced publicly in a 1932 Disney short cartoon, *Flowers and Trees*. Pioneer Pictures, a small independent production firm owned by a major stockholder in Technicolor, produced a live-action musical short, *La Cucaracha*, in 1935 (**Color Plate 10.13**). It demonstrated that Technicolor could render vivid colors with live actors in the studio. That same year, the feature *Becky Sharp* (see Color Plate 10.12) showed that color could add to the appeal of a historical drama. Technicolor's ability to produce bright, saturated colors suggested that, for some films, the extra cost (nearly 30 percent higher than that of black-and-white) was justified. (Color Plates 11.1, 15.1, and 15.10 show other examples of three-strip Technicolor.) The Majors began using color, and the Technicolor company monopolized the process, supplying all cameras, providing supervisors for each production, and processing and printing the film.

Today we regard color as a realistic element in films, but in the 1930s and 1940s, it was often associated with fantasy and spectacle. It could be used for exotic adventures like *The Garden of Allah* (1936), swashbucklers like *The Adventures of Robin Hood* (1939), or musicals like *Meet Me in St. Louis* (1944).

Special Effects

The term *special effects*, used in connection with the 1930s, usually conjures up thoughts of films like *King Kong* and *The Wizard of Oz*. Yet, as the president of the American Society of Cinematographers pointed out in 1943, "Ninety per cent of the trick and special effects shots in Hollywood movies are made with no thought of fooling or mystifying the audience. The great majority of camera trickery is used simply because filming the same action by conventional means would be too difficult, too expensive, or too dangerous."[2] Because special effects promoted ease, efficiency, and safety, they were used frequently and had a considerable impact on films of this period.

Most trick photography in the silent era was done by the cinematographer during shooting. Multiple-camera filming and other complications associated with sound led to trick work's becoming the responsibility of specialists. Studios added special-effects departments that often invented and built equipment to meet the demands of specific scenes.

Special-effects work usually involved combining separately shot images in one of two ways: through *rear projection* (also called back projection) or *optical printing*. In back projection, the actors perform in a studio set as an image filmed earlier is projected onto a screen behind them (**10.4**). In most scenes in which characters ride in cars, for example, the vehicle is filmed in a studio while the background landscape passes on a screen (**10.5**).

10.5 This scene from Fritz Lang's 1936 film *Fury* uses rear projection.

10.6 Only the lower left portion of this shot from *Queen Christina* (1932) was built on the studio backlot; the ships, water, rooftops, and sky were added with a matte painting.

Back projection saved money, since actors and crew did not have to go on location. (A small crew, or *second unit*, would travel to make the back-projection shots.) For example, much of the 1938 MGM film *Captains Courageous* took place on the deck of a fishing schooner, yet the actors worked entirely in the studio, with a tank of water below them and back-projected seascapes.

The optical printer offered more options for rephotographing and combining images. Essentially, an optical printer consisted of a projector aimed into the lens of a camera. Both could be moved forward and backward, different lenses could be substituted, and portions of the image could be masked off and the film reexposed. Images could be superimposed, or portions could be joined like pieces of a jigsaw puzzle; a single image could be enlarged or its speed altered.

Typically the optical printer was used to save money by filling in portions of studio sets. By blocking off a part of a frame with a *matte,* the cinematographer could leave an unexposed portion into which the special-effects expert could later insert a *matte painting* (**10.6**).

Far more complex were *traveling mattes.* Here the effects cinematographer would make two or more masks for each frame of the trick passage and expose the film twice, frame by frame, using complementary masks in turn to cover portions of the film. Traveling mattes were commonly used to make *wipes,* where a line passes across the screen, removing one shot gradually as the next appears. In 1933, wipes became fashionable as a way of replacing *fades* or *dissolves* (two other transitional techniques) when RKO optical-printer expert Linwood Dunn created elaborate transitions, moving in fan, sawtooth, and other shapes, in *Melody Cruise* and *Flying Down to Rio* (**10.7**).

The optical printer was often used to create *montage sequences.* These brief flurries of shots used superimpositions, calendar pages, newspaper headlines, and similar images to suggest the passage of time or the course of a lengthy action (**10.8**).

10.7 A wipe with a zigzag edge provides a transition from one shot to another in *Flying Down to Rio.*

10.8 In *Mr. Deeds Goes to Town,* superimposed newspaper headlines create montage sequences summarizing the public's changing perception of the protagonist.

There were many other types of special effects. Entire scenes could be filmed using miniatures, as in the plane takeoffs and landings in Hawks's *Only Angels Have Wings.* Frame-by-frame three-dimensional animation was used occasionally, most notably to turn small puppets into the giant ape in *King Kong.* Other tricks involved simple mechanical devices, like the trapdoor elevator and dry-ice fumes that make the Wicked Witch seem to melt in *The Wizard of Oz.*

10.9 In *A Farewell to Arms* (1932, Frank Borzage), the romantic scene in which the main characters fall in love consists of soft, glittering images.

10.10 *Shanghai Express* (1932, Josef von Sternberg) employs an extensive range of soft grays to create glamorous images of Marlene Dietrich.

10.11 A depth composition in *Twentieth Century* (1934, Howard Hawks).

10.12, 10.13 Deep-space compositions that keep all planes in focus, from *The Public Enemy* (1931, William Wellman) and *Only Angels Have Wings* (1939).

10.14 Deep focus with one character close to the camera, a second in the middle ground, and a third in extreme depth, in *Citizen Kane*.

Cinematography Styles

During the early 1930s, most cinematographers aimed for a "soft" image, based on the important stylistic trend of the 1920s (p. 147). Now, however, the soft look became less extreme but more pervasive. Camera experts used fewer obvious filters or smeared, distorting glass masks. Instead, studio laboratories typically processed film to make it look grayer and softer. Moreover, in 1931, Eastman Kodak introduced a Super Sensitive Panchromatic stock suitable for use with the more diffused incandescent lighting that the innovation of sound had necessitated (due to the hissing noise emitted by arc lamps). Some films used a sparkling, low-contrast image to convey a sense of glamour or romance (**10.9**). Others went for a clearer focus while still avoiding sharp blacks and whites (**10.10**).

Most Hollywood filmmakers of the 1930s clustered actors together in a relatively shallow area and then cut among them using shot/reverse shot. Others created compositions in greater depth, sometimes with the foreground plane slightly out of focus (**10.11**) but sometimes also using deep focus (**10.12, 10.13**). (Such depth had precedents in the silent era; compare with 7.47.)

Director Orson Welles and cinematographer Gregg Toland took such deep-focus shots further and used them extensively in *Citizen Kane* (1941). Many of *Kane*'s depth shots used optical printing to combine sharply focused planes that had been filmed separately. Some shots, however, placed foreground elements near the lens and background elements at a considerable distance, yet kept everything in sharp focus; this occurs most spectacularly in the long take of the contract-signing scene (**10.14**). Welles went further along the same path in his second film, *The Magnificent Ambersons* (1942), for which cinematographer Stanley Cortez achieved many crisply focused depth shots without using trick photography (**10.15**). The influence of these visually innovative films soon spread throughout the industry. Staging in widely separated planes with deep focus became common practice (**10.16**).

10.15, *left* The ballroom scene of *The Magnificent Ambersons* presents a vast set in clear focus behind the foreground couple.

10.16, *right* A simple shot/reverse-shot situation in *Casablanca* (1943) places Rick close to the camera in front of a sharply focused deep playing space.

10.18 Chaplin expresses Hynkel's lust for power when he dances with an inflatable globe, tossing it about until it bursts.

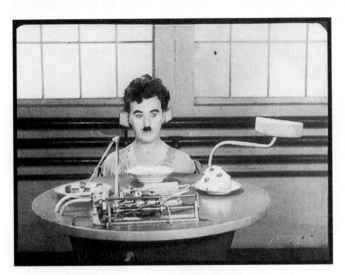

10.17 In *Modern Times*, factory worker Charlie tests a new machine that feeds the workers automatically while they stay on the job.

Overall, technological innovations of the years from 1930 to 1945 did not fundamentally change the classical Hollywood approach to filmmaking. Narrative action and character psychology still remained central, and continuity rules still promoted spatial orientation. Sound, color, deep focus, and other techniques enhanced the style.

MAJOR DIRECTORS

In addition to the established directors working in Hollywood, the introduction of sound brought an influx of stage directors into the film studios; during this era, several screenwriters also joined the ranks of film directors. Moreover, the troubled political situation in Europe brought several émigrés' talents to the United States. We shall survey these directors and discuss the genres in which they worked.

The Older Generation

Charles Chaplin opposed talking pictures. As his own producer and a phenomenally popular star, he was able to go on making "silent" films, with only music and sound effects, longer than anyone else in Hollywood. His output, however, slowed considerably. He made two features without dialogue, *City Lights* (1931) and *Modern Times* (1936). The latter reflected the left-wing views that would get him into trouble with the government and the public after the war. In it, the Little Tramp loses a dreary assembly-line job, gets thrown in jail after being mistaken for the leader of a demonstration, and later joins forces with a poor young woman to seek work. Despite its concentration on Depression-era problems, it is a very funny film (10.17). Oddly enough, so is Chaplin's first talkie, *The Great Dictator* (1940), a comedy on the unlikely subject of Nazi Germany. The resemblance between Hitler's moustache and Chaplin's had often drawn comment, and Chaplin took advantage of their physical similarities to play Hynkel, dictator of Tomania (10.18).

After Josef von Sternberg had directed his second sound film, *The Blue Angel*, in Germany (p. 000), he returned to Hollywood with the film's star, Marlene Dietrich. They made six more films together, including *Morocco* (1930) and *Blonde Venus* (1932). While the stories were conventional melodramas, their style

10.19 Thief and potential victim in one of the gleaming Art Deco sets of *Trouble in Paradise*.

10.20 In *Young Mr. Lincoln*, the climactic courtroom revelation is played out in a carefully arranged framing in depth, with no closer shots to emphasize the characters' emotions.

10.21 Similarly, in *How Green Was My Valley*, a composition reminiscent of D. W. Griffith's films (see 3.48) lingers over the family's silent reaction to bad news.

placed them among the era's most beautiful films. Von Sternberg's fascination with textures and dense compositions intensified. In particular, costume, lighting, and cinematography glamorized Dietrich to an extent that has seldom been equaled (see 10.10). Von Sternberg also made films without Dietrich during this period, including two somber literary adaptations, *An American Tragedy* (1931) and *Crime and Punishment* (1935).

Ernst Lubitsch adjusted quickly to sound with *The Love Parade* (p. 195). He went on to make many popular musicals and comedies. Foremost among these was *Trouble in Paradise* (1932). It begins with a witty scene in which an elegant couple dine together in a Venetian hotel and then discover that each is a thief out to rob the other. They fall in love and continue to ply their trade until a scheme to rob a rich woman almost leads to the man's falling in love with the victim (**10.19**). Lubitsch also directed Greta Garbo's penultimate film, *Ninotchka* (1939). Along with Chaplin's *The Great Dictator*, Lubitsch's *To Be or Not to Be* (1942) was one of the rare comedies about the Nazis.

John Ford continued to be remarkably prolific during the 1930s, signing twenty-six films during the decade, plus several more in the early 1940s before he went into the Navy. Working principally at 20th Century-Fox, he directed some of the studio's most popular stars, making a trio of films with Will Rogers (*Dr. Bull* [1933], *Judge Priest* [1934], and *Steamboat Round the Bend* [1935]) and a costume picture, *Wee Willie Winkie* (1937), starring Shirley Temple. Despite his early concentration on Westerns, he made only one during this era, *Stagecoach* (1939), but it became one of the genre's classics. It traced the trip of a motley group of people through dangerous Indian territory. In this film, Ford first used the unearthly

cliff formations of Monument Valley, a setting that would become his trademark in later Westerns.

That same year Ford directed *Young Mr. Lincoln*, in which a murder case solved by Lincoln suggests the combination of simplicity and shrewdness that will eventually make him President. *How Green Was My Valley* (1941) is a richly nostalgic story of a close-knit Welsh coal-mining family's gradual disintegration. Ford created deeply emotional situations while using great stylistic restraint. Although he used conventional shot/reverse shots and cut-ins in some cases, Ford downplayed the most important or sentimental moments by staying in long shot or holding quietly on a silent scene of the characters in contemplation (**10.20, 10.21**). Ford also used considerable depth in his staging and cinematography, stylistic traits that were to influence Orson Welles, who studied *Stagecoach* before making *Citizen Kane*.

Howard Hawks, who had begun directing in the mid-1920s, became increasingly prominent during this era. Like Ford, he worked in a variety of genres, concentrating on succinct handling of plot and performance and displaying a mastery of rapid pacing and continuity editing. Hawks explained his approach in a typically down-to-earth fashion: "I try to tell my story as simply as possible, with the camera at eye level. I just imagine the way the story should be told and I do it. If it's a scene that I don't want anybody to monkey with or cut, I don't give them any way to cut it."[3]

If Ford's *Stagecoach* is the quintessential Western, then Hawks's *His Girl Friday* (1940) is a model sound comedy. The hilarious script (from Ben Hecht and Charles MacArthur's play *The Front Page*) involves a newspaper editor who tries to prevent his ex-wife from giving up reporting to remarry. He lures her into trying to expose

10.22, *left*   The hero talks down a plane in trouble in *Only Angels Have Wings*.

10.23, *right*   In the famous final scene of *Stella Dallas*, Stella stands outside in the rain, weeping as she watches her daughter's wedding, and then turns to leave forever.

some crooked politicians who plan to execute a mentally incompetent killer in order to swing their election. Cary Grant, Rosalind Russell, and a bevy of character actors delivered the wisecracking dialogue at breakneck speed while Hawks recorded the action primarily with "invisible" shot/reverse shots and reframing movements.

Hawks's aviation adventure film *Only Angels Have Wings* (1939) is set in a small South American port where a flying service tries to get mail through a narrow mountain pass. Using simple resources, Hawks created an intense atmosphere of danger and romance. Much of the action takes place in and around a single building, at night or in a fog, as the characters wait for each returning flight (**10.22**; see also 10.13). As often happens in Hawks films, the characters, male and female alike, have to prove themselves tough and stoic.

William Wyler had begun directing in the late silent era, making mostly inexpensive Westerns. His breakthrough came in 1936, when he began working for independent producer Samuel Goldwyn. He made *These Three* (1936), an adaptation of Lillian Hellman's play *The Children's Hour,* and several other distinguished films over the next few years. These included *Jezebel* (1938), *Wuthering Heights* (1939), and another Hellman adaptation, *The Little Foxes* (1941). On the last two, Gregg Toland was Wyler's cinematographer, and both films display deep-focus imagery similar to that of Ford's and Welles's films.

Veteran director Frank Borzage continued to specialize in sentimental melodramas. *A Farewell to Arms* (1932) adapted Hemingway's novel of an American soldier and a British nurse who fall in love during World War I. Borzage and cinematographer Charles B. Lang filmed the characters in a glimmering soft-focus style that enhanced the intense romanticism (see 10.9). By contrast, King Vidor continued to work in a variety of genres, from Westerns to melodramas. His 1937 remake of *Stella Dallas* is a classic melodrama, telling the story of a working-class woman who marries a factory

owner's son. Her inability to overcome her vulgar upbringing eventually threatens her daughter's marriage to a society man, so she selflessly divorces her husband and gives up her daughter for adoption by his new, and refined, wife (**10.23**).

Raoul Walsh also worked in various genres, making several major action films in the late 1930s and early 1940s. *The Roaring Twenties* (1939), a gangster film, contrasts the lives of three World War I veterans. The film is notable partly for several spectacular montage sequences, including a representation of the stock-market crash as a ticker-tape machine that swells to huge size and shatters. *High Sierra* (1940) is the sympathetic story of a killer fleeing through the mountains to escape the police; he meets a crippled girl whom he befriends. The film was a turning point in the career of Humphrey Bogart, who had previously played mostly villainous supporting roles; the next year he would play tough detective Sam Spade in *The Maltese Falcon*.

New Directors

The introduction of sound brought several stage directors from New York to Hollywood. Among these was George Cukor, who specialized in prestigious literary adaptations, such as *Camille* (1936), with Greta Garbo, and *David Copperfield* (1935), with W. C. Fields. Cukor worked mostly at MGM during this period. Rouben Mamoulian also came from Broadway; his *Applause* (1929) drew attention for its fluid camera movements. Similarly, his adaptation of *Dr. Jekyll and Mr. Hyde* (1932) begins with an unusually extended subjective tracking shot as we watch through Jekyll's eyes as he enters a lecture hall. Another director who came from Broadway was Vincente Minnelli, who specialized in musicals. He joined MGM's musicals unit in 1940. This unit, under producer Arthur Freed, soon gathered some of the finest musical talent in Hollywood, including Judy Garland, Gene Kelly, and Fred Astaire. Minnelli

CITIZEN KANE AND THE MAGNIFICENT AMBERSONS

While still a young man, Orson Welles (born 1915) was directing unusual productions of theatrical and radio plays. For example, in 1936 he staged *Macbeth* with an all-black cast and set it in a Haitian jungle. In 1938, he gained nationwide notoriety with a radio adaptation of H. G. Wells's *The War of the Worlds*, treating it as a news bulletin and panicking thousands of listeners who believed that a Martian invasion was in progress.

In 1939, Welles was put under contract by RKO. His first completed project was *Citizen Kane,* one of the most admired of all films. Welles received an extraordinary degree of control over his work, including the right to choose his cast and to edit the final film. Not surprisingly, the resulting film was controversial. It was a veiled portrait of publishing magnate William Randolph Hearst and his long-term affair with film star Marion Davies. Hearst tried to have *Kane* suppressed, but it was released in 1941, with many audiences being aware of its subtext.

Both the narrative structure and the style of *Kane* are dazzlingly complex. Beginning with the death of Charles Foster Kane, the film switches to a newsreel that sketches out his life. A reporter is assigned to discover the meaning of Kane's mysterious last word, "Rosebud." He interviews people who had known Kane, and a series of flashbacks reveals a contradictory, elusive personality. Ultimately the reporter's quest fails, and the ending retains an ambiguity rare in classical Hollywood films.

Stylistically, *Kane* was flamboyant, drawing extensively on RKO's resources. For some scenes, Welles used quiet, lengthy takes. Other passages, notably the newsreel and several montage sequences, used quick cutting and abrupt changes in sound volume. To emphasize the vast spaces of some of the sets, Welles and cinematographer Gregg Toland worked at achieving deep-focus shots, placing some elements close to the camera, others at a distance (see 10.14). Recent research has revealed that many of these deep shots were made using several types of special effects (**10.24**). Optical-printer work combined several tracking shots imperceptibly into one (as in the crane shot through a nightclub skylight, where a flash of lightning hides the joint between two shots) and made the sets more impressive by combining miniatures and matte paintings with real-size sets. It has been claimed that over half of *Citizen Kane*'s shots contain special effects. The sound track was also altered substantially after filming. All these stylistic as-

10.24   In this shot from *Citizen Kane,* the large objects in the foreground were filmed separately and combined with the set and actors beyond.

pects of *Citizen Kane* proved highly influential during the 1940s.

Welles's second RKO feature was *The Magnificent Ambersons.* The plot does not use flashbacks, but it covers a lengthy period, the decline of a wealthy family as industrialization encroaches on a midwestern town. Welles establishes a nostalgic atmosphere in a prologue, narrated by him, which is a montage sequence depicting turn-of-the-century life. The film gradually adopts a grimmer tone as this genteel lifestyle disappears.

Stylistically, *Ambersons* takes *Kane*'s techniques in less extravagant directions. Still, there are elaborate camera movements, as when Aunt Fannie has hysterics and the camera tracks through several rooms as Georgie tries to calm her. The deep-focus effects were more often done in a single exposure (see 10.15), and a larger budget allowed Welles to build entire sets and downplay optical-printer work.

After adverse audience reactions at previews, RKO took *Ambersons* out of Welles's control and cut it drastically, adding scenes made by the assistant director and editor. This truncated version was given a minor release. No complete version of the film survives, but even so it remains a flawed masterpiece. (See "Notes and Queries" at the end of this chapter.)

did choreography for Busby Berkeley films, including *Strike Up the Band* (1940), and then graduated to directing with *Cabin in the Sky* (1943), a musical with an all-star black cast. His most celebrated film of the war era was *Meet Me in St. Louis* (1944), with Garland.

Other new directors of this era appeared from the ranks of screenwriters. Preston Sturges wrote scenarios during the 1930s, working on *The Power and the Glory* (1933, William K. Howard), a film with a complex flashback structure that was a precursor to *Citizen Kane*. Sturges began directing with *The Great McGinty* (1940), a political satire, and went on to make a string of popular comedies throughout the war years. In *The Miracle of Morgan's Creek* (1944), for example, he poked fun at American prudishness. A young woman winds up pregnant after a wild party and claims that she married the father (whose name she remembers only as being something like "Ignatz Ratskywatsky"). When he proves hard to locate, her mild-mannered boyfriend helps her avoid disgrace by marrying her; she then bears sextuplets, and the family becomes the focus of a media furor. Despite toning down by the MPPDA, the film remains audacious. For a while, Sturges was one of Paramount's most popular directors.

John Huston, who had worked on the screenplays of *Jezebel* and *High Sierra*, was another scriptwriter-turned-director. Later in this chapter we shall discuss his directorial debut, *The Maltese Falcon*, as an early instance of film noir. Huston was in the military for much of the war, making some major war documentaries, and returned to Hollywood after 1945.

Orson Welles, the most influential director to emerge between 1930 and 1945, had already achieved success in a number of other fields including stage and radio (see box p. 227).

New Émigré Directors

Foreign filmmakers continued to come to Hollywood. Some were lured by higher salaries or the chance to work in the world's best-equipped studios. Increasingly, however, the spread of fascism in Europe and the onset of World War II drove filmmakers to seek refuge in the United States.

Dissatisfied with his lack of authority in England and fascinated by the technical possibilities offered in Hollywood, Alfred Hitchcock signed a contract with David O. Selznick. His first American film, *Rebecca* (1940), was a prestigious literary adaptation and won a best-picture Academy Award, but it was not typical of the suspense films he is more famous for. Among his

several wartime films was *Shadow of a Doubt* (1943). A man driven to seduce and kill rich widows visits his sister's family in a small California town. He charms everyone, but his young niece is shattered when she ferrets out the truth about him. Through location shooting, Hitchcock created a sense of small-town normalcy with which to contrast the villain's secret crimes.

The German exodus to Hollywood that had begun in the silent era accelerated after the Nazis gained power in 1933. Fritz Lang arrived in 1934. Although he was able to work fairly steadily (about a film a year up to 1956), Lang seldom had much control over his projects and never gained the prestige he had had in Germany. He worked in many genres, making Westerns, spy pictures, melodramas, and suspense films. *You Only Live Once* (1937) is the affecting story of a young ex-convict who tries to go straight but is falsely accused of a murder; he escapes from jail the night before his execution, but he and his wife are hunted down and shot.

Billy Wilder had been a scriptwriter in Germany and resumed this career in Hollywood, teaming up with Charles Brackett on many screenplays, including those for *Ninotchka* and *Ball of Fire*. His first solo directorial effort was a comedy, *The Major and the Minor* (1942), and his grim study of alcoholism, *The Lost Weekend* (1945) was voted an Oscar as best picture. Although Otto Preminger was Jewish, he was brought to Hollywood to play Nazi villains. He managed, however, to slip into directing in the early 1940s. Wilder and Preminger made two of the period's classic films noirs.

GENRE INNOVATIONS AND TRANSFORMATIONS

Many genres from the silent era continued uninterrupted into the sound period. Technical changes within the industry and social changes in the world at large, however, caused some new genres to arise and some new variants to be introduced into old ones.

The Musical

The introduction of sound promoted the musical as a major genre. Some early *revue musicals* simply strung numbers together. Others, like *The Broadway Melody*, were *backstage musicals*, motivating their numbers as performances by their characters. There were also *operetta musicals,* exemplified by *The Love Parade,* which played out their stories and numbers in fantasy locales.

10.25 Maurice Chevalier sings into three mirrors in *Love Me Tonight*.

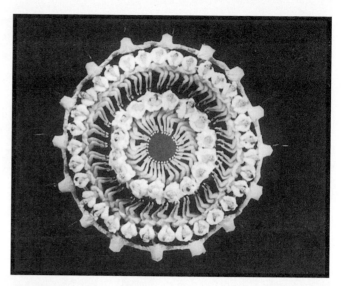

10.26 Busby Berkeley creates an abstract pattern by shooting a dance number from directly overhead in *42nd Street*.

And, there were *integrated musicals,* in which the singing and dancing occurred in ordinary settings. (Backstage musicals often mixed in a few integrated numbers with those performed on stage.) The revue musical soon died out, but the other types all remained prominent.

A delightful example of the operetta subgenre was Rouben Mamoulian's *Love Me Tonight* (1932). The film begins with a sequence influenced by René Clair's early sound films: a Parisian street gradually comes to life in the early morning, with each rhythmic noise contributing to a beat that leads into a musical number. In a celebrated sequence, a song passes from person to person, with the scenes being linked by dissolves. The protagonist, a tailor, sings a song, "Isn't It Romantic?" (**10.25**), which is picked up by a composer, who in turn sings it to soldiers on a train; when the soldiers sing it around their campfire, a gypsy hears it and plays it for his friends; then it makes its way to the heroine, a princess who sings the song on the balcony of her provincial castle.

The backstage musical was typified by a series of films made by Warner Bros. and choreographed by Busby Berkeley. In *42nd Street* (1933, Lloyd Bacon), the film that established many conventions of the genre, a naive chorus girl rises to sudden stardom when the lead player is injured just before the opening of a big Broadway show. The director encourages her: "You *can't* fall down, you *can't,* because *your* future's in it, *my* future, and everything all of us have is staked on you. All right now, I'm through, but you keep your feet on the ground, and your head on those shoulders of yours, and Sawyer, you're going out a youngster, but you've *got* to come back a star!" And, of course, she does become a star. The stage show includes some of Berkeley's elaborate dance numbers, shot using a crane and overhead camera platform (**10.26**).

Among the most popular musicals were those starring Fred Astaire and Ginger Rogers, choreographed by Hermes Pan. In *Swing Time* (1936, George Stevens), for example, Astaire plays a vaudeville hoofer who courts

10.27 The "Let's Face the Music" number in *Follow the Fleet* (1936, Mark Sandrich).

Rogers, a dance instructor. Whether having a backstage plot or an integrated plot, Astaire-Rogers musicals were romances, and many of the dance numbers serve to advance the couple's onscreen courtship. Despite initial misunderstandings and antagonisms, the elegant meshing of their movements shows that they are made for each other (**10.27**).

MGM also made many musicals during this era. Mickey Rooney and Judy Garland were paired in several films about teenagers putting on shows, such as *Strike Up the Band* (1940, Berkeley). Garland became a star in the glossy Technicolor fantasy *The Wizard of Oz* (1939,

10.28 The protagonists compete at throwing theatrical fits in *Twentieth Century*.

10.29 The heiress relaxes as the reporter demonstrates his skill at hitchhiking in *It Happened One Night*.

10.30 In *Mr. Deeds Goes to Town*, the hero is more concerned with playing his tuba than with a lawyer's news of his large inheritance.

10.31, *left* The independent, positive characters in *Holiday* celebrate eccentricity by jokingly awarding the hero a toy giraffe.

10.32, *right* In *The Lady Eve*, brewing heir Charles Pike suffers the comic humiliation typical of the screwball comedy.

Victor Fleming). One of her finest films was Minnelli's *Meet Me in St. Louis*. Another MGM star whose career began during this period was Gene Kelly, whose dance style was often boisterous and athletic, as in the "Make Way for Tomorrow" number in *Cover Girl* (for which Kelly was loaned to Columbia; 1944, Charles Vidor).

The Screwball Comedy

In *screwball comedy,* the romantic couple at the center of the story are eccentrics, often portrayed through slapstick. The films are usually set among wealthy people who can, despite the hardships of the Depression, afford to behave oddly. The romantic couple may initially be antagonistic, as in George Cukor's *The Philadelphia Story* (1940). Or the couple's love may cross class lines; then the wealthy parents must be converted (as in Capra's *You Can't Take It with You,* 1938) or thwarted (as in Cukor's *Holiday,* 1938).

Although eccentric romantic comedies were made during the silent era, screwball comedy gained new prominence in 1934 with two very different films. Hawks's *Twentieth Century* is utterly cynical in its treatment of its lead actors, Carole Lombard and John Barry-

more. A hammy theatrical entrepreneur makes a star of a beautiful store clerk and then seduces her. She soon behaves as theatrically in everyday life as he does; during the film's second half, set on a train, they quarrel and throw tantrums (**10.28**). The other major screwball comedy of 1934, Capra's *It Happened One Night,* is more sentimental. With its spoiled heroine fleeing her father in order to marry a superficial playboy, it popularized the "madcap heiress" character. A down-to-earth reporter aids the heroine in order to get a scoop, and the two fall in love (**10.29**). The image of a spoiled rich woman would be pushed to its limits in Hawks's *Bringing Up Baby* (1938).

The genre developed quickly, and Capra remained one of its main exponents. In his *Mr. Deeds Goes to Town* (1936), a small-town man becomes a national idol when he uses his unexpected inheritance to help dispossessed farmers. Venal lawyers try to have him declared insane, although he is only eccentric, as Capra demonstrates from the start (**10.30**).

Early films in the genre dealt with the Depression. In *It Happened One Night,* the reporter strives to regain his job by writing a story about the fugitive heiress. In *My Man Godfrey* (1936, Gregory La Ceva), a homeless man hires on as a butler to an eccentric wealthy family; the characters frequently mention "forgotten men"—a Depression-era term for the unemployed, many of whom were veterans of World War I. Later in the decade, however, many screwball comedies' plots ignored contemporary social problems, especially those of unemployment. In *Holiday* (1938, George Cukor), the hero longs to quit his lucrative job and find his purpose in life; all the film's positive characters value individualism while despising snobbishness and wealth (**10.31**). *You Can't Take It with You*, a paean to idiosyncracies, concerns a large family who take into their home people who quit dull jobs in order to pursue personal interests.

The comedy of sexual antagonism also continued unabated. In Sturges's *The Lady Eve* (1941), a female cardsharp sets out to fleece the heir to a brewing fortune; instead, they fall in love, and when he discovers her background and rejects her, she vows revenge (**10.32**). Similarly, in *Ball of Fire* (1941, Hawks), a nightclub singer fleeing the law bamboozles a group of naive professors and then falls in love with one of them.

The screwball genre flourished between 1934 and 1945. Sturges contributed a bitter late example with *Unfaithfully Yours* (1948), in which an orchestra conductor believes his wife has a lover and during a concert fantasizes murdering her in three ways, each to an appropriate musical piece. Hawks also made two postwar screwball comedies; in *I Was a Male War Bride* (1948), a French officer suffers a series of humiliations when he must dress as a woman in order to accompany his fiancée to the United States after World War II; *Monkey Business* (1952) portrays the delirious effects of a youth serum on seemingly respectable people. In recent decades, there have been sporadic attempts to revive the screwball formula, as in Peter Bogdanovich's *What's Up, Doc?* (1972) and Garry Marshall's *Runaway Bride* (1999).

The Horror Film

During the early sound era, the horror film became a major genre. Some horror films had been made during the 1920s, mainly by Universal and usually starring Lon Chaney (pp. 156–157). The pattern for many future films was set in 1927 with Paul Leni's popular *The Cat and the Canary*, in which a group of people meet in an isolated mansion to hear a will read.

Universal repeated such successes in its horror cycle, beginning with the vampire film *Dracula* (1931, Tod Browning). Although it betrayed its origins as a stage version of Bram Stoker's original 1897 novel and suffered

10.33 *The Mummy* uses makeup, lighting (including a tiny "pin" light reflected in the eyes), and Boris Karloff's menacing performance to create an eerie atmosphere on a low budget.

from some of the slowness of early sound films, *Dracula* became a hit largely due to Bela Lugosi's performance in the title role. Shortly thereafter, James Whale's *Frankenstein* (1931) made a star of Boris Karloff, who played the monster with the help of heavy makeup. The Universal horror cycle hit its stride from 1932 to 1935. Whale made *The Old Dark House* (1932), which balanced suspense and comedy by trapping a cast of eccentrics in an isolated country home on the proverbial dark and stormy night. He also directed *The Invisible Man* (1933) and *The Bride of Frankenstein* (1935).

One of the most stylish and effective of these films was *The Mummy,* directed in 1932 by Karl Freund, the German cinematographer who had shot *The Last Laugh* and many other important films during the silent era. The mummy of an ancient Egyptian priest returns to life in modern times and attempts to kill a woman he believes to be a reincarnation of his dead love (**10.33**). In later years, the Universal horror cycle was dissipated by formulaic repetition.

A later significant cycle of horror films was made in RKO's B unit during the early 1940s. Producer Val Lewton took charge of production there in 1942. A small number of directors worked under Lewton—Jacques Tourneur, Mark Robson, and Robert Wise—but the producer created a consistent tone and style for the films. Making a virtue of budget necessities, the Lewton films avoided graphic depictions of monsters or violence, concentrating instead on characters threatened by unseen terrors. In Tourneur's *Cat People* (1942), the heroine is obsessed with a black leopard in the zoo and

10.34   The opening scene of *Cat People,* in which the heroine sketches a leopard, typifies the simple, but disturbing, juxtapositions of the Val Lewton horror films.

seems to have inherited a supernatural ability to transform into a killer cat (**10.34**). Tourneur also directed another of the Lewton unit's most effective films, *I Walked with a Zombie* (1943). These titles were chosen by the studio and assigned to Lewton, and he and his collaborators came up with extraordinarily poetic and frightening films to fit them.

The Social Problem Film

The Depression created a new focus on social problems, and many 1930s films dealt with them, frequently adopting a realistic style that was far from the escapism often associated with this era. In 1934, for example, King Vidor independently made *Our Daily Bread,* which portrayed a group of unemployed people who start a cooperative farm. Despite various challenges, including a drought, they eventually succeed. The scene of the group digging a long channel and irrigating their land uses editing and framing to create an exhilarating image of collective triumph somewhat reminiscent of Soviet films of the era.

Warner Bros. was particularly committed to social problem films. In *I Am a Fugitive from a Chain Gang* (1932, Mervyn LeRoy), a World War I veteran is falsely accused of a theft. While a fugitive, he attempts to pawn his war medal, only to be shown dozens of such medals that unemployed veterans had pawned. In the end he disappears into the night, explaining how he now lives: "I steal," an ironic suggestion that the legal system has pushed him into the underworld. *Wild Boys of the Road* (1933, William Wellman) depicts the plight of homeless orphaned and abandoned children.

Fritz Lang made one of the finest social problem films, *Fury* (1936, MGM), on the subject of lynching. While traveling to meet his fiancée, the hero is arrested in a small town and falsely accused of murder. The citizens burn down the jail, and he is apparently killed. In fact, he survives but is so embittered that he nearly allows his attackers to be convicted of his murder before the heroine persuades him to step forward. The film depicts newsreel cinematographers filming the attempted lynching. At the trial, this footage is used as evidence, and the defendants are forced to confront their own actions (**10.35, 10.36**).

John Ford contributed an important social problem film with *The Grapes of Wrath* (1940), an adaptation of John Steinbeck's novel about displaced Oklahoma farmers during the Depression. The Joad family is driven off their land by the great drought that created the dust bowl in the Plains states. Traveling to California for work, they are exploited as migrant workers. They temporarily find a haven in a government-run camp that suggests the benefits of the Roosevelt administration. Near the end, however, the hero leaves to join the struggle for workers' rights, telling his mother, "Wherever there's a fight so hungry people can eat, I'll be there."

After the United States entered the war, increased employment and prosperity led to fewer social problem

10.35, 10.36   A newsreel image of a woman during the lynching scene and the same woman's reaction to the footage in court, in *Fury.*

films. The genre revived in the postwar era with such films as *Gentlemen's Agreement* (1947, Elia Kazan) and *Crossfire* (1947, Edward Dmytryk).

The Gangster Film

Somewhat related to the social problem film was the gangster genre. Although there had been occasional films about small-time street gangs in the silent era, the first major movie with a gangster protagonist was Josef von Sternberg's *Underworld* (1927; p. 157). The genre became more prominent in the early 1930s with *Little Caesar* (1930, Mervyn LeRoy), *The Public Enemy* (1931, William Wellman), and *Scarface* (1932, Howard Hawks). Gangster films were topical, deriving material from the organized crime that grew up during Prohibition (1919–1933).

Gangster films centered on a ruthless criminal's rise to power. Like many films in the genre, *The Public Enemy* hinges on the contrast between two men (friends or brothers), one of whom gets an honest job while the other turns to crime. Typically, the growing status of the gangsters in these films is signaled by their increasingly expensive clothing and flashy cars (**10.37**).

Like other gangster films, *The Public Enemy* was widely criticized for glamorizing violence. The Hays Code forbade the sympathetic depiction of criminals. Producers defended the genre by claiming that they were simply examining a social problem. *The Public Enemy* begins with a title claiming that the film seeks "to honestly depict an environment that exists today in a certain strata [sic] of American life, rather than glorify the hoodlum or the criminal." The protagonists of these films all die violently in the end, so the studios argued that the plots showed that crime does not pay. Tom, in *The Public Enemy*, is gunned down by a rival gang (**10.38**), and his body is dumped ignominiously at his home. Similarly, the main character in *Scarface* is killed during a violent shoot-out with police. Still, pressure groups insisted that such endings did not wipe out the impression that crime was lively and exciting. The release of *Scarface* was delayed, and the producers were forced to add scenes—not filmed by Hawks—of officials and reformers decrying the gangs' power and violence.

The studios tried to avoid censorship pressures while retaining the excitement associated with the gangster genre. As a result, actors closely identified with criminal roles, such as James Cagney and Edward G. Robinson, also played tough, violent cops, as Cagney does in *G-Men* (1935, William Keighley). Or the gangster became less central, with the story focusing on

10.37 After his first big payoff, the protagonist of *The Public Enemy* is measured for a new suit.

10.38 Tom mutters "I ain't so tough" after being shot, a scene designed to deglamorize his criminal career.

other characters tempted toward a life of crime, as in *Dead End* (1938, William Wyler) and *Angels with Dirty Faces* (1938, Michael Curtiz). In the latter, two friends grow up, one becoming a gangster, the other a priest; a group of children idolize the gangster. Finally the priest persuades the gangster to pretend to be terrified just before his execution so that children will be disillusioned and not take him as a role model.

Film Noir

To some extent the cynical, violent narratives of the gangster films were taken over by the *film noir*. This was a term applied by French critics in 1946 to a group of U.S. films made during the war and released abroad in quick succession after 1945. *Noir* means "black" or "dark" but can also imply "gloomy." Less a genre than a stylistic and narrative tendency, film noir is often considered to have started in 1941 with Huston's *The Maltese Falcon* or even earlier with RKO's B film *Stranger on the Third Floor* (1940, Boris Ingster). Most films noirs involve crime, but the tendency crosses genres. It includes social problem films like Wilder's *The Lost Weekend* and spy films like Lang's *Ministry of Fear* (1944).

The film noir tendency derived from the American hard-boiled detective novel, which originated in the

10.39, *left* Our last view of the femme fatale of *The Maltese Falcon*.

10.40, *right* Film noir shadows fall across the set as Walter Neff sneaks up the back stairs to his apartment in *Double Indemnity*.

1920s. In such harsh, tawdry works as *Red Harvest* (1929), Dashiell Hammett reacted against traditional British detective fiction, which often involved staid country-house settings and upper-class characters. Other major authors of hard-boiled fiction included Raymond Chandler, James M. Cain, and Cornell Woolrich. Many of their novels and stories were adapted as films, starting with Hammett's *The Maltese Falcon*. Filmic influences came from German Expressionism, French Poetic Realism (see Chapter 13), and the stylistic innovations of *Citizen Kane*.

Like their literary models, films noirs were mainly aimed at male audiences. Their protagonists are almost invariably men, usually detectives or criminals characterized by pessimism, self-doubt, or a cold, detached view of the world. Women are usually sexually alluring but treacherous, leading the protagonists into danger or using them for selfish ends. A common setting for a film noir would be a big city, especially at night; shiny, rain-slicked pavements, dark alleyways, and sleazy bars are common milieux. Many of the films use distinctive high and low angles, low-key lighting, extreme wide-angle lenses, and location shooting, though some films noirs contain few of these traits.

The Maltese Falcon established many of the conventions of the film noir. Humphrey Bogart became a major star in the role of Sam Spade, a private detective who must decide whether to turn in the treacherous femme fatale who has hired him and whom he (perhaps) loves. In a long take he bitterly explains why he must send her to prison and promises to wait for her during the many years of her sentence. Brigid is taken away in an elevator by the police, marked as the archetypal film noir heroine by the shadow on her face (**10.39**).

Film noir's debt to German film of the 1920s may be reflected in the fact that four important émigrés worked extensively in this tendency. Fritz Lang's *Dr. Mabuse der Spieler*, *M*, and other German works anticipated film

noir, and his Hollywood career developed this tendency. In *Ministry of Fear*, for example, the hero is released from an insane asylum after the mercy killing of his wife. Whiling away time before his train, he wanders into a grim charity fête and accidentally becomes enmeshed in a battle against Nazi spies. Lang's association with independent producer Walter Wanger led to two other notable wartime films noirs: *Woman in the Window* (1944) and *Scarlet Street* (1945). Robert Siodmak began making B films in Hollywood in 1941, achieving a reputation in film noir in 1944 with *Phantom Lady* and *The Suspect* (1945); after the war he would lead this tendency with such films as *The Killers* (1946).

Another German émigré, Otto Preminger, rose to fame with a major film noir. *Laura* (1944) concerns an embittered working-class detective who investigates the murder of a sophisticated advertising executive and falls in love with her through her diary and portrait. *Laura*'s flashbacks, apparent dream sequence, and plot twists are an extreme case of film noir narration.

Perhaps the definitive wartime example of the film noir came from yet another émigré. The script for Billy Wilder's *Double Indemnity* (1944) originated in a unique combination of hard-boiled authors, with Raymond Chandler adapting a James M. Cain novel. A woman seduces an insurance salesman into helping her murder her husband; gradually the scheme unravels in mutual suspicions and betrayals. The film unfolds in a series of flashbacks as the dying salesman speaks into a dictaphone, confessing to his friend, an insurance investigator who is hot on his trail. Many typical traits of the film noir are present: the venality of both the main characters, the voice-over narration by the insurance salesman, the somber urban setting, and the doomed romance. (Film noir was the one type of Hollywood film that permitted an unhappy ending, though abrupt—and often unconvincing—happy endings were sometimes added.) *Double Indemnity* also used a conventional lighting motif: venetian blinds and other parts of the sets cast shadows across the scene (**10.40**).

The War Film

From 1930 to 1945, films about war passed through remarkable changes. The disillusionment of World War I had resulted in a pacifism that dominated films of the 1930s. (Until Pearl Harbor, most citizens opposed American entry into World War II.) Lewis Milestone's *All Quiet on the Western Front* (1930) was one of the most uncompromisingly pacifist films, showing a sympathetic young German hero and ending unhappily with his death. Throughout the decade, war was depicted as tragic and senseless. Warner Bros. made two versions of *Dawn Patrol* (1930, Howard Hawks; 1938, Edmund Goulding), about a commander who agonizes over sending pilots out to be killed. Even the musical *Gold Diggers of 1933* (1933, Mervyn LeRoy) contains a song—"Remember My Forgotten Man"—about World War I veterans impoverished by the Depression.

After Pearl Harbor, however, the film industry supported the war cause wholeheartedly. Combat films were upbeat and often showed Americans from various ethnic backgrounds united in battling the Axis. In Hawks's *Air Force* (1943), men named Winocki, Quincannon, and Weinberg form part of a bomber crew.

Most war films featuring the Nazis treated them simply as cold-hearted killers. Propaganda directed against the Japanese, however, was often more racist in tone, drawing upon stereotypical images. In *Objective Burma* (1945, Raoul Walsh), for example, the hero leads a division of paratroopers to recapture part of Burma from the Japanese (**10.41**), referred to as "monkeys" (a common racial epithet used during World War II). In one scene the GIs discover the bodies of American soldiers tortured and killed by the Japanese forces. A reporter with the group comments on the horrors he has seen in his career: "But this, this is different. This was done in cold blood by a people who, who claim to be civilized. Civilized and degenerate moral idiots! . . . Wipe 'em out! Wipe 'em off the face of the earth!"

One of the few combat films that presented a less gung-ho image was Ford's *They Were Expendable* (1945), a story of PT-boat sailors who fight valiantly but go down to defeat in the Philippines. Some are evacuated, but others, including one of the protagonists, must stay behind to face capture or death. Ford, who had been in the Navy and been injured filming combat footage for his documentary *The Battle of Mid-*

10.41 The hero of *Objective Burma* gives a journalist a captured Japanese flag as a souvenir.

way (1942), made several realistic scenes of PT boats in combat for *They Were Expendable*. Ford later remarked of this film, "I *despise* these happy endings—with a kiss at the finish—I've never done that. Of course, they *were* glorious in defeat in the Philippines—they kept on fighting."[4] As Ford suggests, *They Were Expendable* presents a remarkably unvarnished picture of heroism.

ANIMATION AND THE STUDIO SYSTEM

Before 1910, animated films had been novelties. By the 1930s, however, labor-saving devices had made them a part of nearly every film program. Each of the Majors and Minors regularly released a cartoon series, either under contract with an independent firm or from their own animation units.

Some of these series were highly standardized, turned out by efficient, assembly-line systems. For nearly forty years after 1930, Paul Terry provided his Terrytoons biweekly for Fox/20th Century-Fox. Universal released films by Walter Lantz from 1929 through 1972; Lantz's most famous character, Woody Woodpecker, debuted in 1941. Columbia had its own short-film division, Screen Gems, which made cartoons starring Krazy Kat, Scrappy, and others until 1949.

At the opposite end of the scale from these series were those produced by the Walt Disney Studio, an independent company devoted solely to making cartoons. Disney's enormous success in 1928 with the Mickey Mouse short *Steamboat Willie* had brought animation into the sound age and given it respectability. The studio went on centering cartoons around Mickey but also established a series of "Silly Symphonies," based on musical pieces and containing no continuing characters. *Skeleton Dance* (1928) featured a macabre celebration in a graveyard.

10.42 In *A Dream Walking* (1934), Popeye, Bluto, and Olive Oyl all end up sleepwalking on an unfinished skyscraper.

By 1932, Disney moved from Columbia to distribute through the prestigious United Artists. Critics all over the world suddenly hailed these shorts, with their fluid movements and minimal dialogue, as the answer to the problems of the all-talkie sound film. The studio also was among the first to pick up on three-strip Technicolor, beginning with *Flowers and Trees* in 1932. Disney dominated the cartoon category of the Oscars with such films as *The Three Little Pigs* (1933), whose song "Who's Afraid of the Big Bad Wolf?" became an anthem of Depression-period America. The firm spent a great deal of money on such films, and its huge staff of artists had the leisure to create detailed, shaded backgrounds, lots of figure movement, and bright color schemes (**Color Plate 10.14**).

In 1937, Disney switched to RKO as a distributor—a move that bolstered that shaky firm when it released the first American feature-length cartoon, *Snow White and the Seven Dwarfs* (1937). Despite being terrified by the witch, children were enchanted by the dwarfs, and the film was a huge hit. The studio continued its series of popular short cartoons, starring Mickey Mouse, Donald Duck, Goofy, and Pluto. It also planned several additional features. *Bambi* (1942) took the studio's propensity for realistic backgrounds further, with soft pastel paintings for the natural settings (**Color Plate 10.15**). The film also extensively employed the new *multiplane camera*, an elaborate animation stand introduced in *The Old Mill* (1937). The multiplane permitted the settings and figures to be divided up onto several cels in layers. These could be moved frame by frame at varying rates toward or away from the camera, giving a powerful illusion of gliding through a three-dimensional space.

The Disney studio was working at its peak during the early 1940s, making *Pinocchio* (1940) and *Dumbo* (1941) as well as *Bambi*. Part of the staff was diverted to war propaganda and informational films, but full-time work on both features and shorts resumed after 1945.

Other studios found animators who, with more limited means, could imaginatively exploit the cartoon's potential for absurdist illogic and rapid, distorted movements. In 1927, Paramount began releasing films by Max and Dave Fleischer, inventors of the "Out of the Inkwell" series. In 1931, they introduced Betty Boop, and Koko the Clown became a supporting character. Betty was a sexy innocent wandering through a variety of adventures, sometimes encountering ghosts and monsters. The Fleischers utilized popular songs; in *Minnie the Moocher* (1932), Cab Calloway's band provides the sound track as Betty explores a scary cave.

Betty had to be toned down considerably after the Hays Code was enforced in 1934. A supporting player who had first appeared in *Popeye the Sailor,* a Betty cartoon of 1933, now became the studio's main star. The gravel-voiced Popeye, with his simple credo ("I yam what I yam and that's all what I yam") and his strengthening cans of spinach, rescued girl friend Olive Oyl and adopted child Swee' Pea from the villainous Bluto and other menaces (**10.42**).

After Disney's success with *Snow White and the Seven Dwarfs,* the Fleischers released the feature-length *Gulliver's Travels* (1939), which employed realistic rotoscoped movements for the title character while using caricatural portrayals for the Lilliputians. The other Fleischer feature, *Mr. Bug Goes to Town* (aka *Hoppity Goes to Town,* 1941), achieved a more consistent stylized look. By that point, however, the brothers had overextended themselves. In 1942, Paramount maneuvered them out of their own animation firm and took over the Popeye series, as well as the Superman series (1941 on). The Fleischers were never able to regain their prominence as animators.

In 1930, Warner Bros. launched its own cartoon unit, hiring as its heads former Disney animation team Hugh Harman, Rudolf Ising, and Friz Freleng. Like many early sound cartoons, the Warner Bros. shorts were built around popular songs from the studio's feature musicals. The series was labeled "Looney Tunes," and most of the early entries starred a little black boy named Bosko.

In 1934, Harman and Ising moved to MGM, taking Bosko with them. Over the next few years, Warners hired a new generation of animators who would raise it to the top of the short-cartoon business: Frank Tashlin, Bob Clampett, Tex Avery, and Chuck Jones, who, along with Freleng, each headed a unit within the animation section. The Warners system was more casual than the usual cartoon factory, and this group swapped ideas with a team of writers in informal "jam sessions." They developed superstars Porky Pig, Daffy Duck, Bugs Bunny, and Elmer Fudd.

The Warners group did not have the resources to create detailed backgrounds or elaborate groups of moving figures to match the Disney product. Instead, the animators depended on speed, topicality, and a silly humor that contrasted with the sentimentality and cuteness of most contemporary cartoons. Avery's taste ran to wild visual puns. Clampett specialized in dazzlingly fast motion: in trying to avoid his induction notice in *Draftee Daffy* (1943), Daffy whizzes about his house as a lightning bolt or shower of sparks.

Many Warners cartoons refer self-consciously to the fact that they are cartoons. In *You Ought to Be in Pictures* (1940, Freleng), Porky decides to become a star in live-action features and quits his job with the Warners animation unit (in a scene with the unit's producer, Leon Schlesinger). In several Warners cartoons, a black silhouette rises up from the audience and interrupts the action; in *Thugs with Dirty Mugs*, a spectator who says he has seen the cartoon before calls the police and informs on the gangsters (**Color Plate 10.16**; note also the caricature of Warners star Edward G. Robinson). Warners shorts appealed as much to adults as to children and became immensely popular—an appeal they still retain today on cable TV.

The same adult appeal was injected into MGM's cartoon series when Tex Avery moved there from Warner Bros. in 1942. Avery created a new repertoire of stars, including wisecracking Screwy Squirrel, unlikely superhero Droopy Dog, and an unnamed Wolf, perpetually expressing extravagant (and frustrated) lust for curvaceous heroines. Avery continued his penchant for literalizing dreadful puns, as when the wolf in *The Shooting of Dan McGoo* (1945) has one foot in the grave (a little grave complete with tombstone encloses his boot like a slipper). Avery would continue pushing cartoons to manic limits for a decade after the war.

Hollywood enjoyed great prosperity during the war. That prosperity was to continue briefly after 1945, but later in the decade new challenges would change the film industry profoundly (see Chapter 15).

Notes and Queries

THE CONTROVERSY OVER ORSON WELLES

Orson Welles's career, especially during the making of *Citizen Kane* and *The Magnificent Ambersons*, has remained the subject of controversy. During the 1950s and 1960s, when auteurist criticism began hailing directors as the central creators in the filmmaking process (see Chapter 19), Welles was often singled out as a major example. Critics analyzed the thematic unities of his works. For some samples, see André Bazin, *Orson Welles: A Critical View*, trans. Jonathan Rosenbaum (1972; reprint, New York: Harper & Row, 1978); Ronald Gottesman, ed., *Focus on Orson Welles* (Englewood Cliffs, NJ: Prentice-Hall, 1976); and Joseph McBride, *Orson Welles* (New York: Viking, 1972).

In 1971, Pauline Kael attempted to counter this approach in a long essay, "Raising Kane," which ascribed certain aspects of *Citizen Kane* to other people who had worked on it, especially script collaborator Herman Mankiewicz. See *The Citizen Kane Book* (Boston: Little, Brown, 1971), which also contains the original shooting script. Kael's essay prompted several indignant responses, including Peter Bogdanovich's "The Kane Mutiny" in 1972 (reprinted in Gottesman, *Focus on Orson Welles*).

This controversy, plus the stylistic daring of Welles's two early films, has led historians to examine the films' production circumstances closely. Two detailed accounts of the making of *Citizen Kane* have revealed much about the respective roles of Welles and his collaborators. See Robert L. Carringer, *The Making of Citizen Kane* (Berkeley: University of California Press, 1985) and Harlan Lebo, *Citizen Kane: The Fiftieth-Anniversary Album* (New York: Doubleday, 1990). See also Carringer, The Magnificent Ambersons: *A Reconstruction* (Berkeley: University of California Press, 1993). Welles discusses *Kane* in the second chapter of Orson Welles and Peter Bogdanovich, *This Is Orson Welles*, ed. Jonathan Rosenbaum (New York: HarperCollins, 1992), pp. 46–93.

REFERENCES

1. Martin Quigley, *Decency in Motion Pictures* (New York: Macmillan, 1937), p. 33.
2. William Stull, "Process Cinematography," in Willard D. Morgan, ed., *The Complete Photographer: A Complete Guide to Amateur and Professional Photography,* vol. 8 (New York: National Educational Alliance, 1943), p. 2994.
3. Joseph McBride, *Hawks on Hawks* (Berkeley: University of California Press, 1982), p. 82.
4. Peter Bogdanovich, *John Ford* (Berkeley: University of California Press, 1968), pp. 83–84.

FURTHER READING

Balio, Tino. *Grand Design: Hollywood as a Modern Business Enterprise, 1930–1939.* New York: Scribners, 1993.

Hoberman, J. *Bridge of Light: Yiddish Films between Two Worlds.* New York: Museum of Modern Art/Schocken, 1991.

Jacobs, Lea. *The Wages of Sin: Censorship and the Fallen Woman Film, 1929–1942.* Madison: University of Wisconsin Press, 1991.

Jenkins, Henry. *What Made Pistachio Nuts? Early Sound Comedy and the Vaudeville Aesthetic.* New York: Columbia University Press, 1992.

Maltby, Richard. "'Baby Face' or How Joe Breen Made Barbara Stanwyck Atone for Causing the Wall Street Crash." *Screen* 27, no. 2 (March/April 1986): 22–45.

Schatz, Thomas. *Boom and Bust: American Cinema in the 1940s.* Berkeley: University of California Press, 1997.

Schrader, Paul. "Notes on *Film Noir.*" In Kevin Jackson, ed., *Schrader on Schrader and Other Writings.* London: Faber, 1990, pp. 80–94.

Sikov, Ed. *Screwball: Hollywood's Madcap Romantic Comedies.* New York: Crown, 1989.

Sturges, Sandy, ed. *Preston Sturges by Preston Sturges: His Life in His Hands.* New York: Simon and Schuster, 1990.

Vasey, Ruth. *The World According to Hollywood, 1918–1939.* Madison: University of Wisconsin Press, 1997.

CHAPTER 11

OTHER STUDIO SYSTEMS

During the 1930s and early 1940s, Hollywood's studio system supported the most successful film industry in the world. Film industries elsewhere took other forms. In some countries, such as the USSR and Germany, state-run monopolies developed during this period (see Chapter 12). In others, like France and Mexico, small producers renting studio space put out films, often haphazardly, hoping for quick profits. Still other countries had well-developed studio systems that were either imitations of or variants on the Hollywood models. This chapter examines four countries' studio systems: Britain, Japan, India, and China.

QUOTA QUICKIES AND WARTIME PRESSURES: THE BRITISH STUDIOS

In 1936, a British trade paper commented, "When one recalls the wretched, bleak sheds, barns and huts, the mud and general discomfort of many British studios of 15 years ago, it is possible to realize the strides and opportunities of today, when physical hardships are reduced to a minimum thanks to bold and considerate planning."[1] The occasion was the opening of the Pinewood Studios, part of a construction boom in English production centers during the mid-1930s. Two decades after Hollywood cinema began to consolidate its studio system, British film companies finally expanded into a comparable, if smaller, system.

The British Film Industry Grows

What enabled the British film industry to expand at this relatively late date? Midway through the 1920s, fewer than 5 percent of the features released in Great Britain originated domestically. Responding to this situation, in 1927 the government passed the Quota Act. It required that distributors make at least a certain percentage of British films available and that theaters devote a minimum portion of screen time to such films. The percentages were to rise over ten years, to 20 percent by 1937.

The result was a sharp rise in the demand for British films. American companies distributing their output in the United Kingdom needed to buy or make films there to meet the quota, and English importers also needed to have a certain amount of domestic footage on offer.

The quota was largely responsible for the British cinema's expansion during the early 1930s. In fact, production increased so much that the quota was consistently exceeded. A considerable portion of production, however, was devoted to making *quota quickies*—cheap, short films that barely met the legal requirements for a feature. Many quota quickies sat unseen on distributors' shelves, or made up the second half of double features; spectators often walked out after seeing the American film. One estimate in 1937 suggested that half again as many features were released in the United Kingdom as in America, even though the British market was not even a third the size of the American market.

The British studio system came to resemble a less stable version of Hollywood's. There were a few large,

vertically integrated companies, several midsize firms that did not own theaters, and many small independent producers. Some firms, particularly the smaller ones, concentrated on quota quickies. Other British firms opted to produce films with moderate budgets, aimed at generating a modest profit solely in Britain. A few tried making expensive films, hoping to break into the American market. Although all these companies competed with each other to some extent, they formed a loose oligopoly. Bigger firms commonly rented studio space to each other and to small independents. The quota requirements made room for all.

The two main firms, Gaumont-British and British International Pictures (BIP) had been formed during the silent era but now expanded significantly. BIP's new studio (**11.1**) was the biggest of several in the London suburb of Elstree, which came to be called "the British Hollywood." (As with studios in Los Angeles, British studios were scattered about the outskirts of London.) Both firms practiced a division of labor similar to that used in the Hollywood system, though BIP was particularly noted for rigidly adhering to production roles and discouraging employees' creativity. Both had extensive backlots where large sets could be built (11.1, **11.2**). Gaumont-British and BIP were roughly comparable to the Hollywood Majors in that both were vertically integrated, distributing films and owning theater chains.

11.1 An aerial view of British International Pictures' studio complex, built in 1926 and expanded after the coming of sound.

11.2 Alfred Hitchcock, leaning on the railing in the foreground, directs *Sabotage* (1936) in one of the large street sets built for the film at Gaumont-British's Lime Grove Studios, Shepherd's Bush.

There was also a group of smaller firms, somewhat similar to Hollywood's Minors: British and Dominion (headed by Herbert Wilcox), London Film Productions (Alexander Korda), and Associated Talking Pictures (Basil Dean). All produced, some distributed, but none owned theaters. Wilcox's policy was to make modest films in his studio at Elstree, targeting the British market. Dean called Associated Talking Pictures' Ealing facility "the studio with the team spirit," encouraging filmmakers to make high-quality pictures, often from stage plays.

Export Successes

Korda was the most prominent and influential of these producers in the early 1930s. A Hungarian émigré who had already produced and directed in Hungary, Austria, Germany, Hollywood, and France, he formed London Film in 1932 to make quota quickies for Paramount. Soon, however, he switched to a big-budget approach, hoping to crack the American market. He leased a studio and in 1933 contracted to make two films for United Artists. The first, *The Private Life of Henry VIII* (1933, Korda) provided a breakthrough for Korda and the British film industry. The film was enormously successful at home, and its profits in the United States topped those of any previous British release. Charles Laughton won a best-actor Academy Award and be-

11.3 Impressive sets and crowd scenes re-created the French Revolution in Korda's production of *The Scarlet Pimpernel*.

came an international star. UA signed to distribute sixteen more Korda films.

Korda continued making expensive costume pictures, and some other producers imitated him. Korda's fourth film for UA, *The Scarlet Pimpernel* (1935, Harold Young), was a hit second only to *Henry VIII*. Leslie Howard became known abroad for his portrayal of the seemingly foppish Sir Percey Blakeley, who secretly rescues aristocrats from the guillotine in revolutionary France (**11.3**). At Denham, Korda built Britain's

11.4 *Evergreen* began diminutive song-and-dance star Jessie Matthews's reign as queen of the British musical.

largest studio complex in 1936. Only a few of his epics were spectacularly profitable, however. *Things to Come* (1936, William Cameron Menzies) was set in the space-age after a disastrous war. The high budget required for the fanciful sets and costumes prevented the film from returning its costs.

The Private Life of Henry VIII started a brief boom in British production. Financiers eagerly provided backing, hoping for more American profits. The most significant figure to take advantage of the new prosperity was J. Arthur Rank, one of the entrepreneurs who started British National Films in 1934. He quickly moved toward vertical integration in 1935 by forming General Film Distributors and building the Pinewood Studios. (Pinewood has remained one of the world's major production centers; entries in the James Bond, Superman, Alien, and Batman series were shot there.) Within a decade, Rank's empire would become the most important force in the British film industry.

The production boom made higher-quality filmmaking possible. In 1931, Gaumont-British gained control of a smaller firm, Gainsborough. With it came the talented producer Michael Balcon, who supervised filmmaking for both companies. Despite pressure from the owners to make films with "international" appeal, Balcon favored fostering distinctive stars and directors who could make specifically British films. These often did better than some of the more expensive, but lifeless, costume films. For example, Gaumont-British made musicals starring the popular Jessie Matthews. Her biggest international hit was *Evergreen* (1934, Victor

Saville), in which she plays both the Edwardian music-hall star Harriet Green and her daughter. Years after the mother's retirement and death, the daughter masquerades as the mother, gaining enormous publicity by playing the apparently unaging, "ever green" star (**11.4**).

Alfred Hitchcock's Thrillers

Balcon also signed Alfred Hitchcock to a contract with Gaumont-British. Since his success with the early talkie *Blackmail* (p. 208), Hitchcock had moved from company to company, trying several genres, including comedies and even a musical. At Gaumont-British (and its subsidiary Gainsborough), he returned to his element, making six thrillers, from the *The Man Who Knew Too Much* (1934) to *The Lady Vanishes* (1938). Hitchcock would become identified with this genre throughout his long career.

One of Hitchcock's strengths was his ability to frame and edit shots in such a way as to allow spectators to grasp characters' thoughts. In *Sabotage* (1935), for example, there is a virtuosic scene in which a woman has just learned that her husband is a foreign agent and has accidentally caused the death of her brother. A lengthy series of shots shows her serving dinner, while anguishing over her brother's death (**11.5–11.10**). Hitchcock's use of characters' points of view would remain a defining stylistic trait throughout his career.

Hitchcock's thrillers were also notable for their humor. In *The 39 Steps* (1935), the innocent hero is accused of a murder and flees handcuffed to a woman who believes him guilty. This situation leads to amusing complications and, inevitably, to romance. *The Lady Vanishes* contains similar lighthearted sparring between the hero and heroine, as well as a subplot concerning a pair of obsessive cricket fans who ignore all dangers while trying to learn the outcome of the latest match.

Delightful though Hitchcock's English thrillers are, they betrayed their low budgets and technical limitations. Hitchcock wanted access to better studio facilities and to more dependable financing. In 1939, he signed a contract with David O. Selznick to make films in Hollywood. Beginning with *Rebecca* (1940), which won an Oscar as best picture, Hitchcock did well and stayed in the United States throughout his long career.

Crisis and Recovery

The British production boom suffered a severe setback in 1937. Several producers had received extensive investments and loans but had few profitable films. As a result,

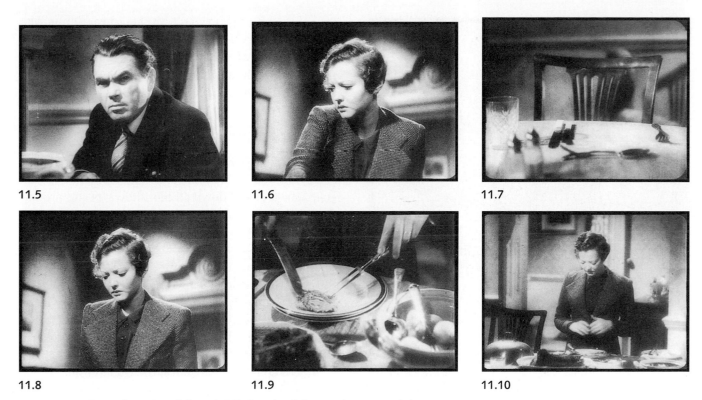

11.5   11.6   11.7

11.8   11.9   11.10

11.5–11.10 Part of a series of shots in Hitchcock's *Sabotage* that uses subtle variations in framing and eyeline direction. The heroine glances at her brother's empty chair and is tempted to stab her husband, who caused the boy's death.

many sources of funding dried up, and responsible production firms suffered along with opportunists. Alexander Korda's policy of big-budget films had been only partially justified. Despite a few notable successes, the American market remained largely closed to British imports. Moreover, the Quota Act of 1927 was due for renewal. There had been much criticism of the original quota for encouraging quickies. Uncertain over what the new quota would require, producers delayed projects. Feature output sank during the crisis from 1937 to 1938.

This crisis triggered changes in the industry. Partly as a result of his extravagance, in late 1938 Korda lost his financial backing. London Film's main asset, the Denham studio, passed into the control of J. Arthur Rank's growing empire. Korda continued producing films, now having to rent space in Denham. During World War II, he spent three years in Hollywood as an independent producer; his films there included Ernst Lubitsch's satire on Naziism, *To Be or Not to Be* (1942). After the war, Korda returned to reorganize London Film Productions. He produced a number of important films up to his death in 1955, but none as influential as some of those he had made in the 1930s.

The crisis also drove Basil Dean out of film production in 1938. Michael Balcon, after spending an unsat-

isfying year supervising quota films for MGM, took over Associated Talking Pictures and renamed it Ealing Studios. He continued producing quality films on a small scale, a practice that would gain prominence after the war with the popular Ealing comedies.

Britain's crisis diminished after Parliament passed the Quota Act of 1938. It specified that higher-budget films would count double or in some cases triple toward satisfying quota requirements. The number of quota quickies dropped as both British and American producers attempted to make or purchase films of higher quality to qualify for extra quota credit.

Film magnate J. Arthur Rank had come through the crisis relatively unscathed, and he rapidly added to his holdings. In 1939, he moved further into vertical integration by purchasing part interest in Odeon Theatres, one of the largest cinema circuits in the United Kingdom. Over the next few years, Rank acquired or built studios until his companies owned over half of Britain's production space. In 1941, he gained controlling interest in Odeon Theatres and Gaumont-British. Rank also formed Independent Producers, an umbrella company to fund the films of several small firms. From 1941 to 1947, companies in Rank's conglomerate financed about half the films made in Britain.

11.11 Michael Redgrave as the hero of Reed's *The Stars Look Down,* in a scene shot in a Cumberland mining village.

Due to the high level of production in Britain during the 1930s, many negligible films were inevitably made. The quota quickies were not entirely pointless, however. For one thing, they kept employment in the film industry high, despite the Depression. For another, they provided a training ground for directors—just as films made in Hollywood's B units and Poverty Row studios did. Michael Powell, one of the most important directors of the 1940s and 1950s, had worked extensively in cheap quota films. In *The Night of the Party* (1934, Gaumont-British), using a script which he later called a "piece of junk,"[2] Powell scraped together a cast from the stars under contract to the studio and created a bizarre and amusing film running a mere sixty-one minutes.

Besides the quota quickies, many solid, middle-budget films were made. These often starred music-hall performers, such as George Formby and Jack Hulbert. They had a huge following in Britain, but their brand of humor was less easily understood elsewhere. These unpretentious pictures also gave rise to significant filmmakers. For example, future director David Lean worked during the 1930s as an editor. Carol Reed got his start making films for Basil Dean's Associated Talking Pictures. His breakthrough came with the more ambitious *The Stars Look Down,* made in 1939 for a small independent firm. It drew on important traditions of British documentary and leftist filmmaking (see Chapter 14) to depict the plight of oppressed coal miners and to advocate the nationalization of the industry. At the beginning, a narrator's voice says, "This is a story of simple working people." Location filming in Cumberland lent the

film authenticity (**11.11**), and the climactic coal-mine disaster was convincing, despite being shot in studio sets.

By the end of the 1930s, Britain's film industry had passed through its crisis, and its situation looked promising. World War II was to give it a further boost.

The Effects of the War

For the United Kingdom, the war began on September 3, 1939. Anticipating immediate German bombing, the government closed down all film showings and production. Soon it became clear that such measures were unnecessary, and theaters reopened. Military officials did, however, requisition many of the country's film studios for such wartime uses as supply warehouses. Some of the industry's personnel also went into military service.

Such problems were balanced, however, by a sharp rise in attendance, as people sought to escape the privations of wartime. Theaters stayed open even during the worst nights of the Battle of Britain in 1940, when many London citizens slept on the Underground's platforms to avoid harm from the bombing. Despite such hardships, weekly attendance rose from 19 million in 1939 to 30 million in 1945.

The Ministry of Information encouraged wartime filmmaking. It required that all film scripts be checked to make sure that they in some way supported the war effort, and producers patriotically cooperated in creating a positive image of Britain. The Ministry of Information even put money into some commercial films. Wartime austerity had made it undesirable to spend money on imported films. Moreover, the new quota was still in effect, and British films were in demand. Due to the lack of studio space and personnel, however, far fewer films were made during the war. From between 150 and 200 annually during the mid-1930s, production sank to just under 70 films a year.

There was little stifling of creativity, however. And, due to cutbacks on quota quickies, the average budget and quality rose. Some films were polished studio productions comparable to Hollywood's. For example, Thorold Dickinson made *Gaslight* (1940) for Rank's main production firm, British National. A melodrama concerning a wife's well-founded fears that her husband is trying to drive her mad, the film used a tight script, three-point lighting, large sets, and other Hollywood-style techniques. Indeed, a version of the same story was made in 1944 at MGM by George Cukor.

Several independent production companies came to prominence during the war. In 1942, an Italian émigré, Filippo del Guidice, formed Two Cities and persuaded

11.12, 11.13   The contrast of a distant aerial combat and an idyllic family picnic in *In Which We Serve.*

11.14, *left*   A parallel low-angle shot implies planes overhead as two women listen anxiously to the unseen attack on their neighborhood.

11.15, *right*   In *49th Parallel*, Leslie Howard plays a British intellectual escaping by camping in the Canadian wilderness. Nazis who invade his camp and burn his Picasso painting and copy of Thomas Mann's *The Magic Mountain* goad him to defend democracy.

the renowned actor and playwright Noel Coward to script, direct, and star in a film. *In Which We Serve* centers on the crew of a British ship sunk by the Germans. While the survivors cling to a life raft, flashbacks tell their stories, focusing on the upper-class captain, a middle-class officer, and a working-class sailor.

In Which We Serve (codirected by David Lean) emphasizes the parallels among these characters. In one scene, as the captain and his wife and children picnic in the south of England, he watches a dogfight between British and German planes in the sky high above (**11.12, 11.13**). The wife wistfully remarks that she tries to think of the fights as games so that they won't bother her. Shortly thereafter, in a scene set in the London home of the middle-class officer, his wife and mother-in-law hear bombers approaching. The wife remarks in an annoyed tone, "Oh, there they are again," but soon a low angle shows the two women listening worriedly to the whine of the bomb that will soon kill them (**11.14**). Such scenes contribute to the film's treatment of the war as a daily presence for all classes, sometimes remote and sometimes suddenly dangerous.

The popular and profitable *In Which We Serve* attracted Rank, who gained control of Two Cities in exchange for an agreement to finance its subsequent films. These included Lean's *This Happy Breed* (1944), an adaptation of Coward's play *Blithe Spirit* (1945), and Laurence Olivier's first directorial effort, a patriotic Technicolor adaptation of Shakespeare's *Henry V* (1945).

Olivier began the film with a "flying" shot over an elaborate model of Renaissance London, moving down into the Globe Theatre. The opening scenes take place on a reconstruction of the Globe's stage (**Color Plate 11.1**); then, as in the play, the narrator's voice urges us to imagine the wider settings of the historical action. The bulk of the film occurs in stylized studio sets based on medieval illuminated manuscripts. The rousing Battle of Agincourt was the only portion shot entirely on location. *Henry V* celebrated England's ability to triumph against superior forces.

One small but important production firm, The Archers, was formed in 1943 by the team of Michael Powell and Emeric Pressburger. After directing quota quickies, Powell had made his first major film, *The Edge of the World* (1937). Shot on a remote island off the western coast of Scotland, it showed how young people's migration to urban areas was depopulating the region. Hungarian-born Pressburger had scripted five Powell-directed films prior to the formation of The Archers. The most prominent of these was *49th Parallel* (1941), a war film financed by the Ministry of Information and J. Arthur Rank. It traces the episodic progress of a band of Nazi infiltrators traveling across Canada. The group's members are gradually killed or captured as they meet resistance from a series of disparate Canadian citizens, including a French-Canadian trapper, a British aesthete (**11.15**), and a Canadian hitchhiker. *49th Parallel* was unusual for wartime propaganda, characterizing the

German soldiers as fallible individuals rather than inhuman beasts and even making one of them a positive figure.

The Archers was financed initially by Rank's new Independent Producers Ltd. Rank offered them considerable freedom. Their first Archers film, *The Life and Death of Colonel Blimp* (1943), followed a model British soldier through three wars. The film was somewhat critical of the current government, positing that the traditional English values of fair play that had served in earlier combats were inadequate to counter the threat of barbaric Nazis. Like *49th Parallel*, it portrayed a German character in a largely sympathetic light, maintaining his friendship with the hero despite their being on opposite sides.

Colonel Blimp was the first of fourteen films that carried the credit "Written, produced and directed by Michael Powell and Emeric Pressburger." Although Powell was the director, the phrase indicated that the two were equal partners. Their films were often extremely romantic and even melodramatic, yet outlandish twists of narrative and style set them apart from conventional studio films. *A Canterbury Tale* (1944), for example, a patriotic story set in the traditional center of the Anglican church, weaves together three episodic narrative strands; one focuses on a local magistrate who creeps about pouring glue into the hair of young girls to keep them from distracting soldiers. The collaboration of Powell and Pressburger would remain fruitful until 1956. Indeed, in general, the strength that the British film industry gained in the 1930s and during World War II continued until the early 1950s.

INNOVATION WITHIN AN INDUSTRY: THE STUDIO SYSTEM OF JAPAN

Britain's studios failed to achieve the stability of Hollywood's, but Japan's film industry succeeded. Its growth after the 1923 Tokyo earthquake and the advent of talking pictures strengthened a studio system much like America's.

Two large, vertically integrated companies, Nikkatsu and Shochiku, dominated several smaller firms. Despite the Depression and the increased expense of sound-film production, feature output remained high (400 to 500 per year in the early 1930s), and new theaters were constantly being built. Most important, Japan was virtually the only country in which U.S. films did not overshadow the domestic product. Nikkatsu and Shochiku could profit from showing Hollywood films in their theaters while limiting American penetration of the market.

A third major player entered the game in 1934. Ichiro Kobayashi, a show-business entrepreneur who mounted extravagant stage revues, formed Toho (Tokyo Takarazuka Theater Company) by buying and merging two small companies specializing in talkies. Along with creating Toho as a production firm, Kobayashi erected movie theaters in Japan's major cities.

While bringing Toho's production up to speed, Kobayashi used imported films to build up attendance at his theaters. He also hired many major directors, such as Teinosuke Kinugasa and the swordfight specialist Masahiro Makino. Toho became Shochiku's chief competitor. Nonetheless, the two vertically integrated companies cooperated to keep Hollywood at bay. Shochiku began to buy up smaller firms to keep pace with Toho, and the expenses of sound filming forced marginal production houses out of business. The industry consequently became more centralized in the course of the 1930s, with three majors and six to ten lesser firms.

The audience's appetite for films remained keen. The Depression was easing by the mid-1930s, and movies had become a central part of urban life. After the 1923 earthquake, the rebuilding of Tokyo had created a westernized popular culture, and the passion for western clothes, jazz, whiskey, and fads continued throughout the 1930s. Japanese moviegoers were as familiar with Harold Lloyd and Greta Garbo as they were with their own stars.

Meanwhile, Japan embarked on ambitious military plans. The nation was Asia's dominant power, having defeated China and Russia in war and having annexed Korea. As political parties proved ineffectual, military factions gained influence in government. Some officers argued that modern Japan had to expand its markets and its sources of labor and materials. In 1932, Japan announced its imperialist aims by invading Manchuria.

The search for "national autonomy" led to government regulation of the economy under a declared "emergency"—one that was to last for thirteen years. At first, however, filmmaking and other aspects of popular culture were comparatively unaffected. Censorship was tightened somewhat, but on the whole the genres that had flourished in the 1920s continued to be exploited.

Popular Cinema of the 1930s

The historical film, *jidai-geki*, was still the realm of swordfights, chases, and heroic deaths. The directors Daisuke Ito and Masahiro Makino continued to contribute to the genre, encouraging filmmakers to use rapid cutting and imaginatively staged fight scenes.

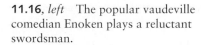

11.16, *left*   The popular vaudeville comedian Enoken plays a reluctant swordsman.

11.17, *right*   The atmospheric tenement setting of the opening discovery of the suicide in *Humanity and Paper Balloons*.

11.18, *left*   A young woman in love with a student discovers that he is not interested in her in *Woman of the Mist*.

11.19, *right*   In *Street without End*, the young wife, spurned by her husband's family, goes to his sickbed.

Among the many satires of the *chambara* (swordfight films) was Toho's *Enoken as Kondo Isamu* (**11.16**).

More psychologically oriented jidai-geki began to come from younger directors. The most prominent member of this group was Sadao Yamanaka. His *A Pot Worth a Million Ryo* (1935) is a warm comedy in which a gruff samurai befriends an orphan. *Humanity and Paper Balloons* (1937), Yamanaka's most famous film, shows a *ronin* (masterless samurai) unable to find work and eventually driven to suicide. Yamanaka filmed this quietly ironic tale in a distinctive manner, with low camera positions, deep perspectival framings, and somber lighting (**11.17**). This was Yamanaka's last film; drafted and sent to the Chinese front, he died there in 1938.

The *gendai-geki,* or contemporary-life film, included many genres: student and salaryman comedies, the *haha-mono* ("mother tale"), and the *shomin-geki,* films about lower-class life. From the early 1930s through the war, these and kindred genres were the bulwark of the major studios. Shochiku's stars Kinuyo Tanaka and Shin Saburi and Toho's Hideko Takamine and Setsuko Hara made their reputations in these unpretentious films portraying work, romance, and family life in Japan's cities and towns.

Yasujiro Shimazu had helped create Shochiku's "*Kamata* flavor," an atmosphere of poignant cheerfulness associated with the gendai-geki made in the firm's suburban Tokyo studio, and he continued it in such lighthearted talkies as *Our Neighbor Miss Yae* (1934). Heinosuke Gosho, formerly Shimazu's assistant, carried on the Shochiku tradition in the early sound comedies *Madam and Wife* (1931; see p. 209) and *The Bride Talks in Her Sleep* (1933), as well as in the melodramas *The Dancing Girl of Izu* (1933) and *Woman of the Mist* (1936; **11.18**). In such films Gosho won fame as a master of the shomin-geki.

Also working in the gendai-geki was Mikio Naruse. He started at Shochiku with salaryman films and contemporary comedies before discovering a more astringent, pessimistic tone. *Apart from You* (1933), *Nightly Dreams* (1933), and *Street without End* (1934) won critical praise despite their bleak look at prostitutes, sailors, and struggling single mothers. These melodramas established Naruse as an outstanding director of actresses and, in lengthy dissolves and brooding close-ups, revealed his ability to build up a sense of society's suffocating pressures on women (**11.19**).

Moving to Toho, Naruse quickly established himself with a series of feminine dramas. The most famous was *Wife, Be Like a Rose!* (1935), an urban comedy that modulates into harsh melodrama. Kimiko has picked out a young man to marry, but she must locate her runaway father. She talks him into returning for her wedding. The confrontation between the father and the high-strung mother, who secretly wants him back, shows Naruse's skill in handling complex emotional

11.20 A high-angle shot of the daughter's grief in *Wife, Be Like a Rose!*

11.21 A characteristic Shimizu track-back from marching students drilling during a country outing in *Star Athlete*.

situations (**11.20**). The film's last shots, tracking in and out on Kimiko and her mother, abandoned by the father once more, intensify our awareness that Kimiko's marriage will be devoted to taking care of her mother. *Wife, Be Like a Rose!*—one of the few Japanese films of the 1930s to be seen in the West—won critical accolades and established Naruse as a major director.

The successes of Yamanaka, Gosho, and Naruse confirmed Japanese studios' policies of encouraging directors to specialize in certain genres and to cultivate personal styles. This practice differentiated each company's product and fed fans' interest. In addition, many of the gendai-geki directors had started in the 1920s, when genre innovations and stylistic originality were prized. As a result, Japanese films of the 1930s experimented with storytelling and technique to a degree not common in most western sound cinema. For example, Tomu Uchida's *Police* (1933) presents a plot straight out of Warner Bros. (two old friends from the neighborhood, one a cop, the other a gangster) but enlivens it with bold compositions, bursts of hand-held camerawork, and rapid intercutting between past and present.

Hiroshi Shimizu, another exponent of humanistic comedy, also displayed a distinctive style. His films centering on children (e.g., *Four Seasons of Children,* 1939) won him the most fame, but he also excelled at adult subjects, as seen in *Arigoto-San (Mr. Thank You,* 1936) and *Star Athlete* (1937). Shimizu's stylistic signature is the shot in which the action moves straight at or away from the viewer while the camera tracks backward or forward to keep up with the figure (**11.21**). Shochiku's flexible policy allowed Shimizu to travel across Japan in search of ideas, shooting films on location from sketchy notes rather than scripts. The arrangement proved productive: between 1924 and 1945 Shimizu directed an astonishing 130 films.

By common consent, the two most influential Japanese directors of the 1930s were Yasujiro Ozu and Kenji Mizoguchi. They contrasted in almost every way. Ozu worked only for Shochiku, whereas Mizoguchi began with Nikkatsu and became a free-lance. Ozu started in comedies and shomin-geki, and he maintained an everyday humor in virtually all of his films. Mizoguchi, whose first films were melodramas, probed every situation for grim psychological and social implications. Ozu was a master of editing and static, closely framed shots, whereas Mizoguchi cultivated a style of long-shot framings, long takes, and camera movements. On the set, Ozu was quietly insistent, while Mizoguchi exploded into demonic tantrums. Ozu and Mizoguchi illustrate how the Japanese studio system permitted directors an enormous range of originality (see box).

Avoiding the strict division of labor practiced in Hollywood, Shochiku and Nikkatsu had cultivated a *cadre system* in which the director and scriptwriter had considerable control over their projects. Supervision tended to be even less stringent at smaller firms. Toho favored a *producer system,* which, like that of Hollywood in the 1930s, placed a producer in charge of several directors at the same time. While Toho films did have a somewhat glossier, mass-manufactured look, directors could still work in idiosyncratic ways at most studios before 1938. After that, they had to face the demands of a nation engaged in total war.

The Pacific War

Japan's all-out attack on China in 1937 marked the beginning of the war in the Pacific. The government banned existing political parties, tightened its alliances with Nazi Germany and fascist Italy, and mobilized the home front around a war-based economy.

YASUJIRO OZU AND KENJI MIZOGUCHI IN THE 1930s

At age twenty-four Yasujiro Ozu began directing with a jidai-geki, but he quickly turned to the gendai-geki. Between 1928 and 1937, he made thirty-five features, running the gamut from the student slapstick (*Days of Youth*, 1929) and the urban comedy of manners (*An Introduction to Marriage*, 1930) to the gangster movie (*Walk Cheerfully*, 1930). He consolidated his fame with three masterpieces in 1933 (*Woman of Tokyo*, *Dragnet Girl*, and *Passing Fancy*). His first sound feature was *The Only Son* (1936), a shomin-geki about a mother following her son to Tokyo to discover that he has not succeeded despite the education she has drudged for years to provide. Ozu characteristically followed this quietly despairing film with a lighthearted satire on the wealthy classes, *What Did the Lady Forget?* (1937).

Ozu was deeply influenced by the Hollywood cinema, particularly the social comedies of Charles Chaplin and Ernst Lubitsch and the gag comedies of Harold Lloyd. Like many Shochiku directors, he adopted the 1920s American comedy style—brief shots of actors and details of setting, edited together crisply and concisely. But Ozu extended this style in several ways. At unexpected moments he inserted shots of unobtrusive objects or adjacent landscapes (**11.22**). In dialogue scenes, he systematically filmed from within a 360-degree circle surrounding the characters, changing the view by multiples of 45 degrees (usually 180 degrees). This strategy consistently violated Hollywood's traditional 180-degree continuity editing. He edited as much for visual pattern as for dramatic emphasis; his 360-degree cutting produces close "graphic matches" between two shapes. A graphically continuous version of shot/reverse shot is shown in **11.23** and **11.24**.

11.22 A boiling teakettle punctuates the drama in Ozu's *Woman of Tokyo*.

Most strikingly, Ozu refused certain resources of film technique. He was the last major director to convert to sound. He also limited his use of camera movements. Above all, he restricted his camera position by filming only from a low height, regardless of the subject. This tactic again allowed him to draw attention to the composition of the shot, balancing the dramatic value of the actor and the milieu with the purely visual design of the frame (**11.25**).

Ozu's style amplified his intimate dramas. His comedies, like those of Lubitsch and Lloyd, are based on embarrassment and psychological revelation, qualities that could be signaled by a judiciously placed close-up of an expression

11.23 In *Passing Fancy*, the man grabs the woman's arm as he faces her from the right.

11.24 Ozu cuts to a position 180 degrees opposite, showing the man now on the left.

(continued)

YASUJIRO OZU AND KENJI MIZOGUCHI IN THE 1930s, continued

11.25 Like the previous illustrations, this frame from *The Only Son* exemplifies Ozu's low-height camera.

11.26 A cutaway to an industrial wasteland in Ozu's *Inn in Tokyo* (1935).

or a gesture. His social dramas, lingering on the cycle of life within an indifferent city, were intensified by enigmatic urban landscapes (**11.26**).

Several of Ozu's films mix comedy and drama so thoroughly that the style alternates between humorous commentary and poetic abstraction. *I Was Born, But . . .* (1931), for instance, is at once a satire on the bootlicking salaryman, a comedy about brattish children, and a sober study of lost illusions. At any moment, Ozu could create a low-key pictorial joke (**11.27**). His films' poignant evocation of missed opportunities, regrets, and foreknowledge of separation is reinforced by a measured style that finds even the most mundane object an occasion for contemplation. Ozu's

distinctive handling of narrative and technique influenced Yamanaka, Shimizu, and Naruse.

Kenji Mizoguchi began directing five years before Ozu. In the high-output 1920s, his forty-two films established him as an eclectic director with artistic pretensions. He made melodramas, crime dramas, even imitations of German Expressionism, but he did not become recognized as a major director until the 1930s.

Across a variety of genres, Mizoguchi concentrated on the social dilemmas facing the Japanese woman. In *White Threads of the Waterfall* (1933), a circus entertainer works to send a poor student to school; in the end, the lovers commit suicide. In *The Downfall of Osen* (1935), a gang-

11.27 Shirts on a clothesline are echoed by the salaryman as he exercises in the morning in *I Was Born, But. . . .*

11.28 In *Sisters of Gion,* Umikichi learns that her sister has been taken to the hospital.

ster's girlfriend sends a young man to medical school; after he has become successful, he finds his benefactor in a railroad station, old and demented. In *Oyuki the Madonna*, modeled on Guy de Maupassant's short story "Boule de suif" ("Tallow Ball"), a prostitute gives her life to save a rebel leader. Mizoguchi's two outstanding melodramas of the mid-1930s, *Naniwa Elegy* (1936, aka *Osaka Elegy*) and *Sisters of Gion* (1936), show women swapping sexual favors for power, only to find that men will not honor their bargains. He later saw these two bitter films as marking the beginning of his maturity: "It is only since I made *Naniwa Elegy* and *Sisters of Gion* that I have been able to portray humanity lucidly."[3]

Mizoguchi was drawn to situations of high emotion—men's sadistic abuse of women and children, women's distraught response to the threat of poverty or solitude, scenes of harsh bargaining and quarrels. But in filming he adopted what would, after World War II, be called a "dedramatizing" approach. His staging and framing put scenes of emotional intensity at a distance, inviting the spectator to react less viscerally to the material.

Mizoguchi thus tended to stage highly charged scenes in long shot (**11.28**). Often the characters turn away from the viewer (**11.29**), or they are hidden by a wall or a shadow (**11.30–11.32**). Only at the end of *Naniwa Elegy* and *Sisters of Gion* does Mizoguchi give us abrupt, intense

11.29 Ashamed, Ayako shrinks away from her lover, and from the viewer, in *Naniwa Elegy*.

11.30 In *The Downfall of Osen*, Osen's gangster lover goes to her with a sword and the shot stands vacant for a moment . . .

11.31 . . . before she backs into the wall . . .

11.32 . . . and he confronts her.

(continued)

YASUJIRO OZU AND KENJI MIZOGUCHI IN THE 1930s, continued

11.33   For the first time in the film, as Ayako is turned out onto the streets by her family, we have a clear frontal view of her in the curt final shot of *Naniwa Elegy*.

close-ups of his protagonists, each woman challenging the audience to reflect on why she must suffer (**11.33**).

Moreover, the camera records the action steadily, refusing to cut in to a character's reaction. To an unprecedented extent, Mizoguchi exploited the long take. There are only 270 shots in *Oyuki*, fewer than 200 in *Naniwa Elegy*, and fewer than 125 in *Sisters of Gion*. Further, these long takes are seldom designed to follow the movements of the actors, as in the work of Max Ophüls and Orson Welles. Mizoguchi's long takes force us to watch painful acts of self-sacrifice unfold at a relentless pace.

Ozu and Mizoguchi were among the most honored directors of their day, one representing the heights of the shomin-geki, the other exemplifying a prestigious cinema of social critique. Their work suggests the richness of what came to be recognized as the first golden age of Japanese cinema.

Government Pressure on the Industry   The film industry was slowly brought into line with the new policies. In this jingoistic atmosphere, western culture became suspect. Studios were ordered not to portray jazz, American dancing, or scenes that might undermine respect for authority, duty to the emperor, and love of family. In April 1939, Japan's Diet passed a law modeled on Goebbel's edicts to the Nazi industry (p. 271). The Motion Picture Law called for nationalistic films portraying patriotic conduct. The Home Ministry established the Censorship Office, which would review scripts before production and order revisions where necessary.

Although American films were still playing in Japan and some Japanese directors dodged the terms of the new law, political constraints were much stronger than ever before. For instance, the Censorship Office rejected Ozu's script for *The Flavor of Green Tea over Rice* because the married couple's parting meal was not the "red rice" traditionally reserved for seeing off a warbound husband.

As the Chinese war intensified, the government forced the film companies to consolidate. In 1941, authorities agreed to a three-part reorganization. One group was dominated by Shochiku, another by Toho, and a third, unexpectedly, by the small firm of Shinko.

Shinko's key executive was Masaichi Nagata (who had produced Mizoguchi's *Naniwa Elegy* and *Sisters of Gion* for his independent firm Dai-Ichi Eiga). Nagata used the consolidation scheme to gain control over Nikkatsu, whose production facilities were absorbed into his group.

Nagata' group was renamed Daiei (for Dai-Nihon Eiga, or "Greater Japan Motion Picture Company"). Nikkatsu was allowed to keep its theater holdings separate, so Daiei initially had difficulties in exhibiting its product. After the war, Daiei would become Japan's major force on the international scene.

All companies participated in the war effort. The government supported the production of newsreels, documentary shorts, and films celebrating the uniqueness of Japanese art. The most elaborate example of the last category is Mizoguchi's *The Story of the Last Chrysanthemum* (1939), an adaptation of a popular Japanese play. Kikugoro Onoe is expected to become a kabuki actor like his father and uncle, but he is a lackluster performer. When he takes up with the maid Otoku, his family disowns him. Her faith enables him to keep trying to perfect his art. At the climax, he gives a devastating performance and is hailed by the audience, while Otoku dies alone. The film won a prize from the Education Ministry.

11.34 In *The Story of the Last Chrysanthemum*, Kikugoro's mother scolds him for associating with the maid Otoku, who watches apprehensively in the background.

11.35 A stupendous gathering of the samurai in *The Abe Clan*.

Mizoguchi's sympathy for women, along with his interest in theatrical performance and stylization, makes *Last Chrysanthemum* one of his most important works. He continued to employ long takes, wide-angle lenses, dramatic chiaroscuro lighting (the use of starkly lit patches in a dark space), and slow rhythm. The camera, poised at a distance, often forces the viewer to scan the frame to pick out the significant action (**11.34**).

Alongside tributes to the purity of Japanese culture were patriotic films supporting the war effort. Tomotaka Tasaka's *Five Scouts* (1939) set the pattern for subsequent efforts, stressing the unity of a fighting group and the quiet heroism of its members. As in many Japanese battle films, the enemy is not seen; war is not a sor-

did struggle among men but a test of the purity of the Japanese spirit. Tasaka's *Mud and Soldiers* (1939) and Kimisaburo Yoshimura's *Story of Tank Commander Nishizumi* (1940) continued to promote the image of the modest, humane Japanese soldier.

The jidai-geki adjusted to the war period by becoming statelier and more grandiose. In *The Abe Clan* (1938, Abe Ichizoku) family honor vies with friendship in a setting that downplays violence and emphasizes the spectacular beauty and power of the martial code (**11.35**). The gendai-geki celebrated national ideals in a more prosaic way. Because of Kobayashi's ties to government agencies, Toho led the charge with stridently patriotic vehicles. Shochiku offered such films as Shimazu's *A Brother and His Younger Sister* (1939), in which a young man abandons petty office politics and carries his sister and mother off to a fresh start in China; a clod of earth clings to their plane wheel, bringing a bit of Japan to the world they are building.

Austerity and Patriotism In attacking American forces at Pearl Harbor in December 1941, Japan declared war on the United States and Britain. Japanese forces seized western colonies throughout the Pacific and soon dominated East and Southeast Asia. By mid-1942, Japan seemed a new imperial power, holding major islands as well as Siam, Burma, Singapore, Vietnam, Hong Kong, Taiwan, and major portions of China. Japan promised to lead the "Greater East Asia Co-Prosperity Sphere," but usually the Japanese occupation was at least as harsh as its colonial predecessors.

Full-scale war reduced resources on the home front. The government cut screenings to two and a half hours, rationed film stock, and limited studios to releasing two features per month. Production dwindled to about a hundred features in 1942, seventy in both 1943 and 1944, and fewer than two dozen in 1945. With most men drafted and most women working in factories or community groups, film attendance fell drastically.

Patriotic efforts became more shrill. Films celebrated kamikaze raids and the struggle against partisans in China. Toho produced the extravaganza *The War at Sea from Hawaii to Malaya* (1942), directed by Kajiro Yamamoto and released on the first anniversary of the Pearl Harbor attack. The film's historical sweep and excellent miniatures and special effects made it an outstanding propaganda piece. Yamamoto exploited the unseen-enemy convention in a chilling scene: on the night before the Pearl Harbor attack, Japanese sailors on a battleship listen quietly to a radio broadcast from an American nightclub.

11.36 The husband in *A Diary of Our Love* watches his wife, framed in a distant window, prepare his food.

11.37 The decentered deathbed scene from *There Was a Father*, determined by Ozu's low camera height.

11.38 Throughout *Brothers and Sisters of the Toda Family*, the changing of households by the mother and daughter is signaled by shots of their plants and bird.

Home-front films continued to emphasize patience, humility, and cheerful stoicism. In Naruse's *Hideko the Bus Conductor* (1941), the gracious heroine (played by the beloved Hideko Takamine) brightens her rural community. *A Diary of Our Love* (1941) shows a husband returning wounded from the war and being nursed back to health by his devoted wife. Shiro Toyoda's direction used Mizoguchi's oblique, long-shot aesthetic to mute the sentimental story (**11.36**).

In such films as *A Diary of Our Love* and Naruse's *Oh, Wonderful Life* (1944), a comic musical that occasionally reverses the sound track, directors continued to explore novel techniques. On the whole, however, most films of the period from 1939 to 1945 are virtually indistinguishable from Hollywood or high-budget European films of the era. The seriousness of the war effort demanded noble, solemn technique, and the daring experimentation of the 1930s was felt to be frivolous. Even Ozu and Mizoguchi toned down their styles for their Pacific War efforts.

Ozu, Mizoguchi, and Kurosawa in Wartime Ozu's output slackened in the war period, when he was repeatedly drafted. His only films were *Brothers and Sisters of the Toda Family* (1941) and *There Was a Father* (1942). The first, quite close in plot to Shimazu's *A Brother and His Younger Sister*, shows an upper-class family recalled to its duty by the youngest members. While carrying a serious message, the film contains Ozu's characteristically quirky comedy. *There Was a Father* proved more severe; not a trace of humor enlivens this tale of a teacher who sacrifices himself to the greater national need.

Toda Family and *There Was a Father* contain much lengthier shots than Ozu had used before; the camera dwells on the actors' moments of deliberation and res-

ignation. Ozu continued to exploit 360-degree shooting space, a quiet handling of dramatic moments (**11.37**), and transitions composed of landscapes and objects (**11.38**). After *There Was a Father,* Ozu was captured in Singapore while planning a battlefront film and spent the remainder of the hostilities as a prisoner of war.

Mizoguchi fared better. He was entrusted with one of the most prestigious projects of the war, a two-part version of a classic tale of self-sacrifice. *Genroku Chushingura* (aka *The Loyal Forty-Seven Ronin,* 1941 and 1942), tells how a lord's retainers patiently suffer indignity before avenging his death.

Earlier film versions told the story with vigorous swordplay and overblown emotions. Predictably, Mizoguchi dedramatized the tale. For three hours he dwells on the ronin's slow preparation for the deed, their calm acceptance of their mission, and their resignation to their ultimate punishment. The long take is carried to extremes, both films totalling only 144 shots (making each shot, on average, over ninety seconds long). The climactic battle takes place offscreen, recounted through a letter read by the lord's widow. Mizoguchi's long takes, monumental compositions, and majestic crane shots ennoble a drama of fidelity to duty (**11.39, 11.40**).

After *Genroku Chushingura*, Mizoguchi returned to direct four films, including the jidai-geki *Musashi Miyamoto* (1944) and *The Famous Sword Bijomaru* (1945). Both betray the industry's paucity of means in the last phase of the war, and except for some very long takes, they are far more orthodox in style than *Genroku Chushingura*.

Of the several directors who made their debuts during the war, the most promising was Akira Kurosawa. A scriptwriter and assistant director at Toho, he worked

11.39   A retainer weeps at the lower left while his lord goes into a garden to be executed in *Genroku Chushingura*.

11.40   In a distant framing reminiscent of Mizoguchi's 1930s work, a woman struggles to keep her brother from assassinating Lord Kira in *Genroku Chushingura*.

11.41, *left*   One of Sanshiro's opponents is hurled endlessly through the air . . .

11.42, *right*   . . . before crashing against a wall, causing a window frame to float down in slow motion (*Sanshiro Sugata*).

for Yamamoto before being entrusted with directing *Sanshiro Sugata* (1943), a tale of martial arts set in the late nineteenth century. *Sanshiro* brings hurly-burly action back to the period film, which had become static and solemn under the influence of wartime ideology. The plot centers on a classic martial-arts conflict: Sanshiro, a hot-headed young judo fighter, must learn restraint under the guidance of a harsh but wise master. Kurosawa handled the combat sequences with a kinetic bravura, using elliptical editing, slow motion, and sudden changes of angle (**11.41, 11.42**). *Sanshiro Sugata* was a major influence on postwar jidai-geki films, and it was the ancestor of Hong Kong martial-arts films and the "spaghetti Westerns" of Sergio Leone.

The film's success led Kurosawa to make a sequel (*Sanshiro Sugata II*, 1945). More significant, however, was his second film, the home-front drama *The Most Beautiful* (1944). Several women are working at a plant that manufactures precision lenses for airplanes' gun-

sights. The plot shows, in episodic fashion, a string of personal dramas, some comic, some intensely serious. Lacking the physical exuberance of the judo films, *The Most Beautiful* reveals Kurosawa's interest in the psychology of stubborn, almost compulsive dedication to a social ideal. Both *Sanshiro* and *The Most Beautiful* fitted wartime ideology, but they also showed Kurosawa to be a virtuosic, emotionally intense director.

Gradually, three years of Allied "island hopping" pushed Japan's forces back. In August 1945, after months of firebombing Tokyo and other cities, U.S. planes dropped atomic bombs on Hiroshima and Nagasaki. Japan surrendered soon afterward.

Like most of the nation's institutions, the film studios were hard-hit, but even the devastation of the war and the reforms of American occupation could not loosen the major companies' stranglehold on the industry. The Japanese studio system would retain control for three more decades.

INDIA: AN INDUSTRY BUILT ON MUSIC

In India, with twelve major languages and twenty secondary ones, the silent cinema was a widely accessible entertainment. The films took their plots from well-known tales in the epics *Ramayana* and *Mahabarata* and the images carried the burden of the story. Although intertitles were in as many as four languages, and sometimes a narrator akin to the Japanese benshi accompanied screenings, the Indian silent film found a national audience. Following the work of D. G. Phalke in the 1910s (p. 51), several production companies sprang up in Bombay and Calcutta. By the mid-1920s, India was producing over a hundred feature films annually, more than England, France, or the USSR.

A Highly Fragmented Business

Indian producers sought to imitate Hollywood's studio system, but they could not achieve oligopolistic vertical integration. In an attempt to do so, Madan Theatres, the most powerful exhibition chain at the end of the 1920s, bought American sound equipment and built a studio in the Calcutta suburb of Tollygunge (soon known by the nickname "Tollywood"). It released the first Indian talking films in 1931, but problems of cash flow forced Madan to sell its studio and most of its theaters. Thereafter, the Indian market would be a free-for-all in which production firms, distributors, and exhibitors vied for power.

The fragmentation of the market was increased by the coming of sound, which broke the national audience into language-based groups. Calcutta firms monopolized Bengali-language production, Bombay controlled production in Marathi, and both cities made films in Hindi, India's principal language. Slowly some production emerged in Madras, specializing in southern languages.

At first, producers controlled the market. The earliest talking feature, the Imperial Film Company's *Alam Ara* ("Beauty of the World," 1931, Ardeshir Irani; Hindi language) proved a huge success, and other producers quickly converted to sound. The major firms were Prabhat, founded in 1929 and operating in a suburb of Bombay; New Theatres, founded in 1930 in Calcutta; and Bombay Talkies, founded in 1934. All were modeled on Hollywood studio complexes, with sound stages, laboratories, and commissaries. Although the producers sought to imitate Hollywood's efficient planning and scheduling, they prided themselves on running friendly, "one-big-family" operations.

11.43 *Chandidas:* The low-caste woman sings with the holy man before his altar.

By the mid-1930s, film companies were turning out a total of about 200 films a year, most of them in Hindi. Although the number of theaters increased throughout the 1930s and 1940s, it did not keep pace with the expansion of production or the growing urban population. Exhibitors competed frantically to show the most popular movies. Production companies manipulated the theater owners through block booking.

Mythologicals, Socials, and Devotionals

The success of the Indian talking picture owed much to its musical sequences. Folk performance and Sanskrit theater were based on music, and these traditions found their way into the cinema. For decades, nearly all films, regardless of genre, contained song and dance interludes. An early and influential example is *Chandidas* (1932, Debahi Bose; Bengali; **11.43**). It featured both songs and a continuous musical background in the manner of Hollywood underscoring. Initially, most stars sang their own parts, but, during the 1940s, firms began to use *playback singers,* who prerecorded the songs for the actors.

The genres of the 1930s had been established in the silent era. The *mythological film,* using a plot derived from legend and the literary epics, had been a mainstay since Phalke's day. More westernized were the *stunt films,* adventure stories modeled on those starring Douglas Fairbanks and Pearl White. Most were cheap productions akin to Hollywood's B pictures; those featuring the masked outlaw woman Nadia were especially popular.

The *social film,* a romantic melodrama set in contemporary times, was introduced in the mid-1920s and

11.44 The bird-chariot that carries the hero to heaven at the climax of *Sant Tukaram*.

became an important genre in the sound era. One of the most famous socials was New Theatres' *Devdas* (1935; Hindi), which used naturalistic dialogue to show the suffering of lovers torn apart by an arranged marriage. Other socials addressed contemporary problems of labor, the caste system, and sexual equality.

Another major genre was the *devotional*, a biographical tale of a religious figure. The most popular was *Sant Tukaram* ("Saint Tukaram," 1936, Moham Sinha; Marathi), made by Prabhat. A poor villager who spends his days singing holy songs is persecuted by the corrupt Brahmin priest. Tukaram's faith creates several miracles, and he is eventually taken to Nirvana in a heavenly chariot (**11.44**). The hero's gentle personality, the understated performances, and the lyrical beauty of the songs, nearly all composed by the historical saint, led many critics to judge *Saint Tukaram* the masterpiece of 1930s Indian filmmaking.

Independents Weaken the System

By 1939, India's film industry was apparently robust. Although the market was still dominated by foreign films, the rise of the talkie had greatly increased audiences for Indian cinema. India had become the third-largest film producer in the world, and *Saint Tukaram* won a prize at the Venice Film Festival. The mobilization for World War II improved the national economy.

The wartime boom also revealed, however, that the film industry was fundamentally unstable. In search of quick profits, entrepreneurs began to form independent production companies, and black marketers used film projects to launder cash. The independents lured stars, directors, and songwriters away from the studios, often paying bonuses in under-the-table deals. Now the older firms had to compete for personnel, and a star might consume half a film's budget. The studios' one-big-family ideology collapsed when stars and creative personnel realized their market value. Moreover, the independents did not have to maintain the massive overhead that encumbered the studios; a producer could simply rent studio space and hire personnel as needed. Now that more companies were offering more films, distributors and theater owners could make the studios compete for screens.

Their failure to achieve vertical integration proved fatal to the big companies. Prabhat, New Theatres, and Bombay Talkies continued to make films throughout the war, but their power ebbed. Only the government's wartime restrictions on investment and raw film stock kept the transient "mushroom producers" from overrunning the market. Once the war was over, black-market profiteering ran unchecked. Although film production expanded and became even more significant internationally, India's studio system was at an end.

CHINA: FILMMAKING CAUGHT BETWEEN LEFT AND RIGHT

For a brief period during the 1930s, Chinese film entrepreneurs struggled to create a small studio system in the face of serious difficulties. During the 1920s, Chinese production had been spread mostly among many small companies that made a few films before going out of business. The market was largely supplied by imports, principally U.S. films. In 1929, only 10 percent of the 500 films released were made in China. The introduction of sound, however, gave a little boost to domestic filmmaking: while educated urban audiences were used to western culture, many workers and peasants wanted more familiar fare that did not require subtitles, which few could read.

There were two relatively large Chinese firms, though neither was vertically integrated. The Mingxing Film Company had been founded in 1922 in Shanghai, the center of Chinese film production. By the 1930s, it was the largest producer. In 1930, a former cinema owner started the Lianhua Film Company, Mingxing's primary competitor. There were also three small producers: Yihua (founded in 1932), Diantong (1934), and Xinhua (1935). These companies mostly turned out melodramas patterned after popular literature.

The political temper of the times, however, injected controversy into this system. Chiang Kai-shek had

11.45, *left* *The Goddess* featured Ruan Lingyu, the wildly popular star whose death at age 25 devastated Chinese audiences.

11.46, *right* An ironic juxtaposition of a doll in a college graduate's gown with a Mickey Mouse figurine in the hero's apartment (*Crossroads*).

seized power in a bloody coup d'état in 1927, establishing the right-wing Guomindong government. The government's forces were engaged in an armed conflict with Mao Zedong's Communist insurgents, who controlled portions of the country outside the largest cities. In 1931, when the Japanese invaded Manchuria and overran other portions of the country, Chiang Kai-shek mistakenly decided that it was more important to fight the Communists than the Japanese. In this atmosphere, a split developed between right-wing nationalists on the side of the Guomindong and leftists who, while not Communists, sympathized with the oppressed working and peasant classes.

These two groups struggled to control the output of the budding studios. In 1932, a Communist cultural group, the League of Left-Wing Writers, formed the Film Group to guide and encourage leftists in the film industry. Although most of the members were scenarists, many important actors and directors also belonged. They were not necessarily Communists but typically came from urban, middle-class backgrounds. They were thoroughly familiar with western filmmaking. Although they never came to dominate the film industry or have any real power, they were to create some of the decade's most significant films.

The right-wing nationalist government of Chiang Kai-shek set up strict censorship to control the cinema. As a result, leftists in the studios had to craft their films subtly to convey their ideas. The leader of the Film Group, scenarist Xia Yan, became head of the script team at the Mingxing company. His adaptation of a novel, *Spring Silkworms* (1933, Cheng Bugao), was the first major left-wing film of the decade. It follows the life of a peasant family during the yearlong cycle of raising worms and harvesting silk. Documentary-style scenes explaining the process are interspersed with scenes of family life; at the end, the family suffers through an unfair drop in silk prices. The emphasis on the dignity of labor and on the plight of peasants made this a controversial film. Although left-wing films were

popular, they created censorship problems. Xia Yan was fired from the Mingxing company the following year and moved to Lianhua.

The owner of Lianhua, the second-largest company, was loyal to Chiang's nationalist cause, and the Film Group found it harder to infiltrate the firm. Nevertheless, one of its three production units was dominated by leftists in the early 1930s. Lianhua released two important liberal films in 1934. The first was *The Goddess*, written and directed by Wu Yonggang. In Chinese, *goddess* was the term for a prostitute, and the story treats the heroine in a straightforward fashion rather than creating a melodrama (**11.45**). She struggles against an unjust society, saving money to send her son through school; when her money is stolen, she kills the thief and her pimp. The second film, *The Highway* (aka *The Big Road*, directed by Sun Yu), follows a group of unemployed men as they get jobs constructing a road that will serve as a defense against the Japanese invaders. The film emphasizes their friendship and the joys of physical labor.

The three small companies reflected the struggle between right-wing and left-wing tendencies in more extreme ways. Yihua was dominated by members of the Film Group from its founding in 1932. The following year, right-wing extremists destroyed its filmmaking facilities, but the company rebuilt, producing more innocuous fare from 1934 on. The Diantong firm was even more overtly leftist in its orientation; after it had produced only four films, the government shut it down. Xinhua, founded in 1935 by right-wing extremists, met no opposition.

In 1937, the left-wing elements of the Chinese cinema seemed to be in resurgence. Xia Yan was rehired by the Mingxing company, which produced two extremely popular, controversial films. *Street Angels* (Yuan Muzhi) combined influences from Frank Borzage melodramas and René Clair musicals to portray the lives of an itinerant trumpet player and his friends, living opposite a prostitute and her sister. The cheerful treatment of the characters' lives is belied by the ending, in which the prostitute is killed by the gang that controls her, and the other characters are left with little hope of a better life.

Crossroads (Shen Xiling) follows the lives of four graduates who cannot find jobs (**11.46**). The protagonist feuds with the unseen woman in the flat next to his, unaware that she is the worker he has been interviewing to write an exposé on factory conditions (and with whom he has fallen in love). The ending implies that the couple will go off to join the Communists in fighting the Japanese.

Such films suggest that the Chinese film industry might have expanded in the late 1930s. In 1937, however, the Japanese overran Shanghai. All the producers except Xinhua ceased production. (Xinhua closed in 1942.) China's filmmakers dispersed, some going to the few areas of the country under Communist control, others fleeing to Guomindong territory. Many of those who had worked at the Mingxing Film Company would become important filmmakers in the era just after the Communist Revolution of 1949.

Our four examples—Britain, Japan, India, and China—illustrate how studio systems of filmmaking took various forms. A group of filmmaking firms could form a solid oligopoly, with some companies being vertically integrated. In Britain and Japan, the larger firms distributed their own films and owned theater chains. The scale of production and the power of domestically made films in the local market helped determine how stable such a system would be. India's studio system was more artisanal, with many producers competing against each other. And, the Chinese industry struggled to develop in a way that imitated western models, only to be overwhelmed by political circumstances. In the next chapter, we shall examine how other film industries functioned under political dictatorships.

. . . .

Notes and Queries

JAPANESE CINEMA REDISCOVERED

Most of the Japanese films discussed in this chapter were unknown in the West before the 1970s. This was largely because the industry's output was almost completely destroyed—junked by the studios, obliterated in wartime bombardment, or burned during the American occupation. We can judge Sadao Yamanaka on only two films. Moreover, several titles by Yasujiro Ozu, Teinosuke Kinugasa, and Kenji Mizoguchi are missing.

What we do know of the prewar Japanese cinema is due to fairly recent interest. After World War II, critics in Europe and the United States knew Japanese cinema principally through Kurosawa's and Mizoguchi's 1950s work. These films quickly became examples of international art cinema (see Chapters 18 and 19). French critics revered Mizoguchi as a director who exemplified the power of mise-en-scène, a quasi-mystical ability to stage a shot with evocative force. "He has," wrote Philippe Demonsablon, "one single aim: to render a note so pure and sustained that the smallest variation will be expressive."[4] In the late 1960s, a few of Ozu's postwar works, notably *Tokyo Story* (1953), joined this select company.

In the early 1970s, more of the 1930s films returned to circulation, along with Kinugasa's *A Page of Madness* (1926; p. 000–000). Retrospectives were held in London, New York, and Paris, while the Japan Film Library Council (later the Kawakita Memorial Film Institute) made prints available to universities and museums. It became evident that Ozu's and Mizoguchi's films of the 1930s and early 1940s were at least the equal of their postwar work and looked startlingly ahead to the "modern" cinema of 1960s Europe.

The reevaluation of the period was crystallized in Noël Burch's book *To the Distant Observer* (Berkeley: University of California Press, 1979). Burch treated the Japanese cinema of the 1920s and 1930s as a critique of western filmmaking, indeed of western conceptions of representation and meaning. His focus on style called attention to the non-Hollywood aspects of the films, which Burch traced to longstanding Japanese traditions in literature and the visual arts.

During the 1980s, retrospectives of Heinosuke Gosho, Mikio Naruse, and Hiroshi Shimizu revived interest in the monumental jidai-geki of the late 1930s. Kurosawa's memoirs of the era were published in *Something Like an Autobiography*, tr. Audie E. Bock (New York: Knopf, 1982). An approach similar to Burch's was developed in David Bordwell's *Ozu and the Poetics of Cinema* (Princeton, NJ: Princeton University Press, 1988) and Donald Kirihara's *Patterns of Time: Mizoguchi and the 1930s* (Madison: University of Wisconsin Press, 1992), though these authors emphasized the films' ties to contemporary popular culture and social change.

Film history remains a provisional discipline, highly dependent on what production companies and archives preserve. Despite gaps in our knowledge, however, Japanese cinema of the interwar era is clearly as important as that of the United States or Europe.

REFERENCES

1. Quoted in Robert Murphy, "A Rival to Hollywood? The British Film Industry in the Thirties," *Screen* 24, nos. 4/5 (July/October 1983): 100.
2. Michael Powell, *A Life in Movies: An Autobiography* (London: Heinemann, 1986), p. 231.
3. Quoted in Peter Morris, *Mizoguchi Kenji* (Ottawa: Canadian Film Archive, 1967), p. 10.
4. Ibid., n.p.

FURTHER READING

Bock, Audie E. *Naruse.* Locarno: Editions de Festival International du Film, 1983.
"Challenge of Sound: The Indian Talkie (I)." *Cinema Vision India* 1, no. 2 (April 1980).
Davis, Darrell William. *Picturing Japaneseness: Monumental Style, National Identity, Japanese Film.* New York: Columbia University Press, 1996.
König, Regula, and Marianne Lewinsky, eds. *Keisuke Kinoshita.* Locarno: Editions de Festival International du Film, 1986.
Low, Rachel. *Film Making in 1930s Britain.* London: Allen and Unwin, 1985.
Murphy, Robert. *Realism and Tinsel: Cinema and Society in Britain, 1939–48.* London: Routledge, 1989.
Nornes, Abé Mark, and Fukushima Yukio. *The Japan/America Film Wars: World War II Propaganda and Its Cultural Contexts.* Chur, Switzerland: Harwood, 1994.
Ryall, Tom. *Alfred Hitchcock and the British Cinema.* London: Croom Helm, 1986.
Zhang, Yingjin. *Cinema and Urban Culture in Shanghai, 1922–1943.* Stanford: Stanford University Press, 1999.

CINEMA AND THE STATE: THE USSR, GERMANY, AND ITALY, 1930–1945

During the 1930s, left- and right-wing dictatorships controlled a few national film industries, most notably in the USSR, Germany, and Italy. The governments treated cinema as a medium of propaganda and entertainment, and both these functions continued during World War II.

Government control took different forms. Under the communist system imposed by the Russian Revolution, the film industries of the various regions that made up the USSR were nationalized in 1919. That centralized control increased during the 1930s. By contrast, the Nazi regime that came to power in Germany in 1933 supported capitalism, so it did not seize the privately owned film industry. Instead, the Nazis nationalized the industry by quietly buying companies. In Fascist Italy, the situation was quite different. There the government supported the industry and censored films, but it did not nationalize production.

THE SOVIET UNION: SOCIALIST REALISM AND WORLD WAR II

The First Five-Year Plan centralized the Soviet film industry under one company, Soyuzkino, in 1930 (p. 140). The purpose was to make the industry more efficient and to free the USSR from having to import equipment and films. In order to dominate the home market, the film industry had to boost the number of films being made. By 1932, new factories were supplying the necessary raw stock, and the conversion to sound had been accomplished with little help from abroad (pp. 204–205). Low production and inefficiency, however, remained problems.

The period from 1930 to 1945 also saw a tightening of controls on the types of films being made. Boris Shumyatsky became head of

Soyuzkino at its formation. He was directly responsible to the country's leader, Joseph Stalin, who took a great interest in the cinema. Shumyatsky favored entertaining and easily comprehensible films, and under his regime the avant-garde Montage movement died out. In 1935, he oversaw the introduction of the doctrine of Socialist Realism into the cinema.

Films of the Early 1930s

Before the introduction of Socialist Realism, several significant films appeared. *Men and Jobs* (1932, Alexander Macheret) combined the Montage style with an emphasis on production reflecting the First Five-Year Plan. An American expert arrives to help build a dam. His initial condescension breaks down, and he decides to stay on and help the new Soviet state (**12.1**). A more unusual film was made by Alexander Medvedkin, who spent the early 1930s traveling in a train, shooting and showing films in villages throughout the Soviet Union. His early shorts made in this fashion do not survive, but his only feature, *Happiness* (1934), does. A peasant, Kymyr, resists the reforms of the Russian Revolution and seeks happiness through personal wealth, while his oppressed wife, Anna, eventually enters a collective farm and persuades Kymyr to join her. Medvedkin uses comic exaggeration to portray the initial poverty of the couple and the stupidity of soldiers and priests (**12.2**). Largely ignored in 1934, *Happiness* was revived in the 1960s, and critics recognized it as an important film.

The Doctrine of Socialist Realism

From 1928, Joseph Stalin ruled the USSR as an absolute dictator, and harsh repression enforced government policy. The secret police ferreted out dissent in all walks of life. The government conducted "purges," whereby party members who were considered not to support Stalin wholeheartedly were expelled, imprisoned, exiled, or executed. This reign of terror peaked during 1936 to 1938, with "show trials" in which party leaders made scripted confessions of their participation in "counterrevolutionary" activities.

Socialist Realism was an aesthetic approach introduced at the 1934 Soviet Writers' Congress. A. A. Zhdanov, a cultural official, explained,

> Comrade Stalin has called our writers engineers of human souls. What does this mean? What duties does the title confer upon you?

12.1   A heroic image of Soviet labor in *Men and Jobs*.

12.2   Stylization in *Happiness:* the hero and heroine's poverty leads their horse to graze on their thatched roof

> In the first place, it means knowing life so as to be able to depict it truthfully in works of art, not to depict it in a dead, scholastic way, not simply as "objective reality," but to depict reality in its revolutionary development.[1]

Writers and artists in all media were required to serve the Communist party's goals in their work and to follow a set of vague official tenets. This policy would remain more or less strictly in force until the mid-1950s.

Artists were forced to accept Socialist Realism as the only correct style. Sergei Eisenstein's early mentor, the foremost theatrical director of the 1910s and 1920s,

SOCIALIST REALISM AND *CHAPAYEV*

The central tenet of Socialist Realism was *partiinost'*—roughly, "party-mindedness." That is, artists had to propagate the Communist party's policies and ideology. The models for this were the European realist novelists of the nineteenth century. Authors like Honoré de Balzac and Stendhal had criticized bourgeois society. Of course, Soviet authors were not supposed to be critical of socialist society. Unlike critical realism, Socialist Realism was based on a second tenet: *narodnost'*. This term (roughly, "people-centeredness") means that artists should depict the life of ordinary people in a sympathetic way.

Socialist Realist artworks were supposed to be free from *formalism,* stylistic experiments or complexities that would make them hard to understand. Thus Socialist Realism ruled out the Montage style of filmmaking. In order to serve the party and the people, art was supposed to educate and provide role models, particularly in portraying a "positive hero."

The *realism* in Socialist Realism was based in part on Frederick Engels's equation of truth with the "reproduction of typical characters in typical circumstances." For Stalinists, *typical* designated traits associated with communist ideals, not with the way things actually are. This means that many Socialist Realist artworks give an optimistic, idealized image of Soviet society, far removed from actual life under Stalin. As party goals changed over the years, so did Socialist Realism, and proper artistic methods were endlessly debated.

Although some traits associated with Socialist Realism had already appeared in cinema, the first film to provide a

12.4   Chapayev's use of potatoes to explain military technique showed how a film could employ familiar means of storytelling that peasants and workers could grasp.

complete model of the new doctrine was *Chapayev* (1934, Sergei and Georgy Vasiliev). Based on a fictionalized account of an actual officer in the civil war, *Chapayev* furnished a hero for audiences to admire. Moreover, Chapayev's cheerful, handsome assistant, Petja, is a "typical" (i.e., idealized) working-class figure with whom people could identify (**12.3**). He provides a romantic subplot as well, flirting with Anna, a female soldier. In an association of romance and work that was common in Soviet films, the two fall in love as Petja teaches Anna to fire a machine gun. *Chapayev* told its story in simple terms. When Chapayev explains a point of military strategy to another officer, he lays out small potatoes to represent the soldiers, with a large potato for the commander (**12.4**).

Chapayev was an enormous success, both with audiences and with film officials promoting Socialist Realism. Shumyatsky praised its concentration on individual characters, contrasting it with the mass heroes in Montage films of the 1920s. He also pointed out that the film does not hide the hero's faults. At first, Chapayev is shown as unschooled in military history, and he follows his own impulses rather than obeying orders calculated to benefit the Bolshevik cause. Shumyatsky declared that Chapayev "presents himself at the beginning of the film as a typical 'innate' bolshevik."[2] Indeed, *Chapayev* follows one of the most common patterns of Socialist Realist narratives, that of a protagonist who learns to subordinate his or her desires to the people's good. *Chapayev* became one of the most influential films in the history of the Soviet cinema.

12.3   This framing of Chapayev and Petja against the sky became the most famous image of the Soviet Socialist Realist cinema.

Vsevolod Meyerhold, disappeared during the 1936–1938 purges. Major writers like Sergei Tretyakov and Isaac Babel were secretly executed. Composer Dmitri Shostakovich chafed under the Socialist Realist doctrine but had to obey it. Film soon took up the new doctrine.

Socialist Realism became official policy in the cinema in January 1935, at the All-Union Creative Conference of Workers in Soviet Cinema. The film *Chapayev,* which had premiered only two months earlier, was referred to throughout the conference (see box). By contrast, Eisenstein was singled out for attack, in an obvious effort to discredit the Montage movement. Other "formalist" directors were forced to admit past "mistakes"; Lev Kuleshov declared, "Like my other colleagues whose names are linked with a whole series of failed productions, I want, whatever the cost, to be, and I shall be, an outstanding revolutionary artist but I shall only be one when my flesh and blood, my whole organism and being are merged with the cause of the Revolution and the Party."[3] Despite this self-abasement, Kuleshov also offered an eloquent defense of the beleaguered Eisenstein.

Filmmakers could not hope to keep a low profile. Stalin was extremely interested in the cinema, viewing many films in his private quarters. Shumyatsky, as Stalin's direct representative, ruled the industry. There was an elaborate censorship apparatus, whereby film scripts had to be reviewed repeatedly before being accepted. After shooting began, films could also be revised or shelved at any stage. This cumbersome bureaucratic system, and the fact that most scripts were rejected, slowed output; throughout the 1930s, the number of finished films remained far below the total planned. A film might take years to make, undergoing minute ideological scrutiny. The most spectacular case of such interference came with Eisenstein's first Soviet sound project, *Bezhin Meadow,* which Shumyatsky shelved in 1937.

Relatively few filmmakers suffered the most extreme penalties of the purges. There were several victims, however. For example, critic and scenarist Adrian Piotrovsky, who had scripted Grigori Kozintsev and Leonid Trauberg's 1926 Montage film *The Devil's Wheel,* was arrested in 1938 and died in a prison camp. Cinematographer Vladimir Nilsen, a student of Eisenstein's, disappeared. Konstantin Eggert, a traditional director, was prevented from making any films after 1935.

Hoping to boost production and create a popular cinema, Shumyatsky decided to build a "Soviet Hollywood." He spent two months touring the American studios in 1935 and determined to replicate their technical sophistication and efficiency. His grand expansion proj-

12.5 Soviet films of the 1930s continued to use the dynamic low-angle framings that had originated in the silent era. This shot from *We from Kronstadt* suggests the protagonist's innate heroism.

ect progressed during 1937, but it was never completed. Indeed, Shumyatsky never raised production to the level called for in the Five-Year Plans. While over a hundred films were scheduled in most years, actual release figures remained modest. After ninety-four films came out in 1930, releases steadily declined to a low of thirty-three in 1936 and averaged about forty-five for the next few years.

Ironically, the final result of Shumyatsky's policies was his own arrest in January 1938. One of the reasons cited for his removal from power was the waste of money and talent in the abandonment of *Bezhin Meadow.* He became the film world's most prominent victim of the purges when he was executed later in 1938. From that point on, Stalin played an even more central role in making decisions about the ideological acceptability of films.

The Main Genres of Socialist Realism

Civil War Films *Chapayev*'s huge success made the *civil war film* an important genre of Socialist Realist cinema. Although the civil war had caused great hardships, many veterans looked back on it as a pre-Stalinist era when communist goals were clear-cut and rapid changes were possible. *We from Kronstadt* (1936, Yefim Dzigan) is virtually a loose remake of *Chapayev,* although its hero is not based on a historical figure. It is set in 1919, during heavy fighting around Kronstadt. The sailor Balachov is initially undisciplined, accosting a woman on the street and only reluctantly sharing his rations with the workers and children of nearby Petrograd. Gradually, after escaping execution by the White troops and enduring hardships in battle, he learns to fit selflessly into the revolutionary cause (**12.5**).

Biographical Films   *Chapayev* also helped make the *biographical film* a major genre. Famous figures of the revolution and civil war eras were often the focus, but films dealt increasingly with great people of the prerevolutionary era, even tsars. Despite the fact that the USSR was supposedly becoming a classless society, this period saw the development of a "cult of personality." Stalin was hailed as the embodiment of communist ideals, and his role in the revolution was exaggerated by historians. Because Stalin saw parallels between himself and great leaders of Russia's past, these men became suitable subject matter for laudatory films.

Important intellectuals who supported the revolution also furnished the basis for biographical films. *Baltic Deputy* (1937, Alexander Zarkhi) is set directly after the October Revolution and gives a fictionalized account of a scientist-professor who welcomed the Bolshevik regime, braving the scorn of his colleagues. In fact, many intellectuals had resisted the revolution, so *Baltic Deputy* was designed to show that all classes could unite under communism. The elderly professor makes friends with a group of sailors (**12.6**). In the end the professor's book is published, and Lenin sends him a congratulatory letter.

Stalinist historians singled out two tsars, Ivan the Terrible and Peter I (known as "the Great"), as "progressive" rulers who carried out reforms that constituted important steps away from feudal society and toward capitalism. Their actions thus helped prepare the way for communism.

Vladimir Petrov's two-part epic, *Peter the First* (1937 and 1938), established some important conventions for "great leader" films. Although a monarch, Peter is also a man of the people. He leads armies in battle and makes shrewd diplomatic moves but is not above carousing in taverns with his men or hammering vigorously in a blacksmith shop. He teaches a class in navigation, dismissing a nobleman's lazy son and promoting a talented servant.

Such conventions appear again in the film that returned Eisenstein to the forefront of the Soviet cinema, *Alexander Nevsky* (1938). Nevsky was a medieval prince who had led a defense of Russia against European invaders. The similarities to the contemporary sit-

12.6   An idealistic image of solidarity across social classes, as the scientist-hero of *Baltic Deputy* lectures on botany to attentive revolutionary sailors.

12.7   Grotesque helmets dehumanize the Teutonic invaders in *Alexander Nevsky.*

uation, with Nazi Germany threatening war, made *Alexander Nevsky* a major patriotic project. The film's anti-German tone was clear (**12.7**). At the end, Nevsky speaks directly into the camera: "Those who come to us with sword in hand will perish by the sword."

Eisenstein's first completed sound film fit into the doctrine of Socialist Realism: its narrative was simple and it glorified the accomplishments of the Russian people. Nevsky, like Tsar Peter, mingles with the peasants and bases his final strategy on a joke he hears by a campfire. Eisenstein also managed, however, to preserve something of the fruits of Montage experimentation in the 1920s. There are frequently several shots of the same action with different framings, and many cuts yield

12.8   Dovzhenko balances a tall sunflower against an explosion in the opening shot of *Shchors*.

12.9   In *Shchors*, a Red officer politely asks for money from a bourgeois theater audience, a machine gun at his side.

12.10   In *Suvorov*, the hero is framed against the sky, towering over his victorious troops.

12.11   The young Gorky walks along the shore, triumphantly holding up a newborn baby. Despite the hardships that he has experienced, the ending implies that this child will grow up in the freedom created by the revolution.

12.12   Shimmering cinematography and a diagonal composition in *Lone White Sail*, as middle-class passengers try to capture a fugitive sailor from the rebellious "Potemkin" battleship.

12.13   This scene of the death of the hero in *Bezhin Meadow* uses a wide-angle lens to achieve an arresting deep-focus composition.

discontinuities. The renowned sequence of the battle on an ice-covered lake is a virtuosic piece of extended rhythmic editing. The music by Sergei Prokofiev helped smooth over the eccentric editing style and enhanced the legendary, larger-than-life qualities of the film.

In early 1935, Stalin remarked to Alexander Dovzhenko, "Now you must give us a Ukrainian *Chapayev*."[4] The subject was to be the Ukrainian civil war hero Nikolai Shchors. Of course Dovzhenko took this suggestion as a mandate. Over the next few years he worked on the project, constantly scrutinized by Stalin and lesser officials. *Shchors* (1939) displays Dovzhenko's typical lyricism, especially in the startling opening scene of a battle erupting in a field of sunflowers (**12.8**). His humor is also evident, as in the scene in which one of Shchors's officers solicits donations in a theater (**12.9**).

Vsevolod Pudovkin contributed to this genre with *Suvorov* (1941), which deals with the late years of a fa-

mous general in the wars against Napoléon. The opening scene is typical of such films (**12.10**). Again, although Suvorov is of noble origins, he fraternizes with the common people. He wins his battles despite the opposition of the stupid tsar, Paul I. In the scene where Suvorov comes to visit the tsar, he slips repeatedly on the polished floor, clearly out of his element at the elegant court. Down-to-earth portrayals of historical figures would continue during the wartime period.

Tales of Everyday Heroes   Stories of "typical," heroic, ordinary people were also common. The exemplar of this approach was Pudovkin's 1926 film *Mother*. It was based on a 1906 novel by Maxim Gorky, who was promoted in the 1930s as the greatest Socialist Realist author. After Gorky's death, Mark Donskoi made three films based on the author's memoirs of his early life (*Childhood of Gorky* [1938], *Among People* [1939], and *My Universities* [1940]). The Gorky trilogy stressed the hero's lack of formal education. Coming from a deprived background, the young Gorky moves from job to job, encountering oppressive aspects of tsarist society but also occasionally finding people who resist—a kindly local chemist arrested for revolutionary activities, a crippled child who treasures the slightest pleasant moment. Near the end of *My Universities*, Gorky helps a peasant woman give birth in a field. The trilogy implies that Gorky's greatness as a writer arose from his close ties with the people (**12.11**).

Another example of this genre is *Lone White Sail* (1937, Vladimir Legoshin), which portrays the adventurous participation by children in the 1905 attempted revolution. (The film is set in Odessa and contains references to *Potemkin*.) It is also an excellent example of Shumyatsky's attempts to make Hollywood films, being shot in a polished continuity style that blended well with Socialist Realism (**12.12**).

Eisenstein's aborted project, *Bezhin Meadow,* would have been the story of a boy who places loyalty to his collective farm above his relationship with his abusive father. Unfortunately, the negative of *Bezhin Meadow* was apparently destroyed in a bombardment during World War II, and all that survives today is a reconstruction made from printing frames from each shot as still photographs. Even this slight record of the film indicates that it would have been one of the era's masterpieces. Eisenstein experimented with an extreme depth of field that looked forward to the films of Gregg Toland and Orson Welles (**12.13**) (see p. 223).

A Member of the Government (1940, Alexander Zarkhi and Josif Heifits) deals with an idealized peasant woman (**12.14**). Alexandra is beaten by her drunken husband, who resents her devotion to their collective farm. The local party official, however, assures her that "you have your role in history." She persists, becoming the presiding officer of the farm. Eventually she is elected her region's deputy to the Supreme Soviet in Moscow and addresses a huge crowd there.

Socialist Musicals   Some of the era's most popular films were musical comedies. Grigori Alexandrov, who had been Eisenstein's assistant, became the master of musicals with *Jolly Fellows* (aka *Jazz Comedy,* 1934). It concerns a cheerful singing farmer who is mistaken for a famous jazz conductor. When a party is held in his honor, his flute lures his animals into the house, and they create havoc (**12.15**). There was criticism of the film's frivolity, but Alexandrov had the ultimate protection: Stalin loved it. Alexandrov's *Volga-Volga* (1938),

12.14   A composition in depth as Alexandra and a friend wait for a boat to pick up the collective farm's milk in *A Member of the Government.*

12.15   *Jolly Fellows* blends slapstick humor and American jazz.

the story of a woman mail carrier who writes a wildly popular song, became Stalin's favorite movie.

The other important director in this genre was Ivan Pyriev, who specialized in *tractor musicals*, which glorified life on collective farms. Both *The Rich Bride* (1938) and *Tractor Drivers* (1939) show cheerful competitions among peasants to exceed work quotas. In 1935, miner Alexei Stakhanov had purportedly set a record for cutting coal, and the government promoted similar accomplishments by workers in all areas. "Stakhanovite" record-breakers were glorified in the press, got special privileges, and even received fan mail.

12.16, *left* The collective farm's mail carrier sings animatedly about the joys of doing his job well as he rides through the broad fields of the Ukraine in *Tractor Drivers*.

12.17, *right* Nurses volunteering for duty in *Front-Line Girl Friends*. The towering white statue of Stalin is typical of the many images of party heroes that appear in Soviet films of this era.

In *The Rich Bride,* a collector's accountant conspires to marry the best female tractor driver in order to share her privileges. He breaks up her romance with the best male driver by falsifying her lover's work record, but the deception is discovered, and the couple is reunited. The notion that Stakhanovite men and women should marry reappears in *Tractor Drivers.* The heroine, Marianne, is so famous for exceeding her plowing quotas that suitors constantly pester her. She pretends to be engaged to Nazar, one of the farm's less productive tractor drivers. The farm's supervisor is appalled at this mismatch and asks Klim, another Stakhanovite, to teach Nazar how to work better. Klim agrees, though he secretly loves Marianne himself. Eventually, Marianne discovers Klim's love for her, and, despite Nazar's improvement, the two best workers marry. Throughout the film, the tone is energetic. Although most peasants on real collective farms spent as much time as possible tilling their private gardens, in *Tractor Drivers* the characters work cheerfully in the fields while performing songs (**12.16**).

Tractor Drivers was made during a period of nervousness about the threat of Nazi Germany. Klim, an exsoldier, undertakes to give the other drivers military training, and the farm supervisor declares, "A tractor is a tank!" Two years after the film's release, the war began.

The Soviet Cinema in Wartime

Uneasy Relations with Germany Before World War II, the United States, England, and other countries avoided making anti-Nazi films since they still exported films to Germany. The USSR was under no such constraints and made several films on the Nazis during the late 1930s. *Professor Mamlock* (1938, Adolf Minkin and Herbert Rappoport), for example, was set in Germany shortly after the Nazi government came to power. It concerns a great Jewish doctor who tries to stay out of politics and disowns his son when the youth joins a Communist group. When the doctor is forced out of his job, he denounces the Nazis and is shot. The Communists vow to fight on.

Despite the fact that the Communists and Nazis were at opposite ends of the political spectrum, on August 23, 1939, a startled world learned that the USSR and Germany were signing a nonaggression pact. Having received no assurances of support from Britain and France, Stalin decided to avoid invasion by negotiating with the Germans. As part of the agreement, Hitler allowed the USSR to seize the Baltic republics and to invade Finland. During the nearly two years that the pact was respected, anti-German films of the 1930s, including *Alexander Nevsky* and *Professor Mamlock*, were withdrawn from circulation.

The first fiction film to deal with the Finnish invasion was *Front-Line Girl Friends* (1941, released abroad as *The Girl from Leningrad*). It focuses on a unit of Red Army nurses. As in many American war films, the central group is made up of such character types as a frivolous party girl who fears the sight of blood and an underage volunteer who insists on being allowed to go to the front (**12.17**). With its spectacular battle scenes and depiction of the nurses' courage, the film was a huge hit in the USSR and was popular abroad as well.

Disruptions of the Early War Period Despite the nonaggression pact, Germany abruptly invaded the USSR on June 22, 1941. By early the next year, it occupied most Soviet territory west of Moscow. In the course of the war, German soldiers pillaged much of this area and committed numerous atrocities. They bombarded Moscow heavily but never managed to capture it. Beginning in October, however, most filmmaking activities were swiftly moved to studios in the unoccupied republics. Mosfilm and Lenfilm, for example, withdrew to Alma-

12.18, *left*   The triumphant end of "Three in a Tank," as a dead German soldier falls into the foreground and victorious Soviet troops rush over him.

12.19, *right*   The heroic partisan in *The Rainbow* refuses to speak, even when the Nazis kill her baby. Carrying its body, she herself is then shot.

Ata, the capital of Kazakhstan. Such an enormous effort caused considerable confusion, and the small studios had to be expanded in order to accommodate the increase in activity. Women workers had to be trained to take the place of male filmmakers who had gone into the military.

These problems interrupted feature filmmaking. Early wartime releases included shorts, newsreels, and features made before the invasion. Newsreel production was centered in the vacated Mosfilm studios. The need for quickly produced films about the war was also met in part by a series of "Fighting Film Albums." These were cheaply made compilations of short segments, combining reports, documentary sketches, satirical scenes, musical numbers, or fictional episodes. Pudovkin made "Feast at Zhirmunka" for *Fighting Film Album 6* (1941). It shows Nazis committing atrocities against women and children in an occupied village where the men have gone off to be guerrilla fighters. One woman lays out a feast for the soldiers and is forced to eat some of it first when they suspect the food has been poisoned. Reassured, they eat and drink, realizing too late that the woman has willingly poisoned herself in order to kill them. This brief, bitter story ends with the woman's husband declaring, "All right, Germany. We're not going to forget." *Fighting Film Album 6* also contained a group of war songs and a documentary on women in the Soviet air force. N. Sadkovich directed a brief fiction segment, "Three in a Tank," for *Fighting Film Album 8* (1942). In it, two Soviet soldiers and their German hostage face being burned alive inside a tank. The German is terrified, but the two Soviet men calmly plan to use dynamite to blow up themselves and the Germans surrounding the tank. Soviet troops arrive in the nick of time (**12.18**).

Although some segments of the "Fighting Film Albums" were effective, they were made far from the actual fighting and the occupied areas. Hence they often

were naïve and unrealistic. Eisenstein commented that they were "more passionate than well planned."[5]

Films of the War Era   Fiction features about the war began appearing in 1942. In order to stress the hatefulness of the German enemy, these often focused on women and children as victims of battles or atrocities. Based on a true incident, *Zoya* (1944, Leo Arnstam) concerns a young guerrilla captured, tortured, and hanged by the Nazis. Most of the film consists of flashbacks to her school days, when an old librarian told her of Nazi book burnings. Victor Eisimont's *Once There Was a Girl* (1945) uses a small girl's viewpoint to give a poignant portrayal of the hardships suffered by the citizens during the long siege of Leningrad.

Mark Donskoi's *The Rainbow* (1944) is set in a Ukrainian village paralyzed by both a heavy snow cover and the occupying German troops. The Nazis continue to commit atrocities among the villagers and to hang captured Soviet partisans, but the occupation has drifted into routine. The German commander has settled comfortably in and taken a mercenary village woman as his mistress. Aside from this woman, the other Ukrainians quietly resist their oppressors. In one powerful scene, a woman partisan who has returned to give birth is questioned under torture (**12.19**). Finally, Soviet troops, camouflaged in white, swoop down on the village and liberate it as a rainbow appears in the sky. Despite its broad character types, *The Rainbow* was considered an unusually realistic war film, and it influenced some filmmakers of the Italian Neorealist movement (see Chapter 16).

The sufferings of the wartime period did not encourage the production of comedies, but a few appeared, especially after the 1943 Battle of Stalingrad brought some hope to the USSR. For example, *Wedding* (1944, Isidor Anensky) was a satire on prerevolutionary provincial pretensions, adapted from a vaudeville

12.20 Two of the caricatural middle-class guests in *Wedding*.

12.21 Eisenstein used lighting to create a looming image of the tsar in *Ivan the Terrible*, part 1.

12.22 Ivan begs forgiveness from the head of the church in *Ivan the Terrible*, part 2.

by Anton Chekhov. It lampooned the middle-class guests at a wedding party; the heavy makeup and broad acting were reminiscent of the "eccentric" style of Soviet comedies of the Montagne movement (**12.20**).

Biographical films continued to be an important genre during the war. Petrov followed *Peter the Great* with *Kutuzov* (1944), depicting the famous general's defense of Moscow against Napoléon in 1812. Shortly after this film was made, Petrov described the contemporary relevance of Socialist Realist biographical films:

> I am not inclined to view *Peter the Great* from a single historical perspective. I think that in some ways it is a contemporary film. The life and activities of the great Reformer of Russia seem to me very close to the life and actions of the Soviet people, who have also from day to day established the basis for a new life. It is the same for *Kutuzov*. The film was made and shown during the war. After the conquest of each village rooted out the enemy, after each new victory, the spectator saw those events as an echo of the old ones.[6]

Because Stalin was the supreme military leader of the USSR during World War II, he could be seen as a parallel both to the progressive tsars and the triumphant generals. Stalin identified in particular with Ivan the Terrible, and during the war Eisenstein worked on a three-part film on that subject. Two parts were completed. They are elaborate, full of exaggerated acting, labyrinthine sets, and richly embroidered costumes (**12.21**). Prokofiev wrote a musical track that emphasizes the heroic nature of the plot's events. The first film (released in late 1944) creates a grandiose image of Ivan, conquering invaders and resisting efforts by the nobility to undercut his unification of Russia. It received the Stalin Prize in early 1946.

The second part of *Ivan the Terrible* fared badly. Eisenstein emphasized Ivan's doubts about his ruthless eradication of the nobility in Russia (**12.22**). Stalin and his officials deplored this depiction of Ivan as hesitating

in his "progressive" actions, and the second part of the film was suppressed in 1946. Eisenstein, suffering from heart disease, concentrated on writing film theory until his death in 1948. The second part of *Ivan the Terrible* was not released until 1958.

From 1943 to 1944, Soviet troops pushed westward, regaining territory and occupying eastern Europe. In early 1945, the Red Army advanced on Berlin, and the German government surrendered on May 8. The war had brought enormous losses to the USSR. The film industry was faced with reestablishing production in the regular studios and rebuilding the Lenfilm facilities, virtually ruined during the Siege of Leningrad. Nevertheless, as one of the victorious powers, the Soviet government retained control of its nationalized film industry. Such would not be the case for Nazi Germany.

THE GERMAN CINEMA
UNDER THE NAZIS

Although Germany emerged from World War I with a relatively liberal government, the political climate moved rightward during the 1920s. In 1933, the fascistic Nationalsozialistische Deutsche Arbeiterpartei ("National Socialist German Workers' party," known as the Nazis) gained parliamentary control, and Adolf Hitler became chancellor. The Nazis became the only legal political party, and Hitler ruled as a dictator.

Nazi ideology was based on extreme nationalism: a belief that Germany was naturally superior to the rest of the world. This notion stemmed from a view that Germans belonged to a pure Aryan race, and that other ethnic groups, especially Jews, were inferior and dangerous. Nazis also held that women were innately subordinate to men and that citizens owed unquestioning obedience to government leaders. Thus, the new German regime opposed not only the communist ideology of the USSR but also the democratic principles of many other nations.

Hitler led his party to power in part by appealing to feelings of humiliation stemming from Germany's defeat in World War I. The country had been forced to disarm its military; soldiers could not carry even rifles. By playing on old prejudices, the Nazis managed to convince many people that the defeat had been caused by Jews. Similarly, the economic problems caused by the Depression were blamed on Jews and communists. Hitler promised to restore both the economy and national pride.

The Nazi Regime and the Film Industry

Like Stalin, Hitler was a movie fan; he cultivated friendships with actors and filmmakers and often screened films as after-dinner entertainment. Even more fascinated with the cinema was his powerful minister of propaganda, Dr. Josef Goebbels, who controlled the arts during the Nazi era. Goebbels watched films every day and socialized with filmmakers. In 1934, he gained control of censorship, and until the end of the war he personally examined every feature film, short, and newsreel that was released. Despite his hatred of communism, Goebbels admired Eisenstein's *Potemkin* for its powerful propaganda, and he hoped to create an equally vivid cinema expressing Nazi ideas.

Goebbels moved to control other aspects of the film industry. The virulently anti-Semitic attitudes of the Nazi party led to an effort in April 1933 to remove all Jews from the film industry. Jews were forbidden to work for any film establishment—even in foreign companies' distribution offices. This precipitated an exodus of filmmaking talent. Many Jews fled, including Max Ophüls, Billy Wilder, and Robert Siodmak. Anyone holding leftist or liberal views was also in danger, and many non-Jews who could not stomach Nazi policies departed. Goebbels wanted Fritz Lang for a high position in the film industry, but Lang went into exile, first in France and then in the United States. Actor Conrad Veidt, though of Aryan origin, reportedly wrote "Jew" on the racial form required of each film worker and left the country. Ironically, in Hollywood he went on to play Nazi villains (most famously, Major Strasser in *Casablanca*).

In April 1935, the Nazis' anti-Semitic campaign expanded with a ban on screenings of all pre-1933 films produced with the involvement of Jews. This move coincided with increasingly harsh measures being enacted by the government; the "Nuremberg laws" in September, among other things, stripped Jews of their citizenship and forbade marriages between Jews and non-Jews. Goebbels later ordered the production of anti-Semitic films.

Goebbels's main effort to control the German cinema came through gradual nationalization of the film industry. When the Nazis came to power, there was no pressing need for the government to take control. Most shares in the largest company, Ufa, belonged to the powerful right-wing media mogul Alfred Hugenberg (who was briefly minister of economics in the new regime). Although many Ufa officials opposed the Nazis, the company made some of the earliest fascist films. Moreover, in June 1933, the government set up the *Filmkreditbank*. The "Film Credit Bank" supported production in the wake of the Depression, but it also allowed the Nazis to oversee filmmaking, since projects had to meet ideological requirements in order to receive loans.

Nationalization was not tried immediately for another reason: Goebbels did not want to alienate other countries. Germany's film industry depended on exports. It also needed imports, primarily from the United States and France, to satisfy German theaters' needs. Some nations, however, resisted dealing with Nazi Germany. Both imports and exports fell sharply during the mid-1930s. At the same time, production costs in Germany were ballooning. The government had two options: to subsidize production (as Fascist Italy did) or to nationalize the industry.

The Nazis chose nationalization because it offered them greater control over the films. The process of nationalization, however, proceeded differently from

12.23, *left*   The hero's zeal for the Nazi cause in *Hans Westmar* sometimes verges on fanaticism. Later propaganda films toned down such extreme behavior.

12.24, *right*   The young hero of *Hitlerjunge Quex* expresses delight as he receives his Hitler Youth uniform.

that in the USSR. Instead of openly seizing private firms, as the Soviet government had done, during 1937 and 1938 the Nazi regime secretly bought controlling interests in the three main film-producing companies (Ufa, Tobis, and Bavaria) and two important smaller firms (Terra and Froelich). By 1939, eighteen independent production firms still existed, but they made fewer than one-third of that year's features.

The nationalization of the film industry was completed in 1942. All German film companies were assembled under a giant holding firm, called Ufa-Film (but abbreviated as Ufi, to distinguish it from the old Ufa). Ufi was vertically integrated, controlling 138 firms in all sectors of the industry. By now, Hitler had seized Austria and Czechoslovakia, and Ufi absorbed their national film industries.

Despite this consolidation, the number of films produced in Germany did not meet the demand, and production declined after the war began in 1939. The Nazis were more successful, however, in controlling the types of films made.

Films of the Nazi Era

Because of the repellent nature of Nazi ideology, modern audiences outside Germany have seen few films from this era. The exceptions tend to be the more heavily propagandistic films like *Triumph of the Will* and *Jud Süss* (see p. 274), which are studied primarily as historical documents. Nevertheless, most films made during the period were intended as entertainment and have little or no overt political content. Of the 1,097 features made from 1933 to 1945, only about one-sixth were banned by postwar Allied censors for containing Nazi propaganda. Since all films had to receive Goebbels's approval, they certainly could not attack Nazi ideology. Many are, however, ordinary studio films not very different from those made in Hollywood or England during the same period. (Indeed, many are shown on Ger-

man television today, as old Hollywood films are in the United States.)

Pro-Nazi Propaganda   Some of the earliest strongly propagandistic films appeared in 1933: *SA-Mann Brand* ("SA-Man Brand," Franz Seitz), *Hans Westmar* (Franz Wenzler), and *Hitlerjunge Quex* ("The Quicksilver Hitler Youth," Hans Steinhoff). These were intended to win adherents to the party by glorifying Nazi heroes. The films take place shortly before the Nazis seized power, and they depict the era as a struggle between vicious Communists and stalwart young Hitler supporters.

Hans Westmar is based loosely on the life of Horst Wessel, one of the first to die for the Nazi cause and author of the party's fighting song. The film portrays late-1920s Berlin as sinking under Jewish, Communist, and decadent foreign influences. Young Westmar disgustedly visits a café that serves only English beer and features a black jazz band. A Jewish play is on at the Piscator-Bühne (a real leftist theater of the day), and a cinema is showing Boris Barnet's 1927 Soviet comedy *The Girl with the Hat Box*. Villainous Communists plot to take over Germany by exploiting working-class poverty. Westmar proves so adept at winning converts to the Nazi cause that the Communists assassinate him (**12.23**).

Hitlerjunge Quex was, like many Nazi films, designed to appeal to adolescents. The protagonist, Heini, is attracted to a Hitler Youth group, despite his drunken Communist father's opposition (**12.24**). The most effective scene shows him visiting a Communist youth camp where the leaders press wine and beer on the young visitors; he then wanders off and encounters a Hitler Youth camp where the children participate in healthy sport. Again, after Heini joins the Hitler Youth, his valiant service leads the Communists to murder him. Although the Communist organizations in both *Hans Westmar* and *Hitlerjunge Quex* contain stereotyped Jewish members, anti-Semitism is a minor part of these propaganda films, which mainly attack the German Communist party.

12.25, 12.26   Facilities for filming *Triumph of the Will* included a camera elevator, visible in 12.25 on the supports of the banners in the giant open-air auditorium. It permitted moving shots of the vast crowds, carefully arranged for the camera, as seen in 12.26.

12.27   Since 1919, German soldiers had been forbidden to bear arms. In *Triumph of the Will* they parade carrying shovels in place of rifles—but the threat posed by Hitler's troops is still clear.

The Reich's Documentarist: Leni Riefenstahl

For modern audiences, the most famous filmmaker of the Nazi era is Leni Riefenstahl. She had started as an actress in the silent era and had directed herself in one sound feature, *The Blue Light* (1932), starring as a mountain sprite. Her two propaganda features, *Triumph of the Will* (1935) and *Olympia* (1938), were made at Hitler's request.

Triumph of the Will is a documentary feature made on the occasion of the Nazi party congress in Nuremberg in 1934. Hitler intended the event to demonstrate his control of a powerful and unified group of followers. Hitler put enormous resources at Riefenstahl's disposal. She oversaw sixteen camera crews, and the huge buildings erected for the event were designed to look impressive in the film (**12.25, 12.26**). Using skillful cinematography, editing, and music, Riefenstahl created an impressive two-hour pageant of Nazi ideology and fervor. She also displayed to a nervous world Germany's military strength (**12.27**).

Made as a record of the 1936 Olympic Games, held in Berlin, *Olympia* contains far less overt Nazi propaganda than *Triumph of the Will*. Nevertheless, it was financed by the government, again on a vast scale. The intention was that the film would show Germany as a cooperative member of the world community and thus quell fears about Nazi aggression. It was also hoped that the games would result in a series of prizes for Aryan participants, demonstrating the racial inferiority of their competitors.

Riefenstahl deployed camera crews to film the events and to catch crowd reactions. The resulting footage required two years to edit, and the final film was released in two feature-length parts. There were glimpses of Hitler and other Nazi officials viewing the games, but Riefenstahl concentrated on creating a sense of friendly

12.28
Riefenstahl juxtaposes a series of shots of bodies soaring against the sky in the diving sequence in the second part of *Olympia*.

competition among the athletes and on the beauty and suspense of the events. At times that sense of beauty became almost abstract, as in the famous diving sequence (**12.28**). The medals won by several non-Aryan athletes, most prominently the black American track star Jesse Owens, also helped undercut the original propaganda purposes of the film.

Attacking the "Enemies" of the Reich

During the Nazi era, films attacking the enemies of the Third Reich continued to appear. Some were anti-British, since Great Britain epitomized the kind of parliamentary democracy that the Nazis opposed. In *Carl Peters* (1941, Herbert Selpin), for example, British secret agents use underhanded means to battle the hero in colonizing parts of Africa. The USSR continued to be a favorite target, since the Nazis aimed to enslave and exterminate Slavic populations. *GPU* (1942, Karl Ritter) associates Soviet communism with women's equality, peace, and disarmament; the GPU (Soviet secret police) acts as a band of assassins furthering the USSR's plans for world domination. (In fact the GPU had been used primarily to persecute Soviet citizens.) After the German defeat at

13.18 One of the most famous images of Poetic Realism: with the police outside, François looks out his window, surrounded by bullet holes.

13.17 The tall, thin set in *Le Jour se lève* emphasizes the isolation of the hero, trapped in his apartment on the top floor.

in Marcel Carné's two major Poetic Realist films: *Quai des brumes* (*Port of Shadows*, 1938) and *Le Jour se lève* (*Daybreak*, 1939).

In *Quai des brumes*, Gabin plays Jean, a deserter from the French Foreign Legion who encounters a beautiful woman, Nelly (played by Michèle Morgan, who formed with Gabin the "ideal couple" of the period). They fall in love, but she is protected by a powerful gangster. Although Jean kills the gangster, he is himself gunned down by a member of the gang and dies in Nelly's arms. The dark, foggy cinematography of German Eugen Schüfftan and the atmospheric sets by Alexandre Trauner, with their rain-dampened brick streets, created a look that typified Poetic Realism.

Le Jour se lève is another major example of Poetic Realism. Again Gabin plays the protagonist, François, a worker who commits a murder in the first scene and is trapped in his apartment by police. Throughout the night he recalls the circumstances leading up to the present; we see them in three flashbacks showing how the villainous Valentin (the murder victim) had seduced the innocent young woman with whom François is in love. The simple story was not as important as the brooding atmosphere, created in part by Trauner's set (**13.17**). This studio-built version of a working-class district illustrates the mixture of stylization and realism in Poetic Realism. Maurice Jaubert's music supplies a simple drumbeat for the opening and closing scenes. Above all, Gabin's portrayal of François pensively awaiting his fate created the ultimate hero of Poetic Realism (**13.18**). *Le Jour se lève* was released just three months before the German invasion of Poland. During the war, Carné would emphasize

doomed romance and downplay realism in two of the most popular films of the era, *Les Visiteurs du soir* and *Children of Paradise* (we shall discuss these films later in the chapter).

The Creative Burst of Jean Renoir

The most significant director of 1930s French cinema was Jean Renoir. Although his filmmaking career stretched from the 1920s to the 1960s, his output during this one decade was a remarkable case of concentrated creativity. He made a wide variety of films, some in the Poetic Realist strain. His first sound film, *On purge Bébé* (roughly, "Baby's Laxative," 1931), was a farce that Renoir made in order to get backing for other projects. His next film was completely different and can be seen as another forerunner of Poetic Realism. *La Chienne* ("The Bitch," 1931) concerns a mild accountant and amateur painter who is unhappily married; he stumbles into an affair with a prostitute whose pimp exploits the hero by selling his paintings. The hero ends up murdering the prostitute and escaping to become a cheerful panhandler. *La Chienne* introduced many elements that would characterize Renoir's work, including virtuosic camera movements, scenes staged in depth, and abrupt switches of tone. The hero's murder of his mistress would seem to be the sort of tragic ending typical of Poetic Realism, yet he simply wanders off into contented poverty. Similarly, despite the film's realistic style, Renoir begins and ends it with a curtain of a puppet theater, thus emphasizing its status as a performance.

Renoir's other notable films of the early 1930s include *Boudu sauvé des eaux* (*Boudu Saved from Drowning*, 1932) and *Toni* (1935). *Boudu* is the comic story of a tramp saved from suicide by a bourgeois bookseller who tries unsuccessfully to reform him. *Toni* is a more somber film dealing with the Italian and eastern European immigrant workers who came to France during the 1920s. It was produced by Marcel Pagnol and was shot

13.19 A typical Renoirian use of deep staging, as Toni bends over Marie after she has tried to drown herself and his friend rushes in from the background.

13.20 Again, Renoir uses deep staging as one of the young men opens a window and watches the wife and daughter swinging in the inn yard in *A Day in the Country.*

13.21 In *Grand Illusion*, Commander von Rauffenstein picks the last flower in his prison camp in tribute to the French officer's death.

entirely on location in the south of France. Its actors were largely unknown and spoke the dialect of the region. Toni is an Italian drifter who comes to France to work in a quarry; he marries his landlady Marie but falls in love with Josefa, who marries another man. When she learns the truth, Marie attempts suicide and then rejects him (**13.19**). Toni takes the blame when Josefa kills her brutal husband. A posse shoots him as a new group of foreign workers arrives. *Toni* was a crucial forerunner of the Italian Neorealist movement (see Chapter 16).

In the mid-1930s, Renoir made a few films influenced by the leftist Popular Front group (we shall examine these shortly). He also made a lyrical short feature, *Une Partie de campagne* (*A Day in the Country,* 1936). This film creates a delicate balance of the humorous and tragic. A Parisian family picnicking at a country inn encounter two young men who seduce the wife and young daughter—to the delight of the wife and the regret of both the daughter and her seducer, who fall in love and must part. Throughout the film, Renoir conveyed both the pleasure of the outing and the sense of loss that would follow it (**13.20**). Due to bad weather, the film was never actually finished, and it was released only in 1946, with two titles summarizing the missing portions.

Renoir's *Grand Illusion* (1937) took a pacifist stance at a time when war with Germany was increasingly probable. This drama of French prisoners in World War I suggests that class ties are more important than national allegiances. The upper-class German camp commander and the French officer understand each other better than do the officer and his French subordinates. When the French officer sacrifices his life so that some of his men may escape, the German commander plucks the only flower in the prison, suggesting that their class is dying out (**13.21**). In contrast, the working-class

13.22 The long hallway set in the château of *Rules of the Game,* where characters enter and exit unpredictably, conveying a sense of bustling activity in all the rooms.

Maréchal and his Jewish friend Rosenthal gain hope by escaping at the end.

This contrast between the declining aristocratic class and the working class reappeared in a more sardonic form in Renoir's last film of the decade, *Rules of the Game* (1939). Here a famous aviator causes confusion by falling in love with the wife of a French aristocrat who is in turn trying to break off with his mistress. These characters form part of a large gathering at the aristocrat's château. The servants' intrigues parallel the romantic confusion among the upper class, as a local poacher gets a job as a servant and immediately tries to seduce the gamekeeper's wife. The many romantic entanglements come to a head in a dazzling party scene at the château, as characters dodge in and out of rooms and forge and break relationships. Despite the characters' foolish actions, no one becomes a villain. As one of them remarks, "In this world, the scary thing is that everyone has his reasons." This line has often been taken as emblematic of Renoir's cinema, where there are seldom villains—only fallible people reacting to each other. In *Rules of the Game*, Renoir employed large, intricate sets and extensive camera movement to convey the characters' constant interactions (**13.22**). He also pioneered a

13.23   As the shot begins, we see the servants at the party, watching the offscreen entertainment. In the center of the frame, the gamekeeper (in cap), who suspects his wife of being unfaithful, looks in through the doorway.

13.24   The camera tracks right to follow a servant with a tray of drinks . . .

13.25   . . . past another doorway, where the gamekeeper, again in the center rear, peers in, hoping to catch his straying wife.

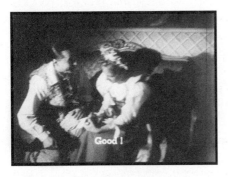

13.26   As the camera moves further, we glimpse the drunken hostess seeming to yield to the seduction of a wealthy neighbor.

13.27   The camera moves further right to reveal the man who loves her, watching this exchange, while at the left the gamekeeper appears again, looking for his wife.

13.28   Finally the hostess and her prospective lover move to leave . . .

13.29   . . . and the camera holds on them until they disappear in the distance.

technique that would become much more common in the 1940s and after: the *long take,* in which the camera holds on a subject without a cut, often moving to follow action, for an unusually long period. For example, in the party scene of *The Rules of the Game,* one shot tracks back and forth to follow two romantic entanglements involving jealous men (**13.23–13.29**). In the end, a death is caused through the confusion and it is covered up by the host. The film implies that the outworn aristocratic class is fading.

Rules of the Game was a failure at the time of its release. Audiences did not understand its mixture of tones, and it was perceived as attacking the ruling classes. The film was released just before France entered World War II, and it was soon banned.

Other Contributors

Despite the weakness of the production sector, the French cinema of the 1930s created a high proportion of important films, thanks partly to the large number of talented people working in the industry. Lazare Meerson designed the sets for Clair's films *Sous les toits de Paris* and *À nous, la liberté!* and for Feyder's *Carnival in Flanders.* He also trained Alexandre Trauner, who worked consistently with Carné. Major French composers worked in the cinema as well; Georges

Auric provided the music for *À nous, la liberté!*; Arthur Honegger scored *Crime and Punishment*; Josef Kosma contributed the haunting music for *A Day in the Country*. Maurice Jaubert composed music for *Zero for Conduct*, *L'Atalante*, *L'Affaire est dans le sac*, *Quai des brumes*, *Le Jour se lève*, and other films before his death in 1940 during the German invasion. Similarly, a surprisingly small number of scriptwriters contributed to many of the significant films of the decade, the two most important being Charles Spaak (several Feyder and Renoir films) and Jacques Prévert (Carné and Renoir films).

BRIEF INTERLUDE: THE POPULAR FRONT

During the 1930s, the gap widened between right-wing and left-wing political parties. Leftists struggled against the rise of Fascist elements in France. Before 1934, leftist parties did not cooperate: the Parti Communiste Français ("Communist Party of France," or PCF) worked against the more moderate Socialists, and both disdained the middle-class Radical Socialists. In various countries, the Communists tried independently to defeat the Fascists. By 1933, however, the German Communist party had failed to prevent Hitler's ascension to power.

In early 1934, the French political scene changed rapidly. Financier Serge Stavisky was revealed as a swindler who had the blessing of high government officials. In February, rightists protested in the violent Stavisky riots, which brought down the Radical Socialist government. The PCF responded with further riots, and several people were killed. The PCF decided to join forces with the rival Socialists, and in July a coalition party called the Popular Front was formed. In the autumn of 1935, even the moderate Radical Socialists were admitted into the Front.

By now the Depression was hitting the working class particularly hard; the number of unemployed reached a record 460,000 by late 1935, and wages had fallen substantially. Economic problems and a fear of fascism led to a Popular Front victory in the elections in the spring of 1936. Socialist Léon Blum became head of the government. In May and June, a massive series of strikes broke out—involving some of the film-producing companies. Blum's government passed important legislation benefiting the working class, including a forty-hour week and paid vacations.

There were soon divisions within the Popular Front, however. When the Spanish Civil War broke out in July 1936, Blum wanted to support the Republican cause against Franco's Fascist troops. Right-wing groups and elements of the Popular Front opposed this move. Controversial economic decisions, such as proposals to nationalize certain industries, led to further dissension, and in June of 1937, Blum's government toppled.

Brief as it was, the Popular Front had a notable effect on the cinema. Although the PCF and the Socialists had each produced a few short propaganda films in the early 1930s, their first joint effort came in 1936. In January, the Popular Front formed a group called Ciné-Liberté to make films and publish a magazine. Members of the group included Jean Renoir, Marc Allégret (who had directed *Fanny* and *Lac aux dames*), Jacques Feyder, and Germaine Dulac. Ciné-Liberté produced a feature film to be used as propaganda in the upcoming spring elections: *La Vie est à nous* ("Life Belongs to Us"). Both the PCF and the Socialists continued to make a few short propaganda and documentary films during the 1930s. The last major left-wing feature was *La Marseillaise* (1938). As Renoir was the most prominent director in Ciné-Liberté, he was a logical choice to supervise the collectively made *La Vie est à nous* and to direct the epic production of *La Marseillaise* (see box).

Aside from its direct participation in the production of a few films, the Popular Front inspired several commercial films. Foremost among these were two about workers' cooperatives. Renoir's *The Crime of Monsieur Lange* (1935) concerns life in a building that houses apartments, a laundry, and a publishing firm. The publisher, Batala, exploits his workers, mismanages the business, and seduces an innocent laundress. When he is forced to flee his creditors and is thought to have been killed in a train wreck, Monsieur Lange, one of his writers, leads the workers in reorganizing the publishing firm into a successful cooperative. When Batala unexpectedly returns, Lange kills him in order to protect the cooperative and flees with his lover, Valentine, the owner of the laundry.

Although Renoir's previous film, *Toni*, had been concerned with the working class, *Monsieur Lange* was his most overtly left-wing film to date and was largely responsible for Renoir's being asked to supervise *La Vie est à nous*. It is one of the rare cases where Renoir included a truly villainous character, the monstrous Batala. Renoir used his distinctive technique to suggest the unity among the people of the entire building by organizing the setting around a central courtyard across

POPULAR FRONT FILMMAKING: *LA VIE EST À NOUS* AND *LA MARSEILLAISE*

La Vie est à nous was made in early 1936, to be used in the Popular Front's election campaign. It was largely financed through collections taken up at PCF meetings, and both the cast and crew donated their labor. It was shot quickly, in about two weeks. Although often referred to as a Renoir film, those who worked on it stressed that *La Vie est à nous* was a collaborative project. Renoir supervised the production and directed a few sequences, and other scenes were directed by Jacques Brunius, Jean-Paul Le Chanois, and Jacques Becker. Completed a few weeks before the May elections, the film was shown at Popular Front meetings and rallies.

La Vie est à nous was innovative in its form as well as in its production circumstances. Taking further the mixture of staged and documentary footage Bertolt Brecht and Slatan Dudow had used in *Kuhle Wampe* (p. 305), Renoir's team mixed scenes and documents in a collage style. What begins as a documentary about France is revealed to be a lecture staged in a classroom; we follow some of the children out into the street as they discuss their poverty, and then a woman directly addresses the camera, giving a straightforward message. Other elements include still photographs, occasional intertitles, newsreel footage, and signs. Several Popular Front officials appear as themselves, yet well-known actors play the workers and peasants who support them. In one scene, a movie screen behind an industrialist illustrates what he is talking about (**13.30**). Later a "family photo album" mocks the "200 families" of France (**13.31**). At one point, the filmmakers show newsreel footage of Hitler speaking but substitute a dog's barking on the sound track.

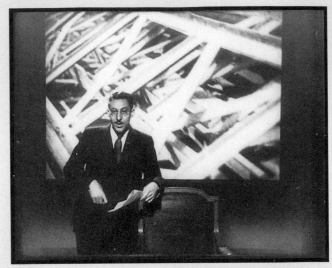

13.30 In *La Vie est à nous,* an industrialist complains of how workers have destroyed equipment and burned farm produce to protest low wages and prices; on the screen behind him, a film shows scenes of the destruction.

La Vie est à nous disappeared after the May elections, and a print resurfaced only in 1969. It was then hailed for its inventive approach and became highly influential.

La Marseillaise is a historical epic depicting the events of the French Revolution surrounding the fall of the monarchy in 1792. Made in support of the Popular Front, the film was to be financed through a subscription system: members of the large labor union, the Confédération Générale du Travail, would buy coupons good toward the cost of

13.31 The "200 families" were the richest in France and were commonly blamed by leftists for the country's financial woes. Here a "family album" lampoons real-life target Eugène Schneider, "cannon merchant."

13.32 In *La Marseillaise,* a group of French aristocrats in exile listen nostalgically to a song about France.

13.33 A tracking shot begins on some children playing leapfrog . . .

13.34 . . . moves to the right past a large crowd looking off right . . .

13.35 . . . pauses on boys playing marbles . . .

13.36 . . . and ends on a group of men battering down the gates of the Tuileries Palace—an event that will lead to the abolition of the French monarchy.

tickets when the film eventually appeared. Not enough tickets were purchased, however, and Renoir had to set up a special company to produce the film. This firm was not much different from the many little one-film production companies in France during this period. *La Marseillaise* had a commercial release in early 1938, but by that time the Popular Front's mass support had dissipated.

The film was praised by the leftist press but proved unpopular, perhaps partly because Renoir refused to make Louis XVI and the aristocrats of his court into stock villains. Instead, he treated them sympathetically, as dignified members of a dying class, rather like the upper-class figures in *Rules of the Game* (**13.32**). Moreover, Renoir

showed only a few of the important events of the revolution; instead, he concentrated on everyday occurrences, focusing primarily on a group of soldiers from Marseille who march to Paris to join the fighting, bringing with them the new song that will become the national anthem. Renoir also used few stars, giving the main roles to minor actors with accents from the south of France.

The film is full of the spectacular tracking shots typical of Renoir's work. One shot exemplifies his "bottom-up" approach to history in this film, encompassing both trivial and momentous events (**13.33–13.36**). This mixture may have made *La Marseillaise* too undramatic for contemporary audiences.

13.37   Deep staging in *The Crime of Monsieur Lange* simultaneously shows characters in the concierge's apartment in the foreground, the courtyard in the middle ground, and the laundry in the background.

which the characters interact. Deep staging juxtaposes events in different parts of the building (**13.37**).

Julien Duvivier's *La Belle équipe* ("The Glorious Team," aka *They Were Five*, 1937) begins with five unemployed workers. An ironic juxtaposition places two of them before a vacation poster (**13.38**), at a time when many working-class people could never afford to leave their grim urban neighborhoods. When the five men win the lottery, they determine to start a cooperative riverside café near Paris. Many little touches indicate the egalitarian quality of the project: each of the five has a sign over his bed with the word "President," and the café's name is Chez Nous ("Our Place"). Yet various problems gradually lead two of the protagonists to drop

out of the project, and one dies in an accident during a party at the unfinished café. By the end, the remaining two have resolved their jealous feud over a woman and preside over Chez Nous's grand opening (**13.39**). In fact, Duvivier had wanted an unhappy ending in which Jean kills Charles over the woman they both love and is arrested while sitting in the empty café (**13.40**). The producer, however, insisted on the happy ending.

Duvivier's original intention for *La Belle équipe*'s ending suggests that the main films inspired by the Popular Front were not very far removed from Poetic Realism. Although the villainous Batala is killed in *The Crime of Monsieur Lange,* Lange and Valentine must pay the price by fleeing from France. *La Belle équipe* would have ended with the cooperative project in a shambles. The aspirations of the Popular Front are evident in a less obvious way in the Poetic Realist films that deal sympathetically, if pessimistically, with working-class heroes.

FILMMAKING IN OCCUPIED AND VICHY FRANCE

The Situation in the Film Industry

When Germany unleashed World War II by invading Poland on September 1, 1939, France and Great Britain honored their diplomatic commitments and declared war on Germany. Many French filmmakers were mobilized, and production of twenty films was suspended.

Poland collapsed swiftly, however, and the British and French did little to prevent it. The period to April 9, 1940, was the *drôle de guerre,* or "phony war." During this time, 2 million French troops remained in the field, but virtually no fighting occurred. It was widely assumed

13.38   Jean and Mario, two of the unemployed heroes of *La Belle équipe,* stand in front of a poster advertising skiing holidays ("Why shiver in Paris? Build your health among the eternal snows").

13.39   Charles and Jean, the remaining protagonists, introduce the triumphal final dance that signals the success of their café.

13.40   The pessimistic final shot of the original ending of *La Belle équipe:* as Jean is arrested for the murder of his partner, he declares, "It's all over. It was a wonderful idea."

that an Allied blockade would eventually defeat Germany. In October 1939, film production had resumed, and it continued throughout the phony war.

In the spring of 1940, Germany attacked again, occupying Denmark on April 9 and moving in quick succession into Norway, the Netherlands, and Belgium. On June 5, Germany invaded France; meeting weak resistance, it occupied Paris on June 14. Two days later a right-wing French government was set up in Vichy, a resort town in central France. The southern portion of France remained an "unoccupied" zone for over two years, with the Vichy government holding power at the pleasure of the Germans.

The film industry was enormously disrupted by these events. Jews, leftists, and others fled into the unoccupied zone or went abroad. Feyder, for example, made one film in the south and then went to Switzerland in 1942; he was unable to direct again until after the war. Renoir worked in the United States during the 1940s. And some refugees returned to the occupied zone after production resumed there in June 1941. Two separate film industries developed.

Vichy France   During late 1940, the Vichy government created the Comité d'Organisation de l'Industrie Cinématographique (COIC) to support and control the film industry. Producers had to go through an elaborate application process to get permission to make a film, and censorship under the Vichy regime was even harsher than that in the German-controlled zone. In addition, the rightist government strove to eliminate Jews from the film industry.

The southern zone had only a few small studios, including Pagnol's in Marseille. Equipment and raw stock were scarce and sometimes had to be obtained on the black market. Producers also faced a lack of funding. Until May 1942, films made in the unoccupied zone were banned from the German zone; thus they showed only in the limited markets of southern France and French North Africa. Moreover, there were few French investors in the area.

Some financing came clandestinely from Jewish and American sources or openly from Italian investors. For example, the French firm Discina was closely linked with the Scalera company of Rome. The two firms coproduced some important films, including Jean Delannoy's *L'Eternel retour* (1943), Carné's *Les Visiteurs du soir* (1942), and Carné's *Les Enfants du paradis* (1945, completed by Pathé after Italy's defeat). (We shall discuss these films shortly.) Italian firms invested in other film enterprises in southern France and also provided a mar-

ket for some French films. Abel Gance's *Le Captaine Fracasse* (1943) was another Italian-French coproduction.

The COIC helped alleviate financial problems by arranging for low-interest government loans for production. Films made with such loans include Grémillon's *Lumière d'été* ("Summer Light," 1943) and *Le Ciel est à vous* ("The Sky Is Yours," 1944) and Robert Bresson's *Les Anges du péché* ("Angels of Sin," 1943). The COIC also attempted to foster quality production with an annual prize of 100,000 francs for the best films of the year. *Les Visiteurs du soir* won in 1942 and *Les Anges du péché* in 1943. Later, once southern films were allowed into the German zone, they shared in the generally high profits of the war period.

Occupied France   The situation in the occupied zone was quite different than in southern France. Initially no French film production was permitted, and a ban on imports of American, British, and French films from the Vichy area gave the Germans a monopoly on screenings. Some German films, especially the infamous *Jud Süss*, were successful. Audiences preferred French films, however, and cinema attendance dropped in 1941. In May of that year, German officials allowed French production to resume. Many filmmakers who had fled returned to the better-equipped studios of Paris. Once new French films began appearing in the cinemas, attendance rose again. With no competition from American films, French production actually became more profitable during the war.

Why did the German authorities permit French production? For one thing, it was widely assumed at that point, by the Germans and many French, that Germany would win the war. Its leaders planned to create a "New Europe," under German control. France, it was assumed, would contribute to that new order. Moreover, strong European production could help Germany break the American domination of world markets, thus fulfilling—though in a less cooperative spirit—the old Film Europe goal of the 1920s. A healthy French film industry could also demonstrate to other occupied countries the benefits of cooperating with the Germans.

In addition, there was considerable German investment in France's film industry. That investment came mainly through the formation in 1940 of a Germany company, Continental, in Paris. Continental was a subsidiary of the giant firm Ufa, which, as we saw in the previous chapter, was becoming the single centralized film company in Germany. Of the approximately 220 features made in both parts of France during the Occupation, 30 were produced by Continental. The largest French producer, Pathé-Cinéma, made only fourteen films during the same period. Most production companies were still small firms, making from one to eight films during the war. However, Continental was vertically integrated, owning its own studios, laboratories, and the biggest French theater chain; it released its films through Ufa's Paris distribution subsidiary. Continental signed up several major French stars and directors and produced some of the most popular—and controversial—films of the Occupation.

German censorship of French films was surprisingly lenient, concentrating on eliminating references to the United States and Great Britain. One area of official control was strict, however. Several regulations were passed to prevent Jews from participating in the film industry, and prewar films with Jewish actors were banned. During the war, about 75,000 French Jews were sent to concentration camps in Germany, and few of them survived. Most Jewish filmmakers, however, managed to flee or hide, and some kept working clandestinely.

France was divided until November 1942, when Germany occupied the southern portion, keeping the Vichy regime as a figurehead government. From then on, the southern production facilities functioned mainly as places for Parisian firms to go for location shooting.

It is sometimes assumed that all French filmmakers who worked in France during the Occupation were collaborating with the enemy. Many, however, felt they were keeping the French film industry alive during an extremely difficult period. While a few films reflected fascist ideals, others were pro-French. Quite a few filmmakers also served secretly in the French Resistance movement. There was a resistance group for cinema, the Comité de Libération du Cinéma Français; members included directors Jean Grémillon and Jacques Becker and actors Pierre Blanchar and Pierre Renoir.

The Allied military push that eventually defeated the Germans began in late 1942. From this point on, the French Resistance expanded. Allied bombing within France damaged some film facilities; five studios were destroyed and 322 theaters damaged or leveled. A shortage of materials hampered production late in the war, and, by July 1944, all production ceased. Filmmakers in the Resistance movement fought in the general uprising during August, while secretly filming the liberation of Paris.

Some filmmakers suspected of collaborating were punished. A few, such as Sacha Guitry and Maurice Chevalier, were briefly imprisoned but then exonerated. Director Henri-Georges Clouzot was briefly barred from filmmaking for having made a supposedly anti-French film, *Le Corbeau*. In order to see why such punishment was meted out, we need to look at the kinds of films made during the Occupation.

Films of the Occupation Period

Most films made during the Occupation were comedies and melodramas of the sort that had appeared before the war. Censorship in the German and Vichy zones forced filmmakers to avoid subject matter relating to the war and other social problems.

The most notable films of this period fit into the prestige category, close to what would later be called the "Tradition of Quality" (see Chapter 17). Belying their straitened circumstances, these films were expert productions, with impressive sets and major stars. Cut off from contemporary reality, they conveyed a mood of romantic resignation. Some films, however—vague allegories of French indomitability—also could be interpreted as suggesting resistance to oppression.

Perhaps the first such film was Christian-Jacque's *L'Assassinat du Père Noël* ("The Murder of Santa Claus," 1941). Set in a snow-covered mountain village, it tells the story of a mapmaker, Cornusse, who plays Santa Claus for the local children every year (**13.41**). On Christmas Eve, odd events occur: a sinister figure steals a saint's relics from the church, and the village's baron, returned from an enigmatic absence, courts Cornusse's ethereal daughter. All ends well, with Cornusse's visit miraculously curing a crippled boy. Cornusse tells him that a French sleeping beauty will someday be awakened by a Prince Charming. Although *L'Assassinat du Père Noël* was the first production by Continental, the German firm, its symbolic message was presumably apparent to many French filmgoers.

Marcel L'Herbier, who had been a major figure in the French Impressionist movement of the 1920s, made his most personal film since that time with *La Nuit fantastique* ("The Fantastic Night," 1942). In it, a poor student works in a Parisian produce market and dreams nightly of an angelic woman in white. One day the woman wanders through the market, taking him on a strange journey through a nightclub, a magic shop, and an insane asylum. When he wakes again, the woman reappears, and they go off together into a permanent dreamlike realm. L'Herbier revived Impressionist subjective techniques for *La Nuit fantastique*, using reversed sound, slow motion, and split-screen effects to convey the hero's dreaming visions. Similarly, Pierre Prévert managed to rekindle something of the anarchic spirit of *L'Affaire est dans le sac* in his 1943 feature *Adieu . . . Leonard!* Leonard, a thief, undergoes a series of comic adventures and then ends up abandoning society and going off with his friends in a gypsy caravan.

Escapist fantasy of a more romantic, yet morbid, kind is apparent in two major films of the midwar pe-

13.41 In *L'Assassinat du Père Noël,* Cornusse plays Santa Claus for the villagers while mysterious events are occurring.

13.42 The Devil's emissaries approach the immense castle set in the opening scene of *Les Visiteurs du soir.*

riod. Marcel Carné's *Les Visiteurs du soir* ("Visitors of the Evening," 1942), a romance set in medieval times, employs elaborate costumes and settings (**13.42**). Yet, because of shortages, many period costumes were made of cheap cloth and the crew injected poison into the fruit in the banquet scenes to prevent hungry extras from eating it. In *Les Visiteurs,* a man and a woman are sent by the Devil to corrupt the inhabitants of a castle. The man falls in love with the princess he is supposed to seduce, and, ultimately, the Devil turns them both into statues (**13.43**). This ending has been widely interpreted as an allegory of France's resistance to German Occupation. Two prominent Jewish film artists, set designer Alexandre Trauner and composer Joseph Kosma collaborated anonymously on the film.

A similar story of doomed love is Jean Delannoy's *L'Eternel retour* ("The Eternal Return," 1943), from a Jean Cocteau script based on the Tristan and Isolde legend. Cocteau set the story in contemporary times but on an isolated island. The hero, Patrice, goes to fetch a young wife, Natalie, for his elderly uncle. Falling in love with her, he lives out a doomed existence in which his evil cousin Achille plots against him. Eventually Patrice and Natalie, both coldly beautiful, idealized characters, accept death as the only way that they can stay together. This sort of fatalism typified much French filmmaking of the Occupation period.

The era was also notable for two films by Jean Grémillon, whose *La Petite Lise* had been a major early sound film and an early entry in the Poetic Realist tendency. In *Lumière d'été* (1943), a love triangle among older people—Cri-Cri, a dancer who now runs a mountain hotel; Patrice, a local nobleman; and Roland, an alcoholic artist—is played off against a more innocent romance between a young engineer, Julien, and a young woman, Michèle. Patrice tries to seduce Michèle, but, after a masked ball and a car crash, the relationships sort themselves out, and Julien and Michèle end up together. The film's settings (**13.44**) and acting were distinctive for the period. Because of its sordid depiction of its characters,

13.43 The Devil hears the heartbeats of his victims and realizes he has failed to completely subjugate them.

13.44 An effective use of a location setting in the mountains in Grémillon's *Lumière d'été.*

13.45, *left*   At the opening of a small airport in *La Ciel est à vous*, French flags are draped conspicuously in the background.

13.46, *right*   Robert Bresson used the nuns' black-and-white clothing, in combination with careful lighting and composition, to create an arresting visual style in *Les Anges du péché*.

the film was nearly banned by the Vichy authorities, who demanded strong, upright French figures.

La Ciel est à vous (1944) is more upbeat. The family of a garage owner sacrifices everything so that the wife, Thérèse, can establish a long-distance solo flying record. The story uses conventional Hollywood-style suspense, showing the family struggling to finance the trip and waiting as Thérèse loses radio contact on her record-breaking flight. Through patriotic motifs (**13.45**), the film lauded French heroism and even revived a bit of the spirit of the Popular Front.

The most important filmmaker to begin a career during the Occupation period was Robert Bresson, whose first feature, *Les Anges du péché*, appeared in 1943. An audacious film noir set in a convent, it deals with nuns who try to reform female criminals. Bresson's characteristic narrative of spiritual redemption emerged in mature form, with a rebellious nun and a murderess unpre-

dictably helping each other find peace. The austere visual style also looked forward to Bresson's later films (**13.46**). Bresson's next film, *Les Dames de Bois de Bologne* ("The Ladies of the Bois de Bologne") began production late in the Occupation period but was not released until 1945, a year after the liberation of France. It shares some traits of the Occupation films, since its narrative is cut off from contemporary society, dealing with a high-society woman who tries to take revenge on her ex-lover by tricking him into marrying an ex-prostitute.

Perhaps the two most famous films of the Occupation period are Carné's *Les Enfants du paradis* ("Children of Paradise," 1945), and Clouzot's *Le Corbeau* ("The Crow," 1943). *Children of Paradise* was made under difficult circumstances, in the lean late-war period. A vast tapestry of the theater world in nineteenth-century Paris (**13.47**), the story traces the romantic entanglements of several characters, centering around the

13.47   Jewish designer Alexandre Trauner, working clandestinely on *Children of Paradise*, created enormous sets reconstructing the theater district of mid-nineteenth-century Paris.

13.48   The bittersweet pantomime involving Pierrot, Columbine, and Harlequin in *Children of Paradise* suggests the sense of lost love that pervades the film's offstage romances.

13.49 At the funeral of one of the "Crow's" victims in *Le Corbeau*, the villagers pass around another poison-pen letter.

mime Baptiste Debureau and the actress Garance, whose thwarted love echoes their onstage roles (**13.48**).

Nothing could be further from the mood of romantic melancholy that pervades *Children of Paradise* than the cynicism of *Le Corbeau*. The film is set in a small French town where a series of poison-pen letters signed "Le Corbeau" reveal various secrets about several of the most respected members of the community. The panicky townspeople react with unreasoning suspicions. The protagonist, Dr. Germain, receives a letter falsely accusing him of having an affair with a married woman and of being an abortionist. He is later seduced by Denise, a young woman whom the community is quick to condemn for her loose morals—despite the fact that she is one of the few to refuse to enter into the hysterical suspicions and accusations prompted by Le Corbeau's letters (**13.49**).

At the time of *Le Corbeau*'s release in 1943, its unpleasant subject matter led to its being widely condemned as anti-French—especially since it had been produced by the German-backed Continental company. Some have argued, however, that *Le Corbeau* was an attack on the sorts of right-wing values that undergirded the Vichy government. The heated debates in the "Clouzot affair" led in 1945 to the filmmaker's being forbidden to work. Clouzot did not direct again until 1947, when the complex and realistic crime film *Quai des orfevres* reestablished his career.

The end of the Occupation brought many changes for French filmmaking, including the renewed competition with imported American films. Yet most of the filmmakers of the wartime period kept working, and the decentralized industrial structures survived into the postwar era.

Notes and Queries

RENEWED INTEREST IN THE POPULAR FRONT

Most surveys of film history written before the 1970s cover René Clair's work, Poetic Realism, and the Occupation—but not the Popular Front. This brief, but important, movement drew attention mainly in the late 1960s and after, when there was a renewed interest in critical political cinema (see Chapter 23). In particular, *La Vie est à nous* and *La Marseillaise*, which had been treated simply as examples of Jean Renoir's work, have been examined in their political contexts.

An early study (1966) of the Popular Front cinema is Geffredo Fofi's "The Cinema of the Popular Front in France (1934–1938)," translated in *Screen* 13, no. 3 (winter 1972/1973): 5–57. A collective text on *La Vie est à nous* appeared in *Cahiers du cinema* in 1970 and has been translated as Pascal Bonitzer et al., "*La Vie est à nous*: A Militant Film" in Nick Browne, ed., *Cahiers du Cinéma: 1969–1971: The Politics of Representation* (Cambridge, MA: Harvard University Press, 1990), pp. 68–88. See also Elizabeth Grottle Strebel's "Renoir and the Popular Front," *Sight and Sound* 49, no. 1 (winter 1979/1980): 36–41, and Ginette Vincendeau and Keith Reader, eds., *La Vie est à nous!. French Cinema of the Popular Front 1935–1938* (London: British Film Institute, 1986).

The most extensive study in English, Jonathan Buchsbaum's *Cinema Engagé: Film in the Popular Front* (Urbana: University of Illinois Press, 1988) takes issue with these earlier studies and deals only with those films actually produced by left-wing French political parties during the 1930s. For a broader overview that treats many films of the 1930s in relation to the Popular Front, see Geneviève Guillaume-Grimaud's *Le Cinéma du Front Populaire* (Paris: Lherminier, 1986).

REFERENCE

1. Quoted in Pierre Lagnan, *Les Années Pagnol* (Renens: Five Continents, 1989), p. 111.

FURTHER READING

Andrew, Dudley. *Mists of Regret: Culture and Sensibility in Classic French Film*. Princeton, NJ: Princeton University Press, 1995.

Bertin-Maghit, Jean-Pierre. *Le Cinéma sous l'Occupation: Le Monde du cinema français de 1940 à 1946*. Paris: Orban, 1989.

Chateau, René. *La Cinéma français sous l'Occupation, 1940–1944*. Paris: La Memoire du Cinéma français, 1996.

Chirat, Raymond. *Le Cinéma français des années de guerre*. Renan, Switzerland: Five Continents/Hatier, 1983.

Clair, René. *Cinema Yesterday and Today*. Trans. and ed. Stanley Appelbaum. New York: Dover, 1972.

Ehrlich, Evelyn. *Cinema of Paradox: French Filmmaking under the German Occupation*. New York: Columbia University Press, 1985.

Faulkner, Christopher. *The Social Cinema of Jean Renoir*. Princeton, NJ: Princeton University Press, 1986.

Garçon, François. *De Blum à Petain: Cinéma et société française (1936–1944)*. Paris: Cerf, 1984.

Siclier, Jacques. *Le France de Pétain et son cinema*. Bourges, France: Veyrier, 1983.

LEFTIST, DOCUMENTARY, AND EXPERIMENTAL CINEMAS, 1930–1945

The era from the early Depression to the end of World War II brought about particularly dramatic changes for filmmakers who worked outside the mainstream commercial industry. Economic hardship and sound technology made it prohibitively expensive for many experimenters and documentarists to work independently. To a considerable extent, the 1920s generation of experimental filmmakers turned in other directions. A new group then took their places, sometimes depending on cheaper, recently developed amateur equipment.

The rise of fascism, civil wars in China and Spain, and the move toward global conflict pushed many filmmakers, often leftist in their sympathies, to politicize their work. The Russian Revolution was still recent enough that Communists in many countries hoped similar uprisings would occur around the world. Some who had begun by making lyrical films turned to documentaries, recording epochal events. At first, political films tended to be pacifist, equating militarism with imperialist aggression. Later, when General Francisco Franco led the attempt to impose a Fascist regime in Spain and the other Axis powers began invading their neighbors, leftists supported the war against them.

THE SPREAD OF POLITICAL CINEMA

During the 1920s and early 1930s, Soviet films, particularly those of the Montage movement, galvanized viewers around the world. Some audiences were interested primarily in these films' stylistic innovations, but others also saw them as models for leftist cinema. Politicized filmmakers displayed the influence of the Soviets. Thus, this era's leftist films, though made in different countries, often resemble each other.

14.1, *left   Workers Newsreel Unemployment Special* (1931, edited by Leo Seltzer) documented widespread hunger and protests against government policy, such as this longshoremen's march.

14.2, *right*   Two homeless men satirize the welfare system in *Pie in the Sky.*

The United States

Politically active filmmakers in the United States started by confronting the issues of poverty and racism. Communist groups had produced a few documentaries during the 1920s, but the first regular association was formed in 1930. Several film enthusiasts in New York joined with a communist still-photographers' organization to create the Workers' Film and Photo League. (The word *Workers* was soon dropped.) Soon a national network of Film and Photo Leagues grew up, cooperating to shoot footage for newsreels that could be shown at socialist gatherings. The filmmakers received no payment, and costs were made up by donations, benefits, and screenings of classic films. The leagues used silent cameras purchased cheaply after the advent of sound. Their early films mainly recorded demonstrations, strikes, and hunger marches that took place around the country (**14.1**).

Members of the Film and Photo League in New York included Paul Strand and Ralph Steiner, who had made lyrical documentaries (Strand's *Manhatta*) and abstract films (Steiner's H_2O) in the 1920s (p. 180). Photographer Margaret Bourke-White joined the group, as did Thomas Brandon, who after the war would become an important 16mm distributor for film societies and classes. The leagues' other activities included providing lecturers to leftist gatherings, writing criticism that denounced Hollywood films and upheld alternative cinema, and protesting screenings of Nazi films.

During 1935, the New York branch published a short-lived newsletter, *Filmfront,* that contained translations of essays by leftist theorists and critics, including Dziga Vertov. A report issued by the leagues in 1934 made explicit the links with his kino-eye theory (p. 185):

> "The Film and Photo Leagues" were rooted in the intellectual and social basis of the Soviet film . . . in the same way as the Soviet cinema began with the kino-eye and grew organically from there on . . . the Leagues started also with the simple newsreel documents, pho-

tographing events as they appeared to the lens, true to the nature of the revolutionary medium, they exploited in a revolutionary cinematic way.[1]

By the mid-1930s, however, some members were moving on to more ambitious projects, and the leagues were moribund by 1937.

In 1935, several filmmakers left to form a loose collective, Nykino (roughly, "cinema now"), whose name suggests a conscious imitation of Soviet cinema. Nykino made only a few films, including documentaries and one notable satire on the sanctimonious promises made to the poor during the Depression. *Pie in the Sky* (1934) was set principally in a dump, where actors improvised gags on church and government institutions (**14.2**). By early 1937, Nykino was transformed into a nonprofit filmmaking firm, Frontier. Frontier was quite successful for a few years in making longer documentaries with impressive photography by, among others, Steiner and Strand. Steiner was cinematographer on *People of the Cumberland* (1938, directed by Sidney Meyers and Jay Leyda), which dealt with unionization in the Cumberland Mountain region.

Frontier's last and longest film was *Native Land*, shot in the late 1930s, though not released until 1942. It was directed by Strand and Leo Hurwitz and photographed by Strand. *Native Land* is a quasi-documentary, restaging actual incidents in which working-class people struggle against oppressive forces of capitalism. In one episode, sharecroppers who try to organize and obtain higher prices for cotton are chased by police; a black farmer and a white one flee together and are both shot down. The incident stresses that workers of different races must cooperate to defend themselves. Other episodes show peaceful union activities broken up by police or company goons (**14.3**).

Leftist cinema declined during the 1940s, due in part to increasing anti-Communist pressures and radical sympathizers' disillusionment after Stalin's purges and show

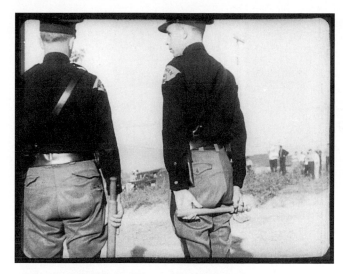

14.3 A staged shot in depth from *Native Land*, showing police looming ominously in the foreground as they break up a peaceful demonstration by strikers.

trials. Fearing the spread of fascism, the Communists also decided to support the American government during the war. Some former members of the Film and Photo Leagues worked on government- and corporate-sponsored documentaries.

Germany

Leftist filmmaking began relatively early in Germany, since that country had been the first to import the Soviet films of the 1920s. Moreover, the Communist party and other left-wing groups in Germany became more active as the influence of right-wing political parties like the Nazis grew in the late 1920s and early 1930s.

In 1926, the International Workers' Relief, a Communist organization concerned with fostering the growth of the USSR, formed Prometheus, a film firm that would distribute Soviet films. It scored a big success in 1926 with *Potemkin* (see Chapter 6) and subsequently released many imported pictures. During the late 1920s, Prometheus also produced German films, including Piel Jutzi's *Mutter Krausens Fahrt ins Gluck* (1929). By this time, Germany was suffering sharply rising unemployment as a result of the Depression. Jutzi's film reveals in grim detail the life of a family trapped in a tiny apartment; when the son is arrested as a thief after losing his job, his mother commits suicide. Only his sister, who joins a Communist demonstration with her fiancé (see 8.7), represents a sense of hope for German society. The film's title was an ironic commentary on the plight of the poor, for whom suicide seems one path to "happiness."

14.4 Brecht's technique of distancing the audience from the action appears after the suicide in *Kuhle Wampe*, when a neighbor woman turns to the camera and repeats the ironic phrase used earlier in an intertitle, "One fewer unemployed."

Prometheus also produced the most prominent German Communist film of this era, *Kuhle Wampe* (1932, Slatan Dudow), named for the workers' camp in which it is set. The script was written by Bertolt Brecht, the leftist playwright who invented the "epic theater" and whose *The Threepenny Opera* had recently been an enormous hit. Brecht believed that theater spectators should be distanced from the actions they witnessed so that they could think through the implications of the events rather than remaining emotionally involved with the story. He applied this idea in *Kuhle Wampe*, which explores unemployment, abortion, the situation of women, and other issues in a series of episodes from the life of a single family. The son commits suicide after failing for months to find a job (**14.4**). Ultimately, the daughter of the family, nearly abandoned by her fiancé after she becomes pregnant, finds help through Communist youth activities, and the family gains a semblance of normal life at the tent city of the unemployed, Kuhle Wampe. Intertitles, songs by composer Hanns Eisler, and a lengthy sequence at a Communist youth sports festival all help give *Kuhle Wampe* the feel of a political tract.

Prometheus went out of business in 1932, and another producer finished the film. By that time, however, the Communist cinema was fighting a losing battle. The Nazis came to power in 1933, and Brecht and Eisler both ended up working in the Hollywood cinema—where their approach fit in uneasily.

Belgium and the Netherlands

In Belgium, which had suffered a lengthy occupation by the Germans during World War I, documentarists and experimentalists were quick to respond to the growth

14.5 A Soviet-influenced composition in *Flamme blanche*, with a dynamic low-angle framing isolating a threatening police officer's head against a blank sky.

14.6, 14.7 Using Soviet-style intellectual montage, Storck compares a yapping lapdog to a pompous politician.

of fascism. Charles Dekeukeleire, who had manipulated narratives in daring ways in his silent films (pp. 183–184), turned to political film with *Flamme blanche* ("White Flame," 1931). He combined documentary footage of a Communist rally with staged scenes of police hunting down a young demonstrator hiding in a barn (**14.5**).

Dekeukeleire's friend Henri Storck had started a ciné-club in his hometown, the Belgian seaside resort of Ostende, in the 1920s. He also had made several poetic documentaries and city symphonies, including *Images d'Ostende* (1929). During the early 1930s, however, his career took a political turn. In 1932, he made an antifascist, pacifist compilation documentary, *Histoire d'un soldat inconnu* ("History of an Unknown Soldier"). Storck's approach to editing was novel, juxtaposing stock footage of government and religious leaders supporting the military with bizarre imagery that created a bitterly ironic comment on warmongering (**14.6, 14.7**).

Dutch filmmaker Joris Ivens, who had also been involved in a ciné-club and made films in abstract and city-symphony genres during the 1920s (p. 182), became more politically oriented. After the success of *The Bridge* and *Rain*, he was invited to make a documentary on the steel industry, *Song of Heroes* (1932), in the Soviet Union. Then, Henri Storck was invited by a left-wing ciné-club in Brussels to make a film exposing the oppressive treatment of coal miners in the Borinage region of Belgium, and he asked Ivens to collaborate with him.

The result was *Misère au Borinage* ("Misery in Borinage," generally known as *Borinage,* 1933). Storck and Ivens made the film clandestinely, dodging authorities to film workers reenacting clashes with police, evictions, and marches (**14.8**). *Borinage*'s powerful treat-

14.8 Workers carry a homemade picture of Karl Marx during a reenacted demonstration scene in *Borinage*.

ment of its subject led to its banning in Belgium and the Netherlands, though it was widely seen in ciné-clubs. Ivens returned to the Netherlands to make another film on the exploitation of workers, *New Earth* (1934), in which he showed how thousands of workers who helped create dikes and new land suddenly ended up unemployed. Thereafter, Ivens's remarkable career took him around the world, as he recorded left-wing activities over the next several decades.

Great Britain

Socialist ciné-clubs and filmmaking groups were particularly active in Britain, in part as a reaction to strict censorship that forbade public screenings of Soviet and other leftist films.

14.9, *left*   *Against Imperialist War—May Day 1932* is an early example of the many films of protests and marches made by British leftists. The filmmakers commonly juxtaposed peaceful marchers and a police presence.

14.10, *right*   Shots taken with a hidden camera made *Construction* (1935) a convincing view of working-class conditions.

In October 1929, a group of communist trade unions created the Federation of Workers' Film Societies to encourage the formation of such clubs. In November, the London Workers' Film Society was established, and, during the 1930s, the movement spread to other British cities. The federation distributed 35mm prints of leftist German and Soviet films to such groups, and it also issued a newsreel, the *Workers' Topical News*.

It soon became apparent, however, that the key to both production and distribution would be 16mm equipment. In 1932, several Communists filmed a May Day demonstration against Japanese aggression in Manchuria (**14.9**). At the time, however, there was no regular distribution mechanism for 16mm films. In 1933, Rudolph Messel formed the Socialist Film Council, the first leftist group in the United Kingdom that systematically used 16mm. Messel asked local groups to submit footage of the oppression of labor. He edited this material into several films, including *What the News Reel Does Not Show* (1933), which juxtaposed footage of the Soviet First Five-Year Plan with scenes in London slums.

In 1934, another socialist group, the Workers' Theatre Movement, formed Kino (Russian for "cinema"), a production-distribution firm that concentrated on 16mm films and distributed Soviet films. Also in 1934, the Workers' Film and Photo League was established to coordinate the activities of leftist film groups. (Following its American prototype, the league soon eliminated the word *Workers* from its name.) Ivor Montagu, one of the main founders of the Film Society in 1925, established the Progressive Film Institute to make documentaries and distribute more Soviet films.

Most films produced by these groups during the 1930s were made by leftist sympathizers who were not themselves members of the working class. One exception was Alf Garrard, a carpenter and amateur filmmaker. After a successful strike by his union, he received support from the Film and Photo League to secretly film scenes of actual construction work and combine them with restaged scenes of the strike enacted by his fellow workers (**14.10**). The film was intended to promote unionism. Dozens of other films of this era documented unemployment, marches, strikes, and other aspects of labor's struggle.

The middle of the decade saw a shift in British political filmmaking. In 1935, the international Communisty party changed its policy. Rather than concentrating on class struggle, it encouraged leftists around the world to oppose the spread of fascism. Partly as a result, during the second half of the 1930s, European groups reacted to two civil wars, in Spain and China. British leftists were to play an important role in documenting the progress of the former. The beginning of World War II caused a severe decline in socialist filmmaking activity in Britain.

International Leftist Filmmaking in the Late 1930s

The Spanish Civil War began in 1936, when Fascist leader Francisco Franco instigated an insurrection against the elected Republican government. Whereas Hitler and Mussolini both backed Franco, the United States, Britain, and France withheld aid. Only the USSR helped those loyal to the Spanish government. This uneven conflict led thousands of volunteers to rally to the Spanish Republican cause either to fight or to succor victims of the war.

Filmmakers supported the cause. Russian cinematographer Roman Karmen shot newsreel footage, which Esfir Shub later edited into a compilation feature, *Spain* (1939). The American leftist production firm Frontier made *Heart of Spain* (1937), shot on the spot and edited in New York by Paul Strand and Leo Hurwitz. Ivor Montagu's Progressive Film Institute made a 16mm civil war film, *The Defense of Madrid* (1936; **14.11**), which Montagu shot in the Spanish capital while it was under

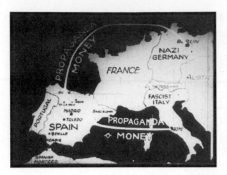

14.11 Montagu's *The Defense of Madrid* used a common convention of newsreels, an animated map. Here, it shows the flow of "propaganda money" among countries that supported Franco's Fascist attacks against the Republican government.

14.12 A shot in *Spanish Earth* juxtaposes defensive barbed wire with more traditional sights of Madrid.

14.13 In *The Four Hundred Million*, Ivens suggests the vast, bleak beauty of China.

attack. Kino distributed *The Defense of Madrid* and raised £6000 for Spanish relief.

After *Borinage* and other films in the early 1930s, Joris Ivens was prominent enough that important leftist writers and artists brought him to the United States. His first assignment was *Spanish Earth* (1937), on the civil war, written and narrated by Ernest Hemingway. Ivens emphasized the juxtaposition of ordinary events—women sweeping a street, men planting a vineyard—with the destruction of war (**14.12**). American composers Virgil Thomson and Marc Blitzstein arranged a score from Spanish folk songs. President and Mrs. Roosevelt viewed and approved the film, but its circulation was limited mainly to film clubs.

The Chinese civil war received less attention, primarily because little was known in the outside world about Mao Zedong's attempt to overthrow Chiang Kai-shek's government—a struggle that had been going on since the 1920s. In 1937, American Harry Dunham managed to reach Mao's forces in their stronghold in Yenan and record events there. The resulting footage was edited in the United States at Frontier Films by Jay Leyda and Sidney Meyers and released as *China Strikes Back* (1937). This film introduced Mao to much of the world. One result was that Joseph Stalin for the first time took Mao seriously as a Communist revolutionary leader. Consequently, cinematographer Roman Karmen, who had filmed the Spanish Civil War, went to China and made a Russian feature documentary, *In China* (1941).

Ever interested in revolutionary struggles, Joris Ivens also went to China, but the official government prevented him from journeying to Mao's stronghold. With American backing, Ivens made *The Four Hundred Million* (1938)—named for China's population at that time.

Unable to show the civil war, Ivens concentrated on the country's struggle against the Japanese invasion and on its vast landscapes (**14.13**). The Maoist revolution would continue to fascinate Ivens, and five decades later he would make his final film in China.

Aside from these major conflicts, oppressed groups around the world attracted the attention of leftist filmmakers. In 1934, for example, the radical administration of Mexican President Lázar Cárdenas financed *The Wave*. Scripted and photographed by Paul Strand and directed by the young Austrian Fred Zinneman, *The Wave* dealt with Indian fishermen who try to resist unfair exploitation by local buyers. Although it was a fiction film,

14.14 Fishermen work on their nets while discussing their plight in *The Wave.*

14.15 By showing a cabin threatened by soil erosion, *The River* suggested the need for government action.

it used nonactors and documentary-style filming to emphasize the reality of the social injustice portrayed (**14.14**). Leftists films became less common during the 1940s, as World War II claimed filmmakers' attention.

GOVERNMENT- AND CORPORATE-SPONSORED DOCUMENTARIES

The United States

After Franklin Roosevelt's inauguration as President in early 1933, the American government sought to alleviate the problems relating to the Depression. As a result, some filmmakers who had started in the early 1930s as members of the leftist Film and Photo Leagues moved into government-sponsored documentary filmmaking.

In the mid-1930s, the Resettlement Administration wanted to disseminate information on the dust bowl, the southern plains states whose drought conditions contributed to the Depression. Pare Lorentz, a young intellectual interested in politics, had never made a film, but he was given a $6,000 budget to make *The Plow That Broke the Plains* (1936). Convinced of the socially beneficial uses of cinema, he wanted to show *The Plow* as a short in commercial-film programs. He hired Ralph Steiner, Paul Strand, and Leo Hurwitz, all members of the New York Film and Photo League, as cinematographers. The group found themselves up against the Hollywood establishment, which regarded their work as government-supported competition. Just finding a firm willing to sell them raw film stock was difficult. No distributor would release *The Plow That Broke the Plains*. A major selling point was achieved when prominent composer Virgil Thomson agreed to write a score for the film, drawing on folk songs.

Despite running over budget, the film proved a success. The manager of New York's Rialto Theater scheduled it and publicized it widely, resulting in bookings at thousands of theaters nationwide. This triumph and

White House approval led to a higher budget for Lorentz's next film, *The River* (1937), photographed by Willard Van Dyke and again provided with a rousing score by Thomson. The filmmakers demonstrated how logging had led to massive erosion in the Mississippi valley (**14.15**). A flood forced them to extend the shooting schedule but the dramatic footage supported arguments for the benefits of the government's Tennessee Valley Authority dam program. After Lorentz's previous triumph, Paramount distributed *The River,* and it also proved widely popular.

Roosevelt admired *The River* and had the U.S. Film Service formed to make films for various government agencies. Lorentz, as head of this service, began to assemble a group of filmmakers to work on several projects. Joris Ivens, for example, was brought in to make *Power and the Land* for the Rural Electrification Agency. Lorentz, however, proved to have little administrative ability, and the service was dissolved in 1940. Its projects were turned over to individual government bodies, so *Power and the Land* (1941) was finally completed by the Rural Electrification Agency. Soon, with the beginning of the war, the military would make some documentaries, while others were commissioned from Hollywood firms.

Some of the filmmakers who worked in the Film and Photo Leagues and for the U.S. government were able to find institutional sponsorship to make significant documentaries. For example, the American Institute of Planners commissioned *The City* for the 1939 New York World's Fair. This film was directed by Ralph

14.16 *The City* emphasizes urban congestion in a sequence of outbound weekenders inching along a road, ironically accompanied by jaunty Aaron Copland music.

14.17 *Drifters* deemphasized the scientific and economic side of British fisheries, stressing the dynamism and dignity of the workers' labor.

Steiner and Willard Van Dyke, from an outline by Pare Lorentz. Again music played a key role, with Aaron Copland composing the score.

The City resembled government documentaries, particularly *The River,* in its presentation of a problem (overcrowded cities) followed by a solution (rebuilding through city planning). Humorous vignettes caught by concealed cameras, combined with fast pace, yielded entertainment value as well as informational content. In one celebrated scene, an automated café serves food to lunch-hour customers as if they were on an assembly line. Other scenes emphasize traffic and congestion (**14.16**). Sponsorship of documentaries by institutions and corporations would become increasingly important in succeeding decades.

Great Britain

While the American government's sponsorship of documentaries was short-lived, in the United Kingdom a major national filmmaking body was built up during the early 1930s. It produced so many classic documentaries that for years historians focused a great deal of attention on this realist streak of British cinema, often to the exclusion of other, more entertainment-oriented filmmaking.

This burgeoning of the documentary mode resulted largely from the efforts of Scottish-born John Grierson. Educated in the United States during the 1920s, Grierson was impressed by how powerfully American cinema and advertising shaped mass audiences' responses.

He deplored, however, the way Hollywood cinema missed its opportunity to combine entertainment with education. And Grierson admired the Soviet cinema, not simply for its artistic innovations but also because the government had sponsored films designed to affect viewers intellectually; he helped prepare the version of *Potemkin* released in the United States. He also strongly approved of Robert Flaherty's tactic of locating corporate funding outside the commercial-film industry for *Nanook of the North* (sponsored by a fur company). At the same time, he thought Flaherty was too fascinated by primitive cultures and too little concerned with influencing modern society.

Grierson returned to Britain in 1927 and encountered a sympathetic supporter in Sir Stephen Tallents, head of the Empire Marketing Board, a government institution charged with promoting British products around the world. Tallents arranged financing to allow Grierson to make a documentary on herring fisheries (supposedly because a key official in the Treasury was an expert on the herring industry). The result was a short feature, *Drifters,* released in 1929. Grierson's interest in Soviet Montage cinema was apparent: he cut quickly among parts of the fishing boats, and his images presented ordinary work as heroic (**14.17**).

British exhibitors were not keen on showing documentaries, so *Drifters* premiered at the Film Society, on a program with *Potemkin.* Its favorable press coverage led to bookings in many commercial theaters. Still, throughout the 1930s, Grierson and his colleagues

ROBERT FLAHERTY: *MAN OF ARAN* AND THE "ROMANTIC DOCUMENTARY"

After the commercial failure of *Moana* in the mid-1920s, Robert Flaherty had briefly collaborated with F. W. Murnau on *Tabu* (p. 161). After withdrawing from that project, he was at loose ends when Grierson asked him to join the Empire Marketing Board's film unit.

Flaherty embarked upon a film on British industries, shooting in factories and mines. He proved too undisciplined for government filmmaking, but some of his voluminous footage formed the basis for *Industrial Britain* (1933), one of the few successes enjoyed by Grierson's Empire Marketing Board unit.

By 1931, Flaherty had conceived a project on the bleak, remote Aran Islands off the west coast of Ireland. Michael Balcon, head of Gaumont-British, Britain's largest film company, agreed to fund a feature. Flaherty and his crew spent years hunting out local people to play roles. Flaherty emphasized the tireless efforts of the Arans' inhabitants to compost seaweed and grow crops on rocky land and to fish among gigantic waves; this drama was embodied in the story of a couple and their young son.

Flaherty also added a scene of the islanders harpooning huge basking sharks from open boats, even though such hunts had ceased long before the current inhabitants had been born. (He had similarly resurrected an obsolete tattoo ritual in *Moana*.) He had harpoons constructed, based on antiques, and the islanders learned how to execute the dangerous shark hunt. Flaherty's insistence on such suspense yielded some dramatic scenes. In particular, there is a haunting moment when the young boy Mikeleen climbs down the cliffs to the water's edge and finds himself looking down into the maw of a huge shark (**14.18, 14.19**).

Man of Aran finally premiered in 1934 and did well, both with critics and audiences. It was picked as best film at the Venice Film Festival. Yet it also stirred up considerable controversy. Many documentarists thought it was escapist fiction. Leftists, including some connected with the Film and Photo League, attacked it for failing to deal with the social situation of the islanders, including their exploitative absentee landlords. Despite his reservations about Flaherty, Grierson defended the film:

> It is of course reasonable for later generations of film-makers to want a documentary tougher, more complex, colder and more classical, than the romantic documentary of Flaherty. It is fitting that it should want a documentary in which both material and theme are found in our own social organization and not in literary idyll. But there are considerations one must watch carefully. The first one is that Flaherty was born an explorer, and that is where his talent is. . . .
>
> Not half-a-dozen commercial films in the year can compare with *Man of Aran* in simple feeling and splendid movement. I am all for congratulating Flaherty on pushing the commercial film brilliantly to its limit. I am all for commending his fortitude in yet another sickening encounter with commercialism.[2]

Nevertheless, *Man of Aran* led to a break between Grierson and Flaherty. Flaherty, unable to find work, returned to the United States, where he would make *The Land* (1942) and *Louisiana Story* (1948).

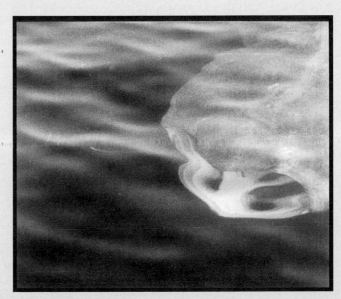

14.18, 14.19   Flaherty used the traditional continuity editing technique of shot/reverse shot to create an unexpected encounter between a young boy and a giant shark in *Man of Aran*.

14.20, *left* The train in *Night Mail*, with accompanying narration: "This is the night mail crossing the border / Bringing the check and the postal order / Letters for the rich, letters for the poor / The shop at the corner and the girl next door."

14.21, *right* Crude location lighting and a direct interview approach emphasize the stark reality of a working-class woman's situation in *Housing Problems*.

faced resistance to commercial screenings of their films, and Grierson increasingly stressed distribution of 16mm prints to schools and educational groups.

In 1930, the Empire Marketing Board hired Grierson to form a permanent film unit. He recruited a number of young, mostly liberal filmmakers, including Paul Rotha, one of the founding members of the Film Society and later the author of an influential early book on the subject, *Documentary Film* (1935). This group tried to foster a positive image of the working class. Most were, however, inexperienced and learned cinematic technique on the job. They shot short, silent films that usually received limited distribution. Many were simply advertisements shown in railway stations. In 1931, attempting to vitalize the board's film unit, Grierson hired Robert Flaherty (see box).

In 1933, before the Empire Marketing Board could turn to more ambitious films, it was dissolved. Tallents moved over to handle public relations for the General Post Office (GPO), a large government institution that oversaw many areas of communications, including radio and early television. Tallents took Grierson and his circle with him, and they became the GPO Film Unit. This unit eventually included several people who would be among the country's most important documentarists: Basil Wright, Arthur Elton, Edgar Anstey, Harry Watt, Alberto Cavalcani, and Stuart Legg.

The GPO Film Unit was prolific. Many of its films were simple didactic works distributed mainly to schools. In some cases, where a more poetic or dramatic approach was taken, the films had wider theatrical circulation. One of the most popular was *Night Mail* (1936, Basil Wright and Harry Watt). Its subject was simple: a typical journey of the daily overnight train from London to Glasgow. Its form, however, was complex and lyrical. A promising young composer, Benjamin Britten, contributed the score, while W. H. Auden wrote a poetic voice-over commentary. A wide variety

of shots moved from such mundane details as a farmer receiving his newspaper to distant views situating the train in the grandeur of the British countryside (**14.20**).

Grierson also sought backing from industry, and the GPO Film Unit's staff made several classic documentaries on diverse subjects. Production of tea in British colonies in India and Ceylon was an important industry, and, in 1934, Basil Wright directed *Song of Ceylon* for the Ceylon Tea Propaganda Board. This film deals only briefly with the tea trade, concentrating instead on the beauties of Ceylonese culture, both past and present. Indeed, the impressive images and dense sound track hint that modern commerce is an intrusion on this society.

In 1935, Arthur Elton and Edgar Anstey directed a different kind of sponsored film. The Gas, Light and Coke Company commissioned *Housing Problems* in hopes of promoting the use of gas heat and light in modern housing. Elton and Anstey responded by experimenting with direct recording of sound on location to interview working-class people in their own grim apartments. This interview approach has since become pervasive in both documentary films and television. Though the subjects apparently were previously interviewed and are repeating their memorized statements for the camera, the effect of real people describing their problems remains poignant (**14.21**). At the end, interviews with satisfied people who have natural gas in their homes suggest that public utilities can improve living standards. Nevertheless, the effect of the earlier interviews with the slum dwellers lingers and creates a pervasive tone of social criticism.

This emphasis on private sponsorship led to a major shift in the GPO Film Unit. Arthur Elton left to form the country's most important corporate film unit, for Shell Oil. Stuart Legg and Basil Wright each set up an independent production firm to make films for commercial sponsors. Grierson himself quit the unit in 1937, creating a firm to match sponsors with filmmakers; in 1939 he went to Canada, where he was instrumental in founding the National Film Board.

Grierson was replaced as head of the GPO Film Unit by Alberto Cavalcanti, the Brazilian-born filmmaker who had helped establish the city-symphony genre in the 1920s with *Rien que les heures* (p. 181). His main film for the GPO was *Coal Face* (1936), a documentary on the coal industry that made use of a complex sound track with a rhythmic commentary and music by Britten. Cavalcanti and the other remaining staff moved away from Grierson's fierce independence and concentration on an educational approach. Under Cavalcanti, the unit produced films that drew more upon the narrative techniques of commercial cinema, as in *North Sea* (1938, Harry Watt). Influenced by Flaherty, the group employed reenactments of events.

In 1940, the GPO Film Unit was absorbed by the Ministry of Information. World War II was in its early stages, and soon the unit became central to wartime documentary filmmaking.

WARTIME DOCUMENTARIES

The beginning of World War II abruptly changed the status of documentary filmmaking. Leftist filmmakers who had criticized capitalist governments recognized the necessity for switching to a position supporting the battle against fascism. Military establishments within the warring countries called on professional filmmakers, and major directors previously associated primarily with fiction films switched to documentaries. Documentaries became far more popular. In those days before television news, families who had members in the military or who were directly endangered could witness wartime events at their local theaters, in newsreels and documentaries.

Hollywood Directors and the War

The United States stayed out of the escalating European conflict until December 7, 1941, when the Japanese launched an unprovoked, devastating attack on the American naval base at Pearl Harbor, Hawaii. Germany declared war on the United States a few days later, and global conflict became inevitable.

The U.S. government called directly upon the Hollywood establishment to make films supporting the war effort. Immediately after Pearl Harbor and the German declaration, the Pentagon asked the prominent Columbia director Frank Capra to make a series of propaganda films. These were to explain to American soldiers and

14.22 In *The Battle of Britain,* animation turns the map of Europe into a Nazi whale about to devour the United Kingdom.

sailors why their country was in the war and why they were obliged to help foreign countries in the fight against Germany, Italy, Japan, and other members of the Axis. It was especially necessary to explain America's new alliance with the USSR, which had previously been portrayed as a threat to the American public.

Capra himself entered the military as a major. He recalled watching Leni Riefenstahl's *Triumph of the Will* and deciding that the best way to motivate soldiers to fight was by drawing upon existing films that portrayed the enemy's power. He created a series called "Why We Fight," based primarily on footage captured from German and other enemy sources, combined with material from the Allies. The directors he supervised compiled this footage, explaining military strategies through animated maps supplied by the Disney studio. A forceful narrator told the audience exactly what to think about the images (**14.22**). The series consisted of seven films: *Prelude to War* (1942), *The Nazis Strike* (1942), *Divide and Conquer* (1943), *The Battle of Britain* (1943), *The Battle of Russia* (1943), *The Battle of China* (1944), and *War Comes to America* (1945). Major Hollywood figures like actor Walter Huston (as narrator) and composer Alfred Newman worked anonymously on some of the films. The series was required viewing for military recruits, but some of the films were also shown publicly.

Other Hollywood directors soon entered the service, recording aspects of the war in powerful documentary films. John Ford joined the Navy as the chief of the Field Photographic Branch. Since military intelligence anticipated the Japanese attack on Midway Island, Ford and his cameraman were there to record this turning point in the war. Using 16mm cameras, they captured the attack and American response, including a memorable shot of the American flag being hoisted amid the turmoil of battle. Ford edited this footage with shots of actors speaking the sentiments of archetypal American people, he also used traditional folk music on the sound track. The result was a paean to American strength, *The Battle*

14.23, *left*   Lightweight 16mm cameras carried during bombing runs created spectacular aerial footage for *Memphis Belle*, including this shot of a plane's tail against the squadron's vapor trails.

14.24, *right*   In *Let There Be Light*, the camera lingers on the jubilant face of a traumatized soldier who has regained his voice under treatment; his therapist is glimpsed in the left foreground.

of Midway (1942, coproduced by 20th Century-Fox and the Navy). Ford was later decorated for wounds received during the attack, and *The Battle of Midway* garnered an Oscar as best documentary.

William Wyler served in the Air Force, where he supervised *Memphis Belle* (1944), a film on bombing runs over Germany (**14.23**). John Huston had established his reputation as a director of fiction films early in the war with *The Maltese Falcon*. He made two exceptionally candid films during the war. In *San Pietro* (generally known as *The Battle of San Pietro*, 1944), he was assigned to show why the Allied advance through Italy was taking so long. He used footage taken by frontline camera operators as the troops moved through Italian villages. The film came close to being banned because Huston juxtaposed soldiers' voices with shots of their body bags. After some revision, the film was released.

Huston ran up against further censorship problems with his next project, *Let There Be Light*. The military initially delegated him to make a film about the rehabilitation of victims of shell shock. Employing direct sound, Huston shot extensive candid interviews with traumatized soldiers undergoing therapy. This film was virtually unprecedented in using unrehearsed, direct recording of people's responses to offscreen questions (**14.24**). *Let There Be Light* captured the soldiers' illnesses so effectively that it was banned by the U.S. government and thus had no influence on the subsequent development of documentary filmmaking. It did not become available to the public until the 1970s. Nevertheless, it anticipated the documentaries of the Direct Cinema era, and especially the "unbiased" approach of Frederick Wiseman (see Chapter 24).

Great Britain

As a result of Germany's invasion of Britain's allies in eastern Europe, primarily Poland and Czechoslovakia, Britain declared war on Germany on September 3, 1939. Just under a year later, on August 13, 1940, the

Germans launched a bombing campaign against Britain, known as the Battle of Britain or the Blitz. Bombers targeted civilian areas as well as military sites, and thousands of Londoners regularly slept on the platforms of Underground stations. Many citizens were killed, and there was massive destruction in the southern and eastern areas of England. Within months, the Britishers' determined resistance led the Nazi military to turn more of its attention to the USSR.

The British documentary cinema contributed to the united front against the Nazi attack. Some films were made by units within the military services. The Army and the Royal Air Force coproduced *Desert Victory* (1943, Roy Boulting), a feature-length account of one of the turning points of the war, the North African campaign and defeat of the Germans at El Alamein. Dozens of camera operators exposed their film in the desert (**14.25**), often in the thick of battle. Stock footage, maps, and staged footage were also used, yielding a clear, dramatic account of the campaign. Rapid editing enhanced the intensity of the battle scenes. *Desert Victory* was popular in many countries, even winning an Oscar as best documentary in the United States.

As soon as the war began, the GPO Film Unit had become the Crown Film Unit, dedicated to making war-related films. Some members of the unit were documentarists who had worked under John Grierson—Harry Watt, for example, who directed *Target for Tonight* (1941), showing a typical bombing raid over Germany. Virtually all the action, from the establishment of the home base and personnel to the return of the planes, is staged; the opening emphasizes, however, that "each part is played by the actual man or woman who does the job." The action goes beyond simple exposition of information, drawing upon conventions of fictional war films. Little touches lend human interest, as when a pilot misplaces his helmet. Similarly, *Target for Tonight*'s bombing unit was a mixture of nationalities (**14.26**). Perhaps in part because of these "fictional" aspects, the film was enormously popular.

14.25 Prime Minister and Minister of Defence Winston Churchill flashes his familiar "V for Victory" sign while visiting the troops in *Desert Victory*.

14.26 An American soldier and a Scot, both members of the bombing team in *Target for Tonight*.

One crucial documentarist came to the fore during this period. Humphrey Jennings, an artist and a poet, had been acting, editing, and scripting for the GPO Film Unit since 1934. He had directed a significant film, *Spare Time* (1939), on Britain's leisure activities. Along with his close collaborator, editor Stewart McAllister, Jennings devised a style that lyrically evokes the lives of ordinary British citizens. The pair frequently cut together shots taken in different locales, but the sound from one locale would continue uninterrupted. The counterpoint invites the viewer to see the connections among events.

Jennings's approach proved suited to depicting the home front once war broke out. Rather than celebrating the dramatic glories of combat, he concentrated on the quiet resilience of the British public. With Watt and Pat Jackson, Jennings made *The First Days* (1939), on London's preparations for the inevitable bombing. The title of *London Can Take It!* (1940, also codirected with Watt), on the Blitz, suggests the determined mood that Jennings captured in his wartime films.

Listen to Britain (1942, codirected with Stewart McAllister) reflects the pair's fascination with sound. Using only music and sound effects, they moved freely among everyday routines continuing incongruously during the reminders of war. A scene inside the National Gallery, for example, shows a concert against a backdrop of empty frames whose paintings have been removed for safekeeping. The concert music continues over views outside the hall, including a girl sitting reading while a barrage balloon floats overhead. As the scene shifts to a factory, the music gives way to loud clanging as a tank is assembled. In other parts of the film, popular songs span a range of shots in different places.

14.27 Staged action in *Fires Were Started* allowed Jennings to cut among details of the firefighting, such as this close shot of two men on a roof.

In 1943, Jennings made a feature documentary, *Fires Were Started,* on the role of the National Fire Service in putting out blazes started by German incendiary bombs during the Blitz. The film was completely staged, using a small group of characters to lend human interest to the story. Jennings portrayed them fighting fires and off-duty—playing pool, drinking beer, listening to music. For the fire scenes, several bombed-out buildings were set ablaze so that Jennings could set up careful compositions and get enough footage to edit scenes in the style of a fiction film (**14.27**). Despite all this manipulation of events, actual firefighters from the Blitz considered the film highly authentic.

Just as Jennings had captured the home front during the war, he meditated on the approaching postwar era in *A Diary for Timothy* (1945). The narration, written by E. M. Forster, addresses a baby born on the fifth anniversary of Britain's entry into the war, attempting to tell him not simply what went on but why the war was fought (**14.28**). The film juxtaposes scenes of the young Timothy along with scenes of wartime events, such as John Gielgud rehearsing *Hamlet* and police coping with a bomb. *A Diary for Timothy* attempted to convey the

14.28 Children walk through the rubble of war as the narrator addresses Timothy: "When you joined us we'd been fighting for exactly five years. We've hated it, but we've kept on at it to save our skins. And also we had a feeling, deep down inside us, that we were fighting for you. For you and all the other babies."

14.29 Walter Ruttman put his flair for abstract images to work for the Nazis in *Deutsche Waffenschmieden* ("German Armaments," 1940), as in this shot of a factory worker inspecting the interior of a new gun barrel.

14.30, *left* The *Deutsche Wochenschau* depicted the hardships of German troops operating during the winter on the Russian-Ukrainian front, as in this shot of an airplane taking off amid heaps of snow and ice.

14.31, *right* In *The Fight for Our Soviet Ukraine,* Dovzhenko used his familiar flower motif, here juxtaposed with real destruction wrought by the Germans (compare with 12.8).

experiences of wartime to the young generation who had to build a new society.

Jennings made a few films after the war's end, but they failed to recapture the poignancy and optimism that had made him the foremost documentarist of the war. He died in an accident while scouting locations in 1950. The Crown Film Unit itself was abolished in 1952, though its alumni continued to work prominently in sponsored documentaries after the war.

Germany and the USSR

Overtly propagandistic films made up a relatively small proportion of German production during the Nazi era (pp. 272–275). Most programs included newsreels and documentary short films, however, and these consistently contained Nazi propaganda. As in other countries, established filmmakers sometimes worked on these. For example, Walter Ruttmann, who had created experi-

mental and documentary films in the 1920s, made a few shorts (**14.29**). In 1940, there were four newsreel series, and these were merged into one, the *Deutsche Wochenschau* ("German Weekly"), under Goebbels's control.

During the early years of the war, theater attendance rose because viewers wanted news from the front. Initially, newsreels portrayed the obstacles German soldiers encountered and overcame abroad (**14.30**); death and suffering were never shown. After the disastrous German defeat at Stalingrad in 1943, however, many spectators dismissed newsreels as mere window dressing. The *Deutsche Wochenschau* became pure agitation in favor of total war, stressing the fearsomeness of the enemy.

Soviet documentaries took a different approach, stressing the suffering and destruction caused by the German invaders. As the war progressed, filmmakers could also inspire the public with genuinely heroic victories. The counterattack against the Fascist forces was shown vividly in *Defeat of the German Armies Near Moscow*

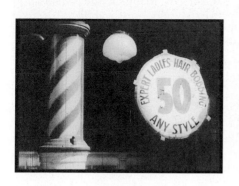

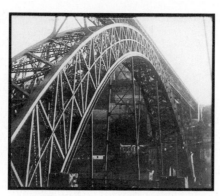

14.32, *left*   *A Bronx Morning* celebrates the charm of ordinary city life.

14.33, *right*   *Douro, Faina Fluvial* returns repeatedly to shots of this dramatic bridge from many angles.

(1942, Leonid Varlamov and Ilya Kopalin; seen in the United States as *Moscow Strikes Back*, it won an Academy Award). *Stalingrad* (1943, Varlamov) depicted the yearlong siege that proved to be the turning point in the war. Alexander Dovzhenko spent the war supervising documentary production, including the heartfelt *The Fight For Our Soviet Ukraine* (1943, Yulia Solntseva and Y. Avdeyenko; **14.31**).

After World War II, documentary films were less frequently seen in theaters. Techniques that had been invented for military cinematography, however, were to affect fiction filmmaking. Also, because documentaries had accustomed audiences to seeing real events depicted in film programs, in some cases a greater realism emerged in entertainment films.

THE INTERNATIONAL EXPERIMENTAL CINEMA

After the heyday of avant-garde cinema in the 1920s, the 1930s was a period of decline. The greater expense of sound production discouraged some filmmakers from experimentation. Some moved toward documentary, often of a political nature. Official policy under the Nazi regime forbade "decadent" modernist styles in the arts, and most German filmmakers either went into exile (as when Hans Richter moved to the United States) or cooperated with the new regime (as we have just seen with Walter Ruttmann).

Nevertheless, experiment did not disappear entirely. Avant-garde narratives and lyrical films, such as the city symphony, remained popular, especially for newcomers to film. The influence of Surrealism lingered, and independent animation saw a resurgence. During the war, the United States and Canada became centers of alternative cinema, both for émigrés and for a new generation of filmmakers.

Experimental Narratives and Lyrical and Abstract Films

During the late 1920s and early 1930s, a small support system for amateur experimental filmmaking developed in the United States. Amateur filmmaking clubs proliferated, and the availability of 16mm film stock made production cheaper. Art cinemas and ciné-clubs rented and showed experimental films. The Film and Photo Leagues distributed some experimental films, along with their leftist films, and the Amateur Cinema League provided another outlet. Some filmmakers rented out their own work through the mail.

Experimental narrative films took many directions. In 1931, Austrian émigré Charles Vidor made *The Spy*, an adaptation of Ambrose Bierce's short story "An Occurrence at Owl Creek Bridge." A man condemned to hang seems to escape, and the long chase culminates in the discovery that the escape was only a hallucination just before his death. Vidor went into the Hollywood industry, where he directed many feature films.

The city symphony was a favorite genre for those working on slim budgets. Aspiring New York photographer and filmmaker Jay Leyda created *A Bronx Morning* (1931). This poetic documentary weaves together simple motifs of actions caught in the streets as shops open and people come outdoors to socialize (**14.32**). The film's photography and editing won Leyda a place at the National Film School in the USSR, where he studied with Sergei Eisenstein and assisted him in the abortive *Bezhin Meadow* project (p. 264). In Portugal, Manoel de Oliveira filmed *Douro, Faina Fluvial* ("Douro, River Work," 1931) at the mouth of the Douro River. Oliveira used the subject as a pretext to experiment with editing dynamic compositions (**14.33**). Although he made only a few films over the next decades, much later Oliveira became a prolific director of features.

Herman Weinberg was a movie enthusiast who worked at an early art theater and wrote reviews. He made experimental short films, the only surviving exam-

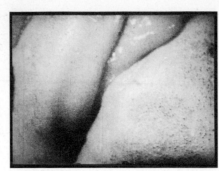

14.34, *left* Many shots in *Autumn Fire* show cityscapes and the countryside without the characters.

14.35, *right* Abstraction through framing in *Geography of the Body*.

ple of which is *Autumn Fire* (1931). It combines lyrical documentary with a slim narrative thread, cutting between estranged lovers: a woman in rural settings and a man in the city (**14.34**). Weinberg went on to a career as a film critic and historian.

The lyrical film could also move into abstraction. One of the most daring films of the war period was the 16mm *Geography of the Body* (1943), by Willard Maas and Marie Menken. Through extreme close-ups, a man's body becomes a sensuous, abstract landscape of hills and crevices (**14.35**).

Surrealism

In 1930, the French poet and artist Jean Cocteau shot his first film, *Blood of a Poet* (released in 1932). His financing came from a rich nobleman, the Vicomte de Noailles (who also backed Luis Buñuel and Salvador Dali's *L'Age d'or* in 1930). *Blood of a Poet* established the dream and psychodrama genres as central to experimental cinema. Cocteau's film was intensely personal, drawing on motifs, like a lyre and a muse figure, that appeared in his poetry and drawings. Developing upon the dreamlike narrative of *Un Chien andalou* (p. 179), Cocteau made his hero an artist whose statue comes to life and sends him through a mirror into a mysterious corridor. Behind its doors he sees bizarre scenes symbolically connected to his art (**14.36**).

After *Un Chien andalou* and *L'Age d'or,* Luis Buñuel spent part of 1930 in Hollywood, hired by MGM as an "observer" to learn filmmaking method. (With dubbing not yet practical, American studios needed Spanish-language directors.) His intractable attitude lost him the job, and he spent the next few years in France, helping dub Hollywood films into Spanish. He also became interested in making a documentary on Las Hurdes, an isolated, extremely primitive area in Spain. With a tiny budget provided by an interested teacher, Buñuel made *Las Hurdes* (aka *Land without Bread*, 1932), emphasizing the region's

stultifying poverty and disease. The catalogue of misery, presented in the dispassionate manner of a travelogue, created an eerie echo of the Surrealism of Buñuel's earlier work (**14.37**). Two decades later, he remarked, "I made *Las Hurdes* because I had a Surrealist vision and because I was interested in the problem of man. I saw reality in a different manner from the way I'd seen it before Surrealism."[3] The film was shot silent and shown in that form privately in 1933. The Spanish government banned it, however, on the grounds that it presented the country in a negative light. In 1937, it was finally released in France, with the music and narrator heard in modern prints.

After this, Buñuel worked as an editor and codirector on several Spanish films and then went back to the United States early in the 1940s, where he did odd filmmaking jobs. His career as a director of feature films did not blossom until after the war.

Another, very different Surrealist completed one film during this era. Self-taught American artist Joseph Cornell had begun painting in the early 1930s, but he quickly became known chiefly for his evocative assemblages of found objects inside glass-sided display boxes. Mixing antique toys, maps, movie-magazine clippings, and other emphemeral items mostly scavenged from New York secondhand shops, these assemblages created an air of mystery and nostalgia. Although Cornell led an isolated life in Queens, he was fascinated by ballet, music, and cinema. He loved all types of films, from Carl Dreyer's *The Passion of Joan of Arc* to B movies, and he amassed a collection of 16mm prints.

In 1936, he completed *Rose Hobart*, a compilation film that combines clips from scientific documentaries with reedited footage from an exotic Universal thriller, *East of Borneo* (1931). The fiction footage centers around *East of Borneo*'s lead actress, Rose Hobart. Cornell avoided giving more than a hint as to what the original plot, with its cheap jungle settings and sinister turbaned villain, might have involved. Instead, he concentrated on repetitions of gestures by the actress, edited together from

14.36 In *Blood of a Poet,* the artist sees a painting with a living head and arm.

14.37 *Las Hurdes* shows victims of genetic defects resulting from inbreeding, one of the chronic problems in the remote Spanish region.

different scenes; on abrupt mismatches; and especially on Hobart's reactions to items cut in from other films, which she seems to "see" through false eyeline matches. In one pair of shots, for example, she stares fascinatedly at a slow-motion view of a falling drop creating ripples in a pool (**Color Plates 14.1, 14.2**). Cornell specified that his film be shown at silent speed (sixteen frames per second instead of the usual twenty-four) and through a purple filter; it was to be accompanied by Brazilian popular music. (Modern prints are tinted purple and have the proper music.)

Rose Hobart seems to have had a single screening in 1936, in a New York gallery program of old films treated as "Goofy Newsreels." Its poor reception dissuaded Cornell from showing it again for more than twenty years. He continued to edit together films—mostly instructional shorts and home movies—in rough form. In the 1960s, he gave these to experimental filmmaker Larry Jordan, who completed some of them as *Cotillion, The Children's Party,* and *The Midnight Party* (1940? to 1968). Many other scraps of films remain unfinished, though Cornell continued his work in painting and assemblage pieces until his death in 1972.

Although relatively few Surrealist films were made during this era, this approach has had an intermittent influence on the cinema ever since.

Animation

Some of the most significant experimental films of the 1930s employed animation techniques. This was partly because animated films required relatively little expenditure for sets, actors, and other necessities of live-action fiction filmmaking. Instead, with a camera, a few simple materials, and a great deal of patience, a single filmmaker or a small group could create richly imaginative works. Moreover, the stylization of animation made it suitable for advertising films, so some artists could support themselves by making both ads and more personal projects.

Most European animators continued to avoid traditional cel animation, perhaps because they associated it with Hollywood commercialism. Instead, they devised ingenious alternative means of creating motion frame by frame.

One of the most dedicated individualists of this period was Berthold Bartosch, a Czech artist who had made animated educational films in Vienna and Berlin during the years just after World War I. He had also assisted Lotte Reiniger on *The Adventures of Prince Achmed,* which gave him skill in shooting layers of translucent material to create land, sky, and sea effects (see 8.18). In 1930, the publishing house of Kurt Wolff (which had discovered Franz Kafka in the 1920s) commissioned Bartosch to make a film based on a book of socialist woodcuts by Frans Masereel. Bartosch set up an animation stand in the Parisian art cinema Théâtre du Vieux-Colombier. Using black-tinted glass, smears of soap, and other materials, over the next two years he created *The Idea* (1932). The film is an allegory of a worker's conception, personified as a nude woman, which he presents to his fellow workers but which is suppressed by corporate and social tyranny. Although the human figures are simple, stiff-jointed cut-outs, they move through atmospheric, subtly shaded cityscapes (**14.38**). Although Bartosch made a few ads over the next few decades, he never completed another major film.

Bartosch's film inspired two important animators to enter filmmaking. Russian-born Alexandre Alexeïeff had become a stage designer and book illustrator in Paris. After seeing *The Idea,* he tried to create the effect of engravings in motion pictures. Around 1934, he and

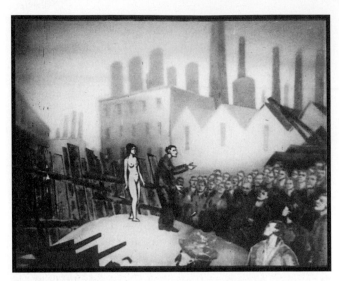

14.38 The hero of *The Idea* speaks to factory workers of his idea. The film was shot on a transparent table with light from below.

his American partner Claire Parker (they married in 1941) invented an animation technique they called the "pinboard." It consisted of a frame around a stretched fabric in which were embedded half a million double-pointed pins. By pushing pins in different areas of the board to various heights and lighting them from the side, Alexeïeff and Parker could create images in shades of gray. Moving some of the pins between each frame generated images textured in ways that no other type of animation could duplicate.

They quickly achieved a masterpiece, *Night on Bald Mountain* (1934), which they set to a tone poem, *Walpurgisnacht,* by Modest Mussorgsky. In keeping with the subject matter of Mussorgsky's work, Alexeïeff and Parker animated a series of weird mutating images (**14.39, 14.40**) that fly toward and away from the camera with dizzying speed. The film was well received by critics and film-society audiences, but the pair had to

turn to advertising films to make a living. These short films, made by animating objects one frame at a time, are today considered classics. Alexeïeff and Parker made one other pinboard film during this period, a charming two-minute piece called *En passant* ("In Passing," 1943), to illustrate a French-Canadian folk song. It was produced by the National Film Board of Canada, after the two had fled the war in France and were living in the United States.

Abstract animation survived into the 1930s. In Germany, Oskar Fischinger attempted to link moving shapes to music. Supporting his small company primarily by doing advertising, Fischinger explored the possibilities of color in abstract animation. For example, *Circles* (1933) was made for an ad agency. The first color film made in Europe, the three-minute short delivered the brief message "Toliras reaches all [social] circles." The bulk of the film consisted of complex patterns of circles rotating and pulsating to music (**Color Plate 14.3**). By 1935, Fischinger was making cigarette and toothpaste commercials while completing *Composition in Blue*, in which three-dimensional objects cavort in an abstract blue space.

Fischinger realized he could not remain in Nazi Germany and moved to Los Angeles. There he was able to make a few animated films, including one short produced by MGM, *An Optical Poem* (1937). It was fairly well received as a novelty, but the animation unit of MGM was not sympathetic to Fischinger's approach. He worked briefly at the Disney studio, and a few touches in the design of *Fantasia* and *Pinocchio* have been attributed to him. Still, most of his work in America was carried on with little support. His most important film after his move to America, however, *Motion Painting No. 1* (1947), was funded by the Guggenheim Foundation. It consists of a single lengthy "shot," lasting roughly ten minutes, of the frame-by-frame brush strokes of a painting gone mad, building up to a whole composition, then

14.39, 14.40 Faces swirling in a void transmute into each other quickly and frighteningly in *A Night on Bald Mountain.*

another composition on top of the first, and so on. Six layers of transparent Plexiglas were successively laid on top of the first to achieve the effect—which Fischinger created in the camera for months on end—without developing it to see if his technique was working. The result, timed to one of Bach's *Brandenburg Concertos,* is a dazzling exercise in continuous extension of lines of color. After the late 1940s, Fischinger could find no financial support, and he turned to abstract painting.

The other major experimenter in abstract animation who had begun work during the silent era was Len Lye. After *Tusalava* in 1929 (p. 177), he tried to make similar films but found no backing. He began painting directly on film. Eventually Grierson's GPO Film Unit assisted Lye by financing his projects or finding backers for him. Like Fischinger, he explored the possibilities of the new color processes that were becoming available in the mid-1930s. *Colour Box* (1935) animated jittery shapes to dance music. It was very popular and influenced the Disney animators who worked on *Fantasia.* In *Rainbow Dance* (1936), Lye took live-action images originally shot on black-and-white stock and manipulated the layers of the color film-stock emulsion to produce extraordinarily vibrant solid hues (**Color Plate 14.4**). The film's only reference to the Post Office, its financial backer, came at the end with the slogan "A Post Office Savings Bank puts a pot of gold at the end of the rainbow for you." Beginning in the late 1930s, when sponsorship declined, Lye directed imaginative documentaries for the GPO Film Unit, such as *When the Pie Was Opened* (1941), a modest short film about making rationed food palatable.

In the United States, painter Mary Ellen Bute began making abstract animated films in the 1930s. Like Fischinger, she used familiar pieces of music and created moving shapes that synchronized to the changes in the tune. Her first films, like *Synchrony No. 2* (1935) and *Parabola* (1937) were in black and white, but with *Escape* (1937), she introduced color (**Color Plate 14.5**) An astute businesswoman, Bute managed to distribute her films directly to ordinary commercial cinemas that ran them as cartoons before the feature. She continued to make occasional shorts until the 1960s.

Several West Coast filmmakers worked in abstract animation. John and James Whitney's *Five Film Exercises* (completed 1944) employed sound tracks consisting of synthesized music (well before the advent of electronic music). The painter Harry Smith explored the *batik* technique, which applied layers of paint to 35mm film strips and controlled the pattern by means of tape or wax. In some of Smith's early abstractions, textured patches

14.41   The animated skeletons of a bird and a fish try to take the hero's hard-won orange in *The Mascot.*

sketchily fill in the constantly changing shapes, while speckles of color overlay the design (**Color Plate 14.6**).

While others were exploring the resources of pictorial animation, the world's foremost puppet animator, Ladislav Starevicz, who had begun in Russia (p. 53) and emigrated to Paris after the Russian Revolution, continued his unique animation style. One of his longest works, *The Mascot* (1934), mixes live action and puppets in a story of a poor seamstress who crafts stuffed toys to support her sick daughter. Some of these come to life, and the protagonist, a toy dog, sets off in search of an orange for the child. Among his many adventures, the dog encounters various grotesque figures at an inn (**14.41**). This scene displays Starevicz's expertise at moving many characters at once and in giving them mobile, expressive faces. Starevicz continued making occasional animated films in Paris until his death in 1965.

The economic and political turmoil of the years from 1930 to 1945 helped foster the documentary cinema, especially that made by leftist filmmakers. After World War II ended, the cold war would create a less receptive atmosphere for such films, and leftists would often face an uphill struggle or outright censorship.

During the 1930s and early 1940s, experimental filmmakers had often worked in near isolation and with little financial support. Their situation improved somewhat, however, after 1945, with the spread of specialized art cinemas, the growth of international film festivals, and new grant support for filmmaking. We shall examine these trends in Chapter 21.

REFERENCES

1. Quoted in Vlada Petric, "Soviet Revolutionary Films in America (1926–1935)" (unpublished dissertation, New York University, 1973), p. 443.
2. Quoted in Paul Rotha, *Robert J. Flaherty: A Biography,* ed. Jay Ruby (Philadelphia: University of Pennsylvania Press, 1983), p. 153.
3. Quoted in Francisco Aranda, *Luis Buñuel: A Critical Biography,* tr. and ed. David Robinson (New York: Da Capo Press, 1976), pp. 90–91.

FURTHER READING

Brecht, Bertolt. *Brecht on Film and Radio.* Trans. and ed. Marc Silberman. London: Methuen, 2000.

Campbell, Russell. *Cinema Strikes Back: Radical Filmmaking in the United States 1930–1942.* Ann Arbor, UMI Research Press, 1982.

Crunow, Wystan, and Roger Horerocks, eds. *Figures of Motion: Len Lye's Selected Writings.* Auckland: Auckland University Press, 1984.

Evans, Gary. *John Grierson and the National Film Board: The Politics of Wartime Propaganda.* Toronto: University of Toronto Press, 1984.

Hodgkinson, Anthony W., and Rodney E. Sheratsky. *Humphrey Jennings: More Than a Maker of Films.* Hanover, NH: University Press of New England, 1982.

Hogencamp, Bert. *Deadly Parallels: Film and the Left in Britain 1929–39.* London: Lawrence and Wishart, 1986.

Kuhn, Annette. "*Desert Victory* and the People's War" *Screen* 22, no. 2 (1981): 45–68.

Macpherson, Don, ed. *Traditions of Independence: British Cinema in the Thirties.* London: British Film Institute, 1980.

Moritz, William. "The Films of Oskar Fischinger." *Film Culture* 58/59/60 (1974): 37–188.

Sitney, P. Adams. "The Cinematic Gaze of Joseph Cornell." In Kynastan McShine, ed., *Joseph Cornell.* New York: Museum of Modern Art, 1980.

Swann, Paul. *The British Documentary Film Movement, 1926–1946.* Cambridge, England: Cambridge University Press, 1989.

FOUR

THE POSTWAR ERA: 1945–1960s

W orld War II created profound changes in many countries and in the balance of power internationally. Europe, Japan, the USSR, and the Far East suffered immense damage during the war, and rebuilding required will and money. The United States, however, had sustained no substantial damages within its own borders after the Pearl Harbor attack; and war spending had ended the Depression and generated a new prosperity that lasted into the postwar years. These circumstances allowed the United States to assist many countries in their reconstruction efforts.

Great political shifts took place whose aftereffects would play out during the rest of the century. The USSR took control of several eastern European countries, dividing that continent with what Winston Churchill dubbed the Iron Curtain. The long struggle between the communist countries within the Soviet sphere and the American-European alliance, organized as the North Atlantic Treaty Organization (NATO) in 1949, dominated international relations until the end of the 1980s. The conflict came to be known as the cold war, since it involved mutual deterrence through the stockpiling of nuclear weapons rather than actual combat.

Another change that would have great consequences involved Jewish refugees' search for a homeland following the horrors of the Holocaust. They moved into Palestine and, in 1948, declared the formation of the state of Israel. After a short war, in 1949 the partition of Jerusalem led to the divided territory that is still being contested.

During the decades following the war, especially the 1950s, many Asian and African countries shed their status as colonies. The Philippines declared its independence from the United States in 1946. The following year, India and Pakistan became separate dominions within the British Commonwealth. And between 1957 and 1962, over two dozen sub-Saharan African countries gained their independence.

Elsewhere, the Chinese civil war resumed and resulted in the revolution of 1949, bringing to power the Communist regime that still rules the country. American occupation helped shape the recoveries of the defeated states of Germany and Japan. Such events could hardly fail to alter the international cinema scene in fundamental ways.

In many of the major film-producing countries, the years after the war saw attendance reach an all-time high. But eventually—soon in the United States, by the end of the 1950s in most European countries—patronage slackened disastrously. The United States pioneered new means of wooing audiences back with color, widescreen, and "bigger," more distinctive pictures, but the golden age of the vertically integrated studio system came to an end (Chapter 15).

The United States was not alone in postwar prosperity. Most European economies recovered quickly, allowing many national cinemas' rise to world prominence. Governments stepped up protection of domestic cinemas, arguing that film was a key representative of national culture. From Europe came a vastly influential film movement—Italian Neorealism—and a self-consciously artistic cinema that borrowed extensively from trends in modernism in the other arts (Chapters 16 and 17). Japanese cinema won international acclaim during the same years (Chapter 18).

The USSR and its eastern European satellites continued to sustain state-controlled production, although countries experimented with degrees of decentralization. Filmmakers from Poland, Czechoslovakia, and Hungary achieved fame in the postwar era. Intermittent thaws in official Soviet policy allowed directors greater latitude. A similar rhythm of freedom and constraint was found in Mao's China (Chapter 18).

Elsewhere, Third World film industries were increasing in power. India led the way in output, while Argentina, Brazil, and Mexico were also major producers. All of these industries produced significant genres and directors (Chapter 18).

The new films of Europe, the Soviet bloc, Latin America and Asia were made more visible through international film trade and accompanying institutions such as coproduction arrangements and festivals. The circulation of these films, along with their roots in artistic traditions, encouraged critics and filmgoers to treat cinema as the art of the director. This new frame of reference, which took the filmmaker as *auteur* ("author"), had profound effects on how films were made and consumed in the postwar era (Chapter 19).

Near the end of the 1950s, a new generation of filmmakers surged to prominence all over the world. Energized by the *auteur* idea of personal expression, they created "new waves" and "young cinemas" that were formally experimental and thematically challenging (Chapter 20).

The art cinema and new waves operated within the commercial film industry, but marginal filmmaking practices continued to offer alternatives. Both documentary and experimental filmmakers sought to express their personal visions in their works, and they pioneered technologies and artistic strategies that influenced mainstream fictional cinema (Chapter 21).

As we saw in previous chapters, the cinema began as an international phenomenon, with films from the main early producing nations circulating freely. During the 1910s and 1920s, distinctive national styles and even movements within nations arose. The development of national cinemas was encouraged by the isolationism practiced by many countries during the Depression, by the rise of authoritarian states whose governments discouraged imports, and by the animosities of the war period.

In the half-century following World War II, however, we can see a move back to an international cinema. Many factors contributed to this phenomenon. Film production became more thoroughly worldwide as smaller nations expanded or commenced film production. This was particularly true in several former colonies. The growth of art cinema, sustained by film criticism and film festivals, allowed films with artistic or cultural interest to circulate more widely. And, resistance to the continued domination of world markets by Hollywood encouraged smaller countries to try coproducing as a competitive tactic. As we shall see in Part 5, these trends accelerated in the last decades of the twentieth century, when the formation of large multinational corporations, the rise of video formats, and the building of many more theaters further encouraged the globalization of the cinema.

CHAPTER 15

AMERICAN CINEMA IN THE POSTWAR ERA, 1945–1960

The United States came out of World War II a prosperous country. Workers had earned good money in military industries but had had little chance to spend it. Returning troops rejoined their spouses or married, ready to set up households and buy consumer goods. The birthrate, increasing during the war, skyrocketed, and the new generation was tagged the "baby boom."

The United States took on the role of a world superpower, helping its allies and former enemies. At the same time, the USSR struggled to assert its authority. President Truman adopted a policy of "containment," trying to counter Soviet influence throughout the world. From 1950 to 1952, the United States fought alongside South Korean troops against the Communist North in an indecisive civil war. The United States and the USSR jockeyed for influence over nonaligned nations. The cold war between the United States and the USSR would last for almost fifty years.

The sense of communist encroachment around the world led to an era of political suspicion in the United States. During the late 1940s, intelligence agencies investigated individuals suspected of spying or subversion. A congressional committee delved into communist infiltration of government and business, and under President Dwight Eisenhower (1953–1961) a cold war policy held sway.

Yet, even as the U.S. government sought to present a united front against communism, American society seemed to fracture into distinct demographic segments. One powerful group was composed of teenagers, who had money to buy cars, records, clothes, and movie tickets. As teenage crime rose, the image of the 'juvenile delinquent' emerged as well. Other social groups also gained prominence. The civil rights movement accelerated, primarily under the guidance of pacifist Martin Luther

King, Jr. In 1954, the Supreme Court decision in the case of *Brown v. Board of Education* took a step toward ending legal discrimination by mandating school desegregation.

1946–1948

During the three years immediately after the war's end, Hollywood experienced pivotal high points and low points. It was a time of transition into a period of decline for the studio system, though no one could have predicted that in 1946. The burst of consumer spending after wartime austerity aided ticket sales, and the year set a box-office record: over $1.5 billion in admissions—a figure that, adjusted for inflation, remains the record. Every week, between 80 and 90 million people went to movies, well over half the total population of 140 million. (In 2001, each week, about 25 million people, out of a population of over 280 million, went to the movies.)

Nonetheless, despite promising box-office figures, Hollywood firms confronted serious problems over the next two years. In 1947, anticommunist investigations by the U.S. government targeted numerous studio personnel, and a legal decision that would help change the very structure of the industry was handed down in 1948.

The HUAC Hearings: The Cold War Reaches Hollywood

During the 1930s, many Hollywood intellectuals had been sympathetic to Soviet communism; some had even joined the American Communist party. Their left-wing leanings had been reinforced during World War II, when the Soviet Union was one of America's allies in the battle against the Axis. America's move toward a staunch anticommunist policy after the war placed many of these leftists in a compromised position. For years the FBI had compiled information on communists or sympathizers in the Hollywood community. By 1947, Congress was investigating communist activities in the United States as part of the nationwide search by the House Un-American Activities Committee (HUAC) for purportedly subversive elements in government and private life.

In May 1947, a number of individuals—among them the actor Adolphe Menjou and the director Leo McCarey—declared in secret interviews with congressional representatives that they were willing to name

Hollywood people with communist ties. In September, Republican J. Parnell Thomas chaired a HUAC hearing that set out to prove that the Screen Writers' Guild was dominated by communists. Forty-three witnesses were subpoenaed.

The "friendly" witnesses, led off by Jack Warner of Warner Bros., labeled several screenwriters communists. Gary Cooper, Ronald Reagan, Robert Taylor, and other stars expressed concern over leftist content in scripts. The "unfriendly" witnesses, most of them screenwriters, were seldom allowed to state their views. Most avoided denying that they had been communists, stressing instead that the First Amendment guaranteed them freedom of expression in their work. Ten who testified were cited for contempt of Congress and briefly jailed. German leftist Bertolt Brecht, who had been working in Hollywood during the war and who had never belonged to any communist party, gave a neutral response and immediately left for East Germany.

Vociferous public protest led Congress to suspend the hearings for four years. The ten unfriendly witnesses who had testified, however, found their careers collapsing as producers blacklisted them. Most of the "Hollywood Ten"—scriptwriters John Howard Lawson, Dalton Trumbo, Albert Maltz, Alvah Bessie, Samuel Ornitz, Herbert Biberman, Ring Lardner, Jr., and Lester Cole; director Edward Dmytryk; and producer Adrian Scott—were unable to work openly in the film industry. Dmytryk later cooperated with HUAC and returned to the Hollywood fold.

The 1947 HUAC hearings concentrated on showing that the subject matter of Hollywood films had been tainted by communist ideas—hence the emphasis on screenwriters. In 1951, the committee resumed its hearings, this time aiming to expose all allegedly communist personnel. Many former communists or sympathizers saved themselves by naming others. Actors Sterling Hayden and Edward G. Robinson and directors Edward Dmytryk and Elia Kazan were among this group. People who were named but who refused to cooperate, such as actress Gale Sondergaard, found themselves on a new blacklist.

Some of the blacklisted filmmakers saved their careers by going abroad. Director Joseph Losey moved to England and Jules Dassin to France. Others worked under pseudonyms. Dalton Trumbo wrote the script for *The Brave One*, which won him an Oscar—under a false name—in 1956. In 1960, Otto Preminger declared that he would give Trumbo screen credit for the script of *Exodus*, and producer Kirk Douglas did the same for

Trumbo's contribution to *Spartacus* (1960). From that point, the blacklist slowly crumbled. Only about one-tenth of its victims, however, were able to resume their film careers. The HUAC hearings had left a legacy of distrust and wasted talent. The resentment felt toward those who had given names during the hearings lingered for decades, resurfacing when Kazan was given a lifetime-achievement Oscar in 2000.

The Paramount Decision

As we saw in Chapters 3 and 7, from 1912 on, the Hollywood studios had expanded to create an oligopoly. Working together, the firms controlled the industry. The largest firms were vertically integrated—making films, distributing them, and showing them in their own theater chains. They benefited from this guaranteed outlet for their products and from a fairly predictable income. The smaller companies also benefited, since their films could fill in the free time in these theaters. The big firms could block-book whole packages of films to theaters they did not own, letting the bigger-budget, star-studded items carry the weaker pictures. In such circumstances, those few big pictures counted for much more than the program pictures—especially the B pictures. During the sound era, the eight main Hollywood firms had continued to keep any competitor from entering the film business.

Almost from the beginning, the U.S. government had investigated this situation. In 1938, the Justice Department initiated a suit, *United States v. Paramount Pictures, Inc. et al.*, usually called the "Paramount case." The government accused the Big Five (Paramount, Warner Bros., Loew's/MGM, 20th Century-Fox, and RKO), and the Little Three (Universal, Columbia, and United Artists), of violating antitrust laws by colluding to monopolize the film business. The Big Five owned theater chains, block-booked films, and used other unfair means to keep independent films out of the big first-run houses. Although the Little Three did not own theaters, they were accused of cooperating to exclude other firms from the market.

After a complex series of decisions, appeals, and legal maneuvers, the U.S. Supreme Court handed down a decision in 1948 declaring that the eight companies had been guilty of monopolistic practices. The Court ordered the Majors to divest themselves of their theater chains. It also directed the eight Hollywood firms to end block booking and other practices that hampered independent exhibitors. To avoid further litigation, the Hollywood companies filed a series of consent decrees, agreements that set up compromises with the Court. Over the next decade, all eight moved to comply with the Court's orders. The Big Five remained production-distribution companies but sold off their theater chains.

Some obvious benefits resulted from the industry's new policy and its resulting increase in competition. With block booking outlawed, exhibitors were free to fill part or all of their programs with independent films. With this new access to exhibitors, independent producers multiplied. Stars and directors broke away to start their own companies. Between 1946 and 1956, the annual number of independent films more than doubled, to about 150. United Artists, which existed solely to distribute independent films, released 50 a year.

The production wing of the industry had been protected the most by the lack of competition in the pre-1948 era. The "Paramount decision's" ban on block booking meant that a producer could no longer count on a few strong films to carry the rest. Every film had to appeal to exhibitors on its own. As a result, studios concentrated on fewer but more expensive films. With access to larger theaters, the small studios could compete better by making bigger-budget films. Among these were Universal's Technicolor biopic *The Glenn Miller Story* (1954, Anthony Mann) and Columbia's all-star *From Here to Eternity* (1953, Fred Zinnemann).

Distribution was still dominated by the eight main companies. Independent producers could not afford to start large distribution circuits with offices in cities around the country. With so little competition among distributors, almost all the independent firms had to distribute their films through the eight established companies. By the mid-1950s, all these big firms, except Universal, had many independent productions on their annual release schedules.

In exhibition, independent theaters, which had previously depended on cheap films from small firms, had access to a wider range of films (though competition from television soon drove many out of business). At the same time, they also had to compete with each other for the smaller pool of films being released. Local theaters continued to cooperate among themselves, however, by keeping a geographic separation within a city and limiting the number of theaters in which the same film could play. As such, theaters historically have not had to compete strongly for moviegoers' business—a fact reflected by today's uniform admission prices among theaters in most towns.

Thus, despite all these changes, the Majors and Minors continued to dominate distribution—the most powerful and lucrative wing of the industry—and to reap the bulk of box-office receipts.

THE DECLINE OF THE HOLLYWOOD STUDIO SYSTEM

Just as Hollywood was enjoying the high box-office receipts of 1946, its international market was also expanding. Late in the war, the studios turned the foreign department of the Motion Picture Producers and Distributors of America (MPPDA) into a new trade organization, the Motion Picture Export Association of America (MPEAA). The MPEAA was responsible for coordinating American exports, negotiating prices, and making sure that Hollywood firms presented a united front abroad. The government, seeing cinema as propaganda for American democracy, assisted film export through Commerce Department initiatives and diplomatic pressures.

Many countries passed protectionist laws, establishing quotas, production subsidies, and restrictions on exporting currency. The benefits were ambivalent at best. In 1947, Britain imposed a tax on imported films, and the MPEAA responded by announcing that the Majors would no longer offer new films to the country. The boycott succeeded: after eight months, the British government repealed the duty and permitted more film revenues to be remitted to the United States. Elsewhere, protectionist action often strengthened American domination. U.S. firms could export currency indirectly by investing in foreign films and importing them to the United States. Alternatively, Hollywood could spend "frozen funds" in shooting films abroad. These *runaway productions* also avoided the high cost of U.S. labor.

While some countries struggled to rebuild their industries domestically, Hollywood came to rely more on exporting its product. Before the war, about one-third of U.S. box-office income had come from abroad, but by the mid-1960s the figure had risen to around half—a proportion that has been constant ever since.

After 1946, however, Hollywood's domestic fortunes began to sag. Attendance steadily shrank, from about 98 million viewers per week in 1946 to about 47 million in 1957. About 4,000 theaters closed during that decade. Output and profits fell. One of the Big Five, RKO, passed through several owners, including Howard Hughes, before ceasing production in 1957. What ended the golden age of the studios, begun so auspiciously during the 1910s?

After the war, the film industry faced a dramatic challenge. As people adopted new lifestyles, leisure-time activities—primarily television—profoundly changed Americans' moviegoing habits.

Changing Lifestyles and Competing Entertainment

During the 1910s and 1920s, theaters had been built near mass-transportation lines in downtown neighborhoods, where they were easily accessible to local residents and commuters alike. After the war, many Americans had enough money saved up to purchase homes and cars. Suburban housing sprang up, and many people now traveled by car to the city center. With small children, however, they had little inclination to make the long trip into town for a film. Thus, changing demographics contributed to the late-1940s slump in moviegoing.

Initially, families stayed home and listened to the radio. Within a few years they were watching television. Americans owned 32 million sets in 1954, and by the end of the decade, 90 percent of homes had television. The suburban lifestyle and broadcast entertainment, along with growth in other leisure activities (such as sports and recorded music), made the film industry's profits plunge by 74 percent between 1947 and 1957.

When suburban couples did decide to go out to the movies, they tended to be more selective than moviegoers in the past. Rather than attending a local theater regularly, they would choose an "important" film—one based on a famous literary work or distinguished by its stars or displaying lavish production values. As the elimination of block booking pushed producers to make higher-budget films, they concentrated on projects that would cater to the more selective moviegoer.

Wider and More Colorful Movies   The television image of the early 1950s was small, indistinct, and black-and-white. Film producers attempted to draw spectators out of their living rooms and back into theaters by changing the look and sound of their movies.

Color filmmaking was an obvious way to differentiate moves from television, and, during the early 1950s, the proportion of Hollywood color films jumped from 20 to 50 percent. Many employed Technicolor, the elaborate three-strip, dye-transfer process perfected in the 1930s (pp. 220–221). Technicolor's monopoly, however, led independent producers to complain that the studios got preferential access. A court agreed, and in 1950 Technicolor was obliged to offer its services more widely. In this same year, however, Eastman introduced a *monopack* (single-strip) color film. Eastman Color could be exposed in any camera and was easy to develop. The simplicity of Eastman's monopack emulsion helped increase the number of films shot in color. Technicolor ceased to be a camera stock in 1955, but the firm continued to prepare release prints in its imbibition process until 1975.

Eastman Color lacked Technicolor's rich saturation, transparent shadows, and detailed textures. (**Color Plate 15.1** is an example of late-1940s Technicolor.) Still, many cinematographers believed that the monopack stock looked better in the widescreen dimensions of the day. Unfortunately, Eastman Color images tended to fade—especially if the footage was hastily processed. By the early 1970s, many prints and negatives had turned a puttyish pink or a sickly crimson (**Color Plate 15.2**).

Nonetheless, at the time, color films provided an appeal that television could not match. So did bigger images. Between 1952 and 1955, many widescreen processes were introduced—or rather revived, since all had been tinkered with in the early sound era.

Cinerama, a three-projector system that created a multipaneled image, premiered in 1952. *This Is Cinerama* was a travelogue in which the audience was treated to a roller-coaster ride, a plane flight through the Grand Canyon, and other thrills. The film played at a single New York theater for over two years at unusually high admission prices, grossing nearly $5 million.

Less elaborate was CinemaScope, introduced by 20th Century-Fox and first displayed in *The Robe* (1953). 'Scope became one of the most popular widescreen systems because it utilized conventional 35mm film and fairly simple optics. Virtually all studios adopted 'Scope; only Paramount clung to its own system, VistaVision, introduced in *White Christmas* (1954). Later, there came processes involving 70mm film (see box for more details on these).

After 1954, most Hollywood films were designed to be shown in some format wider than 1.37:1. Hollywood continued to shoot many films in the Academy sound ratio, but the projectionist had to mask the projector aperture to create a wide image in the theater. In order to compete with America, major foreign industries developed their own anamorphic widescreen systems including Sovscope (the USSR), Dyaliscope (France), Shawscope (Hong Kong), and TohoScope (Japan).

Wider images required bigger screens, brighter projection, and modifications in theater design. Producers also demanded magnetically reproduced stereophonic sound. During the early 1950s, Hollywood studios gradually converted from the optical sound recording introduced in the late 1920s to magnetic sound recording, using ¼-inch audiotape or magnetically coated 35mm film. These innovations permitted engineers to enhance widescreen presentations with multiple-channel sound.

Cinerama used six channels, while CinemaScope used four. But the extra expense, and a conviction that audiences paid more attention to the image than to the sound, kept most exhibitors from installing magnetic projector heads and multichannel sound systems. Although films' music, dialogue, and sound effects were recorded magnetically during production, most release prints encoded the sound information on optical tracks.

Other innovations of the period were transitory fads. Stereoscopic, or "3-D," films had been toyed with since the beginning of cinema, but the process made a reappearance during the postwar recession years. *Bwana Devil* (1952) employed Natural Vision, a system that required two strips of film to be shown one atop the other. The viewer wore polarized glasses that merged the two images into a sensation of depth. *Bwana Devil* attracted large audiences, and all the major studios undertook 3-D projects, the most noteworthy being *House of Wax, Kiss Me Kate* (both 1953), and *Dial M for Murder* (1954). By 1954, however, the craze was over. Even more short-lived was the effort to add odors to films. In 1958, Aromo-Rama and Smell-O-Vision appeared, to largely negative response. Both stereoscope and olfactory processes have been revived occasionally, always as a novelty.

Hollywood Adjusts to Television

Television posed a threat to certain staple products of theaters' programs. Newsreels, for instance, were largely abandoned after television news proved more efficient and immediate. Animated films were edged out more slowly; for two decades after the war, film programs still included short cartoons, and the major animators continued to create works of comic imagination and technical finesse. At MGM, Tex Avery's manic frenzy worked at full heat in *King-Sized Canary* (1947; **Color Plate 15.3**) and *The Magical Maestro* (1952), while William Hanna and Joseph Barbera made the "Tom and Jerry" series perhaps the most bloodthirsty films coming out of Hollywood.

The Warner Bros. cartoon unit became, if anything, even more bizarrely inventive than it had been during the war. Bob Clampett's *The Great Piggy Bank Robbery* (1946) takes Daffy Duck at a breakneck pace through a surrealistic parody of film noir. Chuck Jones, who had begun as a head animator at Warners in the late 1930s, reached the top of his form, combining Wagnerian opera and Bugs Bunny illogic in *What's Opera, Doc?* (1957). He introduced the "Road Runner" series with *Fast and Furryous* (1949; **Color Plate 15.4**) and continued to direct its unpredictable variations on violence until his

SEE IT ON THE BIG SCREEN

Before 1954, American films were almost always shot and shown in a trim rectangle at the proportions of 1.37:1. (The arrival of sound had led studios to modify the common silent ratio of 1.33:1.) The early 1950s' technical innovations drastically widened the image, creating new aesthetic problems and opportunities for filmmakers.

Several incompatible formats competed. Some utilized wider film gauges. Todd-AO, for example, replaced the usual 35mm width with 65mm; the finished film would measure 70mm in width, allowing 5 mm for stereophonic sound tracks. Todd-AO was framed at a 2:1 aspect ratio. Such Todd-AO features as *Oklahoma!* (1955) were released on 70mm prints (**15.1**). Paramount's VistaVision process still used 35mm film but ran it horizontally through the camera. Because the frames were oriented horizontally rather than vertically across the film strip, they could be wider than

35mm, and hence a greater negative area was exposed. When compressed and printed in the normal 35mm format for release, this rendered a rich, dense image.

Cinerama achieved a wider picture by combining separate images. Three adjacent camera lenses exposed three strips of film simultaneously. Theaters showed the film on three mechanically interlocked projectors, yielding a sprawling 2.85:1 image on a curved 146-degree screen (**15.2**). Projectionists faced the constant risk of a reel's breaking and

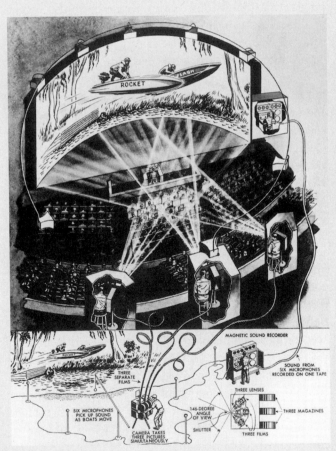

15.2 The Cinerama process (in publicity material).

15.1 Two "fish-eye" Todd-AO lenses, one center left and one on the boom above, were used to shoot *Oklahoma!;* a CinemaScope version was shot simultaneously. (The 'Scope camera is center right.)

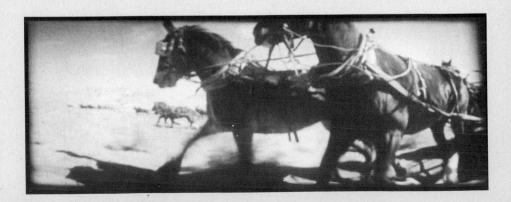

15.3 The curved Cinerama screen and its three panels made horizontal action bulge in perverse ways (*How the West Was Won*, 1963).

15.4   A publicity photograph displays not only Marilyn Monroe but also the "squeezing" and "unsqueezing" of the CinemaScope process (*How to Marry a Millionaire,* 1953).

falling out of synchronization with the others. In addition, odd images resulted from the *blend lines* separating the three panels (**15.3**).

The most popular widescreen system was Cinema-Scope, introduced by 20th Century-Fox in *The Robe* (1953). The CinemaScope camera was equipped with an anamorphic lens that took in a wide angle of view but squeezed it onto a strip of 35mm film. The film could be shown by attaching a comparable lens to the projector, which would unsqueeze the picture to create normal-looking images (**15.4**). CinemaScope was initially standard-ized at 2.55:1 (for magnetic sound) or 2.35:1 (for optical sound). Compared with most other widescreen systems, CinemaScope was inexpensive, technically simple, and fairly easy to use in shooting.

Some widescreen systems mixed these techiques. One process, displayed in the highly praised *Ben-Hur* (1959), combined anamorphic lenses with 65mm film to create im-ages in a 2.76:1 ratio. The process eventually came to be known as Ultra Panavision 70. The Panavision company's improvements in anamorphic optics, its lightweight 70mm cameras, and its sophisticated laboratory techniques for re-

ducing and blowing up different formats established it as the industry's leader in widescreen technology.

At first, Hollywood's creative personnel feared that the wide screen would immobilize the camera and lead to long takes. Some editors were afraid to cut quickly, worrying that viewers would not know where to look in a rapid se-ries of wide compositions. A few early widescreen films, such as *The Robe, Oklahoma!,* and *How to Marry a Mil-lionaire,* were rather theatrical, employing long-shot fram-ings, frontal staging, and simple cutting.

Almost immediately, however, directors applied classi-cal stylistic principles to widescreen composition. They ex-ploited lighting and focus to emphasize the main figures, and they used depth to guide the spectator's eye gracefully across the frame (**15.5**). Orthodox editing returned, com-plete with shot/reverse shots and analytical cuts (**15.6, 15.7**). Alternatively, directors who had already exploited long takes and depth compositions packed the wide frame with significant detail.

By the mid-1960s, three sorts of widescreen systems dominated U.S. production. Anamorphic 35mm was estab-lished at a ratio of 2.35:1, while nonanamorphic 35mm was

15.5   Directors soon learned to leave areas of the widescreen image open in order to guide the audience to the salient information (*Carmen Jones,* 1954).

SEE IT ON THE BIG SCREEN • • • • • • • • • • • • • • • • •

typically shown at 1.85:1. Most 70mm films were non-anamorphic and shown at a ratio of 2.2:1. Wider 70mm movies were usually blow-ups from anamorphic 35mm.

These widescreen systems would remain the principal options available for Hollywood filmmaking during the decades that followed.

15.6, 15.7 Shot/reverse shot in CinemaScope (*Heaven Knows, Mr. Allison*, 1957).

departure from the studio in 1961. During the 1950s, Jones also created several distinctive cartoons without the studio's stars. In *One Froggy Evening* 1955), a construction worker discovers a miraculous singing frog—which he attempts to exploit for money, until realizing that it sings only when alone with him (**Color Plate 15.5**).

Newer and smaller than the units at MGM and Warners was United Productions of America (UPA), formed in 1948 and releasing through Columbia. UPA cartoons placed their recurring characters, Mr. Magoo and Gerald McBoing Boing, in distinctive modernistic backgrounds. One of the founders of UPA, John Hubley, left to form his own company in 1952. Hubley and his wife, Faith, made such films as *Moonbird* (1960; **15.8**) in a decorative style that elaborated on the more spare UPA approach. UPA succumbed to the small screen in 1959, when it was sold and began making cartoons for television.

15.8 Sketchy, distorted figures against a semiabstract background in *Moonbird*.

11.1 *Henry V*

14.1 *Rose Hobart*

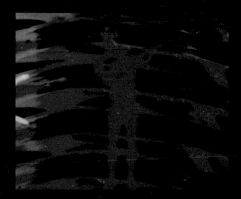

14.2 *Rose Hobart*

14.3 *Circles*

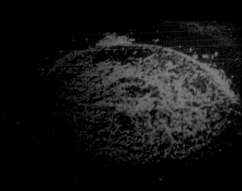

14.4 *Rainbow Dance*

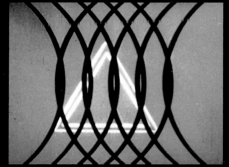

14.5 *Escape*

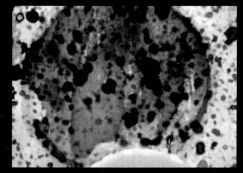

14.6 *Abstraction #2* (1939-46)

15.1 *Sinbad the Sailor* (1947)

15.2 *The Adventures of Robinson Crusoe* (1952)

15.3 *King-Sized Canary*

15.4 *Fast and Furry-ous*

15.5 *One Froggy Evening*

15.6 *Alice in Wonderland*

15.7 *Rio Bravo*

15.8 *Written on the Wind*

.9   *Imitation of Life*

15.10   *On the Town*

5.11   *The Searchers*

15.12   *Rear Window*

15.13   *Rear Window*

15.14   *Vertigo*

16 1   *The Damned*

16 2   *The Rise to Power of Louis XIV*

17.1 *The Golden Coach*

17.2 *Black Narcissus*

18.1 *An Autumn Afternoon*

18.2 *The Fall of Berlin*

18.3 *Liliomfi*

18.4 *Two Stage Sisters*

19.1 *Kagemusha*

9.2 *Amarcord*

19.3 *Red Desert*

9.4 *Red Desert*

19.5 *Lancelot du Lac*

9.6 *L'Argent*

20.1 *Contempt*

20.2 *For a Few Dollars More*

20.3 *Dracula (aka The Horror of Dracula, 1958)*

20.4 *Innocence Unprotected*

20.5 *How Tasty Was My Little Frenchman*

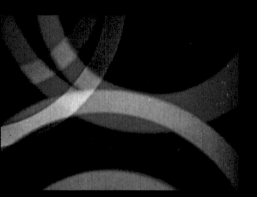

21.1 *No. 5* (1950, Harry Smith)

21.2 *The Long Bodies*

21.3 *Copycat*

21.4 *Blinkety Blank*

21.5 *Lapis* (1966, James Whitney)

21.6 *Allures* (1961, Jordan Belson)

21.7 *Bridges Go Round*

21.8 *Recreation*

21.9 *Fist Fight*

21.10 *The Hand*

21.11 *The Wonder Ring*

21.12 *Anticipation of the Night*

21.13 *The Riddle of Lumen*

21.14 *La Peau de chagrin* (1960, Vladimir Krist)

21.15 *Castro Street*

21.16 *Hold Me while I'm Naked*

21.17 *Chelsea Girls*

21.18 *Chelsea Girls*

22.1 *The Ladies' Man*

22.2 *Fritz the Cat*

Walt Disney continued to distribute his cartoons through RKO until 1953, when he formed his own distribution firm, Buena Vista. Although Disney continued to turn out short films, his most profitable works were his feature-length cartoons, introduced every few years and periodically re-released. These were often sanitized adaptations of children's classics, although *Alice in Wonderland* (1951; **Color Plate 15.6**) displayed a slapstick verve that was missing from more solemn undertakings such as *Cinderella* (1950) and *Sleeping Beauty* (1959). The studio returned to its tradition of combining live action and animation in the enormously successful *Mary Poppins* (1964).

By the mid-1960s, however, broadcast animation had captured the audience. The major studios virtually stopped producing animated shorts; MGM's last Tom and Jerry films (directed by Jones) were released in 1967, and Warner Bros. shut down its animation unit in 1969. Now Bugs, Daffy, Popeye, and their peers could be found on Saturday morning television, not in the local theater.

Yet, in other ways Hollywood accommodated itself to television. The movie industry moved rapidly to take advantage of its new competitor.

For one thing, the networks needed enormous quantities of programs to fill their broadcast hours. In the early 1950s, about one-third of broadcast material consisted of old films, mostly B pictures from Monogram, Republic, and other Poverty Row studios. In 1955, the bigger studios started selling the TV rights to their own libraries. In 1961, NBC launched the first weekly prime-time film series, "Saturday Night at the Movies," and, by 1968, there was a comparable film showcase on every weeknight. Rising fees for this programming made television sales a significant, predictable part of a film's income.

Moreover, the Hollywood studios started creating television shows. In 1949, Columbia converted its short-subject division, Screen Gems, to TV production. Among its products was the hit series "Father Knows Best" (1954–1962). When the networks moved from live broadcasting to showing filmed series in 1953, the demand for material intensified. Independent producers filled the need, as with "I Love Lucy," created by the Desilu company (which took over the RKO studio when that firm ceased production in 1957). As film production declined at the big studios, they generated income by renting out their production facilities for independent filmmaking, for both theatrical release and television broadcast.

Perhaps the shrewdest use of the new medium was made by Walt Disney. Disney adamantly refused to sell his cartoons to television, since their carefully paced theatrical rereleases would yield profits for the indefinite future. In 1954, Disney contracted with ABC to produce an hour-long weekly show, "Disneyland." The series became a hit, running for decades under several names. The show permitted Disney to publicize his theatrical films and his new theme park (opened in 1955). Disney filled his program with shorts and excerpts from the studio library. And, when one of his TV series struck a chord, as did the saga of Davy Crockett, a reedited version of the programs could be released as a profitable theatrical feature.

After the first few years, the Hollywood firms as corporations did not suffer from the competition with television. They simply adjusted by expanding their activities to encompass both entertainment media. The film-based component of the industry, however, did decline. In the 1930s, the Majors released close to 500 features annually, but by the early 1960s the average was under 150. Box-office receipts continued to fall until 1963, when television had effectively saturated the American market. After that, attendance rose a bit and leveled off at around a billion admissions per year. Still, it has never come close to the levels of the pre-TV era.

Art Cinemas and Drive-ins

Many producers responded to the decline in theater attendance by targeting specific segments of the population. Before the 1950s, most studio productions were intended for a family audience. Now films designed specifically for adults, children, or teenagers appeared more frequently.

Aiming at children and adolescents, Disney moved into live-action features with adventure classics (*Treasure Island*, 1950), adaptations of juvenile literature (*Old Yeller*, 1957), and fantasy-comedies (*The Absent-Minded Professor*, 1961). These low-cost films were routinely among each year's top grossers.

In the mid-1950s, the *teenpics* market opened in earnest, as viewers born during World War II began making their consumer strength felt at the box office. Rock-and-roll musicals, juvenile-delinquency films, and science-fiction and horror items attracted the teenage market, with exploitation companies like AIP leading the way (pp. 337–339). The major studios reacted with *clean-teen* comedies and romances featuring Pat Boone and a succession of Tammys and Gidgets. America's burgeoning youth culture, centered on dating, pop music, souped-up cars, and fast food, was soon exported around the world and shaping cinema in other countries.

The demographic-target tactic also created new kinds of exhibition. Although a few little theaters had specialized in showing foreign films since the 1920s, the art-house audience became a more significant force after World War II. With thousands of veterans going to college through the GI Bill, an older, educated audience emerged, many of whose members had traveled in Europe during the war and for whom art films held some appeal.

The film industry had economic reasons for importing more films. American films were flooding into countries whose production was debilitated, but many governments restricted the amount of funds that could be taken out. American companies had to invest their profits in the country or buy goods there for export. Buying the American distribution rights to foreign films proved one way of transferring profits legally.

Moreover, with U.S. production in decline, importing art films provided smaller theaters with low-cost product. Some independent exhibitors, faced with sagging attendance, found that they could fill their houses by booking foreign films and appealing to the local elite. Imported films were not broadcast on television, so these exhibitors suffered no competition.

As of 1950, there were fewer than 100 art theaters in the entire country, but, by the mid-1960s, there were over 600, most in cities or college towns. They were usually small, independent houses decorated in a modernist style calculated to appeal to an educated clientele. The lobbies often displayed art exhibits, and the refreshment counters were more likely to offer coffee and cake than soda and popcorn.

Some offbeat U.S. independent fare got circulation in art theaters, but the staple programming came from Europe. The flow of imports began directly after the war ended, with Roberto Rossellini's *Open City*, released in 1946, earning high grosses and helping to create an interest in films made abroad. Carl Dreyer's *Day of Wrath*, Marcel Carné's *Children of Paradise*, and Vittorio De Sica's *The Bicycle Thief* were among many that accustomed American audiences to reading subtitles. English films consistently dominated the import market. Michael Powell and Emeric Pressburger's *The Red Shoes* broke out of the art-cinema circuit to become one of the top-grossing films of 1948. During the 1950s, some imports, from countries with looser censorship controls, turned sex into an attraction at art cinemas. French director Roger Vadim's *And God Created Woman* (1957) made Brigitte Bardot a star in the United States. Quite often the "sophistication" of imported films owed more to daring subject matter than to complex form or profound themes.

Drive-in theaters presented another attractive alternative for exhibitors during a period of falling box-office receipts. The owner did not need an expensive building—only a screen, a speaker for each parking space, a concession stand, and a ticket booth. Farmland was relatively cheap, and the drive-in's typical location, just outside of town, made it handy for the new suburban population. Now people who seldom frequented the downtown theaters could easily go to the movies. Admission was also affordable, as films playing in drive-ins were often far past their first runs.

The first drive-in dated from 1933, but there were still only two dozen in the whole country in 1945. By 1956, more than 4,000 "ozoners" were operating. This figure was approximately equal to the number of "hard-top" theaters that closed during the postwar era. During the early 1950s, about one-quarter of box-office income came from drive-ins.

Drive-ins were not ideal venues for viewing. The tinny speakers yielded atrocious sound, rain would blur the picture, and cold weather required exhibitors to close down for the season or provide (feeble) heaters. But drive-ins proved successful with their target audiences. Despite the cheap tickets, most showed two or even three features. Parents could bring their children and avoid the cost of a baby-sitter. Since people could circulate during the film without clambering over their neighbors, concession stands did better business in drive-ins than in other theaters. Some drive-ins specialized in teenpics, and the prospect of sharing a dimly lit front seat for several hours brought many adolescent couples to the local "passion pit."

Challenges to Censorship

Exploitation movies, imported films, and independent producers' "adult" themes and subjects inevitably posed problems. Films were failing to win approval from local censorship boards. A turning point in regulation came when an Italian film, Roberto Rossellini's *The Miracle* (1948), was denied an exhibition permit by the New York Board of Censors on the grounds that it was blasphemous. It told the story of a retarded peasant woman who is convinced that her unborn child is the son of God. In 1952, the Supreme Court declared that films were covered by the First Amendment's guarantee of free speech. Later court decisions made it clear that films could be censored only on grounds of obscenity, and even that was narrowly and vaguely defined. Many local censorship boards were dissolved, and few films were banned.

The industry's own self-censorship mechanism, the Motion Picture Association of America (MPAA, formerly the Motion Picture Producers and Distributors of America), also faced problems enforcing its Production Code (pp. 216–217). The MPAA's main weapon for obliging distributors to submit their films for its approval was its rule that no theater belonging to the association would show a movie without a certificate of approval. Once the five Majors divested themselves of their theater chains, however, exhibitors were free to show unapproved films.

The Paramount decision also had the unintended effect of helping to liberalize the Code. The main Hollywood studios had used the requirement of a certificate of approval to keep independent films out of the market, since such films often had riskier subject matter than the mainstream product. Once theaters could show films without certificates, more independent films were exhibited. Inevitably, some of these went beyond what was acceptable under the Code.

Partly in response to this increased competition, the big producer-distributors also began transgressing the Code's boundaries. One way of competing with television, which had extremely strict censorship, was to make films with more daring subject matter. As a result, producers and distributors pushed the Code further and further. When the MPAA refused to approve the mildly risqué *The Moon Is Blue* (1953, Otto Preminger), United Artists released it nevertheless. Preminger was persistent in flaunting the Code, and UA also distributed his film about drug addiction, *The Man with the Golden Arm* (1955), without an MPAA certificate.

Gradually the MPAA softened its position and began awarding seals to films that seemingly violated the original 1934 Code. Billy Wilder's *Some Like It Hot* (1959) put Marilyn Monroe in a nearly transparent dress (decency being maintained only by a few strategically placed bits of embroidery and a shadow) and dealt lightheartedly with transvestism and implied bisexuality (see 15.32). It got a seal from the MPAA, even though the Catholic Legion of Decency nearly gave it a "condemned" rating. *Lolita* (Stanley Kubrick), which dealt with a man's affair with an underage girl, could never have been released in the 1930s or 1940s, but it received a seal in 1962. The Code was obviously outdated, and the stage was set for a switch to a system of rating films, instituted by the MPAA in the mid-1960s (see Chapter 22).

THE NEW POWER OF THE INDIVIDUAL FILM AND THE REVIVAL OF THE ROADSHOW

Before 1948, theater ownership and block booking had guaranteed the big studios that all their films would be exhibited. They planned their production schedules by the year, always making sure to include several special films that would appeal to exhibitors outside the big chains and lure them to book their whole season's films from that studio.

After the Paramount decision, each individual film became more important than the year's overall output. No movie could win its way simply by being slipped into a bundle of better films. Even a studio's cheapest, least prestigious film had to have its own attractions.

In the postwar years, Americans were more prosperous, but they had more types of entertainment to choose from. In 1943, twenty-six cents of every entertainment dollar was spent on going to movies. By 1955, that figure had declined precipitously to eleven cents, and it continued to decline until leveling off at about eight cents in the 1970s. People were less inclined to buy tickets unless the movie was something special, an event. Successful big-budget movies played theaters for longer runs, so fewer movies were needed overall.

As a result, there came to be less distinction between A films and B films. With the Depression over and the high attendance in the immediate postwar years, theaters no longer had to offer a second film to attract customers. The double feature declined, and the B films, which had usually filled the second half of programs in the 1930s, became insignificant to the big producers. Double features continued into the 1950s, but the theaters showing them either booked low-budget films made by small companies or ran two second-run A pictures. As we shall see, the role of making cheaper films was taken over by independent producers who aimed their films at specific segments of the audience.

By making fewer films, the big companies were able to spend more money on each one. Much of this money went into attractions like color and widescreen images, designed to bring audiences back into the theater.

Because some of these films depended on special projection equipment (as discussed on pp. 330–332), distributors revived a tactic used occasionally for special films since the silent era: roadshowing. *The Birth of a Nation* had been a roadshow release in 1915. A *roadshow film* played in only one theater per market, with only two or three screenings each day. Higher-priced tickets for reserved seats, available in advance, compensated for the reduction in showings. In the 1950s the practice became regular.

Starting in 1952, Cinerama films, with their triple images, of necessity played only in the small number of theaters built or remodeled for that purpose. Todd-AO films, with a 70mm width, could only play in about sixty specially equipped theaters, where they were all roadshown. Only after a considerable gap in time were 35mm prints made available to other exhibitors. Twentieth Century-Fox also used roadshow distribution for some of its CinemaScope films.

Most roadshow releases were highly successful. Michael Todd, originally a New York theater producer, formed Todd-AO with Richard Rodgers and Oscar Hammerstein as business partners. They consented to having their hit Broadway musical *Oklahoma!* shot in the new process; the film ran for over a year in some venues. Roadshow pictures continued to be based on big Broadway shows and best-sellers. *Around the World in 80 Days* (1956) had an all-star cast and won several Oscars. During their limited initial releases, such films built up reputations as must-see events, and they later played widely to audiences in a large number of theaters. Roadshowing remained a regular release method through the 1960s (see Chapter 22).

THE RISE OF THE INDEPENDENTS

The increasing importance of individual films went hand in hand with the growth of independent production, a trend that accelerated in the 1950s. An independent firm, by definition, is not vertically integrated; it is not owned by a distribution company and does not itself own a distribution company. An independent could be large and prestigious, like David O. Selznick, or small and marginal, such as the producers of exploitation films, which we shall discuss shortly.

Mainstream Independents: Agents, Star Power, and the Package

Many independent producers were business-people, and some stars and directors had an incentive to turn independent. In the 1930s and early 1940s, studios often signed stars to seven-year contracts, and the producers could put them into as many films as they wanted— whether the stars approved of the projects or not. Simi-

larly, directors were often at odds with their studios over creative matters and longed for freedom.

A radical change that would transform the way films were made began with the help of a small music agency started back in 1924, the Music Corporation of America (MCA). In 1936, MCA hired a dynamic publicist named Lew Wasserman. Loving the movies, Wasserman determined to expand into representing film stars. His first client was the temperamental Bette Davis, who was dissatisfied with her situation at Warner Bros. Despite having won two Oscars during the 1930s, she felt the studio often offered her poor roles. In 1942, Wasserman turned Davis into her own company, B. D. Inc. Thereafter she got her usual acting fee plus 35 percent of the profits from each Warner Bros. film she was in.

In earlier years there had been few stars powerful enough to demand percentages of their films' grosses or profits, including Mary Pickford in the 1910s and Mae West and the Marx Brothers in the 1930s. Wasserman, however, made this practice relatively common. He repeated his success, negotiating a similar deal between Errol Flynn and Warner Bros. in 1947. In fact, the big studios wanted to reduce overhead costs by cutting back on the number of actors they had under long-term contract; yet, they had not planned on doing so by giving actors huge fees on each picture. Other agents adopted this approach, as when the William Morris firm negotiated a deal for Rita Hayworth to receive 25 percent of her pictures' profits as well as script approval.

Wasserman negotiated his most spectacular deal for James Stewart. As a result of a disagreement with MGM, Stewart had found little work in Hollywood after the war. He returned to Broadway theater and at the end of the 1940s scored a success in the comic fantasy *Harvey*. In 1950, Wasserman sold Universal on the idea of a screen adaptation of the play, with Stewart getting a fee plus a percentage. Under the terms of the contract, Universal also had to produce an Anthony Mann Western, *Winchester 73* (1950), with Stewart getting no fee but half the profits. *Winchester 73* was a surprise hit and made Stewart a rich man.

In negotiating this deal, Wasserman also was selling the adaptation rights to the play of *Harvey*. By putting star and project together in one deal, he was "packaging" them. The *package-unit approach* to production, with a producer or agent putting together the script and the talent, came to dominate Hollywood production by the mid-1950s. For example, in 1958, *The Big Country* was made using a bevy of Wasserman's clients: director William Wyler and stars Gregory Peck, Charlton Heston, Carroll Baker, and Charles Bickford.

Wasserman worked similar magic for Alfred Hitchcock, who signed MCA as his agency in the early 1950s. Wasserman moved him from Warner Bros. to Paramount at a large pay raise. Since MCA also produced television programs, Wasserman persuaded Hitchcock to host and occasionally direct episodes for "Alfred Hitchcock Presents." He became the most recognizable filmmaker in the world. Wasserman also negotiated 10 percent of the gross of *North by Northwest* (1959) for Hitchcock. Since producers were reluctant to make the lurid black-and-white thriller *Psycho* (1960), Wasserman arranged for Hitchcock to help finance the film in exchange for 60 percent of the profits. The film's phenomenal success made Hitchcock the richest director in Hollywood, and he stayed loyal to its producer-distributor, Universal, for the rest of his career.

As a result of many such deals, some agents came to have more power than the moguls who founded and headed the big studios. Indeed, MCA brought Universal from its shaky state in the early 1950s to prosperity by decade's end. From 1959 to 1962, Wasserman masterminded MCA's acquisition of Universal, giving up the talent-agency wing of the business to run the studio.

The 1940s saw other directors and stars strike out on their own. After twelve years under contract to Warner Bros., Humphrey Bogart formed the Santana company to produce his own films. Santana lasted six years and produced five films. Most small production firms, however, were vulnerable if they made a single box-office flop. Santana's last film, an eccentric spoof of film noir called *Beat the Devil* (1954), failed at the box office, and its subsequent cult status could not save Bogart's company.

John Ford's creative conflict with Darryl F. Zanuck over his Western masterpiece, *My Darling Clementine* (1946), led him to revive Argosy Pictures, the small production firm he had formed in the late 1930s to make *Stagecoach* (1939) and *The Long Voyage Home* (1940) for distribution by United Artists. In its new incarnation, Argosy produced nine of Ford's next eleven films, from the atmospheric drama *The Fugitive* (1947) to *The Sun Shines Bright* (1953). The company's fortunes reflect the difficulties of independent production. The independents had to distribute their films through the large existing distribution firms that emerged unscathed from the Paramount decision. Argosy's films were distributed through RKO, then MGM, then RKO again. In every case, Ford as producer went deep in debt to make the film. As the

money came in, the banks took their share first, the distributor second, and Argosy third. By 1952, Ford's company was in serious trouble when he made his gently humorous, Technicolor, nostalgic story of Ireland, *The Quiet Man*. Only the small B-film producer Republic would distribute the film—which was a considerable hit. But, Ford's next film, the old-fashioned comedy *The Sun Shines Bright*, killed Argosy Pictures.

Other directors managed independent production with greater long-term success. Having worked extensively for 20th Century-Fox, Otto Preminger began independent production with *The Moon Is Blue* (1953). Through Columbia and United Artists, he released such adaptations of best-sellers as *Anatomy of a Murder* (1959), *Exodus* (1960), and *Advise and Consent* (1962). Stars also managed occasionally to muster sufficient budgets for epic productions. Kirk Douglas produced the Roman Empire-era epic *Spartacus* in 1960, using Technicolor and Super Technirama 70. Its all-star cast included Douglas, Laurence Olivier, Tony Curtis (whose career blossomed during the 1950s under management by Wasserman), and Jean Simmons.

Former moguls could also become independent producers. Hal Wallis, production chief at Warner Bros., left to produce on his own. He struck a long-term deal with Paramount for the films of the most popular stars of the 1950s, comic Jerry Lewis and singer Dean Martin.

Independent production proved to have its own frustrations. Ultimately, independents had to deal with the big distribution firms, which often insisted on some creative input into individuals films—a situation that sometimes differed little from conditions under the big production studios of the 1930s. In later decades, as powerful agents packaged stars and big-name directors into major projects, greater freedom was occasionally achieved (see Chapter 27).

Exploitation

When the major producers cut back their output of cheaper films, the small independent producers filled the gap. As of 1954, 70 percent of American theaters still showed double features, and they needed inexpensive, attention-getting fare. The demand was met by independent companies that produced cheap pictures. Having no major stars or creative personnel, these films cashed in on topical or sensational subjects that could be "exploited." *Exploitation films* had existed since World War I, but in the 1950s they gained new prominence. Exhibitors, now free to rent from any source,

15.9 A publicity still from Corman's *Attack of the Crab Monsters* (1956).

found that the low-priced product could often yield a nicer profit than could the big studio releases, which obliged them to turn back high percentages of box-office revenues.

Exploitation companies cranked out cheap horror, science-fiction, and erotic films. Among the most bizarre were those written and directed by Edward D. Wood. *Glen or Glenda* (aka *I Changed My Sex*, 1953) was a "documentary" about transvestism narrated by Bela Lugosi and starring Wood as a young man confused about his wardrobe preferences. *Plan 9 from Outer Space* (1959), a science-fiction invasion story, was filmed in an apartment, with the kitchen serving as an airplane cockpit. Lugosi died during the filming and was doubled by a chiropractor who scarcely resembled him. Wood's films, ignored or mocked on their release, became cult classics in later decades.

More upscale were the exploitation items made by American International Pictures (AIP). AIP films were targeted at what company head Sam Arkoff called "the gum-chewing, hamburger-munching adolescent dying to get out of the house on a Friday or Saturday night."[1] Shot in a week or two with a young cast and crew, the AIP film exploited high schoolers' taste for horror (*I Was a Teenage Frankenstein*, 1957), juvenile crime (*Hot Rod Girl*, 1956), science fiction (*It Conquered the World*, 1956), and music (*Shake, Rattle and Rock*, 1956). As AIP grew, it would invest in bigger productions, such as beach musicals (*Muscle Beach Party*, 1964) and an Edgar Allan Poe horror cycle beginning with *House of Usher* (1960).

Roger Corman produced his first exploitation film (*The Monster from the Ocean Floor*, 1954) at a cost of $12,000. Soon Corman was directing five to eight films a year, mostly for AIP. They had a rapid pace, tongue-in-cheek humor, and dime-store special effects, including monsters apparently assembled out of plumbers' scrap and refrigerator leftovers (**15.9**). According to Corman, he shot three black comedies—*A Bucket of Blood, Little Shop of Horrors*, and *Creature from the Haunted Sea* (all 1960)—over a two-week period for less than $100,000, at a time when one ordinary studio picture cost $1 million. Corman's Poe cycle won him some critical praise for its imaginative lighting and color, but the films still appealed to teenagers through the scenery-chewing performances of Vincent Price.

Obliged to work on shoestring budgets, AIP and other exploitation companies pioneered efficient marketing techniques. AIP would often conceive a film's title, poster design, and advertising campaign; test it on audiences and exhibitors; and only then begin writing a script. Whereas the major distributors adhered to the system of releasing films selectively for their first run, independent companies often practiced *saturation booking* (that is, opening a film simultaneously in many theaters). The independents advertised on television, released films in the summer (previously thought to be a slow season), and turned drive-ins into first-run venues. All these innovations were eventually taken up by the Majors.

The exploitation market embraced many genres. William Castle followed the AIP formula for teen horror, but he added extra gimmicks, such as skeletons that shot out of the theater walls and danced above the audience (*The House on Haunted Hill,* 1958), as well as electrically wired seats that jolted the viewers (*The Tingler,* 1959).

Independents on the Fringe

Occasionally, independent production took a political stance. Herbert Biberman's *Salt of the Earth* (1954) followed the tradition of 1930s left-wing cinema in its depiction of a miners' strike in New Mexico. Several blacklisted film workers participated, including some of the Hollywood Ten. Most of the parts were played by miners and unionists. The hostile atmosphere of the "anti-Red" years hampered the production, and the projectionists' union blocked its theatrical exhibition.

The "New York School" of independent directors was less politically radical. Morris Engel shot *The Little Fugitive* (1953), an anecdote about a boy's wandering through Coney Island, with a hand-held camera and postdubbed sound. Engel's later independent features, *Lovers and Lollipops* (1955) and *Weddings and Babies* (1958), used a lightweight 35mm camera and on-the-spot sound recording in a manner anticipating Direct Cinema documentary (pp. 483–489). Lionel Rogosin blended drama and documentary realism in *On the Bowery* (1956) and *Come Back, Africa* (1958).

CLASSICAL HOLLYWOOD FILMMAKING: A CONTINUING TRADITION

Even as the industrial base of Hollywood filmmaking began to crack, the classical style remained a powerful model for storytelling. In addition, it underwent some important modifications during the postwar decades.

Complexity and Realism in Storytelling

Citizen Kane's plot had a complexity seldom seen in Hollywood sound cinema, and it created a vogue for subjective narrative techniques (p. 227). This trend intensified in the postwar decade. The first several scenes of *Dark Passage* (1947) are entirely presented through the eyes of the protagonist. In *Hangover Square* (1945), distorted music suggests the demented imagination of a composer who compulsively strangles women, while *Possessed* (1947) conveys a woman's growing madness through exaggerated noises. In *Lady in the Lake* (1946) the image presents detective Philip Marlowe's optical viewpoint for almost the entire film. Characters appear

15.10   *The Lady in the Lake:* "our" mirror image and a subjective point of view.

to punch or kiss the camera, and during his inquiry Marlowe is visible to us only when we glimpse him in a mirror (**15.10**). Such films rely on techniques of camerawork and mise-en-scène pioneered by French Impressionism and German Expressionism.

Similarly, narrative construction became more intricate. *Kane*'s investigation plot, interrupted by flashbacks of people recounting the past, was a model. Some films experimented with flashbacks: *Crossfire* (1947) and *Stage Fright* (1950), for example, incorporate flashbacks that the audience later learns are lies. The melodrama *The Locket* (1946), in which a husband tries to find out about his wife's past, contains a flashback-within-a-flashback-within-a-flashback. None of these innovations threatened the premises of classical narrative filmmaking—a protagonist-centered chain of cause and effect, a "linear" drive toward coherence and closure. Indeed, the fact that most of the experiments with plot time involve a crime to be solved or a mystery to be unveiled suggests that the new complexity of structure was partly motivated by genre conventions.

While some directors were exploring complex storytelling tactics, others were embracing an unprecedented realism of setting, lighting, and narration. The trend toward location shooting, initiated during the war years when the government imposed a limit on budgets for set construction, continued. The semidocumentary film, usually a police investigation or crime tale, staged a fictional narrative in existing locales and was often filmed with the aid of lightweight equipment developed in wartime. For example, *13 Rue Madeleine* (1947) and *The Naked City* (1948) used portable photofloods to

15.11   In *The Asphalt Jungle* (1950), a three-minute sequence shot with movement in depth replaces traditional cutting. Within a deep-focus composition, the truck driver quarrels with Gus, the owner of the diner.

15.12   Gus shoves him out the door . . .

15.13   . . . and continues to berate him . . .

15.14   . . . before coming to the foreground to advise Dix to lie low.

15.15   Dix leaves . . .

15.16   . . . and Gus goes to the rear to make a phone call.

15.17   Deep focus for the gun-obsessed boy in *Gun Crazy* (1949).

15.18   Deep focus for claustrophobic atmosphere (*The Whip Hand*, 1951).

15.19   Cinematographer John Alton's low-key lighting typified film noir (*T-Men*, 1948).

15.20, *left*   *Kiss Me Deadly* (1955): a densely cluttered shot with violence at its center.

15.21, *right*   High-key lighting in *The Bad and the Beautiful* (1952).

light rooms for filming. *The Thief* (1952) was filmed in Washington, D.C., and New York City, often concealing its camera; one shot, with the camera on a cart, tracked for five blocks. Such films, based on actual incidents, frequently featured a thunderous voice-over narration that evoked wartime documentaries and radio broadcasts.

A complex flashback narrative and a semidocumentary feel might be found in the same film. *Sunset Blvd.* (1950), a memory narrated by a dead man, exploits actual Hollywood locations. One of the most intricate examples of artifice in the semidocumentary is Stanley Kubrick's *The Killing* (1956). Several men carry out a precisely timed robbery of a racetrack. Kubrick gives us newsreel-quality images of the track and the races, and the film uses a dry "voice of God" commentator to specify the day and time of many scenes. Yet *The Killing* also manipulates time in a complex way. We see a bit of the robbery, and then the film skips back to show events leading up to that phase. As the film traces different lines of action, events are presented several times.

Stylistic Changes

Kane had reinvigorated the use of long takes and deep-space imagery (p. 223), and these techniques, taken up during the war, became even more prominent during the late 1940s and early 1950s. Scenes might now be filmed in a single shot (the so-called *plan-séquence*, or sequence shot; **15.11–15.16**). Often the long take featured very fluid camera movement, facilitated by new *crab dollies*, which allowed the camera to move freely in any direction. In addition, the vivid deep focus that had been a Welles-Toland trademark was widely imitated (**15.17, 15.18**).

Many of these innovations were associated with film noir, the "dark" style that continued to be important until the end of the 1950s. Adventurous cinematographers pushed chiaroscuro lighting to exaggerated extremes (**15.19**). Noir films became more outrageously baroque, with canted compositions and layers of visual clutter (**15.20**). These stylistic developments attracted enough notice to make them the target of satire. *Susan Slept Here* (1954) mocks the flashback narrative by having an Oscar statuette narrate the film. The "Girl Hunt" ballet in the musical *The Band Wagon* (1953) parodies the excesses of film noir.

In black-and-white dramas, *low-key lighting* schemes continued well into the 1960s, but films in other genres exploited a brighter, *high-key* look (**15.21**). Most melodramas, musicals, and comedies of the 1950s avoided

chiaroscuro. Deep-focus cinematography continued well into the 1960s for black-and-white films, but color films usually cultivated shallow-focus imagery. And for some time, aggressive deep focus of the Wellesian sort proved impossible to achieve with CinemaScope's anamorphic lenses.

New Twists on Old Genres

With greater competition for the entertainment dollar, the major firms gave nearly all genres a higher gloss. And as studios cut back on the number of films produced, each movie had to be more distinctive. Executives enhanced production values with bigger stars, opulent sets and costumes, and the resources of color and widescreen technology. Even minor genres benefited from efforts to turn B scripts into A pictures.

The Western   The postwar Western was set on the "big-picture" trail by David O. Selznick with *Duel in the Sun* (1945). King Vidor was fired from this passion-drenched Technicolor saga before several other directors completed it. It earned large grosses and set the pattern for *Red River* (1948), *Shane* (1953), *The Big Country* (1958), and other monumental Westerns.

More modest Westerns also benefited from enhanced production values, the maturity and range of the directors and stars, and a new narrative and thematic complexity. The genre helped John Wayne and James Stewart consolidate their postwar reputations. Color cinematography enhanced the majestic scenery of *The Naked Spur* (1953, Mann) and the rich costume design of Hawks's *Rio Bravo* (1959; **Color Plate 15.7**). At the same time, social and psychological tensions were incorporated. A Western might be liberal (*Broken Arrow*, 1950), patriarchal (*Red River*; *The Gunfighter*, 1950), youth-oriented (*The Left-Handed Gun*, 1958), or psychopathic (the Ranown cycle directed by Bud Boetticher; Sam Peckinpah's *The Deadly Companions*, 1961).

While the typical B film had run between 60 and 70 minutes, *Duel in the Sun* clocked in at 130 minutes, *Red River* at 133, and *Shane* at 118. Even less epic Westerns tended to run longer; *Rio Bravo*'s charmingly rambling plot filled 141 minutes. Clearly such films were no longer designed to be the second half of a double feature—they *were* the feature.

The Melodrama   Enhanced production values also drove the melodrama to new heights. At Universal, producer Ross Hunter specialized in *women's pictures*, and central to his revamping of the genre was Douglas Sirk.

Sirk was an émigré (p. 274) who had made anti-Nazi pictures and films noirs during the 1940s. Working with cinematographer Russell Metty, Sirk lit Universal's plush sets in a melancholy, sinister low key. Psychologically impotent men and gallantly suffering women (*Magnificent Obsession,* 1954; *All That Heaven Allows,* 1955; *Written on the Wind,* 1956; *Imitation of Life,* 1959) play out their dramas in expressionistic pools of color and before harshly revealing mirrors (**Color Plates 15.8, 15.9**). Critics in later decades believed that Sirk's direction undercut the scripts' pop-psychology traumas and pat happy endings.

The Musical   No genre benefited more from upgrading than the musical, believed to be Hollywood's most durable product. Every studio made musicals, but the postwar decade was ruled by MGM. The studio's three production units mounted everything from operatic biopics to Esther Williams aquatic extravaganzas. Backstage musicals like *The Barkleys of Broadway* (1949) were balanced by folk musicals like *Show Boat* (1951). Adaptations of Broadway hits (e.g., *Kiss Me Kate,* 1953) were matched by original scripts (e.g., *Seven Brides for Seven Brothers,* 1954). A film might be built around a set of career hits from a single lyricist-composer team. *The Band Wagon* (1953), for example, was based on the songs of Howard Dietz and Arthur Schwartz.

The most lauded musical unit at MGM was overseen by Arthur Freed, a top producer since *The Wizard of Oz.* The Freed unit showcased the best talents—Judy Garland, Fred Astaire, Vera-Ellen, Ann Miller, and, above all, Gene Kelly, the wiry, wide-grinning dancer who added athletic modern choreography to the MGM product. *On the Town* (1949, codirected by Kelly and Stanley Donen), a frenetic tale of three sailors on a day pass in Manhattan, was not the first film to stage its numbers on location, but the choreography and the cutting gave the film a hectic urban energy (**Color Plate 15.10**). In *Brigadoon* (1954, Vincente Minnelli) and *It's Always Fair Weather* (1955, Kelly and Donen), Kelly made the musical a sour comment on masculine frustrations in postwar America.

More lighthearted was *Singin' in the Rain* (1952, Kelly and Donen), widely considered the finest musical of the period. Set during the transition to talkies, the film pokes fun at Hollywood pretension while satirizing the style of early musicals and creating gags with out-of-sync sound. The numbers include Donald O'Connor's calisthenic "Make 'Em Laugh"; Kelly's title number, blending swooping crane shots with agile choreography that exploits puddles and umbrellas; and the "Broadway Melody" number, an ebullient homage to MGM's early sound musicals.

Although MGM continued to turn out striking musicals after the mid-1950s, it was no longer the leader. Goldwyn's *Guys and Dolls* (1955), Paramount's *Funny Face* (1956), United Artists' *West Side Story* (1961), Columbia's *Bye Bye Birdie* (1963), and Disney's animated ventures all made the "big musical" a box-office stalwart. Twentieth Century-Fox based several musicals on Broadway hits—*The King and I* (1956), *Carousel* (1956), and *South Pacific* (1958), followed a few years later by the biggest blockbuster of all, *The Sound of Music* (1965). Warners contributed to the genre with George Cukor's *A Star Is Born* (1954) and Doris Day vehicles such as *The Pajama Game* (1957) before dominating the 1960s with *The Music Man* (1962), *My Fair Lady* (1964), and *Camelot* (1967).

Rock and roll brought new dynamism to the postwar musical. *Rock around the Clock* (1956) paved the way, and soon both Majors and independents went after teenage record buyers. After crooning rather than jittering in his debut, *Love Me Tender* (1956), Elvis Presley went on to present a fairly sanitized version of rock and roll in thirty musicals over the next dozen years. The genre was mocked in Frank Tashlin's *The Girl Can't Help It* (1956), which nonetheless managed to include "straight" numbers by popular bands.

Historical Epics   Westerns, melodramas, and musicals had been major genres for several decades, but the inflation of production values and the speculating on big pictures brought another genre to prominence. The biblical spectacle had proved lucrative in the hands of Cecil B. DeMille in the 1920s and 1930s, but it had lain untouched until DeMille revived it in *Samson and Delilah,* the top-grossing film of 1949. When *Quo Vadis?* and *David and Bathsheba* (both 1951) also earned exceptional profits, a cycle of historical pageants was launched. The genre's need for crowds, colossal battles, and grandiose sets made it natural for widescreen processes, and so *The Robe,* its sequel, *Demetrius and the Gladiators* (1954), and *Spartacus* (1960) all showcased widescreen technologies.

"Those who see this motion picture produced and directed by CECIL B. DEMILLE will make a pilgrimage over the very ground that Moses trod more than 3,000 years ago." Thus opens *The Ten Commandments* (1956), one of the most enduringly successful biblical epics. (Some observers noted that the credit gives Moses only second billing.) The film used 25,000 extras and cost over $13 million, a stupendous amount for the time.

Despite ambitious special effects like the parting of the Red Sea, DeMille's staging often harked back to the horizontal blocking of his 1930s films (**15.22**). William Wyler's *Ben-Hur* (1959) proved an equally successful biblical blockbuster; it held the record for the most Oscars won (eleven) for decades, until another historical epic, *Titanic* (1997), tied with it.

Historical epics treated virtually every period. There were Egyptian pageants (*The Egyptian*, 1954; *Land of the Pharaohs*, 1955), chivalric adventures (*Ivanhoe*, 1952; *Knights of the Round Table*, 1953), and war sagas (*War and Peace*, 1956; *The Bridge on the River Quai*, 1957; *Exodus*, 1960). Most of these attracted audiences, but because of budget overruns in production, some proved unprofitable in the long run.

Upscaling Genres   Another genre was revived by the new commitment to big pictures. As the market in science-fiction writing expanded after the war, producer George Pal proved that the atomic age offered a market for science-fiction movies. The success of his *Destination Moon* (1950) gave him access to Paramount budgets for *When Worlds Collide* (1951) and two prestigious productions based on works by H. G. Wells, *The War of the Worlds* (1953) and *The Time Machine* (1960). Using color and sophisticated special effects, Pal's films helped lift science fiction to a new respectability. *Forbidden Planet* (1956), with CinemaScope, electronic music, an "Id-beast," and a plot based on *The Tempest,* was a somewhat more forced effort to dignify the genre. Disney's first CinemaScope feature, *20,000 Leagues under the Sea* (1954), and the precise stop-motion work of Ray Harryhausen (e.g., *The Sev-*

15.22 *The Ten Commandments:* the pharaoh and his counselors, staged in a classic linear medium shot.

enth Voyage of Sinbad, 1959) aided the rebirth of the fantasy film.

Less expensive science-fiction and horror films portrayed technology in a struggle with unknown nature. In *The Thing* (1951), scientists and military men discover an all-devouring monster in the Arctic wastes. In *Invasion of the Body Snatchers* (1955), an average town is overrun by pods who clone the citizens and replace them with unfeeling replicas. Opposed to these paranoid fantasies were pacifist films, exemplified by *The Day the Earth Stood Still,* in which an alien urges earthlings to give up war. Special effects dominated films that portrayed eccentric science and misbegotten experiments, such as *The Fly* (1958) and *The Incredible Shrinking Man* (1957; **15.23**). Such films were interpreted in

15.23 A production still from *The Incredible Shrinking Man.*

15.24 The fight in the Fort Knox set of *Goldfinger,* designed by Ken Adam.

immediate historical terms, often as commentaries on cold war politics or the nightmarish effect of nuclear radiation.

The effect of amplifying B-film material was perhaps most visible in the rise of the big-budget espionage film. Hitchcock's elegant *North by Northwest* (1959) featured an innocent bystander caught up in a spy ring, but the catalyst for genre upscaling was Ian Fleming's fictional British agent James Bond. After two screen adaptations of the novels, 007 became a proven commodity with the phenomenally profitable *Goldfinger* (1964). The Bond films had erotically laced intrigues, semicomic chases and fight scenes, outlandish weaponry, wry humor, and dazzling production design (**15.24**). Over three decades, producers Harry Salzman and Albert Broccoli ran through several directors and main actors. The Bond films, probably the most profitable series in the history of cinema, spawned imitations and parodies throughout the 1960s and 1970s.

Low-budget movies, in order to compete with the new scale of expenditures, had to find their own selling points. The crime film, for instance, became more violent. Menacing films noirs like *Out of the Past* (1947) seemed subdued in comparison to the souped-up sadism of *The Big Heat* (1953) and *Kiss Me Deadly* (1955) and the brutality of a thug running down a little girl in *Underworld USA* (1961).

By the early 1960s, a genre film might be either a lavish blockbuster or a stark, seedy exercise. When the distinguished Hitchcock made a black-and-white thriller called *Psycho* (1960) without major stars and on a B-picture budget, he launched a cycle of grand guignol (e.g., *What Ever Happened to Baby Jane?*, 1962) that continued for decades. After fifteen years of dressing up genre formulas, leading filmmakers began to dirty them up.

MAJOR DIRECTORS: SEVERAL GENERATIONS

A few major directors ceased working or lost impetus fairly soon after the war. Ernst Lubitsch died in 1947. Josef von Sternberg, who had left Paramount in the mid-1930s and worked sporadically through the 1940s, ended his career with two films for Howard Hughes and *The Saga of Anatahan* (1953), a Japan-U.S. coproduction exuding the misty atmosphere of his prewar work. Frank Capra made the perennially popular *It's a Wonderful Life* (1946), a mixture of homespun comedy and astonishingly cruel melodrama, but his few subsequent features had little influence.

The Great Dictator had been the last bow of Charles Chaplin's Tramp. His experiments with other personae, coupled with controversies about his politics and personal life, made his popularity sink. *Monsieur Verdoux* (1947) centered on a quiet gentleman who murders his wives; *Limelight* (1952) was a testament to comic theater. Threatened with political persecution in the United States, Chaplin settled in Switzerland. *A King in New York* (1957) satirized American politics, while *A Countess from Hong Kong* (1967) bade farewell to the urbane comedy of *A Woman of Paris.*

Veterans of the Studio Era

Overall, however, a number of veteran directors continued to be central players in the postwar period. Cecile DeMille, Frank Borzage, Henry King, George Marshall, and others who had started directing during World War I remained surprisingly active into the 1950s and even the 1960s. Raoul Walsh, for example, turned out masculine action films, and *Colorado Territory* and *White Heat* (both 1949) remain models of the trim, understated efficiency of Hollywood classicism.

John Ford was still the most visible director of this generation. His Technicolor Irish comedy-drama *The Quiet Man* (1952) gave its backer, the B-studio Republic, new credibility. The sparkling location photography, the interplay of spirited romance and brawling comedy, and a buoyant epilogue in which the performers gravely salute the audience have made *The Quiet Man* one of Ford's most enduring pictures, a utopian fulfillment of the nostalgic longing for home that permeates *How Green Was My Valley.*

The bulk of Ford's postwar work was in the Western genre. *My Darling Clementine* (1946) is an ode to frontier life, shot in the rich depth and chiaroscuro that Ford had pioneered a decade earlier. His "Cavalry tril-

15.25 In *The Searchers*, the motif is established in the first shot when the mother opens the door onto the desert.

15.26 Later, Ford reminds us of the destroyed home by shooting through the opening of the smokehouse in which the mother's body lies.

15.27 The end of a search: after bringing Debbie back to the settlement, Ethan cannot reenter civilization.

15.28, *left* Moderated deep focus in *The Best Years of Our Lives*.

15.29, *right* In *Adam's Rib* (1949), a long take records the wry interplay between an attorney (Katharine Hepburn) and her district attorney husband (Spencer Tracy).

ogy"—*Fort Apache*, 1948; *She Wore a Yellow Ribbon*, 1949; *Rio Grande*, 1950—pays homage to the close-knit military unit. *Sergeant Rutledge* (1960) and *Two Rode Together* (1961) raise issues of rape and miscegenation in the manner of "liberal Westerns," and each experiments a bit: the former with flashback narrative, the latter with an unmoving long take. *The Man Who Shot Liberty Valance* (1962), widely taken as Ford's elegy for the frontier myth, has the simplicity of a fable: the heroic side of the West dies in the corruption brought by the railroad and Washington politics.

The Searchers (1956), arguably Ford's most complex Western, centers on Ethan Edwards, who pursues the Comanche who have killed his brother's family and carried off his niece Debbie. His saddle partner Martin Pawley gradually realizes that Ethan intends not to rescue Debbie but to kill her for becoming an Indian wife. Seldom had the Western shown such a complex protagonist, in which devotion and pride struggle against violent racism and sexual jealousy. At the film's climax, as Ethan is about to kill Debbie, their shared memory of her childhood links them again in a new bond, and he is purged of his murderous impulse.

The continuity of Ford's style is evident in *The Searchers*. The film's color scheme reflects the changing seasons across Monument Valley (**Color Plate 15.11**).

Fordian depth of space emerges in an evocative motif of doorway framings (**15.25–15.27**). Even John Wayne's final gesture of clasping his forearm is modeled on a gesture Harry Carey had used in *Straight Shooting* (1917). For film critics and young filmmakers of the 1970s, *The Searchers* typified the emotional richness of the Hollywood tradition.

Other veteran directors continued to practice their craft despite the studios' decline. William Wyler directed notable dramas and studio pictures into the 1960s, earning large box-office revenues with *The Best Years of Our Lives* (1946) and *Ben-Hur*. The deep-focus, wide-angle look was already muted in *Best Years* (**15.28**); Wyler seemed content to leave it to directors working in genres more oriented to suspense or action. Howard Hawks made comedies and action-adventure films until 1970. King Vidor turned to spectacles (*War and Peace*) after directing overblown, delirious melodramas such as *The Fountainhead* (1949). George Stevens created several of the era's biggest hits, notably *Shane* (1953) and *Giant* (1956).

Of the directors specializing in melodramas, comedies, and musicals, Vincente Minnelli and George Cukor stand out for their shrewd use of long takes. Cukor's *A Star Is Born* (1954) daringly activates the edges of the 'Scope frame. And his quietly watching

15.30 *The Cobweb* (1955): in a sanitarium, characters confront each other before the controversial drapes.

15.31 The rogue cop finds his way blocked in Lang's *The Big Heat* (1953).

15.32 *Some Like It Hot*: Jack Lemmon, as "Daphne," dances a passionate tango with Joe E. Brown.

camera permits the players full sway in their performances (**15.29**). Minnelli's distant framing emphasizes the characters' interactions with the setting; his melodramas juxtapose characters with symbolic decor (**15.30**).

Émigrés Stay On

Some émigré directors, such as Jean Renoir and Max Ophüls, returned to Europe fairly soon after the Armistice, but others flourished in postwar Hollywood. The most successful was Alfred Hitchcock (see box). Fritz Lang continued to make sober, somber genre pictures that radiated paranoid unease, such as *Rancho Notorious* (1952) and *The Big Heat* (**15.31**). Billy Wilder became a top director noted for irony-laden dramas (*Sunset Blvd.*, 1950; *Ace in the Hole*, 1951; *Witness for the Prosecution*, 1958) and cynical erotic comedies (*The Seven-Year Itch*, 1955; *The Apartment*, 1961; *Irma La*

Douce, 1963). *Some Like It Hot* (1959), less mordant than Wilder's usual work, delighted audiences with its cross-dressing gags (**15.32**).

Another émigré, Otto Preminger, cultivated a distinctive personality both as an actor (in Wilder's *Stalag 17*, 1953) and as a director. His despotic temper was sometimes compared to Erich von Stroheim's, but Preminger was no spendthrift; as his own producer, he counted every penny. Partly to trim shooting time, he pushed the long-take technique even further than Cukor and Minnelli. The average shot in *Fallen Angel* (1945) lasts about half a minute, the same as in his 'Scope musical *Carmen Jones* (1954).

Although Preminger ingeniously composed his CinemaScope frame (**15.35**), most of his long takes refuse expressive effects. There are seldom elaborate camera maneuvers or virtuoso performances; the camera simply observes poker-faced people, most of whom are lying to one another (**15.36**). This impassivity makes

ALFRED HITCHCOCK

Apart from the filmmakers who were also performers (Chaplin, Jerry Lewis), Hitchcock was probably the most publicly recognizable director of the postwar years. The press delightedly reported his remarks: "Actors are cattle"; "A film is not a slice of life but a slice of cake"; "Ingrid, it's only a movie" (after Bergman had sought to understand her role's motivation). His walk-on appearances, quizzically observing the crises his plots set in motion, guaranteed a moment of laughter. His image as the "Master of Suspense" was marketed through shrewd spin-offs: chatty trailers, a mystery magazine, and a television show, with Hitchcock introducing each episode in phlegmatically ghoulish tones.

Above all, the films themselves carried the stamp of his fussy, childish delight in discomfiting the audience. Like his mentors the Soviet Montage directors, he aimed at a pure, almost physical response. His goal was not mystery or horror but suspense. His plots, whether drawn from novels or his own imagination, hinged on recurring figures and situations: the innocent man plunged into a vortex of guilt and suspicion, the mentally disturbed woman, the charming and amoral killer, the humdrum locale with tensions seething underneath. The consistency of his stories and themes furnished evidence for the European critics who proposed that an American studio director could be the creator—the "author"—of his work (p. 416).

Hitchcock flaunted his stylistic ingenuity, embedding into each script a set piece that aroused suspense in the teeth of outrageous implausibility: an assassination is attempted during an orchestra concert (*The Man Who Knew too Much,* 1956), and a crop-dusting airplane tries to shoot down the protagonist (*North by Northwest,* 1959). Sometimes Hitchcock set himself a technical challenge: *Rope* (1948) consists of eight long takes. In *Rear Window* (1951), by contrast, hundreds of shots are assembled to induce the viewer to share the hero's belief that a man living across the courtyard has committed murder (**Color Plates 15.12, 15.13**).

Many critics found Hitchcock's postwar work to be his finest. *Strangers on a Train* (1951) employs taut crosscutting to divide our sympathies between hero and villain (**15.33, 15.34**). The semidocumentary *The Wrong Man* (1956) invests a drab news story with harsh anguish. *Vertigo* (1958) uses location shooting and Bernard Herrmann's haunting score to pull the spectator into a hallucinatory tale of a man obsessed with a woman whom he believes he has killed (**Color Plate 15.14**). Hitchcock's films gave Cary Grant, James Stewart, and Henry Fonda dark, brooding roles suited to their maturing star images.

Hitchcock's calculations of public taste were farsighted. *Psycho* (1960) triggered several cycles of homicidal films, up to the "slasher" movies of the 1980s; *The Birds* (1963) anticipated the "vengeful nature" horror film. Like most veteran directors, he floundered in the mid-1960s, but *Frenzy* (1972) proved that he could still craft a plot that outfoxed the audience and that his technical virtuosity could leave viewers at once anxious and amused.

15.33 *Strangers on a Train:* while the hero desperately tries to finish a tennis match in time . . .

15.34 . . . the villain scrabbles for the lighter he needs in order to frame the hero for a murder. Hitchcock makes the audience root for both.

15.36 A neutral long take in *Anatomy of a Murder* (1959): a defense attorney tries to convince his client's wife to play the role of loyal spouse.

15.35 *Advise and Consent* (1962): in the U.S. Senate, Preminger's 'Scope frame registers different reactions to a blustering speech.

15.37 The final shoot-out in a mirror maze in *The Lady from Shanghai*.

15.38 *Chimes at Midnight:* a deep-space view of a chaotic battle, with the camera flanked by the warriors' furiously scuffling legs.

15.39 In a long take, Terry toys with Edie's glove, keeping her with him while he expresses his reluctant interest in her (*On the Waterfront*).

Preminger's films noirs and adaptations of middlebrow best-sellers intriguingly opaque.

Welles's Struggle with Hollywood

Just the opposite aesthetic strategy was pursued by Orson Welles. Discharged from RKO after *The Magnificent Ambersons* (1942), Welles became a vagabond director. He turned in pictures for Columbia, Republic, and Universal, but he produced most of his films on a shoestring, with funds scraped together from European backers and his film performances (e.g., in Reed's rather Wellesian *The Third Man*, 1949).

Welles directed and starred in versions of *Macbeth* (1948), *Othello* (1952), and *The Trial* (1962), but he also made espionage films (*Mr. Arkadin*, 1955) and crime thrillers (*The Lady from Shanghai*, 1948; *Touch of Evil*, 1958). To all he brought the flamboyant technique he had pioneered in *Kane*—Gothic chiaroscuro, deep-focus imagery, sound tracks of shattering dynamic range, brooding dissolves, abrupt cuts, overlapping and interruptive dialogue, and intricate camera movement. The climax of

The Lady from Shanghai, a shoot-out in a funhouse hall of mirrors, is less a plausible resolution of the drama than a virtuoso display of disorienting imagery (**15.37**). *Touch of Evil*, beginning with one of the most baroque camera movements in Hollywood history, brought the film noir to new heights. In *Chimes at Midnight* (1967), an adaptation of Shakespeare's *Henry IV* plays, Welles presented the most kinetic, harrowing battle sequence of the era (**15.38**). Welles haunted the studios in the 1970s and 1980s, hoping to complete his long-running projects, *Don Quixote* and *The Other Side of the Wind*.

The Impact of the Theater

Welles had come to Hollywood from New York left-wing theater, and several other directors followed him. Jules Dassin started in this vein before turning out harsh crime films (e.g., *Brute Force*, 1947; *The Naked City*, 1948). Joseph Losey worked in the Federal Theatre project and directed Brecht's play *Galileo* (1947) before entering filmmaking with *The Boy with Green Hair* (1948). The HUAC hearings drove Dassin and Losey into exile.

15.40 Judy, Plato, and Jim are brought together unbeknownst to each other in the first scene of *Rebel without a Cause*. The CinemaScope framing tucks them into discrete pockets of the police-station set.

15.41 Deep focus in the wide image, in Ray's *King of Kings*.

During the 1930s, the Group Theatre transplanted to America the naturalistic acting "Method" taught by Konstantin Stanislavsky's Moscow Art Theater. The most influential Group alumnus was Elia Kazan, who established himself in Hollywood while continuing to direct the Broadway premieres of *Death of a Salesman, A Streetcar Named Desire,* and *Cat on a Hot Tin Roof.* After specializing in liberal social-problem films, Kazan moved rapidly to distinguished adaptations of works by Tennessee Williams—*A Streetcar Named Desire* (1951) and *Baby Doll* (1956)—as well as to socially critical films such as *A Face in the Crowd* (1957), which warns of the political abuses of television.

After the war, Kazan and two New York colleagues founded the Actors Studio. They believed that Stanislavsky's Method required the actor to ground the performance in personal experiences. Improvisation was one path to a natural, if sometimes painful and risky, portrayal. Kazan's conception of Method acting found its most famous exponent in Marlon Brando. A prototypical Method exercise occurs in Kazan's *On the Waterfront* (1954), in which Terry picks up and toys with Edie's casually dropped glove. Keeping her glove becomes a pretext for making her linger with him, but—as he straight-

ens the fingers, plucks lint from it, even tries it on—it also expresses his awkward attraction to her and provides an echo of the childhood teasing he recalls (**15.39**). Method acting was to have an enormous influence on Hollywood through Kazan, Brando, James Dean, Karl Malden, and other Actors Studio participants.

Nicholas Ray worked with the Group Theatre before serving as assistant director to Kazan on *A Tree Grows in Brooklyn* (1945). He began directing with a painful tale of a runaway couple drawn into the outlaw life, *They Live by Night* (1948). Always a fringe figure, Ray specialized in films about men whose toughness masks a self-destructive compulsion. *In a Lonely Place* (1950) implicates a Hollywood scriptwriter in a murder, revealing his narcissistic exploitation of others. In the offbeat Western *Johnny Guitar* (1954), the weary gunfighter is dominated by the hard-as-nails saloon lady; the film climaxes with a showdown between two gun-toting women. *Rebel without a Cause* (1954) showcases James Dean as another tormented hero, childishly passive and uncertain; it also demonstrates Ray's forceful use of the CinemaScope frame (**15.40**). After several other "male melodramas," Ray ended his Hollywood career with two historical epics, *King of Kings* (1961; **15.41**) and *55 Days at Peking* (1963).

New Directors

Another group of postwar directors emerged from scriptwriting: Richard Brooks (*The Blackboard Jungle*, 1955; *Elmer Gantry*, 1960), Joseph Mankiewicz (*All about Eve*, 1950; *The Barefoot Contessa*, 1954), and Robert Rossen (*Johnny O'Clock*, 1947; *The Hustler*, 1961). The most idiosyncratic talent was Samuel Fuller, who had been a scenarist for a decade before he directed his first film, *I Shot Jesse James* (1948). A former reporter for New York tabloids, Fuller brought a B-film sensibility to every project. He relied on intense close-ups, off-center framings, and shock editing to underscore his tales of underworld treachery or men facing death in combat.

Fuller went straight for the viscera. During a fist-fight in *Pickup on South Street* (1953), a man is dragged down a flight of stairs, his chin thonking on each step. At the showdown of *Forty Guns* (1957), a cowboy punk uses his sister as a shield. The lawman coolly shoots her. As she falls, he proceeds to fire several rounds into the astonished youth. In *China Gate* (1957), a soldier hiding from an enemy patrol steps on a spike trap, and Fuller cuts from shots of his sweating face to extreme close-ups of spikes protruding from his boot. Fuller enjoyed staging fight scenes that assault the viewer (**15.42**). The opening of *The Naked Kiss* (1963) turns its fury on the audience, with a woman striking directly into the camera.

Other directors had a comparable, if less raw, aggressiveness. Robert Aldrich built *Kiss Me Deadly* (1955) and *Attack!* (1956) out of the hollow dialogue and outrageous sadism of pulp fiction. Don Siegel's police films, along with *Invasion of the Body Snatchers*, show a rapid pace learned during his days as an editor at Warners. Anthony Mann, like Fuller and Aldrich strongly influenced by Welles, staged fight scenes in great depth, hurling his combatants at the audience (**15.43**). "In the films of these hard-edged directors," wrote critic Manny Farber, "can be found the unheralded ripple of physical experience."[2]

Some new directors specialized in grotesque comedy. Frank Tashlin, former animator and children's book illustrator, made several imaginative satires on 1950s culture (*The Girl Can't Help It*, 1956; *Will Success Spoil Rock Hunter?*, 1957), as well as directing Jerry Lewis after Lewis split with his comedic partner, Dean Martin.

The oldest practitioners in the years from 1945 to 1965 learned their craft in the silent cinema or the talkies; the postwar newcomers typically started in theater or in the studio system. The youngest generation,

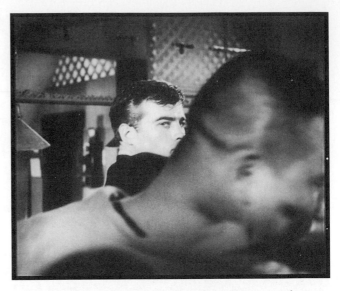

15.42   Using karate on a villain, and the viewer, in *The Crimson Kimono*.

15.43   Thrusting the violence in the audience's face: a fight from Mann's *The Tall Target* (1951).

who began making films in the mid-1950s, often started in television. John Frankenheimer, Sidney Lumet, Martin Ritt, and Arthur Penn directed live broadcast drama in New York before turning to feature films. They brought to cinema a "television aesthetic" of big close-ups, constricted sets, deep-focus cinematography, and dialogue-laden scripts. *The Young Stranger* (1956, Frankenheimer), *Twelve Angry Men* (1957, Lumet), *Edge of the City* (1957, Ritt), and *The Left-Handed Gun* (1958, Penn) exemplified this trend. These directors became significant Hollywood figures in the early 1960s, and they would be among the first to borrow from European art cinema and the new waves.

Despite the upheavals in the industry, directors from several generations and backgrounds made postwar Hollywood films a central force again in world cinema. The system had lost economic stability, but the genres and styles of classical filmmaking supplied a framework within which directors could create idiosyncratic, powerful films. The ambitious young filmmakers who came to prominence in Europe in the early 1960s usually turned to postwar Hollywood for inspiration.

Notes and Queries

WIDESCREEN FORMATS IN SUBSEQUENT HISTORY

Widescreen formats established in the early 1950s have continued to govern theatrical filmmaking, but other technological changes have affected films' presentation.

Since only roadshow theaters had 70mm equipment, wide-gauge films were also released in 35mm copies for neighborhood and suburban theaters. *Ryan's Daughter* (1970) ended the 70mm production cycle, but some big-budget films shot in 35mm, such as *Star Wars* and *Close Encounters of the Third Kind* (both 1977) were released in 70mm, largely to provide bigger images and better sound. Until the mid-1990s, 70mm release prints were common; after that time, improvements in digital sound made them superfluous. *Far and Away* (1992) was the last U.S. feature shot in 70mm.

When films are shown in nontheatrical situations, they often appear in ratios drastically different from those originally intended. A 16mm print of a CinemaScope film may be anamorphic, or it may be *matted* to a widescreen ratio less than the correct 2.35:1, or it may be a *flat* version that fills the 1.37 frame. Matted and flat versions can be projected without a special lens, but they exclude much of the original image.

Broadcast television, which was designed to accord with the Academy film ratio of 1.37:1, routinely shows widescreen films in flat versions. To cover the action in a widescreen original, television engineers devised the *pan-and-scan* process, which introduces camera movements or cuts that were not in the original. To avoid future problems, some cinematographers shoot widescreen films with eventual television presentation in mind. This is easiest when filming "full-frame" (i.e., at the 1.37:1 ratio). This squarer image is more appropriate for versions that will appear on television and videocassette. In filming wider ratios, the cinematographer may take the television frame into account by leaving blank areas in the composition. Currently, many films are released on DVD in a *letterbox format*, which approximates the wider theatrical image, and even cable channels are starting to program such versions of classic widescreen films.

For a discussion of widescreen ratios of the 1950s and their continuation into the present, see John Belton, *Widescreen Cinema* (Cambridge, MA: Harvard University Press, 1992).

REFERENCES

1. Sam Arkoff and Richard Trubo, *Flying through Hollywood by the Seat of My Pants* (New York: Birch Lane, 1992), p. 4.
2. Manny Farber, "Underground Films [1957]," in *Negative Space* (London: Studio Vista, 1971), p. 17.

FURTHER READING

Balio, Tino. "When Is an Independent Producer Independent? The Case of United Artists after 1948." *Velvet Light Trap* 22 (1986): 53–64.

Belton, John. *Widescreen Cinema.* Cambridge, MA: Harvard University Press, 1992.

Bragg, Herbert. "The Development of CinemaScope." *Film History* 2, no. 4 (1988): 359–72.

Carr, Robert E., and R. M. Hayes. *Wide Screen Movies: A History and Filmography of Wide Gauge Filmmaking.* Jefferson, NC: McFarland, 1988.

Ceplair, Larry, and Steven Englund. *The Inquisition in Hollywood: Politics in the Film Community, 1930–1960.* Garden City, NJ: Anchor Press/Doubleday, 1980.

Ciment, Michel. *Kazan on Kazan.* New York: Viking, 1970.

Doherty, Thomas. *Teenagers and Teenpics: The Juvenilization of American Movies in the 1950s.* Boston: Unwin Hyman, 1988.

Finler, Joel W. *Alfred Hitchcock: The Hollywood Years.* London: Batsford, 1992.

Halliday, Jon. *Sirk on Sirk.* New York: Viking, 1972.

Hardy, Phil. *Sam Fuller.* New York: Praeger, 1970.

Hayes, R. M. *3-D Movies: A History and Filmography of Stereoscopic Cinema.* Jefferson, NC: McFarland, 1989.

Huntley, Stephen. "Sponable's CinemaScope: An Intimate Chronology of the Invention of the CinemaScope Optical System." *Film History* 5, no. 3 (September 1993): 298–320.

Johnston, Claire, and Paul Willeman, eds. *Frank Tashlin.* Edinburgh: Edinburgh Film Festival, 1973.

Kindem, Gorham A. "Hollywood's Conversion to Color: The Technological, Economic, and Aesthetic Factors." *Journal of the University Film Association* 31, no. 2 (spring 1979): 29–36.

McCarthy, Todd, and Charles Flynn, eds. *Kings of the Bs: Working within the Hollywood System*. New York: Dutton, 1975.

McDougal, Dennis. *The Last Mogul: Lew Wasserman, MCA, and the Hidden History of Hollywood*. New York: Crown, 1998.

Segrave, Kerry. *Drive-In Theaters: A History from Their Inception in 1933*. Jefferson, NC: McFarland, 1992.

"United States of America v. Paramount Pictures, Inc. et al." Special issue of *Film History* 4, no. 1 (1992).

Waller, Fred. "The Archaeology of Cinerama." *Film History* 5, no. 3 (September 1993): 289–97.

Wilson, Michael, and Deborah Silverton Rosenfelt. *Salt of the Earth*. New York: Feminist Press, 1978.

CHAPTER 16

POSTWAR EUROPEAN CINEMA: NEOREALISM AND ITS CONTEXT, 1945–1959

In 1945, much of Europe lay in ruins. Thirty-five million people were dead, over half of them civilians. Millions of survivors had lost their homes. Factories were obliterated, damaged, or obsolete. Great cities—Rotterdam, Cologne, Dresden—were rubble. All European countries were massively in debt; Britain had lost one-quarter of its prewar wealth, while Denmark's economy had regressed to its 1930 level. This conflagration was the most devastating the world had yet seen.

THE POSTWAR CONTEXT

Europe would have to start again, but according to what principles? Socialists and communists believed that social revolution could start from scratch in this "year zero," and in some countries left-wing parties won substantial popular support. By 1952, however, the left's power had waned, and Europe's most industrially advanced countries were dominated by conservative and middle-of-the-road parties. World War II had demonstrated that a modern government could oversee a nation's economy. Consequently, most European countries introduced centralized economic planning. This mildly "socialistic" reform, along with emerging welfare-state policies pioneered in Scandinavia, blunted some left-wing demands for radical change.

The victory of moderate reconstruction took place in a changed international context. The Allies' victory demonstrated that Europe would no longer enjoy central power in world affairs. The postwar world was bipolar, dominated by the United States and the USSR. The cold war between these two superpowers would affect every nation's internal politics.

The United States helped consolidate the new Europe. In 1947, the European Recovery Plan, popularly known as the Marshall Plan, offered billions of dollars in aid. By the time the plan ended in 1952, industrial and agricultural production in Europe had surpassed prewar levels. Europe's "great boom" in employment, standard of living, and productivity was under way. In exchange for helping Europe rebuild, however, the United States expected political allegiance. In 1949, the United States presided over the formation of the North Atlantic Treaty Organization (NATO), a military alliance that committed members to oppose the USSR and national communist parties. Still, there were many local conflicts with U.S. policy. Many governments resisted the imposition of American will, sometimes by means of legislation that tried to constrain the power of American capital.

The growth of American power after World War I had convinced many Europeans that only a "United States of Europe" could compete in the new arena (p. 168). The "European Idea" was revived in the 1940s, when it became evident that countries would need to cooperate in order to rebuild. Moreover, the United States supported the pan-European idea because it believed a prosperous Europe would resist communism and offer markets for American goods.

The United Nations (founded in 1945), the Organization for European Economic Cooperation, and, in 1957, the European Economic Community (known as the Common Market) certainly constituted steps toward the goal of European unity. Yet the dream of a Europe without national boundaries was not realized. Nations insisted on their distinct cultural identities. Many Europeans argued that in the wake of American economic and political domination had come a cultural imperialism—that in advertising, fashion, and mass media, Europe was already becoming a colony of the United States. In the postwar era, then, we find a complex, often tense interplay among national identity, European unity, allegiance to America, and resistance to it.

FILM INDUSTRIES AND FILM CULTURE

The war had cut the flow of American films to most countries. This cleared space for local industries and nurtured indigenous talent. After the war, however, the American companies strove to reintroduce their product into the lucrative European market.

U.S. foreign aid paved the way for American movies' reentry into European markets. Hollywood's overseas negotiations were conducted by the Motion Picture Export Association of America (MPEAA; p. 328), and the agency used its power forcefully. In France, the U.S. government backed up Hollywood's export agreements. The MPEAA argued that Hollywood films were excellent propaganda against communist and fascist tendencies. This argument carried the most weight in Germany. The American firms could also resort to boycotts, as proved necessary in Denmark between 1955 and 1958.

Hollywood's strategy was to make each country's domestic industry strong enough to support the large-scale distribution and exhibition of American films. Penetration was quick. By 1953, in most countries, American films occupied at least half of screening time. Europe would remain Hollywood's major source of foreign revenue.

West Germany: "Papas Kino"

West Germany offers a case study in how thoroughly the United States could dominate a major market. Between 1945 and 1949, Germany was occupied by the four Allied powers. In 1949, the merged western zones became the German Federal Republic (commonly known as West Germany), and the Russian zone became the German Democratic Republic (East Germany). West Germany received millions of dollars in U.S. aid, a policy justified by American strategists' belief that the country would become a bulwark against communism. By 1952, the German "economic miracle" produced a standard of living almost 50 percent above that of the prewar period.

Superficially, the film industry seemed healthy as well. Production climbed from 5 films in 1946 to 103 in 1953 and did not fall below 100 during the 1950s. Attendance surged and coproductions flourished. Hildegard Knef, Curd Jürgens, Maria Schell, and other German stars gained wide recognition.

Yet the industry failed to foster an internationally competitive cinema. Soon after 1945, American movie companies had convinced the U.S. government to cooperate in making the German market an outpost of Hollywood. The old Ufi monopoly (p. 272) was dismantled and replaced by hundreds of production and distribution companies. Since the German empire was lost, these firms could count only on the domestic market, and this was dominated by American firms. Hollywood controlled a large part of distribution and was permitted to use blind- and block-booking tactics already outlawed in the United States. With no quota restrictions, up to two-thirds of German theaters' screening time was occupied by American films.

16.1, *left*   Echoes of *M*: Peter Lorre's hand dawdling as he is about to kill his wife in *The Lost One*.

16.2, *right*   "Innocent" voyeurism in *The Thousand Eyes of Dr. Mabuse*: a false mirror allows the millionaire to spy on the woman he wishes to seduce.

As in other countries, the bulk of production leaned toward popular entertainment, literary adaptations, and remakes of classics. The most popular genre was the *Heimat* ("homeland") film, the tale of village romance, which represented 20 percent of the domestic output. Much quality production of the era consisted of war films or biographies of statesmen and professionals.

Some postwar cinema critically scrutinized the war and its effects. Peter Lorre's *Der Verlorene* (*The Lost One*, 1951) uses flashbacks to present a doctor haunted by the wartime murders he has committed. The film, like many of its era, makes macabre play with mirrors and shadows, but Lorre also adorned his performance with mildly Expressionist touches (**16.1**). The early postwar years also saw the emergence of the *Trümmerfilm* ("rubble film"), which dealt with the problems of reconstructing Germany (p. 400).

Not until the end of the 1950s did filmmakers suggest that traces of Naziism lingered on. Wolfgang Staudte's *Roses for the State Prosecutor* (1959) and *Fairground* (1960) show ex-SS men prospering under Germany's economic miracle. More oblique in its treatment of the past is Fritz Lang's thriller *The Thousand Eyes of Dr. Mabuse* (1960). Here a criminal doctor uses hidden television cameras to spy on the guests at the Hotel Luxor. By invoking the figure of Mabuse (in the postwar years considered a parallel to Hitler), by suggesting that many characters share his voyeurism (**16.2**), and by stipulating that the hotel was built by the Nazis for espionage purposes, *Thousand Eyes* hints that the Fascist era survives into the present.

The charge could well have been addressed to the industry at large. Although some Nazi-era filmmakers (such as Leni Riefenstahl) were forbidden to work, most were rehabilitated under Allied policy. Some Nazi supporters were given prestigious posts; Veit Harlan, for example, directed eight films in the postwar decades. This continuity with the Fascist era, and the dully complacent film culture that it spawned, would be attacked by young directors of the 1960s, who called for an end to *Papas Kino*, "Papa's cinema."

Resistance to U.S. Encroachment

For U.S. firms, Germany was the model of a quiescent European market, just active enough to permit profitable domination. But most European film industries retained greater independence. This was largely due to a wave of protectionist legislation. As American films flooded the market, producers pleaded for help, and most governments responded.

Protectionist Measures   One strategy, already exercised in the interwar years, was that of setting quotas on American movies or on screen time allotted to the domestic product. In 1948, France limited American imports and required that at least twenty weeks per year be devoted to French films. In the same year, Britain's New Films Act required that at least 45 percent of screen time be reserved for British feature films. Italy's "Andreotti law" of 1949 required that eighty days per year be set aside for Italian films, and numerical quotas on imports soon followed.

Another strategy was to restrict American firms' income. This might be done before the fact by levying charges on each film's expected earnings. Alternatively, a flat rate might be charged. The Andreotti law required that for each imported film, the distributor had in effect to provide Italian film production an interest-free loan of 2.5 million lire. Or a country's legislation might provide for "freezing" American earnings, requiring that they be kept and invested in the country. In France, for instance, a 1948 agreement provided for a freezing of $10 million in earnings per year.

Besides defensive protectionist legislation, most European countries took steps to make their industries competitive. Governments began to finance production. Sometimes, as in Denmark, a tax on movie tickets created a fund that could advance monies to producers judged worthy. In several countries, the national government established an agency through which banks could loan money to film projects; the best-known is Britain's National Film Finance Corporation, established in 1949. A government might also offer cash prizes for scripts or films judged artistically or culturally significant. Sometimes the government subsidized a project outright, through a mechanism that would return to producers a percentage of ticket income or tax. European producing companies soon became dependent on government aid.

Protectionist legislation and government support were somewhat successful. Film output rose significantly in France, Italy, and the United Kingdom after 1950. But the new interventionism aided American firms as well. Most governments encouraged U.S. companies to invest their frozen funds in domestic production, which yielded further profits for Hollywood. The Majors might also earn money from distributing foreign films to American art theaters. Frozen-funds policies encouraged U.S. companies to undertake runaway productions (p. 328). American firms also established foreign subsidiaries. These were eligible for local government assistance and could lobby for Hollywood's interests within each country. In Germany and some other countries, the Hollywood Majors were able to buy distribution outlets, thus controlling the access that domestic films had to their own market. At the same time, quotas became rather insignificant because they coincided with the 1950s downturn in American production: the major companies did not have a great many films to export.

International Cooperation

One tactic for challenging Hollywood's domination moved toward the 1920s goal of Film Europe by creating coproductions, in which producers drew the cast and crew from two or more countries under agreements that allowed the project to qualify for subsidies from each nation. Typically, each coproduction had a majority and a minority partner, and the responsibilities of each were stipulated by the international accords. Thus, in a French-Italian coproduction, if the French company was the primary participant, the director had to be French, but an assistant director, a scriptwriter, one major actor, and one secondary performer had to be Italian. Coproductions spread out financial risks, allowed producers to mount bigger-budget fare that might compete with Hollywood's, and gave access to international markets. The coproduction quickly became central to western European filmmaking.

Technological Innovations

While Hollywood set the international standard in most film technology, a few European innovations competed on the Continent. At the end of the 1940s, Eclair and Debrie introduced lightweight cameras with relatively large magazines and reflex viewing, which allowed the cameraperson to see, during filming, exactly what the lens was recording. These cameras were taken up throughout Europe, as was the German Arriflex (dating back to 1936 but improved in 1956). The Arriflex would become the standard nonstudio 35mm camera of the postwar era. In 1953, a French inventor devised the Pancinor, a zoom lens that retained greater sharpness of focus in all positions.

Specialized Film Exhibition and Film Archives

Some pan-European initiatives created genuine worldwide cooperation. In 1947, the International Federation of Ciné-Clubs was founded in order to join independent film societies in twenty countries. By 1955, there was a European confederation of Cinemas d'Art et d'Essai—theaters that programmed more innovative and experimental films, often aided by tax rebates. An older organization, the International Federation of Film Archives (FIAF), was founded in 1938 but suspended during the war years. FIAF contacts were renewed at a 1945 conference, and in the next decade membership jumped from four to thirty-three archives. The growth in international film consciousness spurred governments to fund archives that would take up the burden of systematically documenting and preserving the world's film culture. Major American archives like the Museum of Modern Art, the International Museum of Photography in Rochester, and the Library of Congress Motion Picture Division joined the international effort.

Film Festivals

Another international initiative of the postwar era was the film festival. It was, most evidently, a competition among productions for prizes awarded by panels of experts. Thus films shown "in competition" would be high-quality representatives of a nation's film culture. The prototype was the Venice festival, run under Benito Mussolini's patronage between 1932 and 1940. In the postwar era, film festivals helped define the public's conception of advanced European cinema. Festivals also showcased films that might attract foreign distributors. Winning a prize gave a film an economic advantage; and the director, producer, and stars gained fame (and perhaps investment for their next ventures). At the same time, many films would be shown "out of competition"—screened for the press, the public, and interested producers, distributors, and exhibitors.

The Venice Film Festival was revived in 1946. Festivals in Cannes, Locarno, and Karlovy Vary began in the same year. The postwar years saw a steady increase in festivals worldwide: Edinburgh (beginning in 1947), Berlin (1951), Melbourne (1952), San Sebastian and Sydney (1954), San Francisco and London (1957), Moscow and Barcelona (1959). There were festivals of short films, animation, horror films, science-fiction films, and experimental films. There also appeared an enormous number of "festivals of festivals," usually noncompetitive events that showcased outstanding works from the major festivals. In North America, festivals began in New York, Los Angeles (known as Filmex), Denver, Telluride, and Montreal. By the early 1960s, a film devotee could attend festivals year-round. In recent decades, festivals have multiplied, forming a distribution and exhibition circuit parallel to commercial theatrical showings (see Chapter 28).

It would be too simple to treat coproductions, technological innovations, and festivals as straightforward European counterattacks on American domination. Just as U.S. companies invested in European cinema, so they also participated in coproductions through their continental subsidiaries. Hollywood filmmakers had access to Arriflexes and used them on occasion, and they had their own zoom lens, the Cooke Zoomar. American films often won both prizes and distribution contracts at European festivals. Hollywood could even pay tribute to its peers by creating (in 1948) a special category of the Academy Awards. A winner of the Oscar for foreign language film stood a good chance of success in the United States, where American firms and theaters would reap a share of the benefits.

Most European film industries enjoyed moderate health during the 1950s. Production increased within a modest range, sometimes exceeding prewar levels. Television and other competitive leisure activities had not yet emerged on a large scale, and the new generation of postwar youth filled the theaters. As a result, in the most populous countries, the period from 1955 to 1958 represented a peak in postwar attendance. Hollywood and its European counterparts had reached a mutually profitable stability.

Art Cinema: The Return of Modernism

Most European films continued popular traditions from earlier decades: comedies, musicals, melodramas, and other genres, sometimes imitative of Hollywood. But now European films competed successfully internationally and won acclaim at film festivals. There was a growing population of young people interested in less standardized fare, as well as a new generation of filmmakers trained during the war. More broadly, European social and intellectual life began to revive. Artists envisaged the possibility of continuing the modernist tradition founded in the early decades of the century. In a rebuilding Europe, modernism, always promising "the shock of the new," became revitalized.

These circumstances fostered the emergence of an international art cinema. This cinema largely turned its back on popular traditions and identified itself with experimentation and innovation in literature, painting, music, and theater. In certain respects, the postwar art film marked a resurgence of the modernist impulses of the 1920s, explored in French Impressionism, German Expressionism, and Soviet Montage. In some ways there were specific links to these earlier movements: the Italian Neorealists followed the Soviet filmmakers in using nonactors in central roles, while some Scandinavian directors had distinct Expressionist leanings. In other ways, though, postwar filmmakers forged a revised modernism suitable to the sound cinema.

Modernism: Style and Form   Postwar modernism can be described by three stylistic and formal features. First, filmmakers sought to be truer to life than they considered most classical filmmakers had been. The modernist filmmaker might seek to reveal the unpleasant realities of class antagonism or to bring home the horrors of fascism, war, and occupation. The Italian Neorealists, filming in the streets and emphasizing current social problems, offered the most evident example.

This _objective realism_ led filmmakers toward episodic, slice-of-life narratives that avoided Hollywood's tight plots. The camera might linger on a scene after the action concluded or refuse to eliminate those moments in which "nothing happens." Similarly, postwar European modernist films favored open-ended narratives, in which central plot lines were left unresolved. This was often justified as the most realistic approach to storytelling, since in life, few things are neatly tied up.

Stylistically, many modernist filmmakers came to rely on the long take—the abnormally lengthy shot, typically sustained by camera movements. The long take could be justified as presenting the event in continuous "real time," without the manipulations of editing. Similarly, new acting styles—halting delivery, fragmentary and elliptical speeches, and a refusal to meet other players' eyes—ran counter to the rapid, smoothly crafted performances of American cinema. Faithfulness to objective reality could also imply a minute reproduction of the acoustic environment. In many postwar French films, for example, silence calls attention to small noises.

Modernist filmmakers' drive to record objective reality was balanced by a second feature: they also sought to represent *subjective reality*—the psychological forces that make the individual act in particular ways. The whole of mental life now lay open to exploration. As in the United States, flashback construction became common, particularly for exploring recent history in a personal way. Filmmakers plunged ever further into characters' minds, revealing dreams, hallucinations, and fantasies. Here the influence of French Impressionism and German Expressionism was often evident (**16.3**). The emphasis on subjectivity increased throughout the 1950s and the 1960s.

The third feature of the European art films of the postwar era is what we might call *authorial commentary*—the sense that an intelligence outside the film's world is pointing out something about the events we see. Here film style seems to be suggesting more about the characters than they know or are aware of. In a shot from *Il Grido* (1957), Michelangelo Antonioni evokes the bleakness of the characters' relationship by framing them, backs to the camera, against a barren landscape (**16.4**). In *Le Plaisir* (1952), Max Ophül's camera pans and tracks down from cherubs in the church to prostitutes in the pews, suggesting that the women are blessed by their attendance at a young girl's confirmation. At the limit, such narrational commentary can become *reflexive*, pointing up the film's own artifice and reminding the audience that the world we see is a fictional construct.

Modernist Ambiguity Narrational commentary is usually far from clear-cut in its implications; one can imagine alternative interpretations of the shots just mentioned. In fact, ambiguity is a central effect of all three features in the postwar modernist European film. The film will typically encourage the spectator to speculate on what might otherwise have happened, to fill in gaps, and to try out different interpretations.

In Michael Cacoyannis's *Stella* (Greece, 1955), for example, the two lovers, Milto and Stella, have quarreled and separated. Each one has picked up another partner, and each couple has gone to a different nightspot. But Cacoyannis crosscuts the two lovers: Milto dancing to Greek music, Stella dancing to bebop (**16.5, 16.6**). The editing makes them appear to be dancing with each other. This might be taken as representing mental subjectivity: perhaps each one would prefer to be with the other. Alternatively, the viewer could inter-

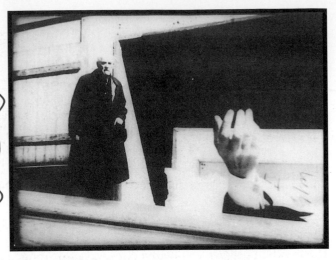

16.3 The bleached-out nightmare in Ingmar Bergman's *Wild Strawberries* (1957).

16.4 Authorial commentary on the characters' lack of feeling in *Il Grido*.

pret the crosscutting as making an external comment: perhaps suggesting that the couple belong together even if they are not aware of it. In a stylistic choice typical of postwar modernism, the film invites the spectator to consider multiple meanings.

Such ambiguities had surfaced in the works of avant-gardists such as Luis Buñuel, Jean Cocteau, and Jean Epstein, but now they were absorbed by directors working in commercial feature production. These directors kept alive classical traditions, such as the post-*Kane* tendency toward deep-space staging and deep-focus shooting (**16.7, 16.8**). Sometimes, however, the modernist film reworked classical devices for the sake of greater realism, subjective depth, narrational commentary, or ambiguity. Our example from *Stella* uses

16.5, 16.6 *Stella:* crosscutting suggests that the separated lovers are dancing with each other.

16.7, *left*   Deep space and deep focus in *The Devil's General* (West Germany, 1955, Helmut Käutner).

16.8, *right*   Hollywood-style depth in *Justice est faite* (France, 1954, André Cayatte).

standard crosscutting in this way. Fantasies and dream sequences were common currency of mainstream cinema; the modernist filmmaker made them more prominent and sometimes even untrustworthy. Films like *Le Jour se lève* and *Citizen Kane* had popularized flashback construction in the 1940s, so the modernist filmmaker could count on audiences being prepared for complicated manipulations of time. Europeans' reliance on continuity editing remained constant, although directors like Jacques Tati and Robert Bresson reworked the technique. The long take with camera movement was already common in Hollywood, but few Americans used it as systematically and intricately as Antonioni and Ophüls.

In all, the modernist cinema located itself between the intelligible, accessible entertainment cinema and the radical experimentation of the avant garde. Often coproduced for a pan-European audience, films of this trend were seen in North America, Asia, and Latin America as well.

Several countries participated in the trend toward cinematic modernism. Italy was the most influential, so we devote most of what follows to it; we close the chapter by examining Spain as an example of Italian Neorealist influence. In the following chapter, we consider other countries that contributed to the European art cinema of the postwar era.

ITALY: NEOREALISM AND AFTER

The most important filmmaking trend of the era appeared in Italy between 1945 and 1951. Neorealism was not as original or as unified a movement as once was thought, but it did create a distinct approach to fictional filmmaking. Moreover, this approach had an enormous influence on cinema in other countries.

Italian Spring

With the fall of Mussolini's government, the Italian film industry lost its organizational center. As in Germany, Allied military forces in Italy cooperated with the American companies in trying to secure U.S. domination of the market. Most production firms became small-scale attairs. While domestic companies struggled, Neorealist cinema emerged as a force for cultural renewal and social change.

During the waning years of the Fascist regime, a realist impulse arose in literature and film (pp. 279–281). *Four Steps in the Clouds, The Children Are Watching Us, Ossessione* and other films led some filmmakers to envision a new cinema. "We are convinced," wrote Giuseppe De Santis and Mario Alicata in 1941, "that one day we will create our most beautiful film following the slow and tired step of the worker who returns

Neorealism and After: A Chronology of Events and Selected Works

1945
Spring: Mussolini is executed; Italy is liberated.
Open City, Roberto Rossellini

1946
June: Popular referendum carries liberal and left-wing parties to government power.
Paisan, Roberto Rossellini
Il Sole sorge ancora ("The Sun Always Rises"), Aldo Vergano
Vivere in pace ("To Live in Peace"), Luigi Zampa
Il Bandito ("The Bandit"), Alberto Lattuada
Shoeshine, Vittorio De Sica

1947
Germany Year Zero, Roberto Rossellini
Caccia tragica (*Fugitive*), Giuseppe De Santis
Senza pietà (*Without Pity*), Luigi Zampa

1948
April: Moderate Christian Democratic party wins election.
La Terra trema ("The Earth Trembles"), Luchino Visconti
The Bicycle Thief, Vittorio De Sica
Bitter Rice, Giuseppe De Santis
Il Mulino del Po (*The Mill on the Po River*), Alberto Lattuada
La Machina ammazzacattivi (*The Machine to Kill Bad People*), Roberto Rossellini
L'Amore (*Love*; episode-film consisting of *Una Voce umana* [*The Human Voice*] and *Il Miracolo* [*The Miracle*]), Roberto Rossellini

1949
December: Andreotti law establishes quotas and subsidies.
Stromboli, Roberto Rossellini

1950
Miracle in Milan, Vittorio De Sica
Francesco, guillare di Dio (*The Little Flowers of Saint Francis*), Roberto Rossellini
Cronaca di un amore (*Story of a Love Affair*), Michelangelo Antonioni
Luci del varietà (*Variety Lights*), Alberto Lattuada and Federico Fellini

1951
Umberto D., Vittorio De Sica
Roma ore 11 (*Rome 11 O'Clock*), Giuseppe De Santis
Bellissima ("The Most Beautiful"), Luchino Visconti
Europa 51, Roberto Rossellini

1952
The White Shiek, Federico Fellini
I Vinti (*The Vanquished*), Michelangelo Antonioni

1953
December: Conference on Neorealism is held in Parma.
Amore in città (*Love in the City*), collective work overseen by Cesare Zavattini
I Vitelloni ("The Young Calves"), Federico Fellini
Stazione termini ("Final Station"), Vittorio De Sica
Signora senza camilie (*The Lady without the Camellias*), Michelangelo Antonioni
Pane, amore e fantasia (*Bread, Love, and Fantasy*), Luigi Comencini

1954
Senso, Luchino Visconti
La Strada ("The Road"), Federico Fellini
Voyage to Italy, Roberto Rossellini

home."[1] Once Italy was liberated in the spring of 1945, people in all walks of life were eager to break with old ways. Parties formed a coalition government, aiming to make left-liberal ideas the basis of a reborn Italy. Film-makers were ready to bear witness to what was called the "Italian Spring." The "new realism" imagined during the war years had arrived (see box).

What made these films seem so realistic? Partly the contrast with many of the films that preceded them. Italian films had become known across Europe for their magnificent studio settings. But the government's Cinecittà studios were heavily damaged in the war and could not support opulent productions. Filmmakers moved into the streets and the countryside. Since Italy had long mastered postsynchronization for dubbing foreign movies, crews could shoot on location and dub in dialogue later.

Another novelty was a critical examination of recent history. Neorealist films presented contemporary stories from a "popular front" perspective. For example, Roberto Rossellini's *Open City* (see p. 365) derived its plot from events of the winter of 1943 to 1944. The principal characters are caught up in the struggle against the German troops occupying Rome. Trust and self-sacrifice bind together the sabotage agent Manfredi, his friend Francesco, Francesco's fiancée Pina, and the priest Don Pietro. The film portrays the Resistance as uniting Communists and Catholics with the populace.

Similarly, Rossellini's *Paisà* (aka *Paisan*) presents a kaleidoscopic vision of the Allied invasion of Italy. The film's six episodes follow the movement of the American forces from Sicily north to the Po valley. More fragmentary and documentary-like than *Open City*, *Paisan* focuses not only on the struggles between the Italian partisans and the occupying forces but also on the frictions, misunderstandings, and occasional affinities that arise between local communities and the Yankee troops. Thematically, *Paisan* is as much about differences of language and culture as it is about the historical events it portrays.

Soon, filmmakers turned from partisan heroics to contemporary social problems, such as party factionalism, inflation, and widespread unemployment. Few Neorealist films represent postwar suffering more vividly than Vittorio De Sica's *Ladri di biciclette* ("The Bicycle Thieves," aka *The Bicycle Thief*). This story of a worker whose livelihood depends on his bicycle shows the brutal rapacity of postwar life (**16.9**). Ricci turns to every institution—police, Church, labor union—but none can recover his stolen bicycle, and most are indifferent to his plight. He and his son Bruno must wander the city in a futile search.

Against this social criticism *The Bicycle Thief* counterpoints the disintegration of trust between Ricci and Bruno. The film's climax comes when, in despair, Ricci tries to steal a bicycle himself. Bruno watches in shock. Their search has stripped away his illusions about his father. Ricci is spared arrest, and Bruno, now sorrowfully accepting his father's frailties, acknowledges his love by slipping his hand into Ricci's. The film's script-

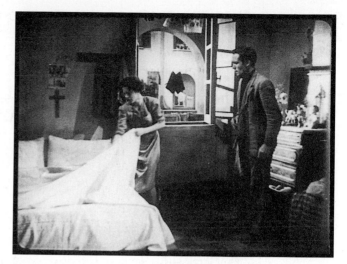

16.9   *The Bicycle Thief:* Ricci and his wife prepare to pawn their sheets in order to reclaim his bicycle.

writer, Cesare Zavattini, often expressed the desire to make a film that simply followed a man through ninety minutes in his life. *The Bicycle Thief* is not that film, but at the time it was seen as a step toward Alicata and De Santis's ideal of following the worker's "slow and tired step."

Some films charted the problems of rural life. *Bitter Rice* depicts, somewhat sensationally, the exploitation of young women driven to low-wage farm work and herded into prisonlike dormitories. The best known of these regional works is Visconti's *La Terra trema* ("The Earth Trembles"). The film portrays the ill-fated rebellion of Sicilian fishermen against the marketers who exploit them. Like other films of the period, it expresses fading hopes for deep social change.

In 1948, the Italian Spring ended. Liberal and left-wing parties were defeated at the polls. At the same time, the country was rebuilding. National income was starting to exceed prewar levels, and Italy was moving gradually into a modernizing European economy. The film industry discovered that it could export films, even to the United States.

Back in 1942, when Vittorio Mussolini, the head of the film industry, saw Visconti's *Ossessione*, he stormed out of the theater shouting, "This is not Italy!" Most Neorealist films elicited a similar reaction from postwar officials. The portrait of a desolate, poverty-stricken country outraged politicians anxious to prove that Italy was on the road to democracy and prosperity. The Catholic Church condemned many films for their anticlericalism and their portrayal of sex and working-class life. Leftists attacked the films for their pessimism and lack of explicit political commitment.

Few Neorealist works were popular with the public. Audiences were more drawn to the American films that came flooding into Italy. The state undersecretary in charge of entertainment, Giulio Andreotti, found a way of slowing the advance of American films while also curbing the embarrassing excesses of Neorealism. The so-called Andreotti law, which went into effect in 1949, not only established import limits and screen quotas but also provided loans to production firms. To receive a loan, however, a government committee had to approve the script, and films with an apolitical slant were rewarded with larger sums. Worse, a film could be denied an export license if it "slandered Italy."[2] The Andreotti law created preproduction censorship.

This move coincided with a general drift away from the "purer" Neorealism of the period from 1944 to 1948. Soon after the war, some filmmakers sought to acquire a Neorealist look by shooting traditional romances and melodramas in regions that would supply picturesque local color. Other directors explored allegorical fantasy (such as in De Sica's *Miracle in Milan* and Rossellini's *The Machine to Kill Bad People*) or historical spectacle (such as Visconti's *Senso*). There also emerged *rosy Neorealism*, films that melded working-class characters with 1930s-style populist comedy. Against this background, De Sica and Zavattini's *Umberto D.*, which depicted the lonely life of a retired man, could only strike officials as a dangerous throwback. The film begins with a scene of police breaking up a demonstration of old pensioners, and it ends with Umberto's aborted suicide attempt. In a public letter to De Sica, Andreotti castigated him for his "wretched service to his fatherland, which is also the fatherland of . . . progressive social legislation."[3]

Defining Neorealism

By the early 1950s, the Neorealist impulse had spent its force. At the 1953 Parma Congress on Neorealism, journalists and filmmakers began to discuss what the movement had been. There had been no Neorealist manifesto or program, only an appeal for greater realism and an emphasis on contemporary subjects and the life of the working class. Soon, however, several critical positions emerged.

One position treated Neorealism as committed reportage, calling for reform in the name of the political unity that had been briefly achieved during the Resistance and the Italian Spring. Another position emphasized the moral dimension of the films, suggesting that the movement's importance lay in its ability to make characters' personal problems gain universal significance.

According to a third position, Neorealism's documentary approach made the viewer aware of the beauty of ordinary life. Cesare Zavattini, De Sica's scriptwriter, was the most tireless advocate of a distinctive Neorealist aesthetic. Zavattini sought a cinema that presented the drama hidden in everyday events, like buying shoes or looking for an apartment. It was his opinion that films should present events in all their repetitive ordinariness. An American producer told Zavattini that a Hollywood film would show a plane passing overhead, then machine-gun fire, then the plane falling out of the sky but that a Neorealist film would show the plane passing once, then again, then again. Zavattini replied, "It is not enough to have the plane pass by three times; it must pass by twenty times."[4] This ideal was seldom realized in Neorealist practice, but Zavattini's formulation allowed filmmakers and film theorists to imagine a radically "dedramatized" cinema that would be approached in the 1960s.

Neorealist Form and Style   Most historians of cinema find Neorealism influential not only for its political attitudes and its worldview but also for its innovations in film form. Many of these had precedents, but the international prestige of the Neorealist movement brought them to attention as never before.

The prototypical Neorealist film is often thought to be shot on location, using nonactors filmed in rough, offhand compositions. Actually, however, few Neorealist films display all these features. Most interior scenes are filmed in carefully lit studio sets (see 16.9). Sound is almost invariably postdubbed, which allows control after filming; the voice of the protagonist in *Bicycle Thief* was supplied by another actor. While, in some films, performers were typically nonprofessionals, more commonly nonactors mixed with such stars as Anna Magnani and Aldo Fabrizi. In sum, Neorealism relies no less on artifice than do other film styles.

Moreover, the films are edited according to the norms of classical Hollywood style. While few Neorealist images are as self-consciously composed as those in *La Terra trema*, shots often aim to impress (**16.10, 16.11**). Even when filmed on location, scenes contain smooth camera movements, crisp focus, and choreographed staging in several planes (**16.12, 16.13**). The Neorealist film typically includes a sweeping musical score that recalls opera in its underlining of a scene's emotional development.

In its conception of storytelling, the Neorealist movement broke fresher ground. Sometimes the films rely extensively on coincidences, as when, in *Bicycle Thief*, Ricci and Bruno happen to spot the thief near the

16.10 *La Terra trema:* Visconti's rich compositional use of seascape.

16.11 Neorealism as historical spectacle in *Il Mulino del Po.*

16.12 In *Bitter Rice*, the camera starts from a close-up of women's striding legs . . .

16.13 . . . and slowly cranes up to reveal the entire rice paddy.

16.14 Edmund pauses in his wanderings when a bombed-out church emits organ music (*Germany Year Zero*).

house of the psychic they have visited. Such plot developments, in rejecting the carefully motivated chain of events in classical cinema, can seem more objectively realistic, reflecting the chance encounters of daily life. Along with this tendency goes an unprecedented use of ellipsis. Neorealist films often skip over important causes for the events we see. In *Paisan,* the Germans' massacre of a farm family is revealed with startling suddenness: at one moment the partisan guerrillas are in the field awaiting a plane, and, in the next scene, the guerrillas discover a baby crying beside the bodies of his parents.

This loosening of plot linearity is perhaps most apparent in the films' unresolved endings. Halfway through *Open City,* Francesco escapes from the Fascists, but the plot does not return to him again. In *Bicycle Thief,* Ricci and Bruno walk off into the crowd without a bicycle. How will the family keep going? The film does not tell us.

Neorealist films employ Hollywoodian deadlines, appointments, and "dialogue hooks" to connect scenes, but the result is likely to seem merely a string of events.

Scene B is apt to follow scene A simply because B happened later, not because scene A made it happen. The bulk of *Bicycle Thief* is organized around the search for the bicycle and traces the chronology of the day, from the morning through lunch to late afternoon.

Similarly episodic are the final sequences of Rossellini's third postwar film, *Germany Year Zero.* Edmund, the boy who exemplifies the moral confusions of defeated Germany, flees his family and wanders the streets of Berlin. The film's final fourteen minutes follow him through a single night and the following morning, concentrating on random events. Edmund watches a prostitute leave her client, plays hopscotch on the empty streets, scuffs through the rubble of buildings, tries to join other boys in a soccer game, and drifts around the city (**16.14**). From high in a shattered building, after he watches his grandfather's coffin carried out, he jumps to his death. While a suicide is a traditional conclusion to a story, Rossellini leads up to it by a string of everyday, accidentally glimpsed events.

UMBERTO D.: THE MAID WAKES UP

The sequence begins with the maid in bed, watching a cat walking across the roof. She rises and goes into the kitchen, where, after several tries, she lights the fire (**16.15**). (The wall bears the marks of many matches scratched there.) She looks out the window again and sees the cat walking on the roof; she looks out another window and then walks back to the kitchen. She goes to the cupboard, then to the table, and finally to the sink, where she sprays ants off the wall (**16.16**). She fills the coffeepot, walks around a bit more, and then returns to the stove, where she checks herself for signs of her pregnancy.

Going to the table, she sits and starts to weep as she grinds the morning coffee (**16.17**). As she grinds, she stretches out her foot to shut the door (**16.18**). Then she sits up, wipes her eyes, and rises to take the coffee to her mistress.

As is often the case with Neorealist films, the realistic details play a narrative role. Bazin rightly praises the sequence for presenting the maid's life in all its "dailiness," but we should also note that a degree of drama is inserted as well. The maid has just discovered that she is pregnant. The force of the scene derives from the tension between her drab routine and her numb anxiety about her future.

16.15

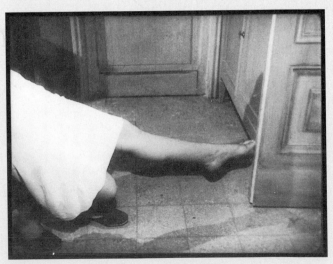

16.16

16.17

16.18

OPEN CITY: THE DEATH OF PINA

Rossellini starts the scene at a pitch of suspense when German soldiers cordon off a block of apartments and begin searching for underground partisans. Don Pietro and Marcello claim to be visiting a dying man. They hide the partisans' munitions in the old man's bed, a ploy that triggers farcical comedy when the old man refuses to pretend to be dying (**16.19**).

The tone shifts again when Pina sees that the Germans have captured her fiancé, Francesco, and are marching him toward their trucks. She breaks free from the guards and runs after his departing truck (**16.20, 16.21**). Don Pietro, watching in horror, presses Marcello's face into his cassock. Francesco shouts, "Hold her back!" (**16.22**). Suddenly there is a burst of machine-gun fire. In the next shot, from Francesco's viewpoint, Pina is hit and falls (**16.23**). Grim music starts. The last four shots of the scene, taken in news-reel fashion with long lenses, show Marcello and Don Pietro running to the dead woman and kneeling by her (**16.24**).

The clarity of Rossellini's style allows him to drive home some unsettling narrative qualities. In a more classical film, Francesco would see who killed Pina and would spend the rest of the film seeking revenge. But here Pina is cut down by an anonymous burst of fire, and the killer's identity is never revealed. In addition, the emotional tone switches abruptly, from suspense to comedy to suspense and finally to shock and sorrow. Even more disturbing, Pina has been established as the film's heroine, and her sudden death constitutes a shock for which few viewers in 1945 would have been prepared. Like the death of André Jurieu in Jean Renoir's *Rules of the Game*, Pina's murder suggests that in real life—as opposed to the movies—good people may die pointlessly.

16.19 *Open City:* to make the old man seem to be dying, Don Pietro has knocked him unconscious with a frying pan.

16.20 Pina breaks free from the guards . . .

16.21 . . . and runs after Francesco; she is seen from his viewpoint on the truck.

16.22 In a reverse shot, Francesco calls out . . .

16.23 . . . just before Pina is shot.

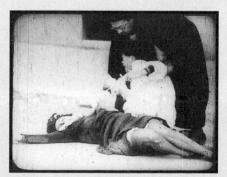

16.24 Don Pietro and Marcello grieve over Pina's body.

Presented with a plot consisting of events that may not be causally connected, the viewer no longer knows which are the "big scenes" and which are simply filler material. Neorealist storytelling tends to "flatten" all events to the same level, playing down climaxes and dwelling on mundane locales or behaviors. The critic André Bazin wrote eloquently about how *Bicycle Thief*'s walk through Rome lets the viewer notice the difference between Ricci's and Bruno's gaits.[5] In *Umberto D.*, one scene is devoted to the maid waking up and starting her day's kitchen work; Bazin praised this for dwelling on trivial "microactions" that traditional cinema never shows us[6] (see box). This unorthodox approach to narrative construction enabled Neorealist filmmakers to draw the viewer's attention to the "irrelevant" details that constitute daily life.

Neorealism sought to embrace the ordinary world in all its varying moods. In *Paisan*, mildly comic or pathetic scenes alternate with scenes full of violence. Probably the most famous example of mixed tone in films of the period is the scene depicting the death of Pina in *Open City*. It reveals how a fairly orthodox film style can convey severe wrenches of emotional timbre (see box).

Neorealism's stylistic and narrative devices influenced the emergence of an international modernist cinema. Location shooting with postdubbing; the amalgam of actors and nonactors; plots based on chance encounters, ellipses, open endings, and microactions; and extreme mixtures of tone—all these strategies would be adopted and developed by filmmakers around the world over the next four decades.

Beyond Neorealism

Apart from works like *Umberto D.*, rosy Neorealism was the dominant form the movement took in the early 1950s. The huge success of Luigi Comencini's *Pane, amore e fantasia (Bread, Love, and Fantasy)* led to a string of imitations that continued well into the 1960s. Rosy Neorealism retained some use of locations and nonprofessional actors, and it occasionally took on social problems, but it absorbed Neorealism into the robust tradition of Italian comedy. As economic recovery continued to move Italy toward greater prosperity, audiences did not welcome Neorealism's focus on poverty and suffering.

Moreover, the domestic film industry was becoming more oriented to an international market. Although hundreds of American films were successfully released in Italy in the late 1940s, the Italian government froze U.S. profits within the country. This encouraged Hollywood studios to reinvest the money in Italian film production,

distribution, and exhibition. Italy also sustained American runaway productions, supplying casts and crews.

Many traditional genres proved exportable. Blasetti's hugely lucrative *Fabiola* (1948) revived the lavish costume picture. Audiences in Europe and America developed a taste for *peplum*, musclemen sagas, such as *Ulysses* (1954) and *Revolt of the Gladiators* (1958). Also successful was the *commedia all'italiana* featuring veteran comic stars like Vittorio De Sica and Totò, along with such postwar arrivals as Sophia Loren, Vittorio Gassman, Alberto Sordi, and Marcello Mastroianni. Among the most successful films were *I Soliti ignoti* ("Suspicious Persons," aka *Big Deal on Madonna Street*, 1956) and *Divorce Italian Style* (1962). Carlo Ponti and Dino de Laurentiis led a new generation of producers who set their sights beyond the Italian border and turned the rebuilt Cinecittà studios into a film factory.

Other filmmakers moved toward more intimate psychological portrayal, focusing on how social circumstances affected the personal relations among individuals. Michelangelo Antonioni, one of the major directors of the period, noted,

> It no longer seems to me important to make a film about a man who has had his bicycle stolen. . . . Now that we have eliminated the problem of the bicycle (I am speaking metaphorically), it is important to see what there is in the mind and in the heart of this man who has had his bicycle stolen, how he has adapted himself, what remains in him of his past experience, of the war, of the period after the war, of everything which has happened to him in our country.[7]

An interest in the effects of war and recovery marks the early 1950s work of both Rossellini and Antonioni. Each director reveals how individuals' lives are altered by a milieu of postwar confusion.

After Rossellini's "war trilogy" of *Open City, Paisan,* and *Germany Year Zero*, his filmmaking attempted to revivify humanism in what he perceived as a decaying society. "We live," he once asserted, "in a world that is scarcely human—in fear and anguish. Humankind drinks whiskey to arouse itself, then takes tranquilizers to calm down."[8] He saw himself as continuing the Neorealist project by bringing people to an awareness of the demands of spiritual truth, self-knowledge, and obligation to others. Rossellini's films became highly didactic, showing how the practical world mistakes sensitive individuals for simpletons, heretics, or lunatics. In *The Miracle*, he presents the story of a bewildered goatherd who believes she is pregnant with a holy child. She is cast out by the villagers and must go into the mountains to bear the

LUCHINO VISCONTI AND ROBERTO ROSSELLINI

The two major directors to emerge from Neorealism were nearly contemporaries. Both grew up in wealthy households, took up film as an amateur pastime, and launched their professional filmmaking under the auspices of Mussolini's fascism. Both men led unorthodox personal lives, Visconti acknowledging his homosexuality and Rossellini getting involved with a number of women (most notably Ingrid Bergman, who bore him a daughter, Isabella, outside marriage).

The aristocrat Visconti became interested in film through assisting Jean Renoir in filming *A Day in the Country* (1936). Visconti took up left-wing causes, and during the war he was drawn into partisan work. His first film, *Ossessione,* played a key part in the realist revival during the last years of fascist cinema. "The term 'neo-realism,'" he declared, "was born with *Ossessione.*"[9] *La Terra trema* started out as a vehicle for the Communist party, but Visconti financed it from his personal fortune.

Visconti was a major theater director, and his films flaunted sumptuous costumes and settings, florid acting, and overpowering music. *Senso* opens at a performance of *Il Trovatore* and uses Giussepe Verdi's music throughout. *The Damned* (1969) was originally to be called *Götterdammerung,* in order to compare the moral decay of Germany under Naziism with Richard Wagner's opera *Twilight of the Gods.* Throughout, the use of color exaggerates the slide from tradition to decadence (**Color Plate 16.1**). Visconti's film version of Thomas Mann's *Death in Venice* (1971) models its hero on Gustav Mahler, and *Ludwig* (1973) makes Wagner a major character. Visconti aimed for intense emotion: "I love melodrama because it is situated right on the border between life and the theater."[10]

La Terra trema, Senso, Rocco and His Brothers (1960), *The Leopard* (1963), *The Damned, Ludwig,* and *Conversation Piece* (1974) all trace the decline of a family in a period of drastic historical upheaval. Visconti evokes the lifestyles of the rich, but he also usually reveals the class conflict that those lifestyles conceal. Foreign powers conspire with the ruling class to oppress the populace (*Senso*); the aristocrats must give way to democracy (*The Leopard*); a bourgeoisie collapses through its own corruption (*The Damned*).

More and more, Visconti relied on a languid, pan-and-zoom shooting style, as if history were a vast stage production and the director were guiding the spectator's opera glasses slowly over its details. As the von Essenbeck family in *The Damned* listen to a Bach sonata, the camera drifts slowly from one face to another, studying the bourgeois self-absorption that the Nazis will exploit (**16.25**). In *Death in Venice,* the camera scans for the boy Tadzio among the pillars, ferns, and silver tea trays of the luxurious hotel.

16.25   Von Essenbeck, with his discreet Nazi badge, lost in contemplation of classical music (*The Damned*).

16.26   Once they fall to the ground, Francesco's spinning followers are to spread the gospel in whatever directions their heads point (*The Little Flowers of St. Francis*).

Rossellini, by contrast, was resolutely antispectacle. "If I mistakenly make a beautiful shot," he once remarked, "I cut it out."[11] His direct approach matched his straightforward faith in rudimentary values. *Open City* turns the partisans into Christlike martyrs, and *The Little Flowers of St. Francis* shows the childlike joy of Christian charity. At the film's end, Francesco instructs his followers to whirl around until they fall to the ground (**16.26**). Rossellini sometimes advocates a more secular humanism that praises fantasy and imagination (*The Machine to Kill Bad People*),

(continued)

LUCHINO VISCONTI AND ROBERTO ROSSELLINI, continued

devotion to good works (*Europa 51*), and acceptance of imperfect love (*Voyage to Italy*). Later, he celebrates the great artists, inventors, and philosophers of the western world (*Socrates*, 1970; *Blaise Pascal*, 1972; *The Age of the Medici*, 1972; *Descartes*, 1974).

However forthright Rossellini's message may have been, his manner of treatment repeatedly led him into modernist ambiguities. His penchant for mixed tone, episodic narratives, ellipses, and open endings often makes the films more evocative than their straightforward themes might suggest. By comparison with Visconti's elegance, Rossellini's style seems awkward. But his simplest effects, in context, often yield complex results, as in his use of *temps morts*, "dead time." Rossellini punctuates his stories with empty intervals of characters simply sitting or walking or thinking. The spectator must infer the characters' attitudes. In *Voyage to Italy*, Katherine pretends to be asleep when her husband returns from Capri, and Rossellini suggests a welter of emotions merely by intercutting shots of each partner.

Like Visconti, Rossellini also came to rely on a pan-and-zoom style after the early 1960s. But Visconti's scanning frame unrolls an endless spectacle, while Rossellini

uses the pan-and-zoom for its simplicity and cheapness and for its ability to present the action neutrally, freeing us from any character's consciousness (**Color Plate 16.2**).

In the last fifteen years of his life, Rossellini launched a series of television films that would introduce the great figures and forces in history. This vast enterprise brought forth *La Prise du pouvoir par Louis XIV* (*The Rise to Power of Louis XIV*, 1966), the Pascal and Medici films, *The Messiah* (1975), and other works. As costume dramas, these films are remarkably unspectacular. Full of talk and dominated by static long takes, they dwell on daily life in each era. Whereas Visconti imagines history as a vast opera, Rossellini dedramatizes it.

Visconti became a model for other Italian directors of an operatic turn, such as Franco Zeffirelli, Francesco Rosi, and Liliana Cavani. Rossellini's version of cinematic modernism, in the name of realism, humanism, and education, centrally influenced the new generation of the 1960s. "Here is our cinema," wrote Jacques Rivette, "those of us who are in our turn preparing to make films (did I tell you, it may be soon)."[12]

child alone. In *Francesco, giullare de Dio* ("Francesco, God's Juggler," aka *The Little Flowers of St. Francis*), Saint Francis of Assisi and his scampering, childlike disciples become models of gentleness and charity in a corrupt world.

In the films starring Ingrid Bergman, Rossellini presents a woman's gradual discovery of moral awareness: A selfish and calculating war refugee comes to quiet acceptance of her husband's love after a mystical experience on the edge of a volcano (*Stromboli*). A mother shattered by her son's suicide devotes her life to relieving the suffering of others; her charity can only seem mad, and she winds up imprisoned in an asylum (*Europa 51*). And an emotionally numb Englishwoman finds Italy frighteningly alive, even in its catacombs. Only after the accidental passing of a religious procession does she—perhaps—begin to love her husband once more (*Voyage to Italy*; see box).

Rossellini concentrates on the extraordinary person who can rediscover time-honored values in the postwar world. By contrast, Antonioni's films focus on how ambition and class mobility make individuals lose their moral sensitivity. In *Story of a Love Affair*, for example,

the heroine and hero accidentally caused the death of a friend years ago. Now, she is the wife of a wealthy industrialist, while he is an itinerant car salesman. Her husband's curiosity about her past leads him to hire a detective, and eventually his investigation reunites the former lovers. As their passion takes hold once more, they begin to plot to murder the husband.

Narratively, many Italian art films of the early 1950s draw on such Neorealist conventions as ellipses and open endings. In particular, the focus on individuals' psychological states led Rossellini and Antonioni toward a dedramatized approach derived from Neorealism's concentration on mundane events. Now a film's plot might mix scenes of banal conversation with scenes showing the characters reacting to their environment or simply walking or driving through a landscape.

The canonical example of the dedramatized tale is Rossellini's *Voyage to Italy*, in which the bickerings between Katherine and her husband alternate with scenes of her excursions to tourist sights around their villa. The excursion episodes suggest her romantic yearnings, her uncertainty about the role of physical pleasure, and her wish for a child (**16.27**), and she gradually recog-

16.27 The celebrated museum scene of *Voyage to Italy:* Katherine comes face-to-face with the striking physicality of ancient statuary.

16.28 *La Strada:* as Gelsomina sits by the roadside, a carnival band strolls out of nowhere.

nizes the sterility of her marriage. *Voyage to Italy* pointed toward a filmmaking that would build scenes not around an intricate plot but around episodes in which casual, "undramatic" incidents would reveal characters' passing moods and barely articulated problems. The museum scene in *Voyage to Italy* is notable for its lengthy camera movements, and in this respect it is characteristic of a stylistic development in Italian films of the early 1950s. More and more, directors used slowly paced tracking shots to explore characters' relations within a concrete environment.

After the early 1950s, much of Italian "quality" cinema would center on individual problems. Instead of documenting a historical moment by depicting group struggles, filmmakers probed middle-class and upper-class characters for the psychological effects of contemporary life.

Alternatively, the filmmaker might treat middle and lower classes in a rather poetic way, as Federico Fellini did in a series of films beginning with *Variety Lights* (1950, codirected with Alberto Lattuada). In Fellini's works of the 1950s, Neorealistic subject matter is given a lyrical, almost mystical, treatment. In *La Strada* ("The Road," 1954), for instance, Fellini's tale of victimized innocence has the simplicity of a parable. The itinerant entertainers Zampano and Gelsomina live in the grim countryside, but occasionally this realm overlaps with a more mysterious one (**16.28**). Marxist critics attacked Fellini for deviating from Neorealism, but he claimed that he remained true to its spirit of "sincerity."[13] In any event, Fellini's work, no less than that of Rossellini and Antonioni, turned Italian filmmaking from the

verisimilitude of Neorealism toward a cinema of imagination and ambiguity. (For discussions of the careers of Fellini and Antonioni, see Chapter 19.)

A SPANISH NEOREALISM?

Spain offers an illuminating case study of the powerful influence of Italian Neorealism. At first glance, no country could have seemed more inhospitable to the Neorealist impulse. Once Francisco Franco's forces won the civil war in 1939, he established a Fascist dictatorship. After World War II, Spain gradually reentered the world community, but it remained an authoritarian country until the mid-1970s.

The film industry was controlled by a government ministry that censored scripts before filming, required dubbing of all films into the "official" Castilian dialect, and created a state monopoly on newsreels and documentaries. The regime demanded pious, chauvinistic films. The result was a procession of civil war dramas (*cine cruzada*), historical epics, religious films, and literary adaptations (including a *Don Quixote de la Mancha*, 1947, that compared the idealistic hero to Franco). At a less prestigious level, the industry turned out popular musicals, comedies, and bullfight films. The domestic industry also furnished locales for coproductions and runaway projects.

In the early 1950s, however, countercurrents became visible. CIFESA, the biggest production company of the 1940s, overinvested in high-budget productions and collapsed. As a reaction to the superproduction approach, several low-budget films, most notably *Furrows* (1951), began to treat social problems, and some used location filming and nonprofessional actors in the Neorealist manner. At the film school IIEC (founded in 1947), students were able to see foreign films that were banned from public exhibition. In 1951, during an Italian film week, IIEC students viewed *The Bicycle Thief, Miracle in Milan, Open City, Paisan,* and *Story of a Love Affair.* Soon afterward, several IIEC graduates founded a journal, *Objetivo,* that discussed Neorealist ideas.

The immediate effect of Neorealism is most evident in the work of the two best-known Spanish directors to emerge in the 1950s, Luis Garcia Berlanga and Juan Antonio Bardem. "B & B," as they came to be known, had been in the first graduating class of IIEC, and in the early 1950s they collaborated on several projects. *Welcome, Mr. Marshall* (1951), scripted by Bardem and directed by Berlanga, is a comic fable reminiscent of De Sica's *Miracle in Milan.* A small town transforms itself into a picturesque stereotype in order to benefit from the Marshall Plan (**16.29**).

Enormously popular in Spain, *Welcome, Mr. Marshall* satirized America's expanding power, took jabs at Hollywood movies and Spanish folk genres, and made a quiet appeal for popular unity. It set the tone for later Berlanga films such as *Calabuch* (1956), which mocked the arms race, and it promulgated what came to be called *la estética franquista* ("the Franco aesthetic"), a sardonic or an ironic treatment of apparently safe subjects.

Welcome, Mr. Marshall was selected as Spain's official entry to the Cannes festival, and, despite controversy about its "anti-American" outlook, it won a special mention. The film launched Bardem's career as a director. Soon, his stature was reaffirmed internationally with *Death of a Cyclist* (1955), which won the best-film prize at Cannes, and *Calle Mayor* (*Main Street,* 1956), which won the Critics' Prize at Venice.

Berlanga blended Neorealist impulses toward regional realism with a penchant for sardonic comedy. Bardem, by contrast, favored a more somber scrutiny of psychological states that owed a good deal to 1950s Italian developments. *Calle Mayor,* a fierce indictment of small-town narrowness and masculine egotism, recalls *I Vitelloni,* but without Fellini's indulgent humor (**16.30**). Similarly, *Death of a Cyclist* derives to some extent from *Story of a Love Affair;* it even stars Lucia Bose, the heroine of Antonioni's film. Bardem's plot shows how an affair between a rich man's wife and a university professor is shattered when their car kills a passing bicyclist. In trying to conceal their crime, the couple break up. The film ends with the woman, perhaps deliberately, running

16.29 The schoolteacher holds classes on how to dress and act like the clichéd Spaniard in *Welcome, Mr. Marshall.*

16.30 Young wastrels in a small town (*Calle Mayor*).

over her lover on the site of the accident. Bardem's editing creates narrational commentary on the affair, and the deep-focus landscape shots isolate his protagonists in compositions that recall Antonioni's (**16.31**).

As the work of Berlanga, Bardem, and others gained international attention, an alternative Spanish film culture began to surface fitfully. The growth of ciné-clubs in various universities led to a conference at Salamanca in 1955. This event assembled filmmakers, critics, and scholars to discuss the future of the nation's cinema. Bardem denounced Spanish film as "politically, useless; socially, false; intellectually, inferior; aesthetically, nonexistent; and industrially, sick."[14] After Bardem's denunciation, he was arrested while filming *Calle Mayor* and was released only after international protests.

16.31 Antonioniesque alienation and anomie in *Death of a Cyclist*.

The Salamanca talks did not sway the industry but did encourage filmmakers to test the limits of government policy. Such resistance was helped by the production company UNINCI, founded in 1951 and responsible for *Welcome, Mr. Marshall*. In 1957, Bardem joined UNINCI's board of directors and soon persuaded Luis Buñuel to return to Spain to make a film. The government welcomed Buñuel's return, and his script was accepted with only one change (which Buñuel claimed was an improvement). *Viridiana* (1961) won the highest award at the Cannes festival, but when Church officials declared it blasphemous, the government banned this most famous Spanish postwar film. UNINCI dissolved. The rebellion of young filmmakers and critics had gone too far, and the experiment in Spanish Neorealism was over.

Notes and Queries

CONTROVERSIES AROUND NEOREALISM

As with most film movements, historians differ about how unified and uniform Italian Neorealism was. At a 1953 conference on Neorealism, Zavattini, Visconti, and other participants could not agree on what characterized the movement. A 1974 conference of scholars saw little coherence; many believed that Neorealism was a loose ethic, not an aesthetic or a political position. A good survey of the range of opinions can be found in chapter 4 of Mira Liehm's *Passion and Defiance: Film in Italy from 1942 to the Present* (Berkeley: University of California Press, 1984).

Historically, Neorealism can be studied from several perspectives. For one thing, the film movement had parallels with a postwar "neorealist" literature, as exemplified in the novels of Elio Vittorini, Pratolini, and Cesare Pavese. These writers' works are discussed in Sergio Pacifici, *A Guide to Contemporary Italian Literature: From Futurism to Neorealism* (Cleveland: Meridian, 1962).

There is also the tricky question of the ties of Neorealism to the political left. In the immediate postwar period, an aesthetic of realism arose within the Communist party. Its proponents sought to create a "national-popular" strategy that would show a progressive, critical realism to be part of Italian cultural history. See David Forgacs, "The Making and Unmaking of Neorealism in Postwar Italy," in Nicholas Hewitt, ed., *The Culture of Reconstruction: European Literature, Thought and Film 1945–1950* (New York: St. Martins, 1989), pp. 51–66. Communist critics at first favored the Neorealist films, and the directors, while not Marxists, often had leftist sympathies. Very soon, however, relations cooled. As early as 1948, *Bitter Rice* was attacked for its sex and its lack of "typical" characters. Between 1950 and 1954, when many directors shifted toward psychological analysis, Marxist attacks intensified.

Since the mid-1950s, the debate about the political underpinnings of Neorealism has continued, and not only in Italy. For a sample, see Liehm, *Passion and Defiance* (cited above), as well as Pierre Sorlin, "Tradition and Social Change in the French and Italian Cinemas of the Reconstruction," in Hewitt, ed., *The Culture of Reconstruction* (cited above), pp. 88–102.

REFERENCES

1. Quoted in Millicent Marcus, *Italian Film in the Light of Neorealism* (Princeton, NJ: Princeton University Press, 1986), p. 16.
2. Quoted in Mira Liehm, *Passion and Defiance: Film in Italy from 1942 to the Present* (Berkeley: University of California Press, 1984), p. 91.
3. Quoted in Marcus, *Italian Film in the Light of Neorealism*, p. 26.
4. Ibid., p. 70.
5. André Bazin, *What Is Cinema?* vol. 2, trans. and ed. Hugh Gray (Berkeley: University of California Press, 1971), pp. 54–55.

6. Ibid., pp. 81–82.

7. Quoted in Pierre Leprohon, *Michelangelo Antonioni: An Introduction* (New York: Simon and Schuster, 1963), pp. 89–90.

8. Quoted in Mario Verdone, *Roberto Rossellini* (Paris: Éditions Seghers, 1963), p. 89.

9. Quoted in Gaia Servadio, *Luchino Visconti: A Biography* (New York: Franklin Watts, 1983), p. 78.

10. Quoted in Marcus, *Italian Film in the Light of Neorealism*, p. 183.

11. Quoted in Peter Brunette, *Roberto Rossellini* (New York: Oxford University Press, 1987), p. 14.

12. Jacques Rivette, "Letter on Rossellini," in Jim Hillier, ed., Cahiers du Cinéma: *The 1950s: Neo-Realism, Hollywood, New Wave* (Cambridge, MA: Harvard University Press, 1985), p. 203.

13. Federico Fellini, "My Experiences as a Director," in Peter Bondanella, ed., *Federico Fellini: Essays in Criticism* (New York: Oxford University Press, 1978), p. 4.

14. Quoted in Virginia Higginbotham, *Spanish Film under Franco* (Austin: University of Texas Press, 1988), p. 28.

FURTHER READING

Armes, Roy. *Patterns of Realism: A Study of Italian Neo-Realist Cinema.* New Brunswick, NJ: Barnes, 1971.

Bernardini, Aldo, and Jean A. Gili, eds. *Cesare Zavattini.* Paris: Pompidou Center, 1990.

Bosch, Aurora, and M. Fernanda del Rincón. "Franco and Hollywood, 1939–56." *New Left Review* 232 (November/December 1998): 112–54.

Brunetta, Gian Piero. "The Long March of American Cinema in Italy from Fascism to the Cold War." In David W. Ellwood and Rob Kroes, eds., *Hollywood in Europe: Experiences of a Cultural Hegemony.* Amsterdam: VU University Press, 1994, pp. 139–54.

"Le Néo-réalisme italien." *Études cinématographiques* 32–35 (1964).

Overbey, David, ed. *Springtime in Italy: A Reader on Neo-Realism.* London: Talisman, 1978.

Rossellini, Roberto. *My Method: Writings and Interviews.* Ed Adriano Aprà. New York: Marsilio, 1992.

Sitney, P. Adams. *Vital Crises in Italian Cinema: Iconography, Stylistics, Politics.* Austin: University of Texas Press, 1995.

POSTWAR EUROPEAN CINEMA: FRANCE, SCANDINAVIA, AND BRITAIN, 1945–1959

Italian Neorealism provided an influential model of social realism and psychological ambiguity, but it was not the only trend in Europe during the postwar era. France achieved recognition for its prestigious "Tradition of Quality," the return of several important prewar directors, and the emergence of modernist experimenters. Scandinavian filmmaking attracted attention with offshoots of theatrical tradition that shaped emerging art-cinema conventions. British filmmaking, on the whole less inclined to experiment, developed new interest in English-speaking countries. Coproductions, export, and festivals helped films find international audiences.

FRENCH CINEMA OF THE POSTWAR DECADE

The Industry Recovers

Before the Nazi Occupation, France's production sector consisted of many small firms, often created solely to make one film. Even Pathé and Gaumont, the major vertically integrated companies, produced few films themselves. They rented studio facilities to other firms and served as distributors and exhibitors. Under the Nazis, however, production was centralized (pp. 297–298).

After the Liberation in 1944, free-for-all competition reemerged. Pathé and Gaumont, while occasionally producing big-budget films, could not supply the market. Filmmakers were forced back to the "artisanal" system of finding smaller production companies or individual producers. In 1947, there were over 200 registered firms, but nearly all had little capital, and banks were reluctant to finance their projects.

POSTWAR FRENCH FILM CULTURE

Since World War I, French intellectuals took a keen interest in cinema (see Chapter 5). After 1945, their enthusiasm, constrained by the war, burst out anew. The German occupation had denied them American movies for five years, but now in a single month they might see *Citizen Kane, Double Indemnity, The Little Foxes,* and *The Maltese Falcon.* The Cinémathèque Française, which had gone underground during the war, began regularly showing older films from around the world. As students gathered in Parisian cafés and lecture halls to argue about Marxism, existentialism, and phenomenology, so too did they flock to movie theaters and spend hours talking and writing about films.

The atmosphere of *cinéphilie* ("love of cinema") must have been heady. The ciné-club movement was revived, and by 1954 there were 200 clubs with approximately 100,000 members. The Catholic Church's lay group on public education formed an agency that arranged screenings for millions of viewers. University courses began to teach cinema, and an academic discipline called "filmology" was developed. Several film journals were launched, most notably *L'Écran français* (published secretly during the Occupation, openly beginning in 1945), *La Revue du cinéma* (founded 1946), *Cahiers du cinéma* (1951), and *Positif* (1952). Soon after the war's end, publishers brought out film histories by Georges Sadoul and theoretical works by André Bazin (**17.1**), Jean Epstein, André Malraux, and Claude-Edmonde Magny.

Certain issues came to the fore. One, central to all thinking about film since the early years, was the question of cinema as an art. Some critics argued that film was analogous to theater; others suggested that it had more in common with the novel. At the same time, many critics proposed fresh ways to think about film style and technique. Bazin, for instance, responded to the revelation of wartime Hollywood films by closely examining the aesthetic potential of deep focus and long takes. Such discussions led to more ab-

17.1 André Bazin, the preeminent French film theorist.

stract speculation too. Film theory, as an inquiry into the nature and functions of cinema, was revived in this philosophical milieu (see "Notes and Queries" at the end of this chapter).

Postwar French film culture has long served as the paradigm of intellectual ferment around cinema. The ideas explored by several brilliant thinkers have permanently shaped the direction of film studies and filmmaking. Out of the debates in ciné-clubs, the screenings of esoteric classics and recent Hollywood products, and the articles in *Cahiers du cinéma* and *Positif,* the New Wave of the 1950s would be born.

Production problems were intensified by government indifference. In May 1946, Prime Minister Léon Blum and U.S. Secretary of State James Byrnes signed an agreement to eliminate prewar quotas on American films. The pact guaranteed that exhibitors would reserve sixteen weeks per year for French films; the rest of the year would be given over to "free competition." Although the Blum-Byrnes accord was defended as a way to encourage production, film workers protested that it actually made France an open market for American films. Immediate results bore out their charge: a year after the accord, the

number of imported American films increased tenfold, and French output dropped from ninety-one features to seventy-eight. With double bills outlawed and with Hollywood companies making deep inroads in other countries that had welcomed French films, there were fewer outlets for the domestic product.

Two government measures responded to the outrage in the industry. In late 1946, the French government established the Centre National de la Cinématographie (CNC, "National Cinema Center"). This agency began to regulate the industry by establishing standards for fi-

17.2, *left* · Many films in the Tradition of Quality dwell on the moment when the male protagonist is captivated by a woman's distant image (*Symphonie pastorale*).

17.3, *right* · *Le Diable au corps:* at night a woman waits for her lover at dockside, and the camera glides toward her while waves of reflections play across her body.

nancial solvency, providing subsidies for filmmaking, and encouraging documentary and artistic efforts. In effect, CNC was a revision of the centralized organization of production under the Vichy regime. By 1949, the agency was regularly subsidizing production, and, in the same year, it founded Unifrance Film, a publicity agency aimed at promoting French film abroad and coordinating the nation's festival entries. The CNC was part of a broader effort toward centralized economic planning, which included nationalization of banks, utilities, and transportation industries.

The government took a second step by enacting protectionist legislation. A 1948 law set a new import quota of 121 American films per year, a figure that remained roughly constant over the next decade. The same law provided for major bank loans to stable companies. The legislation also created an admission tax earmarked for financing future productions. If a film proved successful, ticket surcharges would build up a large fund that would assist the producer in financing his next project. This policy encouraged firms to make popular films with presold stars and stories. A 1953 revision in the law created a development fund for new projects and included a provision for the encouragement of short films.

Government assistance helped feature output rise to about 120 films per year. While the industry never regained the international power it had enjoyed before World War I, it was fairly healthy. Television had not yet penetrated France, and moviegoing remained popular. Although the three major companies—Pathé, Gaumont, and Union Générale Cinématographique—owned or had contractual arrangements with the best first-run theaters, their production output dwindled; Pathé gave up film production altogether and made an arrangement with Gaumont to supply its theaters. The larger production houses—Discina, Cinédis, Cocinor, and Paris Film Production—were able to fill exhibitors' demands, in the process becoming strong distributors. The national film school, Institut des Hautes Etudes Cinématographiques (IDHEC), founded in 1943, trained technicians for industry positions. Coproductions, especially with Italian companies, flourished under the coordination of the CNC.

Throughout the 1950s, as today, international audiences enjoyed French police thrillers, comedies, costume dramas, and star vehicles. The major stars—Gérard Philipe, Jean Gabin, Yves Montand, Fernandel, Simone Signoret, Martine Carol, and Michèle Morgan—gained fame around the world. And France, along with Italy, would become a vanguard for the emerging "modernist currents of the 1950s and 1960s. The audience's interest in cinema as a part of artistic culture (see box), along with the relatively artisanal condition of smaller production companies, enabled some writers and directors to experiment with film form and style.

The Tradition of Quality

The first decade of the postwar French cinema was dominated by what a critic dubbed in 1953 the "Tradition of Quality (also known as the "Cinema of Quality). Originally the term was quite broad, but it was soon identified with particular directors and screenwriters.

The Tradition of Quality aimed to be a "prestige cinema. It relied heavily on adaptations of literary classics. Often the scriptwriter was considered the creative equal or even the superior of the director. Performers were drawn from the ranks of top-flight stars or from leading theaters. The films were often steeped in romanticism, particularly of the sort made famous by Poetic Realism before the war (p. 289). Again and again in these films lovers find themselves in an unfeeling or threatening social environment; most often, their affairs end tragically. The woman is persistently idealized, treated as mysterious and unattainable (**17.2, 17.3**). Stylistically, much of the Tradition of Quality resembles the A-picture romantic dramas of Hollywood and British

17.4 Lovers pause to study the graffiti on a statue while strolling through a murky yard littered with tomb carvings (*Les Portes de la nuit*).

cinema, such as *Arch of Triumph* (1948) and *Brief Encounter* (1945). All the resources of studio filmmaking—lavish sets, special effects, elaborate lighting, extravagant costumes—were used to amplify these refined tales of passion and melancholy (**17.4**).

In certain ways the Cinema of Quality prolonged conventions developed under the Occupation. The French had perfected a literary, studio-bound romanticism that culminated in the Marcel Carné–Jacques Prévert collaboration *Children of Paradise* (p. 300). It is no surprise that among the most famous films in the canon of Quality is the first postwar Carné-Prévert project *Les Portes de la nuit* ("Gates of the Night," 1946). In this allegory of postwar life, a young couple flee the black marketer who has kept the woman as his mistress. In the course of the night they encounter the figure of Destiny, a tramp who continually warns them of their fate. A hugely expensive film, featuring colossal street sets (**17.5**) and a fabricated waterfront, *Les Portes de la nuit* was a financial failure.

Carné and Prévert did not collaborate on a project again, but Carné persisted in his efforts to create a symbolic cinema, notably in *Juliette ou la clef des songes* ("Juliette, or the Key of Dreams," 1951).

More successful was the scriptwriting team of Jean Aurenche and Pierre Bost. After working under the Occupation, they rose quickly in the postwar period, turning out adaptations of classics by Georges Feydeau, Sidonie-Gabrielle Colette, Stendhal, and Émile Zola. Aurenche and Bost became the prototypical scenarists of the Tradition of Quality. Their *Symphonie pastorale* ("Pastoral Symphony," 1946), an adaptation of André Gide's novel, plays up the fateful attraction of a father and son for the same blind girl. In *Le Diable au corps* ("Devil in the Flesh," 1947), Aurenche and Bost use flashbacks to tell another story of lost adolescent love: While crowds joyously celebrate the end of World War I, the teenager François recalls his affair with Marthe, a soldier's fiancée. Just as the soldier returns from the war, Marthe dies giving birth to François's child. *Le Diable au corps* solidified the reputation of its star, Gérard Philipe, and gave director Claude Autant-Lara his first postwar success. Aurenche and Bost were to collaborate frequently with Autant-Lara.

Most English-language audiences encountered Aurenche and Bost through *Jeux interdits* (*Forbidden Games*, 1952), directed by René Clément. Here children form the romantic couple. An orphaned refugee girl is taken in by a farm family. She and the family's youngest son begin to collect dead animals in order to bury them in elaborate graves (**17.6**). The film has a touch of Luis

17.5 A studio set for *Les Portes de la nuit*; like *Children of Paradise*, the film was designed by Alexander Trauner.

17.6   Morbid rituals in *Forbidden Games*.

17.7   Chevalier directs in *Silence est d'or*, Clair's tribute to silent film.

17.8   A ballroom scene in *Les Grands manoeuvres* (1955), with a dancing couple seen in a white iris (a round mask) created by the view through a rolled-up newspaper.

Buñuel in the way that the children's morbid rituals unwittingly satirize the church's own death obsession. On the whole, however, Aurenche and Bost lyricize their subject, contrasting broadly comic rivalries among peasant families with the children's devotion to each other and to the beauty of death.

The Tradition of Quality encompassed other scriptwriter-director teams. One of the most notable was that of Charles Spaak, who had written many of the most famous films of the 1930s, and André Cayatte, a lawyer who began making social-problem films in the 1950s. Like other products of the Quality tradition, the Cayatte-Spaak films, such as *Justice est faite* ("Justice Is Done," 1950) and *Nous sommes tous des assassins* ("We Are All Killers," 1952), are polished studio-bound projects; but, in harshly criticizing the French judicial system, they avoid the usual romanticism and take a didactic, even preachy, attitude.

Most of the Tradition of Quality directors were young men who had launched their careers after the coming of sound, usually during the Occupation. Somewhat detached from this group was their contemporary Henri-Georges Clouzot, who had achieved notoriety with *Le Corbeau* ("The Crow," 1943; p. 300). Clouzot became internationally famous by specializing in mordant suspense films like *Quai des orfèvres* (1957), *The Wages of Fear* (1953), and *Les Diaboliques* (*Diabolique*, 1955). Clouzot, like the director-writer teams, continued the tradition of tightly scripted, fatalistic romances and thrillers associated with the French cinema of the 1930s and 1940s.

The Return of Older Directors

While young directors were achieving prominence, much older men like Marcel L'Herbier, Abel Gance, and Jean Epstein continued their work in film. With the pos-

sible exception of Epstein's *Le Tempestaire* ("Master of the Winds," 1947), however, no films by these directors had much influence on the course of French cinema. More influential was a middle generation of directors who had begun their careers in the late 1920s and early 1930s. Julien Duvivier, René Clair, Max Ophüls, Jean Renoir, and others had fled to Hollywood, but, after the war ended, they returned to their homeland.

Repatriation failed to revive Duvivier's career, but other exiled directors reestablished their reputations. They came to embody a postwar alternative to the Tradition of Quality—that of the veteran director not beholden to screenwriters but to a trusted cadre of assistants and technicians who could enable him to express his own personality.

Clair, for example, returned from a mildly successful stay in England and Hollywood to direct seven features. For nearly all of these, he relied on Léon Barsacq for set design (much as he had frequently turned to Lazare Meerson in the 1930s). Upon his return, Clair established continuity with his native tradition with *Le Silence est d'or* ("Silence Is Golden," 1947). Maurice Chevalier plays a turn-of-the-century film producer-director who oversees a love affair (**17.7**). Later films continued Clair's work in light comedy, but several were dramas in keeping with prevailing Cinema of Quality tastes. Throughout, Clair retained some of the playful exuberance of his early works, often paying homage to silent cinema (**17.8**).

Max Ophüls directed four films in Hollywood before returning to Paris, where he had worked a decade earlier. He renewed his career with four films: *La Ronde* (1950), *Le Plaisir* (1952), *Madame de . . .* (*The Earrings of Madame de . . .* , 1953), and *Lola Montès* (1955). For each film Ophüls called upon virtually the same collaborators: scriptwriter Jacques Natanson, cinematographer Christian Matras, costume designer Georges Annenkov, and set designer Jean d'Eaubonne. All four films were literary adaptations set in picturesque locales and periods; they featured international stars, gorgeous sets, appealing music, and extravagant costumes.

Yet these were not ordinary prestige pictures. *La Ronde* aroused controversy for its casual treatment of promiscuity, and *Lola Montès* provoked such a storm of attacks that several prominent directors signed a public letter defending it. Refusing to moralize or preach, Ophüls detachedly observes courting rituals at all levels of society. Sexual conquest usually brings no lasting pleasure, especially for the predatory and foolish males who fill Ophüls's films. Instead, Ophüls emphasizes the subterfuges through which women satisfy their desires. The romantic tales of deceived love that he presented in his American films gave way to a more explicit treatment of feminine sexual identity. In *Lola Montès,* the title character is a courtesan who rises through society and ends up as a performer in a circus, an object of fantasy but lifeless, withdrawn, and wholly artificial.

The films center on casual liaisons, extramarital affairs, and seduced innocence—all topics betraying Ophüls's roots in theater and operetta of the 1920s. Yet he complicates stock situations by means of episodic plot construction, presenting the film as a set of sketches (three in *Le Plaisir*), offering sharply separated flashbacks (*Lola Montès*), recycling characters across distinct episodes (in *La Ronde*), or following an object passed among characters (the earrings in *Madame de . . .*). This construction echoes the rhythm of arousal, brief fulfillment, and long-term dissatisfaction that is central to the theme of unconsummated love.

Ophüls distances us from his characters by several means—through irony, through a sense of a predetermined plot pattern that the characters do not realize, and especially through a narrator who addresses us directly. In *Lola Montès,* the ringmaster becomes a master of ceremonies who leads the circus audience, and us, into episodes from Lola's past. In *La Ronde,* the narrator strolls through what seems to be a street, mounts a theater stage to address us, and then is revealed to be in a film studio, turning the carousel that is the film's symbol of the endless dance of love (**17.9**). This reflexivity made Ophüls's works seem highly modernist to many young French critics.

A comparable self-consciousness pervades the films' style. In a period when other directors were following the Neorealist impulse toward simplicity in staging and shooting, Ophüls required all the artifice of the French studio cinema to create his rococo world of restaurants, parlors, ballrooms, artists' lofts, and cobblestone streets. The lines of his compositions are sweeping arabesques

17.9 The *meneur de jeu* ("master of ceremonies") in *La Ronde.*

that recall the frilly curves of the writing in the credit sequences. His camera sweeps as well, following characters as they stroll, dance, flirt, or race to their destinies. Even more than his Hollywood films, his French efforts return to the tradition of the *entfesselte camera,* the "unfastened camera,   of the German studio cinema of his youth (p. 203).

These tendencies of Ophüls's work are evident in a single shot from *La Ronde* (**17.10–17.14**; compare with 9.22–9.24). At one level, the play of hiding and revealing the action repeats the rhythm of frustration and satisfaction of desire in the narrative's episodes; but the sheer zest in the graceful dance of the camera with the characters is itself a source of the audience's—and director's—pleasure. James Mason wrote in a poem about Ophüls, "A shot that does not call for tracks / is agony for poor dear Max. . . . / Once, when they took away his crane / I thought he'd never smile again. [1]

Jean Renoir was the last of the exiled prewar directors to return to France, and he did so only sporadically. He continued to live in Beverly Hills, occasionally teaching at Los Angeles universities, until his death in 1979. After two postwar features made in Hollywood, he undertook an American-British coproduction shot on location in India, *The River* (1951). There Renoir claims to have learned a more serene and accepting vision of life: "The only thing that I can bring to this illogical, irresponsible, and cruel universe is my love. [2] His work from this point on was balanced between a worship of the sensuality of nature and a meditation on art as the repository of human values.

The themes of art and nature intermingle in *The River*. Three teenage girls are growing up in a Bengali

17.10 *La Ronde:* when the guilty wife comes to call on the young poet, he rushes to greet her.

17.11 In a reflexive gesture that announces the sheer artificiality of the set, the camera passes through the wall to show her entering.

17.12 As the couple move toward the parlor, Ophüls "loses" and then "finds" them through a play of props that momentarily block our view.

17.13, *left* She sits on the divan, and the camera draws a bit closer each time the poet tremblingly lifts a layer of veiling from her face.

17.14, *right* As he removes the hat, her face is finally revealed.

17.15, *left* *The River:* three girls reflect on new life . . .

17.16, *right* . . . and Renoir's camera moves serenely to the enduring river.

river town. Harriet, who narrates the film from the vantage point of adulthood, writes poetry and dreams up stories. Valerie, the oldest girl, becomes infatuated with a wounded American veteran, while Melanie, daughter of a British father and an Indian mother, quietly accedes to her role in Indian society and urges the tormented soldier to "accept everything." Renoir delicately balances two cultures, western and Indian, counterposing the girls' fantastic intrigues with the Indian community's seasonal rituals. The girls are initiated into adulthood through the cycle of life: the death of a little brother, the birth of a sister. In the last shot, the camera rises past the three girls reacting apprehensively to the baby's first squalls (**17.15**). The ceaselessly flowing river

becomes the center of the image (**17.16**), as the rhythms of nature frame the ongoing passions of everyday life. Yet westerners can learn this acceptance only through art, as embodied in Harriet's poem:

> The river runs, the round world spins;
> Dawn and lamplight; midnight, noon.
> Sun follows day, night, stars, and moon;
> The day ends, the end begins.

During the 1940s, Renoir's reputation was in eclipse. France ciné-clubs began a Renoir revival late in the decade, and the January 1952 issue of *Cahiers du cinéma* timed a reevaluation of his work to coincide

17.17   The last shot of Renoir's last film, *The Little Theatre of Jean Renoir*.

with the French release of *The River*. André Bazin's major essay, "The French Renoir," argued that he had made unique contributions to the nation's cinema. The 1950s saw a steady rise in Renoir's critical stock. A critics' forum at the 1958 Brussels World's Fair voted *Grand Illusion* one of the twelve best films of all times. Since the reconstructed version of *The Rules of the Game* was released in 1965, many critics have declared Renoir cinema's supreme artist.

Yet few critics would have rested that evaluation on Renoir's postwar work. Ironically, while many directors—some of them inspired by Renoir—exploited the sort of deep-space staging and complex camera movements that he had favored in the 1930s, he largely abandoned such techniques. He developed instead a simple, direct, at times theatrical style centered on the performer. His next film after *The River,* the French-Italian coproduction *The Golden Coach* (1953), pays homage to Italian classical theater (**Color Plate 17.1**). His first fully French-made—and most popular—film after the war, *French Cancan* (1955), dealt with the production of musical numbers in the Moulin Rouge in Paris. With *The Testament of Dr. Cordelier* (1959), he explored the television technique of shooting with multiple cameras to avoid interrupting the actor's performance. *Picnic on the Grass* (1959) made extensive use of zooms and telephoto framings, giving the actors considerable freedom of movement while the cameraman panned to follow them.

These post-*River* films continue Renoir's new concern with nature and art. *Picnic on the Grass* mocks artificial insemination and celebrates the joy of unbridled passion, while *Dr. Cordelier* shows the grotesque results

of tampering, Dr. Jekyll-like, with nature. *The Golden Coach* treats the theater as a supreme achievement: a sharing of experience through sensuous artifice. Renoir's Technicolor contrasts the pale pastels of the viceroy's court with the bright, saturated hues of the sixteenth- to eighteenth-century Italian *commedia dell'arte* plays (**Color Plate 17.1**). Such theatricality continued into Renoir's late career: his last film, *The Little Theatre of Jean Renoir* (1970; made for French and Italian television) concludes with a shot in which the cast bows to the camera (**17.17**). Indeed, while not filming, Renoir (like Luchino Visconti and Ingmar Bergman) was active in the theater, writing and directing plays.

If Renoir saw art as an entryway to nature, Jean Cocteau treated it as a path to myth and the supernatural. Cocteau considered himself above all a poet, even though his creative output included novels, plays, essays, drawings, stage designs, and films. He was centrally involved with many of the most important avant-garde developments in France after World War I: Sergey Diaghilev's ballets; Pablo Picasso's paintings; the music of Erik Satie, Igor Stravinsky, and *Les Six;* and the experimental cinema of the early sound era (p. 317). After a decade of stage work, Cocteau began writing scripts during the Occupation (for Jean Delannoy's *L'Eternal retour,* 1943, and Robert Bresson's *Dames du bois du Boulogne,* 1945).

After the war, Cocteau returned to filmmaking in earnest. Working frequently with the composer Georges Auric and the actor Jean Marais, Cocteau directed *Beauty and the Beast* (1945), *L'Aigle à deux têtes* (*The Eagle with Two Heads,* 1947), *Les Parents terribles* (1948; from his own play), *Orphée* (*Orpheus,* 1950), and *Le Testament d'Orphée* (*Testament of Orpheus,* 1960). Most are self-consciously "poetic" works, seeking to create a marvelous world sealed off from ordinary reality and to convey imaginative truths through evocative symbols.

While *Beauty and the Beast* remains an exemplary case of rendering a fairy tale on film, *Orphée* has proved the most influential of Cocteau's work of this period. The film freely updates the myth of Orpheus, the poet who tries to rescue his wife Eurydice from death. Cocteau's Orphée lives in contemporary Paris, with a cozy bourgeois home and a loving wife. But he becomes fascinated with the Princess, who roars through the city in a black limousine and who seems to have captured Cégeste, a dead poet whose cryptic verses are broadcast on the car radio. The Princess, an emissary of death, falls in love with Orphée and captures Eurydice. In Cocteau's personal mythology, the Poet becomes a charmed being, courting death in an attempt to discover enigmatic beauty.

17.18 *Orphée:* the mirror as threshold and curtain.

17.19 *Antoine et Antoinette* (1947, Becker): location shooting in the Paris Métro.

17.20 Simone Signoret as Marie, seen through her lover's eyes in *Casque d'or.*

In *Orphée* Cocteau creates a fantasy world through striking cinematic means. The afterlife, *la Zone,* is a maze of factory ruins raked by searchlights—at once a bombed-out city and a prison camp. The dead return to life in reverse motion, while slow motion renders the trip to death's world as a floating, somnambulistic journey. Mirrors become the passageways between death and life. When Orphée dons the magic gloves, he penetrates the quivering liquid curtain of the mirror (**17.18**).

Cocteau conceived rich images that could be translated into many media, confirming his belief that the poet is not merely a writer but rather someone who creates magic through any imaginative means. His career typifies the intense interest that creative writers like Jean-Paul Sartre, Claude Mauriac, Françoise Sagan, and Raymond Queneau took in the cinema. In addition, Cocteau's commitment to a cinema of private vision, even obsession, influenced New Wave directors and the American avant-garde.

Although Clair, Ophüls, Renoir, and Cocteau reasserted their distinctive identities in the postwar period, none represented a radical challenge to the prestige cinema. Two other directors struck a compromise with the Tradition of Quality while also reviving aspects of the 1930s realist tradition. Roger Leenhardt's first feature, *Les Dernières vacances* ("The Last Vacations," 1947) resembles the contemporary Aurenche Bost output in its treatment of a young man's lost love, but the plot also brings economic factors to the fore in a way atypical of the Cinema of Quality. Jacques Becker gave the neighborhood film of the 1930s a new realism of setting (**17.19**). His *Casque d'or* ("Golden Cask," 1952) is a turn-of-the-century drama of life among petty thieves and criminals. The doomed romance of Marie and the carpenter Jo, heightened by a radiant romanticization of the enigmatic woman (**17.20**), creates an ambience not far from the Cinema of Quality. *Le Trou* ("The Hole,"

1960), the story of a prison break, concentrates both on the mechanics of escape and on the need for trust among the prisoners as they cooperate in their flight. Many critics saw Becker's film as a humanistic call for collective unity reminiscent of 1930s Popular Front cinema.

New Independent Directors

One provision of the 1953 aid law encouraged the production of short films of artistic quality, and several filmmakers benefited from this. The veteran Jean Grémillon and the older Roger Leenhardt and Jean Mitry made several shorts in this period, but the most notable talents to emerge belonged to a younger generation. Alain Resnais, Georges Franju, and Chris Marker got their start making short poetic documentaries (see Chapter 21). Alexandre Astruc launched his career with *Le Rideau cramoisi* ("The Crimson Curtain," 1952), a symbolic Poe-like short containing no dialogue. Agnès Varda's short feature *La Pointe courte* (1954) has a regional realism recalling *La Terra trema,* but it also presents abstract compositions and a stylized, discontinuous editing of conversations (p. 443). In the work of Astruc and Varda we find the first stirrings of the New Wave.

More central to mainstream cinema at the time was the eccentric, Stetson-wearing Jean-Pierre Melville. (An ardent lover of American culture, he changed his name in honor of Herman Melville.) In 1946, he became a producer in order to direct. He worked as an independent, eventually owning his own studio. He produced, directed, wrote, edited, and occasionally starred in his films, once claiming that he never had enough employees to make up a decently long credits list.

Melville's first film, *Le Silence de la mer* ("The Silence of the Sea," 1949), now seems one of the most experimental works of its day. During the German Occupation, an officer is assigned to live with an old man

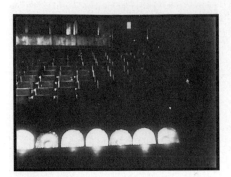

17.21 *Les Enfants terribles:* a scene begins with a shot facing an auditorium . . .

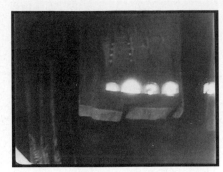

17.22 . . . the camera pulls back to reveal a curtain as seen through a window . . .

17.23 . . . then pans left to show us the children's bedroom.

17.24 An off-the-cuff shot from *Two Men in Manhattan* (1958), where Melville acted as his own cinematographer.

17.25, 17.26 Alternative versions of the robbery in *Bob le flambeur.*

and his niece. The officer tries, in halting French, to engage them in conversation; but they ignore him and never speak in his presence. A tense silence envelops almost every scene. The most minute sounds, particularly the ticking of a clock, become vivid. The voice-over narration often daringly reiterates what the images show, and even introduces dialogue with such lines as "And he said. . . ." As the German becomes more worn down by the pair, he too lapses into silence and is unable to talk freely with his friends outside the household. At last he leaves. The niece, looking at him blankly, finally speaks: "Adieu."

A similar freedom of treatment dominates *Les Enfants terribles* ("The Terrible Children," 1950), Melville's adaptation of Cocteau's novel. Again there is a voice-over commentary (spoken by Cocteau), which slips in and out between characters' lines and almost becomes a participant in the dialogue. Melville respects Cocteau's personal mythology—the film opens with a snowball fight reminiscent of that in *Blood of a Poet* (1932)—while giving the piece a self-consciously theatrical quality. Characters look at or speak to the camera, and Melville occasionally treats

the action as if it occurred on a stage (**17.21–17.23**). *Les Enfants terribles* exemplifies the rethinking of the relation between film and other arts of postwar modernism.

Melville gained most fame for such dry, laconic gangster films as *Bob le flambeur* (1955), *Le Doulos* (1962), *Le Deuxième souffle* ("Second Breath," 1966), and *Le Samourai* ("The Samurai," 1967). Expressionless men in trenchcoats and snap-brim hats stalk through gray streets to meet in piano bars. Almost completely impassive, they behave as if they have watched too many Hollywood films noirs—driving American sedans, pledging loyalty to their pals, dividing duties for a caper they intend to pull. Melville dwells on long silences as gunmen size each other up, stare at their reflections, or stoically realize that a deal has failed.

The films teem with bravura techniques—hand-held camerawork, long takes, and available-light shooting (**17.24**). Melville often experimented with narration. The plot of *Le Doulos* leaves out crucial scenes, leading us to misjudge the hero's motives as severely as do the gang members he seems to have betrayed. *Bob le flambeur* has a "hypothetical" sequence, introduced by the

17.27   In *Le Silence de la mer,* Melville paid homage to the deep focus of *Citizen Kane* (compare with 10.24).

17.28   Chiaroscuro lighting and slow performance in *Day of Wrath*.

voice-over narrator: "Here's how Bob planned it to happen.   We then see the robbery of the casino, played silently (**17.25**). This is very different from the way the heist turns out (**17.26**).

Melville loved to watch movies. ("Being a spectator is the finest profession in the world. [3]) Many of his films are tributes to American cinema (**17.27**), and he brought to French film some of the audacious energy of Hollywood B pictures. If Renoir fathered the New Wave, Melville was its godfather.

SCANDINAVIAN REVIVAL

Denmark and Sweden proved to have the two most influential Scandinavian national cinemas. As with Italian Neorealism and French postwar cinema, their first contributions to 1940s art cinema were made during the war.

Denmark had a strong film industry in the 1910s, but it lost its international standing during World War I. Late in the 1930s, Danish cinema regained some ground, thanks partly to generous government policies that taxed ticket prices to create a fund for artistic and cultural filmmaking.

The Germans invaded Denmark in 1940. As elsewhere, the Nazis' ban on film imports from the Allied countries spurred domestic production. Documentary and educational films continued to be made under the Occupation, but the most important film, made for the country's major firm, Palladium, was Carl Theodor Dreyer's *Day of Wrath* (1943). This somber study of witchcraft and religious dogma in a seventeenth-century

village marked Dreyer's return to Danish feature filmmaking after almost two decades. The film caused a sensation and was widely interpreted as an anti-Nazi allegory. When it was shown abroad after the war, it proved no less controversial, but more for its solemn tempo, its restrained technique (**17.28**), and its teasing ambiguities. *Day of Wrath* reestablished Dreyer on the international film scene (see box).

Swedish cinema had been in eclipse since Victor Sjöström and Mauritz Stiller were lured to Hollywood. Sweden was not invaded by the Nazis, but its own policy of neutrality shut out any foreign films considered propagandistic. The lack of competition stimulated the local industry. In 1942, the major studio Svensk Filmindustri hired Carl Anders Dymling as its head. He brought in Sjöström as artistic supervisor of production, a gesture that was considered to symbolize a return to the great Swedish filmmaking tradition.

Once the war ended, Danish and Swedish filmmaking benefited from Scandinavia's rapid recovery. Annual film outputs averaged 15 to 20 features in Denmark and twice that in Sweden—lower figures than the wartime peaks but remarkably high for small countries. Here quality filmmaking was comparatively cheap. Production was dominated by large companies that insisted on small budgets and short shooting schedules. Denmark levied an entertainment tax to subsidize "artistic films, and, in 1951, under pressure from filmmakers, Sweden initiated a comparable policy.

Apart from Dreyer, the most famous Scandinavian filmmakers of the postwar decade were Swedish. Like Sjöström and Stiller, most of these men had ties to a rich

CARL THEODOR DREYER

Between the generation of Sjöström and Stiller, who made their first films in 1912, and the generation who began work in the 1930s, only one Scandinavian director came to worldwide prominence. Dreyer's career prefigured that of the traveling "international" director of the postwar period, making films in Denmark, Sweden, Norway, Germany, and France, notably *The Passion of Joan of Arc* and *Vampyr* (p. 172). There followed a decade of inactivity, broken by some documentary shorts and *Day of Wrath*. After the Swedish *Two People* (1945), Dreyer made *Ordet* (*The Word*, 1954) and *Gertrud* (1964), both in Denmark. He died while planning a film on the life of Jesus.

Dreyer's earliest films revealed his fondness for static, highly pictorial compositions that alternate with intense

17.29 A conversation in *Gertrud*.

close-ups of actors' facial expressions. In *Joan of Arc* and *Vampyr* he also explored unusual camera movements—gymnastic rotations in the former, subtly misleading tracking movements in the latter. After *Vampyr*, Dreyer became convinced that the sound cinema required a more "theatrical" technique. His last four films, all adaptations of plays, are largely confined to interior settings and elaborate their action through lengthy dialogue exchanges. Using very long takes, Dreyer records dialogue in rigid, harmonious compositions (**17.29**). The camera arcs gracefully across parlors as characters slowly move from a sofa to a table, from a doorway to a bedside. "Camera movement," he wrote, "gives a fine soft rhythm."[4] Dreyer's version of modernism acknowledges the film's source in a literary text and creates a "minimal" cinema of minutely varied pace, much more subdued than the aggressive theatricality of Visconti or Bergman.

Through this ascetic style, Dreyer presents the ineffable mystery of faith and love. In *Day of Wrath*, Anne goes to the stake acknowledging she is a witch, but we wonder whether the community has merely convinced her that she is guilty. *Ordet* ends with one of the most daring scenes in film history: a miracle created by a child's faith. In *Gertrud*, the woman who demands absolute devotion retreats into isolation, worshiping an ideal of pure love.

Dreyer's films were not popular successes, but his single-minded tenacity within the commercial film industry and his rigorous exploration of powerful themes won him critical regard. His contributions to modernist technique influenced Jean-Luc Godard, Jean-Marie Straub, and other young directors.

theatrical tradition. During the second half of the nineteenth century, the Norwegian Henrik Ibsen and the Swede August Strindberg had made Scandinavian drama world famous. Both playwrights had a penchant for fantasy and expressionism, and their plays often used complex symbols to suggest characters' emotional states. Strindberg had also developed an intimate psychological drama called the *Kammerspiel*, or "chamber play." Typically, the Kammerspiel was set in a single room and staged in a small theater that would bring the audience close to the actors. (See pp. 109–110 for a discussion of the influence of Kammerspiel on silent German cinema.) Of the filmmakers marked by these modernist trends, the two most influential were Alf Sjöberg and Ingmar Bergman (for more on the latter, see Chapter 19).

After making one film in 1929, Sjöberg became the major director at Stockholm's Royal Dramatic Theatre. He returned to filmmaking in 1939 and completed several films during the war. One of the most original was *The Heavenly Play* (1942), which fused the silent-film traditions of naturalistic landscape and symbolic drama (**17.30**) to create an allegorical fantasy of Protestant redemption.

More influential outside Sweden was Sjöberg's *Torment* (1944), scripted by Bergman. A high-school student tortured by his Latin teacher, nicknamed Caligula, discovers that the man is a lecher, a Nazi sympathizer, and a murderer. *Torment*'s sympathy with teenage rebellion emerges not only from its rather schematic story but also from a visual style derived from German Ex-

17.30, *left*   Chiaroscuro and Expressionist setting in Sjöberg's *The Heavenly Play.*

17.31, *right*   *Torment:* Sinister, endless flights of stairs in the school are similar to those found in the city streets.

17.32, *left*   Caligula as Nosferatu, in *Torment* (compare with 5.16).

17.33, *right*   Two time periods in one shot: Julie, sitting in the foreground, tells of an episode from her childhood; in the background her mother talks with her as a child.

pressionism. Looming architecture and long, sharp shadows turn the entire city into a prison (**17.31**). The pudgy Caligula, with his round spectacles and fussy manner, becomes a wartime Caligari, and his shadow threatens the lovers in a gesture that echoes Murnau's vampire in *Nosferatu* (**17.32**).

After the war, Sjöberg continued to move between theater and cinema. After staging Strindberg's 1888 naturalist play *Miss Julie,* he adapted it to the screen in 1951. The film concentrates upon the performances, especially Anita Björk's skittery Julie, but it also expands the original Kammerspiel. In Strindberg's play, characters recount their memories in monologues. Sjöberg dramatizes the scenes as flashbacks that combine past and present in the same shot (**17.33**). Conventions of what would become art cinema can be found in Strindberg's original Kammerspiel, but Sjöberg adds a modernist ambiguity derived from film's power over space and time.

ENGLAND: QUALITY AND COMEDY

British film output declined during the war, when filmmaking personnel were conscripted and studio facilities were turned to military use. Yet high wartime attendance boosted the industry. The main companies—the Rank Organization, headed by J. Arthur Rank, and the Associated British Picture Corporation—expanded their domains. Associated British owned a major theater chain, while Rank

controlled two others and owned the largest distribution firm, several studios, and two producing companies.

Problems in the Industry

In 1944, a report entitled "Tendencies to Monopoly in the Cinematograph Film Industry" had recommended that the major companies' power be reduced. The "Palache report," as it came to be known, remained the center of debate for years, but it was not acted on soon, partly because the industry seemed robust. High attendance continued, with that of 1946 the highest ever. More British films were being made, and many were of high enough quality to be popular at home and competitive abroad. Moreover, because Rank needed many films for his theater chains, he supported several small independent producers. Rank also had ties with some of the American Majors, and English films began to enter the United States regularly, often becoming successful there. For a few years it seemed as though the intense competition between the British and American firms might diminish.

Yet trouble soon appeared. Production costs were rising, few films made profits, and Hollywood films commanded 80 percent of screen time. The left-wing Labour government, committed to fighting monopolies and protecting British industry from American competition, tackled these problems.

In 1947, the government imposed a 75-percent tariff on all imported American films. When the U.S. industry immediately threatened a boycott, the government compromised and, in 1948, established a quota reminiscent of the prewar era: 45 percent of all screenings in Britain had to consist of British films. Many exhibitors and distributors, dependent on American films, opposed the quota, and it was soon reduced again, to 30 percent.

The Rank Organization was vertically integrated, and only a few firms controlled the industry, so the government could have forced companies to sell part of their holdings, as the American government did in the Paramount decision of 1948 (pp. 327–328). Those trying to cure the industry's woes, however, realized that "divorcement decrees would be suicidal in Great Britain. If firms were forced to sell their theaters, American companies would simply buy them.

The government attempted another solution in 1949. The National Film Finance Corporation (NFFC) was founded for the purpose of loaning money to independent producers. Unfortunately, £3 million, over half the total amount loaned out, went to one of the largest independents, British Lion, which producer Alexander Korda had acquired in 1946. British Lion soon went bankrupt, and its heavy losses weakened the NFFC's ability to support other firms.

In 1950, after a year of financial crisis, the government tried once more to bolster production. It reduced the entertainment tax charged on theater tickets but added a levy against ticket sales, part of which was given to producers. The "Eady levy, named after its planner, thus provided a production subsidy comparable to those that appeared at about the same time in Sweden, France, and Italy.

The Eady levy worked reasonably well and remained in force for several decades. Nevertheless, the film industry continued to decline during the 1950s, as competition with television increased. The problem of monopoly in the industry intensified. Rank and the Associated British Picture Corporation bought up some theaters, and other small, independent exhibitors were forced out of business by declining attendance. Despite industry problems, however, the decade after the war saw a number of important films and trends.

Literary Heritage and Eccentricity

British producers continued to debate whether to produce high-budget prestige films for export or more modest films aimed at home audiences. As always, many films were literary adaptations featuring famous actors. Laurence Olivier followed up his wartime success *Henry V*

17.34 *Oliver Twist:* an elaborate set re-creates Victorian London.

(1945) by directing and starring in *Hamlet* (1948) and *Richard III* (1955). Gabriel Pascal continued his association with the plays of George Bernard Shaw by making a lavish version of *Caesar and Cleopatra* (1946), with Vivien Leigh and Claude Rains. This approach to filmmaking was comparable to the French Tradition of Quality. In addition, two major British directors achieved international reputations during this period.

David Lean had his start during the war codirecting *In Which We Serve* (1942) with Noel Coward. His postwar career began with the release of *Brief Encounter* (1945), a story of a middle-aged man and woman, both trapped in unexciting marriages, who fall in love. They meet repeatedly but resist having a sexual affair. Lean's restrained romanticism centers around Celia Johnson's portrayal of the heroine.

Lean went on to make two popular adaptations of Dickens novels, *Great Expectations* (1946) and *Oliver Twist* (1948). Both featured Alec Guinness, who within a few years became the most popular actor in exported British films. *Oliver Twist* is typical of Lean's postwar films, containing large, dark sets, deep-focus compositions, and film-noir lighting (**17.34**). Lean also made comedies, such as *Hobson's Choice* (1953), in which a strong-willed heroine defeats her tyrannical father. Lean later gained wider renown with costume epics such as *Lawrence of Arabia* (1962) and *Doctor Zhivago* (1965).

The other prominent director of the postwar years was Carol Reed. Reed had begun directing in the late 1930s, but his international reputation was built upon *Odd Man Out* (1947), *The Fallen Idol* (1948), *The Third Man* (1949), *An Outcast of the Islands* (1951), and *The Man Between* (1953). Like Lean, Reed favored

17.35 Location shooting in *Odd Man Out*.

17.36 The wounded hero stares down at the table . . .

17.37 . . . and we see his point of view of a pool of beer, with various characters from earlier scenes of the film superimposed in the bubbles.

dramatic lighting, often intensified by flashy camera techniques. Thus *The Third Man* (probably influenced by Orson Welles, who plays the villain) is full of canted framings and uses an unusual instrument, the zither, for its musical accompaniment.

Reed's awareness of emerging art-cinema norms is evident in one of his most important films, *Odd Man Out*. An Irish Republican Army unit steals payroll money to fund its terrorist activities. During the robbery, the hero (James Mason) is wounded. As he flees, he encounters a series of people who try to save him or to exploit him. While Reed shot some scenes in Irish slums (**17.35**), several passages stress a more subjective realism (**17.36, 17.37**).

Less famous than Lean and Reed, Michael Powell and Emeric Pressburger were undoubtedly the most unusual British filmmakers of the era. They had created their production company, The Archers, in 1943, and supported it with Rank's help. Writing, producing, and directing in collaboration, the pair made modest dramas in black and white and elaborate Technicolor productions.

Typical of their offbeat approach is *I Know Where I'm Going!* (1945). A strong-willed young woman engaged to a rich industrialist attempts to join him on a Scottish island. As she waits for the weather to clear, she struggles against falling in love with a pleasant, but impoverished, Scottish landowner. Powell and Pressburger display their characteristic feeling for the British countryside, as well as their sympathy for eccentric characters. They even make the headstrong, greedy heroine sympathetic. Another intimate drama, *A Small Back Room* (1948), deals with the intriguing subject of an alcoholic whose job is to defuse unexploded bombs left in England after the war.

Powell and Pressburger directed some of the most opulent color films ever made. Their most popular film,

The Red Shoes (1948), and its successor, *The Tales of Hoffmann* (1951), use ballet to motivate deliriously stylized decors and cinematography. *A Matter of Life and Death* (aka *Stairway to Heaven,* 1946) centers on a British pilot who impossibly survives a potentially fatal crash and argues in a heavenly courtroom (in his dream?) that he should be sent back to earth to join the woman he loves. Color film stock used for the sequences on earth contrasts with black-and-white film used for heaven.

One of Powell and Pressburger's color masterpieces is *Black Narcissus* (1947), a story of nuns trying to run a dispensary and school in a Tibetan palace formerly used as a harem. Sexual frustrations, a lack of understanding of local customs, and the general ambience of the setting drive some of the nuns to dereliction of duty, nostalgic fantasies, madness, and even attempted murder before the convent is finally abandoned. The directors created a vivid sense of the Himalayas, even though they shot the film wholly in the studio (**Color Plate 17.2**).

Powell and Pressburger's most extravagant works contrast strongly with the modest product of Michael Balcon's Ealing Studios. Balcon, a veteran of the industry since the early 1920s, became head of Ealing in 1938. In the postwar period Ealing prospered because the Rank Organization helped finance production and released the studio's films through its distribution network. Balcon achieved a consistency of tone across the studio by making decisions democratically (allowing the studio staff to vote at roundtable meetings) and by giving filmmakers an unusual degree of independence.

Today, Ealing Studios is usually associated with comedies starring Alec Guinness, Stanley Holloway, and other major British actors, but only about one-third of the company's output was in this genre. Indeed, one of the most successful Ealing films is a realistic drama about police life, *The Blue Lamp* (1950). Scenes in

17.38 The Ealing Studios, nestled in a suburban neighborhood, had no backlot on which to build sets. Directors filmed scenes on location, as in *The Blue Lamp*.

17.39 A landscape of bombed-out London in *The Lavender Hill Mob*.

which a veteran cop explains the job to a new recruit give a systematic account of police procedure, in the tradition of the 1930s and wartime British documentaries. As in other Ealing films, many scenes were shot on location in poor or bombed-out areas of London (**17.38**).

Ealing's reputation for comedies was established with three 1949 releases, *Passport to Pimlico* (directed by Henry Cornelius), *Whiskey Galore!* (aka *Tight Little Island*, directed by Alexander Mackendrick), and *Kind Hearts and Coronets* (directed by Robert Hamer). *Kind Hearts*, in which Guinness plays eight different characters, swept him to international stardom. While many Hollywood-style comedies depended on slapstick or on sophisticated screwball situations, Ealing's humor was built on injecting a single fantastic premise into an ordinary situation. *Passport to Pimlico*, for example, takes place in the drab working-class London district of Pimlico, and much of the film was shot on location in realistic style. Yet the plot depends on a zany premise: researchers discover that the suburb is actually not part of England at all but belongs to the French district of Burgundy. As a result, following a maddeningly linear logic, Britishers must have a passport to enter Pimlico, and the residents are no longer subject to London's rationing restrictions. Like other Ealing comedies, *Passport to Pimlico* presents an imaginary escape from postwar austerity.

Another typical Ealing comedy is Charles Crichton's *The Lavender Hill Mob* (1951). The hero, played by Guinness, works guarding gold shipped to London banks. With a gang of mild-mannered crooks, he plans and executes a massive heist. The Ealing fantasy emerges when the gang disguises the bullion as souvenir

17.40 When the Lavender Hill Mob plot their crime, the low-key lighting and deep-focus composition suggest Hollywood gangster films of the 1940s (compare with 15.18–15.20).

Eiffel Towers. The film mixes realism with stylization. The near-documentary opening sequence depicts the hero's daily routine. Scenes shot on location (**17.39**) contrast with scenes that parody film noir and even Ealing's own *Blue Lamp* (**17.40**). Crichton returned to prominence decades later with *A Fish Called Wanda* (1989), which many critics considered an updating of the Ealing tradition.

The Ealing comedies depend on a notion of English eccentricity: in *The Lavender Hill Mob*, the hero entertains a sweet elderly woman by reading lurid crime thrillers to her. The last major film from the studio, *The Ladykillers* (1955), revolves around a dotty old lady who discovers that the string quintet players renting her spare room are actually a gang of robbers.

Art-House Success Abroad

Distinctive though the Ealing and Archers films were, they fall into recognizable commercial genres and employ classical storytelling techniques. Yet the success of these films abroad depended largely on the same art theaters that showed Italian Neorealist or Scandinavian films. Although the films were not themselves modernist, they reinforced the trend toward international film circulation that fostered art-cinema trends elsewhere. In particular, they showed that the U.S. market could support European filmmaking to an unprecedented extent.

The pattern was set quietly by *I Know Where I'm Going!*, which became an unexpected hit in a New York art house. Soon afterward Olivier's *Henry V* (U.S. release 1946) ran for thirty-four weeks in a small Manhattan theater at high admission prices. In 1948, his *Hamlet* became such a hit in small theaters that it moved into wide release and won several Oscars. *Brief Encounter, Blithe Spirit*, and other British films prospered in the art-house circuit, with *The Red Shoes*, astonishingly, becoming the top U.S. box-office attraction of 1948. An Ealing comedy could make more money in art houses than in limited release to larger theaters.

In the mid-1950s, most of the older creative figures of the early postwar era lost momentum. Powell and Pressburger broke up The Archers in 1956; Powell's career was nearly curtailed by the scandal aroused by *Peeping Tom* (1960). (Although it was a thoughtful examination of a serial killer's psyche, *Peeping Tom* was denounced as lurid trash by British critics; feminists protested its revival in the early 1970s.) Heavy losses forced Balcon to sell Ealing's studio facilities in 1955, though he made a few more films before losing the company. Some of the most successful directors of this era, such as Lean and Reed, went on to make big-budget, American-financed projects. These developments cleared the way for a generation of filmmakers who would turn against the polished cinema of the postwar decade.

· ·

Notes and Queries

POSTWAR FRENCH FILM THEORY

Postwar Paris saw a revival of theoretical writings about film as art. Some writers suggested that film aesthetics owed less to the theater than to the novel. In her book *The Age of the American Novel*, trans. Eleanor Hochman (New York: Ungar, 1972; originally published 1948), Claude-Edmonde Magny argued that the work of Hemingway and Faulkner showed strong affinities with the style of American cinema. She also suggested that the camera lens was like the organizing consciousness of the narrator in literary works. Alexandre Astruc spoke of the "camera-pen," *la caméra-stylo*, and predicted that filmmakers would treat their works as vehicles of self-expression much as writers did (Alexandre Astruc, "The Birth of a New Avant Garde. La Caméra-Stylo," in Peter Graham, ed., *The New Wave* [New York: Doubleday, 1968], pp. 17–24).

André Bazin also pointed out that a "novelistic" cinema seemed to be emerging in France and Italy. In his opinion, films by Bresson, Clément, Leenhardt, and other directors went beyond the theater's depiction of character behavior. These directors either plunged into the depths of psychology or moved beyond the individual to portray, in a realistic fashion, the world in which the characters lived. Many of Bazin's essays are collected in Hugh Gray, trans. and ed., *What Is Cinema? I* (Berkeley: University of California Press, 1967), and *What Is Cinema? II* (Berkeley: University of California Press, 1971); see also Bazin's *Jean Renoir*, trans. W. W. Halsey II and William H. Simon (New York: Simon and Schuster, 1973).

The comparison of film to literature also called attention to style and narrative construction. Theorists began to reevaluate the traditional analogy between film style and language by developing a notion of *écriture cinematographique*, or "filmic writing." Bazin revolutionized film criticism by his detailed discussions of how editing, camerawork, and deep-space staging offered expressive possibilities to the filmmaker. He and his peers were also sensitive to how filmic storytelling could create ellipses and could shift point of view. And, by assuming the filmmaker to be a novelist-on-film, the critic could examine even a popular film as the vehicle of a personal vision. There arose debates about whether the filmmaker could be considered an *auteur*, or author, of his works (see Chapter 19).

At the same time, Bazin and others began to ponder the possibility that cinema might be radically unlike all traditional arts. They argued that the film medium has as its basic purpose to record and reveal the concrete world in which we find ourselves. This line of thought treated cinema as a "phenomenological" art, one suited to capture the reality of everyday perception. For thinkers like Bazin (p. 374) and Amédée Ayfre, the Italian Neorealist films exemplify cinema's power to reveal the ties of humans to their surroundings.

Discussions of the theoretical trends of this era can be found in Dudley Andrew, *André Bazin* (New York: Oxford University Press, 1978), and Jim Hillier, ed., Cahiers du Cinéma: *The 1950s: Neo-Realism, Hollywood, New Wave* (Cambridge, MA: Harvard University Press, 1985), especially pp. 1–17. A related development, the academic discipline of filmology, emerged at the same period. For a discussion, see Edward Lowry, *The Filmology Movement and Film Study in France* (Ann Arbor: UMI, 1985).

THE POWELL-PRESSBURGER REVIVAL

For several years, Michael Powell and Emeric Pressburger remained marginal figures, but their reputations have risen substantially since the late 1970s.

The team made some films that were widely popular, but much of their work was so eccentric that it earned unfavorable reviews. Their baroque melodramas and fantasies lay outside the documentary tradition long considered the strength of British cinema. After the breakup of their production company in 1956 and the scandal surrounding Powell's *Peeping Tom* in 1960, most historians treated them as minor filmmakers. British auteurism tended to focus on Hollywood directors and treat English filmmaking as pallid and stodgy. Raymond Durgnat (writing as O. O. Green) presented an intelligent defense in "Michael Powell," *Movie* 14 (autumn 1965): 17–20 (also in his *A Mirror for England* [New York: Praeger, 1971], in revised form). This was, however, largely ignored.

By the mid-1960s, *Peeping Tom* had acquired cult status. The National Film Theatre in London presented a Powell retrospective in 1970, and the National Film Archive and BBC restored a few important films. In 1977, Powell received an award at the Telluride Film Festival in Colorado. American director Martin Scorsese helped fund a rerelease of *Peeping Tom,* and the film showed at the 1979 New York Film Festival, with Powell in attendance, to a sell-out crowd. See John Russell Taylor, "Michael Powell: Myths and Supermen," *Sight and Sound* 47, no. 4 (autumn 1978): 226–29; and David Thomson, "Mark of the Red Death," *Sight and Sound* 49, no. 4 (autumn 1980): 258–62. British historian Ian Christie has helped both in the restoration of Powell and Pressburger's films and in the dissemination of information on the pair. See his *Arrows of Desire: The Films of Michael Powell and Emeric Pressburger* (London: Waterstone, 1985). See also Christie's "Powell and Pressburger: Putting Back the Pieces," *Monthly Film Bulletin* 611 (December 1984): back cover, for an account of how their films have been cut and, in some cases, restored. See also Scott Salwolke, *The Films of Michael Powell and the Archers* (Lanham, MD: Scarecrow, 1997) and James Howard, *Michael Powell* (London: B. T. Batsford, 1996).

Powell and Pressburger have influenced Martin Scorsese, Francis Coppola, Brian De Palma, George Lucas, and Derek Jarman. *Scorsese on Scorsese,* ed. David Thompson and Ian Christie (Boston: Faber and Faber, 1990) contains numerous references to Powell. Powell tells his own story in *Michael Powell: A Life in Movies* (London: Heinemann, 1986) and *Million Dollar Movie* (New York: Random House, 1994).

REFERENCES

1. Quoted in Andrew Sarris, ed., *Interviews with Film Directors* (Indianapolis: Bobbs-Merrill, 1967), p. 295.
2. Quoted in Christopher Faulkner, *The Social Cinema of Jean Renoir* (Princeton, NJ: Princeton University Press, 1986), p. 170.
3. Quoted in Rui Nogueira, ed., *Melville on Melville* (New York: Viking, 1971), p. 64.
4. Quoted in Sarris, *Interviews with Film Directors,* p. 111.

FURTHER READING

Barrot, Jean-Pierre. "Une Tradition de la qualité." In H. Agel et al., *Sept ans de cinema français.* Pais: Cerf, 1953, pp. 26–37.

Bellour, Raymond. *Alexandre Astruc.* Paris: Seghers, 1963.

Bergery, Benjamin. "Henri Alekan: The Doyen of French Cinematography." *American Cinematographer.* 77, no. 3 (March 1996): 46–52.

Braucourt, Guy. *André Cayette.* Paris: Seghers, 1969.

Farwagi, André. *René Clement.* Paris: Seghers, 1967.

Jarvie, Ian. "The Postwar Economic Policy of the American Film Industry: Europe 1945–1950." *Film History* 4, no. 4 (1990): 277–88.

Jeancolar, Jean-Pierre. "L'Arrangement Blum-Byrnes à l'épreuve des faits. Les relations (cinématographiques) franco-américaines de 1944 à 1948." *1895* 13 (December 1992): 3–49.

Nogueira, Ruy, ed. *Melville on Melville.* New York: Viking, 1971.

Passek, Jean-Loup. *D'un cinéma l'autre: notes sur le cinéma français des années cinquante.* Paris: Centre Georges Pompidou, 1988.

Turk, Edward Baron. *Child of Paradise: Marcel Carné and the Golden Age of French Cinema.* Cambridge, MA: Harvard University Press, 1989.

Willemen, Paul, ed. *Ophüls.* London: British Film Institute, 1978.

Zimmer, Jacques, and Chantal de Béchade. *Jean-Pierre Melville.* Paris: Edilig, 1983.

CHAPTER 18

POSTWAR CINEMA BEYOND THE WEST, 1945–1959

In the mid-1950s, the world was producing around 2,800 feature films per year. About 35 percent of these came from the United States and western Europe (termed the "First World"). Another 5 percent were made in the USSR and the eastern European countries under its control. Although quantitatively small, the output of this "Second World" dominated the Soviet bloc (where few films were imported from the West) and had notable influence in other regions.

Sixty percent of feature films were made outside the western world and the Soviet bloc. Japan accounted for about 20 percent of the world total. The rest came from India, Hong Kong, Mexico, and other less industrialized nations. Such a stunning growth in film production in the developing countries is one of the major events in film history.

This chapter examines postwar filmmaking in selected nonwestern regions: Japan, the USSR and its satellites, and areas of what was coming to be called the "Third World."

GENERAL TENDENCIES

After World War II, international affairs were dominated by two superpowers, the United States and the USSR. In the postwar settlements, the United States brought Japan into the western alliance while the USSR took control of portions of eastern Europe. For the next several decades, the bipolar power split created competing spheres of influence.

Over the same period, colonies began to break away from the western European empires. Through negotiation or insurrection, Indonesia, the Philippines, India, Pakistan, Burma, Egypt, Cuba, and other countries gained independence in the 1940s and 1950s. Western policymakers feared that resources and markets would be lost if these new nations aligned themselves with the USSR. The 1949 Chinese revolution, which installed a government allied with Moscow, demonstrated that communism could take power in an underdeveloped nation.

Most decolonized nations joined the western camp, since local leaders had been trained there and conditions for investment and trade were firmly established. Under this "neocolonialism," such countries were politically sovereign but economically dependent on the western powers. Many countries in Latin America were prime examples of neocolonialism.

The Third World, where cities were growing fast and television had hardly penetrated, presented a huge market for films. The USSR and its satellite countries virtually banned American films, but in almost every other market Hollywood cinema ruled. As in Europe, U.S. firms established powerful regional distribution companies throughout the Third World, and exhibitors often favored the popular and cheap Hollywood product. The Motion Picture Export Association of America (MPEAA) negotiated favorable quotas and fiscal policies with local governments (p. 328). Soon, prewar conditions returned, with Hollywood movies occupying between 50 and 90 percent of screen time in most countries.

Yet as Hollywood cut back its output in the 1950s, it could not fill the appetites of Third World urban populations who might go to the movies once a month or even once a week—a far higher average than that in the United States or much of Europe. And, in most countries, indigenous stars, locales, and music remained powerful attractions.

Despite the U.S. companies' dominance of world markets, then, film production grew in the developing countries. Burma, Pakistan, South Korea, and the Philippines had had virtually no film production before the war, but in the 1950s each produced more films annually than almost any European country. In postwar Egypt, the growth of cities and an economic upturn created a film-making boom that made Egyptian films the most widely circulated Middle Eastern product. The most spectacular rise occurred in Hong Kong; film output grew from about 70 features in 1950 to over 250 in 1962—more than that of the United States and Britain combined.

Nonwestern film enterprises organized production in various ways. In the Soviet sphere of influence, the centralized vertical monopoly system established in the USSR was put in place. Directors, writers, and technicians were kept on salary whether working or not. At every step a film was subjected to financial and ideological scrutiny. The system was at its most inflexible in the

Soviet Union and China; in the USSR, output dropped dramatically after the war. The major eastern bloc nations, however, managed to increase production during the 1950s, thanks to more decentralized creative policies, a weakening of ideological controls, increased export possibilities, and overall growth in the economies.

Outside the eastern bloc, the most common option was artisanal, small-company production on the postwar European model. In India and South Korea, where the government refused to support the industry, independent production created chaos, with speculators using cinema to turn a quick profit. In Mexico, where the state protected the industry, independent production proceeded in a somewhat more orderly fashion.

Some countries sought to imitate Hollywood's vertically integrated studio system. This strategy failed in Argentina and succeeded only partially in Brazil, but it proved successful in East Asia. Japan sustained its strong vertical oligopoly throughout the postwar era. A similar structure appeared in Hong Kong, when the major companies formed the "Big Eight" combine. By 1961, the prosperous Shaw Brothers company surpassed even Hollywood's "factory system" by building Movieland, a 46-acre complex of studios, sets, laboratory facilities, and dormitories where 1,500 performers and 2,000 staff worked around the clock.

New countries earned some international notice. The Asian Film Festival (established in Tokyo in 1954) and the Moscow International Film Festival (1959) brought nonwestern cinemas greater worldwide recognition. By and large, however, the rich film traditions of the Middle East, the Far East, Latin America, and the Indian subcontinent remained almost completely unknown in the West. Even today, archives and distribution companies do not hold many such films, and many nations have been unable to preserve representative examples of their own output. Thus any generalizations about tendencies in theme, structure, and style must remain tentative.

As in the West, most production was in popular genres: action and adventure films, romances, comedies, musicals, melodramas, and adaptations of literary classics. More "serious" works often concentrated on episodes of national history or depicted contemporary social problems. Some filmmakers sought to create a cinema that would be more realistic than mainstream production. Many directors were strongly influenced by documentary practices and Italian Neorealism. In addition, some countries brought forth a sector of filmmaking inspired by western art cinema.

Filmmakers in Japan, the Second World, and the Third World were also influenced by formal trends of

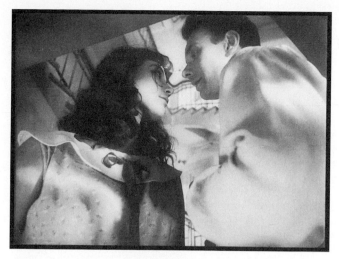

18.1 The distorting effect of the wide-angle lens in *The Cranes Are Flying* (USSR, 1957).

the West. Scriptwriters made flashback construction common. Directors began using wide-angle lenses to create deep-space staging and deep-focus cinematography (**18.1**). The zoom lens, revived in late-1940s Hollywood, gained wider international currency through its extensive use in Hungarian and Polish films of the late 1950s. In all, the postwar decades saw a return to the cross-national stylistic influences and the circulation of technology that World War II had momentarily halted.

JAPAN

World War II devastated Japan. American firebombing laid waste to the largest cities, and the dropping of atomic bombs on Hiroshima and Nagasaki left casualties on an unprecedented scale. By the time Japan surrendered on August 15, 1945, it had lost almost 8 million soldiers and over 600,000 civilians. U.S. forces moved to occupy Japan, directing it toward allegiance with the First World.

The Occupation was administered by General Douglas MacArthur; both he and his official bureaucracy were known as Supreme Commander of the Allied Powers (SCAP). SCAP's goal was to remake Japanese society. The large, family-run conglomerates, known as *zaibatsu*, were dissolved. Rural landlords' estates were given to tenant farmers. Universities were created, and the country had a new constitution. Women were granted the vote, and divorce and inheritance laws were liberalized.

As the 1949 Chinese revolution made the American government fear the spread of communism throughout Asia, Japan was designated Asia's bulwark of western

capitalism and democracy. In this cold war atmosphere, some SCAP reforms, such as the encouragement of labor unions, were rapidly scaled back. With American economic assistance the economy was rebuilt. When the Korean War (1950–1953) gave Japan a crucial strategic role and a source of war-related business, the country began a period of unprecedented economic growth.

Industry Recovery under the Occupation

SCAP officials took a keen interest in the film industry. They reviewed wartime productions for "feudalistic" and "nationalistic" content. Hundreds of films were banned, many of them burned. SCAP encouraged films on democratic themes, such as women's rights and the struggle against militarism, and even insisted that modernization should include kissing scenes (long forbidden by Japanese tradition). But not wishing to strengthen left-wing sentiments, SCAP also discouraged films criticizing Japanese militarism or the wartime suppression of civil rights.

During the war, the film industry had consolidated its forces under three companies: Shochiku, Toho, and Daiei (see p. 252). Under Occupation auspices, independent production grew considerably, but the three vertically integrated firms controlled distribution and exhibition. The companies worked with SCAP authorities to plan films that followed the new policies. In turn, SCAP restrained labor activities that threatened to disrupt the studios.

With relative stability in the production sector, other companies could enter the market. During a 1946 strike at Toho, one union faction went off to form an alternative company, Shintoho ("New Toho"). At first, Shintoho shared distribution and theaters with the parent company, but, in 1950, the units formally split into two vertically integrated firms. In 1951, Toei ("Eastern Film Company") also entered the field. By building theaters in the center of urban traffic and by winning control of the cheaper double-feature market, Toei became in 1956 the most profitable studio in the industry. And in 1954 the moribund Nikkatsu was revitalized. It refurbished its studios and lured disaffected employees away from other firms. Soon it was, like its competitors, turning out a film a week.

The postwar era saw a rapid recovery and expansion of the industry. SCAP had admitted hundreds of American films to Japan, but, despite their popularity, the domestic industry kept firm control of the market. By the mid-1950s, Japanese companies could count on 19 million viewers per week—nearly half the attendance in the United States and five times that in France. Overall, the decade brought unprecedented prosperity, with production increasing to almost 500 films a year by 1960. Thanks to this success, the industry was able to invest in the Fujicolor process (first seen in *Carmen Comes Home,* 1951) and in widescreen technology, which quickly became standard in Japanese studios.

Japanese cinema also burst onto the international scene. Masaichi Nagata, head of Daiei, began to concentrate on foreign markets. His breakthrough was *Rashomon,* which won the Golden Lion at the Venice Film Festival of 1951 and the Academy Award for the best foreign film. Though hardly a typical Japanese film, *Rashomon* immediately drew worldwide attention. Nagata began producing high-quality costume pictures suitable for export. "America was making action pictures," he explained. "France had love stories, and Italy realism. So I chose to approach the world market with the appeal of Japanese historical subjects. Old Japan is more exotic than Westernized Japan is to Westerners."[1] Such Daiei films as *Ugetsu Monogatari* (1953), *Sansho the Bailiff* (1954), and *Gate of Hell* (1954) won festival awards and increased western audiences' appetite for Japanese cinema.

Banned during the Occupation, *jidai-geki* (historical films) reappeared soon after the Americans had departed in 1952. The *chambara* (swordfight movie) remained the staple product, while more dignified jidai-geki, principally Teinosuke Kinugasa's *Gate of Hell* and Akira Kurosawa's *Seven Samurai* (1954), renewed the genre.

Still, Japanese production concentrated on the broad category of *gendai-geki* (films set in the contemporary period). These included extreme leftist films, pacifist and antinuclear films, salaryman comedies, musicals, films about delinquent youths, and monster movies (e.g., *Godzilla,* 1954). Most popular were the *shomin-geki* (films of ordinary daily life). These melodramas of family crises or young romance sustained entire studios and often became sensational hits. Such films were seldom exported because they were regarded as too mundane and slowly paced for the international audience.

The Veteran Directors

Directors who had made their initial successes in the 1920s and 1930s continued to play central roles in the postwar era. For example, Kinugasa continued to be known for his quality jidai-geki. His postwar production of *Actress* (1947), based on the life of a pioneer of modern Japanese theater, is less typical of his output than the

18.2   A high-angle shot in *Gate of Hell* recalls the "floating perspective" of Japanese prints.

florid *Gate of Hell* (1954). Shot on Eastman Color stock, the film self-consciously borrowed techniques of Japanese scroll painting, not only in its color schemes but also in its high-angle views (**18.2**). Less well known than Kinugasa's films was the work of Hiroshi Shimizu, who continued to produce excellent films about children. His *Children of the Beehive* (1948) used nonprofessional actors and real locations to portray the plight of war orphans. Shimizu founded an orphanage and used many of the children as players in subsequent films.

Mikio Naruse, who had worked for various studios in the 1930s, made several outstanding shomin-geki films for Toho, Shintoho, and Daiei. *Repast* (1951), *Lightning* (1952), *Mother* (1952), *Floating Clouds* (1955), and *Flowing* (1956) center on relations between mother and daughter, aunt and niece, sister and sister. In these dark melodramas, set in working-class neighborhoods, characters are plagued by sickness, debt, and jealousy. Hideko Takamine, one of the most accomplished actresses of the postwar period, often appears in the role of the suffering heroine.

Less bleak is the postwar work of Heinosuke Gosho, who tempers the shomin-geki with muted lyricism. *Where Chimneys Are Seen* (1953), for example, tells a tale of marital mistrust, but Gosho lightens it with a wry motif: from different vantage points in the neighborhood, the same group of chimneys seems to be two, or three, or four. This hint that one's situation may seem different from various standpoints makes the married couple's tribulations seem less tragic than they believe.

The two most distinguished old masters of the postwar period were Kenji Mizoguchi and Yasujiro Ozu. As in the 1930s, Mizoguchi was drawn to social-problem

18.3 A characteristic Mizoguchi interior, with doorways and windows framing characters in depth (*Street of Shame*).

films centering on women's suffering, and SCAP authorities were highly encouraging. *Victory of Women* (1946) presents a female attorney defending a woman who in a burst of mad despair has killed her child. *Women of the Night* (1948) portrays the life of prostitutes, a subject Mizoguchi was to take up again in his last work, *Street of Shame* (1956). In the same period, Mizoguchi launched a string of historical films with *The Life of Oharu* (1952), a somber adaptation of a literary classic. Mizoguchi's old associate Nagata saw the export possibilities in such prestigious fare, so under the auspices of the Daiei company, Mizoguchi went on to make *Ugetsu Monogatari* ("A Tale of Ugetsu," 1953), *Sansho the Bailiff* (1954), *Chikamatsu Monogatari* (*The Crucified Lovers*, 1954), and *New Tales of the Taira Clan* (1955).

In his earliest postwar films, Mizoguchi continued to place figures at a considerable distance from the cam-

era. In more intimate scenes, Mizoguchi tended to film from a slightly high angle and used wide-angle lenses to set the characters in depth, often framed by doorways and walls (**18.3**). Mizoguchi also persisted in using abnormally long takes. The average shot runs between forty and fifty seconds, and some takes last minutes. Unlike Max Ophüls or Michelangelo Antonioni, however, Mizoguchi often used little or no camera movement. This has the effect of creating enormous dramatic pressure. For example, in *Victory of Women*, when the mother confesses to murdering her child, Mizoguchi staged the action as a frontal scene in which the gradual, frequently halted movement of the mother and her attorney toward the camera provides an accumulated dramatic effect (**18.4, 18.5**).

After 1950, Mizoguchi began to make more explicit use of Japanese aesthetic traditions. Still working with his long-time screenwriter Yoshikata Yoda, Mizoguchi adapted famous works of literature, both classic and modern. He also began to present landscapes and vistas in ways that echoed Japanese pictorial styles (**18.6**). The picturesque elegance of Mizoguchi's 1950s historical films made them the prototype of "Japaneseness" for western audiences.

In later decades, Yasujiro Ozu's postwar films would take on the same aura. After some shomin-geki in a realist vein (such as *Record of a Tenement Gentleman*, 1947), Ozu began a collaboration with screenwriter Kogo Noda that was to result in a string of major works. These films usually center upon family crises: marriage, separation, and death. In *Late Spring* (1949), a dutiful daughter faces the necessity of leaving her widowed father alone. In *Early Summer* (1951), several generations of a family are shaken by a daughter's impulsive decision to marry. *Tokyo Story* (1953) chronicles an elderly couple's visit to their grown, unfeeling children. In

18.4 Two stages of a single shot: a mother confesses . . .

18.5 . . . to killing her child (*Victory of Women*).

18.6 The frightening kidnapping scene in *Sansho the Bailiff* relies on atmospheric effects of water and mist.

18.7, 18.8 Ozu's version of shot/reverse shot in *Late Autumn* (1960).

18.9 Ozu reveals in an urban landscape the mysterious beauty of a still life (*Early Summer*).

Equinox Flower (1958) and *An Autumn Afternoon* (1962), a father must accept his daughter's wish to leave the household. Ozu and Noda explore a few dramatic issues from various angles. Usually the film is suffused with a contemplative resignation to life's painful changes—an attitude embodied in the gentle smile and sigh of Chishu Ryu, Ozu's perennial actor of this period.

A comparable calm pervades the director's style. The films adhere to the "rules" he set for himself in the 1930s: low camera position, 360-degree shooting space, cutting for graphic effects, transitional sequences that obey a logic of similarity and difference rather than strict spatial continuity. Avoiding the comparative flamboyance of his 1930s experiments, the late films rely on the more muted technique he had developed in the wartime films *Brothers and Sisters of the Toda Family* (1941) and *There Was a Father* (1942, p. 254). Now, Ozu forswears dissolves and fades entirely. He stages conversations with the characters facing the camera head-on and looking over the lens (**18.7, 18.8**). His color design turns mundane settings into abstract patterns (**Color Plate 18.1**). As ever, his camera is attracted by humble objects in the corner of a room, down a hallway, or on a thoroughfare (**18.9**). The peaceful contemplation at the heart of the drama finds its correlative in a style that allows us time to look closely at the characters and their world. This quietude, sometimes broken by sly humor, makes Ozu's films seem undramatic. But he came to be recognized as one of the cinema's most sensitive explorers of everyday life.

The War Generation

As in other countries, many of Japan's most notable directors of the postwar decade began their career during the war. Keisuke Kinoshita's wartime efforts, notably *The Blossoming Port* (1943) and *Army* (1944), were home-front dramas lacking the strident nationalism sometimes seen in the genre. *Army*'s ending, in fact, is ambiguous

enough to suggest a critique of militarist ideology. During the Occupation, Kinoshita made one of the first SCAP-approved pictures, *Morning for the Osone Family* (1946). Here, 1930s militarism brings on a family's suffering, but the war's end promises them a bright future. Over the next four decades, Kinoshita directed many gendai-geki. His most widely seen film in the West is *Twenty-Four Eyes* (1954), a heartrending tale of a dedicated teacher in a rural school during the war.

Kon Ichikawa's first film, a puppet adaptation of a kabuki play, was made near the end of the war but banned by SCAP. Trained as a cartoonist, Ichikawa acquired a reputation as an efficient craftsman, turning out several films for every major company. Ichikawa never specialized in a genre, but his postwar reputation rested largely on satirical and grotesque comedies like *Odd Obsession* (1959) and on several intense dramas: In *The Burmese Harp* (1956), a soldier forced to disguise himself as a monk is eventually won over to a humanistic pacifism. *Fires on the Plain* (1958) presents the Philippine front in the grim last days of the war, when starving soldiers resort to cannibalism. Immensely prolific and commercially successful, Ichikawa adroitly varied his style. Many of his films indulge in flamboyant technical tricks (direct address to the audience in *Odd Obsession*, decentered widescreen compositions in *Conflagration*, 1958, and *An Actor's Revenge*, 1963), while others, such as *The Burmese Harp*, are far more subdued.

The most widely acclaimed talent to come to prominence in the postwar period was Akira Kurosawa. He had made several features during the war (p. 255), one of which, *The Men Who Tread on the Tiger's Tail* (1945), was a satiric jidai-geki made at the very end of the war and was banned by SCAP. It was a rare setback for Kurosawa, who remained prolific for many decades. The international success of his *Rashomon* made him for decades the best-known Japanese director outside the country. We shall consider his career in Chapter 19.

POSTWAR CINEMA IN THE SOVIET SPHERE OF INFLUENCE

After the Allied victory in Europe, the United States and the USSR began to establish spheres of influence. The Soviet Union had acquired the Baltic republics in the 1939 pact with Hitler. In 1945 at Yalta, Joseph Stalin was granted preliminary control over territories held by Soviet troops, which included eastern Germany, most of eastern Europe, and Mongolia. China's 1949 revolution brought Communists to power and initially aligned the country with the USSR. By 1950, several countries had become Soviet satellites.

Most of those nations had worse economic and social problems than western Europe. Over 25 million Soviet citizens had been killed, and as many were now homeless. Hitler had resettled or massacred millions of Germans and eastern Europeans. Towns, bridges, waterways, and rail lines were destroyed. A 1947 famine took almost a million lives in Russia alone. Because Stalin distrusted American aid, no Marshall Plan funds helped rebuild eastern Europe. Eastern bloc leaders followed Moscow's example in developing heavy industry and collectivized farms.

A pattern of cultural activity also emerged in the Soviet bloc countries. First there would be a period of tight political control. Writers and artists would be faced with strict demands for doctrinaire Communist art. This repression would be lifted by a moment of liberalization. But then this liberality would be perceived as threatening stability, and the government would enforce new restraints. This cycle of "freeze" and "thaw" would recur throughout the postwar era, and it emerged first in the Soviet Union.

The USSR: From High Stalinism to the Thaw

The Soviet people lived in wartime stringency well into the 1950s. Leaders exhorted the workers to sterner sacrifices, insisting that the new enemy was the western alliance. Political repression returned in full force. Into prison camps poured captured soldiers, refugees, religious believers, and political prisoners.

Obstacles of the Postwar Years   The Communist party quickly reasserted its domination of the arts. In 1946, Minister of Culture Alexander Zhdanov, who had led the cultural purges of the late 1930s, launched a new campaign. The policy of Socialist Realism became, if anything, even more constraining than it had been in the 1930s. The writer or dramatist had to affirm Com-

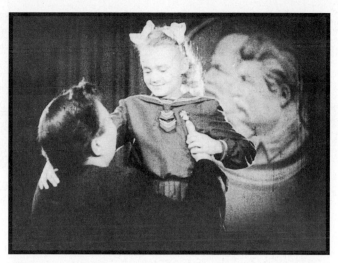

18.10   The scientist receives his reward under the benevolent gaze of the leaders (*In the Name of Life*, 1947, Alexander Zharki and Josef Heifits).

munist heroism and patriotism; there could be no ambiguity about characters' motives or purposes. The party harassed artists, charging them with disloyalty and neglect of political duty. Admitting to western influences, as Grigori Alexandrov did in acknowledging his debts to American comedy, brought accusations of "kowtowing to bourgeois culture." Just as Socialist Realism had stifled Soviet modernism in the early 1930s, Zhdanov's new policies ensured that western European trends, particularly Neorealism, would have no influence on postwar Soviet film.

Film production was already a cumbersome bureaucratic process, and Zhdanov's campaign for ideological purity brought the studios to a virtual standstill: a script might wend its way through the bureaucracy for two years before getting approval. Alexander Dovzhenko's *Michurin* (1948) and Sergei Gerasimov's *Young Guard* (1948) were "corrected" during scripting and after filming. Other films, notably the second part of Sergei Eisenstein's *Ivan the Terrible* (1946), were banned outright. All the Soviet "film factories" combined produced seventeen features in 1948, fifteen in 1949, thirteen in 1950, and a mere nine in 1951.

Films that survived this system operated within narrow genre constraints. Fairy tales showed off the exotic cultures of the republics, and political dramas attacked American foreign policy. Biographies of artists and scientists continued the 1930s trend of Russian nationalism, with Stalin's image playing a central role (**18.10**). "Artistic documentaries" about the war mixed newsreel footage with restaged scenes, portraying a larger-than-life Stalin deciding the fate of civilization. In all genres, the emphasis was on exceptional protagonists.

18.11 An indomitable pose of youthful courage climaxes a long take in a prison scene.

18.12 In Yutkevich's *Tales of Lenin* (1957), old-fashioned technique sanctifies the leader.

18.13 A subdued presentation of wartime homecoming: while the populace celebrates with fireworks, a soldier's greatcoat is draped over a chair and a reunited couple embrace offscreen (*The House I Live In*).

Although such characters were said to derive their strength from the people, the ordinary person usually served only to inspire or assist the hero.

Most of the pioneering 1920s filmmakers became inactive. Lev Kuleshov continued teaching but made no films. Poor health kept Eisenstein from revising *Ivan the Terrible*, and he died in 1948 without making another film. Vsevolod Pudovkin made two films after the war, and Dovzhenko, just one. Only Alexandrov, Sergei Yutkevich, Fridrikh Ermler, and Grigori Kozintsev worked steadily. A younger generation, consisting of Gerasimov, Mark Donskoi, Mikhail Romm, and Josef Heifits, became the central figures of postwar filmmaking. All had launched their careers in the early 1930s and had produced major Socialist Realist works. Particularly adept in adapting to policy was the Georgian Mikhail Chiaurelli, whose *The Vow* (1946) and *The Unforgettable Year 1919* (1951) took Stalin worship to dizzying heights.

Even top directors were vulnerable to official reprimand, however, and so they retreated into a uniformity of style. The inflated tendencies of the wartime cinema (p. 270) were carried to extremes. The "artistic documentaries" showed the nation's leaders brooding in huge offices or striding down colossal corridors. In Chiaurelli's *The Fall of Berlin* (1949), the reunion of the couple takes place before a huge crowd, with Stalin towering above all (**Color Plate 18.2**). Even the more intimate *Young Guard* uses lengthy takes and deep focus to present its young people as a monumental ensemble (**18.11**). Postwar Socialist Realist cinema was even more rigid and academic than the 1930s version.

The ponderousness of this approach soon became evident. In 1952, party spokesmen complained that most films lacked conflict; the fear of censorship had created blandness. At the party congress of the same year, the leadership demanded an increase in film output. The production process smoothed out. Now scripts about ordinary persons could be accepted, as long as the Communist party still played a positive role in the story. There emerged the short-lived genre of the *three-person film*, centering on a husband-wife-lover conflict that is ultimately resolved by the intervention of a sympathetic party representative. Pudovkin's last film, *The Return of Vasily Bortnikov* (1954), exemplifies this trend.

Stalin's Death and the New Humanism   Stalin's death in March 1953 triggered a power struggle that five years later would carry Nikita Khrushchev to leadership. In the course of the years from 1953 to 1958, known broadly as the "thaw," the party undertook some reforms. Taxes were lowered, thousands of political prisoners were freed from the camps, and the government invested in education and research. Most improvements were aimed at securing popular support, but in comparison with Stalin's reign, the thaw proved liberating.

Reform crept into the film industry. New screenwriters were recruited; censorship was lightened. The biographical pictures and the artistic documentary went into decline. With "peaceful coexistence" now the official policy, cold war subjects were played down. Comedies and musicals returned to favor. The republics' studios revived. By 1957, production had risen to ninety-two films.

Many directors of the older generation continued to turn out didactic, doctrinaire works (**18.12**). But as "Make room for youth!" became a rallying cry, a number of recent graduates of the film school VGIK launched their careers. For example, Lev Kulidzhanov and Jakov Segel's muted *The House I Live In* (1957) traces the intertwined destinies of families in a housing complex before and during the war (**18.13**).

In 1956, Khrushchev boldly attacked Stalin's dictatorial policies. He singled out the cinema as a prime vehicle of the "cult of personality," denouncing those films that praised Stalin's military genius. As a result, some of the most revisionist films of the thaw treated the war genre in a new light. Grigori Chukhrai's first feature, *The Forty-First* (1956), portrays the developing sexual relation between a female soldier and her prisoner. The actor Sergei Bondarchuk made his directorial debut with *Destiny of a Man* (1959), which questions a Russian soldier's conduct in a Nazi concentration camp.

Near the end of the decade, two other war films represented a trend toward a "new humanism." *The Cranes Are Flying* (1957), directed by the veteran Mikhail Kalatozov, treats the home front unheroically. The protagonist is far from the positive heroine of Socialist Realism. While her fiancé is at the front, she has an affair with his brother, a weak black marketer, and suffers guilt over her infidelity. In the late 1940s, psychological conflicts had usually been considered bourgeois, but *The Cranes Are Flying* shows that they had gained official sanction. Kalatozov relies on the conventional deep-focus style (see 18.1), but he also experiments with hand-held camerawork and slow-motion shots, techniques that would become common in the 1960s. The film's optical subjectivity and imaginary sequences link it to trends in the European art cinema. Its modern look helped *The Cranes Are Flying* win the Grand Prize at the 1958 Cannes Film Festival.

The sense of renewal was strengthened by Chukhrai's World War II drama *Ballad of a Soldier* (1958). The teenage infantryman Alexei is granted a brief furlough to visit his mother. In the course of his trip, he encounters people coping with the problems of the war and falls in love with a refugee girl. He reaches home so late that he must leave immediately. Since Chukhrai opened the film by telling us that Alexei eventually died on the front, his final embrace of his mother (**18.14**) becomes particularly poignant. The effect is strengthened by the shot's visual parallel to the nightmarish tank attack in the film's opening (**18.15**). Alexei's fear of the war, his awkward kindness, and his sexual urges distinguish him from the stiff Bolshevik familiar from high Stalinism.

The Cranes Are Flying and *Ballad of a Soldier* display a conventional patriotism, a trust in paternal leaders, and mammoth battle scenes. Yet these and other films moved beyond the stern puritanism of earlier party dogma, offering "Socialist Realism with a human face." The postwar generation welcomed the sight of youthful sensitivity and passion on the screen, if only in the context of official doctrine and formulaic genres. Such films

18.14   The ending of *Ballad of a Soldier.*

18.15   The opening of *Ballad of a Soldier.*

parallel the teenpics cultivated by Hollywood during the same period (see Chapter 15).

By the end of the decade, films from the USSR had regained worldwide prestige. In 1958, Part II of Eisenstein's *Ivan the Terrible* was released to great acclaim, and an international critics' poll voted *Potemkin* the best film of all time. The works of Dziga Vertov and Alexander Dovzhenko were being revived. New films were winning renown. Although the thaw soon ended, Soviet cinema was rehabilitated in the eyes of the international film community.

Postwar Cinema in Eastern Europe

At the close of the war, the Soviet army occupied Czechoslovakia, Poland, Hungary, Albania, Bulgaria, Romania, Yugoslavia, and the eastern sector of Germany (to become the German Democratic Republic). Between 1945 and 1948, Communist governments arose in all these countries—by first forming coalitions with other parties and then purging the coalitions of non-Communists and dissidents. By 1950, virtually all of eastern Europe had come under Soviet sway. Stalin saw these countries serving as "buffer states" against western invasion. They would also supply the USSR with materials and purchase Soviet goods.

Emergence from Wartime Conditions In these "people's democracies," as in the USSR, one party ruled. The state collectivized agriculture, expanded heavy industry, and controlled wages and prices. Between 1945 and 1948, all the countries' film industries were nationalized, often on the basis of film units within the army, resistance forces, or partisan groups. Many filmmakers who had in the prewar period supported left-wing causes received posts in the new structure.

Some production facilities needed little rebuilding. Czechoslovakian studios had served as the basis for Nazi productions and were able to resume filmmaking easily. In East Germany in 1946, the Soviets established the state monopoly Deutsche Film Aktiengesellschaft (DEFA), taking advantage of the fact that most of the prewar production facilities were located in the eastern zone. By contrast, Bulgaria, Romania, and Yugoslavia had virtually no prewar film tradition. There the governments, with Soviet aid, had to build film production from scratch.

Initially, eastern European industries copied the Soviet structure. Production was centralized, with scripts approved by a single hierarchical agency under the control of the party. Administrators assigned workers to projects. Bureaucrats demanded revisions at stages in the production process. Since distribution and exhibition were also under centralized control, the party might order the banning of a finished film.

One country deviated from this policy when it broke with the Soviet Union. In 1948, Marshal Tito, Communist ruler of Yugoslavia, launched a more decentralized, market-oriented brand of socialism. Yugoslavian production was organized around independent enterprises consisting of artistic and technical workers. State subsidy of filmmaking was supplemented by a tax on admissions. While the party censored finished films, personnel were allowed to initiate projects and move among enterprises. Yugoslavia's industry became the most "commercial" in eastern Europe, entering into coproductions with the West and hosting runaway productions.

Again following Soviet precedent, the eastern European countries emphasized professional film education.

18.16 The "rubble film" *The Murderers Are Among Us.*

18.17 The return of expressionism: *The Murderers Are Among Us.*

Advanced schools were started in Warsaw (in 1945; moved to Lódź in 1948), Budapest (1945), Belgrade (1946), Prague (1947), Bucharest (1950), and Potsdam (1954). Technicians also studied at the Soviet film school VGIK. Such standardized training was believed to guarantee both professional competence and obedience to ideology.

Before the Communist parties achieved full power, left-wing directors worked in a variety of directions. Aleksandr Ford's *Border Street* (Poland, 1948), for example, shows how ordinary people were drawn into becoming Nazi sympathizers. In East Germany, Wolfgang Staudte's *The Murderers Are Among Us* (1946), a major *Trümmerfilm* ("rubble film"), makes almost neorealistic use of the ruins of Berlin (**18.16**) in telling its story of a Nazi sympathizer who remains a powerful businessman. At the same time, however, Staudte draws on the indigenous expressionist tradition (**18.17**).

Left-wing humanism of this sort soon fell into disfavor. Eastern European countries embraced Zhdanov's narrow version of Soviet Socialist Realism. The Soviet Union's Russian chauvinism found its eastern equivalents in patriotic historical epics, revised to suit politically correct policy. Each nation developed its own variant on the war film, the collective-farm film, the factory-sabotage film, and the biography of the great national artist. To help its satellites adhere to the new policy, the USSR sent leading directors to shoot or supervise local productions and to suggest improvements in the domestic product.

Nevertheless, almost every country boasted some films that stretched or evaded the rules of Socialist Realism. In Poland, Ford's *Five Boys from Barska Street* (1954) and Jerzy Kawalerowicz's early work became noted for injecting humanist themes into the formulas. In Hungary, Zoltán Fábri's *Fourteen Lives in Danger* (1954) displayed a neorealist tendency in its account of trapped miners. Some filmmakers found cartoon films to be a haven from Zhdanovism, and in Czechoslovakia and Yugoslavia outstanding animation studios developed (see Chapter 21). Often the nationalistic emphasis of eastern European films of the period offered a degree of distance from Soviet policy: any patriotic film could be taken as asserting local pride in the face of Russian dominance.

Struggles under the Thaw Stalin's death and Nikita Khrushchev's policy of "de-Stalinization" created a thaw within many eastern European governments. But citizens of these countries displayed a stronger spirit of independence and renewal than was common in the USSR. Eloquent intellectuals criticized the Soviet system. Most dramatically, people began to rebel. Strikes and riots broke out in East Germany and Poland; in 1956, Hungary teetered on the edge of revolution. Soviet tanks rolled in to quell the disturbances, but the upheavals revealed popular resentment of Communist rule.

The thaw brought a cultural renaissance to many eastern European countries. Magazines, art groups, and experimental styles came forth to challenge official policies. Young people fresh from film schools could take advantage of the more liberal atmosphere. Intellectuals looked to the cinema to articulate new impulses. Although eastern European film did not pursue western-style modernism until the 1960s, the cinemas of the thaw went further than their Soviet counterpart in loosening traditional narrative structure and in pursuing psychological and symbolic effects. During this period the most innovative and influential work emerged from Czechoslovakia, Hungary, and Poland.

Czechoslovakia's thaw was relatively brief, since many of the liberals who would have pressed for reform had already fallen victim to the Stalinist coup of 1948. Between 1956 and 1958, new trends emerged in the work of two older filmmakers. Ladislav Helge, a committed but critical Communist, made *School for Fathers* (1957), while Ján Kadár's *House at Terminus* (1957) presented a study of social apathy under communism. A younger film school graduate, Vojtech Jasný, presented a poetic treatment of the cycle of seasons in *Desire* (1958), while Václav Krŝka's *Here Are Lions* (1958) offered a modernist use of flashbacks told from the viewpoint of a man on an operating table.

Hungary's response to de-Stalinization was more radical, but in the cinema its thaw lasted only a little longer than that in Czechoslovakia. Between 1954 and 1957, three significant directors received international attention. Karoly Makk's first film, the period comedy *Liliomfi* (1954), not only proved a popular success but displayed technically sophisticated color design (**Color Plate 18.3**). Makk would prove to be one of Hungary's most important directors. Félix Máriássy's *Spring in Budapest* and *A Glass of Beer* (both 1955) introduced strongly neorealistic elements.

Particularly important were two films of Zoltán Fábri, a stage director who had moved into filmmaking after the war. His *Merry-Go-Round* (1955), a tale of reluctant peasants learning the joys of collective farming, displayed an energetic lyricism. Its zoom shots, brief flashbacks (both visual and auditory), quick editing, whirling camera movements, and slow-motion final images put it closer to western modernism than to Socialist Realism. In *Professor Hannibal* (1956), Fábri offered a satirical study of Hungary under right-wing rule in 1921.

The Polish School Of the countries under Soviet sway, Poland proved to be the most hostile to communism. Many Poles remembered that during the war Stalin had refused to back the Polish government in exile, creating instead a puppet regime and using Soviet troops to help the Nazis wipe out the underground Home Army. The Poles resisted agricultural collectivization, and sporadic outbursts of demonstrations and strikes became a regular part of urban life. The moderate leader Wladyslaw Gomulka proposed a series of reforms. Polish filmmakers took advantage of de-Stalinization to reorganize film production and reexamine the nation's history.

In May 1955, the Polish industry established the Creative Film Unit system, a shift away from the Soviet-style centralized bureaucracy. As in Yugoslavia, filmmakers could join a regional production unit, which would rent studio facilities from the government. Each unit would consist of an artistic director (usually a film director), a literary director to develop scripts, and a production manager to oversee filmmaking. The Creative Film Units, bearing such names as Kadr ("Frame"), Start, Kamera, and Studio, proved efficient; they also allowed film-school graduates to gain strong positions in the industry.

During the 1950s, the "Polish School" became the most prominent cinema in eastern Europe. Aleksandr Ford's *Five Boys from Barska Street* (1954) won a major prize at Cannes. A series of documentaries, called the "black series," undertook unprecedented social criticism. Jerzy Kawalerowicz, who had begun his career under Socialist Realism, offered the complexly constructed *Shadow* (1955), which raises the question of a man's death and then only partially explains it through a series of oblique flashbacks. More renowned outside Poland was Kawalerowicz's *Night Train* (1959); another exercise in narrative ambiguity, it has some affinities with the 1960s work of Ingmar Bergman. Many other directors, most of them young, came to form part of the Polish School, but two proved particularly influential.

Andrzej Munk, a Lódź Film Academy graduate, gained fame with *The Man on the Tracks* (1956). An elderly mechanic is run down by a train; a nearby signal lamp is broken; was he a saboteur? The film's plot interweaves the investigation with a series of flashbacks. As a result, events are presented out of chronological order and some actions are shown several times. Common as this plot construction was in Hollywood and western European cinema after *Citizen Kane*, it flouted official Socialist Realist aesthetics. Thematically, the revelation of the mechanic's good intentions makes *The Man on the Tracks* a critique of the Stalinist search for "wreckers."

Munk's *Eroica* (1957), a "Heroic Symphony in Two Parts," offers a similarly demystifying view of the war. The first part, a bitter comedy about a small-time con man during the Warsaw uprising, stands in sharp contrast to the more tragic story of Polish prisoners of war who comfort themselves with illusions about heroism (**18.18**). Munk later undertook a major film about the Nazi concentration camps. He died in an automobile accident early in production, but what remains of *The Passenger* suggests that it might have resembled Alain Resnais's *Hiroshima mon amour*. Apparently the finished film would have moved unpredictably from a

18.18 *Eroica:* comic action in the foreground while a fleeing refugee is shot in the distance.

18.19 The Home Army partisan Jacek in *A Generation.*

woman's memories of serving as an officer at Auschwitz to her attempts to explain her life to her husband.

Andrzej Wajda, the most famous Polish director, was also a graduate of the Lódź film school. After Wajda worked as assistant director to Ford on *Five Boys from Barska Street,* Ford served as artistic supervisor for Wajda's first film, *A Generation* (1954). Roman Polanski, who played a minor role, remarked, "The whole Polish cinema began from it."[2] Wajda's next film, *Kanal* ("Sewers," 1957), created far more controversy, winning a special prize at the Cannes Film Festival. *Ashes and Diamonds* (1959) won a major prize at Venice and became known as the most important film made in eastern Europe.

As a teenager Wajda had served in the non-Communist underground Home Army. In the course of the trilogy, his representation of the underground evolves from ideologically correct criticism of the army (*A Generation*) through a grim celebration of its stubborn heroism (*Kanal*) to an ambiguous affirmation of the non-Communist Resistance (*Ashes and Diamonds*).

In the first film, Jacek, who dies in a crazy flourish standing atop a staircase (**18.19**), is condemned, but he remains attractive in his reckless romanticism. *Kanal,* made at the height of the post-Stalin thaw, is far more sympathetic to its young partisans. After the Warsaw uprising, they take to the sewers. The film's second half intercuts three groups' attempts to escape through the swampy labyrinths. Each band dies heroically. In *Ashes*

18.20, *left   Kanal:* the alternation of pitch darkness and explosions of light.

18.21, *right*   The studio-built sewers enable Wajda to squeeze the characters close to one another or thrust them into the camera lens (*Kanal*).

18.22   *Ashes and Diamonds:* Christianity in wartime.

18.23   Resistance fighters remember their dead.

and Diamonds, an overtly anti-Communist partisan becomes a positive, even seductive figure. Maciek, a young man grown cold-blooded in the Resistance, assassinates the Communist representative arriving in town and dies in a garbage heap, accidentally shot by a policeman. Although he is a political enemy, Maciek, with his machine gun, tight jacket, and dark glasses, became a charismatic figure for young audiences. Because of this role, actor Zbigniew Cybulski was known as "the Polish James Dean."

In the last two films, Wajda found a stylistic flamboyance to match his protagonists' bravado. *Kanal* won notoriety for its suspense, its violence, and its virtuosic style (**18.20, 18.21**). In *Ashes and Diamonds*, Wajda's startling visual effects become symbolic motifs. Maciek's first victim, blasted so fiercely that his back catches fire, collapses against a church door, revealing the bombed altar behind (**18.22**). At the hotel bar, Maciek and his friend honor their fallen comrades by lighting glasses of alcohol, a secular equivalent of votive candles (**18.23**). At the end, killer and victim embrace in a grisly dance while fireworks ironically signal the end of the war (**18.24**).

Critics have contrasted Wajda's romantic celebration of doomed heroes with Munk's more ironic, demystifying attitude. Both directors used the war film to ques-

18.24   The climax of *Ashes and Diamonds*, with the fireworks echoing the fiery wound and the flaming drinks.

tion the official historical record and to address controversial topics—the nature of resistance, the Polish tradition of gallantry. But Wajda's baroque visual effects, his taste for suspenseful plots, and his ambivalent use of religious imagery made his films startlingly different from most of the eastern European products.

As in the Soviet Union, the eastern European thaws lasted only a few years. After Hungary's aborted 1956 revolution, its Union of Film Workers was disbanded, ending hopes for a new production system. In 1957, a Prague filmmakers' conference condemned recent Polish films and demanded that a single ideological line be followed. Polish filmmakers found their works scrutinized and sometimes suppressed. A 1959 conference of Czech filmmakers reorganized production policy and called for major films to be banned. Most governments tightened control of their film industries. Soon, however, even more nonconformist filmmakers would appear.

PEOPLE'S REPUBLIC OF CHINA

During World War II, the Chinese civil war had moderated as both the governmental forces and the Communist revolutionaries battled the occupying Japanese army. After Japan's 1945 surrender, however, the civil war broke out anew. Despite U.S. backing, Chiang Kaishek's forces had to flee to Taiwan in 1949. Under Mao Zedong, the Communists established the People's Republic of China (PRC) on the mainland. While America considered Chiang's Guomindong the legitimate government, the USSR recognized the PRC in 1949, providing it with aid and military assistance.

Civil War and Revolution

During the civil war, film production remained centered in Shanghai. Many scriptwriters and directors were sympathetic to the revolutionary cause, and they frequently ran afoul of strict wartime censorship. Still, some films provided models for the postrevolutionary cinema. Most important of these was the two-part *The Spring River Flows East* (1947–1948, Cai Chusheng and Zheng Junli). The film proved immensely popular, partly because it encapsulated the experiences of many Chinese citizens under the oppressive Japanese occupation.

Three hours long, *The Spring River Flows East* covers the years from 1931 to 1945 as it traces the fortunes of a husband and wife separated by war. Like many Chinese films, *The Spring River Flows East* resembles Hollywood films in its use of a lush symphonic score, skillful editing, and careful script construction. Scenes contrasting the husband's and wife's situations are carefully timed, as when a housewarming party for his new mansion is intercut with a scene of his family being evicted from their shack.

Shanghai filmmaking yielded another major film during the civil war, Fei Mu's *Spring in a Small Town* (1948). Fei had made some important films for the Lian-

hua company in the 1930s, including Ruan Lingyi vehicles (p. 258). His *Backstage/Frontstage* (1937), set among an opera troupe, presents the performances in a tableau style but depicts the personal dramas offstage with bold cutting and remarkable depth. *Spring in a Small Town* is even more daring. A wife and her sickly husband live with his sister in a mansion now ruined by war. The husband's old friend, who is also the wife's former lover, comes to visit. As the friend and the wife are drawn to each other again, Fei presents their growing passion in distant, often chiaroscuro framings. They approach and withdraw through small gestures that only intensify our sense of their irresistable attraction (**18.25**). Although made for a left-wing studio, the film avoids propagandistic critique. Because of Fei's muted handling of the love triangle, as well as his free use of voice-over suggesting the wife's train of thought, many critics consider *Spring in a Small Town* the finest Chinese film ever made.

Two other important films spanned the transition between the civil war era and the postrevolutionary era. Zheng Junli's *Crows and Sparrows* (1949) offers a cross section of prerevolutionary Chinese society by portraying the various inhabitants of an apartment block. The story contrasts the "sparrows," honest working-class people (**18.26**), with the "crows," the decadent right-wing party boss and his wife who exploit them (**18.27**). *San Mao, the Little Vagabond* (1949, Zhao Ming and Yang Gong), like *Crows and Sparrows*, encountered censorship barriers under the Guomindong government and was finished after the revolution. Based on a comic strip, it centers on a suffering street urchin who gains hope when the revolution occurs. *San Mao* uses location shooting reminiscent of Italian Neorealism, and the boy's presence in actual celebrations of revolutionary victory lends the film a documentary power.

The Communist party quickly nationalized the Chinese film industry. Many filmmakers welcomed the victory of the Communists in 1949 and provided a continuity of personnel. The Beijing Film Studio was established in April 1949; its head was Yung Muzhi, who in 1937 had made the important left-wing film *Street Angels* (p. 258) and had studied filmmaking in Moscow for six years. The new Ministry of Culture also formed the Film Bureau. Between 1949 and 1950, plans were made to centralize production, censorship, distribution, and exhibition. Although western films were popular, theaters gradually eliminated them from their programs. Since Chinese production could not meet the demand, films were brought in from the USSR and other communist countries.

18.25 Former lovers meet in *Spring in a Small Town*.

18.26 Two of the positive characters in *Crows and Sparrows*, a leftist clerk and a maid, lead a group of children in a song.

18.27 Fashionable clothes, liquor, and cigarettes mark the right-wing couple of *Crows and Sparrows* as corrupt.

Despite the propaganda value of film, officials in charge of the industry faced a problem. China was mainly agricultural, with 80 percent of the population living in rural districts. In 1949, the nation had only about 650 theaters, concentrated in the port cities and catering to a middle-class, educated audience. Millions of Chinese had never seen a movie and could not assimilate the ideas depicted in Soviet films.

Like the Bolsheviks after the 1917 Russian Revolution, the Chinese government worked to expand the exhibition network and to make films that peasants, workers, and soldiers could enjoy. Directly after the Chinese revolution, the government created mobile projection units that could tour films throughout distant regions. By 1960 there were about 15,000 such units. As filmgoers gained access to films, the number of annual admissions grew enormously, from 47 million in 1949 to 4.15 billion in 1959.

China was largely untouched by western-style modernism. On the whole, Communist Chinese cinema reworked popular genres into political message films. Due to changes in government policy, periods of control alternated with periods of relaxation, a cycle reminiscent of the freeze-and-thaw rhythm of culture in the USSR.

Right after the Chinese revolution, officials obliged filmmakers to take Soviet Socialist Realism as their model. Soviet specialists lent their expertise as they did in eastern European countries, and Chinese filmmakers traveled to Moscow to study the industry there. New personnel were trained, initially at a school attached to the Beijing Film Studio (opened in 1952) and later at the Beijing Film Academy (1956). One noteworthy film of the era is *My Life* (1950, Shi Hui), structured as a series of flashbacks as an old beggar recalls his career as a policeman loyally serving various regimes since 1911. This panorama of his life provides the opportunity for

18.28 A Chinese officer who serves the Japanese occupation government is seen surrounded by his instruments of torture, in *My Life*.

many scenes of prerevolutionary oppression (**18.28**). As the hero dies, his son participates in the revolution.

Strict control was relaxed somewhat during 1956 and 1957. Citing the ancient Chinese saying, "Let a hundred flowers bloom, let a hundred schools of thought contend," Mao Zedong invited constructive criticism of the government. This period of relative openness was comparable to the mid-50s thaw in the USSR and eastern European countries, although Mao quickly used the policy to mark out future "enemies."

Production had been slow to revive in the immediate postwar period, but it expanded under the "Hundred Flowers" movement. Filmmakers adapted literary works by leftist authors of the prerevolutionary "May Fourth School" (named for a major series of 1919 protests). One such film, Sang Hu's *The New Year's Sacrifice* (1956), centers on a woman forced to work as a rich family's servant. Despite its unrelentingly grim story, *The New Year's Sacrifice*, like most Chinese films of the 1950s and 1960s, displays polished production values of a type usually associated with Hollywood, including elaborate studio-built exteriors and rich color cinematography. *Girl Basketball Player No. 5* (1957, Xie Jin) creates a more optimistic mood by focusing on young people learning to work together. Again, however, the unhappy prerevolutionary heritage is stressed, since the team's coach had been fired during the 1930s for refusing to rig the outcome of a game. Such films hinted at a new range of subjects for filmmaking, but as criticism of the government led to a general crackdown, the Hundred Flowers movement ended.

Official policy now declared the need for rapid growth in the Chinese economy, a policy known as the "Great Leap Forward." Among the results of this disastrous campaign was a famine, when peasants were forced onto collective farms and agricultural output plummeted. In the film industry, the Great Leap Forward led to unrealistically high goals for the number of movies to be produced, often on impossibly low budgets. More positively, new emphasis on ethnic diversity led to the establishment of regional film production centers, an action that would have long-range effects on Chinese filmmaking. While Beijing and Shanghai remained the main centers of production, during the years from 1957 to 1960, major regional studios were built: the Pearl River Studio in Guangzhou, the Xi'an Film Studio, and the Emei Film Studio in Chengdu. In addition, some significant films were made during the period. One was *The Lin Family Shop* (1959, Shui Hua), which presents a shopkeeper caught between corrupt Guomindong officials and the invading Japanese. Another polished studio production, *The Lin Family Shop* integrates the family's drama with its examination of 1930s politics.

Mixing Maoism and Tradition

The end of the Great Leap Forward led to another period of openness during the first half of the 1960s. Film production expanded and attendance increased. Prerevolutionary films were revived, and the national film archive (established in 1956) began to preserve them. As the PRC was becoming less dependent on Soviet aid, directors stressed indigenous Chinese traditions.

As a result of this new interest in Chinese life, more films began dealing with the nation's fifty-five distinct minorities. Some films featured these minorities simply to display picturesque cultures. *Ashma* (1964, Liu Qiong), for example, is a pretty widescreen musical

based on a legend of the Bai minority. Other films aimed to show a minority becoming united with the general population. In Li Jun's *Serfs* (1963), Tibetan peasants are oppressed by feudal landowners and religious leaders. The Chinese army liberates the serfs, with one soldier giving his life to save the hero. The hero pays tribute to him by spreading a traditional Tibetan friendship scarf across his corpse (**18.29**). Like many Chinese films, *Serfs* introduces an elaborate metaphor of revolutionary struggle; the protagonist is struck dumb by a Buddhist priest's curse. Only in the final scene, when the victorious crowd cheers Chairman Mao outside the hero's hospital room, does he regain his voice, declaring, "I have so much to say."

There was also a renewal of the historical film. *Naval Battle of 1894* (1962, Lin Nong) is set during the Opium Wars and deals with an admiral trying to lead his men in a patriotic fashion in the face of government corruption. Skillful filming of elaborate miniature ships gives the film an epic quality. In the final scene the hero defiantly steers his ship into the enemy fleet; this is intercut with waves crashing on a coast, metaphorically suggesting the rebellion soon to begin.

Many films continued to glorify the ordinary individual who escapes from oppression by discovering the revolutionary movement. The most important director of this era, Xie Jin, proved adept at combining melodramatic narratives with political concerns. His *The Red Detachment of Women* (1961) tells of a poor serf who escapes from her tyrannical master and joins a revolutionary brigade made up of women. At first driven by revenge, she gradually learns to fight for the good of society. *Red Detachment* is enthusiastically propagandistic, using stirring music and energetic action sequences to create larger-than-life heroes.

Xie's best-known film in the West is *Two Stage Sisters* (1965). When the protagonists become theater stars, Chunhua remains true to her art, while Yuehong succumbs to luxury and drink (**18.30**). After the revolution the sisters bring plays to the peasants. Theater becomes another metaphor for revolution; Chunhua has yearned to have her own stage, but at the end she realizes that "we now have the biggest one"—all of China.

Xie's narrative unfolds in a manner worthy of the glossiest American productions. "*Two Stage Sisters* has a Hollywood quality to it, I think, especially in its structure, the way I shot it, the way I put it together."[3] As in many Chinese films of the period, elaborate camera movements combine with vibrant color design. When Chunhua is pilloried for defending Yuehong from a landowner's lustful advances, a track-back reveals a crowd and a vast set (**Color Plate 18.4**).

18.29, *left* The climactic scene in *Serfs*, as the Tibetan hero honors the Chinese soldier who has saved him.

18.30, *right* Chunhua, right, is shocked when Yuehong shows up backstage late and tipsy in *Two Stage Sisters*.

Such attempts to combine entertainment, high-level production values, diverse subject matter, and ideological education came to an abrupt end in 1966. In that year, the extensive political changes brought about by the Cultural Revolution drove many filmmakers into prolonged inactivity.

INDIA

Of the world's film output in the postwar years, a large share was contributed by India. During this period, Indian films also began to win international renown.

The national independence movement achieved victory when the British government divided its colonial territory into the predominantly Hindu nation of India and the predominantly Moslem one of Pakistan. Although the partition was far from peaceful, India became independent in August 1947. Prime Minister Jawaharlal Nehru undertook many reforms, notably the abolition of the caste system and the promotion of civil rights for women. Nehru also pursued a policy of "nonalignment" that sought to steer a course between the western and Soviet powers.

Even after partition, India remained diverse. As a republic, it was a union of states, each retaining its own culture, languages, and traditions. Most people were illiterate and lived in abject poverty. India's population was increasing, reaching 440 million in 1961. Although most people lived in the countryside, the wartime boom brought many to the cities.

A Disorganized but Prolific Industry

For both farmers and urban workers, cinema quickly became the principal entertainment. But Bombay Talkies, Prabhat, New Theatres, and other established studios owned no theaters and thus could not take advantage of the market (p. 256). After the studios collapsed as production firms, they rented their facilities to the hundreds of independent producers.

Banks avoided investing in motion pictures, so producers often financed their projects with advances from distributors and exhibitors. But this arrangement gave distributors and exhibitors enormous control over scripts, casts, and budgets. The result was a cutthroat market in which many films remained unfinished, hits produced dozens of copies and sequels, and bankable stars worked in six to ten films simultaneously. Nevertheless, annual outputs soared, hovering between 250 and 325 films well into the early 1960s.

The government largely ignored this chaotic situation. Increasing taxes on filmgoing only intensified producers' frenzied bids for hits. A 1951 Film Enquiry Committee report recommended several reforms, including formation of a film training school, a national archive, and the Film Finance Corporation to help fund quality films. It took a decade before these agencies were established. Another initiative of the early 1950s, the creation of the Central Board of Film Censors, had more immediate effect. Coordinating the censorship agencies in the major film-producing regions, the board forbade sexual scenes (including kissing and "indecorous dancing"), as well as politically controversial material.

The Populist Tradition and Raj Kapoor

The exhibition-controlled market, the absence of government regulation, and the strict censorship encouraged standardized filmmaking. Most of the genres established in the 1930s continued (p. 256), but the historicals, mythologicals (stories drawn from Hindu religious epics), and devotionals (tales of gods and saints) became less popular than the socials, which took place in the present and might be a comedy, thriller, or melodrama.

More grandiose was the historical superproduction, initiated by *Chandralekha* (1948), the biggest box-office hit of the decade. *Chandralekha* was produced and directed by S. S. Vasan, who set his tale of adventure and romance in huge sets and amidst massive crowds. Scenes like the spectacular drum dance (**18.31**) sent producers scrambling for even bigger budgets. A decade later, a vogue for *dacoit* (rural outlaw) films appeared in the wake of *Gunga Jumna* (1961), another milestone in big production values.

While regional production grew during the two decades after the war, the national market was dominated by films in Hindi, the principal language. After the war, Bombay was still the center of this "all-India" filmmaking. The India-Pakistan partition had cut the market for Bengali-language films by over half, so Calcutta companies scaled back or began making films in Hindi. After *Chandralekha*, Madras, in southern India, became a production center, and by the end of the 1950s its output surpassed Bombay's; but it too turned out many Hindi-language products.

The postwar Hindi formula centers on a romantic or sentimental main plot, adds a comic subplot, and fin-

18.31 The drum dance in *Chandralekha*, from Vasan, the self-proclaimed Cecil B. De Mille of India.

MUSIC AND POSTWAR INDIAN FILM

It is often difficult to separate the history of cinema from the history of other media. In the United States, film was intricately bound up with theater, literature, radio, and television. Nonwestern cultures displayed the same complex relations between cinema and other media. Indian cinema offers an intriguing example.

Out of the approximately 2,500 Indian sound films made before 1945, only one did not include song sequences. After World War II, music became even more important. Radio disseminated movie songs, advertising forthcoming releases. With the breakup of the studios, independent producers clamored for successful songwriters and lyricists, who were often as well paid as the biggest stars. A composer might write for several dozen films in a single year.

Early on, Indian film scores borrowed western symphonic motifs and orchestration, but it took the Hindi formula film to create the "hybrid score." A song or dance might draw on any musical tradition, from Greece and the Caribbean to Broadway or Latin America. The polyrhythms of Indian dance might blend with American jazz, an Italianate vocal line, and Spanish guitars.

In films of the 1930s and early 1940s, the actor had typically sung her or his own part. After the war, the task was almost always taken up by *playback singers*, professional performers who recorded the songs, which would then be lip-synched by the actors during shooting.

Playback singers became as famous as the stars to whom they loaned their voices. Mukesh (whom Raj Kapoor called "my soul") was preeminent among male playback singers, while the outstanding female singer was Lata Mangeshkar (**18.32**), who recorded 25,000 songs (a world

18.32 Lata Mangeshkar, queen of Indian film music.

record) over a period of forty years. Her chirrupy voice made her powerful enough to dictate terms to producers, directors, and composers.

Comic songs, love songs, songs of friendship or seduction, religious songs—each type had its place in the film and a use for the public. Eight out of ten Indian cassettes and discs sold today are movie music, and film songs are played on religious holidays and at weddings and funerals.

18.33 *Awaara:* the ne'er-do-well Raj Kapoor sings to the rich woman, played by Nargis, another major Hindi star.

18.34 Wandering through a brothel district, the poet Vijay sings of life's suffering (*Thirst*).

ishes with a happy ending. Since the coming of sound, virtually all Indian films had interlarded their plots with song and dance sequences. The Hindi film of the postwar era froze this tendency into a recipe: an average of six songs and three dances. Even melodramas and grim thrillers would have the obligatory musical stretches. The idea was to create a "complete spectacle," an entertainment package that could dazzle an impoverished, illiterate audience. The actor Dilip Kumar and the actress Nargis became stars, while the music used in the films became a major drawing factor (see box).

Virtually all filmmakers worked in this popular tradition. Mehboob Khan specialized in socials before making the biggest Indian box-office success of its era, *Mother India* (1957), a melodrama of a rural woman's struggle to raise her family. V. Shantaram continued the populist tradition of the 1930s with films that criticized social inequities. His most famous film of the 1940s was *Dr. Kotnis* (1946), the story of an Indian physician in China; a typical later work is *Two Eyes, Twelve Hands* (1957), about a humane prison warden. Bimal Roy, the cameraman for the classic *Devdas,* moved to Bombay after the decline of the Calcutta film studios. His Neorealist-influenced *Two Acres of Land* (1953) celebrates the endurance of a rural family, while *Sujata* (1959) tentatively explores the issue of the "untouchable" caste.

Raj Kapoor's third feature, *Awaara* ("The Vagabond," 1951) became a stupendous success from the Middle East to the USSR. Over the next three decades, Kapoor was the master showman of the Hindi film. Kapoor directed and starred in much of his studio's output, becoming in the process probably the most internationally known Indian star of his generation. (It is said that in the Soviet Union parents named their sons after him.) Raj was the most prominent member of a star dynasty including his brothers Shashi and Shammi and his sons Rishi and Bhupendra.

Kapoor gave new formulas to the Hindi film. His scripts, often written by the veteran social critic K. A. Abbas, praise the virtuous poor and satirize the undeserving rich. Kapoor contributes ingratiating comedy as an idealistic, Chaplinesque common man (**18.33**). Heart-wrenching melodrama centering on lovers or orphaned children alternates with farcical humor and erotic scenes. Kapoor portrayed himself as a populist entertainer: "My fans are the street urchins, the lame, the blind, the maimed, the have-nots, and the underdog."[4]

Such show-business hyperbole should not distract from the skill of Kapoor's direction, which displays a mastery of the classical narrative style. He was quick to keep up with western trends: chiaroscuro lighting and low-angle deep focus in the earlier works; a glossier, higher-key look in the late 1950s; vibrant color location shooting in Europe for *Sangam* (1964). *Awaara* has a complicated flashback structure and includes a flamboyant musical fantasy sequence. Kapoor's ingenuity and craftsmanship, no less than his shrewd judgment of public taste, set new standards for the all-India film.

Swimming against the Stream: Guru Dutt and Ritwik Ghatak

A handful of directors pursued an unconventional approach. One major producer-director, Guru Dutt, struggled self-consciously against the conventions of Hindi cinema. After leaving Calcutta's Prabhat company for Bombay, Dutt began as a director of urban romantic drama and comedy and eventually founded his own production company. Like Kapoor, he was in demand as an actor.

Dutt established himself as a major director with *Thirst* (1957). This romantic drama about a sensitive poet (played by Dutt himself) became an unexpected hit (**18.34**). Encouraged, he made *Paper Flowers* (1959),

18.35 The grotesque cabdriver in *Pathetic Fallacy* and his beloved car (production still).

the first Indian CinemaScope film, but this melancholy tale of a film director's decline was a commercial failure. After producing another unpopular film, *Master's Wife and Slave* (1962), he died from an overdose of sleeping pills, either by accident or suicide.

Dutt's dramas are dominated by a brooding romantic fatalism. The filmmaker in *Paper Flowers* fails in marriage, in his love affair with an actress, and finally in his vocation, becoming a drunkard whom his old studio will not even hire as an extra. Dutt's sorrowful depiction of the losing battle of the individual with social forces proved ill-suited to the Hindi formula. His "serious" films are poised between popular genres and "higher" drama.

This somber intensity informs Dutt's song numbers. Long tracking shots pick up the rhythm of the music and move into and away from his characters' sorrowful faces. In *Thirst,* the hero Vijay sings as he stumbles drunkenly through seedy streets, commenting cynically on the exploitation around him: streetwalkers entice him, a mother sells her daughter to a passerby, a teenage prostitute is racked by a cough. Vijay's soliloquy becomes a wail of protest against urban misery. In such sequences, Dutt pushes the Hindi film away from musical comedy toward the pathos of western-style opera.

Like Dutt, Ritwik Ghatak was Bengali, but his background marked him in a different way. Ghatak was shattered to see his homeland become part of Pakistan in 1947, and the experience of exile was at the base of several of his films. He became a member of the Indian People's Theatre Association, a left-wing cultural movement that called for a return to indigenous arts and pro-

test on behalf of the masses. In the early 1950s, Ghatak's interests shifted to cinema, a development intensified by his study of Soviet Montage directors and his viewing of Neorealist films at the Indian Film Festival of 1952.

Out of these impulses came his first film, *The City Dweller* (1953), which failed to get released. Returning to Calcutta after some scriptwriting in Bombay, Ghatak was able to make several films, including *Ajantrik* (*Pathetic Fallacy,* 1958), his children's film *The Runaway* (1959), and a trilogy on the Partition.

Ghatak pushed genre conventions to extremes. In his only comedy, *Pathetic Fallacy,* a cabdriver treats his ancient Chevrolet as more human than the people around him (**18.35**). Ghatak's melodramas turned the Indian social film toward stark tragedy. He relished plot contrivances and lurid action. The climax of *Subarnarekha* (1965) comes when a prostitute learns that her next customer is her drunken brother; she slits her throat with a scythe. Ghatak saw his harsh melodrama as harking back to Indian theater traditions and to mythical archetypes.

Famous for making his sound tracks "thick," Ghatak used music symbolically. In the famous final scene of *The City Dweller,* the Communist anthem "Internationale" is heard playing at a political rally off-screen. Ghatak's later melodramas underscore scenes of suffering with startling whip cracks. In *The Cloud-Capped Star* (1960), the credits sequence establishes a complex matrix of musical associations that are abruptly cut off by the homely sound of rice boiling.

In the mid-1960s Ghatak gave up directing for a time and took a teaching post at the Film Institute of India. "I barged into them," he said of his students. "I tried to win them over in favor of a different cinema."[5] The results would emerge in the 1970s under the rubric "Parallel Cinema."

A third unconventional figure was the Bengali director Satyajit Ray, for decades after the war the only Indian filmmaker widely known in European and Anglo-American film culture. His first film, *Pather Panchali* ("Song of the Little Road," 1955), won a prize at the Cannes Film Festival, and its sequel, *Aparajito* ("The Undefeated," 1956), captured the Grand Prize at Venice. Despite his roots in the broader Indian culture, Ray's films lie closer to the European art film than to the commercial Indian cinema, and most of his films were more popular abroad than at home. We shall examine the career of this international filmmaker in Chapter 19.

LATIN AMERICA

Although Latin American nations had long been politically autonomous, they still depended on the industrialized world, which bought the raw materials and food they produced and sold them manufactured goods. Most of the continent was ruled by dictatorships and military regimes, and there was friction among the intellectuals, businessmen, traditional landowners, urban workers, and indigenous peasants. Populations usually consisted of a mix of indigenous, African, and European elements.

World War II forced many countries in the region to align themselves with the West. Governments formed alliances with the United States while accepting aid under the "Good Neighbor" policy. After the war, the major Latin American countries encouraged cooperation between local entrepreneurs and foreign investors. The state helped by funding or managing companies, and most countries moved back to import-export economies.

In the 1930s, Argentine films had been the most successful Spanish-language product in Latin America. During World War II, the government took a position of neutrality. As a result, the United States refused to ship film materials to Argentina but sent raw stock, equipment, technical advisers, and loans to Mexican firms instead. U.S. policy, along with tactical errors by Argentine producers, enabled Mexico to become the production center of Latin America.

Argentina and Brazil

In the immediate postwar period, Central America and South America were dominated by films from the United States, a few European countries, Mexico, and Argentina. Only Brazil offered any significant competition. Two studios—Atlântida of Rio de Janeiro, and Vera Cruz Studios of São Paulo—dominated postwar production. The vertically integrated Atlântida prospered through exploiting the popular *chanchada,* or musical comedy. Vera Cruz, despite its modern studio complex, went bankrupt in 1954.

Brazil, Mexico, and Argentina relied on genres that were counterparts to Hollywood cinema: musicals, family melodramas, action pictures, and comedies. Each genre, however, was adapted to each nation's culture. The cowboy became the Argentine gaucho; singers and dancers became performers in Rio's Carnival.

Conceptions of an alternative cinema emerged, however haltingly. As in Europe, ciné-clubs sprang up. There was also some influence from Italian Neorealism. Fernando Birrí, after studying at Italy's Centro Sperimentale, founded the Documentary Film School of Santa Fé in Argentina. There he and his students made the documentary short *Throw Me a Dime* (1958; **18.36**). In Brazil, Nelson Pereira dos Santos made *Rio 40 Degrees* (1955), a semidocumentary about boys selling peanuts in the slums, and *Rio Northern Zone* (1957), a biography of a famous samba composer. Pereira dos Santos has stressed that

> Neorealism taught us, in sum, that it was possible to make films on the streets; that we did not need studios; that we could film using average people rather than known actors; that the technique could be imperfect, as long as the film was truly linked to its national culture and expressed that culture.[6]

18.36 *Throw Me a Dime*: child beggars risk their lives running alongside trains.

18.37, *left* *House of the Angel:* gauzy imagery, film-noir lighting, and fluid tracking shots of body parts present the hazy present in which the heroine lives.

18.38, *right* The woman's past, filmed in canted angles and steep perspectives.

Both Birrí and dos Santos would be central figures in Latin American left-wing cinema of the 1960s (see Chapter 23).

A European-style art cinema emerged most visibly in Argentina, where Buenos Aires was a center of cosmopolitan culture. Leopoldo Torre Nilsson, the son of a veteran director, made several features before *House of the Angel* (1957) earned acclaim at the Cannes festival. Told as an ambiguous series of flashbacks, *House of the Angel* reveals a girl's personality stifled by political, sexual, and religious repression. She eventually succumbs to aristocratic decadence, living in a haze of memories and fantasies. Her suffocating life in the present is shot in a misty, mysterious style (**18.37**). Scenes in the past are filmed more crisply, but with an expressionist flavor (**18.38**)—not unexpected in a filmmaker who listed Fritz Lang, F. W. Murnau, and Ingmar Bergman among his favorite directors.

After the success of *House of the Angel*, Torre Nilsson formed his own company. Most of his films were scripted by his wife, Beatriz Guido, a prominent novelist. His most renowned later work was *Hand in the Trap* (1961), which won a prize at Cannes. Of strongly European tastes, Torre Nilsson exemplified the international modernism characteristic of many Argentine artists.

Torre Nilsson's success occurred within the narrow confines of Argentine production. In the late 1940s, Juan Perón's government established protectionist measures, but, in 1950, the government struck a bargain with the Motion Picture Export Association of America that was similar to the pacts negotiated in Europe. U.S. companies and local distributors and exhibitors benefited, but local production was hurt. After a coup overthrew Perón, the military government lifted all control on imports. A 1957 law gave the industry substantial subsidies, which encouraged independent production. Although output dropped to fewer than thirty films per year, conditions encouraged Torre Nilsson's prestige cinema, which attracted elite audiences and foreign prizes.

Mexican Popular Cinema

By contrast, the Mexican government vigorously supported a popular cinema. Thanks to U.S. assistance, the industry came out of the war strong. The government exempted the industry from income taxes and created the National Film Bank to help finance production. In 1954, it created nationalized companies to market films at home and abroad. In 1959, the government bought the country's leading studio facility; in the following year, the major theater chain was nationalized.

For almost twenty years after World War II, the Mexican cinema was second only to that of the United States as a presence in the Spanish-speaking Americas. Working-class audiences in the growing cities were drawn to Mexico's genres: the *comedia ranchera*, featuring the virile singing *charro,* or cowboy; the melodrama; the *pachuco* musical, centering on zoot-suited hustlers; and the *cabaretera,* or brothel film. Cantinflas, "Tin Tan" Germán Valdez, and Dolores del Rio were the best-known Spanish-speaking stars in the world. Mexican feature output ranged from 50 to 100 films per year. By the end of the 1950s, the industry was adapting to competition from television by exploiting the wide screen, color, nudity, and new genre formulas, such as horror films and Westerns.

Mexican films were often cheap, quickly shot formula pictures; the National Film Bank would support only those projects deemed likely to turn a big profit; and the directors' union permitted few young people to enter the profession. Nevertheless, some directors stood out, especially during the golden age from 1946 to 1952. Most notable was Emilio "El Indio" Fernández. His wartime success, *María Candelaria* (1943; **18.39**), was

18.39 Deep-focus staging puts the tolling bell in the foreground of this image from *María Candelaria.*

followed by *Enamorada* ("In Love," 1946), an adaptation of *The Taming of the Shrew,* and *Río Escondido* ("Hidden River," 1947), a didactic film about a teacher sent to reform a backward village. Fernández's melodramatic plots showcased the cinematography of Gabriel Figueroa, who cultivated picturesque, deep-focus landscape shots similar to those in Sergei Eisenstein's *Qué viva Mexico!* Other filmmakers of importance include Mathilde Landeta, the only woman director working in Mexico at the time, and Alejandro Galindo, who made somewhat left-wing social-problem films.

Audiences outside the Spanish-speaking countries knew the postwar Mexican cinema chiefly through the work of Luis Buñuel. After nearly a decade of working in the United States at odd film jobs, Buñuel moved to Mexico. The twenty films he made there between 1946 and 1965 revived his career.

Buñuel quietly accepted the conventions of mainstream cinema. His first Mexican film was a star-filled musical; his second was a comedy. His filming sched-ules were seldom more than four weeks long, his budgets ludicrously small. He developed a straightforward technique that was the antithesis of Fernández's showiness. Buñuel's very poverty of means gave him considerable control; he wrote his own scripts, and he could even slip in bits from his memories or dreams.

By winning a prize at the 1951 Cannes Film Festival, *Los Olvidados* (1950) returned Buñuel to international prominence. Several of his Mexican films were distributed abroad, and in the late 1950s he participated in coproductions with France and Italy. After the scandal of his Spanish production *Viridiana* (1961; see p. 371), he made two prestigious films in Mexico, *The Exterminating Angel* (1962) and *Simon of the Desert* (1965). Both were more modernist than anything he had done since *L'Age d'or,* but even his entertainment films preserved his Surrealist impulses. Yet he remained an international director, and *Los Olvidados* brought him major recognition as part of the postwar art-cinema tradition (see Chapter 19).

Surrealism had flourished in Latin America, and like artists in painting and literature Buñuel showed that it was compatible with indigenous traditions. Unlike Torre Nilsson, he created modernist films within mass-entertainment genres. He sought, as he put it, to make films "which, apart from entertaining the audience, would convey to them the absolute certainty that they do not live in the best of all possible worlds."[7] The unpretentious, high-output Mexican industry enabled him to achieve this goal several times in the postwar decades.

As postwar film culture expanded the international market for movies, many of the directors we have discussed in this chapter won fame outside their regions. A handful, such as Akira Kurosawa, Satyajit Ray, and Luis Buñuel, gained international recognition as innovative artists. The forces that shaped this trend, the search for film "authors," are examined in the next chapter.

Notes and Queries

DE-STALINIZATION AND THE DISAPPEARING ACT

After Khrushchev's "secret speech" denouncing Stalin in 1956, the dictator's image was gradually removed from its place of honor in offices, public squares, and hearthsides. It was also removed from films made during the height of his reign.

During the early 1960s, Soviet archivists produced "revised" versions of 1930s classics that expunged all views of the leader. It was relatively easy to cut out shots in which

18.40, *left* *Lenin in October,* Stalin standing on the left.

18.41, *right* *Lenin in October,* Stalin hidden by a Wellesian foreground supplied by special effects.

Stalin appeared and redub sound tracks to eliminate references to him. But sometimes shots could not be cut without losing story information. Therefore, optical tricks were used to cover portraits of Stalin and his henchmen with large vases of flowers or pictures of Marx and Lenin. When Stalin himself was in the shot, matte work eliminated him, sometimes in bizarre ways. Mikhail Romm revised his *Lenin in October* (1937) by blocking Stalin out with Wellesian foreground elements, such as a head or an elbow (**18.40, 18.41**). See Alexander Sesonske, "Re-editing History: *Lenin in October,*" *Sight and Sound* 53, no. 1 (winter 1983/1984): 56–58.

REFERENCES

1. Quoted in "Industry: Beauty from Osaka," *Newsweek* (11 October 1955): 116.
2. Quoted in Boleslaw Michalek, *The Cinema of Andrzej Wajda,* trans. Edward Rothert (London: Tantivy, 1973), p. 18.
3. George S. Semsel, "Interviews," in Semsel, ed., *Chinese Film: The State of the Art in the People's Republic* (New York: Praeger, 1987), p. 112.
4. Quoted in Bunny Reuben, *Raj Kapoor: The Fabulous Showman* (Bombay: National Film Development Corporation, 1988), p. 380.
5. Quoted in Haimanti Banerjee, *Ritwik Kumar Ghatak: A Monograph* (Pune: National Film Archive of India, 1985), p. 22.
6. Quoted in Robert Stam and Randal Johnson, "The Cinema of Hunger: Nelson Pereira dos Santos' *Vidas Secas,*" in Stam and Johnson, eds., *Brazilian Cinema* (Austin: University of Texas Press, 1982), p. 122.
7. Quoted in Francisco Aranda, *Luis Buñuel: A Critical Biography,* trans. and ed. David Robinson (London: Secker and Warburg, 1975), p. 185.

FURTHER READING

Babitsky, Paul, and John Rimberg. *The Soviet Film Industry.* New York: Praeger, 1955.

Banerjee, Haimanti. *Ritwik Kumar Ghatak: A Monograph.* Poona: National Film Archive of India, 1985.

Chute, David, ed. "Bollywood Rising: A Beginner's Guide to Hindi cinema." *Film Comment* 38, 3 (May/June 2002): 35–57.

Dissanayake, Wimal, and Malti Sahai. *Raj Kapoor's Films: Harmony of Discourses.* New Delhi: Vikas, 1988.

Franco, Jean. *The Modern Culture of Latin America: Society and the Artist.* Harmondsworth, England: Penguin, 1970.

Hirano, Kyoko. *Mr. Smith Goes to Tokyo: Japanese Cinema under the American Occupation 1945–1952.* Washington: Smithsonian Institution Press, 1992.

"Indian Cinema." *Quarterly Review of Film Studies* 11, no. 3 (1989).

Michalek, Boleslaw. *The Cinema of Andrzej Wajda.* Trans. Edward Rothert. London: Tantivy, 1973.

Oms, Marcel. *Leopoldo Torre Nilsson.* Paris: Première Plan, 1962.

Rajadhyaksha, Ashish. *Ritwik Ghatak: A Return to the Epic.* Bombay: Screen Unit, 1982.

Rangoonwalla, Rionze. *Guru Dutt: 1925–1965.* Poona: National Film Archive of India, 1982.

Wajda, Andrzej. *Double Vision: My Life in Film.* Trans. Rose Medina. New York: Holt, 1989.

CHAPTER 19

ART CINEMA AND THE IDEA OF AUTHORSHIP

Individuals and institutions affect history, but so do ideas. One of the most influential ideas in cinema history is the belief that a director is most centrally responsible for a film's form, style, and meanings. Most historians have made this assumption since at least the 1920s, but it was examined and articulated with particular force in postwar European film culture. The debates of that period, along with the films that were drawn into them, shaped filmmaking all over the world.

THE RISE AND SPREAD OF THE AUTEUR THEORY

Since the mid-1940s, French directors and screenwriters quarreled over who could properly be considered the *auteur*, or author, of a film. The Occupation period had popularized the notion that the mature sound cinema would be the "age of the scriptwriter," but Roger Leenhardt and André Bazin claimed that the director was the main source of a film's value. These two critics wrote for the journal *Revue du cinéma* (1946–1949), which championed Orson Welles, William Wyler, and other American directors.

An important statement of this line of thought was Alexandre Astruc's 1948 essay on *la caméra-stylo* ("the camera-pen"). According to Astruc, the cinema had achieved maturity and would attract serious artists who would use film to express their ideas and feelings. "The filmmaker-author writes with his camera as a writer writes with his pen."[1] The modern cinema would be a personal one, and technology, crew, and cast would be no more than instruments in the artist's creative process.

In 1951, Jacques Doniol-Valcroze founded the monthly magazine *Cahiers du cinéma* ("Cinema Notebooks"). Bazin quickly became its central critic. The first issue reviewed *Sunset Boulevard* as a Billy Wilder film, *Diary of a Country Priest* as a Robert Bresson film, *The Little Flowers of Saint Francis* as a Roberto Rossellini film, and so on. Soon younger *Cahiers* critics such as Eric Rohmer, Claude Chabrol, Jean-Luc Godard, and François Truffaut began pushing the auteur approach to the point of provocation. The first scandal came in 1954, with Truffaut's essay, "A Certain Tendency in the French Cinema." He attacked the Cinema of Quality (p. 375) as "scenarists' films," works that revealed a lack of originality and a reliance on literary classics. According to Truffaut, in this tradition the screenwriter hands in the script, and the director simply adds the performers and pictures, thereby becoming only a *metteur en scène*, a "stager." Truffaut named a few genuine auteurs: Jean Renoir, Bresson, Jean Cocteau, Jacques Tati, and others who wrote their own stories and dialogue. Fulfilling Astruc's dream of the caméra-stylo, these directors were true "men of the cinema."

In making the issue of screenwriting central, Truffaut was providing a rationale for *Cahiers*'s tastes. The journal had praised those European and American directors who composed or controlled their scripts. Truffaut's initial conception of authorship was also held by *Cahiers*'s rival magazine *Positif* (founded 1952). Marxist and surrealist in its inclinations, *Positif* shared few of the *Cahiers* writers' tastes, but like them it concentrated primarily on directors who had a great deal of control over the scriptwriting process.

Some of the younger *Cahiers* critics went further, claiming that great directors in Hollywood had managed to express their vision of life without having any say in the screenplay. This hard-core version of auteurism proved most controversial throughout the 1950s and 1960s. Bazin could not accept the extreme views of his young colleagues, but critics elsewhere were quick to take up the *politique des auteurs*—the policy of treating any director with a personal style or a distinct worldview as an auteur. In the early 1960s, American critic Andrew Sarris began promulgating what he called the "auteur theory" as a way of understanding U.S. film history. The British journal *Movie* (founded in 1962) was auteurist from the start. While Sarris and the *Movie* critics were sympathetic to the *Cahiers* European canon, they concentrated chiefly on Hollywood directors (see "Notes and Queries" at the end of this chapter).

Once we have declared, for example, Ingmar Bergman to be an auteur, how does this help us understand a Bergman film? Auteur critics argued that we can examine the film as if it were a piece of "pure" creation, like a novel. The film can be understood as expressing Bergman's view of life.

Moreover, considering Bergman an auteur allows us to look for common elements across his films. One motto of auteur criticism was Renoir's remark that a director really makes only one film and keeps remaking it. Recurrent subjects, themes, images, techniques, and plot situations give the director's films a rich unity. Knowledge of the auteur's other films may thus help the viewer understand the one at hand. In particular, the auteur critic was sensitive to ways in which a director's work developed over time, taking unexpected turns or returning to ideas broached earlier.

Finally, auteur criticism tended to promote a study of film style. If a filmmaker was an artist like a writer or painter, that artistry was revealed not only in *what* was said but in *how* it was said. Like any creator, the filmmaker ought to be a master of the medium, exploiting it in striking and innovative ways. Auteur critics distinguished directors by uses of camerawork, lighting, and other techniques. Some critics drew a distinction between filmmakers who emphasized staging and camera placement (the so-called mise-en-scène directors like Max Ophüls and Renoir) and filmmakers who relied on editing (montage directors like Alfred Hitchcock and Sergei Eisenstein).

AUTHORSHIP AND THE GROWTH OF THE ART CINEMA

Such ideas of authorship meshed smoothly with the growing art cinema of the 1950s and 1960s. Most of the prestigious directors of the period wrote their own scripts; all pursued distinctive themes and stylistic choices in film after film. Film festivals tended to honor the director as the central creator. In a commercial context, Tati, Michelangelo Antonioni, and others became "brand names," differentiating their products from the mass of "ordinary" cinema. Such name recognition could carry a film into foreign markets.

During the 1950s and 1960s, auteurist critics tended to focus on filmmakers who developed the cinematic modernism discussed in the last three chapters. Auteurism sensitized viewers to narrative experiments that expressed a director's vision of life. It also prepared viewers to interpret stylistic patterns as the filmmaker's personal comment on the action. Auteur critics were especially alert for ambiguities that could be interpreted as the director's reflection on a subject or a theme.

This chapter examines the careers of Luis Buñuel, Ingmar Bergman, Akira Kurosawa, Federico Fellini, Michelangelo Antonioni, Robert Bresson, Jacques Tati, and Satyajit Ray. They are not the only auteurs in the history of cinema, of course, but they were considered among the giants by critics promoting the theory of authorship during these decades.

In the Introduction, we stated that films could be important historically because they were good in themselves, because they typified broader trends, or because they were influential. Although each of these directors was significant within his own country's cinema, none was typical of the national trends and movements in filmmaking that came and went during his long career. All remained resolutely individualistic, and, although some (especially Fellini and Antonioni) have been influential, most directors have avoided direct imitation of these auteurs' distinctive films. We treat them here partly to examine their bodies of work as wholes—an approach encouraged by authorship studies—and partly to put them in an international context.

These directors typify broader tendencies in world film production. All made breakthrough films in the 1950s. All triumphed at film festivals and won international distribution, even gaining some foothold in the inhospitable American market. The institutions of film culture helped them to fame, and these directors' successes in turn strengthened the authority of coproductions, national subsidy programs, festivals, and film journals. Some, such as Antonioni and Bergman, made films outside their own country, and several more enjoyed the benefits of international funding. Their careers thereby highlight important trends in the postwar cinema.

In addition, these directors became the most celebrated exponents of 1950s and 1960s modernist filmmaking. Critics considered that each director had enriched film technique while also expressing an idiosyncratic vision of life. The directors' work exercised wide influence on other filmmakers. Since these directors all considered themselves serious artists, they shared auteurist assumptions with audiences and critics. Fellini inadvertently echoed Astruc: "One could make a film with the same personal, direct intimacy with which a writer writes."[2]

During the 1960s and 1970s, auteurism helped create film studies as an academic discipline (see "Notes and Queries" at the end of this chapter). Students and fans soon made the idea of authorship a commonplace in the culture at large. Journalistic reviewers now usually assume that a film's primary maker is its director. Many ordinary moviegoers use a simple version of auteurism as a criterion of taste, not only for art-film directors but also for Hollywood filmmakers like Steven Spielberg, Brian De Palma, James Cameron, and Oliver Stone.

19.1   The nun's crown of thorns becomes kindling (*Viridiana*).

During the late 1960s and the 1970s, not all of our exemplary auteurs sustained their reputations. Most suffered critical and commercial setbacks (often resulting from their incompatibility with post-1968 political cinema). To a considerable extent, however, these directors regained critical acclaim after the mid-1970s, and in the intervening decades their work has continued to command attention.

LUIS BUÑUEL (1900–1983)

The Surrealist films *Un Chien andalou* (1928), *L'Age d'or* (1930), and *Las Hurdes* (1932) established Buñuel's distinctive personal vision, and most critics believed that he continued to express it in Mexico, Spain, and France. Bazin found Buñuel's films deeply moralistic; for Truffaut, they exemplified rigorous scripting and a concern for entertainment; for Sarris, they embodied the mystery of a style without style; and for the critics of *Positif*, Buñuel remained the great, long-lived remnant of cinematic surrealism, attacking bourgeois values with images of savage beauty.

His Mexican films of the postwar decade showed that he could insert his personal obsessions into accessible comedies and melodramas. In *Viridiana* (Spain, 1961), the novitiate Viridiana attempts to establish her uncle's farm as a Christian community, but her plans fall prey to the cynicism of her uncle's son, Jorge, and to the rapacity of the beggars who swarm over the farm. Her ideals chastened, Viridiana joins Jorge and his mistress in a game of cards while a child tosses Viridiana's crown of thorns onto a fire (**19.1**). The protagonist's loss of innocence recalls that of the hero of *Nazarin* (1958), trying vainly to bring grace to a fallen world. As *Los Olvidados* (1950) had put Buñuel back on the

19.2, *left* The dead Julian chortling under the bed: Pedro's dream in *Los Olvidados*.

19.3, *right* *Mort en ce jardin* (1956): in the jungle heat, ants invade the Bible.

map (p. 413), *Viridiana,* which won a major prize at Cannes, revived his fame during the 1960s—especially since he had made this blasphemous film under Francisco Franco's very nose.

In the 1960s, Buñuel moved toward more distinctly modernist experiments that had been partially sketched in *L'Age d'or. The Exterminating Angel* (1962) inexplicably entraps partygoers in a house for days, their polite manners decaying under pressure. With *Diary of a Chambermaid* (1964) Buñuel began his "French phase," in which major stars and the scriptwriter Jean-Claude Carrière became central to his work. As he had used the Mexican commercial cinema for his ends, so he began to exploit the conventions of the European art film: the mixture of fantasy and reality in *Belle de jour* (1967), the episodic narratives in *The Milky Way* (1969), the ambiguous, interwoven dreams of *The Discreet Charm of the Bourgeoisie* (1972), and the device of using two actresses to portray the same character in *That Obscure Object of Desire* (1977). Some of the films became substantial successes on the art-house circuit, and *Discreet Charm* won an Academy Award. At the end of his life, the elderly anarchist became that rarity, a modernist filmmaker whom audiences found entertaining.

In both mass-market films and art films, Buñuel's accessibility was partly due to the sobriety of his technique. Of the major auteurs, he had the least distinctive style. In the Mexican films, he adhered to the conventions of classical Hollywood cinema, including moderate deep focus and restrained camera movements. His third Mexican film, *Los Olvidados* ("The Young and Lost," 1950), depicts juvenile delinquents in a poor neighborhood of Mexico City. Shot largely on location, the film announces in its opening that it is based strictly on facts. These elements encouraged many European critics to see the film as a Mexican version of neorealism. Yet Buñuel offered no warmhearted liberal optimism. Instead of the virtuous poor of *The Bicycle Thief,* he presented vicious youth gangs, unfeeling mothers, bitter vagrants.

Buñuel charged Italian Neorealism with lacking authentic "poetry." In *Los Olvidados*, the poetry is often provided by disturbingly violent or erotic images. Neorealism never generated as unsettling and enigmatic a scene as Pedro's dream, featuring floating chickens, images of his mother bringing him a slab of meat, and a shot of a murdered boy grinning and bleeding under the bed (**19.2**). His more self-consciously modernist films relied on simple staging, long takes, and panning movements to follow the actors.

Buñuel's straightforward style serves to heighten haunting images that disturb received notions of religion and sexuality. In *Un Chien andalou,* Buñuel shows ants crawling out of a man's hand; thirty years later, they are gnawing their way through a Bible (**19.3**). In *Susana* (1950), a spider scuttles across a cross-shaped shadow on the floor of a prison cell. *Nazarin* (1958), based on a classic novel, comments on the ineffectiveness of naive religious faith. The frigid housewife who becomes a prostitute in *Belle de jour* is visited by a Japanese client who shows her a box, from which issue buzzing sounds; the audience never learns what the box contains.

Buñuel gives obsessions to his characters and then insidiously invites the audience to share them. In *The Criminal Life of Archibaldo de La Cruz* (1955), the hero is shown as a young boy, staring at a music box (**19.4**); he comes to associate this with the death of his governess, shot by a stray bullet at the window (**19.5**). As a grown man, he rediscovers the music box (**19.6**). This stirs in him the desire to kill sexually alluring women. He never succeeds, but after he has practiced strangling a mannequin and drags it away, Buñuel calmly shows us the dummy's fallen leg (**19.7**). We, not Archibaldo, make the association with the slain governess and find ourselves firmly within his morbid fantasy.

Buñuel's modernism emerges as well in his experiments with narrative construction. The films are full of repetitions, digressions, and movements between reality and fantasy. ("Don't worry if the movie's too short," he once told a producer. "I'll just put in a dream."[3]) His

19.4

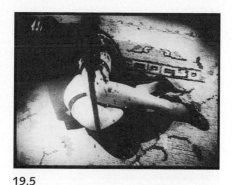

19.5

19.6

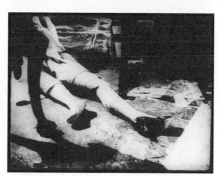

19.7

19.4–19.7   Four shots from *Archibaldo de La Cruz.*

plots depend particularly on outrageous delays. *The Discreet Charm of the Bourgeoisie* is virtually nothing but a series of interrupted dinners. The ostensible action, something about corrupt businessmen smuggling cocaine, is buried in a series of bourgeois rituals gone awry: encountering a restaurant's staff gathered around the corpse of the manager, finding an entire army troop invading one's parlor. The film's surface consists of maddeningly banal conversations about tastes in food, drink, and decor. Whenever the story seems to have reached a climax, a character wakes up, and we realize that previous scenes—how many?—have been imaginary.

Most modernists attack narrative in order to turn the viewer's attention to other matters, but Buñuel treats narrative frustration as itself the basis of pleasure. The very title of *That Obscure Object of Desire* alludes to the impossibility of satisfying one's deepest wishes. Traveling on a train to Paris, the wealthy Fabert tells other passengers of his obsessive pursuit of the virginal Conchita. He gives her money, clothes, even a house of her own, and yet each time he tries to seduce her she eludes him. When he pulls away, she returns to lure him on and humiliate him more brutally. Whenever Fabert pauses in his tale, the passengers urge him to continue; their avid curiosity makes them stand-ins for us. At the end of Fabert's story, Conchita appears on the train, and the cycle of frustrated desire starts again. *Obscure Object*

can be seen as a reflexive parable that makes cinematic narrative akin to sexual flirtation.

If the fun is in the waiting, not the ending, the Buñuel film will often stop arbitrarily. In *Belle de jour*, the supposedly crippled husband miraculously rises from his chair. In *Discreet Charm*, the Mirandan ambassador finally gets to eat a piece of leftover lamb from his refrigerator. And in the final scene of Buñuel's last film, a terrorist bomb destroys the chic shopping arcade through which Fabert still pursues Conchita. Buñuel's films at once criticize social conventions and play cunningly on those narrative conventions that maintain our fascination with storytelling.

INGMAR BERGMAN (1918–   )

Like his mentor Alf Sjöberg (see p. 384), Bergman came from the theater. After a stint as a scriptwriter, this prodigiously energetic man began directing in 1945; by 1988, he had made nearly forty-five films and directed even more plays.

As a filmmaker, Bergman gained a reputation as a serious artist commanding many genres. His earliest films were domestic dramas, often centering on alienated young couples in search of happiness through art or nature (*Summer Interlude*, 1951; *Summer with Monika*,

19.8, *left*   Art as a mysteriously powerful spell (*The Magician*).

19.9, *right*   The ringmaster badgered by his performers in a deep-focus long take (*Sunset of a Clown*).

1953). Soon, with a repertory of skillful performers at his call, he focused on the failures of married love—sometimes treated comically, as in *A Lesson in Love* (1954), but at other times presented in probing, agonizing psychodramas such as *Sawdust and Tinsel* (aka *The Naked Night*, 1953). He moved to more self-consciously artistic works: the Mozartian *Smiles of a Summer Night* (1955); the parablelike *The Seventh Seal* (1957); a blend of expressionist dream imagery, natural locales, and elaborate flashbacks in *Wild Strawberries* (1957; see 16.3). For many viewers and critics, Bergman's career climaxed with two trilogies of chamber dramas: first, *Through a Glass Darkly* (1961), *Winter Light* (1963), and *The Silence* (1963); then, *Persona* (1966), *Hour of the Wolf* (1968), and *Shame* (1968). Bergman was at the height of his fame: critics wrote articles and books on his work; his screenplays were translated; his films won festival awards and Oscars. Even people who usually did not take the cinema seriously as an art form saw him as an exemplar of the film director as artist.

Soon, however, after some ill-judged projects and financial setbacks, Bergman could not get funding for his films. *Cries and Whispers* (1972) was paid for with his savings, some actors' investments, and money from the Swedish Film Institute. It had worldwide success, as did *Scenes from a Marriage* (1973) and *The Magic Flute* (1975). Pursued by tax authorities, Bergman abruptly began a period of exile and poorly received coproductions. He returned to Sweden to make *Fanny and Alexander* (1983), which was an international box-office triumph and winner of four Academy Awards. Following the completion of his television film *After the Rehearsal* (1984), Bergman retired from filmmaking.

Into his films Bergman poured his dreams, memories, guilts, and fantasies. Events from his childhood recur from his earliest works to *Fanny and Alexander*. His loss of a lover shaped *Summer Interlude*, while his domestic life was the basis of *Scenes from a Marriage*. Thus Bergman's private world became public property.

In it dwell the nurturing woman, the severe father figure, the cynical man of the world, and the tormented visionary artist. They enact parables of infidelity, sadism, disillusionment, loss of faith, creative paralysis, and anguished suffering. The setting is a bleak island landscape, a stifling drawing room, a harshly lit theater stage.

Despite the obsessive unity of Bergman's concerns, there are several stages in his career. The early films portray adolescent crises and the instability of first love (e.g., *Summer with Monika*). The major films of the 1950s tend to explore spiritual malaise and to reflect upon the relation between theater and life. The bright spot is often a faith in art—symbolized in *The Magician* (1958) as a conjurer's illusion (**19.8**).

The two trilogies of the 1960s solemnly undercut the religious and humanistic premises of the early work. God becomes distant and silent, while humans are shown to be confused and narcissistic. Even art, *Persona* and *Shame* suggest, cannot redeem human dignity in an age of political oppression. In the deeply pessimistic films of the 1970s, almost every human contact—that between parents and children, husband and wife, friend and friend—is revealed to be based on illusion and deceit. All that is left, again and again, is the memory of infantile innocence. This becomes the basis of *Fanny and Alexander*, a film set in a world that has yet to know the catastrophes of the twentieth century.

"I am much more a man of the theatre than a man of the film."[4] Bergman was able to turn out films quickly partly because he cultivated a troupe of performers—Eva Dahlbeck, Gunnar Björnstrand, Harriet Andersson, Bibi Andersson, Liv Ullmann, and Max von Sydow. His staging and shooting techniques have usually been at the service of the dramatic values of his scripts. His 1950s work applied deep-focus and long-take tactics to scenes of intense psychological reflection (**19.9**). After *Cries and Whispers* he relied more on zoom shots. Throughout his career he drew on the expressionist tradition (**19.10, 19.11**).

19.10   Expressionistic dissolves open *Sunset of a Clown*.

19.11   The Knight questions the "witch" in *The Seventh Seal*.

19.12   *Summer with Monika*: "Have we forgotten," wrote Godard, ". . . that sudden conspiracy between actor and spectator . . . when Harriet Anderson, laughing eyes clouded with confusion and riveted on the camera, calls on us to witness her disgust in choosing hell instead of heaven?"

19.13   At the climax of Cecilia's speech, in a shot lasting almost two minutes, she claws forward into extreme close-up, her face starkly lit . . .

19.14   . . . before falling back exhausted into the nurse's arms.

Perhaps more distinctive is a technique that owes a good deal to the Kammerspiel tradition of August Strindberg and German cinema. Bergman pushed his performers close to the viewer, sometimes letting them challengingly address the camera (**19.12**). In the chamber dramas, Bergman began to shoot entire scenes in frontal close-up, with abstract backgrounds concentrating on nuances of glance and expression.

Brink of Life (1958) illustrates Bergman's adoption of theatrical technique. The plot centers on three women in a maternity ward during a critical period of forty-eight hours. The sense of a Kammerspiel world is reinforced by the first shot, which shows the ward's door opening to admit Cecilia, who is in labor. The film will end with the youngest woman, Hjördis, resolutely departing through the door toward an uncertain future. The women's pasts are revealed through dialogue. In addition, each actress is given one hyperdramatic scene. The first, and perhaps most impressive, presents Cecilia's reaction to the death of her baby. Characteristically, Bergman dwells on this display of shame, anguish, and physical pain, played in virtuosic fashion by one of his regular actors, Ingrid Thulin. In a drugged haze, cradled by a maternal nurse, Cecilia recalls her worries about the delivery, accuses herself of failing as a wife and mother, and alternates among sobs, cries of agony, and bitter laughter. The monologue runs for over four minutes, filmed in long takes and stark frontal close-ups (**19.13, 19.14**).

Persona is perhaps the furthest development of this intimate style. In a little more than sixty minutes, Bergman presents a psychodrama that challenges the audience to distinguish artifice from reality. An actress,

19.15, *left*   *Persona:* Elisabeth and Alma struggle.

19.16, *right*   The mysterious child gropes for an image that is a composite of the film's two protagonists.

Elisabeth Vogler, refuses to speak. Her nurse, Alma, takes her to an island. Having gained Alma's trust, Elisabeth then torments her; Alma retaliates with violence (**19.15**). Several techniques suggest that the two women's personalities have begun to split. A hallucinatory image of a boy groping for an indistinct face further suggests a dissolution of identity (**19.16**).

Bergman frames the story within images of a film being projected, suggesting the illusory nature of a world that can so deeply engross the spectator. At a moment of particular intensity, the film image burns, yanking the audience out of its involvement with the drama. *Persona*'s ambiguity and reflexivity made it one of the key works of modernist cinema.

Bergman's roots in modern theater and his treatment of moral and religious issues helped convince western intellectuals that cinema was a serious art. His films, and his personal image of the sensitive and uncompromising filmmaker, have played a central role in defining the postwar art cinema.

AKIRA KUROSAWA (1910–1998)

Kurosawa began his directorial career during World War II (p. 396), but he quickly adapted to Occupation policy with *No Regrets for Our Youth* (1946), a political melodrama about militarist Japan's suppression of political change. Kurosawa followed this with a string of social-problem films focused on crime (*Stray Dog*, 1949), government bureaucracy (*Ikiru*, "To Live," 1952), nuclear war (*Record of a Living Being*, aka *I Live in Fear*, 1955), and corporate corruption (*The Bad Sleep Well*, 1960). He also directed several successful jidai-geki (historical films), starting with *Seven Samurai* (1954) and including *The Hidden Fortress* (1958) and *Yojimbo* ("Bodyguard," 1961).

It was *Rashomon* (1950) that burst upon western culture, which greeted it as both an exotic and a modernist film. Drawn from two stories by the 1920s Japanese writer Ryunosuke Akutagawa, the film utilized flashback construction in a more daring way than had any European film of the period.

In twelfth-century Kyoto, a priest, a woodcutter, and a commoner take shelter from the rain in a ruined temple by the Rashomon gate. There they discuss a current scandal: a bandit has stabbed a samurai to death and raped his wife. What really happened in the grove during and after the crimes? In a series of flashbacks, the participants give testimony. (Through a medium, even the dead samurai testifies.) But each person's version, shown in flashback, differs drastically from the others'. When we return to the present and the three men waiting out the rain at the Rashomon gate, the priest despairs that humans will ever tell the truth. The woodcutter abruptly reveals that he had witnessed the crimes and relates a fourth contradictory version.

Kurosawa's staging and shooting sharply demarcate the film's three major "time zones" (**19.17–19.19**). These stylistic differences make for great clarity of exposition, but they do not help the viewer determine exactly what happened in the grove. As with *Paisan* and other neorealist works, the film does not attempt to tell us everything; like *The Bicycle Thief*, *Voyage to Italy*, and some of Bergman's works, Kurosawa's film leaves key questions unanswered at the end. *Rashomon*'s unreliable flashbacks were a logical step beyond 1940s Hollywood experimentation in flashback technique and beyond European art cinema as well. By presenting contradictory versions of a set of events, *Rashomon* made a significant contribution to the emerging tradition of art cinema.

In the years after *Rashomon* was introduced to European audiences, Kurosawa became the most influential Asian director in film history. His use of slow-motion cinematography to portray violence eventually become a cliché. Several of his films were remade by Hollywood, and *Yojimbo* spawned the Italian Western. George Lucas's *Star Wars* (1977) derived part of its plot from *Hidden Fortress*.

Throughout his career, he had been considered the most "western" of Japanese directors, and, although this

19.17 *Rashomon*'s "three styles": the present-day scenes in the temple during the cloudburst rely on compressed wide-angle and deep-focus compositions.

19.18 The scenes of testimony in the hot, dusty courtyard employ frontal compositions. Witnesses address the camera as if the audience were the magistrate.

19.19 The sensuous forest flashbacks emphasize close-ups, dappled sunlight, and mazelike tangled brush.

19.20 The bureaucrat Watanabe waiting for death in *Ikiru*.

19.21 In *Red Beard*, the young intern and a cook (both in the foreground) watch a disturbed girl try to make friends with a little boy amid a forest of quilts hung out to dry. The long lens flattens the space and creates an abstract pattern of slots and undulations.

is not completely accurate, his films proved highly accessible abroad. He drew many of his stories from western literature. *Throne of Blood* and *Ran* ("Chaos," 1985) are based on Shakespeare; *High and Low* (1963), on a detective novel by Ed McBain. Kurosawa's films have strong narrative lines and a good deal of physical action, and he admitted that John Ford, Abel Gance, Frank Capra, William Wyler, and Howard Hawks influenced him.

Critics looking for an authorial vision of the world found in Kurosawa's work a heroic humanism close to western values. Most of his films concentrate on men who curb selfish desires and work for the good of others. This moral vision informs such films as *Drunken Angel* (1948), *Stray Dog*, and *Ikiru*. It is central to *Seven Samurai*, in which a band of masterless swordfighters sacrifice themselves to defend a village from bandits. Often Kurosawa's hero is an egotistical young man who must learn discipline and self-sacrifice from an older, wiser teacher. This theme finds vivid embodiment in *Red Beard* (1965), in which a gruff, dedicated doctor teaches his intern devotion to poor patients.

After *Red Beard*, however, Kurosawa's films slide into pessimism. *Dodes'kaden* (1970), made after he attempted suicide, presents the world as a bleak tenement community holding no hope of escape. *Kagemusha* and *Ran* depict social order as torn by vain struggles for power. Yet *Dersu Uzala* (1975) reaffirms the possibility of friendship and charitable commitment to others, and *Madadayo* (1993) becomes a poignant farewell to a teacher's humanistic ideals.

The first few years of Kurosawa's postwar career established him in three genres: the literary adaptation, the social-problem film, and the jidai-geki. To all these he brought that pluralistic approach to cinematic technique typical of Japanese filmmakers. His first film, *Sanshiro Sugata* (1943), displays immense daring in editing, framing, and slow-motion cinematography (p. 255). Soon after the war, perhaps as a result of exposure to a variety of American films, Kurosawa adopted a Wellesian shot design, with strong deep focus (**19.20**). He later explored ways in which telephoto lenses could create nearly abstract compositions in the widescreen format (**19.21**).

19.22   In the opening sequence of *Record of a Living Being*, the supposedly mad Kiichi is brought in for his court hearing. A camera from one side of the set shows him in medium shot arguing with his sons.

19.23   A second shot, taken by a camera with a less long lens, establishes them in a more frontal view.

19.24   A third camera, from the right side of the set, uses a very long lens to supply a close-up of the old man's rage.

19.25–19.27   Axial cutting enlarges an image abruptly in *Sanshiro Sugata*.

He also experimented with violent action. In *Seven Samurai*, the combat scenes were filmed with several cameras. The cameramen used very long telephoto lenses and panned to follow the action, as if covering a sporting event. Kurosawa began to apply the multiple-camera technique to dialogue, as in *Record of a Living Being* (**19.22–19.24**). His revival of multiple-camera shooting (a commonplace of the early sound era; see p. 196) allowed the actors to play the entire scene without interruption and to forget that they were being filmed. Both telephoto filming and the multiple-camera technique have become far more common since Kurosawa began using them.

Throughout his career, Kurosawa was noted for his frantically energetic editing. In *Sanshiro Sugata* he boldly cuts into details without changing the angle, yielding a sudden "enlargement" effect (**19.25–19.27**). When using the multiple-camera, telephoto-lens strategy, however, he has a penchant for disjunctive changes of angle. These editing strategies can dynamize tense or violent confrontations.

There is a more static side to Kurosawa's style as well. His 1940s films exploit extremely long takes, and his later works often utilize rigidly posed compositions, as in the startling opening of *Kagemusha*, which holds for several minutes on three identical men (**Color Plate 19.1**). This tendency toward abstract composition can be seen in his settings and costumes. Early in his career, Kurosawa depicted environments in extremely naturalistic ways; no film was complete without at least one scene in a downpour and another in a gale. But this tendency steadily yielded to a more stylized mise-en-scène. After *Dodes'kaden*, the orchestration of color in the image became Kurosawa's primary concern. Originally trained as a painter, he lavished attention upon vibrant costumes and stark set design. In *Kagemusha* and *Ran*, the precise compositions of the early works give way to sumptuous pageantry captured by incessantly panning cameras.

It was Kurosawa's technical brilliance and his kinetic treatment of spectacular action in particular that won the reverence of Hollywood's "movie brat" generation. (George Lucas and Francis Ford Coppola helped finance *Kagemusha* and *Ran;* Martin Scorsese portrayed Vincent Van Gogh in *Akira Kurosawa's Dreams* [1990]). In addition, his preoccupation with human values comprehensible to audiences around the world has made him a prominent director for almost fifty years.

19.28, *left*   The holy fool worships the stolen statue in *I Vitelloni.*

19.29, *right*   *La Strada:* Gelsomina and the acrobatic angel.

19.30, *left*   *La Strada:* Gelsomina mimes a tree.

19.31, *right*   Teenagers scamper out of the forest to console the heroine of *Nights of Cabiria* (1956).

FEDERICO FELLINI (1920–1993)

In 1957, after Fellini had made five feature films, André Bazin could already detect a web of recurring imagery. He pointed out that the angel statue of *I Vitelloni* ("The Young Calves," 1953, **19.28**) reappears as the angelic wire-walking Fool in *La Strada* ("The Road," 1954; **19.29**). In other films, the angel's wings are associated with bundles of sticks carried on people's backs. Bazin's conclusion—"There is no end to Fellini's symbolism"[5]—is amply proved by the director's whole career. The films return compulsively to the circus, the music hall, the desolate road, deserted squares at night, and the seashore. *La Strada* begins by the seashore and ends there as well, with Zampano, who has left Gelsomina for dead, sobbing alone. In *La Dolce Vita* ("The Sweet Life," 1960), Marcello is in almost exactly the same posture as dawn breaks over the sea and he cannot reply to the little girl who is calling him.

There are recurring characters as well, such as the holy fool, the narcissistic male, the nurturing mother figure, the sensual whore. There are invariably parades, parties, shows—all usually followed by bleak dawns and dashed illusions. And there are the odd, privileged moments that offer a glimpse of mystery (**19.30, 19.31**). Echoing Renoir, Fellini admits, "I seem to have always turned out the same film."[6]

Fellini's ability to create a personal world on film was central to his fame during the 1950s and 1960s.

I Vitelloni brought him to international attention, and *La Strada* became a huge success, winning the Academy Award in 1956. *La Dolce Vita* received the grand prize at Cannes, and its depiction of the orgiastic lifestyles of the idle rich shocked and tantalized audiences around the world. It quickly became one of the most profitable films Italy ever exported. With *8½* (1963), another Oscar winner, Fellini created perhaps the most vivacious modernist film of the era, a reflexive study of a film director unable to make the film he has planned. After *Juliet of the Spirits* (1965), a counterpart to *8½* told from a woman's viewpoint, Fellini adapted Petronius's *Satyricon* (1969). This loose, episodic spectacle established the new Fellini mode: teeming, grotesque spectacle reminiscent of commedia dell'arte, often lacking a linear narrative. He continued to work steadily throughout the 1970s and 1980s, always to a chorus of controversy. With Bergman, he became the most widely seen and intensively interpreted of European filmmakers.

The films are frankly autobiographical. Fellini's school days inform the flashback scenes in *8½*; his adolescence in Rimini shapes *I Vitelloni*, the story of a band of young loafers, and *Amarcord* (1974), a lyrical treatment of a small town. His childhood fascination with Charles Chaplin, Buster Keaton, Stan Laurel, Oliver Hardy, and the Marx Brothers emerges again and again, notably in the mimed comedy of Giulietta Masina's performances. Yet like Guido, the hero of *8½*, Fellini claimed not to know where memory leaves off and fantasy begins. He offers not literal autobiography but personal mythology: a life mixed with fantasy. This expressive side of Fellini, seen most clearly in *8½*, influenced other directors, such as Paul Mazursky (*Alex in Wonderland*, 1970), Bob Fosse (*All That Jazz*, 1979), and Woody Allen (*Stardust Memories*, 1980; *Radio Days*, 1986).

Up to *La Dolce Vita*, the films were firmly rooted in the real world, albeit one that harbored mysteries. With *8½* and *Juliet*, the realm of dream and hallucination opened up. In an important sense, the protagonist of each Fellini film became Fellini himself—or, rather, his imagination. *Satyricon* is a series of fragments unified by a phantasmagoric vision. He launched extravagant spectacles—*The Clowns* (1970), *Roma* (1972), *Casanova* (1976), *City of Women* (1980), *The Ship Sails On* (1983), each announcing itself as revealing more of the director's obsessions, fears, aspirations. For some critics, the films became increasingly narcissistic exercises; for others, they carried the consistent theme that only through the creative imagination could people find freedom and happiness.

There is also a less personal side to Fellini's work. Several of the films since the late 1950s fused autobiography and fantasy with an examination of social history. *La Dolce Vita* juxtaposes ancient Rome, Christian Rome, and modern Rome, and it judges contemporary life decadent. *Satyricon* draws the same analogy, comparing the emotionally empty protagonists to hippies. For Fellini, *Amarcord* is not simply a placid look back at his boyhood but also an attempt to show how Benito Mussolini's regime fulfilled Italians' immature needs. *Casanova*'s obsessed, mechanical sexuality can be seen as portraying the protagonist as a proto-fascist. *City of Women* reacts to the feminist movement, while *Orchestra Rehearsal* (1980) presents contemporary life collapsing under oppressive authority and random terrorism. As did Bergman, Kurosawa, and Ray, Fellini offers social criticism in the name of artistic sensitivity and human values. This attitude emerges clearly in *Ginger and Fred* (1986), which attacks the superficiality of television and celebrates the more intimate performance associated with a dancing team from the 1930s (consisting of Fellini's definitive couple, Giulietta Masina and Marcello Mastroianni).

Fellini's images depend on intricately staged action, and he proved a master of flamboyant costume, decor, and crowd movement (**Color Plate 19.2**). He happily continued the Italian tradition of total postsynchronization, preferring to control all dialogue and sound effects after filming. The canonical Fellini scene—a vast procession accompanied by lilting Nino Rota music—does not permit the direct sound recording favored by Bresson.

19.32 Cabiria shares a look of hope with the viewer.

19.33 One of *Amarcord*'s many storytellers.

Like many of the auteurs who came to prominence in the 1950s, Fellini steadily turned away from interesting the audience in a story to interesting them in the very act of storytelling. At the end of *Nights of Cabiria*, the heroine, rescued by the dancing youths, smiles shyly at the camera (**19.32**) and then glances away, as if uncertain of our existence. By *Amarcord*, Fellini structures the film around characters openly and casually chatting with us (**19.33**). "It seems to me that I have invented almost everything: childhood, characters, nostalgias, dreams, memories for the pleasure of being able to recount them."[7]

MICHELANGELO ANTONIONI (1912–   )

Antonioni's fame emerged somewhat later than Fellini's, and his pessimistic, cerebral films stood out in sharp contrast to Fellini's life-affirming extravagance. Nonetheless, throughout the 1960s, he helped define European cinema's "high modernism."

Antonioni served his apprenticeship in Italian Neorealism with several short films and five features running from *Story of a Love Affair* (1950) to *Il Grido* ("The Outcry," 1959). His most famous film was *L'Avventura* ("The Adventure," 1960); though booed at the Cannes Film Festival, it became an international success. *L'Avventura* was followed by *La Notte* ("The Night," 1961), *L'Eclisse* (*Eclipse*, 1962), and *Red Desert* (1964), the entire tetralogy constituting an exploration of contemporary life. By the mid-1960s, as one of the half-dozen most prominent directors in the world, Antonioni accepted a contract

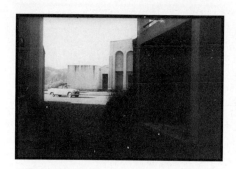

19.34   The modern city becomes a labyrinth that dominates human beings (*L'Avventura*).

19.35   A reminder of the fatal elevator looms over the couple in *Story of a Love Affair*.

19.36   The itinerant worker confronts his wife in *Il Grido*.

with MGM to make three films in English. The first, *Blow-Up* (1966), amply justified Hollywood's faith, earning praise and profits around the world. But *Zabriskie Point* (1969), Antonioni's rendition of student activism, was a financial disaster. After *The Passenger* (1975), Antonioni returned to Italy, breaking several years of silence with *The Mystery of Oberwald* (1981), *Identification of a Woman* (1982), and *Beyond the Clouds* (1995, co-directed with Wim Wenders).

Antonioni's historical significance rests principally on his early and middle-period films. During the first decade, he helped turn Italian Neorealism toward intimate psychological analysis and a severe, antimelodramatic style. The films depicted an anomie at the center of Europe's booming economy, an indifference also portrayed in postwar Italian fiction. Antonioni's early portrayals of the rich could be seen as extending the social criticism inherent in the idea of Neorealism. But Antonioni found numb, aimless people in the working class as well. The sluggish, inarticulate drifter of *Il Grido* is far from the struggling hero of *The Bicycle Thief*, who at least has his wife and son to sustain him.

With the tetralogy of the early 1960s, what Andrew Sarris called "Antoniennui" deepens. *L'Avventura* undertakes a panoramic survey of the upper classes' alienation from the world they have made (**19.34**). Vacations, parties, and artistic pursuits are vain efforts to conceal the characters' lack of purpose and emotion. Sexuality is reduced to casual seduction, enterprise to the pursuit of wealth at any cost. Technology has taken on a life of its own; an electric fan or a toy robot has a more vivid presence than the people who use it. ("It is things, objects, and materials that have weight today."[8]) One cliché of Antonioni criticism—the "lack of communication"—takes on its significance within his broader critique of how all personal relations have shriveled in the contemporary world.

These thematic preoccupations are expressed in innovative narrative forms and stylistic patterns. After an increasingly episodic treatment of narrative in *I Vinti* (1952) and *Il Grido*, *L'Avventura* moved sharply toward pure modernist storytelling. Wealthy vacationers descend on a Mediterranean island, and Anna wanders off. Her friends cannot find her. Her lover, Sandro, and her friend, Claudia, return to the mainland to continue the search. Gradually, as they become attracted to one another, Anna is forgotten. What starts as a detective story becomes the tale of an ambivalent love affair haunted by guilt and uncertainty.

Other films in the tetralogy take different narrative paths. *La Notte* covers a twenty-four-hour period, tracing the ways in which a couple's random encounters illuminate their disintegrating marriage. *Red Desert* presents an industrial landscape pervaded by ambiguity, in which the washed-out color schemes may be attributed either to the disturbed psyche of the heroine, Giuliana, or to Antonioni's vision of the blighted modern world. All the films utilize a slow rhythm, with many *temps morts* (intervals of "dead time") between events. Scenes begin a bit before the action starts and linger after the action has ended. And all four films conclude with "open endings"—perhaps most notably *L'Eclisse*'s series of empty urban spaces where the two lovers might yet meet.

From the start of his career, Antonioni demonstrated a mastery of deep focus (**19.35**) and the long take with camera movement. The early works also pioneered the possibility of concealing the characters' reactions from the audience, often by means of setting (**19.36**; see also 16.4). *L'Avventura* systematically extends this strategy (**19.37**). The film's last image is an extreme long shot of the couple dwarfed by a building, staring out at Mount Etna, their backs resolutely to the viewer (**19.38**). The viewer can hardly feel close to characters presented so dispassionately.

A similar detachment results from Antonioni's increasingly abstract compositions. He reduces human beings to masses and textures, figures on a ground (**19.39**).

19.37 *L'Avventura* often presents characters turned from the camera, rendering emotional states uncertain.

19.38 *L'Avventura:* the ending.

19.39 *L'Avventura:* two strong diagonals divide the frame and isolate Claudia.

With *Red Desert*, Antonioni's first color film, he pushed his abstraction further. He painted fruit gray (**Color Plate 19.3**); objects became blobs or slabs of color. In some scenes, space is flattened by long lenses; in others it becomes cubistic, as blocks and wedges of color fracture the shot (**Color Plate 19.4**).

In *Blow-Up*, the distancing effects of the previous films cooperate with a full-scale reflexivity. Thomas accidentally photographs a couple in the park; has he also filmed a murder? The more he enlarges his pictures, the more granular and abstract they become. Within a detective-story framework, the film probes the illusory basis of photography and suggests that its ability to tell the unvarnished truth is limited. Like *8½* and *Persona*, *Blow-Up* became a central example of modern cinema's interrogation of its own medium.

Antonioni's muted dramatization of shallow or paralyzed characters found a sympathetic response in an era that also welcomed existentialism. Perhaps more than any other director, he encouraged filmmakers to explore elliptical and open-ended narrative. Juan Bardem, Miklós Jancsó, and Theo Angelopoulos learned from his distinctive style. Francis Ford Coppola's *The Conversation* (1974) and Brian De Palma's *Blow-Out* (1981) derive directly from *Blow-Up*. An entire generation identified film artistry with the silences and vacancies of Antonioni's world, and many viewers saw their own lives enacted there.

ROBERT BRESSON (1907–1999)

Bresson's reputation rests upon a comparatively small body of work. After his first two significant films, *Les Anges du péché* (1943) and *Les Dames du Bois du Boulogne* (1945; p. 300), he made only eleven films in forty years, most notably *Diary of a Country Priest* (1951), *A Man Escaped* (1956), *Pickpocket* (1959), *Au Hasard Balthasar* ("At Random Balthasar," 1966), *Mouchette* (1967), *Four Nights of a Dreamer* (1972),

Lancelot du Lac (*Lancelot of the Lake,* 1974), and *L'Argent* ("Money," 1983). Yet, from the early 1950s on, Bresson was one of the most respected directors in the world. Championed by the *Cahiers* critics, praised by Sarris and the *Movie* group, his rigorous, demanding films display an internal consistency and a stubbornly individualistic vision of the world.

Bresson's reliance on literary texts gave him some credibility in the period when the Cinema of Quality reigned. His films are often structured around letters, diaries, historical records, and voice-over retellings of the action. Yet there is nothing particularly literary about the finished product. His work perfectly exemplifies Astruc's caméra-stylo aesthetic: he took literary works as pretexts, but he composed by purely filmic means. Bresson was fond of contrasting what he called "cinematography"—"writing through cinema"—with "cinema," or the ordinary filmmaking that is, he insisted, merely photographed theater.[9]

Bresson concentrated on sensitive people struggling to survive in a hostile world. His two 1940s features weave vengeful intrigues around innocent victims. With *Diary of a Country Priest* and on through the early 1960s, a long second phase emerged in his work. The films presented austere images and subdued acting. In most of these works, suffering is redeemed to one degree or another: the country priest dies with the realization "All is grace"; in *A Man Escaped*, Fontaine breaks out of a Nazi prison by trusting in his cellmate; after a fascination with crime, the pickpocket learns to accept a woman's love. Bresson's interest in religious subjects struck a strong chord during the revival of Catholicism in postwar France. During this phase, he gained his international reputation as the great religious director of postwar cinema.

After the mid-1960s, his films became far more pessimistic. Viewers who had identified Bresson as a "Catholic" director were puzzled by his turn to the secular, even sexual, problems of young people in modern society. Now his protagonists are led to despair and even suicide. In *Balthasar*, Marie dies after a juvenile gang has stripped and beaten her. Mouchette and the protagonists of *Une Femme douce* ("A Gentle Woman," 1969) and *The Devil Probably* (1977) kill themselves. In *L'Argent,* an unjust accident hurls a young man in and out of prison and toward unreasoning murder. Now Christian values offer no solace: the quest for the Grail in *Lancelot du Lac* fails; chivalry becomes a heap of bloodied armor.

However bleak they may be, Bresson's films radiate mystery. It is difficult to understand his characters because they are typically examined from the outside. The performers—Bresson called them his "models"—are often nonactors or amateurs. They are preternaturally still and quiet, breaking their silence with a clipped word or a brief gesture. In this cinema, a sudden raising of the eyes becomes a significant event: a shared look, a climax. The models are often filmed from behind, or in close-ups that fragment their bodies (**19.40**). In addition, Bresson's abrupt cutting, short scenes, bright track-ins or track-

19.40 *Pickpocket:* Michel's hand seems almost cut free from his arm as it moves freely into purses and pockets.

outs, and laconic sound tracks demand the viewer's utmost concentration. The reward is a markable balance between a penetration of the characters' experiences and a sense that their inner states remain elusive and mysterious, as in a scene from *Diary of a Country Priest,* when the protagonist discovers information about the author of a cruel anonymous letter to him (**19.41–19.46**).

19.41 *Diary of a Country Priest:* as the priest walks into the church, he picks up a fallen prayerbook and discovers that the inscription is in the same handwriting as a cruel anonymous letter he has received. We make the discovery with him and share his curiosity to learn who has been persecuting him. But then we hear a door opening. He quickly puts the book in front of a pew and walks out of the frame.

19.42 Bresson holds on the book for eleven seconds, tracking in as the offscreen steps approach.

19.43 The suspense is resolved when the governess from the manor house comes into medium shot, kneels, and opens the book.

19.44 She looks up.

19.45 Bresson cuts to a medium-close shot of the priest walking into the chapel and looking briefly at her . . .

19.46 . . . before he makes his way to the altar, eyes lowered. As he kneels, the scene fades out. Her motivations, and his reactions, have been suppressed.

19.47, 19.48   Oblique eyeline matches in *Four Nights of a Dreamer:* "To set up a film is to bind persons to each other and to objects by looks."

19.49, *left*   Most directors would show Mouchette going to school by establishing the locale with a long shot and then cutting in to a direct view of her walking along the street and joining her schoolmates. Instead, Bresson starts with a downward angle on the children's feet . . .

19.50, *right*   . . . lets Mouchette come in, her back to us . . .

19.51, *left*   . . . tracks a short way to follow her . . .

19.52, *right*   . . . and then stops before the school gate. The effect is to cut characters free of locale for a brief moment, suspending our knowledge of where they are in order to concentrate on their physical behavior.

After *Diary of a Country Priest,* Bresson began to avoid long shots. He typically created a scene's space by showing small portions of it and linking shots through characters' eyelines (**19.47, 19.48**). At other times his tightly framed camera movements suggest action by concentrating on details. In one scene from *Mouchette,* for instance, by showing no faces, Bresson calls attention to Mouchette's discouraged gait and her shabby clothes (**19.49–19.52**).

Bresson also needs no long shot of Mouchette's school because he has evoked the setting through the sounds of the school bell and the students' chatter. "Every time that I can replace an image by a sound I do so."[10] Against a background of pervasive silence, every object in a Bresson film takes on a distinct acoustic flavor: the scrape of the bedstead in Fontaine's cell, the clank of the knights' armor in *Lancelot du Lac,* the rusty bray of the donkey Balthasar. Offscreen sound will establish a locale or will provide a motif that recalls other scenes. Bresson's intense concentration on physical details and isolated sounds often fills in for psychological analysis. The mystery and ambiguity of Bresson's style

proved suited to his treatment of solitary individuals who struggle to survive a spiritual or physical ordeal.

These enigmatic gestures, textures, and details are presented in a highly sensuous way. Bresson's images may be severe, but they are never drab. In *Les Anges du péché,* the nuns' habits create an angular geometry and lustrous range of tonalities (see 13.45). His color films achieve vivid effects by minute means: a knight's armor stands out slightly by its sheen; a mail basket in a prison office becomes a vibrant blue (**Color Plates 19.5, 19.6**).

Bresson moved toward abbreviated, elliptical storytelling. From *Pickpocket* on, and especially in *Au Hasard Balthasar,* so much is left to the spectator's imagination that the very story events—"what happens"—become almost opaque. ("I never explain anything, as it is done in the theatre."[11]) What gives the Bresson film a sense of ongoing structure are the subtly varied, almost ceremonial repetitions—daily routines, replayed confrontations, returns to the same locales. The spectator suspects, as the individuals involved do not, that the apparently random action is part of a vast cycle of events governed by God, fate, or some other unknown force.

19.53–19.55 *Jour de fête:* the camera arcs around the farmer to keep François in the background as a persistent bee plagues them both.

Bresson never sought the commercial success enjoyed by Antonioni, Bergman, and Fellini. Yet he influenced filmmakers as varied as Jean-Marie Straub (who saw political implications in ascetic images and direct sound) and Paul Schrader (whose *American Gigolo* reworks *Pickpocket*). Although Bresson never made his long-cherished version of the biblical book of Genesis, he remains one of the most distinctive auteurs of the past fifty years.

JACQUES TATI (1908–1982)

With true auteurist fervor Truffaut once declared that "a film by Bresson or Tati is necessarily a work of genius *a priori,* simply because a single, absolute authority has been imposed from the opening to 'The End.'"[12] The similarities between the two directors are enlightening. Both made tentative starts on their film careers during the 1930s, worked on films during the war, and became prominent in the early 1950s. Both spent years on each film; Tati's output, with only six features between 1949 and 1973, was even slimmer than Bresson's. Both directors experimented with fragmented, elliptical narratives and unusual uses of sound.

Unlike Bresson, however, Tati made some very popular films. Since he was a performer as well as a director, he also became an international celebrity. From this perspective, Tati resembled Buñuel in pushing modernist tendencies toward accessible, mainstream tradition. At one level, Tati's films are satiric commentaries on the rituals of modern life—vacations, work, housing, travel. Declaring himself an anarchist, he believed in freedom, eccentricity, and playfulness. His films lack strong plots: things simply happen, one after the other, and nothing much is ever at stake. The film accumulates tiny, even trivial events—like the microactions of Italian Neorealism (p. 364), only treated as gags.

Jour de fête ("Holiday," 1949) set the pattern for most of Tati's subsequent works. A small carnival comes to a village, the townsfolk enjoy a day off, and the carnival leaves the next day. In the midst of the celebration, the local postman, François, played by Tati, continues to deliver the mail and decides to adopt American methods of efficiency. The circumscribed time and place, the contrast between humdrum routine and bursts of zany amusement, the bumbling character who disrupts everyone else's life, and the recognition that only children and eccentrics know the secret of fun—all these elements would reappear throughout Tati's later work. The loose plot, built out of elaborately staged gags and motifs rather than a strong cause-and-effect chain, would become a Tati trademark.

Jour de fête also inaugurated Tati's characteristic style. The comedy is not verbal (very little is said, and that often in a mutter or mumble) but visual and acoustic. A stiff-legged beanpole capable of outrageously mechanical gestures, Tati was one of the cinema's great clowns. Like Keaton, he was also one of its most innovative directors, relying on long shots that spread elements across the frame or in depth. Changes in sound source or level shift our attention from one aspect of the shot to another. In *Jour de fête,* for example, a depth shot shows a farmer staring at François on the road, thrashing his arms about (**19.53**). As François moves on, we hear a buzzing noise and see the farmer begin flapping away at the invisible bee (**19.54**); then the buzzing fades, and, as the shot ends, François begins flapping his arms again (**19.55**).

An even bigger success was *Mr. Hulot's Holiday* (*Les Vacances de M. Hulot,* 1953). The scene is a seaside resort to which various middle-class city people repair; the action consumes the one week of their stay. The disruptive force is Mr. Hulot, who insists on making the most of his vacation. He shatters the routine meals,

19.56 A non-gag in *Mr. Hulot's Holiday:* the painter suspects Hulot of accidentally releasing his boat into the sea; both stand awkwardly for several moments.

19.57 Two women greet one another in *Mon Oncle:* the winding pathway keeps them from walking straight toward each other. (Note the fish fountain, turned on only when a guest arrives.)

arranged outings, and quiet evenings playing cards. His splenetic car disturbs the guests, his outrageously unprofessional tennis game defeats all comers, and his antics on the beach bring woe to bystanders. Tati's performance captivated audiences around the world and was credited with single-handedly reviving the pantomime tradition of Chaplin and Keaton. Again, sound guides our eye and characterizes people and objects, from the percussive chugging of Hulot's car to the musical thunk of the hotel restaurant's door to the harsh ricochet of a ping-pong ball as it invades the hotel parlor. Just as im-

portant, Tati the director had composed a film with a firm structure that owes little to traditional plotting. By alternating strong visual gags with empty moments that invite the spectator to see ordinary life as comic, *Mr. Hulot's Holiday* points forward to the more extreme experiments of *Play Time* (**19.56**).

Back in Paris, Hulot launches a hilarious attack on modern work and leisure on *Mon Oncle* (*My Uncle,* 1958). The windows of a modernistic house seem to spy on passersby; plastic tubing extruded from a plant becomes a giant serpent. Again, Tati's long shots show in-

19.58 A production still showing a portion of Tativille.

dividuals at the mercy of the environment they have created (**19.57**). The result is a comic version of Antonioni's portrayal of urban alienation.

The international success of *Mon Oncle,* which won the Academy Award for best foreign film, encouraged Tati to undertake his most ambitious project. On the outskirts of Paris he built a false city, complete with paved roads, water and electricity, and traffic (**19.58**). He shot the film in 70mm, with five-track stereophonic sound.

The result was *Play Time* (1967), one of the most audacious films of the postwar era. Aware that audiences would watch for Hulot, Tati played down his presence. Knowing that viewers rely on close-ups and centered framings to guide their attention, Tati built the film almost completely out of long shots and scattered his gags to all corners of the frame (**19.59**). Sometimes, as in the lengthy sequence of the disintegration of the Royal Garden restaurant, he packs simultaneous gags into the frame, challenging the spectator to spot them all (**19.60**). Tati's satire of tourism and urban routine encourages us to see all of life as play time.

Since Tati initially insisted that *Play Time* be shown in 70mm, it did not get wide distribution and quickly failed. Tati went into bankruptcy, and his career never recovered. To the end of his life, he hoped to establish one theater somewhere in the world that would show *Play Time* every day, forever.

He made two more films. In *Traffic* (1971), Hulot helps a young woman deliver a recreational vehicle to an Amsterdam auto show. Simpler than *Play Time* or *Mr. Hulot's Holiday, Traffic* satirizes car culture. *Parade* (1973), shot for Swedish television, is a pseudo-documentary celebration of the circus and its audience. As usual, Tati blurs the boundary between performance and the comedy of everyday life (**19.61**).

Before his death, Tati was planning another Hulot film, *Confusion,* in which his hero would work in television and be killed on camera. But the debts of *Play Time* haunted him, and in 1974 his films were auctioned off at an absurdly low price. Over the next two decades, however, rereleases of all his films demonstrated to new audiences that Tati had left behind a rich body of work that invites the spectator to see ordinary life as an endless comedy.

SATYAJIT RAY (1921–1992)

Throughout the postwar era, European and Anglo-American film culture took the Bengali director Satyajit Ray as the preeminent Indian filmmaker. He made

19.59 *Play Time:* the principal joke is on the left side of the frame, where M. Giffard has collided with the glass door. On the far right, the businessman is frozen mannequinlike in midstride; he will start to walk only at the end of the shot.

19.60 *Play Time:* while the millionaire orders his meal from the splotches on the waiter's jacket, the restaurant owner (foreground left) prepares to calm his nerves with an antacid; this sets up a later joke, when Hulot accidentally drinks the fizzy potion, thinking it is champagne.

19.61 The audience in *Parade:* all but the three women in the foreground row are photographic cut-outs.

19.62, *left*   Durga dances in the rain in *Pather Panchali.*

19.63, *right*   The beginning of the girl's song in *Three Daughters.*

19.64, *left*   *Three Daughters:* as Amulya walks home through the mud, the tomboy Puglee mocks him from behind a tree.

19.65, *right*   Much later, Amulya marries Puglee, somewhat against her will. Unhappy, Puglee flees him, and when he goes out searching for her, Ray repeats the earlier camera setup, emphasizing Amulya's realization of his loss.

almost thirty feature films and triumphed in other media as well. As a commercial graphic artist, he revolutionized Indian book design. He wrote children's books, science-fiction novels, and detective stories. He also became an acclaimed musician, scoring his own films and those of other filmmakers.

Most of Ray's film work runs counter to the commercial Indian cinema. His artistic roots lie in the Bengali renaissance of the nineteenth century, associated with the Tagore family. The most famous Tagore, the poet Rabindranath, turned the young Ray toward the liberal humanism that is the hallmark of his work. In addition, Ray's own family boasted distinguished inventors, teachers, writers, and musicians. He brought this westernized humanistic culture of his youth to all his activities.

After youthful training in drawing at Tagore's cultural center, Ray worked as an artist in a British advertising agency. In 1947, he founded the Calcutta Film Society, which brought European and American films to India. His cinematic influences crystallized in the late 1940s: the films of John Ford, William Wyler, and Jean Renoir, whom he met during the filming of *The River* (p. 378), as well as the body of Italian Neorealist cinema, especially *The Bicycle Thief.* He criticized the contemporary Indian cinema for its exaggerated spectacle and inattention to reality. To Ray, the central purpose of filmmaking is "the revelation of the truth of human behavior."[13] His films' refusal to single out villains links him to Renoir, and his reluctance to endorse collective political

solutions testifies to an individualistic approach to life. His film work would render Indian life through the subtle drama of naturalistic European cinema.

Pather Panchali, which took two years to make, was a turning point in postwar Indian film. A sober adaptation of a literary classic, it was shot extensively on location and used restrained acting. The film tells the story of a boy, Apu, and his life in a rural area; the movie culminates in the death of his aunt and his sister. Ray continued Apu's story with *Aparajito* ("The Undefeated," 1956), which depicts his teenage years and the death of his parents. The trilogy concludes with *The World of Apu* (1960), in which Apu marries, confronts the death of his wife in childbirth, and comes to accept his son.

The trilogy's leisurely, "undramatic" action is based more on chronology than causality. Ray avoids dwelling on sentimental moments. In *Aparajito*, for instance, Apu hurries home to his dying mother. In most 1950s Indian cinema, this would provide the occasion for a touching deathbed scene, but here he simply arrives too late. In *The World of Apu*, the death of Apu's wife is kept offscreen. Ray's subdued approach to dramatic moments adhered to western standards of subtle, realistic filmmaking. "At last," declared Vittorio De Sica's scriptwriter Cesare Zavattini, "the neorealist cinema that the Italians did not know how to do."[14]

Ray's earliest period, running from *Pather Panchali* to *Charulata* (1964), centers on rudimentary human problems. In the Apu trilogy (*Pather Panchali, Aparajito,*

19.66 Alive, the old aunt dominates a composition of the porch (*Pather Panchali*).

19.67 After she has died, the composition seems hollow.

19.68 Apu offers his mother the globe (*Aparajito*).

and *The World of Apu*), the problems are those of growing up and accepting responsibility in a world filled with frustration and death. In his works on the landowning aristocracy (most notably *The Music Room*, 1958), he portrays individuals who cling unreasonably to dying traditions. His "awakening woman" trilogy (most famously *Mahanagar*, or "The Big City," 1963, and *Charulata*) present women confined by Indian tradition and struggling to create their own identities. Whether the setting is a rural area or a city, Ray concentrates on the domestic life of families, courtship, and daily work.

Ray's films slowly accumulate moments that reveal characters' feelings. In *Pather Panchali*, Apu and his sister Durga are caught in a monsoon. He takes shelter under a tree, but she spins excitedly, washing herself in the pounding rain (**19.62**). Most Indian films would have made this the excuse for a song sequence, but here, without dialogue, Ray conveys both Durga's childish exuberance and her awakening sensuality. The moment has a dramatic consequence too: Durga will die from the cold she catches. Similarly, in the episode film *Three Daughters* (1961), tradition would have dictated an elaborate number when the little girl Ratan sings to her employer, the haughty young postmaster assigned to her remote village. Instead, Ray stages the scene with subdued simplicity. The postmaster has just finished reading a letter from his sister, and, as Ratan starts to sing, the camera tracks slowly in on him (**19.63**). Ray quietly suggests that through Ratan's song, the young man recalls his sister.

As in a novel by Henry James, Ray's characters are judged by their eagerness to learn and their sensitivity to their surroundings. Apu observes the life around him before plunging into reading and, eventually, writing.

At the beginning of *Charulata*, the wife, virtually imprisoned in the household, rushes from window to window, watching the world through binoculars.

Despite their quiet pace and realism, the films of this first period reveal a craftsman's approach. Ray gained a sense of firm structure from his study of western cinema and of western music, with its dramatic sonata form so different from the open forms of Indian ragas. Ray also developed his style along European and Hollywood lines. Often his shot compositions draw parallels between situations in a before-and-after fashion (**19.64, 19.65**).

The entire Apu trilogy is bound together by motifs of setting and camera placement (**19.66, 19.67**). The most prevalent motif in the films is the train: glimpsed by the children in *Pather Panchali*, running in the background as the mother weakens in *Aparajito*, chugging through the neighborhood of Apu's apartment in *The World of Apu*. Sometimes the train symbolizes the great world that Apu craves to explore. When he wins a globe as a school prize, he thrusts it at his mother, loftily demanding, "Do you know what this is?"; offscreen the distant train is heard (**19.68**). At other times the train is an impersonal force shuttling the family from the countryside to Benares, from a village to Calcutta. By the end, when Apu has reconciled with his son, the train is no more than a toy that can be left behind.

Ray's international preeminence doubtless distorted western conceptions of Indian filmmaking. Still, he was not completely cut off from the popular tradition. His films were often successful with Bengali audiences. He made several popular comedies and children's films, and he even attempted a historical epic in Hindi (*The Chess Players*, 1977). His early works also had considerable influence on Indian cinema, turning filmmakers toward location shooting and a more understated acting style.

After the political upheavals of the late 1960s, Ray's work began to confront social issues more directly. A trilogy of "city films" portrays weak men trying to survive in a corrupt business world. In *The Middleman* (1975), for instance, Somnath is expected to provide a client with a woman. He is shocked when he learns that she is a friend's sister. Ray's conception of the cost of success is conveyed by cutting from Somnath's playing the pimp to a shot of his father at home, listening to a Tagore song on the radio: "Darkness is gathering over the forest."

Ray became more deliberately "modern." He adapted contemporary fiction by young writers and utilized flashbacks, negative footage, and freezeframes. Yet he was uncomfortable with self-conscious technique: "As if being modern for a film-maker consisted solely in how he juggles with his visuals and not in his attitude to life that he expressed through the film."[15]

Many of the films of this period reflect the growing inability of Ray's humanism to comprehend the political uncertainties of modern India. His cinema was identified with the liberal politics of Prime Minister Nehru, and as Nehru's legacy faded, so did Ray's belief in India's moral progress. His optimism is more evident in the fantasy films he made for children, such as the lively *Goopi Gyne Bagha Byne* (1969).

At the end of his career, Ray seems to have synthesized individual concerns with contemporary political problems. *The Home and the World* (1984), a Tagore adaptation, presents the 1907 anticolonialist struggle by centering on a wife who breaks with her reclusive domestic life. *Public Enemy* (1989) is an updating of Henrik Ibsen's *Enemy of the People* and depicts the youth of a community rallying to the defense of a doctor who finds cholera-infested water in a temple. The film was relevant to an India still suffering from the disaster at the Bhopal chemical plant. Ray's 1980s work persists in asserting that any significant action, political or otherwise, can spring only from the consciousness and conscience of the sensitive individual.

- -

Notes and Queries

THE IMPACT OF AUTEURISM

To a great extent, the academic study of film in English-speaking countries arose from auteurism. The premise of individual artistic expression proved congenial to scholars trained in art, literature, and theater. Moreover, auteurism's emphasis on the interpretation of a film called on skills already cultivated by literary education.

During the 1960s, auteur-based courses began to appear in the American college curriculum. Trade publishers launched book series that translated French monographs and gave a forum to the *Movie* critics and their American counterparts. University presses started publishing academic studies such as Donald Richie's *The Films of Akira Kurosawa* (Berkeley: University of California Press, 1965) and Charles Higham's *The Films of Orson Welles* (Berkeley: University of California Press, 1970). In the mid- to late 1960s, colleges and universities started film study programs, often emphasizing individual directors. The process by which auteurism helped lay the groundwork for contemporary film study is discussed in David Bordwell, *Making Meaning: Inference and Rhetoric in the Interpretation of Cinema* (Cambridge, MA: Harvard University Press, 1989).

AUTEURISM AND THE AMERICAN CINEMA

Only certain versions of auteurism proved controversial. Critics had been ascribing films to their directors since at least World War I. In the 1950s, no one doubted that the films of our eight auteurs could be treated as "personal expression" in some sense. But the young critics of the British journal *Sequence* and of the French magazines *Cahiers* and *Positif*, and later writers like Andrew Sarris and the *Movie* group, urged that Hollywood filmmakers who might have no input into their scripts could also be treated as expressive artists. Look at the body of their work, the critics urged, and you will see recurrent themes, stylistic patterns, and narrative strategies. In this light, not only Howard Hawks and John Ford but Otto Preminger and Vincente

Minnelli could be revealed as sophisticated filmmakers with distinctive artistic visions. The "French revolution" in critical thought revealed artists in what most English-speaking intellectuals disdained as uniform, mass-produced entertainment.

By the early 1960s, French publishers were devoting entire volumes to Minnelli, Anthony Mann, and other American filmmakers. The breakthrough in English-language criticism came with Sarris's special 1963 issue of *Film Culture* on American cinema. Here he constructed a vast reference text on Hollywood directors, modeled on *Cahiers*'s encyclopedic special issues on American cinema. Sarris grouped filmmakers, ranking them as "Pantheon Directors" (John Ford, Alfred Hitchcock, D. W. Griffith, Josef von Sternberg, et al.), "Second Line" (George Cukor, Nicholas Ray, Douglas Sirk, et al.), "Fallen Idols" (Elia Kazan, Fred Zinnemann, et al.), and so on. Each entry was accompanied by a brief discussion of the director's career.

The *Film Culture* issue was expanded into Sarris's book *The American Cinema: Directors and Directions* (New York: Dutton, 1968), one of the most influential volumes on film ever published. Sarris's career surveys provided the point of departure for many in-depth analyses, and auteurism became the overwhelmingly dominant approach to studying the history of the Hollywood cinema—a status it has never lost. The most diversified revision of the Sarris approach is Jean-Pierre Coursodon and Pierre Sauvage's two-volume collection *American Directors* (New York: McGraw-Hill, 1983).

Auteurism changed in the late 1960s. A group of writers associated with the British Film Institute sought to make the approach more rigorous by incorporating insights from structuralist linguistics and anthropology. Now an auteur's themes could be seen as organized around oppositions (e.g., desert versus garden). The oppositions might then be reconciled by mediating images or narrative actions. An early example of "auteur structuralism" is Geoffrey Nowell-Smith's *Visconti* (London: Secker and Warburg, 1967); the theory was most fully systematized in chapter 2 of Peter Wollen's *Signs and Meaning in the Cinema* (London: Secker and Warburg, 1969; rev. ed., 1972).

Auteur structuralism was soon surpassed by a revision in *Cahiers*'s policy during the late 1960s (see Chapter 23). The new generation of *Cahiers* critics adopted a Marxist position that treated auteur films as unwitting expressions of social ideology. The most influential formulation of this view was a 1970 essay by the *Cahiers* editors on John Ford's *Young Mr. Lincoln*. Here John Ford's direction was said to "rewrite" a script that could have simplistically celebrated the Lincoln myth. The conflict between the script and Ford's personal themes and motifs resulted in a film full of discordances; these in turn expressed contradictions within dominant ideology. For a general account of the *Cahiers* position, see Jean Narboni and Jean-Louis Comolli, "Cinema/Ideology/Criticism," a 1969 essay reprinted in Bill Nichols, ed., *Movies and Methods* (Berkeley: University of California Press, 1976), pp. 22–30. The *Young Mr. Lincoln*

study has been widely reprinted. (See Nichols, *Movies and Methods*, pp. 493–529.)

Cahiers's new approach to authorship was extended during the 1970s by writers in the British journal *Screen* and other publications of the British Film Institute. Examples are several essays in Laura Mulvey and Jon Halliday, eds., *Douglas Sirk* (Edinburgh Film Festival, 1972); Phil Hardy, ed., *Raoul Walsh* (Edinburgh Film Festival, 1974); and Claire Johnston, ed., *The Work of Dorothy Arzner* (London: British Film Institute, 1975).

Some historians have accused the auteur approach of concentrating on individual innovation rather than institutional processes. Nonetheless, some notion of directorial authorship has remained central to most film scholarship. The development of auteur debates is traced in John Caughie's anthology *Theories of Authorship* (London: Routledge and Kegan Paul, 1981). For personal accounts of the rise of auteurism in the United States, see Emanuel Levy, *Citizen Sarris, American Film Critic* (Lanham, MD: Scarecrow Press, 2001).

1950s AND 1960s MODERNIST CINEMA

As we have seen, non-American auteurs were often identified with a modernist trend in postwar cinema. During this period, several English-language critics examined this trend. Their discussions document art cinema's rise to authority in western film culture.

Penelope Houston's *The Contemporary Cinema* (Harmondsworth, England: Penguin, 1963) and John Russell Taylor's *Cinema Eye, Cinema Ear: Some Key Filmmakers of the Sixties* (New York: Hill and Wang, 1964) typify the response of mainstream British criticism to European and Asian auteurs. David Thomson's more offbeat *Movie Man* (New York: Stein and Day, 1967) incorporates both American and European auteurs within a tradition of inquiry into the nature of the "visual society." More explicitly than many of his contemporaries, Thomson made the issue of reflexivity central to modernist cinema. In addition, Parker Tyler recast modernist arguments for an American readership; see his essay "*Rashomon* as Modern Art" in *The Three Faces of the Film* (Cranbury, NJ: Barnes, 1967) and his influential popularization *Classics of the Foreign Film* (New York: Bonanza, 1962).

More recent and historically framed surveys of modernist cinema are Roy Armes's *The Ambiguous Image: Narrative Style in Modern European Cinema* (London: Secker and Warburg, 1976) and Robert Phillip Kolker's *The Altering Eye: Contemporary International Cinema* (New York: Oxford University Press, 1983). Armes's discussion stops around 1968, while Kolker's moves into the late 1970s. Both retain an auteurist approach in tracing distinct strands within the modernist cinematic tradition. See also John Orr's *Cinema and Modernity* (Cambridge: Polity Press, 1993).

REFERENCES

1. Alexandre Astruc, "The Birth of a New Avant-Garde: *La Caméra-Stylo,*" in Peter Graham, ed., *The New Wave* (Garden City: Doubleday, 1967), p. 23.
2. Federico Fellini, *Comments on Film,* ed. Giovanni Grazzini and trans. Joseph Henry (Fresno: California State University Press, 1988), p. 64.
3. Luis Buñuel, *My Last Sigh,* trans. Abigail Israel (New York: Knopf, 1983), p. 92.
4. Quoted in Lise-Lone Marker and Frederick J. Marker, *Ingmar Bergman: Four Decades in the Theatre* (Cambridge: Cambridge University Press, 1982), p. 6.
5. André Bazin, *What Is Cinema? II,* trans. and ed. Hugh Gray (Berkeley: University of California Press, 1971), p. 89.
6. Fellini, *Comments on Film,* p. 77.
7. Quoted in Peter Bondanella, *Italian Cinema: From Neorealism to the Present* (New York: Ungar, 1983), p. 230.
8. Quoted in Andrew Sarris, ed., *Interviews with Film Directors* (Indianapolis: Bobbs-Merrill, 1967), p. 9.
9. See Robert Bresson, *Notes on Cinematography,* trans. Jonathan Griffin (New York: Urizen, 1977).
10. Quoted in "The Question," *Cahiers du Cinéma in English* 8 (February 1967): 8.
11. Quoted in Sarris, *Interviews with Film Directors,* p. 26.
12. François Truffaut, *The Films of My Life,* trans. Leonard Mayhew (New York: Simon and Schuster, 1975), p. 235.
13. Quoted in Chidananda Das Gupta, ed., *Satyajit Ray: An Anthology of Statements on Ray and by Ray* (New Delhi: Directorate of Film Festivals, 1981), p. 136.
14. Ibid., p. 61.
15. Quoted in Marie Seton, *Portrait of a Director: Satyajit Ray* (Bloomington: Indiana University Press, 1971), p. 283.

FURTHER READING

Bellos, David. *Jacques Tati: His Life and Art.* London: Harvill Press, 1999.
Bergman, Ingmar. *Images: My Life in Film.* Trans. Marianne Ruuth. New York: Arcade, 1990.
———. *The Magic Lantern: An Autobiography.* Trans. Joan Tate. New York: Viking, 1988.
Bondanella, Peter, ed. *Federico Fellini: Essays in Criticism.* New York: Oxford University Press, 1978.
Brunette, Peter. *The Films of Michelangelo Antonioni.* Cambridge: Cambridge University Press, 1998.
Buñel, Luis. *My Last Sigh: The Autobiography of Luis Buñuel.* Trans. Abigail Israel. New York: Knopf, 1983.
———. *An Unspeakable Betrayal: Selected Writings of Luis Buñuel.* Trans. Garrett White. Berkeley: University of California Press, 1995.
Chatman, Seymour. *Antonioni, or, the Surface of the World.* Berkeley: University of California Press, 1985.
Das Gupta, Chidananda. *The Cinema of Satyajit Ray.* New Delhi: Vikas, 1980.
Gado, Frank. *The Passion of Ingmar Bergman.* Durham, NC: Duke University Press, 1986.
Hanlon, Lindley. *Fragments: Bresson's Film Style.* Rutherford, NJ: Associated University Presses, 1986.
Hardy, James. *Jacques Tati: Frame by Frame.* London: Secker and Warburg, 1984.
Kurosawa, Akira. *Something Like an Autobiography.* Trans. Audie E. Bock. New York: Knopf, 1982.
Nyce, Ben. *Satyajit Ray: A Study of His Films.* New York: Praeger, 1988.
Prince, Stephen. *The Warrior's Camera: The Cinema of Akira Kurosawa.* 2nd ed. Princeton, NJ: Princeton University Press, 1999.
Quandt, James, ed. *Robert Bresson.* Toronto: Toronto International Film Festival Group, 1998.
Ray, Satyajit. *Our Films, Their Films.* Bombay: Orient Ltd., 1976.
Reader, Keith. *Robert Bresson.* Manchester: Manchester University Press, 2000.
Robinson, Andrew. *Satyajit Ray: The Inner Eye.* Berkeley: University of California Press, 1989.
Sandro, Paul. *Diversions of Pleasure: Luis Buñuel and the Crises of Desire.* Columbus: Ohio State University Press, 1987.
Wood, Robin. *The Apu Trilogy.* New York: Praeger, 1971.
———. *Ingmar Bergman.* New York: Praeger, 1969.
Yoshimoto, Mitsuhiro. *Kurosawa: Film Studies and Japanese Cinema.* Durham, NC: Duke University Press, 2000.

CHAPTER 20

NEW WAVES AND
YOUNG CINEMAS, 1958–1967

The decade after 1958 saw extraordinary ferment in the international art cinema. Not only were major innovations introduced by older auteurs, but a host of "new waves," "young cinemas," and "new cinemas," criticized and rejuvenated the modernist tradition. Many of the younger filmmakers became the major figures of later decades.

THE INDUSTRIES' NEW NEEDS

Industrial conditions favored the arrival of fresh talent. Whereas American film attendance had declined after 1947, elsewhere audiences did not significantly dwindle until the late 1950s. Then, with television providing cheap entertainment, producers aimed at new audiences—sometimes through coproductions, sometimes by making erotic films. They also tried to attract the "youth culture" that emerged in most western countries in the late 1950s. In western Europe, sexual liberation, rock music, new fashions, the growth of soccer and other sports, and new forms of tourism such as Club Med became hallmarks of the generation coming to maturity around 1960. Trends toward an urban, leisure-class lifestyle were strengthened by an economic boom after 1958 that raised European living standards. Similar patterns emerged in Japan and eastern Europe.

Who could better attract this affluent audience than young filmmakers? Film companies began to open up production to beginning directors. These opportunities coincided with the expansion of professional film training. After the late 1950s, existing film academies in the USSR, eastern Europe, France, and Italy were joined by national film schools founded in the Netherlands, Sweden, West Germany, and Denmark. Throughout Europe, young directors (around their thirties) made their

20.1, *left*   István Szabó's *The Age of Daydreaming* (1964): shooting on the street, using a long lens that flattens perspective.

20.2, *right*   Shallow depth in a closer view, yielded by the telephoto lens (*Walkover*, 1965, Jerzy Skolimowski).

first features in the years 1958 to 1967. Brazil, one of the most westernized countries in South America, also reflected this trend in its Cinema Nôvo group.

Youth culture accelerated the internationalizing of film culture. Art theaters and ciné-clubs multiplied. The list of international film festivals now included San Francisco and London (both begun in 1957), Moscow (1959), Adelaide and New York (1963), Chicago and Panama (1965), Brisbane (1966), and San Antonio and Shiraz, Iran (1967). Festivals in Hyères, France, and Pesaro, Italy (both begun in 1965) were deliberately created as gathering points for young filmmakers.

FORMAL AND STYLISTIC TRENDS

Each nation's new cinema was a loose assortment of quite different filmmakers. Typically their work does not display the degree of unity that we find in the stylistic movements of the silent era. Still, some broad trends link the young cinemas.

The new generation was the first to have a clear awareness of the overall history of cinema. The Cinémathèque Française in Paris, the National Film Theatre in London, and the Museum of Modern Art in New York became shrines for young audiences eager to discover films from around the world. Film schools screened foreign classics for study. Older directors were venerated as spiritual "fathers": Jean Renoir, for François Truffaut; Fritz Lang, for Alexander Kluge; Alexander Dovzhenko, for Andrei Tarkovsky. In particular, young directors absorbed the neorealist aesthetic and the art cinema of the 1950s. Thus the new cinemas extended several postwar trends.

Most apparent were innovations in technique. In part, Young Cinema identified itself with a more immediate approach to filming. During the late 1950s and throughout the 1960s manufacturers perfected cameras that did not require tripods, reflex viewfinders that

showed exactly what the lens saw, and film stocks that needed less light to create acceptable exposures. Although much of this equipment was designed to aid documentary filmmakers (p. 484), fiction filmmakers immediately took advantage of it. Now a director could film with direct sound, recording the ambient noise of the world outside the sealed studio. Now the camera could take to the streets, searching out fictional characters in the midst of a crowd (**20.1, 20.2**). This portable equipment also let the filmmaker shoot quickly and cheaply, an advantage for producers anxious to economize in a declining industry.

The 1960s fictional cinema gained a looseness that put it closer to Direct Cinema documentary (see Chapter 21). Directors often filmed from a distance, using panning shots to cover the action and zoom lenses to enlarge details, as if the filmmaker were a journalist snooping on the characters (**20.3**). It was during this period that close-ups and shot/reverse-shot exchanges began to be shot almost entirely with long lenses—a trend that would dominate the 1970s (**20.4, 20.5**).

Yet this rough documentary look did not commit the directors to recording the world passively. To an extent not seen since the silent era, young filmmakers tapped the power of fragmentary, discontinuous editing. In *Breathless* (France, 1960), Jean-Luc Godard violated basic rules of continuity editing, notably by tossing out frames from the middle of shots in order to create jarring *jump cuts* (**20.6**). A film by the Japanese Nagisa Oshima might contain over a thousand shots. Older directors favored smooth editing, considering Soviet Montage unrealistic and manipulative, but now montage became a source of inspiration. At the limit, 1960s directors pushed toward a *collage* form. Here the director builds the film out of staged footage, "found" footage (newsreels, old movies), and images of all sorts (advertisements, snapshots, posters, and so on).

Yet young filmmakers also extended the use of long takes, one of the major stylistic trends of the postwar

20.3   A moment in the pan-and-zoom shot covering a conversation (*Es*, 1965, Ulrich Schamoni).

20.4, 20.5   Shot/reverse shot employing a long lens in Milos Forman's *Black Peter* (1963).

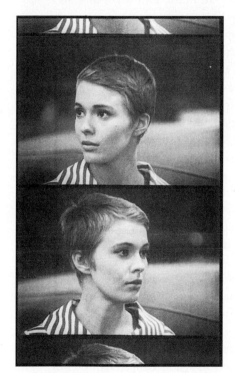

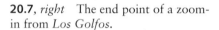

20.6, *left*   In *Breathless*, Godard's jump cuts create a skittery, nervous style.

20.7, *right*   The end point of a zoom-in from *Los Golfos*.

era (p. 341). A scene might be handled in a single shot, a device that quickly became known by its French name, the *plan-séquence* ("sequence shot"). The lightweight cameras proved ideal for making long takes. Some directors alternated lengthy shots and abrupt editing; French New Wave directors were fond of chopping off a graceful long take with sudden close-ups. Other directors, such as the Hungarian Miklós Jancsó, developed the Ophüls-Antonioni tradition by building the film out of lengthy, intricate traveling shots. Across the 1960s, telephoto filming, discontinuous editing, and complex camera movements all came to replace the dense staging in depth that had been common after World War II.

The narrative form of the postwar European art film relied on an objective realism of chance events that often could not be fitted into a linear cause-and-effect story line. The objective realism of the Neorealist approach was enhanced by the use of nonactors, real locations, and improvised performance. The new techniques of Direct Cinema allowed young directors to go even further on this path. Accordingly, young filmmakers set their stories in their own apartments and neighborhoods, filming them in a way that traditional directors considered rough and unprofessional. For instance, in *Los Golfos* ("The Drifters," 1960), Carlos Saura uses nonactors and improvisation to tell his story of young men's lives of petty crime. Saura incorporates hand-held shots and abrupt zooms (**20.7**) to give the film a documentary immediacy.

The art cinema's subjective realism also developed further during this period. Flashbacks had become common in the postwar decade, but now filmmakers used them to intensify the sense of characters' mental states. Alan Resnais's *Hiroshima mon amour* (1959) led many filmmakers to "subjectivize" flashbacks. Scenes of fantasy and dreams proliferated. All this mental imagery became far more fragmentary and disordered than it had been in earlier cinema. The filmmaker might interrupt the narrative with glimpses of another realm that only gradually becomes identifiable as memory, dream, or fantasy. At the limit, this realm might remain tantalizingly obscure to the very end of the film, suggesting how reality and imagination can fuse in human experience.

20.8, *left   Daisies:* the long lens flattens women and man.

20.9, *right   Everything for Sale* joins the new cinemas in its self-conscious references to film history—a history that includes Wajda's early work. In a direct echo of *Ashes and Diamonds*, the mysterious young actor lights drinks while remarking that the partisans were symbols for his generation (compare with 18.23).

The art-cinema tendency toward authorial commentary likewise continued. François Truffaut's lilting camera movements around his characters suggested that their lives were a lyrical dance. In *Daisies* (1966), Vera Chytilová uses camera tricks to comment on her heroine's mocking view of men (**20.8**).

Directors combined objective realism, subjective realism, and authorial commentary in ways that generated narrative ambiguity. Now the spectator could not always tell which of these three factors was the basis for the film's presentation of events. In Federico Fellini's *8½* (1963), some scenes indiscernibly blend memory with fantasy images. Younger directors also explored ambiguous uses of narrative form. In Jaromil Jireš's *The Cry* (1963), events may be taken as either objective or subjective, and the question is left open as to whose subjective point of view might be represented. Open-ended narratives also lent themselves to ambiguity, as when we are left to wonder at the end of *Breathless* about the heroine's attitude toward the hero.

As films' stories became indeterminate, they seemed to back away from documenting the social world. Now the film itself came to seem the only "reality" the director could claim. Combined with young directors' awareness of the history of their medium, this retreat from objective realism made film form and style self-referential. Many films no longer sought to reflect a reality outside themselves. Like modern painting and literature, film became *reflexive*, pointing to its own materials, structures, and history.

Reflexivity was perhaps least disturbing when the film built its plot around the making of a film, as in *8½*, Godard's *Contempt* (1963), and Andrzej Wajda's *Everything for Sale* (1968), a memorial to Zbigniew Cybulski, the deceased star of *Ashes and Diamonds* (**20.9**). Even when filmmaking is not an overt subject, reflexivity remains a key trait of new cinemas and of 1960s art cinema generally. Erik Løken's *The Hunt* (1959) starts with a voice-over commentary remarking, "Let's begin," and ends with the narrator asserting, "We can't let it end like this." In *Breathless,* the hero talks to the audience, and Truffaut's *Shoot the Piano Player* (1960; **20.10**) affectionately echoes silent cinema.

The collage films, which juxtapose footage from different sources or periods, contribute to a similar awareness of the artifice of film. And new cinemas could even cite each other, as when Gilles Groulx's *Le Chat est dans le sac* ("The Cat Is in the Bag," 1964) deliberately echoes a French New Wave film (**20.11, 20.12**). In all, the films acknowledge the mechanisms of illusion-

20.10 Irises in *Shoot the Piano Player* pay homage to silent film.

20.11, 20.12 *Le Chat est dans le sac* cites Godard's *Vivre sa vie.*

making and an indebtedness to the history of the medium. This made the new cinemas major contributors to postwar cinematic modernism.

Many countries sustained new waves and new cinemas, but this chapter concentrates on the most influential and original developments in western and eastern Europe, Great Britain, the USSR and Brazil.

FRANCE: NEW WAVE AND NEW CINEMA

In France during the late 1950s, the idealism and political movements of the immediate postwar years gave way to a more apolitical culture of consumption and leisure. The rising generation was dubbed the *Nouvelle Vague,* the "New Wave" that would soon govern France. Many of these young people read film journals and attended screenings at ciné-clubs and *art et essai* ("art and experiment") cinemas. They were ready for more offbeat films than those of the Cinema of Quality.

The film industry had not fully tapped these new consumers. In 1958, film attendance started to decline sharply, and several big-budget films failed. At the same time, government aid fostered risk taking. In 1953, the Centre National du Cinéma established the *prime de la qualité* ("subsidy for quality"), which allowed new directors to make short films. A 1959 law created the *avance sur recettes* ("advance on receipts") system, which financed first features on the basis of a script. Between 1958 and 1961, dozens of directors made their first full-length films.

Such a broad development naturally included quite different trends, but two major ones are crucial. One centers on the *Nouvelle Vague,* or New Wave, group. The other trend, often identified with the Left Bank group, involves a slightly older generation who now moved into feature production. Both groups are represented in the following box.

The New Wave

The French New Wave (Nouvelle Vague) is largely responsible for the romantic image of the young director fighting to make personal films that defy the conventional industry. Ironically, most directors associated with the New Wave quickly became mainstream, even ordinary, filmmakers. But certain members of the group not only popularized a new conception of personal cinema but also provided innovations in film form and style.

The principal Nouvelle Vague directors had been film critics for the magazine *Cahiers du cinéma* (p. 374). Strong adherents of the auteur policy, these men believed that the director should express a personal vision of the world. This vision would appear not only in the film's script but also in its style. Most of the *Cahiers* group started by directing short films but, by the end of the decade, most turned to features. They helped each other by financing projects and sharing the services of two outstanding cinematographers, Henri Decae and Raoul Coutard.

The New Wave's initial impact came from four films released in 1959 and 1960. Claude Chabrol's *Le Beau Serge* and *Les Cousins* explored the disparity between rural and urban life in the new France. The first film almost became the French entry at Cannes; the second won a major prize at the Berlin festival. François Truffaut's *The 400 Blows,* a sensitive tale of a boy becoming a thief and a runaway, won the director's prize at Cannes and gave the New Wave great international prestige. The most innovative early New Wave film was Jean-Luc Godard's *Breathless,* a portrait of a petty criminal's last days. As Chabrol, Truffaut, and Godard followed up their debuts, other young directors launched first features.

Many New Wave films satisfied producers' financial demands. Shot on location, using portable equipment, little-known actors, and small crews, these films

French New Cinema and the Nouvelle Vague: A Chronology of Major Releases

1959
Le Beau Serge ("Good Serge"), Claude Chabrol
Les Cousins (*The Cousins*), Claude Chabrol
Les Quatre cents coups (*The 400 Blows*), François Truffaut
Hiroshima mon amour ("Hiroshima My Love"), Alain Resnais
Les Yeux sans visage (*Eyes without a Face*), Georges Franju

1960
À bout de souffle (*Breathless*), Jean-Luc Godard
Les Bonnes femmes ("The Good Girls"), Claude Chabrol
Tirez sur le pianiste (*Shoot the Piano Player*), François Truffaut
Zazie dans le metro ("Zazie in the Subway"), Louis Malle

1961
Lola, Jacques Demy
Une Femme est une femme (*A Woman Is a Woman*), Jean-Luc Godard
L'Année dernière à Marienbad (*Last Year at Marienbad*), Alain Resnais
Paris nous appartient (*Paris Belongs to Us*), Jacques Rivette

1962
Jules et Jim (*Jules and Jim*), François Truffaut
Le Signe du lion ("The Sign of the Lion"), Eric Rohmer
Vivre sa vie (*My Life to Live*), Jean-Luc Godard
Cléo de 5 à 7 (*Cléo from 5 to 7*), Agnès Varda
L'Immortelle ("The Immortal One"), Alain Robbe-Grillet

1963
Le Petit soldat ("The Little Soldier"), Jean-Luc Godard
Ophélia, Claude Chabrol
Les Carabiniers ("The Riflemen"), Jean-Luc Godard
Le Mépris (*Contempt*), Jean-Luc Godard
Muriel, Alain Resnais
Judex, Georges Franju
Adieu Philippine, Jacques Rozier

1964
La Peau douce (*The Soft Skin*), François Truffaut
Bande à part (*Band of Outsiders*), Jean-Luc Godard
Une Femme mariée (*A Married Woman*), Jean-Luc Godard
Les Parapluies de Cherbourg (*The Umbrellas of Cherbourg*), Jacques Demy

1965
Alphaville, Jean-Luc Godard
Pierrot le fou ("Crazy Pierrot"), Jean-Luc Godard
Le Bonheur ("Happiness"), Agnès Varda

1966
Masculin-Feminine, Jean-Luc Godard
Fahrenheit 451, François Truffaut
La Guerre est finie ("The War Is Over"), Alain Resnais
Suzanne Simonin, la Réligieuse de Denis Diderot ("Suzanne Simonin, the Nun by Denis Diderot"),
Jacques Rivette
Les Créatures ("The Creatures"), Agnès Varda
La Collectionneuse ("The Collector"), Eric Rohmer

1967
Made in USA, Jean-Luc Godard
Deux ou trois choses que je sais d'elle (*Two or Three Things I Know about Her*), Jean-Luc Godard
La Chinoise ("The Chinese Woman"), Jean-Luc Godard
Weekend, Jean-Luc Godard
Les Demoiselles de Rochefort (*The Young Girls of Rochefort*), Jacques Demy
Trans-Europe Express, Alain Robbe-Grillet
Ma nuit chez Maud (*My Night at Maud's*), Eric Rohmer

20.13   Antoine Doinel, at the edge of the sea, turns to the audience in world cinema's most famous freeze-frame (*The 400 Blows*).

20.14   In Chabrol's *Les Cousins*, a browser finds a book on Alfred Hitchcock, written by Eric Rohmer and . . . Claude Chabrol.

could be made quickly and for less than half the usual cost. Often a film would be shot silent and postdubbed. And, for three years, several New Wave films made high profits. The trend brought fame to Jean-Paul Belmondo, Jean-Claude Brialy, Anna Karina, Jeanne Moreau, and other stars who would dominate the French cinema for decades. Moreover, Nouvelle Vague films proved more exportable than many bigger productions.

As the very name *New Wave* indicates, much of the group's success can be attributed to the filmmakers' rapport with their youthful audience. Most of the directors were born around 1930 and were based in Paris. By concentrating on urban professional life with its chic fashions and sports cars, all-night parties, bars and jazz clubs, this cinema suggested that the café scene was being captured with the immediacy of Direct Cinema. The films also have thematic affinities. Authority is to be distrusted; political and romantic commitment is suspect. The characters' gratuitous actions bear traces of pop existentialism. And in an echo of Poetic Realism, the Tradition of Quality, and American crime movies, the films often center on a femme fatale.

The New Wave directors also share some basic narrative assumptions. Like Michelangelo Antonioni and Federico Fellini, these filmmakers often build their plots around chance events and digressive episodes. They also intensify the art-cinema convention of the open-ended narrative; the famous ending of *The 400 Blows* made the freeze-frame technique a favored device for expressing an unresolved situation (**20.13**). At the same time, the mixture of tone characteristic of Italian Neorealism gets pushed to the limit. In the films of Truffaut, Godard, and Chabrol, farcical comedy is often only an instant away from anxiety, pain, and death.

Further, the Nouvelle Vague was the first group of directors to refer systematically to prior film traditions. For these former critics, film history was a living presence. In *Breathless*, the hero imitates Humphrey Bogart, while the heroine comes from Otto Preminger's *Bonjour Tristesse* (1958). Partygoers in *Paris Belongs to Us* screen *Metropolis*, while in *The 400 Blows* the boy steals a production still from Ingmar Bergman's *Summer with Monika*. Celebrating their own notoriety, the directors cited each other or their friends at *Cahiers du cinéma* (**20.14**). Such awareness of a film's debt to history helped usher in the reflexive filmmaking of the 1960s.

Since the *Cahiers* critics favored a cinema of personal vision, it is not surprising that the New Wave did not coalesce into a unified stylistic movement like German Expressionism or Soviet Montage. The development of the directors' careers during the 1960s suggests that the New Wave was only a brief alliance of varied temperaments. The two most exemplary and influential directors were Truffaut and Godard (see box), but several of their colleagues also made long-term careers in the film industry.

"You become a director," Claude Chabrol wrote, "when you find the money to make your first film."[3] His wife's inheritance financed *Le Beau Serge*, which won a *prime de la qualité* that nearly covered its costs before it was released. The success of *Les Cousins* allowed Chabrol to make several films quickly. His admiration for Hitchcock turned him toward moody psychodramas, often with touches of grotesque humor (*Les Bonnes femmes*,

FRANÇOIS TRUFFAUT AND JEAN-LUC GODARD

Friends, *Cahiers* critics, codirectors (on a 1958 short), and eventual adversaries, Truffaut and Godard usefully define the poles of the New Wave. One proved that the young cinema could rejuvenate mainstream filmmaking; the other, that the new generation could be hostile to the comfort and pleasure of ordinary cinema.

A passionate cinéphile, François Truffaut grew up as a ward of the critic André Bazin. After a notable short film, *Les Mistons* ("The Brats," 1958), Truffaut managed to finance a feature, *The 400 Blows*. This film about a young runaway established an autobiographical strain in Truffaut's work. His next features revealed two more tendencies that would recur over his career: the offhand, affectionately parodic treatment of a crime plot (*Shoot the Piano Player*) and the somber but lyrical handling of an unhappy love affair (*Jules and Jim*). For many worldwide audiences, these three films defined the New Wave.

Stylistically, Truffaut's early films flaunt zoom shots, choppy editing, casual compositions, and bursts of quirky humor or sudden violence. Sometimes such devices capture the characters' vitality, as in Antoine Doinel's frantic rush around Paris in *The 400 Blows* or in the waltzlike camera movements that surround Jules, Jim, and Catherine during their country outings. The extreme shifts of mood in *Shoot the Piano Player* are accented by abrupt cutaways; when a gangster swears, "May my mother die if I'm not telling the truth," Truffaut cuts to a shot of an old lady keeling over. But Truffaut's technique increasingly injected a subdued romanticism, as when he dwells on Charlie's numb face at the end of *Shoot the Piano Player* or turns Catherine's image into a freeze-frame (**20.15**).

Truffaut remained true to the *Cahiers* legacy by inserting into each film references to his favorite periods of film history and his admired directors (Lubitsch, Hitchcock,

20.15   A snapshot image, thanks to the freeze-frame (*Jules and Jim*).

Renoir). *Jules and Jim,* set in the early days of cinema, provided an occasion to incorporate silent footage and to employ old-fashioned irises.

Truffaut sought not to destroy traditional cinema but to renew it. In the *Cahiers* spirit he aimed to enrich commercial filmmaking by balancing personal expression with a concern for his audience: "I have to feel I am producing a piece of entertainment."[1] Over two decades he made eighteen more films. As if seeking more direct contact with the viewer, he took up acting, performing in his own works and in Spielberg's *Close Encounters of the Third Kind* (1977). His output includes light entertainments (*Vivement dimanche!* ["Finally Sunday!"], 1983), bittersweet studies of youth (*Stolen Kisses*, 1968), and more meditative films (*The Wild Child*, 1970). Late in his life, he created intense studies of psychological obsession (*The Story of Adele H.*, 1975; *The Green Room*, 1978; see Color Plate 26.9). Of Truffaut's last films only *The Last Metro* (1980) achieved international success, but he remained the most popular New Wave director.

Far more abrasive was the work of Jean-Luc Godard. Like Truffaut, he was a stormy and demanding critic. He soon became the most provocative New Wave filmmaker.

Ophélia). Chabrol churned out lurid espionage pictures before embarking on a series of psychological thrillers: *La Femme infidèle* ("The Unfaithful Wife," 1969), *Que la bête meure* (*This Man Must Die*, 1969), *Le Boucher* ("The Butcher," 1970), and others. Like Hitchcock, Chabrol traces how the tensions of middle-class life explode into madness and violence. By 2001, Chabrol had made over fifty features and several television episodes, remaining the most commercially flexible and pragmatic of the directors to emerge from *Cahiers*.

Although Eric Rohmer was nearly ten years older than most of his *Cahiers* friends, his renown came somewhat later. A reflective aesthete, Rohmer adhered closely to André Bazin's teachings. *Le Signe du lion* is akin to

The Bicycle Thief, consisting largely of a homeless man's meanderings through the hot Parisian summer (**20.17**).

After this work, Rohmer embarked on his "Six Moral Tales," wry studies of men and women struggling to balance intelligence with emotional and erotic impulses. In the first feature-length tale, *La Collectionneuse*, the nymphlike Haydée tempts the overintellectual Adrien but remains just out of his reach (**20.18**). After the success of this film, Rohmer was able to complete his first series with *My Night at Maud's* (1967), *Claire's Knee* (1970), and *Love in the Afternoon* (1972). In the 1980s, he completed a second series, "Comedies and Proverbs," and launched another, "Tales of Four Seasons" (1990–1998). Rohmer has continued directing

Of his early works only *Breathless* had notable financial success—due in part to Belmondo's insolent performance and Truffaut's script. The film was also recognizably New Wave in its hand-held camerawork, jerky editing, and homages to Jean-Pierre Melville and Monogram B pictures. Over the next decade, Godard made at least two features per year, and it became clear that he, more than any other *Cahiers* director, was redefining film structure and style.

Godard's work poses fundamental questions about narrative. While his first films, such as *Breathless* and *A Woman Is a Woman,* have fairly straightforward plots, he gradually moved toward a more fragmentary, collage structure. A story is still apparent, but it is deflected into unpredictable paths. Godard juxtaposes staged scenes with documentary material (advertisements, comic strips, crowds passing in the street), often with little connection to the narrative. Far more than his New Wave contemporaries, Godard mixes conventions drawn from popular culture, such as detective novels or Hollywood movies, with references to philosophy or avant-garde art. (Many of his stylistic asides are reminiscent of Lettrist and Situationist works; p. 493.) The inconsistencies, digressions, and disunities of Godard's work make most New Wave films seem quite traditional by comparison.

Breathless identified Godard with the hand-held camera and the jump cut (see 20.6). His subsequent films explore film style more widely, interrogating conventional film techniques. Compositions are decentered; the camera moves on its own to explore a milieu. One of Godard's most influential innovations was to design shots that seem astonishingly flat (**20.16**).

Nothing could be further from Truffaut's accommodating attitude to his audience than Godard's assault on sense and the senses. In Truffaut's *La Nuit américaine* (*Day for Night,* 1973), filmmaking becomes a merry party, after

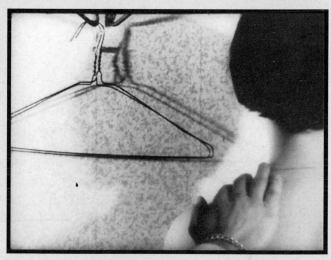

20.16 The painterly flatness of the Godard frame (*Vivre sa vie*).

which everyone can be forgiven. Godard's *Contempt,* by contrast, treats filmmaking as an exercise in sadomasochism. To secure his job, a scriptwriter leaves his wife alone with a venal producer and then taunts her with his suspicions of infidelity. His games and her contempt for him lead to her death. Fritz Lang, playing himself as the director, is seen to be a slave in exile. Ironically, Godard's critique of the film world uses the resources of the big-budget film to create ravishing color compositions (**Color Plate 20.1**).

Such works aroused passionate debate. After the mid-1960s Godard continued to develop, always in ways that aroused attention. Even his detractors grant that he is the most widely imitated director of the French New Wave, perhaps the most influential director of the entire postwar era. With characteristic generosity Truffaut remarked, "There is the cinema *before* Godard and the cinema *after* Godard."[2]

20.17 Parisian landscapes and a weary man's gait in *Le Signe du lion.*

20.18 Flirtation among the intelligentsia: Rohmer's characteristic world already formulated in *La Collectionneuse.*

20.19 A theater rehearsal with sinister overtones (*Paris Belongs to Us*).

20.20 Filming the theater rehearsal in *L'Amour fou*.

into his eighties, embracing 16mm and digital video (*The Lady and the Duke*, 2001). Deflating his characters' pretensions while still sympathizing with their efforts to find happiness, Rohmer's cinema has the flavor of the novel of manners or of Renoir's films.

Whereas Rohmer favors the concise, neatly ironic tale, the films of Jacques Rivette, another *Cahiers* critic, struggle to capture the endlessness of life itself. *L'Amour fou* (1968) runs over four hours, *Out I* (1971) twelve. Such abnormal lengths allow Rivette gradually to unfold a daily rhythm behind which intricate, half-concealed conspiracies are felt to lurk.

Paris Belongs to Us initiated this paranoid plot structure. A young woman is told that the unseen rulers of the world have driven one man to suicide and will soon kill the man she loves. The film owes much to Lang, whose parables of fate and foreboding Rivette admired. *Paris Belongs to Us* also introduces Rivette's fascination with the theater. In one plot strand, an aspiring director tries to stage *Pericles* in makeshift circumstances (**20.19**). *L'Amour fou* develops the motif more elaborately by following a 16mm film crew documenting a theater troupe's production (**20.20**). Considered marginal in the prime Nouvelle Vague period, Rivette's work strongly influenced the French cinema of the 1970s.

More stylized in technique are the films of Jacques Demy, whose career was launched with *Lola* (dedicated to Max Ophüls in memory of *Lola Montès*). This and *Baie des anges* ("Bay of Angels," 1963) introduced the artificial decor and costumes that became Demy's trademark. With *The Umbrellas of Cherbourg*, Demy broke even more sharply with realism by having all the dialogue sung. Michel Legrand's pop score and Demy's vibrant color schemes helped the film achieve a huge commercial success. In *Les Demoiselles de Rochefort,* an homage to MGM musicals, Demy created the sense that an entire city's population was dancing to the changing moods of his protagonists (**20.21**). Most of Demy's films disturbingly contrast sumptuous visual design with banal, even sordid, plot lines.

The *New Wave* label was often applied to directors who had little in common with the *Cahiers* group. Niko Papatakis's savage *Les Abysses* (1963), for instance, seems chiefly indebted to the Theater of the Absurd in its depiction of two housemaids' frenzied psychodrama (**20.22**). By contrast, the mainstream Louis Malle could appropriate a New Wave style for his *Zazie dans le métro* (**20.23**). In general, the New Wave rubric allowed a variety of young filmmakers to emerge.

20.21 The rapture of a city dancing: *Les Demoiselles de Rochefort*.

20.22 *Les Abysses:* an adaptation of the story of the murderous Papin sisters. Here they savagely peel away wallpaper.

20.23, *left* Joviality echoing the Marx Brothers (*Zazie dans le métro*).

20.24, *right* In *La Pointe courte*, the couple declaim philosophically while in the background fishermen go about their work.

20.25, 20.26 *Hiroshima mon amour:* as the couple lie in bed, Resnais cuts abruptly to a shot of the woman's German lover. The grayer tonality of the film stock helps mark the distant past.

New Cinema: The Left Bank

The late 1950s brought to prominence another loosely affiliated group of filmmakers—since known as the *Rive Gauche*, or "Left Bank," group. Mostly older and less movie-mad than the *Cahiers* crew, they tended to see cinema as akin to other arts, particularly literature. Some of these directors—Alain Resnais, Agnès Varda, and Georges Franju—were already known for their unusual short documentaries (pp. 481–482). Like New Wave filmmakers, however, they practiced cinematic modernism, and their emergence in the late 1950s benefited from the youthful public's interest in experimentation.

Two works of the mid-1950s were significant precursors. Alexandre Astruc, whose caméra-stylo manifesto had been an important spur to the auteur theory (p. 415), made *Les Mauvaises rencontres* ("Bad Meetings," 1955), which uses flashbacks and a voice-over narration to explain the past of a woman brought to a police station in connection with an abortionist. More important is Agnès Varda's short feature *La Pointe courte* (1955). Much of the film consists of a couple's random walks. But the non-actors and real locales conflict with the couple's archly stylized voice-over dialogue (**20.24**). The film's elliptical editing was without parallel in the cinema of its day.

The prototypical Left Bank film was *Hiroshima mon amour,* directed by Alain Resnais from a script by Marguerite Duras. Appearing in 1959, it shared the limelight with *Les Cousins* and *The 400 Blows*, offering more evidence that the French cinema was renewing itself. But *Hiroshima* differs greatly from the works of Chabrol and Truffaut. At once highly intellectual and viscerally shocking, it juxtaposes the present and the past in disturbing ways.

A French actress comes to Hiroshima to perform in an antiwar film. She is attracted to a Japanese man. Over two nights and days they make love, talk, quarrel, and gain an obscure understanding. At the same time, memories of the German soldier she loved during the Occupation well up unexpectedly. She struggles to connect her own torment during World War II with the ghastly suffering inflicted in the 1945 atomic destruction of Hiroshima. The film closes with the couple's apparent reconciliation, suggesting that the difficulty of fully knowing any historical truth resembles that of understanding another human being.

Duras builds her script as a duet, with male and female voices intertwining over the images. Often the viewer does not know if the sound track carries real conversations, imaginary dialogues, or commentary spoken by the characters. The film leaps from current story action to documentary footage, usually of Hiroshima, or to shots of the actress's youth in France (**20.25, 20.26**). While audiences had seen flashback constructions throughout the 1940s and 1950s, Resnais made such temporal switches sudden and fragmentary. In many cases they remain ambiguously poised between memory and fantasy.

20.27 *Last Year at Marienbad*: people cast shadows but trees don't.

In *Hiroshima*'s second part, the Japanese man pursues the French woman through the city over a single night. Now her inner voice takes the place of flashbacks, commenting on what is happening in the present. If the film's first half is so rapidly paced as to disorient the spectator, the second part daringly slows to the tempo of their walking, her nervous avoidance, his patient waiting. The rhythm, which forces us to observe nuances of their behavior, anticipates that of Antonioni's *L'Avventura*.

Hiroshima mon amour was shown out of competition at Cannes in 1959 and awarded an International Critics' Prize. It caused a sensation, both for its scenes of sexual intimacy and for its storytelling techniques. Its ambiguous mixture of documentary realism, subjective evocation, and authorial commentary represented a landmark in the development of the international art cinema.

Hiroshima lifted Resnais to international renown. His next work, *Last Year at Marienbad*, pushed modernist ambiguity to new extremes. This tale of three people encountering each other in a luxurious hotel mixes fantasy, dream—and reality, if there is any to be discovered (**20.27**). Resnais's next film *Muriel*, uses no flashbacks, but the past remains visible in a young man's amateur movies of his traumatic tour of duty in Algeria. Even more explicitly than *Hiroshima*, the film takes up political questions; the Muriel of the title, never seen, is an Algerian tortured by French occupiers. Resnais emphasizes the anxiety of the present through a jolting editing far more precise than the rough jump cuts of the New Wave (**20.28, 20.29**).

The success of *Hiroshima mon amour* helped launch features by other Left Bank filmmakers. Georges Franju's *Eyes without a Face* (**20.30**) and *Judex* offered cerebral, slightly surrealist reworkings of classic genres and paid homage to directors like Fritz Lang and Louis Feuillade. Resnais's editor Henri Colpi was able to make *Une Aussi longue absence* (1960), a tale of a café keeper who believes that a tramp is her returning husband. With its fragmentary scenes and unexpected cuts, it anticipates *Muriel*. Marguerite Duras, who wrote Colpi's film as well as Resnais's, was eventually drawn to filmmaking (see Chapter 25).

The fame of Resnais's work enabled another literary figure to move into directing. After scripting *Last Year at Marienbad*, the novelist Alain Robbe-Grillet debuted as a director with *L'Immortelle*. It continues *Marienbad*'s rendition of "impossible" times and spaces (**20.31, 20.32**). Robbe-Grillet's second film, *Trans-Europe Express*, is self-consciously about storytelling, as three writers settle down in a train to write about international drug smuggling. The film shows us their plot enacted, with all the variants and revisions that emerge from the discussion.

The *Hiroshima* breakthrough also helped Agnès Varda make a full-length feature, *Cléo from 5 to 7*. Despite its title, the film covers ninety-five minutes in the life of an actress awaiting the results of a critical medical test. Varda distances us from this tense situation by breaking the film into thirteen "chapters" and by including various digressions (**20.33**). The film's exuberance, in surprising contrast to its morbid subject, puts it close to the New Wave tone, but its experiment in manipulating story duration has an intellectual flavor typical of the Left Bank group.

Varda's films after *Cléo* include the controversial *Le Bonheur*, which disturbed viewers by suggesting that one woman can easily take the place of another. In a typically modernist attack on traditional morality, Varda quotes Renoir's *Picnic on the Grass*, in which a character remarks, "Happiness may consist in submitting to the order of Nature."

Both the New Wave and the Left Bank groups had only a few years of success. French film attendance continued to decline. Some works by novice directors, notably Jacques Rozier's *Adieu Philippine*, ran up huge production costs. By 1963, the New Cinema was no longer selling, and it was as difficult for a young director to get started as it would have been ten years earlier. Tenacious producers such as Georges de Beauregard, Anatole Dauman, Mag Bodard, and Pierre Braunberger assisted the major filmmakers, but far more bankable were directors like Claude Lelouch, whose *A Man and a Woman* (1966) used New Cinema techniques to dress up a traditional romantic plot.

Nevertheless, the French cinema of the 1960s was one of the most widely admired and imitated in the world. The Tradition of Quality had been supplanted by a vigorous cinematic modernism.

20.28, 20.29 *Muriel:* when Alphonse rises from a table, Resnais cuts to him in a different locale but in the same part of the frame.

20.30 A dead-white mask echoing silent-film makeup in Franju's *Eyes without a Face.*

20.31, 20.32 The protagonist of *L'Immortelle* peers out through a blind, and the phantom woman he pursues, in still photograph, peers back.

20.33 Cléo sings to the camera.

ITALY: YOUNG CINEMA AND SPAGHETTI WESTERNS

During the late 1950s and early 1960s, the Italian film industry fared much better than the French. Higher ticket prices offset the decline in attendance, American imports were decreasing, and Italian films were gaining a large share of domestic revenues. The international market proved accessible to horror films, comedies like *Divorce Italian Style* (1961), and revived "mythological" epics like *Hercules Unchained* (1959). U.S. and European firms continued to seek Italian coproductions. Cinecittà churned out films, and in 1962 Dino De Laurentiis built a huge studio outside Rome. By the early 1960s, Italy had become western Europe's most powerful production center.

The most visible directors were Fellini and Antonioni, whose early 1960s films solidified their reputations as auteurs (see Chapter 19). Expansion in the industry also enabled dozens of new directors to embark on careers. Most went immediately into the popular genres, but a few became more celebrated and influential. As we might expect, they were often characterized in relation to the Neorealist tradition.

A straightforward updating of Neorealism occurred in the work of Ermanno Olmi. From the first scene, which shows a young man waking up while his parents

20.34 *Il Posto:* an older employee's death allows the protagonist to move into the office amid a scramble for the slightly better empty desk at the front of the row.

prepare breakfast, *Il Posto* ("The Job," aka *The Sound of Trumpets,* 1961) seems to continue the patient observation of daily life conducted in *Umberto D.* (p. 364). *Il Posto* is also characteristic of international Young Cinema in the way it loosens its narrative beyond the Neorealist norm. The young man's application for a civil service job, the petty office routines, and the melancholy lives of the clerks are presented in an anecdotal, digressive fashion (**20.34**). The romance plot line remains

20.35 *Salvatore Giuliani:* soldiers line a street in a village that has aided the hero.

20.36 Hand-held shots give a sense of war reportage as the camera follows soldiers invading an apartment block in *Battle of Algiers.*

unfulfilled. Olmi's alternation of satiric touches with quiet sympathy resembles the attitude of young Czech filmmakers like Jiří Menzel.

Neorealism's socially critical impulse was intensified by new filmmakers identified with the left. Perhaps closest to the Neorealist source was the work of the Taviani brothers, Vittorio and Paolo, who would gain international prominence in the 1970s. Francesco Rosi, who had assisted Visconti on *La Terra trema,* merged a semidocumentary inquiry into a Sicilian bandit's death with nonchronological flashbacks in *Salvatore Giuliano* (1961). Avoiding a concentration on its protagonist, the film explores the Mafia and government forces that defeat the populist rebel (**20.35**). Marco Bellocchio brought a New Left critique of orthodox communism to the screen with *Fists in the Pockets* (1966) and *China Is Near* (1967). Gillo Pontecorvo, older than these filmmakers, made one of the most important contributions to the trend in *Battle of Algiers* (1966). This restaged semidocumentary drew upon the conventions of cinema vérité to render the immediacy of the Algerian war for independence (**20.36**); but, in using a complex flashback construction, Pon-

tecorvo, like Rosi, showed the influence of Resnais and other experimenters.

The Neorealist impulse also encountered a radical modernism in the work of Pier Paolo Pasolini. An unorthodox Marxist, a homosexual, and a nonbeliever steeped in Catholicism, Pasolini generated a furor in Italian culture. He was already famous as a poet and novelist when he entered filmmaking. He worked on several scripts, notably for Fellini's *Nights of Cabiria,* and he cast his own films on a principle that Vittorio De Sica could have accepted: "I choose actors for what they are and not for what they pretend to be."[4] Yet Pasolini claimed to take from Charles Chaplin, Carl Dreyer, and Kenji Mizoguchi the idea that the filmmaker could reveal the epic and mythic dimensions of the world.

The bleak examination of urban poverty in *Accatone* (1961) and *Mama Roma* (1962) was hailed as a return to Neorealism. Yet Pasolini's treatment of the milieu seems to owe more to Luis Buñuel's *Los Olvidados,* not only in the scenes of savage violence but in the disturbing dream imagery. Pasolini criticized Neorealism as being too tied to Resistance politics and too attached to a surface veracity. "In neorealism things are described with a certain detachment, with human warmth mixed with irony—characteristics which I do not have."[5]

Pasolini's first films also display what he called *pasticchio,* the "jumbling together" of a wide range of aural and visual materials. In compositions reminiscent of Renaissance paintings, characters spew forth vulgar language. Cinéma-vérité street scenes are accompanied by Bach or Mozart. Pasolini explained these disparities of technique by claiming that the peasantry and the lowest reaches of the urban working class retained a tie to preindustrial mythology, which his citation of great artworks of the past was meant to evoke.

The tactic of stylistic "contamination," as Pasolini called it, was perhaps least disturbing to audiences in *The Gospel According to St. Matthew* (1964), which—unlike his previous writings and films—won praise from the Church. The biblical tale was presented with greater realism than would be found in Hollywood or Cinecittà epics. Pasolini made Jesus a fierce, often impatient, preacher, and he dwelt on the characters' gnarled features, wrinkled skin, and broken teeth. *The Gospel,* however, is not simply a Neorealist scripture. Techniques are jumbled together. Bach and Prokofiev vie with the African *Missa Luba* on the sound track. Faces out of Renaissance paintings are filmed in abrupt zoom shots. Jesus' trial before Pilate is viewed by a hand-held camera within a crowd of onlookers, as if a news reporter could not get closer (**20.37**).

20.37 *The Gospel According to St. Matthew:* from Judas's point of view, we glimpse the trial past the heads of other onlookers.

Pasolini, the experimental writer turned filmmaker, somewhat resembles Alain Robbe-Grillet, while Bernardo Bertolucci represents an Italian parallel to the directors of the Nouvelle Vague. At age nineteen Bertolucci was assistant director on *Accatone,* and Pasolini supplied the script for his first film, *La Commare secca* ("The Grim Reaper," 1962). A devoted cinéphile, he spent his teenage vacations watching movies at the Cinémathèque Française. Although Bertolucci identified strongly with the New Wave filmmakers, the careful construction and technical elegance of his films put them closer to the world of older modernists like Resnais. In *La Commare secca,* offscreen detectives interrogate murder suspects, and flashbacks supply each suspect's version of events.

This familiar modernist device, exploited in *Citizen Kane* and *Rashomon,* is here applied to a classic Neorealist situation—a purse theft that recalls both *The Bicycle Thief* and *Nights of Cabiria.*

Bertolucci's most celebrated film of the era was the autobiographical *Before the Revolution* (1964). A tale of a young man who falls in love with his aunt, it parades references to *Cahiers du cinéma* and Hollywood directors and displays the director's mastery of art-cinema procedures of disorientation (20.38–20.42). Avoiding the radical disjunctions of Godard, Bertolucci made mildly modernist films of great technical polish, a quality that he would exploit in his successes of the 1970s and 1980s.

The industry's prosperity allowed Olmi, Pasolini, Bertolucci, and many other directors to enter filmmaking. As in France, however, the period of opportunity was rather brief. A crisis emerged during 1963 and 1964, when the costume epic fell out of favor and major companies suffered from expensive failures, principally Luchino Visconti's *The Leopard* (1963) and Robert Aldrich's *Sodom and Gomorrah* (1963). In 1965, the government intervened and offered an aid policy resembling that of France: prizes for quality efforts, guaranteed bank loans, credits from special funds.

While this policy led to a new filmmaking boom, producers turned to low-budget production in new genres, such as sex films and James Bond imitations. Mario Bava introduced new eroticism, baroque set designs, and bizarre camera movements into fantasy-based thrillers

20.38 Disorienting time juggling in *Before the Revolution:* the aunt sorts photographs from her life on her bed.

20.39 After a close-up of some of the pictures . . .

20.40 . . . Bertolucci cuts to the bed, empty, and tracks in; she comes into the room in the background.

20.41, *left* Then Bertolucci resumes showing pictures, again spread on the bed . . .

20.42, *right* . . . before the aunt slowly turns the pictures over one by one. The shot of the empty bed presents an ambiguity of time: Is the shot out of order, or does it mark a new occasion on which the aunt returned to the bed and laid out the photos once again?

20.48 Morgan imagines his execution in a junkyard decorated with pictures of famous Marxists.

fashionable, and London came to be seen as the capital of trendiness, social mobility, and sexual liberation. A series of films probing the shallowness of the "mod" lifestyle found success in art theaters around the world.

For example, in *Darling* (1965, John Schlesinger) a thoughtless, trivial model rises in society through a string of love affairs and finally marries an Italian prince. *Darling* uses many techniques derived from the Nouvelle Vague, such as jump cuts and freeze-frames. *Alfie* (1966, Lewis Gilbert) offers a male reversal of *Darling,* in which a selfish charmer seduces a series of women, ducking all problems until confronted with the illegal abortion of one of his victims. *Alfie* follows *Tom Jones* in letting the hero share his thoughts with the viewer by means of asides to the camera.

Reisz's *Morgan, a Suitable Case for Treatment* (1966) joined the working-class hero of the Kitchen Sink period with a comic critique of swinging London. A man from a Marxist family tries desperately to prevent his wife from divorcing him and marrying a snobbish art-gallery owner. *Morgan* assimilates art-cinema conventions in its fantasy scenes, in which the hero compares people to gorillas and envisions his execution (**20.48**).

Apart from the new prominence of the London lifestyle, creative talents left Kitchen Sink realism behind. The success of *Tom Jones* led Richardson to Hollywood, while Albert Finney, Tom Courtenay, Richard Harris, and Michael Caine became international stars. Hollywood's tactics in financing British films changed as well. The intimate, realistic film would often be associated with a more overtly political cinema, while many notable later British works were either expensive prestige films (often made with American backing) or inventive genre pictures.

YOUNG GERMAN FILM

In February 1962, at the Oberhausen Film Festival, a new impulse in West German cinema was articulated. Twenty-six young filmmakers signed a manifesto declaring the old film dead. In the face of a decaying industry and a dwindling audience, the signatories promised to help German cinema regain international renown. After three years of lobbying and public debate, the central government established the Kuratorium Junger Deutsch Film ("Commission for Young German Film") in early 1965. This agency provided interest-free loans on the basis of scripts by directors who had proved themselves with notable short films.

During its brief existence, the Kuratorium financed nearly two dozen feature films. All were low-budget projects, in which the filmmaker paid the actors little and filmed almost completely on location. But many of these *Rücksackfilme* ("backpack films") had the shock of novelty. They depicted contemporary Germany as a land of broken marriages, soured affairs, rebellious youth, and casual sex. They suggested that the legacy of Naziism lingered into the present. And, after nearly two decades of respectful adaptations of classics, the Young German Film forged alliances with experimental writing. This was a cinema of *Autoren*. Unlike the French auteur critic-filmmakers, the young Germans sought a cinema of literary quality.

Later the Oberhauseners would admit that the manifesto was largely a bluff, but several signatories, such as Edgar Reitz and Volker Schlöndorff, managed to sustain careers. From a long-range international perspective, the two most noteworthy debuts of the period were those of Alexander Kluge and Jean-Marie Straub.

Trained as a lawyer, Kluge moved into experimental writing and—after seeing *Breathless*—filmmaking. He became the most tireless advocate of the Young German Film. A signer of the Oberhausen manifesto, Kluge played a central role in lobbying for the Kuratorium. He also helped establish West Germany's first film production school, at Ulm. During the same period, he made a series of shorts. In 1965, he was given Kuratorium funding for what became *Abscheid von Gestern* ("Departure from Yesterday," aka *Yesterday Girl*, 1966). Kluge's stylistic flourishes—jump cuts, fast motion, interruptive titles, hand-held tracking shots—and his fragmented, elliptical storytelling firmly locate *Yesterday Girl* in the 1960s Young Cinema. Anita G. might be a French New Wave heroine: she drifts though cities, tries to hold a job, indulges in petty theft, has love affairs, and winds up pregnant and in prison.

Unlike his French contemporaries, though, Kluge sought to give Anita a historical significance. Her story is intermingled with a host of documents: a children's story from the 1920s, Direct Cinema interviews, old photographs and songs. Anita's plight illustrates the continuity between the old Germany and the new; the film's epigraph is "We are separated from yesterday not by an abyss but by the changed situation." Although Kluge's narrative technique does not encourage the audience to identify wholly with Anita, there are moments of subdued pathos (**20.49**). After the international recognition granted *Yesterday Girl,* Kluge became the Young German Film's most articulate theorist, championing films that would free the audience's imagination in new ways.

Far less public a figure was the French-born Jean-Marie Straub. As a youth he was deeply impressed by Robert Bresson's *Les Dames du Bois du Boulogne* and the films of Lang and Dreyer. With his wife, Danièle Huillet, Straub adapted two works of Heinrich Böll as *Machorka-Muff* (1963) and *Nicht versöhnt* (*Not Reconciled,* 1965).

Like Kluge, Straub juxtaposed fictional and documentary materials. *Machorka-Muff,* which points up the rise of militarism in postwar Germany, is presented in snippets of dialogue, action, and internal monologue, all intercut with landscapes and newspaper headlines. The film squeezes Böll's novelette *Berlin Diary* into eighteen minutes.

Not Reconciled is even more daringly compressed. In only fifty minutes, Straub and Huillet trace a continuity between World War I, World War II, and the present through the story of three generations of a family. The deliberately inexpressive, even stilted acting, the great number of characters, the unsignaled switches between present and past, and the staccato fragmentation of the scenes make *Not Reconciled* almost incomprehensible on a first viewing. The plot complexities are accompanied by a self-conscious visual beauty (**20.50**) and direct sound—a rarity among young filmmakers, who typically kept costs low by using postdubbing. Although German distributors refused to handle *Not Reconciled,* it enabled Straub and Huillet to win Kuratorium funding for a feature on the life of Bach. This film and subsequent efforts would have considerable international influence.

By the end of 1967, the Young German Film could point to many successes. *Yesterday Girl* and Volker Schlöndorff's *Young Törless* (1966) each won eight festival prizes, and other films did well on the international market. But directors, differing on principles and forced to compete for scarce resources, became divided. The

20.49 *Yesterday Girl:* On the run, Anita must change her clothes at the roadside.

20.50 Depth and decentering in *Not Reconciled.*

mainstream industry successfully lobbied for a new form of subsidy, and, in January 1968, the Film Promotion Law went into effect. It shut out first-time directors and favored producers who turned out quick, low-budget commercial series. In addition, the new law controlled content with a provision that refused sponsorship to films that were "contrary to the constitution or to moral or religious sentiments."[7]

Some beginning filmmakers used Kuratorium money and producers' interest in the young audience to make espionage thrillers and bedroom comedies. Eckhardt Schmidt, director of *Jet-Generation* (1967), remarked, "I prefer filming a naked girl rather than chattering about problems."[8] But many young filmmakers critical of the German "economic miracle" would make their voices heard throughout the decade.

NEW CINEMA IN THE USSR AND EASTERN EUROPE

Young Cinema in the Soviet Union

The "thaw" after Stalin's death in 1953 ended quickly: in the political sphere, with the 1956 crushing of the Hungarian Revolution; in the artistic domain, with the 1958 attacks on Boris Pasternak's novel *Dr. Zhivago*. But, in 1961, Nikita Khrushchev launched a new de-Stalinization campaign, calling for openness and greater democracy. Intellectuals and artists responded eagerly, and a Soviet youth culture began to emerge.

In the cinema, most older directors continued to work in traditional ways. Joseph Heifits's *Lady with the Little Dog* (1960), for example, continued the stolid 1950s deep-focus technique in telling its story of a love affair in a declining class (**20.51**). Still exploiting the monumental style, Mikhail Romm displayed a more liberal stance in *Nine Days of One Year* (1962), a social-problem film about nuclear radiation. Although Romm had been a major Stalinist filmmaker, he proved a progressive force after the thaw, training and encouraging several of the important directors of the postwar decades.

A new emphasis on youth could be seen in several films about children. Other filmmakers, like their counterparts abroad, concentrated on young adults in the contemporary world. Vasily Shukshin, a fiction writer, directed *There Was a Lad* (1964), in which a good-natured trucker encounters teenage life in the USSR (**20.52**).

The most celebrated young director was Andrei Tarkovsky. The son of a major poet, he studied under Romm at VGIK. Like many of his contemporaries, Tarkovsky became interested in European art cinema, particularly the work of Bergman, Bresson, and Fellini. His first feature was *Ivan's Childhood* (1962). After winning the Grand Prize at Venice, it became one of the most widely admired Soviet films of the 1960s.

The plot of *Ivan's Childhood* adheres to many conventions of the Soviet World War II film. A boy vows to avenge his parents' deaths and becomes a scout for a band of partisans. But Tarkovsky treats this material with an unusual lyricism (**20.53, 20.54**). The wordless opening sequence, a dream in which Ivan floats through the trees to greet his mother and take a drink of water, establishes a cluster of visual motifs. After Ivan has died at the hands of the Nazis, the film concludes with a glowing sequence of fantasy images. The ambiguity is characteristic of 1960s art cinema; the sequence could be Ivan's final reverie, or it could be the filmmaker's free elaboration and comment. The authorities resented

20.51   The continuation of deep-focus shooting in the prestigious literary adaptation *The Lady with the Little Dog.*

20.52   Youth culture in socialist humanism: in *There Was a Lad*, a disdainful Muscovite confronts locals at a club dance.

Tarkovsky's effort "to replace narrative causality with poetic articulations."[9]

The new liberalization soon ended. After Khrushchev denounced *I'm 20* (1963, Marlen Khutsiev) for insulting the older generation, the Young Cinema encountered greater resistance. In 1964, Khrushchev was forced to resign, and the conservative Leonid Brezhnev took over as party secretary. Under the rubric "harmonious development," Brezhnev halted reforms and tightened control of culture. Nonconformist films were reshot or banned. Andrei Konchalovsky's *Asya's Happiness*, finished in 1966, was withdrawn for its supposed insults to the peasantry. Alexander Askoldov's *Commissar* (1967) was suppressed for its positive portrayal of Jewish characters. After Grigori Chukhrai's *Beginning of an Unknown Era* (1967) was shelved, he closed his experimental studio.

The fate of Tarkovsky's second feature exemplifies the difficulties filmmakers faced. *Andrei Rublev* (1965), a long, somber drama of the life of a fifteenth-century icon painter, followed the strategy Tarkovsky had pursued in *Ivan's Childhood*. Once more he took a formu-

20.53, 20.54 Tarkovsky's battle-scarred landscapes in *Ivan's Childhood* have a Bergmanesque starkness and stand in contrast to the lush tranquility of nature in Ivan's imagination.

20.55 The mystical tactility of Tarkovsky in *Andrei Rublev:* a bloody hand slumping into a stream produces a milky stain.

20.56 As Tartars pillage a town, geese float down from the sky (*Andrei Rublev*).

laic genre—here, the biography of the great artist—and infused it with mysteriously poetic imagery (**20.55, 20.56**). *Andrei Rublev* also had disturbing contemporary overtones. Surrounded by viciousness and cruelty, Rublev gives up speaking, stops painting, and abandons religious faith. Some viewers saw Tarkovsky's film as an allegory of art crushed by social oppression. Goskino administrators denied it a release.

Despite political pressures, several films of the Brezhnev era broached issues of importance to youth and intellectuals. Two significant women directors emerged. Larissa Shepitko centered *Wings* (1966) on a

20.57, *left* A Godard-style shot from *Brief Encounters*.

20.58, *right* A man is struck by an axe, and blood dribbles down the camera lens (*Shadows of Forgotten Ancestors*).

female pilot learning to become a school supervisor. Kira Muratova's *Brief Encounters* (1968) shows a man from the viewpoints of the two women who love him (**20.57**).

The studios of the Soviet republics, closer to folk traditions and less vulnerable to official reprimands, produced some oblique, poetic films. Older than the "new" directors, Serge Paradzhanov grew up in Georgia, graduated from VGIK in 1951, and during the 1950s made several films in the Ukraine. His *Shadows of Forgotten Ancestors* (1965) tells of a man haunted by the death of the woman he loved. The folklike story, however, is rendered in a flurry of hysterically modernist techniques. Jerkily hand-held, the camera races through landscapes. Paradzhanov gives us shots taken from treetops, ceremonially still compositions, and abrupt subjective images (**20.58**). Paradzhanov's aggressive style made authorities limit the film's distribution in the USSR but also helped it garner over a dozen international prizes.

Once Brezhnev's regime was firmly in place, Paradzhanov, Tarkovsky, and other innovative directors found it difficult to launch projects. Instead, the industry and the Party made Sergei Bondarchuk's massive *War and Peace* (1967) the official emblem of Soviet film. The film was trumpeted as the most costly production in history and was widely successful in the export market. Bondarchuk cautiously inserted a few self-consciously contemporary techniques (slow-motion, hand-held camera), but on the whole he revived the monumental tradition. A new period of "stabilization"—later to be known as "stagnation"—set in, and not until the early 1970s would Soviet cinema and other arts have the chance to explore new avenues.

New Waves in Eastern Europe

The USSR's resistance to cinematic experimentation had its parallels in some eastern European countries. Still, in the early 1960s new waves sprang up in Poland, Czechoslovakia, Yugoslavia, and Hungary.

During the late 1950s, eastern Europe's economy strengthened, and countries sought to enter western mar-

kets. Films proved to be valuable export items. In addition, economic reforms led many governments to increase artistic freedom. Each new wave typically participated in a broader cultural renaissance including literature, drama, painting, and music.

Several eastern European countries simultaneously developed production structures that were more decentralized than the rigidly controlled Soviet hierarchy. In 1955, Poland had pioneered the system of "creative film units"; in each one directors and scriptwriters worked under the supervision of a senior filmmaker. In 1963, both Czechoslovakia and Hungary adopted variants of the film-unit system. Yugoslavia's decentralized system, in place since 1950, was revised in 1962 to allow filmmakers to form independent companies to make a single film. Since nearly all these countries were threatened by the advance of television, the reorganization offered ways of competing with the new rival.

Consequently, filmmakers in these countries were freer to try fresh subjects, themes, forms, and styles than were their Soviet counterparts. The films that emerged linked eastern European cinema to the art cinema that had been flourishing in western Europe since the war. Because eastern Europe had always imported more foreign films than had the Soviet Union, directors and audiences were more aware of other new cinemas. And, as eastern European films entered festivals and international distribution circuits, western viewers encountered innovative examples of cinematic modernism.

Young Cinema in Poland In the early 1960s it might have seemed that Polish filmmaking had lost none of its force. Andrzej Wajda's *Innocent Sorcerors* (1960) adapted his style to an intimate subject, a couple's night together. *Mother Joan of the Angels* (1961), by Jerzy Kawalerowicz, offered a daring tale of possession in a convent. By 1960, the Polish system of producing films by independent units was working smoothly, and strict Socialist Realism was firmly in the past.

Yet political pressures were intensifying. Films were seldom banned, but they might be denounced by critics and politicians, and this slowed the progress of older directors. After *Innocent Sorcerors*, Wajda made no film in Poland for several years, opting instead for international coproductions. His Polish historical epic, *Ashes* (1965), did not find much favor. Similarly, Kawalerowicz made the long, brooding *Pharaoh* (1966) after six years of preparation. On the whole, the older directors of the Polish School seemed to have run out of energy.

In the early 1960s, there was the possibility that Poland's younger directors would cultivate a modest, realistic approach in contrast to the "baroque" tendencies of Wajda and Kawalerowicz. A few intimate films based on sociological observation did appear, but the two most celebrated young directors avoided such realism and moved toward a strongly dramatic, technically flamboyant approach to youthful subjects.

Roman Polanski was an actor before going to film school and attracting international attention with a short, *Two Men and a Wardrobe* (1958). After spending a few years in Paris, he returned to Poland to make *Knife in the Water* (1962). At one level, the film is an intimate suspense drama. An unhappily married couple take a young hitchhiker along on a sailing trip, and the tension builds as the husband taunts the young man mercilessly. *Knife in the Water* could be defended as politically accurate in attacking the new "red bourgeoisie" who lived in western luxury. But the young man can hardly be a positive hero, since he is at best naively confused and at worst somewhat cynical.

Polanski avoids most of the technical innovations of the European new cinemas, relying on orthodox cutting and vivid deep-focus shots that keep the characters in tense confrontation (**20.59**). Yet in other ways *Knife in the Water* relies on art-cinema conventions. The opening derives from *Voyage to Italy*, although by 1962 Polanski needed none of the expository dialogue that Roberto Rossellini required: we can infer that the couple are quarreling when the wife gets out of the car to let her husband drive. The film's finale, with the couple reunited in their car and the husband wondering if the young man is really dead, became an emblem of the lack of closure in 1960s cinema.

Jerzy Skolimowski, scriptwriter for *Innocent Sorcerors* and *Knife in the Water*, became the Polish director closest in style and theme to the Parisian Nouvelle Vague. *Identification Marks: None* (1964), assembled out of student footage, shows a draft-dodger moving through Polish youth culture. *Walkover* (1965) centers on a prizefighter who eventually wins a factory boxing match. *Barrier* (1966) draws upon Felliniesque fantasy to portray contemporary Polish youth rebelling against cynicism and bureaucracy. In each film, Skolimowski's

20.59 Harsh, Wellesian depth in *Knife in the Water.*

20.60 Dazzling reflections in *Identification Marks: None.*

20.61 False depth and flatness, in *Walkover.*

hero (usually played by the director) is a sensitive drifter disillusioned by society but still hoping to find happiness in a woman's love.

Skolimowski's films exhibit the casual improvisation we find in early Truffaut or Godard. They also have a flashy, almost exhibitionist style. There are long takes, with complex camera movements and zooms; abstract, often perplexing compositions (**20.60**); and surreal images of the contemporary city (**20.61**). In *Identification Marks: None*, after a traffic accident a hand covers the lens, only then do we realize that the shot represents the protagonist's optical point of view.

The late 1960s marked an end to the Polish School. After *Knife in the Water*, Polanski went into exile. Skolimowski made *Le Départ* (1967), a Nouvelle Vague echo, in Belgium; the banning of his next Polish production, *Hands Up!* (1968), led him to work in England and western Europe.

The Czech New Wave Czechoslovakia offered more favorable conditions for a New Cinema. The years from 1962 to 1966 saw steps toward "market socialism" and

20.62 After a hospital is bombed, Menzel's flat, Keaton-esque shot shows Milos, miraculously unscathed, lifting his coat off the rack.

20.63 The final shot of *Intimate Lighting*: obstinate eggnog.

a mood of reform. The cinema took an active part in cultural renewal. A decentralized production system placed a director-scriptwriter team at the head of each unit. As television became the main source of popular entertainment, the cinema became subsidized by the state. By 1968, production units had become independent and censorship had diminished.

The Czech New Wave crested in the period between 1963 and 1967, winning international prizes and even Academy Awards. Although some nations in the Soviet sphere disapproved of the new Czech films, elsewhere they were almost as influential as the Nouvelle Vague.

The younger directors, most of them graduates of the film school FAMU, made their entry with short films in the early 1960s. All the filmmakers knew Italian Neorealism, the Polish School, and the French New Wave, and all to some degree felt the effects of Direct Cinema. But, like most new waves, the Czech phenomenon can only loosely be considered a stylistic movement. For the most part filmmakers shared only conditions of work, thematic concerns, and an urge to move beyond Socialist Realist formulas.

One tendency was toward an art-cinema realism. Jaromil Jireš's *The Cry* (1963), often considered the first manifestation of the Czech New Wave, used nonactors and Direct Cinema technique to explore the life of a couple expecting a baby. Ewald Schorm's *Courage for Every Day* (1964) and *Return of the Prodigal Son* (1966) owed more to Antonioni in their probing of the problems of the middle-class professional.

Jiří Menzel, who found international success with *Closely Watched Trains* (1966) and *Capricious Summer* (1967), took to an extreme the shifting of tone that

Neorealism made a major principle of postwar cinema. In *Closely Watched Trains,* Menzel mixes solemn issues with erotic jokes, satire on authority, and moments of sheer absurdity. The film shifts instantly from mocking the young hero's petty ambitions to appreciating his courage, however inadvertent, in participating in partisan sabotage. Individual images display reflexive wit (**20.62**).

The single Czech feature made by Ivan Passer presents a gentler blend of comedy and social criticism. A sketch of the reunion of two musicians, *Intimate Lighting* (1965) contrasts city and country manners, amateur and professional music making, and traditional and modern conceptions of women's roles. The fragmentary incidents have a muted pathos and humor: a hen hoping to hatch a car, hosts and guests patiently trying to drink eggnog that will not leave their glasses (**20.63**).

Milos Forman was also influenced by Neorealism and Direct Cinema, but his films present more caustic social criticism than do those of Menzel and Passer. His first feature, *Black Peter* (1963), centers on a teenager similar to Menzel's Milos. Barely holding down a job, constantly at odds with his father, clumsily seeking romance, Peter becomes a comic emblem of confused Czech youth. In the first half of *Loves of a Blonde* (1965), Forman focuses with cruel hilarity on the effects of an army unit assigned to a factory town where women vastly outnumber men. In the second half, the heroine pursues a traveling piano player to Prague, where she learns that neither he nor his parents care for her. The film's grim undertones blend with Forman's satire of meaningless work and official morality.

At the center of *Black Peter* and *Loves of a Blonde* are long seriocomic scenes of couples flirting at a dance. In *The Firemen's Ball* (1967), Forman builds an entire plot around such a situation. Concentrating on the single evening of a party honoring a retiring fire chief, Forman does not develop characters in depth. Instead, he fills his film with incisive running gags and revelations of human vanities. As the ball goes on, prizes are stolen, an impromptu beauty contest creates a scandal, couples make love, and

20.64 The long lens picks out details in documentary fashion (*The Firemen's Ball*).

20.65 Harsh Direct Cinema techniques rendering the boys' escape in *Diamonds of the Night*.

20.66 The central fantasy of the empty tramcar in Nemeć's *Diamonds of the Night*.

20.67, 20.68 In *Something Different*, Vera's meeting with the bike boy cuts to another vertical and centered shot in Eva's practice session.

an old man's home burns down. Stylistically, *The Firemen's Ball* exemplifies the emerging worldwide tendency to use long lenses and documentary techniques to film staged material (**20.64**). Forman's portrait of socialist society, with its frustrated sexuality, incompetent bureaucracy, and petty pilfering, drew torrents of criticism.

Besides impulses toward satiric realism, there were efforts to find a more formally complex approach on the model of Resnais, Fellini, or Robbe-Grillet. Jan Nemeć's first feature, *Diamonds of the Night* (1964), takes as its situation two young men's escape from a train carrying them to a concentration camp. This incident, a likely basis for a Socialist Realist war film, triggers an exercise in 1960s modernism. The physical frenzy of the boys' flight is rendered via documentary techniques: hand-held camera, high-contrast cinematography (**20.65**), and a sound track dominated by gasping and thrashing noises. Nemeć goes on to interrupt the action with fragmentary, jumbled flashbacks that mix indiscernibly with fantasy scenes (**20.66**).

If *Diamonds of the Night* owes something to *Hiroshima mon amour*, Nemeć's next film, *Report on the Party and the Guests* (1968), echoes *Last Year at Marienbad*. As if to compensate for the virtual absence of dialogue in *Diamonds of the Night*, Nemeć fills this film with talk—the empty absurdities of bourgeois life. These

are only the prelude to a symbolic critique of a Stalinist police state. Banned upon completion and released two years later, *Party and the Guests* proved to be the most controversial film of Czech New Cinema.

The New Wave pushed toward even purer fantasy. In Vojtech Jasný's *Cassandra Cat* (1963), a magical cat wreaks havoc when its special eyeglasses turn people different colors. Jan Schmidt's *End of August in the Hotel Ozone* (1966), about survivors of an atomic war, also became an abstract political allegory. Nemeć's third feature, *Martyrs of Love* (1966), consists of a trio of three surrealistic tales on the border between fantasy and reality. In a remark that would have provoked the wrath of Communist officials a few years before, Nemeć summed up the attitude of many Czech filmmakers: "The director must create his own world, a world independent of reality."[10]

The work of Vera Chytilová partakes of several of these trends. Her *Something Different* (1963) intercuts the lives of Eva, a gymnast who trains arduously, and Vera, a bored housewife. Since Eva and Vera never meet, the viewer is obliged to compare their situations. Chytilová also links the stories through film style. The piano music accompanying Eva's training is heard over scenes of Vera's life, while shots in one story graphically resemble those in another (**20.67, 20.68**). Eva's story is filmed in a modified Direct Cinema style, while Vera's is presented as a more conventional fiction, setting up an interplay between two trends in the Czech New Wave itself.

With *Daisies* (1966), Chytilová moves into symbolic fantasy, satirizing a society of consumption and waste. Like *Something Different,* the film concentrates on two women, but now their personalities are robotically identical. Taking them through a string of sight gags and escalating bouts of eating and mayhem, Chytilová mocks female stereotypes when special effects reduce the heroines to cut-outs and pin-ups (**20.69**).

Menzel, Passer, Forman, Nemeć, and Chytilová were the most widely known filmmakers of the New Wave, but many others played a role in reviving Czech production. During 1966 and 1967, the government attempted to retighten cultural policy. Authorities attacked liberal writers and banned several films, including *Daisies* and *Report on the Party and the Guests.* The year 1968, an important benchmark in cinemas around the world, would put the Czech New Wave to a crucial test.

Yugoslavian New Film   Since 1948, Yugoslavia had evolved its own nationalistic, market-based version of socialism. In the years 1960 to 1961, and 1966 to 1967, workers' councils gained more power over industrial production, and this tendency benefited cinema workers. A revised film law (1962) gave regional republics greater autonomy in filmmaking and allowed filmmakers to create independent enterprises. Such companies could compete for generous state subsidies. Soon the number of production units tripled.

These conditions encouraged Yugoslavia's *Novi film* ("New Film"). Influenced by Neorealism, the Nouvelle Vague, and recent eastern European cinemas, young directors advocated experimenting with film form in the name of socialist humanism. As in other countries, filmmakers and critics wrote for periodicals and translated articles from foreign journals.

The peak period of New Film, from 1963 to 1968, revealed active groups in Belgrade, Zagreb, and Ljubljana. Two directors had particularly strong influence outside Yugoslavia.

Aleksandar Petrović, whose *Two* (1961) helped launch New Film, represented an "intimate cinema" that examined personal problems in contemporary society. His *Days* (1963) portrays the empty life of a young urban couple. *Three* (1966) is a triptych of World War II stories. Petrović called for "personal films" that "claimed the right to subjective interpretations of the lives of individuals and society, the right to 'open metaphors,' leaving room for viewers to think and feel for themselves."[11]

20.69   *Daisies:* the interchangeable heroines as disassembled parts.

20.70   Armed with a knife, the protagonist enters the mattress-stuffing room at the climax of *I Even Met Happy Gypsies.*

Petrović's most widely known film, *I Even Met Happy Gypsies* (1967), is an open-ended study of a tough gypsy merchant of goose feathers whose romantic involvement with two women leads him to murder (**20.70**). Petrović relies on long lenses and hand-held shots, and he uses nonactors speaking their various native languages. The overall effect is of pseudo-documentary realism in the portrayal of an oppressed minority.

Far more freewheeling, close to the flamboyant experimentation of the Czech fantasists, are the works of Dušan Makavejev. Makavejev's first feature, *Man Is Not a Bird* (1965), announced his penchant for deflating the pretensions of politics with earthy humor. In one scene, lovers copulate to Beethoven's Ninth Symphony, played for the edification of workers. In *Love Affair, or the Tragedy of a Switchboard Operator* (1967) he utilizes a collage form which owes something to Resnais and

Godard but which is treated with Makavejev's bawdy humor. While Chytilová's *Something Different* crosscuts two simultaneous lines of action, Makavejev alternates the progress of a love affair with flashforwards that show the affair's grisly outcome. The film also includes newsreel footage and lectures on criminal behavior. The viewer learns quickly that the affair ends in the death of Isabella. But which of her two lovers killed her? The film mixes gruesome scenes (an autopsy, a search for rats) with racy comedy and satire on socialist ideals.

At one level, Makavejev's next film, *Innocence Unprotected* (1968), is a Direct Cinema inquiry into the life of Aleksic Dragoljub, a professional acrobat who also made the first Serbo-Croatian sound movie. Interviews with Aleksic and his surviving collaborators are interrupted by intertitles, newsreels, and extracts from the original film (also called *Innocence Unprotected*). Makavejev further "decorates" the found footage with tinting, toning, hand-coloring (**Color Plate 20.4**), and ironic musical accompaniment. The collage strategy allows Makavejev to mock Nazi and Communist politics, satirize show business, celebrate naive filmmaking, and pay tribute to the national pride expressed in Aleksic's "very good old film." Through their collage form, *Love Affair* and *Innocence Unprotected* create the sort of "open metaphors" Petrović had called for in New Film.

New Cinema in Hungary   The French New Wave had a strong influence on Hungarian cinema. As one filmmaker put it, "Everybody went to Paris to see Truffaut's and Godard's films. . . . At the time, people imitated them but that was liberating."[12] Such influences would not have had much consequence, however, without favorable production circumstances.

As the political scene liberalized and television became more popular, production became decentralized. In 1958, the Béla Balázs studio (named after the pioneer film theorist and scriptwriter) was created to give graduates of the film academy a chance to make shorts and first features. In 1963, the industry adopted the Polish "creative film unit" system, which assigned each director a place in a unit but also allowed him or her to propose a project to another unit. The units were coordinated by MAFILM, which also allocated studio facilities. The industry's reorganization yielded an output of twenty or more films per year, twice the 1950s average.

Like other new cinemas, Hungary's included two generations. In the early 1960s, older directors such as Karoly Makk, Zoltán Fábrí, and István Gaal seized new opportunities. Most widely seen was the work of Miklós Jancsó, who made his first feature in 1958, when he was thirty-seven, and who achieved fame with the films he made after he turned forty (see box).

MIKLÓS JANCSÓ

Miklós Jancsó graduated from the Hungarian Film Academy in 1950, at the age of twenty-nine. After making some short films, he directed a fairly orthodox feature in 1958. His second feature, *Cantata* (1962), a story of a young doctor seeking to rekindle his relationship with his peasant father, was filmed in the manner of Antonioni, a key influence on Jancsó. Not until the mid-1960s did he emerge as a distinct auteur.

Jancsó's major films concentrated on upheavals in Hungary's tumultuous history: World War II, military coups, and popular rebellions. He follows Soviet Montage cinema in creating drama out of collective action and historical movements. In Jancsó films, individuals have little psychological identity. Instead, they become emblematic of social classes or political factions. The drama emerges out of the ways in which they are caught in a historical process.

Distancing us from the characters, the films avoid subjective devices like fantasy and refuse flashbacks and flashforwards. What comes to the fore are naked displays of power. In *The Red and the White* (1967), after a peasant

woman has numbly obeyed a Cossack officer's order to strip, a superior appears and curtly orders the troops to execute the officer. In *The Round-Up* (1965), the occupying Austrians promise a peasant that he can escape execution if he can find a partisan who has killed more men than he has. Before suffering torture or execution, victims must march in file, form circles, strip or lie down or swim a river—that is, undergo absurd ceremonies that merely display their subjection to the will of authority. Coming from a generation appalled by the revelation of wartime atrocities and the Nazi death camps, Jancsó suggests that power is exercised through public humiliation and minute control of the victim's body.

Jancsó's manner of treatment suits his dramas. After *My Way Home* (1965), he exploited abnormally long takes; the average shot in *Silence and Cry* (1968) runs two and a half minutes. Jancsó presents the moment-by-moment oscillations in power by means of a dynamic camera that renders every situation fluid and filled with tension. To illustrate even a single Jancsó shot would require several

(continued)

MIKLÓS JANCSÓ, continued

pages. In *The Round-Up,* the camera often emphasizes geometrical patterns in the Austrians' search for partisans (**20.71**). *The Red and the White* uses both immense landscape views and medium shots, sometimes tracking, panning, and zooming all at once (**20.72–20.77**).

In few auteurs' work do structure, style, and theme mesh so precisely as in Jancsó's. His narrative construction and cinematic technique present a spectacle of power that is at once abstractly symbolic and concretely historical. He became the principal example of the artistic originality and seriousness that could be achieved in an eastern European film industry.

20.71   *The Round-Up:* geometric figures of power fill the wide screen.

20.72   The floating fluidity of Jancsó's long takes in *The Red and the White:* the youth flees the White soldiers at the river . . .

20.73   . . . comes up to the hospital cabin . . .

20.74 . . . and hides among the wounded . . .

20.75 . . . before a nurse comes out . . .

20.76 . . . and the camera follows her to the edge of the cabin . . .

20.77 . . . where she and the other nurses discover the Whites' atrocities at the river's edge.

20.78 Szabó cuts from newsreel shots of the 1956 Hungarian rebellion . . .

20.79 . . . to shots of his heroes marching with a crowd, in *Father*.

The younger generation of directors consisted largely of those who had graduated from the Academy for Theatre and Cinematography during the late 1950s. Entranced not only by the Nouvelle Vague but also by the Polish Young Cinema and European auteurs like Bergman and Antonioni, Hungarian directors pursued the goals of most new cinemas: to rethink their country's past and to present a portrait of contemporary youth.

For example, István Szabó presented his films as "the autobiography of a generation."[13] *The Age of Day-dreaming* (1964) portrays a new socialist technocracy: confident young people wear western sports clothes, take beach vacations, and talk of their love affairs while watching footage of Nazi horrors. Szabó sometimes romanticizes their lives with Nouvelle Vague techniques, as in lyrical slow-motion shots or citations of Truffaut, but as the film goes on, it questions material success.

Szabó's next film, *Father* (1966), probes the main character's mind in a way typical of the European art cinema generally. As in the films of Kluge and Straub, a play with time serves to pose questions about politics and history. Tako believes his father to be a war hero, but upon investigating his life, the son finds that history is more complicated. An interplay of memory, dreams, fantasy, and history in the hero's experience creates the ambiguity so characteristic of 1960s modernism. Just as *Hiroshima mon amour* treats newsreels as both documents and symbolic commentary, Szabó inserts footage of the 1956 uprising into his story, generating both a mild collage effect and a plausible sense that the characters are involved in the historical event (**20.78, 20.79**). In his attempt to fuse the concerns of contemporary youth with a critical study of his nation's past, Szabó typified the efforts of most directors in eastern Europe's new waves.

THE JAPANESE NEW WAVE

After a high-school girl is raped by a thuggish student, she agrees to seduce older men so that he can shake them down. When she becomes pregnant, the student gets money for her abortion by sleeping with an older woman. As the student is beaten to death by a gang, the young woman, riding with a man who has picked her up, tries to escape and is dragged to her death.

Aptly titled *Cruel Story of Youth* (1960), this film by the young Nagisa Oshima would scarcely have been recognizable as Japanese to western connoisseurs of Akira Kurosawa, Kenji Mizoguchi, and Yasujiro Ozu. Yet it is a typical product of the Japanese New Wave. The movement is all the more remarkable in being one of the few new cinemas deliberately created by a film industry.

The Japanese studios had jumped on the youth bandwagon early. During the mid-1950s, the newly revived swordfight movie catered to adolescent boys, while romantic melodramas were aimed at teenage girls. In 1956, *Season of the Sun*, adapted from a scandalous best-seller, brought forth a series of *taiyozoku* ("sun-tribe") movies, which depicted spoiled young people living an amoral, licentious lifestyle. Crime thrillers, rock-and-roll musicals, and swordplay films were ground out relentlessly, particularly at less prestigious studios like Nikkatsu and Toei. Thanks to the new strategy, 1958 movie attendance rose to just over a billion, a postwar high.

Shochiku, the most conservative Japanese studio, noted its rivals' triumphs with youth fare and observed the box-office success of French Young Cinema. The company decided to launch a Japanese New Wave. In 1959, the firm promoted a young assistant director, Nagisa Oshima, and allowed him to direct his own scripts. The success of his first films led Shochiku to promote other assistants. Nikkatsu followed suit, giving newly appointed directors substantial assignments.

At first, New Wave films attracted critical praise and proved somewhat popular with young audiences. But they could not halt a downturn in the box office. By 1963, the popularity of color television had pulled attendance to half its 1958 level. The studios tried desperately to win back the audience by lowering ticket prices, by making more violent swordplay films (e.g., the *Zato-*

ichi "blind swordsman" series), and by pioneering new genres—the *yakuza* (gambler-gangster) film and the "pink film" (soft-core pornography). Some of the New Wave directors contributed interestingly to these trends, but soon most of the filmmakers quit their studios.

Only a few years earlier this would have meant leaving filmmaking. Unlike European countries, Japan had a strong, vertically integrated studio system, and until the 1960s no one could easily work outside it. Moreover, the government did not encourage new talent through subsidies and prizes. But theaters' habits of showing double features created a larger appetite for releases than the studios could profitably satisfy. As a result, many New Wave directors were able to create independent production companies. While young directors' films were sometimes distributed by the big studios, a central role was played by the Art Theater Guild (ATG), a chain of specialized theaters. In 1964, the ATG began financing and distributing films, and it became the mainstay of the New Wave generation.

Like young cinemas elsewhere, the Japanese New Wave attacked mainstream cinematic traditions. Complex flashback structures, intrusions of fantasy and symbolism, and experiments with shot design, color, cutting, and camerawork became common. Directors splashed jarring compositions across the wide screen, and the hand-held camera and disjunctive editing came to the fore. But since mainstream Japanese films had explored such techniques before, they were perhaps less disruptive than the subjects, themes, and attitudes portrayed in the New Wave works.

No films had so savagely criticized Japanese society, revealing oppression and conflict behind the image of a tranquil, prosperous nation. Theft, murder, and rape were rendered casually. The directors flaunted the vulgarity of their heroes and heroines, and often the critique was framed in political terms. The Japanese directors went further than even their German contemporaries in showing that authoritarian forces continued to rule their country long after democracy had supposedly come.

All these qualities are evident in the work of Nagisa Oshima. Like his contemporary Truffaut, before getting into directing he wrote inflammatory film criticism. But, as a former student activist, he gave his articles a political slant alien to the French auteur critics. Oshima complained that Japanese society stifled the individual in the name of superficial harmony. He called for a personal cinema of the "active subject," in which the director expressed his deepest passions, anxieties, and obsessions. This view, a cliché in the West and one basis of postwar art cinema, was a breakthrough in Oshima's group- and

tradition-dominated nation. He and his New Wave peers created Japan's postwar modernist cinema.

Oshima saw flickers of active subjectivity in the wave of late 1950s student demonstrations against renewing the U.S.-Japan Security Treaty (known as "Ampo"). For the first time, the Japanese abandoned their time-honored role of obedient sufferer and saw themselves as able to change their fate. But Oshima quickly came to believe that the Ampo demonstrations led only to disillusionment. He traces this process in *Night and Fog in Japan* (1960), a scathing critique of the Communist party and the student left. Oshima intercuts student political activities from the 1950s with Ampo treaty demonstrations during 1960, rearranging their order to bring out parallels. He frames the two time schemes within a wedding ceremony that symbolizes a cynical surrender of political ideals. Shochiku shelved *Night and Fog in Japan* almost immediately after release, claiming that it was failing, but Oshima charged that the studio bowed to political pressures after the recent assassination of a Socialist leader. In protest he quit Schochiku, though several of his later films were produced with the company.

Throughout these films and others, Oshima pursued the question of how individual desires of the active subject, however warped, reveal the rigidity of political authority. His two major representations of these desires—criminality and eroticism—films that remain disturbing today. Moreover, Oshima refused to cultivate an identifiable style. *Cruel Story of Youth* frames most scenes in medium shots and tight, decentered close-ups (**20.80**). *Night and Fog in Japan,* comprising only forty-five shots, relies on disorienting camera movements that whip across theatrically poised tableaux (**20.81**). *Violence at Noon* (1966), by contrast, uses naturalistic staging and around 1,500 shots. Each film's style, Oshima maintained, sprang from his feelings and attitudes of the moment.

Other directors created more conventional methods of stylization while still expressing a degree of social criticism. Hiroshi Teshigahara, associated with a surrealist group and the novelist Kobo Abe, found international success with *Woman in the Dunes* (1963). This tale of a man trapped in a gigantic sandpit with a mysterious woman was widely interpreted as an allegory of how an arid society could be overcome by a primal eroticism (**20.82**).

More central to the New Wave was Yoshishige Yoshida, whom Shochiku promoted to director when Oshima's earliest work became successful. Yoshida admired Resnais and Antonioni, whose emphasis on pictorially

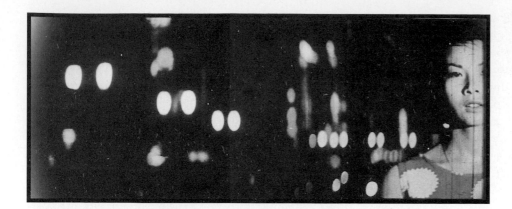

20.80 Just before the ending of *Cruel Story of Youth*, with the heroine's face split by the wide frame.

20.81 The quarreling leftists, framed in cramped, telephoto shots (*Night and Fog in Japan*).

20.82 In *Woman in the Dunes*, the protagonist's attempt to dig his way out of a sandpit results in an impressive avalanche.

striking images shows up in his work. His sensuous camera movements in *Akitsu Springs* (1962) owe less to Oshima than to *Last Year at Marienbad*. The film's concerns, however, remain resolutely historical, suggesting that, in the postwar era, Japan lost its chance for true democracy. Another Shochiku alumnus was Masahiro Shinoda, an assistant to Ozu and an admirer of Mizo-

guchi. Shinoda's films have a fastidiousness of visual design that echoes 1930s Japanese classicism (**20.83**).

Closer to Oshima's political perspective was the other major director to emerge from the New Wave, Shohei Imamura. Declaring his interest in "the lower part of the human body and the lower part of the social structure,"[14] Imamura sought to record Japan's forgotten regions, oppressed classes, and lustful impulses.

As a young director at Nikkatsu, Imamura became identified with the New Wave principally through his outrageously satiric *Pigs and Battleships* (1961). This story of a teenage thug whose gang raises pigs on black-market garbage is less stylized than Oshima's work of the period, but the political critique remains sharp. Presenting a society of petty racketeers, prostitutes, and mothers anxious to sell their daughters to GIs, Imamura equates the Japanese with the pigs feeding off refuse from U.S. warships. The hero dies in a moment of rebellion, cut down as he machine-guns a row of buildings (**20.84**).

Like Oshima's men, Imamura's are typically driven by perverse antisocial desires, but he often regards his heroes more mockingly, as in *The Pornographers* (1966). The final scene of *Pigs and Battleships* establishes the central Imamura character as the tough woman who fights for herself in a world dominated by men. *The Insect Woman* (1963) celebrates the pragmatism of three

20.83 This shot from Shinoda's *Assassination* (1965), echoes the poise of Mizoguchi displayed in the swordfight film.

20.84 *Pigs and Battleships:* the rage of youth against the world.

generations of postwar women who use prostitution and theft to win a measure of independence. In *Intentions of Murder* (1964), a woman, impregnated by her rapist, abandons him to death and lives for the sake of her son.

The Japanese New Wave brought recognition to many other filmmakers, both older directors like Kaneto Shindo (notable for *The Island*, 1960) and younger talents like Susumu Hani (*Bad Boys*, 1960; *She and He*, 1963). In addition, it created a climate of acceptance for experimentation. Koji Wakamitsu exploited the "pink" genre in gruesome, stylized films like *Violated Women in White* (1967). Seijun Suzuki's Nikkatsu films, with their eccentric black humor and comic-book exaggerations, made him a cult figure with young audiences. Executives were distressed to find that the New Wave they had created led young audiences to expect outrageous formal innovations and attacks on authority in even routine studio products.

BRAZIL: CINEMA NÔVO

In the late 1950s, young cinéphiles in Rio de Janeiro began meeting at movie theaters and coffeehouses. Intrigued by both Hollywood classics and contemporary European art films, the young men wrote articles calling for a change in filmmaking. Given opportunities in the commercial industry, they launched a movement: *Cinema Nôvo*, the Portuguese term for "New Cinema."

In outline, Cinema Nôvo's history conforms to that of many young cinemas, particularly the Parisian Nouvelle Vague. Yet the differences are striking. Although Brazil was in many ways a westernized country, it remained firmly a part of the underdeveloped Third World. The cinéphiles, far more politically militant than their counterparts in France, wanted their films to speak for the disenfranchised people of their country—the ethnic minorities, the peasants and landless laborers. Influenced by Italian Neorealism as well as the New Wave, the directors sought to record their nation's dilemmas and aspirations.

Cinema Nôvo films combined history and myth, personal obsessions and social problems, documentary realism and surrealism, modernism and folklore. In mixing populist nationalism, political criticism, and stylistic innovation, Cinema Nôvo recalled the Brazilian Modernist movement of the 1920s. It also chimed well with contemporary literary experiments and Augusto Boal's Theater of the Oppressed. The young directors became a link between the western new cinemas of the early 1960s and later Third World movements (see Chapter 23).

20.85   *Barravento* is filmed with a hand-held, zooming camera that dynamizes the *capoeira* fight/dance between Firmino and Aruan.

20.86   Hired by a landowner and a priest to kill the religious agitator Sebastião, Antonio das Mortes takes aim at his real target in *Black God, White Devil*.

20.87   The hand-held camera is used to follow the family's endless search for a home in *Vidas secas*.

The most populous country in South America, Brazil had a topography stretching from drought-parched areas to tropical beaches. Its population included groups of African, Amerindian, European, and Far Eastern descent. Through a policy of "developmental nationalism," President João Goulart sought to unify and modernize the country. His plan for achieving industrial capitalism required that people recognize the country's backwardness. Although under fire from both right and left, Goulart supported many liberal cultural initiatives.

Cinema Nôvo was one such effort. Nelson Pereira dos Santos had already made his mark with the neorealistic *Rio 40 Degrees* (1955) and was to serve as producer, editor, and inspiration to a group of younger men who came from film schools and film criticism. Like many New Wave directors before them, Brazil's filmmakers first tried their hands at short films. Ruy Guerra, Glauber Rocha, and Joaquim Pedro de Andrade made shorts while they were in their teens and early twenties. The anthology film *Slum Times Five* (1962) included episodes by Carlos Diegues, de Andrade, and others. Within a year, distinctive Cinema Nôvo features began to appear. Drawing on stylistic resources of other new cinemas—hand-held camera, zoom shots, plans-séquences, underplayed dramatic moments, temps morts, ambiguous leaps between fantasy and reality—these directors turned out politically critical works.

Many films concentrated on life outside the cities. Glauber Rocha's *Barravento* ("The Turning Wind," 1962) is set in Bahia. Firmino returns from the city and tries to persuade the fishermen to free themselves from bondage to the owner of their nets. He also comes into conflict with Aruan, a local holy man (**20.85**). Eventually Aruan becomes the new force of social consciousness.

Rocha's next film, *Black God, White Devil* (1963), is more disjunctive. Set in the *sertão*, Brazil's harsh northwestern plain, it shows the oppression of the peasants by messianic religious leaders and vicious bandits. Between the two forces stand the credulous follower Manuel and the gunman Antonio das Mortes (**20.86**). The story is modeled on folk ballads, and songs comment ironically on the action. When Antonio kills the bandit Corisco, a choir sings "The power of the people is the strongest power," followed immediately by a lengthy take of Manuel and his wife fleeing across the wastelands. "Sad, ugly films . . . screaming, desperate films where reason does not always prevail"[15]— Rocha's description of Cinema Nôvo's style of this period fits his own work perfectly.

Nelson Pereira dos Santos dealt with peasant life more austerely in *Vidas secas* ("Barren Lives," 1963). Adapted from a classic novel, the film traces the attempts of Fabiano to find work during the 1940s drought. The dedramatized, almost wordless opening sequences introduce his family's trek across the arid sertão (**20.87**). In the course of the film, the family picks up scraps of work, but Fabiano is unjustly arrested and beaten. The film ends as it began, with quasi-documentary images of the family on the move.

Ruy Guerra made one of the earliest Cinema Nôvo films, *Os Cafejestes* ("The Loafers," 1962), but his fame arrived with *Os Fuzis* ("The Guns," 1963). Soldiers arrive in a famine-ridden town to guard a landlord's warehouse. As the starving peasants pray for miracles, the soldiers idle away their time drinking, firing their rifles, and chatting with the truck driver Gaucho. At the film's climax, Gaucho leads an aborted rebellion. Guerra uses striking wide-angle close-ups as well as long shots, which dramatize the alignment of political forces (**20.88**).

These films' stylistic differences reveal the influence of the European auteur theory. Guerra's crisp deep-focus imagery, the bleached dedramatization of Pereira dos

Santos, and the flamboyant zooms and jerky cutting of Rocha mark each film as the product of a distinct sensibility. Most Cinema Nôvo directors followed Rocha in seeing the auteur theory as a vehicle of political critique. He considered cinematic authorship a reaction to the dominance of Hollywood; making idiosyncratic films was itself a revolutionary act.

The worldwide popularity of samba and bossa nova music and the building of the modernistic capital Brasília helped promote Cinema Nôvo as the expression of an energetic, modernizing country. More concretely, the films were oriented toward Goulart's ideology of consciousness raising. They show peasant Brazilians oppressed by illiteracy, subsistence living, and military and clerical rule. The sertão films exemplify what Rocha called an "aesthetics of hunger," the revelation of how centuries of suffering could burst into cathartic rebellion. "Cinema Nôvo shows that the normal behavior of the starving is violence."[16]

President Goulart's reforms aroused fears in conservative circles. In 1964, the military seized power. For more than two decades afterward, Brazil was ruled by generals. Guerra, who left the country soon after the coup, declared that Cinema Nôvo ended in 1964; however, the movement was not yet interrupted. Despite the authoritarian regime, politically critical art flourished. Cinema Nôvo directors continued to work, and new filmmakers entered the industry.

Several Cinema Nôvo directors reflected on the failure of the Goulart government. Their films often focus on the tormented intellectual, cut off from both the bourgeoisie and the people. Gustavo Dahl's *The Brave Warrior* (1967) ends with an idealistic politician about to shoot himself in the mouth. Rocha gave this despair an extravagant treatment in *Terra em transe* ("Land in Anguish," 1967). In the country of Eldorado, a political myth is played out within the delirious consciousness of a revolutionary poet. *Terra em transe* is a surrealistic interrogation of the artist's political role, culminating in an Eisensteinian sequence: while police fire at the poet, churchmen and businessmen hold a raucous celebration.

Despite the new regime, Brazilian film culture was advancing. Universities were starting film courses, an annual festival was begun in Rio, and new magazines appeared. The collapse of the Atlântida and Vera Cruz companies (p. 411) had seemed to end all prospects for a national film industry, but both Goulart and his military successors sponsored state initiatives aimed at rebuilding it. Legislation dictated tax exemptions, uniform ticket prices, and bigger screen quotas for the local product. The Grupo Executivo da Indústria Cine-

20.88 *Os Fuzis:* a truckload of onions in the right foreground is off-limits to the peasants, kept passive and frightened by the soldiers.

20.89 *Antonio das Mortes:* in the town square, Antonio and the bandit reenact the battle that climaxed *Black God, White Devil.*

matográfica (GEICINE) was created in 1961 to coordinate film policy. In 1966, GEICINE was absorbed into the Instituto Nacional do Cinema (INC), which supported production through loans and prizes. Cinema Nôvo had a strong influence on the agency. The INC also assisted coproductions, which sharply increased national film output.

This expansion was aided by an abrupt turn of political events. As inflation increased in 1967 and 1968, so did strikes and protests. A second coup took place, installing hard-line generals. They pushed through legislation curtailing civil liberties and dissolving political parties. Leftist forces launched urban guerrilla war, and, between 1969 and 1973, Brazil was a battleground between terrorists and the military regime.

As usual, Rocha was quick to comment on contemporary conditions. *O Dragão da maldade contra o santo guerreiro* ("The Evil Dragon versus the Holy Saint," aka *Antonio das Mortes*, 1969) revisits the subject of *Black God, White Devil,* but now the mystic and the bandit are seen as affirmative forces. No longer are the peasants benighted victims; revolution arises out of folk rituals, such as theater and festival. Accordingly, Rocha's technique is more stylized. The people become the audience as the antagonists play out their conflicts in a bare, semitheatrical arena (**20.89**). In asking spectators to consider his films as part of an evolving personal vision,

Rocha continued to take European auteur cinema as a model. Yet he also pushed toward political militancy. He saw *Antonio das Mortes* as an instance of "guerrilla filmmaking" in which the cold-blooded killer had obvious analogies with the new regime.

As part of the military government's plan to centralize cultural activities, film policy was recast. Censorship became much stiffer. In 1969, an agency was created to control filmmaking. Empresa Brasileira de Filmes (Embrafilme) was charged with organizing film export and financing production, much as France's CNC did. Through low-interest loans to successful firms, Embrafilme helped boost production to a postwar high of ninety-one films in 1971. The agency would eventually absorb the INC and fuel Brazil's export success in the 1980s.

Although production was flourishing, political repression drove many artists out of the country. Rocha and Diegues made films elsewhere, while Guerra returned to make a film in 1970 and then departed once more. The Cinema Nôvo directors who stayed altered their filmmaking in distinctive ways.

One trend, which encompassed music and theater as well, was called "tropicalism." This was a comic and grotesque celebration of indigenous popular culture. Instead of Cinema Nôvo's didactic insistence on the backwardness of rural life, tropicalism treated folk culture as brimming with vitality and wisdom. Joaquim Pedro de Andrade's *Macunaíma* (1970), for example, is an exuberant comic epic blending Brazilian myths with contemporary satire. Filmed in brilliant color, full of surreal gags and sudden switches of tone, *Macunaíma* became the first Cinema Nôvo film to win large audiences.

Throughout *Macunaíma* the lazy, deluded hero is confronted with cannibalism as a way of avenging oneself on enemies. This motif, an echo of 1920s literary movements, became another element of Cinema Nôvo work of the period. The metaphor of cannibalism showed authentic Brazilian culture ravenously incorporating colonial influences. In *How Tasty Was My Little Frenchman* (1972), Pereira dos Santos's Direct Cinema technique and voice-over narration show a French colonialist captured by a tribe of Tupinamba. He is allowed to live among them before he is executed and eaten. The film dwells satirically on the cultural and economic dynamics of imperialism, as when the greedy colonist and the white trader open a grave in their search for treasure (**Color Plate 20.5**).

Both tropicalism and cannibalism were in the tradition of Brazil's "festive left," which traditionally paid homage to popular culture. Rocha saw in these qualities a way for filmmakers to connect with myth and to guide people toward "anarchic liberation."[17] These trends could win a wider audience than did the astringent realism or flamboyant experiments of earlier Cinema Nôvo efforts. The competition of television serials and erotic comedies (the *pornochanchada*) also pushed filmmakers toward more accessible, spectacle-centered works.

As Cinema Nôvo became a prestige cinema, winning financial support from INC and Embrafilme, a more extreme avant-garde arose to challenge it. Colleges, ciné-clubs, and archives began to screen samples from the *udigrudi*, or "underground." Rogerio Sganzala's *Red Light Bandit* (1968), Andrea Tonacci's *Bla Bla Bla* (1968), and Julio Bresanne's *Killed the Family and Went to the Movies* (1969) were all-out assaults on good taste. Gruesome scenes of murder and vomiting were recorded in deliberately sloppy technique. This self-proclaimed "aesthetics of garbage" savagely mocked the aesthetics of hunger, and many scenes parodied films by Rocha, Guerra, and their peers. Cinema Nôvo, its edge blunted by exile or cooperation with the state-controlled film industry, was no longer a disruptive force.

Diegues and Guerra continued to make politically critical films in exile. Rocha became even more militant. He denounced Cinema Nôvo's formative influences—Neorealism and the Nouvelle Vague—declaring that Third World revolution would overturn both Hollywood and the tradition of European authorship represented by Jean-Luc Godard, Roberto Rossellini, and Sergei Eisenstein. In this he echoed the manifestos of "imperfect cinema" and "Third Cinema" elsewhere in the hemisphere.

Years before, Rocha and his colleagues had been, as Diegues put it, "making political films when the [French] New Wave was still talking about unrequited love."[18] The young Rio cinéphiles had helped launch a tradition of political modernism that swept through the world during the next decade, as we shall see in Chapter 23.

Cinematic modernism, revived in the decade after World War II, became even more prominent between 1958 and 1967. While established directors consolidated the trend, young auteurs experimented with novel techniques and applied them to new subjects. Now art-cinema films were likely to be fragmentary and nonlinear in their time and space, provocative and puzzling in their storytelling, ambiguous in their thematic implications.

Moreover, many young cinemas were explicitly, and critically, political. In this respect, the Nouvelle Vague, influential in so many ways, lagged behind. Outside France, many filmmakers assaulted myths about national history, cast a severe eye on contemporary social conditions, celebrated rebellions against authority, and dissected the mechanisms of repression. Older directors like Resnais and Jancsó and youthful talents like Godard, Pasolini, Straub, Kluge, Chytilová, Makavejev, and Oshima were laying the groundwork for a "political modernism." This trend would become central to international cinema in the decade after 1968.

Notes and Queries

CENSORSHIP AND THE FRENCH NEW WAVE

The Nouvelle Vague was not socially or politically critical in the fashion of most young cinemas, partly because French censorship remained strong throughout the period. Films treating France's colonial wars (in Indochina until 1954, and Algeria until 1962) were suppressed. After some mayors had banned Vadim's *Les Liaisons dangereuses* (1960), the Centre National de la Cinématographie strengthened its power over controversial scripts and films. According to a 1961 decree, no film could be shot unless the script was approved by the president of the CNC, and the Ministry of Information had final say over which films could be shown. Politically critical films circulated clandestinely, and police began raiding political meetings and ciné-clubs. As a result of the new policy, films by Resnais (*Muriel*, 1963) and Godard (*Le Petit soldat*, 1960) were delayed or banned because of their references to the Algerian war.

NEW FILM THEORY

The success of Fellini, Bergman, and the other postwar directors discussed in Chapter 19 encouraged the auteur theory developed in France, Britain, and America. Similarly, the young or first-time directors of the late 1950s and early 1960s triggered new ways of thinking about cinematic meaning in general and modernist filmmaking in particular.

The most influential trend in film theory of this period was that of *semiology*. The ancient study of signs in culture, or "semiotics," was revived in the twentieth century by the linguist Ferdinand de Saussure and taken up in Europe in the postwar era. One of the most influential codifications of semiological doctrine was Roland Barthes's book *Elements of Semiology* (1964). Soon this perspective was applied to film, most notably by Christian Metz. (See *Film Language: A Semiotics of the Cinema*, trans. Michael Taylor [Chicago: University of Chicago Press, 1990; originally published 1968].) Italian proponents of semiology include Umberto Eco (notably his *La Strutture assente* of 1968, revised as *A Theory of Semiotics* [Bloomington: Indiana University Press, 1976]) and Pier Paolo Pasolini, who proposed the controversial idea that cinema uses nonlinguistic signs to duplicate our perception of everyday reality and psychological states. Pasolini, like Metz and others, felt a special need to explain the innovativeness of the second phase of postwar film modernism. He proposed that the Young Cinema depended heavily on a "free indirect discourse" that combines the author's point of view with that of a character. (See Pasolini, "The Cinema of Poetry," in Louise K. Barnett, ed., *Heretical Empiricism* [Bloomington: Indiana University Press, 1988], pp. 167–86.) As this line of argument suggests, the new film theory did not immediately seek to overturn the auteur approach to criticism; rather, it often promised to put auteurism on a more rigorous, even "scientific" basis.

REFERENCES

1. Quoted in Peter Graham, ed., *The New Wave* (Garden City, New York: Doubleday, 1968), p. 92.
2. Quoted in Jean-Luc Douin, *Godard* (Paris: Rivages, 1989), p. 26.
3. Claude Chabrol, *Et Pourtant je tourne . . .* (Paris: Laffont, 1976), p. 181.
4. Quoted in Oswald Stack, *Pasolini on Pasolini* (Bloomington: Indiana University Press, 1969), p. 49.
5. Ibid., p. 109.
6. Quoted in Noël Simsolo, *Conversations avec Sergio Leone* (Paris: Stock, 1987), p. 93.
7. Quoted in "Young German Film," *Film Comment* 6, 1 (spring 1970): 44.
8. Quoted in " . . . Preferably Naked Girls," in Eric Rentchsler, ed., *West German Filmmakers on Film: Visions and Voices* (New York: Holmes & Meier, 1988), p. 42.
9. Andrei Tarkovsky, *Sculpting in Time: Reflections on the Cinema*, trans. Kitty Hunter-Blair (London: Faber and Faber, 1989), p. 30.
10. Quoted in Peter Hames, *The Czechoslovak New Wave* (Berkeley: University of California Press, 1985), p. 187.
11. Quoted in Daniel J. Goulding, *Liberated Cinema: The Yugoslav Experience* (Bloomington: Indiana University Press, 1985), p. 72.
12. Quoted in Jean-Pierre Jeancolas, "Le Cinéma hongrois de 1963 à 1980," in Jean-Loup Passek, ed., *Le Cinéma hongrois* (Paris: Pompidou Center, 1979), p. 48.

13. Quoted in Graham Petrie, *History Must Answer to Man* (Budapest: Corvina, 1978), p. 107.
14. Quoted in Audie Bock, *Japanese Film Directors* (Tokyo: Kondansha, 1978), p. 293.
15. Quoted in Randal Johnson and Robert Stam, eds. *Brazilian Cinema* (Austin: University of Texas Press, 1982), p. 70.
16. Ibid.
17. Quoted in Sylvia Pierre, *Glauber Rocha* (Paris: Cahier du Cinéma, 1987), p. 139.
18. Quoted in Johnson and Stam, *Brazilian Cinema*, p. 33.

FURTHER READING

"Agnès Varda." *Études cinématographiques* 179–186 (1991).
"Alexander Kluge." *October* 46 (fall 1988).
Armes, Roy. *The Films of Alain Robbe-Grillet.* Amsterdam: John Benjamins, 1981.
Benayoun, Robert. *Alain Resnais: Arpenteur de l'imaginaire.* Paris: Stock, 1980.
Brown, Royal S., ed. *Focus on Godard.* Englewood Cliffs, NJ: Prentice-Hall, 1972.
Desser, David. *Eros Plus Massacre: An Introduction to the Japanese New Wave Cinema.* Bloomington: Indiana University Press, 1988.
Gerber, Jacques, ed. *Pierre Braunberger: Producteur; Cinémémoire.* Paris: Pompidou Center, 1987.
Godard on Godard. Trans. and commentary by Tom Milne. New York: Viking, 1972.
Greene, Naomi. *Pier Paolo Pasolini: Cinema as History.* Princeton, NJ: Princeton University Press, 1990.
Hill, John. *Sex, Class and Realism: British Cinema 1956–1963.* London: British Film Institute, 1986.
Johnson, Randal. *Antônio das Mortes.* Trowbridge, England: Flicks Books, 1998.
———. *Cinema Novo X 5: Masters of Contemporary Brazilian Cinema.* Austin: University of Texas Press, 1984.
Lutze, Peter C. *Alexander Kluge: The Last Modernist.* Detroit: Wayne State University, 1998.
Murphy, Robert. *Sixties British Cinema.* London: British Film Institute, 1986.
Rohmer, Eric. *The Taste for Beauty.* Trans. Carol Volk. Cambridge, England: Cambridge University Press, 1989.
Siclier, Jacques. *Nouvelle Vague?* Paris: Cerf, 1961.
Stoil, Michael J. *Balkan Cinema: Evolution after the Revolution.* Ann Arbor: UMI Research Press, 1982.
Truffaut, François. *The Film in My Life.* Trans. Leonard Mayhew. New York: Simon and Schuster, 1975.
Van Wert, William F. *The Film Career of Alain Robbe-Grillet.* Pleasantville, NY: Redgrave, 1977.

CHAPTER 21

DOCUMENTARY AND EXPERIMENTAL CINEMA IN THE POSTWAR ERA, 1945–MID-1960s

In the two decades after World War II, documentary and avant-garde filmmaking underwent enormous changes around the world. New technologies and institutions altered the basis of independent filmmaking. These developments were often connected to the rise of the commercial art cinema and the emergence of new waves.

Both documentarists and avant-gardists renewed the idea of a personal cinema. In the 1930s, the Spanish civil war, Stalin's rigged trials of his former associates in Moscow, and the rise of fascism and militarism had led to genocide and a world war. Now many artists turned from political commitment (see Chapter 14) to a conception of individual expression. This impulse, most notable in the rise of Abstract Expressionist painting in the United States and Europe, was also visible in experimental film. Even the postwar documentary film became more of a vehicle for the filmmaker's beliefs and feelings than had been usual before.

Another prevailing idea was a new interest in capturing unpredictable events on film. Before 1950, most documentary cinema had sought to control chance to a great degree. The filmmaker might record a casual action, but that would be smoothly absorbed into a larger structure of meaning by virtue of editing and voice-over commentary. Most major documentarists, from Dziga Vertov and Robert Flaherty to Pare Lorentz and Humphrey Jennings, had resorted to even more strongly controlling techniques, such as staging scenes for the camera. But Neorealism, particularly in Cesare Zavattini's pronouncements, had seen truth in the uncontrolled event. In the 1950s lightweight cameras and sound equipment allowed documentarists to eliminate the artifice of voice-over commentary and preplanned structure, creating a cinema centered on the spontaneous moment.

At the same time, avant-gardists revived dada and surrealist conceptions of the revelatory accident. John Cage, for example, composed

21.1, *left*   *The Silent World*: this view toward the ocean's surface suggests the new freedom given divers by Cousteau's invention, the aqualung.

21.2, *right*   Flirtation on the stoop (*In the Street*, Helen Levitt, Sidney Loeb, and James Aree).

musical pieces that incorporated chance and environmental sounds. His *Imaginary Landscape no. 4* (1951) consisted of twelve radios tuned to different stations according to chance. Postwar experimental filmmakers, as well as workers in other arts, often adapted Cagean ideas by incorporating accidents as part of self-expression. Lucky aberrations of light or color could become part of a larger form. By the late 1950s and early 1960s, the sort of objectivity courted by documentarists entered the avant-garde as well. In the work of the Fluxus group and of Andy Warhol, the artist no longer expressed personal feelings but rather invited the spectator to scrutinize a process or witness an improvised scene. Because this approach risked boring the audience, these avant-gardists, like their documentary counterparts, in effect asked audiences to accept a cinema that refused to arouse and fulfill the narrative appetites to which Hollywood catered.

TOWARD THE PERSONAL DOCUMENTARY

At the end of the war, most documentary filmmaking remained in the hands of large institutions. Pathé, news organizations, and the Hollywood studios issued newsreels and informational films for theatrical exhibition. Government agencies in many countries supported documentary units, which produced informational and propaganda films for schools and civic organizations. Corporations sponsored films that promoted products, as when Shell Oil backed Flaherty's lyrical *Louisiana Story* (1948).

After the early 1950s, fewer documentaries appeared on theater programs. Television journalism displaced the weekly newsreels, and studios ceased to produce them. Yet television also provided a new market. For example, before the war the feature-length documentary had been rare, but by the early 1960s it became more common, aimed at television broadcast or occasional theatrical exhibition.

In the postwar era, most of the older documentarists slackened their pace. Vertov supervised a newsreel series

until his death in 1954. After *Louisiana Story*, Flaherty was unable to complete a film, though before his death in 1951 he produced several shorts. John Grierson left the National Film Board of Canada in 1945 but then presided over several efforts to make documentary-style fiction films and documentary television series. Only Joris Ivens remained active as a director, teaching and making films in Poland, China, Cuba, and other nations aligned with the USSR.

Innovative Trends

A new generation of documentarists appeared during the first decade after the war. Although some had begun their careers during the war, the freer circulation of films in peacetime helped their work become known internationally. Most of these individuals worked within well-tried genres, but others innovated more significantly.

In the film of nature and exploration, for example, the Swede Arne Sücksdorff used telephoto lenses and hidden cameras to bring the viewer into the midst of wildlife in *The Great Adventure* (1954). Oceanographer Jacques Cousteau perfected undersea photography in a series of films exploring marine life (*The Silent World*, 1956; **21.1**; *World without Sun*, 1964).

The film of social observation also attracted idiosyncratic talents. The tabloid photographer Weegee toured the seamy side of city life in *Weegee's New York* (1950). Less sensationalistic was *In the Street* (1952), an unpolished evocation of the world of the New York poor (**21.2**). Perhaps the most important observational film of the period was Georges Rouquier's *Farrebique* (1946), a chronicle of the struggles of a French peasant family during 1944 and 1945. Much of the film was staged and drew on conventions of fictional cinema (**21.3, 21.4**). Yet Rouquier minimizes voice-over commentary in order to savor the regional dialect, and he skillfully evokes the routines and travails of the Farrebique farm.

The film of reportage, though largely replaced by television coverage, still held a place, especially when it could present an event in fresh ways. Kon Ichikawa's

21.3, 21.4 *Farrebique:* During labor, Berthe clutches the sheet, and Rouquier dissolves to a flower opening as a shriek is heard and her baby is born.

21.5 Haanstra pokes fun at the gestures of salesmen in a Dutch auto show (*Alleman*).

21.6 Labor-camp inmates are fed in *Le Retour.*

21.7 The compilation film as an investigation of the past: the Spanish civil war in *To Die in Madrid.*

21.8 *Point of Order:* after accusing Senator Joseph Welch's associate of espousing communism, Senator Joseph McCarthy tries to shrug off Welch's rebuke ("Until this moment, Senator, I never truly gauged your cruelty or your recklessness").

21.9 Boys of the Kalihari desert practice archery (*The Hunters*).

Tokyo Olympiad (1965), for example, did not try to duplicate television coverage of the 1964 Olympics but instead used over 150 cameramen and a virtuosic barrage of techniques to capture the human toil of the games. Similarly, the city symphony (see Chapter 8) continued in such works as Frank Stauffacher's *Sausalito* (1948), Francis Thompson's *N.Y., N.Y.* (1957), and Bert Haanstra's *Alleman* (*Everyman*, 1960; **21.5**).

The compilation documentary had become a staple of the wartime film diet, and it retained its importance in the years that followed. One of the most powerful was Henri Cartier-Bresson's *Le Retour* (1946), using U.S. military footage to show the liberation of the Nazi POW camps and the prisoners' return to their homes (**21.6**). The feature-length compilation film flourished in the

hands of a new generation of filmmakers. Frédéric Rossif's *To Die in Madrid* (1962; **21.7**) marked the mainstream success of a politically critical use of the genre. With *Point of Order* (1964), a recapitulation of the U.S. Senate's 1954 investigation of charges against Senator Joseph McCarthy, Emile De Antonio established himself as one of the most skillful exponents of the compilation genre (**21.8**).

Ethnographic cinema was rejuvenated as anthropologists began to employ more professional standards. Flaherty's approach to exotic societies—a search for drama, an emphasis on the clash of humans and nature, a willingness to restage events—gave way to an attempt to record remote cultures more neutrally and accurately. During the 1950s, the American John Marshall filmed customs of the Bushmen of the Kalihari desert, and anthropologist Robert Gardner helped him assemble the footage into *The Hunters* (1956). Following four men hunting a giraffe, the film adheres to the Flaherty tradition, but it marked an important stage in the sober recording of folkways (**21.9**). Gardner went on to make the most famous American anthropological film, *Dead Birds* (1963), in which he recorded, with a minimum of interference, the Dani people of Indonesia as they fought a war.

The National Film Board and Free Cinema

Most innovative documentarists of the postwar era worked on an artisanal basis or on a film-by-film arrangement with a funding group. The National Film Board of Canada (NFB) had been formed in 1939 by John Grierson, and it concentrated on short animated and documentary films. Despite its government funding, the board sought to institutionalize innovation—to give idiosyncratic talents a bureaucratic structure that could help them express individual viewpoints. A typical NFB documentary is *City of Gold* (1957, Colin Low and Wolf Koenig). Ostensibly a historical view of the gold rush in Dawson City, it was framed as a meditation on the contrasts between the town as it had been in the 1890s and the modern town, in which the narrator had been raised (**21.10**). Of those who stayed in the town despite finding no gold, he concludes, "These men found their El Dorado."

The trend toward individual innovation was most evident in the work of several filmmakers who found ways to express their personal attitudes via the documentary. This trend arose simultaneously with *Cahiers du cinéma*'s auteur policy, which emphasized the director's personal vision in fictional and commercial film. Not surprisingly, many of the directors of *personal documentaries* moved into mainstream fiction production.

In Great Britain, the personal documentary came to prominence in a short-lived movement called Free Cinema. Karel Reisz, Lindsay Anderson, and other members of the group had been associated with the film magazines *Sequence* (1947–1952) and *Sight and Sound*. In these forums they had expressed hostility to both commercial filmmaking and the current state of British documentary. They called for a "free" cinema that would express the director's commitment to deep personal views. Thanks to the British Film Institute's Experimental Film Fund and to occasional corporate sponsorship, several of the Free Cinema filmmakers were able to make short documentaries before becoming the core filmmakers of the British Kitchen Sink cinema (see Chapter 20).

Most of the films expressed the directors' attitudes toward contemporary, urbanizing Britain. Popular culture formed a central subject. Anderson's *O Dreamland* (1953) reflected on the public's need for a cheap night out, while Tony Richardson's *Momma Don't Allow* (1956) and Reisz's *We Are the Lambeth Boys* (1958) ren-

21.10 In *City of Gold,* old-timers from gold-rush days gossip, with a modern Coca-Cola ad in the background.

21.11 Reisz's Lambeth boys drive back through Whitehall, the framing juxtaposing their youthful rowdiness with a postcard London cityscape.

21.12 A deaf child learns about speaking by touching her teacher's jaw in *Thursday's Children.*

dered teenagers' lifestyles with considerable affection (**21.11**). More traditional subjects were treated with a new restraint. Anderson's film about Covent Garden's markets, *Every Day Except Christmas* (1957), emphasized work routines and earthy language, while his

21.13 "No description, no image can restore their true dimension: endless, uninterrupted fear": the barracks in *Night and Fog*.

21.14 A book shut into its cell in *Toute la mémoire du monde*.

21.15 A junkyard yields surrealist icons in *Le Sang des bêtes*.

Thursday's Children (1954) offered an optimistic view of a school for deaf children by capturing the pupils' spontaneous cheerfulness (**21.12**).

France: The Auteurs' Documentaries

In France as well, personal expression emerged in the documentary. The government funded films about art and culture, both subjects that traditionally allowed filmmakers to inject their own viewpoints. By 1953, the government was actively encouraging short quasi-experimental films. In addition, *Cahiers du cinéma*, like *Sequence*, considered artistic cinema to depend on directorial expression (following the auteur idea; see Chapter 19). Pierre Braunberger, Anatole Dauman, Paul Legros, and other producers gave directors a free hand in the making of poetic or essayistic documentaries.

Alain Resnais achieved his reputation as a documentarist with a series of films on art. *Van Gogh* (1948), which won a prize at Venice and an Academy Award, set forth a new method of portraying a painter's work. Instead of considering each painting as a whole and in chronological order, Resnais delineated Van Gogh's private world across his entire career. He panned over a canvas to show the rhythm of a line and intercut details from different paintings without supplying an orienting long shot. Resnais modified his tactic for *Guernica* (1951), intercutting Picasso's sketches and notes with photographs and headlines from the Spanish civil war. More controversial was *Les Statues meurent aussi* ("Statues Also Die," 1953), which Resnais codirected with his friend Chris Marker. This study of African art in western museums implies that the colonizers destroyed the cultures of the lands they invaded. The film was banned.

Resnais's two most honored documentaries explore the nature of historical memory. *Nuit et brouillard* (*Night*

and Fog, 1957) gives a clipped, unsensationalized image of the Nazi concentration camps akin to Resnais's treatment of the atomic bomb in *Hiroshima mon amour*. He cuts between a deserted prison seen today—in a bright countryside, filmed in full color—and newsreel footage of the camps in operation. Instead of playing up the horror, *Night and Fog* dwells upon the impossibility of ever truly capturing the past. As the camera probes the ruins, the commentator asks, "How to discover what remains of the reality of these camps?" (**21.13**). At the end, the commentary suggests that the impulses that created the holocaust are far from extinguished today.

More optimistic is *Toute la mémoire du monde* ("All the World's Memory," 1957), a study of the French national library. Resnais's camera glides through the gloomy storerooms and stacks, creating a series of metaphors: the library as labyrinth, as prison (**21.14**), and as gigantic brain. The film's somber lyricism celebrates the desire to know the truth and to remember the past.

Resnais's work ran parallel to that of Georges Franju. Both men were born in 1912, made their first significant film in 1948, and moved to fiction features after the explosion of the New Wave in the late 1950s. Of Franju's numerous documentaries, the most influential were *La Sang des bêtes* (*Blood of the Beasts*, 1948) and *Hôtel des Invalides* (1951). In these films Franju set out to disturb his audiences in a way reminiscent of the Surrealists and of Luis Buñuel's *Las Hurdes*.

Le Sang des bêtes records a day in a slaughterhouse. It emphasizes the casual professionalism of the butchers and the violence necessary to put meat on plates. But Franju also juxtaposes images of suffering animals with the homes and churches surrounding the slaughterhouse. Accidental details of this quiet neighborhood take on bizarre aspects (**21.15**). In this context, a shot of calves' heads stacked like cabbages exudes the disturbing poetry sought by Buñuel and Salvador Dalí.

21.16, *left*   The juxtaposition of the military past and its consequences in *Hôtel des invalides*.

21.17, *right*   "But first, look at her—to the point where she becomes an enigma, as words endlessly repeated become unrecognizable": the closing of Marker's *Description of a Struggle*.

21.18, *left*   *Les Maîtres fous*: the celebrants stalk up and down in a frenzy. At this point in his career, Rouch used a long lens, which allowed him to stay at a distance from the action, an approach he would later abandon.

21.19, *right*   In a dance hall, Edward G. Robinson is "in" the story action and so ignores Rouch's camera, while Eddie Constantine and the others frankly acknowledge it.

Hôtel des invalides does much the same for a national war memorial. In this monument to war's glory, the film discloses images of suffering (**21.16**). Franju dwells on the ominous overtones of military memorabilia, as when a general's bust resembles a shattered skull. Franju later brought this vision of the disquieting aspects of everyday life to feature films.

The films of Chris Marker, more cerebral and freely structured than those of Resnais and Franju, epitomize the use of documentary for personal expression. A professional photographer and a world traveler, Marker produced a series of essayistic documentaries expressing complex opinions and ironic wit.

Marker explores two documentary modes. One is the travelogue, which he treats as a pretext for a free-ranging reflection on western ideas of exotic cultures. *Dimanche à Pekin* (*Sunday in Peking*, 1956) and *Lettre de Sibérie* (*Letter from Siberia*, 1958) take banal, almost tourist-movie images and, through a dense poetic commentary, meditate on the storybook clichés representing non-European cultures. *Letter from Siberia* is both a parody of the travelogue and a highly formalized reflection on documentary film's inability to capture the truth of a culture. In the film's most famous sequence, Marker demonstrates the power of voice-over commentary by running the same series of shots three times, each time changing the narration to create different meanings.

Marker also made political documentaries. In *Cuba Sí!* (1961), he appraises Castro's revolution in the face of U.S. attacks. *Le Joli mai* (1963) brought a political critique to bear on the new trend of Direct Cinema. But Marker's highly personal stance often confounds orthodox leftist positions. His reflections on Israel (*Description of a Struggle*, 1961) mix praise, criticism, humor, and a tourist's fascination (**21.17**).

Jean Rouch and Ethnographic Documentary

While Resnais, Franju, and Marker were defining varieties of the personal documentary, another French filmmaker was bringing this attitude to the ethnographic film. In 1946, the young anthropologist Jean Rouch took a 16mm camera on his first field trip to Niger, and on a later visit he took along a portable tape recorder. The short ethnographic documentaries he made led to his being named head of the newly created International Commission of Sociological and Ethnographic Film.

Rouch's influence began to be felt with his controversial *Les Maîtres fous* ("The Mad Masters," 1957). While in Ghana in 1955, he was asked by priests of the Hauka cult to film their ceremonies of possession. Rouch recorded cult members in a trance, pacing frenziedly, foaming at the mouth, and eventually eating a dog. What differentiates this film from sensationalized portraits of "primitive" Africa is the fact that the participants adopt the identities of the colonialists who rule them. By day the cultists are dockers and cattle herders, but, at the ritual, one becomes an army captain, another the governor, a third an elegant French lady (**21.18**). Rouch's doctoral thesis argued that in parodying their rulers, the Hauka release their feelings of imperialist oppression. "This violent play," the film's commentary warns, "is only the reflection of our civilization."

Les Maîtres fous caused a scandal. Many African countries banned it, and both Europeans and Africans urged Rouch to destroy it. Nonetheless, it won a prize at the Venice Film Festival and reinforced Rouch's desire to document the effects of colonialism in the Third World. His next film, *Moi un noir (Treichville)* ("Me, a Black Man [Treichville]," 1959), shows people in the Ivory Coast consciously imitating western life. Surrounded by the trappings of European culture, menial laborers take new names: Edward G. Robinson, Tarzan, Dorothy Lamour. The hand-held camera follows them drinking, searching for jobs, and drifting through dance halls. Rouch also displays their aspirations, notably the dream of Ivorian Edward G. Robinson to become a prizefighter. *Moi un noir* becomes an intriguing mixture of fiction and documentary (**21.19**). Rouch showed the edited film to Robinson, whose comments during the screening were added to the sound track.

Ethnographic film, in Rouch's eyes, was of paramount importance for westerners because it showed the differences among societies, preventing Europeans from "trying to transform [other cultures] into images of ourselves."[1] Rouch was criticized for delineating the psychological effects of colonialism without presenting Africans who seek to change their lives through social action. But he saw his project in less political terms. He sought to give ethnographic film a human dimension, not only by showing westerners other cultures, but also by using the filmmaking act to create a bond between the researcher and the subject. Having brought Edward G. Robinson into the movies, he made him his assistant. (Years later, under his given name, Oumarou Ganda, Rouch's protagonist became one of Niger's most important filmmakers.) Rouch made films, he claimed, primarily for the people he filmed and for himself, to preserve his experiences in the culture. His involvement with his subjects, and his willingness to break technical rules if they interfered with human immediacy, also led him toward another documentary trend, Direct Cinema.

DIRECT CINEMA

Between 1958 and 1963, documentary filmmaking was transformed. Documentarists began to utilize lighter and more mobile equipment, to work in smaller crews,

and to reject traditional conceptions of script and structure. The new documentary sought to study individuals, to reveal the moment-by-moment development of a situation, to search for instants of drama or psychological revelation. Instead of staged scenes dominated by a voice-over narration, the new documentary would let the action unfold naturally and permit people to speak for themselves.

Called *candid cinema, uncontrolled cinema, observational cinema,* and *cinéma vérité* ("cinema truth"), this trend was most generally known as Direct Cinema. The name suggests that the new technologies recorded events with an unprecedented immediacy and that the filmmaker avoided the more indirect documentation—restaging, narrational commentary—of earlier documentarists.

Several factors influenced the new approach. Most generally, Italian Neorealism had intensified documentarists' urge to capture everyday life. Technological innovations, such as the growth of 16mm production and the emergence of sound-on-tape, provided a new flexibility (see box). Moreover, television needed motion pictures to fill airtime, and network news organizations sought a fresh approach to audiovisual journalism. In the United States, Canada, and France, documentarists affected by these conditions forged distinct versions of Direct Cinema.

The United States: Drew and Associates

In the United States, Direct Cinema emerged under the auspices of the photojournalist Robert Drew. Drew wanted to bring to television reporting the dramatic realism he found in *Life* magazine's candid photography. In 1954, he met Richard Leacock, who had worked on *Native Land* (p. 304) and had been cinematographer for Flaherty's *Louisiana Story*. With the backing of Time, Inc., Drew hired Leacock, Don Pennebaker, David and Albert Maysles, and several other filmmakers.

Drew produced a series of short films aimed at television broadcast, including the ground-breaking *Primary* (1960), a report on the Wisconsin primary contest between John Kennedy and Hubert Humphrey. Leacock, Pennebaker, the Maysleses, and Terence Macartney-Filgate all worked as cinematographers. Although the film contained some lip-sync sound, its visual authenticity attracted more attention. The camera followed the politicians working the streets, riding from town to town, and nervously relaxing in hotel rooms (**21.20–21.22**). *Primary*'s drama was heightened by crosscutting between the two candidates and by voice-over news reports, which largely replaced explanatory commentary.

NEW TECHNOLOGY FOR THE NEW DOCUMENTARY • • • • • • • • • •

Eastman Kodak introduced the 16mm gauge in 1923, chiefly for home movies and educational films. During the 1930s, some American avant-gardists began using the gauge for experimental work (p. 318). During World War II, 16mm came into wider use. It was well suited for combat filming, and 16mm prints of educational and propaganda films circulated among military stations and on the home front. The U.S. government donated 16mm projectors to schools and civic organizations so they could screen government releases. After the war, documentary and experimental filmmakers around the world eagerly took up the format.

Television arrived in Europe and North America in the early 1950s. In those prevideotape days, the cheapness and flexibility of 16mm made it the standard gauge for reportage, commercials, and TV films. Manufacturers began to produce professional 16mm cameras. These usually had zoom lenses and reflex viewfinders, which allowed the filmmaker to sight directly through the lens during filming. In 1952, the Arriflex 16 established a new standard for ease of operation and became the model for most professional 16mm. In addition, Eastman and other companies developed a range of 16mm film stocks, often "fast" emulsions that permitted filming in relatively low light.

Two further developments led to Direct Cinema. Before the mid-1950s nearly all professional 16mm cameras were so heavy that steady shots could be obtained only if the camera was anchored to a tripod. Yet attaching a standard camera to a tripod was time-consuming; by the time the camera was set up, the action had usually passed. The drawbacks of using a tripod encouraged documentarists to restage events. In addition, the bulky camera made subjects aware of the act of filming. Only filmmakers using amateur equipment, such as Rouch in his ethnographic shorts and Stan Brakhage in his experimental *Desistfilm* (1953), could easily shoot hand-held.

Around 1958, several manufacturers introduced lighter 16mm professional cameras. The Auricon Cinevoice and the Eclair Cameflex each weighed around sixty pounds, light enough to be anchored on a shoulder brace. An improved model of the Arriflex 16 weighed just twenty-two pounds. The prototype KMT Coutant-Mathot Eclair, made available to Rouch for *Chronique d'un été* (1961), weighed

21.20 The most famous shot in *Primary:* Albert Maysles's camera, held above his head, follows Kennedy through a crowd of supporters . . .

21.21 . . . into a corridor (note the distortions created by the wide-angle lens) . . .

21.22 . . . and onto the stage, where another Drew cameraman can be glimpsed waiting to capture a reverse angle.

Shortly afterward, Drew and Leacock were commissioned to make several films for ABC television, notably *Yanki, No!* (1960), an examination of anti-U.S. feelings in Latin America, and *The Children Were Watching* (1960), a study of school integration. Between 1961 and 1963, Drew Associates made twelve more films, including *Eddie* (1961), *Jane* (1962), and *The Chair* (1962). Ten of these films became known as the "Living Camera" series. By now they fully exploited direct sound.

Drew, who exercised editorial control over most of the films made by the company, saw documentary as a way of telling dramatic stories. "In each of the stories there is a time when man comes against moments of tension, and pressure, and revelation, and decision. It's these moments that interest us most."[2] For Drew, Direct Cinema gripped audiences through what came to be called its *crisis structure.* Most Drew-unit films center on a high-stakes situation to be resolved in a few days or hours. The film arouses the viewer's emotion by showing

less than twenty pounds. Holding such a camera, the film-maker could pan quickly, walk with the subject, ride in a car, follow the situation wherever it led.

Just as important were improvements in sound recording. Documentaries had relied on voice-over narration partly because filmmakers could not easily record lip-synchronized sound outside the studio. It was far less trouble to add music, background noise, and commentary to a string of images than to let the participants speak for themselves. Only in highly prepared circumstances—a politician giving a speech before a microphone, a person interviewed in a studio—was it possible to record lip-sync sound during filming. Even the relatively spontaneous Free Cinema films suffered from the limitations of sound recording.

During the early 1950s, both fiction and documentary filmmakers began to replace optical sound-on-film recording with magnetic sound, recorded on tape. Documentarists consequently tried to capture sound on-site with a portable tape recorder. The Swiss company Nagra introduced a tape recorder for filmmaking in 1953 and made an improved version available four years later.

The problem now was synchronizing the picture track with sound recorded on the spot. Around 1958, engineers devised the Pilotone system, by which an electric pulse is sent from the camera to the recorder and registered on one track of the tape. In playback, the pulse automatically adjusts the speed of the tape to correspond to the picture. Most early versions of the Pilotone system used a cable to connect the camera to the recorder. This umbilical cord hampered the freedom of movement that Direct Cinema sought, so engineers created radio-transmission systems. A quartz crystal or a tuning fork in the camera emitted a pulse that the recorder picked up and recorded as a guide for synchronization. The wireless system, first used extensively in the United States, became standard internationally by the mid-1960s.

Although synchronization and camera noise still posed problems, by 1958 portable 16mm cameras and recorders, along with smaller microphones and faster film stocks, had triggered a revolution in filmmaking practice.

conflict, suspense, and a decisive outcome. *Primary* exploits the crisis structure, as does *The Chair*, which shows lawyers' struggles to save a rehabilitated convict from execution. The crisis puts the participants under stress and reveals their personalities. Often, as in *Eddie* or *Jane*, the protagonist fails to achieve the goal, and the film ends with a scrutiny of his or her emotional reaction.

Drew used multiple crews on most films, tracing out several lines of action and intercutting between different forces racing against the clock. He encouraged each cameraman to efface himself, to accustom the subjects to his presence, and to respond intuitively to the developing drama. The approach was that of feature journalism, in which the reporter balances respect for the facts with subjective judgments about selection and emphasis.

Soon Drew's filmmakers left the unit to form their own companies. The Maysles brothers departed to make *Showman* (1962), a study of film producer Joseph E. Levine, and *What's Happening! The Beatles in New York* (1964). Far more episodic than the Drew films, the Maysleses' projects avoided the crisis structure and offered casual, sketchy portraits of show-business celebrities. *What's Happening!*, the first Direct Cinema film in the United States to omit voice-over narration entirely, was simply a diary of the Beatle's tour, rousing one pro-

fessional television producer to complain, "As most documentary filmmakers understand the film, it was hardly a film at all."[3]

Don Pennebaker and Richard Leacock also left Drew Associates, forming their own firm. Pennebaker made a study of handicapped twins (*Elizabeth and Mary*, 1965) and specialized in films documenting American popular music (*Don't Look Back*, 1966; *Monterey Pop*, 1968; *Keep on Rockin'*, 1970). Leacock went on to make *Happy Mother's Day* (1963), showing how the birth of quintuplets disrupts a small town; *A Stravinsky Portrait* (1964); and *Ku Klux Klan—The Invisible Empire* (1965).

Leacock, the most proselytizing of U.S. Direct Cinema filmmakers, advocated what he called "uncontrolled cinema." The filmmaker would not interfere with the event; the filmmaker simply observed, as discreetly and responsibly as possible. Leacock believed that a self-effacing crew could become so integrated into a situation that people would forget they were being filmed.

The purpose of uncontrolled cinema, Leacock claimed, is "to find out some important aspect of our society, by *watching how things really happen* as opposed to the social image that people hold about the way things are *supposed* to happen."[4] Leacock's concern for Direct Cinema's power to reveal social institutions through

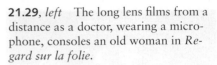

21.29, *left* The long lens films from a distance as a doctor, wearing a microphone, consoles an old woman in *Regard sur la folie.*

21.30, *right* Referring to the end of *Chronique d'un été*, Ruspoli's camera leaves a conversation behind and confronts the viewer.

21.31, *left* *Le Joli mai:* "The others don't count much for you, do they?" "The others? What others?"

21.32, *right* In the shooting-gallery scene that opens "The Return of Fantomas," *Le Joli mai* builds up the atmosphere of political menace pervading "happy" Paris.

Ruspoli's films lie midway between the American "observational" method and the Rouch-Morin "provocational" one. At times, the camera style is discreet, even surreptitious (**21.29**). Yet, even more than Rouch, Ruspoli flaunts the act of recording, showing his crew and ending *Regard sur la folie* with the camera turning from a conversation between doctors to advance toward us (**21.30**). We are continually aware of the filmmaker's presence even if the subjects are not.

A direct criticism of Rouch and Morin's method is to be found in Chris Marker's *Le Joli mai* ("The Pretty May," 1963). Marker could not embrace the Direct Cinema trend, preferring always to retain the voice of a narrator who reflects on the images before us. *Le Joli mai* absorbs Direct Cinema techniques into a larger meditation on freedom and political awareness.

The first part of the film inquires into the state of happiness in Paris in May 1962, the moment when the Algerian war ended. Marker's aggressive questioning of smug or oblivious people pushes the camera-as-catalyst tactic to the point of rudeness. He also criticizes the limited, apolitical notion of happiness from which *Chronique* began. (Marker ironically dedicates his film "To the happy many.") A clothes salesman says that his goal in life is to make as much money as possible; a couple in love are indifferent to social issues (**21.31**). Part two, opening with mysterious evocations of terrorism and right-wing reprisals (**21.32**), consists of interviews with people who seek political solutions to contemporary problems.

Harsh and acerbic, shot through with Marker's quirky humor and poetic digressions, *Le Joli mai* asks cinema vérité to recognize the complexity of life and the political forces governing French society at a historical turning point. Yet Marker's meditation has its base in Direct Cinema; his evidence consists partly of his lip-sync interviews. "Truth is not the destination," he conceded, "but perhaps it is the path."[7]

The American, Canadian, and French exponents of Direct Cinema were keenly aware of each others' work. Many of them first met at a 1958 seminar. At a conference at Lyon in 1963, Direct Cinema documentarists debated their differences. Should the camera observe, empathize, or challenge? Is it more authentic to film with several cameras at once? Should the director be the camera operator? Above all, what is the responsibility of the director to the people, their lives, and the event recorded? Direct Cinema, apart from its technical and technological innovations, raised perennial issues of the ethics of documentary film.

By the mid-1960s, several sophisticated 16mm and 35mm cameras offered all filmmakers the flexibility of Direct Cinema. The trend revolutionized documentary; after the early 1960s, most documentarists utilized the hand-held camera to snatch bits of arresting action (**21.33**). Direct Cinema also gave ethnographic filmmaking a new flexibility. It shaped the course of several national cinemas: the French Canadians Groulx and

21.33, *left*   A "snapshot" made possible by the lightweight 16mm camera: Kazimierz Karabasz's *Musicians* (1960).

21.34, *right*   In Peter Watkins's *The War Game* (1966), the staging of a nuclear attack on Britain gains intensity through use of Direct Cinema; here, a hand-held shot captures a fireman collapsing by a child.

Jutra moved into features on the basis of their NFB work, while directors in Third World countries made Direct Cinema central to their style (see Chapter 23).

The open-ended, episodic narratives of Direct Cinema also reinforced tendencies in the fiction films of the art cinema. Stylistically, most of the new waves from 1958 to 1967 pledged themselves to the hand-held camera, available light, and apparently off-the-cuff shooting (see Chapter 20). (Few directors, however, undertook the harder task of recording direct sound.) More mainstream films, such as *Dr. Strangelove; or, How I Learned to Stop Worrying and Love the Bomb* (1963), *Seven Days in May* (1964), and *A Hard Day's Night* (1964) invoked Direct Cinema techniques when a sense of spontaneous action was required. Even fiction films set in the distant past or the future could intensify their realism (**21.34**). And Direct Cinema became a central tool of western militant cinema of the 1960s, which relied on unstaged interviews, footage shot on the fly, and the ease of taped sound. In both technology and technique, Direct Cinema exercised a powerful international influence throughout the 1960s and 1970s.

EXPERIMENTAL AND AVANT-GARDE CINEMA

The experimental film also renewed itself after World War II. The wider availability of 16mm equipment made experimental filmmaking more feasible for the nonprofessional. Most schools, universities, and museums in the United States had 16mm projectors and could show experimental films. Foreign classics had been available on 16mm from the Museum of Modern Art, but after the war new companies began to circulate experimental films in that gauge. In Europe, which largely lacked 16mm distribution, newly founded or reopened film archives screened classic experimental films.

A growing number of institutions nurtured experimental cinema. Hundreds of ciné-clubs sprang up in cities and universities throughout Europe; because of censorship laws, avant-garde works barred from general screenings could only be shown in such venues. An international federation of ciné-clubs was created in 1954. International festivals appeared as well, most significantly the Experimental Film Competition at Knokke-le-Zoute, Belgium, begun in 1949. Occasionally European governments offered funding for imaginative "cultural films." In France, theaters designated to show *art et essai* (artistic and experimental) films received some government subsidy.

The most dramatic growth of an experimental film culture occurred in the United States. Here 16mm film stock and equipment were available, universities and art schools began film production departments, and the wartime work of Willard Maas, Marie Menken, brothers John and James Whitney, and other experimentalists started to circulate. Moreover, Hans Richter, Oskar Fischinger, and other older avant-gardists had emigrated to America. Experimental film acquired a public identity with Richter's feature-length *Dreams that Money Can Buy* (1946), a batch of vaguely surrealist sketches by prominent avant-gardists.

Throughout the period, most filmmakers funded their work in the time-honored ways: from their own pocketbooks or from a patron. Although the U.S. government and private foundations stepped up support for the fine arts generally, only a few filmmakers won grants. Still, in the postwar era, a number of new exhibition venues emerged. Frank Stauffacher's "Art in Cinema" series, presented at the San Francisco Museum of Art immediately after the war, crystallized interest on the West Coast. The New York City film society Cinema 16 was founded in 1949 and grew to a membership of 7,000. In 1960, Canyon Cinema in San Francisco became a similar venue. Students at Dartmouth, Wisconsin, and other universities founded campus film societies, and many were eager for alternatives to commercial fare. A national association of film societies, the Film Council of America (later the American Federation of Film Societies), began in 1954.

THE FIRST POSTWAR DECADE: MAYA DEREN

The figure of Maya Deren dominated the first decade of postwar experimental film in the United States. She achieved recognition with two films made in wartime, won a prize at the Cannes Film Festival, and became the emblematic figure of the American avant-garde. Renting a New York theater for her screenings, sending flyers to film societies to advertise her work, lecturing mesmerically, she inspired an intellectual public with a new respect for artistic film.

Deren initially studied literary criticism and then became interested in dance. She worked as secretary to the choreographer Katherine Dunham, who inspired in Deren an enduring interest in Caribbean cultures, particularly the dance and religion of Haiti.

In 1943, Deren and her husband, Alexander Hammid, collaborated on what would become the most famous American avant-garde film, *Meshes of the Afternoon*. A woman (played by Deren) has a series of mysterious encounters with a hooded figure whose face is a mirror. She passes through chambers (**21.35**), splits into several personalities, and eventually dies.

The drifting protagonist and the dream structure were conventions of what came to be called the *trance film*. Strong cues that the images are projections of the heroine's anxieties also initiated a long line of "psychodramas" in American experimental film. Stylistically, *Meshes* creates a nonrealistic spatial and temporal continuity through false eyeline matches of the sort already exploited in the avant-garde tradition.

Hammid (whose original name was Hackenschmied) had made some experimental narratives himself in his native Prague, and *Meshes* has strong resemblances to *Un Chien andalou*, *Blood of a Poet*, and *Vampyr*. But Deren disavowed

21.35   Air and space as gauzy barriers in *Meshes of the Afternoon*.

any connection with the European tradition of experiment, rejecting the continental version of Surrealism for relying too much on the unconscious. "Creativity," she noted, "consists in a logical, imaginative extension of a known reality."[8] Moreover, making a woman the protagonist alters the implications of the role changes (**21.36, 21.37**).

Deren went on to make another psychodrama, *At Land* (1944), in which she plays a woman emerging from the sea and crawling across a variety of landscapes. This film was almost completely Deren's creation, with Hammid serving occasionally as a technical adviser.

Deren's postwar films marked a new phase in her creative development. She initiated a series of dance films with *A Study in Choreography for Camera* (1945), an exploration

21.36, *left*   *Meshes of the Afternoon:* the abject figure of the early sequences . . .

21.37, *right*   . . . becomes a cool assassin.

21.38 *A Study in Choreography for Camera:* the dancer lifts a leg in a forest . . .

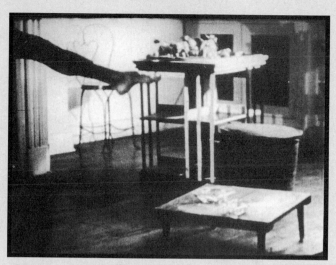

21.39 . . . and through a match-on-action cut, the movement continues in a studio.

of the unique ways in which framing and editing could create an "impossible" time and space (**21.38, 21.39**). A similar examination of movement dominates *Meditation on Violence* (1948), a choreographic study of Chinese boxing.

Ritual in Transfigured Time (1946) combines techniques of the dance films with the trancelike narrative of psychodrama. A woman whose identity shifts across two bodies drifts through three rituals—domestic work (**21.40**), flirtatious socializing, and sexual pursuit. Slow motion, freeze-frames, and Deren's elliptical match cuts "transfigure" the time of these social rites. Deren saw deep affinities between artistic form and the rote gestures of social ceremonies. "Historically, all art derives from ritual. In ritual, the form is the meaning."[9]

Supported by a Guggenheim grant, Deren went to Haiti to make a film on Voudoun dance and ritual. Although she never competed the film, she did publish a book, *Divine Horsemen: The Voodoo Gods of Haiti* (1953). Before her death in 1961, she finished another dance film, *The Very Eye of Night* (1959).

In New York, Deren adopted the image of a Voudoun priestess, gifted with the power to bless her friends and curse her enemies. An extroverted, dynamic organizer, she formed a community of filmmakers in 1953, eventually named the Independent Film Foundation, which held monthly meetings for screenings, lectures, and heated disputes.

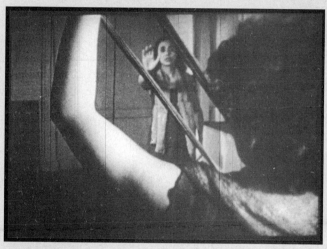

21.40 *Ritual in Transfigured Time:* winding yarn as an image of both unwinding time and women's domestic rituals.

In specialized journals and the general press, Deren promoted avant-garde cinema. She also elaborated a provocative theory of film form and expression. She distinguished between a "horizontal" cinema that emphasizes action and plot and a "vertical" cinema that "probes the ramifications of the moment," emphasizing not what is happening but "what it feels like or means."[10]

21.41 Poets Gregory Corso and Allen Ginsberg spar in *Pull My Daisy*.

Distribution, always a problem for independent American cinema, also expanded considerably. Amos Vogel started a Cinema 16 distribution library, and other companies followed. The founding of the Film-Makers' Cooperative in New York in 1962 marked a milestone. The cooperative accepted all work, making no judgment of quality, and received a flat percentage for rentals. A year later, the Canyon Cinema Cooperative was established on the West Coast.

The United States had developed an infrastructure for supporting the avant-garde cinema. Tastemakers had emerged: Maya Deren, Amos Vogel, the critic Parker Tyler, and Jonas Mekas, editor of the key New York journal *Film Culture* (founded in 1955), organizer of the Film-Makers' Cooperative, and film reviewer for the *Village Voice*. By 1962, anyone with access to 16mm or even 8mm equipment could make a film, and it had a chance of being distributed and discussed. While New York was displacing Paris as the capital of modern painting, the United States had become the leading force in avant-garde cinema. In the postwar decade, the filmmaker most responsible for establishing experimental cinema in the United States was Maya Deren (see previous box).

As in earlier epochs, experimental filmmakers were more closely tied to the world of the fine arts than to the commercial film industry. Some filmmakers continued to animate abstract paintings or illustrate passages drawn from classical music (e.g., Jean Mitry's *Pacific*

231, 1949). Stylistically, several postwar filmmakers were influenced by Surrealism and Dada. During the 1950s, others found inspiration in contemporary trends that favored an intuitive, personal approach to creation. Abstract Expressionist painting had centered on the spontaneous creativity of the artist, who might splatter and drip paint as Jackson Pollock did. Critics compared this "gestural painting" to the writings of Jack Kerouac and other "Beats," who advocated an impulsive, nonintellectual approach to experience.

Some avant-garde painters and poets moved into film. In Paris, the Lettrist movement of the late 1940s experimented with the pure sound of verse and the arrangement of letters on the printed page; it soon made filmmaking integral to its program. A breakaway Lettrist group eventually founded the "antiart" Situationist International, which also produced several films. In the early 1960s in the United States, experimental films were made by artists associated with Pop Art and the Fluxus group. Avant-garde composers, such as Steve Reich and Terry Riley, assisted their filmmaker friends by scoring films or performing live accompaniment.

At certain moments, experimental filmmaking spread beyond the fine-arts world and made contact with wider audiences. Typically, this occurred when the filmmakers addressed a distinct subculture of viewers. For example, *Pull My Daisy* (1959) attracted attention because of its ties to the Beat milieu; its narration was written and recited by Jack Kerouac, and its veneer of loose improvisation reflected the "hip" attitude to life (**21.41**). Soon afterward, experimental films drew audiences in the worldwide "counterculture."

Abstraction, Collage, and Personal Expression

The new avenues of expression encouraged the continuation of many tendencies of the prewar period. Dada and surrealist influences continued throughout the postwar era. For example, Dada's antiart impulses can be seen in the films made by the French Lettrists. Their leader, Isidore Isou, argued that linguistic signs were more important than images. In an updating of the strategy of Marcel Duchamp's *Anémic cinema* (1926; p. 178), he argued for a *cinéma discrépant* ("cinema of discrepancy"), in which the sound track dominates the image. Guy Debord's Lettrist film *Hurlements en faveur de Sade* ("Howls for de Sade," 1952) carried out Isou's program by eliminating all images. A silent black screen alternates with a white screen that is accompanied by a voice-over harangue.

Surrealist imagery pervaded the work of the Polish animator Walerian Borowczyk. His *Les Jeux des anges* ("Games of Angels," 1964), made in France, presents a series of undefinable objects and nonsense syllables flying past the camera before what seem to be disembodied human organs start to fight. *Renaissance* (1963) uses stop-motion in reverse to make messy heaps of material on a floor assemble into a series of ordinary but disquieting objects: a table, a stuffed owl, an antique doll (**21.42**). In the end, a grenade explodes the still life.

Besides dada and surrealist tendencies, four major trends dominated avant-garde filmmaking between the late 1940s and the early 1960s: abstract film, experimental narrative, the lyrical film, and the experimental compilation film.

Abstract Film The abstract film had emerged in the 1920s with such works as Walter Ruttmann's *Lichtspiel Opus 1* and Viking Eggeling's *Diagonal Symphony* (p. 176). Several Americans who made abstract films during the war (p. 321) continued their experiments in the postwar decades. Harry Smith, who created his early abstractions directly on the film strip, began to use a camera to shoot painted imagery (**Color Plate 21.1**). Douglass Crockwell employed cut-outs, frame-by-frame painting, and color-veined blocks of wax in *Glens Falls Sequence* (1946) and *The Long Bodies* (1947; **Color Plate 21.2**). Marie Menken painted designs on film that present one pattern onscreen and another when one examines the film strip (for example, *Copycat*, 1963; **Color Plate 21.3**).

21.42   The reassembly process nears completion in *Renaissance*.

The Canadian Norman McLaren practiced a great many forms of animation, including Cohl's technique of animating three-dimensional objects (dubbed by McLaren "pixillation"). It was, however, principally his abstract animation that garnered praise for his unit at the National Film Board. Soon after Len Lye, McLaren mastered painting and scratching directly on film, and his hand-painted *Begone Dull Care* (1949) and *Blinkety Blank* (1955; **Color Plate 21.4**) were shown and admired in art cinemas throughout North America.

Two other exponents of abstraction, John and James Whitney, won a prize for their *Variations* (1943) at Knokke in 1949. John went on to experiment with computer imagery, while James devised a dot-painting method that could generate mandala shapes and kinetic patterns reminiscent of Op Art (**Color Plate 21.5**). In a similar vein was the abstract animation of Jordan Belson, who sought to induce Zen-like states (**Color Plate 21.6**).

Smith, McLaren, the Whitneys, and Belson presented rich, elaborate works, but other filmmakers took a more reductive approach to abstraction. The Viennese filmmaker Dieter Rot created his "Dots" series (1956–1962) by punching different-size holes in black leader. When projected, the holes appeared as shifting or expanding white disks. Perhaps the height of such reduction was reached in *Arnulf Rainer* (1960). Here the Austrian Peter Kubelka created a film wholly out of clumps of pure white and black frames, which created a rhythmic flicker onscreen and produced spectral afterimages in the viewer's eye (**21.43**).

All these experiments relied on filming purely abstract designs, often frame by frame. The filmmaker could also shoot objects in ways that brought out their abstract qualities. This approach, earlier identified with cinéma

21.43 Peter Kubelka before a wall to which strips of his flicker film *Arnulf Rainer* are attached.

pur (p. 179), had been launched by Fernand Léger and Dudley Murphy's *Ballet mécanique* (1924), and it was taken up throughout the postwar era. Charles and Ray Eames's *Blacktop* (1950) recalls Joris Ivens's *Rain* in its scrutiny of the patterns formed by foaming water. In Kubelka's *Adebar* (1957), printing processes turn footage of people dancing in a café into a flow of negative images, inverted or flipped end for end. Shirley Clarke's *Bridges Go Round* (1958) employs more complicated laboratory effects, including tinting and superimposition to bring out the bridges' soaring arcs (**Color Plate 21.7**).

Pure pictorial design and the abstract handling of familiar objects mix frantically in the witty films of the American Robert Breer. While in Paris in the early 1950s, he experimented with single-frame filming. The technique was established in animation, but, instead of changing a single object or drawing frame by frame, Breer hit on the idea of making each frame a completely different image. In *REcreation* (1956), abstract images swirl together with close-ups of tools, writing utensils, toys, photos, and drawings (**Color Plate 21.8**). Breer went on to incorporate animated footage, handwriting, and other material, as in *Fist Fight* (1964; **Color Plate 21.9**). His films establish a new threshold of minimal clarity: in the context of single-frame images, a shot of four or five frames becomes distinct and vivid. The avant-garde equivalent of cartoons, Breer's works exude the gentle humor and childlike wonder that we find in the paintings of Paul Klee.

Some European films were abstract in yet another sense. Their makers organized the images into rigorous patterns according to formulaic rules. Whether the shot displayed a pure design or a distinct object, the filmmaker could build the shots into an unfolding structure that owed nothing to narrative. The most evident precursor of this approach is Charles Dekeukeleire's *Impatience* (1929; p. 183), with its few motifs inexorably reiterated. In postwar Austria, avant-garde artists were under the sway of formalistic painting and the serial music of Arnold Schoenberg and Anton von Webern, so it is not surprising that the two major proponents of structural abstraction were the Viennese Peter Kubelka and Kurt Kren.

Building on the discoveries of Breer, as well as on the rhythmic cutting of the French Impressionists and the Soviet Montage directors of the 1920s, Kubelka formulated a theory of "metrical" film: "Cinema is not movement. Cinema is a projection of stills—which means images which do not move—in a very quick rhythm."[11] Kubelka concluded that the basic units of cinema were not shots but the single frame and the interval between one frame and the next. The director could assemble frames into a fixed series and then build the film out of variations and manipulations of that series. For example, because the musical phrase to be used in *Adebar* lasted twenty-six frames, Kubelka decided that all his shots of dancing couples would be either thirteen, twenty-six, or fifty-two frames. These shots would combine to form "phrases."

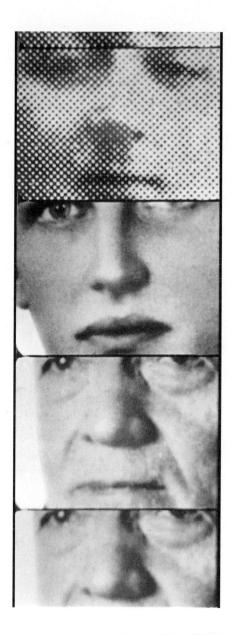

21.44 Kren's *2/60:* the effect onscreen is that of turning heads, blinking eyes, and transformed features.

21.45 *Mother's Day:* mother's "lovely boys and girls" are frozen in childish postures recast by adult fantasy.

21.46 A game of hopscotch in *The Lead Shoes,* with the lens enhancing the quality of heaviness evoked by the title.

Kubelka then varied the phrases according to a set of self-imposed rules; for example, a cut could link only positive and negative images. *Adebar* ends when all the combinations of shots have been exhausted. The process consumes a mere ninety seconds.

Like Kubelka, Kurt Kren worked with shot units of only a few frames, but his exercises in structural abstraction paid more attention to the imagery. His frame-by-frame patterning is applied to material that is more recognizable despite the brevity of each shot. For example, *2/60 48 Köpfe aus dem Szondi Test* ("2/60 48 Heads from the Szondi Test," 1960 [Kren numbers and dates his films]) atomizes a set of photo-cards from a psychological test (**21.44**). His *5/62 Fenstergucker, Abfall, Etc.* ("5/62 Window Watchers, Garbage, Etc.," 1962) teases the viewer with repeated shots ordered according to strict rules. At the start, each shot of the window watchers lasts only a single frame. As the film goes on, each image extends to two frames, then three, then five, and so on. Kren's formulas are less mathematically intricate than Kubelka's, but their patterning is more geared to the spectator's memory of specific images.

Experimental Narrative   In *Entr'acte, Un Chien andalou, Histoire de détective,* and other films, the 1920s experimentalists had challenged the storytelling conventions already developed by the world's film industries. After World War II, filmmakers continued to create narratives that differed significantly from those produced by mainstream film industries.

Deren's *Meshes of the Afternoon* and *At Land* (p. 490) had crystallized the tendency toward psychodrama that emerged in the symbolic dramas of the Surrealists and French Impressionists of the 1920s. American filmmakers found the psychodrama a congenial form for expressing personal obsessions and erotic impulses. In its fluid mixture of subjective and objective events, the genre anticipated the exploration of narrative ambiguities that characterizes the postwar European art cinema.

Psychodramas commonly present fantasy tales through highly stylized techniques. James Broughton's *Mother's Day* (1948) offers an adult's fantasy projection of childhood. Adults play children's games, framed in striated, off-center tableaux (**21.45**). By contrast, distorting lenses intensify the grotesque plot of Sidney Peterson's *The Lead Shoes* (1949; **21.46**).

21.47 *Bells of Atlantis*: a super-imposition reminiscent of French Impressionism (compare with 4.8).

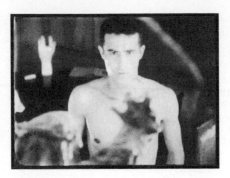

21.48 In *Fireworks*, the protagonist, played by Anger himself, stares at himself in a shot that recalls the mirror imagery in Jean Cocteau's films.

21.49 Photos of pain/ecstasy burn in *Fireworks*.

21.50 *Un Chant d'amour*: prisoners share smoke through a straw.

21.51 Tensions between a couple in Brakhage's *Reflections on Black*.

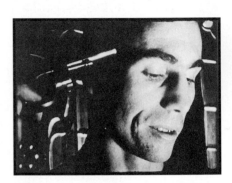

21.52 John takes his life in Maclaine's tense and brooding *The End*.

21.53, *left* A U.S. missile targets Khrushchev in *Science Friction*.

21.54, *right* Esoteric imagery in *Heaven and Earth Magic*.

As in *Meshes* and surrealist works, postwar psychodramas are often presented as dreams. Ian Hugo's *Bells of Atlantis* (1952) uses languorous superimpositions to create an underwater world (**21.47**), but, according to Anaïs Nin's voice-over commentary, "This Atlantis could only be found at night by the route of the dream." Similarly, Kenneth Anger's *Fireworks* (1947) elaborates a dream structure reminiscent of *Blood of a Poet* (p. 318; **21.48**). The story of a young man drawn to a sailor and then beaten by a gang of sailors ends with the hero awakening alongside his lover as flames consume photographs of dream images (**21.49**).

Gregory Markopoulos also used dreams and hallucinations to motivate erotic fantasy. Like Anger, he structured his films around protagonists who stood in for himself; like Cocteau, he filled his narratives with references to classical mythology. He made *Psyche* (1947) while a student at the University of Southern California and then completed several films (*Lysis*, 1948; *Charamides*, 1948) in his hometown of Toledo, Ohio. In *Swain* (1950), an inmate of a mental hospital fantasizes escape from his prison and from confining masculine roles.

Anger and Markopoulos brought male homosexual themes and imagery into films with an explicitness not

21.55 The improvised "hanging-out" narrative: Jack Smith as the Spirit of Listlessness in *Little Stabs at Happiness*.

21.56 In *The Invention of Destruction*, real people are dwarfed by animated machines in a style that recalls nineteenth-century engravings.

previously seen in the avant-garde. So did French poet Jean Genet in *Un Chant d'amour* ("Song of Love," 1950), which presents desire among prisoners and guards with surrealist touches but without the abili of dream or hallucination (**21.50**). Psychodramatic narratives express heterosexual drives as well. Stan Brakhage's *Reflections on Black* (1955) presents a series of variations on male-female relationships through a mysterious blind man's visit to an apartment house (**21.51**).

Apart from dramas of erotic longings and personal anxiety, postwar experimental films offered large-scale narratives. Some, like Christopher Maclaine's sepulchral *The End* (1953), warned against nuclear holocaust (**21.52**). Several filmmakers offered satiric or mystical fables. Stan VanDerBeek's Pop-flavored *Science Friction* (1959) stages the cold war through animated cut-outs taken from TV imagery and news-media caricature (**21.53**). Harry Smith's cut-out animations, culminating in *Heaven and Earth Magic* (1958), present bizarre narratives dominated by occult symbolism (**21.54**).

Far more loosely organized are the anecdotal, almost home-movie, narratives cultivated by filmmakers influenced by the Beat and hipster milieus. *Pull My Daisy* is an example of this genre; another is Ken Jacobs's *Little Stabs at Happiness* (1959), featuring Jack Smith, founder of a vaudeville act called "The Human Wreckage Revue" (**21.55**). Ron Rice's *Flower Thief* (1960) follows the misadventures of the roguishly goofy Taylor Mead, one of the "stars" of American experimental film.

European animators were particularly noteworthy for their experiments with narrative. After the war, several of the newly socialist eastern European countries formed small, state-supported animation units that often allowed filmmakers a considerable degree of creative freedom. In Czechoslovakia, for example, the puppet animator Jiří Trnka started working in 1945. As with many eastern European animators, his work made veiled comments on the contemporary political situation while celebrating national culture, especially folklore. The latter tendency is evident in *Old Czech Legends* (1953). Trnka's last film, *The Hand* (1965), is an allegory of artistic freedom. A little artisan who makes flowerpots is pressured by a huge, officious hand into making a sculpture of it; when he finally agrees, he must work in a giant cage (**Color Plate 21.10**). Ironically, Trnka was able to make this fable of state-controlled art in a Communist-supported studio.

Another major Czech animator, Karel Zeman, seemed to comment on the nuclear-arms race in his feature *The Invention of Destruction* (aka *The Fabulous World of Jules Verne*, 1957), which combines live action, special effects, and animation to create an elaborate science-fiction film about a menacing factory hidden inside a mysterious island (**21.56**).

The most prominent of the eastern European animation units was in Yugoslavia. Founded in 1956, the Zagreb studio gained a reputation for highly stylized cartoons, most of them specifically aimed at an adult, art-cinema audience. The films, with simple or lyrical stories that needed little or no dialogue, had considerable international appeal. The comedies usually satirized modern life, as in *Ersatz* (1961, Dušan Vukotić), in which a man's visit to the beach ends when everything—

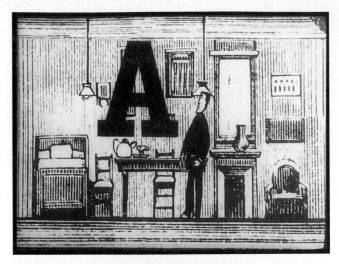

21.57 The protagonist confronts his nemesis in *A*.

21.58 The discomfited hero tries to retrieve his nose, now grown into a government official.

including the hero and the scenery—turn out to be inflatable imitations.

Jan Lenica began work in Poland, moved to France, and also worked in Germany. His French-made *A* (1964) typifies much European narrative animation by combining the humorous and the threatening. A writer is tyrannized by an enormous letter "A" that invades his home (**21.57**); then, just as he thinks he has finally gotten rid of it, a giant "B" appears.

Alexandre Alexëieff and Claire Parker, back in France after the war, continued to support themselves by doing advertisements. They also made more pinboard films (p. 320). *The Nose* (1963), an adaptation of a tale by Nikolay Gogol, alludes evocatively to the original story rather than presenting it in linear fashion (**21.58**).

The Lyrical Film   As continuations of prewar genres, abstract film and experimental narrative appealed to well-established avant-garde conventions. But new genres were created as well. The most influential is called the poetic, or lyric, film. Here the filmmaker seeks to capture a personal perception or emotion, much as a poet conveys a flash of insight in a brief lyric. The film lyric aims to convey a sensation or a mood directly, with little or no recourse to narrative structure.

Stan Brakhage, one of the most influential avant-garde filmmakers of the postwar era, established the genre of the lyrical film (see box). Other filmmakers followed him, including Charles Boultenhouse in *Hand Written* (1959) and Bruce Baillie in *To Parsifal* (1963). Brakhage's footage of his family, pets, and household showed that the lyric form could work with intimate, home-movie material. The lyric mode led filmmakers to explore the film journal or diary, in which the filmmaker records impressions of daily existence (e.g., Jonas Mekas's *Walden,* completed 1969). There was also the film "portrait," such as Markopoulos's *Galaxie* (1966), which consists of thirty brief films depicting friends.

The experimental narrative and the lyric film incorporate abstract imagery and structure. Broughton's hard-edged compositions emphasize the design of the shot, while Anger's play with lighting and focus to soften outlines and make the image fairly abstract. Brakhage's films exploit reflections, spectral diffusion, and hand-painting on the film strip. Markopoulos interrupts his erotic quest tales with brief clusters of single-frame shots, film phrases that recall the abstract modules of Kren and Kubelka. And the animators who worked in narrative often used abstraction; Zagreb films display flat, painterly backgrounds (**Color Plate 21.14**). In most narrative and lyric works, however, abstraction carries symbolic overtones, enhances expressive qualities, or conveys that direct perception that Brakhage believed to be the mission of art.

The Experimental Compilation Film   This postwar trend also has few antecedents in earlier years, though Joseph Cornell's *Rose Hobart* (1939; p. 318) is an important one. In this genre, the filmmaker either gathers footage from a variety of sources and cuts it together or trims and rearranges someone else's finished film. The result conveys an emotion or builds up metaphorical associations. Unlike the compilation documentary, the avant-garde compilation, or assemblage, film avoids an overt message and uses the original footage in satiric or shocking ways.

Perhaps the earliest postwar assemblage films came from the Lettrist movement in Paris. Isidore Isou's *Traité*

THE SECOND POSTWAR DECADE: STAN BRAKHAGE

The possibility that cinema could dwell on the imaginative resonance of the instant, manifested in Deren's *Meshes* and in Markopoulos's psychodramas, was taken in nonnarrative directions by Brakhage. During his stay at the Institute of Fine Art in San Francisco and in his travels between Colorado, California, and Manhattan, Brakhage came to know experimentalists of the older generation—Broughton and Peterson on the West Coast; Deren, Menken, Maas, and Joseph Cornell (p. 318) in New York. He absorbed ideas from all of them but quickly forged his own personal style.

Brakhage defined the film lyric in his work from the mid-1950s: *The Wonder Ring* (1955), *Flesh of Morning* (1956), *Nightcats* (1956), and *Loving* (1956). For Brakhage, the lyrical film records the act of seeing and the flow of imagination. In his "first-person" filmmaking, a jerky pan becomes a glance; a flash frame, a glimpse; a flurry of cuts, sensory transport. Brakhage's films capture light as it radiates, reflects, refracts, dapples, and dazzles. *The Wonder Ring*, commissioned by Cornell when he heard that the New York City elevated train was about to be destroyed, gives us the city as a stream of layers, warped and fractured by the glass of the train windows (**Color Plate 21.11**). The abstract patterns suggest light hitting the eye and stirring associations.

Brakhage continued to explore the lyric in his "domestic" films, such as *Window Water Baby Moving* (1959) and *Thigh Line Lyre Triangular* (1961); his "cosmic" cycle *Dog Star Man* (completed in 1964); his 8mm series *Songs* (1964–1969); and his cycle *Scenes from Under Childhood* (completed in 1970) defined the genre. His output was prodigious—over fifty films in the 1960s and nearly a hundred in the 1970s.

The most elaborate of Brakhage's films of this period is *Anticipation of the Night* (1958). Here a sketchy psychodrama about a man hanging himself is recast by the lyric approach. The protagonist is not even a body, only a shadow. Most of the film is an exploration of surface, hue, and movement in the visible world. An aggressive hand-held camera makes light smear and blur across the frame. Brakhage links shots by texture or color, as when a light-streaked stretch of night footage is cut to a burst of light through treetops (**Color Plate 21.12**). *Anticipation of the Night* established the lyrical film as one of America's central contributions to avant-garde cinema.

Brakhage pursued the genre with a series of films about his family. In *Window Water Baby Moving*, Jane Brakhage's pregnancy and childbirth is rendered in flashbacks and a weave of pictorial motifs (**21.59**).

Brakhage conceived of the artist as a visionary who perceives and feels more deeply than others. He sought to capture on film untutored vision, a sense of space and light unspoiled by knowledge and social training:

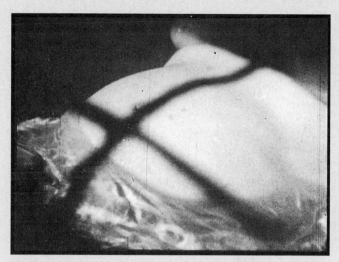

21.59 Motifs of light, fertility, merge in *Window Water Baby Moving*.

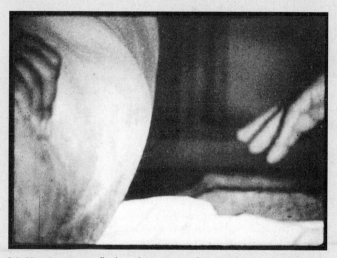

21.60 A corpse's flesh as lyric material in Brakhage's *The Act of Seeing with One's Own Eyes*.

Imagine an eye unruled by man-made laws of perspective, an eye unprejudiced by compositional logic, an eye which does not respond to the name of everything but which must know each object encountered in life through an adventure of perception. How many colors are there in a field of grass to the crawling baby unaware of "Green"? . . . Imagine a world alive with incomprehensible objects and shimmering with an endless variety of movement and innumerable gradations of color. Imagine a world before the "beginning was the word."[12]

Brakhage believed that even unpleasant sights—a rotting dog in *Sirius Remembered* (1959), autopsies in *The Act of Seeing with One's Own Eyes* (1970; **21.60**)—become

(continued)

THE SECOND POSTWAR DECADE: STAN BRAKHAGE, continued

revelatory visual experiences when seized by the artist's innocent eye.

This Romantic trust in the creative imagination went along with a modernist insistence on abstraction and intricate formal play. Brakhage's transformation of everyday objects into sheer patterns puts him in the tradition of cinéma pur (p. 179; **Color Plate 21.13**). His work bears traces of currents outside the cinema as well—the poetry of Kenneth Rexroth and Robert Duncan, the photography of his teacher Minor White, and the painting of Abstract Expressionism. Critics found in Brakhage's roaming camera the spontaneity of Jackson Pollock's gestural painting.

Brakhage's work encouraged filmmakers to trust their immediate impressions and to make even editing and laboratory work serve direct emotional expressiveness. By "deprofessionalizing" film craft—refusing sharp focus and "correct" exposure, exploiting light-struck footage, showing the splices, filming everyday surroundings with an amateur camera obedient to the movements of the body—he exemplified the notion of the caméra-stylo in a way that would have surprised Alexandre Astruc (p. 415). Making a film was now as personally expressive as writing a poem on a piece of paper.

de bave et d'éternité ("Treatise on Slime and Eternity," aka Slime and Eternity, 1951) incorporates casual footage, scratched film, black screen, and flicker. Isou's unflagging commentary in Traité is deliberately out of synchronization. Maurice Lemaître's Le Film est déjà commencé? ("Has the Film Already Started?" 1951) portrays a phantasmagoric visit to the movies. Anticipating many of the devices that avant-gardists would exploit in coming years, Lemaître pulled together clips from Intolerance, coming attractions, and previous Lettrist films and then mixed these bits with negative and tinted footage, perforation strips, and flash frames—all accompanied by snatches of classical music and the sneering voice of a commentator reading the critical reviews that the film will receive.

Other European avant-gardists produced such assemblage films during the 1950s and early 1960s. Guy Debord's Sur le passage de quelques personnes à travers une assez courte unité de temps ("On the Passage of a Few People through a Rather Brief Moment in Time," 1959) combines news footage, advertising shots, and snatches of fiction films with scenes staged and shot by Debord himself, thus becoming a kind of avant-garde parallel to Night and Fog and preparing a path for the collage features of European modernism of the 1960s.

In the United States, the sculptor Bruce Conner brought the avant-garde compilation film to notice with A Movie (1958). Conner juxtaposes thrilling scenes from Westerns and jungle pictures with eerie newsreel shots of death-defying stunts and man-made disasters, interspersed with intertitles repeating the film's title. The four-minute Cosmic Ray (1961) is an orgiastic montage of reportage and stock footage, linking sexual-

ity and violence and timed to Ray Charles's song, "What'd I Say."

Success and New Ambitions

Encouraged by the support for experimental filmmaking, avant-gardists in all these genres moved toward works of ambitious length and thematic breadth. Gregory Markopoulos's Twice a Man (1963) takes nearly an hour to unfold the interwoven points of view of four characters. Bruce Baillie's Mass: For the Dakota Sioux (1964) uses the Roman Catholic liturgy as a framework for a series of lyrical films portraying the degradation of contemporary America (**21.61**). Stan Brakhage extended the lyrical form in Dog Star Man, a five-part cycle of films that seeks to fuse nature, everyday human life, the necessity of death, and the rhythms of the cosmos (**21.62**). Brakhage also separated out all the footage in the film, peeling away the layers of superimposition, and called the four and a half hours that resulted another film, The Art of Vision (1965). The avant-garde film was laying claim to the monumentality of the Joycean novel, Picasso's "Guernica," and modernist works in other arts.

In a similar effort toward a broad statement, Bruce Conner made Report (1965), a complex meditation on the assassination of John Kennedy. By means of television news material, Academy "countdown" leader, and advertising footage, Conner not only evokes the nation's horror and grief but also suggests that the assassination and funeral became media events. His sound track, drawn from news broadcasts, creates unsettling echoes with the image (**21.63**). Conner completed Report on a Ford Foundation grant; that he and eleven

21.61 Baillie's richly textured superimpositions in *Mass* evoke an America choked by technology and mournful routine.

21.62 Cosmic superimpositions in *Prelude: Dog Star Man*.

21.63 "And here it comes—the gun-metal gray limousine . . .": commentary as counterpoint in Conner's *Report*.

other experimental filmmakers received such funding attests to the status experimental film had achieved within American culture.

Work was done on a more intimate scale too. As 16mm became a semiprofessional gauge, 8mm (introduced by Kodak in 1932) became the most popular home-movie format. Jacobs and Conner began shooting in 8mm in the early 1960s, and Brakhage made an 8mm series, *Songs*, notably the optically dense *23rd Psalm Branch* (1967). Throughout the decade, the personal film lyric proved well suited for 8mm and its offspring, super 8mm (introduced in 1965). Some filmmakers hoped to sell their films in 8mm editions, as fine artists sold prints;

in the smaller gauge, the avant-garde film might become a respectable, and collectible, artistic commodity.

By the early 1960s, all the genres of experimental cinema were thriving. In the United States, a small, active infrastructure—magazines, distribution cooperatives, exhibition venues—supported and promoted avant-garde filmmaking. A canon of recognized masterworks and major directors was starting to form. At the same time, experimental trends were swept up within a broader social phenomenon. Avant-garde cinema became increasingly affiliated with the fine arts, with the mass culture of youth, and with a nonconformist counterculture. The result came to be called *underground cinema*.

Underground and Expanded Cinema

While the experimental film culture was consolidating in the late 1950s and early 1960s, strange things were happening in the art world. William Burroughs created his novel *Naked Lunch* by cutting and pasting together his manuscript at random. Cellists performed suspended from wires. La Monte Young's musical piece *Composition 1960 no. 2* consisted of building a fire in the auditorium. In Paris, sculptors constructed elaborate machines whose sole purpose was to self-destruct. A Japanese artist laid a clean canvas on the floor and called the result "Painting to be Stepped On" (1961, Yoko Ono). Choreographers were making entire dances out of natural movements, while painters reworked comic strips, advertisements, and magazine illustrations. "Happenings" offered theatergoers plotless, often random, pieces of activity that might continue indefinitely.

Under the influence of John Cage and others, avant-garde art was blurring the line between the order of art and the disorder of life (which might reveal an unpredictable order of its own).

Boundaries among the media were also dissolving. Painters staged theater pieces and turned musical scores into graphic designs. Composers collaborated with poets and dancers in what came to be called the Theater of Mixed Means. Computers made it possible to compose music, generate sounds, create imagery, and merge the results. Multimedia shows coordinated painting, film, music, light, and performance. George Brecht's "Drip Event" (1962), which consisted of letting water drip from any source into any empty vessel, could be regarded as music, theater, or even kinetic sculpture.

This nonconformist, vaguely threatening, art intrigued the public outside the art world. American newspapers and magazines began discussing avant-garde art, and, with the arrival of Pop Art in 1962, the new experiments came to public consciousness as never before. At the same time, the youth culture of the late 1950s was becoming the counterculture of the 1960s. Many young people rejected traditional values and embraced rock and roll, "mind-expanding" drugs, and Zen and Hindu religious doctrines. For a time, avant-garde artists were automatically taken as part of this social tendency, and experimental filmmakers found themselves in the "underground." In the theater, underground experiments were associated with sexual explicitness, as in the bacchanals of the Living Theatre, or with political critique, as in the work of San Francisco's Bread and Puppet troupe.

Stretching the Limits of Taste and the Medium Within the film community, *underground* initially meant "independent" and "anti-Hollywood." Stan VanDerBeek popularized the term in a 1961 collage-essay that referred to a diverse group of filmmakers (Brakhage, Clarke, Mekas, Hugo, Breer, Lye, and others). Soon, almost all experimental films were called underground movies, since they offered glimpses of a world that Hollywood ignored.

Films intended for quite different purposes were absorbed into the underground aesthetic. Conner's compilations became successful shorts at midnight showings. Abstract films formed part of light shows or were screened as *head movies*, supposedly enhancing the effects of drugs. Harry Smith suggested that film societies play Beatles songs while showing his early abstractions. Avant-garde institutions encouraged this manner of appropriating the films. In 1961, Mekas began setting up midnight screenings at New York theaters, and some theaters started exhibiting the more notorious films. In 1964, Mekas opened the Film-makers' Cinematheque as a venue for experimental work. Independent film festivals became underground meeting points. A chain of West Coast theaters regularly showed midnight programs of avant-garde films.

Some experimental films fit the underground label reasonably well. A film lyric might evoke the mellow spirituality and cosmic consciousness promised by eastern religions and marijuana or LSD. Brakhage's domestic films, with their presentation of childbirth and lovemaking, achieved some underground currency, while Baillie's polished lyrics were taken to embody the serene affirmation popularly associated with California lifestyles. In *Castro Street* (1966), slow dissolves through switch engines and oil refineries reflect what Baillie called "the essential image of *consciousness*"[13] (**Color Plate 21.15**).

Most audiences expected that underground films would flaunt a raunchy eroticism. The expectation was met in the films of George and Mike Kuchar, twins who began collaborating on 8mm films when they were twelve. *A Tub Named Desire* (1960), *Born of the Wind* (1961), *A Town Called Tempest* (1961), *Lust for Ecstasy* (1963)—the very titles indicate the high trashiness of the brothers' ambitions. Their cast lists parody "Coming Attractions" taglines: "Steve Packard as Paul—who made love with his body, waste with his bowels." At age nineteen the Kuchars began to work separately, and throughout the 1960s both turned out lurid extravaganzas of frustrated male sexuality. The garish mise-en-scène of George Kuchar's *Hold Me while I'm Naked* (1966) becomes a travesty of the rich colors of Douglas Sirk and Vincente Minnelli (**Color Plate 21. 16**).

Quite different from the Kuchars' neurotic parodies of Hollywood melodramas, and even more closely identified with the cinematic underground, is Kenneth Anger's *Scorpio Rising* (1963). Anger links motorcycle culture to homoeroticism, diabolism, the death wish, and the desires aroused by the mass media (**21.64**). He creates an aggressive montage of staged scenes, off-the-cuff documentary shots, and imagery drawn from comic strips, movies, and mystical traditions. In addition, each episode is accompanied by a rock-and-roll song, anticipating the structure of music videos.

The most notorious underground movie was Jack Smith's *Flaming Creatures* (1963). In about forty minutes, transvestites, naked men and women, and other "flaming creatures" enact a rape and an orgy (**21.65**). Shot in a jerky, awkward style and harshly overexposed, *Flaming Creatures* created the underground's noisiest scandal. After the first screening, the theater management

21.64 Scorpio in his lair, surrounded by pop-culture imagery of rebellion.

21.65 Transvestites at the orgy in *Flaming Creatures*.

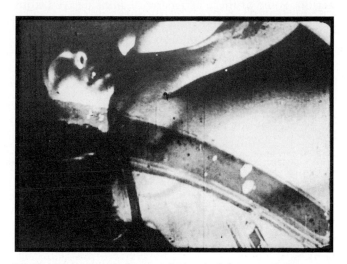

21.66 Distortion and overpainting in Schneeman's *Fuses*.

canceled all underground shows. *Flaming Creatures* could not pass New York City censorship requirements, so it was screened free at the Gramercy Arts Theater while donations were solicited. At the 1963 Knokke-le-Zoute festival, the film was denied a screening, but Mekas seized the projection booth and ran the film until authorities cut the power. In 1964, New York police shut down the Gramercy. When Mekas changed to another venue, detectives burst in and seized *Flaming Creatures*. Coinciding with this crackdown was the arrest of a Los Angeles exhibitor for showing *Scorpio Rising*. In court, both cases ended in a victory for the prosecution, with Mekas and Smith given suspended sentences. The underground cinema had lived up to its name.

Women filmmakers also helped establish the underground mode. Barbara Rubin's *Christmas on Earth* (1963) portrays a largish orgy, with characters in masks or painted faces. The film's two reels are projected simultaneously, with one image inserted inside the other. An equally controversial piece was Carolee Schneeman's *Fuses* (1967), which presents copulation through an ecstatic burst of film-lyric superimpositions, applied paint, and rephotographed imagery (**21.66**).

Underground cinema drew upon new modes of visual arts and performance. Some experimentalists followed the cross-media pollination of the art world and postulated an *expanded cinema*. The phrase included computer-generated films (e.g., VanDerBeek's *Collideoscope*, 1966, made at Bell Laboratories) as well as multimedia performances integrating dance, music, and theater, Expanded-cinema adherents began to revive Abel Gance's idea of triptychs (p. 94) in multiscreen events. Stan VanDerBeek's *Movie-Movies* (1965) used hand-held

projectors to present film images and slide projections. In Stony Point, New York, VanDerBeek built a "Movie-Drome," which projected films on a dome while spectators lay back to watch.

Avant-gardists were questioning the specific identity of their media, and filmmakers began to ask what counted as cinema. Nam June Paik's *Zen for Film* (1964) consisted of clear film that accumulated scratches and dirt as it was replayed; on some occasions Paik projected it on his body. When presenting *March of the Garter Snakes* (1966), Standish Lawder began with slides that contained paint and wax; in the heat of the projection lamp, the colors ran, producing movement. Ken Jacobs performed shadow plays in which "close-ups" and "long shots" mimicked film technique. At this point, expanded cinema merged with light shows and even the behavior of light in the everyday world.

21.67 Red Grooms's *Fat Feet* (1966) creates a circuslike atmosphere through slapstick comedy and exaggerated cut-outs, recalling his 1959 Happening "The Burning Building."

21.68 Sequential variations on an image in Warhol's *Self-Portrait* (1964) . . .

As filmmakers borrowed ideas from multimedia artists, so painters and performance artists moved into film. The Pop artists Claes Oldenburg, Rudy Burckhardt, and Red Grooms had staged Happenings, theater events jammed with shocking, puzzling, or frantic action. Some of these artists made films derived from their performance pieces (**21.67**). Fluxus, a neodada group, presented more minimal theatrical works, typified by George Brecht's "Drip Event."

Andy Warhol and Pop Cinema   The most significant underground filmmaker to come from the art world was Andy Warhol. A 1962 gallery exhibit brought to public notice a group of painters who took their material from mass culture and treated it in ambiguously straight-faced ways. Roy Lichtenstein presented blown-up, hand-painted comic-strip panels; James Rosenquist painted still lifes of housewares and detergents; Claes Oldenburg built oversize, inflated, sagging hamburgers. Warhol portrayed row upon row of Campbell's soup cans and portraits of Marilyn Monroe and Elvis Presley. All this Pop Art could be seen as ironically criticizing American life or as cheerfully celebrating the energy of the mass media.

As Warhol became famous as a Pop painter and printmaker, he took up cinema. He made a variety of films, but the ones that made him notorious were stunningly simple. A man sleeps (*Sleep,* 1963); a man eats a mushroom (*Eat,* 1963); couples kiss (*Kiss,* 1963). Some of the films were related to procedures Warhol used in his graphic art (**21.68, 21.69**); but transposed to cinema, his artistic strategies caused a furor.

Warhol's first films were unnerving largely because of what they did not do. They lacked credit lists and titles. They were silent, even when they showed people talking. They told no stories. There was typically no cutting within the scene, and only occasionally would the camera pan or zoom. Usually Warhol or the camera-person simply loaded the camera, turned it on, and let it record action until the film ran out. The only editing consisted in splicing the camera rolls together, so light flares and punched footage appeared in the finished film (**21.70**). Astonishingly long (*Sleep* consisted of three hours of footage; *Empire,* 1964, was designed to be shown over eight), Warhol's films posed so many challenges that most viewers took them as put-ons—an attitude encouraged by his own comments. "They're experimental films; I call them that because I don't know what I'm doing."[14]

Warhol took up sound films in 1965 and turned toward performance and rudimentary narratives. For *The Life of Juanita Castro, Vinyl,* and *Kitchen* (all 1965), playwright Ronald Tavel provided the actors with semiscripted situations; Warhol had told him he wanted "not plot, but incident."[15] Narcissistic amateur performers chatter aimlessly and aggressively, each one vying to control the scene while parading what she or he perceives as "star quality." Most scenes are rendered in very long takes, with gaps sometimes signaled by *strobe cuts* (flashes of bright light) and disconcerting zaps on the sound track. In 1966, always alert for new opportunities, Warhol joined the expanded-cinema trend with *Up Tight,* two side-by-side films with music provided by a rock group, the Velvet Underground. This led to *The Chelsea Girls* (1966), a three-hour feature that presented a string of scenes on two screens (**Color Plates 21.17, 21.18**).

During the next two years, Warhol moved toward more recognizable narrative form in *I, a Man, Bike Boy, Nude Restaurant,* and *Lonesome Cowboys* (all 1967). After being seriously wounded when one of his circle shot him, Warhol gave up film directing, although he lent his name to films conceived and directed by Paul Morrissey and he signed some later video work.

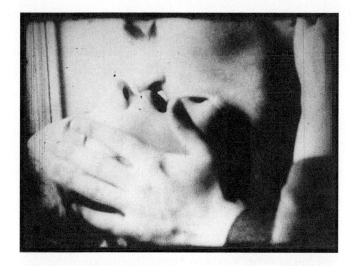

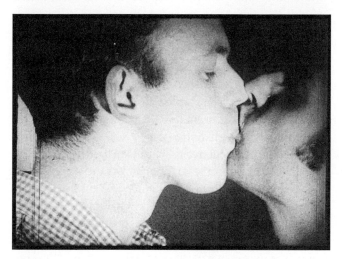

21.69 . . . and in *Kiss*.

21.70 *Eat:* the punch marks at the beginning and the end of a raw roll of film deface Robert Indiana as he chews a mushroom.

Warhol's cinema was an extension of his celebrity lifestyle and the group-manufacture process behind his pictures. Just as many "Warhol" silk screens were made by his staff and merely signed by him, he came up with ideas for his films but the staging and shooting were usually carried out by others. Hovering on the fringes of the Factory, his silver-foil-lined studio and social gathering point, Warhol presented himself as a bland, passive onlooker, naively enthusiastic about everything. "The world fascinates me. It's so nice, whatever it is."[16] His films had the impassive ambiguity of Pop paintings, but they also encapsulated several broader qualities of 1960s avant-garde art.

They manifested in a deadpan way the eroticism that had made a scandal of *Flaming Creatures* and *Scorpio Rising*. *Couch* (1964), for instance, consists of seventy minutes of couples engaging in sexual activity in one corner of the Factory. Moreover, the films' nonchalant depiction of sadomasochism and male homosexuality marked a stage beyond the oblique and overwrought imagery of *Fireworks* and Markopoulos's works. The second half of *My Hustler* (1965) takes place entirely in a cramped bathroom, where gay prostitutes discuss their

21.71 Good grooming and flirtation in *My Hustler*.

careers, indulge in casual caresses, and groom themselves painstakingly (**21.71**).

Related to the films' eroticism was Warhol's investment in the "camp" sensibility. *Camp,* as defined in a well-known essay by Susan Sontag, "is the love of the exaggerated, the 'off,' of things-being-what-they-are-not."[17] Associated with the gay subculture, camp taste elevated the excessive and extravagant. Kenneth Anger and Jack Smith both manifested camp, but Warhol celebrated it forthrightly in his parodies of Hollywood genres and in the performances of several of his "superstars," notably the transvestites Holly Woodlawn and Jackie Curtis.

Eroticism and campiness gave Warhol's work an underground cachet, but he also won attention with more radical qualities. For example, the idea of reflexivity, already important in European art cinema (p. 442), had been significant in American art criticism since the rise of Abstract Expressionist painting. Many experimental films of the period exploited reflexivity quite literally; Stanton Kaye's *Georg* (1964), for instance, presents its fictional story as a film diary, so we are constantly aware of the frame, the cuts, and the sound recording.

The early films' offhand, plotless shapes also manifested the ideal of indeterminacy in art. Cage had pioneered this attitude in the 1940s, as had the Happenings and the Fluxus events a decade later. Warhol, an apt borrower, gave his films a random, unfinished quality. Often the camera reels could be cut together in any sequence. On initial release of *The Chelsea Girls,* the order of the reels was determined by the projectionist, although an orthodox sequence has subsequently been developed.

Also, in its passive rendering of objects and events, Warhol's work embodied an avant-garde aesthetic of boredom. Cage and other artists had insisted that repeti-

tion of even the most trivial action would eventually yield a deeper interest. But Warhol seemed to value boredom in itself. "The more you look at the same exact thing, the more the meaning goes away, and the better and emptier you feel."[18] By projecting the early silent films at sixteen frames per second (although they were shot at the normal twenty-four), Warhol guaranteed that his slight material would be stretched to the limit of endurance.

Warhol ascended into Manhattan's world of discothèques and celebrity parties at the moment when the avant-garde was becoming part of the "art business." Dealers, critics, museums, collectors, and news media turned the art world into a realm of rapid changes in fashion and a market that demanded stylistic innovation and fresh talent. Warhol's films participated in this cultural change and helped bring the underground above ground. By embracing more structured narrative situations, he bid for a broader audience. *The Chelsea Girls* achieved some commercial distribution and attracted unprecedented media attention. His "superstars"—the jittery and shrill Edie Sedgwick; the vacantly beautiful Nico and Joe Dalessandro; the amphetamine-driven Ondine; the perpetually spacy Viva, retelling anecdotes from her Catholic girlhood—had a screen presence that gave the late films entertainment value.

Warhol's rise in the art world certainly helped the films achieve fame, but their influence went beyond the shifts of fashion. His early work was praised for a refreshing simplicity that revived the tradition of Auguste Lumière. More generally, his work signaled a reaction against the expressive psychodramas and rich, dense imagery of the 1940s and 1950s. The films' awkwardness, superficiality, and self-mockery seemed an antidote to an avant-garde that was becoming too serious and pretentious. Further, by attracting dealers, curators, and critics, Warhol raised hopes that avant-garde cinema might find a home in museums and galleries, gaining prestige and funding. In all, Warhol became as important to the world of avant-garde cinema as Jean-Luc Godard was to the art cinema.

International Underground The work of Smith, Anger, and Warhol, as well as the continuing traditions typified by Brakhage, Conner, Jacobs, and others, played a central role in creating an international underground. American experimental films had won recognition at the Brussels Experimental Film Competition of 1958 and elsewhere. In 1963, after the Belgian scandal of *Flaming Creatures,* Mekas and the critic P. Adams Sitney toured Europe with the Exposition of the New American Cinema. Two years later the tour went to South America and Japan. Independent cooperatives sprang up in Lon-

21.72 A typically enigmatic image from Iimura's *Dance Party in the Kingdom of Lilliput* (1964).

scratched, and dubbed clips from American Cinema-Scope films. The filmmakers cut their snippets together in ways that expose Hollywood clichés and create purely formal disjunctions, as when, distorted by the anamorphic squeeze (p. 331), Gregory Peck closes the door twice. An even greater expansion of European avant-garde cinema would take place in the late 1960s and throughout the 1970s.

In Japan, powerful and scandalous underground works appeared quite early, notably *Love* (1962) and *Onan* (1963), by Takahiko Iimura (**21.72**). On the whole, though, the freedom of directors like Oshima and Suzuki in the commercial cinema delayed a broad underground movement. The arrival of U.S. work intensified interest. Soon, many taboo-breaking films were being shown in art galleries, cafés, and universities.

don and Toronto (both 1966), Holland, Montreal, Italy (1967), and Hamburg (1968), and many of these distributed canonical works of the American avant-garde.

Underground cinema outside the United States explored recognizable genres and styles. In Vienna, Kurt Kren filmed Otto Muehl's "Material-Actions," aggressive and shocking spectacles in which people were rolled in mud and apparently tortured and mutilated. Kren subjected the footage to the same rigorous organization he had applied in his earlier structure-based works. In *La Verifica incerta* ("Uncertain Verification," Italy, 1964), Gianfranco Baruchello and Alberto Grifi developed the avant-garde compilation film by scavenging worn, faded,

Between 1958 and 1968, international experimental filmmaking enjoyed a period of vitality and variety without parallel since the first avant-garde epoch of the 1920s. Through its alliance with a worldwide youth-based counterculture, experimental film also prepared the way for the politically active roles that mainstream filmmakers were soon to play.

· ·

Notes and Queries

WRITING THE HISTORY OF THE POSTWAR AVANT-GARDE

The experimental film in America has benefited from strong polemicists and critics with a vivid sense of history. Parker Tyler proved one of the sharpest observers of emerging trends, identifying the "trance film" and dubbing the film of hipsters hanging out the "pad movie." Tyler produced an astute chronicle of the avant-garde in essays collected in *The Three Faces of the Film* (New York: Barnes, 1967) and *Sex Psyche Etcetera in the Film* (New York: Horizon, 1969). Later he accused underground filmmakers of infantile exhibitionism (*Underground Film: A Critical History* [New York: Grove, 1969]).

The assimilation of avant-garde cinema to the underground aesthetic is evident in Sheldon Renan's *An Introduction to the American Underground Film* (New York: Dutton, 1967). *The New American Cinema: A Critical Anthology*, ed. Gregory Battcock (New York: Dutton, 1967), collects important manifestos and critical essays. From the West Coast came Gene Youngblood's *Expanded Cinema* (New York: Dutton, 1970), a fund of technical information as well as a document of the 1960s merger of electronics, space exploration, parapsychology, Zen, and cosmic consciousness.

P. Adams Sitney, who became a devotee of experimental cinema before leaving high school, emerged as the most scholarly critic of the avant-garde. In *Film Culture* and his periodical, *Filmwise*, he printed interviews with filmmakers and close critical discussions of films. In the early 1970s, he elaborated a comprehensive history of the postwar American avant-garde, plotting a shift from the trance film through the lyric to the "mythopoeic" form (*Dog Star Man, Scorpio Rising*). Sitney saw the filmmakers as part of a Romantic tradition, with each movement seeking to represent an essential aspect of the human mind: dream in the psychodramas, perception in the lyric, and the collective unconscious in the myth films. Sitney elaborated this argument in "The Idea of Morphology," *Film Culture* 53–55 (spring 1972): 1–24, and developed it at full length in *Visionary Film: The American Avant-Garde 1943–1978*, 2nd ed. (New York: Oxford University Press, 1979; originally published 1974). Sitney's wide-ranging scheme, as well as his sensitive scrutiny of films, became the standard historical account. His framework is utilized in Marilyn Singer, ed., *A History of the American Avant-Garde Cinema* (New York: American Federation of the Arts, 1976).

Four other monographs offer different treatments. Steven Dwoskin's *Film Is: The International Free Cinema* (Woodstock, NY: Overlook, 1975) supplies essays on the international avant-garde. Dominique Noguez provides an institution-based account in *Une Renaissance du cinéma: Le cinéma "underground" américain: Histoire, économique, esthétique* (Paris: Klincksieck, 1985). David James situates experimental filmmaking in relation to Hollywood cinema and militant film in *Allegories of Cinema: American*

Film in the Sixties (Princeton, NJ: Princeton University Press, 1989). James Peterson examines various types of postwar avant-garde cinema and the cognitive strategies spectators may use to understand them in *Dreams of Chaos, Visions of Order: Understanding the American Avant-Garde Cinema* (Detroit: Wayne State University Press, 1994).

· ·

REFERENCES

1. Quoted in Mick Eaton, ed., *Anthropology—Reality—Cinema: The Films of Jean Rouch* (London: British Film Institute, 1979), p. 63.
2. Quoted in Gideon Bachmann, "The Frontiers of Realist Cinema: The Work of Ricky Leacock," *Film Culture* 22–23 (summer 1961): 18.
3. Quoted in Stephen Mamber, *Cinéma Vérité in America: Studies in Uncontrolled Documentary* (Cambridge, MA: MIT Press, 1974), p. 146.
4. Quoted in James Blue, "One Man's Truth: An Interview with Richard Leacock," *Film Comment* 3, no. 2 (spring 1965): 18.
5. Quoted in Louis Marcorelles, *Living Cinema* (New York: Praeger, 1973), p. 82.
6. Quoted in "Jean Rouch," *Movie* 8 (April 1963): 22.
7. Quoted in Mark Shivas, "New Approach," *Movie* 8 (April 1963): 13.
8. Quoted in Vè Vè A. Clark, Millicent Hodson, and Catrina Neiman, *The Legend of Maya Deren: A Documentary Biography and Collected Works.* Vol. 1, pt. 2: *Chambers (1942–1947)* (New York: Anthology Film Archives/Film Culture, 1988), p. 566.
9. Maya Deren, "An Anagram of Ideas on Art, Form, and Film," in Clark, Hodson, and Neiman, *The Legend of Maya Deren.* Vol. 1, pt. 2: *Chambers (1942–1947)*, p. 629.
10. Quoted in "Poetry and the Film: A Symposium," in P. Adams Sitney, ed., *The Film Culture Reader* (New York: Praeger, 1970), p. 174.
11. Peter Kubelka, "The Theory of Metrical Film," in P. Adams Sitney, ed., *The Avant-Garde Film: A Reader of Theory and Criticism* (New York: New York University Press, 1978), p. 140.
12. Stan Brakhage, *Metaphors on Vision*, ed. P. Adams Sitney (New York: Film Culture, 1963), n.p.
13. Quoted in *Film-Makers' Cooperative Catalogue* no. 4 (New York: Film-Makers' Cooperative, 1967), p. 13.
14. Quoted in "Nothing to Lose," *Cahiers du cinéma in English* 10 (May 1967): 42.
15. Quoted in Stephen Koch, *Star-Gazer: Andy Warhol's World and His Films* (New York: Praeger, 1973), p. 63.
16. Quoted in "Nothing to Lose": 42.
17. Susan Sontag, "Notes on Camp," in *Against Interpretation and Other Essays* (New York: Delta, 1966), p. 279.
18. Andy Warhol and Pat Hackett, *POPism: The Warhol '60s* (New York: Harcourt Brace Jovanovich, 1980), p. 50.

FURTHER READING

Banes, Sally. *Greenwich Village 1963: Avant-Garde Performance and the Effervescent Body.* Durham, NC: Duke University Press, 1993.

Blistene, Bernard, et al. *Andy Warhol, cinéma.* Paris: Pompidou Center, 1990.

Brakhage, Stan. *Brakhage Scrapbook: Collected Writings 1964–1980.* Ed. Robert A. Haller. New Paltz, NY: Documentext, 1982.

"The Cinema of Jean Rouch." *Visual Anthropology* 2, nos. 3–4 (1989).

Devaux, Frédérique. *Le Cinéma lettriste (1951–1991).* Paris: Experimental Editions, 1992.

Dixon, Wheeler Winston. *The Exploding Eye: A Re-visionary History of 1960s American Experimental Cinema.* Albany: State University of New York Press, 1997.

Jaffe, Patricia. "Editing *Cinéma Vérité.*" *Film Comment* 3, no. 3 (summer 1965): 43–47.

Jenkins, Bruce. "Fluxfilms in Three False Starts." In Janet Jenkins, ed., *In the Spirit of Fluxus.* Minneapolis: Walker Art Center, 1993, pp. 122–39.

Lebrate Christian, ed. *Peter Kubelka.* Paris: Experimental Editions, 1990.

Levin, Thomas Y. "Dismantling the Spectacle: The Cinema of Guy Debord." In Elisabeth Sussamn, ed., *On the Passage of a Few People through a Rather Brief Moment in Time: The Situationist International 1957–1972.* Boston: ICA, 1989, pp. 72–123.

Markopoulos, Gregory. "Towards a New Narrative Film Form." *Film Culture* 31 (winter 1963/1964): 11–12.

Marsolais, Gilles. *L'Aventure du cinéma direct.* Paris: Seghers, 1974.

Mekas, Jonas. *Movie Journal: The Rise of a New American Cinema, 1959–1971.* New York: Macmillan, 1972.

———. "Notes after Reseeing the Movies of Andy Warhol." In John Coplans, ed., *Andy Warhol.* New York: New York Graphic Society, 1968, pp. 139–95.

O'Pray, Michael, ed. *Andy Warhol: Film Factory.* London: British Film Institute, 1989.

Rouch Jean. "The Camera and Man." In Paul Hockings, ed., *Principles of Visual Anthropology.* Paris: Mouton, 1975, pp. 83–102.

Ruby, Jay, ed. *The Cinema of John Marshall.* Chur, Switzerland: Harwood, 1993.

Stan Brakhage: An American Independent Film-Maker. London: Arts Council of Great Britain, 1980.

VanDerBeek, Stan. "The Cinema Delimina: Films from the Underground." *Film Quarterly* 14, no. 4 (summer 1961): 5–15.

PART
FIVE

· ·

THE CONTEMPORARY CINEMA SINCE THE 1960s

B y the mid-1960s, film was widely recognized as not only a mass entertainment medium but also a vehicle of high culture. The achievements of postwar European modernism, the increasing influence of the auteur idea, and new developments in documentary and experimental film had established cinema as a vital contemporary art.

Very quickly, however, this art form faced challenges. In the 1960s, Hollywood's attempts to compete with television and other types of entertainment led to a series of big-budget failures that left the industry in crisis. During the 1970s, filmmakers tried to appeal to youth by borrowing from art cinema. A new generation of directors, the movie brats, helped turn American film toward an updated version of the classical Hollywood cinema (Chapter 22).

Internationally, from the early 1960s to the mid-1970s, the world was shaken by a series of political crises. The Third World, home to three-quarters of the world's population, had been the site of most political strife since 1945. The violence intensified during the 1960s and 1970s. African states were torn by ethnic conflict and civil wars. Rightwing juntas seized power in Latin America, and guerrilla movements arose to fight them. Egypt and Israel went to war in 1967 and again in 1974, while Palestinian resistance groups embarked on military actions throughout the Middle East.

Western leaders sought to contain communist expansion in newly independent nations. The first notable failure was Cuba: after Castro's 1959 revolution, the country quickly aligned itself with the USSR. Leftwing regimes, many identified with the Soviet Union, also sprang up in Africa and Latin America. Most dramatically, the war in Vietnam demonstrated the extent to which a western power would go to block the formation of another communist state. The United States, which committed

Convention in Chicago, and President Nixon widened the Vietnam War. Campuses exploded; 400 closed or held strikes during 1970.

The withdrawal of U.S. forces from Vietnam in 1973 could not heal the deep divisions in American society that the war had created. The New Left collapsed, partly due to internal disputes and partly because the shooting of students at Kent State University in 1970 seemed to prove the futility of organized action. Nixon's successful bid for the presidency resulted from middle-class voters' resentment of eastern liberals, the left, and the counterculture.

The upheavals of this period led to an international critical political cinema (see Chapter 23). In America, Emile De Antonio, the Newsreel group, and other filmmakers practiced an "engaged" filmmaking of social protest. At the same time, with diminishing profits from blockbusters, the Hollywood industry tried to woo the younger generation with countercultural films. The effort brought forth some experiments in creating an American art cinema.

Responding to the U.S. government's turn to the right in the early 1970s, left and liberal activists embraced a micropolitics: they sought grassroots social change by organizing around concrete issues (abortion, race- and gender-based discrimination, welfare, and environmental policy). Many American documentary filmmakers participated in these movements (p. 584). At the same time, however, this activism was fiercely opposed by the rise of the New Right, conservative organizations that organized local support for school prayer, the abolition of newly won abortion rights, and other issues. The struggle between reform movements and New Right forces was to become the central political drama of the 1970s, and many films (*Jaws, The Parallax View, Nashville*) bear traces of it.

The drama was played against the backdrop of a waning U.S. economy, fallen prey to oil embargoes and brisk competition from Japan and Germany. The 1970s ended the postwar era of prosperity. This period coincided with Hollywood's reinvention of the blockbuster and the rise to power of the movie brats, the most pragmatic and influential young filmmakers who became the new creative leaders of the industry.

THE 1960s: THE FILM INDUSTRY IN RECESSION

Superficially, Hollywood might have seemed healthy in the early 1960s. The Majors—MGM, Warner Bros., United Artists, Paramount, 20th Century-Fox, Colum-

bia, Disney, and Universal—still controlled distribution, and nearly all money-making films passed through their hands. *Lawrence of Arabia* (1962), *Cleopatra* (1963), *Dr. Zhivago* (1965), and other historical epics played for months. Broadway musicals continued to yield such hits as *West Side Story* (1961), *The Music Man* (1962), and *The Sound of Music* (1965), the decade's top-grossing film. Independent *teenpics* such as *Beach Blanket Bingo* (1965) catered to the drive-in audience with the lure of clean fun in the sun. The Disney studios dominated the family market with hugely successful films like *101 Dalmatians* (1961), *Mary Poppins* (1965), and *The Jungle Book* (1967). Although stars were free agents, many signed long-term production deals with studios. Paramount had Jerry Lewis, Universal had Rock Hudson and Doris Day, MGM had Elvis Presley. Each studio's output stabilized at between twelve and twenty feature releases per year—a pattern that would hold for several decades. The Majors had made peace with television. Networks were paying high prices for the rights to broadcast films, and the studios began making "telefeatures" and series programs.

The Studios in Crisis

Despite all the evidence of prosperity, the 1960s proved to be a hazardous decade for the studios. Movie attendance continued to drop, leveling out at about 1 billion per year. Studios were releasing fewer films, and many of those were low-budget pickups or foreign productions that would have been passed over in earlier years. Most of the Majors were stuck with large facilities, forcing them to lease sound stages to television. Big stars proved a mixed blessing. Once they joined a package they usually insisted on control of the script and direction, along with a percentage of a film's grosses, yet most star vehicles did not yield profit to the studios.

The bulk of the films released by the Majors were independent productions, often cofinanced by the studio. What films did the Majors finance, plan, and produce on their own? More and more these tended to be roadshow movies of the sort that had proved enticing during the 1950s. During the 1960s, six films were roadshowed per year, and most proved lucrative. *The Sound of Music* roadshowed at 266 theatres, running for as long as twenty months on some screens. Only 1 percent of films released between 1960 and 1968 grossed over $1 million, but a third of the roadshow pictures surpassed that figure. The success of roadshow films like *West Side Story, El Cid* (1961), *How the West Was Won* (1962), and *Lawrence of Arabia* drove the studios to risk millions on epic movies. Soon, however, the investments were in peril. In 1962, MGM lost nearly $20 million, thanks largely to cost overruns on *Mutiny on the Bounty* (1962), and *Cleopatra*'s protracted production pushed Fox to a loss of over $40 million.

By the late 1960s, every studio faced a financial crisis. Most releases lost money, and executives proved slow to understand that the big picture was no longer a sure thing. Despite *Cleopatra*'s high box-office intake, its production costs guaranteed that it would lose money on theatrical release—as did many other expensive historical epics, such as *The Fall of the Roman Empire* (1964) and *The Battle of Britain* (1969). Nor was the musical film a guaranteed winner. Although *The Sound of Music* was a hit, *Doctor Dolittle* (1967), *Thoroughly Modern Millie* (1967), *Star!* (1968), and *Paint Your Wagon* (1969) were expensive fiascos.

The only bright spots were a few low-budget films, usually aimed at the college audience, that yielded remarkable returns. *Bonnie and Clyde* (1967) cost $3 million and returned $24 million domestic rental income to Warner Bros., while *Midnight Cowboy* (1969) cost $3 million and yielded $20 million to United Artists. The winner in the low-budget sweepstakes was the independent release *The Graduate* (1967). It cost $3 million and returned $49 million to its small distributor, Embassy Pictures. This scale of profits made the sophisticated young adult film very attractive to studio decision makers. Soon an entire cycle of *youthpics* tried to capitalize on campus activism and counterculture lifestyles.

The Majors, at their weakest point since World War II, were ripe for absorption into healthier companies. In 1962, Universal was acquired by the Music Corporation of America, but at least the deal remained in the Hollywood family, since MCA was a former talent agency (pp. 336–337). But now conglomerates began circling the studios. In 1966, Gulf + Western industries (a firm with holdings in auto parts, metals, and financial services) acquired the ailing Paramount Pictures. Warner Bros. was bought by Seven Arts in 1967, which two years later was absorbed into Kinney National Services (an owner of parking lots and funeral parlors). United Artists was bought by the Transamerica Corporation (car rentals, life insurance) in 1967. In 1968, financier Kirk Kerkorian gained control of MGM, downsized it, and funneled its assets into building the MGM Grand Hotel in Las Vegas. Studios that were used to operating as freestanding companies now found themselves small slices of large corporate pies.

The conglomerates could help the ailing studios by injecting money from other businesses and guaranteeing lines of bank credit. But nothing seemed to stem the flow of red ink. Between 1969 and 1972, the major film companies lost $500 million. The studios quickly brought in new executives, often with little experience in film production. Banks forced companies to trim the number of releases, avoid big-budget films, and partner with other studios in coproductions (as when Warners and Fox joined forces for *The Towering Inferno,* 1974). In 1970, unemployment in Hollywood rose to over 40 percent, an all-time high. As recession gripped the industry, the roadshow era ended. Exhibitors began splitting their houses into two or three screens and building *multiplexes* (cheaper shopping-mall theaters). The result was a generation of narrow auditoriums with poor sightlines and garbled sound.

Styles and Genres

With the decline of the studios and the continuing drop in attendance, 1960s Hollywood was unsure about what the public wanted. When a performer won a loyal audience, he or she could count on studio support. Perhaps the most obvious example is Jerry Lewis. After teaming with Dean Martin on several hugely successful Paramount releases in the 1950s, Lewis set out on a solo career—writing, directing, and performing in his own comedies. In most of his films, Lewis gave his idiot-child character a spasmodic, demonic frenzy. In *The Nutty Professor* (1963), he portrayed not only a geeky simpleton but also a suave lady-killer modeled on Dean Martin. Lewis displayed considerable visual flair: *The Ladies' Man* (1961) presents a women's boardinghouse as a colossal dollhouse (**Color Plate 22.1**).

Studios looked for ways to lure people away from their television sets. Not every movie endorsed family values; the same theaters that played Disney films also featured more risqué fare. Universal's Doris Day comedies (including *Pillow Talk,* 1958, and *Lover Come Back,* 1962) celebrated women's sexual stratagems, often at the expense of the male ego (usually incarnated in Rock Hudson). Other films snickered at promiscuity (*A Guide for the Married Man,* 1967), suburban adultery (*Boys' Night Out,* 1962), and aggressive women (*Sex and the Single Girl,* 1964).

Audiences were also intrigued by films from outside the Hollywood mainstream. Studios distributed films from Europe, not just quickly made costume pictures like *Hercules* (1959), but also ambitious and polished efforts like *Zorba the Greek* (1965). British imports were particularly successful. The erotic period comedy *Tom Jones* (1963) and the edgy drama *Alfie* (1966), which traded

anxiety is charted through dreams and fragmentary flashbacks. The murder is presented in disorienting shards, as Harry glimpses and overhears it. Eventually, the audience discovers that parts of the original conversation have been filtered through Harry's mind. As Harry realizes the true situation, Coppola intercuts shots of him with shots of the murder, perhaps as he now imagines it to have taken place (**22.15–22.17**).

22.15 *The Conversation:* as Harry watches the mysterious younger people leave the corporation under press scrutiny . . .

PERSONAL CINEMA: ALTMAN AND ALLEN

After the mid-1970s, efforts to maintain a Hollywood art cinema were much less common. One director who persisted was Robert Altman. Altman directed some fairly orthodox features before his career was energized by the late 1960s recession, the youthpics cycle, and the vogue for Hollywood art cinema. His films travesty their genres, from the war film *M*A*S*H* to the antimusical *Popeye* (1980). They radiate a distrust of authority, a criticism of American pieties, and a celebration of energetic, if confused, idealism.

Altman also developed an idiosyncratic style. He relied on shambling, semi-improvised performances, a restless pan-and-zoom camera style, abrupt cutting, multiple-camera shooting that kept the viewpoint resolutely outside the character action, and a sound track of unprecedented density. His long lenses crowd characters in on one another and lock them behind reflecting glass (**22.18**). *Nashville* (1975), for many critics Altman's major achievement, follows twenty-four characters over a weekend, often scattering them across the widescreen frame (**22.19**). In Altman's films, characters mumble, interrupt each other, talk simultaneously, or find themselves drowned out by the droning loudspeakers of official wisdom.

Without a major hit after *M*A*S*H*, Altman found himself adrift in the 1980s, but he still managed to be quite prolific, skewering American values in bare-bones play

adaptations (*Secret Honor,* 1984; *Fool for Love,* 1985). His career was rejuvenated through his handling of the dark Hollywood comedy *The Player* (1992), which allowed him to return to more mainstream production and continue his off-kilter, bitterly anarchic handling of theme, genre, image, and sound.

Altman's contemporary Woody Allen created a personal cinema from a production base in New York. A television gag writer and a stand-up comedian, Allen wrote plays and starred in films during the 1960s. His first directorial effort, *Take the Money and Run* (1969), became an immediate success, sustaining the wisecracking absurdist tradition of the Marx Brothers and Bob Hope. Allen's early films also appealed to young audiences through their cinematic in-jokes, such as the homage to *Potemkin*'s Odessa Steps in *Bananas* (1971).

With *Annie Hall* (1977), Allen launched a series of films that blended his interest in the psychological problems of the urban professional with his love for American film traditions and for such European filmmakers as Fellini and Bergman. "When I started making pictures, I was interested in the kind of pictures I enjoyed when I was younger. Comedies, real funny comedies, and romantic comedies, sophisticated comedies. As I got a little more savvy, that part of me which responded to foreign film started to take over."[4]

22.18 In *The Long Goodbye,* a dense window reflection shows the detective Philip Marlowe on the beach while inside the house novelist Roger Wade quarrels with his wife.

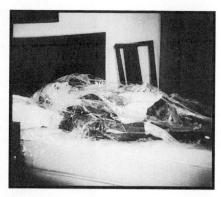

22.16, *left*   . . . Coppola interrupts the scene with glimpses of the murder . . .

22.17, *right*   . . . and suggests that these images could be either Harry's imaginings or fragments of the real action.

22.19   Several major characters pass each other unawares in the bustling airport scene at the beginning of *Nashville*.

Allen's most influential films have thrown his comic persona—the hypersensitive, insecure Jewish intellectual—into a tangle of psychological conflicts. Sometimes the plot centers on the Allen figure's confused love life (*Annie Hall; Manhattan*, 1979). In *Hannah and Her Sisters* (1986) and *Crimes and Misdemeanors* (1990), the plot consists of intertwined romantic relationships among several characters, played for contrasts between verbal comedy and sober drama. *Hannah*, for instance, mixes marital infidelity, a cancer scare, and satiric observation of New York intellectual life (**22.20**). Allen built many of his films around the questions that preoccupied him, and he unabashedly recorded his loves (jazz, Manhattan), dislikes (rock music, drugs, California), and values (love, friendship, trust).

A unique production arrangement allowed Allen to retain control over the script, casting, and editing; he was even permitted extensive reshooting of portions of his films. He explored a range of styles, from the pseudo-documentary realism of *Zelig* (1983) to the mock German Expressionism of *Shadows and Fog* (1992). Allen also paid homage to a number of his favorite films and auteurs. *Stardust Memories* (1980) is an overt reworking of Fellini's *8½*; *Radio Days* (1987), in its glowing evocation of period detail, recalls *Amarcord*. *Interiors* (1978) and *September* (1987) are Bergmanesque chamber dramas, while the holiday family

22.20   Middle-class couples debate artificial insemination: romantic satire in *Hannah and Her Sisters*.

gatherings of *Hannah and Her Sisters* evoke *Fanny and Alexander*. Few of his films made a profit, but into the 2000s Allen attracted major stars willing to take part in his personal universe.

Hollywood Strikes Gold

During the 1970s, new forces were at work to salvage the U.S. film industry. In 1971, a new law allowed film companies to claim tax credits on investments in U.S.-made films and to recover tax credits from the 1960s. This legislation not only returned hundreds of millions of dollars to the Majors, it also allowed them to defer tax on subsidiaries' activities. In addition, a tax-shelter plan allowed investors in films to declare up to 100 percent of their investment as exempt from taxes. The latter provision helped successful, offbeat films like *One Flew Over the Cuckoo's Nest* (1975) and *Taxi Driver* (1976) to be made. The tax-shelter provision was rescinded in 1976, and the studios' tax-credit benefits were abolished in the mid-1980s, but they had been crucial to the industry's recovery.

A more visible force was a fresh burst of highly successful films. Although many of the new generation of Hollywood directors—especially the movie brats—considered themselves artists, few wanted to be esoteric. Most enjoyed satisfying the demands of a large audience. And some made not just ordinary hits but films that broke records year after year. The top-grossing films of 1970 and 1971 (*Love Story, Airport, M*A*S*H, Patton, The French Connection, Fiddler on the Roof*) had yielded between $25 million and $50 million to the studios from U.S. box-office returns—strong profits, but lackluster in comparison with what was to come. *The Godfather* ushered in an era of box-office income on a scale no one had imagined. The following figures are rentals, not box-office grosses; the rentals are the revenues returned to the studio after the theaters have taken their percentages of gross ticket sales:

1972: *The Godfather,* directed by Francis Ford Coppola, returned over $81 million to Paramount in the U.S. market. Two years later, its global rentals and TV sales amounted to $285 million.

1973: William Friedkin's *The Exorcist* (Warners; **22.21**) surpassed *The Godfather's* U.S. rentals by $3 million. In the same year, Universal reluctantly released a small-budget film called *American Graffiti,* directed by George Lucas; it reaped over $55 million.

1975: *Jaws* (Universal), directed by Steven Spielberg, earned $130 million in domestic rentals.

1976: *Rocky,* made without major stars and by little-known director John Avildson, earned United Artists $56 million at the U.S. box office.

1977: Steven Spielberg's *Close Encounters of the Third Kind* (Columbia; $82 million) and John Badham's *Saturday Night Fever* (Paramount; $74 million) generated

22.21 *The Exorcist,* an adaptation of a best-selling horror novel, aroused controversy with its blasphemous language and its shocking special effects. Here, thanks to a life-sized puppet, the possessed Regan mockingly rotates her head.

very healthy profits, but records were broken again by George Lucas's *Star Wars* (Fox). Costing $11 million, it began as a summer movie, ran continuously into 1978, and was rereleased in 1979. *Star Wars* earned over $190 million in U.S. rentals and about $250 million worldwide, on a total ticket sales of over $500 million.

No cluster of films had ever made so much money on initial release.[5] Studios on the brink of bankruptcy found their profits hitting unprecedented levels. Richard F. Zanuck, the son of long-time 20th-Century Fox boss Darryl F. Zanuck, produced *The Sting* and *Jaws.* When the receipts came in, he realized that "I had amassed more money with one or two pictures than my father had in a lifetime of work."[6] During the boom of the early and mid-1970s, most Majors had at least one top hit, so the industry as a whole maintained its stability. Overall rentals from domestic and foreign release increased about $200 million per year, reaching $2 billion in 1979. Television networks and cable companies began paying large sums for rights to broadcast the new blockbusters. The 1970s resurgence catapulted several filmmakers to fame, with three becoming major producer-directors (see box).

The Return of the Blockbuster

The 1970s blockbusters made producers far less willing to let filmmakers experiment with plot, tone, and style. During the recession of the early 1970s, studios welcomed even a small hit; directors were not expected to create big pictures. By the late 1970s, however, companies did not want to risk money on untried subjects or approaches.

THE 1970s BIG THREE: COPPOLA, SPIELBERG, AND LUCAS

Three directors who emerged at the beginning of the 1970s became powerful producers and redefined what Hollywood cinema might be. Like other novices of the time, they were less directors than "filmmakers" who had tried their hand at every aspect of the craft, from writing to postproduction. They understood movies as total creations, and they sought to put their personal stamp on everything they did. They were also well acquainted with each other: Francis Ford Coppola acted as producer and mentor for George Lucas on *American Graffiti*, and later Lucas and Steven Spielberg collaborated on several projects, notably *Raiders of the Lost Ark* (1980). Still, their paths diverged. With *The Godfather*, Coppola proved that he could turn out a mainstream masterpiece, but he wanted to go further, to turn Hollywood into a center of artistic cinema. Lucas and Spielberg wanted to modernize the system without disturbing it.

Coppola broke through first. His youth comedy *You're a Big Boy Now* (1967) borrowed the flashy techniques of Richard Lester's Beatles films and the swinging-London pictures. Coppola came to know the collapsing studio system from the inside, moving from Corman's American International Pictures to screenwriting (the Oscar-winning script for *Patton*, 1970) and then to directing, with the unsuccessful Broadway musical *Finian's Rainbow* (1968). *The Godfather* yielded him great financial rewards, but instead of promptly parlaying his success into a commercial career, he plunged into an intimate, ambivalent art movie, *The Conversation*. He turned *The Godfather, Part II* (1974) into a complex, time-juggling piece. Then he embarked on the vast, exhausting, budget-shattering *Apocalypse Now* (1979).

Coppola's was bravura filmmaking on a grand scale. In college he wanted to direct theater, and in many respects he remained an actor's director. For *The Godfather* he fought Paramount to hire Marlon Brando and Al Pacino and gave prime roles to James Caan, Robert Duvall, his sister Talia Shire, and other little-known actors. During rehearsals he had actors improvise scenes that would not be

in the film, and he held dinners in which the actors ate and drank and talked in character. For *The Godfather, Part II* he added New York stage legends like playwright Michael Gazzo and Lee Strasberg, the dean of the Actors Studio.

This interest in performance was balanced by a risk-taking cinematic sensibility. *The Godfather* was remarkably poised, partly because it refused the fast cutting and camera movements of the early 1970s. Coppola and his cinematographer, Gordon Willis, settled upon a "tableau" style that emphasized a static camera and actors moving through rich, often gloomy, interiors (**Color Plate 22.3**). In contrast, the fragmentary montage of sound and image in *The Conversation* sets the audience adrift in alternative times and mental spaces. In *Apocalypse Now*, Coppola would strive to give the Vietnam War an overpowering visual presence, with psychedelic color, surround sound, and slow, hallucinatory dissolves.

Coppola had founded his company, American Zoetrope, in 1969 in order to nurture his personal projects. After years of yearning for a facility, he bought the Hollywood General studio in 1979, renamed it Zoetrope Studios, and announced that it would be a center of new technology for feature films, an "electronic cinema" based on high-definition video sent out by satellite. He rebuilt the stages and directed performances from his trailer via video feeds. The main result was *One from the Heart* (1982), a flamboyantly artificial musical drama filled with stunning pictorial effects (**Color Plate 22.4**). *One from the Heart* would influence the French *cinéma du look* of the 1980s (p. 620), but the cost overruns and public indifference led to a massive failure. Soon Coppola was forced to sell his facility to satisfy his creditors.

What followed were twenty years of difficulty. Coppola launched some intriguing projects such as the teenage dramas *The Outsiders* (1983) and *Rumble Fish* (1983), as well as the brash *Tucker: The Man and His Dream* (1988, produced by Lucas). He never ceased to experiment with eye-catching compositions (**22.22**) and offbeat storytelling techniques, such as the use of a fake publicity film in *Tucker* and

(continued)

22.22 *Tucker*: an in-camera optical effect connects Tucker with his wife as they talk on the phone.

THE 1970s BIG THREE: COPPOLA, SPIELBERG, AND LUCAS, continued

22.23 Ingenious depth staging in Spielberg's *Jaws*.

22.24 The heroes of *Star Wars* rewarded.

the silent-film-style special effects in *Bram Stoker's Dracula* (1992). Yet he failed to restart his career. Even a sequel, *Godfather III* (1990), to his biggest hit did not redeem him, and he became a director for hire. Coppola began to be known not for his movies but for the wine cultivated at his Napa Valley vineyard.

By contrast, Lucas and Spielberg sought to recover their boyhood pleasure in movies. They tried to re-create the uncomplicated fun of space opera (*Star Wars*), action-packed serials (*Raiders of the Lost Ark*), and fantasy (*Close Encounters, E.T.: The Extraterrestrial*, 1982). In making *Star Wars*, Lucas pulled together the most exciting portions of several air battles from Hollywood combat pictures, storyboarded the compiled sequence, and then shot his space dogfights to match the older footage. As producers, Lucas

and Spielberg revived the family film of adventure (*Willow*, 1988), fantasy (*Gremlins*, 1984), and cartoon comedy (*Who Framed Roger Rabbit?*, 1988; **Color Plate 22.5**). While the Disney studio was floundering, two baby boomers recaptured the old magic. Many critics noted that Walt himself would have loved to make *Star Wars* or *E.T.*

Spielberg divided his attention between what he called "fast-food movies" (*Jaws*, the "Indiana Jones" series) and more upscale directorial efforts (*The Color Purple*, 1985; *Empire of the Sun*, 1987). These dignified adaptations of best-selling novels had a nostalgic side, too, recalling the Hollywood prestige picture of the 1930s and 1940s. Looking back to the great tradition, Spielberg filled his films with reverent allusions to the studio program picture (*Always*, 1989, is a remake of Victor Fleming's *A Guy Named Joe*,

It had become clear that the industry's success was based on very few films. In any year, only ten or so "must-see" pictures comprised the bulk of admissions, while most of the Majors' releases failed to break even. The industry therefore sought to minimize the risks. Companies

began releasing their big-budget films in the peak leisure periods, summer and Christmas. Following the lead of exploitation companies like AIP, Universal filled television with ads for *Jaws* and released the film to hundreds of theaters simultaneously. In the decades to come, most

1943) and to Disney (*Close Encounters; Hook,* 1991; and *A.I.: Artificial Intelligence,* 2001).

In one respect, Spielberg proved himself heir to the studio directors; with the right material, he could make a story come grippingly alive for his audience. The cleverly constructed *Jaws* balanced its thrills with a skeptical attitude toward political leadership. Against the money-grubbing businesspeople of Amity, the film offers three versions of male heroism: the grizzled man of action Quint, the scientific rationalist Hooper, and the reluctant pragmatist Sheriff Brody. Each sequence hits a high pitch of emotional tension, and scene by scene the audience's anxiety is ratcheted up through crisp editing, inventive Panavision compositions (**22.23**), and John Williams's ominous score. Likewise, in the "Indiana Jones" and "Jurassic Park" series, Spielberg revamped the traditions of Raoul Walsh and Jacques Tourneur for the blockbuster age.

Spielberg's New Age–tinted spirituality, often expressed as mute wonder at glittering technological marvels, proved even more popular. Over and over the young man from divorced suburban parents replayed the drama of a family's breakup and a child's yearning for happiness. He found emblematic images—spindly aliens communicating through music, a boy bicycling silhouetted against the moon—that verged on kitsch but also struck a chord in millions. Spielberg became New Hollywood's reliable showman, recalling Cecil B. DeMille, Alfred Hitchcock, and the director whom he claimed he most resembled, Victor Fleming, the contract professional who had a hand in both *Gone with the Wind* and *The Wizard of Oz.*

Less of a movie fan than Coppola and Spielberg, Lucas spent his youth watching television, reading comic books, and tinkering with cars. The world of cruising and rock'n'roll was lovingly depicted in *American Graffiti,* whose meticulously designed music track and interwoven coming-of-age crises presented the real teen picture that studios had been craving. *Star Wars* offered chivalric myth for 1970s teens, a quest romance in which young heroes could find adventure, pure love, and a sacred cause (**22.24**). Not surprisingly, *Star Wars* was published as a comic book before the film was released. Coppola loved working with actors, but Lucas avoided talking with them except for the occasional "Faster!" He looked forward to creating his scenes digitally, shooting isolated actors against blank screens, or creating characters wholly on computer. This dream, the ultimate film extension of the comic-book aesthetic, was realized first in *Star Wars Episode I: The Phantom Menace* (1999), in which Jar Jar Binks was the first wholly computer-generated character in a major live-action feature film.

Lucas often called himself an independent filmmaker, and in some sense he was. The triumph of *Star Wars* allowed him to dictate terms to any studio in town. After frequent clashes with Fox on *The Empire Strikes Back* (1980), which ran over schedule and budget, he vowed that he would never compromise again. Retreating to his own fiefdom, Skywalker Ranch, Lucas oversaw a high-tech wonderland based on a saga that gripped the imagination of millions around the world and spawned *Star Wars* novels, toys, games, action figures, and video games. Skywalker staff maintained a volume, "The Bible," that listed all the events occurring in the *Star Wars* universe.

Yet Lucas continued to believe that he was spinning a simple tale grounded in basic human values. Like Spielberg, Lucas hit on a resonant New Age theme: the Force, representing God, the cosmos, or whatever the viewer was comfortable with. Beneath all the hardware, he claimed, *Star Wars* was about "redemption." Spielberg remarked, hyperbolically, that *Star Wars* marked the moment "when the world recognized the value of childhood."[7]

All three directors had colossal hits in the 1970s, but only Spielberg and Lucas continued to rule over the next twenty years. At one point in the early 1980s, the pair were responsible for the six top-grossing films of the postwar period. Coppola foresaw the multimedia future but believed that Zoetrope Studios could become a vertically integrated firm on its own. His two peers saw deeper, letting the studios remain distributors while they provided content. Lucasfilm and LucasArts produced theatrical films, television series, commercials, interactive games, computer animation, and special effects, as well as new editing and sound systems. Spielberg's Amblin Entertainment produced some of the era's most popular films (*Back to the Future,* 1985; *Twister,* 1996). Later, DreamWorks SKG, which Spielberg founded with Jeffrey Katzenberg and David Geffen, churned out features and television shows to be distributed by Universal. By 1980, Lucas and Spielberg had become the most powerful director-producers in the industry, and they remained at the top into the new century.

major releases would receive saturation advertising and booking, pinning their fates on one opening weekend.

When viewers returned to *Jaws* over and over, studios learned that it was profitable to extend runs for big films. In planning productions, studios opted for sequels and series that were based on successes, such as the *Rocky* films and the *Star Trek* saga. Moreover, *Jaws* had been made with little concern for merchandising, but in negotiating his stake in *Star Wars,* Lucas had shrewdly obtained a large percentage of the rights to toys,

T-shirts, and other tie-ins. Studios watched as the *Star Wars* merchandising income exceeded its box-office take, and they subsequently created their own merchandising divisions.

Despite some inroads made by independent distributors, the market was ruled by familiar players. The major distribution companies garnered 90 percent of all theater revenues. A film financed outside the studios could not get widely screened unless it was distributed by a top company. The standard distribution fee, 35 percent, came directly from gross rentals, so *Jaws* and *Star Wars* earned distribution income for Universal and 20th Century-Fox over and above any investments the studios made in the productions. The major distributors also controlled international circulation of U.S. films.

Still, the Majors needed filmmakers. While some studios, notably Disney, prided themselves on generating their own projects, most came to rely on directors and producers with strong track records. Spielberg and Lucas became powerful producers who could find financing easily and could even demand reductions in distribution fees. Studios cultivated long-term relationships with producers who could bring together a script, a director, and stars. Increasingly, agents were functioning as quasi-producers by gathering their clients into packages, a strategy pioneered by Lew Wasserman (p. 336–337) and developed by Sue Mengers in assembling Ryan O'Neal, Barbra Streisand, and director Peter Bogdanovich for *What's Up, Doc?* (1973). The year 1975 saw the formation of two powerful talent agencies, International Creative Management and Creative Artists Agency, both of which would become prime packagers in the 1980s.

Many of the most adept moguls were TV-trained, like Paramount's Barry Diller and Michael Eisner, and understood how to broker talent. Studios also hired agents as executives because they had show-business experience though they lacked corporate MBAs. Accordingly, the 1970s initiated an era dominated by "the deal." *Development deals* generated income for the agents, producers, scriptwriters, and stars, but few films resulted. *Overall deals* paid stars and directors to develop "vanity projects" for studios, and *housekeeping deals* gave their production companies an office on the studio lot. Every participant in a package tried to hold out for the maximum, so a project might take years to reach the screen. Filmmakers complained that shooting pictures had become secondary to deal making.

As successful filmmakers gained more control over their projects, budgets often inflated. Coppola's *Apocalypse Now* took three years to shoot and cost over $30 million. Even highly successful directors were not immune to cost overruns, as Spielberg's *1941* (1979)

showed. The most notorious failure of the system involved Michael Cimino's ambitious Western, *Heaven's Gate* (1980). The budget rose to $40 million, the highest production cost of the 1970s. After the director's cut had a disastrous premiere, United Artists released a shortened version. It earned less than $2 million in rentals, and soon UA collapsed as a Major, eventually to be absorbed by MGM.

Studio executives began to complain that every young director wanted to be an auteur, free of all financial constraints (see "Notes and Queries" at the end of this chapter). Ironically, the rise of the New Hollywood, a director-centered trend, led to a general mistrust of directors. The 1980s would see studios strain to keep the filmmaker on track. Executives would provide notes on scripts and rushes, and test screenings would sample audiences' reaction to the director's cut.

A new era of blockbusters, built on packages and deals and bolstered by stars and special effects, had begun. *Superman: The Movie* (1978) was two years in the making. This independently produced film wound up costing somewhere between $40 million and $55 million. Gene Hackman demanded a salary of $2 million, while Marlon Brando received $3 million for two weeks' work. Mario Puzo, author of *The Godfather*, was paid $350,000 for the *Superman* script plus 5 percent of the gross receipts. Millions more were invested in the elaborate sets and special effects, prepared at England's Pinewood Studios. Aware of the value of a franchise series, the producers shot two films in one stretch of studio time so as to have a sequel ready. The film featured a score by the certified mega-hit composer John Williams (*Jaws, Star Wars, Close Encounters*). Released in December, *Superman: The Movie* eventually grossed over $80 million in its U.S. run, becoming the top hit of 1979 and Warner Bros.' most profitable film to date. It spawned three sequels and millions in merchandising, along the way spurring new interest in superhero comic books. Directed by Richard Donner, a man with no auteurist pretensions, it pointed the way to the *megapicture* strategy of the 1980s and 1990s.

Hollywood Updated

No 1970s studio could afford to concentrate completely on big-budget pictures. Each firm made only two or three of these per year. But since the studio's distribution wing needed from twelve to twenty pictures each year to pay for itself, the rest of the program was filled out with less costly items—often, genre fare revamped for young audiences. Comedy was pushed toward gross-out slapstick by directors and performers associated with *Na-*

22.25   The return of wide-angle shots: *Close Encounters of the Third Kind*.

22.26   Debt collecting in Little Italy: the "mook" scene from *Mean Streets*.

22.27, 22.28   In *Catch-22* (1970), Mike Nichols intercuts exaggerated deep-focus shots with images taken with a much longer lens.

tional Lampoon magazine and television's "Saturday Night Live" in *Animal House* (1978). Musicals were updated to incorporate disco (*Saturday Night Fever*, 1977) or to playfully mock 1950s teen culture (*Grease*, 1978).

Now that simply updating genres occasionally provided hits, many directors steered away from the experimentation encouraged by the art-cinema vogue of the late 1960s and early 1970s. Most young directors did not try to challenge mainstream storytelling. Instead, they followed Spielberg and Lucas in reworking established genres and referencing hallowed classics and directors. In several ways, the New Hollywood defined itself by remaking the old. "We were very much concerned with making the Hollywood film," recalled John Milius, "not to make a lot of money, but as artists."[8]

Many films became ironic or affectionate tributes to the studio tradition. John Carpenter's *Assault on Precinct 13* updates Hawks's *Rio Bravo*, pitting a stoic code of conduct against contemporary urban violence. Brian De Palma became famous for his pastiches of Hitchcock: *Obsession* (1976) is *Vertigo* with an incestuous twist; *Dressed to Kill* (1980) confronts *Psycho* with contemporary sexual mores. John Milius sought to revive the

swashbuckling action film in *The Wind and the Lion* (1975). These directors often cultivated a style that recognizably borrows from the masters. Carpenter's rhythmic cutting in *Assault on Precinct 13* is indebted to Hawks's *Scarface*. De Palma's overhead shots, startling deep-focus imagery, and split-screen handling of action recall Hitchcock's swaggering ingenuity. In *Jaws*, Spielberg borrowed Hitchcock's zoom-in/track-out technique from *Vertigo*, a device that was to be used commonly in 1980s film to show a background eerily squeezing around an unmoving figure.

During the late 1960s and early 1970s, directors had become reliant on long lenses; entire scenes might be shot with the depth-flattening telephoto. By contrast, Spielberg, De Palma, and other New Hollywood directors reintroduced wide-angle-lens compositions reminiscent of Orson Welles, William Wyler, and film noir. The results were often striking depth of focus and distortion of figures (**22.25, 22.26**). Yet directors did not abandon long lenses. From the 1970s onward, they mixed occasional deep-focus shots with flatter telephoto shots (**22.27, 22.28**). As the films' scripts often gave 1940s and 1950s genres a contemporary treatment, so their style became a synthesis of techniques derived from many eras.

Several films of the New Hollywood revisited traditional genres. *The Godfather* movies revived the classic gangster film but gave the formula some fresh twists. *The Godfather* (1972) emphasizes the genre's conventional ethnic divisions (Italian/Irish/Jewish/WASP) and its machismo values but adds a new stress on family unity and intergenerational succession. Michael Corleone, at first remote from the "family business," becomes his father's rightful heir, at the cost of distancing himself from his wife Kay. *The Godfather, Part II* (1974) shows how Michael's father became a success, harking back to another genre formula, the emigrant gangster's rise to power. This earlier time period is intercut with Michael's expanding authority and ruthlessness in the 1950s. Whereas the first *Godfather* ends with Michael's full assimilation into the male line of the family, *Part II* closes with him locked in autumnal shadow, alone and brooding, unable to trust anyone.

The Godfather did not lead to a renaissance of the gangster film, but two other genres were revived on a major scale. The horror film, long associated with low-budget exploitation, was given a new respectability in *The Exorcist* and became an industry mainstay for twenty years. Carpenter's *Halloween* (1978) spawned a long cycle of stalker-slasher films in which the victims, usually voluptuous teenagers, meet gory ends. Adaptations from best-selling novels by Stephen King yielded *Carrie* (1976, De Palma) and *The Shining* (1980, Stanley Kubrick).

The other significant genre to be revived was science fiction. Kubrick's *2001: A Space Odyssey* was the major forerunner, but it was Lucas and Spielberg who impressed Hollywood with the profit possibilities of a genre previously identified with kiddie matinees and teenage exploitation. *Star Wars* showed that space adventure, mounted with updated special effects, could attract a new generation of moviegoers, and its unprecedented success triggered not only its own film series but one based on the television program *Star Trek*. *Close Encounters of the Third Kind* turned the 1950s "invasion film" into a cozy, quasi-mystical experience of communion with extraterrestrial wisdom. After these films, science fiction would remain a dominant Hollywood genre, often as a showcase for new filmmaking technology.

The young directors acquired a taste for tradition from film school or late-night television, but an older figure came to it more spontaneously. Starting as a studio contract player, Clint Eastwood moved from movie bit-parts to a successful 1960s television series (*Rawhide*) and then to movie stardom in Sergio Leone's spaghetti Westerns (p. 454). Returning to Hollywood, Eastwood deepened his star image by working with veteran action director Don Siegel in *Coogan's Bluff* (1968) and *Dirty Harry* (1972). Eastwood's screen persona had a cynical, even sadistic, cast that set him apart from Paul Newman and John Wayne, his main box-office rivals. He turned to directing with *Play Misty for Me* (1971), which cast him as a late-night disc jockey stalked by an obsessive fan. Eastwood directed conventional action fare like *The Eiger Sanction* (1975), but he also brought a sour, mythic feel to the Western in *The Outlaw Josie Wales* (1976) and experimented with his image in *The Gauntlet* (1977) and *Bronco Billy* (1980). He shrewdly starred in other directors' genre efforts, which gave him big hits like *Any Which Way But Loose* (1978).

Eastwood shot his films fast and cheap, which yielded solid profits but sometimes made them look staid in an age of hyper-produced extravaganzas. Yet his respect for genre conventions and the trim efficiency of his style stood as a reminder of the solidity of the classic studio picture. During the 1980s and 1990s, Eastwood was the most prolific major director in Hollywood, and he represented its traditions at their purest, in his sober treatment of the military film (*Heartbreak Ridge,* 1986), the Western (*Pale Rider,* 1985; *Unforgiven,* 1992), the romance (*The Bridges of Madison County,* 1995), and the crime drama (*True Crime,* 1999). He also won acclaim for *Bird* (1988), a testament to his love of jazz.

Eastwood's calm craftsmanship seemed distinctly unhip alongside the satires and parodies pouring out of the studios in the 1970s. Woody Allen parodied the caper film (*Take the Money and Run,* 1969) and the science-fiction film (*Sleeper,* 1973). Mel Brooks made raucous, bawdy farces of the Western (*Blazing Saddles,* 1973), the Universal horror film (*Young Frankenstein,* 1974), the Hitchcockian thriller (*High Anxiety,* 1977), and the historical epic (*History of the World, Part I,* 1981). David and Jerry Zucker, along with Jim Abrahams, savaged the disaster film in *Airplane!* (1980). Such zany treatment of genre conventions had already been employed in silent slapstick and in the comedies of Bob Hope and Bing Crosby and Dean Martin and Jerry Lewis. Mocking Hollywood was itself a Hollywood tradition.

Scorsese as Synthesis

A few filmmakers managed to express personal concerns by adapting aspects of the European art film, and several more did so by reviving the studio tradition. Very few, however, were able to do both. Coppola managed

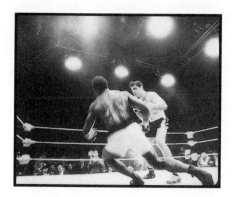

22.29, 22.30 Two different fights in *Raging Bull*, each with a distinct cinematic texture.

for a time, but Martin Scorsese blended both possibilities more consistently. Brought up on Hollywood features, Italian Neorealism, and "Million Dollar Movie" TV broadcasts, Scorsese studied filmmaking at New York University. He made an underground reputation with several shorts and two low-budget features before his *Mean Streets* (1973) drew wide attention. *Alice Doesn't Live Here Any More* (1974) and *Taxi Driver* (1975) propelled him to fame. *Raging Bull* (1980), a biography of prizefighter Jake LaMotta, won still greater notice; many critics consider it the finest American film of the 1980s. Scorsese's later films (notably *King of Comedy,* 1982; *The Last Temptation of Christ,* 1988; *GoodFellas,* 1989) cemented his reputation as the most critically acclaimed American director of his generation.

As a movie brat, Scorsese was heavily indebted to the Hollywood tradition. *Taxi Driver* was scored by Bernard Herrmann, Hitchcock's composer, and, as preparation for shooting *New York, New York* (1976), Scorsese studied 1940s Hollywood musicals. Later, with *Cape Fear* (1991), he would remake a classic thriller. Like Altman and Allen, however, he was also influenced by European cinema. A shot change in *Raging Bull* is as likely to derive from Godard as from George Stevens's *Shane,* and the exploration of Rupert Pupkin's world in *King of Comedy* creates a Felliniesque ambiguity about what is real and what is fantasy.

Scorsese's film consciousness also emerges in his virtuosic displays of technique. His films alternate intense, aggressive dialogue scenes designed to highlight the skills of performers such as Robert De Niro with scenes of physical action served up with dazzling camera flourishes. The action sequences are often abstract and wordless, built out of hypnotic imagery: a yellow cab gliding through hellishly smoky streets (*Taxi Driver*), billiard balls ricocheting across a pool table (*The Color of Money,* 1986). Each of the boxing scenes in *Raging Bull* is staged and filmed differently (**22.29, 22.30**). Whereas

other movie brats created spectacle through high-tech special effects, Scorsese engaged the viewer by a bold, idiosyncratic style.

Like Allen's films, Scorsese's had strong autobiographical undercurrents. *Mean Streets* drew upon his Italian American youth (see 22.26). After years of self-destructive behavior, he felt ready to tackle *Raging Bull:* "I understood then what Jake was, but only after having gone through a similar experience. I was just lucky that there happened to be a project there ready for me to express this."[9] Perhaps as a result of his emotional absorption in his stories, Scorsese's films center on driven, even obsessed, protagonists, and his technique often puts us firmly in their minds. Rapid point-of-view shots, flickering glances, slow-motion imagery, and subjective sound heighten our identification with the prizefighter Jake LaMotta, the taxi driver Travis Bickle, and the aspiring stand-up comedian Rupert Pupkin (**22.31**). For many critics, Scorsese showed that a filmmaker could skillfully

22.31 In his basement, aspiring talk-show host Rupert Pupkin interviews cardboard cut-outs of Liza Minnelli and Jerry Lewis (*King of Comedy*).

blend experimental impulses with the renewed crafts-manship that characterized the 1970s.

OPPORTUNITIES FOR INDEPENDENTS

The difficulties and recovery of the Majors were bound up with the fate of independent production in the United States during this period. The 1948 Paramount decision and the rise of the teenage market gave independent companies like Allied Artists and American International Pictures (AIP) an entry into the low-budget market (p. 338).

During the late 1960s, the low-budget independents grew stronger, partly through the relaxing of the Production Code and partly through the decline of the Majors. With the slackening of censorship controls, the 1960s saw growth in erotic exploitation. *"Nudies"* surfaced from the 16mm *stag film* world and could be seen in decaying picture palaces in America's downtown neighborhoods. Eroticism became mixed with gore in Herschell Gordon Lewis's *Blood Feast* (1963) and *2000 Maniacs* (1964). Russ Meyer began in nudies before discovering his idiosyncratic blend of hammering editing, gruesome violence, and parodically overblown sex scenes (*Motorpsycho*, 1965; *Faster Pussycat, Kill! Kill!*, 1966). Meyer blazed the trail for "mainstream" 1970s pornography with films such as *Vixen* (1968).

The youthpics craze was fed by AIP's cycle of motorcycle-gang movies and *Wild in the Streets* (1968). The films of AIP's main director, Roger Corman, had a strong influence on young directors of the late 1960s, and AIP gave opportunities to Coppola, Scorsese, Bogdanovich, John Milius, De Palma, Robert De Niro, and Jack Nicholson. The low-budget independent film *Night of the Living Dead* (1968), rejected by AIP as too gory, went on to become a colossal cult hit and launched the career of director George Romero.

During most of the 1970s as well, independent production proved a robust alternative to the Majors. As the studios cut back production, low-budget films helped fill the market. Firms began to specialize in certain genres—martial-arts films, action pictures, erotic pictures (*sexploitation*). Films aimed at African Americans (*blaxploitation*) showcased young black performers and, sometimes, black creative personnel like directors Gordon Parks, Sr. (*Shaft*, 1971) and Michael Schultz (*Cooley High*, 1975; *Car Wash*, 1976). In the wake of *Night of the Living Dead* and *The Exorcist*, the teenage horror market was tapped with films like Tobe Hooper's grotesque *Texas Chainsaw Massacre* (1974) and John Carpenter's more sober and expensive *Halloween*. Corman's

new company, New World Pictures, created cycles and trained new directors (Jonathan Demme, John Sayles, James Cameron).

In some venues, the cheaper films could find an audience denied to the glossier studio product. Sunn International discovered, to the Majors' surprise, that there was still a family audience who could be lured from the television set with wildlife adventures and quasi-religious documentaries. Tom Laughlin, the enterprising director-producer-star of *Billy Jack* (1971), showed that small-town viewers would still come to films that mixed sentiment, action, and populist themes. Meanwhile, teenagers and college students began flocking to outrageous movies like John Waters's *Pink Flamingos* (1974). Theaters found that *midnight movies* would attract a young crowd; *The Rocky Horror Picture Show* (1975) and *Eraserhead* (1978) became profitable almost solely through such shows.

The Majors responded by absorbing the sensational elements that had given independent films their edge. Big-budget films became more sexually explicit, and for a time Russ Meyer, exploiter of erotica, found himself working for a studio (*Beyond the Valley of the Dolls*, 1970). *The Exorcist* traded on blasphemy and visceral disgust to a new degree. *Star Wars* and *Close Encounters* incorporated elements of low-budget science fiction (*Silent Running*, 1971; *Dark Star*, 1974), while *Alien* (1979) and other films reflected the new standards of gory violence established by independent directors such as Carpenter and David Cronenberg (*Rabid*, 1977; *The Blood*, 1979). "'Exploitation' films were so named because you made a film about something wild with a great deal of action, a little sex, and possibly some sort of strange gimmick," wrote Corman. "[Later] the majors saw they could have enormous commercial success with big-budget exploitation films."[10]

Apart from the mass-market independents, there emerged a more artistically ambitious independent sector. New York sustained an "off-Hollywood" tendency. Shirley Clarke, known for her dance and experimental shorts, adapted the play *The Connection* (1962) and made the semidocumentary *The Cool World* (1963; **22.32**). Jonas and Adolfas Mekas modeled *Guns of the Trees* (1961) and *Hallelujah the Hills* (1963) on the experiments of European new waves.

The most famous member of this off-Hollywood group was John Cassavetes. A New York actor committed to Method acting, Cassavetes made a career on the stage and in films and television. He scraped up donations to direct *Shadows* (1961). "The film you have just seen was an improvisation": this curt closing title announced Cassavetes's key aesthetic decision. The story,

22.32 Shirley Clarke directing *The Cool World*.

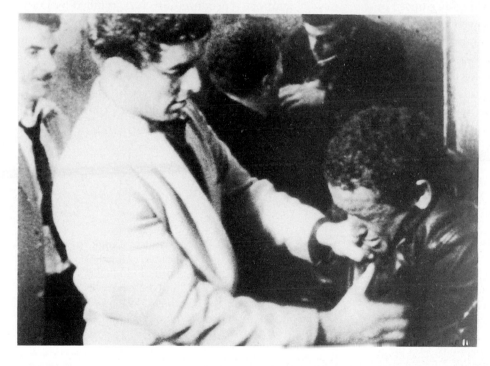

22.33 The roughly shot beating of Ben (*Shadows*).

about two black brothers and their sister in the New York jazz and party scene, was unscripted; the actors shared creative choices about dialogue and delivery with the director. Although shooting in a semidocumentary style, with a grimy, grainy look (**22.33**), Cassavetes also relied on deep-focus compositions and poetic interludes familiar from contemporary Hollywood cinema. *Shadows* won festival prizes and led Cassavetes to undertake

a pair of ill-fated Hollywood projects. He returned to independent cinema, financing his films by acting in mainstream pictures, and became an emblematic figure for younger filmmakers.

Basing his aesthetic on a conception of raw realism, Cassavetes created a string of films featuring quasi-improvised performances and casual camerawork. *Faces* (1968) and *Husbands* (1970), with their sudden zooms to close-up and their search for revelatory detail, use Direct Cinema techniques to comment on the bleak disappointments and deceptions of middle-class American couples. Characteristically, his counterculture comedy *Minnie and Moskowitz* (1971) centers on the love affair of a middle-aged hippie and a lonely museum curator. In *A Woman under the Influence* (1974), *Opening Night* (1979), and *Love Streams* (1984), the drama alternates between mundane routines and painful outbursts that push each actor to near-hysterical limits. This spasmodic rhythm, and his focus on the anxieties underlying adult love and work, made Cassavetes's midlife melodramas seem experimental by 1970s and 1980s Hollywood standards.

The New York scene received a further burst of energy from Joan Micklin Silver's *Hester Street* (1975), a drama of Jewish life in late-nineteenth-century New York. Filmed for less than $500,000, it was released nationwide and earned more than $5 million. When it received an Academy Award nomination, the film sparked a new awareness of off-Hollywood filmmaking.

The independent impulse spread to regional filmmakers, who managed to make low-budget features centered on territories seldom brought to the screen. John Waters revealed Baltimore as a campy Peyton Place (*Female Trouble*, 1975), while Victor Nuñez's *Gal Young 'Un* (1979) took place in Florida during the Depression. Another historical drama was John Hanson and Rob Nilsson's *Northern Lights* (1979), set in 1915 North Dakota during labor unrest. It won the best first-film award at the Cannes Film Festival.

Slowly, alternative venues were emerging for independent film. In addition to New York's Anthology Film Archive (founded in 1970), several festivals were established in Los Angeles (known as Filmex, 1971), Telluride, Colorado (1973), and Toronto and Seattle (1975), as well as the U.S. Film Festival (1978), later known as Sundance. At the same time, enterprising filmmakers organized the Independent Feature Project (IFP) as an association of independent film artists, and the IFP established, in 1979, the Independent Feature Film Market as a showcase for finished films and works in progress. The American independent cinema was poised for takeoff.

During the 1960s, the failing studios searched for new corporate identities and business models. After some winnowing, the 1970s set in place patterns that would dominate American film for the rest of the century. A new generation of moguls would partner with a new generation of producer-directors, typified by Lucas and Spielberg, under the auspices of a conglomerate. The studios would concentrate on funding and making must-see movies. Alongside the expanding industry was an independent sector whose fortunes fluctuated but whose commitment to alternative stories and styles increased the variety of U.S. film culture.

· ·

Notes and Queries

THE AMERICAN DIRECTOR AS SUPERSTAR

The auteur theory of film criticism and history held the individual director to be the primary source of the film's formal, stylistic, and thematic qualities. This theory, reinforced by the prominence of postwar directors in Europe and Asia, was applied by *Cahiers du cinéma* to Hollywood directors as well, and Andrew Sarris introduced it to English-language readers (see "Notes and Queries," Chapter 19). Collections of interviews such as Sarris's *Interviews with Film Directors* (Indianapolis: Bobbs-Merrill, 1967) and Joseph Gelmis's *The Film Director as Superstar* (New York: Doubleday, 1970) reinforced the impression that the director was the central figure in the creation of a film. By the 1980s, this belief was taken for granted even in mass journalism and fan magazines.

Many directors who came to prominence in America during the 1970s and 1980s knew the auteur theory through its promulgation in film schools and the popular press. Young directors self-consciously sought to create personal films modeled on European art cinema or the Hollywood classics of Hitchcock, Ford, and Hawks. The results of this strategy are discussed in Noël Carroll, "The Future of Allusion," *October* 20 (spring 1982): 51–81, and David Thomson, *Overexposures: The Crisis in American Filmmaking* (New York: Morrow, 1981), pp. 49–68.

FILM CONSCIOUSNESS AND FILM PRESERVATION

American filmmakers' new awareness of film history coincided with a growing need to safeguard the country's motion-picture heritage. During the 1970s and 1980s, nitrate copies were decomposing and Eastman Color prints began to fade. There were new efforts to *preserve* films (that is, keep good negatives and prints in archival conditions), to *restore* films (to bring deteriorated material back to something approaching its original quality), and to *reconstruct*

CHAPTER 23

POLITICALLY CRITICAL CI
OF THE 1960s AND 1970s

Tensions between the
lessen during the 1960
model was fracturing. Gr
Union led to an open brea
eastern European peoples s
time, the Third World appe
came sovereign states, and
and western ways. Third-W
that these developing coun
use the experience of oppre

Economic developmen
moving at an uneven pace. N
were briskly becoming mar
ever, were not developing f
populations.

Political violence intens
from the major confrontatio
nam, and the Middle East—
ternal aggression, civil wars,
rise to revolutionary hopes.
gested that sovereignty, nat
enough to help the developir
tries' class systems, holdover
structured by means of socia
persistent guerrilla warfare of
fied many resistance moveme

Film history was profou
World. As industrialization

films (to gather lost or discarded footage to enable viewers to see more complete or more original versions of films).

The American Film Institute, founded in 1967, took as part of its charter the preservation and restoration of films. The Library of Congress, the Academy of Motion Picture Arts and Sciences, the Museum of Modern Art, the George Eastman House, and other archives saved hundreds of films with the financial assistance of the AFI. During the 1980s, the UCLA Film Archive restored *Becky Sharp* and *For Whom the Bell Tolls,* and MoMA reconstructed *Intolerance.* (See Robert Gitt and Richard Dayton, "Restoring *Becky Sharp,*" *American Cinematographer* 65, no. 10 [November 1984]: 99–106, and Russell Merritt, "D. W. Griffith's *Intolerance*: Reconstructing an Unattainable Text," *Film History* 4, no. 4 [1990]: 337–75.) Individual specialists also took part. Ronald Haver found new footage for a longer version of *A Star Is Born* (1954; see **A Star Is Born:** *The Making of the 1954 Movie and Its 1983 Restoration* [New York: Knopf, 1988]), and Robert Harris restored *Lawrence of Arabia* and *Spartacus* ("HP Interviews Robert Harris on Film Restoration," *Perfect Vision* 12 (winter 1991/1992): 29–34). Martin Scorsese helped finance the 1993 restoration and rerelease of *El Cid* (1961, Anthony Mann).

The 1980s also saw a new public for older films, made available at special events or on video. Kevin Brownlow's series of silent films for Thames television led to gala theatrical showings of new prints of *The Wind, Greed,* and other classics. Brownlow and David Robinson discovered precious material from Charles Chaplin's outtakes and made them available in video formats as *The Unknown Chaplin.* Studios, recognizing the financial benefits of rereleases, cablecasting, and video versions, have become somewhat more willing to preserve and restore their films.

EXPLOITATION FILMS AND CONNOISSEURS OF "WEIRD MOVIES"

Since the 1970s, exploitation movies have become cult items. Some fans find hilarity in the overblown dialogue, stiff performances, and awkward technique. This so-bad-it's-good attitude was popularized in Harry and Michael Medved, *The Golden Turkey Awards* (New York: Putnam, 1980). Other aficionados consider the exploitation films a direct challenge to the idea of normality presented by the Hollywood mainstream. Arising at the time of Punk and No Wave music, this notion of the subversive potential of rough technique and bad taste was exemplified in the "fanzines" *Film Threat* and *That's Exploitation!* With the new availability of exploitation items on video, a "psychotronic" subculture grew up around violent films, both old and more recent.

"Incredibly Strange Films," *Re/Search* 10 (1986) gathers information on exploitation items of the 1960s. The magazine *Video Watchdog* specializes in comparing versions of exploitation horror films. Rudolph Grey's *Nightmare of Ecstasy: The Life and Art of Edward D. Wood, Jr.* (Los Angeles: Feral, 1992) compiles attractively odd interviews. Autobiographies of more successful exploitation filmmakers include William Castle, *Step Right Up! I'm Gonna Scare the Pants Off America: Memoirs of a B-Movie Mogul* (New York: Pharos, 1992 [originally published in 1976]); Roger Corman (with Jim Jerome), *How I Made a Hundred Movies in Hollywood and Never Lost a Dime* (New York: Random House, 1990); and Sam Arkoff (with Richard Trubo), *Flying through Hollywood by the Seat of My Pants* (New York: Birch Lane, 1992).

REFERENCES

1. Quoted in Peter Bogdanovich, *Who the Devil Made It* (New York: Knopf, 1997), p. 250.
2. Quoted in Tag Gallagher, *John Ford: The Man and His Films* (Berkeley: University of California Press, 1986), p. 437.
3. Quoted in Peter Cowie, *Coppola* (London: Faber and Faber, 1990), p. 61.
4. Quoted in Eric Lax, *Woody Allen: A Biography* (New York: Knopf, 1991), p. 255.
5. *Gone with the Wind* and the Disney animated classics had higher all-time returns, but they were rereleased at intervals over many years. Still, if rentals are adjusted for inflation, *Gone with the Wind* remains the highest-earning film of all time.
6. Quoted in Stephen M. Silverman, *The Fox That Got Away: The Last Days of the Zanuck Dynasty at Twentieth Century-Fox* (Secaucus NJ: Lyle Stuart, 1988), p. 303.
7. Quoted in Bernard Weinraub, "Luke Skywalker Goes Home," in Sally Kline, ed., *George Lucas Interviews* (Jackson: University Press of Mississippi, 1999), p. 217.
8. Quoted in Michael Goodwin and Naomi Wise, *On the Edge: The Life and Times of Francis Coppola* (New York: Morrow, 1989), p. 30.
9. Quoted in David Thompson and Ian Christie, eds., *Scorsese on Scorsese* (London: Faber and Faber, 1989), pp. 76–77.
10. Roger Corman and Jim Jerome, *How I Made a Hundred Movies in Hollywood and Never Lost a Dime* (New York: Random House, 1990), p. 34.

FURTHER READING

Bach, Steven. *Final Cut: Dreams and Disasters in the Making of* **Heaven's Gate.** New York: New American Library, 1986.
Biskind, Peter. *Easy Riders, Raging Bulls: How the Sex-Drugs-and-Rock'n'Roll Generation Saved Hollywood.* New York: Simon and Schuster, 1998.
Gomery, Douglas. "The American Film Industry of the 1970s: Stasis in the 'New Hollywood.'" *Wide Angle* 5, no. 4 (1983): 52–59.
Hoberman, J., and Jonathan Rosenbaum. *Midnight Movies.* New York: Harper and Row, 1983.

Jenkins, Gary. *Empire Building: The Remarkable Real Life Story of* **Star Wars.** 2nd ed. New York: Citadel, 1999.

Kline, Sally. *George Lucas Interviews.* Jackson: University Press of Kentucky, 1999.

Lax, Eric. *Woody Allen: A Biography.* New York: Knopf, 1991.

Lebo, Harlan. *The* **Godfather** *Legacy.* New York: Simon and Schuster, 1997.

Levin, Lear. "Robert Altman's Innovative Sound Techniques." *American Cinematographer* 61, no. 4 (April 1980): 336–39, 368, 384.

Lewis, Jon. *Hollywood v. Hard Core: How the Struggle over Censorship Saved the Modern Film Industry.* New York: New York University Press, 2000.

———. *Whom God Wishes to Destroy . . . : Francis Coppola and the New Hollywood.* Durham, NC: Duke University Press, 1995.

McBride, Joseph. *Steven Spielberg: A Biography.* New York: Simon and Schuster, 1997.

Patterson, Richard. "The Preservation of Color Films." *American Cinematographer* 62, no. 7 (July 1981):

growth of Third World cities—at the rate of 10 million to 11 million people per year in the 1960s—expanded audiences. Significantly, this occurred as filmgoing was declining in Europe and the United States. A larger proportion of the world film audience was made up of Indians, Africans, and Asians.

The Third World was at the forefront of revolutionary cinema, foreshadowing trends that would emerge in the developed countries. People were pushing for social change—through protest, through resistance to authority, and sometimes through violent confrontation. Between the mid-1960s and the mid-1970s, filmmaking and film viewing became political acts to a degree not seen since World War II. The first part of this chapter examines how filmmakers treated cinema as a tool of social change and a weapon of political liberation.

In the Soviet bloc countries, many citizens strained to liberalize communist societies, and the most politically provocative works of eastern European and Soviet cinema often asserted the individuality of the artist's imagination. In western Europe and North America, unorthodox left-wing groups criticized government policies, educational institutions, and economic conditions. Radical politics entered daily life. As was often said, the personal had become political.

Many western radicals were suspicious of the very democratic humanism that Soviet bloc reformists craved. Capitalist society, many believed, maintained an "illusory democracy" and "repressive tolerance." Radicals often took Third World leaders like Mao Zedong, Che Guevara, and Fidel Castro as models of popular revolution. By the mid-1970s, however, militancy gave way to a micropolitics that focused pragmatically on particular issues. What one historian has called "the political culture of dissent" began to permeate everyday life in the western countries.[1] The second part of this chapter looks at how this culture shaped filmmaking in the First and Second Worlds.

POLITICAL FILMMAKING IN THE THIRD WORLD

Brazil's Cinema Nôvo (pp. 471–475) had struck a compromise between auteur cinema and political critique. Its films were addressed primarily to cultivated viewers who appreciated European art cinema. In the late 1960s, Third World directors began making politically critical films aimed at broader audiences.

In some countries, politicized cinema arose from the same concerns for social critique that had propelled filmmakers in the 1950s. Actors or directors who had

23.1   A smooth crane shot reflects the technical prowess of Egypt's well-established film industry (*The Land*).

23.2   *Umut:* as Djabbar (played by Güney) and his customer talk of finding buried treasure, they drive through a neighborhood whose wealth mocks their dreams.

found success in a well-organized industry were in a strong position to make critical films. The Egyptian Youssef Chahine, for instance, was able to exploit his commercial reputation to direct such populist films as *The Land* (1969; **23.1**). In Turkey, the actor Yilmaz Güney also benefited from a growing national industry. His popularity enabled him to direct *Umut* ("Hope," 1970), in which Güney stars as a taxi man hoping to strike it rich in the lottery. The film's emphasis on daily routine and its episodic structure put it in the lineage of Neorealism and the early 1960s art cinema, while its slow pace and use of *temps morts* exemplify a resistance to action-filled plotting (**23.2**). *Umut* inspired a new, "engaged" filmmaking in Turkey.

23.3 Bhuvan Shome, a cold bureaucrat on vacation in a village, learns about life outside the office from a warm-hearted rural woman (production still).

In India, Mrinal Sen's *Bhuvan Shome* (1969) sprang largely from the individual filmmaker's urge to launch a social critique. Sen had participated in the left-wing Indian People's Theatre Movement and had made films since 1956, but *Bhuvan Shome*, a comic satire on neocolonialist bureaucrats (23.3), led him to what he called "a taste for pamphleteering."[2] Along with Ritwik Ghatak, the leftist director who had gone into teaching (p. 410), Sen helped create the New Indian Cinema of the early 1970s.

Revolutionary Aspirations

Chahine, Güney, and Sen exemplify the general politicized tendency of Third World filmmaking in the late 1960s. But Third Worldism called for a more militant film practice. Many believed that Third World revolution was in the offing. In 1962, Algeria won a war of independence from France. African colonies, newly liberated, showed promise of indigenous rule. Some guerrilla wars in Latin America were initially successful. The Palestine Liberation Organization, founded in 1964, promised to win Palestinians a homeland. Fidel Castro had led a revolution in Cuba, and the U.S.-backed Bay of Pigs invasion had been easily repelled. China's split with Moscow in 1960 seemed to signal the emergence of a non-Soviet-style communism, and Mao Zedong's pronouncements carried enormous authority among radicals throughout the 1960s. In Vietnam, Ho Chi Minh's National Liberation Front had managed to resist U.S. intervention in the war with the corrupt regime in the South.

Such developments seemed to point toward a mass revolution of oppressed peoples. The writings of Algerian psychiatrist Frantz Fanon argued that all colonized people had to recognize that their minds had been restructured by western domination. "People of the world," Mao urged in 1964, "unite and defeat the U.S. aggressors and all their running dogs!"[3] At the 1966 Conference of Solidarity in Havana, speakers advocated that Asia, Africa, and Latin America organize to fight western imperialism and neocolonialism.

The possibility of tricontinental revolution inspired many filmmakers. In the Middle East, for instance, there grew up a New Cinema movement dedicated to Third World revolution. Egyptian anticolonialist films such as Salah Abou Seif's *Cairo '30* (1966) and Tewfik Saleh's *The Rebels* (1968) inspired filmmakers in Lebanon, Tunisia, and Egypt to make more-militant features. Palestinian and Algerian resistance organizations made short propaganda pieces. Moroccans established a journal, *Cinema 3* (the "3" standing for Third World). In December 1973, concurrent with a conference of nonaligned countries, Algiers hosted a meeting of Third World filmmakers. Similar activities took place in Asia, Africa, and Latin America.

The fundamental premise of revolutionary Third World film was that all art, even that purporting to be only entertainment, is deeply political. The stories that are told, the views with which the viewer is asked to sympathize, the values implicit in the action, and even the way in which the story is told—all were held to reflect political ideologies. The domination of Hollywood films in the Third World thus provided an obvious target. Revolutionary cinema would not only reject the politics that masqueraded as entertainment, not only attack the imperialist ideology carried by American movies, but also offer the viewer a politically liberating film experience.

Political Genres and Style

To some extent revolutionary cinema employed traditional genres, such as documentary or socially critical films set in the present day. But in Latin America and Africa, filmmakers forged new genres of fictional films.

One common genre was the historical examination of mass struggles against imperialism. In almost every country, filmmakers found incidents of resistance or rebellion that could be made relevant to the contemporary scene. There was also the *exile film,* which portrayed the experiences of individuals cut off from their roots and reflecting on their native country from abroad. African filmmakers studying abroad in the 1960s often made films in this genre; Latin American filmmakers also used it to examine their political exile in the 1970s. Yet another genre was one that plumbed indigenous cultures, seeking to reveal a national identity untainted by colonialism. In this genre (known in African cinema as the *return to the sources*), filmmakers drew upon folklore, myth, and ritual and then transformed such elements so as to reflect critically upon native traditions or contemporary politics.

Stylistically, militant Third World filmmakers refused the technical gloss identified with Hollywood spectacle. The lightweight cameras and informal lighting of Direct Cinema enabled them to make films cheaply and quickly. Such techniques also created a sense of a direct, intimate encounter with the event. The rawness of style was itself a political statement. Yet the filmmakers were also open to aesthetic subtleties. Cuban and Chilean directors followed the lead of Glauber Rocha in making the hand-held camera an aggressive, kinetic force. Moreover, since little sound recording was done during filming, postsynchronization offered rich possibilities for manipulating the sound track in relation to the image. Cuban directors, Argentina's Cine Liberación, and the New Chilean Cinema directors also revived Soviet Montage techniques as part of their rejection of Hollywood continuity style.

Most militant Third World filmmakers came from the middle classes, and many had been trained in Europe. Most were intellectuals with deep knowledge of American and European film traditions. As a result, their films often blend formal innovation with direct emotional appeal. Many films of this tradition challenged western conceptions of cinematic art by showing that mass audiences were not as intolerant of experimentation as Hollywood and Europe had trained them to be. An aesthetically rich film could also address the audience's political concerns.

Latin America

In 1963, the Mexican novelist Carlos Fuentes wrote, "South of your border, my North American friends, lies a continent in revolutionary ferment—a continent that possesses immense wealth and nevertheless lives in a misery that you have never known and barely imagine."[4] It was this revolutionary ferment, and the challenge it flung at Europe and the United States, that many Latin American filmmakers sought to advance.

Throughout most of the century, Latin America had been economically dependent on the western-controlled world market. Most countries exported natural resources in order to develop their industrial infrastructures. But the 1960s saw a stagnation in trade throughout Latin America. This in turn encouraged the growth of authoritarian military regimes, which sought to attract northern investment and repress political dissent. Many activists went underground. During the early 1970s, Brazil was only one of several South American countries to be assailed by guerrilla warfare and urban terrorism.

In addition, the United States sought to stifle left-wing activity that could disrupt business. President Kennedy sponsored the Cuban exiles who invaded at the Bay of Pigs in 1961, President Johnson quashed a 1964 uprising in the Dominican Republic, and the Central Intelligence Agency sought to subvert uncooperative regimes, notably that of Salvador Allende in Chile. Such actions only intensified the sense of Latin America as a battleground between economic imperialism and mass insurgence.

Outside Cuba, the only country to undergo a left-wing revolution, few artists took sides in this conflict. Latin American novelists of the 1960s were more famous for their evocative "magical realism" than for partisan positions. Some painters were more socially critical: the Argentine Antonio Berni made disturbing collages out of junked First World commodities, and the Colombian Fernando Botero mocked authority in his eerie paintings of inflated, vacantly staring priests and generals. Closer to cinema was the *nueva canción* ("new song") movement, which began in Chile as a mix of indigenous sources with politically critical lyrics. The music spread throughout Latin America, becoming internationally popular through the Cuban singer Silvio Rodríguez. Film

23.4, *left* In a nervous hand-held shot, the Indian Corachi confronts his land-lord (*Tarahumara*).

23.5, *right* Intellectual montage in *The Hour of the Furnaces:* the bull, evoking the slaughter of the workers in Eisenstein's *Strike*, represents the oppression of Argentines working in the beef-export industry.

played an equally important role in presenting revolutionary ideology through popular art.

In Cuba, filmmaking was sponsored by Fidel Castro's regime, but elsewhere militant filmmakers usually gathered in twos or threes, often working with political groups or labor unions. It might happen, as in Argentina and Chile, that a new government would support or at least tolerate their activities, but the resurgence of right-wing regimes drove filmmakers into exile. By the mid-1970s, many worked outside their native countries.

More than other Third World filmmakers, Latin American directors were haunted by Hollywood cinema. American films had dominated southern markets since the mid-1910s. Hollywood's flirtation with South American locales and music during the 1930s and 1940s, although presenting stereotyped images, intensified audience interest in U.S. genres and stars. The dreamlike glamour of the studio cinema profoundly influenced the countries' cultures. The Argentine novelist Manuel Puig has recalled that for him the American films shown on his small town's movie screen created a "parallel reality . . . which, I was convinced, existed somewhere beyond my town, and in all three dimensions."5

Politicized Latin American directors sometimes assimilated elements of the Hollywood product they knew so well, but they also turned to foreign models of socially critical cinema. As in the 1950s, Italian Neorealism was a pervasive influence, particularly in the handling of nonprofessional actors and location shooting. Direct Cinema documentary was also an important source, as it had been for the Cinema Nôvo group. In *Tarahumara* (1964), for instance, the Mexican Luis Alcoriza uses the hand-held camera much as Ruy Guerra had in *Os Fuzis* (**23.4**). For both aesthetic and economic reasons, most Latin American directors shot on location with nonprofessional performers, using a lightweight camera and post-synchronizing dialogue.

In editing, filmmakers usually relied on the principles of Hollywood continuity. There were, however,

some experiments that harked back to Soviet silent cinema, particularly Sergei Eisenstein's "intellectual montage." For example, the Argentine *La Hora de los hornos* (*The Hour of the Furnaces,* 1968) crosscuts a soft-drink ad with the slaughter of a bull (**23.5**). Similarly, the use of sound could intensify thematically pointed editing. In the Cuban film *Memories of Underdevelopment* (1968), newsreel shots of victims of military torture are intercut with society women applauding.

All these stylistic tendencies, along with elements drawn from European young cinemas, led Latin American film to blur the boundaries between documentary and fiction. The use of nonactors, the immediacy of the handheld camera, the interpolation of newsreel footage, and the focus on topical issues gave the films the urgency of reportage, even if their action was set in the past. At the same time, by assimilating modernist techniques— fragmentary flashbacks, elliptical narration, to-camera address—directors avoided the stolidity of Soviet Socialist Realism.

Driven by a desire to capture the continent's political aspirations, new directors sought a more immediate contact with the public than was characteristic of most other young cinemas. In Cuba, directors merged experimental form with entertainment. Like the tropicalist Cinema Nôvo works (p. 474), some films drew on folklore traditions, particularly oral storytelling. Other films were designed to provoke discussion after the screening. For a time, the Latin American cinema sustained the political modernism of Cinema Nôvo and other movements while addressing a wider public than the Brazilian directors reached.

Latin American filmmakers also resembled the Soviet Montagists and the Italian Neorealists in their eagerness to connect theory and practice. In the late 1960s, critical discussion of political cinema generated essays and manifestos, notably Fernando Solanas and Octavio Getino's "Towards a Third Cinema" (1969) and Julio Garcia Espinosa's "For an Imperfect Cinema"

 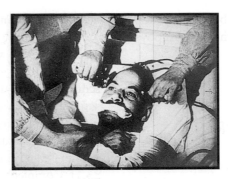

23.37, *left*   The calculated effrontery of Makavejev's *WR*: in a cult-of-Stalin fiction feature, the leader declaims that the USSR will fulfill Lenin's legacy. This is followed by . . .

23.38, *right*   . . . a shot of a patient receiving electroshock therapy.

opposition to any social institutions "which cripple human beings, arrest their development, and impose on them patterns of simple, easily predictable, dull, stereotyped behavior."[14] In the same period, the Central Committee of the Yugoslavian party demanded economic reform. During the events of the spring of 1968, students occupied Belgrade University. Tito intervened to break the strike, and government repression intensified. By 1972, the rising Croatian nationalist movement provoked the government to arrest, try, and purge political dissenters.

Yugoslavian film culture of the late 1960s strongly resembled that of western Europe. Politically and erotically outspoken, Yugoslavian New Film infuriated conservative factions. Zika Pavlović's *Ambush* (1969) and Krsto Papić's *Handcuffs* (1969) saw traces of the Stalinist past continuing into the present, while Aleksandar Petrović's *The Master and Margarita* (1972) compared current attacks on cinema to Stalinism. The Zagreb Film Festival of 1970 took as its theme "Sexuality as an Effort to Achieve a New Humanism." As pressures increased after 1968, official critics labeled the New Films "black films" because of their "defeatism" and "nihilism."

Dušan Makavejev offered the most scandalous black film of the era in *WR: Mysteries of the Organism* (1971). Like his earlier works, it juggles newsreel footage, extracts from older fiction films, and a story; it is also, centrally and explicitly, about sex. A biography of Wilhelm Reich, a psychoanalyst and radical sex theorist, is mixed with Direct Cinema footage of current erotic practices in the United States, newsreels of the Chinese revolution, and a grotesque story about Milena, a Yugoslavian woman who believes that "communism without free love is a wake in a graveyard." *WR* epitomizes counterculture irreverence, not least in its outrageous juxtapositions (**23.37, 23.38**). In suggesting that erotic freedom would revitalize Marxism, Makavejev was attacking Communist prudery head-on.

In the early 1970s, the government denied distribution to *WR*, *The Master and Margarita*, and other black films. Petrović, who had won worldwide fame with

I Even Met Happy Gypsies (1967), was forced out of his post at the Film Academy. The party expelled Makavejev and Pavlović; Makavejev joined the band of wandering directors exiled from eastern Europe.

Polish cinema experienced a government crackdown like that in Czechoslovakia, but it recovered more easily. In the spring of 1968, the Polish government was debating the need for economic reform. In May, an uprising at Warsaw University was suppressed. The Creative Film Unit system, which had operated since the mid-1950s, was replaced by a centralized organization. Venerated figures like Aleksander Ford were removed from their supervisory positions.

After workers' strikes in the early 1970s, however, Wladyslaw Gomulka lost control and was replaced by a more concessive leadership. The freer atmosphere reanimated Polish cinema. The production units were reorganized in 1972, with filmmakers having even more control than they previously had. A literature-based cinema won favor with audiences and solidified the production units. Andrzej Wajda returned to the center of Polish cinema with *Landscape after Battle* (1970), *Wedding* (1972), and *Land of Promise* (1975). Several new talents appeared, most notably Krzysztof Zanussi, a former physics student who brought his scientific training to bear on contemporary dramas in *The Structure of Crystals* (1969), *Illumination* (1972), and *Balance* (1974).

Other eastern European cinemas flourished in the postinvasion era. In Romania, which had only loose ties to the USSR, the late 1960s saw a liberalization. More experimentation was permitted, and in the early 1970s decentralized production units were formed. The Bulgarian government created a production-unit system in 1968, and three years later it installed new management in the industry. The nation's most celebrated film was Todor Dinov and Hristo Hristov's *Iconostasis* (1969), somewhat similar to Andrei Tarkovsky's *Andrei Rublev* in its echoes of folk and religious art (**23.39**). After 1971, Bulgarian cinema underwent a renaissance, with several films winning international recognition.

It was Hungary, however, that moved to the forefront of eastern European cinema in the aftermath of the Prague Spring. The economic reforms created in the late 1960s remained intact, and decentralized planning and a mixed economy continued well into the mid-1970s. A critical political cinema continued in Hungary, and the four production units were each making about five films per year. Because directors such as Miklós Jancsó, Marta Mészáros, and István Szabó were closely tied to western trends, they are considered later in this chapter.

Dissent and Stagnation in the USSR   While there was no "Moscow Spring," the early 1960s spawned a USSR youth movement of sorts. Students scrutinized the history of communism and debated party conduct. Liberals and religious believers formed dissident and pro-democracy organizations. Writers circulated *samizdat* ("self-published") articles and books. When Soviet tanks rolled into Czechoslovakia, protesters crowded Red Square.

Facing a declining economy and a conflict with China, Party Secretary Leonid Brezhnev sought détente with the West while dealing harshly with dissent on the home front. Christians and intellectuals were imprisoned or sent to mental hospitals. Physicist Andrei Sakharov's Human Rights Committee was steadily undermined by the secret police. In 1970, Aleksandr Solzhenitsyn won the Nobel Prize for literature, but when his novel *The Gulag Archipelago* (1973) revealed the horrors of Stalin's prison camps, he was deported and forbidden to return. (He moved to Vermont in 1976 and finally returned to Russia in 1994.)

In cinema, production averaged about 130 features annually. But the new freeze demanded a return to Socialist Realism, now called "pedagogical realism." Energetic factory workers and World War II heroes came back to the screen. Some of the more idiosyncratic directors of the New Wave, such as Vasily Shukshin, produced well-crafted literary adaptations. In the late 1960s, Andrei Konchalovsky had proposed a film on Che Guevara, but he too turned to safe sources, such as novelist Ivan Turgenev for *A Nest of Gentlefolk* (1969).

In the regional republics, however, intense anti-Russian nationalism created a "poetic cinema." Alexander Dovzhenko's peasant lyricism offered filmmakers a distant precedent (p. 129), and Sergei Paradzhanov's *Shadows of Forgotten Ancestors* (1965) reopened the way toward a personal treatment of folk material. Georgy Shengelaya's *Pirosmani* (1969) used the artist-biography genre to treat a folk painter, a subject that carried nationalistic connotations but also justified experi-

23.39   *Iconostasis:* the icon painter and his creation.

23.40   In *Solaris*, the hero kneels before his father as the camera retreats to a God's-eye perspective.

ments in abstract shot design (**Color Plate 23.2**). Similar efforts were Ukrainian Yuri Ilienko's *White Bird with a Black Mark* (1972) and Georgian Otar Ioseliani's *Pastorale* (1977).

Two other directors associated with the poetic tendency emerged as central to the new Soviet cinema. Andrei Tarkovsky's *Andrei Rublev*, suppressed in 1966, premiered in Paris in 1969. After widespread acclaim abroad it was released in the USSR. By then Tarkovsky had completed his third feature, *Solaris* (1972), widely touted as Russia's answer to *2001: A Space Odyssey* (p. 627). Its ambiguous depiction of the hero's delusions is motivated by its space-travel premise, but typically Tarkovskian are passages of mystical contemplation: weeds coiling under water, an endless freeway, and the awesome final images (**23.40**). Tarkovsky wanted to avoid an ideological message: "The image is not a certain *meaning*, expressed by the director, but an entire world reflected as a drop of water."[15]

The reflection of the artist's world is carried to an extreme in *The Mirror* (1975), a poetic blend of childhood memories, documentary footage, and fantastic imagery. As Tarkovsky's voice recites his father's poetry offscreen, the camera slides across a room, moving from a cat lapping a puddle of milk to the mother at the window,

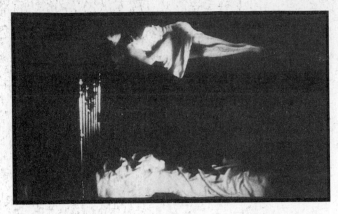

23.41 *The Mirror:* the enigma of memory and fantasy.

23.42 In *The Color of Pomegranates,* the tableau shot recalls folk art.

23.43 Sayat Nova's death in *The Color of Pomegranates.*

tearfully watching the rain. A barn burns in a downpour; a man is almost blown over in a windy landscape; a woman levitates (**23.41**). While the mainstream *Slave of Love* (Nikita Mikhalkov, 1976) was enjoying worldwide success, Soviet authorities declared *The Mirror* incomprehensible and gave it a cramped, unprofitable release.

Paradzhanov remains the most vivid example of how the personal became political in the Soviet cinema. After his Ukrainian feature *Shadows of Forgotten Ancestors* (p. 460) won international success, Paradzhanov used his new fame to protest the treatment of dissidents. In 1968, he was arrested on charges of "Ukrainian nationalism"; after his release he was transferred to an Armenian studio, where he made *The Color of Pomegranates* in 1969. Although the script is based on the life of the Armenian poet Sayat Nova, a prologue tells us that the film will not be a conventional biography. Long-take shots frame characters, animals, and objects in rigid frontal tableaux (**23.42**). Editing serves merely to link these shots or to cut jarringly into the static portraits. The film's mise-en-scène presents Sayat Nova's poetic imagery: waterlogged books opened out to dry on rooftops, carpets bleeding as they are washed, chicken feathers scattering over the dying poet (**23.43**). Although Paradzhanov's style differs drastically from Tarkovsky's, both directors contemplate the changing textures of objects through time.

The Color of Pomegranates was probably the most shockingly experimental film made in the USSR since the late 1920s. It was immediately shelved, although a shorter, revised version (the one currently available) achieved limited release in 1971. Forbidden to direct, Paradzhanov fought back. He wrote a pamphlet on his problems and those of Soviet cinema. In January 1974, he was accused of homosexuality, trafficking in stolen art objects, and "incitement to suicide." He was sentenced to several years at hard labor.

In the eastern bloc, Socialist Realist policy obliged the artist to serve society—or rather its representative, the Communist party. The major eastern European directors such as Chytilová, Jancsó, and Makavejev believed that their visions were in harmony with some socialist position, even if that position was not currently in favor. But the poetic cinema of Tarkovsky and Paradzhanov presented the artist's vision as independent of all needs of the collective. Their highly personal films thus boldly challenged the Soviet orthodoxy and echoed trends in the West that sought political liberation in the unconstrained imagination of the individual.

Political Cinema in the West

The year of the Prague Spring, 1968, also marked the height of social protest in western countries. As in the Third World and eastern Europe, young people played a key role.

22.3 The Godfather

2.4 One from the Heart

23.1 Larks on a String

23.2 Pirosmani

23.3 Viva la muerte!

23.4 *The Lost Honor of Katherina Blum*

24.1 *Field Diary*

24.2 *The Thin Blue Line*

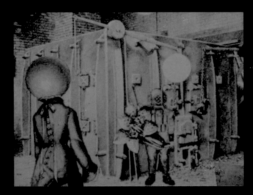

24.3 *Our Lady of the Sphere*

24.4 *Dimensions of Dialogue*

24.5 *Surfacing on the Thames*

24.7 *Street of Crocodiles*

24.8 *Quasi at the Quackadero*

24.6 *T,O,U,C,H,I,N,G*

24.9 *Lineage*

24.10 *Journeys from Berlin/1971*

24.11 *One Way Boogie Woogie*

24.12 *Pharoah's Belt*

24.13 *Triste*

24.14 *Cinderella*

25.1 *Chicken Run*

25.2 *Mona Lisa*

25.3 *Landscape in the Mist*

25.4 *Le Bal*

25.5 *Flower of My Secret*

25.6 *Night of the Shooting Stars*

25.7 *Topsy Turvy*

25.8 *Toute une nuit*

25.9 *Appletrees*

25.10 *Beau Travail*

25.11 *The Green Room*

25.12 *Barry Lyndon*

25.13 *The Draughtsman's Contract*

25.14 *El Sur*

25.15 *Distant Voices, Still Lives*

25.16 *The Goalie's Anxiety at the Penalty Kick*

25.17 *Wings of Desire*

25.18 *Un Chambre en ville*

25.19 *Mauvais sang*

25.20 *Parsifal*

25.21 *Act of Spring*

25.22 *Caravaggio*

25.23 *The Quince Tree Sun*

25.24 *Freak Orlando*

25.25 *Passion*

25.26 *Détective*

25.27 *Element of Crime*

25.28 *Stalker*

25.29 *Nostalgia*

25.30 *The Legend of Suram Fortress*

25.31 *Taxi Blues*

25.32 *Mother and Son*

26.1 *Tangos: The Exile of Gardel*

26.3 *Frida*

26.2 *Tango*

26.4 *Cantata de Chile*

26.5 *Hum Aapke Hain Koun*

26.6 *In the Realm of the Senses*

26.7 *Akira*

26.8 *Maboroshi*

26.9 *Sonatine*

26.10 *Princess Mononoke*

26.11 *The Black Cannon Incident*

26.12 *Life on a String*

26.13 *Ju Dou*

26.14 *A touch of Zen*

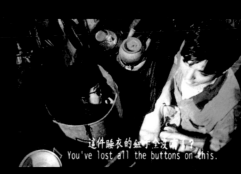

26.15 *Shangai Blues*

26.16 *Rouge*

26.17 *Chungking Express*

26.18 *A Brighter Summer Day*

26.19 *City of Sadness*

26.20 *Flowers of Shanghai*

26.21 *Why Has Bodhi-Dharma Left for the East?*

26.22 *Picnic at Hanging Rock*

26.23 *An Angel at My Table*

26.24 *Yol*

26.25 *Life and Nothing More*

26.26 *The Apple*

27.2 *Dick Tracy*

27.3 *Boyz N the Hood*

27.4 *Terminator 2*

27.5 *Who Framed Roger Rabbit?*

27.6 *Do The Right Thing*

27.7 *Mars Attacks!*

27.8 *Heat*

27.9 *Beauty and the Beast*

27.10 *Blue Velvet*

27.12 *Monsters, Inc.*

27.11 *O Brother Where Art Thou?*

28.2 *julien donkey-boy*

28.1 *The Fifth Element*

28.3 *Crouching Tiger, Hidden Dragon*

28.4 *Waking Life*

By 1966, many students were questioning authority and rejecting traditional American values. Some were drawn to the New Left, a diverse movement propounding a spontaneous, libertarian Marxism opposed to orthodox Soviet varieties. University students were central to the New Left in the United States, Britain, France, Japan, West Germany, and even Franco's Spain. Another element in youth politics was loosely known as the counterculture. It spanned a range of alternative lifestyles, free-flowing eroticism, immersion in rock music, experiments in communal living, and drug use in the name of expanded consciousness. Although some counterculture bohemians considered themselves apolitical, many felt allied with the New Left.

The international politics of youth focused on several issues. A central one was America's role in the Vietnam War, which steadily intensified after American planes began bombing North Vietnam in 1965. U.S. organizations such as Students for a Democratic Society actively opposed the war. This opposition began as protest but hardened into resistance, as young men refused the draft and activists blocked induction centers. Between 1967 and 1969, resistance turned to confrontation, with activists occupying buildings and fighting police in the streets.

By then, the issue of Vietnam had become part of a broader push for social change. Throughout the First World, the student movement launched a critique of post–World War II capitalist society. The university was seen as a machine of social control, cranking out well-behaved managers and technicians. Around the world, students protested crowded classes, poor facilities, impersonal teaching, and irrelevant programs. The Berkeley free-speech movement of 1965 became a prototype of campus rebellion around the world.

The Vietnam War, the weakness of traditional left parties, the consumption-based economies of the West, and the specter of neocolonialism led students to question their culture. Many charged that western society created an artificially "normal" life in order to restrain impulses toward freedom and self-management. Wilhelm Reich, who saw fascism as springing from sexual repression, and philosopher Herbert Marcuse, who attacked the irrationality of "one-dimensional society," introduced the generation of the 1960s to a wide-ranging social critique. Yippies and other countercultural groups attacked "Amerika" in less theoretical terms. "The left," declared Jerry Rubin, "demands full employment for all—we demand full unemployment for all."[16]

Other social movements shaped the radical politics of the period. In the United States, the black-power movement emerged around 1965. While the civil rights movement stressed legal and nonviolent reform, black power called for a more aggressive stance—crystallized in the public mind by the militant Black Panther party, founded in 1966. African American students protested segregation and demanded black studies programs. During the same period the women's liberation movement reemerged in the United States and Britain, influenced by the civil rights movement and reacting against sexism, found even within the New Left leadership. Gay and lesbian groups, which had become more outspoken in the early 1960s, often joined the New Left and the counterculture.

By the end of 1967, many social-protest movements had converged. There began two years of political upheaval unparalleled in the West since World War II. The events of 1968 led many to believe that western society was on the brink of social revolution.

In that year, when students in Madrid closed the university, over a thousand were sent to military service. In Germany, student leader Rudi Dutschke was shot in the head. In the insurrection that followed, police killed two people and arrested a thousand. In London, a peace march sparked a battle between police and 20,000 demonstrators. At Japan's Nihon University, students locked administrators in their offices and shut down classes. Italian students' seizure of universities was supported by strikes among workers and high school students.

Similar tremors shook 200 U.S. campuses, notably Columbia, San Francisco State, Wisconsin, and Michigan. In April, Martin Luther King, Jr., was assassinated and riots broke out in scores of ghettos. Two months later, Robert Kennedy, widely perceived as America's best hope for moderate social change, was also assassinated. At the Democratic Convention in Chicago, police assaulted thousands of demonstrators protesting President Johnson's prosecution of the Vietnam War. By the end of the year, armed black students were occupying Cornell University buildings, and 400,000 American students claimed to be revolutionaries.

For many historians, events in Paris during May 1968 typify the radical energies and frustrations of the period. The Stalin worship of the 1950s had turned many French students against the Communist party. Trotskyite and Maoist factions quarreled. Other groups, such as the Situationist International, injected a freewheeling critique of the consumer society. Housing shortages, unemployment, the unions' collusion in keeping wages down, and vastly overcrowded universities led to an explosive situation.

At Nanterre and the Sorbonne, students confronted administrators and police, demanding university reforms and social change. Mass marches were met with tear gas

FILM ACTIVITIES DURING THE MAY EVENTS IN PARIS

French film culture was deeply involved in the upheavals of 1968. Early in February, the government tried to remove Henri Langlois as curator of the Cinémathèque Française. Resnais, Truffaut, Godard, Bresson, Chabrol, and others coordinated demonstrations of hundreds of filmmakers. On February 14, 3,000 people demonstrating in support of Langlois clashed with police. Thanks to press coverage and threats from film companies, Langlois was reinstated.

As the May uprising unfolded, Godard spearheaded an effort to halt the Cannes Film Festival, leading demonstrators to occupy the theaters. Truffaut called on all to support the events in Paris: "The colleges are occupied! The factories are occupied! The stations are occupied! It's political action on an unprecedented scale! And you want this activity to stop at the doors of the festival? . . . There must be solidarity!"[17] After Godard and Truffaut halted a screening by holding the curtains closed, the Cannes festival shut down.

In Paris, students at the state film school IDHEC quickly began making newsreels and ciné-tracts (p. 563). The issues broadened as cinéastes and cinéphiles launched a critique of film under capitalism. A large number of professional film workers established the États Générales du Cinéma (EGC). The EGC aimed to create an alternative French system of production, distribution, and exhibition.

Members, many of them technicians and projectionists, went on strike "to denounce and destroy the reactionary structures of a cinema which has become a commodity."[18]

The EGC called for public ownership of the film industry, workers' control of production, abolition of censorship, and elimination of the government's Centre Nationale de Cinématographie (p. 374). The EGC prepared several projects, involving Malle, Resnais, and other influential figures, and it laid plans for autonomous production units (akin to those in eastern Europe) that could undertake noncommercial projects. Members also stressed the need for educating viewers in new ways of watching film.

Throughout May and June, the EGC held sessions. It quickly became a filmmaking cooperative, turning out documentaries over the following two years. But without government support there was no way to implement the ambitious EGC proposals. As Charles de Gaulle regained power, most film personnel resumed work as usual. In July, many of the filmmakers involved in the EGC formed the Société des Réalisateurs ("Society of Film Directors"), which took as its goal the defense of artistic freedom. Beyond this, the May movement created some long-term political commitment, a "parallel cinema" of militant engagement, and alternative production and distribution structures.

---

and truncheons. On May 10, 20,000 demonstrators built cobblestone barricades and battled charging police. Three nights later, 500,000 students, workers, and professionals marched through Paris, forcing the government to reopen the Sorbonne and release arrested student leaders. Students occupied the universities anew, seeking to create models of a just, nonexploitative society. In solidarity, 10 million French citizens went out on strike. The beginning of 1968 saw French film culture also embroiled in politics (see box).

The May events led many to think that de Gaulle's government might fall in the June elections, but he won in a landslide. Life gradually returned to routine as the government cracked down on extreme-left groups.

In April 1970, President Nixon's widening of the Vietnam War into Cambodia touched off a new wave of protest in the United States. Nearly 400 colleges went on strike, students on many campuses burned their ROTC buildings, and sixteen states called out the National Guard. Two students were shot and killed at Mississippi's Jackson State University, and four more were killed at Ohio's Kent State University.

Already, however, the radical movement was losing unity. By 1970, the student left in most countries had failed to ally itself with working-class issues. In the United States, the Black Panthers and the New Left fell out. Many feminists, gays, and lesbians saw the New Left as oppressive and formed their own organizations. During 1969 and 1970, some radicals, convinced that only violence could defeat "the system," formed terrorist cadres, such as the Weathermen in the United States, the Red Brigade in Italy, and the Red Army Faction (Baader-Meinhof) in Germany. Often modeling themselves after Third World guerrillas, these groups brought bombing, kidnapping, and political assassination to western capitals in the 1970s.

Radical political movements steadily lost their authority as New Left ideas were incorporated into more mainstream socialist and communist parties. The excesses of the Chinese Cultural Revolution (p. 551) and the revelations of Solzhenitsyn's *Gulag Archipelago* suggested that communism led to totalitarian rule. With the middle class governing the western democracies, there was a growing awareness that social change was more likely to come through issue-oriented, grassroots activism..

The militancy of the late 1960s thus evolved into a micropolitics. Activists concentrated on particular lifestyles and issues—cooperatives, communes, squatters' movements, and the ecology movement. "Working within the system" ceased to be a reproach. German leftists adapted a Maoist phrase, calling for social change by "the long march through the institutions."

The growth of gay and lesbian movements shows how radical energies could change concrete situations. In 1969, gay men in New York City fought off a police raid on the Stonewall bar. Throughout the period from 1969 to 1973, gay and lesbian activism flourished in Britain, Canada, Australia, West Germany, and France. Groups changed laws and altered attitudes toward homosexuality.

During the 1970s, women's liberation broadened into the feminist movement. Some participants hoped for a radical restructuring of social consciousness, but others emphasized step-by-step progress toward equality and justice. Italian feminists helped liberalize divorce laws, while throughout Europe and North America similar groups altered abortion statutes. In country after country there arose women's shelters, clinics, legal services, childcare centers, and bookstores—an alternative "woman's culture."

Most broadly, both the militant radicalism of the late 1960s and the micropolitics of the 1970s changed fundamental attitudes. The goals of universities, the social and sexual inequality within western democracies, and matters of sexual orientation became part of public awareness as never before.

Filmmakers participated vigorously in the politicization of culture. We can identify three broad tendencies from the late 1960s to the mid-1970s. First, "engaged cinema" uncompromisingly aligned itself with revolutionary social change. Its purpose was explicitly propagandistic, and its favored genre was the documentary. Second, alongside engaged cinema there emerged a political modernism. This tendency, an outgrowth of the postwar art cinema and Third World trends such as Cinema Nôvo (see Chapter 20), created a radical aesthetic that fused left-wing politics with innovative forms and styles. And, third, even the commercial fictional film and the mainstream art cinema bore the traces of the emerging political culture.

Engaged Cinema: Collective Productions and Militant Films

During the 1960s and early 1970s, a cinema of political engagement, addressing itself to concrete social problems and arguing for radical social change, emerged

on a scale not seen since the 1930s. A project might be financed by a political organization, as when the Vietnam Veterans Against the War supported *Winter Soldier* (United States, 1972). Sometimes an individual filmmaker or small group might scrape up funding from donors; this occurred with Noriaki Tsuchimoto's series of films on Japan's Minamata pollution tragedy (e.g., *Minamata: The Victims and Their World*, 1972). In rare cases, independent producers arranged funding for radical work. In France, Marin Karmitz's MK Productions had supported militant cinema since 1964.

Particularly characteristic of the era was the attempt to create filmmaking collectives. Militant filmmakers would band together and work in subgroups on separate projects. Rental fees helped finance more films. Britain's Cinema Action and Berwick Street Collective, Italy's Militant Cinema Collective, Denmark's Workshop, Sweden's New Film, Belgium's Fugitive Cinema, Greece's Band of 6, the Chicago-based Kartemquin, and other groups utilized the collective mode of production. Often the group's collective structure itself embodied left-wing ideals of equality and shared responsibility.

The prototype of the engaged-cinema collective was the U.S. group Newsreel. In late 1967, students aligned with Students for a Democratic Society decided to make films that would counter the mainstream media's representation of protests against the Vietnam War. This group became New York Newsreel. Early in 1968, another group formed San Francisco Newsreel.

The Newsreel logo—the flickering word synchronized with machine-gun fire—announced the militant, confrontational quality of the films. The Newsreel groups specialized in coverage of individual events, such as the occupation of a campus, a strike, or a demonstration. Beginning as a "full democracy," the Newsreel collective soon adopted a steering-committee system whereby every film was screened for the entire membership and was released only if a majority supported it.

A parallel development took place in France. During May 1968, striking film workers created ciné-tracts, short 16mm films made simply and circulated for a few weeks. These sometimes led to the formation of collectives. For example, the SLON Group made its first film, *A bientôt j'éspère* ("Soon, I Hope"), codirected by Chris Marker and Mario Marret, in 1967; it dealt with a strike at La Rhodia, a textile factory in Besançon. When the factory's workers were dissatisfied with the result, they formed their own cooperative, the Medvedkin Group, and made their own film, *Classe de luttes* ("Class of Struggle"), released in 1969. SLON (later ISKRA) remained robust, however. Godard teamed up with Jean-Pierre Gorin to form the Dziga-Vertov Group. Other production units sprang up, each with its own ideological alignments. Such collectives formed France's "oppositional," or "parallel," cinema.

Collectives usually depended on alternative distribution and exhibition structures. Marin Karmitz created a distribution company and ran three Parisian theaters. In the United States, New Day Films and Women Make Movies circulated feminist works, while Newsreel distributed films from Third World countries along with its own projects. Holland's alternative distribution network, The Free Circuit, led to the creation of production collectives. Other independent distribution agencies included Belgium's Cinélibre, Holland's feminist Cinemien, Sweden's Cinema of the People, and Britain's The Other Cinema.

Like Solanas and Getino of Cine Liberación, engaged filmmakers in the West sought to change the context in which their work was shown. Some avoided traditional theaters and preferred that the films be screened in clubs, union meetings, and campus or community centers. Many filmmakers also hoped that the audience would discuss the film. In some countries, these alternative venues created a parallel outlet for films. In France, the festival of Hyères, created as a showcase for young directors, became an international meeting place for engaged cinema. In 1972, the first New York Women's Film Festival was held, quickly followed by similar events in Toronto and elsewhere.

New film journals—*Jump Cut* and *Women and Film* in the United States, *Champ libre* in Canada, *Filmkritik* and *frauen und film* in West Germany, and *Cinéthique* in France, among many others—also promoted radical filmmaking. Older magazines, such as the U.S. *Cineaste* and the Parisian *Cahiers du cinéma*, moved to a left political position. Most of these journals became central sources of information about new films.

Even though radical leftism declined in the mid-1970s, engaged filmmaking remained central to the micropolitics of the era. A June 1979 alternative-cinema conference in New York assembled over 400 political activists working in film and video in the United States. In some countries, government liberalization led to funding for militant film. The new Labor government in Britain assisted Liberation Film and Cinema Action, while in France the regional Maisons de la Culture allotted money for local media groups. Some parallel distribution and exhibition circuits proved successful in promoting films about nuclear power, day care, ethnic rights, and similar issues.

In the United States and Great Britain, feminist filmmaking pioneered the turn to issue-centered, grassroots problems. By 1977, 250 women's films had been produced in the United States alone. Although some feminist films were made under the auspices of New York Newsreel between 1968 and 1969, the first major Newsreel effort came from the San Francisco wing. *The Women's Film* (1970) was followed by New York Newsreel's *Janie's Janie* (1971). Other feminist engaged films of the period were Julia Reichert and Chuck Klein's *Growing Up Female* (1970) and Kate Millett's *Three Lives* (1970). British feminist cinema was initiated by the London Women's Film Group (founded 1972), and it often sought to link women's concerns with labor issues.

As the international women's movement grew, films on rape, self-defense, and housekeeping were paralleled by explorations of women's history, the latter most widely seen in the U.S. films *Union Maids* (1976) and *With Babies and Banners* (1978) by the Women's Labor History Project. Women's filmmaking groups emerged in other countries as well, with France's Musidora, Italy's Feminist Film Collective, and Australia's Sydney Women's Film Collective being among the most active.

Techniques and Forms of Engaged Cinema   In general, engaged filmmakers adopted the techniques and forms established by Direct Cinema documentary in the late 1950s. The new 16mm technology of lightweight cameras, portable tape recorders, and faster film stocks could be used for agitational moviemaking, often by people without formal training. But the engaged filmmakers typically avoided purely descriptive observation of the type advocated by Richard Leacock (p. 483). Direct Cinema technique supplied evidence, but the film as a whole was likely to be defiantly rhetorical in confronting its audience.

The typical engaged film draws upon both spontaneously shot reportage and more or less staged interviews. Most Newsreel films, such as *Break and Enter* (1971), combine street footage of demonstrations and interviews with participants. A film might strongly emphasize reportage, as does *Some of Your Best Friends* (1972), which records gay activists' invasion of a psychiatric conference. The filmmaker's reliance on candid footage could go beyond the single event, the normal province of Direct Cinema, and suggest broader trends, as does Pierre Perrault in his survey of political agitation in Québec, *A Country without Good Sense!; or, Wake Up, My Good Friends!!!* (1970). As in any compilation film, reportage could be enhanced by the sound track (in Newsreel films, often rock and roll) or interpolated footage, as in Newsreel's *Oil Strike* (1969), which included a company promotional film to mock management's public relations face.

23.44 *Word Is Out:* an interviewee sits by a poster indicating her feminist position.

23.45 On the sound track, Lyndon Johnson reviews his trip to Saigon: "We never heard a hostile voice, and we never shook a hostile hand"; on the image track, he presides over the crowd (*In the Year of the Pig*).

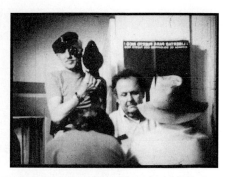

23.46 Filming into a mirror, Lampson, Wexler, and De Antonio interview Weathermen fugitives who went into hiding after their Greenwich Village bomb factory exploded.

During the 1970s, engaged filmmakers also explored the interview technique. Now entire films were built around talking heads. In feminist filmmaking, this led to a genre of "film portraits," often in an effort to create positive role models of women. *The Women's Film* consists of intercut interviews with five women, talking about work and married life, followed by footage of them meeting in consciousness-raising groups. *Three Lives, Growing Up Female,* and *Union Maids* all render the individual's report on her experience through lengthy close-ups. This tendency recalls Shirley Clarke's *Portrait of Jason* (p. 580) and probably owes something to the central role of the consciousness-raising group in the women's liberation movement. A similar strategy is at work in the lesbian or gay "confessional" film, such as *Lavender* (1972). In *Word Is Out* (1977; **23.44**) the accumulation of many interviews seeks to provide a panoramic view of various aspects of gay and lesbian life.

Throughout the 1970s, some feature-length engaged documentaries played commercial theaters. In the United States, Peter Davis's *Hearts and Minds* (1974), Cinda Firestone's *Attica* (1974), Jill Godmilow's *Antonia* (1974), *Word Is Out, Union Maids,* and *With Babies and Banners* drew broad audiences.

De Antonio and Radical Scavenging The engaged filmmaker who consistently achieved commercial recognition was Emile De Antonio. His first film, *Point of Order* (1963; p. 479) was devoted to the congressional hearings investigating Senator Joseph McCarthy. *Point of Order* showed that mainstream news-footage shots could sustain a politically critical film with no nudging from an anonymous voice-over narrator. *Rush to Judgment* (1966), a brief for a multiple-assassin theory of

President John Kennedy's death, brought interviews into the compilation mix.

"Radical scavenging" allowed De Antonio to include footage that was too controversial for its original users. *In the Year of the Pig* (1969), an analytical history of the Vietnam War, drew upon material shot for television that was too grisly or embarrassing to broadcast. ("Outtakes," De Antonio commented at the time, "are the confessions of the system."[19]) *In the Year of the Pig* makes its case through a variety of techniques. In the hallucinatory opening, brief, almost subliminal images of battle and peasants' suffering interrupt a black screen while the drone of airplanes and helicopters rises chillingly. The rest of the film puts the argument in analytical terms, juxtaposing expert and eyewitness testimony with news footage of speeches, ceremonies, battles, and Vietnamese life. De Antonio's editing uses one interview to contradict another and undercuts official accounts by contrary evidence. Although the film has virtually no voice-of-God narration, interviewees' remarks become voice-over commentary for the images (**23.45**).

In the Year of the Pig gained a wide audience on campuses and in some theatrical venues. So did *Millhouse: A White Comedy* (1971), in which De Antonio's compilation technique satirizes Richard Nixon. The more serious *Underground* (1976) provided an opportunity to reflect on developments since the 1960s. In 1975, while five Weathermen members were sought by the FBI, De Antonio, Mary Lampson, and Haskell Wexler filmed lengthy interviews with them, interspersing their memories and reflections with biographical and newsreel footage (**23.46**).

A comparable sense of stocktaking informs *Milestones* (1975), by Robert Kramer and John Douglas. Kramer was a founder of New York Newsreel who also

BRECHT AND POLITICAL MODERNISM

Although Bertolt Brecht (**23.47**) was closely identified with Soviet communism in his lifetime, his creative work contributed to a strong "unorthodox Marxist" tradition in the arts. For thirty years his plays explored many forms of theater, some explicitly political, others closer to musical, parable, and "problem drama": *The Threepenny Opera* (1928), *The Rise and Fall of the City of Mahagonny* (1929), *Mother Courage and Her Children* (1941), *The Good Woman of Szechuan* (1943), and others.

Brecht's film *Kuhle Wampe* (1932, directed by Slatan Dudow; p. 305) was not as influential for western cinema as were his theatrical productions and his writings. The hugely successful 1950s tour of his East German troupe, the Berliner Ensemble, introduced European audiences to Brecht's theater. When he died in 1956, his influence was still growing.

In a pungent, often humorous, style, Brecht attacked traditional, or "Aristotelian," theater, on the grounds that it tries to absorb the audience completely. The spectator is supposed to identify with individual characters, feel their emotions, and accept the premises of the play's world. A committed Marxist, Brecht saw art as inevitably political. Impressed by Eisenstein's *Potemkin,* he also believed that playwrights would cease to focus on individuals and would eventually represent mass movements.

Brecht contrasted the drama of hypnotic empathy with Asian theater and the boxing match, which encourage spectators to take a more detached attitude to what they see. Brecht proposed several techniques that might accomplish this: breaking the play into episodes, interspersing titles, separating text from music or performance, and letting the performers speak the lines as if quoting them. These and other devices created the *Verfremdungseffekt,* often translated as "alienation effect" but better rendered as "estranging" or "distancing." Through this effect, the spectator would evaluate the action critically and see larger historical forces at work behind it. The spectator could then

23.47 A shot in Godard's *La Chinoise* shows a photo of Brecht

start to understand how to change the world that created the characters' problems.

Brecht's influence emerged in cinema in the early 1960s, notably in Godard's *Vivre sa vie* (1962; see 20.16). His ideas energized a generation of political modernist filmmakers who sought to break the "illusion of reality" that classical fiction films created for the spectator. Filmmakers used collage structures, disjunctive editing, stylized framing and acting, and interspersed titles to achieve "anti-illusionist" works that would provoke reflection.

Brecht's influence also extended to less avant-garde films, such as *How I Won the War* (1967), *Oh What a Lovely War!* (1969), and *O Lucky Man!* (1973). Some critics claimed that even Sirk, Hitchcock, and Ford were "Brechtian." In many cases, filmmakers and critics recast and distorted the dramatist's ideas. Nevertheless, the versions of Brechtian theory in circulation during the 1960s and 1970s remain central to understanding critical political cinema of the era.

---

developed a semifictional approach to New Left politics in the independent features *In the Country* (1966), *The Edge* (1968), and *Ice* (1970). Like the earlier features, *Milestones* was shot in Direct Cinema fashion, using improvised performances. Featuring several protagonists and running over three hours, the film is a broad assessment of the successes and failures of the New Left.

Political Modernism In seeking to rouse the viewer to political reflection or action, the engaged filmmaker drew upon Direct Cinema technology and the tradition of left-

ist documentary. Other militant filmmakers explored modernist traditions. These directors combined politically radical themes and subjects with aesthetically radical form, pushing further the impulses of Brazil's Cinema Nôvo and Cuba's postrevolutionary cinema.

The political modernists took inspiration from the Soviet Montage cinema of the 1920s. Eisenstein and Vertov became models of political consciousness and formal innovation. Even more pervasive was the influence of the Marxist playwright Bertolt Brecht (see box). In addition, many radical filmmakers sought to surpass

23.48 In *Un Film comme les autres*, Godard appropriates advertising imagery and then attacks it through his own graffiti-like comments.

23.49 Godardian flattening of space put at the service of political critique in *Luttes en Italie* ("Struggles in Italy," 1969).

the postwar art cinema. Its techniques had become fairly familiar and its mildly critical liberalism seemed reformist, not revolutionary. The political modernist director would transform character subjectivity, reflexivity, and ambiguity in the name of radical critique. At the forefront of this political modernism stood Jean-Luc Godard and Nagisa Oshima.

Godard and the Dziga-Vertov Group   Before the May events, Godard was already fusing political criticism with modernist aesthetics. His films mounted an almost sociological examination of French life, accompanied by harsh attacks on American foreign policy (for example, *Masculin-Feminine*, 1966, and *Two or Three Things I Know about Her,* 1967). In *La Chinoise* ("The Chinese Girl," 1967) a Maoist study group turns into a terrorist cadre. *Weekend* (1967) shows the bourgeoisie, preoccupied with greed, murder, and gruesome sexuality, overtaken by an absurd guerrilla band while Third World emigrants stand by awaiting their chance for revolt. With the eruptions of 1968, Godard turned his energies to a more severe and cerebral political modernism.

During the May events, he produced several ciné-tracts, consisting of demonstration footage and still photographs, usually with a few words scribbled over each one (**23.48**). His films of 1968 alternate such material with dialogues of characters exploring political positions: a young man and a woman in a black vacuum in *Le Gai savoir* ("Joyful Wisdom," 1968), a group of workers and students (all barely visible in tall grass) in *Un Film comme les autres* ("A Film Like the Others," 1968). After *One Plus One* (aka *Sympathy for the Devil*, 1968),

which juxtaposes a Rolling Stones rehearsal with staged scenes depicting political repression and black revolution, Godard joined the young Communist Jean-Pierre Gorin in forming the Dziga-Vertov Group.

The collective marked itself as politically modernist, declaring that it would struggle not only against political repression but also against "the bourgeois concept of representation."[20] Renouncing his previous films, Godard converted to Maoism and support for Third World revolution. Because his name guaranteed funding, usually from European television, the Dziga-Vertov Group turned out several films quickly, notably *British Sounds* and *Wind from the East* (both 1969). The group dissolved when Godard had a severe motorcycle accident, but after his recovery he and Gorin made *Tout va bien* ("Everything's Fine") and *Letter to Jane* (both 1972), which are linked with the earlier work.

Each Dziga-Vertov Group film is an assemblage of diverse material, juxtaposing Direct Cinema footage (street scenes, labor actions, conversations) with titles and highly stylized tableaux (**23.49**), often with direct address to the camera. Unlike Godard's earlier works, where such material interrupts a more or less coherent narrative, the Dziga-Vertov Group films largely lack stories. Rapid montages of still photos and blank frames alternate with long takes, either completely static or slowly tracking right or left. On the sound track, voices read extracts from Marx or Mao or exhort the viewer to criticize the image. Noises, as in the lengthy tracking shot down an auto assembly line in *British Sounds,* also assault the audience. Impossible to consume as entertainment or as engaged documentary, the films carry the modernist project to an abrasive extreme.

23.50 *Tout va bien:* a factory on strike, rendered as a dollhouse set.

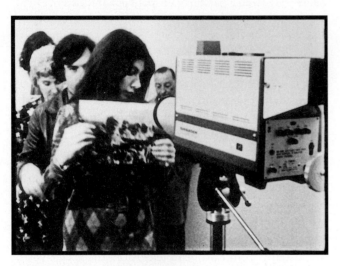

23.51 "Each time, one image comes to replace the other . . . keeping, of course, the memory": images of Palestinian struggle presented in a personification of the process of montage (*Ici et ailleurs*).

Tout va bien withdraws from this forbidding extreme, subscribing instead to Brecht's notion of "culinary"—that is, pleasurable—political art. The film has, for one thing, a fairly clear story. A radio journalist (Jane Fonda) and her lover (Yves Montand), a director of TV commercials, accidentally get locked into a factory occupied during a strike. The experience makes them rethink their relation to each other, to the aftermath of May 1968, and to French society in 1972. Yet this story is "estranged" by a host of Brechtian devices: male and female voice-overs that plan how the film is to be made, hands signing checks to the stars, to-camera interviews by the characters, a cutaway set (**23.50**), virtuoso left-and-right tracking shots along supermarket checkout counters, and alternate versions of scenes. *Tout va bien* remains a prototypical Brechtian film; its reflexivity in-

vites the audience to consider the political implications of film form and style.

After 1972, Godard created a media facility, Sonimage, in Grenoble, France, with the photographer Anne-Marie Miéville. The male-female dialogue of *Tout va bien* became central to their mid-1970s work. *Ici et ailleurs* ("Here and Elsewhere," 1976), for example, returns to the assemblage form of the Dziga-Vertov Group work, while Godard and Miéville in voice-over reflect on the Palestinian liberation movement and discuss visual and auditory representation (**23.51**). Several Godard-Miéville films include video imagery, which allows for still more varied juxtapositions of image, sound, and written language.

The Radical Oshima For most critics of the decade from 1967 to 1977, Godard personified the political modernist, creating a formally and ideologically exploratory cinema. The work of the Japanese director Nagisa Oshima was not as widely seen, but it was no less aggressive and disturbing.

The Japanese New Wave filmmakers had begun producing politically critical films in the late 1950s (p. 469). A decade later, Oshima and other directors recorded and supported current social activism against the Vietnam War, education policies, and renewal of the American-Japanese security treaty. Oshima made several films about student politics, notably *Diary of a Shinjuku Thief* (1968) and *He Died after the War (Story of a Young Man Who Left His Will on Film)* (1970). He also turned his attention to the social problems of Koreans (in *Death by Hanging*, 1968) and of Okinawans (in *Dear Summer Sister*, 1972), groups who were suffering discrimination at Japanese hands.

Oshima also continued to explore modernist techniques of disjunction and distancing. He became especially drawn to strategies of repetition, replaying actions or episodes from different perspectives and offering none as definitively true or accurate. Twenty minutes into *Three Resurrected Drunkards* (1968), the film begins again, as if the projectionist has put on the wrong reel, and continues, repeating each shot before slight diversions from the original slowly appear. The device makes the three Japanese students "become" Koreans. In *He Died after the War* (known in English-language distribution as *The Man Who Left His Will on Film*), the militant student Motoki tries to decipher the footage left behind by a friend. Visiting the sites his friend filmed, Motoki sees each one trigger violence.

Repetition is also central to *Death by Hanging*, based on an actual criminal case. R, a young Korean con-

23.52 In an abstract, purified set, R is about to be executed (*Death by Hanging*).

victed of rape and murder, is about to be hanged. To convince him of his guilt, police and bureaucrats stage elaborate reenactments of his crime until they (perhaps) kill an innocent victim themselves. Only then does R accept his guilt, "for the sake of all Rs." The film's stylized sets (23.52) and grotesque comedy stress its central issues: Koreans as an oppressed minority, capital punishment as political control, and sexual murder as an inevitable outcome of social repression. Oshima urged that the original criminal's letters become high school reading.[21]

Unlike Godard, Oshima alternated very experimental films like *Three Resurrected Drunkards* and *Death by Hanging* with more accessible works like *Boy* (1969), the story of parents who make a living by shoving their child into traffic and then collecting payment for his injuries. *Ceremonies* (aka *The Ceremony*, 1971) is likewise fairly traditional in its treatment of the familiar Oshima theme of how society frustrates young people's sexual drives. The story plots the political and erotic intrigues within a family ruled by a rapacious father. The relatives gather only at funerals and weddings. Oshima's insistence that exploitation, incest, and guilt pervade the Japanese extended family forms a critique of the serene domestic life presented in Ozu's work.

Stylistic Trends of Political Modernism The works of Godard and Oshima are central cases, but they do not exhaust all the tendencies within political modernism. There were at least four other trends: collage construction, fantasy and parable, a stylized presentation of myth and history, and minimalism.

An exemplary modernist strategy, *collage construction* has origins in Cubist painting. Most broadly, the collage film assembles bits of footage that are not intrinsically connected. Instead of trying to make the linkage seem natural or even "invisible," as in Hollywood's use of stock footage, the modernist filmmaker emphasizes the disparities among the images or sounds, forcing the viewer to make an imaginative leap. We have already seen this strategy used for metaphorical or poetic effect in Joseph Cornell's *Rose Hobart* (ca. 1936), Chris Marker's *Letter from Siberia* (1957), and Bruce Conner's short films; but in the late 1960s many filmmakers exploited it for political critique.

Radical filmmakers working with fictional narrative typically employ the collage principle in a more linear fashion. Such films set up a story and then elaborate on it with footage drawn from other realms. Brecht and Dudow's *Kuhle Wampe* pioneered this approach in a mild way, and we have already seen it in Makavejev's films (p. 464). Very similar to *WR: Mysteries of the Organism* is Vilgot Sjöman's *I am Curious (Yellow)* (1967) and *I Am Curious (Blue)* (1967). Sjöman's story of a young woman seeking sexual liberation is treated in Direct Cinema terms (with a good deal of reflexivity), but it is interrupted by titles and cutaways (23.53, 23.54).

Political modernism after 1967 also embraced *fantasy* and *parable*. The return of Luis Buñuel to international fame rekindled interest in the Surrealist tradition, which had nursed revolutionary aspirations since the 1920s. Many viewers considered *The Discreet Charm of the Bourgeoisie* (1972) and *The Phantom of Liberty* (1974) to be sly comments on official repressions of the 1968 rebellions. Closer to the ferocity of Buñuel's first

23.53, 23.54 Through editing, Martin Luther King, Jr., seems to be looking at Lena, heroine of *I Am Curious (Yellow)*.

films is *Viva la muerte!* ("Long Live Death!" 1971), by the Spanish playwright Ferdinand Arrabal. A Spanish boy fantasizes his father's torture at the hands of the Church and the army. The boy is also obsessed with his mother, whom he imagines bathing in the blood of a slaughtered bull. Arrabal's cheerfully perverse fantasies put the film in the modernist tradition, and he savors gruesome imagery. A shot of the father being tortured is rendered peculiarly beautiful through tinting (**Color Plate 23.3**). Traces of the Surrealist impulse are also evident in Alexander Jodorovsky's grotesque *El Topo* ("The Mole," 1971) and his mystical *The Holy Mountain* (1973).

Less indebted to Surrealism in the use of fantasy was Pier Paolo Pasolini. *Hawks and Sparrows* (1965) initiated his interest in contemporary political parables, but his subsequent work in this vein was more scathing. *Teorema* (1968) shows a blankly handsome young man taken in by a bourgeois family; one by one, their lives are changed in ways at once sordid and miraculous. *Pigpen* (1969) sets side by side two stories about perverse appetites: a young mountain climber becomes a cannibal, and an industrialist is eaten by pigs. In these films, Pasolini's technique has a Buñuelian objectivity, throwing into relief the absurd spectacle of a disintegrating society.

Political modernist filmmakers also employed a stylized presentation of *history* and *myth*. Instead of portraying a past event neutrally, or simply retelling a myth, the radical filmmaker might treat it through nonrealistic techniques and then draw analogies with contemporary political struggles. For example, Yoshishige Yoshida's trilogy—*Eros plus Massacre* (1969), *Heroic Purgatory* (1970), and *Martial Law* (1973)—uses decentered framing and stylized lighting to show how Japanese activism in different eras parallels that of the late 1960s.

Similarly, Pasolini consistently teased a political critique out of his adaptations of classical myths and contemporary history. In *Medea* (1969), among masked choristers and pink rocks, the classical heroine embodies the conflict between colonization and the people it dominates. Pasolini's last film, *Salò, or the 120 Days of Sodom* (1975), stages the final days of Italian fascism as a spectacle out of the Marquis de Sade. Here Pasolini's technique of *pasticchio* ("mixing"; p. 452) frames mutilation and sexual assault in classical compositions and sets them to the music of Carl Orff's *Carmina Burana*.

In the wake of 1968, Miklós Jancsó's treatment of history also became more defiantly unrealistic. *The Confrontation* (1969) centers on left-wing debates in Hungary during the immediate postwar period. As usual, Jancsó concentrates on group dynamics. Activists ransack a university library, bully other students, argue with their opponents, and purge a leader on orders from the party. Jancsó's sinuous camera movements and very long takes are now accompanied by a more stylized mise-en-scène. Characters sing and dance spontaneously, and, although the events are set around 1948, the students wear the sport shirts and blue jeans of the sixties.

Jancsó began to create political allegories fusing past, present, and future events. *Agnus Dei* (1970) shows the 1919 Hungarian revolution in the countryside, concentrating on an epileptic priest and a mysterious White officer who may represent the fascism that will overtake Europe. Jancsó's subsequent films extend his examination of power to the entire history of the West. Attila's murder of his brother (*Technique and Rite*, 1971), the plot against Julius Caesar (*Rome Wants Another Caesar*, 1973), and Elektra's legendary struggle with Aegisthos (*For Elektra*, 1974) become ritualized dialogues and ceremonial encounters, rendered in elaborate choreography and long takes. (*For Elektra* is composed of only ten shots.)

Red Psalm (1971), for many critics Jancsó's masterpiece, balances these generalizing tendencies with national elements and more idiosyncratic symbolism. Although no actual event or period is designated, the story portrays a struggle of Hungarian peasants against landowners and soldiers. Followed by a zooming, panning, and tracking camera, victims and oppressors float through an abstract, expanding and contracting, space (**23.55–23.60**). Beginning with a peasant woman holding a dove and ending with the same woman brandishing a rifle, *Red Psalm* draws on revolutionary symbols. When someone is killed, the victim may return to life, now wearing a red flower. *Red Psalm* becomes a pageant that restages the revolutionary tradition in the light both of Brecht and of art-cinema modernism.

A stylized treatment of history and myth was also explored by the Greek director Theo Angelopoulos. Influenced by Mizoguchi, Antonioni, and Dreyer, Angelopoulos began his career under the dictatorship of the Greek generals in the late 1960s. His first feature, *Reconstruction* (1970), displayed a by-then conventional reshuffling of present and past, as flashbacks interrupt the investigation of a murder. But the cryptic dialogue, which supplies little information about character relations, and the camera's dwelling on still compositions and landscapes (**23.61**) make the film seem dedramatized even by art-cinema standards.

Like the early Jancsó, Angelopoulos plumbed his nation's history for political lessons for the present. Despite censorship under the military regime, *Days of '36* (1972), a film about the murder of a militant union leader, shows how the government protected the assassin. The result,

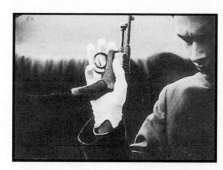

23.55 One phase of one shot in *Red Psalm:* from a woman with a dove . . .

23.56 . . . the camera pans left to a soldier's pistol . . .

23.57 . . . before glimpsing a balladeer drifting into the background.

23.58 The camera follows him to a group of peasants . . .

23.59 . . . who surround the soldier . . .

23.60 . . . and entice him into a dance.

shot in long takes and 360-degree panning movements, became an allegory of political repression. Under the same regime, Angelopoulos produced *The Traveling Players* (1975), a four-hour panorama of Greek political strife between 1939 and 1952. Over the years a theater troupe performs the same play, a mythical piece that comments upon the changing political situation. As he did in *Reconstruction,* Angelopoulos rearranges the time sequence, but

now he blends historical periods within a single shot. The soliloquies and performances, along with Angelopoulos's long-shot framings, yield a dry anti-illusionism consistent with early-1970s interpretations of Brecht (**23.62**).

The spareness of Angelopoulos's technique relates him to another trend of post-1968 political modernism. Some filmmakers pursued a strategy of *minimalism—* sparse narratives rendered in a rigorous, ascetic style.

23.61 Bus passengers stop to relieve themselves in *Reconstruction.*

23.62 Moving through history and staging a classic play in small towns, the traveling players become the conscience of Greek culture.

23.63 *Jeanne Dielman:* household routine made unfamiliar through use of static long takes.

Outstanding examples are found in the work of Chantal Akerman, one of the most influential women directors of the era. Akerman's minimalism derived less from European sources than from encounters with Warhol's work (p. 504) and North American Structural cinema (see Chapter 24). *Je, tu, il, elle* (1974) was a stripped-down narrative of sexual encounters rendered in long takes. Her most influential film was *Jeanne Dielman, 23, Quai du commerce, 1080 Bruxelles* (1975; the title gives the main character's name and address in Brussels).

Over 225 minutes, Akerman presents three days in the life of a housewife who works as a prostitute in her home. The film's first half presents Jeanne's life in a style as meticulous as her housekeeping. The low-height camera, centered down a corridor or across a kitchen table, records every bit of business—dressing, washing dishes, greeting a customer, making a meatloaf. After one client's visit, however, Jeanne's routine mysteriously breaks down and she starts to make errors. Finally, she stabs a client and goes to sit at the dining table—virtually the only time we see her relax.

Jeanne Dielman is a landmark in feminist modernism. By slowing plot action to a standstill, Akerman obliges the viewer to look at the empty intervals and domestic spaces that mainstream cinema skips over. In one sense, *Jeanne Dielman* moves toward fulfilling Neorealist Cesare Zavattini's dream of recording eight hours in a person's life; the film could even be considered an expansion of the sequence of the maid's awakening in *Umberto D.* (p. 364). But Akerman treats domestic space as harboring sexual repression and financial exploitation. Housekeeping is woman's work, as is prostitution (as Jeanne's address on "Commerce Pier" indicates).

Akerman's minimalist style recalls Bresson, Ozu, Mizoguchi, and experimental cinema, but she uses spare technique for purposes of political critique. The static camera and the rectilinear, low-height compositions estrange the viewer from the action while dignifying household chores as aesthetically and socially significant (**23.63**).

Despite the diversity within political modernism, the mid-1970s saw the trend drop off, at least in 35mm filmmaking. Although the exploration of myth and history continued, the collage form and surrealist fantasy virtually vanished. Minimalism was adapted to less formally radical ends. As left-wing positions became assimilated into mainstream politics, radical production groups were difficult to sustain. Oshima disbanded his company Sozosha in 1973, a year after the end of Godard and Gorin's Dziga-Vertov Group. The scandals surrounding Makavejev's *Sweet Movie* (1974) and Oshima's *In the Realm of the Senses* (1975) were triggered by their sexual content, not modernist technique or political stance. Godard announced his return to more accessible narrative in *Sauve qui peut (la vie)* ("Let one who can save [one's life]," aka *Every Man for Himself,* 1979). By the end of the 1970s, most political modernists were making less radical, and less radically experimental, works.

The Politicization of Mainstream Narrative and the Art Film During the 1960s and 1970s, mainstream European and Asian cinema became politicized to some degree. In Italy, directors were more willing to investigate the fascist past; even spaghetti Westerns became more partisan (for example, Sergio Leone's *Duck, You Sucker!,* 1972). In Sweden, Bo Widerberg made *Adalen 31* (1969), a study of labor strife. In Japan, the pink films of Koji Wakamitsu became frenzied studies of sexual repression and terrorism. The British *Sunday, Bloody Sunday* (1971) inserted male homosexuality into a domestic melodrama.

Political Genres The most commercially successful integration of left-wing politics and classical narrative cinema took place in the genre of the *political thriller.* Here a plot would be built around the investigation of an actual government scandal, mentioned by name or thinly disguised. The political thriller offered the excitement of a detective film and the shock of an exposé. The inclusion of major stars also ensured a film's wide circulation.

The political thriller had been pioneered by Francesco Rosi in *Salvatore Giuliano* (1961), and he continued to exploit it in *The Mattei Affair* (1972), *Lucky Luciano* (1974), and *Exquisite Corpses* (1975). Rosi's films intercut the inquiry with key events in the past while drawing upon documentary techniques, such as newsreel footage, dates, and explanatory captions (**23.64**). Although the genre was almost exclusively male territory, Nadine Trintignant's *Défense de savoir* ("Right to Know," 1973) was a comparable study of collusion between police and the extreme right. The most famous exponent of the political thriller was Costa-Gavras. A Greek who became a French citizen, Costa-Gavras started as a director of thrillers (*The Sleeping Car Murder,* 1965) before he made *Z* (1969), one of the most widely seen political films of the era.

"Any similarity to actual events, or persons living or dead, is not coincidental. It is intentional." Signed by Costa-Gavras and scriptwriter Jorge Semprun, the opening title of *Z* announces a political agenda. The film retells the events surrounding the assassination of a popular opponent of the dictatorial Greek colonels. The investigating magistrate, a political moderate, exposes the right-wing conspiracy, but then he falls victim too. By 1969, many New Cinema techniques—glimpsed flashbacks, slow motion, freeze-frames, hand-held shots (**23.65**)—had become easily understood, and Costa-Gavras used them to create suspense and rapid-fire action. The presence of the star Yves Montand helped *Z* gain international recognition.

Costa-Gavras then made *The Confession* (1970), a re-creation of a political purge in postwar Czechoslovakia; *State of Siege* (1973), an attack on American attempts to oust the Tupamaro guerrillas of Uruguay; and *Special Section* (1975), an exposé of French collaboration with the Germans during World War II. The films rested upon a body of research, but critics from all political persuasions faulted the action-packed intrigues and the schematic hero/villain characterizations. Costa-Gavras replied that only by working within mainstream conventions could he bring information to a broad audience. He refused the slow pace and intellectual demands of political modernism:

> The general public is not sufficiently trained to reflect upon a film while it is being projected. They have become accustomed to the rapid pace of American cinema, and I have to confess that I feel closer to this rhythm too. It's only after the film that the spectator can truly reflect upon it. Or reject it.[22]

For two decades, Costa-Gavras remained the dean of the political thriller (*Missing,* 1982; *Betrayed,* 1988; and *Music Box,* 1989).

Other genres became political vehicles. Louis Malle's period drama *Lacombe Lucien* (France, 1974) shows a young peasant seduced by fascist politics, while in the

23.64 Pseudo-documentary touches in *The Mattei Affair.*

23.65 A hand-held shot follows the dissident to his assassination in *Z.*

23.66 Spanish peasant life as a breeding ground for political rebellion (*Pascal Duarte*).

more elliptical *Pascal Duarte* (Spain, 1975) Ricardo Franco traces how an equally violent youth becomes a rebel during the Spanish civil war (**23.66**). Comedy also assimilated left-wing themes. In France, Diane Kurys made the highly popular *Diabolo Menthe* (1977), an affectionate portrait of post-1968 youth, following it two years later with *Cocktail Molotov,* set in the days of May. Political subjects were taken up in Italian comedies

23.67 *Seven Beauties:* the street hustler forced to bargain for his comforts in a prison camp.

23.68 In *Dillinger Is Dead,* the husband takes a fantasy swim "inside" a movie.

23.69 The imaginary life of the upper class, attacked in *The Garden of Delights.*

tler must humble himself to survive in a Nazi prison camp (**23.67**).

Marco Ferreri's grotesque comedies offer a more deadpan, enigmatic attitude. *Dillinger Is Dead* (1969) builds enormous suspense as it observes a businessman coming home late, preparing a meal, watching home movies, and murdering his wife. In this masculine version of Akerman's *Jeanne Dielman,* the minute depiction of the husband's habits reveals the pettiness of his business ethos (**23.68**). In Ferreri's *La Grande bouffe* ("The Big Blowout," 1973), a batch of businessmen literally kill themselves through gorging and fornication.

Politicizing the Art Film Along with such mainstream filmmakers, directors working within the art cinema were affected by the climate of the era. Avoiding the extremes of Brechtian alienation and stylization, many established directors nevertheless continued the tradition of postwar modernism while incorporating political material. Carlos Saura, for instance, had already made *The Hunt* (1965), an attack on the machismo ethos in Spain. *The Garden of Delights* (1970) took a more Buñuelian slant, showing a perverse ruling class living between fantasy and reality (**23.69**).

In *If . . .* (1968), Lindsay Anderson intensified the critique of British society that had driven the Kitchen Sink films (p. 454). An upper-middle-class boys' school becomes a microcosm of social revolution as four radical students rebel against repressive officials. *If . . .* adopts Godardian techniques by introducing major segments with intertitles; its alternation of color and black-and-white film stock (though used out of economic necessity) becomes a mildly Brechtian distancing device. The final scene, in which the boys fire from a roof into a crowd, refers to the ending of Jean Vigo's anarchistic *Zero for Conduct.* With its fantasy sequence and concluding freeze-frame, *If . . .* invoked conventions of the contemporary art cinema.

Postwar European films had used strongly demarcated flashbacks to compare past and present; *Hiroshima mon amour* had made the time shifts more rapid and ambiguous; directors of the 1960s had pushed the technique to fragmented extremes. In the 1970s, the flashback continued to be a tool for exploring political change across history. The Hungarian Istvan Szabó employed the device to chronicle the lives of people in an apartment building in *25 Firemen's Street* (1973). Through a rhythmic alternation of eras, André Téchiné's *Souvenirs d'en France* ("Memories of France," 1974) chronicles the effects of labor struggles on a family over several decades. Karoly Makk's *Love* (Hungary, 1970) uses swift montage and abrupt flashbacks to con-

as well, most famously in Lina Wertmuller's *The Seduction of Mimi* (1972), *Love and Anarchy* (1973), and *Swept Away* (1974). *Seven Beauties* (1976) offers a critique of Italian male pride, showing how a cocky hus-

trast the lives of two women waiting for the return of a political prisoner.

Bernardo Bertolucci, always in touch with contemporary trends, employed flashbacks in more innovative ways in *The Spider's Stratagem* (1970). Here characters look exactly the same "now" as they did thirty years before, and from the past they speak to someone in the present (**23.70**). Bertolucci's *The Conformist* (1971) is perhaps the exemplification of the politicized art film. It presents a precise play among memory, fantasy, and reality in its portrayal of a sexually repressed man driven to become a fascist political assassin. A simpler flashback structure frames *1900* (1975), a sweeping fresco of the rise of fascism presented through the parallel lives of two friends, one a leftist peasant and the other a weak-willed son of the gentry.

Directors of the postwar generation reflected on the new era in distinct ways. Federico Fellini's *Satyricon* (1969) was widely interpreted as his sour commentary on current social decline, and in *Amarcord* (1973) he produced a half-nostalgic, half-mocking portrayal of fascist spectacle. A colossal steamship holds the villagers spellbound, and a gigantic head of Mussolini looms frowning over a parade (see Color Plate 19.2). Michelangelo Antonioni's *Zabriskie Point* (1970) made common cause with student revolution through a hallucinatory love-in at Death Valley and a series of shots detailing the slow-motion explosion of an American home. *The Passenger* (aka *Profession: Reporter*, 1975) shifted to the Third World, where Antonioni's characteristic questions about identity are played out in a political intrigue involving arms shipments.

The Swiss director Alain Tanner declared himself also stirred by the May events, and throughout the ensuing decade his films reflected upon the legacies of 1968. With Michel Soutter, Claude Goretta, and others, Tanner founded the Groupe Cinq ("Group 5") in 1968 in order to make films for Swiss television. Tanner's early features, influenced by British Free Cinema and the Nouvelle Vague, lay firmly in the European art-cinema tradition, using reflexivity (*Charles mort ou vif* ["Charles Dead or Alive," 1969]) and the investigation-via-flashbacks structure (*The Salamander*, 1971). Thereafter he specialized in wistful studies of how the absence of radical change blocked personal relationships. His most famous film was *For Jonah, Who Will Be 25 in the Year 2000* (1976). Here eight "children of May" (*Max, Marco, Marguerite, Madeline,* and so on) form a commune in the era of dashed hopes and political "normalization." Black-and-white images represent their utopian desires, and Tanner ends the film with an ambivalent image of the future (**23.71**).

23.70 *The Spider's Stratagem:* standing in the past, Draifa tells the young Athos in the present about his father (the man at the window in the background); the technique serves the thematic purpose of questioning the need for sanctified historical heroes.

23.71 In an epilogue set in the future, Jonah scribbles on the commune's mural (*For Jonah, Who Will Be 25 in the Year 2000*).

If Tanner focuses on middle-class characters longing for change, the brothers Paolo and Vittorio Taviani concentrate on the revolutionary aspirations of the peasantry and the working class. The Tavianis undertook a populist retelling of Italian revolutionary history in *Subversives* (1967), *Under the Sign of Scorpio* (1968), *St. Michael Had a Cock* (1971), and *Allonsanfan* (1974). Their first international success was *Padre padrone* ("Father-Boss," 1977), the story of an illiterate shepherd boy who becomes a scholar of linguistics through an obstinate revolt against his father. The film begins with the author of the original autobiography whittling a branch as he introduces the tale. He then hands the stick to the actor playing the father (**23.72**), who enters the schoolroom to fetch his son, and the fictional story begins. Apart from introducing a Brechtian distance, the scene

23.72 *Padre padrone:* the stick is transferred.

suggests that the son, now grown, realizes that harsh authority is necessary if youth is to define itself.

A New Prominence for Female Directors Attention to women's concerns gave a new impetus to the careers of female art-cinema directors. The Hungarian Marta Mészáros had made several short films during the 1960s. Her first feature, *The Girl* (1968), was followed by several others, notably *Riddance* (1973), *Adoption* (1975; winner of a grand prize at the Berlin Film Festival), and *Nine Months* (1976). Mészáros's work balances a consideration of women's relation to social forces, particularly class structure, with a probing of intimate relationships. Taken together, her films dramatize a vast range of feminine experience, from school, dating, and marriage to work, childbirth, and family life. She particularly explores mother-daughter relationships. Her style emphasizes realism and authorial commentary, both inflected by close-ups of her heroines' bodies; in *Adoption* she builds an entire sequence out of women's hands at work in a factory.

Agnès Varda had been directing since the early 1950s, though her fame came only with the rise of the Nouvelle Vague (p. 450). She was active in the cinematic left, making a short on the Black Panthers and contributing to the collective film *Far from Vietnam* (1967). After *Lions Love* (1969), a relaxed celebration of the American counterculture, Varda made several short films before her next feature, *One Sings, the Other Doesn't* (1976). Like many political films of the mid-1970s, it takes stock of the previous decade—here, by tracing the course of two women's friendship from 1962 to 1974. Wanting to focus attention on abortion and childbearing as seen from her liberal feminist viewpoint, Varda deliberately aimed *One Sings* at a wide audience. "In France, our film has already been seen by 350,000

people. . . . If the meaning of the film and its feminist point of view is even half or two-thirds as strong as that of a more radical film, at least we've gotten a lot of people *thinking,* and not in the wrong direction."[23]

The late 1960s and early 1970s saw new women directors emerge within the art cinema. In France, Nelly Kaplan, who had been Abel Gance's assistant since 1954, made her first feature. *The Pirate's Fiancée* (aka *A Very Curious Girl,* 1969) shows a young village woman exploited by the local men until she begins blackmailing them with tape recordings of intimate secrets. Liliane de Kermadec's *Aloïse* (1974) launched the career of Isabelle Huppert, who plays a woman imprisoned for opposing World War I. Several French actresses took up directing, notably Diane Kurys, Anna Karina, and Jeanne Moreau. In Canada, the experimental filmmaker Joyce Wieland made the reflexive melodrama *The Far Shore* (1976). Some filmmakers focused on particular feminist issues, while others dealt with subjects of broader political concern, including the "politics of everyday life."

On the whole, mainstream cinema and art cinema adapted to the political culture of the post-1968 era. Classical narrative conventions assimilated political themes and subject matter, especially in the political thriller and the comedy. Art-cinema directors who retreated from the extreme experimentation of political modernism nevertheless took micropolitics and the culture of dissent to be fruitful subjects. Tanner, calling himself "marginal" within commercial filmmaking, spoke for many: "My position is not to be as radical as Godard, but to try to force the commercial world to open their doors to outside experiences."[24] As radical political modernism left the realm of 35mm commercial filmmaking in the late 1970s, most politicized fictional filmmaking in the western world worked within the bounds of classical or art-cinema narrative. Political modernism survived longer in the experimental 16mm sector (see Chapter 24).

New Cinema in West Germany: The Political Wing
The "New German Cinema," a phrase coined in the early 1970s, denotes an even more amorphous group than most new cinemas. The label covers filmmakers pursuing very different agendas. Several directors did not practice critical political cinema (see Chapter 26). But those who took up left-wing filmmaking vividly illustrate the trends of the late 1960s and after.

The Oberhausen manifesto of 1962 (p. 456) stimulated some socially critical filmmaking, particularly for television, but not until 1968 did left-wing students at Berlin's Institute of Film and Television launch a series of engaged documentaries and fiction films aimed at working-class audiences. More ambitious were the films of the "Berlin School," which echoed the German proletarian films of the late 1920s (p. 305) in their focus on working-class life. Rejecting the idealized realism of the Berlin School, the feminist Helga Reidemeister concentrated on documenting the domestic life of the working class, notably in *The Purchased Dream* (1977), a compilation from four hours of super-8mm material that a family had shot.

Political Modernism: Kluge, Syberberg, and Straub/Huillet
Political modernism was also a strong force in the New German Cinema. The 1968 upheavals and their political culture strengthened the Brechtian documentary drama practiced by playwrights Peter Weiss and Rolf Hochhuth. In film, political modernists continued the social critique implicit in much Young German Film of the early 1960s, but they gave it a more radical edge in response to the rise of the counterculture and the New Left.

Alexander Kluge, a moving force in the Young German Film (pp. 456–457) exemplifies the collage trend in political modernism. By intercutting fiction, documentary, written titles, and other material, his films continued the strategies of *Yesterday Girl* (1966), confronting the spectator with gaps "in which fantasy can take root." "The film is composed in the head of the spectator; it is not a work of art that exists on the screen by itself."[25] Kluge hoped that this countercultural openness would permit the film to become less a preplanned message and more the basis of an ongoing dialogue between filmmaker and audience.

Artists at the Top of the Big Top: Perplexed (1968) was a reaction to the radical students at the Berlin Film Festival who pelted Kluge with eggs and charged him with elitism. The story of Leni Peickert's attempt to create a new kind of circus is interrupted by news photos, newsreels, shots from Eisenstein's *October,* color footage, and references to current ideas that only through a "work of mourning" could Germany come to terms with its Nazi past. The circus of Leni's imagination (**23.73**) never comes to pass, and she winds up working as a television producer. In its open-textured way, *Artists at the Top of the Big Top* presents the difficulty of utopian political change and suggests that only a "long march through the institutions"—here, existing media conditions—will lead to social change.

The alternation of documentary and fiction within Kluge's films takes place in a more theatrical fashion in the work of Hans-Jürgen Syberberg. Syberberg came to notice with a series of Direct Cinema documentaries in

23.73 *Artists at the Top of the Big Top: Perplexed:* a circus acrobat pirouettes on Leni's head, thanks to Kluge's framing.

23.74 The phantasmagoric blend of cinema, music, and German history (*Hitler: A Film from Germany;* production still).

the late 1960s, but his most famous films are the trilogy *Ludwig: Requiem for a Virgin King* (1972), *Karl May* (1974), and the eight-hour *Hitler: A Film from Germany* (1977). The spirit of Brecht, whom Syberberg has called his "foster father," mingles with a Wagnerian giganticism in the first and last of these works. Swirling smoke, vast auras of colored light, and mournful music enfold monumental tableaux representing the twilight of German culture (**23.74**). The *Hitler* film's reflexivity, with references running from Thomas Edison and Leni Riefenstahl to *Citizen Kane,* makes it a history of the cinema in which Hitler, turning politics into mythical drama, becomes "the greatest filmmaker of all time."

Probably the most controversial practitioners of political modernism in the New German Cinema were Jean-Marie Straub and Danièle Huillet. After *Not Reconciled*

23.75 Impersonally rendered musical performance in *The Chronicle of Anna Magdalena Bach.*

(1965), they made the feature-length *The Chronicle of Anna Magdalena Bach* (1968). In one sense it employs the collage aesthetic, setting together shots of documents from Bach's day, brief staged narrative scenes, and lengthy performances. But for most of its length it is a remarkable effort in minimalism. Straub and Huillet present elliptical, fragmentary episodes from Bach's life and use static shots or a slightly moving camera to record lengthy stretches of performances, never showing the audience (**23.75**). As in *Not Reconciled* and later works, they counter most production practice in fictional film by using direct sound, thereby capturing the specific auditory character of each space. From one perspective, the film resembles *Artists at the Top of the Big Top* in being a "materialist" study of artistic labor, with Straub and Huillet suggesting that Bach's music arose in part from particular social and political conditions.

The combination of collage construction, direct sound, and ascetic treatment of narrative and style returns in *History Lessons* (1972), an adaptation of a Brecht novel, and *Sinai Dogs: Fortini Cani* (1977). Straub

and Huillet also explore minimalist ways of adapting theater pieces: *Othon* (1969) uses the hand-held camera to present a classical French play staged in contemporary Rome, while the opera *Moses and Aaron* (1974) is played out in a desert arena with stylized arrangements of solo singers and chorus (**23.76**). Opposed to all forms of entertainment cinema, Straub and Huillet's films interrogate artistic tradition, probing classic novels and plays for contemporary political implications. (*The Chronicle of Anna Magdalena Bach* is dedicated to the people of Vietnam; *Moses and Aaron,* to a terrorist.)

Mainstream Politicized Cinema   The more commercially successful New German films adapted political commentary to the conventions of mainstream cinema. The most prominent genres were the *Arbeiterfilm* ("worker film"), which used realistic storytelling technique to portray the life of the contemporary working class, and the *Heimatfilm* ("homeland film"), which focused on rural life.

Among the many directors working within the art cinema, Volker Schlöndorff stands out. His 1970 *The Sudden Wealth of the Poor People of Kombach* draws on mildly Brechtian techniques to trace the capture and execution of a gang of peasant bandits. Schlöndorff attracted international attention by codirecting *The Lost Honor of Katherina Blum* (1975) with his wife, Margarethe von Trotta. The film shows a woman accused of aiding a terrorist and hounded by the police and the scandalmongering press. Throughout most of the film, the viewer is led to believe Katherina is an innocent victim (**Color Plate 23.4**). Once she has gained the viewer's sympathy, the plot reveals that love led her to help the young man. The narrational processes of classical filmmaking coax the audience to sympathize with a subversive act.

After another film with Schlöndorff, von Trotta began directing on her own. *The Second Awakening of Christa Klages* (1977) pursues the narrative strategy of *Katherina Blum* by aligning the audience with a feminist robber on the run. In a period when terrorism, plane hijackings, and assassinations created headlines,

23.76, *left*   *Moses and Aaron:* the protagonists sing, backed by an invisible chorus.

23.77, *right*   *The Little Chaos:* Fassbinder plays a robber in his first film.

23.78   *Katzelmacher* (1969): loafing couples, shot in a flat, frontal manner.

23.79   *The Bitter Tears of Petra von Kant* takes place entirely in the luxurious apartment of a fashion designer; Fassbinder's filming of the richly decorated set recalls Josef von Sternberg.

such a focus on a criminal woman had a vivid political impact.

Von Trotta's career exemplifies the extent to which West Germany's production subsidy system enabled women directors to work in numbers unparalleled in other nations. Many of them produced politically inflected art films. For example, Helga Sanders-Brahms's *Violence* (1971) is an "anti-road movie," alternating static road maps with a tale of how two assembly-line workers kill an immigrant. In an Arbeiterfilm, *The Employee* (1972), Sanders-Brahms traces a computer programmer's descent into madness, while her *Last Days of Gomorrah* (1974) shows a future society in which television gratifies all desires.

Fassbinder: The Provocateur   Rainer Werner Fassbinder was perhaps the best-known director of the New German Cinema, partly because of his aggressive personality and self-destructive lifestyle. Fassbinder was influenced by the French New Wave and the political modernism that intensified in the late 1960s. Beginning as an actor, playwright, and theater director, Fassbinder revealed a taste for grotesque comedy, splashy violence, and strong realism of characters' regional dialects. Yet he rejected the Brechtian theory that was important for Kluge, Straub, and others. He insisted that politically critical art had to engage the spectator's feelings. "With Brecht you see the emotions and you reflect upon them as you witness them but you never feel them. . . . I let the audience *feel and think.*"[26]

After his early, strongly Godardian short *The Little Chaos* (1966; **23.77**), Fassbinder made eleven films with

the Antiteater, a troupe of actors and technicians. Some of the films recast Hollywood genres, while others show the influence of the Nouvelle Vague and Straub and Huillet. Fassbinder then acquainted himself with Douglas Sirk's Hollywood melodramas (p. 341), which he took as a model of a socially critical cinema that was also emotionally engaging. He was struck by the arbitrarily upbeat endings (he called them "unhappy happy ends") and by the way that Sirk blocked full identification with the characters. With *The Merchant of Four Seasons* (1971) Fassbinder initiated a second phase in his work, that of domestic melodramas. Once more he proved highly prolific, using rapid shooting schedules and low budgets to turn out several features, notably *The Bitter Tears of Petra von Kant* (1972), *Fear Eats the Soul* (1973), *Effie Briest* (1974), and *Fox and His Friends* (1974).

Early in his career Fassbinder often framed figures in a sober, mug-shot fashion (**23.78**). In his "Hollywood revisionist" phase, he accepted the conventions of continuity editing in order to keep the drama paramount, yet much of the fascination of these films derives from Fassbinder's dwelling on gazes or distant views or his using elements of decor to veil characters' emotional states (**23.79**).

The early Antiteater films experiment with narrative, while the later political melodramas are gripping, emotion-laden stories aimed at a broader public. Most of Fassbinder's films are about power. He often focuses on victimization and conformity, showing how members of a group exploit and punish outsiders. Fassbinder insists that the victim often accepts the standards the group applies, so he or she comes to believe that the punishment

23.80   *Far from Vietnam:* the director as laconic and detached commentator.

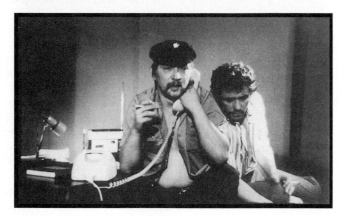

23.81   *Germany in Autumn:* the director as confused and dispirited participant.

is deserved. Ali in *Fear Eats the Soul* literally internalizes the racial prejudice he suffers, collapsing from an ulcer— a common illness of immigrant workers.

Coming after the failures of 1968, Fassbinder's work is often interpreted as acknowledging the impossibility of radical change. No Brechtian aesthetic could promise a social revolution. The movement of Fassbinder's career from anarchistic and severe political modernism to works that use the less disturbing conventions of Hollywood and the art cinema reflects a general trend within European critical political cinema during the 1970s.

The same change is conveniently summarized in two European films from the beginning and the end of the period. In 1967, thirteen left-wing directors, mostly French, collaborated on *Far from Vietnam*. The film sought to mobilize intellectuals against the war by a series of episodes—some fictional (e.g., Resnais's), some compiled from newsreel footage (e.g., Marker's), one essayistic (Godard's; **23.80**). In 1978, fourteen German directors, coordinated by Kluge, made *Germany in Autumn*. Like *Far from Vietnam* it brings together disparate tendencies within current filmmaking. But now the hope is not to change international policy; the goal is to understand national life in a climate of terrorism and right-wing oppression. Certain episodes, particularly Fassbinder's drug-hazed confrontation with his lover, dramatize the extent to which the political had become personal (**23.81**). *Germany in Autumn* exemplifies the turn from broad activism toward a micropolitics, while indicating that critical filmmaking remained central to the 1970s political culture of dissent.

Notes and Queries

DEFINING THIRD WORLD REVOLUTIONARY CINEMA

Three essays set the agenda for Third World political filmmaking: Rocha's "Aesthetics of Hunger" (1965), Espinosa's "For an Imperfect Cinema" (1969), and Solanas and Getino's "Third Cinema" manifesto (1969). The authors all subsequently reconsidered their ideas. Espinosa explained that he conceived "imperfection" not as clumsiness but as an acknowledgment of the filmmaker's political position (Julio Garcia Espinosa, "Meditations on Imperfect Cinema . . . Fifteen Years Later," *Screen* 26, nos. 3–4 [May–August 1985]: 94). Solanas explained that not all big productions were necessarily First Cinema, just as not all auteur-based films were necessarily Second Cinema. Third Cinema did, however, support anticolonialism and

social change (quoted in "L'Influence du 'Troisième Cinéma' dans le monde," *Revue tiers monde* 20, no. 79 [July–September 1979]: 622). Writing later in the 1970s, Getino noted ruefully that "the force and cohesion of the popular movements in these countries—and in Argentina—were not as strong as we had imagined" (Octavio Getino, "Some Notes on the Concept of a 'Third Cinema,'" in Tim Barnard, ed., *Argentine Cinema* [Toronto: Nightwood, 1986], p. 107).

Most expansively, in a 1971 essay, "The Aesthetics of the Dream," Rocha defined three types of revolutionary art: that useful for immediate political action (e.g., *The Hour of the Furnaces*), that which opens up political discussion (e.g., most of Cinema Nôvo), and a revolutionary art based on the people's dreams, as reflected in magic and myth (quoted in Sylvie Pierre, *Glauber Rocha* [Paris: Cahiers du Cinéma, 1987], pp. 129–30). This art of the dream had been ignored by the traditional left, Rocha claimed, although he glimpsed it in the 1968 youth revolutions.

As the force of Third World cinema was waning, film scholars began to study the phenomenon extensively. Some took the position that there was a tricontinental Third Cinema, characterized by recurrent political themes and formal conventions. The most extensive argument for this view is set forth in Teshome Gabriel, *Third Cinema in the Third World: The Aesthetics of Liberation* (Ann Arbor, Michigan: UMI Research Press, 1982). A condensed statement of his position is "Towards a Critical Theory of Third World Films," in Jim Pines and Paul Willemen, eds., *Questions of Third Cinema* (London: British Film Institute, 1989), pp. 30–52. The view is criticized by Julianne Burton in "Marginal Cinemas and Mainstream Critical Theory," *Screen* 26, nos. 3–4 (May–August 1985): 2–21. Gabriel replies in "Colonialism and 'Law and Order' Criticism," *Screen* 27, nos. 3–4 (May–August 1986): 140–47.

FILM STUDIES AND THE NEW FILM THEORY

The era this chapter surveys witnessed the enormous growth of academic film studies in Britain, Europe, and North America. The political movements of the late 1960s influenced many film courses; instructors and students often analyzed the ideological implications of mainstream Hollywood film and considered critical political films as "oppositional" cinema.

Along with these developments went major changes in film theory. Building on semiological ideas of the early 1960s (see "Notes and Queries," Chapter 20), film theorists in the wake of 1968 sought to explain how cinema functioned politically while providing pleasure. The newly radicalized editors of *Cahiers du cinéma* proposed a taxonomy that distinguished films wholly in the grip of dominant ideology from those that use political critique opportunistically (e.g., *Z*). The editors left a space for committed works, for modernist efforts, and for those mainstream films that could be read "symptomatically," as if they were "splitting under an internal tension" (see Jean-Luc Comolli and Paul Narboni, "Cinema/Ideology/Criticism," in Bill Nichols, ed., *Movies and Methods*, vol. 1 [Berkeley: University of California Press, 1976], p. 27). Another early theoretical effort, drawing upon current psychoanalytic ideas, was Jean-Pierre Baudry's 1970 essay "Ideological Effects of the Basic Cinematographic Apparatus." Baudry suggested that the very technology of film—camera shutter, screen, light beam—manifested a bourgeois worldview.

Feminists also posed theoretical questions about film's role in promoting patriarchal values. Journals like *Camera Obscura* and *frauen und film* took as part of their task the elaboration of a feminist film theory. The most influential essay in this direction was Laura Mulvey, "Visual Pleasure and Narrative Cinema" (1975), which generated a vast range of comment. By the end of the 1970s, not only had film study established itself as a discipline, but women's cinema found an audience among feminists.

These and other important essays can be found in Nichols, ed., *Movies and Methods,* vol. 1 (cited above) and vol. 2 (Berkeley: University of California Press, 1985); Philip Rosen, ed., *Narrative, Apparatus, Ideology: A Film Theory Reader* (New York: Columbia University Press, 1986); Constance Penley, ed., *Feminism and Film Theory* (London: Routledge, 1988); and Nick Browne, ed., *Cahiers du cinéma 1969–1972: The Politics of Representation* (Cambridge: Harvard University Press, 1990). Historical overviews can be found in introductions to the above volumes, as well as in Christine Gledhill, "Recent Developments in Feminist Film Theory," in Mary Ann Doane, Patricia Mellencamp, and Linda Williams, eds., *Re-Vision: Essays in Feminist Film Theory* (Frederick, MD: University Publications of America, 1984), pp. 18–48; and David Bordwell, *Making Meaning: Inference and Rhetoric in the Interpretation of Cinema* (Cambridge, MA: Harvard University Press, 1989), pp. 43–104.

- -

REFERENCES

1. See H. Stuart Hughes, *Sophisticated Rebels: The Political Culture of European Dissent, 1968–1987* (Cambridge, MA: Harvard University Press, 1988), pp. 3–14.
2. Quoted in Aruna Vasudev, *The New Indian Cinema* (Delhi: Macmillan, 1986), p. 29.
3. *Quotations from Chairman Mao Tse-Tung* (Peking: Foreign Languages Press, 1967), p. 82.
4. Quoted in Jean Franco, "South of Your Border," in Sohnya Sayres et al., eds., *The 60s without Apology* (Minneapolis: University of Minnesota Press, 1984), p. 324.
5. Manuel Puig, "Cinema and the Novel," in John King, ed., *On Modern Latin American Fiction* (New York: Noonday, 1987), p. 283. See also Puig's novel *Betrayed by Rita Hayworth*, trans. Suzanne Jill Levine (New York: Vintage, 1981).
6. Quoted in Julianne Burton, "Revolutionary Cuban Cinema, First Part: Introduction," *Jump Cut* 19 (1978). 18.
7. "Film Makers and the Popular Government: Political Manifesto," in Michael Chanan, ed., *Chilean Cinema* (London: British Film Institute, 1974), p. 84.
8. Quoted in Sylvie Pierre, *Glauber Rocha* (Paris: Cahiers du Cinéma, 1987), p. 180.
9. Jorge Sanjinés and the Ukamau Group, *Theory and Practice of a Cinema with the People,* trans. Richard Schaaf (Willimantic, CT: Curbstone, 1989), p. 43.
10. Quoted in Noureddine Ghali, "An Interview with Sembene Ousmane," in John D. H. Downing, ed., *Film and Politics in the Third World* (New York: Autonomedia, 1987), p. 46.

one of the most important American cinéma-vérité films, *Salesman* (1969), a dogged chronicle of an unsuccessful Bible salesman begging, cajoling, and bullying prospective customers. For Allan King's *A Married Couple* (Canada, 1969), the director and crew lived with a Toronto family and shot over seventy hours of film; observing a string of quarrels, the filmmakers documented the marriage's disintegration.

The most widespread use of Direct Cinema was in the emerging genre of *rockumentaries.* With the success of Don Pennebaker's Bob Dylan film *Don't Look Back* (1966) and *Monterey Pop* (1968), filmmakers realized that lightweight cameras and direct sound recording made it possible to shoot appealing films quickly and comparatively cheaply. *Woodstock* (1970) and *Let It Be* (1970) were records of single, memorable events, while other films were structured around tours. Both tendencies met in the most provocative instance of the genre, the Maysleses' *Gimme Shelter* (1970). The film intercuts a Rolling Stones tour with a single concert in which the camera records a Hell's Angel fatally stabbing a member of the audience. The whole action is framed by the Maysles brothers' reviewing of the footage at the editing machine while Mick Jagger looks on.

Mercilessly parodied in *This Is Spinal Tap* (1984), the rockumentary proved to be the most theatrically successful documentary genre. Aimed at young moviegoers, it offered performances and sound quality unavailable on broadcast television. By the time Jonathan Demme made *Stop Making Sense* (1984), the concert had become secondary to the filming; David Byrne storyboarded the Talking Heads' performance for the shooting. Finnish fiction filmmaker Aki Kaurismäki pushed the rockumentary to its absurdist limit, scheduling a real rock band, the Leningrad Cowboys ("the worst rock 'n' roll band in the world"), alongside the prestigious Soviet Red Army Ensemble in a concert filmed as *Total Balalaika Show* (1993).

The dominance of Direct Cinema techniques led filmmakers to extend and interrogate them. Norman Mailer's *Beyond the Law* (1968) and *Maidstone* (1970) were semi-improvised narratives in the tradition of John Cassavetes's *Shadows,* with Direct Cinema veteran Pennebaker supplying the cinematography. Some rockumentaries also included staged fictional scenes, as in *200 Motels* (1971), *Renaldo and Clara* (1977), and *Pink Floyd—The Wall* (1982).

Jim McBride's *David Holtzman's Diary* (1967) was more critical: by using Direct Cinema techniques to treat a fictional man's life, McBride suggests that they are purely conventional. Similarly, Shirley Clarke's *Por-*

24.1 Assailed by his friends for "acting," Jason breaks down (*Portrait of Jason*).

trait of Jason (1967) at first seems an instance of pure Direct Cinema. Clarke records long monologues of a black homosexual prostitute, and, in the manner of Jean Rouch, she hovers offscreen asking Jason increasingly probing questions. But Clarke also criticizes Direct Cinema's selectivity and invisible editing by keeping to a single camera position, using long takes, and acknowledging shot changes by letting the screen lose focus and fade to black. Thus *Portrait of Jason* resembles the work of Warhol: an exhibitionistic performer is berated by others (here, his friends offscreen) and collapses in psychic pain (**24.1**).

McBride and Clarke were exceptional in criticizing Direct Cinema, and standardized uses of the approach continued throughout the 1970s and 1980s. The technology and techniques proved well adapted to capturing the filmmaker's personal experiences. Kazuo Hara's *My Intimate Eros: Love Song 1974* (Japan, 1974) records the filmmaker's obsessive search for the woman who has left him. In *Best Boy* (1979), Ira Wohl traces how his cousin, a middle-aged man with a learning disability, leaves his family to enter a hospital. Michael Moore's ironic *Roger & Me* (1989) chronicles his attempts to confront the chairman of General Motors with the effects of Michigan plant closings.

Direct Cinema attracted other directors because of its ability to capture the immediate texture of social and political processes. The most famous filmmaker to exploit this capacity was Frederick Wiseman, whose Direct Cinema documentaries since the late 1960s essentially defined the pure form of the style (see box).

The observational tradition of Direct Cinema was sustained by France's Raymond Depardon. Beginning at

FREDERICK WISEMAN AND THE TRADITION OF DIRECT CINEMA

In the spring of 1966, a middle-aged lawyer produced and directed a film about conditions at a Massachusetts hospital for the mentally ill. He filmed everyday activities as well as a show put on by the patients. The result, titled *Titicut Follies* after the patients' name for their show, was released in 1967 and set off a storm of protest. Since that directorial debut, controversy has pursued Wiseman through over thirty feature-length documentary films. In the process, his work has become emblematic of Direct Cinema.

Whereas the Drew unit concentrated upon situations of high drama and the Rouch-Morin approach to cinéma vérité emphasized interpersonal relations (see Chapter 21), Wiseman pursued another path, focusing on the mundane affairs of social institutions. His titles are indicative: *Hospital* (1970), *Juvenile Court* (1972), *Welfare* (1975), *Sinai Field Mission* (1978), *Racetrack* (1985). *Law and Order* (1969) records police routine, while *The Store* (1983) moves behind the scenes of a Dallas department store.

Wiseman typically does not follow individuals facing a crisis or solving a problem. He assembles a film out of slices of day-to-day life in a business or government agency. Each sequence is usually a short encounter that plays out a struggle or expresses the participants' emotional state. Then Wiseman moves to another situation and other participants. He has called this a "mosaic" structure, the result of assembling tiny pieces into a picture of an institution. Using no narrator, Wiseman creates implications by making shrewd juxtapositions between sequences and by repeating motifs across the film (**24.2, 24.3**). The meaning, he insists, is in the whole.

His first films reflect a conception of institutions as machines for social control. He declared himself interested in "the relationship between ideology and practice and the way power is exercised and decisions rationalized."[1] Wiseman records the frustrations of ordinary people facing a bureaucracy, and he captures the insular complacency of those used to exercising power. In his most famous film, *High School* (1968), secondary education becomes a confrontation between bewildered students and oppressive or obtuse teachers: schooling as control and conformity.

In his later work, Wiseman claimed to take a more flexible and open-minded approach reminiscent of Richard Leacock's "uncontrolled cinema" (p. 483).

> You start off with a little bromide or stereotype about how prison guards are supposed to behave or what cops are really like. You find that they don't match up to that image, that they're a lot more complicated. And the point of each film is to make that discovery.[2]

This concern for complexity, plus decades of support from the Public Broadcasting System (PBS), led Wiseman to expand his mosaics to vast proportions, shown as miniseries. *Canal Zone* (1977) runs almost three hours, the pair *Deaf* and *Blind* (both 1988) total eight hours, and *Belfast, Maine* (1999), a portrait of a community, lasts about six hours. It is as if his search for comprehensiveness and nuance forced Wiseman to amass more and more evidence, searching for all sides of the story. In later decades, Wiseman expanded his subject matter beyond micropolitical struggles for survival, investigating instead artistic creation in *Ballet* (1995; on the New York City Ballet) and *La Comédie-Française* (1996). Despite Wiseman's increasing emphasis on television, his films are also shown in museums and in marathon retrospectives at film festivals.

24.2, 24.3 The controlling hand as a motif in *High School*.

(continued)

FREDERICK WISEMAN AND THE TRADITION OF DIRECT CINEMA, continued

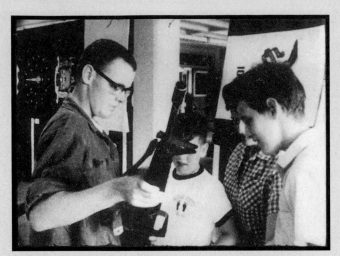

24.4 A trainee's family admires his rifle during a visit to boot camp (*Basic Training*, 1971). As in a fiction film, the participants seem oblivious to the presence of the filmmakers.

Wiseman carries on the Leacock tradition of fly-on-the-wall observation. The cameraman and the recordist (Wiseman) efface themselves (**24.4**). The filmmakers ask no questions and hope that the subjects never look into the lens. Wiseman creates classical continuity through eyeline matches, cutaways, and sound overlaps. We seem to be on the scene, invisible observers of social rituals of authority and humiliation. Yet Wiseman insisted that his documentaries were subjective creations, "reality fictions" expressing highly personal judgments. Many of his targets agreed.

Wiseman showed that the apparently neutral methods of Direct Cinema could create strong reactions through selection and emphasis. Yet some filmmakers believed that his films hid their "fictional" side. The films exemplified a transparency that documentarists would react against in the name of anti-illusionism and skepticism about the truth claims of Direct Cinema.

---

age eighteen as a photojournalist, he quickly combined still photography with filmmaking. His first feature, *Reporters* (1981), conveys the routines of press photographers like himself. Like Wiseman, Depardon explored social roles and institutions; his hand-held camera follows neighborhood policemen in *Faits divers* ("News Items," 1983) and studies psychiatric patients in *Urgences* ("Emergencies," 1987). Also like Wiseman, Depardon avoids talking heads and scene-setting montages, preferring to plunge the viewer directly into a situation. But Depardon occasionally includes his own voice-over commentary, and *Délits flagrants* ("Misdemeanors," 1994) experiments with more overt artifice: the camera is fixed to a tripod, framing police interrogations of suspects in dry profile compositions.

While Wiseman and Depardon adhered to the American tradition of Direct Cinema, effacing the presence of the filmmaker, other directors adopted the Rouch-Morin model of provocation (p. 487). *Field Diary* (1982), by the Israeli documentarist Amos Gitai, begins with a very long take as the filmmakers move through a town in the Gaza Strip and try to interview its Palestinian mayor. They continually confront Israeli soldiers, who cover the lens and demand identity papers from the sound recordist (**Color Plate 24.1**). Kazuo Hara's *The Emperor's Naked Army Marches On* (1987) follows a Japanese veteran who insists that the emperor take the blame

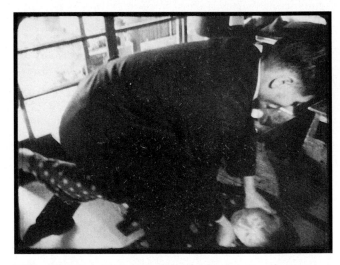

24.5 *The Emperor's Naked Army Marches On:* the vengeful veteran assaults another ex-soldier when he refuses to acknowledge his role in wartime atrocities.

for war crimes. Tracking down witnesses, the veteran invades their homes (**24.5**).

Claude Lanzmann's *Shoah* (1985), a nearly nine-hour study of the Nazis' extermination of the Polish Jews, recalls Alain Resnais's *Night and Fog* (p. 481) in studying bland contemporary landscapes that were the sites of unspeakable cruelty (**24.6**). Here, however, no stock footage takes us into the past; Lanzmann presents

24.6, *left*   The extermination camp at Belzic, seen today (*Shoah*).

24.7, *right*   Dr. Franz Grassler, former Nazi officer: "We at the Commission tried to maintain the ghetto for its labor force" (*Shoah*).

24.8   *Harlan County USA*: in a moment worthy of the Drew unit, the cameraman and sound recordist follow a sheriff reluctantly serving a warrant on a strikebreaker.

24.9   Archival footage used to create Soviet-style montage: a newsreel shot of soldiers moving in to break a strike in the 1930s . . .

24.10   . . . gives way to a shot of present-day police arriving to clear the roads, matched in frame position and direction of movement (*Harlan County USA*).

only what he called "traces of traces," interviews with witnesses, Jewish survivors, and former Nazis (**24.7**). In the provocateur tradition of Edgar Morin and Chris Marker, Lanzmann is present throughout, guiding, goading, and challenging his interviewees.

Veteran documentarist Don Pennebaker and his younger collaborator Chris Hegedus carried on the tradition of *Primary* (1960) by codirecting *The War Room* (1993); this vérité study of Bill Clinton's 1992 campaign headquarters "starred" spin doctors George Stephanopoulos and James Carville. In 1999, Canadian documentarist Peter Wintonick explored the importance and pervasive effect of this approach to documentary in his film *Cinéma Vérité: Defining the Movement*.

Synthesizing Documentary Techniques

Shoah, Wiseman's films, and most of the others mentioned above, are quite pure instances of Direct Cinema. Each is built principally out of the filmmaker-recordist's immediate confrontation with a concrete situation. Usually no narrator or nondiegetic music guides the audience's attention. The standard documentary format of the 1970s, however, was less stringent. It blended Direct Cinema interviews (often including an offscreen questioner), scenes shot on the fly (often without direct sound), and compilation footage, the whole glued together by commentary and music. Emile De Antonio's *In the Year of the Pig* (1969) pioneered this synthetic format, which dominated well into the 2000's.

A highly visible example is Barbara Kopple's *Harlan County USA* (1976). Chronicling a thirteen-month strike of Kentucky coal miners, much of the film is in the Direct Cinema vein. The camera crew records the strikers' changing tactics, with particular attention given to the wives who form a strong picket line and block the entry of scab workers. The film has as much drama as any crisis-structure film from the Drew unit—quarrels among the strikers, thugs firing at picketers, and a confrontation between the women and the strikebreakers (**24.8**).

Kopple frames the immediate drama, however, with background history concerning struggles in the mining industry. She draws upon archival footage and interviews with older citizens. And Kopple, a former member of Newsreel (p. 559), suggests broader points in the manner of De Antonio. There is no voice-over commentator, but superimposed titles supply basic information; regional folk music comments sympathetically on the action; and editing patterns make points in a manner that Leacock would find judgmental (**24.9**, **24.10**). The

24.11   Advertising imagery tapping pornographic appeals (*Not a Love Story*).

result has the immediacy of Direct Cinema but supplies historical context and leaves no doubt about the film-maker's sympathies.

The synthesis of Direct Cinema material, archival footage, titles, and music proved especially apt for examining controversial figures of the recent past, as in *Lenny Bruce without Tears* (1972), *The Times of Harvey Milk* (1984), *What Happened to Kerouac?* (1985), *Let's Get Lost* (1988, Bruce Weber), and similar portrait documentaries. Other filmmakers began to use the synthetic format to record lengthy processes. The makers of *So That You Can Live* (UK, 1981) revisited a Welsh family over five years, and the film chronicles not only the maturing of the family members but also the growing sensitivity of the filmmakers. Michael Apted's *28 Up* (UK, 1985) interviews people at ages 7, 14, 21, and 28. Over the years of its making, the filmmakers increasingly stress the ways in which social class shaped their subjects' lives.

The synthetic documentary format also dominated critical political cinema. By putting "talking heads" into context, filmmakers constructed oral histories of social movements in *Union Maids* (1976) and *With Babies and Banners* (1978). *The Wobblies* (1979) traces the history of a left-wing party, while *Before Stonewall* (1984) does the same for gay culture and activism in the United States. Other filmmakers used the synthetic format to report on contemporary political struggles: nuclear power accidents (*We Are the Guinea Pigs*, 1980), civil wars in Latin America (*When the Mountains Tremble*, 1983), and apartheid (*We Are the Elephant*, South Africa, 1987).

When mixing archival footage with interviews, film-makers oriented toward social criticism and change fol-lowed Newsreel and De Antonio in using individual testimony to challenge accepted positions or images. In *The Life and Times of Rosie the Riveter* (1980, Connie Field)—a study of women who worked in the defense industry during World War II—information films about plant safety are undercut by women's accounts of accidents on the job. *Common Threads: Stories from the Quilt* (1989, Robert Epstein and Jeffrey Friedman) juxtaposes media coverage of AIDS with the personal stories of five people afflicted with the disease. The interviews in Bonnie Sherr Klein's *Not a Love Story* (Canada, 1981), a study of pornography, move along a spectrum of opinions, ending with an attack upon erotic advertising (**24.11**). Mark Achbar and Peter Wintonick explored the controversial ideas of linguist and political commentator Noam Chomsky in *Manufacturing Consent: Noam Chomsky and the Media* (Canada, 1992) by combining their interviews with Chomsky with clips from his lectures and TV appearances.

The synthetic format proved central to the work of Marcel Ophüls (son of Max Ophüls). His four-and-a-half-hour film about the Nazi Occupation, *The Sorrow and the Pity* (Switzerland, 1970), identified him with the investigative political documentary. Ophüls brought to light a history that many French preferred to hide behind heroic Resistance legends. Newsreels and interviews portray citizens acquiescing comfortably to their German masters and turning a blind eye to the holocaust.

Either in its pure form or in the synthetic version, Direct Cinema, along with its goal of recording social and political processes "behind the scenes," sustained political filmmaking throughout the 1970s and 1980s. At the same time, however, another trend was gathering force, and this called into question the idea that cinema could directly record any reality.

The Questioning of Documentary Actuality

Political modernism, as practiced by Jean-Luc Godard, Nagisa Oshima, Jean-Marie Straub, Danièle Huillet, and others, set many documentary filmmakers to thinking about their work. Throughout film history, and particularly since the advent of Direct Cinema, documentarists claimed to offer immediate access to reality. If the Brechtians' critique of "transparent" and "illusionist" filmmaking (p. 562) was right, though, documentary could appear even more manipulative than the Hollywood fiction film. Perhaps documentary only *seemed* to capture reality.

The problem was not that of the filmmaker's bias. Many documentarists had acknowledged their own sub-

24.12   A cold war film uses animation to cure a pessimistic citizen of "nuclear blindness" (*The Atomic Cafe*).

24.13   In Ruiz's *Of Great Events and Ordinary People,* an unidentified looker reminds us of the convention of over-the-shoulder views.

24.14   Decentered framings and jerky editing accentuate the "invisible" conventions of the ethnographic film (*Reassemblage*).

jectivity, and directors like Georges Franju and Chris Marker had made it integral to their essayistic films (p. 481). What came to the fore now was the idea that perhaps the very forms and techniques of documentary were invisible conventions, no more inherently valid than the conventions of fictional narratives. Most documentaries presented themselves as descriptions or stories; yet these very forms carried a persuasive effect, asking the audience to accept a tacit social or political perspective. Most documentaries used voice-over commentary, but from whence came the voice's authority? Documentaries showed archival footage or on-the-spot interviews, but what gave these images any power to penetrate reality, to present not only facts but truths?

The Meta–Documentary   This line of thought was most explicitly posed by film theorists and critics (see "Notes and Queries" at the end of this chapter), but it was not merely academic. Documentaries became more reflexive, turning a critical eye on documentary tradition itself. A rudimentary instance is *The Atomic Cafe* (1982, Kevin Rafferty, Jayne Loader, and Pierce Rafferty). This compilation film reviews the history of the testing and deployment of nuclear weapons by the United States, from Hiroshima to the mid-1960s. In the De Antonio vein, commentary is reduced simply to subtitles identifying place, time, and occasionally sources of the footage. But much of the footage does not function as a transparent record of events. Since the shots come from educational and propaganda films, *Atomic Cafe* dwells on the ways in which these documentary genres spread oversimplified ideas of nuclear war (**24.12**). The film implies that the public's acceptance of cold war policies was strengthened by the conventions of popular media.

The reflexive film might go further and scrutinize its own use of documentary conventions. Raul Ruiz's

Of Great Events and Ordinary People (France, 1978) takes its title from John Grierson's remark: "We wait for the cinema to give us an event, a great event which can show us ordinary people." Yet, in this film, events and people are visible only through the distorting lenses of the media. "What I am calling the everyday," remarks Ruiz the narrator, "is a parody of TV documentary." Ruiz mocks news broadcasts, Marker's *Le Joli mai,* and the talking-heads convention. Titles announce what we will see, promising "stock footage" and "shots which block the view" (**24.13**). The film's ostensible subject—political attitudes in a Paris neighborhood before an election—is all but lost in tangents and rambling anecdotes. *Of Great Events and Ordinary People* delights in a digressive reflexivity that shows how much of reality the traditional documentary must ignore.

Chris Marker, an old hand at reflexivity and the essayistic form, contributed to the new *meta-documentary* with *Sans soleil* (aka *Soleil noir, Sun Less,* 1982), perhaps his most obscure and challenging film. A whimsical examination of the byways of Japanese city life is set against glimpses of other nations, while a woman's voice reads extracts from a man's letter about visiting a foreign country. In the vein of his *Letter from Siberia,* Marker's *Sans soleil* questions current documentary clichés ("global culture," "the rise of Asia") while also interrogating assumptions of ethnographic cinema.

This interrogation paralleled work by others. Trinh T. Minh-Ha's *Reassemblage* (1982) films village life in Senegal in ways that refuse to transmit standard forms of anthropological knowledge (**24.14**). Laleen Jayamanne's *Song of Ceylon* (1985) presents tableaux of western leisure activities and courting rituals, accompanied by an anthropological description of a Sri Lankan exorcism (**24.15**). Invoking Basil Wright's *Song of Ceylon* (1935), made for John Grierson's GPO Film Unit

The IMAX firm specialized in films with spectacular wildlife, scenery, and events, such as *Mountain Gorilla* (1991, Adrian Warren), *Fires of Kuwait* (1992, David Douglas), and *T-REX: Back to the Cretaceous* (1998, Brett Leonard). Although the films were costly to produce, their short length (usually around 40 minutes) permitted numerous showings per day; this and higher ticket prices meant a per-screen income much higher than in ordinary theaters. Despite the firm's emphasis on the educational value of its films, they were also sold as viscerally exciting adventures. It is no wonder that IMAX started a small side business of designing simulator rides, including the *Back to the Future* attraction at Universal Studios in Los Angeles and Orlando.

There was still a place for the feature documentary at film festivals and in art theaters in the United States, but such films tended to fall into a limited number of genres. Not surprisingly, documentaries involving sex or violence unacceptable for television airing often found an audience. Joe Berlinger and Bruce Sinofsky's *Paradise Lost: The Child Murders at Robin Hood Hills* (1996) investigates the trial of teenagers accused of brutally murdering three children; while not attempting to assess the boys' guilt, the film emphasizes the flimsiness of the evidence on which they were convicted. *Sick: The Life and Death of Bob Flanagan, Supermasochist* (1996, Kirby Dick) graphically depicts the self-mutilation of a performance artist during his act. *Sex: The Annabel Chong Story* (1999, Gough Lewis) reveals the self-destructive behavior of its sex-worker subject, and *American Pimp* (1999, Albert and Allen Hughes) interviews African American pimps and the prostitutes they manage.

Another genre of commercial nonfiction film that became more prominent in the 1990s was the *portrait documentary*. Such films usually went beyond the popular, straightforward *Biography* series on the Arts & Entertainment channel. Using a less stringent version of Direct Cinema, filmmakers could profile an eccentric individual whose activities provided the same sort of entertainment value as a fictional character. Terry Zwigoff blended interviews and candid footage in *Crumb* (1994), which deals with his friend, the underground comic artist Robert Crumb (**24.16**), as well as with his dysfunctional family. In Bennett Miller's *The Cruise* (1998), a tour-bus guide's patter reflects his idiosyncratic enthusiasm for New York City. For *American Movie* (1999), Chris Smith spent two years following the struggles of an obsessive Wisconsin filmmaker to produce a horror film on a microbudget. Films such as these often blend humor and pathos to create the sort of ambiguity of tone appreciated by art-house audiences.

24.16 *Crumb*: visiting a comics shop, the antisocial artist refuses to sign an autograph for a long-time fan.

24.17 *Hoop Dreams* creates drama not only from the two boys' aspirations but also from their families' emotions.

24.18 In *Frantz Fanon*, Fanon's sister-in-law dusts his portrait before recalling his life.

On a more serious note, films with such themes as the holocaust or African American Life have proven modest hits. One of the most acclaimed American documentaries of the decade, *Hoop Dreams* (1993, Peter Gilbert, Frederick Marx, and Steve James), follows the contrasting fortunes of two black Chicago teenagers dreaming of careers playing professional basketball (**24.17**). The portrait documentary could also be used to reveal the significance of overlooked historical personages. Isaac Julien's *Frantz Fanon: Black Skin, White Mask* (1995) mixes archival footage and reenactments to chronicle its subject's struggles against the Nazis and later against the French during the Algerian struggle for independence (**24.18**). Such films have a sense of dignity and importance that makes them the nonfiction equivalent of the event film in the world of Hollywood fiction.

FROM STRUCTURALISM TO PLURALISM IN AVANT-GARDE CINEMA

During the late 1960s and early 1970s, experimental filmmaking sustained its postwar renaissance. Established experimental genres and styles continued. Film portraits and diaries were still made—some, like Jonas Mekas's autobiographical series, of mammoth length. The cut-out animation of Larry Jordan recalled the Surrealist collages of Max Ernst (**Color Plate 24.3**), and the Belgian artist Marcel Broodthaers used Dadaist strategies to question the institution of the museum and art history (**24.19**).

Perhaps the most innovative surrealist work was done in Czechoslovakia by the animator Jan Švankmajer. Trained in the marionette section of the Academy of Fine Arts but influenced by Czech Surrealism of the 1930s, Švankmajer turned away from the mainstream animation developed by Jiří Trnka in the 1950s (p. 497). His first short film, *The Last Trick* (1964), combined puppets and frame-by-frame animation in a bizarre duel of two magicians trying to outdo each other.

In Švankmajer's films, images of fear, cruelty, and frustration exude black humor. Every object has a rich texture and tactile appeal, yet the events follow the illogic of dreams. Slabs of meat slither about; antique dolls are ground up and boiled into soup; faces in old prints stare enigmatically as enraged puppets smash each other with mallets. In Švankmajer's first feature, *Alice* (1988), loosely based on Lewis Carroll's *Alice in Wonderland*, the heroine dips her finger into a jar only to find marmalade laced with carpet tacks. *Dimensions of Dialogue* (1981) plays out a repulsive metaphor for communication: heads made of vegetables and tools devour each other and then vomit each other out (**Color Plate 24.4**).

The counterculture underground tendency also flourished after the late 1960s. Soon, however, the more commercially marketable elements of underground cinema obliterated its more experimental aspects. Andy Warhol lent his name as producer to self-consciously

24.19 Marcel Broodthaers interviews the replica of Jeremy Bentham in *Figures of Wax* (1974).

camp features directed by Paul Morrissey (e.g., *Trash*, 1970; *Andy Warhol's Frankenstein*, 1973). Amplifying the Kuchar brothers' parodies of Hollywood melodrama, John Waters produced *Pink Flamingos* (1972), *Female Trouble* (1974), and other low-budget films reveling in bad taste and shock effects. In a comparable vein were the early super-8mm films of the Spaniard Pedro Almodóvar and his first *aboveground* 16mm feature, *Pepi, Luci, Bom and Other Girls in the Neighborhood* (1980). By the mid-1970s, the underground film had become a marketable genre. It became the *midnight movie* or the cult film playing campus film societies, and it provided Morrissey, Waters, Almodóvar, and other directors an entry to commercial features.

Structural Film

As the underground film gained popularity in the late 1960s, a more intellectual approach to experimentation was taking shape. The American critic P. Adams Sitney called this tendency Structural Film. Although Sitney later regretted using this term, it gained wide currency in experimental circles around the world.

If underground filmmakers emphasized shocking subject matter, Structural filmmakers stressed challenging form. They concentrated the spectator's attention on a nonnarrative shape or system that organized the film. Usually this form unfolded gradually, engaging the spectator in a process of noticing fine detail and speculating on the film's overall pattern.

A prime instance is Hollis Frampton's *(nostalgia)* (1971). It consists of twelve shots; in each one, a photograph resting on a hot plate slowly burns to ashes

24.20   A photograph starts to burn on a heating coil in *(nostalgia)*.

24.21   Alternating shots of a corridor, taken with a zoom lens set at different focal lengths, create a rhythmic push-pull effect in *Serene Velocity*.

(24.20). The sound track also consists of twelve units, and, in each, the narrator discusses his memories of each photo. But each chunk of narration describes not the photo onscreen but the photo that is to come next. The spectator imagines what the next photo will look like, but she or he can never directly check the description with the picture. The idea of nostalgia—a longing for a past that cannot be recaptured—is manifested in the very structure of the film.

Frampton's film is also about the process by which images are born and die, and this reflexivity is characteristic of Structural cinema. A Structural film might be "about" camera movement or photographic texture or the illusion of motion. In *Serene Velocity* (1970), Ernie Gehr creates pulsating views down a corridor by alternating shots in which only the focal length of the lens changes (24.21). Structural films were often called anti-illusionist because they drew attention to the ways in which the medium transforms the object filmed. As in *(nostalgia)*, the viewer becomes sharply aware of the act of viewing.

Structural principles had been explored in earlier avant-garde works. *Eat* (1963) and other early Warhol films emphasized stasis and minimal change, while his use of entire camera rolls as the units of the film suggested a modular construction that was explored by Structural filmmakers. During the 1960s, Minimalist sculptors, painters, and composers also concentrated attention on bare-bones forms and slight changes in materials. Yvonne Rainer's dance piece "Trio A" (1966) focused attention on small movements and ordinary, worklike gestures.

Particularly important sources for Structural Film were experiments by the loose group of American painters, composers, and performance artists known as Fluxus. Influenced by Marcel Duchamp's Dada work (p. 177) and John Cage's theories of indeterminacy (p. 477), Fluxus artists sought to dissolve the bounds between art and life. They "framed" mundane events or actions—a dripping tap, a paintbox—as artworks. "Fluxfilms" pioneered the Structural approach, often by recording such banal activities as eating and walking. Mieko Shiomi's *Disappearing Music for Face* (1966) records a fading smile at 2,000 frames per second, creating onscreen movement so slow as to be imperceptible. Conceptual artist Yoko Ono made several Fluxfilms (24.22) and with her husband, John Lennon, continued on a minimalist line. Their forty-five minute *Fly* (1970) follows a fly crawling over a woman's body.

Structural films vary in their organizing principles. Some center completely on a single process of gradual change, inviting the spectator to notice minute differ-

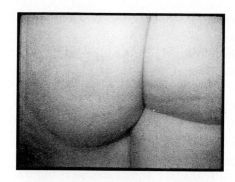

24.22, *left*   One of Yoko Ono's Fluxfilms consists exclusively of walking buttocks (*No. 4 [Bottoms]*, 1966).

24.23, *right*   *Film in Which There Appear Sprocket Holes, Edge Lettering, Dirt Particles, Etc.*: loops of a laboratory test in which the woman on the right blinks but the woman on the left does not.

24.24, *left*   Name the boat: one of the quiz shots in Robert Nelson's *Bleu Shut*.

24.25, *right*   The camera zooms in on a distant wall, oblivious to the dead man in the foreground (*Wavelength*).

ences from moment to moment. For example, Larry Gottheim's *Fog Line* (1970) shows, from a fixed long shot and over an interval of eleven minutes, a field with fences and cattle gradually becoming visible as a fog lifts. This gradual-change approach usually relies on the static camera setup, the long take, or some form of rephotography. In David Rimmer's *Surfacing on the Thames* (Canada, 1970), an optical printer reduces riverboats to slightly changing granular patches reminiscent of Impressionist painting (**Color Plate 24.5**).

Other Structural films complicate their form through repetition. George Landow's *Film in Which There Appear Sprocket Holes, Edge Lettering, Dirt Particles, Etc.* (1966) takes a strip of test footage featuring a woman's face, copies it so that four shots fill the frame, and then loops the result so that the strip accumulates scratches and dirt in successive printings (**24.23**). Paul Sharits's films alternate solid-colored frames and tableaux of aggressive actions. The result bombards the viewer with flickering colors and subliminal imagery (**Color Plate 24.6**). Ken Jacobs's *Tom, Tom the Piper's Son* (1969) employs rephotography to dissolve a 1905 American Mutoscope & Biograph film into frozen gestures and patches of light and dark.

Several Structural filmmakers organized their work around a rigorous, almost mathematical, set of rules. Kurt Kren's and Peter Kubelka's early 1960s work (p. 494) anticipated this tendency. In *Serene Velocity*, Gehr adjusted focal length according to a strict set of pro-

cedures, moving from the least distinct changes to the most radically noticeable ones. J. J. Murphy's *Print Generation* (1974) is guided by a similar plan. After reprinting casual footage until it became blobs and smears of light, Murphy arranged the shots into arithmetical patterns that develop from dimly visible imagery to recognizable figures and then back into abstraction. *Bleu Shut* (1970), a comic Structural film, contains an absurd system—a game in which contestants guess the names of boats—that is interrupted by looped imagery and concluded by people making grotesque faces at the camera (**24.24**).

The most famous Structural film, *Wavelength* (1967), by the Canadian Michael Snow, offers a rich mixture of techniques. It begins as a descriptive study of a single loft apartment, with the camera fixed at a distance from the windows. People enter and leave, and a death seems to occur, but the camera refuses to budge, preferring to register the slight changes in illumination in the apartment. At the same time, the film flaunts a technique: the zoom, which abruptly and spasmodically enlarges the frame at intervals, indifferent to the action in the room. Over the forty-five minutes of the film, as the lens enlarges the back wall (**24.25**), it reveals a photograph of waves on the ocean. (So the film traces a literal "wavelength.") In addition, bursts of color periodically wash out the shot, serving as reflexive reminders of the flatness of the cinematic image.

Several of Snow's films reflexively display the resources of the moving frame. *Wavelength* exhibits the

24.26   The camera's movement across the table pushes the food against the wall, creating a cubistic flattening (*Breakfast*).

perceptual effects of the zoom; ↔ (called *Back and Forth*, 1969) explores pan shots; *Breakfast* (1976) emphasizes how the tracking shot alters space (**24.26**). For the majestic *La Région centrale* (*Central Region*, 1971), Snow filmed a rocky wasteland with a multiple-jointed machine that executes pans, crane shots, and other movements (**24.27**).

In the United States, perhaps the most versatile exponent of Structural Film was Hollis Frampton. Trained in science and mathematics but steeped in the history of painting and literature, Frampton declared his opposition to the romantic sensuousness of his predecessors.

According to Frampton, to understand an artwork a viewer had to recover its "axiomatic substructure"[3]— a notion that made Stan Brakhage shudder.

Frampton's celebrated *Zorns Lemma* (1970) merges several strains within Structural cinema. The film's first section, over a blank screen, consists of a woman's voice reading an ABC rhyme taken from a colonial American primer. The second portion consists of one-second shots showing single words, usually found on signs (**24.28**), arranged in alphabetical order. Gradually, as Frampton runs through the alphabet again and again, every time using a different set of words, each letter's slot is filled by an image—fire, ocean waves, grinding hamburger. By the end of this section, the film has created a unique pictorial alphabet, each image correlated with one letter.

The film's final section consists of several long takes of a man, a woman, and a dog slowly crossing a snowy field as voices read a medieval text about light. While the middle section exemplifies the rigorously systematic side of Structural Film, the fixed camera and final long takes present a gradual change in the manner of Gottheim's *Fog Line* and other meditative works. The formal complexity of *Zorns Lemma* has invited a broad range of interpretations. Is it about the child's acquisition of language, the rivalry between sight and sound, or the superiority of nature and human relations to artificial systems like the alphabet?

Frampton's films, like other Structural works, often invite the spectator to watch himself or herself undergoing the very experience of the film. This "participatory"

24.27   Snow adjusts his filming machine in the Canadian landscape; during shooting, the camera's gyrations were operated by remote control (*Central Region*).

24.28 *Zorns Lemma*: an "A" word.

24.29 A 9.5mm home movie, with its central perforations, askew frame lines, and other Structural essentials, whizzes through the frame in Le Grice's *Little Dog for Roger*.

relation between the viewer and the film led Sitney to suggest that the Structural trend was fundamentally about human consciousness, the ways in which the mind builds patterns and draws conclusions on the basis of sensory information.

British filmmakers drawn to the Structural idea found this psychological approach disagreeable. At the London Co-op, "Structural/Materialist" filmmakers such as Peter Gidal and Malcolm Le Grice insisted that the most honest film was about only the medium itself. By drawing the spectator's attention to filmic qualities, the films produced knowledge about the "material" processes of cinema. Le Grice's *Little Dog for Roger* (1967), which subjects old home movies to a dizzying range of printing techniques (**24.29**), exemplifies this stance. Structural/Materialist ideas influenced many British filmmakers, including Chris Welsby (*Seven Days*, 1974) and John Smith (**24.30**), who turned landscapes into formal systems far stricter and more elaborate than those visible in *Fog Line* and *Central Region*.

Outside the English-speaking countries, the Structural impulse had a less cerebral tint. Many filmmakers applied Structural techniques to erotic material. In Paul de Nooiyer's *Transformation by Holding Time* (Netherlands, 1977), a man photographs a nude woman in Polaroid snapshots and then mounts each one on a grid close to us. The film's distinct shape is concluded when the photos fill the frame, reconstructing the woman's body from several vantage points. Other filmmakers used the static camera and rephotography of the Structural approach to evoke emotions recalling the film lyric. Through this hedonistic treatment of Structural premises, many avant-gardists kept the tendency alive through the 1980s.

Underground film reached a broad public through accessible humor and shock value, but most Structural films were aimed at a sophisticated audience interested in reflexivity and other rarefied aesthetic issues. The films' affinities with art-world movements carried them into museums and art galleries. Art schools and film de-

24.30 Editing turns goalposts into purely material configurations in John Smith's *Hackney Marshes —November 4th 1977* (1977).

partments also welcomed the intellectual rigor of Structural Film. As the discipline of film studies gained ground in the 1970s, Structural Film won academic support, and filmmakers moved into teaching positions.

24.31   Between 1970 and 1974, New York's Anthology Film Archives held screenings in the "Invisible Cinema," an auditorium designed to enhance each individual's absorption in the film experience. Here, Andy Warhol sits in one of the auditorium's partitioned and shielded seats.

Structural Film further benefited from an expansion of avant-garde institutions. In 1966, the Millennium Film Workshop of New York began as a production cooperative and screening venue. Jonas Mekas opened the Anthology Film Archives (**24.31**) in 1970 as a repository for a canon of masterpieces, including many from the postwar avant-garde. In response, the Collective for Living Cinema (founded in 1973) offered younger artists a venue. During the same period, filmmakers began to receive funding from the National Endowment for the Arts (established in 1965), state arts councils, and the Jerome Foundation (established by railroad heir and experimental filmmaker Jerome Hill).

Cooperatives and collectives grew stronger. In Britain, Cinema Action and The Other Cinema were formed to distribute experimental work. Bruce Elder in Canada, Peter Gidal in England, Birgit Hein in Germany, and other Structural filmmakers wrote essays that attracted public attention and helped fund work in this vein. The British Film Institute expanded its aid to experimental production, as did the Canadian Arts Council. The Goethe Institute of West Germany and the Alliance Française offered touring packages of experimental films. In all these countries, Structural Film played a central role in making experimental film culturally respectable.

Reactions and Alternatives to Structural Film

As institutional support expanded for the Structural project, North American filmmakers launched ambitious, even epic works. Michael Snow's *Rameau's Nephew by Diderot (Thanx to Dennis Young) by Wilma Schoen* (1974) runs four and a half hours. Its segments systematically explore paradoxes of language and sound effects in the cinema. Hollis Frampton conceived *Magellan,* a thirty-six-hour film to be shown in installments over 371 days. It remained unfinished at Frampton's death in 1984.

For many filmmakers, however, Structural Film was an overintellectual, apolitical dead end. Its acceptance as "high art" meant that the avant-garde had lost its critical edge. In addition, a younger generation who had not lived through the innovations of the 1960s had little sympathy with modernism, particularly in its purist guises. As a result, new experimental tendencies manifested themselves in the 1970s and 1980s. Some filmmakers revisited narrative. Others turned experimental techniques toward political criticism or theoretical debate. Still others embraced a harsh and passionate personal expression.

Structural Film, especially in North America, had been dominated by men, but the reactions to the Structural movement were led by women. This tendency paralleled the growth of feminist documentary and feature filmmaking during the 1970s. During the next decade, in the United States and Great Britain, minority women also played an increasing part in the changes in experimental cinema.

Deconstructive Film and the New Narrative   Perhaps the most direct development out of Structural Film was the "Deconstructive Film." The term (originally referring to a type of philosophical analysis) became applied to a certain kind of reflexive experimental work. Avant-garde films had for decades called attention to the cinema as a medium, from Vertov's *Man with a Movie Camera* (1928) through Conner's *A Movie* (1958) and the technique-centered Structural films. Deconstructive filmmakers went a step further. They targeted mainstream moviemaking, and they aimed to reveal its illusory artifice.

An early example is Hellmuth Costard's *Fussball wie noch nie* ("Football as Never Before," 1970). Here an entire soccer match is shown by concentrating on one player; we see the ball only when it comes near him. Inevitably, long stretches of empty time alternate with bursts of action. Costard's approach recalls that of Warhol and the gradual-process Structural film, but it

INDEPENDENT ANIMATION OF THE 1970s AND 1980s

With the decline of studio animation in the late 1960s, the cartoon became identified with children's entertainment, on television or in Disney's occasional theatrical features. But the sales of underground comics, the revival of interest in superheroes, the "graphic novels" produced in Europe and Japan, and the growing appetite for offbeat newspaper comics like Nicole Hollander's "Sylvia," Matt Groening's "Life in Hell," Lynda Barry's "Ernie Pook's Comeek," and Gary Larson's "The Far Side" showed that comic-strip art still attracted young adults and aging baby boomers. In this atmosphere, new film animators came to the fore.

Some had clearly European sources. *Heavy Metal* (Canada, 1981, Gerald Potterton) derived from a French magazine of sword-and-sorcery fantasy. The twin brothers Steve and Tim Quay, Americans working in Britain, modeled their puppet animation on Jan Švankmajer's surrealist fantasies. In the Quays' evocative *Street of Crocodiles* (1986), an emaciated figure explores a Victorian street whose buildings house decaying dolls, sawdust, writhing screws, and sinister machinery (**Color Plate 24.7**).

Other animators took their inspiration from the American tradition. Sally Cruikshank's cel-animation satires of American consumerism recall 1970s "headcomix" and *Yellow Submarine*, but the jazzy music and the incessantly pulsing backgrounds also evoke Fleischer's Betty Boop films (**Color Plate 24.8**). George Griffin's reflexive *Lineage* (1979) allows Mr. Blockhead to dial up any genre of animated film. Griffin's punning title refers not only to the history of the animated film but also to the "lines" with which he creates virtuosic parodies of early silent animation and the minimal abstract film (**Color Plate 24.9**).

More women began drawing comic strips in the 1970s, and more also took up animation. Often they expressed feminist concerns through evocative imagery or symbolic narratives. Susan Pitt's *Crocus* (1971) shows a couple's lovemaking interrupted by a baby's offscreen cries and by birds, a Christmas tree, and phallic objects floating above them (**24.32**). In Kathy Rose's *Pencil Booklings* (1978), the animator tries to discipline her errant characters (**24.33**) and then joins them in their fantasy world.

In the West, most independent animators came from art schools and funded their work through grants and tele-

24.32   A cucumber hovers over the couple in *Crocus*.

24.33   The realistically rotoscoped heroine confronts her cartoonish creation in *Pencil Booklings*.

vision commissions. The new animated shorts, no longer able to serve as theatrical fillers, were shown on alternative television and in film societies, museum programs, and touring programs such as the annual "Tournée" package of festival prizewinners.

primarily encourages the viewer to reflect upon the conventions of normal television coverage.

Deconstructive films often rework footage from an existing film, as does Ken Jacobs's *The Doctor's Dream* (1978), which reorders shots of a 1930s Hollywood fic-

tional short according to an arbitrary numerical principle. The filmmaker may also create new scenes that display conventions of orthodox style. In Manuel De Landa's *The Itch Scratch Itch Cycle* (1976), a couple's argument is refilmed and recut to survey shot/reverse-shot options.

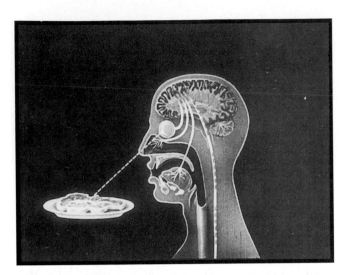

24.51 *Mongoloid:* Conner applies his associational compilation skills to a Devo tune.

films (particularly combat footage) and how-to documentaries (sports training, exercise tapes, language lessons). The cassette format encouraged schools, libraries, and businesses to acquire documentaries.

The rise of video had a more complex effect on the experimental cinema. Throughout the 1970s, fairly strict lines separated avant-garde film from video art, which was largely confined to performance pieces and gallery installations. In the early 1980s, George Kuchar and Punk filmmakers embraced video when portable video cameras using $\frac{1}{2}$-inch tape became available in Beta and VHS cassette formats. Some experimentalists clung to the vanishing super-8mm gauge, but, by the end of the decade, avant-garde film and video art had grown much closer together. Festivals exhibited the two side by side; cooperatives distributed works in both formats; artists moved between them; and some works, such as Thornton's *Peggy and Fred in Hell*, employed both. Moreover, video distributors made avant-garde classics available to the general public. Video fulfilled Brakhage's dream that average citizens could collect experimental films to watch at home.

At the level of form and style, the two media intertwined. Music videos borrowed from the avant-garde tradition, with many reworking conventions of the trance films. Some experimentalists' song-based films looked forward to the music-video format: Kenneth Anger's *Scorpio Rising* furnished an early model, while Bruce Conner's *Mongoloid* (1978; **24.51**) and Derek Jarman's *Broken English: Three Songs by Marianne Faithful* (1979) also pointed the way.

In the late 1980s, documentarists and avant-garde filmmakers freely incorporated television and video materials. Stylized reenactments in *The Thin Blue Line* refer as much to "true-crime" reportage as to Flaherty's restagings; Todd Haynes's *Poison* (1991) cites not only Anger's *Fireworks*, Genet's *Chant d'amour,* and film noir but also soap operas and "unsolved-mysteries" programs.

Structural Film continued the tradition of *cinéma pur* launched by Henri Chomette and Germaine Dulac in the 1920s (p. 180). It aimed to expose "film as film"—its ultimate materials, its essential procedures. Yet Michael Snow remarked in 1989, "'Film as film' is reaching its end. . . . Film will continue as a video representation/reproduction."[4] This prophecy is probably too absolute, but certainly experimental filmmakers, faced with the discontinuation of super 8mm and the great expense of 16mm, turned increasingly to the video format. By the end of the 1980s, Japan's New Cinema and the USSR's necro-realism had become largely video movements. Film-based works also found ways to cross over. *Tribulation 99* attracted "psychotronic" video fans, and Erica Beckman incorporated video games into *Cinderella* (1986; **Color Plate 24.14**). In various ways, avant-garde filmmakers were appropriating the electronic media in order to expand their audience.

REFERENCES

Notes and Queries

RETHINKING DOCUMENTARY

Direct Cinema, the documentaries of the 1960s and 1970s, and the more reflexive works of those and later years triggered a burst of interest in the history and practice of documentary cinema. Wiseman generated an enormous amount of attention, while certain films— *Salesman, A Married Couple, Gimme Shelter, Hearts and Minds* (1974)—became focal points of controversy. Alan Rosenthal's *The New Documentary in Action* (Berkeley: University of California Press, 1971) and *The Documentary Conscience* (Berkeley: University of California Press, 1980) present interviews with influential practitioners. His anthology, *New Challenges for Documentary* (Berkeley: University of California Press, 1988), gathers useful essays.

As documentary practice was changing from pure Direct Cinema to a more synthetic form derived from the work of De Antonio and others, film academics turned their attention to matters of style and structure. Scholars built taxonomies, distinguished trends, noted rejections of tradition, and explored questions of practice (reenactment, continuity editing) and ethics (the exploitative dimensions of Direct Cinema). For examples, see Bill Nichols, *Ideology and the Image* (Bloomington: Indiana University Press, 1981), and *Representing Reality: Issues and Concepts in Documentary* (Bloomington: Indiana University Press, 1992); Thomas Waugh, ed., *"Show Us Life": Toward a History and Aesthetics of the Committed Documentary* (Metuchen, NJ: Scarecrow Press, 1984); Noël Carroll, *Theorizing the Moving Image* (Cambridge: Cambridge University Press, 1996), pp. 224–252; and Willem De Greef and Willem Hesling, eds., *Image Reality Spectator: Essays on Documentary Film and Television* (Leuven: Acco, 1989).

THE IDEA OF STRUCTURE

Structural Film was one manifestation of a growing interest in film form during the 1960s and 1970s. But the label *Structural* has diverse sources in the social sciences and the fine arts.

The wide-ranging intellectual movement known as Structuralism originated in France in the 1950s. Its proponents, such as the anthropologist Claude Lévi-Strauss and the linguist Émile Benveniste, argued that human thought was patterned somewhat as languages are. Consciousness and all its products—myth, ritual, and social institutions—were traceable not to individual minds but to collective "structures" manifested in language or other cultural systems. Although as a philosophical position Structuralism had largely collapsed by the late 1960s, its influence in the arts grew. Structuralist studies led film theorists to examine mythical patterns in Westerns and other genres. Examples of this approach are Jim Kitses, *Horizons West: Studies of Authorship within the Western* (Bloomington: Indiana University Press, 1970), and Rick Altman, *The American Film Musical* (Bloomington: Indiana University Press, 1987).

At about the same time, the issue of structure was broached by a competing tradition stemming from experimental music. Serial composition, as initiated by Arnold Schoenberg and Anton von Webern, posited that the artist could control all "parameters"—melody, harmony, rhythm, and so on—by devising a single generative system. This serial conception of structure was elaborated more generally in Umberto Eco's *La Struttura assente* (1968) and was applied to film in Noël Burch's *Theory of Film Practice*, translated by Helen R. Lane (Princeton, NJ: Princeton University Press, 1973; originally published 1969). Whereas the mythic approach emphasizes the organization of social meanings, the serial approach stresses the "purer" process of sheer pattern making.

Thus by 1969, when Sitney dubbed certain American films "Structural," the term had already taken on several meanings. He added yet another. In the Structural film, "the *shape* of the whole film is predetermined and simplified,

and it is that shape that is the primal impression of the film" (P. Adams Sitney, "Structural Film," in Sitney, ed., *The Film Culture Reader* [New York: Praeger, 1970], p. 327). Here "structure" means neither deep organization of meaning (the French Structuralist concept) nor serialist control of part-whole relations. Other critics found other terms (*minimalist film, literal cinema*) more apt, but Sitney's formulation crystallized the movement in the minds of viewers and filmmakers. Many subsequent films owe as much to his definition as to any films in the movement.

Important recastings of the idea of Structural Film can be found in a 1972 essay by Paul Sharits, "Words Per Page," in Richard Kostelanetz, ed., *Esthetics Contemporary* (Buffalo: Prometheus, 1978), pp. 320–32, and in two anthologies: Annette Michelson, ed., *New Forms in Film* (Montreux: 1974), and Peter Gidal, ed., *Structural Film Anthology* (London: British Film Institute, 1976). Malcolm Le Grice's *Abstract Film and Beyond* (Cambridge, MA: MIT Press, 1977) tells the history of experimental film from the standpoint of British Structural aspirations.

THE AVANT-GARDE AND POSTMODERNISM

Postwar experimental cinema, like the international art cinema, operated under the auspices of modernism in the arts (pp. 357–359). Frampton, for example, often invoked James Joyce's *Ulysses* as a model for his *Magellan* project. But the rise of Pop Art led many art historians toward a new tolerance of mass culture and a rejection of the grand ambitions of "high modernism." Artists in all media began to draw upon popular culture, to emphasize fragmentation, to acknowledge the power of the art market in the creation of trends, and to regard all styles of the past as equally available for parody and pastiche. These were some of the traits identified as postmodernism. The term itself, initially applied to a new style of architecture, spread quickly to the other arts and even became a name for the postwar era of "finance capitalism."

Russell Ferguson et al., eds., *Discourses: Conversations in Postmodern Art and Culture* (New York: New Museum of Contemporary Art, 1990) includes interviews with many filmmakers, some of whom work under the postmodern label. Noël Carroll argues that postmodernism in film is better understood as "post-Structural Film." (See "Film in the Age of Postmodernism" in *Interpreting the Moving Image* (Cambridge: Cambridge University Press, 1988), pp. 300–332. For other views, see *Millennium Film Journal* 16–18 (fall/winter 1986/1987) and J. Hoberman, *Vulgar Modernism: Writing on Movies and Other Media* (Philadelphia: Temple University Press, 1991). The literature on postmodernism is voluminous, but one of the most accessible accounts is Robert Hughes, *The Shock of the New* (New York: Knopf, 1981), pp. 324–409. See also Margot Lovejoy, *Postmodern Currents: Art and Artists in the Age of Electronic Media* (Upper Saddle River, NJ: Prentice-Hall, 1992). An important statement is Frederic Jameson's *Postmodernism; or, the Cultural Logic of Late Capitalism* (Durham, NC: Duke University Press, 1991).

TELEVISION AND AARDMAN ANIMATION

Aardman Animations, based in Bristol, England, began in 1972 as a small firm making commissioned shorts for television. Its founders, Peter Lord and David Sproxton, concentrated on Plasticine ("clay") animation. Their first successful series was "The Amazing Adventures of Morph" (1981–1983), twenty-six five-minute shorts made for *Lip Sync,* a BBC program for the deaf. Sound became a more central component of two subsequent series for Channel 4, *Conversation Pieces* (1981–1983) and *Lip Sync* (1989). For these, brief interviews with ordinary people were recorded, and then stories were written and animated to fit them.

The breakthrough year was 1989. Aardman made the classic music video for Peter Gabriel's *Sledgehammer*. One contributing animator was Nick Park, who had been working part-time for Aardman while attending the National Film and Television School. He also directed a *Lip Sync* short called *Creature Comforts*, a parody of talking-heads documentaries that interviewed zoo animals about their living conditions. After seven years of work, Park finished his college project, *A Grand Day Out*, the first of a series of wildly popular shorts starring eccentric inventor Wallace and his put-upon dog Gromit.

In the mid-1980s, the firm branched into television advertising, including a series of spots for Heat Electric featuring animals from *Creature Comforts*. These were so popular that they were released on video. Park won Academy Awards for his next two Wallace and Gromit films, *The Wrong Trousers* (1993), a film-noir parody starring a villainous penguin, and *A Close Shave* (1995), in which Gromit saves a herd of sheep. Although the series was commissioned by the BBC (which broadcast it repeatedly to record viewership), the films had theatrical release as well.

Aardman produced many other animated shorts, including Peter Lord's *Wat's Pig* (1996) and Peter Peake's send-up of sickly sweet children's programs, *Pib and Pog* (1994). Feature-length collections of Aardman films circulated theatrically throughout Europe.

Aardman's first feature, *Chicken Run* (2000), moved the company out of television commission and into studio filmmaking when the young DreamWorks company signed Lord and Park to a five-picture contract. Although the age of computer animation had begun (see Chapter 27), the Aardman team stuck to Plasticine and created elaborate scenes parodying prisoner-of-war movies (**Color Plate 25.1**). Despite some doubts about whether British clay animation could succeed with a broad public, *Chicken Run* was one of the top twenty grossing films in the United States that year.

---

successes as *The Draughtsman's Contract* (1982) and *My Beautiful Laundrette* (1985; **25.1**). Eventually British television's early support of Aardman Animations would yield global hits (see box).

In France, Canal Plus, a cable company like the U.S. Home Box Office, transmitted hundreds of feature films, but unlike its U.S. counterparts, it was required by law to invest in production. In 1987, Canal Plus was the major funding source for French filmmaking; by 2001 it had helped finance over 700 films around the world.

Throughout Europe, the burden of film finance shifted from individual investors and national governments to media conglomerates, private investment groups, and banking concerns. Canal Plus, Berlusconi of Italy, Prisa of Spain, Britain's Thorn-EMI (which had absorbed the Rank theater chain), PolyGram of the Netherlands, and Bertelsmann of West Germany began backing films made outside their own countries. Crédit Lyonnais, an international bank, became a principal source of loans to European and American companies during the 1980s.

25.1 Stephen Frear's *My Beautiful Laundrette* was originally intended as a television film, but its depiction of racism, homosexuality, and class struggle led to a successful release in theaters. Here the young Pakistani and white lovers confront a hostile gang.

The Return of Film Europe   New forms of international funding also became available under the auspices of the European Community. In 1987, with its twelve member nations looking toward European integration at the end of the century, the EC founded MEDIA, a program to do velop the continent's audiovisual industries. MEDIA funded EC production projects through loans and created the European Film Distribution Office, which offered financial incentives for national distributors to handle imported films. Another EC commission, Eurimages, offered an avance sur recettes for coproductions. Four years after its founding in 1988, Eurimages had backed *Cyrano de Bergerac* (1990), *Prospero's Books* (1991), *Europa* (1991), and over a hundred other films.

Since the 1950s, coproductions and internationally financed projects had been accused of being bland "Eurofilms," lacking any distinctive national qualities. This was, in the cinematic domain, the equivalent of many Europeans' worries that a Single Europe would iron out differences between cultures. Doubts about Eurofilms intensified as international investment and television participation expanded. The big international film, following the tradition of the Sam Spiegel–David Lean epics of the 1950s and 1960s, was epitomized in Bertolucci's *The Last Emperor* (1987), but diversified financing was necessary for less grandiose projects as well. Companies in London, St. Petersburg, Rome, Paris, and Amsterdam cofinanced Sally Potter's *Orlando* (1992). Bille August's *Best Intentions* (1992) was wryly described as a Swedish-Danish-Norwegian-Icelandic-Finnish-British-German-French-Italian film.

Now even a first film was likely to be an international product. Jaco Van Dormaël's *Toto le héros* ("Toto the Hero," 1991) was funded by the Belgian government's avance sur recettes, as well as by Germany's ZDF, French public television, Belgian public television, and Canal Plus. *Toto* also benefited from MEDIA, Eurimages, and the EC's European Script Fund. Van Dormaël spent three years conferring about where the film should be shot and what language should be used. After winning a major prize at Cannes, the film attracted audiences in Europe, Japan, and even the United States. Some observers criticized it as "Europudding" or called it *Toto l'Euro*, but others saw it as an emblem of how a small first feature could find an audience through the concerted effort of pan-European government agencies and private venture capital.

"Unless all European producers work together," prophesied one producer, "we will soon have zero percent of the market."[1] In the heyday of the Eurofilm, however, distinctive national film movements were unlikely to emerge, and some observers believed that their time had passed.

During the 1920s, producers had laid the groundwork for a Film Europe market that could compete with the United States (p. 617). In the late 1980s, something

25.2 The protagonist of *Croupier* focuses unemotionally on his job until being drawn in to a heist scheme.

like that began to emerge out of the cooperation of national governments, television companies, investment concerns, and EC agencies. In tempo with these developments were the creation of the European Film Academy, which gave annual achievement awards modeled on the American Oscars, and the establishment of Lumière, a Lisbon-based agency coordinating the activity of European archives.

Despite these initiatives, European production remained far from healthy. Only 5 percent of films recouped their investments in theatrical runs; 80 percent of them were never screened outside their country of origin. Even bright signs, such as a slight upsurge in attendance or the popularity of multiplex theaters, helped American films more than the local product.

The Art Cinema Revived: Toward Accessibility

In a climate presenting few opportunities for magnificent success, European popular genres maintained their stability. International audiences were drawn to Italian comedies, from Franco Brusatti's *Bread and Chocolate* (1973) to Maurizio Nichetti's *Icicle Thief* (1990) and Roberto Begnini's *Life Is Beautiful* (1997). French sex comedies (e.g., *Cousin Cousine*, 1975) and British eccentric humor (e.g., the Monty Python films) also kept their place in both domestic and foreign markets. French and British crime films often evoked the shadowy traditions of Poetic Realism and film noir, as in *Mona Lisa* (1986, Neil Jordan; **Color Plate 25.2**), *Lock, Stock and Two Smoking Barrels* (1998, Guy Ritchie), *Croupier* (1999, Mike Hodges; **25.2**), and *Sexy Beast* (2001, Jonathan Glazer).

At the other extreme, experimental political modernism did not entirely vanish. Alexander Kluge, after his more straightforward narrative *Strongman Ferdinand*

25.3, *left*   In Kluge's *Female Patriot* (1979), a persistent researcher, sickle in hand, exhumes the German past.

25.4, *right*   Characteristically static framings and a range of performance styles in Straub and Huillet's *Class Relations* (1983).

(West Germany, 1975), returned to fragmented historical allegories that inquired into the continuing effects of Nazism and the war (**25.3**). Jean-Marie Straub and Danièle Huillet continued to make both static, text-centered films (*Fortini/Cani*, 1976; *Too Early, Too Late*, 1981) and narratively oriented literary adaptations (**25.4**). The Chilean exile Raul Ruiz created labyrinthine modernist puzzles. *La Vocation suspendu* ("The Suspended Vocation," 1977) purports to present two unfinished films, one intercut with the other, about intrigues within a religious order. *Memory of Appearances: Life Is a Dream* (1987) drops a political agent into a dictatorship where police interrogate suspects behind the screen of a movie theater (**25.5**).

Of all directors in the tradition of political modernism, the one who gained the most stature during the 1980s was the Greek Theo Angelopoulos. He replaced Michelangelo Antonioni and Miklós Jancsó as the major representative of the long-take approach to film style. His distant camera emphasizes characters moving through landscapes, delineating the force of location on action or contrasting a milieu with the event (as when a lengthy, extreme long shot intensifies the shocking rape of the adolescent girl in *Landscape in the Mist*, 1988; **Color Plate 25.3**). Still prepared to play time-shifting games with history and memory, Angelopoulos represented a monumental version of the postwar modernist tradition.

But even Angelopoulos moved toward personal, psychologically driven tales. His frescoes of Greek history such as *Traveling Players* (1975; p. 567) gave way to more intimate dramas. *Voyage to Cythera* (1984) shows an elderly communist exile returned to Greece. Angelopoulos also took up the problems of European migration and the dissolution of national borders. In *Landscape in the Mist,* children leave home in search of the father they believe to be in Germany, while *The Suspended Step of the Stork* (1991) centers on a famous novelist who abandons middle-class comforts for the precarious life of a refugee.

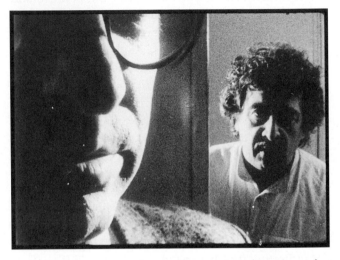

25.5   Ruiz accentuates the cryptic narrative of *Memory of Appearances: Life Is a Dream* with colossal wide-angle shots.

Charming Rebels and a New Tradition of Quality   The decline of attendance and export markets, the conservatism of investors, and competition from Hollywood drove producers and directors toward a more accessible, less challenging and disruptive cinema than had been seen during the era of political modernism. Social commentary and formal experiment could be presented ingratiatingly in comedies. In Italy, for instance, Ettore Scola's *We All Loved Each Other So Much* (1974) established him as an astringent commentator on the political disillusionments of postwar Italian history. With that film, *A Special Day* (1977), and *Le Bal* ("The Ball," 1983), he won international success. Each project wittily merges art-cinema modernism with accessible comedy. *Le Bal* is set entirely in a French dance hall at different eras, and the whole film is played without dialogue. Scola's close-ups heighten the caricatural performances, and he cleverly manipulates color design, as when the Popular Front sequence drains all color from the shot save that of the Communist flag (**Color Plate 25.4**).

Another Italian talent, Nanni Moretti, began his career with anarchic, pseudo-underground comedies (*Ecce*

Bombo, 1978) before developing his distinctive brand of bemused, wistful humor speaking for a generation disenchanted by the failure of left-wing ideals. Moretti typically plays a slightly neurotic hero encountering the frustrations of modern life. In *Palombella Rossa* (1989), a young Communist-party official suffers amnesia and must relearn correct doctrine; his naive questions satirize a spectrum of political opinions. To add to the humor, most of the film is set in a swimming pool during a game of water polo. In the poignant *Caro Diario* (*Dear Diary,* 1993), Moretti shares his pleasure in riding his Vespa through Rome and his fear in discovering that he has a mysterious disease (**25.6**). *Aprile* ("April," 1998) celebrates the birth of his child as he is planning a new movie. Moretti surprised many by making a straight drama, *The Son's Room* (2001). Like many filmmakers who started in the 1970s, Moretti turns from large-scale politics to the intimacy of friendship and family devotion.

A similar move to the mainstream was seen in the career of Pedro Almodóvar, who shifted from gay underground films to more mainstream productions that fused melodrama, camp, and sex comedy. In Almodóvar's world, nuns become heroin addicts (*Sisters of Night,* aka *Dark Habits,* 1983), a downtrodden wife slays her husband with a hambone (*What Have I Done to Deserve This?,* 1984), a newscaster confesses to murder on television (*High Heels,* 1991), a woman is attracted to a man because he slays bulls (*Matador,* 1986), and another falls for a man who has abducted her (*¡Atame!,* aka *Tie Me Up! Tie Me Down!,* 1989). As in some Mexican works of Luis Buñuel, scandalous situations and imagery are handled with a casual, ingratiating lightness (**25.7**). Almodóvar also parodies ordinary movies, often through a film within a film.

Almodóvar achieved international notoriety with the sex farce *Women on the Verge of a Nervous Breakdown* (1988), but his later films turn toward straight drama and melodrama. Like Fassbinder, Almodóvar admired Douglas Sirk, and he began to mount convoluted plots of erotic rivalries and pathetic twists of fate. *The Flower of My Secret* (1995) centers on an intellectual woman who secretly writes trashy romances. *All About My Mother* (1999) builds an unlikely family out of a single mother, a pregnant nun, a transvestite prostitute, and an HIV-infected baby. Like Douglas Sirk and Rainer Werner Fassbinder, Almodóvar delighted in treating flamboyant plots with bold color design (**Color Plate 25.5**).

During the same period, Finland's Aki Kaurismaki won worldwide notice with the Wendersian *Ariel* (1989) and the Bressonian *Match Factory Girl* (1989). His cruel, deadpan mockery, born partly of a passion for hard-rock

25.6 Poking fun at his own health problems, Moretti shows himself checked by two physicians in *Caro Diario.*

25.7 *Women on the Verge of a Nervous Breakdown:* comedy on the edge of hysteria.

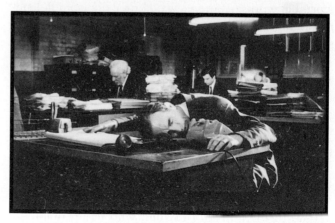

25.8 No one in the office notices the death of a drab London bureaucrat in Kaurismaki's *I Hired a Contract Killer.*

music, is most unadulterated in *Leningrad Cowboys Go America* (1989), while it is tempered with ironic sentiment in *I Hired a Contract Killer* (1990) and *Vie de bohème* ("Bohemian Life," 1991). Kaurismaki's celebration of bizarre, marginal characters, his wide-ranging film references, and his satire of middle-class values (**25.8**) made him a cult director across 1990s Europe.

Many European directors returned to the comfortable mode of prestige pictures, literary adaptations, and the milder modernism forged in the 1950s and 1960s. French critics pointed out that literary values and elegant style seemed to be creating a new "tradition of quality" (p. 375). The success of Bertrand Blier as a novelist led him to adapt his own work in *Les Valseuses* ("The Waltzers," 1974). His *Get Out Your Handkerchiefs* (1978) earned an Academy Award, while *Too Beautiful for You* (1989) won prizes both at home and abroad. Similarly, the critic-turned-director Bernard Tavernier evoked the golden years of the postwar French cinema by hiring Jean Aurenche (p. 376) as scenarist and by making such films as *Un Dimanche à la campagne* (*Sunday in the Country*, 1984) in homage to Jean Renoir. *Tous les matins du monde* (*All the Mornings of the World*, 1991), by Alain Corneau, portrayed seventeenth-century court life while presenting exquisite baroque music. Olivier Assayas, former editor of *Cahiers du cinéma* and son of a prestigious screenwriter, revamped romantic realism in films like *Fin août, début septembre* ("End of August, Beginning of September," 1999). Even Raul Ruiz abandoned bizarre experimentation for a handsomely mounted costume picture, *Les Temps retrouvé* (*The Past Recaptured*, 1999).

The Pan-European Film   Established directors participated in the new Eurofilm by creating distinguished, exportable works. Andrezej Wajda, in exile from Poland, made films in France (*Danton*, 1982) and West Germany (*A Love in Germany*, 1983). Ermanno Olmi's *Tree of the Wooden Clogs* (Italy, 1978) marked a return to neorealism, re-creating the life of nineteenth-century peasants in their original dialect but also giving them the dimension of legend. Carlos Saura's prodigious output drew on Spanish culture: *Blood Wedding* (1981), *Carmen* (1983), and *El Amor brujo* ("Love, the Magician," 1986) employed indigenous dance, while *El Dorado* (1988), a lavish coproduction with Italy, presented Spanish colonialism as a brutal political game.

Vittorio and Paolo Taviani, who had promoted a humanistic, populist political cinema during the 1960s and early 1970s, became acclaimed directors with the success of *Padre padrone* (1977). They sealed their reputation with a mythic recasting of the Neorealist tradition, *Notte di San Lorenzo* (*Night of the Shooting Stars*, 1982; **Color Plate 25.6**), and a luxuriant adaptation of Luigi Pirandello stories, *Kaos* (1984). *Good Morning Babylon* (1987) returns in both theme and structure to the romantic simplicity of the American silent cinema. The Tavianis, along with many others, forged an international tradition of quality for the 1970s and 1980s.

That the new international cinema could also present political critique was demonstrated when, in the 1970s, with New German Cinema gaining respect around the world, Rainer Werner Fassbinder came onto the international stage with a series of big-budget films featuring renowned stars. When *The Marriage of Maria Braun* (1978) proved an international success, Fassbinder moved quickly to large-scale coproductions such as *Lili Marlene* (1980), *Lola* (1981), and *Querelle* (1982). These late films all employ the resources of color, costume, soft focus, and spectacle to stylize the characters' worlds: unrealistic strips of pink light falling across a face (*Lola*) or a tangerine glow emanating from a wharf (*Querelle*). Extreme close-ups of historically exact details interrupt the action of *Maria Braun* (**25.9**). Yet Fassbinder did not wholly abandon his experimental impulses. Unlike Straub and Huillet, he preferred postdubbing, which allowed him to make his sound tracks no less baroque than the settings. *In a Year of 13 Moons* (1978) and *The Third Generation* (1979) overlay radio broadcasts, television commentary, and conversations to create dense acoustic ambiences.

Fassbinder sought to remind viewers that their country retained close ties to its Nazi past. His late films presented an epic history of Germany, from the 1920s (*Bolweiser* and *Despair*, both 1977) through the Fascist era (*Lili Marlene*) to the rise of postwar Germany (*Maria Braun*; *Veronika Voss*, 1981; *Lola*). He was also concerned with contemporary history, as in his controversial treatment of homosexual relations in *Fox and His Friends* (1974), his critique of leftists in *Mother Kusters' Journey to Happiness* (1975), and his mockery of chic terrorism in *The Third Generation*. By contrast, Maria Braun, "the Mata Hari of the Economic Miracle," survives by coolly separating her devotion to her husband from her shrewd manipulation of others. Fassbinder's last films continued, in muted form, the vein of melodrama plus social critique he had explored earlier.

Socially Critical Naturalism   As directors retreated from the radical extremes of politically critical modernism, several sought to reveal social conflicts in a more realistic way. In Great Britain, Ken Loach used nonprofessional actors, shooting in a quasi-documentary style on location in the industrial north for *Kes* (1969). The film depicts a working-class boy who is miserable in school and whose only interest in life is his ill-fated fascination with training a falcon (**25.10**). In the early 1970s, the British Film Institute Production Board, which had been formed in 1966 and had concentrated on independent shorts, began funding features as well. One of the first was an autobiographical trilogy by Bill Douglas: *My*

25.9, *left* A pack of cigarettes evokes the privations of postwar Germany in *The Marriage of Maria Braun*.

25.10, *right* The hero of *Kes* shows a flicker of interest in school: asked to tell about his pet falcon, he writes falconry terms on the board.

25.11, *left* *My Childhood* explores the small events of youth as the hero's brother rushes to stand exultantly in the smoke above a passing train.

25.12, *right* Jean-Pierre Léaud (Antoine Doinel of *The 400 Blows*) as the shifty and selfish protagonist of Eustache's *The Mother and the Whore*.

25.13, *left* *À nos amours:* Sandrine Bonnaire as the middle-class teenager avid for excitement.

25.14, *right* Provincial realism: in Lille, romantic rivalry and financial stresses shatter a friendship in *The Dream Life of Angels*.

Childhood (1972), *My Ain Folk* (1974), and *My Way Home* (1977). In an elliptical, unsentimental fashion, these trace a boy's loveless life in a northern industrial town (**25.11**).

The British Film Institute (BFI) also funded the first film of theater director Mike Leigh, *Bleak Moments* (1971), a story of a female office worker living with her mentally handicapped sister. Its conversation mixed sad, amusing, and quiet incidents in a manner that was to become typical of Leigh's work. His subsequent dialogue-based depictions of working-class life, produced by the BBC and later Channel 4, balance humor and pathos in depicting social problems, as in *Life Is Sweet* (1991). *Naked* (1993) takes a much bleaker look at poverty in modern Britain through the eyes of an intelligent but violent and disillusioned man. In 2000, Leigh surprised his admirers with *Topsy-Turvy*, a ripe portrayal of London in the 1880s, when W. S. Gilbert and Arthur Sullivan were mounting the operetta *The Mikado* (**Color Plate 25.7**). Despite the musical numbers and lush design, however, Leigh stuck to realism by displaying authentic reconstructions of Victorian stagecraft and by injecting social criticism in references to British imperialism, slum life, and the treatment of women.

In France, Jean Eustache offered a withering portrait of the self-centered young male, lying and quarreling his way through women's lives, in *The Mother and the Whore* (1972; **25.12**). Maurice Pialat's *Nous ne viellrons pas ensemble* ("We Won't Grow Old Together," 1972) and *Passe ton bac d'abord* ("First Get Your Degree," 1978) harshly depict middle-class problems such as divorce, unwanted children, and cancer. Pialat's brand of domestic realism won international acceptance in *Loulou* (1980) and *À nos amours* (1983), a story of a girl's coming of age in an era of sexual liberation (**25.13**).

The continental tradition of naturalistic observation continued through to Bruno Dumont's *L'Humanité* (1999) and Erick Zonca's *The Dream Life of Angels* (1998; **25.14**). Among the most noted new naturalists of the 1990s were the Belgian brothers Luc and Jean-Pierre Dardenne. In *La Promesse* (1996), a father and son rent rooms to illegal immigrants; *Rosetta* (1999) tells a grim tale of a girl driven to crime by unemployment and an alcoholic mother.

DURAS, VON TROTTA, AND THE EUROPEAN ART CINEMA

Two of the most important women directors of the era exemplify several trends. Marguerite Duras, established in the 1950s as a major novelist, also wrote film scripts, most notably for *Hiroshima mon amour* (1959). She began to direct in 1966 and made a strong impression with *Détruire dit-elle* (*Destroy, She Said,* 1969). Her fame increased considerably with *Nathalie Granger* (1973), *La Femme du Gange* ("Woman of the Ganges," 1974), *Le Camion* ("The Truck," 1977), and particularly *India Song* (1975).

Duras's writing had ties to the avant-garde Nouveau Roman ("New Novel"), and she carried literary conceptions of experimentation over to her films much as Jean Cocteau and Alain Robbe-Grillet had earlier. Like Germaine Dulac, Maya Deren, and Agnès Varda, though, she also explored a "feminine modernism." Her slow, laconic style, using static images and minimal dialogue, searches for a distinctively female use of language. Duras also developed a private world set in Vietnam during the 1930s. Several of her novels, plays, and films tell recurring and overlapping stories about colonial diplomats and socialites entangled in complex love affairs.

India Song remains a landmark in 1970s modernist cinema. It is set mostly in a French embassy in Vietnam, mostly during a long evening party. Couples dance to languid tangos, drifting through the frame or gliding out of darkness in the huge mirror that dominates the sitting room (**25.15**). But there is no synchronized dialogue. We hear anonymous voices who seem to be commenting on the image, even though the voices are in the present and the action occurs in the past. Moreover, most of the dramatic action—seductions, betrayal, and a suicide—takes place offscreen or in the mirror.

India Song is an experiment in sustained tempo: Duras timed every gesture and camera movement with a stopwatch. We cannot be sure that the action we see took place or is a kind of emblematic staging of the characters' relations. Murmurs on the sound track suggest that the party is crowded, but the vacant long shots show only the principal characters. The film pulls the spectator into a hypnotic reverie while also meditating upon the insular routines of colonialist life.

Margarethe von Trotta belongs to a younger generation. Born in 1942, she worked as an actress in several Young German films. She married Volker Schlöndorff in 1971 and collaborated with him on several films. The popular success of their codirected effort, *The Lost Honor of Katherina Blum* (1975; p. 574), enabled von Trotta to direct several films herself: *The Second Awakening of Christa Klages* (1977), *The German Sisters* (1981), *Friends and Husbands* (1982), *Rosa Luxembourg* (1986), and *Three Sisters* (1988).

25.15 The parlor mirror in *India Song:* class relations doubled.

Not as experimental as Duras or Chantal Akerman, von Trotta exploits more accessible conventions of the art cinema. Somewhat like Varda, she poses questions of women's problems in society. Her earliest works show women breaking out of their domestic roles and becoming scandalous public figures: Katherina Blum aids a terrorist on the run; Christa Klages becomes a bank robber. Von Trotta's later films concentrate on the conflicting pulls of work roles, family ties, and sexual love. She is keenly interested in the ways in which mothers, daughters, and sisters, sharing key moments of family history, slip into situations in which they exercise power over one another.

Sisters, or the Balance of Happiness (1979), for example, contrasts two women. The crisp, efficient Maria is an executive secretary geared to career advancement. Her younger sister Anna, halfheartedly pursuing a degree in biology, lives in her imagination, lingering over memories of childhood. Anna commits suicide, partly because of Maria's demand that she succeed. Maria responds by finding a substitute sister, a typist whom she tries to mold into a professional. Eventually, however, Maria realizes that she has been too rigid: "I will attempt to dream in the course of my life. I will endeavor to be Maria and Anna."

Fassbinder would have turned *Sisters* into a sinister melodrama of sadomasochistic domination, but von Trotta presents a character study that refuses to portray Maria as a monster. Von Trotta manipulates point of view to create a gradual shift of sympathies. At first the audience enters Anna's memories and reveries (**25.16**) and stays at a distance from Maria. After Anna's suicide, von Trotta takes us more into Maria's guilt-ridden mind (**25.17**). At the end,

25.16 Mirrors define Anna's fantasy world in *Sisters, or the Balance of Happiness*. Here, she recalls herself and Maria putting on lipstick as children.

25.17 After Anna's death, von Trotta presents her "haunting" of Maria through a hallucinatory mirror vision.

25.18 Mirror as window, playing perceptual tricks (*India Song*).

the characteristic art-cinema blend of memories, fantasies, and ambiguous images suggests that Maria has gained something of her sister's imagination: she seems to envision the mysterious forest that had formed part of Anna's daydreams.

The two directors' uses of mirrors neatly encapsulate the differences in their approaches. The luxurious geometry of *India Song*'s parlor illustrates Duras's emphasis on form, with the mirror sometimes resembling a window to another realm (**25.18**). Duras's experimental impulses led her into esoteric explorations of sound and image relations. *Son nom de Venise dans Calcutta désert* ("Her Name, Venice, in the Desert of Calcutta," 1976) uses *India Song*'s

soundtrack but shows entirely different shots of the embassy, all empty of human presence. Thirty of the forty-five minutes of *L'Homme atlantique* ("The Atlantic Man," 1981) consist of a black screen.

By contrast, von Trotta's mirrors link and contrast characters, intensifying story issues. "If there is such a thing at all as a female form of aesthetics in film, it lies for me in the choice of themes, in the attentiveness as well, the respect, the sensitivity, the care, with which we approach the people we're presenting as well as the actors we choose."[2] The poles of rarefied formal experiment and accessible subjects and themes typified the range of art cinema of the 1970s and 1980s.

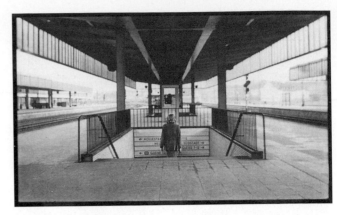

25.19 Directorial detachment in *Vagabond:* while the yuppie researcher complains to his wife, the protagonist Mona collapses in the background.

25.20   The road movie, filmed in Akerman's dry, rectilinear manner (*Les Rendez-vous d'Anna*).

New Women Filmmakers   The most extensive wave of politically oriented films came from women. As political commitment turned from revolutionary aspirations to micropolitics (see Chapter 23), the 1970s and 1980s saw female filmmakers gain wider recognition. In the popular cinema, the Italian Lina Wertmuller, the German Doris Dörrie, and the French Diane Kurys and Colline Serreau found success with comedies on women's friendship and male-female relations.

Other women directors expressed feminine or feminist concerns through art-cinema conventions. Two major examples are Marguerite Duras and Margarethe von Trotta (see box). Another is Agnès Varda, who won a major prize at the Venice festival with *Sans toit ni loi* ("Neither Roof nor Law," aka *Vagabond*, 1985). Through the countryside tramps an enigmatic young woman, self-destructively bent on living in an unorthodox way. The film obeys the art-cinema norm of flashing back from the investigation of Mona's death to her life in the past. Varda traces Mona's breakdown with a spare, detached camera technique (**25.19**) that suggests both respect for her self-reliance and a sense of a life wasted.

In line with the general move toward more accessible filmmaking, Chantal Akerman of Belgium followed her demanding *Jeanne Dielman* (1975, p. 568) with films closer to familiar models. *Les Rendez-vous d'Anna* ("Anna's Appointments," 1978) follows a filmmaker through Europe in a female version of the road movie (**25.20**). *Toute une nuit* ("All Night Long," 1982) is a cross section of a single night in which nearly three dozen couples meet, wait, quarrel, make love, and part (**Color Plate 25.8**). *The Golden 80s* (aka *Window Shopping,* 1983) offers a high-gloss musical in the Demy manner, with romantic intrigues crisscrossing a shopping mall, bubbly song numbers, and bitter reflections on sexual stratagems and the failures of love (**25.21**). *Nuit et jour* ("Night and Day," 1991) is something of a feminist rethinking of the Nouvelle Vague, as if the love triangle of *Jules and Jim* were told from the woman's point of view. In all these, the fragmented narrative of the postwar art-cinema enables Akerman to dwell on

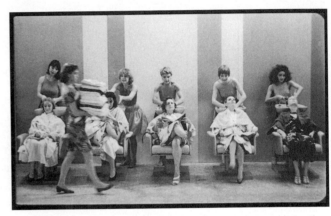

25.21   Akerman revises the musical: hairdressers deflate romantic aspirations with bawdy lyrics about male duplicity (*The Golden 80s*).

casual encounters and accidental epiphanies, as well as her consistent interest in women's work and their desire for both love and physical pleasure.

Women directors created a virtual wing of the New German Cinema, thanks partly to the ambitious funding programs launched by television and government agencies. Von Trotta was only the most visible representative of a boom in films that used art-cinema strategies to investigate women's issues. For example, Helke Sander was a student activist in 1968 and a cofounder of the German women's liberation movement. After several short films linked to the women's movement, including one on the side effects of contraception, Sander made *The All-Around Reduced Personality: Redupers* (1978), the story of a photographer who shows unofficial images of West Berlin and encounters opposition to publishing them. Helma Sanders-Brahms, who came to prominence at the same time as von Trotta, also concentrated on contemporary social controversies such as migrant workers and

25.22 *Years of Hunger:* older women explain menstruation to Ursula; later her mother will tell her father Ursula had a stomachache.

25.23 The rat race as a fight between executive mice in *Mon oncle d'Amérique.*

25.24 The hero's glimpse of his mourning wife and two mysterious women may be a fantasy or a premonition of the future in *Don't Look Now.*

women's rights. Her *Apfelbäume* (*Appletrees,* 1991) tells of an East German woman who is tempted by the Communist elite but who must remake her life when the two Germanies unite (**Color Plate 25.9**).

One of the most forceful recastings of art-cinema modernism was Jutta Brückner's *Hungerjahre* (*Years of Hunger,* 1979). In a voice-over from the present, a woman recalls growing up in the politically and sexually repressive 1950s. Cold war ideology and a strict family life confuse Ursula as she grows to sexual maturity (**25.22**). Unexpected voice-overs and an uncertain ending—in which Ursula may or may not commit suicide—create ambiguities of space and time reminiscent of Resnais and Duras. Brückner's goal recalls the fragmentation of *Hiroshima mon amour* and later art-cinema experiments; she sought a psychoanalytic narrative in which scenes combine "disparately, in uncoordinated juxtapositions, because memory tends to make leaps by association."[3]

In the 1990s, women's cinema took a "postfeminist" turn, most visibly in France, where many female directors emerged. They often dramatized childhood fantasy, adolescent pangs, and youthful romance (e.g., Patricia Mazuy's *Travolta et Moi,* 1994; Pascale Ferran's *Petits arrangements avec les morts,* 1994). Others took a hard-edged line. Catherine Breillat, who had been making films since the 1970s, offered audacious studies in female sexual desire in *Romance* (1999) and *À Ma Soeur!* ("To My Sister," aka *Fat Girl,* 2001). Claire Denis, who tackled brother-sister relations in *Nénette et Boni* (1996), turned her attention to masculine fantasies of heroism in the sumptuous *Beau Travail* ("Nice Work," 1999; **Color Plate 25.10**).

The Return of Art-Cinema Modernism   Despite the work of the few political modernists and the many feminist filmmakers, most significant European films avoided the direct engagement with political issues that had characterized the period from 1965 to 1975. Established directors continued to produce moderately modernist films

for the international market. François Truffaut, for instance, won great success with *La Nuit américain* (*Day for Night,* 1973) and *The Last Metro* (1980), but the fierce melancholy of *The Green Room* (1978) proved less popular (**Color Plate 25.11**). Alain Resnais became increasingly concerned with exposing the artifices of storytelling, often with a light touch seldom displayed in his official masterpieces *Hiroshima mon amour* and *Muriel.* In *Mon oncle d'Amérique* ("My American Uncle," 1980) human beings' careers illustrate theories of animal behavior (**25.23**). *Providence* (1976), with its scenes halted and revised in midcourse, lays bare the arbitrariness of fictional plotting.

Two older directors, based in Britain, helped revive the European art cinema. Stanley Kubrick brought a cold detachment to his 1975 adaptation of William Thackeray's *Barry Lyndon,* treating it as an occasion for technical experimentation with a lens that could capture candlelit images (**Color Plate 25.12**). Nicholas Roeg, a distinguished cinematographer, made his reputation with the ambiguous, aggressive *Performance* (1970) before creating Resnais-like flashes of subjectivity in *Don't Look Now* (1974; **25.24**) and *Bad Timing: A Sensual Obsession* (1985).

Somewhat later, the Georgian director Otar Iosseliani came to France, where he produced films of wry fantasy. In *Favorites of the Moon* (1984), Russian émigrés wander through Paris, caught up in gang wars and love affairs. *Chasing Butterflies* (1992) satirizes efforts to modernize the countryside. *Farewell Home Sweet Home* (1999) is a tangled tale of an aristocratic family and their interactions with their small-town neighbors. Iosseliani admitted that he was influenced by Jacques Tati not only in his dry physical humor but also in his use of sustained long shots packed with intersecting characters and plotlines. "As soon as I see a film that begins with a series of shots and reverse shots, with lots of dialogue and well-known actors, I leave the room immediately. That's not the work of a film artist."[4]

A great many younger directors arose to sustain the new pan-European art cinema. From the experimental realm came Peter Greenaway, who moved squarely into the art cinema with *The Draughtsman's Contract* (1982), coproduced by Channel 4 and the British Film Institute. A lush seventeenth-century costume drama, *The Draughtsman's Contract* (**Color Plate 25.13**) retains the gamelike labyrinths of Greenaway's early films in tracing how an artist discovers the secrets of a wealthy family while preparing drawings of their estate. Elaborate conceits underlie Greenaway's later work, as when he systematically works numerals into the settings of his dark sex comedy *Drowning by Numbers* (1988) or brings to life the twenty-four texts of *Prospero's Books* (1991), a free adaptation of Shakespeare's *The Tempest*.

The Spaniard Victor Erice was far less prolific than Greenaway, but his films attracted attention for their calm beauty and their exploration of childhood as a time of fantasy and mystery. *Spirit of the Beehive* (1972), set in 1930s Spain, follows a little girl who believes that the criminal she hides is a counterpart to the monster in her favorite film, *Frankenstein*. *El Sur* ("The South," 1983) is centered on an adolescent who discovers her father's love affair. Through chiaroscuro cinematography, Erice creates a twilight world between childhood and adulthood (**Color Plate 25.14**).

Another director working with family relationships in an art-cinema framework was the Englishman Terence Davies. Davies's highly autobiographical films combine a post-1968 sense of the political implications of personal experience with a facility in art-cinema conventions. Thanks to BFI production initiatives, Davies broke through to international markets with *Distant Voices, Still Lives* (1988). Here the anguish of family life under a psychopathic, abusive father is tempered by the love shared among mother, daughters, and son. The painful

25.25 Unexpected viewpoints, rapidly cut together, are hallmarks of the music-video look of *Run Lola Run*.

material is intensified by a rigorous, rectilinear style akin to Akerman's in *Jeanne Dielman*. Davies dwells on empty hallways and thresholds and treats family encounters and sing-alongs as if they were portrait sittings (**Color Plate 25.15**). In *The Long Day Closes* (1992), a lusher style recreates the bittersweet atmosphere in a family after the father's death. Slow camera movements, dissolves synchronized with lighting changes, and bridging songs slide the action imperceptibly from one time to another and between fantasy and reality.

The use of complex, fragmentary flashbacks in Davies's films typified a trend that was still being sustained in the early 2000s. Directors often returned to the sort of free-floating time shifts pioneered by Fellini, Buñuel, and others. Jaco Van Dormaël's *Toto le héros*, the prototype of 1990s Eurofilm, creates a Resnais-like interplay between reality, memory, and fantasy. Lars von Trier's *The Element of Crime* (Denmark, 1983) and *Europa* (aka *Zentropa*, Germany, 1991) sketch ominous landscapes hovering between history and dream. Tom Tykwer's *Run Lola Run* (1998) offers its heroine alternative fates in three parallel universes, all shot in music-video style and set to a techno beat (**25.25**). In opposition to Socialist Realism, new directors adopted the formal artifice and thematic ambiguity characteristic of 1960s art cinema while drawing, as Van Dormaël and Tykwer did, on popular culture to make things more audience-friendly.

The Arresting Image

Along with a new acknowledgment of artifice in narrative went a "return to the image." As Steven Spielberg, George Lucas, and Francis Ford Coppola dazzled audiences with visual pyrotechnics, many European directors also gave their films a captivating surface. Hollywood's hyperkinetic spectacle of chases, explosions, and special effects was countered by European directors' efforts to let the beautiful or startling image be the ultimate spectacle, to absorb the spectator in a rapt contemplation of the picture. Both the Europeans and the New Hollywood were offering images of a scale and intensity not to be found on television. In addition, the new pictorialism of the art cinema had local sources, many of them distinctly modernist.

Herzog, Wenders, and Sensibilist Cinema Two Munich-based directors manifested this tendency in the early 1970s: Werner Herzog and Wim Wenders. Because of their concentration on the revelatory shot, they were identified as "sensibilist" directors. Trusting to the beauty of the image and the sensitivity of the viewer, they turned away from the political concerns of other New German filmmakers. Their introspective cinema was also in tune with a "new inwardness" trend in German literature of the period.

Herzog made his reputation with a string of cryptic dramas: *Signs of Life* (1968), *Even Dwarfs Started Small* (1970), *Aguirre, the Wrath of God* (1972), *Every Man for Himself and God against All (The Enigma of Kaspar Hauser)* (1975), and *Heart of Glass* (1976). All flaunt Herzog's highly romantic sensibility. He fastens on the heroic achiever (the conquistador Aguirre out to rule the world; **25.26**), the marginal and innocent (dwarfs, the feral child Kaspar Hauser), and the mystic (the entire community in *Heart of Glass*). "That's why I want to make films. . . . I want to show things that are inexplicable somehow."[5]

Herzog sought to capture the immediacy of experience, a purity of perception unhampered by language. He often celebrated the encounter of people with the sheer physicality of the world: the world's most determined "ski flier" (*The Great Ecstasy of the Sculptor Steiner,* 1974), blind and deaf people visiting a cactus farm or taking their first airplane trip (*Land of Silence and Darkness,* 1971). Film images, he believed, should return people to the world as it is, but as we seldom see it. "People should look straight at a film. . . . Film is not the art of scholars, but of illiterates. And film culture is not analysis, it is agitation of the mind."[6]

In order to increase this agitation, Herzog conjured up bizarre images, often suspending the narrative so that the viewer could "look straight" at them. The camera observes impassively as an empty car circles a barnyard while a little man laughs maniacally. Conquistadors floating through the Peruvian jungle stare at a ship nestled in a treetop. Slow motion far more excruciating than in any sports reportage follows the soaring arc of the skier

25.26 *Aguirre, the Wrath of God:* the conquistador, holding his dead daughter, still vows to rule the globe.

25.27 The final images of *Heart of Glass* illustrate a character's parable about men who set out for the edge of the world.

Steiner as he launches himself into space. A door about to close mysteriously stops, and this tiny event becomes an occasion for contemplation.

Herzog's images open onto the infinite through visions of water, mists, and skies (**25.27**). In the opening of *Heart of Glass*, clouds flow like boiling rivers through mountain valleys. Periodically *Aguirre* contemplates the hypnotic pulsations of the turbulent Amazon. The deserts of *Fata Morgana* (1970) dissolve into teeming speckles of film grain, flickers akin to those that interrupt *Kaspar Hauser* and invite us to share the protagonist's vision.

Herzog declared himself the heir of W. F. Murnau; he made a new version of *Nosferatu* (1978), and he recaptured Expressionist acting style by hypnotizing the cast of *Heart of Glass*. His allegiance to the silent cinema was evident in his belief that sheerly striking images could express mystical truths beyond language; but the evocative power of his cinema also depended on the throbbing scores supplied by the art-rock group Popol Vuh. The loosening of cause and effect characteristic of the art cinema enabled Herzog to dedicate himself to the rapt contemplation of the pure, timeless image.

Wim Wenders began with similar antinarrative impulses, making a series of minimalist experimental shorts during the late 1960s. When Wenders turned to features, his sensibilist side found expression in loose journey narratives that halted for contemplation of locales and objects. Strongly influenced by American culture, he found as much sensuous pleasure in pinball, rock and roll, and Hollywood movies as Herzog found in mountains and sports of nature.

Wenders praised the moments in films that are "so unexpectedly lucid, so overwhelmingly concrete, that you hold your breath or sit up or put your hand to your mouth."[7] In *The Goalie's Anxiety at the Penalty Kick* (1971), a young man drifts about, moves in with a woman, murders her, drifts some more, and waits for the police to find him. The plot, based on a novel by the new-inwardness writer Peter Handke, crumbles into a series of "overwhelmingly concrete" moments, as when a cigarette tossed from a bus showers sparks in the road while the radio plays "The Lion Sleeps Tonight" (**Color Plate 25.16**). Similarly, in Wenders's "road" trilogy—*Alice in the Cities* (1973), *The Wrong Move* (1974), and *In the Course of Time* (aka *Kings of the Road,* 1976)—the wanderings of displaced characters are punctuated by long landscape shots, silences, and images that invite intense study. Not surprisingly, Wenders declared Yasujiro Ozu his favorite director, making a documentary in homage to him (*Tokyo-Ga,* 1985).

"I totally reject stories," Wenders wrote in 1982, "because for me they only bring out lies, nothing but lies, and the biggest lie is that they show coherence where there is none. Then again, our need for these lies is so consuming that it's completely pointless to fight them and to put together a sequence of images without a story—without the lie of a story. Stories are impossible, but it's impossible to live without them."[8] Wenders's films enact an ongoing struggle between the demand for narrative and a search for instantaneous visual revelation.

Wenders's *Himmel über Berlin* ("Heavens over Berlin," aka *Wings of Desire,* 1987) again searches for the overwhelmingly concrete—this time by means of the angel Damiel, who is captivated by the transient beauty of the world. He decides to join the human race; like Dorothy entering Oz, he falls into a world of color (**Color Plate 25.17**). He eventually unites with a trapeze artist, while his fellow angel must watch from the celestial, black-and-white world. Yet this initiation into the

25.28 The artificial image in Rohmer's *Perceval le gallois.*

everyday is a fall into narrative and history, emblematically represented by Homer, the elderly storyteller who links Berlin to its past. *Wings of Desire* is dedicated to "all the old angels, especially Yasujiro [Ozu], François [Truffaut], and Andrei [Tarkovsky]"—all directors who reconciled narrative significance with pictorial beauty.

France: The Cinéma du Look   In France, the new pictorialism surfaced in an uncharacteristic film by Eric Rohmer, *Perceval le gallois* (1978; **25.28**). It emerged in a glossier form in André Téchiné's *Barocco* (1976), a pastiche of film noir. Jacques Demy's most important 1980s contribution, the "musical tragedy" *Un Chambre en ville* ("A Room in Town," 1982), presents saturated colors and busy wallpaper patterns that frame a grim story of lovers' betrayal and a workers' strike (**Color Plate 25.18**).

In the early 1980s, a younger generation of French filmmakers began to steer this visual manner in fresh directions. They turned away from the political modernism of the post-1968 era and the grubby realism of Jean Eustache and Maurice Pialat toward a fast-moving, highly artificial cinema. They drew inspiration from the New Hollywood (especially Coppola's *One from the Heart* and *Rumble Fish*), late Fassbinder, television commercials, music videos, and fashion photography. Characteristic examples of the new French trend are Jean-Jacques Beineix's *Diva* (1982), *Moon in the Gutter* (1983), *37°2 le matin* (aka *Betty Blue,* 1985), and *IP5* (1992); Luc Besson's *Subway* (1985), *Big Blue* (1988), and *Nikita* (aka *La Femme Nikita,* 1990); and Leos Carax's *Boy Meets Girl* (1984), *Mauvais sang* ("Bad Blood," aka *The Night Is Young,* 1986), and *Les Amants du Pont-Neuf* ("The Lovers of the Pont-Neuf," 1992).

25.29 A photocopy store becomes a dizzying play of shadows, moving light, and reflections (*Boy Meets Girl*).

25.30 Divas freeze into histrionic poses (*Death of Maria Malibran*, 1971).

Parisian critics called this the *cinéma du look*. The films decorate fairly conventional plot lines with chic fashion, high-technology gadgetry, and conventions drawn from advertising photography and television commercials. The directors fill the shots with crisp edges and stark blocks of color; mirrors and polished metal create dazzling reflections (**25.29**). The slick images of Beineix and Besson evoke publicity and video style, as well as *Blade Runner* and *Flashdance*. Carax, the most resourceful of the group, creates sensuous imagery through chiaroscuro lighting, unusual framings, and unexpected choices of focus (**Color Plate 25.19**). Several critics diagnosed this trend as a postmodern style that borrowed from mass-culture design in order to create an aesthetic of surfaces. In a broader perspective, the cinéma du look was a mannerist, youth-oriented version of that post-1968 tendency toward abstract beauty seen in less flashy form in Herzog and Wenders.

Theater and Painting: Godard and Others The fascination with images was shared by German directors outside the sensibilist trend. For some, theater provided another way to return to the image and spectacle. Werner Schroeter, a distinguished opera director, created several stylized, baroque films (**25.30**). Hans-Jürgen Syberberg followed *Hitler* (see 23.74) with *Parsifal* (1982), an adaptation of Richard Wagner's music drama as a colossal allegory of German history and myth (**Color Plate 25.20**).

Further manifestations of the new pictorialism came from the Portuguese Manoel Oliveira. Born in 1908, Oliveira directed only sporadically after his 1931 city symphony *Douro, Faina Fluvial* (see 14.33). His second feature, *Act of Spring* (1963) was a quasi-documentary about a village reenactment of Christ's passion. Oliveira went on to make a string of films whose visual beauty often arose from a transformation of theatrical traditions.

Oliveira perpetuated conventions of art-cinema narration; *Act of Spring*, for instance, displays the act of filming according to then-current conventions of reflexivity and cinéma vérité. Once the passion play begins, however, he treats it as a self-contained ritual, eliminating the audience and dwelling on the tensions between theatrical conventions and the open-air space, where stylized costumes and props stand in sunlight and landscape (**Color Plate 25.21**). In other films, Oliveira adapted plays written by himself or by other Portuguese dramatists. All his work displays a sumptuous mise-en-scène, often acknowledging theatricality through direct address to the camera or tableau shots incorporating prosceniums, backdrops, and curtains.

For other directors inclined to return to the image, theater did not provide as much inspiration as did painting. Derek Jarman's first mainstream feature, *Caravaggio* (1986), not only portrays the master creating his paintings (**Color Plate 25.22**) but also employs a painterly style in the dramatic scenes. In Raul Ruiz's *Hypothèse du tableau volé* ("Hypothesis of the Stolen Painting," 1978), the camera wends its way around figures frozen in place and representing missing paintings by an obscure artist. Jacques Rivette's *La Belle noiseuse* ("The Beautiful Flirt," 1991) and Victor Erice's *The Quince Tree Sun* (1992) center on painters, and in each the plot is secondary to quiet observation of the meticulous process by which an image is born (**Color Plate 25.23**).

Ulrike Ottinger, a West German photographer and graphic artist, was a central participant in the new pictorialism. Her *Ticket of No Return* (1979) portrays a rich woman alcoholic on a binge through Berlin, dogged by three sociologists who interject lectures on the dangers of drink. The unrealistic staging is interrupted by several of the woman's daydreams. *Freak Orlando* (1981) confronts Virginia Woolf's dual-gendered time traveler Orlando with "freaks" at various points in history. Ottinger's outlandish costumes intensify the fantasy (**Color Plate 25.24**).

Jean-Luc Godard also took inspiration from painting. His video work had concentrated on the relations among images, dialogues, and written texts, but when he returned to cinema he was calling himself a painter who happened to work in film. However much Wenders believed he gave up the story for the sake of the singular image, Godard went much further. *Passion* (1982), one of the most pictorially rich films of his career, centers on an East European filmmaker who replicates famous paintings on video by shooting tableaux of actors. As Godard's camera glides over these groupings, a two-dimensional image becomes voluminous, as if the cinema had the power to revivify clichéd masterpieces (**Color Plate 25.25**).

Godard's films of the decade—*First Name armen* (1983), *Hail Mary* (1985), *Détective* (1985), *King Lear* (1987), *Soigne ta droite* ("Keep Up Your Right," 1987), *Nouvelle Vague* (1990)—while not relaxing his usual demands on the viewer, suggest a new serenity. There is a lyrical treatment of foliage, water, and sunlight. Rejecting the frontal, posterlike shots of the late 1960s, Godard builds his scenes out of oblique, close views of the human body and its surroundings. He uses available light, without fill, to create rich shadow areas. His angles split the scene into planes of sharp detail and out-of-focus action (**Color Plate 25.26**). In all, the "painterly" Godard has a calm radiance that softens the abrasiveness of the narrative construction. In his characteristically radical way, he shows the rewards of a return to the arresting image.

Rough Edges The tendency toward the ravishing image did not dwindle in the 1990s, with Lars von Trier's *Element of rime* yielding a trancelike view of a frightening netherworld (**Color Plate 25.27**) and Claire Denis's *Beau Travail* presenting sun-baked images of Foreign Legionnaires tidily ironing their uniforms (see Color Plate 25.10). In *Delicatessen* (1991) and *The ity of Lost hildren* (1995) Jean-Pierre Jeunet and Marc Caro revealed comic-book grotesquerie, half Terry Gilliam, half Tim Burton (**25.31**). Yet, as if in response to the beautification of the image, other European filmmakers seemed prepared to assault the viewer with shocking material in a raw state. French filmmakers began presenting sexual imagery previously seen only in hard-core pornography,

25.31 Wide-angle deformations in *The City of Lost Children*.

25.32 In *Code Inconnu*, the selfish French boy throws a crumpled sack into the lap of a Romany beggar woman. The gesture starts to spin a web of painful human relations.

as in Catherine Breillat's *Romance*, Bruno Dumont's *La vie de Jésus* (1997), Patrice Chéreau's *Intimacy* (2001), and Virginie Despentes and Coralie Trinh Thi's *Baise-moi* (2000), about two women who embark on a road trip mixing sex with murder. Gaspar Noë's *Seul ontre Tous* (*I Stand Alone*, 1999) is no less brutal in its portrayal of a sociopathic butcher.

The Austrian filmmaker Michael Haneke typified this trend. In calm and clinical detail, refusing to aestheticize the emotional coldness he finds in modern life, he follows his people beyond the limit of civilized behavior. Haneke found his distinctive tone with *The Seventh ontinent* (1989), a dispassionate portrayal of a family's collective suicide. *Benny's Video* (1992) shows a rich schoolboy seducing and murdering a classmate, all of it recorded on tape. In *La Pianiste* (aka *The Piano Player*, 2001), a middle-aged piano teacher becomes fascinated by one of her pupils, whom she entices into a sadomasochistic relationship. In *ode Inconnu* ("Code Unknown," 2000) Haneke plays a harsh variant on the intersecting-story plotline. Several Parisians—an aspiring actress, an African family—are connected to the Bosnian war through a gesture of casual cruelty (**25.32**).

EASTERN EUROPE AND THE USSR

Eastern Europe: From Reform to Revolution

"It is time to relegate to the archives the postulates of the cold war, when Europe was viewed as an arena of confrontation divided into 'spheres of influence.' . . . Any interference in internal affairs and any attempts to restrict the sovereignty of states—either friends and allies or anyone else—are inadmissible."[9] These remarks, made by Soviet President Mikhail Gorbachev in June 1989, went beyond the Soviet platitudes about the independence of its satellites. Gorbachev's glasnost policy included a greater degree of self-determination for the eastern European countries.

In the months before and after Gorbachev's speech, these countries astonished the world—and Gorbachev himself—by throwing off their governments. Throughout 1989, East Germany, Hungary, Poland, Czechoslovakia, Bulgaria, and Romania cast out their Communist leaders and demanded democracy and economic reform along capitalist lines. Joyous crowds, gathering from all over Europe, tore down the Berlin Wall. Less than two years later, an aborted coup against Gorbachev triggered the collapse of the Communist party in the Soviet Union itself.

Twenty years before, few would have predicted such a dramatic death for eastern European communism. The 1968 Prague Spring had been aborted by an invasion of Soviet troops (p. 553), and all hopes of democracy seemed stilled. Poland, Hungary, and some other eastern countries pacified their citizens with economic reforms and boosts in the standard of living that suggested that "socialist consumerism" had finally arrived.

Yet the prosperity of eastern Europe was artificial, sustained by price controls. OPEC's 1973 oil-price increase, along with domestic shortfalls in agriculture and consumer goods, led to the beginning of discontent. "A spectre is haunting Eastern Europe," wrote Václav Havel in 1979, "the spectre of what is called in the west 'dissent.'"[10] New forces for change—labor unions, nationalist groups, and even religious bodies—began to chip away at the Communist regimes.

Velvet Revolutions and National Cinemas The most decisive events took place in Poland. During 1976 and 1977, the government's attempt to raise fixed prices was met by a rash of strikes. In 1980, more strikes erupted

when thousands of workers occupied the shipyards of Gdansk. With the aid of the Catholic Church, Lech Walesa and other workers founded a new union, Solidarity. Solidarity rapidly became a kind of popular front, claiming that it was working to turn Poland into a "self-governing republic." The regime responded by outlawing Solidarity and declaring martial law. Leaders of Solidarity were arrested, and the organization went underground. When Gorbachev announced in 1985 that the Soviet government would not sponsor an invasion of a sovereign nation, the Polish government began negotiations with Solidarity. Eventually, in the summer of 1989 in open elections, Solidarity won a stunning victory over Communist incumbents and Walesa became president of the new Poland.

Popular movements toward liberalization emerged in Hungary and Czechoslovakia as well. In Yugoslavia and other Balkan States, the collapse of communism was accelerated by new leaders who played on nationalistic feelings. The failures of eastern Europe's planned economies made people eager to move toward democracy, free- or mixed-market economies, and access to agricultural produce, modern housing, and up-do-date consumer goods. The "velvet revolutions" of 1989 were partly responses to the inability of communism to deliver social services and to guarantee citizens a modern lifestyle.

Political freedom, however, eventually hurt film production. East European cinema, galvanized by growing dissent after the mid-1970s, was battered by the economic crises and political upheavals of the late 1980s. In the staunch Soviet ally East Germany, for example, Socialist Realism had held firm, counterbalanced by more progressive trends toward "youth films" and "outsider films" centering on nonconformist women. The end of Erich Honecker's regime in 1989, followed by reunification with West Germany the following year, left old-line Communist filmmakers stranded. After reunification, German films claimed only 10 percent of the national box office.

In Bulgaria, expensive historical spectacles made in the late 1970s and early 1980s ate up the nation's film funds, just before the economic crisis in all Communist satellites let to massive cutbacks in state industries. In Yugoslavia, an emergent independent film movement, strongly decentralized production aided by television funding, and a move toward privatization were cut short by the country's economic collapse in the mid-1980s. After the fall of communism, an ethnic war started in 1991 and destroyed the nation's civil society. The war was grinding to a close at the end of the century, but with the creation of Serbia, Croatia, Bosnia, and other states, Yugoslavian cinema was ended. Its wilder traditions

25.33 In a memoir as cinéphiliac as any offered by the French New Wave, Márta Mészáros recalls sharing her mother's love at a village movie show (*Diary for My Children*).

25.34 *Werckmeister Harmonies:* shot in an intricate long take, a young man teaches the inebriated tavern patrons to dance in a pattern that mimics the solar system.

were recalled in Emir Kusturica's Felliniesque black comedy *Underground* (1995), which traces the history of Yugoslavia from 1941 to the Bosnian war.

Hungary: Old and New Auteurs   Events in Hungary, Czechoslovakia, and Poland illustrate further how eastern European film moved from the stagnant years of the mid-1970s to the bleak conditions of the 1990s. Hungarian cinema suffered the least radical changes. In the 1970s, Hungary became a crucible for reform within a socialist economy, and the state's "New Economic Mechanism" successfully raised living standards through a mixture of centralized control, private businesses, and joint ventures with the capitalist West. The Communist party, though firmly in control, had tolerated multicandidate elections, and censorship was relatively relaxed. After the fall of communism, Hungary was able to recover somewhat faster than its neighbors. Yet, as in most former Soviet satellites, U.S. films captured the market. The government's Motion Picture Foundation, created in 1991 to ease the transition to a free market, was still funding most local films ten years later.

Both before and after the fall, Hungary turned out between twelve and twenty features per year, many of

them signed by major directors. The most internationally visible director was István Szabó, whose *Confidence* (1979) led him to the high-budget, high-profile German-financed *Mephisto* (1981), *Colonel Redl* (1983), and *Sunshine* (1999). Arguably the most consistent and accomplished senior director in Hungary was Márta Mészáros. "I tell my own life story in most of my films. The search for Mother and Father is a determining experience in my own life."[11] Mészáros dramatized her quest in *Anna* (1981) and the fictionalized series of her memoirs of growing up under Stalinism: *Diary for My Children* (1984; **25.33**), *Diary for My Loves* (1987), and *Diary for My Father and Mother* (1991). Mészáros's former husband Miklós Jancsó remained prolific, but none of his 1980s films aroused the acclaim that had greeted his 1960s work. He eventually recaptured his home audience with absurdist comedies featuring two popular clowns playing gravediggers (e.g., *Damn You! The Mosquitoes*, 1999).

In the 1990s, a group of younger Hungarian directors came to attention with black-and-white films that were sour in tone, enigmatic in subject matter, and extravagantly stylized in execution. Gyorgy Feher's *Passion* (1998) is a dank, grainy story of rural adultery, shot in long takes. The most famous exponent of the grimy style was Béla Tarr. Tarr came to international attention with *Satan's Tango* (1994), an adaptation of a classic Hungarian novel. In a bleak, muddy village, the relations among characters unfold with aching slowness, all observed by a doctor sitting at a window and trying to write down everything he sees. The film runs for seven and a half hours. In *Werckmeister Harmonies* (2000), a seedy small town plays host to a traveling circus, complete with a stuffed whale.

An admirer of the early Jancsó, Tarr relied on tightly choreographed long takes but kept them at a lugubrious pace, as if the characters are laboring with every movement (**25.34**). Why is everything so slow? Tarr answered that a shot had to respect many protagonists, not just the characters: "Scenery, the weather, time, and locations have their own faces and they are important."[12] Recalling the German sensibilist trend, Tarr reinvigorated the tradition of contemplative cinema.

Slovakia and the Czech Republic   Czechoslovakian filmmakers had a less equable time during these decades. The crackdown after the Prague Spring of 1968 kept pressure firm. The government tightened control over film units, where byzantine bureaucracies and corps of "literary advisers" steered production away from political subjects and toward popular entertainment. Many

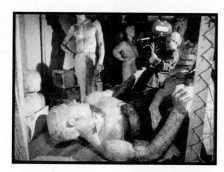

25.35, *left   Man of Marble:* Birkut's triumphs as a bricklayer staged for the "documentary" camera.

25.36, *right   Man of Marble:* Agnieszka discovers the statue glorifying Birkut.

directors emigrated to the United States, Canada, and western Europe.

Of the New Wave directors who stayed, Jiří Menzel did not make a film until 1976 and thereafter turned out several characteristically bittersweet comedies, notably *Seclusion Near a Forest* (1976), *Cutting It Short* (1980), and *My Sweet Little Village* (1986), which was a triumph at home and a foreign art-house success. Vera Chytilová, after campaigning for years against the sexism of the regime's film policy (p. 553), returned to directing with *The Apple Game* (1976), a farce about sexual relations that earned official disapproval but was marketed abroad. She followed this with films that mixed commercial narrative forms with eroticism and social satire.

After the 1989 revolts, major banned films came off the shelf. Audiences around the world saw what the censors had forbidden, and the vivacity of the Prague Spring was recaptured. Menzel's *Larks on a String* (1969; p. 553), taken out of the vaults, won the main prize at the Berlin Film Festival twenty years after it was finished. More recently banned works, such as Dušan Hanák's *I Love, You Love* (1980), also received international notice.

In 1993, the country split peacefully in two, creating the Czech Republic and Slovakia. The significantly more active Czech industry was growing at the start of the new century, while Slovakia relied on coproductions, chiefly with Czech funding.

Poland: From Solidarity to Kieślowski   The most energetic eastern European cinema of the 1970s and 1980s was to be found in Poland. Neither as liberated as Hungary nor as repressive as Czechoslovakia, Poland offered filmmakers some latitude for social criticism. Although production units had been dissolved in the wake of the 1968 demonstrations (p. 554), they were soon reconstituted, and filmmakers acquired greater freedom. Each production unit consisted of an artistic director (usually a major filmmaker) and a literary director (usually a screenwriter). During the early 1970s, filmmakers

adhered to safe literary and historical subjects. Midway through the decade, in synchronization with popular discontent with economic policy, there arose the "cinema of moral concern."

A prime example was Andrzej Wajda's *Man of Marble* (1976), a fictionalized investigation of a "model worker" from the 1950s. The filmmaker Agnieszka tries to find out why Birkut, a loyal bricklayer, was erased from history. In a knowing echo of *Citizen Kane,* her interviews with people who knew Birkut frame extensive flashbacks. Wajda's exposure of Stalinist and post-Stalinist political intrigue reflexively invokes cinema's ability to create ideology (**25.35**). At first, Agnieszka trusts the camera as a documentary tool (**25.36**), but by the end of the film, denied raw stock and a camera, she must discover the truth directly, through human contact with Birkut's son.

Along with Krzysztof Zanussi's *Camouflage* (1976), a depiction of conformity and idealism at a summer camp for college students, *Man of Marble* signaled a disaffection with the regime. A harder-line vice-minister of culture for films came to power, and the filmmaking community protested. Directors pointed out that the public was treating film as the conscience of Poland, the only witness to the conditions of social life. Feliks Falk's *Top Dog* (1977), Zanussi's *Spiral* (1978), and other films of "moral concern" countered the regime's boasts about improved living standards with charges that Poles had sacrificed their honor and conscience. Many of the younger directors, born after the war, grew up in Stalinist culture and were alert for its signs in contemporary life.

When Solidarity's strikes galvanized the nation in 1980, film workers rallied to the cause. As Solidarity won initial concessions from the government, the annual national film festival in Gdansk announced a new socially critical cinema. The filmmaker, Wajda declared in 1980, "can succeed only if he makes an honest scrutiny of contemporary realities and the scale of the human effort and suffering they contain . . . and explores them for the chances they offer of man's spiritual victory."[13]

25.37 In *The Decalogue 1,* young Pawel embarks on his search for the soul—which his father will deny exists—with tragic results.

From the production units supervised by Wajda and Zanussi came several films reflecting the new realism. The most celebrated was Wajda's *Man of Iron* (1980), a sequel to *Man of Marble* in which Agnieszka and Birkut's son press their investigation into the 1960s and 1970s. It was shot during the Solidarity strike and incorporated documentary footage of contemporary events. Attacking the government with unprecedented audacity, *Man of Iron* quickly became the most widely seen Polish film in history.

When the gains of Solidarity were overturned by the government, the outspoken filmmakers felt the counterblows. But Gorbachev's new policies toward eastern Europe led the government to open negotiations with Solidarity, and Polish filmmakers returned to the cinema of moral urgency. The most significant director from an international prospective was Krzysztof Keiślowski. He had made his name during the 1970s with barbed television documentaries and *The Scar* (1976), an acerbic study of an ineffectual factory foreman. In *Camera Buff* (1979), a worker tries to make an amateur film about his factory but runs into problems of honesty and bad faith.

Kieślowski's skepticism about political answers led him to probe more essential questions: "What is the true meaning of life? Why get up in the morning? Politics don't answer that."[14] *Chance* (1981) presents three hypothetical plots, tracing out the life choices available to a man: becoming a party leader, an opposition fighter, or an apolitical bystander. *No End* (1984) was the boldest film about martial law. In a pungent mixture of the religious and the secular, Kieślowski's series of television films, *The Decalogue* (1988), offers a story for each of

the Ten Commandments (**25.37**). Two of these somber tales were expanded into features (*A Short Film about Killing* and *A Short Film about Love,* both 1988).

After 1989: The Threat of Hollywood Just before the 1989 revolutions, reform was brewing in several film industries. Yugoslavia made its regional studios autonomous. Hungary and Poland abolished the state monopoly on film and gave the production units their independence, urging them to pursue financing and create joint productions with capitalist nations. After the 1989 events, Czechoslovakia dissolved its central film bureau. Throughout eastern Europe, film companies were privatized, and western money was welcomed. Censorship was virtually abolished. Hungary made a distribution arrangement with American companies in 1989, and soon other countries opened their markets.

The new conditions created a fresh barrage of problems. Under Communist regimes, ticket prices had been absurdly low (usually less than a dollar), but open-market conditions required a price rise, which drove audiences away. Theaters had lacked maintenance for years, but without state subsidy there was no money for renovations. Home video, late in penetrating eastern Europe but offering unrestrained (often pirated) access to popular western films, further cut theater attendance.

Worst of all, post-1989 freedom put filmmakers head to head with Hollywood. The results were predictable. American films, long barred from eastern Europe, flooded the market much as they had deluged western Europe after 1945. In 1991, 95 percent of the films playing in Poland were from U.S. companies, and Czechoslovakian films attracted less than one-fourth of domestic box-office revenues. In the same year, the audience for Hungarian films was only one-seventh of what it had been two years before. The local product played in small art theaters and barely broke even.

Eastern European governments sought to imitate western Europe by offering loans, subsidies, and prizes, but funds remained pitifully small. With eastern countries struggling to heal fractured economies and inflation running high, art cinema could no longer expect much help. Filmmakers had little choice but to pursue international cinema. "We want to make films for viewers in Paris, New York, Tokyo," announced one Polish director. "We cannot make films only for Poland."[15]

Doubtless most directors dreamed of a success such as that met by Kieślowski's *Double Life of Véronique* (1991). Its plot, involving two apparently identical women living in different countries, found a ready audience around the world. Shot in Poland and France, it was funded by a French production firm and Canal Plus.

Even more successful was his "three colors" trilogy on contemporary Europe: the mournful *Blue* (1993), the satiric *White* (1993), and the spiritually mysterious *Red* (1994), which ends by showing how the protagonists of the other two films have fared. Unabashedly humanistic, teasing the viewer with secret doublings and fateful coincidences, wrapped in thrilling musical scores by Zbigniew Preisner, these films convinced critics that the tradition of postwar modernism could still flourish. Kieślowski died in 1996, honored by all.

After dissolving the Warsaw Pact in 1991, eastern Europe sought to join the European Community. Some filmmakers began to receive funds from Eurimages, but most would take many years just to achieve the defensive, beleaguered position of most of their western European counterparts.

The USSR: The Final Thaw

From 1964 to 1982, Leonid Brezhnev served as secretary of the Communist party of the Soviet Union. Opposed to reform, favoring rule by elderly officials, Brezhnev's regime presented an image of solidity and apparent growth. During the 1970s, citizens acquired televisions, refrigerators, and cars. At the same time, Brezhnev committed himself to a policy of military intervention, assisting revolts in Angola and Ethiopia and invading Afghanistan.

Although consumer comforts increased, culture suffered another "freeze." Aleksandr Solzhenitsyn, Andrei Sakharov, and other dissidents were silenced by exile or imprisonment. Sergei Paradzhanov, the director of *Shadows of Forgotten Ancestors* and *The Color of Pomegranates,* was released from prison in 1977, but he was forbidden to emigrate or to work in cinema. Goskino, the agency overseeing cinema, had become a bloated bureaucracy, encouraging popular entertainment in tune with the new socialist consumerism. The strategy was rewarded by the international success of *Moscow Does Not Believe in Tears* (1980), the first Soviet film to win an Academy Award. As in Hollywood during the same period, the bulk of box-office income was supplied by relatively few films.

Despite the conservatism of the Brezhnev era, some slice-of-life films gave voice to the problems of daily existence, especially among Soviet youth. Dinara Asanova (*The Restricted Boy,* 1977), Lana Gogoberidze (*Some Interviews on Personal Matters,* 1979), and other women directors created distinctive psychological studies. The lyrical, or poetic tendencies associated with the republics' studios continued in the work of Tengiz Abuladze (e.g., the banned *Repentance,* 1984).

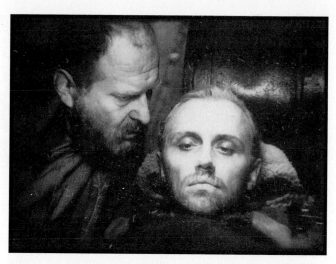

25.38 In the course of *The Ascent,* Sotnikov becomes paralleled to Christ in his willingness to sacrifice himself for other Russians captured by the Germans.

Tarkovsky and the Ethics of Art In addition, several directors created idiosyncratic, self-consciously artistic works that reflected both European art cinema and Russian traditions. In the massive *Siberiade* (1979; banned), Andrei Mikhalkov-Konchalovsky offered a personalized historical epic, while in *A Slave of Love* (1976) and *Unfinished Piece for Player Piano* (1977) his brother Nikita Mikhalkov experimented with reflexivity in the manner of Fellini and other European directors. Larissa Shepitko's films emphasize individual conscience and moral choice in the vein of Fyodor Dostoyevsky and contemporary anti-Stalinist literature. Her World War II film *The Ascent* (1977) shows two partisan soldiers captured by the Germans and forced to decide between collaboration and execution. The intellectual Sotnikov, having conquered his fear of death in an earlier skirmish, bears up under torture and accepts death with an eerie, Christ-like gentleness (**25.38**).

The most visible exponent of an artistic cinema opposed to mass genres and propaganda films remained Andrei Tarkovsky. *Solaris* (1972) had somewhat mitigated the scandal of *Andrei Roublev* (1966, p. 458), but the obscure, dreamlike *The Mirror* (1975) confirmed that he worked in a mystical vein fiercely opposed to the mainstream.

Considered a "reactionary," Tarkovsky insisted on the family, poetry, and religion as central forces in social life. He declared himself against cinema with a political message and argued for a cinema of direct, evocative impressions—a position that put him close to the sensibilist German directors. But his somber films seek to engage the spectator in a weightier way than do those of Herzog and Wenders. *Stalker* (1979) presents an allegorical

25.39, *left*   The hard, westernized Soviet teenagers of *Scarecrow*.

25.40, *right*   To-camera address intensifies the brutality of *Come and See*. Here the young hero returns to his village and is told that his family has been massacred.

expedition through a wrecked postindustrial landscape into "the Zone," a region where human life can be fundamentally changed. Filmed in a blue murk, *Stalker* uses hypnotic, achingly slow camera movements to create what the director called "the pressure of the time" running through the shots (**Color Plate 25.28**).[16]

Tarkovsky went to Italy to make *Nostalghia* (1983), a melancholy, virtually nonnarrative meditation on memory and exile (**Color Plate 25.29**). He decided not to return to the USSR. He directed some stage productions, and in Sweden he filmed the Bergmanesque *The Sacrifice* (1986), which won the special jury prize at Cannes. By the time of his death in 1986, Tarkovsky had become an emblem of the cinema of artistic conscience. His prominence abroad had saved his films from shelving, and, even if they went unseen in the USSR, they were salable foreign exports. He influenced the pictorialist strain of European cinema during the 1970s and 1980s, and his Soviet contemporaries gathered courage from his resistance to official policies. A self-conscious auteur on the European model, Tarkovsky demanded that art be a moral quest: "Masterpieces are born of the artist's struggle to express his ethical ideals."[17]

During Tarkovsky's silence and exile, Soviet cinema was changing. Rolan Bykov's *Scarecrow* (1983), a film about a village girl despised by her classmates, quietly celebrates indigenous tradition and historical memory over the harsh selfishness of the new consumerist Russia (**25.39**). Alexei Guerman's *My Friend Ivan Lapshin* (1983; banned until 1985) eclectically mixes newsreels and abstractly staged footage to criticize Stalinist conceptions of political crimes. The World War II movie was given a new savagery in Elem Klimov's *Come and See* (1985), a harrowing portrayal of the German occupation of Byelorussia (**25.40**). Based on an idea of Klimov's wife, the deceased Larissa Shepitko, *Come and See* presented the naive young hero as something less than the Socialist Realist ideal. During the same period, Paradzhanov returned to feature filmmaking. *The Legend of Suram Fortress* (1984) recalls *The Color of Pomegranates* in its stylized simplicity and vibrant textures (**Color Plate**

25.30). Even a "parallel cinema" shot on 16mm and super 8mm was beginning to lurk in students' apartments and artists' basements (p. 598).

Behind the façade of Brezhnev's regime, the USSR had stagnated. Agricultural and industrial production had declined, and so had health and living standards. Corruption, inefficiency, and overextended military commitments were draining the state's resources. Neither Brezhnev nor the two elderly general secretaries who succeeded him faced up to the challenges. A younger politician, Mikhail Gorbachev, assumed leadership in 1985 and revealed that the USSR was on the verge of financial collapse. His announcement that the USSR would no longer sustain its satellites in eastern Europe led to the overthrow of Communist regimes there. Gorbachev also called for a policy of glasnost, which was to initiate a long-overdue rebuilding of Soviet institutions, or *perestroika* ("restructuring"). Another "thaw" had begun.

Glasnost and Perestroika in the Cinema   At first Gorbachev sought to implement reforms through the chain of party command, but in 1987 he began to call for fundamental changes. Glasnost meant confronting the errors of the past. Stalin's regime was excoriated, and citizens were encouraged to discuss the failures of the economy, the rise of crime and drug use, and the sense that the Soviet system bred people to be hard and selfish.

Glasnost gave filmmakers an unprecedented freedom. Stalin's policies were attacked in *The Cold Summer of '53* (1987), a sort of Soviet Western that shows a village terrorized by a gang of released political prisoners. Valery Ogorodnikov's *Prishvin's Paper Eyes* (1989) portrays the early days of Soviet television, with jabs at propaganda filming and a remarkable sequence that mixes newsreels and Eisenstein's Odessa Steps massacre to suggest that Stalin is selecting the victims from a balcony.

Youth films dwelt upon student rebellion, often laced with rock music and a post-Punk anomie (e.g., Sergei Solovyev's *Assa*, 1988). *Chernukha*, or "black cinema," rubbed audiences' noses in the sordidness of daily life and predatory politics. Satiric films mocked party tradition and current fashions. Even mass entertainment exploited the new attitudes, as when the enormously successful gangster film *King of Crime* (1988) showed the KGB, the state, and criminals conspiring to defraud the public. Internationally, the hallmark of glasnost cinema was Vasily Pichul's *Little Vera* (1988). Vera's cynical amorality and casual promiscuity once and for all deflated the myth of the virtuous heroine who could sacrifice all for the collective.

Most of these films would not have been made had not perestroika opened up the film industry. In May 1986, at the Congress of Soviet Filmmakers, Elem Klimov, director of *Come and See* and a friend of Gorbachev's, was elected head of the union. The same congress set in motion the restructuring of Goskino. Under the new policy, Goskino would serve principally as a conduit for funds and a source of facilities. Filmmaking would be in the hands of free creative production units on the eastern European model. In addition, censorship was markedly liberalized.

One of Klimov's major reforms was the establishment of the Conflict Commission, aimed at the review and release of banned films. Soon critical works such as the humanistic war dramas *My Friend Ivan Lapshin* and *Commissar* (1967) and the surreal Ukrainian satire *Repentance* (1984) were unshelved. In the year after his death, Tarkovsky was honored with a complete retrospective in his homeland.

Glasnost and perestroika gave more autonomy to the republics as well. In Kazakhstan, quasi-Punk directors offered films like *The Needle* (1988, Rashid Nugmanov), a drug movie bearing the influence of Hollywood melodrama, Fassbinder, and Wenders's road sagas. In Georgia, Alexander Rekhviashvili made *The Step* (1986), a structurally adventurous, wryly absurd film about the meaningless routines of Soviet life. Before Paradzhanov's death in 1990, he directed *Ashik Kerib* (1989), a literary adaptation transformed by his ritualized treatment of Georgian legend and ethnic custom.

While international circles grew interested in the "New Soviet Cinema," Gorbachev's attempt to reform communism from the top down was proving unworkable. He pressed for a more rapid shift to individual initiative and a market system. In 1989, the government demanded that film studios become profitable and encouraged filmmakers to form private companies and independent cooperatives. Formerly Goskino had sole distribution power, but now independent producers could distribute their own products.

The decline in state funding came at a bad time, since technology was in disrepair. The thirty-nine Soviet

25.41   Ramshackle structures and a sea of mud: the landscape of Soviet life in *Freeze, Die, Come to Life!*

studios badly needed renovation. Only one had Dolby sound equipment, a necessity for western markets, and Soviet film stock was still the world's worst.

Cinema and Market Bolshevism   The free market was an anarchic one. No legislation regulated film activity. Video piracy flourished. Clandestine companies churned out pornography, often as diversions for black-market funds. Before glasnost, national production averaged 150 features per year; in 1991, 400 features were made. A year later, there were fewer than 100.

As in India and other countries of unpredictable production, very few completed films found their way into theaters. Attendance dropped to around one-tenth of theater capacity, as were most of the upstart entrepreneurs. The devaluation of the ruble increased production costs tenfold, and top directors could not get their films released. Although the Hollywood Majors refused to release new films until the USSR took antipiracy measures, old or cheap Hollywood pictures dominated the market, capturing 70 percent of audiences.

The final years of Soviet cinema were nevertheless prestigious ones. Filmmakers joined writers and composers as representatives of a vigorous, eclectic culture. Not since the 1960s had so many Soviet films won praise in the West. *Taxi Blues* (1990, Pavel Loungine), a Soviet-French effort, portrays a decaying urbanism and amoral, rudderless characters (**Color Plate 25.31**). Vitaly Kanevsky's *Freeze, Die, Come to Life!* (1990), a "black film," suggests the savagery and spite pervading contemporary Soviet life by means of a story about children's corruption in a village during World War II (**25.41**). The Ukrainian-Canadian production *Swan Lake: The Zone* (1990), directed by the veteran Yuri Ilienko from a story by Paradzhanov, renders a political fable with Bressonian asceticism. An escapee from a prison camp hides in a gigantic, hollow hammer-and-sickle sign. The ponderous symbolism of the looming, rusting emblem is counterbalanced by a rich sonic texture and a painstaking rendering of the man's cramped, dank shelter.

The End of the Soviet System   An aborted coup against Gorbachev in August 1991 triggered the dissolution of the Communist party. Boris Yeltsin ascended to leadership, and the USSR was replaced by the Commonwealth of Independent States (CIS). Now Russia, the Ukraine, Armenia, and other former Soviet republics would function as separate nations. The cold war that had ruled world political strategy since World War II was ended.

Like their counterparts in eastern Europe, CIS filmmakers were eager for productions with the West. Yet the "common European home" envisaged by Gorbachev, a huge market stretching from the Atlantic to the Ural Mountains, was not taking shape. The CIS had a collapsed economy, a steeply declining standard of living, and modern problems of crime and drug addiction. The European Community proved reluctant to aid or assimilate CIS nations.

Communism may have failed as a political ideology, but well-connected party officials grew rich in the frenzy of privatization. In Russia, organized crime moved into government and major industries. Amidst charges of corruption, Yeltsin was succeeded in 2000 by former KGB agent Vladimir Putin, who continued the punitive war against breakaway region Chechnya. As Russia defaulted on its debts, the economy stumbled from crisis to crisis, crashing in 1998 and only slightly recovering in 2000. Buildings and streets were crumbling, and the population, among the sickest in the world, was shrinking fast. In light of all this, foreign investors stayed out.

The CIS film industries moved in synchronization with the boom-and-bust cycle. British, French, and Italian film companies launched "international" pictures featuring prominent western stars in CIS locales. Mosfilm, Lenfilm, and other studios became service facilities for runaway productions. Because the studios attracted cash, the state resisted privatizing them, but it did foster tax concessions for film investment. Cowboy capitalism reigned. In the mid-1990s, Vladimir Gusinsky's Media-Most emerged as the dominant private force, funding several films and seeking, unsuccessfully, to take over the state-protected Mosfilm studios. A few years later, Gusinsky was hiding in Spain, resisting extradition to Russia to answer charges of fraud.

Despite overwhelming video piracy, the Hollywood studios cautiously sent films in, but Russia hardly constituted a major market. In 1999, even though they dominated the theaters, Hollywood releases took in less than $9 million at the box office. Most of the twenty to forty Russian films made each year played only at state-funded local festivals. A few Russian films earned overseas attention, with several being nominated for Academy Awards and one, Nikita Mikhalkov's *Burnt by the Sun* (1994), winning an Oscar. Returning to 1953, Alexei Guerman's *Khroustaliov, My Car!* (1998), shows a doctor caught up in the paranoia of Kremlin leaders right after Stalin's death. With the camera squeezing through overstuffed parlors and kitchens, it presents a comic phantasmagoria of a bloated and decaying society.

Sokurov and the Tarkovsky Tradition   Aleksandr Sokurov had been making films for twenty years before he attracted strong attention outside Russia. His first feature, *The Solitary Voice of a Man* (1978; shelved until 1987), harks back to the 1920s avant-garde in its elliptical narrative and crisp montage, but it also has a disturbingly dreamlike quality that would typify much of his work. Sokurov initially became known for his literary adaptations, but after glasnost, usually with foreign financing, he was able to develop his expressionistic side. *The Second Circle* (1990), a stark black-and-white exercise, examines the minutiae of a primal ritual: in the space of ninety-two minutes, a son prepares his father's corpse for burial. *Whispering Pages* (1992) meditates on Nikolay Gogol and Fyodor Dostoevsky, with an apparently entranced hero drifting along murky canals and through cavernous tunnels. We glimpse the action dimly, through drifting haze; occasionally white birches are superimposed on the scene.

Sokurov's most widely seen expressionist exercise was *Mother and Son* (1997). A companion piece to *The Second Circle*, it shows a young man visiting his ailing mother. He carries her out from her farmhouse and reads to her. He takes her back inside. He wanders out into a vast, phantasmic landscape. He returns to find her dead, and he lays his face on her hand. Almost completely without dialogue, *Mother and Son* creates a piercing sense of loss through the simplicity of its situation and Sokurov's daring use of distorting lenses and filters. He films the landscape through paint-streaked glass, a "special effect" that creates an unearthly realm halfway between realism and abstraction (**Color Plate 25.32**).

Sokurov had Tarkovsky's unswerving seriousness in exploring a mournful spirituality. He maintained, however, that Tarkovsky's influence on his generation was not wholly beneficial: "A director [today] doesn't think of himself as a professional who can make a drama, a comedy, a thriller, et cetera. . . . It's called Tarkovschina [the Tarkovsky syndrome]—to be great philosophers and make unwatchable films."[18] Sokurov may have thought his later films, emblematic dramas involving major historical figures (Hitler in *Moloch*, 1999; Lenin in *Tauris*, 2001), would reach wider audiences, but the true populist was Alexei Balabanov. His gritty action film *Brother* (1997) centered on a soldier returning from Chechnya who becomes a hired killer. It became the most popular Russian film of the post-Soviet period. Balabanov produced a sequel called, in true Hollywood fashion, *Brother II* (2000).

As the market for U.S. films expanded in the 1970s, Hollywood's European competitors were forced to rely on export markets and cross-national financing. During the postwar decades, European filmmakers relied on governmentally overseen coproductions, but in the 1970s and 1980s, coproductions were also funded by the EU and media empires. Soviet and central European directors like Tarkovsky, Kieślowski, and Tarr also benefited from these initiatives. More broadly, European film production was torn between individual nations' demands for films that reflected their uniqueness and pressures toward EU solidarity in order to fight Hollywood.

The strengthening of European unity and the collapse of communism accelerated pressures toward less overtly political, more accessible cinema—the pan-European film. Some filmmakers, like Germany's von Trotta, Spain's Almodóvar, and France's Jeunet, sought to entice audiences with variants upon the popular genres and art-cinema conventions pioneered in earlier eras. Yet other directors, from Loach and Pialat to Duras and Sokurov, remained wedded to more difficult cinema, offering either uncomfortable realism or formal experiment. By maintaining the gap between auteur cinema and popular film, they consigned many European products, from West or East, to the festival circuit.

Notes and Queries

THE NEW GERMAN CINEMA

French Impressionist or Italian Neorealist cinema can be discussed as a group of filmmakers sharing broad assumptions about film form, style, and subject. After the early 1960s, however, most new cinemas in both West and East were not clear-cut stylistic movements. During this era, a new cinema often consisted of younger filmmakers who happened to make films that won international recognition.

The New German Cinema offers an example. Most historians consider it to be a development out of Young German Film (pp. 456–457). It includes several diverse trends: the political wing we discussed in Chapter 23 (pp. 572–576), the sensibilist trend (pp. 618–620), and diverse works of female, gay, and lesbian directors (pp. 597–599). By the late 1980s, New German Cinema had become a broad term for all independent filmmaking in West Germany since the 1960s, and many historians believed it continued into the 1990s.

The term itself played a concrete historical role. In the 1970s, international film culture took young filmmakers as representatives of a "new German cinema" as yet unacknowledged in their homeland. The New York Film Festival, the Cannes festival, the Museum of Modern Art, and other institutions helped build up the sense of a new trend in international art cinema. After directors such as Fassbinder, Herzog, and Wenders won recognition outside Germany, their reputations became elevated at home. State support of production was accompanied by initiatives from cultural agencies such as the Goethe Institute, which helped promote the director-based Autorenfilm in other countries by circulating films and subsidizing filmmakers to tour with their works.

For some historians, the radical edge of the 1960s and 1970s films was blunted as the films became absorbed into the European art cinema. By 1979, when Schlöndorff's *Tin Drum*, Fassbinder's *Marriage of Maria Braun*, Herzog's *Nosferatu*, and von Trotta's *Sisters* won international acclaim, the process of assimilation had become evident. During the 1980s, new directors—particularly women—received government and television funding, and several of them gained international recognition. Once in place, the idea of a "new" national cinema could be developed and exploited by the nation as a sign of cultural prestige.

For extensive discussions of how the New German Cinema came to be treated as a distinctive trend in film history, see Eric Rentschler, *West German Film in the Course of Time* (Bedford Hills, NY: Redgrave, 1984), and Thomas Elsaesser, *New German Cinema: A History* (New Brunswick, NJ: Rutgers University Press, 1989).

REFERENCES

1. René Cleitman, director of Hachette Premiere Films, quoted in Peter Bart, "Too Little or Too Much?" *Variety* (24 May 1993): 5.
2. Margarethe von Trotta, "Female Film Aesthetics," in Eric Rentschler, ed., *West German Filmmakers on Film: Visions and Voices* (New York: Holmes & Meier, 1988), p. 89.
3. Quoted in Marc Silberman, "Women Filmmakers in West Germany: A Catalog," *Camera Obscura* 6 (fall 1980): 128.
4. Quoted in "Iosseliani on Iosseliani," in *The 24th Hong Kong International Film Festival Catalogue* (Hong Kong: Urban Council, 2000), p. 138.
5. Quoted in Timothy Corrigan, *New German Film: The Displaced Image* (Austin: University of Texas Press, 1983), p. 146.
6. Quoted in Alan Greenberg, *Heart of Glass* (Munich: Skellig, 1976), p. 174.
7. Wim Wenders, "Three LPs by Van Morrison," in Jan Dawson, ed., *Wim Wenders* (New York: Zoetrope, 1976), p. 30.
8. Wim Wenders, "Impossible Stories," in *The Logic of Images: Essays and Conversations*, trans. Michael Hofmann (London: Faber, 1991), p. 59.
9. Mikhail Gorbachev, "A Common European Home," in Gale Stokes, ed., *From Stalinism to Pluralism: A Documentary History of Eastern Europe since 1945* (New York: Oxford University Press, 1991), p. 266.
10. Quoted in Vladimir Tismaneau, *Reinventing Politics: Eastern Europe from Stalin to Havel* (New York: Free Press, 1992), p. 134.
11. Quoted in Barbara Koenig Quart, *Women Directors: The Emergence of a New Cinema* (New York: Praeger, 1988), p. 193.
12. Quoted in "*Damnation:* Jonathan Romney Talks to Béla Tarr," *Enthusiasm* 4 (summer 2001): 3.
13. Andrzej Wajda, "The Artist's Responsibility," in David W. Paul, ed., *Politics, Art and Commitment in the East European Cinema* (New York: St. Martin's, 1983), p. 299.
14. Quoted in Danusia Stok, *Kieślowski on Kieślowski* (London: Faber, 1993), p. 144.
15. Waldemar Dziki, quoted in Andrew Nagorski, "Sleeping without the Enemy," *Newsweek* (19 August 1991): 56.
16. Andrei Tarkovsky, *Sculpting in Time: Reflections on the Cinema,* trans. Kitty Hunter-Blair (London: Faber, 1989), p. 117.
17. Ibid., p. 27.
18. Quoted in George Faraday, *Revolt of the Filmmakers: The Struggle for Artistic Autonomy and the Fall of the Soviet Film Industry* (University Park: Pennsylvania State University, 2000), p. 165.

FURTHER READING

Austin, Guy. *Contemporary French Cinema: An Introduction.* Manchester: Manchester University Press, 1996.
Corrigan, Timothy. *New German Film: The Displaced Image.* Austin: University of Texas Press, 1983.
———. *The Films of Werner Herzog: Between Mirage and History.* New York: Methuen, 1986.
Dale, Martin. *The Movie Game: The Film Business in Britain, Europe and America.* London: Cassell, 1997.
Dibie, Jean Noël. *Les mecanismes de financement du cinéma et de l'audiovisual en Europe.* Paris: Dixit, 1992.
Elsaesser, Thomas. *Fassbinder's Germany: History, Identity, Subject.* Amsterdam: Amsterdam University Press, 1996.
Finney, Angus. *The State of European Cinema: A New Dose of Reality.* London: Cassell, 1996.
Forbes, Gill. *The Cinema in France after the New Wave.* London: Macmillan, 1992.
Goulding, Daniel J. *Post New Wave Cinema in the Soviet Union and Eastern Europe.* Bloomington: Indiana University Press, 1989.
Hjort, Mette, and Ib Bondebjerg. *The Danish Directors: Dialogues on a Contemporary National Cinema.* Bristol, England: Intellect, 2001.
Horton, Andrew, ed. *The Last Modernist: The Films of Theo Angelopoulos.* Westport, CT: Praeger, 1997.
Horton, Andrew, and Michael Brashinsky. *The Zero Hour: Glasnost and Soviet Cinema in Transition.* Princeton, NJ: Princeton University Press, 1992.
Kolker, Robert Phillip, and Peter Beicker. *The Films of Wim Wenders: Cinema as Vision and Desire.* Cambridge: Cambridge University Press, 1993.
Kotkin, Stephen. *Armageddon Averted: The Soviet Collapse, 1970–2000.* (New York: Oxford University Press, 2001).
Magny, Joël. *Maurice Pialat.* Paris: Cahiers du Cinéma, 1992.
Menashe, Louis. "Moscow Believes in Tears: The Problems (and Promise?) of Russian Cinema in the Transition Period." *Cineaste* 26, no. 3 (summer 2001): 10–17.
Portuges, Catherine. *Screen Memories: The Hungarian Cinema of Márta Mészáros.* Bloomington: Indiana University Press, 1993.
Prédal, René. *Le Cinéma français contemporain.* Paris: Cerf, 1984.
Silberman, Marc. "Women Filmmakers in West Germany: A Catalogue." *Camera Obscura* no. 6 (fall 1980): 123–51; no. 11 (fall 1983): 133–45.
Smith, Paul Julian. *Desire Unlimited: The Cinema of Pedro Almodóvar.* London: British Film Institute, 2000.

CHAPTER 26

BEYOND THE INDUSTRIALIZED WEST: LATIN AMERICA, THE ASIA-PACIFIC REGION, THE MIDDLE EAST, AND AFRICA SINCE THE 1970s

Since cinema's invention, Europe and the United States have dominated world filmmaking by their influence but not, however, by sheer numbers. In the 1960s, while filmgoing was in decline in the industrialized West, the audience expanded in most other regions, largely because of steady migration from the countryside to the cities. To satisfy this growing urban public, film production expanded in many countries. In 1950, the world was releasing about 2,000 features per year, but by 1980 Asia alone was producing that many. Needless to say, most of these films would never be seen in the West. The larger national industries, such as India, Japan, and the People's Republic of China, aimed to satisfy domestic tastes. Moreover, some films, such as those of India and Hong Kong, were also able to move across national boundaries and become powerful regional forces.

In the early 1970s, Japan was the world's most prolific filmmaking country, but in 1975 India surpassed it with 450 films. (By the early 1990s, output would level off at an astonishing 900 films per year.) The romantic, colorful Hindi films, always adorned with exuberant music, won a huge audience across the developing world. Production in South Korea, Pakistan, and the Philippines also expanded. By 1975, Asian countries outside India and Japan yielded one-quarter of the world's entire feature output.

Most other countries could not match this scale of production, but all catered to local audiences and nearly all tried to send their films abroad. In Latin America and Africa, government support was as volatile as the regional politics. Australia and New Zealand were stabler, and their filmmakers benefited from government support and interest from Hollywood. Some Middle Eastern states, though isolated by politics and religion, could sustain an industry and some regional export. For all, the

633

burgeoning film festival scene provided some distribution of quality cinema. Several countries—notably Australia, mainland China, Taiwan, Iran, and South Korea—achieved worldwide renown at various times after 1970.

FROM THIRD WORLD TO DEVELOPING NATIONS

Japan, Australia, and New Zealand, the mature economies and social democracies of the Pacific area, did not face the problems of their Asian neighbors or of Africa and Latin America. As radicals' hopes for social change faded in these poorer countries, belief in the Third World as a distinct political force seemed less plausible. Nonetheless, economists began to describe these regions as the "developing world," pointing out that life expectancy and literacy had increased, employees' earnings were growing, and the "green revolution" in agricultural practices had expanded food productivity. Some economies began to thrive. South Korea, Hong Kong, Singapore, and Taiwan, for example, became energetic manufacturing and investment centers.

Overall, however, prospects for the developing world were even grimmer than they had been in the period before 1975. Many nations were ruled by military juntas or charismatic dictators. The gap between rich and poor countries widened catastrophically: by 1989, the top fifth of the world's population had become sixty times richer than the bottom fifth. Mechanized farming increased rural unemployment, forcing families to migrate to urban areas. The developing countries had fifteen of the world's biggest cities, usually ringed by shantytowns and squatters' camps.

Most countries failed to substitute new products for the exports they had relied on in the colonial era, and their debt to the West rose dizzyingly. Simultaneously, the industrial countries, shaken by the oil shocks of 1973 and 1979, began to cut foreign aid. A world recession in the early 1980s only intensified developing nations' financial problems. As the International Monetary Fund (IMF) imposed austerity measures on debtor nations, hunger riots erupted in Brazil, Tunisia, Algeria, and Venezuela.

The underdeveloped nations were also torn by wars—conflicts with neighbors, as in the Middle East and Southeast Asia, or civil struggles, as in the guerrilla wars of Latin America and the ethnic and religious strife of Africa. Disease began to spread; in 1988, one out of thirteen people in Zaire carried HIV. Perhaps most alarming,

populations were expanding unchecked. In 1977, three-quarters of the world's population lived in the developing nations. Based on the same rate of increase, estimates projected that these countries would be home to nearly 90 percent of the human race by 2026.

Huge as these social problems were, the developing world continued to play an important role in world cinema. Audiences remained large—200 million per year in Africa, nearly 800 million in Latin America, and several billion in India. At the end of the 1980s, the nations in the developing world were producing about half of the 4,000 or so features made globally. Even where the Hollywood product commanded the lion's share of box-office receipts, cinema remained an important aspect of national cultures throughout the nonindustrialized Western world. In Asia, Latin America, and Africa, filmmakers gave voice to indigenous conceptions of national history, social life, and personal conduct. Cinema displayed a sense of regional, cross-national identity as well, as when some directors sought to express pan-African themes. In addition, some films from developing countries commanded the attention of industrialized nations, which made room for both popular entertainment and more unusual fare from its former colonies.

As in Europe, developing-nation governments discovered that if they wanted a national cinema, they would have to help pay for it. Most new cinemas were the result of state funding. Filmmakers also relied on coproduction arrangements with neighboring countries or with European firms—often countries that had been colonial rulers. Euzhan Palcy's *Rue cases nègres (Sugar Cane Alley*, Antilles, 1983) was financed by French concerns, while Japanese firms eagerly invested in the national cinemas of its former colonies Taiwan and South Korea.

The new cinemas that emerged from the developing world had virtually none of the stylistic or thematic coherence that characterized silent-film movements or Italian Neorealism. The New Argentine Cinema, India's Parallel Cinema, the Hong Kong New Wave, China's Fifth Generation—each rubric often lumped together very different directors.

Still, there were a few recurring elements. Because of the problems of developing nations, new cinemas often proposed political critiques. The heritage of revolutionary cinema lived on in films about dictators' abuse of power, the plight of families, ethnic conflict, and other sensitive issues. One of the more important realms of human rights involved women, long oppressed in developing countries. The United Nation's designation of the years 1975 to 1985 as the international "Decade

LATIN AMERICAN LITERATURE AND CINEMA

During the 1960s, Latin American writing became renowned throughout the world. The Mexican Carlos Fuentes (*The Death of Artemio Cruz,* 1962), the Argentine Julio Cortázar (*Hopscotch,* 1963), the Peruvian Mario Vargas Llosa (*The Green House,* 1966), and the Colombian Gabriel García Marquez (*One Hundred Years of Solitude,* 1967) were recognized as masters of a literature that mingled European influences with indigenous cultural sources.

Working in a vein of *lo real maravilloso* (Magical Realism), these writers spiced social realism with myth, fantasy, and fairy tales taken from popular culture. Episodic folktale plots might turn suddenly into symbolic labyrinths, full of images as disconcerting as those of European Surrealism. But whereas the Surrealists sought the liberation of the individual psyche, the fantastic imagery of Magical Realism sought to reflect the collective imagination of colonized peoples, for whom everyday reality was only one step away from the supernatural.

Latin American filmmaking had already been influenced by this strain in literature, as when Brazilian films took inspiration from the tropicalism of the prewar period (p. 474). During the 1980s, filmmakers began to develop the Magical Realist trend further. Often this involved adapting literary works, as in the six-part series *Difficult Loves* (1988); each film was derived from a story by García Marquez and signed by a major director from a different country. Other directors opted for more original mixtures of realism and fantasy, as in Eliseo Subiela's Borgesian *Conquest of Paradise* (Argentina, 1981) and *Man Looking Southeast* (1986).

A key example of Magical Realist film is Ruy Guerra's *Erendira* (Mexico, 1982), with a script by García Marquez. The beautiful Erendira undergoes a series of grotesque adventures, mostly involving the efforts of her Gorgon-like

26.1 Senator Onesimo's campaign is adorned by a huge billboard ship that mysteriously spouts smoke (*Erendira*).

grandmother to gain money from prostituting the girl. They travel across a vaguely modern Latin America, teeming with smugglers, corrupt police, and cynical politicians. Their home is a vast circus tent, housing statues, a huge boat, and a labyrinth of veiled and curtained corridors. The film leaps from the brutality of Erendira's exploitation to lyrical fantasy: handbills turn into birds, blue fish swim through the air, a political rally becomes a fairy-tale spectacle (**26.1**).

The dynamic relations between film and fiction were also seen in the ways in which Latin American writers absorbed the lessons of popular cinema. Gabriel Cabrera Infante's novels sought to capture the raucous vulgarity of movies. Manuel Puig's novel *Kiss of the Spider Woman* (1976) drew plots from Hollywood B pictures; the process of appropriation came full circle when the novel was filmed in 1984. Latin American cinema won a place in world film markets partly through its ties with a prestigious literary trend.

---

of the Woman" helped groups address day care, abortion, rape, and other pertinent issues. In the same period, female filmmakers began to enter production, often focusing on women's concerns.

Even when directors took on political subjects or themes, most continued the movement of the early 1970s away from radical experimentation. Politically critical films from the developing world tended to rely on conventions of classical narrative or of art-cinema modernism (particularly the interplay between objective realism, subjective realism, and authorial commentary). These strategies enabled filmmakers to reach wider audiences. By abandoning extreme political modernism, they gained some access to festivals and distributors in the First World.

LATIN AMERICA: ACCESSIBILITY AND DECLINE

During the 1970s, military governments took power in much of South and Central America. Brazil, Bolivia, Uruguay, Chile, and Argentina all fell under military dictatorships. After 1978, pluralist democracy returned to most Latin American countries, but the new governments faced colossal inflation rates, declining productivity,

26.12 *The Funeral:* a family member takes a snapshot. "Get a little closer to the coffin. Look sad."

actor, a screenwriter, and an author since the 1960s. Itami's *The Funeral* (1985; **26.12**), *Tampopo* (1986), and *A Taxing Woman* (1987) are mordant satires of contemporary Japanese life. Full of physical comedy and mockery of the new consumerist Japan, they became highly exportable items and made Itami the most visible Japanese director of the 1980s.

The success of the "New Japanese Cinema" was undergirded by industrial factors. As in the United States, the decline in attendance leveled off; by the late 1970s, it stabilized at around 150 million annually. The market could support about 250 films per year, although at least half of these would be low-budget, soft-core pornography. Producers sought filmmakers willing to turn out inexpensive films attuned to the free-spending younger audience.

Yet even offbeat films faced increasingly stiff competition from U.S. firms. In 1976, for the first time, receipts from foreign films surpassed those from Japanese films. By the end of the 1980s, most of each year's top-grossing films were American, and Japanese films made up only about one-third of all features released. Japan replaced Britain as Hollywood's biggest foreign market.

The film industry, facing few export prospects and sharper competition at home, drew some hope from its new directors and from favorable tax laws that encouraged motion-picture investments. In addition, the studios' control of exhibition guaranteed them a share of Hollywood's income. Yet even this security was shaken in 1993, when Time Warner, in partnership with a Japanese supermarket chain, opened a chain of multiplex theaters. Slowly the Big Three launched multiplexes of their own.

In the meantime, Japanese business was coming to terms with Hollywood in another arena. By 1980, the country was supreme in manufacturing automobiles, watches, motorcycles, cameras, and electronic goods. Japan replaced the United States as the world's major creditor, holding the largest banks and insurance companies and investing billions of dollars in foreign companies and real estate. During the same period, investment companies began funneling hundreds of millions of dollars to Hollywood firms. With the launching of pay television and high-definition television, Japanese media companies needed attractive material of the sort that Hollywood could provide.

Most spectacularly, Japanese manufacturers of consumer electronics were buying Hollywood studios. Sony purchased Columbia Pictures Entertainment for $3.4 billion in 1989, while Matsushita Electric Industrial Company paid $6 billion for Music Corporation of America, the parent company of Universal Pictures. The latter was the largest investment any Japanese company had ever made in a U.S. firm. Matsushita eventually pulled out, selling MCA/Universal to Seagram. After purchasing Columbia, Sony had a rocky time of it at first, eventually writing off over $1 billion in debt. Still, Japanese firms had shown their desire to operate as global media players.

The 1990s: The Punctured Bubble and a New Surge of Talent

Japan's boom decades were followed by a steep and prolonged recession, with falling stock prices and real estate values bringing the economy to a halt. The long-ruling Liberal Democratic party, repeatedly exposed as corrupt, could respond only by sinking more money into the construction industry. In this climate, the vertically integrated movie companies became even more stagnant. They preserved their power at the box office through superior distribution power and the tradition of forcing employees of the studios or of allied businesses to buy movie tickets. For the world outside Japan, the interesting films were largely independent products, and fresh talent began to attract festival prizes and foreign distribution.

Young directors, many of whom started with 8mm student films, began to win acclaim. Shinji Aoyama's melancholy and disturbing *Eureka* (2000) galvanized festivals. The film begins with a brother and sister taken hostage on a bus, but the film is not a conventional action picture (**26.13**); instead it focuses on the efforts of the bus driver to heal the teenagers' wounded lives after the crisis. Shunji Iwai directed the offbeat romance *Love Letter* (1995) and the dystopian fantasy *Swallowtail Butterfly* (1996). The tirelessly self-promoting Sabu (Hiroyuki Tanaka) made post-Tarantino genre exercises

26.13 *Eureka:* the bus driver and a policeman at the mercy of the hijacker.

26.14 A team of sumo misfits and their cheerful cheerleader (*Sumo Do, Sumo Don't*).

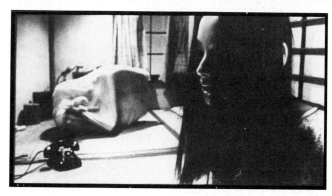

26.15 In *Audition*, the salaryman's chosen woman answers his call; unbeknownst to him, a mysterious sack (containing a previous lover?) thrashes helplessly behind her.

26.16 A typical Kitano "clothesline" composition (*Sonatine*).

like *Dangan Runner* (1996), about three men chasing through Tokyo, and *Sunday* (2000), about a young salaryman dragged into a gang war. Several filmmakers examined gay sexuality; Ryosuke Hashiguchi's *Like Grains of Sand* (1995) presented a sensitive study of schoolboys exploring their affection for each other.

More in the mainstream was Masayuki Suo, who sought to revive early-Ozu comedy in a series of films about young people, notably *Shiko Funjatta* (aka *Sumo Do, Sumo Don't*, 1992), centering on the adventures of a college Sumo team (**26.14**). Suo found international success with his wistful salaryman comedy *Shall We Dance?* (1995). Likewise, Hirokozu Koreeda won attention with *Maborosi* (1995), a subdued drama of a widow learning to love her second husband. The stately, often distant, compositions celebrate the beauty of everyday life (**Color Plate 26.8**) and the forbidding but fascinating seaside landscape of the community in which the wife finds herself. Koreeda's *After Life* (1998) presents a benevolent limbo in which the dead are allowed to record their most precious memory on film.

Many of the most intriguing directors worked in downscale genres. Kyoshi Kurosawa (no relation to Akira Kurosawa) loosed a barrage of enigmatic and shocking works, using crime plots or horror conventions in quirky ways. *Cure* (1997) is about a detective tracking a killer who is able to control his victim's minds. *Kairo* (aka *Pulse*, 2001) suggests that ghosts haunt the Internet. Takeshi Miike, Kurosawa's contemporary, also reworked pulp material, turning out movies at a pace no less frantic than that of the plots. *Fudoh: The New Generation* (1996) centers on schoolboy gangsters and schoolgirl assassins. *Dead or Alive* (1999) is a hard-driving crime movie, while *Audition* (1999) begins as a slightly perverse romance (a salaryman auditions women as girlfriends) and ends in carnage (when he gets more than he bargained for; **26.15**).

The most significant director of the 1990s was Takeshi Kitano (aka "Beat" Takeshi). Japanese audiences loved him as a TV comedian but turned away from his movies. It was on the international scene that he won praise for brutal yakuza movies such as *Boiling Point* (1990), *Sonatine* (1993), and *Hana-bi* (1997). Kitano cultivated a deadpan style of performance and image design, with characters often facing the camera, lined up like figures in a simple comic strip (**26.16**). They speak seldom, stare at each other, and remain strangely frozen when violence flares up. Kitano's films compel attention by unashamedly alternating brusque rhythm with almost childish poignancy, especially when he returns to his favorite motifs—sports, adolescent pranks, flowers, the sea. His sense of color has a naive immediacy (**Color Plate 26.9**), and he warms his spare visuals with the cartoonish tinkle of Joe Hisaishi's musical scores. Kitano's work outside the yakuza genre includes *A Scene at the Sea* (1991), a wistful tale of a deaf-mute couple, and his coming-of-age movie *Kids Return* (1996).

In the late 1990s, Japanese horror won new audiences with a cycle of mystical Japanese films about a videocassette that kills anyone who watches it (*Ring*, 1998, and its sequels). The Asian craze for *Ring* resembled the western response to *The Blair Witch Project* (1999). Still, anime remained Japan's most popular film export, with 250 hours of it produced each year. The new god of anime was Hayao Miyazaki. His charming features *My Neighbor Totoro* (1988) and *Kiki's Delivery Service* (1989) made their way to Europe and North America slowly, but they became perennials of video rental. *Princess Mononoke* (1997) blends Miyazaki's splendid linear style with selective use of computer techniques to enhance cel animation (**Color Plate 26.10**).

Miyazaki's works broke local box-office records; *Spirited Away* (2001) became the top-grossing Japanese film to date and the first non-U.S. film to earn more than $200 million outside the United States. But such rare hits could not revive the Japanese industry. At the end of the 1990s, 250 or more features were being made each year, most going unseen. Average yearly attendance hovered at one visit per person, and the Big Three studios clung to power. Nonetheless, the scale of Japanese investments overseas ensured the nation a central place in international film commerce, and a surge of excellent films brought new attention to one of the world's most venerable national cinemas.

MAINLAND CHINA: THE FIFTH GENERATION AND BEYOND

"To make money is glorious!" With this slogan, Deng Xiaoping announced the Chinese government's intention to redeem China's economy and encourage mildly capitalistic reforms. Marketing of privately grown agricultural produce, joint ventures with foreign companies, and other types of free enterprise were introduced. Yet China's leadership tried to promote these economic reforms without liberalizing individual rights.

During China's Cultural Revolution (1966–1976), few films were made (p. 551) and the Beijing Film Acad-

emy was closed. Under the new and more open policies, the cinema began slowly to recover.

To supply the theaters while production was geared up, hundreds of banned pre-1966 films were rereleased. Foreign films were again imported, and Chinese filmmakers could see works from the European art cinema of the 1960s and 1970s.

Production climbed steadily, from 19 features (1977) to 125 (1986). Most films made soon after the Cultural Revolution tended to revert to the polished studio style. *Rickshaw Boy* (1982, Ling Zifeng), a melodrama set in the prerevolutionary period, concerns a man who loses his rickshaw and must rent one from his boss, whose daughter pressures him into marrying her. Meanwhile, a young woman living in the same courtyard has to become a prostitute in order to support her brothers. All the characters in the film meet unhappy endings. This glossy studio picture recalled *The New Year's Sacrifice* and other 1950s works (p. 405).

A few films, however, began to imitate European models. Yang Yanjin and Deng Yimin's *Bitter Laughter* (1979), set during the Cultural Revolution, centers on a journalist forced to write inaccurate stories. *Bitter Laughter*'s style reflects art-cinema influences, using flashbacks, vision scenes, and many special effects to convey subjectivity. Yang, who had graduated just before the Beijing Film Academy closed in 1968, went on to make *The Alley* (1981), a film that offers three alternative endings. Wu Yigong's *My Memories of Old Beijing* (1980) consists of three stories in flashback, filtered through a little girl. While Cultural Revolution policies had favored films with simple character types and unambiguous meanings, these films utilized psychological depth, symbolism, and ambiguity.

The Fifth Generation

Chinese film historians have typically slotted filmmakers into generations associated with major political events. The Fourth Generation of filmmakers began their careers following the Revolution of 1949. Their most prominent member was Xie Jin, who directed *Two Stage Sisters* (p. 406).

The Beijing Film Academy reopened in 1978, admitting a new class into the four-year program. In 1982, the graduates, along with a few directors who worked their way up the studio ranks, formed what was known as the Fifth Generation. Several of these became the first Chinese filmmakers whose work was widely known abroad. These students had had unusual training. During the Cultural Revolution, education had emphasized

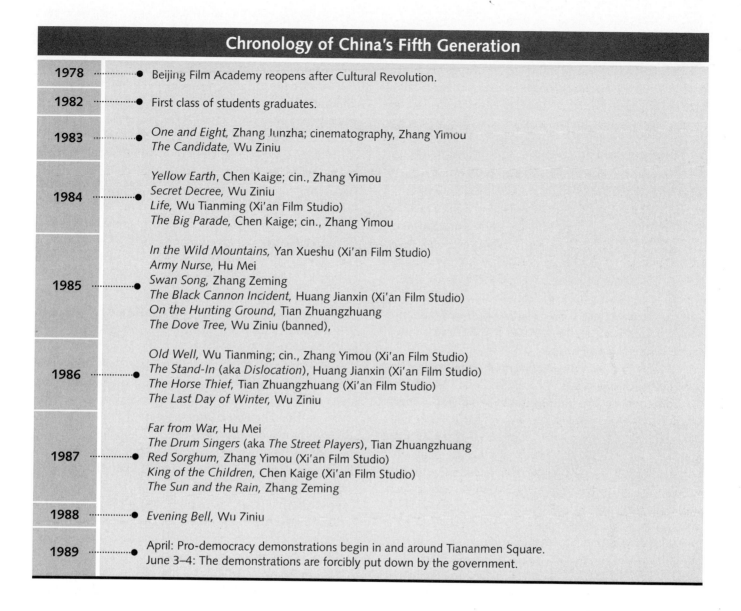

Chronology of China's Fifth Generation

1978 ....● Beijing Film Academy reopens after Cultural Revolution.

1982 ....● First class of students graduates.

1983 ....● *One and Eight*, Zhang Junzha; cinematography, Zhang Yimou
The Candidate, Wu Ziniu

1984 ....● *Yellow Earth*, Chen Kaige; cin., Zhang Yimou
Secret Decree, Wu Ziniu
Life, Wu Tianming (Xi'an Film Studio)
The Big Parade, Chen Kaige; cin., Zhang Yimou

1985 ....● *In the Wild Mountains*, Yan Xueshu (Xi'an Film Studio)
Army Nurse, Hu Mei
Swan Song, Zhang Zeming
The Black Cannon Incident, Huang Jianxin (Xi'an Film Studio)
On the Hunting Ground, Tian Zhuangzhuang
The Dove Tree, Wu Ziniu (banned),

1986 ....● *Old Well*, Wu Tianming; cin., Zhang Yimou (Xi'an Film Studio)
The Stand-In (aka *Dislocation*), Huang Jianxin (Xi'an Film Studio)
The Horse Thief, Tian Zhuangzhuang (Xi'an Film Studio)
The Last Day of Winter, Wu Ziniu

1987 ....● *Far from War*, Hu Mei
The Drum Singers (aka *The Street Players*), Tian Zhuangzhuang
Red Sorghum, Zhang Yimou (Xi'an Film Studio)
King of the Children, Chen Kaige (Xi'an Film Studio)
The Sun and the Rain, Zhang Zeming

1988 ....● *Evening Bell*, Wu Ziniu

1989 ....● April: Pro-democracy demonstrations begin in and around Tiananmen Square.
June 3–4: The demonstrations are forcibly put down by the government.

---

rote learning, mostly based on Mao's writings. Fifth Generation filmmakers, however, were not taught exactly what to think. Chen Kaige, one of the most famous members of the group, recalled his education:

> I really appreciated my teachers because they didn't know how to teach us. They hadn't taught anybody for ten years. They were very openminded. They said they would not teach the old way they used to, the old-fashioned way. We would see films, work nights, and have discussions.[3]

These students saw many imported films and proved susceptible to their influence. By 1983, the works of these Fifth Generation filmmakers were being released (see box).

Traditionally, each academy graduate was permanently assigned to a studio in Beijing, Shanghai, or the provinces. Several Fifth Generation filmmakers broke this pattern, moving about to find interesting work. Chen Kaige, for example, was assigned to the Beijing Film Studio, but he went instead to join a fellow graduate, cinematographer Zhang Yimou, at the Guangxi studio, where they made *Yellow Earth* and *The Big Parade*. Tian Zhuangzhuang, also delegated to the Beijing Film Studio, could get no directional work, and so he went to the tiny Inner Mongolia Film Studio to make *On the Hunting Ground*.

Virtually all the Fifth Generation films were made at such provincial studios. The most significant was the Xi'an Film Studio, a medium-size facility in central China. It had had a poor record before Wu Tianming took over as its head in 1983. Wu, an actor who had begun directing in 1979, became a patron to the Fifth Generation, hiring young filmmakers and giving them artistic freedom. As the chronology in the box indicates, over a third of the Fifth Generation films were made at Xi'an. Wu also asked cinematographer Zhang Yimou to come from Guangxi to photograph *Old Well*. Zhang agreed on condition that he then be allowed to direct. His film, *Red Sorghum*, became the most popular early Fifth Generation work, both in China and abroad.

The Fifth Generation filmmakers, influenced by European art films, reacted against the Cultural Revolution. Whereas Cultural Revolution films used character types, the younger directors favored psychological depth. Instead of presenting simple tales with clear-cut meanings, they adopted complex narratives, ambiguous symbolism, and vivid, evocative imagery. Their films remained political, but they strove to explore issues rather than restate approved policy.

Huang Jianxin's *The Black Cannon Incident* is a bitter satire on bureaucracy. A German adviser supervising the assembly of heavy equipment in China needs a translator with technical expertise. The best translator happens to send a telegram concerning a "black cannon," a game piece. Mistaking the phrase for a code, party officials remove him from the job and launch an elaborate inquiry that eventually damages expensive equipment. Huang uses a series of flashbacks to follow the investigation. His color design aids the satire, as in a stylized set where the officials meet (**Color Plate 26.11**).

King of the Children, by Chen Kaige, also exemplifies how some of the Fifth Generation filmmakers emphasized narrative subtlety and striking visual design. A young man, sent to work in the countryside during the Cultural Revolution, is suddenly assigned to teach at a rural school. Trying to inspire the students to think for themselves rather than learn by rote, he runs afoul of his superiors and is dismissed. At the end, his departure from the village is interrupted by imagery of a fire sweeping over the countryside—perhaps symbolizing the devastation of the Cultural Revolution or the purifying effects of ending it. Such an ambiguous scene suggests the influence of European art cinema. Motifs of setting and color in *King of the Children* contrast the enclosed world of the school and the vast terrain surrounding it.

Some Fifth Generation films make even fewer concessions to popular entertainment. Tian Zhuangzhuang's *The Horse Thief*, for example, simply follows a horse thief and his family as they roam Tibet for a year. Tian does not explain Tibetan rituals and customs. The film's interest lies in its very exoticism and in its handsome shots of barren plains, mountains, and temples.

Most Fifth Generation films were criticized for being too obscure for peasants, who made up 80 percent of the Chinese population. China had no tradition of art theaters where specialized audiences could see such films. Whereas a popular film might circulate in a hundred or more copies, only six prints of *The Horse Thief* were made. Few Fifth Generation films did well financially, so Wu Tianming produced more popularly oriented films at Xi'an to balance the losses. In addition, because these films drew on foreign influences, they could be appreciated abroad more easily than most other Chinese films. The money earned by exporting Fifth Generation films helped the group to keep working.

Even as it was gaining fame abroad, however, the group began encountering more difficulties at home. During late 1986, a series of student protests for greater political reforms led the government to tighten control. It conducted a campaign against "bourgeois liberalization," including foreign influences. In cinema, officials demanded accessible, profitable films. As a result, during 1987 and 1988, some Fifth Generation filmmakers undertook more commercial projects. Tian Zhuangzhuang switched from the austere style of *The Horse Thief* and made a slick film called *Rock Kids*. Huang Jianxin and others worked in television. In 1987, Chen Kaige left for New York.

The government's violent suppression of the pro-democracy movement of 1989 brought an end to the Fifth Generation as a cohesive unit. Wu Tianming emigrated to California, while Huang Jianxin went to teach in Australia. Most of those who remained in China worked in popularly oriented film and television.

The Sixth Generation and Illegal Films

Directors who managed to keep working in their own styles often depended on foreign financing. Chen Kaige's *Life on a String* (1991) was produced with German, British, and Chinese backing. A legendlike story of a wandering blind musician and his apprentice, the film contains even more symbolism and ambiguities than Chen's earlier films. Filmed in China, it continues his reliance on expressionistic, overpowering landscape (**Color Plate 26.12**). Chen followed with the international art-house hit *Farewell My Concubine* (1993), *Temptress Moon* (1996), and *The Emperor and the Assassin* (1999), all international coproductions using Chinese facilities and labor but not made available to Chinese audiences.

Zhang Yimou stayed in China and made *Ju Dou* (1990) with Japanese funding. Its yellow-suffused cinematography evokes the dye shop in which the action is set (**Color Plate 26.13**). Zhang's sumptuous explorations of eroticism and the repression of women, such as *Raise the Red Lantern* (1991) and *Story of Qiu Ju* (1992), carried his films into art theaters abroad, but they were usually banned in China. Only after they won acclaim in the West would the government permit them to be released at home. The prolific Zhang continued balancing the tastes of the festival circuit with pressures from the government while making such films as *To Live* (1994) and *Not One Less* (1999).

Other Fifth Generation veterans eventually resumed ambitious projects. Huang Jianxin returned from exile to make a series of pointed social comedies. *Back to Back, Face to Face* (1994) uncovers the jockeying for power at a cultural affairs office. *Signal Left, Turn Right* (1996) centers on a group of people taking a drivers' training course, sympathetically surveying a range of social types from the drug-addicted young man to the ambitious executive and the mother who seeks to better life for her family.

Foreign funding often provided leverage. Wu Tianming, godfather to the Fifth Generation, came back to direct the poignant *The King of Masks* (1996), about an elderly street performer. The script was Taiwanese, bought by Shaw Brothers of Hong Kong. Tian Zhuangzhuang found European and Hong Kong financing for *The Blue Kite* (1994), a chronicle of a mother's search for her husband through the years 1953 to 1967, from the Great Leap Forward to the Cultural Revolution. In bold pictorial juxtapositions, Tian questions Maoist ideology and the sacrifices it demanded of the Chinese people (**26.17**).

While Tian, Chen, Zhang and other Fifth Generation directors remained internationally visible, a Sixth Generation came to the fore in the early 1990s. Most were not Beijing Film Academy graduates. Rather, they were independent directors who pursued their own visions of cinema. Their movement surfaced just as China began to back off from subsidizing its film studios. Studios that produced profitable films would be rewarded with the rights to attractive foreign imports. This was a compelling offer, since foreign imports, chiefly from Hong Kong and the United States, counted for as much as 40 percent of the urban box office.

The dilemma was that, although filmmakers no longer had to be attached to a studio, only studios could release films. Independent films, made without a distribution or exhibition permit, became *dixia dianying* ("il-

26.17   Mao oversees the life of the couple in *The Blue Kite*.

26.18   *Postman:* static, rectilinear framings create a bureaucratic world.

legal films"). One of the pioneers of illegal cinema was Zhang Yuan, who began his first film, *Mama* (1990), under studio auspices. After the Tiananmen Square assault, he raised completion money from businesses, edited the movie in a hotel room, and persuaded the Xi'an Studio to release it. His second feature, *Beijing Bastards* (1993), traveled to festivals without any studio imprimatur. *The Days* (1993), made underground for $14,000, was distributed abroad but not in China.

Centered on young people and social problems, Sixth Generation films did not fit into the government-sanctioned forms. Marital difficulties were at the center of *The Days*, while the Chinese rock culture was on display in *Beijing Bastards*. In *Postman* (1995), He Jianjun created a sparse, unsettling drama based on the premise—shocking to official ideology—that a postman might interfere with people's lives by reading and withholding their letters (**26.18**). Zhang Yuan's controversial *East Palace West Palace* (1996) portrays Beijing's gay cruising scene.

As illegal films triumphed at festivals, the government took sterner measures, raising obstacles to coproductions and foreign investment. After Zhang Yimou's *To Live* (1994) competed at Cannes without permission, authorities demanded that any film made in China, official or not, had to pass censorship to be shown abroad. Zhang had to offer a "self-criticism" in order to finish the French-financed *Shanghai Triad* (1994). After *The Blue Kite*, Tian Zhuangzhuang was blacklisted from any studio-based production. Directors were denied permission to leave the country, and the negatives of films shot in China were required to be deposited there until censors found them satisfactory. After *Postman*'s negative was smuggled out for completion in the Netherlands, the government also began to withhold approved films from any festivals that showed unapproved films.

This government suppression continued into the new century. Jiang Wen, one of China's most popular comedians, ran afoul of officialdom with his World War II film *Devils on the Doorstep* (2000). The film begins as a humorous portrayal of wartime culture clash, as a villager keeps two Japanese soldiers prisoner in exchange for food. When the Japanese retake the village, a Chinese horse mounts a Japanese donkey, and the tone switches instantly from comedy to horror as an evening feast turns into a massacre. *Devils on the Doorstep* won the Jury Prize at Cannes, but that seemed only to deepen Jiang's difficulties. As punishment for not submitting his work to censors, the film was forbidden to be shown at home or abroad, and Jiang was banned from filming or acting in China for seven years.

China's long-standing studio system of production was finished, supplying only facilities and a trademark to independent films and foreign coproductions. The most successful films were usually foreign imports, and thanks to pirated video the public could avoid the official didactic films. In this climate, directors were encouraged to create audience-pleasing commercial products, such as He Ping's *Red Firecracker, Green Firecracker* (1994). Feng Xiaogang became China's most popular filmmaker by concentrating on amusing fare showcasing the comedian Ge You. His *Be There or Be Square* (1998) centered on two mainland conmen who move to a crime-ridden Los Angeles in search of the good life. Funded by private investors, the film became the second-highest grossing film in Chinese history (following *Titanic*). Feng baited critics by declaring that he loved making money and scorned art-house movies.

Yet art-house-oriented filmmakers found ways to dodge sanctions. Lou Ye's dreamlike *Vertigo* homage, *Suzhou River* (2000; **26.19**), plunges young drifters into kidnapping, but the lyrical handling (reminiscent of Hong

26.19 The mysterious kidnapped girl seems reincarnated (*Suzhou River*).

Kong's Wong Kar-wai, p. 658) softens its harsh portrayal of Shanghai street life. Like *The Blue Kite*, *Platform* (2000) undertook an ambitious survey of recent Chinese history. Director-writer Jia Zhang-ke follows a provincial acting troupe through the post-Mao period, tracing how traditions erode and young people start to question their elders' authority. *Platform*'s long-take style suggested that Chinese cinema was being influenced by Taiwanese masters like Edward Yang and Hou Hsiao-hsien (p. 660).

For two decades, the Chinese government tantalized the U.S. Majors, suggesting that the door was about to open wider. At the end of 2001, in accord with China's entry into the World Trade Organization, the government promised to privatize distribution by assigning rights among several provincial firms. But officially sanctioned output was down to about 30 features per year, and foreign pictures now claimed up to 80 percent of the box office. If Hollywood were to bring in more than the ten or so pictures per year already permitted, the local product would vanish. As a result, there were signs that the principal agency, China Film Import/Export, would reorganize in such a way as to keep tight control over what was shown. China was far from an open market, either for western companies or its own filmmakers.

NEW CINEMAS IN EAST ASIA

By 1975, of the 4,000 or so feature films made worldwide, half came from Asia. Although the bulk of these were produced in India and Japan, other countries contributed a surprising number. Malaysia, for instance, developed a significant film industry thanks to government encouragement. Similarly, Indonesian cinema benefited from protectionist legislation, allowing companies to produce an average of 70 films a year, many in a distinctive horror genre featuring "snake women." Thailand be-

26.20 The slum dwellers' plight emphasized by the name of the street (*Manila: In the Claws of Neon*).

26.21 *My Country: Clinging to a Knife Edge:* a worker forced into a robbery meets a gang member under portraits of the Philippines' first family.

came another major force, producing over 600 films between 1983 and 1987. Although most of these countries' output dropped when the video boom decimated Asian attendance in the mid-1980s, they produced some significant works, such as Teguh Karya's *Mementos* (Indonesia, 1986) and Cherd Songsi's *The Scar* (Thailand, 1978).

The Philippines

The Philippines established a small, vertically integrated studio system during the 1930s, but the companies declined in the postwar era and most production was in the hands of independents. Under the rule of Ferdinand Marcos and his wife Imelda (1965–1986) production rose, leveling off at about 150 features per year in the mid-1970s. Most of these were in the popular genres of romantic melodrama, musicals (*zarzuela*), comedies, religious films, and soft-core eroticism (*bomba*). A star system was firmly in place, and many plots were derived from action- or romance-based comic books. The audience was proportionately large: 1,300 theaters lured in over 66 million viewers per year.

In the early 1970s, a new generation of Filipino filmmakers began to tackle social subjects. Their films retained the rapes, beatings, and other lurid conventions of mainstream genres but framed these as part of social criticism. Ishmal Bernal's *Speck in the Water* (1976), Eddie Romero's *We Were Like This Yesterday, How Is It Today?* (1976), and Mike De Leon's *Black* (1977) dwell on poverty, crime, and corruption in a manner reminiscent of American film noir.

One of the most noteworthy efforts was *Manila: In the Claws of Neon* (1975). Lino Brocka had begun making films in 1970, most of them exploiting the conventional love triangles, rapes, and violent action in order to make points about contemporary Filipino life. In *Manila*, Ligaya is lured to the city by a procuress, who sells her to a Chinese. When Ligaya's fiancé Julio finds her, the Chinese kills Ligaya, and Julio murders him before being slain by a mob. Alongside the passion-

driven plotline, however, runs an indictment of economic exploitation. Julio's search for Ligaya becomes a cross section of Manila's unemployed men and women, and collateral scenes, such as some dockers' brutal attack on bourgeois men in a movie theater, define the city as a class battleground. Brocka underlines the suffering of slum dwellers with symbolic compositions (**26.20**).

Just as the "New Filipino Cinema" was emerging, President Marcos's government installed much stricter censorship. Scripts were reviewed before production, and completed films could be either cut or banned. De Leon, Brocka, and others aroused censors' ire: not particularly popular at home, their films were winning praise abroad and calling attention to the seamy side of Marcos's regime. Brocka, the most outspoken of the group, spent time in prison for fighting censorship and participating in strikes. Yet he and his peers were still allowed to make films merging social criticism and entertainment conventions. One of the most stinging is Brocka's *My Country: Clinging to a Knife Edge* (1982), which criticizes the regime's inequities with remarkable bluntness (**26.21**).

In 1986, an urban insurrection overthrew Marcos's regime and installed President Corazon Aquino, widow of an assassinated opposition leader. The revolution raised hopes for a new, dynamic cinema, but mass entertainment ruled the market as intensely as before. Aquino's government passed no measures to protect the industry, and the Marcos censorship apparatus remained in place. Many filmmakers expressed bitter disappointment with Aquino's policies; Brocka's *Fight for Us* (1989), produced by Pathé, suggested that repression and militarism had not left the islands.

In other respects, however, the Philippines' commercial industry prospered. Attendance and feature output rose sharply, and several local productions proved to be huge successes. New laws gave more rights to women, and several female directors began careers, notably Marilou Diaz-Abaya (*Milagros*, 1997). Aquino's daughter Kris found stardom in a series of romantic comedies in 1991—the same year that an auto accident killed Brocka, who was planning another film critical of the post-Marcos era.

In the early 1990s, with Aquino's former defense chief, Fidel Ramos, now president, popular film stars were being elected to government posts. The industry won some favors from Ramos's regime, chiefly a liberalization of censorship. Producers continued to release between 120 and 200 films each year, many of which were *pito-pito* ("seven-seven") films, shot in seven to ten days and aimed at recouping quickly their minimal costs. Few films made money, and most were quickly pirated on video.

In May 1998, film actor Joseph Estrada was elected president, and censorship was further weakened. Producers began cranking out lucrative sex pictures. Soon, however, terrorist attacks by Muslim separatists discouraged filmgoing and reduced production output. At the start of the new century, despite the perseverance of Mike De Leon and other veteran directors, the Filipino cinema was facing a grim future.

Hong Kong

The most successful and influential Asian cinema outside Japan and India was located in the British Crown Colony of Hong Kong. During the 1930s, Hong Kong had been a refuge for Chinese filmmakers fleeing the war-torn mainland, and by the 1950s several studios were operating there. Hong Kong's was a regional industry, providing comedies, family melodramas, Cantonese opera films, and swordfight movies to South China and Chinese populations throughout East and Southeast Asia.

Shaw Brothers and the New Wuxia Pian One company emerged to rule the market. The Shaw Brothers firm had established an entertainment empire in Singapore. The indefatigable entrepreneur Run Run Shaw decided to use Hong Kong as his production base and in 1958 built a studio there. The Movietown complex held ten shooting stages, numerous backlots (including an artificial lake), an actor's training school, laboratory and sound facilities, and even dormitories and apartments for the employees. Shaw Brothers was vertically integrated, owning distribution agencies and theater chains throughout East Asia. The firm emphasized production in Mandarin, the most common regional Chinese dialect.

During the 1960s, Shaw pioneered the revision of the martial-arts film (the *wuxia pian*, or "film of martial chivalry"). Borrowing from Peking-opera acrobatics, Japanese samurai films, spaghetti Westerns, and even James Bond films, Shaw's swordplay film became a dazzling spectacle. Zhang Che, the most successful practitioner of the genre, turned *The One-Armed Swordsman*

(1966), *The Assassin* (1967), and *Golden Swallow* (1968) into violent spectacles (**26.22**). Zhang's assistant directors and instructors went on to become important directors in the 1970s.

More innovative and widely renowned was King Hu, whose *Come Drink with Me* (1965) marked the emergence of the new martial-arts trend. Set almost wholly within an inn, *Come Drink with Me* builds its action out of intrigues, masquerades, and flare-ups among the guests. Hu's rapid editing, sweeping widescreen compositions, and Peking-opera acrobatics shaped the martial-arts film for decades. "Working on that film," he recalled, "I began to realize that if the plots are simple, the stylistic delivery will be even richer."[4]

Hu left Shaw Brothers for Taiwan, where he produced *Dragon Inn* (1967) and *A Touch of Zen* (1970). The latter project was on a scale unprecedented in the wuxia pian. Three years in the making and based upon intricacies of Buddhist philosophy, the original version ran three hours. *A Touch of Zen* pushes stylization to new extremes. While "flying swordsmen" were already a convention of martial-arts films, Hu intensified the urgency of the action. His warriors execute fantastic leaps, hovering to slash or punch before landing gracefully, already coiled for a new encounter (**Color Plate 26.14**).

Hu's later films, such as *The Valiant Ones* (1975, co-produced in Hong Kong), and *Raining in the Mountain* (1979) amplify the balletic excitement of *A Touch of Zen*. Nimble performers hurl themselves over rocks, ricochet off walls and tree trunks, and swoop down from the sky. In Hu's work, the martial-arts film achieved a new kinetic grace, and his Taiwanese productions had an enduring influence on Hong Kong directors.

Bruce Lee and the Kung-Fu Film A new martial-arts cycle developed under the auspices of Raymond Chow, who served as head of production for Run Run Shaw. In 1970, Chow broke away to found his own company, Golden Harvest. Chow aimed his product at a broad international market. He found immediate success in films starring the Asian martial artist Bruce Lee.

Born in California, Lee had been a popular child and teenage actor in Hong Kong, but he found only minor roles in U.S. films and television. Then Golden Harvest's *The Big Boss* (aka *Fists of Fury*, 1971) burst onto screens. It propelled Lee to stardom and made kung fu, the art of punching and kickboxing, a worldwide fad. Chow built upon Lee's success with *Fist of Fury* (aka *The Chinese Connection*, 1972) and *The Way of the Dragon* (aka *The Return of the Dragon*, 1972), each of which broke Hong Kong box-office records. Lee appeared with minor Hollywood actors in the bigger-budget *Enter the Dragon*

26.22 The villain is punished appropriately in *The New One-Armed Swordsman* (1970).

26.23 In *Enter the Dragon*, Bruce Lee licks his own blood to fuel his rage.

26.24 *Fist of Fury:* in slow motion, Lee leaps into the air and kicks to pieces a sign reading "No Dogs or Chinese Allowed."

(1973), a coproduction with Warner Bros. Lee's death under mysterious circumstances in 1973 made him a cult hero.

The most famous Chinese star in history, Lee played a key role in opening foreign markets to Hong Kong films. He also saw himself as an emblem of the excellence of Chinese martial arts, a point made explicit in *Fist of Fury*, which celebrates Shanghai's resistance to Japanese occupation during World War II. Lee's films, enjoyed throughout the Third World, were often taken as symbolizing the rebellious pride of insurgent Asia.

Although Lee directed only one film, *The Way of the Dragon*, he controlled his star image carefully. Typically he played a superman, unquestionably the best fighter around but keeping his full force in reserve until the explosive climax (**26.23**). Lee insisted on more realistic combat scenes than were the norm in Hong Kong films, displaying his skills in longish takes and long shots. Some moments of spectacle, however, are intensified by camera tricks and editing (**26.24**).

After Lee's death, producers cast about for substitutes (often named Bruce Le, Leh, or Li), but the kung-fu

26.25 Michael Hui gets the better of his brother Sam in *The Private Eyes* (1976).

26.26 In *Snake in the Eagle's Shadow,* Jackie Chan practices his "snake" attack on unsuspecting eggs.

film rapidly declined in quality. Nevertheless, foreign audiences had embraced the genre, and Raymond Chow's enterprise grew. By the mid-1970s, Golden Harvest and Shaw Brothers produced about one-third of Hong Kong films. Chow controlled the largest theater circuit in the colony and 500 other theaters across Asia. The martial-arts film, as developed under Shaw and Chow, contributed conventions to action-based genres around the world and won Hong Kong films a high place in international markets.

Breakthroughs in the 1980s Even with the expansion of output in small Asian countries, Hong Kong films dominated the region. In the colony, the local product overwhelmed imports at the box office. The genres and stars were hugely popular throughout Asia, as well as in Africa, Latin America, and Asian communities in Europe and North America. Vertically integrated companies like Shaw Brothers and Chow's Golden Harvest kept production costs down while supplying their own theaters with a staple product.

Some directors, such as Lau Kar-leung, sustained the martial-arts genre in *Spiritual Boxer* (1975) and *The Eight-Diagram Pole Fighter* (1984), but, on the whole,

swordplay and kung-fu films declined. Police thrillers, contemporary comedies, and underworld action films became the major genres of the 1980s. For many critics and audiences, the new genres reflected the city's modernizing, westernizing culture. New stars also emerged. The television comedian Michael Hui formed his own company with Golden Harvest for a string of successful slapstick films (*Games Gamblers Play,* 1974; *Security Unlimited,* 1981; *Chicken and Duck Talk,* 1988). Hui played grasping merchants and boorish professionals, types readily associated with the new mercantile Hong Kong (**26.25**).

The success of Hui's comedies accelerated the rise of another performer, Jackie Chan. Chan began his career as a Bruce Lee imitator before mixing acrobatic kung fu with breakneck comedy in *Snake in the Eagle's Shadow* (1978; **26.26**), *Fearless Hyena* (1979), and *Young Master* (1980). Chan soon became the biggest star in Asia. Refusing to use a double, he executed astonishingly risky stunts while giving himself a screen persona reminiscent of Buster Keaton and Harold Lloyd—the diminutive, resourceful, never-say-die average man. Chan also shifted genres rapidly. Sensing that pure martial art was waning in popularity, he combined it and physical comedy with histori-

26.27 Chan in an awkward defensive position (*Armour of God*).

26.28 The Hong Kong journalist with the Vietnamese children he tries to rescue in *Boat People*.

cal intrigue (*Project A*, 1983), the cop thriller (*Police Story*, 1985), and swashbuckling adventure modeled on *Raiders of the Lost Ark* (*Armour of God*, 1986; **26.27**).

The Hong Kong New Wave The sense of a cosmopolitan Hong Kong identity was an important ingredient in the New Wave of the late 1970s. A new film culture emerged with the establishment of the Hong Kong Film Festival (1977), industry-related magazines, and college courses. Several directors, often trained abroad and starting out in local television production, won international recognition. Some remained independent filmmakers, while others quickly became central forces in the industry—the Hong Kong equivalents of the Hollywood movie brats of the 1970s.

After directing in television, Ann Hui entered feature production with *The Secret* (1979), a murder mystery using an unprecedented number of women in production roles. Her *The Spooky Bunch* (1980) helped revive the ghost-story genre, and *The Story of Woo Viet* (1981) looked forward to the "hero" crime films. Hui's interna-

tional reputation rested upon more somber dramas reflecting on postwar Asian history. *Boat People* (1982) explains the political oppression that drives Vietnamese to emigrate to Hong Kong (**26.28**). *Song of the Exile* (1990) traces how a young woman comes to understand the complex past of her mother, a Japanese woman sent to become a prostitute in China during the war.

Other filmmakers contributed to the New Wave. Shu Kei's *Sealed with a Kiss* (1981) details a love affair between two handicapped adolescents. Allen Fong, who studied filmmaking at the University of Southern California, also specialized in intimate human dramas. Rejecting the flamboyant spectacle of commercial cinema and often obliged to shoot in 16mm, Fong made *Father and Son* (1981) in a bittersweet vein reminiscent of François Truffaut.

The sobriety of such works identified the Hong Kong New Wave with social commentary and psychological nuance. But this side of the trend was quickly overwhelmed by a rapid-fire revamping of popular genres. Central to this development was Tsui Hark. Tsui studied film in the United States before taking directing jobs in television. He entered theatrical features with a futuristic wuxia pian, *The Butterfly Murders* (1979). After some violent satires, Tsui turned abruptly toward family entertainment. He helped launch a cycle of "supernatural kung fu" with *Zu: Warriors of the Magic Mountain* (1982), and he gained still more recognition with *Shanghai Blues* (1984) and *Peking Opera Blues* (1986).

These dazzling, frantic mixtures of action, comedy, and sentimental romance borrow openly from the New Hollywood. Tsui's scenes are busy to the point of exhaustion: the camera rushes up to the actors, wide-angle setups multiply rapidly, and fighters soar endlessly through space. In a characteristic scene from *Shanghai Blues*, several characters dodge one another, popping up in unexpected crannies of the frame (**Color Plate 26.15**).

Like Steven Spielberg and George Lucas, Tsui became a powerful producer. His company, Film Workshop, produced several of the all-time successes of the Hong Kong cinema. John Woo's gory *A Better Tomorrow* (1986) made television star Chow Yun-Fat sensationally popular and founded a cycle of hero films featuring sensitive, romanticized gangsters (**26.29**). Tsui also produced Ching Siu-Tung's *A Chinese Ghost Story* (1987), an extravaganza of supernatural martial arts, and the key Jet Li vehicle *Once upon a Time in China* (1991)—both of which spawned numerous sequels and clones. Tsui's success with spectacle-centered entertainment signaled the end of the New Wave and created a vogue for flashy, fast-paced movies.

26.29 In the midst of a gunfight, two gangsters join forces with the cop, bound to them by blood and love (*A Better Tomorrow*).

26.30 Chow Yun-Fat and Danny Lee discuss matters in *The Killer*.

Films like Tsui's, with their flamboyant style and an unapologetic appeal to emotion, began to be recognized in western film circles. European and North American distributors circulated Woo's *The Killer* (1989), in which the gangster-hero cycle reaches delirious heights. In the middle of almost unremitting carnage and sentimental scenes of manly devotion, conversations are conducted at gunpoint (**26.30**). The U.S. Majors began hiring Woo (*Hard Target*, 1993), Tsui (*Double Team*, 1997), and other Hong Kong directors. (Only Woo became an A-list Hollywood presence, helming megapics like *Face/Off*, 1997, and *Mission: Impossible 2*, 2000.) Ironically, the worldwide appreciation of Hong Kong cinema coincided with a downturn in the industry's fortunes.

The 1990s: A Better Tomorrow? In the early 1980s, the United Kingdom had agreed to return Hong Kong to the People's Republic of China in 1997. The movie industry shifted into high gear, pumping out films to make as much money as possible in the face of an uncertain future. A star might perform in over a dozen pictures per year, shooting one in the morning and another in the afternoon. The criminal gangs known as "triads" intensified their involvement in the industry by forcing stars to play in quickies. By the early 1990s, production soared to over 200 features per year—a reflection of the popularity of the films throughout East Asia. Hong Kong producers accordingly raised their budgets, paying for the films by presales to overseas distributors.

In the flurry of production, several unusual films were made, including "art films" like Stanley Kwan's graceful ghost romance *Rouge* (1988; **Color Plate 26.16**) and his biography of Ruan Lingyu (p. 258), *Actress* (aka *Centre Stage*, 1991). The most original art movies came from the former scriptwriter Wong Kar-wai. After a success with the *Mean Streets* variant *As*

Tears Go By (1988), Wong made *Days of Being Wild* (1990), a milestone in Hong Kong cinema. The film used a retro-1960s look to tell the linked stories of several people whose lives are touched by a cold, manipulative young man. No Hong Kong film before had been so formally daring and psychologically dense.

However, the expensive *Days of Being Wild* was a fiasco and drove Wong out of directing for several years. He returned with a string of films that won him worldwide attention at film festivals: *Ashes of Time* (1994), *Chungking Express* (1994), *Fallen Angels* (1995), *Happy Together* (1997), and *In the Mood for Love* (2000). Honored with several Cannes prizes, Wong became the most artistically respected Hong Kong director. He drew upon the elements of commercial cinema—big stars, pop sound tracks, romantic situations, violent confrontations—but poeticized them with a freewheeling, lyrical style. Writing his script day by day, he improvised on the set, discarded previously shot scenes, used a free-roaming hand-held camera, and played music during filming to evoke an emotional atmosphere.

The result is a sketchy, digressive, sometimes self-indulgent, but often exhilarating cinema. Plotlines split off and converge unexpectedly. In *Chungking Express*, the story starts with one couple and segues to another, never returning to the first but inviting us to compare their attitudes to time and love (**Color Plate 26.17**). Against the frantic pacing and ultraviolence of 1980s Hong Kong film, Wong favored languid scenes and wistful imagery reminiscent of French Impressionist cinema (**26.31**). Even *Ashes of Time*, his version of a wuxia pian, dwells on swordsmen meditating on the women they have lost. Wong's innocents yearn for romance, all the while sensing life's transience. Through muted dramas and vivid images Wong seemed to be seeking a cinema of pure, instantaneous rapture.

26.31 *Chungking Express:* the fast-food countergirl, now a flight attendant, waits for the man of her dreams.

Wong's films, widely distributed in Europe, Japan, and North America, were not local hits; the domestic audience preferred Jackie Chan, still turning out top-grossing adventures, as well as comedian Stephen Chiau and action star Jet Li. But even the popularity of these foolproof stars began to wane as the regional market felt a surfeit of Hong Kong films, and Hollywood films spread through the Pacific. The 1997 handover of Hong Kong to the PRC coincided with an economic crisis throughout Asia, leaving Hong Kong cinema in perilous condition.

Even while the industry was faltering, however, new forces emerged. Peter Chan, a U.S.-trained director, developed a strong following with his comedy *He's a Woman, She's a Man* (1994) and the drama *Comrades: Almost a Love Story* (1996). Tsui Hark, ever the entrepreneur, provided *The Blade* (1995), a shattering remake of Zhang Che's *The One-Armed Swordsman*, and a computer-animated version of *A Chinese Ghost Story* (1997). And new, robust production companies began turning out stylish genre films. Most notable was Milky-

way Image, led by veteran Shaw Brothers director Johnnie To, and writer-director Wai Ka-fai. Together they produced a string of piercing, neo-noir crime dramas: *The Longest Nite, Expect the Unexpected,* and *A Hero Never Dies* (all 1996). To's *The Mission* (1999), with its cryptic plot centering on hitmen hired to guard a triad boss, promised to redefine the Hong Kong action film (**26.32**). Once again, this hyperkinetic cinema refused to stand still.

Taiwan

In 1982, Taiwan was an unlikely source of innovative filmmaking. Its products were notorious for being either stultifyingly propagandistic or rudimentary, low-budget entertainment. Yet, in the 1980s, Taiwanese cinema became one of the most exciting areas of international film culture.

Taiwan was colonized by the Japanese in 1895, and not until World War II were they driven out. But native Taiwanese were not to enjoy independence long. In 1949, Jiang Jie-shi's (Chiang Kai-shek's) Guomindong troops fled Mao's revolution, bringing 2 million mainland Chinese to the island. The mainland emigrants took control and created an authoritarian state, on the grounds that Jiang, China's rightful leader, would someday retake the mainland. Martial law was declared for the indefinite future.

Initially, filmmaking was under control of the government, principally through the Central Motion Picture Corporation (CMPC). The CMPC and other agencies concentrated on anti-Communist documentaries. Commercial firms copied the costume operas, comedies, and love stories brought in from Hong Kong.

During the 1960s, the success of imported martial-arts films spurred Taiwanese producers to imitate them, sometimes by welcoming Hong Kong directors such as

26.32 Shootout in a shopping mall: suspenseful and dynamic use of wide-screen space in *The Mission.*

EDWARD YANG AND HOU HSIAO-HSIEN   •

Both born in China in 1947 to families who then emigrated to Taiwan, the island's two major filmmakers pursued paths that often diverged and occasionally converged. Both were given a key opportunity through the government's "New Cinema" initiative, but their films became significantly different.

Edward Yang went to college in the United States, studying computer science, before returning to Taiwan in the 1980s. After doing some scriptwriting and television directing, he was chosen to direct an episode of *In Our Times*, which led to his first feature, *That Day, on the Beach* (1983). Following the success of that film, Yang went on to make *Taipei Story* (1985) and *The Terrorizers* (1986).

With these films, Yang established his area of concern as the anomie and frustration of young urban professionals. Wearing chic fashions and living in modern apartments, his characters fall prey to mysterious forces rippling through the metropolis. *The Terrorizers*, for instance, intercuts two stories: that of a Eurasian woman involved with terrorists and that of a young novelist who eventually separates from her husband. A fan of comic books, Yang relied on striking imagery, staccato cutting, and a minimum of dialogue. He used urban architecture to frame his yuppies in static, foreboding shots (**26.33**).

The Terrorizers won acclaim at festivals, but with the decline of the New Wave, it took Yang several years to win support for the film many regard as his masterpiece. *A Brighter Summer Day* (1991) took its title from an Elvis Pres-

ley song and told the story of a 1960s teenage gang. Nearly four hours long, with dozens of speaking parts, the film pivots on what one boy saw—or didn't see—one evening in a schoolroom; that glimpse leads eventually to murder. Yang's technique is at its most refined in his gang confrontations, staged in long takes and rich depth (**Color Plate 26.18**).

Hou Hsiao-hsien started in the film industry by another route, becoming an assistant director after studying at the Taipei Academy of Dramatic Art. His first solo efforts were ingratiating teenage musicals. His episode in *The Sandwich Man*, however, turned him toward a more personal and contemplative cinema. His major New Wave films—*A Summer at Grandpa's* (1984), *The Time to Live and the Time*

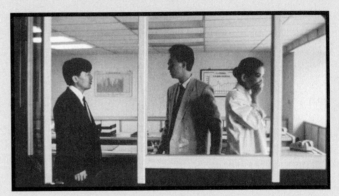

26.33   Architecture and office adultery in *The Terrorizers*.

King Hu. Hong Kong companies also set up studios in Taiwan. The CMPC, now obliged to support itself, moved toward fictional films no less didactic than its earlier documentaries had been. Production soared, reaching over 200 features per year, and moviegoing increased dramatically.

Then came the crash. The new Hong Kong stars and genres attracted Taiwanese audiences, and profits from the domestic product plummeted. Output sank from 100 films at the beginning of the 1980s to fewer than 30 ten years later. At the same time, Taiwan was shifting from a rural economy to one based on manufacturing and modern technology. For many young people, Jiang's promise to recapture the mainland was meaningless; like Hong Kong youth, they sought a distinct cultural identity. College-educated and urban white-collar workers disdained the action pictures and romances that were the staples of Taiwanese production.

The Taiwanese New Wave   During this period, a new film culture emerged. The government created a national archive in 1979, and three years later an annual film festival began showcasing new works. Film magazines appeared, and European classics were screened in universities and small theaters. As with many new waves—in 1950s France, in 1960s eastern Europe, in 1970s Germany—an educated, affluent audience was ready for a national art cinema.

So, too, was the industry. By 1982, the box-office decline pressed the CMPC and commercial producers to recruit young, largely western-trained, directors. The success of the anthology films *In Our Times* (1982) and *The Sandwich Man* (1983) and of a host of new features proved that low-budget films could attract audiences and win prestige at festivals. Like many other young cinemas, the Taiwanese New Wave benefited from a crisis in the industry that encouraged cheap, quickly made films by newcomers.

to Die (1985), and *Dust in the Wind* (1986)—dedramatize the narrative. Coming-of-age stories, usually taking place in a rural milieu, the films recall Satyajit Ray's "Apu" trilogy in building up a rich texture of daily life through dwelling on mundane routines. The story emerges not out of dramatic climaxes but out of details, observed in a painstaking, slow rhythm. Hou also obliquely evokes the history of Taiwan through the interplay among generations (**26.34**).

In *Dust in the Wind* and *City of Sadness* (1990), Hou applied this dedramatizing strategy to film technique through extreme long shots, long takes, static framing, and almost no shot/reverse-shot cutting (**Color Plate 26.19**). Like Kenji Mizoguchi and Jacques Tati, he subordinates character action to a large-scale visual field. The viewer's eye roams around the frame, led into depth and often to the very limits of visibility. Hou punctuates these long-take scenes with Ozu-like shots of landscapes or objects.

With *City of Sadness,* Hou launched a trilogy on Taiwanese history, which included *The Puppetmaster* (1993) and *Good Men, Good Women* (1995). In these films, past and present mingle unpredictably, sometimes in the same shot, and Hou meditates on the mixture of languages and cultures that constitute modern Taiwan. One of his most striking accomplishments is *Flowers of Shanghai* (1998), a sumptuous re-creation of nineteenth-century Chinese brothel society. Lit by lanterns, observed in long takes by a gently arcing camera, the sexual intrigues and drinking games become mesmeric (**Color Plate 26.20**).

26.34 A characteristic sustained long shot from *Dust in the Wind:* the young man returns from the army to talk with his grandfather.

Hou and Yang earned worldwide fame. They tried to form a cooperative production company and an alternative distribution network. But the troubles of the domestic industry blocked their efforts to consolidate the gains of the New Wave. Their films had virtually no audience in Taiwan, but international financing and the film-festival circuit gave them vigorous international careers. Yang won a Cannes prize for his family drama *Yi Yi* (2000), while Hou was widely considered the world's finest director of the 1990s. Apart from their individual achievements, they were a powerful influence on young filmmakers throughout Asia.

Most of the New Wave films reacted against studio-bound spectacles characteristic of Taiwanese cinema. Like the Neorealists, the Nouvelle Vague, and others before them, New Wave directors took their cameras on location to film loose, episodic narratives, often enacted by nonprofessional performers. Many of the films were autobiographical stories or psychological studies. Since government policy banned overt political comment, social criticism was left implicit. Directors cultivated an elliptical approach to storytelling, using flashbacks, fantasy sequences, and dedramatized situations—all owing something to European art cinema of the 1960s. Two very different directors stood out: Edward Yang and Hou Hsiaohsien (see box).

A New Generation of Filmmakers   By 1987, Taiwan's New Wave had ended. The colossal success of video entertainment in Taiwan (a center of videocassette piracy) drove production to abysmal lows, and Hong Kong imports ruled the market. At the same time, however, martial law was lifted, censorship was relaxed, and those filmmakers still practicing could broach sensitive issues of Taiwanese history and identity. Hou's *City of Sadness,* which won the main prize at the Venice Film Festival, portrays in muted form how the events from 1945 to 1949 tear a family apart—a topic filmmakers could not have treated a few years earlier.

The international renown of Hou and Yang led filmmakers from a younger generation to explore new ways of defining Taiwanese culture. The most prominent of the newcomers was Tsai Ming-liang. Like Hou and Yang, he favored long takes and tangled storylines, but he brought to his films of dysfunctional families and grim eroticism an anxious humor. In *Vive l'amour* (1994), a boy hiding under a bed while a couple make love on top becomes embarrassingly aroused. In *The River* (1997), a

26.35 A glitzy musical number played out in a decaying apartment building (*The Hole*).

26.36 Sumptuous costumes and sets and solemn performance highlight Im's *Chunhyang*.

gay father searching for lovers in a darkened bathhouse inadvertently makes overtures to his son. *The Hole* (1998) is perhaps Tsai's most ingratiating film: as an apartment house crumbles and floods during a rainstorm, one of the tenants unpredictably breaks into full-scale musical production numbers (**26.35**). Tsai's bizarre humor and murky sexuality played better abroad than locally, but with the collapse of the industry, the brightest future of the Taiwanese cinema lay in the international festival scene.

South Korea

Hong Kong cinema gained momentum in the 1970s, while Taiwanese and mainland cinema did so in the early 1980s. South Korean cinema began to claim festivals' attention in the late 1980s, and by the end of the 1990s it was becoming a strong commercial player in the region as well.

Like Taiwan, Korea had been a Japanese possession until the end of World War II. It was divided at the thirty-eighth parallel when the Korean War (1950–1953) ended in a stalemate. North Korea's Communist regime maintained autocratic control over its populace even after the fall of the USSR. For decades, South Korea was ruled by military juntas, and a moderately democratic system was not installed until the late 1980s. Economically, South Korea shot forward, its entry into electronics and computer technology steered by the family conglomerates known as *chaebols*.

Since the 1950s, the film industry had specialized in melodramas, historical spectacles, and, during the 1980s, films of graphic sex. Many film studios flourished. But in 1973, the government passed stricter laws regulating them, effectively turning control of distribution over to a handful of companies. Domestic production ran to between 100 and 200 titles per year, supported by a ban on most foreign imports. In 1986, authorities bowed to a U.S. boycott and allowed more foreign titles to enter, which decreased the audience for local product. The opening of the market also increased the number of production companies, which yielded fresh opportunities for young filmmakers.

South Korea's breakthrough to the western art-house market was through an utterly atypical film, Bae Yong-kyun's *Why Has Bodhi-Dharma Left for the East?* (1989). Shot over three years, the film tells a Zen-inspired story of a boy's initiation into Buddhist wisdom by an older master. Bae deliberately avoided the Hollywood-derived style that dominated his national cinema and instead lingered on tranquil, meditative images (**Color Plate 26.21**).

Bae's film paved the way for other Korean filmmakers. Im Kwon-taek had made nearly 100 costume films and melodramas since 1962, but it was his later films that commanded attention on the festival circuit. *The Taebek Mountains* (1994) traces the effects of war on friendship and trust in a village. The often-told historical drama *Chunhyang* (2000) features lush, detailed sets and costumes (**26.36**). Im respects the story's roots in oral narrative by interspersing shots of the narrator's performance (*pansori*) with the filmed drama.

Younger directors began gaining recognition as well. Pak Kwang-soo's *A Single Spark* (1996) treats a 1960s incident in which suicide was used for political protest. The American-trained Yi Kwangmo created a minimalist, Hou-like study of the U.S. presence during the Korean War in *Spring in My Hometown* (1998). Far wilder was Kim Sangjin's *Attack the Gas Station!* (1999), a hip-hop-flavored story of aggressive and restless youth. Jang San-woo aroused international contro-

26.37, *left* *The Power of Kangwon Province:* the first scene of the film centers on the young woman riding the train to the resort. The man passing her is, as far as we know now, a stranger.

26.38, *right* Much later in the film, the man whom we now know as a friend of the hero passes her again, and we realize that the film has returned to an earlier time frame.

versy with the sadomasochistic sexual encounters of *Lies* (1998).

One of the most intriguing young directors was Hang Sang-soo, a fastidious experimenter with narrative form. In *The Day a Pig Fell in the Well* (1996) and *The Bride Stripped Bare by Her Bachelors* (aka *Oh, Soo-jung!*, 2000), Hang explored multiple-viewpoint stories, often presenting the same scene differently at two points in the film. *The Power of Kangwon Province* (1998) starts by centering on a female student traveling to a resort area with two girlfriends (**26.37**). Returning to Seoul, she tries to find her lover, a college professor. The film then shifts to the lover's viewpoint. He goes about his business in Seoul and decides to visit the resort with a friend. Aboard the train, the friend goes to get a snack, and he passes the woman (**26.38**). Suddenly we realize that Hang is "starting the film over." The two men's ensuing rambles through the countryside coincide with the women's trip, which the viewer now senses offscreen.

Alongside such festival favorites came deftly made action films and supernatural thrillers (*The Gingko Bed*, 1996; *Swiri*, 1999; *Tell Me Something*, 2000; *Joint Security Area*, 2000) that beat Hollywood imports at the local box office and swept through regional markets. Protected by a strong quota, South Korean films attracted millions of dollars in venture capital from abroad, and the Pusan Film Festival, founded in 1996, became the Pacific's most talked-about showcase. South Korea became the rising cinema of Asia for the new century.

AUSTRALIA AND NEW ZEALAND

Australia and New Zealand entered the international scene thanks largely to government subsidies akin to those supporting western European cinema. Each was able to create a New Cinema for the festival circuit. In addition, Australian film won some successes in mainstream popular film. As local films won notice abroad,

Australian and New Zealand filmmakers were sought by Hollywood. By the end of the 1990s, both countries also depended financially on local production facilities and talent being used on American and other foreign films being shot down under.

Australia

Australian production reached a low ebb in the 1950s and early 1960s. One of the first indications that the country could again make commercially viable films came when Michael Powell, forced to work in television after the scandal resulting from *Peeping Tom* (p. 454), made an Australian feature film. *They're a Weird Mob* (1966), a low-budget comedy about an immigrant worker, proved hugely popular. In 1971, Canadian director Ted Kotcheff made *Wake in Fright* (aka *Outback*).

During the early 1970s, the Australian government tried to foster the establishment of a national identity. The arts enjoyed new support. In 1970, the Liberal government formed the Australian Film Development Corporation, which funded Bruce Beresford's *The Adventures of Barry McKenzie* (1972), Peter Weir's *The Cars That Ate Paris* (1974), and other films by directors who would soon create a "New Australian Cinema." The Australian Film and Television School was also formed. In 1972, a Labor government came to power and intensified these efforts, replacing the Film Development Corporation with the Australian Film Commission (AFC). The AFC helped finance about fifty features in its first five years, outperforming its European counterparts by recovering about 38 percent of its investments.

Television had come to Australia in 1956, siphoning off cinema audiences but also fostering a generation of young filmmakers who longed to make theatrical features. Australian film critics of the 1970s favored films of the French New Wave and of auteurs like Ingmar Bergman and Luis Buñuel. This combination of government support and interest in European-style art cinema

26.39 The hero and his companions find a sacred spot covered with graffiti left by white tourists (*The Chant of Jimmie Blacksmith*).

26.40 In a shot reminiscent of the wide-angle images of Spielberg and De Palma, *The Road Warrior* uses a bold depth composition to show the wounded Max flown into the besieged camp.

led Australian directors toward international elite audiences. The breakthrough film was Peter Weir's *Picnic at Hanging Rock* (1976), in which a group of schoolgirls mysteriously disappear during an outing. The film proceeds at a leisurely pace, creating intense atmosphere through actual locations, haunting music, and luminous cinematography (**Color Plate 26.22**).

Although the New Australian Cinema included several genres, including low-budget exploitation films, historical films became the most visible internationally. Bruce Beresford made another film set in a Victorian girls' school, *The Getting of Wisdom* (1977), and a Boer War story about an absurd court-martial, *Breaker Morant* (1980). Weir's World War I drama *Gallipoli* (1981) and *The Year of Living Dangerously* (1982), re-creating the overthrow of Sukarno in Indonesia, construct a comparably rich historical context. One of the rare historical films devoted to the plight of Aborigines, *The Chant of Jimmie Blacksmith* (1978, Fred Schepisi) shows a young black man striving to succeed in a white world, only to be driven to murderous rebellion (**26.39**). Gillian Armstrong used the Victorian era to make a feminist study in *My Brilliant Career* (1979), and Philip Noyce admiringly portrayed newsreel filmmakers of the 1940s and 1950s

in his *Newsfront* (1978). Weir, Beresford, Schepisi, Noyce, and other major directors were eventually lured to Hollywood.

Aside from its prestige pictures, the Australian industry also had some international popular successes. Independently of government funding, a small production firm called Kennedy-Miller made a pair of violent futuristic road movies, *Mad Max* (1978) and *Mad Max II* (aka *The Road Warrior*, 1982). Producer-director George Miller, influenced by the spaghetti Westerns of Sergio Leone and by Roger Corman's low-budget action films, peopled a savage, postnuclear Australian outback with bizarre warriors. Miller's aggressive, visceral style owed a good deal to the New Hollywood (**26.40**). Somewhat later, *Crocodile Dundee* (1986), a simple action comedy featuring Australian star Paul Hogan, became a surprise hit around the world.

The successes of both art films and popular movies led to a concentration on more foreign investment, coproductions, and export. *Mad Max beyond Thunderdome* (1985) was financed by Warner Bros., distributor of *The Road Warrior,* and *Crocodile Dundee 2* (1988) was also a foreign production. By the late 1980s, Australian cinema had moved heavily into an international mode, often depending on foreign stars (e.g., Meryl Streep in Schepisi's *Evil Angels* [aka *A Cry in the Dark*], 1990).

In 1988, the government support agency, renamed the Film Finance Corp. (FFC), linked funding to greater commercial viability, especially on the world art-house market. Soon came a string of successes that seemed to revive the golden era of the 1970s. In 1992, Baz Luhrman's first feature, *Strictly Ballroom,* became an international hit. As with English films, eccentric comedies were often attractive abroad. *Muriel's Wedding* (**26.41**) and *Priscilla, Queen of the Desert* were both on the domestic top-ten chart in 1994 and succeeded abroad as well. The enormous international popularity of *Babe* (Chris Noonan, 1995; **26.42**) and *Shine* (1996) seemed to confirm that local production was prospering. Yet *Babe* was entirely American-financed, while *Shine* was an Australian-British coproduction. More and more, production depended on foreign funding.

In 1996, a conservative Liberal-National party coalition took power, and FFC budgets were cut the following year. Imported American independent films were increasingly competing for box-office dollars with small-budget local productions. No films of the late 1990s were hits on the level of *Shine,* and an expensive failure, Gillian Armstrong's *Oscar and Lucinda* (1997), made higher government subsidies seem unjustified. The sequel *Babe: Pig in the City* (George Miller, 1998), produced by Kennedy-Miller but financed by Universal, was an even bigger disappointment. Local production slumped, drawing only 4 percent of domestic box-office receipts.

In mid-1998, 20th Century Fox, owned by ex-Australian Rupert Murdoch, opened Fox Studios Australia in Sydney. The Australian dollar was low, and American producers reckoned it was 40 percent cheaper to film there than in Hollywood. Such savings, the equipment of the huge Fox facility, and access to many experienced, English-speaking film personnel also made Australia extremely attractive for runaway production. Portions of the *Matrix* and *Star Wars* series were shot at Fox, as was *Mission: Impossible 2.* European producers wanting to make English-language films also invested in Australian projects.

The American influx made successful Australian directors realize they could stay in their native country and still benefit from U.S. funding. *Dark City* (1998), coproduced by New Line Cinema and Australian director Alex Proyas's own production company, was one of the first films shot there. Luhrman decided to stay, making Australian-American coproductions *Romeo and Juliet* (1996) and *Moulin Rouge!* (2001) at Fox Studios Australia. Moreover, Australian stars could be lured

26.41 Toni Collette's vibrant performance as the marriage-obsessed heroine of *Muriel's Wedding* made the film a hit and led to her departure for Hollywood.

26.42 *Babe*: new computer technology allowed animals' lips to move as they conversed.

back from Hollywood, as when Nicole Kidman starred in *Moulin Rouge!*

Australians weighed the benefits of large-scale foreign income for the industry and its workers against the decline in films with local themes. In 2000, a low-key entry in the eccentric-comedy genre, *The Dish,* about the role played in the 1969 moon landing by a small tracking station in western Australia, found modest international success. By the turn of the century, however, government funding was targeted at projects more likely to win global audiences than to reflect Australian culture.

New Zealand

New Zealand followed a similar, though shorter, path to national film production. Sporadic filmmaking had gone on since the early silent era, but there was no organized industry until the 1970s. In 1978, the government established the New Zealand Film Commission to support films at the preproduction stage and to help them find private investment. By the 1980s, a low, if fluctuating, level of production had been established.

Because the population of New Zealand numbered only about 3 million people during the 1980s, films had to be exported in order to recoup their costs. As usual, directors' best opportunities often lay with art-house audiences. For example, Vincent Ward's *The Navigator: A Mediaeval Odyssey* (1988) transports its characters from England in the Middle Ages to a modern Australian city. Ward later made the international coproductions *A Map of the Human Heart* (1992) and *What Dreams May Come* (1998).

Another major director, Jane Campion, was born in New Zealand but studied at the Australian Film and Television School. Her first feature, *Sweetie* (1989), was produced in Australia. By contrasting two sisters with differing mental problems, the film explores the boundaries between madness and sanity and between art cinema and melodrama. *An Angel at My Table* (1990) was planned as a three-part miniseries for New Zealand television but was released to theaters internationally. Based on the autobiographical works of poet Jane Frame, it attracted art-cinema audiences through its subtle performances depicting the heroine's struggle against being labeled "insane." Campion used many close shots to emphasize her grubby daily existence, punctuating the scenes with breathtaking landscapes that suggest her lyrical vision (**Color Plate 26.23**). Campion's third feature, *The Piano*, a French-Australian-New Zealand coproduction, won the Grand Prize at the 1993 Cannes Festival. Her adaptation of *The Portrait of a Lady* (1996) was a British vehicle, but she returned to Australia for an American coproduction, *Holy Smoke*, in 1999.

During the mid-1990s, film attendance more than doubled, thanks to the spread of multiplex theaters. The Film Commission was still supporting four films a year, and there were private producers as well. In 1994, Lee Tamahori's *Once Were Warriors* proved a surprise hit, eventually beating out *Jurassic Park* to become the highest-grossing film ever in New Zealand. Its tale of domestic violence in a working-class urban Maori family both reflected local life and had an appeal abroad (**26.43**) That same year, shlock-horror director Peter Jackson broke into art-house circles with *Heavenly Creatures*, a stylish depiction of two teenage girls and their fantasies leading up to murder.

Tamahori went to Hollywood, where he directed crime films like *Mulholland Falls* (1996) and *Along Came a Spider* (2001). Jackson, however, like the Aus-

26.43 The resilient mother and daughter of the Maori family in *Once Were Warriors*.

tralian Luhrman, chose to stay at home, making *The Frighteners* (1996), coproduced by Universal and Jackson's own firm, WingNut Films. Jackson also developed Weta Digital, a major digital postproduction studio in Wellington somewhat parallel to Fox Studio Australia in its creation of a local facility appealing to foreign producers. He created a worldwide stir by successfully undertaking the three-feature adaptation of J. R. R. Tolkien's *The Lord of the Rings* (2001, 2002, 2003; see Chapter 28). Filming and postproduction were done in New Zealand, pumping a large portion of the films' reputed $300 million budget into the local industry. Other filmmakers took advantage of the country's mountainous beauty, as when parts of *The Vertical Limit* (2001) were shot there. With such outside income and continued government funding for a few local films per year, the industry in New Zealand moved into the new century with strong prospects.

FILMMAKING IN THE MIDDLE EAST

From the 1960s into the 2000s, Middle Eastern politics were pervaded by the friction between Israel and the Arab states. Hostilities intensified after Israel's victory in a 1967 war with Egypt, Syria, and Jordan. In 1973, Egypt and Syria launched a new attack. This Yom Kippur War triggered a fourfold increase in oil prices set by the oil-producing countries, and the United States and the USSR began to supply arms to the combatants. President Jimmy Carter coaxed Egypt and Israel to accept a peace plan in 1979, but the 1991 assassination of Egypt's President Anwar Sadat, as well as Israel's refusal to cede captured territory, ensured continued conflict in the region. Arabs in territories under Israeli occupation carried on the struggle begun in the 1960s by the Palestine Liberation Organization, which sought an autonomous homeland for Palestinians. Despite Jordan's recognition of the state of Israel, most Arab nations remained neutral or hostile. Palestinian militants in the West Bank and Lebanon continued their struggle through the 1990s and into the new century, while Israel refused to grant Palestine its own territory.

The cinemas of the region were very diverse. Egypt, Iran, and Turkey had large-scale industries, exporting comedies, musicals, action pictures, and melodramas. Other nations' governments created film production that would promote indigenous cultural traditions. Some filmmakers aligned themselves with Third Cinema developments (p. 536), but, after the mid-1970s, many filmmakers undertook to broaden their audiences, participating in the international art cinema of the West. Video, recession, and competition from foreign films led to declines in production throughout the region from the mid- to late 1990s, with the most internationally famous auteurs seeking coproduction support in Europe. Iran maintained a relatively high level of production, and won respect around the world for its disarmingly and deceptively simple dramas.

Israel

Israel had a very small film industry. In the 1960s, Menahem Golan and his cousin Yoram Globus began producing musicals, spy films, melodramas, and the ethnic romantic comedies known as *bourekas*. During the 1970s, Israel also hosted a Young Cinema that focused on psychological problems of the middle classes. Then, in 1979, the Ministry of Education and Culture offered financial support for "quality film," thus stimulating low-budget films of personal reflection (e.g., Dan Wolman's *Hide and Seek*, 1980) or political inquiry (Daniel Wachsmann's *Transit*, 1980). Soon the quality fund was supporting about half of the fifteen or so features produced annually. The subsidy dwindled in the early 1980s but was revived and increased later in the decade.

As the Middle Eastern country most closely aligned with the West, Israel became part of that international market. The films of Moshe Mizrahi and the teenage nostalgia comedy *Lemon Popsicle* (1978) found release abroad. There were coproductions with European countries, and several films were nominated for Academy Awards. Israeli directors shot English-language films with U.S. stars, and Warner Bros. distributed Uri Barbash's *Beyond the Walls* (1984), a story of Arabs and Israelis in prison. The quality fund encouraged foreign companies to invest in internationally oriented projects.

26.44 In a remarkable 7½-minute take in *Kippur,* four increasingly desperate members of a rescue team manhandle a wounded soldier through deep mud.

Golan and Globus made a bid for international prominence in 1979 by acquiring control of Cannon Pictures, an independent production company. The pair produced both international entertainment movies (e.g., *Cobra*, 1986) and art films by Robert Altman, John Cassavetes, Andrei Konchalovsky, and Jean-Luc Godard. Cannon also bought theaters and gained control over half of Israeli film distribution. In addition, Cannon helped bring runaway productions to Israel, bolstering the local industry as a service sector. Although Globus left Cannon in 1989 to found his own company, the Israel industry continued to have strong western affiliations.

Throughout the 1990s, Israeli production continued to decline, averaging around ten films a year. In 1995, the only film-processing laboratory, an American-owned firm, closed down, requiring producers to ship film to Paris for development. The government slashed the budget of its Fund for Promotion of Quality Films in 1996, and many filmmakers sought work in television. By 1999, local films attracted only 1 percent of the national box office, most of the rest going to American imports.

Despite such problems, Israel's most prominent filmmaker, the documentarist Amos Gitai, who had been working abroad, returned to make a series of fiction features, beginning with *Devarim* (1995). Gitai's films were politically provocative, but he could draw funding from Canal Plus and other French sources. Gitai's *Kadosh* (1999) was the first Israeli film to compete at Cannes in twenty-five years, but the Fund refused to reimburse its share of the costs. *Kippur* (2000), Gitai's graphic drama of helicopter rescue teams in the Yom Kippur War (**26.44**), was also refused government funding and was not released in Israel.

In late 2000, the government began applying 50 percent of taxes paid by commercial television stations to subsidizing Israeli film culture—schools, the archive, and festivals, as well as production—and the new century began on a hopeful note.

Egypt

Other Middle Eastern countries were more closely tied to the Third World circuits of film export and personnel flow. In the early 1970s, Syria had a robust industry, sending films to Lebanon, Kuwait, and Jordan. There was a "new Syrian cinema" of social protest, as well as the biannual Damascus Film Festival showcasing Third World products. Lebanon also had a vigorous film industry before the outbreak of civil war in 1975 forced most personnel to emigrate.

Cairo had once been the Hollywood of Arab cinema, but in the 1970s Egyptian production declined. Major director went into exile; after making *The Betrayed* (1972) in Syria, Tewfik Saleh became head of the Iraqi film institute. The Egyptian industry's output rose during the 1980s, chiefly because of hospitable Arab Gulf markets and the popularity of Egyptian films on video. Yet soon the industry fell on hard times. Video piracy ran rampant, and the government withdrew all financial assistance to producers. U.S. films conquered the market, leaving the local product to fend for itself.

While some new Egyptian directors (including women) emerged during the period, the most famous filmmaker remained the veteran Youssef Chahine. An early proponent of Egyptian President Nasser's pan-Arab nationalism, Chahine later examined Egyptian history from a critical perspective. *The Sparrow* (1973) explores the causes of Egypt's defeat in the 1967 war. Later, his films became at once more personal and more transnational. *Alexandria, Why?* (1978) intercuts events of 1942 with Hollywood films of the era; in *Memory* (1982), a filmmaker facing a heart operation recalls his career over thirty years. Both films are autobiographical, but Chahine joined many political filmmakers of the era in seeking a broader audience by means of more intimate dramas. "I would like to be able to communicate with all of humanity and not only with the narrow parents-children-country group."[5] Chahine continued to direct regularly into the twenty-first century; notable among his films is *The Emigrant*, released in 1994. He received a life achievement award at Cannes in 1997.

During the 1990s, Egyptian production fell sharply, from fifty-three films in 1993 to only sixteen in 1997. A new production company, Sho'aa (Cultural Media Company) started up, however, boosting production and allowing new young directors a chance. Directors found the "fish out of water" comedy a huge draw. Sudanese

director Said Hamed made *An Upper Egyptian at AUC* (1998), about a provincial scholarship student attending the American University in Cairo and coping with city life. The film was the top grosser of the year, and Hamed followed it with *Hammam in Amsterdam* in 1999, a year in which the top nine box-office hits were all Egyptian films.

Turkey

Turkish cinema came to international notice in the late 1960s with such films as Yilmaz Güney's *Umut* ("Hope," 1970; p. 536). Turkey already boasted the highest output in the region. Erotic films, comedies, historical epics, melodramas, and even Westerns drew in an audience of over 100 million per year. But production and attendance were already declining when a military contingent seized power in 1980.

The government's oppression of suspect directors was little short of terroristic. Güney became the most visible target. A popular actor who had become a left-wing sympathizer, he fell under suspicion in the mid-1970s. When the military took power, Güney was already serving a twenty-four-year prison sentence. During his prison stay, he wrote scripts that were filmed by others. The most famous of these, *Yol* (*The Way*, 1982) follows five prisoners given a week's release to visit their families, and its forlorn landscapes hint at the oppressiveness of contemporary Turkey (**Color Plate 26.24**). In 1981, Güney escaped to France, where he made his last film. *The Wall* (1983) is a bitter, dispirited indictment of a prison system that oppresses men, women, and children alike. The prison wall, filmed in different sorts of light and weather, becomes an ominous presence throughout. When Güney died in 1984, the Turkish government sought to erase every trace of him. Police burned all his films and arrested anyone who possessed his photo.

Despite stifling censorship, the film industry gradually rebuilt itself, and production grew to almost 200 films. Only half of these, however, were released to theaters; the rest were destined for the increasingly powerful video market. At the same time, the government sought to attract western capital, and U.S. companies reappeared on the scene in the late 1980s. Their expanding hold on the market drove production to a mere 25 films in 1992, most made with European cofinancing.

During the 1990s, Turkey gradually liberalized, planning to become the only Asian country in the European Union. In 1993, censorship was all but abolished. At the same time, however, a recession continued to push down production to around ten films a year. The surprising local success of Yavuz Turgul's *The Bandit*, which beat out *Braveheart* for number one at the box office in 1996, inspired new attempts at production. In 1998, *Yol* finally received a commercial release in Turkey. By 2000, a young generation of directors seemed to be emerging. One of these, Nuri Bilge Ceylan, used his own family as actors in the contemplative and lyrical *The Town* (1998) and *Clouds of May* (2000).

Iraq and Iran

Filmmakers fell under comparable constraints in two nearby states on the Arabian Peninsula. In 1979, a revolt drove the shah of the Pahlavi dynasty out of Iran, and the Ayatollah Khomeini took over the government. While Khomeini was consolidating a fundamentalist Islamic state, his country was attacked by Iraq, led by Saddam Hussein. The war proved costly for Iran. At the cease-fire of 1988, Khomeini's leadership was shaken and Saddam had gained stature.

Iraq's cinema had long been inconsequential; Iraqi dialect was incomprehensible in other Middle Eastern countries, and no stars or genres were worth exporting. But as Saddam bid for leadership of the Arab community, his government launched a patriotic film program. It established a monopoly on production and began inviting Arab filmmakers to work on big-budget features. The $15 million battle epic *Al-Qadissa* (1981) was the most expensive film ever made in the Arab world. Directed by the Egyptian veteran Salah Abou Seif, it utilized a crew drawn from all over the Middle East. In celebrating a seventh-century Iraqi victory over Persian forces, *Al-Qadissa* suggests parallels to Saddam's war with Iran. His next military venture, against the much smaller neighboring Arab country of Kuwait, led to the U.S. launching the Gulf War against Iraq. Driven out of Kuwait, Saddam resisted peace with western nations. The resulting long-standing boycott decimated the country's filmmaking.

Iran: Before and after the Revolution   Iran's cinema, much more significant than Iraq's, underwent more severe fluctuations. Under the shah, Tehran boasted a major film festival and a commercial industry releasing up to seventy films a year. In the early 1970s the mass-entertainment cinema was counterbalanced by the *cinema motefävet* ("New Iranian Cinema"), exemplified by films such as Dariush Mehrjui's *Gav* ("The Cow," 1970; **26.45**). Some directors left the film workers' union to establish the New Film Group, which received limited government funding. Mehrjui's *The Cycle* (1976) and Bahman Farmanara's *Tall Shadows of the Wind* (1978)

26.45   The regional realism of *Gav:* Hassan returns to his village, unaware that his beloved cow has died.

were among several films criticizing social conditions, including the shah's secret police.

After Khomeini's 1979 revolution many filmmakers went into exile, and film production slackened. Only about a hundred features were made between 1979 and 1985. Censorship, confined largely to political topics under the shah, now also focused on sexual display and western influences. Foreign films were drastically cut and shown with dubbed commentary. Soon Khomeini's regime drove out foreign cinema altogether.

Iran's theocracy condemned many western traditions, but government officials quickly recognized that film could mobilize citizens to support the regime. Movies were powerful in a nation in which nearly half the population was under the age of fifteen. Khomeini's government created a film industry that reflected his interpretation of Iranian culture and the Shi'ite Muslim tradition. The Farabi Cinema Foundation (FCF), established in 1983, offered government financial aid to producers willing to back directors' first films. Although the war with Iraq was depleting the country's resources, the regime encouraged a new generation of filmmakers, and production rose steadily. Even women directors entered the industry.

A Film Renaissance in Iran   The Ayatollahs' restrictive regime would seem an unlikely source of creative cinema, yet soon a series of imaginative, affecting films began to appear not only in Iranian theaters but at film festivals abroad. One reason for such apparent freedom was the Children and Young Adults' Unit of the FCF. Films for or about children were unlikely to contain political messages offensive to the government, and they received easy funding. As a result, some of the most original directors took this route, and many of the earliest films to gain international attention centered on children.

26.46 In *Under the Olive Trees*, tensions between local nonactors repeatedly ruin a simple scene.

The first filmmaker to gain wide acclaim was the veteran Abbas Kiarostami. His unpretentious story of a child searching for his classmate in a distant village, *Where Is My Friend's Home?* (1986), brought attention to New Iranian Cinema. As a sequel, Kiarostami made *And Life Goes On* (1992), an autobiographical fiction film showing a film director and his son driving through the regions devastated by the 1991 earthquake, searching for the boy who had performed in the earlier film. Kiarostami uses imaginative framings to dedramatize the quake's horror and display the determination of the survivors, as when the son pours a drink for an unseen baby in an adjacent vehicle (**Color Plate 26.25**).

Kiarostami completed this boxes-within-boxes trilogy in 1994 with *Under the Olive Trees* (aka *Through the Olive Trees*), a film about a movie crew camping near a small village in the earthquake region. They are apparently making *And Life Goes On*. Kiarostami creates a humorously maddening scene: multiple takes of the same shot break down when the young actress refuses to speak to the actor who is courting her in real life (**26.46**). Kiarostami went on to deal with the forbidden subject of suicide in *The Taste of Cherry*, the 1997 Grand Prize–winner at Cannes. His *The Wind Will Carry Us* (1999) takes another media professional on a contemplative, faintly comic journey into the countryside. By the early 1990s, Kiarostami was obtaining his funding from outside Iran, but his films were still subject to government censorship.

Kiarostami's prominence drew the world's attention to other talented Iranian filmmakers. Jafar Panahi, who had assisted on *Under the Olive Trees*, inspired Kiarostami to write *The White Balloon* (1995), which Panahi made as his first feature. Coaxing a remarkable performance out of the child lead, Panahi then cast her sister in *The Mirror* (1997), about a little girl who tries to make

her way home from school in crowded Tehran. Along with *Where Is My Friend's Home?*, such films established what the Iranians called the "child quest" genre, in which a determined child doggedly overcomes obstacles to achieve a goal. Not only were such films relatively safe fare politically, but they charmed audiences abroad.

Like Kiarostami, Mohsen Makhmalbaf had been directing since the 1970s, but his international breakout film was *Salaam Cinema* (1994), a good-humored documentary about film lovers. He swiftly turned out many lyrical films, including *Moment of Innocence* (1996), like *Under the Olive Trees*, about the ways in which romance disrupts filmmaking; *Gabbeh* (1996), a mystical drama about a weaver of Persian carpets; and the rapturous *The Silence* (1998), centered on a blind boy who must find work. Makhmalbaf also appeared as himself in Kiarostami's *Close-Up* (1990), which investigates a bizarre swindle: a film buff impersonated Makhmalbaf and promised to put people into movies. Kiarostami intercuts documentary footage of the culprit's trial with staged scenes in which participants reenact the event. Makhmalbaf's 2001 film *Kandahar*, a tale of Afghan oppression under the Taliban, became unintentionally timely and popular abroad after the United States began its campaign against terrorism in Afghanistan.

On the basis of his successes, Makhmalbaf established his own firm, the Makhmalbaf Film House, for which his 17-year-old daughter Samira directed *The Apple* (1997), using him as scriptwriter and editor. Basing her film on the true story of a couple who had never let their two 12-year-old daughters out of the house until forced to by social workers, Samira Makhmalbaf recruited the family themselves to reenact their story, which they do so with remarkable naturalness and unconcern for the camera's presence (**Color Plate 26.26**). Her second feature, *Blackboards* (2000), used mostly nonactors to portray unemployed teachers on the roads near the Iraqi border, struggling to educate refugees too concerned with staying alive to respond. Mohsen Makhmalbaf's wife, Marziyeh Meshkini, worked as assistant director to her daughter and then took up directing herself with *The Day I Became a Woman* (2000), examining the situation of women in Iran through tales of three generations.

In comparison to its Middle Eastern neighbors, Iran proved notably successful in building its film industry. While in 1980, the year after the downfall of the shah, only twenty-eight features were made, by 2001 the number had risen to eighty-seven. Many nations were like Iran in providing some form of government subsidies for filmmaking, but in Iran there was one enormous advantage: American films were banned. In fact, bootleg videotapes of foreign films, mostly from Hollywood, circulated widely and clandestinely. After copies of *Titanic* appeared in Tehran, Leonardo DiCaprio's face appeared on the fronts of magazines and of Iranian teenagers wearing knock-off T-shirts. But theatergoers were limited mostly to domestically produced fare. Most films were in popular genres like melodramas and historical pageants, and these seldom circulated to festivals.

Few countries, however, won such acclaim on the world's film-festival circuit. While to the West Iran might seem a closed society, the Farabi Cinema Foundation monitored the international scene carefully. An English-language quarterly called *Film International* ranked films and directors by the number of their successes at festivals. With the FCF now coordinating all national film activities, more money was poured into production. The average film budget rose from $11,000 in 1990 to $200,000 in 1998—still, of course, absurdly low by western standards.

In 1997, Iran elected a more liberal president, Mohammed Khatemi. As a former minister of culture, he had played a role in helping filmmakers achieve some relative freedom. His desire to open Iran to a dialogue with the West was strongly opposed by more conservative officials, but Khatemi had a powerful ally in his country's cinema.

AFRICAN CINEMA

Of all Third World regions, Africa remained the most underdeveloped. Although about 10 percent of the world's population lived there, the continent represented only 1 percent of world productivity and trade. Already poor in arable land, the region suffered from devastating droughts. As people fled the villages, the cities became the fastest-growing in the Third World. Of the thirty poorest countries in the world, twenty-five were in Africa.

Because of this poverty, most African countries did not produce a feature-length film before the mid-1970s. Many nations had small populations, few theaters, and virtually no technical facilities. Distribution was controlled by foreign companies, and they had little to gain from promoting competition within Africa. And governments living on IMF austerity measures were unlikely to support much domestic production.

As a result, African filmmakers moved toward international cooperation. In 1970, they created the Fédération Pan-Africaine des Cinéastes (FEPACI), an association of over thirty countries that aimed to solve common problems. In 1980, the United Nations helped film workers found a continent-wide distribution network, the Consortium Interafricain de Distribution Cinematographique (CIDC), to assist the dissemination of African films. To the festivals of Carthage, Tunisia (established in 1966) and Ouagadougou, Burkina Faso (1969) was added another in Mogadishu, Somalia (1981).

Such initiatives generated a little state support. Senegal, Algeria, and Tunisia nationalized film import and distribution. Some countries also nationalized production. Burkina Faso, despite its tiny size, became an administrative center of black African film, increasing the importance of the annual Ouagadougou festival and creating a film school and a well-equipped production facility. New directors emerged, including Senegal's Safi Faye, the first black African woman filmmaker (*Letter from My Village*, 1976).

On the whole, however, regional continental associations and state support failed to raise production or enhance distribution possibilities. The CIDC halted its work in 1984; of the 1,200 titles it distributed, only about 60 were African. The Cinafric studio in Burkina Faso remained the only indigenous production facility. Filmmaking was still an artisanal activity, with the director forced to raise funds, arrange publicity, and negotiate distribution. Few filmmakers completed second films, and those who did waited many years between projects.

The late 1980s saw little cooperation among African states. The continent's production outside Egypt and South Africa amounted to fewer than twenty features annually. Senegal, the leader of Francophone filmmaking on the continent, had produced around two dozen features, most notably the works of Ousmane Sembene (p. 548). Most countries had made fewer than ten features since achieving independence. The production of short films and documentaries was more robust, however, especially in Anglophone countries like Ghana and Nigeria, which were bequeathed documentary film units by the British colonists.

North Africa

The Francophone North African countries known as the Maghreb were in a position to develop filmmaking somewhat. In Morocco, private producers made a few popular entertainments on the model of Egyptian melodramas and musicals. One Moroccan filmmaker, Souhel Ben Barka, attracted attention with accessible dramas of social criticism, such as *A Thousand and One Hands* (1972), about the carpet industry and *Amok* (1982), a treatment of South African apartheid filmed on a big budget and starring singer Miriam Makeba. In Tunisia,

26.47 *Chronicle of the Years of Embers:* the hero, wheeling the corpses of his plague-ridden family to the graveyard, follows the wise fool.

a mixture of government funding and private investment turned out a few coproductions.

The most significant film industry in the Maghreb was Algeria's. After winning its independence from France in 1962, Algeria nationalized all aspects of its film industry and successfully resisted a Hollywood boycott. The government also established a national film archive. Throughout the late 1960s and the early 1970s, the most influential films were dramas of the revolutionary struggle, such as Mohamed Lakhdar Hamina's *Wind of Aurès* (1965).

In the early 1970s, Algeria's government shifted to the left, and social criticism emerged in a *Cinema djidid* (New Cinema), seen in Mohamed Bouamari's *The Charcoal Maker* (1973) and other works. Within two years, however, the New Cinema declined as the government began subsidizing big-budget historical dramas. The most famous of these, Hamina's *Chronicle of the Years of Embers* (1975; **26.47**), treats the history of the country between 1939 and 1954. Hamina's saga of village life under colonialism cost $2 million and became the first African film to win the Grand Prize at the Cannes Film Festival. Much criticized for his mainstream style, Hamina echoed Youssef Chahine in asserting that political modernism could not reach large audiences: "I believe that good films are distinctive by their universality."[6]

Algeria had the second-highest film output in the Arab-African world, and its 300 theaters gave it a fairly strong audience base. Popular cinema underwent a revival with satiric comedies and political thrillers reminiscent of Costa-Gavras, while some directors explored the everyday life of ordinary Algerians. In the early 1980s, filmmakers took up new themes, notably women's emancipation and workers' emigration to Europe. At the same time, however, the government relinquished central control of filmmaking. As private companies began producing mass-market films, Algerian filmmakers pursued projects abroad and embarked on Francophone coproductions featuring European actors. Even militant members of the New Cinema generation found themselves, like Latin American and European proponents of critical political cinema, making more mainstream and accessible works.

Sub-Saharan Africa

Comparatively little black African production was in a mass-market vein. The Nigerian director Ola Balogun produced musical films based on Yoruba theater (**26.48**). Cameroon turned out police thrillers as well as very successful comedies by Danial Kamwa (*Boubou cravate,* 1972; *Pousse-pousse,* 1975) and Jean-Pierre Dikongue-Pipa (*Muna moto,* 1975; *The Price of Liberty,* 1978). Ghana generated commercial action pictures, while in Zaire *La Vie est belle* (*Life Is Beautiful,* 1986) became a box-office hit by capitalizing on the charisma of music star Papa Wemba.

Less mass-oriented films, principally from Francophone countries, claimed worldwide attention. Shown at festivals during the 1970s and 1980s, black African films suggested avenues for a postcolonial cinema. International audiences might miss indigenous details and specific references, but the films' recurrent thematic oppositions—tradition versus modernity, country versus city, native lore versus westernized education, collective values versus individuality—were evident. They posed questions of authorship and Third Cinema with particular acuteness. And because most directors had been trained in Europe and had grown up watching American films, their works displayed a dynamic interaction between western filmmaking conventions and explorations of African aesthetic traditions.

One of the most significant traditions was that of oral storytelling (see "Notes and Queries" at the end of

26.48 Balogun's *Ajani Ogun* (1976) exemplifies his popular adaptations of Nigerian theater and dance.

26.49 In *Jom*, the griot moves through history, appearing at various moments of crisis to aid his people; here he joins women on their way to force their husbands to join a strike.

26.50 Women storytellers in *Faces of Women*.

this chapter). Sometimes a film includes a storyteller as part of its action, as when Fadiko Kramo-Lancine makes the griot a main character in *Djeli* ("Blood," Ivory Coast, 1981). A film might also employ the storyteller as an omniscient narrator, as in Ababakar Samb's *Jom* ("Dignity,"

1981; **26.49**). Chiek Oumar Sissoko's *Guimba* (1995) has a griot as its hero, as does Dani Koouyate's *Keita: The Heritage of the Griot* (1995). Or a film might draw from folklore character types such as the trickster or plot action such as the initiation or quest. Oumarou Ganda's *The Exiled* (Niger, 1980) links an ambassador's adventures in an episode folktale pattern. More recently, Jean-Pierre Bekolo's *Quartier Mozart* (Cameroon, 1992) combines elements of folk magic with music-video editing.

For the most part, black African filmmaking since the mid-1970s followed the trends of political commentary and social criticism characteristic of Third World cinema of the late 1960s. There were comparatively few films of exile, but films dramatizing colonial conflict continued to be made. In *West Indies* (1979), Med Hondo staged an operatic treatment of the slave trade within a vast set, built in an abandoned Paris auto factory. Hondo returned to Africa to film *Sourraouina* (1987), an epic of anticolonial rebellion. After a ten-year hiatus, Ousmane Sembene resumed filmmaking with *Campe de Thiaroye* (Senegal, 1987; codirected by Thiemo Faty Sow), a drama treating the clash between French and Senegalese infantrymen at the end of World War II.

Studies of contemporary conditions continued as well. Souleymane Cissé's *Finye* (*The Wind,* 1982) criticizes a military regime by dramatizing the growth of student protest. At the climax of the action, a young man's grandfather, committed to ancestral magic, joins the political struggle. Cissé's sumptuous images—the product of his belief that too many African films were technically awkward—enhance the drama's mixture of politics and supernatural forces.

One of the most widely seen films portraying contemporary African life was Désiré Écaré's *Visages de femmes* (*Faces of Women,* Ivory Coast, 1985). Although his earlier films (p. 548) had won prestigious festival prizes, Écaré took twelve years to finance and film *Faces of Women*. The film's first story centers on two village women's attempts to outwit their husbands. The film then shifts to present a prosperous, middle-aged city woman seeking to expand her business while taking care of her lazy husband, spoiled daughters, and demanding rural kinfolk.

Écaré emphasizes the tension between tradition and modernization through contrasting film styles—a rough Direct Cinema approach for the village story, a more polished technique for the urban tale. The first story is interrupted by shots of women at a festival reciting it and commenting on it (**26.50**), in the manner of oral performance, while in the second story voice-over commentary is supplied by the heroine herself. This narrational

27.5 Digital special effects create the fated *Titanic* at dockside.

Six Directors Steven Spielberg and George Lucas were the only top-grossing directors of the 1970s to make top-ten films in the next two decades. Nearly all the 1970s major directors, from Woody Allen and Robert Altman to Brian De Palma and Clint Eastwood, were outstripped by newer names willing to turn out megapics. Leaving risk-taking to the independent sector, Hollywood wanted movies to be dominated by stars, special effects, and recognizable genre conventions. Ambitious filmmakers often had to find some creative spark in genre exercises, sequels, or remakes. Still, some directors blended distinctive personal styles with the demands of event films.

James Cameron was perfectly suited to the new demands for megapics. Beginning in special-effects jobs, he became adept at every phase of the filmmaking process, from scriptwriting to editing and sound effects. Science fiction and fantasy came naturally to him, as did the sort of striking, powerful ideas that succeeded in the high-concept 1980s. Above all, Cameron realized that a successful film could be built around nonstop physical action. His breakthrough, *The Terminator* (1984), displayed ingenious chases and gunplay, sketching in its time-travel premise without halting the breathless pace. *The Terminator* proved that Cameron could squeeze high quality out of a small budget while yielding catchphrase dialogue ("I'll be back," "Come with me if you want to live") and a career-making performance from robotic Arnold Schwarzenegger. *Terminator 2: Judgment Day* (1991), with even more grandiose action set-pieces also pushed computer-generated visual effects to new levels in the presentation of a liquefying Terminator (**Color Plate 27.4**). Cameron was comfortable with sequels and spinoffs, injecting adrenaline into every plot. *Aliens* (1986) gave *Alien* (1979) a military twist, emphasizing firepower and squad camaraderie. *The Abyss* (1989) inserted into a *Close Encounters* premise more thrills than Spielberg had felt necessary, and *True Lies* (1994), a tongue-in-cheek spy piece, sought to out-Bond the Bonds.

With *Titanic,* Cameron produced the perfect date movie: doomed love between a spunky heroine and a boyish hero, a long prologue featuring high-tech gadgetry, and a costume romance that culminated in an hour packed with action, suspense, and spectacular visual effects (**27.5**). Although *Titanic* was scheduled as a summer blockbuster, production delays pushed it to December, which gave a prestigious David Lean quality to the film. Opening on nearly 2,700 screens, it played for months, sometimes increasing its audience from week to week. Although the production had cost $200 million, one of the studios backing it profited by at least $500 million. *Titanic*'s stupendous success and its spillover benefits (such as luring in older viewers who had given up on modern movies) reconfirmed Hollywood's faith in event pictures.

Robert Zemeckis lacked Cameron's reputation as an obsessive taskmaster, but he became just as adept at exploiting new technologies. Trained under Spielberg, Zemeckis made two comedies before directing *Romancing the Stone* (1984), a wryly feminist version of *Raiders of the Lost Ark.* He created the ingenious *Back to the Future* films (1985, 1989, 1990), which mixed science fiction, comedy, and teenpic appeals. Zemeckis proved a skillful storyteller, able to lay out the convolutions of Marty McFly's time travels with amusing economy.

Like Cameron, Zemeckis sought out technical challenges: blending live action with animation (*Who Framed Roger Rabbit?*, 1988; **Color Plate 27.5**) and inserting contemporary actors into historical footage (*Forrest Gump,* 1994; **27.6**). His films' relentless cheerfulness often seemed to leave a zone of ambiguity, as when *Forrest Gump*'s celebration of mindless optimism veers toward mocking American values. Zemeckis embraced top box-office stars but subsumed them to each production's over-

27.6 Digital compositing inserts Forrest Gump into a Kennedy photo opportunity.

all concept. In *Cast Away,* Zemeckis presented a modern Robinson Crusoe, building a story out of fine detail, crisply articulated turning points, the star acting of Tom Hanks, and an austere and evocative sound track.

Not all films, though, had to have a high-end budget if a director could create an event aura around the project. Oliver Stone proved adept at doing so as he moved from the independent realm to mid-budget studio filmmaking. Gifted with a flair for promoting both his films and himself, he attracted top stars to controversial topics: America's new business climate (*Wall Street*, 1987), the legacy of the Vietnam War (*Born on the Fourth of July*, 1988; *Heaven and Earth*, 1993), recent presidential history (*JFK*, 1991; *Nixon*, 1995), the power of the media (*Natural Born Killers*, 1994). Assiduously working the talk-show circuit, Stone made his name synonymous with passionate social-problem filmmaking. His 1990s films became flamboyant and jarring—rapidly cut, full of jolting camera movements, and mixing color with black-and-white footage, 35mm with super 8mm, naturalistic shooting with outrageous special effects (**27.7**). For *Natural Born Killers*, the actors sometimes filmed scenes themselves. Yet Stone also worked pragmatically, such as building stadium signs to allow product placement in the football drama *Any Given Sunday* (2000).

Another emigrant from independent filmmaking was Spike Lee, one of the most prolific directors of the period. Race, he remarked, was "America's biggest problem, always has been (since we got off the boat), always will be."[9] He often addressed his films to black audiences, using "Wake up!" as a signature line to emphasize the need to take the initiative in solving African Americans' problems. *School Daze* (1988) is a drama-musical about life in a traditionally black college. *Mo' Better Blues* (1990) centers on the development of jazz as a

27.7 *Natural Born Killers* inserts wide-angle, black-and-white shots into its media mix.

business and a way of life, and *Jungle Fever* (1991) deals with interracial romance. *Malcolm X* (1992), a biography of the Black Muslim leader, was scaled as an event movie and required complicated historical re-creations. *Do The Right Thing* (1989), which many regard as Lee's masterpiece, offers a panoramic portrayal of racial and sexual tensions in a Harlem neighborhood in a single day. Faced with shrinking budgets, Lee turned to more intimate subjects (*Girl 6*, 1996), docudrama (*Get on the Bus*, 1996), and straight documentary (*4 Little Girls*, 1997). He constantly experimented with color schemes (**Color Plate 27.6**), camerawork (distorted lenses in *Crooklyn*, 1994), and sound; the hip-hop track of *Do The Right Thing* was a major ingredient in its success.

Also steering a course between megapics and lower-budget projects was Tim Burton. Of all the Hollywood talents of the 1980s and 1990s, Burton created the most

27.8 Tim Burton makes Beetlejuice (aka Betelgeuse) a cross between a ghoul and a circus clown.

distinctive visual world. He filled familiar American landscapes with grotesque, absurdist imagery. The New England town of *Beetlejuice* (1988), a haven for yuppies and bored New York gentry, harbors a clownish but dangerous "bio-exorcist" (**27.8**). The suburbia of *Edward Scissorhands* (1990) is invaded by an awkward young monster resembling a Goth rocker. The trailer parks and Las Vegas streets of *Mars Attacks!* (1996) fall prey to ruthless, brainy aliens (**Color Plate 27.7**) who can be stopped only by the yodeling of Slim Whitman. The films' playful ominousness is enhanced by Danny Elfman's scores.

Burton started as an animator, and he never stopped seeing human beings as cartoon characters or puppets, so the rise of special-effects driven movies played directly into his talents. He was drawn to perverse exercises such as *Ed Wood* (1994), a celebration of "the world's worst director;" and he wrote and produced *The Nightmare before Christmas* (1993, Henry Selick), full of astringent songs and unsettling gags (a little boy finds a python under his Christmas tree). But Burton was careful to establish himself as bankable with megapics like the top-grossing *Batman* (1989) and *Planet of the Apes* (2001).

Refusing to woo the teen audience, Michael Mann created traditional films of unusual purity: the neo-noir pieces *Thief* (1981), *Manhunter* (1986), and *Heat* (1995); the romantic historical adventure *The Last of the Mohicans* (1992); the social-problem exposé *The Insider* (1999). Mann's brilliant cinematographer Dante Spinotti helped him cultivate a spare, cool style, turning characters' surroundings into abstract color designs (**Color Plate 27.8**). Fascinated by the group dynamics of planning a heist or investigating a cover-up, Mann became one of the most detached directors since Otto Preminger.

But any tendency to coldness was modified by his daring scores (perhaps a vestige of the music montages of *Miami Vice,* the television series Mann created). The rhythmically cut climax of *Mohicans* staged a clifftop fight to a Scottish dance, while *Heat*'s eclectic sound track, ranging from Moby to the Kronos Quartet, deepened the melancholy tale of two loners bent on self-destruction. Mann showed that even in the New New Hollywood, traditions could be soberly and sensitively updated.

Genres

Continuing trends set in the 1960s, American films tested the boundaries of taste. Whatever the genre, an ordinary movie was likely to include sensational violence, sexuality, or obscene language. When even the family-friendly Spielberg experimented with more shocking material in *Gremlins* (1984, directed by Joe Dante) and *Indiana Jones and the Temple of Doom* (1984), the MPAA rating system was revised to include a PG-13 category.

Aided by the new frankness, the 1970s upgrading of exploitation genres like horror, science fiction, and fantasy continued. These highly artificial and visceral genres could exploit cutting-edge special effects and could spin off into comic books, television series, and videogames. Ridley Scott's noir/science-fiction crossover *Blade Runner* (1982) proved to be one of the most influential films of the period. Its detailed creation of a rainy, rusty dystopia would become the norm for portrayals of the future, and its mix of cultural icons (Asian, retro American, Punk) set a new standard for film design (**27.9**). Many of the 1970s generation—Steven Spielberg, Brian De Palma, John Carpenter, and George Romero—continued in the horror genre; even Francis Ford Coppola (*Bram Stoker's Dracula,* 1992) and other prestigious directors had a fling with it. David Cronenberg emphasized horrific deformations of the body in *Scanners* (1981), *Videodrome* (1983), and *The Fly* (1986). The former Monty Python animator Terry Gilliam displayed a Rabelaisian grotesquerie in his dark comic fantasies *Brazil* (1985) and *Twelve Monkeys* (1995). M. Night Shayamalan extracted a mournful anxiety from fantasy conventions in *The Sixth Sense* (1999; **27.10**) and *Unbreakable* (2000).

Comedy proved equally durable. The romantic comedy, usually star-driven, furnished many hits—from *Tootsie* (1982) through *When Harry Met Sally* (1989), *Pretty Woman* (1990), and *Jerry Maguire* (1995) to *What Women Want* (2000). Romantic comedy sustained the careers of two women directors, Penny Marshall (*Big,* 1988) and Nora Ephron (*Sleepless in Seattle,* 1993), and

27.9 *Blade Runner:* Los Angeles as Metropolis and Tokyo.

27.10   The young hero of *The Sixth Sense* picks up a dead child's anguish.

27.11   *Se7en:* the serial killer neo-noir at its most morbid.

many female stars, notably Julia Roberts, Meg Ryan, and Sandra Bullock. The farce, typified by the collaborations of Jerry and David Zucker and Jim Abrahams on *Airplane!* (1980) and *The Naked Gun* (1988), later served as a vehicle for comedians extending the Jerry Lewis tradition of spasmodic performance, such as Jim Carrey and Adam Sandler. The teen comedy was initially developed in a relatively innocent form by John Hughes (*The Breakfast Club*, 1985) and Amy Heckerling (*Fast Times at Ridgemont High*; *Clueless*, 1995), but the most enduring brand proved to be the gross-out sex farce, emerging in *Animal House* (1978) and successfully cloned in *Porky's* (1981) and *Revenge of the Nerds* (1984). The raunch factor increased dramatically in *There's Something about Mary* (1998) and *American Pie* (1999).

While the Western and the live-action musical, staples of the 1960s and 1970s, virtually died, other genres became more prominent. The neo-noir crime thriller, traceable to Polanski's *Chinatown* (1974), came into its own with many exercises in lust, murder, and betrayal, including *Body Heat* (1981) and *L.A. Confidential* (1997). Serial killers became central to neo-noir, since their predations could add a touch of horror or morbid fantasy, as in *The Silence of the Lambs* (1991), *Se7en* (1995; **27.11**), and *The Cell* (2000).

The newly supreme genre was the blood-filled action film, initially built around pneumatic stars like Schwarzenegger and Stallone (*First Blood*, 1982, and two *Rambo* sequels). The action film of heroic adventure

27.12 Bold rack-focus in anamorphic Panavision: from the TV announcer . . .

27.13 . . . to the reporter in the foreground (*Die Hard*).

was established as a winning formula by *Raiders of the Lost Ark* (1980) and continued in such films as *Rambo: First Blood 2* (1985) and *The Mummy* (1999). The interracial cop-buddy picture, sparked by *48HRS*, was sustained in the *Lethal Weapon* franchise (1987–1999) and innumerable other efforts. John McTiernan emerged as the most skillful practitioner of the new action picture; his fluent direction of *Die Hard* (1988) set a standard for elegant camera movement and well-timed staging (**27.12, 27.13**), while also establishing Bruce Willis as a major star. Many megapics of these two decades would mix breakneck action with comedy, fantasy, horror, and science-fiction elements, as in *Batman, Ghostbusters, Jurassic Park, Independence Day* (1996), and *Men in Black* (1997).

During the 1980s and 1990s, the animated film reestablished itself as a viable genre. Disney lost momentum when some of the studio's former animators broke away under the leadership of Don Bluth to make *The Secret of NIMH* (1982) and *An American Tail* (1986), the first cartoon produced by Steven Spielberg. Bluth's success led to a proliferation of features with rich textures and fully articulated movements. But Disney reasserted its preeminence with *The Little Mermaid* (1989), incorporating lively songs by Howard Menken and Howard Ashman. The Disney team went further in *Beauty and the Beast* (1991), in which rotoscope techniques were applied to the sets, giving space a fresh volume and solidity (**Color Plate 27.9**). Disney's new cartoon features were aimed at all ages, offering simple stories for children, and romance and verbal comedy for teenagers. *Aladdin* (1992) used Robin Williams's free-associative patter as a basis for the genie's frenzied shape-shifting. The tuneful and splendidly designed *Lion King* (1994) became the top-grossing film in animation history. Disney's 1990s triumphs proved that animation could still attract the entire family—a lesson driven home by the phenomenal success of computer animated features from the mid-1990s.

A NEW AGE OF INDEPENDENT CINEMA

Video income allowed low-budget companies like Troma to continue turning out the sort of gross comedies and exploitation horror (*The Toxic Avenger,* 1985) that had surfaced in the 1970s. Soon, however, films made and distributed outside the major companies began to attract wide audiences. How many people who saw *Platoon*

(1986), *Dirty Dancing* (1987), *Mystic Pizza* (1988), *The Player* (1992), *Leaving Las Vegas* (1995), and *Pleasantville* (1998) realized that these were independent movies? More daring films pushed the boundaries of style and subject matter. *Stranger than Paradise* (1984) and *Blue Velvet* (1986) presented off-center, avant-garde visions of the world. "Independent film" took on an outlaw aura, with *Pulp Fiction* (1994) and *Killing Zoe* (1995) marketed as the last word in hipness. Part of the buzz around *The Brothers McMullen* (1995), *The Tao of Steve* (2000), and other fairly conventional romantic comedies came from the sense that they were indie movies. The Hollywood conglomerates realized that they could diversify their output and reach young audiences by teaming up with independents.

Support Systems

By the late 1980s, there were between 200 and 250 independent releases per year, over three times the number of studio-based releases. What enabled the independents to become so active? For one thing, new labor policies. In the early 1980s, an "East Coast Contract" permitted union technicians to work on independent productions without losing their union membership. The Screen Actors Guild wrote special agreements to allow performers to work for lower pay scales on low-budget and nontheatrical projects. There also emerged new venues for independent work, such as the Independent Feature Film Market, an annual round of screenings for press and distributors. In 1980, Robert Redford established the Sundance Film Institute in Utah, where aspiring filmmakers could meet to develop scripts and get coaching from industry professionals.

Fresh funding sources also appeared. The Public Broadcasting System's *American Playhouse* series financed theatrical features in exchange for first television rights. Independents could also draw production money from the new ancillary markets. Specialized U.S. cable companies had a voracious appetite for niche fare, and European broadcasting companies were eager to acquire low-cost American films. The German firm ZDF was the most prominent, funding such films as *Stranger than Paradise* and Bette Gordon's *Variety* (1984). Above all, in the early years of the home video market, cassette presales could cover a large part of an independent film's budget.

While the Majors had enormous publicity machinery, the independents relied on press reviews and film festivals. Overseas festivals were important showcases, but the prime venue turned out to be in Utah. In 1978,

the U.S. Film Festival began in Salt Lake City, featuring some independent work alongside retrospectives of classic cinema. Redford's Sundance Institute took over the event and moved it to Park City, renaming it the Sundance Film Festival in 1990. In the early years, Sundance programming leaned toward humanistic rural pictures ("granola movies"), but the screening of Steven Soderbergh's *sex, lies, and videotape* (1989) changed the festival's image drastically. This polished tale of yuppie angst won the top prize and went on to gross nearly $100 million in worldwide theatrical release, a staggering amount for a low-budget drama. From then on, Park City swarmed with Hollywood agents and distributors looking for the next big hit.

The Sundance Film Festival became the preeminent indie brand name. It attracted over a thousand submissions for its 100 or so annual screening slots, was covered extensively in the press, and established its own cable television channel. Soon many U.S. communities founded festivals showcasing independent film. Sundance was thus central to the "mainstreaming" of independent cinema. Redford explained that Sundance's concentration on personal films did not constitute a criticism of Hollywood. "What we have tried to do is to eliminate the tension that can exist between the independents and the studios. . . . Many industry people participate, and it's a great place for independent filmmakers to make contacts."[10]

Mini-Majors such as Orion sometimes underwrote independent productions, but the biggest players on the independent scene were New Line Cinema and Miramax. Both these "art-house indies" began as small companies acquiring finished films and distributing them with flair. By the early 1990s, they were themselves Mini-Majors, financing and producing films.

New Line, established in 1967, became a premiere distributor of European films and low-budget horror (*Texas Chainsaw Massacre,* 1974), as well as the showcase for John Waters's outrageous oeuvre, from *Pink Flamingos* (1972) to *Hairspray* (1988). New Line eventually became an important conduit for more highbrow independent films (*The Rapture,* 1991; *My Own Private Idaho,* 1991; *My Family,* 1995; *Wag the Dog,* 1997). The company started its Fine Line division to deal in edgier fare such as *The Unbelievable Truth* (1990) and *Gummo* (1997). At the same time, New Line found large-scale success with *Teenage Mutant Ninja Turtles* (1990) and the *Nightmare on Elm Street* and *House Party* franchises, Jim Carrey comedies, and other lucrative genre items. Said Mike De Luca, production head, "I always thought of us as a Hollywood studio."[11]

Miramax was founded in 1979 by two brothers, the former rock-concert promoters Bob and Harvey Weinstein. Buoyed by the Oscar-crowned U.S. release of *Cinema Paradiso* (1988), the Weinsteins discovered their first indie blockbuster in *sex, lies, and videotape*. Miramax went on to triumph with *Reservoir Dogs* (1992), *Clerks* (1994), *Pulp Fiction, The English Patient* (1997), and *Shakespeare in Love* (1998). Directors complained that "Harvey Scissorhands" was too quick to trim their movies, but no one doubted the advantages of doing business with a company that could offer $11 million at Sundance for the rights to an unknown movie (*Happy, Texas*, 1999). The company became an indie empire, setting up long-term relations with preferred actors and expanding into television, music, and publishing. Miramax also started its own downscale line with Dimension, which found wide success with the perennial low-budget genre, teen horror, in the *Scream* and *Scary Movie* franchises.

The revenues earned by *sex, lies, and videotape* and *Pulp Fiction* were exceptional for the indie world. In 1995, independent films represented only about 5 percent of U.S. box-office income. The sector still attracted investors, however, because a moderately successful film could return a handsome profit relative to outlay. In 1998, *Sliding Doors* cost $7 million and returned nearly ten times that in worldwide box office, while π (*Pi*, 1998) yielded $4 million, thirteen times its $300,000 budget.

Such profit potential made the Majors start shopping. In 1993, the Disney corporation purchased Miramax, and a year later Ted Turner acquired New Line and Castle Rock, just before Time Warner bought out Turner's media holdings. The Majors also relaunched classics divisions (Fox Searchlight, Sony Pictures Classics) to handle independent product. The most successful independent companies became branches of the studios, catering to specialized tastes. Just as important, by acquiring independent companies, the Majors could scout for young directors who might bring fresh talent to the synergy mix.

The Arty Indies

The diversity of independent work makes it hard to categorize, but three main trends can be identified, running from the most experimental to the most traditional.

In 1984, a grainy, bleached-out black-and-white film made for $110,000 became the emblem of a new trend in independent filmmaking. It seemed to reject just about everything that Spielberg-Lucas Hollywood stood

27.14   Hipsters hanging out in *Stranger than Paradise*.

for. Its tempo was slow, and every scene consisted of a single shot, usually a static one. In place of a sumptuous score, the sound track mixed discordant string music with the wailing beat of Screamin' Jay Hawkins. There were no stars, and the actors' performances were dry and deadpan. The plot, split into three long parts, seemed utterly undramatic. Two men in Sinatra fedoras meet a young woman who has just arrived from Hungary. They float and drift, mostly quarreling or playing cards. It was the ultimate hanging-out movie: the three losers hang out in Manhattan, then in Cleveland, and finally in a Florida motel, where they get caught up in a drug deal (**27.14**).

Yet this understated chamber drama/road movie proved strangely compelling. The director, Jim Jarmusch, finished the first section as a short film (using film stock loaned by Wim Wenders), but after strong festival screenings in Europe, he found enough funding to spin the tale out to two more parts. As a full-length feature, *Stranger than Paradise* won the prize for best first film at Cannes and became a highlight of Filmex, Telluride, and Sundance. The National Society of Film Critics named it the best film of the year, and it grossed over $2 million in U.S. art theaters.

In its dedramatized approach to its characters, *Stranger than Paradise* recalled the European art cinema of the 1960s, a tradition that Jarmusch (who studied filmmaking at NYU) knew well. His portrayal of cool bohemians also recalled Beat cinema of the 1950s. Yet in its respectful treatment of people struggling to hide their emotions, his film had an affinity with Robert Bresson, Yasujiro Ozu, and other minimalist masters whom Jarmusch admired. Still, *Stranger than Paradise* was more than the sum of its influences, bringing a tone of ironic affection to the post-Punk New York scene.

27.15, *left*   *Simple Men:* Hartley often uses deflected glances and deep medium shots, as characters talk without listening to each other.

27.16, *right*   A mad housewife? Alienated staging in Todd Haynes's *Safe.*

The success of *Stranger* launched an indie trend toward artifice and stylization. Hal Hartley brought a Jarmusch-like detachment to his tales of Long Island anomie, such as *Trust* (1991) and *Simple Men* (1992), but Hartley tended to be more philosophical and literary. His characters deliver hyperarticulate dialogue in unnervingly flat tones, the scenes captured in ingeniously staged long takes (**27.15**). *Stranger*'s loose structure, opposed to Hollywood's strongly plotted script, encouraged filmmakers to explore fractured storytelling, as in the daisy-chain monologues of Richard Linklater's *Slacker* (1991). In the same spirit, Todd Haynes's first feature, *Poison* (1991), presents three distinct AIDS-related stories, each in a different cinematic or televisual style. Like many filmmakers in this trend, Haynes's projects have a European art-cinema sensibility. His most acclaimed feature, *Safe* (1995), traces the plight of a mysteriously ailing housewife in static long shots reminiscent of Michelangelo Antonioni (**27.16**).

Not least, *Stranger than Paradise* showed that microbudgeted films had a chance to play theaters. (Producers considered a "microbudget" anything under $2 million.) The minimal means available to Jarmusch, Hartley, Linklater, and Haynes prodded their imaginations and allowed them to take chances with subject and style. The films, to use Jarmusch's term, were "hand-made."

Off-Hollywood Indies

Stranger than Paradise, Poison, Slacker, and *Safe* could never have been released by Hollywood companies, but other independent films were less avant-garde. They used recognizable genres and even stars. What pushed them off-Hollywood were their comparatively low budgets and risky subjects, themes, or plots. The careers of Woody Allen and Robert Altman exemplify this trend. Highly praised studio filmmakers in the early years, both were forced to work as independents in the 1980s and

1990s. Under the same conditions, Altman protégé Alan Rudolph continued the quest for an Americanized art cinema in the ambiguous fantasy/flashback sequences of *Choose Me* (1984) and the enigmatic motivations of *Trouble in Mind* (1985).

A key example of the off-Hollywood trend is *Blue Velvet* (1986). After the avant-garde midnight movie *Eraserhead*, the historical piece *The Elephant Man* (1980), and the big-budget science-fiction epic *Dune* (1984), David Lynch made one of the most disquieting films of the decade, a small-town murder mystery wrapped around a young man's sexual curiosity (**Color Plate 27.10**). Nighttime scenes of erotic obsession alternate with sunny picket-fence normality, at the center of it all a voyeuristic college boy, a femme fatale nightclub singer, and a terrifying bully inhaling a mysterious drug through a mask. In the hallucinatory prologue, a man collapses over his garden hose and the camera plunges into the grass, where beetles and ants swarm. At the end, with a perky robin on a windowsill gnawing a beetle, the narration suggests that perhaps everything we have seen has been the repressed hero's fantasy. *Blue Velvet* revived Lynch's career and opened up the anxious, dread-filled landscape he explored in *Wild at Heart* (1990), *Lost Highway* (1997), *Mulholland Drive* (2001), and the television series *Twin Peaks* (1990–1991).

Steven Soderbergh likewise skewed genre conventions in *sex, lies, and videotape* (1989). A husband is having an affair with the sister of his slightly neurotic wife; so far, a standard domestic melodrama. But into the triangle comes the husband's old friend, who confesses that he records women's sexual fantasies on video and then masturbates while replaying them. Gradually both women are drawn toward him, and his boyish passivity becomes a challenge to the swaggering husband. In technique, the film displayed a Hollywood polish. Soderbergh engineered a clever psychodrama while

27.17 The disturbingly passive hero of *sex, lies, and videotape* records women's sexual confessions.

27.18 *Pulp Fiction:* Vincent and Jules on the job.

pushing the envelope of sexual frankness beyond what the Majors would have allowed (**27.17**).

For the 1990s, the milestone off-Hollywood movie was *Pulp Fiction.* In *Reservoir Dogs,* Quentin Tarantino had given the caper film a zestful viciousness and vulgarity. His follow-up was a stew of old genres—gangster film, prizefight film, outlaw movie. Tarantino, a self-admitted movie geek, gave several stars showcase roles. Bathing nearly every character in world-weary cool, he shuffled chronology and interwove storylines. He wrote

scenes of arch wit and visceral violence (a hypodermic to the heart, an auto interior spattered with blood and brains), sprinkling in references to movies and television shows. His chatty hitman duo quickly entered popular culture (**27.18**), as did taglines like "Royale with cheese" and "Did I break your concentration?" At a cost of $8 million, *Pulp Fiction* grossed $200 million worldwide, becoming the most financially successful off-Hollywood independent film of the decade.

On a lesser scale, many 1980s and 1990s independent directors took Hollywood traditions in daring directions. Lizzie Borden's *Working Girls* (1986) offered a spare but sympathetic portrayal of women in the sex industry. Gus Van Sant mixed seedy realism and film-noir stylization in *Drugstore Cowboy* (1989) and *My Own Private Idaho* (1991), a gay/grunge road movie based on Shakespeare. David Fincher brought a visceral grimness to a serial-killer tale in *Se7en* (1995).

Genre conventions could be inflated or deflated. Joel and Ethan Coen offered hyperbolic versions of film noir (*Blood Simple,* 1984), Preston Sturges comedy (*Raising Arizona,* 1987), the Warners gangster film (*Miller's Crossing,* 1989), and the Capraesque success story (*The Hudsucker Proxy,* 1994). While the Coens delighted in pushing genres to the brink of absurdity, playwright David Mamet's tense psychodramas of swindling and misdirection, such as *House of Games* (1987) and *Homicide* (1991), stripped noir conventions down to bare plot mechanics and laconic, repetitive dialogue. The Coens cultivated comic-book visuals (**27.19**) and howling, corny sound tracks, but Mamet's images and sound effects were Bressonian in their austerity (**27.20**).

Soderbergh, Van Sant, the Coens, and other off-Hollywood directors eventually worked, regularly or sporadically, for the studios. The fastest move to the

27.19 A failed executive finds that jumping through a skyscraper window is not as easy as he had thought (*The Hudsucker Proxy*).

27.20 Joseph Mantegna as the wary Jewish cop of Mamet's *Homicide.*

27.21 Spike Lee as Mars Black-mon, talking in-cessantly to Lola Darling.

27.22 In a long take characteristic of *Sling Blade*, the boy meets the man who will change his life.

27.23 Hallucinatory distortion for a pill-popping matron in *Requiem for a Dream*.

Majors was made by Jarmusch's NYU contemporary Spike Lee. In outline, *She's Gotta Have It* (1986) is a classic romantic comedy, with three men pursuing a self-reliant woman. But the men are black, and the woman makes no secret of her sexual appetites. In the long run, Nola Darling is revealed as more liberated than her lovers. Lee revels in African American slang and courtship rituals, as well as his own frenetic perfor-mance as the unstoppable jive artist Mars Blackmon (**27.21**). To-camera monologues show a domesticated Godard influence, particularly in the hilarious montage of strutting men trying out seduction lines. *She's Gotta Have It* proved a perfect indie crossover, earning $30 million in domestic theatrical grosses. Lee was immedi-ately taken into the studios, for which he made many provocative films.

Another politically committed independent was John Sayles, whose low-key but nuanced scrutiny of the political dimensions of everyday life brought a 1970s concern with community into the next two decades (*The Return of the Secaucus Seven*, 1980; *Matewan*, 1987; *City of Hope*, 1991; *Lone Star*, 1996). Oliver Stone of-fered a more strident critique, expressing his sense that 1960s liberal idealism lost its way after the death of Kennedy. In *Salvador* (1986) and *Platoon* (1986), he consciously sought to meld political messages with en-tertainment values. After *Platoon* won three Academy Awards and grossed $160 million, Stone became a high-profile Warner Bros. director.

Off-Hollywood filmmakers also designed their fare for overlooked audiences. On the whole, the Majors neglected the tastes of minority audiences. The gay and lesbian films of the 1980s and 1990s were nonstudio pro-ductions, adapting traditions of melodrama and comedy to alternative lifestyles (*Parting Glances,* 1986; *Desert Hearts,* 1986; *Longtime Companion,* 1990; *Go Fish,* 1994). Similarly, most of the African American, Asian American, and Hispanic directors eventually cultivated by the studios started as independents. Reginald Hudlin moved from *House Party* (1990) to *Boomerang* (1992),

while Wayne Wang's microbudgeted *Chan Is Missing* (1982) led him eventually to *The Joy Luck Club* (1993).

To the very end of the 1990s, off-Hollywood film-makers continued to win attention. Billy Bob Thornton's *Sling Blade* (Miramax, 1998) achieved acclaim despite its slow pace, thanks largely to Thornton's performance as a feeble-minded innocent (**27.22**). In *Happiness* (1998), Todd Soloudz offered a cross section of middle-class misery, from phone sex to pedophilia. Darren Aronofsky's hectic π proved but a prelude to the frenzied drug trip *Requiem for a Dream* (2000; **27.23**). Paul Thomas Anderson used a grant from the Sundance Insti-tute to transform a short film into his first feature, *Hard Eight* (1997). *Boogie Nights* (1997), a jolting New Line vehicle, offers an Altmanesque portrait of the 1970s porn-movie industry, treating scandalous scenes (explicit couplings, a final revelation of the hero's penis) with deli-cate framing and sweeping camera movements. Like Alt-man, Anderson became known as an actor's director, showcasing performances by 1970s icon Burt Reynolds and recurring players Philip Baker Hall, Philip Seymour Hoffman, John C. Reilly, and Julianne Moore. *Magnolia* (1999) was even more ambitious, charting a day in the San Fernando Valley that is interrupted by a meteorolog-ical miracle. Few melodramas have put angry suffering

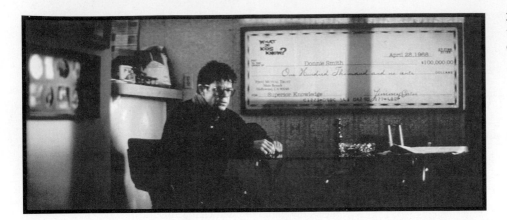

27.24 *Magnolia:* Donny Smith, washed-up quiz kid, broods on a crime while singing "Wise Up."

27.25 The ambivalent beauty of nature in war (*The Thin Red Line*).

so centrally on display, portraying men cracking under physical and emotional strain, endlessly wounding themselves and their loved ones (**27.24**).

Anderson grew up admiring Altman, Scorsese, and films like *Network* (1976). David O. Russell, director of *Spanking the Monkey* (1994) and *Flirting with Disaster* (1996), likewise recalled "all those great 1970s Hollywood movies that had stars and were commercial; yet they were original and subversive."[12] For some, the return of Terrence Malick (*Badlands*, 1973; *Days of Heaven*, 1978) with his lyrically spiritual war film *The Thin Red Line* (1998; **27.25**) signaled a revival of ambitious American filmmaking at the end of the century. The aspirations of 1970s Hollywood, now abandoned by the studios, had been taken up by the off-Hollywood independents.

Retro-Hollywood Independents

Hollywood had purged not only the controversial trends of the 1970s; it had also narrowed its genre base. Studios focused on special-effects extravaganzas, action pictures, star-driven melodramas and romances, and gross-out comedy. This left several traditional genres unexplored, and independent filmmakers were prepared to take up

the slack. For example, most Majors had failed to capitalize on the low-budget horror trend, and so the Mini-Majors and smaller players could develop profitable franchises around *The Evil Dead* (1983), *Nightmare on Elm Street* (1984), *Scream* (1996), and *I Know What You Did Last Summer* (1997). Indie neo-noir could be edgier than studio fare, as seen in John Dahl's *Red Rock West* (1993) and *The Last Seduction* (1994), Bryan Singer's *The Usual Suspects* (1995), Larry and Andy Wachowski's *Bound* (1996), and Alex Proyas' *Dark City* (1998). There also remained the unpretentious, intimate drama, which Hollywood had largely left to television but which offered opportunities for independents: Victor Nuñez's lyrical Florida tales (*Ruby in Paradise*, 1993; *Ulee's Gold*, 1997), Gus Van Sant's *Good Will Hunting* (1997), Kimberly Peirce's *Boys Don't Cry* (1999), and Kenneth Lonergan's *You Can Count on Me* (2000).

After the 1960s crisis, Hollywood had abandoned most historical drama and literary adaptations—those prestige pictures like *Lawrence of Arabia* (1962) and *Who's Afraid of Virginia Woolf?* (1966), which garnered not only profits but awards. As the Majors moved away from middle-budget projects, there opened a market that independents could fill. Costume pictures, for example, did well on video and suited the independents' mid-range budgets. Director James Ivory and his producer Ismail Merchant had made small, urbane films since the 1960s, but the new market enabled them to make prestigious adaptations of Edwardian novels (*The Bostonians*, 1984; *Howard's End*, 1992; *The Remains of the Day*, 1993). The independents pursued this path even more aggressively after Miramax triumphed with *The English Patient* and *Shakespeare in Love*. Likewise, several modestly budgeted films were based on theatrical works by David Mamet, Sam Shepard, and other contemporary playwrights. Top stars (Alec Baldwin and Al Pacino for *Glengarry Glen Ross*, 1992; Dustin Hoffmann for *American Buffalo*, 1996) proved willing to sacrifice pay to be in high-quality adaptations.

All three trends can be plotted along a spectrum, from the most avant-garde (arty indies) to the most traditional (retro-Hollywood), but occasionally an independent film came along whose main selling point was its lack of budget. Two of the most noteworthy were Robert Rodriguez's gunfest *El Mariachi* (1992) and Kevin Smith's day-in-the-slacker-life comedy *Clerks* (1994). *El Mariachi* is a showcase for resourceful camerawork and dynamic cutting, while *Clerks*, as grainy as a surveillance video, features casually scabrous humor. Both draw on classic genres (the crime thriller, the romantic comedy), but the resolutely cheap look also puts both outside the off-Hollywood tradition. These were the cinematic equivalents of garage-band CDs. Similarly, although it offers only a minor twist on the teen-horror genre, *The Blair Witch Project* (1999) attracted an audience through its defiantly amateurish style. Brilliantly marketed on the Internet, it proved a spectacular hit (and probably the most profitable film ever made). If films this low-tech could be released theatrically, one might conclude that the "age of independents" had indeed arrived. Kevin Smith remarked of Jarmusch's breakthrough film, "You watch *Stranger [than Paradise]*, you think 'I could really make a movie.'"[13] Thousands of young people watching *Clerks*, *El Mariachi*, and *The Blair Witch Project* thought exactly the same thing.

Since the 1970s, Hollywood hunted for talent in the independent realm. Joe Dante (*The Howling*, 1980; *Innerspace*, 1987), Sam Raimi (*The Evil Dead*, 1983; *A Simple Plan*, 1998), Penelope Spheeris (*The Decline of Western Civilization*, 1981; *Wayne's World*, 1992), and Katherine Bigelow (*Near Dark*, 1987) all learned their craft in low-end genres. In the 1990s, Kevin Smith and Richard Rodriguez were snapped up by the Majors, and

the latter had a mainstream hit with *Spy Kids* (2000). Sometimes directors were hired to work on action blockbusters, in the hope that indie edginess would appeal to young audiences. Bryan Singer moved from *The Usual Suspects* to *X-Men* (2000), while Darren Aronofsky was hired to reinvigorate the *Batman* franchise.

The independent companies had developed a new auteurism in order to market films. One producer claimed, "I'm in the business of selling directors."[14] As the Majors sought to enliven their schedules in the late 1990s, they courted young nonstudio auteurs who could offer something different. From two indie comedy-dramas, David O. Russell moved to Warners for the unconventional combat picture *Three Kings* (1999). David Fincher made *Se7en* and *The Game* (1997) for New Line, but his most daring film, *Fight Club* (1999), was released through Twentieth Century Fox. At the beginning of the 2000s, commentators were predicting that the studios would be hiring Paul Thomas Anderson, Spike Jonze (*Being John Malkovich*, 1999), Wes Anderson (*Rushmore*, 1998; *The Royal Tennenbaums*, 2001), and other independents. Yet the rewards heaped on Steven Soderbergh's star-friendly *Erin Brockovich* and *Traffic* (both 2000), far less daring films than his thrillers *Out of Sight* (1998) and *The Limey* (1999), suggested that independents were not expected to break many rules when they were given big-budget projects.

DIGITAL CINEMA

For most of its first century, cinema was an analog medium. Through photochemistry, it captured on a strip of film a continuous imprint of light and sound waves. Since the 1980s, film has become more and more a digital medium—sampling information in the binary form of ones and zeros. In principle, any sight or sound can be recorded adequately in either format, but digital capture required the enormous storage capacity of modern computers, and so it was slow to emerge.

Commercial cinema's earliest digital technology involved *motion-control systems*, computer-governed cameras that could repeat, frame by frame, movements over miniatures or models. The first extensive use of motion control was in *Star Wars* (1977), and the system quickly became vital to make special-effects shots more three-dimensional. Sound recording and reproduction became digital as well. Digital audio tape (DAT), which sampled and stored sound waves in binary form, emerged as the audio engineer's standard for both music and film sound. Just as digital sound was becoming normal for film

A TIMELINE OF 3-D COMPUTER ANIMATION

Applied to traditional cel animation, computer technology speeded up production by executing repetitive drawing and coloring tasks. It also created more textured objects and intricate movements than would be feasible in drawn animation. Disney's *Tarzan* (1999) enhanced backgrounds with a program called "Deep Canvas," and DreamWorks' *The Prince of Egypt* (1998) used Computer Graphics Imaging (CGI) in fully half of its shots, including the parting of the Red Sea.

In cel animation, CGI enhanced drawings and thus blended in with a traditional look. A more spectacular change in the style of animated films came with the creation of so-called 3-D CGI, generating characters and settings with volume and depth, as in puppet or clay animation. During the 1980s and early 1990s, limitations in computer technology confined animators to smooth surfaces and simple shapes, resulting in toys and insects used as characters in early CGI films. As computer memory and flexibility grew, animators could add complex textures and control hundreds of different points on a figure. By the end of the 1990s, fur, waving grass, and human faces were becoming more realistic. The development of 3-D computer animation was pioneered largely by two firms: Pixar and Pacific Data Images. Following is a timeline of events leading up to the development of 3-D computer animation.

1978   George Lucas founds Lucasfilm Computer Development Division (LCDD, later Pixar) to develop digital applications in filmmaking.

1980   Independent CG studio Pacific Data Images (PDI) is founded to design TV logos, credit sequences, etc.

1981   Working in Disney's computer unit, John Lasseter sees CGI scenes from *TRON*, then in production. *Dilemma*, CGI short by John Halas for Computer Creations.

1982   *TRON* is released, with 15 minutes of pure CGI and 25 minutes of CGI and live action mixed. *The Abyss* moves Industrial Light and Magic toward special effects for live-action films.

1984   Lasseter leaves Disney to work for LCDD. Apple fires Steve Jobs (who had cofounded the computer firm). Three CGI shorts receive festival screenings: *The Wild Things,* a short from Disney and Lasseter's first CGI project; *The Adventures of André and Wally B,* an animated short from LCDD that introduces

motion-blur into CGI, designed by Lasseter; *Snoot and Muttly,* a CGI short by Susan Van Baerle.

1985   Lucasfilm spins LCDD off as Pixar.

1986   Jobs buys Lucas's controlling interest in Pixar for $10 million. *Luxo Jr.,* Pixar's first CGI short, directed by Lasseter, is nominated for an Oscar for best animated short.

1987   *Red's Dream,* the second Pixar CGI short, is released.

1988   Lasseter's *Tin Toy* is released; it's the first CGI film to win an Oscar as best animated short.

1989   *Knickknack,* Pixar's fourth short, employing stereoscopic CGI.

1991   Disney signs a three-feature contract with Pixar (raised to five after the success of *Toy Story*).

1994   After leaving Disney, Jeffrey Katzenberg forms DreamWorks SKG with Steven Spielberg and David Geffen.

1995   *Toy Story,* first completely CGI feature, directed by Lasseter, released by Disney.

1996   DreamWorks buys 40% interest in PDI.

1997   *Gerri's Game*, Pixar short by Lasseter; wins Oscar for best animated short.

1998   *Antz,* second completely CGI feature, produced by PDI, released by DreamWorks. *A Bug's Life,* second Pixar feature, directed by Lasseter, released by Disney.

1999   *Toy Story 2,* third Pixar feature, directed by Lasseter, released by Disney.

2000   *Dinosaur,* first feature from Disney's new in-house CGI unit, Secret Lab. CGI animals against live-action backgrounds. *For the Birds,* directed by Ralph Eggleston. Short film first using "Geppetto" system of character control; wins Oscar for best animated short.

2001   *Shrek,* second completely CGI feature from PDI/DreamWorks; also employs Geppetto system. *Final Fantasy: The Spirits Within.* First CGI feature with realistic humans, released by Sony/Columbia. *Monsters, Inc.* fourth Pixar feature, released by Disney (**Color Plate 27.12**).

production in the mid-1980s, it spread to the consumer market through the audio compact disc. Then multiplexes and megaplexes upgraded to digital multichannel systems, encouraging filmmakers to use evocative surround effects and greater dynamic ranges, from a whisper to a bone-shaking explosion.

TRON (1982) showed that computers could generate rudimentary imagery, but detailed figures and locales remained hard to render. So for several years filmmakers clung to miniatures, matte shots, and other camera-based optical effects. As computer memory and speed increased, however, more effects were handled digitally. Digital dinosaurs replaced many of the miniatures and puppets initially planned for *Jurassic Park* (1993). The Gotham City set devised for the animated film *Batman: Mask of the Phantasm* (1993) was revised for the live-action *Batman Forever* (1995). By the late 1990s, filmmakers were routinely using software to clean up shots or to generate imagery, as when a small group of people was multiplied into a huge crowd in the football stadium of *Forrest Gump*. For *O Brother Where Art Thou?* (2000), cinematographer Roger Deakins painstakingly "repainted" every shot to resemble 1930s tinted postcards, turning green foliage into brilliant yellow and bathing the characters in tobacco-brown light (**Color Plate 27.11**).

Digital technology also reshaped animation (see box), but its implications for live-action film were equally radical. Throughout the 1990s, commentators began to suggest that film—photographic, celluloid-based cinema—was dying. Actors would be replaced by cyberstars, and a director could translate his or her vision directly into sound and images. The most famous director to be identified with this view was, not surprisingly, George Lucas (see "Notes and Queries" at the end of this chapter). In this view, cinema would become less like photography and more like painting or literature—a pure act of imaginative creation.

Once films were produced digitally, they could be distributed in the same way. Digital satellite and cable systems produced acceptable quality for home monitors, and in the late 1990s several theaters experimented with digital projection. The Majors would benefit most from the cost-savings of digital exhibition, so they began planning to help exhibitors pay for installing the new projection systems. At the same time, studios dreamed of "video on demand." Thousands of digitized movies awaited a simple dial-up, to be delivered through phone or cable lines, probably with help of the Internet. Bypassing the movie theater and the rental store, video on demand would ensure maximum profit to the content provider.

As a new century dawned, the U.S. film industry faced many difficulties. The multiplex building spree of the 1990s collapsed, forcing eleven theater circuits to file for bankruptcy. Film piracy exploded, thanks to digital copying and Internet access. Box-office revenues swelled due to increased ticket prices—not to larger audiences; in real terms, theaters were earning less from ticket sales than they had in the 1980s. In the meantime, the costs of filmmaking and marketing were rising faster than income.

Nonetheless, theatrical motion pictures remained central ingredients in the media mix. Films spawned television series, videogames, comic books, and straight-to-video releases. Old films could be released on DVD, in some cases repeatedly, adding new special features each time. The press tracked top-grossing films as if they were sports teams, and the Academy Awards ceremony remained an international ritual. Fan magazines, infotainment television, and websites catered to an apparently insatiable appetite for gossip about moviemaking. The industry might have been riddled with economic problems, but film was securely at the center of America's, and the world's, popular culture.

Notes and Queries

VIDEO VERSIONS

Video release became more than another window for a film; it also gave filmmakers a chance to alter the film. Music could be added, scenes could be trimmed, and dialogue could be rerecorded. Some films were released in longer "director's cuts." When Disney's *Aladdin* was criticized by Arab Americans for stereotyped characters and dialogue, the song lyrics were changed for the video release. Joe Dante used the video venue to reshape a gag in *Gremlins 2: The New Batch* (1990). The theatrical release included a scene in which it appears that the movie we're watching is breaking down in the projector. Since that gag did not work on video, Dante reshot the scene to make it seem that the viewer's VCR is mangling the movie.

GEORGE LUCAS: IS FILM DEAD?

George Lucas led the digital revolution. His Lucasfilm computer division innovated digital hardware for editing picture and sound, an effort followed by Avid and other firms. Lucas also established the THX standard, which certified superior digital theater sound. His Industrial Light & Magic was at the forefront of computer-generated visuals, working on almost every major special-effects film of the 1990s.

Characteristically, Lucas was eager to screen *Star Wars: Part I: The Phantom Menace* digitally. More radically, he shot part 2 of his saga wholly on Sony high-definition video: sets existed only in the software, and actors performed individually before *bluescreen,* to be pasted into the same shot together. Lucas was even able to erase unwanted expressions

and eyeblinks. He envisioned digital tools as allowing more people to take up filmmaking. "It's going to be more like novels or plays: if you have the talent, you can express yourself" (quoted in Benjamin Bergery, "Digital Cinema, By George," *American Cinematographer* 82, no. 9 [September 2001]: 73).

Did this mean that film was dead? Lucas compared the shift from photographic to digital cinema to the shift from black-and-white to color cinema. The new medium offered different creative options, not a cancellation of what went before. "I still love black-and-white movies. I don't believe silent movies are dead, either—any more than the pencil is dead" (ibid.: 74). Interestingly, Lucas did not write the Star Wars scripts on a computer but on yellow legal pads, in longhand.

. . . .

REFERENCES

1. Stephen Prince, *A New Pot of Gold: Hollywood under the Electronic Rainbow, 1980–1989.* Vol. 10: *History of the American Cinema* (New York: Scribners, 2000), p. 84.
2. Bill Mechanic, quoted in Don Groves, "Global Vidiots' Delight," *Variety* (15–21 April, 1996): 43.
3. Quoted in Justin Wyatt, *High Concept: Movies and Marketing in Hollywood* (Austin: University of Texas Press, 1994), p. 13.
4. Michael D. Eisner, with Tony Schwartz, *Work in Progress* (New York: Random House 1998), pp. 100–101.
5. Quoted in Mark Litwak, *Reel Power: The Struggle for Influence and Success in the New Hollywood* (New York: William Morrow, 1986), p. 73.
6. Quoted in Bruce Handy, "101 Movie Tie-Ins," *Time* (2 December 1996): 68.
7. Peter Bart, "By George, They've Got It . . . Wrong," *Variety* (23–29 July, 2001): 4.
8. Walter Murch, *In the Blink of an Eye: A Perspective on Film Editing* (Los Angeles: Silman-James, 1995), 88.
9. Spike Lee, with Lisa Jones, *Do The Right Thing* (New York: Fireside, 1989), p. 33.
10. Quoted by Lory Smith, *Party in a Box: The Story of the Sundance Film Festival* (Salt Lake City: Gibbs-Smith, 1999), p. 103.
11. Quoted in Paul Cullum, "Deconstructing De Luca," *Fade In* 6, no. 2 (2000): 44.
12. Quoted in Emanuel Levy, *Cinema of Outsiders: The Rise of American Independent Film* (New York: New York University Press, 1999), p. 206.
13. Quoted in John Pierson, *Spike, Mike, Slackers, & Dykes: A Guided Tour Across a Decade of American Independent Cinema* (New York: Hyperion, 1995), p. 31.
14. James Schamus, personal interview, 26 February 1998.

FURTHER READING

Andrew, Geoff. *Stranger Than Paradise: Maverick Film-Makers in Recent American Cinema.* London: Prion, 1998.

Bordwell, David. "Intensified Continuity: Visual Style in Contemporary American Film." *Film Quarterly* 55.3 (Spring 2002): 16–28.

Compaine, Benjamin M., and Douglas Gomery, *Who Owns the Media? Competition and Concentration in Mass Media Industry.* 3rd ed. Mahwah, NJ: Erlbaum, 2000.

Croteau, David, and William Hoynes. *The Business of Media: Corporate Media and the Public Interest.* Thousand Oaks, CA: Pine Forge Press, 2001.

Kent, Nicolas. *Naked Hollywood: Money and Power in the Movies Today.* New York: St. Martin's, 1991.

Lewis, Jon, ed. *The New American Cinema.* Durham, NC: Duke University Press, 1998.

Litman, Barry. *The Motion Picture Mega-Industry.* Needham Heights, MA: Allyn and Bacon, 1998.

Schatz, Thomas. "The New Hollywood." In Jim Collins, Hilary Radner, and Ava Preacher Collins, eds., *Film Theory Goes to the Movies* (New York: Routledge, 1993), pp. 8–36.

Thompson, Kristin. *Storytelling in the New Hollywood: Understanding Classical Narrative Technique.* Cambridge, MA: Harvard University Press, 1999.

Wasko, Janet. *Hollywood in the Information Age: Beyond the Silver Screen.* Cambridge: Polity, 1994.

Wasser, Frederick. *Veni, Vidi, Video: The Hollywood Engine and the VCR.* Austin: University of Texas Press, 2001.

CHAPTER 28

TOWARD A GLOBAL FILM CULTURE

In 1970, an American visiting Paris or Tokyo would have seen few signs of U.S. culture—perhaps only Coca-Cola and a few Ford autos. But over the last decades of the twentieth century, national cultures were transformed by *globalization*, the emergence of networks of influence that tightened the ties among all countries and their citizens.

Perhaps the most apparent sign of the trend was the prominence of multinational corporations, from Exxon and IBM to Toyota and Benetton. Multinational corporations created regional subsidiaries, bought smaller firms, and entered into joint ventures with other multinationals. Before the 1980s, mergers and acquisitions across national borders were fairly rare, but waves of deregulation encouraged transnational enterprises in banking, the automotive industry, information technology, and telecommunications. In many cases, the creation of intellectual property—brands, logos, and "content"—became more important than the manufacture of products, which might take place anywhere. Nike's shoes were assembled from components made across Asia, but the product was defined by a casual swoosh and the hard-driving slogan "Just Do It."

Globalization became evident in other ways. When worldwide financial markets were deregulated in the late 1980s, they began to play a crucial role in national economies. People became more mobile, through migration and tourism. All these changes created new worldwide regulatory agencies, such as the World Bank, as well as transnational social organizations, such as Greenpeace and Doctors without Borders.

The West, plus some Asian-Pacific nations, led globalization, announcing it as the dawning of a new age of free-market capitalism and universal democracy. Its effects, however, were varied. Corporations could subcontract production to countries with low wages, and then, when those countries raised their standard of living, pull out and head for cheaper labor markets—the "race to the bottom." A fluid global market often disrupted communities, while the demands of the International Monetary Fund made poorer nations, typically in Africa and Latin America, even more dependent on richer ones. In most countries, real wages declined over the 1980s and 1990s. The disparity between rich and poor sharpened: in 1996, the combined income of the world's 400 richest people exceeded the total income of 45 percent of the earth's population.

Globalization was not a completely new phenomenon; from 1850 to 1920, western European countries' overseas empires had bound together nations and peoples in a similar way. The international spread of cinema was one sign of this process (see Chapters 1 and 2). Penetrating virtually every society, movies became the first globalized mass medium. Still, after World War II, and especially after the 1960s, globalization intensified, based not on colonialism but rather on social and economic ties. Popular culture spread via new technologies. Television (which became global in the 1970s and 1980s), communications satellites (1970s), audio cassettes (1970s), CDs (1980s), videotape (1980s), and digital media (1990s) sent music, television, and films throughout the world. During the 1980s and 1990s, cinema became more widely available than it had ever been before.

Globalization's effects on film can be examined from several angles. Most evident was Hollywood, which created a global cinema. As a counterthrust, regional impulses responded to Hollywood's international power. At the same time, filmmakers living outside their place of origin created a "diasporic" cinema that linked new homes to old. All of these tendencies were visible at film festivals, which emerged as an alternative distribution network to that of the U.S. Majors. In addition, new, globally dispersed subcultures of viewers began to appear. Further, film played a central part in the worldwide convergence of digital media.

HOLLYWORLD?

From early on, U.S. studios created a worldwide popular culture that people of many societies enjoyed. During the 1990s and 2000s, the sheer pervasiveness of American cinema became even more evident. Films from the seven major distributors—Warner Bros., Universal, Paramount, Columbia, 20th Century Fox, MGM/UA, and Disney (Buena Vista)—reached nearly every coun-

try on earth. Between 1970 and 1980, Hollywood received about 40 percent of its film rentals from foreign countries. In the 1980s, over half of the Majors' theatrical income began to flow in from overseas.

In part, Hollywood globalized by becoming a wing of foreign corporations. As we have seen (p. 682-683), the Australian firm News Corporation acquired Twentieth Century-Fox, and Sony bought Columbia. Universal was absorbed first by the Japanese electronics firm Matsushita, then by Canada's Seagram, and finally by the French company Vivendi. These acquisitions were part of a larger general trend. Throughout the 1990s, companies outside the United States spent hundreds of billions of dollars buying American firms. Daimler-Benz of Britain bought Chrysler, and British Petroleum bought Amoco.

In addition, all the Majors routinely drew financing from foreign sources, ranging from large companies like France's Canal Plus to investment circles formed for the purpose of speculating in movies. As wings of multinational conglomerates, the studios attracted high-powered international investment. In 2000, 98 percent of film funds raised by German tax shelters went to finance Hollywood pictures, and about one-fifth of studio pictures drew on them.

Always international, the Majors depended more than ever on their standing as the main source of popular cinema. Since the 1970s, U.S. films routinely won over half of box-office receipts in western Europe and Latin America. Some countries held off total defeat through protectionist legislation or through canny maneuverings of the local industry, but, in the 1990s, Hollywood gained the edge. It won supremacy in Hong Kong, South Korea, and Taiwan, while Japan became the Majors' biggest overseas national market. Although Hollywood produced only a small fraction of the world's feature films, it garnered about 75 percent of theatrical motion picture revenues and even more of the video rentals and purchases.

The Media Conglomerates

How did Hollywood cinema strengthen its hold on world culture? We have already seen that many film industries declined in the 1970s and 1980s, often because of competition from television and other leisure activities. Hollywood films, particularly megapictures, offered stiff competition to the local product. U.S. companies had often stayed out of markets where admission prices were very low, since they could not recoup much of their investment there. As living standards rose in the 1980s and 1990s, particularly in Asia, moviegoers could afford higher ticket prices and the U.S. firms moved in.

The U.S. studios also benefited from the vast power of the conglomerates to which they now belonged. The entertainment conglomerates that had acquired most of the Hollywood firms in the 1980s and 1990s were among the world's top-ten media companies. In 2001, the combined revenue of the six giants came to $130 billion. Each conglomerate, linked to international funding and audiences, could act globally. Viacom, parent to Paramount, owned MTV, which broadcast in eight languages throughout the world, and the company programmed over 2,600 movies and series per year for international television. Viacom also owned the Blockbuster video rental chain. Similarly, News Corporation owned not only 20th Century Fox but also newspapers, book publishers, and the rights to broadcast major sports events, such as NFL football and Manchester United rugby. News Corporation's television holdings, particularly its satellite outlets BskyB and Asian Star TV, reached three-quarters of the world's population.

By owning more media outlets in many countries, a conglomerate gained access to new markets, competing with smaller-scale local companies. The conglomerate could also reap economies of scale. The modern media empire, dependent on "content providers," sought synergy (p. 682) between a novel, a movie, or a television series and other divisions, such as record companies.

The Disney Empire   For many companies, the model was the Walt Disney Company. Its revenues placed it in the top tier of global entertainment companies, second only to AOL Time Warner. In the 1980s Disney wisely diversified its filmmaking, entering the adult market with its Touchstone and Hollywood labels. Later it bought Miramax, so that films as varied as *Pulp Fiction* (1994), *Shakespeare in Love* (1998), and *Scary Movie* (2000) contributed their share to the Magic Kingdom. Apart from theatrical filmmaking, Disney held a commanding place in the U.S. market through publishing, cable television (The Disney Channel, ESPN), network television (Capital Cities/ABC), theme parks, and merchandising (highlighted by a chain of Disney Stores).

On all these fronts and more, Disney expanded into the world. It established cruise lines, launched Disneyland parks in Japan and France, and placed its stores in major European and Asian capitals. Disney employed people from eighty-five different countries at its parks and retail outlets as well as in its filmmaking divisions.

It outsourced much of its animation work to Asia, where inkers and colorists worked for low wages.

Disney invested in cable and satellite television companies, licensed merchandising to an estimated 3,000 firms worldwide, and dubbed its entire film and television library into thirty-five languages. At the end of the 1990s, nine of the world's ten top-selling home videos were Disney animated features. By buying Capital Cities/ABC in 1995, Disney could bundle its cartoon and live-action programs along with the immensely popular sports programs exported on ESPN. In 1999, revenues from overseas came to nearly $5 billion, or 20 percent of the company's total income.

The key to the Kingdom was branded content. The Disney name, like famous brands of soap or automobiles, guaranteed quality and consistency. Trademarked characters Mickey Mouse and Simba the Lion could be poured into many media molds—a film, a TV show, a comic book, a song, a Broadway play, or merchandise. The Disney company understood synergy long before the term became fashionable. Although it floundered in the 1960s and 1970s (chiefly through failing to exploit its assets), the firm took off again in the early 1980s, particularly after Michael Eisner became president in 1984. Eisner started his job by seeking "to formalize the role of synergy and brand management."[1]

Cooperation and Cooptation

The Disney company taught Hollywood to keep the world market in mind at all times. Directors brought from abroad, such as Hong Kong's John Woo and Germany's Roland Emmerich, supposedly knew how to please foreign audiences. Stars had to tour the world with their movies. Above all, producers sought a "global film." *Batman* (1989), *The Lion King* (1994), *Independence Day* (1996), *Men in Black* (1997), *Titanic* (1997), *The Lord of the Rings* (2001–2003)—these were mega-events that aimed to attract every viewer, everywhere. *Jurassic Park* (1993) is a particularly compelling model of the global film (see box).

It was not only home-grown movies that allowed Hollywood to penetrate other countries. For decades the Majors had invested in the overseas film trade, a process that began to intensify in the 1980s. The studios sank money into cable and satellite television, theater chains, and theme parks. Because of the power of the Majors' distribution network, many local films were marketed, either nationally or internationally, by a Hollywood company. The most noted instance was *The Full Monty*

JURASSIC PARK, GLOBAL FILM

Jurassic Park was an unprecedented financial success. It earned a worldwide box-office gross of $913 million and yielded millions more from cable, broadcast television, and home video. Revenues from merchandising ran to over $1 billion. Until *Titanic* (1997) surpassed it, *Jurassic Park* defined how large the market for a megapicture could be.

To a greater degree than earlier blockbusters, *Jurassic Park* set out to be a global hit. Two years before the film opened, Steven Spielberg's Amblin Entertainment mounted a careful strategy with Universal's international distribution arm. They branded the film with a red-yellow-black dinosaur silhouette that would provide instant recognition all over the world. Publicists trumpeted the technical advances that had led to computer-generated velociraptors and gallimimuses (**28.1**). But, for most of the campaign, Spielberg showed no images featuring the dinosaurs. Months before release, theaters screened coming-attractions trailers showing only evocative bits of the background story. Eventually Spielberg released one image of a tyrannosaurus tipping over a jeep, but to see more monsters, audiences would have to pay.

Internationally, the film rolled out very quickly. It was released in the United States and Brazil in June 1993, most of Latin America and Asia in July and August, and Europe in September and October. This schedule ensured that *Jurassic Park* would be featured in the world's press throughout the summer and fall. France, the country that protested most loudly against Hollywood imperialism, was one of the last countries to see the movie; ironically, the opening-week grosses there were the highest outside the United States. After the film had played out in most countries, it opened in India and Pakistan, becoming the top-earning western film in both countries.

Worried that he had missed some chances to exploit *E.T.* (1982), Spielberg coordinated *Jurassic*'s tie-ins with great care. Multinational companies like McDonald's, Coca-Cola, Shell Oil, and Marks & Spencer plunged in. Amblin and Universal assembled a merchandising team for each region, licensing hundreds of items, from schoolbags to dinosaur-shaped cookies. A French computer-game firm spent as

28.1 Realistic blur for computer-generated dinosaurs roaming Jurassic Park.

much publicizing the video game as Universal spent promoting the film. Relying on children's fascination with dinosaurs, marketing teams synchronized the release with special museum displays and television documentaries.

Universal drove a hard bargain with exhibitors, demanding larger than usual shares of ticket sales. But the pressure paid off. *Jurassic Park* widened markets for U.S. films. It helped break the hold of Hong Kong films on East Asia, and it showed that there was a large Indian audience for Hindi-dubbed Hollywood films. As the biggest film to enter the emerging markets of eastern Europe, it taught exhibitors western-style marketing techniques, such as blasting the public with TV spots, comic books, and souvenirs.

In all, the marketing blitzkrieg set a new standard for comprehensiveness. Some critics wondered if Spielberg was having a laugh on everyone. By using the film's trademark as the logo for the park in the story, did he suggest that very little separated the movie's world from ours? Were we in fact the suckers whom the lawyer in the film hopes to entice into the park? Was the movie just the last piece of merchandise in the chain? And when Spielberg's digital creatures went prowling for victims past a souvenir shop featuring *Jurassic* toys, had movies reached the limit of product placement?

(1997), a British-made film funded and distributed worldwide by Fox. U.S. studios also stepped up the number of coproductions they mounted. With the 1990s boom in international movie receipts, studios wanted bigger pieces of regional markets.

One advantage in going global was that certain activities were less strictly regulated outside the United States. Even when vertical integration was forbidden at home, the studios had owned foreign theaters and local distribution companies. Block booking and blind bidding, outlawed in the United States, were routine in foreign markets, and they continued into the 1990s. These practices carried even more clout with multinational media empires backing them up.

Battles over GATT

The U.S. majors had long protected their international interests through their trade association, the Motion Picture Export Association of America. In the 1990s, the MPEAA had branches in sixty nations, where 300 employees worked to increase the local market for the Majors. MPEAA employees monitored legislation that might create barriers to American media, and they lobbied politicians and government decision makers. Since the mid-1960s, Jack Valenti, the head of the MPEAA's parent organization, the Motion Picture Association of America, had fought fiercely to limit censorship, to persuade U.S. politicians to look kindly on the media industry, and to keep Hollywood films supreme throughout the world.

Just as Hollywood's grip on the market tightened in the early 1990s, Valenti faced rebellion. Film and television became flashpoints in the long-running negotiations on the General Agreement on Tariffs and Trade (GATT, later to become the World Trade Organization). Nations signing on to GATT pledged to eliminate subsidies and tariffs, allowing other nations' products to compete equally with domestic ones. The Majors fought to have films defined as services, which would have required European countries to cut their subsidies to local filmmaking and eliminate levies and taxes on U.S. movies.

In 1992, the French led a counterattack against any effort to include "audiovisual industries" in GATT. They pointed out that Hollywood already dominated the region; to dissolve the protectionist measures in place would virtually eliminate European film production. The announcement that *Jurassic Park* would play on one-quarter of France's major screens strengthened the case against the Majors. The MPEAA fought hard, but when GATT was signed in December 1993, film and television were not included. The Europeans were jubilant.

The Majors tried to make amends by muffling free-trade rhetoric and donating money for European film education. Still, the next year proved how well founded the Europeans' fears had been. In 1994, for the first time, the Majors earned more rental income from overseas theaters than from domestic ones. Meanwhile, films from all other countries received a still thinner slice of the world market. *Variety*'s headline ran "Earth to H'wood: You Win."[2]

During the rest of the decade, all film revenues for the Majors rose, with nearly every year notching record returns. Overseas grosses were increasing faster than domestic ones, which only confirmed the belief that the global movie market still had room to grow.

Multiplexing the Planet

At the start of the 1990s, the United States contained 30 percent of the world's movie screens, about one screen for every 10,000 people. Most of western Europe had far fewer screens per capita, and Japan had only one theater for every 60,000 people. Since Americans visited movies more frequently than nearly any other people—four to five times on average each year—the Majors believed that most regions were "underscreened" and failed to tap the potential market. In addition, the studios and the U.S. independents were pumping out many films, but, in most countries, there were comparatively few places to show them.

Multiplexing seemed the natural solution. Because multiscreen cinemas had increased attendance in North America by reinforcing the moviegoing habit, observers reasoned that they might spur more demand in other markets. The advantages of many screens under one roof, a single box office, centralized concession sales, and other economies of scale would apply abroad. By increasing the number of screens, multiplexes would also allow more films to come in faster. As in the United States, where films opened wide and played off quickly, the distributors would benefit by getting a large share of the first-week receipts. Moreover, if the new theaters were more luxurious than the aging competition, ticket prices could be boosted. This was an important consideration in developing countries, where a ticket often cost less than one dollar. And, if the Majors owned or operated the multiplex, then they could compete with local exhibitors, monitor box-office receipts accurately, and control access to prints, thus limiting piracy.

The idea was too tempting to resist, especially since European exhibitors had already started building multiplexes on their own. Soon American firms launched multiplexes in the United Kingdom, Germany, Portugal, Denmark, and the Netherlands. Warner Bros. was a leader in the effort, often in alliance with Australia's Village Roadshow circuit. Paramount and Universal launched a joint venture, United Cinemas International. Because European exhibition firms were well-entrenched, the U.S. companies usually partnered with regional chains. By the 1990s, western Europe was blanketed with multiplexes. The fever spread to Asia. Warners joined with Village Roadshow to erect a complex in Taiwan and partnered with a department-store chain to build thirty multiplexes in Japan.

Now Hollywood was exporting not just American movies but the American moviegoing experience. Snacks were adapted to local tastes, but popcorn, previously a

U.S. specialty, proved surprisingly popular. European multiplexes were usually on the edge of town, providing ample parking and adjacent malls with restaurants, bars, and shops. Some cineplexes went beyond the American standard. A Canadian venue offered a lobby with game stations, lounges serving alcohol, and a food court. Warsaw's Silver Screen cinema boasted a bar, a café, and an Internet-access lounge—and the "Platinum Club," three 100-seat theaters where, for a $9 ticket, the patron could drink champagne and nibble on caviar.

Wherever multiplexes were introduced, attendance rose dramatically. In the early 1990s, European box-office returns jumped after a decade of decline. Germany, which began building 'plexes in the early 1990s, had its biggest surge in attendance of the post-1945 period. Customers proved willing to pay more for a bright, comfortable, modernized venue. The Golden Village complex in Bangkok, with only ten screens, grossed nearly as much as all other screens in Thailand combined. Just as in the United States, however, multiplex saturation set in. The United Kingdom and Germany could not sustain so many screens, and East Asia's post-1997 economic slowdown cut attendance there. By the early 2000s, many multiplex giants were trying to sell off their overseas theaters.

Still, in emerging markets such as Russia, eastern Europe, and Latin America, as well as in "under-screened" Japan, the multiplex boom continued. The single-screen cinema would soon be defunct. The future of mass-market movies was the multiplex, an entertainment center for the public and a profit center for major companies—many of them affiliated with Hollywood.

REGIONAL ALLIANCES AND THE NEW INTERNATIONAL FILM

Of the 4,000 or so features made worldwide in the mid-1970s, only 8 percent were released by the U.S. Majors. Europe, Asia, and Latin America made many more films, but those seldom left their country of origin. The most successful of these industries, such as India's and Hong Kong's, did manage to reach neighboring countries. As Hollywood began to penetrate these remote markets, filmmakers became more aware of the need to create regional affiliations.

Although it may sound paradoxical, globalization tended to promote stronger ties within regions. As money, products, and ideas flowed across national boundaries, regions with existing affinities of culture or language began to forge trade alliances and security arrangements. In film, several regional forces, defined both by language and culture, emerged to challenge Hollywood's global reach.

While there were some important Latin American media conglomerates, the most powerful competition to the Majors came from Europe and Asia. A prosperous and heavily populated region, western Europe (including the United Kingdom) was Hollywood's most important overseas market. At the end of the 1990s, the principal European countries were annually yielding the studios $7 billion to $8 billion from television, theatrical film, and video. The Asia-Pacific region yielded significantly less, but it was a fast-growing market. Together, western Europe and Asia generated three-quarters of Hollywood's overseas revenue. Naturally, many Europeans and Asians began asking, If nations cooperated, could they gain ground in their regional markets? Might they even create global films of their own?

Europe and Asia Try to Compete

As a first measure, the Europeans banded together to protect their markets against further American encroachment. In the wake of GATT, national film institutes stepped up film financing, still promoting national diversity but also favoring films that proved accessible to international audiences. Between 1996 and 2000, the European Union shifted its MEDIA program (p. 608) from funding production to training filmmakers, developing projects, and expanding distribution. Another EU program, Eurimages, financed coproductions. On the exhibition side, MEDIA and Eurimages helped fund theaters that pledged to screen at least 50 percent European films. The affiliation, called Europa Cinemas, had nearly 900 screens in fifty-one countries, including some in the Middle East and the former Soviet states.

Exhibition chains went international too, chiefly by building multiplexes. Since many European theaters needed drastic upgrades, it made sense to rebuild the large single-screen houses as multiplexes. As more Europeans acquired cars, exhibitors could move outside the high-priced real estate of city centers. In 1988, Kinepolis opened on the outskirts of Brussels, with 24 screens, an Imax theater, and 7,400 seats—at that time, the largest movie house in the world. The Kinepolis company was formed to build cineplexes throughout Belgium, France, Spain, Switzerland, and the Netherlands. In the 1990s, other European exhibition firms, such as Germany's Cinemaxx, followed.

Attendance at both Hollywood and European films leaped sharply upward in the late 1990s, and most observers believed that multiplexes were partly responsible. Local movies appeared to benefit; playing alongside Hollywood hits made them seem more like event films. By 2000, although many countries were becoming over-'plexed, films from the fifteen EU-member countries accounted for about a quarter of all EU theater admissions.

On the production front, however, local films could not stand up to the American onslaught. Europe was turning out about 700 films a year, many more than came in from Hollywood. Yet only 300 or so would play theaters; most were relegated to late-night television. They seldom recouped the funds invested in them. Export possibilities were similarly slight. Only about 20 percent of European productions were aimed at international audiences, and the United States, the world's biggest market, resisted non-English-language films. Relying on national subsidies, regional funding, and private investment but seldom traveling beyond a single nation's borders, European film could not really compete with the Majors.

Media Empires

Several western European media conglomerates pursued a strategy of mixing competition and cooperation. As in the United States, during the 1980s, European antitrust legislation began to relax and large media concentrations began to emerge. The key players included Bertelsmann of Germany, the largest media combine in Europe; Germany's Kirch company; Italy's Berlusconi Group; and Havas of France (eventually to be acquired by Vivendi). The former giants of French film, Gaumont and Pathé, were now small companies by comparison. Conglomerates acquired them in order to move into film distribution, television, and theatrical exhibition.

Until Vivendi purchased MCA/Universal, European media companies displayed comparatively little interest in film production. Gaumont financed half a dozen films per year, while Havas supported local production through Marin Karmitz's MK2 company, France's leading art-film producer-distributor. Bertelsmann had a stake in Germany's revamped Ufa company. For the most part, however, the conglomerates concentrated on other media, like publishing and music, and on delivery systems and licensing rights. Kirch, for example, controlled television rights to over 15,000 feature films.

When it came to filmmaking, the media companies preferred to bet on Hollywood. In the late 1990s, the continental conglomerates sank about $150 million in European films versus $450 million to $600 million in U.S. films. After purchasing MCA/Universal, Vivendi

downsized its Canal Plus branch, the major private funding source for French filmmaking. It seemed likely that Vivendi would shift the bulk of its investment to Universal projects.

PolyGram: A European Major?

The most ambitious effort to create a powerful European production company was made by PolyGram. The Dutch company was the world's third largest producer of recorded music. After investing in some successful U.S. films (*Flashdance*, 1983; *A Chorus Line*, 1985), PolyGram launched a production slate and a distribution network in 1988. Each year the firm hoped to produce a few local Dutch films, a few French-language films that could travel abroad, and several U.S. and UK titles that could sell around the world. PolyGram bought or contracted with energetic production companies such as Working Title and Interscope, and then gave them the individualized identity of record labels within a music company.

Most of PolyGram's successes came from Working Title's lively British films: *Four Weddings and a Funeral* (1994), *Shallow Grave* (1994), *Trainspotting* (1996), and *Bean* (1997). PolyGram also supported many independent American films (*The Usual Suspects*, 1995; *Fargo*, 1996). These hits were outweighed by many costly failures, such as the $80 million digital-imaged *What Dreams May Come* (1998). Ultimately, PolyGram could not generate enough films to feed its distribution outlets, and its boutique companies did not spawn megapics. In 1998, Seagram, already owner of MCA/Universal, bought PolyGram for its music library and sold the film unit to USA Films, a partial subsidiary of MCA. The only viable European studio had been swallowed by Hollywood.

Global Films from Europe

When European films traveled abroad, they usually played small art-house venues. But a film might find a wider market if it satisfied two conditions. The film had to be in English, and the production had to be cofinanced by a North American company, preferably a Major. It also helped if the film had U.S. stars. *House of the Spirits* (1993), directed by the Dane Bille August and financed by several European companies and Miramax, featured Jeremy Irons, Meryl Streep, and Glenn Close. The French production *1492: Conquest of Paradise* (1992) starred Gérard Depardieu but included U.S. actors like Sigourney Weaver and Frank Langella. While

28.2   One of dozens of cameras catches Björk off-center as she climbs aboard a train, singing "I've Seen It All" (*Dancer in the Dark*).

these films did stronger business outside the United States than in it, Luc Besson's Gaumont-financed *The Fifth Element* (1997) also succeeded in North America. Shot in English, distributed by Columbia, starring Bruce Willis and Chris Tucker, the film presents a science-fiction extravaganza festooned with special effects reminiscent of European comic books (**Color Plate 28.1**).

While several European filmmakers began shooting in English, the most celebrated efforts came from the Danish director Lars von Trier. Turning away from the fastidious and polished look of his early work, von Trier won even more fame with *Breaking the Waves* (1996). When a man is rendered impotent by a job accident, he urges his wife to have sex with other men and tell him about it. The result could have been sordid, but von Trier's sketchy, cinéma-vérité treatment and some hallucinatory landscape interludes create a moving account of shared love in the face of community scorn. Von Trier filmed in 35mm, transferred the footage to video in order to drain out most of the color, then transferred it back to film. *Breaking the Waves* won the Grand Prize at Cannes and made von Trier one of the world's most noteworthy directors.

The look of *Breaking the Waves* was inspired by the loose camerawork in the U.S. television series *Homicide: Life on the Streets*. "The hand-held camera gives quite a different feeling of intimacy," von Trier remarked. "A film must be like a pebble in your shoe."[3] He pushed still further in another English-language feature, *Dancer in the Dark* (2000), which took two Cannes prizes. This somber musical fable set in the United States starred pop singer Björk and an international cast. Its bumpy hand-held technique was accentuated, as in *Breaking the Waves*, by the anamorphic wide-screen image. Shot on digital video, *Dancer* used as many as 100 cameras for its musical numbers, allowing von Trier to cut among

peculiar angles with jarring effect (**28.2**). The nervous, almost irritating, style worked against the fluidity traditionally associated with song and dance.

Although he claimed to take Dreyer as a model, von Trier was far more uninhibited and publicity-conscious. (He added the "von" to his name as a tribute to Erich von Stroheim and Josef von Sternberg). For *Dimension*, a film begun in 1992, he filmed two minutes each year; he estimated that it would take thirty years to complete. He was also a founder of the Dogme 95 movement (see box). The success of *Breaking the Waves* allowed von Trier to expand his company, Zentropa, into a microstudio. Stationed at a former military base, Zentropa opened divisions specializing in children's films, pornography, TV commercials, music videos, Internet films, and international productions. By 2001, Zentropa and its affiliates were turning out several features and many hours of film and television each year. Whereas Poly-Gram could not succeed with megapics, von Trier's brainchild found a modest but steady market for the global art movie.

East Asia: Regional Alliances and Global Efforts

Asia had its own regional political association, ASEAN (Association of Southeast Asian Nations). Like the EU, it moved toward creating a fully integrated trade market, and trade among nations boomed throughout the 1990s. Such regional initiatives set the stage for stronger links among Asia's film industries.

Since Chinese emigrants had moved to Hong Kong, Singapore, Taiwan, Indonesia, and other countries, East Asian cinema had been strongly regional for years. Widespread use of the Chinese language helped Hong Kong films to enter many national markets (p. 656). During the 1980s and 1990s, Chinese affiliations grew stronger.

BACK TO BASICS: DOGME 95

Late one night in 1995, after serious drinking, Danish directors Lars von Trier and Thomas Vinterberg took twenty-five minutes to jot down a manifesto calling for a new purity in filmmaking. The new waves of the 1960s had betrayed their revolutionary calling, and now new technology was going to democratize cinema. "For the first time, anyone can make cinema."[4] But some discipline was necessary, so von Trier and Vinterberg laid down an "indisputable set of rules" for the new avant-garde: a "Vow of Chastity."

The vow required that the film be shot on location (using only props naturally found there). The camera had to be hand-held and the sound recorded directly, so music could arise only from within the scene itself. The film had to be shot in the 1.33:1 format, in color, and without filters or laboratory reworking. It could not be set in another period of history nor be a genre film (apparently ruling out police and action pictures, science fiction, and other Hollywood genres). The film could not include "superficial action": "Murders, weapons, etc. must not occur." The director must not be credited. Above all, a director had to pledge that the film would be not an artwork but "a way of forcing the truth out of my characters and settings." Soon thereafter two other Danish filmmakers signed on. The four created the Dogme 95 collective.

Distributed in a Paris symposium devoted to cinema's hundredth anniversary, the manifesto attracted little notice until 1998. That year the film labeled Dogme #1, Vinterberg's *The Celebration*, won the Jury Prize at Cannes, and Dogme #2, von Trier's *The Idiots*, won a critics' award at the London Film Festival. *Mifune* (1999), by Søren Kragh-Jacobsen, was Dogme #3. After winning a major prize in Berlin, it went on to gross $2 million internationally. Dogme began issuing certificates for projects that adhered to the Vow of Chastity, while directors who strayed from it (as most did) made public confession on the Dogme website.

Since the Dogme films were closely tied to von Trier's Zentropa company, many critics dismissed Dogme 95 as a publicity stunt. If it was, it succeeded spectacularly. Danish cinema became a center of critical attention. On New Year's Eve 2000, each Dogme director shot a live film and broadcast it on a different television channel. Viewers were encouraged to switch among the films and create their own Dogme 95 movie. One-third of Denmark tuned in.

The Dogme brethren insisted that they were serious. They held that film's increasingly complex technology and bureaucracy hampered genuine creation. One could, however, fight Hollywood's globalization by going back to basics; Kragh-Jakobsen compared the group to rockers rediscovering "unplugged" music. Like John Cassavetes and the Direct Cinema filmmakers, they sought to capture the

28.3 Liberation from city conventions in *Mifune*.

unrepeatable here and now. The vow declared that the director must "regard the instant as more important than the whole."

Central to the movement was a collaboration between director and performers. In the typical Dogme film, the actors and directors worked out the scene, often without a script, and then shot it in catch-as-catch-can fashion. For *The Celebration*, the actors sometimes operated the camera, and all were present to witness each scene. Dogme directors favored digital video; Vinterberg noted that actors tended to forget the presence of small cameras. Dogme #4, Kristian Levring's *The King Is Alive* (2001), used three cameras so that none of the actors knew when she or he was being filmed.

Von Trier claimed that the formal rigidity of his earlier films dissatisfied him, and the vow provided a rationale for the freer-form shooting that emerged in *Breaking the Waves*. Vinterberg agreed: "I had the impression that my way of filming was imprisoned by conventions: returning to standard techniques to make people cry, use artificial light for a night scene. . . . There are things in cinema that you're supposed to do, and you do them without asking questions."[5] All the Dogme directors stressed that filmmakers had to start reflecting on why they made certain choices; by working under a self-imposed simplicity they could relearn how to tell stories on film. Although the vow attacked the idea of the auteur, most directors found their Vow projects becoming highly personal.

Some Dogme films were structured as fairly traditional dramas (*The Celebration, The Idiots*) or romances (*Mifune*; **28.3**). The most experimental early Dogme effort came

(continued)

from the United States. Harmony Korine's *julien donkey-boy* (1999) is a disjointed tale of a dysfunctional family. Overseen by a tyrannical father, the schizophrenic Julien tries to help his pregnant sister, who may be carrying his child. Korine filmed scenes with up to twenty digital-video cameras, placing them on tabletops and in hats and occasionally even using infrared cameras. The digital imagery, blown up first to 16mm reversal and then to 35mm, yields radiantly unearthly colors and layers of abstract shapes, linking Korine with Stan Brakhage and other experimentalists (**Color Plate 28.2**). Korine claimed he wanted to "decompose" the image, "losing some details but finding a texture."[6] Because it included nondiegetic music and many

optical effects, *julien donkey-boy* seemed to stray from the vow, but the Dogme group agreed to certify it.

By 2001, the Dogme impulse showed no signs of slackening. Two dozen projects in France, Korea, Argentina, Sweden, Italy, Switzerland, Belgium, Spain, and the United States were certified. Lone Sherfig's *Italian for Beginners*, the first Vow of Chastity film made by a woman, won a major prize at Berlin and looked likely to become an international hit. Reliant on video, promoted on the Internet, and consecrated by film festivals, Dogme 95 had launched something at once local and international—a film movement suited to a global age.

Although the People's Republic of China forbade direct investment from Taiwanese businesses, Taiwanese producers set up companies in Hong Kong to fund mainland films. *Raise the Red Lantern* (1991) was produced by Hou Hsiao-hsien's firm, and Hou became one of the first Taiwanese directors to film in China. Chen Kaige shot *Farewell My Concubine* (1993) and *Temptress Moon* (1996) in Beijing; both projects were financed by Hsu Feng, a Taiwanese producer who had starred in King Hu's swordplay films of the 1970s (p. 660). On video, Hong Kong films flowed into China, and Tsui Hark, Wong Kar-wai, and other Hong Kong directors began shooting on the mainland. Although Hong Kong films still counted as "foreign" pictures and faced an import quota, companies in the former colony hoped to tap the enormous Chinese market eventually.

Other countries got aboard. South Korea exported sleek, high-grossing thrillers and action pictures. Japanese stars appeared in Chinese and Korean movies, and Japanese companies financed major works by Hou Hsiao-hsien, Edward Yang, and Wong Kar-wai. Spurred by the international success of Thailand's *Nang Nak* (1999), Hong Kong director Peter Chan founded a company to create international Asian coproductions. More generally, East Asian tastes were blending. Japanese pop music was the rage in Taipei and Seoul, and television soap operas spoke to all: Japanese romance series were huge successes in Taiwan and Hong Kong, and South Korean soaps drew large audiences in the PRC. Film was firmly part of a pan-Asian popular culture.

28.4   The view from inside a pool in the wholly computer-generated *Final Fantasy: The Spirits Within* (2001).

Still, Asian filmmakers had little luck mounting a global film, either mass-market or art-house. Media Asia of Hong Kong, which invested in films made in Singapore and Taiwan, sought to make a blockbuster out of *The Soong Sisters* (1997), but it failed to attract attention outside the region. Square, a Japanese company, tried to turn its *Final Fantasy* videogame into a photorealistic computer-generated feature. Despite remarkable imagery (**28.4**), the film flopped spectacularly. The most promising eastern initiative came from Hollywood. Sony Asia was formed as an attempt to underwrite Asian films that could capture an international audience. Two of the first three projects, Tsui Hark's frenzied Hong Kong action film *Time and Tide* (2000) and Takeshi Kitano's gangster bloodbath *Brother*

(2000), did not score, but Ang Lee's *Crouching Tiger, Hidden Dragon* (2000) did.

Lee, born in Taiwan but trained and based in New York, had proven himself highly bankable. *The Wedding Banquet* (1993) and *Eat Drink Man Woman* (1994) were among the top-ten best-grossing foreign-language films in the United States. Producer James Schamus of the independent company Good Machine cowrote the script for *Crouching Tiger* and stitched together financing from the United States, Europe, Taiwan, and Hong Kong. The resulting film contains romance, intrigue, exotic locations, and graceful airborne martial arts (**Color Plate 28.3**). *Crouching Tiger* was marketed shrewdly, using film festivals to build word of mouth slowly and aiming advertising at a wide range of audiences, from art-film devotees to teenagers and kung-fu fans. Budgeted at only $15 million, it wound up grossing over $200 million internationally, making it the most financially successful Asian film of all time. With dialogue in Mandarin, *Crouching Tiger* also proved that a global triumph did not have to be in English.

DIASPORAS AND THE GLOBAL SOUL

Globalization sent millions of people on the road. Decolonization after World War II brought people from India, Asia, and the Caribbean to England, from Algeria and West Africa to France, from Indonesia to the Netherlands. Latin Americans and Asians immigrated to Australia and North America, while the fall of the USSR sent people from the former Soviet states to seek their fortunes in western Europe, Israel, and the United States. People fled Mao's China for other parts of East Asia, while Filipinos searched for work in Hong Kong. The world became a web of crisscrossing diasporas, with people trying to sink new roots while still yearning for the lands they had left. "A world with a hundred kinds of home," writes Pico Iyer, "will accommodate a thousand kinds of homesickness."[7]

This migration of populations created a form of "world film" quite far from the dreams of the U.S. Majors. Ever since cinema began, directors and other creative personnel traveled among countries, but the heightened pace and greater dispersion of migration after 1980 created something new. Hollywood émigrés like Fritz Lang and Maurice Tourneur did not make films about leaving Germany or France. In the closing years of the twentieth century, though, filmmakers began to explore the experience of migration, the sense of floating among

28.5 Turkish lovers in *Lola and Billy the Kid* (production still).

cultures, speaking minority languages, being shut off from the mainstream, and living divided social lives.

The result were films of dispersion and displacement, a cinema of diaspora. In Paris, the Peronist Fernando Solanas filmed *Tangos: Exile of Gardel* (1985), a reflection on Argentine popular culture as recalled from afar (p. 637). Tony Gatlif, a Romany living in France, made *Latcho Drom* (1993) as a tribute to gypsy music. Several Iranians who had fled the Muslim fundamentalist revolution cooperated with director Reza Allamehzadeh to film *The Guests of Hotel Astoria* (1989), which portrays exiled Iranians waiting to find asylum in Europe.

Much diasporic filmmaking sprang from second- or third-generation immigrants who had lived in the host culture long enough to grasp its customs but who also participated in a mature immigrant subculture. In Paris, *beurs* (second-generation Arabs from North Africa) created novels and films about their society, as in Mehdi Charif's portrait of a transvestite, *Miss Mona* (1986). The Moroccan director Philippe Faucon based *Samia* (2001) on a coming-of-age novel about beur life. Turks became a significant minority in Germany when they were invited in as guest workers during the 1960s; over the next forty years, Berlin became a center of Turkish life. Kutlig Ataman's *Lola and Billy the Kid* (1999) portrays a young German Turk who learns that the brother whom he believed dead is actually a transvestite performing in gay nightclubs (**28.5**).

Often the second-generation character gains access to his or her roots not through direct memory but through popular culture. Gurinda Chadha grew up in England watching Indian cinema with her father, so her

28.6 *Bhaji on the Beach:* a middle-aged woman romps with her lover in a sequence reminiscent of a Bollywood musical.

Bhaji on the Beach (1993) uses dazzling imagery reminiscent of Bollywood romances (**28.6**) to portray the adventures of Indian women visiting the seaside resort of Blackpool.

As each nation became more ethnically mixed, filmmakers of all origins were attracted by the dramatic possibilities of populations confronting or blending. In *La Haine* ("Hatred," 1996), Mathieu Kassovitz, himself an emigrant from Hungary, filmed suburban housing-project gangs that throw together beurs and white youths. Because Italian filmmaker Roberta Torre believed that migration would become the great theme of the new century, her *South Side Story: The Real Story of Julietto and Romea* (2000) made Shakespeare's hero a Sicilian youth and his beloved a Nigerian girl. Such films could record and express the displacement felt by migrating populations. When everyone seemed to be living in a new place, traveling to another place, forming part of what Iyer calls "the global soul," diasporic cinema was another way in which national and regional cultures gained a wide resonance.

THE FESTIVAL CIRCUIT

The film festival emerged soon after World War II (p. 356), reflecting the growing internationalization of cinema, the decline of the Hollywood studio system, and the expansion of independent filmmaking. In the decades after Cannes, Berlin, and Venice established their events, the film festival quickly became a central institution within world film culture. Most of the non-Hollywood feature films discussed in Parts 4 and 5 of this book, from Italian Neorealism to the cinemas of the postcolonial world, gained international stature through festi-

vals. Festivals brought to attention the influential auteurs of the 1950s and 1960s, the various new waves and young cinemas, Third World political filmmaking, and most new trends since the 1970s.

After videotape allowed filmmakers to submit films for previewing, festivals proliferated. In 1981, there were around 100 annual festivals. By 2001, there were over 700. By the end of the century, film festivals had provided a global distribution system, perhaps the only one rivaling Hollywood's.

Most festivals are purely local affairs, giving audiences in small cities a chance to see films that would never appear there otherwise. Some festivals last two days, others two weeks. Some aim to promote tourism, others to celebrate regional filmmaking. Many are thematic festivals, concentrating on certain genres (science fiction, fantasy, films for children) or themes (ethnic identity, religion, sexuality). Feminist and gay filmmaking became dependent on special-interest festivals, such as San Francisco's Tranny Fest for films about transgendered life. Austin, Texas created a festival for films made in super 8mm, and Philadelphia boasted a festival for films rejected by other festivals.

Festivals sometimes became powerful and moving assertions of community. Locarno, Switzerland, is famous for its nighttime screenings in the Piazza Grande, where 7,000 viewers seated on plastic chairs before a temporary screen applaud and cheer. Sarajevo, a city shattered by the Balkan war, created its first film festival in 1995, when snipers and shellfire were constant threats. The festival gave people a chance to rebuild a public life outside the bomb shelters. In such ways, festivals can reshape a nation's culture. The Sydney International Film Festival began fighting Australian film censorship in the 1960s and eventually won the right to show all its films unaltered.

Festivals also allow national cultures to present themselves in a good light. There can be little doubt that westerners' attitudes toward Iran were softened by the humanistic films (p. 670) that took so many prizes on the festival circuit. Likewise, most governments denied Taiwan diplomatic recognition, and so its films would have had little chance to be seen abroad had not festivals made them available. Thanks to Cannes and Venice, Hou Hsiao-hsien and Edward Yang (p. 660) found international funding and distribution. Indeed, the films of some major directors were better known in festivals than in their home countries.

The fifty to sixty most prestigious festivals are accredited by the International Federation of Film Producers Associations (FIAPF). These are "A-list" festi-

THE TORONTO INTERNATIONAL FILM FESTIVAL ● ● ● ● ● ● ● ● ● ● ● ● ● ● ●

The North American market, with its large number of screens and its affluent, movie-addicted population, is the principal target for most filmmakers around the world. Two festivals, the Sundance Film Festival and the Toronto International Film Festival, dominate North America, and in many respects the Toronto event is a prototype of the truly global festival.

Starting in 1976 as a local "festival of festivals," it hosted 140 films from thirty countries. In the years afterward, it found creative ways to enhance local cinema: a trade forum that by the turn of the century attracted 2,000 people in the film business, retrospective and competitive sections devoted to Canadian film, and a sales office to help sell Canadian films. The festival also established sidebars and screenings devoted to children's films, other national cinemas, major directors, first-time directors, documentaries, and experimental film. The festival has a popular midnight screening schedule, and it provides rooms for directors to program their favorite films and then discuss them with audiences. It also celebrated its twenty-fifth anniversary by producing ten short films by Canadian directors and inviting twenty-five attending directors to bring digital shorts. Apart from FIPRESCI (International Federation of Film Critics) prizes, the festival gives audience awards and prizes to outstanding Canadian cinema.

What made Toronto a top international festival was its flair for spotting talent. It hosted the North American premieres of *Chariots of Fire* (1981); *The Big Chill* (1983); *Women on the Verge of a Nervous Breakdown* (1988); *Drugstore Cowboy*, *Blood Simple*, and *Roger and Me* (all 1989); *Reversal of Fortune* (1990); *Reservoir Dogs* (1992); *Welcome to the Dollhouse* and *Leaving Las Vegas* (both 1995); *Boogie Nights* (1997); *Life Is Beautiful* (1998); and *Run Lola Run* (1998). In 1999, many films that would be nominated for Oscars the following spring were introduced at Toronto, from *American Beauty* to *Boys Don't Cry*. Toronto became the primary North American launching pad for serious films for the fall season. The festival's programmers were also among the first to notice important trends in taste, such as Hong Kong cinema, gay and queer cinema, and new Latin American filmmaking.

The Toronto festival illustrates the global dimensions of festival activity. Many screenings in its "Masters" section are sponsored by MEDIA's European Film Promotion agency. It conducts a series of press and industry screenings running parallel to the public ones. What started as a city-based festival now attracts thousands of programmers, critics, film executives, stars, and movie buffs to a feast of over 500 screenings. At the same time, it has established offshoot institutions. It created The Film Circuit, a distribution agency for circulating films to other Canadian cities, and it joined forces with Cinémathèque Ontario, an excellent year-round screening program. Few film gatherings have so powerfully altered their national culture while enhancing the dynamism of the international festival network.

---

vals, although some are more significant than others. Many A-list festivals include prize competitions. Other festivals are "noncompetitive," but they may still give awards, such as sponsors' prizes. "Audience awards," based on viewers' votes, are a staple of many festivals. An event may seek out premieres, as Cannes does, or cull its offerings from other festivals, as do the New York and London festivals.

Festivals are crucially important in marketing movies made outside Hollywood, throwing the media spotlight, however briefly, on small-budget films. If the critics speak favorably of the film, or if it wins a prize, it is still further publicized. For films made with subsidies from national governments, earning a slot in a prestigious festival confirms the funding agency's decision to support the project.

With publicity come business deals. A few festivals finance films; Rotterdam's Tigers and Dragons Award supports young Asian cinema, while Sundance offers a prize to turn a promising script into a film. (One prominent winner was *Central Station*, p. 636). More commonly, festivals put filmmakers in contact with distributors. Parallel to festival screenings, Cannes runs a market that allows hundreds of companies to show films to potential buyers. Since 1970, the Berlin festival's European Film Market has become the central meeting place for the German industry. Sundance is notorious for its feeding frenzy, with studio representatives phoning in bids from their theater seats before the film has finished screening.

Once a film has sold its rights for a region, the producer can use a festival to launch the film. Hollywood studios use Berlin, Cannes, and Venice to introduce their blockbusters to Europe, but less prominent films can also get a boost from festival screenings. Cannes, held in May and attracting about 30,000 visitors, is the most stunning showcase. It created worldwide awareness of *The Piano* (1993), *Pulp Fiction, Breaking the Waves,* and *Crouching Tiger, Hidden Dragon.* Rotterdam (held in January and February) and Berlin (February) can position a noteworthy film for spring and summer release in Europe. Venice (August and September) plays the same role for Europe's fall season. Sundance (January) helps launch spring and summer titles, while Toronto (September) has become important for fall art-house releases and Academy Award contenders (see box).

As festivals have become more numerous and varied, they have become a diffuse but powerful distribution system. Who are the key players? The world-class filmmakers are sought after by every festival—the established old guard, the recent prizewinners, the emerging talents. Just as important are the festival directors. In the early years of festivals, each participating country appointed a committee to pick films. During the 1960s, festival directors gained control of programming, and the films shown reflected the tastes of the directors and their staffs. Programmers cultivate relationships with established filmmakers while also sniffing out talented newcomers. The biggest A-list festivals send scouts around the world, visiting other festivals and watching rough cuts and works in progress.

Critics are also key players, since the media call public attention to new films. Festivals give reporters access to celebrities and a pressroom from which they can send stories home. The International Federation of Film Critics (FIPRESCI) has established its own awards, including several honoring beginning filmmakers. Critics sit on juries and help determine prizes, and both festival programmers and distributors may consult critics about promising titles. "The scene is surprisingly tight," notes one filmmaker. "There is a network of people who go from festival to festival all over the world, and gossip is in large part the glue of the circuit."[8]

Although the system is informal, it has become increasingly powerful. As Hollywood tightens its grip on commercial distribution, films not bought by the studios' classics divisions depend on festival screenings not just for publicity but for audiences. After the festival ends, most local audiences will never have a chance to see the films again. The festival has in effect distributed the film, giving it one or two screenings in its city. Multiply this film by the thousands of titles needed to fill festival slots, and festivals become crucial circulation mechanisms for films with scant commercial prospects.

Filmmakers obviously benefit from this network. Gay and lesbian films (such as Todd Haynes's *Poison,* 1991), feminist cinema, and films from ethnic minorities would receive few screenings if not for the festival circuit. Asian cinema came to global prominence in the 1990s thanks partly to energetic programmers at Locarno, Toronto, and Vancouver. Hong Kong films often gained recognition through midnight screenings at Rotterdam and elsewhere. Festivals are also the primary paths to parallel film circulation, where buyers for video distributors or cable-television networks find new material to fill the pipeline.

Now that festivals have become a distribution network, however, they can hurt a film's chances for commercial release. After a film has screened once or twice in a major city's festival, local distributors may feel that it has reached its maximum audience. As critic Roger Ebert has pointed out, most films receive their only screenings at festivals: "A good film will play seventy festivals and then that's it. It never gets picked up by a distributor, and it never plays in any theaters, and the people who made the film are expected to pay for the shipping costs and to send over the press kits and maybe send in a star or a director."[9] Despite their drawbacks, however, festivals remain the main mechanism for selecting, from all the thousands of films made outside Hollywood, those that might find international audiences.

GLOBAL SUBCULTURES

Since the 1910s, films—particularly U.S. films—have won international fans. Around the world, magazines and newspapers have catered to moviegoers' fascination with stars and, more recently, celebrity directors. Books and magazines have targeted cults devoted to Marilyn Monroe, James Dean, Bruce Lee, and other charismatic figures. *Famous Monsters of Filmland,* first published in 1958, fed the love of classic horror. The science-fiction and fantasy boom of the 1970s triggered a burst of publishing, with periodicals like *Cinefantastique, Starlog, Fangoria,* and many magazines devoted to *Star Wars.* With the arrival of videotape and the Internet, fandom changed dramatically. Isolated and diverse fans became a true community, interacting with each other on a worldwide scale.

Video Piracy: An Efficient Distribution System?

By the mid-1980s, about 130 million videocassette recorders were in use around the world. Video became to film what audiotape and CDs were to music: a dramatically new phase in the globalization of entertainment. With video, however, came piracy. Legal tapes were copied and sold at a discount. Recently released films could be available on the street immediately, thanks to cooperative projectionists or laboratory workers, who would smuggle out a print for duplication. Street copies might also be "auditorium versions," shot furtively during a theater screening.

Piracy was everywhere, spreading out from copying centers in Italy, Turkey, Taiwan, Russia, and New York. One Manhattan gang earned $500,000 a week from counterfeit tapes. Illegal sales constituted one-quarter to one-half of the video revenues in Europe, and up to 90 percent of those in China, India, and South America. Throughout Asia, dupe copies were shown publicly in "video parlors." In India, pirated films filled cable channels (themselves often outlaw operations). Reflecting on the speed and efficiency of the illegal video trade, a Hong Kong film producer once remarked, "Piracy is the best distribution system."

The arrival of digital reproduction only exacerbated the problem. In East Asia, the Video CD (VCD), a digital format using low-level compression, began to replace tape in the mid-1990s. Illegal disks were cheaper to make and transport than videotapes. Working from cable broadcasts, legal tapes, or laserdiscs, factories in mainland China stamped out thousands of VCDs a day and shipped them all over Asia, to sell at one to two dollars each. The higher-quality imagery offered by Digital Video Discs (DVDs) proved even more attractive. Although the United States studios coded DVDs by region, the codes were quickly broken, region-free players went on sale, and bootleg discs appeared. The ultimate buccaneering frontier was the Internet, where hundreds of movies were available for free.

Fan Subcultures: Appropriating the Movies

Alongside the legal and illegal circulation of films on video was a gray zone of video exchange, where fans of certain genres were buying and trading copies. Before videotape, fans were forced to hunt down the films they loved in cinemas and late-night television broadcasts. Now, a fan could own copies of beloved titles and, equipped with two VCRs, copy tapes obtained from other fans. A community of fans grew up, dedicated to swapping and discussing their favorites. In some countries, small companies formed to circulate hard-to-find tapes, often in defiance of copyright laws.

As more unusual movies flashed across national borders via cable, satellite, and rental tapes, fans' tastes diversified. During the 1960s and 1970s, marginal film industries had exported cheap, sometimes wild, genre

28.7   Two of the Empire's troops reflect on killing Jawas in Kevin Rubio's Internet movie *Troops* (1998).

films—women-in-prison movies from the Philippines, Mexican masked-wrestler dramas, Turkish vampire films, Singapore spy adventures. Discovered on video, these "mondo" movies seemed cool to many young people looking for thrills beyond Hollywood. Kung-fu sagas, Bollywood musicals, and Japanese animation found a niche in mainstream youth culture thanks largely to the fans who tirelessly circulated video copies in the 1980s and 1990s.

Whatever their preferences, fans found their voice in fanzines. These photocopied cut-and-paste magazines were labors of love, distributed through the mail and the increasingly popular fan conventions. Cult films like *Blade Runner* and *Blue Velvet* were common 'zine subjects. Some fanzines achieved newsstand distribution, such as Damon Foster's *Oriental Cinema*, lovingly devoted to obscure Japanese monster movies. By the mid-1990s, the Internet took the place of fanzines. Now fans could build websites as shrines to their favorites, and chatrooms let fans swap opinions and video copies.

Fan communities have been called "participatory cultures" in that they often rework the media texts they love.[10] Offered the chance, fans will spin the original movie or TV show in new directions—clipping out scenes to make best-moments tapes, writing poems and songs about their favorite characters, even circulating new stories about them. The fan frenzy around *Star Wars* made film companies realize that if they did not form authorized fan clubs and crack down on the dozens of 'zines in circulation, they were forfeiting rights to their intellectual property. The Internet only increased the risk, as fans would not hesitate to recycle anything and even post videos derived from originals (**28.7**). Music and coming-attractions trailers might

28.8 A New Zealand vista becomes Middle Earth in *The Lord of the Rings: The Fellowship of the Ring.*

show up on fan sites before they hit the open market, and images might be reworked, footage recut, sound redubbed. Yet the fans were the most loyal sector of the audience, and the studios could not afford to alienate them entirely. As a result, the Majors constantly oscillated between wooing the fans and threatening them if they were perceived as going too far.

Some studios decided to bring fans into the creative process. New Line's *The Lord of the Rings: The Fellowship of the Ring* (2001; **28.8**), designed as a global film, became a fan fetish as soon as it was announced. Chatrooms buzzed about the best casting, aware that director Peter Jackson was monitoring them; the discussions may have shaped the final decision, as fan favorite Cate Blanchett was awarded a crucial role. Many fans believed that protesting against changes to the original novel encouraged Jackson to shoot a more faithful version. One devotee trekked to New Zealand to observe the shooting and post reports; at first the producers saw her as a spy, but then they invited her to visit the set. In the meantime, New Line allowed one actor, Ian McKellen, to leak hints about the production on his website, www.mckellen.com. Just as cleverly, the first trailer for the film was released online, before it was seen in theaters, and it drew over 1.6 million hits in its first day.

In the case of *The Lord of the Rings,* fans helped stir up interest in the movie. By contrast, fans helped thwart the release of MGM/UA's remake of the 1975 film *Rollerball.* During production, a script leaked out and was reviewed, devastatingly, by net guru Harry Knowles on his aint-it-cool-news.com site. When the film was ready to preview in spring of 2001, director John McTiernan flew to Austin, picked up Knowles and some friends, and took them to New York for a test screening. The exercise in damage control failed. After the preview, Knowles and his pals posted detailed critiques of the film, confessing their admiration for the original and for McTiernan but declaring the movie virtually unreleasable. Other disastrous previews were reported to Knowles's site. In August, MGM/UA pulled *Rollerball* from its summer lineup. Although the movie was released in early 2002, its theatrical chances were irreparably damaged, and it failed at the box office. Before the Internet, *Rollerball*'s poor testing would have been insider knowledge. Now, the once-marginal fan subculture was shaping the opinions of many thousands of viewers.

DIGITAL CONVERGENCE

Digital technology entered cinema in the 1970s through computer-driven special effects, then in the 1980s through computerized editing and sound mixing (pp. 701, 703). In the 1990s, digital video emerged as a practical recording medium, and inexpensive editing software became available on laptop computers. At the same time the World Wide Web gave easy access to the Internet. In 1993, only 1.3 million people used the Internet; by 2000, over 300 million people did. Soon the DVD was introduced as a consumer entertainment format and seemed likely to replace videotape. These developments pointed toward complete convergence between film and digital media. Why couldn't a filmmaker make, market, distribute, and exhibit movies wholly in digital form?

The Internet as Movie Billboard

An obvious use of the Internet was movie advertising. In 1994, one of the first movie-dedicated sites was set up for *Stargate,* using little more than press-kit materials. Other sites sprouted soon, mostly for fantasy and science-fiction films like *Casper* and *12 Monkeys* (both 1995). The studios began adding more erotic and violent material in order to attract browsing viewers. In 1998, the MPAA established a committee to review websites for objectionable content, such as the image from *Rush Hour* (1998) showing Chris Tucker and Jackie Chan pointing guns in each other's faces. Studios quickly realized that the best advertising was interactive, so sites started to include games, film clips, and links to other sites. By 2000, studios were spending between $1 million and $3 million for a film's website.

In 1977, George Lucas published a *Star Wars* comic book before releasing the film. Years later the Internet could generate a fan subculture in a far more interactive way. It could create a virtual world that extended the movie's story. Artisan Entertainment built up anticipation for *The Blair Witch Project* (1999) by providing an online dossier, treating the Blair Witch as a real phenomenon and barely mentioning the film. Most observers credited the film's stunning success to the cult interest generated by the site. For Spielberg's *A.I.: Artificial Intelligence* (2001), a parallel universe was created around Dr. Jeanine Salla, a "sentient machine therapist" listed in the film's trailer and apparently involved in a mysterious murder. Months before the film was released, clues and secret passwords were strewn among a maze of websites, and participants could receive faxes and emails related to the investigation. As fans speculated online about the meaning of it all, the web designers incorporated fans' ideas into further twists of the action.

Digital Moviemaking from Script to Screen

Shooting a film on digital video (DV) could cut costs drastically, and Vinterberg's Dogme 95 film *The Celebration* (p. 713) showed that a transfer to film could be of acceptable theatrical quality. The earliest DV cameras were fairly lightweight, and soon there were palm-sized digital recorders (miniDV), opening up a new flexibility of camera placement seen in such films as *julien donkeyboy* (see **Color Plate 28.2**). U.S. companies began funding production arms specializing in digital features (Blow Up Pictures; Next Wave Films, funded by the Independent Film Channel). More and more independent films were shot digitally (the documentary *The Cruise*, 1998; *Chuck and Buck*, 2000; *The Anniversary Party*, 2001). Well-established directors began using DV: Hal Hartley for *Book of Life* (2000), Allison Anders for *Things Behind the Sun* (2000), and Spike Lee for *Bamboozled*

28.9 "Video has arrived," says the woman in the lower left frame, "and is demanding new expressions, new sensations" (*TimeCode*).

(2000). Wim Wenders, one of the oldest filmmakers to take up digital filming (*The Buena Vista Social Club*, 1999), remarked that video was "reconstructing cinema from scratch. . . . The future of cinema no longer lies in its past."[11]

Other established filmmakers took advantage of DV's cheapness to experiment with storytelling and visual style. Richard Linklater shot *Waking Life* (2001) on digital video, then used a computer program to create rotoscope-like animation (**Color Plate 28.4**). Agnès Varda, still filming at age 73, returned to her roots as a photographer in the essayistic, pictorially rich *The Gleaners and I* (2000), drawing analogies between people who collect the remains of the harvest and the filmmaker who scavenges scraps of reality. For another New Wave director, 81-year-old Eric Rohmer, shooting in digital allowed him to graft actors onto paintings in his *The Lady and the Duke* (2001). Using digital Betacam, Peter Watkins (p. 489) presented another of his "anachronistic" historical re-creations in *La Commune (Paris 1871)* (2001). Mike Figgis's *TimeCode* (1999) follows four story strands simultaneously and presents them on the same screen (**28.9**).

Cinematographers complained that compared to film, digital imagery yielded too few true blacks, too much depth of field, and too little latitude in lighting. It seemed to encourage an offhand approach to shooting that worked against giving the film a distinctive visual design. Still, no one doubted that the technology would improve. Thanks largely to George Lucas's prodding of Sony and Panavision, high-definition video was advancing quickly, offering imagery approaching the prized "film look." In 2001, 24-frame high-definition video promised even richer results, as seen in the French Gothic thriller *Vidocq* (2001). It seemed likely that quite soon many mainstream productions would be shot on high-definition formats.

Once feature films were shot in digital processes, they were usually transferred to film for theatrical showing. The Majors still controlled distribution, the pipeline to the multiplexes and the ancillary markets. With the growth of the Internet, however, independent filmmakers reasoned that films shot on digital video could bypass the studios and be offered to the public directly. The model was the home-made music scene, whereby kids with a basement synthesizer could post samples of their music on the web. Beginning in 1998, dot-com companies like iFilm and AtomFilms offered short films online. Nibblebox, cofounded by Doug Liman (*Swingers*, 1996; *Go*, 2000), made equipment available to college students on a competitive basis, assigned them to mentors, and then sent their films to student television stations, film clubs, and other campus venues.

The Majors were no less intrigued by the web as an outlet. Their idea was video on demand, which would provide a catalogue of films for downloading to a computer, television, or mobile display unit. Thus the industry began trying to upgrade compression and decompression processes to allow for high-quality streaming video. But putting theatrical, mass-audience films on the web posed problems: digital piracy was easy, and kids thought it was cool. With horror, the Majors watched as millions of users swapped files on music sites like Napster. What would stop people from doing the same with movies? There were technical problems as well: streaming video suffered from poor resolution, network congestion, and software players (QuickTime, Windows Media, and the like) that were not "open source." To truly exploit the entertainment potential of the web, television screens, not computer screens, were the most likely destinations, and somehow cable and satellite systems would have to become the pipeline. At the beginning of the 2000s, many companies were scrambling to lay the groundwork for true digital convergence, but no one knew exactly how that would take shape.

The Majors also dreamed of digital exhibition. From a satellite or the Internet, a film would be downloaded to a theater chain's screens. This would eliminate film prints, the cost of shipping, and the risk of piracy. It would allow companies to monitor where and when any film was projected. It might also open the way to using theaters for transmitting live sporting events, concerts, quiz shows, and other material now available on television. Some observers prophesied that digital projection would kill cinema. The image's quality would be compromised, and serious films would be driven out of the market by special events that were inflated versions of television. One film critic asked, "If you were the executive in charge of exploiting *Seinfeld*'s last episode and you had the chance to beam it into thousands of theaters and charge, say, $25 a seat, why in the hell would you *not* do that?"[12]

Instead of framing digital convergence as "film versus video," many cinematographers and directors insisted that the two were distinct media, each good for certain expressive purposes. They might blend in certain ways, but neither would vanquish the other. Across history, some media technologies have vanished, but many competing technologies have flourished side by side. After television arrived, people still listened to the radio. Videotape and the Internet did not kill theatrical cinema.

At the beginning of the twenty-first century, there is more diversity of taste than in many earlier eras. As Hollywood's power has tightened, the number of festivals showing offbeat films has shot up. Thanks to cable and home video, a person outside major cities can see films that would never have played local theaters. Fan subcultures are promoting films far from Hollywood's idea of the global blockbuster. In addition, there are hundreds of important films that will never be transferred to digital formats, and there will always be a need for machines to project them and places to see them. Today, there are more theater screens than at any other time in history, and films remain a global industry and art form. Moving images—analog or digital, in theaters or in the home or on the palm—are likely to retain their power to arouse and enchant viewers for many years to come.

Notes and Queries

AKIRA, GUNDAM, SAILOR MOON, AND THEIR FRIENDS

The momentum of global fan culture is exemplified by the accelerating interest in Japanese animation, or anime (p. 645). During the 1960s, Japanese companies began selling original anime television programs to overseas channels. Children throughout the world grew up adoring *Atom Boy*, *Speed Racer*, and *Gigantor*. Fan clubs sprang up in the late 1970s. The community expanded rapidly with the coming of videotape, allowing fans to dub shows off-air or to copy tapes from Japan. Fans began studying Japanese in order to understand the dialogue, and some created their own subtitled versions. From the United States and England, anime fever spread to Europe, with one French television channel programming anime heavily. Because Japanese studios turned out 250 hours of anime each year, the fan base had plenty to look forward to.

The feature films *Akira* and *My Neighbor Totoro*, released in western theaters in the early 1990s, brought anime into the mainstream. Although fan piracy continued, legitimate companies began distributing dubbed and subtitled tapes. Video rental chains began to include anime sections. Newsletters and 'zines were replaced by reference books and glossy magazines like *Protoculture Addicts* (first published in 1988). The fans migrated to the Web, and soon hundreds of sites offered pictures, essays, streaming video, music, chatrooms, and online superstores. Fans were spread throughout Asia (where imported anime often stifled the development of local animation), Europe, and

South America. With international audiences for the robots in the *Gundam* series and the team of fighting schoolgirls in *Sailor Moon*, anime, like the Hollywood megapic, had become a global cinematic form. One distributor called it "the Punk rock of the 1990s" (quoted in Helen McCarthy, "The Development of the Japanese Animation Audience in the United Kingdom and France," in John A. Lent, ed., *Animation in Asia and the Pacific* [London: John Libbey, 2001], p. 77).

AUTEURS ON THE WEB

One prototype of Internet filmmaking was launched in spring of 2001, when BMW announced "The Hire," a collection of five brief digital films shown exclusively online at bmwfilms.com. The films were made by John Frankenheimer (*The Manchurian Candidate*), Ang Lee (*Crouching Tiger, Hidden Dragon*), Wong Kar-wai (*Chungking Express*), Guy Ritchie (*Snatch*), and Alejandro González Iñárritu (*Amores perros*). Each spot cost about $2 million, becoming on a per-minute basis the most expensive films most of the directors had made. BMWs featured prominently in each plot, but the company claimed that these were not commercials but rather "short films" with true plots. Lee showed a chase to carry a young Buddhist lama to sanctuary, while Wong explored hints of an illicit love affair. "The Hire" suggested that the Web might provide a convenient showcase for film sketches that would have no other venue.

REFERENCES

1. Michael Eisner, with Tony Schwartz, *Work in Progress* (New York: Random House, 1998), p. 238.
2. *Variety* (13–19 February 1995): 1.
3. Quoted in Stig Björkman, "Preface," in Lars von Trier, *Breaking the Waves* (London: Faber and Faber, 1996), p. 8.
4. The Dogme 95 manifesto can be found at www.dogme95.dk.
5. Quoted in Romaine Johais, "Zydogmatique," *Cinéastes* 1 (October–December 2000): 32.
6. Quoted in Richard Kelly, *The Name of This Book is Dogme 95* (London: Faber and Faber, 2000), p. 107.
7. Pico Iyer, *The Global Soul: Jet Lag, Shopping Malls, and the Search for Home* (New York: Knopf, 2000), p. 93.
8. Kirby Dick, quoted in Holly Willis, "Indie Influence," in Steven Gaydos, ed., *The* Variety *Guide to Film Festivals* (New York: Perigee, 1998), p. 27.
9. Quoted in "Screen to Shining Screen," *Variety* (24–30 August 1998): 51.
10. Henry Jenkins, *Textual Poachers: Television Fans and Participatory Culture* (New York: Routledge, 1992).
11. Quoted in Shari Roman, *Digital Babylon: Hollywood, Indiewood, and Dogme 95* (Hollywood, CA: iFilm, 2001), p. 36.
12. Godfrey Cheshire, "The Death of Film/The Decay of Cinema," www.nypress.com/coll.cfm?content_id=243.

FURTHER READING

Billups, Scott. *Digital Moviemaking: The Filmmaker's Guide to the 21st Century.* Hollywood, CA: Michael Wiese, 2001.

Björkman, Stig. *Lars von Trier: Entretiens.* Paris: Cahiers du Cinéma, 2001.

Castells, Manuel. *The Rise of the Networked Society.* 2nd ed. Oxford: Blackwell, 2000.

Dubet, Éric. *Économie du cinéma européen: de l'interventionnisme à l'action entrepreneuriale.* Paris: L'Harmattan, 2000.

Held, David, Anthony McGrew, David Goldblatt, and Jonathan Perraton. *Global Transformations: Politics, Economics, and Culture.* Stanford: Stanford University Press, 1999.

Hjort, Mette and Scott MacKenzie, ed. *Purity and Provocation: Dogme 95.* London: BFI, 2002.

Hoskins, Colin, Stuart McFadyen, and Adam Finn. *Global Television and Film: An Introduction to the Economics of the Business.* Oxford: Oxford University Press, 1997.

Klein, Naomi. *No Logo.* Hammersmith: HarperCollins, 2000.

Knowles, Harry, with Paul Cullum and Mark Ebner. *Ain't It Cool? Hollywood's Redheaded Stepchild Speaks Out.* New York: Warner, 2002.

Miller, Toby, Nitin Govil, John McMurna, and Richard Maxwell. *Global Hollywood.* London: British Film Institute, 2001.

Moran, Albert, ed. *Film Policy: International, National, and Regional Perspectives.* London: Routledge, 1996.

Naficy, Hamid. *An Accented Cinema: Exilic and Diasporic Filmmaking.* Princeton: Princeton University Press, 2001.

Tombs, Pete. *Mondo Macabro: Weird and Wonderful Cinema Around the World.* New York: St. Martin's, 1998.

Turan, Kenneth. *Sundance to Sarajevo: Film Festivals and the World They Made.* Berkeley, CA: University of California Press, 2002.

Wasko, Janet. *Understanding Disney: The Manufacture of Fantasy.* Cambridge: Polity, 2001.

BIBLIOGRAPHY

This is a select bibliography, emphasizing book-length studies and special issues of journals. Most of the works listed are comprehensible to the nonspecialist. Each chapter's "Notes and Queries" and "Further Reading" sections supply additional bibliographical information about particular topics.

General Reference Works

Under the editorship of Michael Singer, Lone Eagle Publishing (Los Angeles, California) publishes a series of reference books compiling information on directors, screenwriters, film composers, and other creative personnel. The directors volume is updated annually.

The American Film Institute Catalogue: Feature Films, 1911–1920. 2 vols. Berkeley: University of California Press, 1988.

The American Film Institute Catalogue: Feature Films, 1921–1930. 2 vols. New York: Bowker, 1971.

The American Film Institute Catalogue: Feature Films, 1931–1940. 3 vols. Berkeley: University of California Press, 1993.

The American Film Institute Catalogue: Feature Films, 1941–1950. 3 vols. Berkeley: University of California Press, 1999.

The American Film Institute Catalogue: Film Beginnings, 1883–1910. 2 vols. Metuchen, NJ: Scarecrow, 1995.

Atkins, Robert. *Artspeak: A Guide to Contemporary Ideas, Movements, and Buzzwords.* New York: Abbeville, 1989.

Barnard, Timothy, and Peter Rist, eds. *South American Cinema: A Critical Bibliography 1915–1994.* Austin: University of Texas Press, 1998.

Câslavský, Karel. "American Comedy Series: Filmographies 1914–1930." *Griffithiana* 51/52 (October 1994): 9–169.

Charles, John. *The Hong Kong Filmography, 1977–1997.* Jefferson, NC: McFarland, 2000.

Cherchi Usai, Paolo, ed. *The Griffith Project.* 5 vols to date. London: British Film Institute, 1999–2001.

Clements, Jonathan, and Helen McCarthy. *The Anime Encyclopedia: A Guide to Japanese Animation Since 1917.* Berkeley: Stone Bridge, 2001.

Cowie, Peter, ed. *International Film Guide.* London: Tantivy; later, Variety, Inc., 1964–present.

Elsaesser, Thomas, and Michael Wedel, eds. *The BFI Companion to German Cinema.* London: British Film Institute, 1999.

The Film Daily Yearbook of Motion Pictures (Initially *Wid's Year Book*). New York: Film Daily, 1918–1969.

The Film/Literature Index. Albany: Filmdex, 1973–present.

Gerlach, John, C., and Lana Gerlach. *The Critical Index: A Bibliography of Articles on Film in English, 1946–1973, Arranged by Names and Topics.* New York: Teachers College Press, 1974.

Gifford, Denis. *The British Film Catalogue 1895–1985: A Reference Guide.* Newton Abbott, England: David & Charles, 1986.

Houston, Penelope. *Keepers of the Frame: The Film Archives.* London: British Film Institute, 1994.

The International Index of Film Periodicals. Brussels: International Federation of Film Archives, 1972–present.

Jihua, Cheng, Li Shaobai, and Xing Zuwen. "Chinese Cinema: Catalogue of Films, 1905–1937." *Griffithiana* 54 (October 1995): 4–91.

Katz, Ephriam. *The Film Encyclopedia.* New York: Crowell, 1979.

Konigsberg, Ira. *The Complete Film Dictionary.* New York: New American Library, 1987.

Lauritzen, Einar, and Gunnar Lundquist. *American Film-Index 1908–1915.* Stockholm: Film-Index, 1976.

———. *American Film-Index 1916–1920.* Stockholm: Film-Index, 1984.

Lyon, Christopher. *The International Dictionary of Films and Filmmakers.* 4 vols. Chicago: St. James Press, 1984.

MacCann, Richard Dyer, and Edward S. Perry. *The New Film Index: A Bibliography of Magazine Articles in English, 1930–1970.* New York: Dutton, 1975.

The Motion Picture Almanac. New York: Quigley, 1933–present.

Passek, Jean-Loup, ed. *Dictionnaire du cinéma.* 2nd ed. Paris: Larousse, 1991.

Plazola, Luis Trelles, *South American Cinema: Dictionary of Film Makers.* Rio Pideras: University of Puerto Rico, 1989.

Rajadhyaksha, Ashish, and Paul Willeman, eds. *Encyclopedia of Indian Cinema.* 2nd ed. Chicago: Fitzroy Dearborn, 1999.

Russell, Sharon A. *Guide to African Cinema.* Westport, CT: Greenwood Press, 1998.

Taylor, Richard, Nancy Wood, Julian Graffy, and Dina Iordanova. *The BFI Companion to Eastern European and Russian Cinema.* London: British Film Institute, 2000.

Unterburger, Amy L. *The St. James Women Filmmakers Encyclopedia.* Farmington Hills, MI: Visible Ink, 1999.

Vincendeau, Ginette, ed. *Encyclopedia of European Cinema.* New York: Facts on File, 1995.

Vincent, Carl. *General Bibliography of Motion Pictures.* Rome: Ateneo, 1953.

Workers of the Writers' Program of the Work Projects Administration in the City of New York. *The Film Index: A Bibliography.* Vol. 1: *The Film as Art.* New York: Museum of Modern Art, 1941. Vol. 2: *The Film as Industry.* White Plains, NY: Kraus, 1985. Vol. 3: *Film in Society.* White Plains, NY: Kraus, 1985.

Historiography

Allen, Robert C., and Douglas Gomery. *Film History: Theory and Practice.* New York: Random House, 1985.

Bordwell, David. *On the History of Film Style.* Cambridge, MA: Harvard University Press, 1997.

Cherchi Usai, Paolo. *Silent Cinema: An Introduction.* London: British Film Institute, 2000.

———, ed. "Film Preservation and Film Scholarship." Special issue of *Film History* 7, no. 3 (autumn 1995).

Lagny, Michèle. *De l'histoire: Méthode historique et histoire du cinema.* Paris: Colin, 1992.

Pierce, David. "The Legion of the Condemned: Why American Silent Films Perished." *Film History* 9, no. 1 (1997): 3–22.

Sadoul, Georges. "Materiaux, méthodes et problèmes de l'histoire du cinéma." In his *Histoire du cinéma mondial des origines à nos jours.* 9th ed. Paris: Flammarion, 1972, pp. v-xxix.

Sklar, Robert, and Charles Musser, eds. *Resisting Images: Essays on Cinema and History.* Philadelphia: Temple University Press, 1990.

World Cinema Surveys

Kindem, Gorham, ed. *The International Movie Industry.* Southern Illinois University Press, 2000.

Luhr, William, ed. *World Cinema since 1945.* New York: Ungar, 1987.

Pratt, George, ed. *Spellbound in Darkness: A History of the Silent Film.* Rev. ed. Greenwich, CT: New York Graphic Society, 1973.

Sadoul, Georges. *Histoire du cinéma mondial des origines à nos jours.* 9th ed. Paris: Flammarion, 1972.

———. *Histoire générale du cinéma.* Vols. 1–4, 6. Paris: Denoël, 1946–1975.

Thompson, Kristin. *Exporting Entertainment: America in the World Film Market, 1907–1934.* London: British Film Institute, 1985.

Regional and National Cinema Surveys

Apart from the works listed here, an excellent set of national cinema histories has been published in the French series "Cinéma/pluriel" by the Pompidou Center under the general editorship of Jean-Loup Passek. As of 2001, volumes have been devoted to Armenia, Australia, Brazil, Canada, Soviet Central Asia, China, Cuba, Czech Republic/Slovakia, Denmark, the Republic of Georgia, Germany (1913–1933), Hungary, India, Italy (1905–1945), Korea, Mexico, Poland, Portugal, Russia and the USSR, Scandinavia, Turkey, and Yugoslavia.

Aberdeen, J. A. *Hollywood Renegades: The Society of Independent Motion Picture Producers.* Los Angeles: Cobblestone Entertainment, 2000.

Anderson, John. *Sundancing: Hanging and Listening In at America's Most Important Film Festival.* New York: Spike, 2000.

Anderson, Joseph, and Donald Richie. *The Japanese Film: Art and Industry.* Expanded ed. Princeton, NJ: Princeton University Press, 1982.

Andrew, Dudley. *Mists of Regret: Culture and Sensibility in Classic French Film.* Princeton, NJ: Princeton University Press, 1995.

Armes, Roy. *Third World Filmmaking and the West.* Berkeley: University of California Press, 1987.

Bachy, Victor. *Pour une histoire du cinéma africain.* Brussels: OCIC, 1987.

Balio, Tino, ed. *The American Film Industry.* 2nd ed. Madison: University of Wisconsin Press, 1985.

———. *Hollywood in the Age of Television.* Boston: Unwin Hyman, 1990.

Balski, Grzegorz. *Directory of Eastern European Film-Makers and Films, 1945–1991.* London: Flicks, 1992.

Banerjee, Shampa, and Anil Srivastava. *One Hundred Indian Feature Films: An Annotated Filmography.* New York: Garland, 1988.

Barbas, Samantha. *Movie Crazy: Fans, Stars, and the Cult of Celebrity.* New York: Palgrave, 2001.

Barnouw, Erik, and S. Krishnaswamy. *Indian Film.* 2nd ed. New York: Oxford University Press, 1980.

Barr, Charles, ed. *All Our Yesterdays: 40 Years of British Cinema.* London: British Film Institute, 1986.

Bergan, Ronald. *The United Artists Story.* New York: Crown, 1986.

Bernardi, Joanne. *Writing in Light: The Silent Scenario and the Japanese Pure Film Movement.* Detroit: Wayne State University Press, 2001.

Bertellini, Giorgio, ed. "Early Italian Cinema." Special issue of *Film History* 11, no. 3 (2000).

Billard, Pierre. *L'Age classique du cinéma français: Du cinéma parlant à la Nouvelle Vague.* Paris: Flammarion, 1995.

Bock, Audie. *Japanese Film Directors.* New York: Kodansha, 1978.

Bondanella, Peter. *Italian Cinema from Neorealism to the Present.* New York: Ungar, 1983.

Bonnell, René. *Le Cinéma exploité.* Paris: Seuil, 1978.

Bordwell, David, Janet Staiger, and Kristin Thompson. *The Classical Hollywood Cinema: Film Style and Mode of Production to 1960.* New York: Columbia University Press, 1985.

Brunet, Patrick J. *Les Outils de l'image: Du cinématographe au caméscope.* Montreal: Université de Montréal, 1992.

Buehrer, Beverly Bare. *Japanese Films: A Filmography and Commentary, 1921–1989.* Jefferson, NC: McFarland, 1990.

Burch, Noël. *To the Distant Observer: Form and Meaning in the Japanese Cinema.* Berkeley: University of California Press, 1978.

Chabria, Suresh, ed. *Light of Asia: Indian Silent Cinema 1912–1934*. Pordenone: Le Giornate del Cinema Muto, and New Delhi: National Film Archive of India, 1994.

Chakravarty, Sumitra S. *National Identity in Indian Popular Cinema, 1947–1987*. Austin: University of Texas Press, 1993.

Chanan, Michael. *Chilean Cinema*. London: British Film Institute, 1974.

———. *The Cuban Image*. London: British Film Institute, 1985.

———. *The Dream That Kicks: The Prehistory and Early Years of Cinema in Britain* 2nd. ed. London/New York: Routledge, 1996.

"Les Cinémas arabes et Grand Maghreb." *CinémAction* 43 (1987).

Clark, Paul. *Chinese Cinema: Culture and Politics since 1949*. Cambridge, England: Cambridge University Press, 1987.

Courtade, Françis. *Les Malédictions du cinéma français: Une Histoire du cinéma français parlant (1928–1978)*. Paris: Moreau, 1978.

Cowie, Peter. *Swedish Cinema*. London: Tantivy, 1966.

Crisp, Colin. *The Classic French Cinema, 1930–1960*. Bloomington: Indiana University Press, 1993.

Curran, James, and Vincent Porter, eds. *British Cinema History*. London: Weidenfeld and Nicolson, 1983.

Dabashi, Hamid. *Close-Up: Iranian Cinema Past, Present and Future*. London: Verso, 2001.

Davay, Paul. *Cinéma de Belgique*. Gembloux: Duculot, 1973.

Dennis, Jonathan, and Jan Beringa, eds. *Film in Aotearoa New Zealand*. Wellington, New Zealand: Victoria University Press, 1992.

Dermody, Susan, and Elizabeth Jacka. *The Screening of Australia: Anatomy of a National Cinema*. 2 vols. Sydney: Currency, 1988.

Diawara, Manthia. *African Cinema: Politics and Culture*. Bloomington: Indiana University Press, 1992.

Dick, Bernard F. *City of Dreams: The Making and Remaking of Universal Pictures*. Lexington: University Press of Kentucky, 1997.

Dickinson, Margaret, and Sarah Street. *Cinema and State: The Film Industry and the British Government 1927–1984*. London: British Film Institute, 1985.

D'Lugo, Marvin. *Guide to the Cinema of Spain*. Westport, CT: Greenwood, 1997.

Dyer, Richard, and Ginette Vincendeau, eds. *Popular European Cinema*. London: Routledge, 1992.

Eames, John Douglas. *The MGM Story*. New York: Crown, 1976.

———. *The Paramount Story*. New York: Crown, 1985.

Elsaesser, Thomas. *New German Cinema: A History*. New Brunswick, NJ: Rutgers University Press, 1989.

———, ed. *A Second Life: German Cinema's First Decades*. Amsterdam: University of Amsterdam Press, 1996.

Feldman, Seth. *Take Two: A Tribute to Film in Canada*. Toronto: Irwin, 1984.

Feldman, Seth, and Joyce Nelson, eds. *Canadian Film Reader*. Toronto: Peter Mastin, 1977.

FEPACI. *Africa and the Centenary of Cinema*. Paris: Présence Africain, 1995.

Finler, Joel W. *The Hollywood Story*. New York: Crown, 1988.

Frodon, Jean-Michel. *L'Age moderne du cinéma français: De la Nouvelle Vague à nos jours*. Paris: Flammarion, 1995.

Gokulsing, K. Mott, and Wimal Dissayanke. *Indian Popular Cinema: A Narrative of Cultural Change*. Stoke-on-Trent: Haffordshire, 1998.

Gomery, Douglas. *The Hollywood Studio System*. New York: St. Martin's, 1986.

———. *Shared Pleasures: A History of Movie Presentation in the United States*. Madison: University of Wisconsin Press, 1992.

Haghighat, Mamad. *Histoire du cinéma iranien*. Paris: Bibliothèque public d'information, 1999.

Hanan, David. *Film in South East Asia: View from the Region*. Manila: SEAPAVAA, 2001.

Hayward, Susan, and Ginette Vincendeau, eds. *French Film: Texts and Contexts*. London: Routledge, 1990.

Hershfield, Juanne, and David R. Maciel. *Mexico's Cinema: A Century of Films and Filmmakers*. Wilmington, DE: Scholarly Resources, 1999.

Hibon, Danièle, ed. *Cinémas d'Israël*. Paris: Galerie Nationale du Jeu de Paume, 1992.

Higginbotham, Virginia. *Spanish Film under Franco*. Austin: University of Texas Press, 1988.

Hirschorn, Clive. *The Columbia Story*. New York: Crown, 1990.

———. *The Universal Story*. New York: Crown, 1983.

———. *The Warner Bros. Story*. New York: Crown, 1979.

Hollis, Richard, and Brian Sibley. *The Disney Studio Story*. New York: Crown, 1988.

Issari, M. Ali. *Cinema in Iran, 1900–1979*. Metuchen, NJ: Scarecrow, 1989.

Jarvie, Ian. *Hollywood's Overseas Campaign: The North Atlantic Movie Trade, 1920–1950*. Cambridge, England: Cambridge University Press, 1992.

Jewell, Richard B., and Vernon Harbin. *The RKO Story*. New York: Arlington House, 1982.

Johnson, Randal. *The Film Industry in Brazil: Culture and the State*. Pittsburgh: University of Pittsburgh Press, 1987.

Johnson, Randal, and Robert Stam, eds. *Brazilian Cinema*. Austin: University of Texas Press, 1982.

Juin, Rikhab Dass. *The Economic Aspects of the Film Industry in India*. Delhi: Atma Ram, 1960.

Kabir, Nasreen Munni. *Bollywood: The Indian Cinema Story*. London: Channel 4, 2001.

Kenez, Peter. *Cinema and Soviet Society: From the Revolution to the Death of Stalin*. London/New York: I. B. Tauris, 2001.

King, John, *Magical Reels: A History of Cinema in Latin America*. London: Verso, 1990.

King, John, and Nissa Torrents, eds. *The Garden of Forking Paths: Argentine Cinema*. London: British Film Institute, 1987.

"Latin American Cinema." *Iris* 13 (summer 1991).

Lawton, Anna, ed. *The Red Screen: Politics, Society, Art in Soviet Cinema*. New York: Routledge, 1992.

Lent, John A., ed. *The Asian Film Industry*. London: Helm, 1990.

Leprohon, Pierre. *The Italian Cinema*. Trans. Roger Greaves and Oliver Stallybrass. New York: Praeger, 1972.

Lever, Yves. *Histoire générale du cinéma au Québec*. Montreal: Boréal, 1988.

Leyda, Jay. *Kino: A History of the Russian and Soviet Film*. 3rd ed. Princeton, NJ: Princeton University Press, 1983.

Liehm, Mira. *Passion and Defiance: Film in Italy from 1942 to the Present*. Berkeley: University of California Press, 1984.

Liehm, Mira, and Antonin J. Liehm. *The Most Important Art: Soviet and Eastern European Film after 1945*. Berkeley: University of California Press, 1977.

"Lightning Images: Société Eclair 1907–1920." Special issue of *Griffithiana* 47 (May 1993).

Litman, Barry R. *The Motion Picture Mega-Industry*. Boston: Allyn and Bacon, 1998.

Low, Rachel. *The History of the British Film*. 6 vols. London: Allen & Unwin, 1948–1979.

Marcus, Millicent. *Italian Film in the Light of Neorealism*. Princeton, NJ: Princeton University Press, 1986.

Merritt, Greg. *Celluloid Mavericks: A History of American Independent Film*. New York: Thunder's Month Press, 2000.

Michalek, Boleslaw, and Frank Turaj. *The Modern Cinema of Poland*. Bloomington: Indiana University Press, 1988.

Mora, Carl J. *Mexican Cinema: Reflections of a Society 1896–1988*. Berkeley: University of California Press, 1989.

Neale, Steve, and Murray Smith, eds. *Contemporary Hollywood Cinema*. New York: Routledge, 1998.

Neergaard, Ebbe. *The Story of Danish Film*. Copenhagen: The Danish Institute, 1963.

Nemeskurty, István. *A Short History of the Hungarian Cinema*. Budapest: Corvina, 1980.

Noletti, Arthur, and David Desser, eds. *Reframing Japanese Cinema: Authorship, Genre, History*. Bloomington: Indiana University Press, 1992.

Park, James. *British Cinema: The Lights That Failed*. London: Batsford, 1990.

Prédal, René. *Le Cinéma français depuis 1945*. Paris: Nathan, 1991.

———. *50 ans de cinéma français*. Paris: Nathan, 1996.

Prince, Stephen. *A New Pot of Gold: Hollywood under the Electronic Rainbow, 1980–1989*. New York: Scribner's, 2000.

Ramachandran, T. M., ed. *Seventy Years of Indian Cinema (1913–1983)*. Bombay: Cinema India, 1983.

Rayns, Tony, ed. *Eiga: 25 Years of Japanese Cinema*. Edinburgh: Film Festival, 1984.

Rayns, Tony, and Scott Meek, eds. *Electric Shadows: 45 Years of Chinese Cinema*. London: British Film Institute, 1980.

Reid, Nicholas. *A Decade of New Zealand Film: Sleeping Dogs to Came a Hot Friday*. Dunedin: John McIndoe, 1986.

Rimberg, John David. *The Motion Picture in the Soviet Union: 1918–1952*. New York: Arno, 1973.

Rist, Peter Harry. *Guide to the Cinema(s) of Canada*. Westport, CT: Greenwood, 2001.

Roberts, Graham. *Forward Soviet! History and Non-fiction Film in the USSR*. London: Tauris, 1999.

Rockett, Kevin, Luke Gibbons, and John Hill. *Cinema and Ireland*. Syracuse: Syracuse University Press, 1988.

Rose, Frank. *The Agency: William Morris and the Hidden History of Show Business*. New York: HarperCollins, 1995.

Russell, Sharon A. *Guide to African Cinema*. Westport, CT: Greenwood, 1998.

Sabria, Jean-Charles. *Cinéma français: Les Années 50*. Paris: Pompidou Center, 1987.

Schmidt, Nancy J. *Sub-Saharan African Films and Filmmakers*. Bloomington: Indiana University African Studies Program, 1986.

Schnitman, Jorge A. *Film Industries in Latin America: Dependency and Development*. Norwood, NJ: Ablex, 1984.

Segrave, Kerry. *American Films Abroad: Hollywood's Domination of the World's Movie Screens*. Jefferson, NC: McFarland, 1997.

Shiri, Keith, ed. *Directory of African Film-Makers and Films*. London: Flicks, 1992.

Shirley, Graham, and Brian Adams. *Australian Cinema: The First Eighty Years*. Sydney: Angus and Robertson, 1983.

Shohat, Ella. *Israeli Cinema: East/West and the Politics of Representation*. Austin: University of Texas Press, 1989.

Silberman, Marc. *German Cinema: Texts in Context*. Detroit: Wayne State University Press, 1995.

Slater, Thomas J. *Handbook of Soviet and East European Films and Filmmakers*. New York: Greenwood, 1992.

Slattery, Margaret, ed. *Modern Days, Ancient Nights: Thirty Years of African Filmmaking*. New York: Film Society of Lincoln Center, 1993.

Sobański, Oscar. *Polish Feature Films: A Reference Guide 1945–1985*. West Cornwall, CT: Locust Hill, 1987.

Solomon, Aubrey. *Twentieth Century-Fox: A Corporate and Financial History*. Metuchen, NJ: Scarecrow, 1988.

Street, Sarah. *British National Cinema*. London/New York: Routledge, 1997.

Taylor, Richard, and Ian Christie, eds. *The Film Factory: Russian and Soviet Cinema in Documents 1896–1939*. Cambridge, MA: Harvard University Press, 1988.

Teo, Stephen. *Hong Kong Cinema: The Extra Dimension*. London: British Film Institute, 1997.

Thomas, Tony, and Aubrey Solomon. *The Films of 20th Century-Fox*. Secaucus, NJ: Citadel, 1979.

Thompson, Kristin. "Early Alternatives to the Hollywood Mode of Production: Implications for Europe's Avant-gardes." *Film History* 5, no. 4 (December 1993): 386–404.

Thoraval, Yves. *The Cinemas of India (1896–2000)*. New Delhi: Macmillan, 2000.

———. *Regards sur le cinema égyptien*. Paris: L'Harmattan, 1988.

"Le Tiers monde en films" *CinémAction* special number (1981).

Ukadike, Nwachukwu Frank. *Black African Cinema.* Berkeley: University of California Press, 1994.

Vasudev, Aruna, ed. *Frames of Mind: Reflections on Indian Cinema.* New Delhi: UBS, 1995.

Vasudev, Aruna, and Philippe Leuglet, eds. *Indian Cinema Superbazaar.* Delhi: Vikas, 1983.

Vincendeau, Ginette. *Stars and Stardom in French Cinema.* London/New York: Continuum, 2000.

Wayne, Mike. *Political Film: The Dialectics of Third Cinema.* London: Pluto Press, 2001.

Willemen, Paul, and Behroze Gardhy, eds. *Indian Cinema.* London: British Film Institute, 1982.

Williams, Alan. *Republic of Images: A History of French Filmmaking.* Cambridge, MA: Harvard University Press, 1992.

Zglinicki, F. V. *Der weg des Films.* 2 vols. Reprint. Hildesheim: Olms Press, 1979.

Figures and Personalities

These sources pertain to individuals whose activities are discussed in several chapters of this book. For other major figures, see "Further Readings" sections in each chapter.

G. K. Hall (Boston) publishes a useful series of annotated reference guides to major filmmakers.

Aranda, Francisco. *Luis Buñuel: A Critical Biography.* Trans. and ed., David Robinson. London: Secker and Warburg, 1975.

Arnaud, Phillippe, ed. *Sacha Guitry, cinéaste.* Crisnee, Belgium: Editions Yellow Now, 1993.

Aumont, Jacques, ed. *Jean Epstein: Cinéaste, poète, philosophe.* Paris: Cinémathèquc française, 1998.

Bachy, Victor. *Alice Guy-Blaché (1873–1968): La première femme cinéaste du monde.* Perpignan: Institut Jean Vigo, 1993.

Beauchamp, Cari. *Without Lying Down: Frances Marion and the Powerful Women of Early Hollywood.* New York: Scribner's, 1997.

Bellour, Raymond, ed. *Jean-Luc Godard: Son + Image.* New York: Museum of Modern Art, 1992.

Bendazzi, Gianalbert, ed. *Alexeieff: Itinerary of a Master.* Paris: Dreamland, 2001.

Bertin, Celia. *Jean Renoir: A Life in Pictures.* Trans. Mireille Muellner and Leonard Muellner. Baltimore: Johns Hopkins University Press, 1991.

Bordwell, David. *The Cinema of Eisenstein.* Cambridge, MA: Harvard University Press, 1993.

———. *The Films of Carl Theodor Dreyer.* Berkeley: University of California Press, 1981.

———. *Ozu and the Poetics of Cinema.* Princeton, NJ: Princeton University Press, 1988.

Brakhage, Stan. *Film at Wit's End: Eight Avant-Garde Filmmakers.* Kingston, NY: McPherson, 1989.

Cazals, Patrick. *Serguei Paradjanov.* Paris: Cahiers du Cinéma, 1993.

Cerisuelo, Marc. *Jean-Luc Godard.* Paris: Lherminier, 1989.

Custen, George F. *Twentieth Century's Fox: Darryl F. Zanuck and the Culture of Hollywood.* New York: BasicBooks, 1997.

Danvers, Louis, and Charles Tatum, Jr. *Nagisa Oshima.* Paris: Cahiers du Cinéma, 1986.

Dumont, Hervé. *Frank Borzage: Sarastro à Hollywood.* Milan: Mazzotta, 1993.

Durgnat, Raymond, and Scott Simmon. *King Vidor, American.* Berkeley: University of California Press, 1988.

Eyman, Scott. *Ernst Lubitsch: Laughter in Paradise.* New York: Simon & Schuster, 1993.

Fraigneau, André. *Cocteau on the Film: Conversations with Jean Cocteau.* Trans. Vera Traill. New York: Dover, 1972.

Gallagher, Tag. *John Ford: The Man and His Films.* Berkeley: University of California Press, 1986.

Goodwin, James. *Eisenstein, Cinema, and History.* Urbana: University of Illinois Press, 1993.

Hardt, Ursula. *From Caligari to California: Eric Pommer's Life in the International Film Wars.* Providence/Oxford: Berghahn Books, 1996.

Insdorf, Annette. *François Truffaut.* New York: Morrow, 1979.

King, John, Sheila Whitaker, and Rosa Bosch, eds. *An Argentine Passion: María Luisa Bemberg and Her Films.* London: Verso, 2000.

McBride, Joseph. *Searching for John Ford: A Life.* New York: St. Martin's Press, 2001.

McCarthy, Todd. *Howard Hawks: The Grey Fox of Hollywood.* New York: Grove Press, 1997.

McDonald, Keiko. *Mizoguchi.* Boston: Twayne, 1984.

Morton, Lisa. *The Cinema of Tsui Hark.* Jefferson, NC: McFarland, 2001.

Petty, Sheila, ed. *A Call to Action: The Films of Ousmane Sembene.* Westport, CT: Greenwood, 1996.

Prinzler, Hans Helmut, and Enno Patalas, eds. *Lubitsch.* Munich: C. J. Bucher, 1984.

Quandt, James, ed. *Kon Ichikawa.* Toronto: Cinémathèque Ontario, 2001.

Rabinovitz, Lauren. *Points of Resistance: Women, Power and Politics in the New York Avant-Garde Cinema, 1943–71.* Urbana: University of Illinois Press, 1991.

Renoir, Jean. *My Life and My Films.* Trans. Norman Denny. New York; Atheneum, 1974.

Richie, Donald. *Ozu: His Life and Films.* Berkeley: University of California Press, 1974.

Robinson, David. *Chaplin: His Life and Art.* New York: McGraw-Hill, 1985.

Rotha, Paul. *Robert J. Flaherty: A Biography.* Philadelphia: University of Pennsylvania Press, 1983.

Sarris, Andrew, ed. *Interviews with Film Directors.* Indianapolis: Bobbs-Merrill, 1967.

Seton, Marie. *Sergei M. Eisenstein.* London: John Lane, The Bodley Head, 1952.

Sikov, Ed. *On Sunset Boulevard: The Life and Times of Billy Wilder.* New York: Hyperion, 1998.

Spoto, Donald. *The Art of Alfred Hitchcock.* Garden City: Doubleday, 1979.

Tarkovsky, Andrey. *Sculpting in Time: Reflections on the Cinema.* Trans. Kitty Hunter-Blair. London: Faber, 1989.

Turovskaya, Maya. *Tarkovsky: Cinema as Poetry.* London: Faber, 1989.

Van Cauwenberge, Geneviève. "Chris Marker and French Documentary Filmmaking: 1962–1982." Ph.D. dissertation, New York University, 1992.

"Youssef Chahine, l'Alexandrin." *CinémAction* 33 (1985).

Genres, Movements, and Other Trends

The Aurum Film Encyclopedia (London: 1985–present), edited by Phil Hardy, has published reference volumes on horror, science fiction, and the Western.

Altman, Rick. *The American Film Musical*. Bloomington: Indiana University Press, 1987.

———. *Film/Genre*. London: British Film Institute, 1999.

Barsam, Richard M. *Nonfiction Film: A Critical History*. Rev. ed. Bloomington: Indiana University Press, 1992.

Bendazzi, Giannalberto. *Cartoons: Il Cinema d'animazione 1888–1988*. Venice: Marsilio, 1988.

Brenez, Nicole, and Christian LeBrat, eds. *Jeune, dure et pure! Une histoire du cinéma d'avant-garde et experimental en France*. Paris: Cinémathèque française, 2001.

Coe, Brian. *The History of Movie Photography*. London: Ash and Grant, 1981.

Copjec, Joan, ed. *Shades of Noir: A Reader*. London/New York: Verso, 1993.

Cornwell, Regina. *The Other Side: European Avant-Garde Cinema 1960–1980*. New York: American Federation of the Arts, 1983.

Crafton, Donald. *Before Mickey: The Animated Film 1898–1928*. Cambridge, MA: MIT Press, 1982.

Crawford, Peter Ian, and David Turton, eds. *Film as Ethnography*. Manchester, England: Manchester University Press, 1992.

Cripps, Thomas. *Making Movies Black: The Hollywood Message Movie from World War II to the Civil Rights Era*. New York: Oxford University Press, 1993.

———. *Slow Fade to Black: The Negro in American Film, 1990–1942*. New York: Oxford University Press, 1977.

Dixon, Wheeler Winston, ed. *Film Genre 2000*. Albany: State University of New York Press, 2000.

Drummond, Philip, et al. *Film as Film: Formal Experiment in Film, 1910–1975*. London: Hayward Gallery, 1979.

Dyer, Richard. *Now You See It: Studies on Lesbian and Gay Film*. New York: Routledge, 1990.

Flitterman-Lewis, Sandy. *To Desire Differently: Feminism and the French Cinema*. Urbana: University of Illinois Press, 1990.

Frayling, Christopher. *Spaghetti Westerns; Cowboys and Europeans from Karl May to Serigo Leone*. London: Routledge, 1981.

German Experimental Films from the Beginnings to the 1970s. Munich: Goethe Institute, 1981.

Gili, Jean A. *La Comédie italienne*. Paris: Veyrier, 1983.

Gledhill, Christine, ed. *Home Is Where the Heart Is: Studies in Melodrama and the Woman's Film*. London: British Film Institute, 1987.

Green, Stanley. *Encyclopedia of the Musical Film*. New York: Oxford University Press, 1981.

Heider, Karl G. *Ethnographic Film*. Austin: University of Texas Press, 1976.

Hennebelle, Guy, and Raphael Bassan. *Cinémas d'avant-garde: Expérimental et militant*. CinémAction 10–11 (spring–summer 1980).

Hirsch, Foster. *Detours and Lost Highways: A Map of Neo-Noir*. New York: Limelight Editions, 1999.

"The History of Black Film." *Black Film Review* 7, no. 4 (1993).

James, David. *Allegories of Cinema: American Film in the Sixties*. Princeton, NJ: Princeton University Press, 1989.

Jancovich, Mark. *Rational Fears: American Horror in the 1950s*. Manchester: Manchester University Press, 1996.

Jones, G. William. *Black Cinema Treasures: Lost and Found*. Denton: University of North Texas Press, 1991.

Kalinak, Kay. *Settling the Score: Music and the Classical Hollywood Film*. Madison: University of Wisconsin Press, 1992.

Kuhn, Annette, and Susannah Radstone, eds. *Women in Film: An International Guide*. New York: Fawcett Columbine, 1990.

Lamartine, Thérèse. *Elles: Cinéastes ad lib 1895–1981*. Paris: Remne-Ménage, 1985.

Lovell, Alan, and Jim Hillier. *Studies in Documentary*. New York: Viking, 1972.

Maltin, Leonard. *Of Mice and Magic: A History of American Animated Cartoons*. New York: New American Library, 1980.

Martin, Michael T. *Cinemas of the Black Diaspora: Diversity, Dependence, and Oppositionality*. Detroit: Wayne State University Press, 1995.

McCarthy, Helen. *Manga Manga Manga: A Celebration of Japanese Animation at the ICA Cinema*. London: Institute for Contemporary Art, 1992.

Neale, Steve. *Genre and Hollywood*. New York: Routledge, 2000.

Noguez, Dominique. *Éloge du cinéma expérimental: Définitions, jalons*. Paris: Pompidou Center, 1979.

Quart, Barbara Koenig. *Women Directors: The Emergence of a New Cinema*. New York: Praeger, 1988.

Rollwagen, Jack R., ed. *Anthropological Filmmaking*. Chur, Switzerland: Harwood, 1988.

Rubin, Martin. *Thrillers: Genres in American Cinema*. Cambridge: Cambridge University Press, 1999.

Russett, Robert, and Cecile Starr. *Experimental Animation: An Illustrated Anthology*. New York: Van Nostrand Reinhold, 1976.

Russo, Vito. *The Celluloid Closet: Homosexuality in the Movies*. Rev. ed. New York: Harper & Row, 1981.

Scheugl, Hans, and Ernst Schmidt, Jr. *Eine Subgeschichte des Films Lexikon des Avantgarde-, Experimental- und Undergroundfilms*. 2 vols. Frankfurt: Suhrkamp, 1974.

Silver, Alain. *The Samurai Film*. South Brunswick, NJ: Barnes, 1977.

Silver, Alain and Elizabeth Ward. *Film Noir: An Encyclopedic Reference to the American Style*. Woodstock, NY: Overlook, 1979.

Sitney, P. Adams. *Visionary Film: The American Avant-Garde 1943–1978*. 2nd ed. New York: Oxford University Press, 1979.

Sobchak, Vivian. *Screening Space: The American Science Fiction Film*. 2nd ed. New York: Ungar, 1987.

Stauffacher, Frank, ed. *Art in Cinema: A Symposium on the Avant-Garde Film together with Program Notes and References for Series One of Art in Cinema*. San Francisco: San Francisco Museum of Art, 1947.

Swedish Avantgarde Film 1924–1990. New York: Anthology Film Archives, 1991.

Tudor, Andrew. *Monsters and Mad Scientists: A Cultural History of the Horror Movie*. Oxford: Blackwell, 1989.

Waugh, Thomas, ed. *"Show Us Life": Toward a History and Aesthetics of the Committed Documentary*. Metuchen, NJ: Scarecrow, 1984.

Wees, William. *Recycled Images: The Art and Politics of Found Footage Films*. New York: Anthology Film Archives, 1993.

Weis, Elisabeth, and John Belton, eds. *Film Sound: Theory and Practice*. New York: Columbia University Press, 1985.

Weiss, Andrea. *Vampires and Violets: Lesbians in the Cinema*. London: Jonathan Cape, 1992.

Weisser, Thomas. *Spaghetti Westerns—The Good, the Bad, and the Violent: 558 Eurowesterns and Their Personnel, 1961–1977*. Jefferson, NC: McFarland, 1992.

GLOSSARY

Academy ratio In the silent era, the film frame was customarily 1⅓ times as wide as it was high (1.33:1). When a sound track was added, however, the image became nearly square. The 1.33:1 silent *aspect ratio* was standardized by the Academy of Motion Picture Arts and Sciences in 1932. (In practice, the sound-film ratio was closer to 1.37:1.)

actualities An early term for documentary films.

anamorphic lens A lens for making widescreen films using regular *Academy ratio* frame size. The camera lens takes in a wide field of view and squeezes it onto the frame, and a similar projector lens unsqueezes the image onto a wide theater screen. The most famous anamorphic widescreen processes are CinemaScope and Panavision.

animation Any process whereby artificial movement is created by photographing a series of drawings (see *cel animation*), objects, or computer images one by one. Small changes in position, recorded frame by frame, create the illusion of movement.

art cinema (1) A critical term used to describe films that, while made within commercial circumstances, take an approach to form and style influenced by modernist trends (see *modernism*) within "high art" and that offer an alternative to mainstream entertainment. (2) A term used in the U.S. film industry to describe imported films of interest principally to upper-middle-class, college-educated audiences.

artisanal production The process in which a filmmaker, producer, and crew devote their energy to making a single film, often with no expectation of collaborating on another project in the future. This is in contrast to the mass production and division of labor of *studio production*.

aspect ratio The relationship of the frame's width to its height. The standard international ratio was 1.33:1 until the early 1950s, when *widescreen formats* became more common.

auteur The presumed or actual "author" of a film, usually identified as the director. The term is also sometimes used in an evaluative sense to distinguish good filmmakers (auteurs) from bad ones. Identifying the director as the film's "author" and evaluating the film as the work of an auteur has a long history, but it became a prominent issue after the 1940s, particularly in French- and English-language film criticism.

avance sur recettes ("advance on receipts") A government policy of loaning money to a film project on the basis of anticipated ticket sales. The system came into use in France after World War II and provided a model for other countries' film-financing policies.

axis of action In the *continuity editing* system, the imaginary line that passes from side to side through the main actors, defining the spatial relations of all the elements of the scene as being to the right or left. The camera is not supposed to cross the axis at a cut and thus reverse those spatial relations. The axis is also called the "180-degree line" (see *180-degree system*).

backlighting Illumination cast onto the figures in the scene from the side opposite the camera, usually creating a thin outline of light on the figures' edge.

block booking An arrangement in which the distributor forces exhibitors to rent several films in order to get the most desirable ones. Common in the U.S. film industry after the 1910s, the practice was declared illegal in the "Paramount decision" of 1948.

camera angle The position of the frame in relation to the subject it shows: above it, looking down (a high angle); horizontal, on the same level (a straight-on angle); looking up (a low angle).

camera movement The onscreen impression that the framing is changing with respect to the scene being photographed. This is usually caused by the camera's being physically moved, but it may also be caused by a *zoom lens* or certain *special effects*. See also *crane shot*, *pan*, *tilt*, *tracking shot*.

canted framing A view in which the frame is not level; either the right or the left side is lower, causing objects in the scene to appear tipped.

cel animation Animation that uses a series of drawings on pieces of celluloid, called "cels" for short. Slight changes between the drawings combine to create an illusion of movement.

cinematography A general term for all the manipulations of the film strip by the camera in the shooting phase and by the laboratory in the developing phase.

close-up A *framing* in which the scale of the object shown is relatively large. Most commonly, a close-up shows a person's head from the neck up, or a medium-size object.

closure The degree to which the ending of a narrative film reveals the effects of all the causal events and resolves (or "closes off") all lines of action.

collage A film style that assembles footage from widely disparate sources, often juxtaposing staged fictional scenes with newsreel, animation, or other sorts of material. Explored by experimental filmmakers such as Joseph Cornell in the 1930s, it became a major resource for the avant-garde and political filmmaking of the 1960s.

compilation film A genre of documentary cinema that draws together news footage from various sources in order to convey a large-scale process, such as a war or a social change. Widely used in government and public-affairs documentaries of the sound era, the compilation film was also subjected to experimental treatment by the French Lettrists and Bruce Conner.

continuity editing A system of cutting to maintain continuous and clear narrative action. Continuity editing relies upon matching action, screen direction, and figures' positions from shot to shot. For specific techniques of continuity editing, see *axis of action, cut-in, establishing shot, eyeline match, intercutting, match on action, reestablishing shot, screen direction, shot/reverse shot.*

crane shot A shot in which a change of framing is accomplished by having the camera above the ground and moving up, down, or laterally through the air.

crosscutting. See *intercutting.*

cut (1) In filmmaking, the joining of two strips of film together with a splice. (2) In the finished film, an instantaneous change from one framing to another. See also *jump cut.*

cut-in An instantaneous shift from a distant framing to a closer view of some portion of the same space.

cycle A relatively short-lived fashion for certain subgenres within a genre: e.g., the "adult" Westerns in Hollywood during the 1950s or the films about heroic gangsters in the 1980s Hong Kong cinema.

dedramatization In narrative filmmaking, the strategy of minimizing suspense, emotional high points, and physical action in favor of low-key character portrayal, *temps morts,* and an emphasis on surroundings. Commonly used in European *art cinema* of the post–World War II era, often to explore character psychology, evoke mood, or bring out environmental details.

deep focus A use of the camera lens and lighting that keeps both the close and distant planes in sharp focus.

deep space An arrangement of *mise-en-scène* elements so that there is a considerable distance between the plane closest to the camera and the one farthest away. Any or all of these planes may be in focus.

depth of field The measurements of the closest and farthest planes in front of the camera lens between which everything will be in sharp focus. A depth of field from 5 to 16 feet, e.g., would mean everything closer than 5 feet and farther than 16 feet would be out of focus.

diegetic sound Any voice, musical passage, or sound effect presented as originating from a source within the film's world. See also *nondiegetic sound.*

diorama A nineteenth-century entertainment in which the spectators sat in a circular room and viewed long transparent paintings that seemed to move as the lighting changed.

direct sound Music, noise, and speech recorded from the event at the moment of filming; the opposite of *postsynchronization.* Early sound films and Direct Cinema documentaries emphasized direct sound.

dissolve A transition between two shots during which the first image gradually disappears while the second image gradually appears. For a moment the two images blend briefly in *superimposition.*

distance of framing The apparent distance of the frame from the mise-en-scène elements; also called "camera distance" and "shot scale." See also *close-up, extreme close-up, medium shot.*

distribution One of the three branches of the film industry; the process of supplying films to the places where they will be shown. See also *exhibition, production.*

dolly A camera support with wheels, used in making *tracking shots.*

dubbing The process of replacing part or all of the voices on the sound track in order to correct mistakes or rerecord dialogue. See also *postsynchronization.*

editing (1) In filmmaking, the task of selecting and joining camera *takes.* (2) In the finished film, the set of techniques that governs the relations among *shots.*

ellipsis In narrative, the omission of certain scenes or portions of the action.

elliptical editing Editing that omits portions of the action often with the purpose of startling the viewer or creating questions about what occurred in the missing stretches.

establishing shot A shot, usually involving a distant framing, that shows the spatial relations among the important figures, objects and setting in a scene.

exhibition One of the three branches of the film industry; the process of showing the finished film to audiences. See also *distribution, production.*

experimental cinema Filmmaking that avoids the conventions of mass-entertainment film and seeks to explore unusual aspects of the medium and/or suppressed or taboo subject matter. When experimental films present plots, these are frequently predicted upon dreams or symbolic journeys, but often experimental films avoid narrative form altogether, exploring lyric, associational, descriptive, or other formal means.

extreme close-up A framing that enlarges a small detail, such as an eye or a line of newsprint.

eyeline match A *cut* obeying the *axis of action* principle, in which the first shot shows a person looking off in one direction and the second shows a nearby space containing what he or she sees. If the person looks to the left, the following shot should imply that the looker is offscreen right.

fade (1) Fade-in: A dark screen that gradually brightens as a shot appears. (2) Fade-out: A shot that gradually darkens as the screen goes black. Occasionally fade-outs brighten to pure white or to a color.

fill light Illumination from a source less bright than the *key light,* used to soften deep shadows in a scene. See also *three-point lighting.*

film noir ("dark film") A term applied by French critics to a type of American film, usually in the detective and thriller genres, with low-key lighting and a somber mood. Film noir was most prevalent in the 1940s and 1950s, though it was revived occasionally later.

film stock The strip of material upon which a series of film frames is registered. It consists of a clear base coated on one side with a light-sensitive emulsion.

filter A piece of glass or gelatin placed in front of the camera or printer lens to alter the light striking the film in the aperture.

flashback An alteration of story order in which events occurring in the present are interrupted by the showing of events that took place earlier.

flashforward An alteration of story order in which the plot presentation moves forward to future events and then returns to the present.

focal length The distance from the center of the lens to the point at which the light rays meet in sharp focus. The focal length determines the perspective relations of the space represented on the flat screen. See also *normal lens, telephoto lens, wide-angle lens.*

focus The degree to which light rays coming from the same part of an object through different parts of the lens converge at the same point on the film *frame*, creating sharp outlines and distinct textures.

frame A single image on the strip of film. When a series of frames is projected onto a screen in quick succession, the spectator sees an illusory movement.

framing The use of the edges of the film frame to select and to compose what will be visible onscreen.

front projection A composite process whereby footage meant to appear as the background of a shot is projected from the front onto a screen. Figures in the foreground are filmed in front of the screen as well. See also *rear projection.*

frontality In staging, the positioning of figures so that they face the viewer.

gauge The width of the film strip, measured in millimeters. The standard gauges in film history are 8mm, 16mm, 35mm, and 70mm.

genres Various types of films that audiences and filmmakers recognize by their recurring conventions. Common genres are horror films, gangster films, and Westerns.

graphic match Two successive shots joined so as to create a strong similarity of compositional elements, such as color or shape.

hand-held camera The use of the camera operator's body as a camera support, either holding it by hand or using a harness. Seen in some silent films, such as Abel Gance's *Napoléon*, but more common in Direct Cinema documentaries and fiction films from the 1960s on.

hard lighting Illumination that creates sharp-edge shadows.

height of framing The distance of the camera above the ground, regardless of its angle to the horizontal.

high-key lighting Illumination that creates comparatively little contrast between light and dark areas of the shot. Shadows are fairly transparent and brightened by *fill light.*

horizontal integration A practice in which a company in one sector of the motion-picture industry acquires or gains control over other companies in that sector. For example,
a production company may expand by purchasing other production firms. See also *vertical integration.*

intellectual montage The juxtaposition of a series of images to create an abstract idea not suggested by any one image. Pioneered by Soviet Montage directors, particularly Sergei Eisenstein, it returned to widespread use in *experimental cinema* and left-wing cinema of the 1960s.

intercutting Editing that alternates shots of two or more lines of action occurring in different places, usually simultaneously. Used synonymously with *crosscutting.*

iris A round, moving *mask* that can (1) close down to end a scene (iris-out) or emphasize a detail or (2) open to begin a scene (iris-in) or reveal more space around a detail.

jump cut An elliptical cut that appears to be an interruption of a single shot. Either the figures seem to change instantly against a constant background or the background changes instantly while the figures remain constant. See also *elliptical editing.*

key light In the *three-point lighting* system, the brightest illumination coming onto the scene. See also *backlighting, fill light.*

linearity In a narrative, the clear motivation of a series of causes and effects that progress without significant digressions, delays, or irrelevant interpolations.

long shot A framing in which the scale of the object shown is small. A standing human figure would appear nearly the height of the screen.

long take A shot that continues for an unusually lengthy time. Rare in silent cinema, the long take became more significant in the 1930s and 1940s, especially as used by Jean Renoir and Orson Welles. It soon became a common technique in films throughout the world. See also *plan-séquence.*

low-key lighting Illumination that creates strong contrast between light and dark areas of the shot, with deep shadows and little *fill light.*

Majors A term for the most powerful film companies in the U.S. industry. In the 1920s, the Majors were also knows as the "Big Three" and consisted of Paramount-Publix, Loew's (MGM), and First National. During the 1930s, the Majors (now the "Big Five") were MGM, Paramount, 20th Century-Fox, Warner Bros., and RKO. Before 1948, the Majors achieved their status because they had a high degree of *vertical integration.* Today the Majors consist of several production-distribution companies owned by media conglomerates, such as Universal Vivendi and AOL Time-Warner.

mask An opaque screen placed in the camera or printer that blocks part of the frame and changes the shape of the image. As seen on the screen, most masks are black, although they can be white or colored. See also *iris.*

masking In exhibition, stretches of black fabric that frame the theater screen. Masking may be adjusted according to the *aspect ratio* of the film to be projected.

match on action A continuity cut that joins two shots of the same gesture, making it appear to continue uninterrupted.

matte shot A type of *process shot* in which different areas of the image (usually actors and setting) are photographed separately and combined in laboratory work.

medium shot A framing in which the scale of the object shown is of moderate size. A human figure seen from the waist up would fill most of the screen.

Minors From the 1920s to the 1950s, significant Hollywood production companies that did not own theaters. Also known as the "Little Three," the Minors consisted of Universal, Columbia, and United Artists. See also *Majors.*

mise-en-scène All the elements placed in front of the camera to be photographed: the settings and props, lighting, costumes and makeup, and figure behavior.

mixing Combining two or more sound tracks by rerecording them onto a single track.

modernism A broad trend in twentieth-century art and literature emphasizing aesthetic innovation and themes that comment upon contemporary life. Modernist are flaunts difficult, often aggressive or disruptive, forms and styles; it frequently challenges traditional "realistic" art and criticizes mass popular entertainment. Thematically, modernism displays a fascination with technology, city life, and problems of personal identity. It embraces both political critique and spiritual exploration. Expressionism, surrealism, and atonal music are some typical manifestations of modernism. Modernism's impact has been felt in *experimental cinema*, *art cinema*, and some mainstream commercial filmmaking.

montage (1) A synonym for *editing*. (2) An approach to editing developed by the Soviet filmmakers of the 1920s. Soviet Montage emphasizes dynamic, often discontinuous, relationships between shots. It also emphasizes *intellectual montage*.

montage sequence A segment of a film that summarizes a topic or compresses a passage of time into brief symbolic or typical images. Frequently *dissolves*, *fades*, *superimpositions*, and *wipes* are used to link the shots in a montage sequence.

motif An element in a film that is repeated in a significant way.

movement A group of filmmakers working in a common period and place who share some distinctive presumptions about how films should be made. Typically, the films of a movement share formal, stylistic, and thematic features. Some movements, such as French Surrealism of the 1920s, can be seen as fairly unified; others, such as the French New Wave of the late 1950s, are comparatively loose.

nickelodeon boom Beginning in 1905, a period of rapid expansion in the number of small, inexpensive store-front theaters showing programs of short films. During the 1910s, nickelodeons disappeared as larger theaters were built.

nondiegetic sound Sound, such as mood music or a narrator's commentary, represented as coming from a source outside the world of the narrative (the "diegesis").

normal lens A lens that shows objects without severely exaggerating or reducing the depth of the scene's planes. In theatrical filmmaking, a normal lens is 35mm to 50mm. See also *telephoto lens*, *wide-angle lens.*

oligopoly An economic situation in which a few companies control a market, often cooperating with each other to keep out new firms. In the U.S. film industry after the 1920s, the *Majors* and the *Minors* constituted an oligopoly.

180-degree system In the continuity approach to editing, the dictate that the camera should stay on one side of the action to ensure consistent spatial relations between objects to the right and left of the frame. The 180-degree line is the same as the *axis of action*. See also *continuity editing*, *screen direction.*

overlapping editing Cuts that repeat part or all of an action, thus expanding the duration of the action on screen.

pan A *camera movement* in which the camera body swivels to the right or left. The onscreen effect is of scanning the space horizontally.

pan-and-zoom technique A way of substituting for cutting into and out of a scene; continuous *pans* and zooms concentrate attention on significant aspects of a scene. Rossellini pioneered this technique in the late 1950s, and it became widespread during the 1960s. Often the pan-and-zoom technique enables the director to create a *long take*. See also *zoom lens.*

pixillation A form of animation in which three-dimensional objects, often people, are made to move in staccato bursts through the use of stop-action cinematography.

plan-séquence ("sequence shot") A French term for a scene handled in a single shot, usually a *long take*.

point-of-view (POV) shot A shot taken with the camera placed approximately where a character's eye would be, showing what the character would see. A POV shot is usually preceded or followed by a shot of the character looking.

postsynchronization The process of adding sound to images after they have been shot and assembled. This can include *dubbing* voices, as well as inserting *diegetic* music or sound effects. Contemporary fiction films are often postsynchronized. The technique is the opposite of *direct sound.*

process shot Any shot involving rephotography to combine two or more images into one or to create a special effect; also called "composite shot." See also *front projection*, *matte shot*, *rear projection*, *special effects.*

production One of the three branches of the film industry; the process of creating a film. See also *distribution*, *exhibition.*

protectionism A government policy that defends national filmmaking from competition by foreign imports. Typical protectionist policies are quotas on the number of films that may be imported or shown, requirements that theater time be set aside for the domestic product, and forms of financial aid to domestic production.

racking focus Shifting the area of sharp focus from one plane to another during a shot. The effect on the screen is called "rack focus."

rear projection A technique for combining a foreground action with a background action filmed earlier. The foreground is filmed in a studio, against a screen; the background imagery is projected from behind the screen. The technique is the opposite of *front projection*.

reestablishing shot A return to a view of an entire space after a series of closer shots following the *establishing shot*.

reflexivity A tendency, characteristic of cinematic modernism, to call attention to the fact that the film is an artifact or an illusion. Advocates of reflexivity often suggest that while mainstream cinema encourages the viewer to see the onscreen world as real, a more self-conscious cinema will expose the ways in which movie makers create this effect of reality.

reframing Using short *pan* or *tilt* movements of the camera to keep figures onscreen or centered.

rotoscope A machine that projects live-action motion-picture film frames one by one onto a drawing pad or *cel* so that an animator can trace the figures in each frame. The aim is to achieve more realistic movement in an animated cartoon.

run A distinct period during which a film is exhibited following its release. In Hollywood's studio era, a film's "first run" in major urban theaters would be followed by subsequent runs in neighborhoods or small towns. Today, after a film's first theatrical run, later runs include in-flight screenings, screenings in budget theaters, 16mm nontheatrical screenings, cable television premieres, and videocassette release.

runaway production The practice of Hollywood film companies shooting their films abroad after World War II. This was done partly to save money and partly to utilize the rental income ("frozen funds") that European governments had forbidden U.S. companies to withdraw from the country.

scenics Early nonfiction short films that displayed picturesque or exotic locales.

screen direction The right-left relationships in a scene, set up in an establishing shot and determined by the position of characters and objects in the frame, the directions of movement, and the characters' eyelines. *Continuity editing* attempts to keep screen direction consistent between shots. See also *axis of action, eyeline match, 180-degree system.*

sequence shot See *plan-séquence.*

shallow focus A restricted *depth of field*, which keeps only those planes close to the camera in sharp focus; the opposite of *deep focus.*

shallow space An arrangement in which the action is staged with relatively little depth; the opposite of *deep space.*

shot (1) In shooting, one uninterrupted run of the camera to expose a series of frames. Also called a *take*. (2) In the finished film, one uninterrupted image with a single static or mobile framing.

shot/reverse shot Two or more shots edited together that alternate characters, typically in a conversation situation. In *continuity editing*, characters in one framing usually look left, in the other framing, right. Over-the-shoulder framings are common in shot/reverse-shot editing.

side lighting Lighting coming from one side of a person or object, usually in order to create a sense of volume, to bring out surface textures, or to fill in areas left shadowed by light from another source.

soft lighting Illumination that avoids harsh bright and dark areas, creating a gradual transition from highlights to shadows.

sound-over Any sound that is not represented as being directly audible within the space and time of the images on the screen. A spoken narration (called "voice-over") is a common example.

sound perspective The sense of a sound's position in space, yielded by volume, timbre, pitch, and, in multichannel reproduction systems, binaural information.

special effects A general term for various photographic manipulations that create illusory spatial relations in the shot, such as *superimposition*, a *matte shot*, and *rear projection.*

storyboard A tool used in planning film production, consisting of comic-strip-like drawings of individual shots, with descriptions written below each drawing.

studio production A manner of filmmaking in which an enterprise creates motion pictures on a mass scale. Usually labor is divided on the basis of extensive preparation, guided by the shooting script and other written plans. Typically, some personnel, such as directors and cinematographers, work on one film at a time, while other staff, such as screenwriters or specialized technicians, work on several films more or less simultaneously. The Hollywood companies between the 1920s and 1950s exemplify studio production.

style The systematic and salient uses of film *techniques* characteristic of a film or a group of films (e.g., a filmmaker's work or a film *movement*).

superimposition The exposure of more than one image on the same film strip.

synchronous sound Sound that is matched temporally with the movements occurring in the images, as when dialogue corresponds to lip movements.

take In filmmaking, the *shot* produced by one uninterrupted run of the camera. One shot in the final film may be chosen from among several takes of the same action.

technique Any aspect of the film medium that can be manipulated in making a film.

telephoto lens A lens of long focal length that affects a scene's perspective by enlarging distant planes and making them seem close to the foreground planes. In 35mm filming, a telephoto lens is 75mm or more in length. See also *normal lens, wide-angle lens.*

temps morts ("dead moments") A French phrase used to describe a manner of staging and filming that stresses long intervals between actions or lines of dialogue in which no major narrative development takes place. A temps mort might be a lengthy pause in a dialogue scene or an extended sequence showing a character walking through a landscape. Usually temps morts are used to suggest realism, characterization, or mood. The device, seen occasionally in silent films and exploited by Italian Neorealism after World War II, has become widely used in the European *art cinema* since the 1950s.

three-point lighting A common arrangement using three directions of light on a scene: from behind the subjects (*backlighting*), from one bright source (*key light*), and from a less bright source (*fill light*).

tilt A *camera movement* in which the camera body swivels upward or downward on a stationary support. It produces a mobile framing that scans the space vertically.

top lighting Lighting coming from above a person or object, usually in order to outline the upper areas of the figure or to separate it more clearly from the background.

topicals Early short films showing current events, such as parades, disasters, government ceremonies, and military maneuvers. Most topicals recorded the action as it was occurring, but many restaged the event.

tracking shot A *camera movement* in which the camera body moves through space in a horizontal path. On the screen, it produces a mobile framing that travels through space forward, backward, or to one side.

typage A performance technique of Soviet Montage cinema in which an actor is given features believed to characterize a social group, often an economic class.

underlighting Illumination from a point below the figures in the scene.

vertical integration A practice in which a single company engages in two or more of the activities of the film industry (*production, distribution,* and *exhibition*). In the U.S. film industry, the *Majors* were vertically integrated from the 1920s on, owning production facilities, distribution companies, and theaters. The industry's vertical integration was judged monopolistic by the Supreme Court in the Paramount decision of 1948. In the 1980s, the practice reemerged when production and distribution companies began acquiring interests in theater chains and cable television concerns.

whip pan An extremely fast movement of the camera from side to side, which causes the image to blur briefly into a set of indistinct horizontal lines. Often an imperceptible cut will join two whip pans to create a transition between scenes.

wide-angle lens A lens of short focal length that affects a scene's perspective by bulging straight lines near the edges of the frame and exaggerating the distance between foreground and background planes. In 35mm filming, a wide-angle lens is 30mm or less. See also *normal lens, telephoto lens.*

widescreen formats Screen ratios wider than the *Academy ratio*, which is standardized at 1.37:1 in the United States. Important widescreen formats are the U.S. standard of 1.85:1, the CinemaScope and anamorphic Panavision ratio of 2.35:1, and the 70mm ratio of 2.2:1. See also *anamorphic lens, aspect ratio.*

wipe A transition between shots in which a line passes across the screen, gradually eliminating the first shot and replacing it with the next one.

zoom lens A lens with a *focal length* that can be changed during a shot. A shift toward the telephoto range (zoom-in) enlarges the central portions of the image and flattens its planes together. A shift toward the wide-angle range (zoom-out) deenlarges the central portions of the image and separates planes more. See also *telephoto lens, wide-angle lens.*

Grateful acknowledgment is made for use of the following illustrations:

Color plate figure 5.1 Ernst Ludwig Kirchner, *Dodo with a Feather Hat*. Ernst Ludwig Kirchner Dodo with a Feather Hat (Dodo mit Federhut), 1911 Oil on canvas 31 1/2 × 27 1/8″ Milwaukee Art Museum, Gift of Mrs. Harry L. Bradley M1964.54; *Color plate figure 5.2* Lyonel Feininger, *In a Village near Paris*. The Univeristy of Iowa Museum of Art, Gift of Owen and Leone Elliott (1968.16); *Color plate figure 6.1* El Lissitsky's, *Beat the Whites with the Red Wedge H* © 2003 Artist Rights Society (ARS), New York/VG Bild-Kunst, Bonn; *text page 504* Andy Warhol, *Self-Portrait*, 1964 © 2003 Andy Warhol Foundation for the Visual Arts/ARS, NY/Art Resource, NY.

INDEX